5th
*Canadian
edition*

Operations
Management

William J. Stevenson
Rochester Institute of Technology

Mehran Hojati
University of Saskatchewan

James Cao
University of Saskatchewan

 McGraw-Hill
Ryerson

Operations Management
Fifth Canadian Edition

ISBN-13: 978-0-07-133959-9
ISBN-10: 0-07-133959-0

2 3 4 5 6 7 8 9 WEB 1 9 8 7 6 5

Printed and bound in Canada.

Director of Product Management: Rhondda McNabb
Senior Product Manager: Kimberley Veevers
Marketing Manager: Cathie Lefebvre
Product Developer: Erin Catto
Senior Product Team Associate: Marina Seguin
Supervising Editor: Jessica Barnoski
Photo/Permissions Editor: Derek Capitaine
Copy Editor: Karen Rolfe
Plant Production Coordinator: Scott Morrison
Manufacturing Production Coordinator: Emily Hickey
Cover Design: David Montle, Pixel Hive Studio
Cover Image: James Brey/Getty Images
Interior Design: David Montle, Pixel Hive Studio
Page Layout: Aptara®, Inc.
Printer: Webcom

Library and Archives Canada Cataloguing in Publication

Stevenson, William J., author
        Operations management / William J. Stevenson, Rochester
Institute of Technology, Mehran Hojati, University of Saskatchewan,
James Cao, University of Saskatchewan.—Fifth Canadian edition.
Includes index.
ISBN 978-0-07-133959-9

        1. Production management—Textbooks. I. Hojati, Mehran, 1958–, author
II. Cao, James, author III. Title.

TS155.S785 2015   658.5   C2014-906833-6

About the Authors

William Stevenson
Saunders College of Business
Rochester Institute of Technology

This book is dedicated to you.

Dr. William Stevenson is an associate professor of Decision Sciences in the Saunders College of Business at Rochester Institute of Technology. He teaches graduate and undergraduate courses in operations management, management science, quality concepts, and quality applications.

He is the author of textbook/eBooks in management science and statistics, as well as operations management. His articles have appeared in *Management Science, Decision Sciences, Quality Progress*, and other journals.

Dr. Stevenson received a bachelor's degree in industrial engineering, an M.B.A. and a Ph.D. in production/operations management from Syracuse University.

Mehran Hojati
Edwards School of Business
University of Saskatchewan

I dedicate this book to my parents, Hossein Hojati and Zahra Hedayati.

Dr. Hojati is an associate professor of operations management in the Edwards School of Business at the University of Saskatchewan. He teaches operations management, purchasing and supply management, and supply chain management. He has taught and prepared teaching materials for the Purchasing Management Association of Canada (now Supply Chain Management Association). His articles have appeared in *International Journal of Production Economics, Production & Inventory Management Journal*, and others. His research interests are in the applications of operations research techniques in operations.

Dr. Hojati received a bachelor's degree in economics and a master's degree in operational research from London School of Economics, and a Ph.D. in management science from the University of British Columbia. He is certified in Production and Inventory Management (CPIM), awarded by APICS (the Association for Operations Management).

James Cao
Edwards School of Business
University of Saskatchewan

I dedicate this book to my dearest wife, Vivian, whose love and support has given my life both meaning and direction.

Dr. Cao is an assistant professor of operations management in the Edwards School of Business at the University of Saskatchewan. He teaches undergraduate and graduate classes in operations management, statistics, management science, and quality management. Dr. Cao received bachelor's degrees in mathematics, economics, and psychology as well as a doctorate degree in operations management from the University of California at Irvine. His research interests lie in the field of supply chain management, which deals with both matching supply with demand and the coordination of multi-party decision making.

Brief Contents

Contents

PART THREE System Design

Preface

This textbook/eBook is intended as an introduction to operations management in Canada, and demonstrates its applications to service and manufacturing operations. We've included 8 chapter supplements (some are in text and others accessible online), which offer a comprehensive and flexible amount of content that can be selected as appropriate for different courses and formats, including undergraduate, graduate, and executive education. This allows instructors to select the chapters, or portions of chapters, that are most relevant for their purposes. That flexibility also extends to the choice of relative weighting of the qualitative or quantitative aspects of the material and the order in which chapters are covered because chapters do not depend on sequence. For example, some instructors cover project management early, others cover quality or JIT/lean early, etc. The topics covered include both strategic issues and planning/control decisions. Activities such as capacity, designing production process and work methods, inventory management and control, and assuring and improving quality are core issues in organizations. Some of you are or will be employed directly in these areas, while others will have jobs that are indirectly related to operations. So, whether this is your field of study or not, knowledge of operations management will certainly benefit you and the organization you work for.

The advantages of using a Canadian offering for your operations management learning resource are numerous, including:

- A focus on Canadian data for context
- Canadian locations and companies are showcased
- Examples of Canadian organizations and their decisions are highlighted
- Issues important for Canadian instructors and reviewers are addressed
- International examples are framed and reflected from a Canadian perspective

What's New in the Fifth Canadian Edition?

We are excited to introduce a **second Canadian author, Dr. James Cao**, for this edition. Dr. Cao was responsible for revision of chapters 3, 4, 4S, 6S, 8–10, 8S, 10, 15, 15S, 17, and 18. His contributions were instrumental in bringing a fresh perspective to a classic text.

New and Updated Canadian Content. The new Canadian edition features a chapter opener Canadian story, with many of the topics requested by the Canadian reviewers. We've also increased the number of end-of-chapter solved problems, and overall questions and problems. A new set of relevant Canadian readings (OM in Action boxes) and mini-cases fill the textbook/ eBook with real-world applications. There are over **55** new Canadian readings (OM in Action boxes) and mini-cases replacing dated material; there are over **10** other new OM in Actions; all the other OM in Actions and mini-cases have been updated. In addition, there are several new photos and captions, the majority of which are Canadian. These updates provide students with a realistic understanding of Canadian manufacturing and service organizations and the problems they face today.

Tightened Exposition. The fifth Canadian edition of *Operations Management* has been further revised to bring you a tighter, shortened text while maintaining the wide topical coverage and student-friendly style.

Below are some important chapter-by-chapter changes to note:

Chapter	Title	Important Changes/Additions
1	Introduction to Operations Management	Added a problem-solving guide.
5	Strategic Capacity Planning	Break-even point in dollars and multiple items has been added. Several capacity determination problems have been added.
6	Process Design and Facility Layout	IDEF method is deleted. Service blueprinting is added. An in-class assembly line design game, Lego car, is added.
7	Work/Job Design and Measurement	Maynard Operation Sequence Technique (MOST) is added. Random number generation for work sampling is added.
9	Management of Quality	Cost of quality is expanded.
10	Statistical Quality Control	The statistical theory behind control charts is expanded.
11	Supply Chain Management	Rearranged the chapter: moved logistics to the end and e-commerce between purchasing and supplier management. Sections on information systems and transportation management were added.
12	Inventory Management	Expanded warehouse management. Added multi-echelon inventory management.
13	Aggregate Operations Planning and Master Scheduling	Added an example for rough-cut capacity planning.
14	Material Requirements Planning and Enterprise Resource Planning	Added a solved problem: MRP setup guide.
15	Just-in-Time and Lean Production	Added lean services section.
16	Job and Staff Scheduling	Added the assignment model and Hungarian solution method.
17	Project Management	The section on Using Microsoft Project has been updated from the 2010 to the 2013 version.

Features Retained from Previous Edition

Balanced Content. The textbook/eBook strives to achieve a careful balance in the presentation of operations management. Care has been taken to balance definitions and concepts with quantitative, hands-on problems; to balance theoretical material with real-life applications; and to balance classical topics in operations management with new developments that particularly interest students.

Problem-Solving Approach. To further students' hands-on experience of OM, the textbook/eBook contains examples with solutions throughout. At the end of most chapters is a group of solved problems to illustrate concepts and techniques. Some of the end-of-chapter problems have answers at the end of the book.

Easy to Read. The writing style is clear, concise, and student friendly, while maintaining the technical rigour necessary for the subject matter. From step-by-step problem solving, to theoretical exposition, to in-depth mini-cases and readings, the book is designed to promote student understanding of the role of operations management in successful businesses—which, in turn, promotes student success in class.

Pedagogy and Learning Tools

A number of key features in this textbook/eBook have been specifically designed to help introductory students learn, understand, and apply operations concepts and problem-solving techniques. All of these have been carefully developed over five Canadian editions and twelve U.S. editions and have proven successful.

Learning Objectives. Every chapter lists the learning objectives as a short guide to studying the chapter. These objectives are linked to each section and to the questions and problems at the end of the chapter.

Opening Vignettes. Every chapter has an opening vignette that illustrates the importance of the topic, usually highlighting a company.

Figures and Photos. The fifth Canadian edition includes extensive photographs and graphic illustrations to support student study and provide interest and motivation for all types of learners.

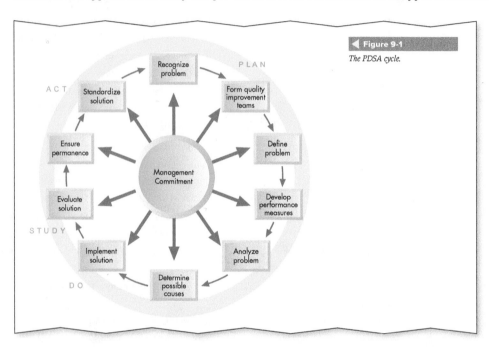

◄ **Figure 9-1**

The PDSA cycle.

OM in Action. Throughout the new edition are readings about applications of OM. These OM in Action boxes highlight important real-world applications, provide examples of operations issues, and/or offer further elaboration of the content. They also provide a basis for classroom discussion and generate interest in the subject matter.

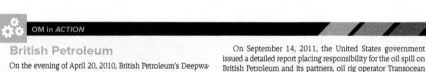

OM in *ACTION*

British Petroleum

On the evening of April 20, 2010, British Petroleum's Deepwater Horizon offshore oil platform was drilling an exploratory well at a record depth of more than 4,000 metres below the ocean surface. At approximately 9:50 p.m., the protective cement barrier around the well suddenly failed, allowing high-pressure methane gas to rise up onto the oil platform. The escaped gas ignited and began a chain reaction that culminated in a series of catastrophic explosions. Eleven men tragically lost their lives that evening, and an unprecedented amount of oil began to pour into the Gulf of Mexico.

Immediately after the oil was released underwater, it rose to the surface of the ocean as a foamy mousse. As the oily mousse approached shorelines, it began to engulf sensitive aquatic ecosystems such as coral reefs, oyster beds, marshes, and mangrove stands that lay in its path. Within hours, hundreds of oil-coated birds, dolphins, sea turtles and other marine animals, some of which are endangered, began to wash ashore. Over the next 87 days, nearly five million barrels of oil were discharged into the Gulf of Mexico, affecting more than 10,000 kilometres of pristine coastline in Texas, Louisiana, Mississippi, Alabama and Florida, resulting in the largest and most devastating oil spill in history.

On September 14, 2011, the United States government issued a detailed report placing responsibility for the oil spill on British Petroleum and its partners, oil rig operator Transocean and contractor Halliburton. The report attributes the central cause of the blowout to the failure of the cement barrier around the well, which allowed the pent-up gas and oil to gush out of the oil platform. BP and its partners failed to perform the cement job in accordance with industry-accepted standards. In addition, they attempted to work faster and more cheaply by cancelling an independent diagnostic test used to test the strength of the cement. The test would have detected the problems with the cement seal at a cost of only C$140,000. In sharp contrast to this modest sum, BP had to ultimately pay out more than C$46 billion in fines, costs to restore the damaged shoreline, and settlements to compensate the millions of people who lived and worked in the region. The tragic loss of life and the subsequent pollution of the Gulf of Mexico were the results of poor management decisions, based on a lack of understanding of the costs of poor quality.

Source: http://docs.lib.noaa.gov/noaa_documents/DWH_IR/reports/dwhfinal.pdf (accessed February 12, 2014).

Examples with Solutions. Throughout the new edition, wherever a quantitative technique is introduced, an example is included to illustrate the application of that technique. These are designed to be easy to follow.

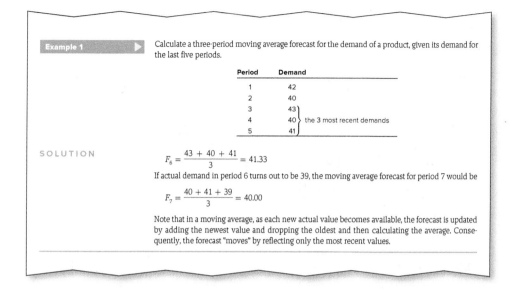

Example 1 ▶ Calculate a three-period moving average forecast for the demand of a product, given its demand for the last five periods.

Period	Demand
1	42
2	40
3	43
4	40 } the 3 most recent demands
5	41

SOLUTION

$$F_6 = \frac{43 + 40 + 41}{3} = 41.33$$

If actual demand in period 6 turns out to be 39, the moving average forecast for period 7 would be

$$F_7 = \frac{40 + 41 + 39}{3} = 40.00$$

Note that in a moving average, as each new actual value becomes available, the forecast is updated by adding the newest value and dropping the oldest and then calculating the average. Consequently, the forecast "moves" by reflecting only the most recent values.

Service Icons. Where **operations management service** topics are addressed in the new edition, a service icon appears in the corresponding margin to flag the attention of both students and instructors.

ervice

Web Links. Web addresses of relevant web sites are highlighted in the margin with a Web icon.

Global Icons. Where a concept or example has international effect, it is flagged with a globe icon.

End-of-Chapter Resources

For student study and review, the following items are provided at the end of each chapter.

Summary. An overview of the material covered in point form.

Key Terms. Key terms are highlighted in the text, repeated in the margin with brief definitions for emphasis.

Solved Problems. At the end of most chapters, solved problems illustrate problem solving and the core concepts of the chapter. These have been carefully prepared to enhance student understanding, as well as to provide additional examples of problem solving.

Problem 1

Forecasts based on averages. Given the following data:

Period	Number of Complaints
1	60
2	65
3	55
4	58
5	64

Prepare a forecast using each of these approaches:

a. The appropriate naïve approach.

b. A three-period moving average.

Excel Spreadsheet Solutions. Where applicable, the solved problems include screen shots of a spreadsheet solution. These are taken from the Excel templates, which can be found on *Connect*.

Discussion and Review Questions. These are intended to serve as a student self-review or as class discussion starters.

Taking Stock, Critical Thinking, Experiential Learning, and Internet Exercises. These activities encourage analytical thinking and help broaden conceptual understanding.

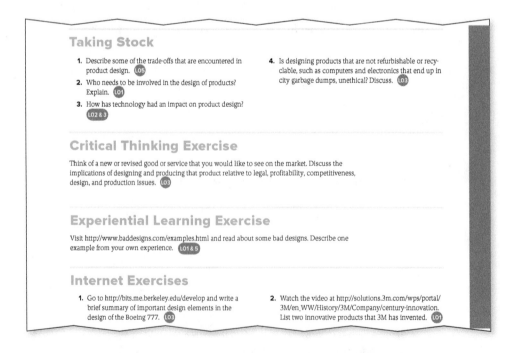

Problems. Most chapters have numerous problems, ranging from simple practice problems that apply techniques to more difficult conceptual problems that provide a challenge and require students to integrate concepts (these are marked with an asterisk).

Operations Tours. These readings give students a descriptive look at operations in action at manufacturing or service organizations. These real-life illustrations show direct application to reinforce the importance of the concepts described in the textbook/eBook.

Mini-Cases. Many chapters include short cases, selected to provide a broader, more integrated thinking opportunity for students.

MINI-CASE http://www.harveys.ca

Open Wide and Say "Ultra"

In fourth place behind McDonald's, A&W, and Burger King, Harvey's, the Canadian quick-service hamburger chain with more than 340 restaurants, needed a new idea in the mid-1990s. Harvey's is part of Cara Operations Ltd., the airline food-services company that also owns the Swiss Chalet chain of restaurants, approximately 100 Air Terminal Restaurants, and Summit Food Services Distributors. Harvey's had had new ideas before (open grill and fresh vegetables, for one), but these had become old hat by 1995. Gabe Tsampalieros, Cara's new president, who was a major franchisee with 60 Harvey's and Swiss Chalet restaurants, started working on the idea in October 1995, and by the following month the mission was clear: "Create Canada's best-selling hamburger." Tsampalieros and Harvey's vice-president planned the launch of the new burger for May 1996.

Harvey's began polling burger lovers across Canada in January 1996, first by telephone and later in focus groups of 8 to

this simple idea to life, Harvey's brought in chef Michael Bonacini, whose upscale Toronto restaurants had been a big hit.

Bonacini's challenge was not only to produce a tasty burger, but also to produce a burger that could handily survive the fast-food process (mechanically produced, frozen for weeks, and shipped around the country). Bonacini produced 12 "taste profiles"—from the bland to the bizarre—and introduced them to the Harvey's executives at a suburban Harvey's training centre. This would be the first in a long series of tasting exercises. (Bonacini thinks he ate 275 bite-sized burgers in a four-month period.)

Each of Harvey's executives tasted a portion of the 12 unlabelled patties and ranked it for "mouth feel," taste, linger, fill factor, and bite. Exotic offerings (Cajun, Oriental, falafel, and so forth) were rejected, leaving three simply seasoned burgers on the short list.

McCormick Canada Inc., Harvey's spice supplier, was employed to determine the final proportions of seasonings and secret ingredients to replicate the taste of Bonacini's samples in a way that could survive the fast-food process. "They

Technology Solutions

McGraw-Hill Connect™ is a Web-based assignment and assessment platform that gives students the means to better connect with their coursework, with their instructors, and with the important concepts that they will need to know for success now and in the future.

With Connect, instructors can deliver assignments, quizzes, and tests online. Nearly all the questions from the text are presented in an auto-gradeable format and tied to the text's learning objectives. Instructors can edit existing questions and author entirely new problems. Track individual student performance—by question, assignment, or in relation to the class overall—with detailed grade reports. Integrate grade reports easily with Learning Management Systems (LMS).

By choosing Connect, instructors are providing their students with a powerful tool for improving academic performance and truly mastering course material. Connect allows students to practise important skills at their own pace and on their own schedule. Importantly, students' assessment results and instructors' feedback are all saved online—so students can continually review their progress and plot their course to success.

Connect also provides 24/7 online access to an eBook—an online edition of the text—to aid students in successfully completing their work, wherever and whenever they choose. Our new edition Connect study resources were created by **Robert Shepherd**, *Niagara College*.

Key Features

Simple Assignment Management

With Connect, creating assignments is easier than ever, so you can spend more time teaching and less time managing.

- Create and deliver assignments easily with selectable end-of-chapter questions and test bank material to assign online.
- Streamline lesson planning, student progress reporting, and assignment grading to make classroom management more efficient than ever.
- Go paperless with the eBook and online submission and grading of student assignments.

Smart Grading

When it comes to studying, time is precious. Connect helps students learn more efficiently by providing feedback and practice material when they need it, where they need it.

- Automatically score assignments, giving students immediate feedback on their work and side-by-side comparisons with correct answers.
- Access and review each response; manually change grades or leave comments for students to review.
- Reinforce classroom concepts with practice tests and instant quizzes.

Instructor Library

The Connect Instructor Library is your course creation hub. It provides all the critical resources you'll need to build your course, just how you want to teach it.

- Assign eBook readings and draw from a rich collection of textbook/eBook/eBook-specific assignments.
- View assignments and resources created for past sections.
- Post your own resources for students to use.
- Access instructor resources:
  - **Instructor's Manual.** Prepared by the authors, the instructor's manual includes a brief description of the McGraw-Hill OM video series, "teaching notes" for each chapter and supplement, complete solutions to all text problems, mini-cases, and cases.
  - **Computerized Test Bank.** Prepared by **Paul Callaghan,** *Acadia University*, the computerized test bank includes over 2,000 questions and problems for exams. The computerized test bank is available through EZ Test Online—a flexible and easy-to-use electronic testing program—which allows instructors to create tests from book-specific items. EZ Test accommodates a wide range of question types and allows instructors to add their own questions. Test items are also available in Word format (rich text format). For secure online testing, exams created in EZ Test can be exported to WebCT and Blackboard. EZ Test Online is supported at www.mhhe.com/eztest where users can download a Quick Start Guide, access FAQs, or log a ticket for help with specific issues.
  - **Microsoft® PowerPoint® Lecture Slides.** Prepared by **Laurel Donaldson,** *Douglas College*, the PowerPoint slides draw on the highlights of each chapter and provide an opportunity for the instructor to emphasize the most relevant visuals in class discussions.
  - **Data files and Excel templates.**
  - **Video Library.** The MH OM Video Series includes professionally developed videos showing students real applications of key manufacturing and service topics. Each video contains plant tours to help students see how companies are using operations management concepts and techniques to be productive and competitive.
  - **The OM Centre.** The OM Centre, edited and maintained by Byron Finch, provides additional operations management resources for both students and instructors. Consider this as your site for pedagogical support or reference and for students seeking current OM information. Among its features, the site covers OM resources by topic, contains links to the "top 50" company tours, offers Internet-published articles and business news, and lists OM publications and organizations.

eBook

Connect reinvents the textbook learning experience for the modern student. Every Connect subject area is seamlessly integrated with Connect eBooks, which are designed to keep students focused on the concepts key to their success.

- Provide students with a Connect eBook, allowing for anytime, anywhere access to the textbook/eBook.

- Merge media, animation, and assessments with the text's narrative to engage students and improve learning and retention.
- Pinpoint and connect key concepts in a snap using the powerful eBook search engine.
- Manage notes, highlights and bookmarks in one place for simple, comprehensive review.

LearnSmart

LEARNSMART®

No two students are alike. Why should their learning paths be? LearnSmart uses revolutionary adaptive technology to build a learning experience unique to each student's individual needs. It starts by identifying the topics a student knows and does not know. As the student progresses, LearnSmart adapts and adjusts the content based on his or her individual strengths, weaknesses, and confidence, ensuring that every minute spent studying with LearnSmart is the most efficient and productive study time possible.

SmartBook

SMARTBOOK™

As the first and only adaptive reading experience, SmartBook is changing the way students read and learn. SmartBook creates a personalized reading experience by highlighting the most important concepts a student needs to learn at that moment in time. As a student engages with Smart-Book, the reading experience continuously adapts by highlighting content based on what each student knows and doesn't know. This ensures that he or she is focused on the content needed to close specific knowledge gaps, while it simultaneously promotes long-term learning.

Connect Insight

connect INSIGHT

New to the Fifth Canadian Edition of Stevenson! Visualized data tailored to your needs as an instructor makes it possible to quickly confirm early signals of success, or identify early warning signs regarding student performance or concept mastery—even while on the go.

Superior Learning Solutions and Support

The McGraw-Hill Ryerson team is ready to help you assess and integrate any of our products, technology, and services into your course for optimal teaching and learning performance. Whether it's helping your students improve their grades, or putting your entire course online, the McGraw-Hill Ryerson team is here to help you do it. Contact your Learning Solutions Consultant today to learn how to maximize all of McGraw-Hill Ryerson's resources!

For more information on the latest technology and Learning Solutions offered by McGraw-Hill Ryerson and its partners, please visit us online: **www.mheducation.ca/he/solutions.**

McGraw-Hill Ryerson | **Solutions that make a difference. Technology that fits.**

| **MH-Campus** | **Connect** | **LearnSmart** | **Tegrity** | **Custom** |
| LMS Integration | Course Management | Adaptive Learning | Lecture Capture | Print & Digital |

Acknowledgements

We gratefully acknowledge the input of reviewers and contributors who so vitally helped to shape the fifth Canadian edition, including:

Mohammed Fazle Baki,
University of Windsor

Paul Callaghan,
F.C. Manning School of
    Business

Kelly Halliday,
Georgian College

Burchell C. Hanson,
Humber College

Elkafi Hassini,
McMaster University

Shanling Li,
McGill University

Janet Porter,
Humber College

Raul Valverde,
Concordia University

Navneet Vidyarthi,
Concordia University

John H. Walker,
Brock University

We would like to thank the McGraw-Hill Ryerson staff, including Senior Product Manager, Kimberley Veevers; Product Developer, Erin Catto; Supervising Editor, Jessica Barnoski; and freelance Copy Editor, Karen Rolfe for their excellent work.

Mehran Hojati
James Cao
William J. Stevenson

Part 1

CHAPTER 1

Introduction to Operations Management

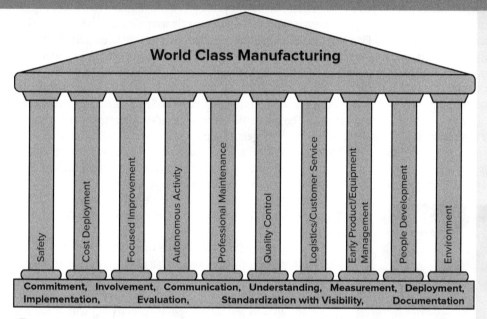

World Class Manufacturing

Safety | Cost Deployment | Focused Improvement | Autonomous Activity | Professional Maintenance | Quality Control | Logistics/Customer Service | Early Product/Equipment Management | People Development | Environment

Commitment, Involvement, Communication, Understanding, Measurement, Deployment, Implementation, Evaluation, Standardization with Visibility, Documentation

Chapter 1 introduces operations management. It describes the nature and scope of operations management and why it is important, how it relates to other functions of the organization, contents of the book, production of goods versus performance of services, the operations manager's job, approaches to decision-making, a brief history of operations management, and major trends that affect operations.

Chapter 2 discusses operations management in a broader context, and presents the issues of competition, strategic planning, and productivity.

Learning Objectives

After completing this chapter, you should be able to:

LO1 Define the term *operations management* and identify operations management jobs.

LO2 Identify the three major functional areas of organizations and describe how they interrelate.

LO3 Describe the scope of operations management and provide an overview of this book, including differentiating between design and planning/control decisions.

LO4 Compare goods and services.

LO5 Discuss the operations manager's job.

LO6 Describe the key aspects of operations management decision making.

LO7 Briefly describe the historical evolution of operations management.

LO8 Identify some of the major trends that affect operations management.

World Class Manufacturing (WCM) is closely related to just-in-time (JIT) manufacturing, total quality management (TQM), total productive maintenance (TPM), and total industrial engineering (TIE). WCM was developed by Fiat Group and Professor Yamashina of Kyoto University. JIT is based on the Toyota Production System and aims to produce components and products only as needed, thus reducing inventories. TQM involves all levels of personnel in an organization in quality assurance and statistical quality control including root-cause analysis. TPM is the use of both operator (called autonomous maintenance) and maintenance technicians (called professional maintenance) to reduce machine downtimes. TIE is the use of industrial engineering to reduce worker injuries and increase productivity. The power of WCM comes from employee involvement and teams.

Fiat started implementation of WCM at Case New Holland (now CNH Industrial) in 2008 and at Chrysler Group soon after becoming the majority shareholder in 2009.

The progress of a plant toward perfection (zero injuries, zero waste/loss/defects/breakdowns, and zero inventories) is measured by 10 technical criteria (called technical pillars) and 10 managerial criteria (these are displayed on the diagram on the previous page). Cost Deployment is costing each loss/waste, and Focused Improvement is selecting the most costly waste/loss to study and eliminate (according to Deming's Plan-Do-Check-Act continuous improvement method). Early Equipment Management is designing machines that are easy to run and reliable. People Development involves measuring skill level of employees and training them as required. This is usually done by supervisors/managers. Chrysler (together with the UAW union) even has a WCM Academy that offers hands-on fun exercises to develop advanced skills in its employees. Setting standards and standard methods is also a major part of WCM. The managerial criteria includes deployment and alignment of goals from plant manager down to area managers, supervisors, and workers. Performance is measured using Key Performance Indicators (KPI) which include weekly measures for safety, quality, absenteeism, suggestions per employee, delivery, manufacturing hours, inventory, etc. The KPIs are regularly communicated to employees using various types of displays and boards in the plant.

Many other companies have adopted WCM, including Lucerne Foods, Magna International, Otis Elevator, Michelin, Celestica, and ArcelorMittal.

CNH Industrial Saskatoon is the only CNH Industrial plant in Canada. It produces planters, headers, air carts, and other equipment for the agriculture division of CNH Industrial, Case IH, and New Holland Agriculture. Over 70 percent of its products are sold in the United States. In order to remain competitive, including with other CNH Industrial plants in the United States, the Saskatoon plant started to implement WCM in 2009. Since then there has been constant improvement in its WCM score. The Saskatoon plant's score ranks them No. 7 in the CNH Industrial family which is comprised of 58 plants worldwide practicing WCM. In five years, its productivity is up approximately 30 percent and it has had no lost-time injury for 3 million hours.

 ## Introduction

operations management
The management of activities and resources that create goods and/or provide services.

Operations management is the management of activities and resources that create goods and/or provide services.

We use an airline to illustrate the activities and resources involved. The resources include staff, airplanes, airport facilities, and maintenance facilities, sometimes spread out over a wide territory. Most of the activities performed by management and administrative employees fall into the realm of operations management:

Forecasting things such as seat demand for flights, the growth in air travel, and weather and landing conditions.

Capacity planning such as deciding the number of planes and where to use them.

Scheduling of planes for flights and for routine maintenance; scheduling of pilots and flight attendants; and scheduling of ground crews, counter staff, and baggage handlers.

Managing inventories of items such as food and beverages and spare parts.

Assuring quality, essential in flying and maintenance operations, where the emphasis is on safety. It is also important in dealing with customers at ticket counters and check-in, and during telephone and electronic reservations and in-flight service, where the emphasis is on efficiency and courtesy.

Employee motivation and training in all phases of operations.

Location of facilities according to top managers' decisions on which cities to provide service for, where to locate maintenance facilities, and where to locate major and minor hubs.

Buying materials such as fuel, food, and spare parts, and buying aircraft and maintaining it.

Now consider a bicycle factory. This might be primarily an *assembly* operation: buying components such as frames, tires, wheels, gears, and other items from suppliers, and then assembling bicycles. The factory might also do some of the *fabrication* work itself (forming frames, making the gears and chains) and buy mainly raw materials and a few parts and materials such as paint, nuts and bolts, and tires. Among the key operations management activities in either case are deciding on the style of bicycle to produce and how many, deciding which components to make and which to buy, scheduling production, ordering parts and materials, purchasing new equipment to replace old or worn-out equipment, maintaining equipment, motivating workers, and ensuring that quality standards are met.

Obviously, an airline and a bicycle factory are completely different types of operations. One is a service operation, the other a producer of goods. Nonetheless, these two operations have much in common. Both involve scheduling of activities, motivating employees, ordering and managing supplies, selecting and maintaining equipment, and satisfying quality standards. And in both businesses, the success of the business depends on planning.

Many companies use operations management strategies, tactics, and actions in order to improve their efficiency and effectiveness. **Efficiency** refers to operating at minimum cost and time, whereas **effectiveness** refers to achieving the intended goals (quality and timeliness). This text contains many practical and real-life examples of operations management in the form of chapter opener, photo with caption, reading in the form of OM in Action, mini-case, problem, and tour. For example, Porter Airlines' operations strategy (Ch 2), Draganfly's product design (Ch 4), Oil Sands capacity planning (Ch 5), Lavergne's process design (Ch 6), UPS's work method design (Ch 7), Toyota's quality problems (Ch 9), Grower Direct's supply chain (Ch 11), Federated Cooperatives' inventory management (Ch 12), Future Shop's workforce planning (Ch 13), Kitchen Partners' material requirements planning (Ch 14), and Sivaco Wires' scheduling (Ch 16).

efficiency Operating at minimum cost and time.

effectiveness Achieving quality and timeliness.

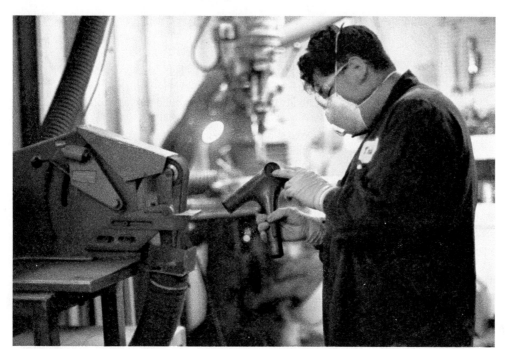

A worker is making the bottom bracket lug for a Trek OCLV carbon road bike at Trek Bicycle Company. Trek is a world leader in bicycle products and accessories, with 1,500 employees worldwide. Designers and engineers incorporate the most advanced technology into Trek products, resulting in award-winning bikes and components.

Two Operations Management Job Ads

Manufacturing Operations Manager

London (ON)

Salary: Yearly: min. $80,000 max. $100,000 for 40.0 hours per week

Education: Completion of college/CEGEP/vocational or technical training

Experience: 5 years or more

Staff Responsibility: 21–50

Budgetary Responsibility: $500,001–$1,500,000

Type of Industry: Chemical

Specific Skills: Plan, organize, direct and control daily operations; Evaluate efficiency of production; Determine adequacy of personnel, equipment and technologies used for operations; Maintain inventory; Prepare work schedules; Schedule and oversee the maintenance of plant equipment; Plan and manage budgets; Direct quality control inspections; Develop production reporting procedures; Oversee the analysis of data and information; Analyze cost and quality data

Additional Skills: Train staff; Arrange training for staff; Conduct performance reviews; Establish and implement safe work practices and procedures

Work Conditions and Physical Capabilities: Fast-paced environment; Work under pressure; Tight deadlines; Attention to detail; Large workload

Other Information: 5+ yrs exp. as Operations Manager for large-scale Silicon products manufacturer.

Inventory Team Lead

Location: Calgary, Alberta

JOB OVERVIEW: As the Inventory Team Lead, you will lead a team of Inventory Analysts while managing and optimizing composition and replenishment of a portion of inventory held at all operating locations using standard SAP based processes and tools.

KEY ACCOUNTABILITIES

- Manage staff and participate in setting Inventory Management function objectives
- Apply advanced SAP knowledge to execute complex tasks in daily work and makes professional judgment based on industry standards, internal guidelines, and best practices
- Analyze business plans and utilize inventory forecasting and modelling techniques to set inventory targets and control levels, develop short-term supply plans, and determine the impact of inventory control issues on service levels
- Lead the analysis of inventory status reports and develop inventory performance plan and strategies utilizing total cost of ownership analysis including, but not limited to, inventory levels, inventory turns, Critical Spare Parts Management (CSPM), and fill rates
- Assess risk, identify trends and opportunities, and make recommendations to develop contingency plans and improve (CSPM) processes, policies, and procedures
- Communicate with internal and external stakeholders on day-to-day inventory management and CSPM issues to initiate stock purchase and disposal processes, and to align inventory management strategies with other company initiatives
- Consult with senior specialists on complex issues and resolve or escalate Inventory Management issues
- Proactively recommend ways to improve Inventory Management activities
- Identify issues in standards, methods and tools for analysis and control of inventory
- Participate in regular Inventory Management, Material Management and Logistics meetings to evaluate business unit requirements and expectations, and evaluate process and performance optimization opportunities

REQUIRED QUALIFICATIONS

Education and Experience:

- 5+ years of experience in Supply Chain Management with increasing levels of responsibility
- Post-secondary business or Supply Chain and Operations Management degree/accreditation
- SAP Inventory Management experience required
- Inventory modelling and forecasting experience required
- Oil & Gas, Mining or Utilities industry experience preferred
- Supervisory experience preferred

Skills and Knowledge:

- Strong analytical skills required
- Ability to be adaptable and build trust and confidence in colleagues and customers preferred
- Solid experience around Inventory Management including Critical Spare Parts Management, Supply/Demand Planning and Inventory Modelling and forecasting is required
- Possess a strong knowledge in ERP (SAP preferred), Spend Analysis, Business Performance Management (KPIs), as well as Critical Spare Parts Management
- Good understanding on SCM Development, Sourcing Strategy, Supplier Integration, Category Management, Total Cost of Ownership (TCO) and Reverse Logistics is preferred

Working Conditions: Office environment and infrequent business travel will be required to operating locations and third parties.

Why Study Operations Management?

There are a number of good reasons. First, because a large percentage of a company's expenses occur in the operations area, such as purchasing materials and workforce salaries, more efficient operations—even a small reduction in operations costs—can result in large increases in profits. Second, a number of management jobs are in operations management—including related areas such as purchasing, quality assurance, production planning and control, scheduling, logistics, inventory management, and many more (see the "Two Operations Management Job Ads" OM in Action). Third, activities in all the other areas of organizations, such as finance, accounting, human resources, management information systems (MIS), and marketing are all interrelated with operations management activities. So it is essential for people who work in these areas to have a basic understanding of operations management.

Careers in Operations Management

If you are thinking of a career in operations management, you can obtain relevant information from one or more of the following associations.

- Supply Chain Management Association (SCMA)
- Canadian Institute of Traffic and Transportation (CITT)
- Canadian Supply Chain Sector Council (CSCSC)
- American Production and Inventory Control Society (APICS)
- American Society for Quality (ASQ)
- Project Management Institute (PMI)

Most of these offer certification programs and a job bank.

http://www.scmanational.ca
http://www.citt.ca
http://www.supplychaincanada.org
http://www.apics.org
http://www.asq.org
http://www.pmi.org

Functions within Organizations

Organizations are formed to pursue goals that are achieved more efficiently and effectively by the concerted efforts of a group of people rather than by individuals working alone. Organizations are devoted to producing goods and/or providing services. They may be for profit (i.e., businesses) or nonprofit (e.g., hospitals). Their goals, goods, and services may be similar or quite different. Nonetheless, their functions and the way they operate are similar.

A typical organization has three basic functions: operations, finance, and marketing (see Figure 1-1). These three functions, and other supporting functions, perform different but related activities necessary for the organization. The functions must interact to achieve the goals and objectives of the organization, and each makes an important contribution. For instance, unless operations and marketing work together, marketing may promote goods or services that operations cannot profitably deliver, or operations may turn out goods or services for which there is no demand. Similarly, unless finance and operations work closely, funds for materials, building expansion, and new equipment may not be available when needed.

Let's take a closer look at these functions.

Figure 1-1

The three basic functions of an organization and flows between them.

Operations

The operations function manages all the activities *directly* related to producing goods or providing services. Hence, it exists both in manufacturing operations, which is *goods oriented*, and in industries such as health care, transportation, restaurant, and retailing, which are *service oriented* (see Table 1-1).

Industries	Examples
Goods producing	Farming, mining, construction, manufacturing
Services	Warehousing, trucking, airlines
	Retailing, wholesaling, banking
	Films, radio, television
	Telephone

The operations function is the core of most organizations; it is responsible for the creation of an organization's goods or services. Inputs are used to obtain finished goods or services using one or more *transformation/conversion process(es)*. A process is a sequence of activities/operations, e.g., cutting, welding, and assembly. To ensure that the desired outputs are obtained, measurements are taken at various points (*feedback*) and then compared with previously established standards to determine whether corrective action is needed (*control*). Figure 1-2 shows the conversion process. Table 1-2 provides two examples of inputs, transformation process, and outputs.

Figure 1-2 ▶

The operations function involves the conversion of inputs into outputs.

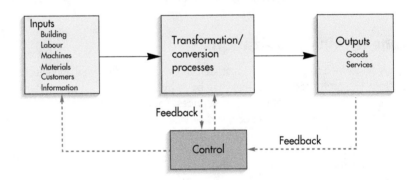

Table 1-2 ▶

Illustrations of the transformation process.

Food Processor	Inputs	Process	Output
	Raw vegetables	Cleaning	Canned vegetables
	Metal sheets	Making cans	
	Water	Cutting	
	Energy	Cooking	
	Labour	Packing	
	Building	Labelling	
	Equipment		
Hospital	**Inputs**	**Process**	**Output**
	Sick patients, doctors, nurses	Examination	Healthy patients
	Building	Surgery	
	Medical supplies & drugs	Monitoring	
	Equipment	Medication	
	Laboratories	Therapy	

It is important to note that goods and services often occur jointly. For example, having the oil changed in your car is a service, but the new oil is a good. Similarly, house painting is a service, but the paint is a good. The goods–service package is a continuum. It can range from primarily goods with little service to primarily service with few goods (see Figure 1-3).

Figure 1-3

The goods–service continuum.

The essence of the operations function is to *add value* during the transformation process: **Value added** is the term used to describe the difference between the cost of inputs and the value or price of outputs. In nonprofit organizations, the value of outputs (e.g., highway construction, police and fire protection) is their value to society; the greater the value added, the greater the efficiency of these operations. In for-profit organizations, the value of outputs is measured by the prices that customers are willing to pay for those goods or services. Companies use the money generated by value added for research and development, investment in new facilities and equipment, workers' salaries, and owners' *profits*. Consequently, the greater the value added, the greater the amount of funds available for these purposes.

value added The difference between the cost of inputs and the value or price of outputs.

One way that organizations attempt to become more productive (i.e., make more output with the same or fewer inputs) is to critically examine whether any of their activities adds value. Those that do not add value are wasteful. Eliminating or improving such wastes decreases the cost of inputs or transformation, thereby increasing the value added. For instance, a company may discover that it is producing an item much earlier than the scheduled delivery date to a customer, thus requiring the storage of the item in a warehouse until delivery. In effect, additional costs are incurred by storing the item without adding to the value of the item. Reducing storage time would reduce the transformation cost and, hence, increase the value added. A similar comment applies for receiving raw material/parts too early. This is the concept called just-in-time (more in Chapter 15). Obviously, working with suppliers and customers can lead to increased productivity for all sides. This is called supply chain management (more in Chapter 11).

Finance

The finance function performs activities related to securing funds at favourable prices and allocating those funds throughout the organization. Finance and operations management personnel cooperate by exchanging information and expertise in activities such as:

1. *Provision of funds.* The necessary funding of operations and the amount and timing of funding can be important and even critical when funds are tight. Careful planning can help avoid cash flow problems. Most for-profit companies obtain the majority of their funds through the revenues generated by sales of their goods and services.

2. *Economic analysis of capital investment proposals.* Evaluation of alternative investments in plant and equipment requires inputs from both operations and finance people.

Marketing

Marketing is responsible for assessing customer wants and needs, and for communicating those needs and feedback to operations and to product design (usually engineers). That is, operations needs information about demand so that it can plan accordingly (i.e., purchase materials and schedule production), while product design people need information that relates to improving current goods and services, and designing new ones. Marketing, design, and production must work closely together to successfully implement design changes and to develop and produce new products. One important piece of information marketing needs from operations is the production **lead time** in order to give customers realistic estimates of how long it will take to fill their orders.

Thus, marketing, operations, and finance must interface on product and process design, forecasting, setting realistic schedules, and quality decisions.

lead time The time between ordering a good or service and receiving it.

Other Functions

There are many other supporting functions that interface with operations (see Figure 1-4).

Accounting supplies information to management on costs of labour, materials, and overhead, and provides reports on items such as scrap, downtime, and inventories. Accounting includes accounts payable and accounts receivable. Accountants gather the information needed for financial statements as well.

Management information systems (MIS) is concerned with providing management with the information it needs to effectively manage. This occurs through computer and communication systems (hardware and software) that capture relevant information and prepare reports.

Purchasing has responsibility for procurement of materials, supplies, equipment, and services. Close contact with operations is necessary to ensure correct quantities and timing of purchases. The purchasing department identifies appropriate suppliers and facilitates close relationships. Purchasing may also be involved in arranging incoming transportation.

The *personnel* or *human resources* department is concerned with recruitment and training of personnel, labour relations, contract negotiations, wage and salary administration, and ensuring the health and safety of employees.

Manufacturing engineering is responsible for the machines and equipment needed in the production process. Also called process engineers, they are mainly trained as mechanical engineers, but other fields such as electrical and chemical may also be needed.

Maintenance and facility management is responsible for the upkeep and repair of equipment, buildings and grounds, and heating and air-conditioning; removing wastes; parking; and perhaps security.

Product design in manufacturing companies is done by design engineers, but in other companies it could be done by people such as architects, scientists, chemists, and chefs. Designers create goods and services from information given to them by marketing people and provide product specifications to operations to make the products.

Logistics involves the transportation of raw material to the plant; storage and warehousing; and transportation of goods to warehouses, retail outlets, or final customers.

Some of these interfaces are elaborated on in later chapters.

Figure 1-4 ▼

Operations interfaces with a number of supporting functions.

LO3 The Scope of Operations Management

We have already noted that operations management is responsible for the creation of goods and services. This encompasses acquisition of resources and the conversion of raw material into outputs using one or more transformation processes. This involves designing, planning, scheduling, executing, and controlling the activities/operations that make up the processes.

A primary function of operations management is decision making. Certain decisions affect the *design* of the system, and others are *planning/control*. Design decisions are usually strategic and long term (1–5 years ahead), whereas planning decisions are tactical and medium term (1–12 months ahead), and control decisions (including scheduling and execution) are short term (1–12 weeks ahead).

Design involves product design, production capacity, the location of facilities, arrangement of departments and placement of equipment within physical structures (i.e., layout), acquisition of equipment, and work/job design. Planning/control *activities* include quality planning and control, inventory planning and control, production planning, scheduling, and project management. Operations management is more involved in day-to-day operating decisions and planning than design. However, operations management has a vital stake in design because *design determines limitations of operations*. For example, costs, space, and quality are affected by design. Even though operations management is not solely responsible for design, it can provide information that will have a bearing on design. Table 1-3 provides additional details on the design and planning/control decisions, and indicates in which chapter each topic is discussed.

One factor that influences these decisions is whether the output is a good or a service.

Decision Area	Basic Questions	Chapter
Forecasting	What will the demand be?	3
Design		
Product Design	What do customers want? How can products be designed?	4
Capacity (long term)	How much capacity will be needed? How can the organization best meet capacity requirements?	5
Process design	What processes should the organization use?	6
Layout	What is the best arrangement for departments, machines, and equipment, in terms of work flow?	6
Work design	How to improve work methods? How to measure work?	7
Location	What is a satisfactory location for a facility (factory, warehouse, etc.)?	8
Planning/control		
Quality	How is quality defined? How is quality achieved and improved?	9
Quality control	Are processes performing adequately (i.e., are in control and capable)?	10
Supply chain management	Which supplier to choose? How to transport goods?	11
Inventory management	How much to order? When to reorder?	12
Aggregate planning	How much capacity will be needed over the medium term? How can capacity needs best be met?	13
Material requirements planning	What material, parts, and subassemblies will be needed, and when?	14
Just-in-time	How to manage production so that it is fast and lean?	15
Scheduling	How can jobs best be scheduled? How to schedule staff?	16
Project management	Which activities are the most critical to the success of a project? What resources will be needed, and when will they be needed?	17
Waiting lines	What service capacity is appropriate?	18

◀ **Table 1-3**

Design and planning/control decisions.

Differentiating Production of Goods and Services

Production of goods results in a *tangible output,* such as an automobile, a building, or wheat–anything that we can see or touch. Production includes manufacturing, construction, agriculture, forestry, fisheries, mining, and oil and gas. Among these, manufacturing is the largest sector. Manufacturing produces food and beverage, textile and clothing, wood products and furniture, paper and printing, petroleum, chemicals, plastics, primary metals and nonmetals, fabricated metals and nonmetals, machinery, computer and electronic products, electrical equipment and appliances, and transportation equipment.

Service, on the other hand, implies an *act.* A physician's examination, auto repair, lawn care, and theatre are examples of services. The majority of services fall into these categories: government services (federal, provincial, and municipal), wholesale/retail (clothing, food, appliances, stationery, toys, etc.), finance and insurance (banking, stock brokerage, insurance, etc.), real estate, rental, and leasing, health care (doctors, dentists, hospitals, etc.), professional and technical services (lawyers, accountants, architects, auto mechanics), personal services (laundry, dry cleaning, hair/beauty, lawn care, etc.), business support services (data processing, e-business, advertising, employment agencies, etc.), education (schools, colleges, universities, etc.), hotels and restaurants, information, culture, and recreation, transportation and warehousing, and utilities.

Production of goods and performance of services are often similar in terms of *what* is done but different in terms of *how* it is done. They are similar in that both involve design and planning/control decisions, and decide what size facility is needed, and make decisions on location, scheduling and control of operations, and allocation of scarce resources.

Production of goods and performance of services differ in:

1. Customer contact, use of inventories, and demand variability.
2. Uniformity of input.
3. Labour content of jobs.
4. Uniformity of output.
5. Measurement of productivity.
6. Quality assurance.

Let us consider each of these differences.

1. Often, by its nature, service involves a much higher degree of customer contact. The performance of a service often occurs at the point of consumption. For example, repairing a leaky roof must take place where the roof is, and surgery requires the presence of the patient. On the other hand, goods production allows a separation between production and consumption, so that it may occur away from the consumer. This permits a fair degree of latitude in selecting work methods, assigning jobs, scheduling work, and exercising control over operations. In addition, goods producers can build up inventories of finished goods, enabling them to absorb some of the shocks caused by variable demand. Services, however, cannot build up inventories and are much more sensitive to demand variability–banks and supermarkets alternate between lines of customers waiting for service and idle tellers or cashiers waiting for customers.

2. Services are subject to greater variability of inputs than typical goods producers. Each patient, each lawn, and each auto repair presents a specific problem that often must be diagnosed before it can be remedied. Goods producers often have the ability to carefully control the amount of variability of inputs.

3. Services often require a higher labour content whereas goods production typically can be more capital intensive (i.e., mechanized).

4. Because high mechanization generates products with low variability, goods production tends to be smooth and efficient; service activities sometimes appear to be slow and awkward, and output is more variable. Automated services such as ATMs are an exception to this.

5. Measurement of productivity (i.e., ratio of outputs to inputs) is more straightforward in goods production due to the high degree of uniformity of produced items. In services, variations in demand intensity and in requirements from job to job make productivity measurement considerably more difficult. For example, compare the productivity of two doctors. One may have a large number of routine cases while the other deals with complications, so their productivity appears to differ.

6. Quality assurance is more challenging in services because performance and consumption occur at the same time. In goods production, errors can be corrected before the customer receives the output.

The service indusrty and the goods-producing industry are both important to the economy. However, the service industry has been growing faster and now accounts for more than 78 percent of jobs in Canada. See Figure 1-5.

Figure 1-5

Percentage of total labour force by industry.

Source: Adapted from Statistics Canada CANSIM database, Table 282–0094, various series.

The Operations Manager's Job

The operations manager has the ultimate responsibility for the creation of goods or performance of services. Note that the person performing this job may have a different title. For example, a fast-food chain's restaurant manager is essentially the restaurant's operations manager. At the district level, the district manager is essentially the operations manager, and at the executive level there is usually a VP of operations. In an independent restaurant, the manager also performs finance and marketing activities. Even if a job's title is the operations manager, it may involve other activities such as technical product-specific aspects of production, finance/accounting, project management, engineering, etc.

The kinds of jobs that operations managers oversee vary tremendously from organization to organization, largely because of the different goods or services involved. Thus, managing a banking operation obviously requires a different kind of expertise than managing a steelmaking operation. However, they are both essentially *managerial*. In every case, the operations manager must co-ordinate the use of resources through the management activities of planning, organizing, directing, and controlling. Note that these activities are defined a little differently than in Table 1-3. Examples of the responsibilities of operations managers according to these classifications are given in Table 1-4.

In a survey of operations managers of 114 Canadian companies,[1] the following characteristics were discovered: 87 percent of companies were manufacturers, 80 percent employed under

---

[1] A.S. Sohal et al, "The Roles and Responsibilities of Production/Operations Managers in SMEs: Evidence from Canada," *Technovation* 21, pp. 437–448.

Table 1-4

Responsibilities of operations managers.

Planning	Organizing
Capacity	Degree of centralization
Location	Departments
Mix of products	Subcontracting
Production process	Suppliers
Layout	Staffing
Controlling	**Directing**
Inventory control	Scheduling
Quality control	Issuance of work orders
Production pace	Job assignments
Motivation	Purchasing
Cost control	Logistics

100 employees, average age of the operations manager was 45, 91 percent were men, and 47 percent had a university/college degree. Approximately a third were deficient in business management, accounting/finance, and computer skills. Most started their full-time job in another area and had an average of four jobs before transferring into operations. But, when in operations, they stayed (average OM experience was 10 years). Ninety percent of salaries were between $40,000 and $110,000. Approximately half had total authority over planning, quality, and maintenance, whereas the other half provided major inputs into these decisions. Approximately half would have liked more control over planning decisions. Ninety-five percent were responsible for cost reduction and productivity, 90 percent for work and worker organization, and 85 percent for quality and technology. They spent 25 percent of their time on operations, 18 percent on planning, 12 percent on quality, 11 percent on customer liaison, 8 percent on labour relations, and 8 percent on improvements. Most operations managers were given targets for improvement. A list of job content and satisfaction of respondents is given in Figure 1-6. Most enjoy these challenges, whereas more than half are not happy with the heavy hours of work. Further questions revealed that most are happy with their compensation, work variety, work importance, autonomy, benefits, social interaction, feedback from top management, and advancement opportunity.

Figure 1-6

Level of job satisfaction.

OM in *ACTION*

Seth Beytien

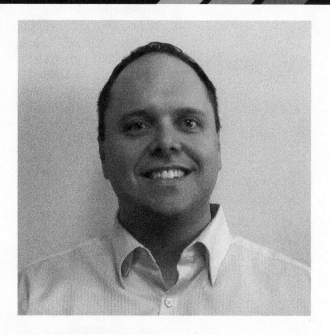

Seth is a graduate of Iowa State University majoring in Operations and Supply Chain Management. After working for a few companies and a consulting firm in process improvement, he joined CNH Industrial in 2011 and later moved to Saskatoon as the Operations Manager of CNH Industrial plant. After two years, Seth was promoted to the plant manager job at the Saskatoon plant.

As the operations manager, Seth was responsible for the manufacturing side of the plant. The three area managers who are responsible for fabrication, welding, and assembly, as well as the maintenance manager, reported to him. Seth, along with the materials manager, the manufacturing engineering manager, and the quality manager reported to the plant manager providing updates on employees and production.

A typical day for Seth began with meetings with staff and managers, discussing issues from the previous day, making sure they won't happen again, and identifying issues (safety, quality, and cost) for the current day. Then, Seth walked through the plant observing and discussing the progress of projects (25–50) with employees in charge. Later in the day, there was another meeting with managers to discuss achievement of daily targets (KPI).

Seth was concerned with the location's turnover of skilled workers due to higher wages offered at the oil patch in Alberta. He participated in monthly meetings about the level of

workforce needed. Also, there were strategic issues to be addressed such as the introduction of new products and continuation of existing products in the plant.

Source: http://www.theomsa.com/events/2013-10.

Operations Managers and Decision Making

 LO6

The chief role of an operations manager is that of a decision maker. In this capacity, the operations manager exerts considerable influence over the degree to which the goals and objectives of the organization are realized.

Throughout this book, you will encounter the broad range of decisions that operations managers must make, and you will be introduced to the tools necessary to handle those decisions. This section describes general approaches to decision making, including the use of models, quantitative approaches, analysis of trade-offs, the systems approach, establishing priorities, and ethics.

Models

A **model** is an abstraction of reality, a simplified representation of something. For example, a child's toy car is a physical model of a real automobile. Mathematical models represent important characteristics of the object by mathematical symbols and their relationship by mathematical equations and inequalities. Schematic models are graphs, charts, and drawings. Common statistical models include Normal distribution and regression equations.

model An abstraction of reality; a simplified representation of something.

Real life involves an overwhelming amount of detail, much of which is irrelevant for any particular problem. Models ignore the unimportant details so that attention can be concentrated on the most important aspects of a situation, thus increasing the opportunity to understand a problem and find its solution.

Because mathematical, schematic, and statistical models play a significant role in operations management decision making, they are heavily integrated into the material of this textbook. For each model, try to learn (1) its purpose, (2) how it is used to generate results, (3) how these results are interpreted and used, and (4) what assumptions and limitations apply.

Quantitative Techniques

Quantitative techniques to problem solving often embody an attempt to obtain optimal solutions to the mathematical models of managerial problems. This is sometimes done by solving a set of equations. A popular technique is *linear programming*, which is widely used for optimal allocation of scarce resources. *Queuing techniques* are useful for analyzing situations in which waiting lines form. *Inventory techniques* are widely used to control inventories. *Project scheduling techniques* such as PERT (program evaluation and review technique) are useful for planning, co-ordinating, and controlling large-scale projects. *Forecasting techniques* are widely used in forecasting demand. *Statistical techniques* are used in many areas of decision making, including quality control.

Many of these quantitative techniques require computers and are time consuming. In contrast, a heuristic approach is a quick way to find a good solution. For example, in designing the work of an assembly-line worker, a good heuristic is to choose the longest possible (eligible and will-fit) activity first. For many decisions, a heuristic may be the only practical solution technique.

Analysis of Trade-Offs

One type of heuristic approach is *trade-off* analysis. For example, (a) in deciding on the amount of inventory to stock, the manager may take into account the trade-off between the increased level of customer service (availability) that the additional inventory would yield and the increased costs required to stock that inventory; (b) in selecting a piece of equipment, a manager may evaluate the merits of extra features relative to the cost of those extra features; (c) in the scheduling of overtime to increase output, the manager may weigh the value of the increased output against the higher costs of overtime.

Throughout this textbook you will be presented with solution methods that reflect these kinds of trade-offs. Managers sometimes deal with these decisions by listing the advantages and disadvantages—the pros and cons—of a course of action to better understand the consequences of the decisions they must make. In some instances, managers add weights to the items on their list that reflect the relative importance of various factors. This can help them "net out" the potential impacts of the trade-offs on their decision. An example of this is the factor-rating approach described in Chapter 8 on location planning and analysis.

The Systems Approach

system A set of interrelated parts that must work together.

A **system** is a set of interrelated parts that must work together. The systems approach emphasizes interrelationships among these parts. Hence, from a systems viewpoint, the output and objectives of the organization as a whole take precedence over those of any one department.

The systems approach is essential whenever something is being designed, redesigned, implemented, improved, or otherwise changed. It is important to take into account the impact on all parts of the system. For example, to investigate if the upcoming model of a vehicle will have anti-lock brakes, a designer must take into account how customers will view the change, instructions for using the brakes, chances for misuse, the cost of producing the new brakes, and procedures for installing, repairing, and recycling worn-out brakes. In addition, workers will need training to make and/or assemble the brakes, production scheduling may change, inventory procedures may have to change, quality standards will have to be established, advertising must be informed of the new features, and parts suppliers must be selected.

Establishing Priorities

Pareto phenomenon A few factors account for a high percentage of results achieved.

In virtually every situation, managers discover that certain elements are more important than others. Recognizing this fact of life enables the managers to direct their efforts to where they will do the most good and to avoid wasting time and energy on insignificant elements. This is referred to as the **Pareto phenomenon**, which means some things (a few) will be very important for achieving an objective or solving a problem, and other things (many) will not. This is also known as 80–20 rule, meaning that approximately 20 percent of factors will impact approximately 80 percent of the results achieved. The implication is that a manager should examine each situation, searching for the few factors that will have the greatest impact, and give them the highest priority. This is one of the most important and pervasive concepts in operations management. In fact, this concept can be applied to all decision making, both professional and personal.

Ethics

Operations managers, like all managers, have the responsibility to make ethical decisions. Ethical issues arise in:

- Worker safety: providing adequate training, maintaining equipment in good working condition, maintaining a safe working environment.
- Product safety: providing products that minimize the risk of injury to users or damage to property or the environment.
- The environment: not doing things that will harm the environment.
- Closing facilities: taking into account the impact on the community, and honouring commitments that have been made.

In making decisions, managers must consider how their decisions will affect shareholders, employees, customers, suppliers, the community at large, and the environment. Finding solutions that will be in the best interest of all of these stakeholders is not always easy, but it is a goal that all operations managers should strive to achieve.

The Historical Evolution of Operations Management

In the earliest days, goods were produced using **craft production**: highly skilled workers using simple, flexible tools produced goods according to customer specification. Goods were produced in small shops by craftsmen and their apprentices. Under that system, it was common for one person to be responsible for making a product, such as a horse-drawn wagon or a piece of furniture, from start to finish. Only simple tools were available; the machines that we use today had not been invented.

craft production Highly skilled workers using simple, flexible tools to produce small quantities of customized goods.

Craft production had major shortcomings. Because products were made by skilled craftsmen who custom-fitted parts, production was slow and costly. And when parts failed, the replacements also had to be custom made, which was also slow and costly. Another shortcoming was that production costs did not decrease as volume increased; there were no *economies of scale*, which would have provided a major incentive for expansion.

Prior to the 1700s, business activities in Canada were limited to fishing and fur trade. Under a practice called *mercantilism*, raw materials were exported to Europe for further processing and manufacturing. Companies such as the Hudson's Bay Company imported British-made goods to trade with local populations. All manufactured products came from Europe. The modern factory system has its roots in the Industrial Revolution.

The Industrial Revolution

The Industrial Revolution began in the 1770s in England and spread to the rest of Europe and to North America during the nineteenth century. A number of innovations changed production forever by substituting machine power for human or animal power. Perhaps the most significant of these was the steam engine, made practical by James Watt around 1769, because it provided a source of power to operate machines in factories. The spinning jenny (1770) and power loom (1785) revolutionized the textile industry. Machines, made of iron, replaced simple wooden machines. Two concepts assisted in large-scale production: division of labour and interchangeable parts.

Division of labour, which Adam Smith wrote about in *The Wealth of Nations* (1776), means that the production process is divided up into a series of small tasks and individual workers are assigned to each one of those tasks. Unlike craft production, where each worker was responsible for doing many tasks and thus required skill, with division of labour the tasks were so narrow that virtually no skill was required.

division of labour Breaking up a production process into small tasks so that each worker performs a small portion of the overall job.

The **interchangeable parts** concept is attributed to Eli Whitney, an American inventor who applied the concept to assembling muskets in the late 1700s. The basis for interchangeable parts is to standardize parts so that any part in a batch of parts would fit. This meant that parts did not have to be custom fitted, as they were in craft production. The standardized parts could also be used as replacement parts. The result was a tremendous decrease in assembly time and cost.

interchangeable parts Parts of a product made to such precision that they do not have to be custom fitted.

Soon after their invention in Britain, the iron-making and steam engine technologies were imported into North America. In Canada, a few small mills began operating in the first half of the 1800s. By the second half of the 1800s, canals and railways were built, and timber was being exported.

The discovery of electricity by Edison in the late 1800s allowed replacement of electricity for steam as a power source, improving the efficiency and working environment of factories.

Despite the major changes that were taking place, management theory and practice had not progressed much from early days. What was needed was a systematic approach to management.

Scientific Management

Scientific management was spearheaded by American efficiency engineer and inventor Frederick Taylor. Taylor believed in a "science of management" based on observation, measurement, analysis and improvement of work methods, and economic incentives. He studied work methods in great detail to identify the best method for doing each job.

Taylor's methods emphasized maximizing output. They were not always popular with workers, who sometimes thought the methods were used to unfairly increase output without a corresponding increase in compensation. Certainly some companies did abuse workers in their quest for efficiency. Eventually, the public outcry reached the halls of the U.S. Congress, and hearings were held on the matter. Taylor himself was called to testify in 1911, the same year in which his classic book *The Principles of Scientific Management* was published. The publicity from those hearings actually helped scientific management achieve wide acceptance in industry.

A number of other pioneers also contributed to this movement, including the following:

Frank Gilbreth was an industrial engineer who is often referred to as the father of time and motion study. He developed the principles of motion economy that could be applied to small portions of a task.

Lillian Gilbreth, a psychologist and the wife of Frank Gilbreth, worked with her husband, focusing on the human factor in work. (The Gilbreths were the subject of a classic 1950 film, *Cheaper by the Dozen*, remade in 2003.) Many of her studies in the 1920s dealt with worker fatigue.

Henry Gantt developed a widely used tool for scheduling, called a Gantt chart, a horizontal bar chart.

During the early part of the twentieth century, automobiles were just coming into vogue in North America. Ford's Model T was such a success that the company had trouble keeping up with orders for the cars. In an effort to improve the efficiency of operations, Henry Ford introduced the *moving assembly line*, a type of assembly line in which the car is pulled along the line at a fixed speed while the workers assemble its parts.

Row of "Tin Lizzies," or Model T's, being manufactured on an early Ford assembly line.

Ford's production system is an example of **mass production**, a system of production in which large volumes of standardized goods are produced by low-skilled or semiskilled workers using highly specialized, and often costly, equipment.

The Industrial Revolution and scientific management allowed some industrialization in Canada in the beginning of the twentieth century. These changes allowed for more effective exploitation of Canada's resources, such as minerals and agriculture. Import tariffs encouraged foreign entrepreneurs and companies, mainly Americans, to set up factories and sales offices in Canada; the transfer of technology helped both countries. For example, Massey Ferguson was established and grew as one of the world leaders in agricultural harvesting machinery, and McLaughlin Motor Co. was established in partnership with Buick and later became General Motors of Canada. The United States replaced Britain as the largest trading partner and investor in Canada in 1926.

> **mass production** System in which lower-skilled workers use specialized machinery to produce high volumes of standardized goods.

The Human Relations Movement

Whereas scientific management emphasized the technical aspects of work design, the human relations movement emphasized the importance of workers in work design. There was much emphasis on motivation. During the 1930s, Elton Mayo conducted studies at the Hawthorne division of Western Electric. His studies revealed that in addition to the physical and technical aspects of work, giving special attention to workers is critical for improving productivity. During the 1940s, Abraham Maslow developed motivational theories that Frederick Hertzberg refined in the 1950s. Douglas McGregor added to this in the 1960s. In the 1970s, William Ouchi combined the Japanese approach, with features such as lifetime employment, employee problem solving, and consensus building, and the traditional Western approach that features short-term employment, specialists, and individual decision making and responsibility.

Decision Models and Computers

The factory movement was accompanied by the development of several quantitative models and techniques. F.W. Harris developed one of the first models in 1913: a mathematical model for inventory management. In the 1930s, three coworkers at Bell Telephone Labs—Dodge, Romig, and Shewart—developed statistical procedures for sampling and quality control.

At first, these quantitative models were not widely used in industry. However, the onset of the Second World War changed that. The war generated tremendous pressures on manufacturing output, and specialists from many disciplines combined efforts to achieve advancements in the military and in manufacturing. This area became known as operations research. After the war, efforts to develop and refine quantitative tools for decision making continued, facilitated by the advent of the mainframe computer in 1951. This resulted in decision models for forecasting, production planning (using the linear program of Dantzig), project management, and other areas of operations management.

During the 1960s and 1970s, quantitative techniques were highly regarded (these modelling and solutions for business are called *management science*); in the 1980s, they lost some favour. However, the widespread use of personal computers (invented in the late 1970s by Apple Computers) and user-friendly software in the workplace is causing resurgence in the popularity of these techniques. In 1975, Orlicky proposed Material Requirements Planning (MRP), mainly for assembly operations.

The advent of the computer resulted in its use in machine automation starting in the 1960s. In the middle to late 1980s, network computing began to increase, with applications such as electronic data interchange (EDI) and the ability to instantaneously receive point-of-sale data. This has led to more co-operation with the suppliers in the form of partnering, and formation of supply chains. In the mid-1990s, the Internet began to play a major role in operations, and more and more companies now use enterprise resources planning (ERP) software to co-ordinate their sales, materials management, production planning/manufacturing, and accounting/finance activities. The vast amount of data available now, e.g., customer purchases in a supermarket, have led to popularity of powerful business analytics software that look for unusual patterns and relationships in data. For example, Walmart has discovered that just before a storm, sales of granola bars peak in its affected stores.

The Influence of Japanese Manufacturers

A number of Japanese manufacturers have developed or refined management practices that have increased the productivity of their operations and the quality of their products. This has made

total quality management
Involving every employee in a continual effort to improve quality and satisfy the customers.

lean production System that uses minimal amounts of resources to produce a high volume of high-quality goods with some variety.

them very competitive, sparking interest in their approaches by companies outside Japan. One of their approaches, **total quality management (TQM)**, emphasizes quality and continuous improvement, worker teams and empowerment, and achieving customer satisfaction. A related approach is lean production system and just-in-time (JIT) manufacturing.

Lean production systems use much fewer resources than mass production systems—less space, less inventory, and fewer workers—to produce a comparable amount of output. They use a highly skilled workforce and flexible equipment. In effect, they incorporate advantages of both mass production (high volume, low unit cost) and craft production (high variety and flexibility). And quality is higher than in mass production. Lean production is a broad approach to just-in-time manufacturing. World Class Manufacturing (WCM) is a combination of TQM and JIT with some worker-initiated maintenance (called total productive maintenance) and industrial engineering. WCM is recently being used by the Fiat group, Chrysler, CNH, and others to improve their productivity.

The skilled workers in lean production systems are more involved in maintaining and improving the system than their mass production counterparts. They are taught to stop production if they discover a defect, and to work with other employees to find and correct the cause of the defect so that it won't recur. This results in an increasing level of quality over time, and eliminates the need to inspect and rework at the end of the line.

Because lean production systems operate with lower amounts of inventory, additional emphasis is placed on anticipating when problems might occur *before* they arise, and avoiding those problems through careful planning. Even so, problems still occur at times, and quick resolution is important. Workers participate in both the planning and correction stages. Technical experts are still used, but more as consultants rather than substitutes for workers. The focus is on designing a system so that workers will be able to achieve high levels of quality and quantity.

Compared to workers in traditional systems, much more is expected of workers in lean production systems. They must be able to function in teams, playing active roles in operating and improving the system. Individual creativity is much less important than team success. Responsibilities are also much greater, which can lead to pressure and anxiety not present in traditional systems. Moreover, a flatter organizational structure means career paths are not as steep in lean production organizations. Workers tend to become generalists rather than specialists, another contrast to more traditional organizations.

Unions often oppose conversion from a traditional system to a lean system because they view the added responsibility and multiple tasks as an expansion of job requirements without comparable increases in pay. In addition, workers sometimes complain that the company is the primary beneficiary of employee-generated improvements.

Table 1-5 provides a comparison of craft production, mass production, and lean production. Keep in mind that all three of these systems of production are in existence today.

Table 1-5 ▼

A comparison of craft, mass, and lean production.

	Craft Production	Mass Production	Lean Production
Description	High variety, customized output, with one or a few skilled workers responsible for an entire unit of output.	High volume of standardized output, emphasis on volume. Capitalizes on division of labour, specialized equipment, and interchangeable parts.	Moderate to high volume of output, with more variety than mass production. Less inventory. Emphasis on quality. Employee involvement and teamwork are important.
Examples of goods and services	Home remodelling and landscaping, tailoring, portrait painting, diagnosis and treatment of injuries, surgery.	Sugar, steel, movie theatres, airlines, hotels, mail sorting, paper.	Automobiles and their components, electronics, industrial equipment.
Advantages	Wide range of choice, output tailored to customer needs.	Low cost per unit, requires mostly low-skilled workers.	Flexibility, variety, high quality of goods.
Disadvantages	Slow, requires skilled workers, few economies of scale, high cost, and low standardization.	Rigid system, difficult to accommodate changes in output volume, product design, or process design. Volume may be emphasized at the expense of quality.	No safety nets to offset any system breakdowns, fewer opportunities for employee advancement, more worker stress, requires higher-skilled workers than mass production.

Table 1-6 provides a chronological summary of some of the key developments in the evolution of operations management.

Approximate Date	Contribution/Concept	Originator
1769	Steam engine	James Watt
1776	Division of labour	Adam Smith
1790	Interchangeable parts	Eli Whitney
1911	Principles of scientific management	Frederick W. Taylor
1911	Time and motion study	Frank Gilbreth
1912	Chart for scheduling activities	Henry Gantt
1913	Moving assembly line	Henry Ford
1913	Mathematical model for inventory management	F.W. Harris
1930	Hawthorne studies on worker motivation	Elton Mayo
1935	Statistical procedures for sampling and quality control	H.F. Dodge, H.G. Romig, W. Shewhart
1940	Operations research applications in warfare	Operations research groups
1947	Linear programming	George Dantzig
1951	Commercial digital computers	Sperry Univac
1960s	Computer-aided automation	Numerous
1970s	Personal computers	Apple
1975	Material requirements planning	Joseph Orlicky
1980s	Total quality management and lean production/just-in-time	Quality gurus; Toyota, and Taiichi Ohno
1990s	Internet and e-business, globalization, supply chains, and outsourcing	Numerous
2000s-	Business Analytics, World Class Manufacturing, Sustainability	Numerous

◀ Table 1-6

Historical summary of operations management.

Major Trends

Organizations must constantly monitor current trends and take them into account in their strategies and operations. It appears that the slowdown in the world economy that started in 2008 is coming to an end. The following are current major trends:

1. *The Internet and e-commerce.* The *Internet* has altered the way companies compete in the marketplace. Electronic commerce, or **e-commerce**, involves the use of Internet to buy and sell goods and services. E-commerce has changed the way organizations interact with their customers and their suppliers. It has also resulted in significant efficiencies.

2. *Technology.* Technological advances have led to a vast array of new products and processes. Undoubtedly the computer has had—and will continue to have—the greatest impact on organizations. It has revolutionized the way companies operate. Applications include computer-aided product design, computer numerically controlled machining centres, ERP (enterprise software), and electronic (data) communication.

3. *Globalization.* Global competition, global markets, global supply chains, and global operations are having a growing impact on the strategies and operations of organizations, large and small, around the world. The General Agreement on Tariffs and Trade (GATT) of 1994 and later agreements of the World Trade Organization have reduced the tariffs and subsidies in many countries, expanding world trade. China has become the factory of the world. This has led to long international supply chains and the importance of managing them. The implication is the need for improved efficiency and increased quality.

e-commerce Use of the Internet to buy and sell goods and services.

supply chain A sequence of organizations involved in producing and delivering a product.

4. *Supply chains.* A **supply chain** is the sequence of organizations that are involved in producing and delivering a product. The sequence begins with basic suppliers of raw materials and extends all the way to final consumers. Facilities might include warehouses, factories, distribution centres, and retail outlets.

Figure 1-7 provides an illustration of the bread supply chain: it begins with wheat growing on a farm and ends with a customer buying a loaf of bread in a grocery store. Notice that the value of the product increases as it moves through the supply chain. Obviously, if members of a supply chain work together and coordinate their activities, they can all benefit. This is called supply chain management (see Chapter 11).

Figure 1-7 ▶

A supply chain for bread.

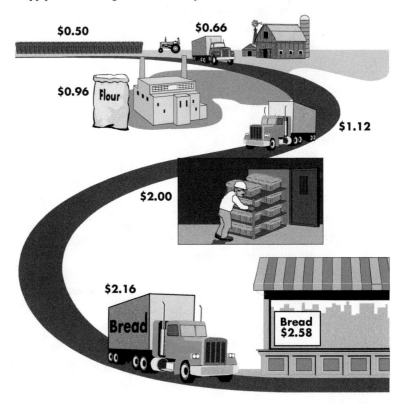

5. *Sustainability.* Concern about global warming and pollution has had an increasing effect on how businesses operate. Governments are imposing stricter environmental regulations. Furthermore, businesses are coming under increasing customer pressure to reduce their carbon footprint. Sustainability refers to reduced use of resources and reduced harm to the environment so that future human existence is not threatened. Activities that are most affected are product design, purchasing and supply chain management, production process, and disaster preparation and response. Note that purchasing of goods from overseas increases not only transportation costs, but also fuel consumption and carbon released into the atmosphere. Green initiatives include reducing packaging, materials, water and energy use, and buying locally. Other initiatives include refurbishing used equipment (e.g., printers and copiers) and recycling.

These trends are having a major influence on organizations, as well as on operations. Their impact on operations management is discussed throughout the book.

Summary

- Operations management is responsible for planning and co-ordinating the use of the organization's resources to convert inputs into outputs.

- The operations function is one of three primary functions of organizations; the other two are marketing and finance. The operations function is present in both service- and goods-producing organizations.

- Operations decisions involve design decisions and planning/control decisions. Design decisions relate to capacity planning, product design, process design, layout of facilities, work design, and selecting locations for facilities. Planning/control decisions relate to quality assurance, production planning, scheduling and control, inventory management, and project management.
- Service differs from goods production in customer contact and labour content, lack of inventories, variation in inputs and outputs, and difficulties in productivity measurement and quality assurance.

- Operations managers plan, organize, control, and direct.
- They use models, trade-off analysis, systems approach, priorities, and ethics in decision making.
- The chapter provides a brief discussion of the historical evolution of operations management, including craft, mass, and lean production systems, and recent trends in the field.
- Among these trends are e-commerce, technology, globalization, supply chains, and sustainability.

Key Terms

craft production	lead time	supply chain
division of labour	lean production	system
e-commerce	mass production	total quality management
effectiveness	model	value added
efficiency	operations management	
interchangeable parts	Pareto phenomenon	

Discussion and Review Questions

Note: An asterisk indicates that a question or problem may be more challenging.

1. Briefly describe the term *operations management*. **LO1**
2. Name the title of three jobs in operations management. **LO1**
3. Why is operations management important to any organization? **LO1**
4. Identify the three major functional areas of organizations and briefly describe how they interrelate. **LO2**
5. Describe the operations function and the nature of the operations manager's job. **LO2 & 5**
6. Explain the difference between design and planning/control decisions. **LO3**
7. List five important differences between producing goods and performing services. **LO4**
*8. Give an example of a pure service (i.e., one where no goods are exchanged). What do you think is being transformed? **LO2 & 4**
9. Give three specific activities an operations manager is likely involved in. *Hint:* use Figure 1-6. **LO5**
10. Briefly discuss each of these terms related to the historical evolution of operations management: **LO7**
    a. Industrial Revolution.
    b. Scientific management.
    c. Interchangeable parts.
    d. Division of labour.
11. Why are services important? Why is manufacturing important? **LO4**
12. What are models and why are they important? **LO6**
13. Name three people who have contributed to the development of operations management. **LO7**
*14. List the trade-offs you would consider for each of these decisions: **LO6**
    a. Driving your own car versus using public transportation.
    b. Buying a computer now versus waiting for an improved model.
    c. Buying a new car versus buying a used car.
    d. Speaking up in class versus waiting to get called on by the instructor.
15. Describe each of these systems: craft production, mass production, and lean production. **LO7**
16. Why might some people prefer not to work in a lean production system? **LO7**
*17. How have technological changes affected you? Are there any downsides to technological change? Explain. **LO8**

18. Identify some of the current trends in operations management and relate them to recent news or to your personal experience. **LO8**

19. Give an example of an unethical behaviour you have observed. **LO6**

20. Explain the term *value added*. **LO2**

*21. What is a supply chain and what is supply chain management? **LO8**

22. What is sustainability and why is it important? **LO8**

Taking Stock

This item appears at the end of each chapter. It is intended to focus your attention on four key issues for organizations in general, and operations management, in particular. These issues are trade-off analysis, collaboration among various functional areas of the organization, the impact of technology, and ethical issues. You will see four questions relating to these issues.

1. What are trade-offs? Why is careful consideration of trade-offs important in decision making? **LO6**

2. Why is it important for the various functional areas of an organization to collaborate? **LO2**

3. In what ways has technology impacted operations? **LO8**

4. Why is employing child labour (10- to 16-year-olds) in developing countries unethical? **LO6**

Critical Thinking Exercises

This item also will appear in every chapter. It allows you to critically apply information you learned in the chapter to practical situations.

1. Many organizations offer a combination of goods and services to their customers. As you learned in this chapter, there are some key differences between production of goods and delivery of services. What are the implications of these differences relative to managing operations? **LO4**

2. Some people who work in knowledge or arts sectors and whose jobs involve creativity argue that the operation of their organization cannot be defined as a process, i.e., a sequence of predetermined activities. Discuss. **LO1**

Experiential Learning Exercises

These exercises also appear at the end of each chapter. They are designed to help you see the relevance of operations management firsthand. **LO3**

Visit a fast-food restaurant and answer these questions:

1. In what ways is quality, or lack of quality, visible?

2. What items must be stocked in addition to the food?

3. How important do you think employee scheduling is? Explain.

4. How might capacity decisions affect the success or failure of the restaurant?

Internet Exercises

This item will appear at the end of each chapter. It allows you to use the Internet to gain additional knowledge about chapter material. Here are the first exercises.

1. Visit the Web page of one of the associations listed under Careers in Operations Management and briefly list the targeted members and the services that they provide to their members. **LO1**

2. Visit http://www.dofasco.ca/bins/content_page. asp?cid=339-342-352 and watch the video of steel making by Dofasco. Answer the following questions. (a) What are the inputs, process, and outputs of ArcelorMittal Dofasco? (b) Where in the process is quality determined? (c) What inventories are kept? **LO2 & 3**

MINI-CASE

Lynn

Lynn had worked for the same major Canadian company for almost 15 years. Although the company had gone through some tough times, things were starting to turn around. Customer orders were up, and quality and productivity had improved dramatically from what they had been only a few years earlier due to a companywide quality improvement program. So it came as a real shock to Lynn and about 400 of her coworkers when they were suddenly terminated following the new CEO's decision to downsize the company.

After recovering from the initial shock, Lynn tried to find employment elsewhere. Despite her efforts, after eight months of searching she was no closer to finding a job than the day she started. Her funds were being depleted and she was getting more discouraged. There was one bright spot, though: She was able to bring in a little money by mowing lawns for her neighbours. She got involved quite by chance when she heard one neighbour remark that now that his children were on their own, nobody was around to cut the grass. Almost jokingly, Lynn asked him how much he'd be willing to pay. Soon Lynn was mowing the lawns of five neighbours. Other neighbours wanted her to work on their lawns, but she didn't feel that she could spare any more time from her job search.

However, as the rejection letters began to pile up, Lynn knew she had to make an important decision in her life. On a rainy Tuesday morning, she decided to go into business for herself—taking care of neighbourhood lawns. She was relieved to give up the stress of job hunting, and she was excited about the prospect of being her own boss. But she was also fearful of being completely on her own. Nevertheless, Lynn was determined to make a go of it.

At first, business was a little slow, but once people realized Lynn was available, many asked her to take care of their lawns. Some people were simply glad to turn the work over to her; others switched from professional lawn care services.

By the end of her first year in business, Lynn knew she could earn a living this way. She also performed other services such as fertilizing lawns, weeding lawns and gardens, and trimming shrubbery. Business became so good that Lynn hired two part-time workers to assist her and, even then, she believed she could expand further if she wanted to. During winter months (January and February), Lynn takes her vacation in Florida.

Questions

1. Lynn is the operations manager of her business. Among her responsibilities are forecasting, inventory management, scheduling, quality assurance, and maintenance.
   a. What kinds of things would likely require forecasts?
   b. What inventory items does Lynn probably have? Name one inventory decision she has to make periodically.
   c. What scheduling must she do? What things might occur to disrupt schedules and cause Lynn to reschedule?
   d. How important is quality assurance to Lynn's business? Explain.
   e. What kinds of maintenance must be performed?

2. What are some of the trade-offs that Lynn probably considered relative to:
   a. Working for a company instead of for herself?
   b. Expanding the business?
   c. Launching a website?

3. Lynn decided to offer the students who worked for her a bonus of $25 for ideas on how to improve the business, and they provided several good ideas. One idea that she initially rejected now appears to hold great promise. The student who proposed the idea has left, and is currently working for a competitor. Should Lynn send that student a cheque for the idea?

4. Lynn is thinking of making her operations sustainable. Name one or two ideas she might consider.

OPERATIONS TOUR

Sobeys

Sobeys Inc. is one of the two national grocery store chains in Canada (the other is Loblaw). Sobeys distinguishes itself from Loblaw by offering just food (Loblaw also sells general merchandise such as electronics).

Sobeys grew out of Nova Scotia mostly through acquisition of other grocery chains and now owns (or franchises) over 1,500 grocery stores all over Canada. Sobeys has revenues of over $21 billion and over 125,000 employees. The latest acquisition is Safeway Canada (over 200 stores in Western Canada).

Sobeys offers different-size stores in different locations based on market size. The stores are also targeted to different customer demographics, although all formats primarily emphasize quality and freshness of products and customer service. There is large full-service format such as Sobeys, IGA extra, Safeway and Thrifty Foods; fresh service format such as Sobeys Urban Fresh and IGA in Quebec; small community service format such as Foodland, Marché Bonichoix, and Les Marchés Tradition; price service format such as FreschCo and Price Chopper; and convenience service format such as Needs Convenience.

(continued)

Sobeys also has a chain of drug stores (Lawtons Drugs) in the Atlantic Canada. In 2012, Sobeys purchased over 200 Shell retail gas stations and related convenience stores in Quebec and Atlantic Canada.

In addition to national brands, Sobeys has its own private label brands Compliments and Signal. In addition, Sobeys also has its own manufacturer—Big 8 Beverages—for its private label soft drinks and water in Atlantic Canada.

Sobeys is a wholly-owned subsidiary of Empire Company Limited which also has a 41.6% equity accounted interest in Crombie REIT, a real estate development and management company. Crombie owns the buildings and shopping plazas that Sobeys stores occupy, as well as other properties.

Sobeys has implemented SAP (an ERP or enterprise software) nationwide. This has enabled reorganization of Sobeys from regional-based (Atlantic Canada, Quebec, Ontario, West Canada) to format-based. Now, there's Sobeys Multi-Format, IGA Operations in Quebec and Safeway Operations, each with their own business unit presidents.

Most products are bought centrally and distributed to the stores through 27 regional distribution centres (DCs) located throughout the country.

Operations management activities and decisions are split between corporate office, Distribution and Logistics, and store operations.

The corporate office initiates and manages various programs to increase the number of customers, including constant evaluation of performance of stores, closing low-profit stores and opening new stores, including modernization of stores. It also manages the computer technology, performs data analytics to improve category management, initiates training programs, and performs accounting and finance activities. Directors of Operations (i.e., district managers) interact with the store managers in their district to implement improvement programs such as sharing best practices.

A store manager manages all facets of the store and ensures operational excellence in retail merchandising, inventory management, and customer relations. He/she ensures superior execution of the retail programs by communicating the operational requirements and/or changes and store vision to the employees. This includes occupational health and safety, food safety, and other regulatory requirements and procedures. The store manager also oversees recruitment, orientation, training, and performance management.

Questions

1. What are the inputs, processes, outputs, and feedback/control for a grocery store such as Sobeys?

2. What are the operations decisions for running a grocery store such as Sobeys?

Sources: Sobeys, Inc., http://www.sobeyscorporate.com; http://www.sobeyscorporate.com/en/video.aspx; http://www.sobeyscorporate.com/en/Careers.aspx.

Here is a procedure that will help you solve most of the end-of-chapter problems in this book and on exams:

1. Identify the question to be answered. This is critical.

2. Summarize the information given in the problem statement using the appropriate symbols.

3. Determine what type of problem it is so you can select the appropriate problem-solving tools such as a formula or table. Check your notes from class, chapter examples, and the Solved Problems section of the chapter, and any preceding chapter problems you have already solved for guidance.

4. Solve the problem and indicate your answer.

Department A can produce parts at a rate of 50/day. Department B uses those parts at the rate of 10/day. Each day unused parts are added to inventory. At what rate does the inventory of unused parts build up?

Example 1

1. The question to be answered: At what rate does inventory of unused parts build up (i.e., increase) per day?

Solution

2. The given information: Production rate = 50 parts/day
                            Usage rate   = 10 parts/day

3. For this simple problem, no formula or table is needed. Inventory buildup is simply the difference between the production and usage rates.

4. Production rate   = 50 parts/day
   Usage rate   = 10 parts/day
   ————————————————————————————————————
   Inventory buildup = 40 parts/day

Companies often use this formula to determine how much of a certain item to order: $Q = \sqrt{\dfrac{2DS}{H}}$

Example 2

where

Q = order quantity S = ordering cost
D = annual demand H = annual holding cost per unit

   If annual demand is 400 units, ordering cost is $36, and annual holding cost is $2 per unit, what is the order quantity?

1. The question to be answered: What is the order quantity, Q?

Solution

2. The information given in the problem: D = 400 units/year, S = $36, H = $2 per year

3. To solve the problem, substitute the values given in the problem into the formula.

4. Solution: $Q = \sqrt{\dfrac{2(400\ units/yr.)\$36}{\$2/unit/yr.}} = 120$ units

connect   **LEARNSMART**   **SMARTBOOK**™

For more information on the resources available from McGraw-Hill Ryerson, go to www.mheducation.ca/he/solutions.

CHAPTER 2
Competitiveness, Strategic Planning, and Productivity

Learning Objectives

After completing this chapter, you should be able to:

LO1 List and briefly discuss the primary ways that organizations compete.

LO2 Describe a company's strategic planning, mission/vision/values, strategies, and operations strategy, and list the steps involved in formulating an operations strategy.

LO3 Define and measure the term *productivity*, describe factors affecting productivity, and explain why measuring the productivity of services is difficult.

The Canadian airline industry is littered with bankrupt airlines. Competition is fierce. Air Canada is the major player, itself on the verge of bankruptcy. WestJet, based in Calgary, has managed to compete using a low-cost strategy (modelled after Southwest Airlines) initially aimed at leisure travellers. Another company that has found a way to compete is Porter Airlines. In 2006, the founder, Bob Deluce, used a product differentiation strategy. Why not use the Billy Bishop Toronto City Airport as the hub, providing a quick and hassle-free alternative for Toronto business travellers? This small regional airport is within five minutes of downtown Toronto on an island on Lake Ontario (but only 120 metres from the shore on a ferry), whereas Pearson International Airport is one hour away on a busy highway. Deluce bought the small old airport and spent $50 million to renovate and expand it. Just like WestJet which uses only one type of plane (Boeing 737), Porter uses only the Bombardier Q400 turboprop. Its range is limited but sufficient to reach major cities around Toronto. In particular, Porter started having 10 to 15 daily scheduled flights between Toronto, Ottawa, and Montreal. No jets are permitted on the airport so WestJet can't currently compete (although it has started off a small regional subsidiary in the West with a handful of Q400 turboprops). Deluce managed to terminate the landing right of Jazz, Air Canada's regional subsidiary, thus protecting his competitive advantage, the airport (However, recently Jazz has been allowed to return to the airport, but is not competing on the Toronto–Ottawa route). To compensate for the disadvantage of turboprop airplanes (relative to jets), Porter offers a lounge with free WiFi and beverages, courteous service, and leather seats with plenty of leg room and free beverages in the planes. More than a million travellers used Porter in a year. Now, Porter flies to more than 18 cities, most within 1,000 km of Toronto, including four to five in the United States. It appears that Porter has found a way to survive in the tough airline business.[1]

This chapter discusses competitiveness, strategic planning, and productivity: three related topics that are vitally important to organizations. **Competitiveness** relates to the ability and performance of an organization in the market compared to other organizations that offer similar goods or services; **strategy** is the long-term plans that determine the direction an organization takes to become (or remain) competitive; **strategic planning** is the managerial process that determines a strategy for the organization; and productivity is a measure of how efficiently the resources are being used.

Slumping productivity gains in recent years and the impressive successes of foreign competition in the market have caused many North American companies to rethink their strategies and to place increased emphasis on operations.

Competitiveness

Companies must be competitive to sell their goods and services in the market. Competitiveness is the reason a company prospers, barely gets by, or fails. Competitiveness depends on the capabilities and performance of the company in its market. Capabilities can be developed over time by focusing on a limited range of goods or services, and/or on a technology, using teamwork and rewards (also called core competencies). Companies should use past experience and expertise in design, operations/manufacturing, or marketing, and leverage them to introduce new goods and services.[2]

An organization's performance in the market also depends on the expectation of its customers for the purchase of goods or services, mainly price, quality, variety, and timeliness. These are **key purchasing criteria**. A customer can be a consumer (i.e., the final customer) or another company.

Price is the amount a customer must pay for the good or service. If all other factors are equal, customers will choose the good or service that has the lowest price.

Quality refers to characteristics of a good or service determined by its design, material, workmanship, performance, and consistency. Most customers desire high-quality goods and services, but are willing to settle for goods or services that serve their intended purpose (specification) as long as the quality is consistent. We will use this interpretation of quality throughout the book.

Variety refers to the choices of models and options available to customers. The more variety, the wider the range of potential customers.

Timeliness refers to the availability of goods or services when they are needed by the customer. This means being delivered on time (as in just-in-time purchasing) or quickly.

Other purchasing factors include customer service (e.g., easy and fast returns, warranty repairs, response to requests, etc.) and convenient location.

competitiveness Ability and performance of an organization in the market compared to other organizations that offer similar goods or services.

strategy The long-term plans that determine the direction an organization takes to become (or remain) competitive.

strategic planning The managerial process that determines a strategy for the organization.

key purchasing criteria The major elements influencing a purchase: price, quality, variety, and timeliness.

[1] J. D'Cruz, Case Study: Porter Airlines, FT.com, April 6, 2011; https://www.flyporter.com/About/Philosophy
[2] R.H. Hayes, et al., *Strategic Operations—Competing through Capabilities*, New York: The Free Press, 1996.

OM in ACTION

Amazon's Customer Service

Amazon received the top spot in customer service in a recent *BusinessWeek* ranking. Although most Amazon customers never talk with an employee, when something goes wrong, Amazon excels in dealing with the problem. In one case, when a New Jersey woman received a workbook she ordered that was described as "like new," she was surprised to discover that it wasn't even close to new—worksheets had already been filled in. She complained to the merchant but didn't get a response. Then she complained to Amazon. She promptly received a refund, even though she had paid the merchant, not Amazon. And she wasn't asked to return the book.

Amazon sees its customer service as a way to enhance customer experience, and as a way to identify potential problems with merchants. In fact, if merchants have problems with more than 1 percent of their orders, that can get them removed from the site.

Source: Based on "How Amazon Aims to Keep You Clicking," *BusinessWeek*, March 2009, p. 34.

Amazon's service helped propel the company to double-digit sales growth. Amazon started same-day shipping in major cities, launched a program to urge manufacturers to drop frustrating packaging, and extended its service reach by acquiring free-shipping pioneer shoe etailer Zappos.com.

Most customers tend to trade off price against the other purchasing criteria and choose the "best buy" or best "value":

$$\text{value} = \frac{\text{quality, timeliness, etc.}}{\text{price}}$$

order qualifiers Purchasing criteria that customers perceive as minimum standards of acceptability to be considered for purchase.

In complex purchases, customers may use two categories of purchasing criteria: order qualifiers and order winners.[3] **Order qualifiers** are those purchasing criteria that customers perceive as minimum standards of acceptability for purchase. However, these may not be sufficient to get a customer to purchase from the selling organization. **Order winners** are those purchasing criteria that cause the selling organization to be perceived as better than the competition.

order winners Purchasing criteria that cause the selling organization to be perceived as better than the competition.

Purchasing criteria such as price, on-time delivery, delivery speed, and quality can be order qualifiers or order winners. Over time, a characteristic that once was an order winner may become an order qualifier, and vice versa. For example, in the past certain percentage of defective items was acceptable to most buyers but not now. This means that quality was not an order qualifier before but has become one now.

Obviously, it is important to determine the set of order qualifiers and order winners, and the relative importance of each for each market so that appropriate attention can be given to them. Marketing must make that determination and communicate it to operations. For example, for business air travellers, comfort/convenience (customer service) and being on time are most important (i.e., are order qualifiers) whereas for economy air travellers price is most important (i.e., is the order qualifier). Also, for new products such as an iPad, innovative features (variety) is most important but for mature products price, quality, and availability/on-time delivery are.

---

[3] T. Hill, *Manufacturing Strategy: Text and Cases*, 3rd ed. New York: McGraw-Hill, 2000.

Organizations compete by emphasizing one or more of the key purchasing criteria in their goods or services. From an organization's point of view, these are called **competitive priorities**:

Cost is the unit production cost of a good or performance of a service to the organization. Organizations that compete based on cost (i.e., price from a customer's perspective) emphasize lowering their operating costs.

Quality from an organization's perspective means determining customers' quality requirements, translating these into specifications for goods or services, and consistently producing goods or performing services to these specifications. Producing products free of defect (unacceptable to customer) is the goal of all organizations.

Flexibility refers to being able to produce a variety of goods or services. This also includes customization, which is modifying goods or services to meet the requirements of individual customers. It may also refer to being able to easily increase or decrease the production quantity of goods or services (quantity flexibility). Flexibility is usually achieved by having general-purpose equipment, excess capacity and/or inventory, and multi skilled workers, resulting in easy changeover between products.

Delivery reliability and speed refer to being able to consistently and promptly meet promised due dates by producing/delivering goods or performing services on time and quickly. Delivery reliability and speed is achieved by using faster and more reliable resources/processes.

If an organization is far from being competitive, it may be able to improve many or all of its competitive priorities simultaneously. However, as the organization becomes more competitive, it tends to reach a point where improving one priority can be achieved only by reducing the emphasis on another priority, i.e., a trade-off is required. The result of this is a focus on only one priority at a time. It has been observed that most companies first emphasize quality, and only after their quality has reached a competitive level focus on delivery reliability, next on low-cost operations, and finally on flexibility.

Table 2-1 lists the competitive priorities and examples of companies that emphasize them. Understanding competitive issues can help managers develop successful strategies.

competitive priorities The importance given to operations characteristics: cost, quality, flexibility, and delivery.

Competitive Priority	Emphasis	Examples of Organization
Cost	Low cost	The Great Canadian Superstore (Loblaw), WestJet, Walmart
Quality	Meeting customer requirements consistently	Sony, Sobeys, Amazon.com, CNH, Porter Airlines, Apple, Coca-Cola, Toyota, Pizza Hut
Flexibility	Variety	Dell Computers
		Hospital emergency room
	Quantity flexibility	Potash Corp, Air Canada
Delivery	Rapid delivery	McDonald's, Purolator, Domino's Pizza
	On-time delivery	WestJet
		Just-in-time parts suppliers, e.g., Magna International

◀ **Table 2-1**

Examples of competitive priorities used by companies.

Strategic Planning

Strategic planning is the process of determining a strategy, i.e., a long-term plan that will set a new direction for an organization, and implementing it through allocation of resources and action plans. Some companies perform strategic planning only when they face a crisis, e.g., when they face a significant drop in their sales. More progressive organizations perform strategic planning on a regular basis, usually annually.

Briefly, strategic planning starts with top management soliciting the performance of current strategy from stakeholders (department managers and employees, shareholders, customers, suppliers, and society), and commissioning a market research study of the industry and where it is headed in the next five years. Then, the management team may form/adjust the organization's mission and vision, based on the organization's values, determine a set of goals, and brainstorm and evaluate alternative ways (strategies) to achieve them. Finally, the chosen strategy is implemented by determining a set of action plans at the department level. A related framework is called Balanced Scorecard (see Figure 2-1).

Figure 2-1 ▶

The Balanced Scorecard.

Source: Reprinted with permission of Harvard Business School Press from Robert Kaplan and David Norton, *Balanced Scorecard: Translating Strategy into Action.* Copyright © 1996 by the Harvard Business School Publishing Corporation. All rights reserved.

The analysis usually concerns the competitiveness of the organization. A well-known decision aid is the SWOT (Strengths, Weaknesses, Opportunities, and Threats) analysis. The organization will try to identify these and to use/build up its strengths (relative to its competitors) to take advantage of market opportunities, and to avoid/neutralize its weaknesses (relative to its competitors) to defend against the threats.

A more detailed strategic planning process for a business has been proposed.[4] It involves answering the following questions:

1. Getting started
   a. What is the scope of business?
   b. Is the current strategy working?
   c. What are the issues/problems?

2. Analyze the industry and source of competitive advantage (i.e., earning above-average profit)
   a. How intense is the competitive rivalry?
   b. How large is the bargaining power of suppliers?
   c. How hard is it for new entrants to enter the industry?
   d. How easily can substitute goods or services be developed?
   e. How large is the bargaining power of customers?
   f. How would trends and changes (demand, technology, regulation, etc.) affect the industry?
   g. How can generic strategies of niche market, low cost, and product differentiation be used in this industry?
   h. How can we gain and sustain competitive advantage?

3. Analyze customers
   a. What are the market segments?
   b. What are customers' key purchasing criteria?

---

[4] S. Early, "Issues and Alternatives: Key to FMC's Strategic Planning System," *Planning Review* 18(3), May/June 1990, pp. 26–33.

4. Analyze competitors
   a. What are the strategies and positions (i.e., relative competitive comparison of products) of winners and losers?
   b. Why do competitors behave as they do? Can we influence them?
   c. How has their strategy been changing through time?

5. Assess our relative position
   a. What are our products' strengths and weaknesses as customers see them? Profitability?

6. Assess the state of our business
   a. What are the major issues (in order of importance)?
   b. What should our goals be?
   c. Should we grow, maintain, or sell off part of our business?

7. Develop and evaluate alternative strategies
   a. Can strategies be found for each major issue?
   b. What investments should we make? What actions should we take?
   c. For each alternative, do financial returns justify it?

8. Choose and refine the recommended strategy
   a. What strategy should we choose?
   b. What actions and policies are required? Do they fit together? Are they reinforcing?
   c. What resources are required? Timetables? Expected results?

9. Identify major actions and implement them
   a. How can we co-ordinate the actions and monitor overall progress?

BC Frozen Food Ltd.

◀ Example 1

BC Frozen Food Ltd. (BCFF) is a small processor of fruits (e.g., berries) and vegetables (e.g., cauliflower) located in Mission, BC. Most BCFF products are grown locally within 40 miles of the plant. The best products are sold fresh to local markets and inferior products are made into jam, but most products are individually quick frozen (IQF). Founded in 1989, the owners, the Shah family, have been working very hard to keep BCFF profitable. Initially, BCFF sold frozen products in bulk to distributors such as Sysco. But throughout the years an increasing number of local processors as well as some large companies, such as Lucerne and General Mills, have opened processing plants close by in Abbotsford. The response from the Shah family has been to diversify, both in products and in distribution markets. They expanded the plant to be able to process green beans and acquired a vacuum pack machine to be able to package the products in small vacuum plastic bags. To be able to convince their partner farmers to grow green beans, BCFF had to purchase seven bean harvesting machines. After several years, BCFF house-brand and private-label fruit and vegetable bags are now sold in retail stores such as Federated Co-op members and Krogers, largest grocery chain in the United States. Also, cases of 1 or 2 kilogram bags of BCFF house brand are sold to food service & restaurants such as Dairy Queen. The retail and foodservice sectors now provide the majority of BCFF's revenue.

Sources: S. Shah and I.A. Ghazzawi, BC Frozen Food Limited: Challenges and Change, *Journal of the International Academy for Case Studies*, Volume 18, Number 7, 2012; http://www.bcfrozenfoods.com.

Mission, Vision, and Values

Some organizations determine and use a mission, vision, and values statement during their strategic planning process. This may help build consensus within the organization as well. An organization's **mission** is where the organization is going now, its products, and its markets. **Vision** is where the organization desires to be in the future. Vision has to be realistic. **Values** are the shared beliefs of the organizations' stakeholders that should drive everything else such as culture, mission/vision, and strategy.

It is important that an organization has a clear and simple mission/vision/values statement. Table 2-2 provides some sample mission/vision/values/strategy statements.

mission Where the organization is going now, its products and markets.

vision Where the organization desires to be in the future.

values Shared beliefs of the organization's stakeholders.

Table 2-2 ▶

Selected company mission/vision/ values/strategy statements.

http://www.flyporter.com

http://www.westjet.ca

http://www.cpr.ca

Porter Airlines

Mission:

Porter's philosophy is to make travel easier by lightening the load. Porter embodies this philosophy by reintroducing convenience, speed, and service to air travel. As the airline of choice for discerning short-haul passengers, our warm and effortless approach to hospitality, combined with our spotless service brings dignity and refinement back to flying. This extends throughout the travel experience, beginning on the ground with our modern, comfortable airport lounges, and service-oriented team members, continuing seamlessly aboard aircraft with spacious interiors and well-appointed crew.

Source: Based on https://www.flyporter.com/About/Philosophy?culture=en-CA

WestJet

Our mission:

To enrich the lives of everyone in WestJet's world by providing safe, friendly and affordable air travel.

Our vision:

By 2016, WestJet will be one of the five most successful international airlines in the world, providing our guests with a friendly and caring experience that will change air travel forever.

Our values:

- Commitment to safety
- Positive and passionate in everything we do
- Appreciative of our people and guests
- Fun, friendly and caring
- Align the interests of WestJetters with the interests of the company
- Honest, open and keep our commitments

Source: http://www.westjet.ca/guest/en/about/index.shtml

Canadian Pacific

Strategy:

Canadian Pacific is driving change as it moves through its transformational journey to become the best railroad in North America, while creating long-term value for shareholders. The Company is focused on providing customers with industry-leading rail service; driving sustainable, profitable growth; optimizing our assets; and reducing costs, while remaining a leader in rail safety.

Looking forward, CP is executing its strategic plan to become the lowest-cost rail carrier. This plan is centred on five key foundations, which are the Company's performance drivers.

Provide Service: Providing efficient and consistent transportation solutions for the Company's customers. "Doing what we say we are going to do" is what drives CP by providing a reliable product with a lower-cost operating model. Centralized planning aligned with local execution is bringing the Company closer to the customer and accelerating decision making.

Control Costs: Controlling and removing unnecessary costs from the organization, eliminating bureaucracy, and continuing to identify productivity enhancements are the keys to success.

Optimize Assets: Through longer sidings, improved asset utilization, and increased train lengths, the Company is moving increased volumes with fewer locomotives and cars while unlocking capacity for future growth potential.

Operate Safely: Each year, CP safely moves millions of carloads of freight across North America while ensuring the safety of our people and the communities through which we operate. Safety is never to be compromised. Continuous research and development in state-of-the-art safety technology and highly focused employees ensure our trains are built for safe, efficient operations across our network.

Develop People: CP recognizes that none of the other foundations can be achieved without its people. Every CP employee is a railroader and the Company is shaping a new culture focused on a passion for service with integrity in everything it does. Coaching and mentoring managers into becoming leaders will help drive CP forward.

Source: Canadian Pacific Rail, *Management's Discussion & Analysis* documents, "Strategy" section. http://www.cpr.ca/en/investors/financial-reports.

Goals and Objectives. Mission/vision provides a general direction for an organization and should lead to organizational *goals*, which provide substance to the overall mission/vision. For example, one goal of an organization may be to capture more market share for a product; another goal may be to achieve profitability. An objective is a specific goal containing numerical values. For example, an objective of a company may be a 25 percent reduction in operating costs.

Strategies, Tactics, and Action Plans. A strategy comprises the long-term plans that will determine the direction an organization will take to become (or remain) competitive. A strategy is determined during the strategic planning process. An organization usually has an overall organizational *strategy*. In the past, organizational strategies were dominated by long-term financial and marketing plans, but recently long-term operations plans have dominated. Examples of strategy include branding, growth, niche market, product differentiation, first-to-market, innovation, e-commerce, low cost, global selling and operations, partnership, and sustainability. The long-term functional plans are sometimes called *functional strategies*, e.g., financial strategy or marketing strategy or operations strategy. The functional strategies, if different from organizational strategy, should obviously be congruent with it.

Tactics are medium-term plans used as components of a strategy. They are more specific in nature than a strategy, and they provide guidance for determining policies and carrying out **action plans**. An action plan is a medium- or short-term project to accomplish a specific objective, assigned to an individual, with a deadline and the resources needed.

It should be apparent that the overall relationship that exists from the mission/vision down to actual policies and action plans is *hierarchical* in nature. This is illustrated in Figure 2-2. However, a strategy should also reflect the day-to-day experience of employees (bottom up) and performance data. The action plans should not only improve the performance of an organization to meet its customers' needs, but also increase the organization's long-term capabilities. Note that radical changes will face resistance and should be implemented carefully.

A simple example may help to put these concepts into perspective.

tactics Medium-term plans used as components of a strategy.

action plan A medium- or short-term project to accomplish a specific objective, assigned to an individual, with a deadline and the resources needed.

Figure 2-2

Strategic planning is hierarchical in organizations.

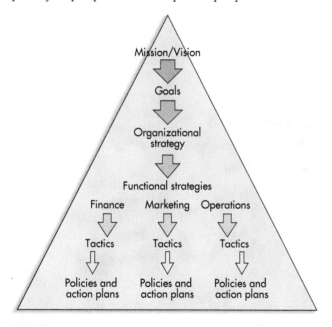

David is a high school student. He would like to live comfortably. A possible scenario for achieving his mission/vision might look something like this:

Example 2

- Mission/vision: Live a good life.
- Goal: Successful career, good income.
- Strategy: Obtain a college/university education.
- Tactics: Select a college/university and a major; decide how to finance the education.
- Action plans: Register, buy books, take courses, study.

The following example shows the use of a goal, improvement objectives, and an action plan.

Example 3 ▶

The management of Wilson Sporting Goods decided to become the leader in the special-order golf-ball business (golf balls that have personalized logos). This goal was to be accomplished over a five-year period by improving quality and delivery. Specific improvement objectives were decided for each competitive priority, and these objectives were cascaded down the organization to appropriate departmental teams, where action plans were established for each needed activity. The objectives and an example of an action plan are shown in Figure 2-3.[5]

Figure 2-3 ▶

An example of objectives and an action plan.

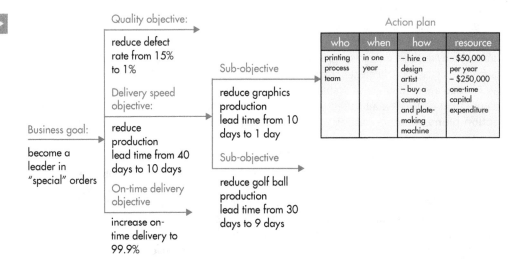

The difficulty of implementing a strategy (the set of action plans, etc.) depends on its scale (size), complexity (the part of organization/organizations it affects), and uncertainty (how novel it is). Powerful stakeholders should be kept informed and managed. Informal/unwritten practices also play a role.

Indian operators take calls at Quatro call centre in Gurgaon on the outskirts of New Delhi. Companies take advantage of communications and software support offshore to drive down costs. This industry in India already provides over 1 million jobs.

---

[5] Based on J.H. Sheridan, "America's Best Plants: Wilson Sporting Goods," *Industry Week* 241(20), October 19, 1992, pp. 59–62.

Operations Strategy

In large organizations the operations function can play a proactive role in strategic planning by helping shape the operations strategy (as opposed to the reactive role of just fixing operations problems). **Operations strategy** comprises a set of well-co-ordinated policies, objectives, and action plans, directly affecting the operations function, which is aimed at securing a long-term sustainable advantage over the competition.[6] In order to formulate an operations strategy, the operations function has to co-operate with all the other functions of the business to collectively monitor the external markets. For example, marketing should be aware of competitors' new product development and customers' expectations in the product markets, and engineering/R&D should be aware of new processing technologies in the technology markets.

The role of operations should be identified. Usually, operations' objectives/performance measures are determined in terms of competitive priorities such as cost (e.g., unit cost, labour productivity, inventory turnover), quality (e.g., percentage of products defective, cost of quality), delivery (e.g., percentage of on-time deliveries, lead time), and flexibility (e.g., response to product/quantity changes). As mentioned earlier, trade-offs must be made among these priorities because operations cannot excel in all of them simultaneously. For example, a flexible operation cannot produce the products at minimum cost.

The operations policies, objectives, and action plans can be classified into nine strategic decision categories.

Nine Strategic Decision Categories.

Facility. The number and location of facilities influence the operations and marketing strengths of the organization. A major operations decision for multifacility organizations is how to specialize or focus each facility: by market, product group, or production process type. This usually depends on the economics of production and distribution.

Capacity. This decision is related to facility decision. Long-term capacity decisions relate to size of plants and major equipment (which affect economies of scale and unit production costs). The main issue is whether and how to change the capacity in anticipation of future demand. Capacity underutilization/shortage affect operating/opportunity costs. Inventory can be held to address medium-/short-term capacity imbalances.

Vertical Integration/Outsourcing. Vertical integration is ownership of a major part or the whole of the supply chain. Outsourcing is letting a supplier perform some of production/service. Cost, co-ordination, and control are the important decision factors. Operations is expected to play a more important role in the supply chain.

Supplier Relationship/Partnership. The two extremes are using competitive arm's-length or co-operative close relationships (i.e., partnership). This decision also determines how the quality of purchased goods will be assured: either work with a supplier to assure/control its production processes or inspect the incoming parts. The purchasing agent's knowledge and effective performance are important for operations' strength.

Product Mix and New Products. The challenge of operations management increases as the variety of products and the rate of new product introduction increase. These require flexible production systems. Products designed for easy manufacturing and assembly and effective product development process increase operations' strength.

Process Types and Technology. There are four generic process types: job shop, batch flow, assembly line, and continuous flow. The product-process matrix (described in Chapter 6) can be used to relate product characteristics to process characteristics (and technologies). The matrix also shows the important trade-offs required in process choice. The process type determines the appropriate technologies and degree of process automation. In-house process-technology knowledge, using new/efficient technologies and good facility layout are important for operations' strength.

operations strategy comprises a set of well-co-ordinated policies, objectives, and action plans, directly affecting the operations function, which is aimed at securing a long-term sustainable advantage over the competition.

---

[6] C.H. Fine and A.C. Hax, "Manufacturing Strategy: A Methodology and an Illustration," *Interfaces* 15(6), November/December 1985, pp. 28–46.

Visioneering

Visioneering Corp (VC) of Toronto is engaged in the extremely competitive LED and florescent lighting business. At one time the firm manufactured standard 4- and 8-feet florescent lights. But the imports of cheap products from China caused a decline in its revenues. VC's management realized that these competitors relied on mass production of standard items, which were shipped in ocean containers and took months to arrive. As a result, VC's strategy focused on building low-volume nonstandard bulkier products on short notice. VC invested in high-precision, programmable machines that reduced labour cost, shortened changeover times, and improved quality. VC's lead time to its customers has been reduced to a few days.

Source: Based on C. Piper, Reversing the Tide in Canadian Manufacturing, *Ivey Business Journal Online* 72.5 (Sep/Oct 2008).

Human Resources. With co-operation of the personnel department, workers/staff are appraised, selected, developed/trained, motivated, promoted, and rewarded to work as a team to achieve the company's goals. Various types of compensation and incentives can be used. Organizational learning and flexible organizational structure also play important roles in gaining competency.

Quality. Product quality is determined during the design and production. Conformance to specification during production requires quality assurance/planning, control, and improvement. The tools that can be used include statistical process control and continuous improvement/Six Sigma. A major decision is whether to assign the responsibility of quality control to the workers.

Operations Infrastructure and Systems. These decisions include effective planning and control (including forecasting, material requirements planning, and scheduling), using a software program for planning and control, whether to use just-in-time production, operations policies, and the type of production/delivery system used (make-to-stock or make-to-order).

These nine strategic decision categories are described in detail in the following chapters. The following steps can be used to formulate an operations strategy.

Formulation of an Operations Strategy.

1. Link the organizational goals (e.g., becoming a leader in a sector) to the operations strategy: determine operations requirements of the organizational goals.

2. Categorize/segment the customers into types: for example, major customers (with whom closer relationship is desirable) and others (with whom transactional relationship is adequate). For each category, determine which of the four competitive priorities (cost, quality, delivery, and flexibility) should be emphasized.

3. Group product lines into types: for example, classify the product lines into low volume and high volume.

4. Conduct an operations audit to determine the strengths/weaknesses of the current operations strategy in each of the nine strategic decision categories. Also, for each customer category, assess the relative standing of products (relative to desired competitive priorities) against those of most relevant competitors.

5. Assess the degree of focus at each plant: note that a focused plant is more efficient. We can use the product-process matrix (described in Chapter 6) to detect the degree of congruence between a product line and its "natural" process. For example, a low volume–high variety product line should be produced using a job shop process.

6. Develop an operations strategy and reallocate product lines to plants if necessary. For each of the nine strategic decision categories, state the objectives, policies, and action plans. Deploy these policies and action plans.

The following example illustrates the formulation of an operations strategy.

◀ **Example 4**

Rohm and Haas (R&H) is a major North American producer of specialty chemicals such as polymer emulsions used in water-based paint.[7]

In the-mid 1990s, R&H was being squeezed between suppliers (petrochemical companies) and major customers such as Walmart and Home Depot. Furthermore, competitors were taking market share. R&H's selling price had remained the same for five years whereas costs were going up. In addition, the production and order fulfillment was chaotic and stressful. The 11 plants each made all of the approximately 800 products. All customers, approximately 4,000, received the same service such as customized certificate of analysis or packaging/labelling. There was no fixed lead time; the due date was negotiated between the customer service rep (CSR) and the schedulers. The production schedule kept changing, with less than a day's notice.

To fix these problems, R&H spent $100 million on an Enterprise Resource Planning (ERP) software, but after three years of implementation, there was no real change to its business processes. Then, a management team was formed consisting of sales, marketing, manufacturing, operations, and logistics managers, and some internal consultants. The team analyzed R&H's customer base, dividing them into four categories/tiers: (1) partners or potential partners, (2) strategically important, (3) important, and (4) others.

It was decided that the approximately 3,200 customers in Tier 4 would be supplied by three exclusive distributors and not by R&H directly. This would save CSRs/schedulers' time and save production/transportation costs as larger batches to the distributors would be cheaper per unit.

Sales and marketing people interviewed Tier 1 customers to find out what service they valued most and what R&H's competitors were offering. The services were categorized, their cost estimated, and a matrix was formed that related each tier with the service categories it would receive. For example, Tier 1 customers would receive special services such as customized packaging/labelling, Tier 2 would receive standard services, and Tier 3 would receive limited services.

Also, the team studied the demand characteristic of the approximately 800 products. The results showed that most high-volume products were ordered regularly, whereas most low-volume products were ordered irregularly. The team mathematically modelled one of the facilities and performed a simulation study to find out the effect of dedicating chemical reactors to either high-volume or low-volume products, given various lead times. The results showed that the capacity would increase by 20 percent and on-time delivery would improve.

The team recommended specializing some of the plants/reactors to make the high-volume products and the others to make the low-volume products. Also, the high-volume products, which can be forecasted accurately, are to be made to stock, with a lead time of two days. On the other hand, it was decided not to carry any stocks of the low-volume variable-demand products. These are made to order with a lead time of seven days, and a minimum-order quantity equal to the production batch size. Tier 1 customers have accepted the increase in lead time for low-volume products because it is certain.

As a result of these changes, R&H has saved millions of dollars, increased its production capacity, and improved its on-time delivery rates.

[7] A.J. D'Alessandro and A. Baveja, "Divide and Conquer: Rohm and Haas' Response to a Changing Specialty Chemicals Market," *Interfaces* 30(6), November/December 2000, pp. 1–16.

Generic Operations Strategies. Generic operations strategies are theme-based operations improvement programs and plans such as just-in-time production and total quality management/continuous improvement. These are generic because they have been frequently used irrespective of the market conditions and competitive situation. If every company in an industry pursues the same generic strategy, every company becomes more efficient and/or more effective without gaining competitive advantage. Therefore, these are, strictly speaking, not strategies, though they are commonly considered so.

The popular generic operations strategies have been changing over time. To illustrate, the generic operations strategies some Japanese manufacturing companies have used since the Second World War are:

- *Low labour-cost strategy.* Immediately after the war, exploited the (then) inexpensive labour pool.
- *Scale-based strategy.* During the 1960s, used capital-intensive methods to achieve higher labour productivity and lower unit costs.
- *Focused factories strategy.* During the 1970s, used smaller factories that focused on narrow product lines to take advantage of specialization and achieve higher quality.
- *Flexible factories strategy.* During the 1980s, reduced the time needed to add new product and process designs. Used flexible equipment that allowed volume and design changes, as well as product variety. Continued to stress quality.
- *Continuous improvement strategy.* In the 1990s, introduced new product features and continuous improvement of both products and processes.

Another generic strategy used by some organizations in 1990s was Business Process Reengineering (BPR). This is a radical process redesign that involves process reorientation, breaking up functional silos and integrating operations into customer-focused processes.

Another generic strategy related to BPR occurred just before year 2000, when many organizations changed their legacy computer systems and installed Enterprise Resource Planning (ERP) software. ERP automates business processes and can reduce cost and data entry errors but requires data to be entered in a central database as soon as a transaction occurs anywhere in the organization.

We will briefly describe two generic operations strategies that are still popular.

quality-based strategy
Strategy that focuses on quality of an organization's goods and services.

Quality-based strategies focus on maintaining or improving the quality of an organization's goods or services. Quality is generally a factor in both attracting and retaining customers. Quality-based strategies may be motivated by a variety of factors. They may reflect an effort to overcome an image of poor quality, a desire to catch up with the competition, a desire to maintain an existing image of high quality, or some combination of these and other factors. Interestingly enough, quality-based strategies can be part of another strategy such as cost reduction, increased productivity, or time reduction, all of which benefit from higher quality.

Recently, some organizations are using a quality improvement initiative called Six Sigma which uses more advanced statistical methods than continuous improvement as well as BPR approach. Chapters 9 and 10 cover more details of quality and Six Sigma.

time-based strategy
Strategy that focuses on reduction of time needed to accomplish tasks.

Time-based strategies focus on reducing the time required to accomplish various activities (e.g., develop new products and market them, respond to a change in customer demand). By doing so, organizations seek to improve service to the customer and gain a competitive advantage over rivals that take more time to accomplish the same tasks. Also costs are generally less, productivity is higher, and quality tends to be higher. Just-in-time production is a special case.

An example of a Canadian company using a time-based strategy is Standard Aero, based in Winnipeg. By redesigning its processes into U-shaped cells, and controlling the activities using a visual system, Standard Aero performs repairs/overhauls of small airplane engines in only two weeks, much faster than its competitors. More on just-in-time and lean production appears in Chapter 15.

Minimizing operating costs through becoming more efficient is a common strategy for most organizations. A topic related to efficiency is productivity.

A major key to Apple's continued success is its ability to keep pushing the boundaries of innovation. Apple has demonstrated how to create growth by dreaming up products so new and ingenious that they have upended one industry after another.

Productivity

One of the primary responsibilities of an operations manager is to achieve *productive use* of an organization's resources. The term *productivity* is used to describe this. **Productivity** measures output (goods and services) per unit input (machine, labour, materials, energy) used to produce them. It is usually expressed as the ratio of output to input:

$$\text{Productivity} = \frac{\text{Output}}{\text{Input}} \qquad (2\text{-}1)$$

A productivity ratio can be computed for a worker, a department, an organization, or an entire country.

A related measure is the rate of *productivity growth*. Productivity growth is the increase in productivity from previous period to the current period relative to the productivity in the previous period. Thus,

$$\text{Productivity growth} = \frac{\text{Current period productivity} - \text{Previous period productivity}}{\text{Previous period productivity}} \qquad (2\text{-}2)$$

For example, if productivity increased from 80 to 84, the growth rate would be

$$\frac{84 - 80}{80} = .05 \text{ or } 5\%$$

Productivity growth is a key factor in a country's standard of living. Productivity increases add value to the economy while keeping inflation in check.

Measuring Productivity

Productivity measures can be based on a single input (partial productivity), on more than one input (multifactor productivity), or on all inputs (total productivity). Table 2-3 lists some examples

productivity A measure of productive use of resources, usually expressed as the ratio of output to input.

Partial measures	$\dfrac{\text{Output}}{\text{Labour}}$	$\dfrac{\text{Output}}{\text{Machine}}$	$\dfrac{\text{Output}}{\text{Material}}$	$\dfrac{\text{Output}}{\text{Energy}}$
Multifactor measures	$\dfrac{\text{Output}}{\text{Labour} + \text{Machine}}$		$\dfrac{\text{Output}}{\text{Labour} + \text{Material} + \text{Energy}}$	
Total measure	$\dfrac{\text{Goods or services produced}}{\text{All inputs used to produce them}}$			

◀ **Table 2-3**

Some examples of different types of productivity measures.

of different types of productivity measures. The choice of productivity measure depends primarily on the purpose of the measurement. If the purpose is to track improvements in labour productivity, then labour becomes the obvious input.

Partial measures are often of greatest use in operations management. Table 2-4 provides some examples of partial productivity measures.

Table 2-4 ▶

Some examples of partial productivity measures.

Labour productivity	Units of output per labour hour
	Units of output per shift
	Value-added per labour hour
	Dollar value of output per labour hour
Machine productivity	Units of output per machine hour
	Dollar value of output per machine hour
Material productivity	Units of output per unit material input, e.g., kilometres per gallon. Note: litres per 100 km is the inverse of the productivity measure we have defined, but it is still used to measure productivity.
	Dollar value of output per unit material input
Energy productivity	Units of output per kilowatt-hour
	Dollar value of output per kilowatt-hour

The unit of output used in productivity measure depends on the type of job performed. The following are examples of labour productivity:

$$\frac{\text{Square metres of carpet installed}}{\text{Labour hours}} = \text{Square metres of carpet installed per labour hour}$$

$$\frac{\text{Number of offices cleaned}}{\text{Number of shifts}} = \text{Number of offices cleaned per shift}$$

$$\frac{\text{Board feet of lumber cut}}{\text{Number of weeks}} = \begin{array}{l}\text{Board feet of lumber cut per week (Board foot = volume} \\ \text{of lumber that covers 1 foot} \times \text{foot} \times \text{1 inch)}\end{array}$$

Similar examples can be listed for *machine productivity* (e.g., the number of pieces turned out by a machine per hour).

Example 5 ▶

Determine the productivity for these cases:

a. Four workers installed 720 square metres of carpet in eight hours.

b. A machine produced 68 usable (i.e., good quality) pieces of a part in two hours.

SOLUTION

a. $\text{Productivity} = \dfrac{\text{Square metres of carpet installed}}{\text{Labour hours worked}}$

$= \dfrac{720 \text{ square metres}}{4 \text{ workers} \times 8 \text{ hours}}$

$= \dfrac{720 \text{ square metres}}{32 \text{ worker hours}}$

$= 22.5 \text{ square metres/worker hour}$

b. $\text{Productivity} = \dfrac{\text{Usable pieces}}{\text{Production time}}$

$= \dfrac{68 \text{ pieces}}{2 \text{ hours}}$

$= 34 \text{ pieces/hour}$

Calculations of inputs in a multifactor productivity measure use a common unit of measurement, such as dollars. For example:

$$\frac{\text{Quantity of production}}{\text{Labour cost (\$) + Materials cost (\$) + Machine overhead (\$)}} \qquad (2\text{-}3)$$

Determine the multifactor productivity for the combined inputs of labour, materials, and machine time using the following data:

◀ **Example 6**

Output: 7,040 units

Input costs:

Labour (line and support staff, including benefits): $1,000

Materials: $520

Machine overhead: $2,000

$$\frac{\text{Multifactor}}{\text{productivity}} = \frac{\text{Output}}{\text{Labour + Materials + Machine overhead}} = \frac{7,040 \text{ units}}{\$1,000 + \$520 + \$2,000}$$

SOLUTION

$$= 2 \text{ units/dollar input}$$

Even though labour cost as a proportion of total cost has been decreasing in manufacturing, labour productivity is still the main measure used to gauge the performance of individuals, processes, and plants. In addition, its use in services has been increasing as services are employing more workers.

We should not confuse productivity with *efficiency*. Efficiency is a narrower concept that pertains to getting the most out of a *fixed* set of resources; productivity is a broader concept that pertains to better use of overall resources. For example, an efficiency perspective on mowing a lawn if given a hand mower would focus on the best way to use the hand mower; a productivity perspective would include the possibility of using a power mower.

Labour productivity and average operation time for tasks are inversely related. For example, if it takes an average of five minutes to produce one unit, this implies a productivity of (60 minutes per hour)/(5 minutes per unit) = 12 units per hour.

Productivity can be enhanced by the use of robotic equipment. Robots can operate for long periods with consistent precision and high speed.

Productivity measures are useful on a number of levels. For an individual, process, department, or organization, productivity measures can be used to track performance *over time*. This allows managers to judge performance and to decide where improvements are needed. For example, if a manager finds that productivity has slipped in a certain area, the manager can examine the factors used to compute productivity to determine what has changed and then devise a means of improving productivity in subsequent periods. Labour productivity is sometimes used in labour wage negotiations where wage raises are tied to productivity growth.

Total productivity and profit of a company are directly related: Total productivity is revenue/total cost, whereas profit is revenue − total cost.

Productivity measures can also be used to judge the performance of an entire industry or a country as a whole. These productivity measures are *aggregate* measures.

In essence, productivity measurements serve as scorecards of the efficient use of resources. Business leaders are concerned with productivity as it relates to *competitiveness*: if two companies both have the same level of output, but one requires less input because of higher productivity, that one will be able to charge a lower price and consequently increase its share of the market, or it might elect to charge the same price, thereby reaping a greater profit.

Productivity Measurement of Services

Service productivity measurement is more problematic than manufacturing. In some services where there is also a large goods component, a measure of output is not hard to find. For example, in the transport (hauling) sector ton-miles is used, in the power sector KWH is used, and in the communication sector number of phone calls is used. In other situations, it is more difficult to measure output because it is partly intangible (e.g., state of health of a patient), involves intellectual activities (e.g., learning operations management), or the output has a high degree of variability (e.g., getting legal advice). Because the outcome is usually an improved state of customer, and customers start off in different states, the inputs can also be variable. Think about medical diagnosis, surgery, consulting, legal services, education, hotels and restaurants, and recreation.

OM in ACTION

Examples of Health Care Productivity Measurement

Diabetes, the imbalance of blood sugar, has no cure. The patient has to monitor his diet and blood sugar, and possibly use insulin to restore it to normal range. Hospital visits are usually confined to outpatient care, but if not in check, diabetes results in serious complications that require inpatient care in hospitals. The output of health care system can be measured as quality-adjusted life years, i.e., the expected life years minus complication rates × their impact. The complication rate depends on clearly identifying serious cases and assisting them intensively. The input cost is measured as cost of staff (doctors, nurses, etc.) at hospitals for both outpatient and inpatient needs (which depend on staffing level and length of stay), plus cost of insulin. Cost of diagnosis (blood test) is not significant; neither is the cost of continuous monitoring of blood sugar (usually self-paid).

Gallstones develop in the gallbladder, and result in abdominal pain. If the case is serious enough, the only treatment is surgery, by removing the gallbladder. Then, patient is cured for life. Because seriousness of this disease is subjective, the choice of surgery is also rather subjective. There are two types of surgery: traditional surgery of opening the stomach and laparoscopic surgery (which results in only three small incisions). Using laparoscopic surgery will result in a considerably shorter hospital stay, which reduces the input cost (cost of the surgery and hospital stay) significantly. The output, quality-adjusted life years, depends on the timing of the decision to go for surgery.

Breast cancer is the most common type of cancer among women. The only treatment is removing the malignant lump, and likely the whole breast, before it spreads. This requires identifying it first. The screening is done by physical exams and mammography. If the initial test indicates possible cancer, a biopsy is performed. Biopsy and surgery can be performed together in one step, or sequentially in two steps. The two-step procedure is less costly because (a) biopsy can be done on outpatient basis, and (b) some biopsies indicate no cancer, thus making step two redundant. Cost of screening and diagnosis can be significantly reduced if only 50-year-old or older women are targeted. Output can be measured in percentage of diagnosed patients who survive at least five years. This depends on how early cancer is detected.

Lung cancer is fatal in approximately 25 percent of the cases. The diagnosis may use expensive CT scanners. If it is treatable, surgery and chemotherapy are used. Chemotherapy is usually done on an outpatient basis. Output can be measured by a five-year survival rate. Input costs include cost of diagnosis, surgery, hospital stay, and chemotherapy.

Source: M.N. Bailey et al., "Healthcare Productivity," *Brookings Papers on Economic Activity*, 1997, pp. 143–202.

As an illustration, consider the "Examples of Health Care Productivity Measurement" OM in Action, which considers productivity measurement for treating/managing four common diseases.

Sometimes measures of output used in services could result in misleading conclusions about productivity growth. For example, a hospital's aggregate output is usually measured by the number of patient-days of care provided. Suppose that the hospital becomes more productive, resulting in faster patient discharge. This reduces number of patient-days, which will reduce the productivity measure of the hospital!

Factors That Affect Productivity

Numerous factors affect productivity. Generally, they are methods and management, equipment and technology, and labour. Consider a student who plans to type a lengthy term paper. The student is an average typist and can turn out about three pages per hour. How could the student increase her productivity (i.e., turn out more pages per hour)? One way would be to enrol in a short course to improve typing skills (labour). Another way might be to replace her old computer with a more expensive computer and word-processing package (equipment and technology). Still other productivity improvements might be achieved through improving organization and preparation for the actual typing (methods and management). The incentive of receiving a good grade and the pride of doing a good job might also be important. The point is that all these factors are potential sources of productivity, not only for typing papers but also for any kind of work, and it is generally up to the manager to see that they are fully exploited.

A commonly held misconception is that workers are the main determinant of productivity. According to that theory, the route to productivity gains involves getting employees to work harder. However, the fact is that many productivity gains in the past have come from *equipment and technological* improvements. Familiar examples include machine automation and computers, text processing, spreadsheets, CAD software, bar codes and scanners, and Internet and e-mail.

Effective management and methods result in better design, planning, and operating decisions, standardizing and improving processes, improving quality, reducing waste (as in just-in-time production), providing better layout, and using technology, equipment, and labour more effectively and efficiently.

Summary

- Competition is the driving force in many organizations. Companies compete by emphasizing one or more competitive priorities, such as cost, quality, flexibility, and delivery.

- From a customer's perspective, these competitive priorities are price, quality, variety, and timeliness. These are called key purchasing criteria.

- To develop an effective strategy for the organization, it is essential to determine the key purchasing criteria of customers, and to identify which are order qualifiers and which are order winners.

- Strategies are plans for directing the organization to achieve its mission/vision/goals.

- Mission/vision is what the company wants to achieve, its products and services, and its markets (now and in the future, respectively).

- Organizations generally have overall strategies that pertain to the entire organization and functional strategies that pertain to each of the functional areas. Functional strategies are narrower in scope and should be linked to overall strategy.

- An operations strategy is a co-ordinated set of policies, objectives, and action plans directly affecting the operations function.

- An operations strategy can be classified into nine strategic decision categories: facility, capacity, vertical integration/outsourcing, supplier relationship/partnership, process types and technology, product mix and new products, human resources, quality, and operations infrastructure and systems.

- Quality-based and time-based strategies are among the most widely used generic operations strategies.

- Productivity is a measure of efficient use of resources. Organizations want higher productivity because it yields higher profits and helps them become more competitive.
- Productivity is measured as output/input.
- The most common productivity measure is labour productivity, e.g., number of units produced per hour.

- Productivity of services is harder to measure because outputs are usually intangible and variable, and inputs are variable, too.
- Factors affecting productivity include methods and management, equipment and technology, and labour.

Key Terms

action plan
competitive priorities
competitiveness
key purchasing criteria
mission
operations strategy

order qualifiers
order winners
productivity
quality-based strategy
strategic planning
strategy

tactics
time-based strategy
values
vision

Solved Problems

Problem 1

A company that processes fruits and vegetables is able to produce 400 cases of canned peaches in one-half hour with four workers. What is labour productivity?

Solution

$$\text{Labour productivity} = \frac{\text{Quantity produced}}{\text{Labour hours}} = \frac{400 \text{ cases}}{4 \text{ workers} \times 1/2 \text{ hours}}$$

$$= 200 \text{ cases per worker hour}$$

Problem 2

A wrapping paper company produced 2,000 rolls of paper in one day. Labour cost was $160, material cost was $50, and overhead was $320. Determine the multifactor productivity.

Solution

$$\text{Multifactor productivity} = \frac{\text{Quantity produced}}{\text{Labour cost} + \text{Material cost} + \text{Overhead}}$$

$$= \frac{2,000 \text{ rolls}}{\$160 + \$50 + \$320}$$

$$= 3.77 \text{ rolls per dollar input}$$

A variation of the multifactor productivity incorporates the price in the numerator by multiplying the units by the price.

Problem 3

A pottery manufacturer that sells to flower stores and department stores had the following output and costs during the last three weeks. Average labour cost is $10 per hour during regular time (first 40 hours of a week) and $15 per hour during overtime (any hours in excess of 40 hours a week), and pottery clay cost was $2/kg. Calculate the multifactor productivity for each week and comment on the results.

Week	1	2	3
Units produced	1,000	1,500	1,500
No. of workers	2	2	3
Hours per week per worker	40	60	40
Material (kg)	150	250	300

Solution

Multifactor productivity = units produced/(labour cost + material cost)

Week	1	2	3
Units produced	1,000	1,500	1,500
Labour cost	2(40)($10) = $800	$800 + 2(20)($15) = $1,400	3(40)($10) = $1,200
Material cost	150($2) = $300	250($2) = $500	300($2) = $600
Total cost	$1,100	= $1,900	= $1,800
Multifactor productivity	1,000/$1,100	= 1,500/$1,900	= 1,500/$1,800
(pots per $ input)	= 0.91	= 0.79	= 0.83

Multifactor productivity decreased as overtime was used in Week 2 but increased as another worker was added in Week 3 and no overtime was used. However, material cost increased in Week 3 due to mistakes of the new worker.

Problem 4

A health club has two employees who work on lead generation. Each employee works 40 hours a week, and is paid $20 an hour. Each employee identifies an average of 400 possible leads a week from a list of 8,000 names. Approximately 10 percent of the leads become members and pay a one-time fee of $100. Material costs are $130 per week, and overhead costs are $1,000 per week. Calculate the multifactor productivity for this operation in fees generated per dollar of input.

Solution

$$\text{MFP} = \frac{(\text{Possible leads})(\text{No. of workers})(\text{Fee})(\text{Conversion percentage})}{\text{Labour cost} + \text{Material cost} + \text{Overhead cost}}$$

$$= \frac{(400)(2)(\$100)(.10)}{2(40)(\$20) + \$130 + \$1,000} = \frac{\$8,000}{\$2,730} = 2.93$$

Discussion and Review Questions

Note: An asterisk indicates that a question or problem may be more challenging.

1. How do you use the four key purchasing criteria personally when buying goods and services? Give an example. **LO1**

2. List the four ways that organizations compete, and give an example for each. **LO1**

3. Explain the difference between order qualifiers and order winners. **LO1**

*4. Explain how a company can gain competitive advantage. **LO1**

5. What is strategic planning and why is it important? **LO2**

6. Briefly list the steps used in strategic planning. **LO2**

7. Describe what an operations strategy is. **LO2**

8. List the nine strategic decision categories. **LO2**

9. Describe how an operations strategy is formulated. **LO2**

10. Give an example of a policy and an action plan. **LO2**

11. Explain the term *time-based competition* and give two examples of companies using it. **LO2**

*12. Boeing's strategy appears to focus on its 787 mid-to-large size plane and its ability to fly into smaller, non-hub airports. Rival European Airbus's strategy appears to focus on its very large A380 plane. What assumption about future demand for air travel is each company making? **LO2**

13. What is productivity and why is it important? **LO3**

14. List some factors that can affect productivity and an example of each that should improve productivity. **LO3**

15. A typical Japanese automobile manufacturing plant in North America produces more cars with fewer workers than a typical Big 3 North American plant. In other words, total manufacturing labour hours per vehicle (body stamping, engine, transmission, and assembly hours) is lower for Japanese transplants (30 vs. 33 hours); see, for example The Harbour Report in the bottom of http://www.autonews.com/article/20080605/OEM01/306059997/harbour-report:-chrysler-toyota-tie-for-2007-efficiency-title. What are some possible explanations for this? **LO3**

16. A century ago, most people worked in agriculture, but now less than 4 percent of workers work in agriculture in Canada. Yet due to mechanization and automation, the agricultural output is much more now than a century ago. The majority of people now work in other industries. Also, the standard of living is much higher now than a century ago. Discuss the statement "if productivity increases, fewer workers will be needed." **LO3**

17. Explain the difference between productivity and efficiency. **LO3**

18. Give two reasons that productivity measurement in health care, e.g., treatment of diabetes, is difficult. **LO3**

Taking Stock

1. Who needs to be involved in formulating organizational strategy? **LO2**

2. Name some of the competitive trade-offs that might arise in a fast-food restaurant. **LO1**

3. How does technology improve each of these?
   a. Competitiveness. **LO1**
   b. Productivity. **LO3**

4. How can ethics be included in strategic planning? *Hint:* see http://www.scu.edu/ethics/practicing/focusareas/business/strategic-plan.html **LO2**

Critical Thinking Exercise

A company has two manufacturing plants, one in Canada and another in China. Both produce the same product. However, their labour productivity figures are quite different. The analyst thinks that this is because the Canadian plant uses more automated equipment for production while the Chinese plant uses a higher percentage of labour. Explain how that factor can cause labour productivity measures to be misleading. Is there another way to compare the two plants that would be more meaningful? **LO3**

Experiential Learning Exercises

1. Select one store that you shop at regularly. What advantage does this store have over its competitors that causes you to shop there? Try to use a purchasing criterion or competitive priority given in the chapter. **LO1**

2. Name one of your personal goals. Determine a plan to reach it (this is the strategy). **LO2**

3. Pick an organization and determine one of its goals and the associated strategy. *Hint:* Its goal may be discerned from its mission/vision statement. Its strategy may be discerned from its strategic actions. **LO2**

Internet Exercises

1. Find the mission/vision/goals/strategy of a company (e.g., Canadian Pacific). Try to relate them to the concept of this chapter. **LO2**

2. Visit http://www.timbuk2.com/. What is Timbuk2's competitive priority? **LO1**

3. View McDonald's "Made for you" video at http://bevideos.mhhe.com/business/video_library/0072917776/swf/Clip_08.html and answer the following questions: **LO1 & 2**
   a. What competitive priority is McDonald's trying to maintain (according to the video)?
   b. Identify the goal and the associated strategy/actions of McDonald's as shown in the video.

4. Visit http://www.jiffylube.ca/about/historyandmission.aspx and answer the following questions: **LO1**
   a. What market niche is Jiffy Lube filling?
   b. What is its competitive priority?

5. Visit http://www.canadapost.ca/cpo/mc/assets/pdf/aboutus/5_en.pdf and answer the following questions: **LO1 & 2**
   a. Why is Canada Post in trouble financially? Give two reasons.
   b. Does Canada Post have a competitive priority? Briefly explain.
   c. Name four action plans that are aimed to reduce Canada Post's operating costs.

Problems

1. A company produced 300 standard bookcases last week using seven workers and 240 standard bookcases this week using five workers. In which period was labour productivity higher? Explain. **LO3**

2. The manager of a crew that installs carpets has tracked the crew's output over the past several weeks, obtaining these figures: **LO3**

Week	Crew Size	Square Metres Installed
1	4	960
2	3	702
3	4	968
4	2	500
5	3	696
6	2	500

Calculate the labour productivity for each of the weeks. On the basis of your calculations, what can you conclude about crew size and productivity?

3. Calculate the multifactor productivity measure for each of the weeks shown below. What do the productivity figures suggest? Assume 40-hour weeks and an hourly wage rate of $12. Overhead is 1.5 times weekly labour cost. Material cost is $6 per kilogram. Selling price is $140 per unit. **LO3**

Week	Output (units)	Workers	Material (kg)
1	300	6	45
2	338	7	46
3	322	7	46
4	354	8	48

4. A company that makes shopping carts for supermarkets and other stores recently purchased some new equipment that reduces the labour content of the jobs needed to produce the shopping carts. Prior to buying the new equipment, the company used four workers, who produced an average of 80 carts per hour. Labour cost was $10 per hour and machine cost was $40 per hour. With the new equipment, it was possible to transfer one of the workers to another department. Machine cost increased by $10 per hour while output increased by four carts per hour. **LO3**
   a. Calculate labour productivity before and after the new equipment. Use carts per worker per hour as the measure of labour productivity.
   b. Calculate the multifactor productivity before and after the new equipment. Use carts per dollar cost (labour plus machine) as the measure.
   c. Comment on the changes in productivity according to the two measures. Which one do you believe is more pertinent for this situation?

5. An operation has a 10 percent scrap rate. As a result, only 82 good pieces per hour are produced. What is the potential increase in labour productivity that could be achieved by eliminating the scrap? **LO3**

6. A manager checked production records and found that a worker produced 160 units while working 40 hours. In the previous week, the same worker produced 138 units while working 36 hours. Calculate the labour productivity growth. Explain. **LO3**

*7. Teradyne Connection Systems makes "backplanes" (large printed circuit-board assemblies) for communication and storages devices. Recently, the company converted its production process from batch into assembly line. It also used computers to assist the workers at workstations. As a result, productivity has shot up. The site manager, Mark Galvin, says: "Operators made 300 backplanes in seven days using three shifts by the batch process (i.e., 7 days, 24 hours a day). Later, they assembled 500 backplanes in five days using just two shifts with the new assembly-line approach (i.e., 5 days, 16 hours a day)." Assuming that the same number of workers worked during each shift, and before and after the conversion, what is the percentage growth in labour productivity? **LO3**

8. A land title search office had a staff of three, each working eight hours per day (for a total payroll cost of $480/day) and overhead costs of $300 per day. This office processed an average of seven titles each day. The office recently purchased a computerized title-search system that will allow the processing of an average of 12 titles per day. Although the staff, work hours, and pay will be the same, the overhead costs will be $600 per day. **LO3**
   a. Calculate the labour productivity in the old and the new systems. How much (in percentage) has the labour productivity grown?
   b. Calculate the multifactor productivity in the old and the new systems. How much (in percentage) has the multifactor productivity grown?
   c. Which productivity measure is more appropriate for the land title search office?

9. When Henry Ford introduced moving assembly lines in his Ford Motor Company plants in 1913, the productivity soared.[8] An example of this is the coil line. A coil is an electrical component that makes high voltage for ignition. Before, a skilled worker took approximately 20 minutes to make a coil from start to finish. After an assembly line was set up and the job was divided into 29 different tasks performed by 29 workers, it took only approximately 13 minutes to assemble one coil. (*Note:* Because workers work simultaneously, approximately every 0.5 minute a coil is produced.) **LO3**
   a. Calculate the labour productivity before and after the conversion into an assembly line.
   b. Calculate the percentage increase in labour productivity due to the assembly line.

10. (i) One person using a hammer will take five days to nail new shingles on the roof of a 300 m² house.
    (ii) Two persons using a hammer but working together (one holds a shingle, the other swings the hammer) will take two days to do the same job.

---

[8] J.C. Wood and M.C. Wood, eds., *Henry Ford: Critical Evaluations in Business and Management*, London: Routledge, 2003.

(iii) One person using a nail gun will take one day to do the same job. **L03**

    a. Define a labour productivity measure and determine its value for each of the above cases.

    b. Calculate the percentage increase in productivity due to method improvement, i.e., from (i) to (ii).

    c. Calculate the percentage increase in productivity due to using technology, i.e., from (i) to (iii).

11. Southwest Tube of Oklahoma[9] is a small fabricator of specialty tubes used in boilers and other equipment. Southwest buys the tubes in long segments and cuts, bends, cold draws, and welds the pieces to make what is needed for the products. A few years ago Southwest Tube was facing tough competition. The prices were falling while the costs were rising. To improve productivity, consultants were brought in. They pointed out problems with labour turnover, absenteeism, weak supervision, staffing mismatch, lack of performance goals, and a dislike for the weekly rotating schedule as causes of the problem. One of the solutions tried, in addition to other improvements, was changing the work schedule to four 12-hour days followed by three days off. The productivity seemed to improve gradually. To ascertain this, the following data for two physically demanding work centres were collected starting the year before the change in work schedule. **L03**

Question: Has workers' productivity in the two work centres increased? Explain.

Cold Draw Dept			Weld Mill Dept		
	Labour	**Output**		**Labour**	**Output**
Year	(1,000 hr)	(1,000 ft)	Year	(1,000 hr)	(1,000 ft)
0	228	18,269	0	132	22,434
1	234	19,576	1	157	34,777
2	183	17,633	2	102	26,715
3	150	18,870	3	77	25,227

*12. The following data (all in billion $) were the sales and profit of Hudson's Bay Company (parent of The Bay and Zellers) during a three-year period. **L03**

	3	**2**	**1**
Total Sales & Revenue	7.1	7.3	7.3
EBIT	0.13	0.17	0.18

EBIT = earnings before interest and tax

Hint: Inputs = Total cost = Total Sales & Revenue − EBIT

The following data (all in billion $) were the sales, cost of sales (= cost of goods sold), and operating and overhead expenses of Walmart during the same three-year period:

	3	**2**	**1**
Net Sales	285	256	230
Cost of Sales (COS)	220	199	178
Operating, selling, general & admin costs (OSGA)	51	45	40

Hint: Inputs = Total cost = COS + OSGA

Calculate an appropriate measure of productivity for each company and compare. Which company was more productive? Explain.

*13. The following data (all in billion $) were the sales and costs (excluding selling and general and administrative costs) of McDonalds for company-operated restaurants (i.e., excluding franchise restaurants) during a three-year period. **L03**

    a. Calculate the labour productivity (in $ sales over $ payroll & benefits costs) and its growth over time. Interpret your results.

    b. Calculate the multifactor productivity (in $ sales over $ all operating costs given) and its growth over time. Interpret your results.

	1	**2**	**3**
Sales	16.6	16.6	15.5
Operating costs Food & paper	5.5	5.9	5.2
Payroll & benefits	4.3	4.3	4.0
Occupancy (lease, etc)	3.9	3.8	3.5

*14. The following data were the production of potash (KCl), in 1,000 tonne units, and number of active mine-site employees for two mine/mill facilities of the Potash Corp (of Saskatchewan) during a four-year period. **L03**

Calculate the labour productivity (in 1,000 tonnes per employee per year) and its changes over time for each facility, and interpret your results (over time and across the two facilities).

	Lanigan		Rocanville	
Year	Production	Employees	Production	Employees
1	2,025	364	1,833	328
2	2,023	378	2,573	340
3	1,471	402	1,897	343
4	1,907	441	2,647	354

15. Frank Gilbreth is the "father" of motion study. One of the first operations he studied was bricklaying. He noticed that there was unnecessary stooping, walking, and reaching. Also some bricks were damaged, which required the bricklayer to inspect each brick and find the better side before laying it. Stooping per brick laid was

---

[9] J.M. Shirley and T.M. Box, "Productivity Gains at Southwest Tube," *Production and Inventory Management Journal*, Fourth Quarter 1987, 28(4), pp. 57–60. Also see http://www.webcoindustries.com. Reprinted with permission of the APICS, The Association for Operations Management.

once for the mortar, and another for the brick. Gilbreth designed a nonstooping scaffolding platform that was raised by a lifting jack as work progressed up the wall so that the mortar and bricks were always at easy reach of the bricklayer. Motions per brick were reduced from 18 to 5, and average time went down from approximately 29 seconds per brick laid to approximately 10 seconds per brick laid. Calculate the labour productivity before and after the improvement, and the percentage of increase. **LO3**

16. A company offers identity-theft protection. It obtains client leads from banks. Three employees work 40 hours a week on the leads, at a pay rate of $25 per hour per employee. Each employee identifies an average of 3,000 potential leads a week from a list of 5,000. An average of 4 percent actually sign up for the service, paying a one-time fee of $70. Material costs are $1,000 per week, and overhead costs are $9,000 per week. Calculate the multi-factor productivity for this operation in fees generated per dollar of input. **LO3**

17. The following are the performance measures used by Canadian Pacific Railways (http://www.cpr.ca/en/investors-site/Lists/FinancialReports/cp-2013-q4-er.pdf, page 14). Determine which is a productivity measure (output/input) and describe what type of productivity measure (labour, machine, material, energy, multifactor) it is. (FRA = Federal Railroad Administration) **LO3**

Fourth Quarter

2013	2012	Operations Performance
68,531	66,204	Freight gross ton-miles ("GTM") (millions)
9,341	10,046	Train miles (thousands)
7,844	7,014	Average train weight—excluding local traffic (tons)
6,668	6,198	Average train length—excluding local traffic (feet)
7.9	7.4	Average terminal dwell (hours)
17.6	17.6	Average train speed (mph)
223.2	197.1	Locomotive productivity (daily average GTMs/active horsepower ("HP"))
1.06	1.14	Fuel efficiency (U.S. gallon of fuel consumed/1,000 GTMs)
71.4	74.4	U.S. gallons of locomotive fuel consumed (millions)
3.51	3.47	Average fuel price (U.S. dollars per U.S. gallon)
14,677	16,369	Total employees (average)[1]
14,506	15,713	Total employees (end of period)[1]
14,977	16,907	Workforce (end of period)[2]
		Safety
1.77	2.05	FRA personal injuries per 200,000 employee-hours
1.35	1.68	FRA train accidents per million train-miles

[1] An employee is defined as an individual, including trainees, who has worked more than 40 hours in a standard biweekly pay period. This excludes part time employees, contractors, and consultants.

[2] Workforce is defined as total employees plus part time employees, contractors and consultants.

 MINI-CASE

Canadian Pacific

CP is one of the two major railways in Canada and its history goes back as far back as Canada itself. However, it is second to CN in terms of size and was having a hard time competing with CN before 2012 when a major institutional investor, unhappy with its performance, removed its head and some of its directors through a proxy contest, and brought in Hunter Harrison, the ex-CEO of CN, as the new CEO, despite a legal challenge by CN.

In less than six months, Mr. Harrison turned CP around by accomplishing the following tasks:

- Closed four of the five hump yards (classification yards using gravity) in Toronto, Winnipeg, Calgary, and Chicago; combined the pair of intermodal yards in each of Chicago and Toronto into a larger one, converted the Winnipeg yard to a local switching yard, and closed Milwaukee intermodal yard.

- Increased train speed by 15 percent and reduced yard dwell time by 12 percent, allowing CP to reduce the number of its locomotives, railcars, and workers, and to offer a fast four-day intermodal service from Vancouver to Toronto or Chicago, which is faster than CN's.

(continued)

- Negotiated five-year agreements with major CP unions.
- Moved the CP HQ from downtown to Ogden railyard in Calgary.
- Taught 700 managers how to run locomotives and railyards.
- Reduced the number of customer service staff from 800 to 200.
- Lengthened some of its trains from approximately 2 km to 3–4 km.

Questions

a. What is CP's competitive priority?
b. Are the above actions consistent with your answer to part *a.* Briefly explain.

CASE http://www.loblaw.ca

Competing the Loblaw Way

Loblaw is Canada's largest national grocery store chain with annual revenue of approximately $31 billion. Its mission is to provide consumers with the best in one-stop shopping for everyday household needs. Besides food, some stores sell housewares, electronics, clothing, beauty products, pharmacy, photo finishing, toys, and gasoline. Loblaw also offers financial services, including a MasterCard. Loblaw is one of the largest companies in Canada, with over 134,000 full-time and part-time employees.

When Richard J. Currie was appointed president of Loblaw in 1976, Loblaw was only a regional chain (mainly in Ontario), with low profits and cash flow problems. Most store buildings were leased on a long-term basis and the company had no strategic direction.

Currie closed some unprofitable stores and concentrated on maximizing sales per square foot of the other stores. Loblaw did not open new stores. Although it appeared weak to its competitors, this strategy allowed Loblaw to survive.

Currie believed that Loblaw should own its stores, rather than lease them; the leases were long term and inflexible. This frequently resulted in the company having to pay for the building well after the store was closed. Also, changing a leased building to accommodate new departments was problematic. So, Loblaw gradually reduced its leases and increased its real estate ownership. Loblaw now owns more than 70 percent of the buildings it uses.

Currie also believed that controlling the buying activities and labour costs were most important. Given that cost of goods is approximately 90 percent of the selling price in the grocery business, there is not much margin for labour and overhead costs. Also, he believed that union workers were much more costly than non union workers. Given that most stores were already unionized, the way around the low margin was to expand the high-volume large stores.

Another problem in the food retailing business was that competitors competed using periodic sales (promotions), following a "high-low" pricing strategy. Currie believed that selling anything below cost was absurd, but he could not convince his competitors. He believed that customers just needed "quality products, reliably available, and priced competitively."

His solution was to introduce the No-Name private label brand in 1978. This way, Loblaw could provide reasonable quality products at reduced prices every day. This was very successful. Later Loblaw continued its private brand (or "control label" products as it calls them) with President's Choice in 1984, and 8 others later, including the Joe Fresh Style line of clothing in 2006, for a total of approximately 5,000 items.

Currie also believed in the advantage of an online in-store computerized information system. The use of bar codes and scanners allowed efficient data gathering that was used to identify profitability of items. This allowed Loblaw to control costs back up its supply chain.

Throughout the years, Loblaw has grown immensely through buying smaller regional chains and opening new stores. It now owns approximately 580 and franchises approximately 470 grocery stores (approximately 4.8 million m² of floor space) in Canada under 22 different banners, including large superstores such as The Real Canadian Superstore in the West and Ontario, Dominion in Newfoundland, and Atlantic Superstore; medium-size food-focused stores (called "Great Foods") such as Loblaw's and Zehrs (mainly in Ontario), and Provigo (in Quebec); discount food stores such as Extra Foods (in the West), No Frills (franchised), and Maxi and Maxi & Co in Quebec; wholesale stores such as Real Canadian Wholesale Club, Cash & Carry, and Presto; and ethnic (Chinese) chain T&T Supermarkets.

The different store banners sell basically the same products, approximately 24 percent being Loblaw's private brands. However, the general merchandise is sold only through large superstores. Until recently, pricing was not co-ordinated across different banners and regions. Relations with unions are fairly good. Loblaw has obtained wage cuts from its employees several times.

Loblaw's supply and distribution network is fairly efficient. It has approximately 33 warehouses throughout Canada. It has the largest fleet of trucks in Canada. The information system is gradually being centralized (the purchasing, merchandising, and marketing functions were store banner– and regionally based). Loblaw's revenues are growing annually, and its profit margin is approximately 2.5 percent per year, high for a grocery chain.

Most administrative activities are now centralized in a huge office (for 2,000 employees) in Brampton, Ontario. Information technology (for store ordering, purchasing, and inventory tracking) is being gradually centralized (using SAP).

Control label products are continuously being expanded, with the objective that they constitute 30 percent of sales.

Fresh image, health and beauty products, organics, weekly competitor price checking, and management training are being emphasized.

Net Promoter Score (measuring customer satisfaction) is being measured and is improving for most stores. Approximately 200 stores were renovated recently. Joe Fresh is now sold online, and Loblaw is expanding Joe Fresh's sales internationally through partner store chains such as J.C. Penny. Loblaw recently completed the purchase of Shoppers Drug Mart, the largest pharmacy chain in Canada.

Questions

1. What competitive priority does Loblaw emphasize?

2. List and evaluate Loblaw's operations strategy. Use the nine strategic decision categories.

Sources: Loblaw Annual Reports various years. http://www.loblaw.ca; Richard J. Curry, "Loblaw's: Putting the Super in Supermarket," *Business Quarterly*, Summer 1994, pp. 24–30.

 CASE http://www.westjet.ca

WestJet's Strategy

WestJet is a fast-growing Canadian discount airline headquartered in Calgary. It started in 1996 with three used airplanes targeting short trips in Western Canada (between Calgary, Edmonton, Kelowna, Winnipeg, and Vancouver). Clive Beddoe, one of the founders of WestJet, got the idea for WestJet after having to pay exorbitant fares to Air Canada for his frequent flights between Calgary (his hometown) and Edmonton and Vancouver, where he owned plastic manufacturing plants. According to Beddoe, "the key to expanding the market and luring masses of people who don't travel and those who drive is to charge them bargain-basement fares." He called this market the "visiting friends and relatives" market. In order to be able to offer low prices, WestJet needed to run low-cost operations. WestJet studied successful discount airlines in the United States such as Southwest Airlines, and copied most of their operations principles.

How could WestJet have planned for an operating cost per available seat mile approximately half that of Air Canada? The main principles of WestJet's plan were:

- Short-distance flights.
- Single class of passengers (no first or business class).
- Purchase only one type of aircraft: Boeing 737.
- Fly to smaller cities.
- Recruit young enthusiastic employees whose salary is slightly lower than average, but who receive profit-sharing bonuses.
- Emphasize "fun and friendly culture" and empower the employees (i.e., bottom-up management).
- Use equity financing and tight financial controls.
- Use paperless tickets (first in North America to do so).
- No connecting flights and no baggage transfers.
- No frequent flyer program.

To further motivate its employees, WestJet later introduced an employee share purchase program.

WestJet has gradually and carefully added to its flights. In 2000 WestJet expanded eastward to Hamilton then to Windsor, Halifax, Montreal, Gander, St. John's, and in 2002 to Toronto. Now, WestJet has flights to 88 Canadian, U.S., Mexican, and Caribbean cities. The sun destinations flights are seasonal, offered in winter, when travel inside Canada dips. However, this expansion in flights has resulted in WestJet's flying some medium-distance flights (e.g., to Hawaii), flying to big cities, and performing baggage transfers.

In concert with increased flights, WestJet has been gradually adding to its fleet of planes, simultaneously replacing the old 737-200 (with 125 seats) with new next-generation 737s in three sizes: 737-600 (119 seats), 737-700 (136 seats), and 737-800 (166 seats). Now it has 98 next-generation 737 planes, which are 30 percent more fuel efficient. The average age of WestJet planes is only 3 to 4 years now. New planes can be operated close to 12 hours a day vs. 10 hours for the old planes. Clearly, their maintenance cost is lower than the old planes. The new planes have leather seats and individual live seat-back satellite TV for each passenger. WestJet owns most of its planes. Recently, the legroom in the first three rows of planes haves been expanded (these seats have a higher fare).

WestJet is not afraid to spend money on useful technology. An example is the installation of blended winglets on the end of the wings of new planes, which will increase lift and reduce drag, thus increasing fuel economy by approximately 4 percent. The approximately $600,000 investment per plane pays back in about four years. Another example is the use of dual boarding bridges in certain airports such as Calgary and Vancouver. This allows boarding and un-boarding from both front and back doors simultaneously, halving the time.

WestJet has entered in over 30 interline partnerships with international airlines, 8 of which involve code sharing. It has

(continued)

upgraded its online booking system recently at the cost of $40 million. WestJet has recently started a regional subsidiary called Encore, and uses a handful of Bombardier Q400 turboprops on some flights in BC. Encore plans to expand to the East. Also, WestJet is planning to fly to Europe in the next few years.

WestJet now employs approximately 9,700 employees (still nonunionized, but over 85 percent own WestJet shares) and has about 25 percent of the air travel market in Canada. WestJet's revenue-passenger-miles was approximately 18 billion in 2012 whereas Air Canada's was 56 billion (including overseas flights). WestJet has one of the best on-time (within 15 minutes of the scheduled time) arrival performances and is one of the most profitable airlines in North America, despite the sharp increase in jet fuel cost in recent years. Its load factor (percentage of seats occupied) has been increasing from 70 percent in the late 1990s to 80–85 percent, and its revenue is over $3.4 billion.

Questions

1. What market segment did WestJet originally compete in?

2. What competitive priority did WestJet originally have?

3. What were the advantages of each of the initial principles used by WestJet in 1996 to reduce its operating costs?

4. How has WestJet kept its low operating costs and increased the utilization of its planes, while growing more than 10 percent per year?

Sources: WestJet's Annual Reports, various years, http://www.westjet.com/guest/en/about/index.shtml.

For more information on the resources available from McGraw-Hill Ryerson, go to www.mheducation.ca/he/solutions.

CHAPTER 3
Demand Forecasting

Housing starts in Canada—all areas

Legend:
— Housing starts, SAAR
— Housing starts trend line (6-month moving average)

194,809

183,515

Source: Canadian Mortgage and Housing Corporation, https://www.cmhc-schl.gc.ca/en/corp/nero/nere/2014/2014-05-08-0816.cfm.

This part is devoted solely to demand forecasting. It is presented early in the book because demand forecasts are the basis for a wide range of decisions that are described in the following chapters. In fact, demand forecasts are basic inputs for many kinds of decisions in business organizations. Consequently, it is important for *all* managers to be able to understand and use demand forecasts. Although product demand forecasts are typically developed by the sales/marketing function, the operations function, through production planning, will receive and use the demand forecasts. Also, the operations function develops demand/usage forecasts for supplies and spare parts.

Chapter 3 provides important insights on demand forecasting as well as information on how to develop and monitor demand forecasts.

Learning Objectives

After completing this chapter, you should be able to:

LO1 Identify uses of demand forecasts, distinguish between forecasting time frames, describe common features of forecasts, list the elements of a good forecast and steps of forecasting process, and contrast different forecasting approaches.

LO2 Describe at least three judgmental forecasting methods.

LO3 Describe the components of a time series model, explain averaging techniques, and solve typical problems.

LO4 Describe trend forecasting and solve typical problems.

LO5 Describe seasonality forecasting and solve typical problems.

LO6 Describe associative models (regression) and solve typical problems.

LO7 Describe three measures of forecast accuracy and two ways of controlling forecasts, and solve typical problems.

LO8 Identify the major factors to consider when choosing a forecasting technique.

A home is the single largest investment for an average Canadian household. Consequently, housing affordability has a strong and direct effect on the well-being of all Canadians. The Canada Mortgage and Housing Corporation (CMHC) has recently released a report to address the issue of housing affordability across various metropolitan areas in the country. The housing affordability index depends on the price of homes, the incomes in a region, and the prevailing interest rate. Any household spending less than 30 percent of its income on housing is classified as meeting the affordability standard. Armed with these facts, the CMHC can then provide objective housing research and advice to the Canadian government, consumers, and the entire housing industry. The figure above is a seasonally adjusted forecast of housing starts across all of Canada. How is this forecast made? Are forecasts accurate and reliable in general? Forecasting is the topic of this chapter.

Source: http://www.cmhc.ca/en/corp/about/anrecopl/anre/upload/CMHC_68134_w.pdf

Forecasting

Forecasts are a basic input in the decision processes of operations management because they provide information on future demand. The importance of forecasting to operations management cannot be overstated. The primary goal of operations management is to match supply to demand. Having a forecast of demand is essential for determining how much capacity or supply will be needed to meet demand. For instance, operations needs to know what capacity will be needed to make staffing and equipment decisions, budgets must be prepared, purchasing needs information for ordering from suppliers, and supply chain partners need to make their plans.

Planning is an integral part of an operations manager's job. If uncertainties cloud the planning process, operations managers will find it difficult to plan effectively. Demand forecasts help operations managers by reducing some of the uncertainty, thereby enabling them to develop more meaningful plans. A **demand forecast** is the estimate of expected demand during a specified future period.

People make and use demand forecasts in their everyday life. They forecast e.g., "How much food and drink will I need?" when visiting a grocery store or "How much cash or gas will I need?" when visiting a bank or gas station. To make these forecasts, they take into account two kinds of information. One is current factors or conditions. The other is past experience in a similar situation. Sometimes they will rely more on one than the other, depending on which approach seems more relevant at the time. Demand forecasting for business purposes involves similar approaches. However, more formal methods are used to make demand forecasts and to assess forecast accuracy. Demand forecasting basically involves modelling the past pattern of demand for an item and projecting it into the future while taking new developments into account.

There are three types of uses for demand forecasts in operations. One is to help managers design the system, another is to help them plan the medium-term use of the system, and the third is to schedule the short-term use of the system. Designing the system involves long-term plans about which goods and services to offer; capacities, facilities, and equipment to have; where to locate, and so on. Planning the medium-term use of the system involves tasks such as planning overall inventory and workforce levels, and planning production at the aggregate product family level. Scheduling the short-term use of the system involves scheduling of production, purchasing of parts and raw materials, and staff scheduling.

Business forecasting pertains to more than predicting demand. Financial and economic forecasts are used to predict variables such as profits, revenues, costs, stock prices, and GDP. This chapter will focus on the forecasting of demand (sales of goods/services or usage of spare parts/supplies). Keep in mind, however, that the concepts and techniques presented in this chapter apply equally well to the other types of business forecasting.

In spite of its use of computers and sophisticated mathematical models, forecasting is not an exact science. Instead, successful forecasting often requires a skilful blending of art and science. Experience, judgment, technical expertise, information, and communication all play a role in developing useful forecasts. Along with these, a certain amount of luck and a dash of humility can be helpful, because the worst forecasters occasionally produce a very good forecast, and even the best forecasters sometimes miss completely.

Generally speaking, the responsibility for preparing demand forecasts for finished goods or services lies with the marketing or sales departments rather than operations. Nonetheless, because

demand forecast The estimate of expected demand during a specified future period.

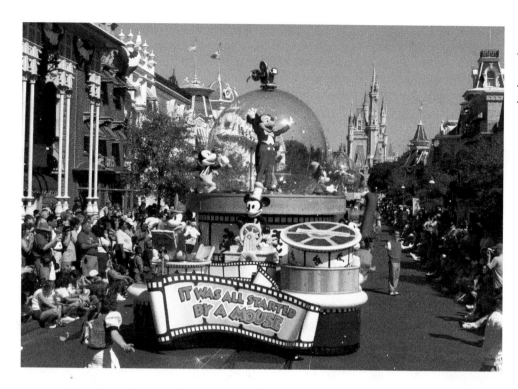

The Walt Disney World forecasting department has 20 employees who formulate forecasts on volume and revenue for the theme parks, water parks, and resort hotels, as well as merchandise, food, and beverage revenue by location.

demand forecasts are major inputs for many operations decisions, operations managers must be knowledgeable about the kinds of forecasting techniques available, the assumptions that underlie their use, and their limitations. Also the operations function provides feedback about the feasibility of producing the demand forecasts. See the "Forecasting in Ocean Spray Cranberries" OM in Action. In addition, inventory managers (see Chapter 12) make forecasts of usage of supplies and spare parts.

Recently, supply chain partners have started to collaborate on the forecasting process. The customer company makes the forecast in consultation with the supplier, allowing for both sides to provide inputs such as the expectation of customers for increased quantities during a promotion, the capacity limitations of the supplier, etc. This is called Collaborative Planning, Forecasting, and Replenishment (CPFR) (more on this in Chapter 11 on supply chain management).

Forecasts affect decisions and activities throughout an organization, in accounting, finance, human resources, marketing, and management information systems (MIS), as well as in operations and other areas. Here are some examples of uses of forecasts in business organizations:

Accounting: New product/process cost estimates, profit projections, cash management.

Finance: Equipment/equipment replacement needs, timing and amount of funding/borrowing needs.

Human resources: Hiring activities, including recruitment, interviewing, and training; layoff planning, including outplacement counselling.

Marketing: Pricing and promotion, e-business strategies, global competition strategies.

MIS: New/revised information systems, Internet services.

Operations: Schedules, capacity planning, work assignments and workloads, inventory planning, make-or-buy decisions, outsourcing, project management.

Product/service design: Revision of current features, design of new products or services.

Features Common to All Forecasts

A wide variety of forecasting techniques are in use. In many respects, they are quite different from one another, as you shall soon discover. Nonetheless, certain features are common to all techniques and forecasts, and it is important to recognize them.

1. Forecasting techniques generally assume that the same underlying causal system that existed in the past will continue to exist in the future.

Comment. A manager cannot simply delegate forecasting to models or computers and then forget about it, because unplanned or special occurrences can wreak havoc with forecasts. For instance, weather-related events, sales promotions, and changes in features or prices of the company's own and competing goods or services can have a major impact on demand. Consequently, a manager must be alert to such occurrences and be ready to override forecasts.

2. Forecasts are rarely perfect; actual results usually differ from predicted values. No one can predict *precisely* how related factors will impinge upon the variable in question; this, and the presence of randomness, preclude a perfect forecast. Allowances should be made for inaccuracies.

3. Forecasts for groups of items tend to be more accurate than forecasts for individual items, because forecasting errors among items in a group usually have a cancelling effect. For example, the forecast for total sales of a new T-shirt will be more accurate than the forecast for each size and colour.

4. Forecast accuracy decreases the farther the forecasted time period is into the future. Generally speaking, short-term forecasts must contend with fewer uncertainties than longer-term forecasts, so the former tend to be more accurate. The **forecasting horizon** is the range of time periods we are forecasting for.

forecasting horizon The range of time periods we are forecasting for.

An important consequence of the last point is that flexible business organizations—those that can respond quickly to changes in demand—require a shorter forecasting horizon and, hence,

OM in ACTION http://www.oceanspray.com

Forecasting in Ocean Spray Cranberries

Ocean Spray is an agricultural cooperative owned by approximately 800 cranberry growers and 100 grapefruit growers in the United States and Canada (British Columbia and Quebec). It produces juices in bottles and cans in different flavour mixes and container sizes. When all the combination of products, sizes, and types of containers are taken into account, the number of different products ranges in the hundreds. For example, a case of eight 1.89 litre Cran-Apple juice drink bottles is a product. The company also keeps track of groups of similar products, called categories, and groups of same-size products, e.g., a group of all 1.89 litre cranberry drink bottles. Also, the products and groups in each of company's four North American manufacturing plants and for the major customers, the retail chains, are tracked separately.

Forecasting is performed by the demand planning group, which is located in the logistics and planning department. It consists of a manager and five demand planners, each responsible for a combination of approximately 300 different products and category/size/manufacturing plant/major customer groupings. Forecasts are primarily used for production planning, purchasing, and shipment of the products. The planning process is called sales and operations planning, and is discussed in more detail later in Chapter 13.

Every month during the first week, the demand planners use a software by Manugistics, which uses the past three years' history of shipments and time series models to forecast shipments for the next six months. These forecasts are shared with local sales managers to check and adjust based on local knowledge of customer intentions, inventory, and promotions. During the second week, the adjusted forecasts are further examined and adjusted by regional and divisional marketing managers in a group meeting, called the Forecast Alignment meeting. During the third week, the aligned forecasts are passed to the production/supply planning for review in the Supply Alignment meeting. Finally, during the last week of the month, upper management from sales, marketing, operations, and finance meet with demand planners (in a Sales and Operations Planning meeting) to review and implement the results of the alignment meetings.

Before setting up the above formal process and using Manugistics in 1998, Ocean Spray did not have one unique forecast for each product and groupings. The accuracy of forecasts was low—mean absolute percentage error (MAPE) was approximately 45 percent at the product level. Now, MAPE is approximately 25 percent.

A challenge for the demand planners is the seasonality of sales of cranberries. Approximately 90 percent of sales occur during the fall, primarily before Thanksgiving and Christmas. Ocean Spray constantly introduces new products such as a new mix of another fruit with cranberry. If a similar product had been introduced before, this product's sales history will be used as a guide for the new product's demand. Otherwise, the services of the consumer research department will be needed.

Sources: http://www.oceanspray.com; P. Gelly, "Managing Bottom Up and Top Down Approaches: Ocean Spray's Experience," *Journal of Business Forecasting Methods & Systems* 18(4), Winter 1999/2000, pp. 3–5; J. Malehorn, "Forecasting at Ocean Spray Cranberries," *Journal of Business Forecasting Methods & Systems* 20(2), Summer 2001, pp. 6–8; H. Landi, "Straight from the Bog to the Bottle," *Beverage World* 124(1757) December 15, 2005, 38–42.

benefit from more accurate short-term forecasts than competitors that are less flexible and must therefore use longer forecasting horizons. Flexibility can be achieved by shortening the lead time required to produce goods/services, and purchase raw materials/parts/supplies, and related approaches such as postponement (i.e., waiting until customer order is received to add differentiating features to standard components or products).

Elements of a Good Forecast

A forecast should fulfill certain requirements:

1. The forecast should be *timely*. The forecasting horizon must cover the time necessary to implement possible changes so that its results can be used.

2. The forecast should be *accurate*, and the degree of accuracy of the forecast should be stated. This will enable users to plan for possible errors and will provide a basis for comparing alternative forecasts.

3. The forecasting method/software chosen should be *reliable*; it should work consistently.

4. The forecast should be expressed in *meaningful units*. Financial planners need to know demand in *dollars*, whereas demand and production planners need to know demand in *units*. The choice of units depends on user needs.

5. The forecast should be *in writing*. Although this will not guarantee that all concerned are using the same information, it will at least increase the likelihood of it. In addition, a written forecast will permit an objective basis for evaluating the forecast once actual results are in.

6. The forecasting technique should be *simple to understand and use*. Users often lack confidence in forecasts based on sophisticated techniques; they do not understand either the circumstances in which the techniques are appropriate or the limitations of the techniques. Misuse of techniques is an obvious consequence. Not surprisingly, fairly simple forecasting techniques enjoy widespread popularity because users are more comfortable working with them.

7. The forecast should be *cost-effective*. The benefits should outweigh the costs.

Steps in the Forecasting Process

There are six basic steps in the forecasting process (only steps 4 to 6 are used on a continuing basis):

1. *Determine the purpose of the forecast*. Determine the level of detail required, the amount of resources (personnel, computer time, dollars) that can be justified, and the level of accuracy necessary.

2. *Establish a forecasting horizon*. The forecast must indicate a time interval, keeping in mind that accuracy decreases as the time horizon increases.

3. *Gather and analyze relevant historical data*. Ensure that the data is of past demand rather than sales or shipments, which will be different if there were stock-outs. Identify any assumptions that are made.

4. *Select a forecasting technique*.

5. *Prepare the forecast*.

6. *Monitor the forecast*. If it is not performing in a satisfactory manner, re-examine the parameters of the technique or use a different technique.

Approaches to Forecasting

There are two general approaches to forecasting: judgmental and quantitative. Judgmental methods consist mainly of subjective inputs, which may defy precise numerical description (but may still depend on historical data). Quantitative methods involve either the use of a time series model to extend the historical pattern of data into the future or the development of associative models that attempt to utilize *causal (explanatory) variables* to make a forecast.

© Mike Baldwin / Cornered

BALDWIN

"I recommend our 'wild' expectations be downgraded to 'great.'"

judgmental methods Use nonquantitative analysis of historical data and/or analysis of subjective inputs from consumers, sales staff, managers, executives, similar products, and experts to help develop a forecast.

time series models Extend the pattern of data into the future.

associative models Use explanatory variables to predict future demand for the variable of interest.

Judgmental techniques permit inclusion of *soft* information (e.g., human factors, personal opinions, hunches) in the forecasting process. Those factors are often omitted or downplayed when quantitative techniques are used because they are difficult to quantify. Quantitative techniques consist mainly of analyzing objective, or *hard,* data. They usually avoid personal biases that sometimes contaminate judgmental methods. In practice, either or both approaches might be used to develop a forecast.

Judgmental methods rely on nonquantitative analysis of historical data and/or analysis of subjective inputs obtained from various sources, such as consumers (surveys), similar products (historical analogies), the sales staff, managers and executives, and panels of experts. Quite frequently, these sources provide insights that are not otherwise available, e.g., for new product development, promotions, etc. Long-term forecasting typically uses judgmental methods because quantitative techniques may be inaccurate in this case.

Some forecasting techniques simply attempt to project past data into the future. These techniques use historical, or time series, data with the assumption that the future will be like the past.

Time series models identify specific patterns in the data and project or extrapolate those patterns into the future, without trying to identify causes of the patterns.

Associative models use equations that consist of one or more *explanatory* variables that can be used to predict future demand for the variable of interest. For example, demand for a particular paint might be explained by variables such as the price, the amount spent on advertising it, and the season, as well as specific characteristics of the paint (e.g., quality).

Overview of Demand Forecasting by Forecasting Horizon

Forecasting *long-term* demand typically involves annual data for, e.g., the next five years. It requires knowledge of the specific market and judgment of experts/managers. For new products, either consumer surveys and test markets are undertaken, or demand for an analogous product is used. A common approach is to forecast the demand for the whole market, estimate the market share for the new product, and multiply the two to get the demand forecast. If historical data are available, the trend is estimated and projected into the future, e.g., using regression.

Forecasting *medium-term* demand typically involves monthly demand, e.g., for the next 12 months. A mix of judgmental and quantitative methods is used. *Seasonal* effects are taken into account.

Forecasting *short-term* demand typically involves daily or weekly demand for, e.g., the next 12 weeks. Usually there are thousands of products/parts to forecast. Therefore, a simple quantitative method, e.g., an averaging technique, is used. Sales promotions are forecasted separately.

LO2 Judgmental Methods

In some situations, forecasters may rely solely on judgment and opinion to make forecasts. The introduction of new products, the redesign of existing products, or sales promotions are situations where judgmental forecasting is needed, as well as when analyzing future actions of customers and competitors. In such instances, forecasts may be based on collective executive opinions, opinions of the sales staff, consumer surveys, historical analogies, or opinions of experts.

Executive Opinions

A small group of upper-level managers (e.g., VPs of marketing, operations, and finance) may meet and collectively develop a forecast. This approach is often used as a part of long-term strategic planning and new-product development. It has the advantage of bringing together the considerable knowledge and talents of various managers. However, there is the risk that the view of one person will prevail, and the possibility that diffusing responsibility for the forecast over the entire group may result in less pressure to produce a good forecast.

Sales Force Opinions

The sales staff or the customer service staff is often a good source of information because of their direct contact with customers. They are often aware of any plans that the customers may be considering for the future, including the current level of customer inventory.

Consumer Surveys

Because it is the potential consumers who ultimately determine sales, it seems natural to solicit input from them. In some instances, every customer or potential customer can be contacted. However, usually there are too many customers or there is no way to identify all potential customers. Therefore, organizations seeking consumer input usually resort to consumer surveys, which enable them to *sample* consumer opinions. This could be in the form of questionnaires conducted by mail or phone to a large sample of potential consumers. It also could be through group meetings with a small number of potential consumers (focus groups).

Historical Analogies

Sometimes the demand for a similar product in the past, after some adjustment, can be used to forecast a new product's demand. For example, the demand for cranberry-apple drink can be used to forecast the demand for cranberry-grape drink.

Expert Opinions

The forecaster may solicit opinions from a number of experts. One way of doing this is called the **Delphi method**. It involves circulating a series of questionnaires among experts. Responses are kept anonymous, which tends to encourage honest responses and reduces the risk that one person's opinion will prevail. Each new questionnaire is developed using the information extracted from the previous one, thus enlarging the scope of information on which participants can base their judgments. The goal is to achieve a consensus forecast.

One application of the Delphi method is for *technological* forecasting, i.e., assessing changes in technology and their impact on an organization. Often the goal is to predict *when* a certain event will occur. For instance, the goal of a Delphi forecast might be to predict when video telephones might be installed in at least 50 percent of residential homes or when a vaccine for a disease might be developed. For the most part, these are long-term, single-time forecasts, which usually have very little hard information to go by.

Delphi method Experts complete a series of questionnaires, each developed from the previous one, to achieve a consensus forecast.

OM in *ACTION*

Barilla SpA

Barilla SpA, a pasta manufacturer, was founded in 1875 when Pietro Barilla opened a small shop in Parma, Italy. Competing in an oversaturated field of over 2,000 pasta manufacturers, Barilla was able to differentiate its products and grow the company using highly innovative marketing programs. Within 100 years, the company had become the largest pasta manufacturer in the world.

Barilla has recently been experiencing problems with large amounts of variability in demand, resulting in significant operational inefficiencies and increased manufacturing costs. Management wondered how there could be large fluctuations in demand for a staple food product—as per capita consumption of pasta does not tend to fluctuate much from month to month.

The reasons for the demand fluctuations are varied but a significant portion of those fluctuations can be traced to the use of sales promotions and lack of collaborative forecasting. Barilla's sales strategy relied heavily on the use of promotions ranging from 1.4 percent all the way up to 10 percent. This would cause a hockey stick effect with low demand in the beginning of each month and high demand at the end of each month as sales representatives pushed harder to clear out inventory. Downstream retailers and distributors were also reluctant to provide proprietary sales data that Barilla needed. With collaborative forecasting, Barilla and its distributors and retailers would work together to forecast demand, which would increase fill-rates while reducing inventories.

Source: Janice H. Hammond, "Barilla SpA (A)," *Harvard Business Review*, Case 9-694-046. Rev. March 25, 2008.

Time Series Models: Introduction and Averaging

Introduction

time series A time-ordered sequence of observations taken at regular intervals of time.

A **time series** is a time-ordered sequence of observations taken at regular intervals over a period of time (e.g., hourly, daily, weekly, monthly, quarterly, annually). Forecasting techniques based on time series data are made on the assumption that future values of the series can be estimated from their own past values. Although no attempt is made to identify variables that influence the series, these methods are widely used, often with quite satisfactory results.

Analysis of time series data requires the analyst to identify the underlying behaviour of the series. This can often be accomplished by merely *plotting* the data and visually examining the plot. One or more patterns might appear: level (i.e., average), trend, seasonal variation, and cycle. In addition, there can be random and irregular (one-time) variations. These behaviours can be described as follows:

level (average) A horizontal pattern of time series.

1. **Level (average)**, or constant, refers to a horizontal pattern of time series.

trend A persistent upward or downward movement in data.

2. **Trend** refers to a persistent upward or downward movement in the data. Population growth, increasing incomes, and cultural changes often account for such movements.

seasonality Regular wavelike variations related to the calendar, weather, or recurring events.

3. **Seasonality** refers to regular repeating wavelike variations generally related to factors such as the calendar, weather, or recurring events. For example, sales of ice cream are higher in the summer. Restaurants, supermarkets, and theatres experience weekly and even daily "seasonal" variations.

cycles Wavelike variations lasting more than one year.

4. **Cycles** are wavelike variations lasting more than one year. These are often related to a variety of economic, political, and even agricultural conditions, such as supply of cattle.

irregular variations Caused by unusual one-time explainable circumstances not reflective of typical behaviour.

5. **Irregular variations** are due to unusual one-time explainable circumstances not reflective of typical behaviour, such as severe weather conditions, strikes, or sales promotions. They do not reflect typical behaviour, and whenever possible should be identified and removed from the data.

random variations Residual variations after all other behaviours are accounted for (also called noise).

6. **Random variations** are residual variations that remain after all other behaviours have been accounted for (also called *noise*). This randomness arises from the combined influence of many—perhaps a great many—relatively unimportant factors, and it cannot be reliably predicted. Time series techniques smooth random variations in the data.

Some of these behaviours are illustrated in Figure 3-1. The small "bumps" in the plots represent random variations. The following sections have descriptions of the various approaches to the analysis of time series data.

Naïve Methods

A simple but widely used approach to forecasting is the naïve method. The naïve method can be used with a stable series (level or average with random variations), with seasonal variations, or with trend. With a stable series, the last data point becomes the **naïve forecast** for the next period. Thus, if the demand for a product last week was 20 cases, the forecast for this week is 20 cases. With seasonal variations, the naïve forecast for this "season" is equal to the value of the series last "season." For example, the forecast for demand for turkeys this Christmas is equal to demand for turkeys last Christmas. For data with trend, the naïve forecast is equal to the last value of the series plus or minus the difference between the last two values of the series. For example, suppose the last two values were 50 and 53:

naïve forecast For a stable series, the next forecast equals the previous period's actual value.

Period	Actual	Change from Previous Value	Naïve Forecast
$t-1$	50		
t	53	$+3$	
$t+1$			$53 + 3 = 56$

Source: Statistics Canada CANSIM 2 database, Series v108517, accessed January 26, 2010.

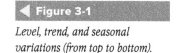 **Figure 3-1**

Level, trend, and seasonal variations (from top to bottom).

Source: Statistics Canada CANSIM 2 database, Series v108612, accessed January 26, 2010.

Source: Statistics Canada CANSIM 2 database, Series v382696; accessed January 26, 2010.

Although at first glance the naïve method may appear *too* simplistic, it is nonetheless a legitimate forecasting tool used by some businesses such as restaurants and retail stores. Consider the advantages: It has virtually no cost, it is quick and easy to prepare, and it is easily understandable. The main objection to this method is its inability to provide highly accurate forecasts.

The accuracy of a naïve forecast can serve as a standard of comparison against which to judge the cost and accuracy of other techniques. One weakness of the naïve method is that the forecast just *traces* the actual data, with a lag of one period; it does not smooth the random variations out at all. But by expanding the number of historical data a forecast is based on, this difficulty can be overcome.

Averaging Methods

Historical data typically contain a certain amount of random variation that tends to obscure systematic movements in the data. This randomness arises from the combined influence of many—perhaps a great many—relatively unimportant factors, and it cannot be reliably predicted. Averaging techniques smooth variations in the data. Ideally, it would be desirable to completely remove any randomness from the data and leave only "real" variations, such as changes in the demand. As a practical matter, however, it is usually impossible to distinguish between these two kinds of variations, so the best one can hope for is that the small variations are random and the large variations are "real."

Averaging techniques smooth fluctuations in a time series because the individual highs and lows in the data offset each other when they are combined into an average. A forecast based on an average thus tends to exhibit less variability than the original data. This can be advantageous because many of these movements merely reflect random variability rather than a true change in the series. Moreover, because responding to changes in expected demand often entails considerable cost (e.g., changes in production rate, changes in the size of a workforce, inventory changes), it is desirable to avoid reacting to minor variations. Thus, minor variations are treated as random variations, whereas larger variations are viewed as more likely to reflect "real" changes, although these, too, are smoothed to a certain degree.

Averaging methods generate forecasts that reflect recent level (i.e., an average) of a time series. They can handle stable series (i.e., a level series with random variations around it), where there is no trend or seasonality. Three techniques for averaging are described in this section:

1. Moving average.
2. Weighted moving average.
3. Exponential smoothing.

moving average Technique that averages a number of recent actual values as forecast for current period. It is updated as new values become available.

Moving Average. The **moving average** technique technique averages a *number* of recent actual data values and uses the average as the forecast for the current period. The moving average forecast is updated as a new value becomes available. The n-period moving average forecast for period t is the average of n most recent actual values.

$$F_t = MA_n = \frac{\sum_{i=t-1}^{t-n} A_i}{n} \tag{3-1}$$

where

i = An index that corresponds to age of the period ($i = t - 1$: last period; $i = t - 2$: two periods back, . . .)

n = Number of periods (data points) in the moving average

A_i = Actual value in period i

MA_n = n period moving average

F_t = Forecast for this period (i.e., period t)

Example 1 ▶

Calculate a three-period moving average forecast for the demand of a product, given its demand for the last five periods.

Period	Demand	
1	42	
2	40	
3	43	
4	40	the 3 most recent demands
5	41	

SOLUTION

$$F_6 = \frac{43 + 40 + 41}{3} = 41.33$$

If actual demand in period 6 turns out to be 39, the moving average forecast for period 7 would be

$$F_7 = \frac{40 + 41 + 39}{3} = 40.00$$

Note that in a moving average, as each new actual value becomes available, the forecast is updated by adding the newest value and dropping the oldest and then calculating the average. Consequently, the forecast "moves" by reflecting only the most recent values.

Figure 3-2 illustrates a three-period moving average forecast plotted against the actual demand during 31 periods. Note how the moving average forecast *lags* behind the actual values and how smooth the forecasted values are compared with the actual values.

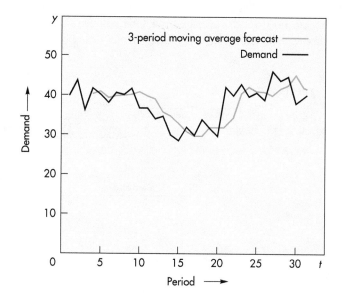

◀ **Figure 3-2**

A moving average forecast tends to smooth the data but lags behind the data.

The moving average forecast can incorporate as many data points as desired. In selecting the number of periods to include, the decision maker must take into account that the number of data points in the moving average determines its sensitivity to each new data point: the fewer the data points in a moving average, the more sensitive (responsive) to most recent data the moving average tends to be. (See Figure 3-3.) If responsiveness is important, a moving average with relatively few data points should be used. This will permit quick adjustment to a change in the data, but it will also cause the forecast to be somewhat responsive even to random variations. Conversely, moving averages based on more data points will be smoother but less responsive to "real" changes. Hence, the decision maker must weigh the cost of responding more slowly to changes in the data against the cost of responding to what might simply be random variations. A review of forecast errors (later in the chapter) can help in this decision.

The advantages of a moving average forecast are that it is easy to calculate and easy to understand. A possible disadvantage is that all values in the moving average forecast are weighted equally. For instance, in a five-period moving average forecast, each value has a weight of 1/5. Hence, the oldest value has the *same weight* as the most recent value.

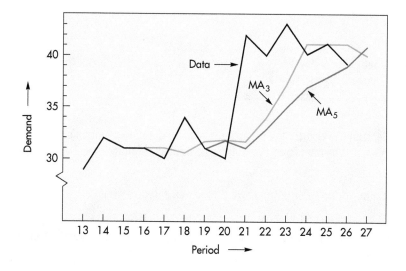

◀ **Figure 3-3**

The fewer time periods in a moving average, the greater the responsiveness of the forecast to the most recent data.

weighted moving average A variation of moving average where more recent values in the time series are given larger weight in calculating a forecast.

Weighted Moving Average. A **weighted moving average** is similar to a moving average, except that it assigns larger weight to the most recent values in a time series in calculating a forecast. For instance, the most recent value might be assigned a weight of .40, the next most recent value a weight of .30, the next after that a weight of .20, and the next after that a weight of .10. Note that the weights sum to 1.00 (because averaging methods assume that there is no trend), and that the heaviest weights are assigned to the most recent values.

Example 2 ▶

Given the following demand data,

a. Calculate a weighted moving average forecast for period 6 using a weight of .40 for the most recent period, .30 for the next most recent, .20 for the next, and .10 for the next.

b. If the actual demand for period 6 is 39, forecast the demand for period 7 using the same weights as in part *a*.

Period	Demand
1	42
2	40
3	43
4	40
5	41

SOLUTION

a. $F_6 = .40(41) + .30(40) + .20(43) + .10(40) = 41.0$
b. $F_7 = .40(39) + .30(41) + .20(40) + .10(43) = 40.2$

Note that if four weights are used, only the *four most recent* demand values should be used to prepare the forecast.

The advantage of a weighted moving average over a simple moving average is that the weighted moving average is more reflective of the most recent observations. However, the choice of weights is somewhat arbitrary and generally involves the use of trial and error to find a suitable weighting scheme.

exponential smoothing Weighted averaging method based on previous forecast plus a percentage of the difference between that forecast and the previous actual value.

Exponential Smoothing. **Exponential smoothing** is a sophisticated weighted averaging method where a new forecast is based on the previous forecast plus a percentage of the difference between that forecast and the previous actual value. That is:

Forecast = Previous forecast + α(Previous actual − Previous forecast)

where (Previous actual − Previous forecast) represents the *forecast error* and α is a proportion less than one. More concisely,

$$F_t = F_{t-1} + \alpha(A_{t-1} - F_{t-1}) \tag{3-2a}$$

where

F_t = Forecast for period t
F_{t-1} = Forecast for period $t - 1$
α = Smoothing constant, $0 < \alpha < 1$
A_{t-1} = Actual demand in period $t - 1$

For example, suppose that the previous forecast was 42 units, previous actual demand was 40 units, and α = .10. The new forecast would be computed as follows:

$$F_t = 42 + .10(40 - 42) = 41.8$$

Then, if the actual demand turns out to be 43, the next forecast would be:

$$F_t = 41.8 + .10(43 - 41.8) = 41.92$$

An alternate form of formula 3-2a reveals the weighting of the previous forecast and the previous actual demand:

$$F_t = (1 - \alpha)F_{t-1} + \alpha A_{t-1} \tag{3-2b}$$

For example, if $\alpha = .10$, this would be

$$F_t = .90F_{t-1} + .10A_{t-1}$$

The quickness of adjustment by forecast error is determined by the smoothing constant, α. The closer its value is to zero, the slower the forecast will adjust by forecast error (i.e., the greater the smoothing). Conversely, the closer the value of α is to 1.0, the greater the responsiveness and the less the smoothing. This is illustrated in Example 3.

The following table illustrates two series of exponential smoothing forecasts for a data set, and the resulting (Actual − Forecast) = Error, for each period. One forecast uses $\alpha = .10$ and the other uses $\alpha = .40$. The following figure plots the actual data and both sets of forecasts. It can be observed that the .10 forecast plot is smoother and less responsive than the .4 forecast plot.

◀ Example 3

Period (*t*)	Actual Demand	$\alpha = .10$ Forecast	$\alpha = .10$ Error	$\alpha = .40$ Forecast	$\alpha = .40$ Error
1	42	—	—	—	—
2	40	42	−2	42	−2
3	43	41.8	1.2	41.2	1.8
4	40	41.92	−1.92	41.92	−1.92
5	41	41.73	−0.73	41.15	−0.15
6	39	41.66	−2.66	41.09	−2.09
7	46	41.39	4.61	40.25	5.75
8	44	41.85	2.15	42.55	1.45
9	45	42.07	2.93	43.13	1.87
10	38	42.36	−4.36	43.88	−5.88
11	40	41.92	−1.92	41.53	−1.53
12		41.73		40.92	

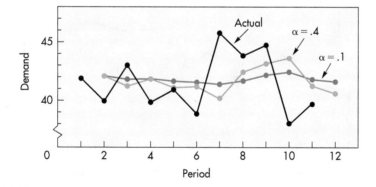

Selecting a smoothing constant is basically a matter of judgment or trial and error (or one can use the forecast errors to guide the decision). The goal is to select a smoothing constant that balances the benefits of smoothing random variations with the benefits of responding to real changes if and when they occur. Commonly used values of α range from .05 to .50. Low values of α are used when the underlying average tends to be stable; higher values are used when the underlying average is susceptible to change.

Some computer packages include a feature that permits automatic modification of the smoothing constant so that the forecast errors do not become unacceptably large. This method is called **adaptive (or variable response) exponential smoothing**.

Exponential smoothing is one of the most widely used techniques in forecasting, partly because of its ease of computation and partly because of the ease with which the weighting scheme can be altered—simply by changing the value of α.

adaptive (or variable response) exponential smoothing A version of exponential smoothing where the smoothing constant is automatically modified in order to prevent large forecast errors from occurring.

Note: A number of different approaches can be used to obtain a starting forecast for period 2, such as the average of the first several periods, a subjective estimate, or the first actual value (i.e., the naïve approach). For simplicity, the naïve approach is used in this book. In practice, using an average of, say, the first three values as a forecast for period 4 would provide a better starting forecast because it would be more stable.

LO4 Techniques for Trend

Analysis of trend involves developing an equation that will suitably describe the trend (assuming that trend is present in the data). The trend component may be linear or it may be nonlinear. Some commonly encountered nonlinear trend types are illustrated in Figure 3-4. A simple plot of the data can often reveal the existence and nature of a trend. We will first focus on *linear* trend because this is fairly common. Linear trend is usually fitted using regression. Microsoft Excel facilitates this, in addition to many types of nonlinear trend.

linear trend equation
$\hat{y}_t = a + bt$, used to develop forecasts when linear trend is present.

Linear Trend Equation. This equation has the form

$$\hat{y}_t = a + bt \tag{3-3}$$

where

t = Index of time periods, starting from $t = 1$ for the first period

$\hat{y}_t$ = Value of trend line at period t

a = Value of trend line at $t = 0$ (intercept)

b = Slope of the trend line

Forecast for period t: $F_t = a + bt$

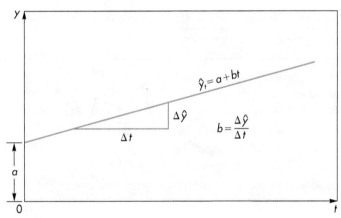

The line intersects the y axis where $\hat{y}_t = a$. The slope of the line $= b$.

For example, consider the trend equation $\hat{y}_t = 45 + 5t$. The intercept (i.e., value of $\hat{y}_t$ when $t = 0$) is 45, and the slope is 5, which means that, on the average, the value of forecast will increase by five units for each time period. If $t = 10$, the forecast, F_t, is $45 + 5(10) = 95$ units. The equation can be plotted by finding two points on the line. One can be found by substituting some value of t into the equation (e.g., $t = 10$). The other point is $(0, a)$ (i.e., $\hat{y}_t$ at $t = 0$). Plotting those two points and drawing a straight line through them yields the graph of the linear trend line.

The coefficients of the line, a and b, can be computed from data using these two equations:

$$b = \frac{n \sum ty - \sum t \sum y}{n \sum t^2 - (\sum t)^2} \tag{3-4}$$

$$a = \frac{\sum y - b \sum t}{n} \text{ or } \bar{y} - b\bar{t} \tag{3-5}$$

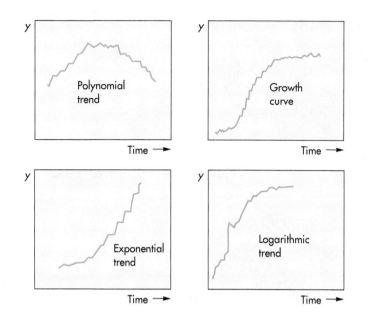

where

n = Total number of periods
y = Value of the demand time series

Note that these equations are identical to those used for computing a linear regression line, except that t replaces x in the equations.

Cellphone sales of a company over the last 10 weeks are shown below. The data appear to have a linear trend. Determine the equation of the linear trend and predict the sales of cellphones for weeks 11 and 12. Plot the data and trend line.

◀ **Example 4**

Week	Unit Sales
1	700
2	724
3	720
4	728
5	740
6	742
7	758
8	750
9	770
10	775

SOLUTION

Week (t)	y	ty	t^2
1	700	700	1
2	724	1,448	4
3	720	2,160	9
4	728	2,912	16
5	740	3,700	25
6	742	4,452	36
7	758	5,306	49
8	750	6,000	64
9	770	6,930	81
10	775	7,750	100
55	7,407	41,358	385

Using formulas 3-4 and 3-5, we can calculate the coefficients of the trend line:

$$b = \frac{10(41,358) - 55(7,407)}{10(385) - 55(55)} = \frac{6,195}{825} = 7.51$$

$$a = \frac{7,407 - 7.51(55)}{10} = 699.40$$

Thus, the trend line is $\hat{y}_t = 699.40 + 7.51t$.

Substituting values of t into this equation, the forecasts for the next two weeks (i.e., $t = 11$ and $t = 12$) are:

$$F_{11} = 699.40 + 7.51(11) = 782.01$$

$$F_{12} = 699.40 + 7.51(12) = 789.52$$

The original data (in blue), the trend line (in red), and the two projections (forecasts) are shown on the following graph. It is evident that the data exhibit a linear trend.

We can use the Excel template on Connect to solve this problem. Alternatively, we can set up our own Excel template. In fact, Excel has a feature that makes fitting a trend line very easy. If you are using Excel 2007, click on the "Insert" tab and follow the instructions to draw a line chart, then click on a white space on the chart ("Layout" tab will appear). Next, click on the "Layout" tab and then "Trendline," and finally in "More Trendline Options" tick "Display Equation on chart."

In Excel 2013, click "Insert" on the command bar and then click "Scatter with Straight Lines and Markers." Next, click on a white space on the chart (Option menu will appear on the right). Click on "+" and choose "Trendline." Click the trendline on the graph and right-click to "Format Trendline . . .," and tick "Display Equation on chart."

Note that the equation computed by Excel has a more accurate value for the intercept.

Nonlinear Trend

Although linear trend is appropriate for some series, it is inadequate for others such as demand for a new product that has a faster growth or for an old product that has a slower growth. Example 5 illustrates an exponential trend.

PHH Fantus Corp. (now part of Deloitte) was involved in facility location and capacity planning consulting work.[1] One project involved a manufacturer of audio products with a production facility in the United Kingdom that needed more production capacity. From this plant, the company was supplying all of Europe. The question was where to locate a second plant and what capacity to build it for. The historical sales for all major European countries were available. From these, Fantus forecasted 1991–95 sales. The largest sales market was in Germany, and it appeared to have exponential trend (see the graph in the margin). We wish to find out the equation for this trend and extend it one year further.

◀ Example 5

Year (x)	Projected Sales in Germany (in million units)
1991	11.3
1992	13.4
1993	16.1
1994	19.2
1995	22.9

SOLUTION

After entering the data in Excel and drawing the time series line plot using "Chart," we use the "Trendline" function to fit the best exponential trend to the data. The equation will also be displayed if you select the "Display equation on chart" option. The exponential trend equation is approximately, $\hat{y}_t = 9.4431\,e^{0.1772x}$, where $e = 2.7182818$. Note that this exponential trend assumes a constant *percentage* increase in sales from one year to the next. This constant growth rate can be determined as follows: take the coefficient of year index x from regression, raise e to the power of the coefficient, subtract 1, and multiply by 100. For this example, $e^{0.1772} = 1.194$, so the constant percentage yearly increase in sales is 19.4 percent. This can be confirmed by subtracting any year's sales from the following year's sales and dividing by the same year's sales. For example (forecast sales 1995 − forecast sales 1994)/forecast sales 1994 = (22.9 − 19.2)/19.2 = 0.193, or 19.3 percent (the difference to 19.4 percent is rounding error). The forecast for 1996 is $F_{96} = 9.4431e^{0.1772(6)} = 27.3$ million units.

Trend-adjusted Exponential Smoothing

A variation of simple exponential smoothing can be used when a time series exhibits trend. It is called **trend-adjusted exponential smoothing** or *double exponential smoothing*. If a series exhibits trend, and exponential smoothing is used on it, the forecasts will all lag behind the trend: if the data are increasing, each forecast will be too low; if the data are decreasing, each forecast will be too high.

trend-adjusted exponential smoothing Variation of exponential smoothing used when a time series exhibits trend.

[1] M.P. Butler, "Facility and Capacity Planning Using Sales Forecasting by Today's Industrial Engineer," *Industrial Engineering* 22(6), June 1990, pp. 52–55.

The trend-adjusted forecast (TAF) for period $t + 1$ is composed of two forecasts:

$$\text{TAF}_{t+1} = S_t + T_t \tag{3-6}$$

where

S_t = Smoothed series at the end of period t

T_t = Smoothed trend at the end of period t

which are in turn estimated by:

$$S_t = \text{TAF}_t + \alpha(A_t - \text{TAF}_t) \tag{3-7}$$

$$T_t = T_{t-1} + \beta(S_t - S_{t-1} - T_{t-1})$$

where α and β are smoothing constants, and A_t = actual value in period t. In order to use this method, one must select values of α and β (usually through trial and error) and make an estimate of starting smoothed series and smoothed trend. We will use the first few data points to estimate the smoothed series and smoothed trend.

Example 6 ▶

Using the cellphone data from Example 4 (where it was concluded that the data exhibited a linear trend), use trend-adjusted exponential smoothing to prepare forecasts for periods 5 through 11, with $\alpha = .4$ and $\beta = .3$. Use the first four weeks to estimate starting smoothed series and smoothed trend.

SOLUTION

Table 3-1 displays the data again in the Actual column. We will use the average of the first four weeks as the starting smoothed series:

$$S_4 = (700 + 724 + 720 + 728)/4 = 718.$$

The starting smoothed trend can be based on the net change of $728 - 700 = 28$ for the *three* changes from week 1 to week 4, for an average of $T_4 = 28/3 = 9.33$.

The trend-adjusted forecast for week 5 is:

$$\text{TAF}_5 = S_4 + T_4 = 718 + 9.33 = 727.33$$

After observing the actual sales in week 5 (740 units), we can calculate the smoothed series and smoothed trend at the end of week 5:

Table 3-1 ▼

Trend-adjusted forecast calculations for Example 6.

$$S_5 = \text{TAF}_5 + \alpha(A_5 - \text{TAF}_5)$$
$$= 727.33 + .4(740 - 727.33)$$
$$= 732.40$$

t (Week)	A_t (Actual)			
1	700			
2	724	Starting values:		
3	720	$S_4 = (700+724+720+728)/4 = 718$, $T_4 = (728-700)/3 = 9.33$		
4	728	$\text{TAF}_5 = 718 + 9.33 = 727.33$		
		$\text{TAF}_t + \alpha(A_t - \text{TAF}_t) = S_t$	$T_{t-1} + \beta(S_t - S_{t-1} - T_{t-1}) = T_t$	$\text{TAF}_{t+1} = S_t + T_t$
5	740	$727.33 + .4(740 - 727.33) = 732.40$	$9.33 + .3(732.40 - 718 - 9.33) = 10.85$	743.25
6	742	$743.25 + .4(742 - 743.25) = 742.75$	$10.85 + .3(742.75 - 732.40 - 10.85) = 10.70$	753.45
7	758	$753.45 + .4(758 - 753.45) = 755.27$	$10.70 + .3(755.27 - 742.75 - 10.70) = 11.25$	766.52
8	750	$766.52 + .4(750 - 766.52) = 759.91$	$11.25 + .3(759.91 - 755.27 - 11.25) = 9.27$	769.18
9	770	$769.18 + .4(770 - 769.18) = 769.51$	$9.27 + .3(769.51 - 759.91 - 9.27) = 9.37$	778.88
10	775	$778.88 + .4(775 - 778.88) = 777.33$	$9.37 + .3(777.33 - 769.51 - 9.37) = 8.90$	786.23

$$T_5 = T_4 + \beta(S_5 - S_4 - T_4)$$
$$= 9.33 + .3(732.40 - 718 - 9.33)$$
$$= 10.85.$$

Therefore, the trend-adjusted forecast for week 6 is:

$$TAF_6 = S_5 + T_5 = 732.40 + 10.85 = 743.25$$

After observing the actual sales in week 6 (742 units), we can calculate the smoothed series at the end of week 6:

$$S_6 = TAF_6 + \alpha(A_6 - TAF_6)$$
$$= 743.25 + .4(742 - 743.25)$$
$$= 742.75$$

and the smoothed trend at the end of week 6 is:

$$T_6 = T_5 + \beta(S_6 - S_5 - T_5)$$
$$= 10.85 + .3(742.75 - 732.40 - 10.85)$$
$$= 10.70.$$

Therefore, the trend-adjusted forecast for week 7 is:

$$TAF_7 = S_6 + T_6 = 742.75 + 10.70 = 753.45.$$

This process is continued until the trend-adjusted forecast for week 11, TAF11 = 786.23, is determined (see Table 3-1).

Although calculations for trend-adjusted exponential smoothing are somewhat more involved than for a linear trend line, trend-adjusted exponential smoothing has the ability to adjust to *changes* in trend. A manager must decide if this benefit justifies the extra calculations.

The following figure shows the graph of the actual demand and the trend-adjusted exponential smoothing forecasts.

Demand for products such as Sea-Doo watercraft and boats, Can-Am roadsters, all-terrain and side-by-side vehicles, Ski-Doo and Lynx snowmobiles, as well as Evinrude outboard engines are subject to seasonal fluctuations. BRP offsets these fluctuations by alternating its manufacturing capacity to deliver a diverse product portfolio.

Techniques for Seasonality

Seasonal variations in time series data or seasonality are regularly repeating wavelike movements in series values that can be tied to recurring events, weather, or calendar. Familiar examples of data with seasonality are retail trade, ice cream sales, and residential natural gas sales. Most seasonal variations repeat annually. However, the term *seasonal variation* is also applied to shorter lengths of repeating patterns. For example, rush-hour traffic occurs twice a day—incoming in the morning and

seasonal variations Regularly repeating wavelike movements in series values that can be tied to recurring events, weather, or calendar.

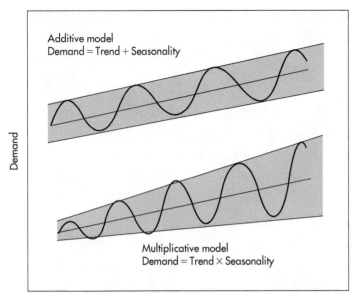

Time

Figure 3-5   ▲

Seasonality: the additive and multiplicative models compared using a linear trend.

seasonal relatives Proportion of average or trend for a season in the multiplicative model.

outgoing in the late afternoon. Theatres and restaurants often experience weekly repeating demand patterns, with higher demand on Fridays or weekend. Banks may experience daily repeating "seasonal" variations (heavier traffic during the noon hour and just before closing), weekly repeating variations (heavier toward the end of the week), and monthly repeating variations (heavier around the beginning of the month because of payroll cheques being cashed or deposited). Most products and services have seasonality.

Seasonality in a time series is expressed in terms of the amount that actual value during a season deviates from the *average* value of a series during the length of a repeating pattern, e.g., a year. If trend is present, seasonality is measured relative to the trend value.

There are two different models of seasonality: additive and multiplicative. In the *additive* model, seasonality is expressed as a *quantity* (e.g., 20 units), which is added or subtracted from the series average (or trend). In the *multiplicative* model, seasonality is expressed as a *proportion* of the average (or trend) amount (e.g., 1.10), which is then multiplied by the average (or trend) of the series. Figure 3-5 illustrates the two models for a linear trend line. In practice, most organizations use the multiplicative model, so we shall focus exclusively on the multiplicative model.

The seasonal proportions in the multiplicative model are referred to as **seasonal relatives** or *seasonal indexes*. Suppose that the seasonal relative for the quantity of toys sold in November at a store is 1.20. This indicates that toy sales for that month are 20 percent above the monthly average (i.e., annual sales/12). A seasonal relative of .90 for July indicates that July sales are 90 percent of the monthly average. Figure 3-6 displays a variety of seasonal variations.

Knowledge of seasonal variations is an important factor in retail planning and scheduling. Moreover, seasonality can be an important factor in capacity planning for systems that must be designed to handle peak loads (e.g., public transportation, electric power plants, highways, and bridges).

Knowledge of the extent of seasonality in a time series can enable one to *remove* seasonality from the data (i.e., to seasonally adjust or deseasonalize the data) in order to discern other patterns. Thus, one frequently reads or hears about, for example, the "seasonally adjusted unemployment rate."

The next section briefly describes how seasonal relatives are used, and the following section describes how seasonal relatives are computed.

Using Seasonal Relatives. Seasonal relatives are used first to *deseasonalize* the data, and later to *incorporate seasonality* in the forecast of deseasonalized data (i.e., to reseasonalize the data).

To deseasonalize the data is to remove the seasonal component from the data in order to get a clearer picture of the nonseasonal components. Deseasonalizing data is accomplished by *dividing* each data point by its seasonal relative (e.g., divide November demand by the November relative, divide December demand by the December relative, and so on).

Reseasonalizing the forecasts of the deseasonalized demand is accomplished by multiplying each forecast by its seasonal relative.

The complete steps of forecasting seasonal demand, called *time series decomposition*, are as follows:

1. Compute the seasonal relatives.
2. Deseasonalize the demand data.
3. Fit a model to the deseasonalized demand data, e.g., moving average or trend.
4. Forecast using this model (to obtain the deseasonalized forecasts).
5. Reseasonalize the deseasonalized forecasts.

Example 7 illustrates steps 3 and 5 of this approach.

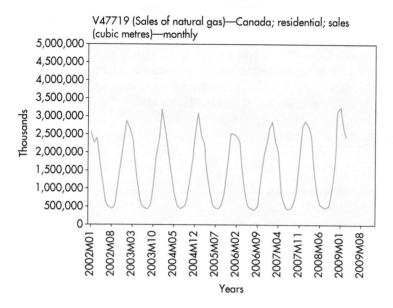

V47719 (Sales of natural gas)—Canada; residential; sales (cubic metres)—monthly

V2452 (New motor vehicle sales, Canada, provinces and territories)—Canada; total, new motor vehicles; units; total, country of manufacture—monthly

V32955919 (Retail trade, sales by trade group based on the North American industry classification system (NAICS))—Canada; general merchandise stores [175]; unadjusted (dollars)—monthly

Figure 3-6

Examples of seasonal variation.

Source: Statistics Canada CANSIM 2 database, Series v47719, accessed January 26, 2010.

Source: Statistics Canada CANSIM 2 database, Series v2452, accessed January 26, 2010.

Source: Statistics Canada CANSIM 2 database, Series v32955919; accessed January 26, 2010.

Example 7

A furniture manufacturer wants to predict quarterly demand for a certain loveseat for quarters 15 and 16, which happen to be the second and third quarters of a particular year. The series has both trend and seasonality. Quarter relatives are $Q_1 = 1.20$, $Q_2 = 1.10$, $Q_3 = .75$, and $Q_4 = .95$. The trend portion of deseasonalized demand data is projected using the equation $\hat{y}_t = 124 + 7.5t$, where t is the index of quarter and $\hat{y}_t$ is the estimate of the trend component of demand in quarter t. Use this information to predict demand for quarters 15 and 16.

SOLUTION

The trend values at $t = 15$ and $t = 16$ are:

$$\hat{y}_{15} = 124 + 7.5(15) = 236.5$$
$$\hat{y}_{16} = 124 + 7.5(16) = 244.0$$

Multiplying the trend value by the appropriate quarter relative yields a forecast that includes both trend and seasonality. Given that $t = 15$ is a second quarter and $t = 16$ is a third quarter, the forecasts are:

$$F_{15}: 236.5(1.10) = 260.15$$
$$F_{16}: 244.0(0.75) = 183.00$$

Computing Seasonal Relatives. We need to first compute the average (or trend) of all periods during the length of a repeating pattern, e.g., a year. A simple method is to just use the average of all periods. However, this ignores any trends. If there is a linear trend, then regression can be used to model it. However, seasonality could influence the slope of the line. A better way is to use **centred moving average (CMA)**. The computations are similar to those for a moving average forecast. However, the values are not projected as in a forecast; instead, they are *positioned in the middle* of the set of periods used to compute the moving average. The implication is that the CMA is most representative of that point in the series. For example, consider the following time series data where the length of a repeating pattern is three periods:

centred moving average (CMA) A moving average positioned at the centre of the data that were used to compute it.

Period	Demand	Three-Period Centred Average	
1	40		
2	46	42.67	Average $= \dfrac{40 + 46 + 42}{3} = 42.67$
3	42		

The three-period average is 42.67. As a centred average, it is positioned at period 2; the average is most representative of the series at that point.

The ratio of demand at period 2 to this centred average at period 2 is an estimate of the seasonal relative at that point. Because the ratio is $46/42.67 = 1.08$, the series is 8 percent above average at that point. However, to achieve a reliable estimate of seasonality for any season, it is necessary to compute seasonal ratios for a number of seasons and then average these ratios. For example, average the ratios of two or three Fridays for the Friday relative, average two or three Saturdays for the Saturday relative, and so on.

Example 8

The manager of a parking lot has calculated the daily relatives for the number of cars per day in the parking lot. The length of a repeating pattern is a week. The calculations are displayed below (about three weeks are shown for illustration). A seven-period centred moving average is used because there are seven days (seasons) per week.

Day	No. of Cars	Centred MA_7	No. of Cars/CMA_7
Tues	67 ⎫		
Wed	75 ⎪		
Thur	82 ⎪		
Fri	98 ⎬	71.86	98/71.86 = 1.36 (Friday)
Sat	90 ⎪	70.86	90/70.86 = 1.27
Sun	36 ⎪	70.57	36/70.57 = .51
Mon	55 ⎭	71.00	55/71.00 = .77
Tues	60	71.14	60/71.14 = .84 (Tuesday)
Wed	73	70.57	73/70.57 = 1.03
Thur	85	71.14	85/71.14 = 1.19
Fri	99	70.71	99/70.71 = 1.40 (Friday)
Sat	86	71.29	86/71.29 = 1.21
Sun	40	71.71	40/71.71 = .56
Mon	52	72.00	52/72.00 = .72
Tues	64	71.57	64/71.57 = .89 (Tuesday)
Wed	76	71.86	76/71.86 = 1.06
Thur	87	72.43	87/72.43 = 1.20
Fri	96	72.14	96/72.14 = 1.33 (Friday)
Sat	88		
Sun	44		
Mon	50		

The estimated Friday relative is (1.36 + 1.40 + 1.33)/3 = 1.36. Relatives for other days can be calculated in a similar manner. For example, the estimated Tuesday relative is (.84 + .89)/2 = .87. The sum of average ratios of the seven days of the week should be 7 (because an average day has a seasonal relative of 1 and there are 7 average days in a week). If it is not, the average ratios should be adjusted by rescaling them.

The number of periods needed in a centred moving average is equal to the number of "seasons" involved. For example, with quarterly data, a four-period centred moving average is needed. When the number of periods is even, one additional step is needed because the middle of an even set of periods falls between two middle periods. The additional step requires taking a centred two-period moving average of the even-numbered centred moving average, which results in averages that "line up" with data points and, hence, permit determination of seasonal ratios. The following example illustrates this case, as well as the other steps of the time series decomposition.

Below are quarterly data for production of ice cream in Canada from quarter 1 of 2006 to quarter 3 of 2009.[2]

 Example 9

a. Calculate the quarterly relatives using the centred moving average method.
b. Deseasonalize the data, fit an appropriate model, project it four quarters ahead, and reseasonalize to obtain forecasts for ice cream demand for the 4th quarter of 2009 and Q1 to Q3 of 2010.

---

[2] Adapted from CANSIM 2, Series v382696. Note that timing of production of a perishable product such as ice cream is close to its sales.

SOLUTION

a.

Quarter	Production (million litres)	CMA₄	CMA₂	Production/CMA₂
2006 1	66			
2	96			
		79.75	78.875	91/78.876 = 1.154
3	91			
		78	77.375	66/77.375 = 0.853
4	66			
		76.75	75.875	0.778
2007 1	59			
		75	74.250	1.226
2	91			
		73.5	73.000	1.151
3	84			
		72.5	71.375	0.841
4	60			
		70.25	69.500	0.791
2008 1	55			
		68.75	66.875	1.226
2	82			
		65	63.875	1.221
3	78			
		62.75	59.750	0.753
4	45			
		56.75	54.875	0.838
2009 1	46			
		53		
2	58			
3	63			

			QUARTER			
Year	1	2	3	4	Total
2006			1.154	0.853	
2007	0.778	1.226	1.151	0.841	
2008	0.791	1.226	1.221	0.753	
2009	0.838				
Average	0.802	1.226	1.175	0.816	4.019
Adjusted	.802(4/4.019)=0.798	1.226(4/4.019)=1.220	1.170	0.812	4.000

b.

Quarter	Production (million litres)	Seasonal Relatives	Deseasonalized Production
2006 1	66	0.798	66/.798=82.707
2	96	1.220	96/1.220=78.689
3	91	1.170	77.778
4	66	0.812	81.281
2007 1	59	0.798	73.935
2	91	1.220	74.590
3	84	1.170	71.795
4	60	0.812	73.892
2008 1	55	0.798	68.922
2	82	1.220	67.213
3	78	1.170	66.667
4	45	0.812	55.419
2009 1	46	0.798	57.644
2	58	1.220	47.541
3	63	1.170	53.846

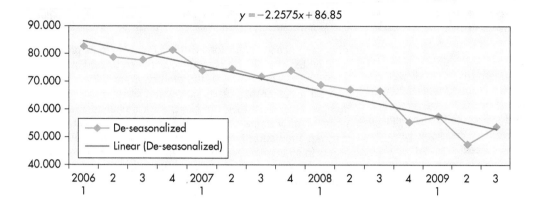

$$y = -2.2575x + 86.85$$

The deseasonalized data has a (decreasing) linear trend. Therefore, a linear trend is fitted to the deseasonalized data using regression, and its equation is displayed at the top of the chart above.

Using the regression equation, the trend forecasts for periods 16 to 19 (Q4 of 2009 and Q1 to Q3 of 2010) are:

$$Y_{16} = -2.2575(16) + 86.85 = 50.730$$
$$Y_{17} = -2.2575(17) + 86.85 = 48.473$$
$$Y_{18} = -2.2575(18) + 86.85 = 46.215$$
$$Y_{19} = -2.2575(19) + 86.85 = 43.958$$

The reseasonalized forecasts for the fourth quarter of 2009 and Q1 to Q3 of 2010 are:

$$F_{16} = 50.730(0.812) = 41.193$$
$$F_{17} = 48.473(0.798) = 38.681$$
$$F_{18} = 46.215(1.220) = 56.382$$
$$F_{19} = 43.958(1.170) = 51.431$$

Techniques for Cycles

Cycles are wavelike movements, similar to seasonal variations, but of longer duration—say, two to six years between peaks. When cycles occur in time series data, their irregularity makes it difficult or impossible to project them from past data because turning points are difficult to identify. A short moving average or a naïve approach may be of some value, although both will produce forecasts that lag cyclical movements by one or several periods.

The most commonly used approach is associative models: Search for another variable that relates to, and *leads*, the variable of interest. For example, the number of housing starts (i.e., permits to build houses) in a given month often is an indicator of demand a few months later for products and services directly tied to construction of new homes (e.g., sales of new major appliances; new demands for shopping, transportation, schools). Thus, if an organization is able to establish a high correlation with such a *leading variable* (i.e., changes in the variable precede changes in the variable of interest), it can develop an equation that describes the relationship, enabling forecasts to be made. It is important that a persistent relationship exist between the two variables. Moreover, the higher the correlation, the better the chances that the forecast will be accurate.

Associative Models

LO6

Associative models rely on identification of related variables that can be used to predict values of the variable of interest. For example, sales of beef are related to the price of beef and the prices of substitutes such as chicken, pork, and lamb; sales during promotions depend on the discount and size of the ad; and crop yields are related to soil conditions and the amounts and timing of rain and fertilizer applications.

Mark's Work Wearhouse

Mark's Work Wearhouse is a large chain of work wear in Canada. The demand for most of Mark's products, such as winter clothing and boots or summer shorts, is affected by the season. Mark's uses a software called Inforem to forecast demand for its products and to make inventory decisions. Here, we describe the forecasting module of Inforem, whereas the Mini-Case at the end of Chapter 12 provides information on inventory decisions in Mark's.

Inforem facilitates adoption of a seasonal-relatives profile for each product by providing typical profiles for each product family. The forecasting method deseasonalizes the past demand, fits adaptive exponential smoothing (a variation of exponential smoothing where the smoothing constant α is automatically adjusted after each period to best fit the data) to the deseasonalized data, forecasts using the fitted model, then reseasonalizes the forecasts.

Recently, Mark's has started using weather intelligence information from Planalytics to fine-tune its seasonal merchandising, assortment, and allocation planning for some of its products. Mark's buyers have found this information useful. For example, recently a men's buyer had to decide the

discount price for shorts for a Father's Day flyer to be printed in May. Usually, all shorts would have been offered at a 50 percent discount. However, the prediction from Planalytics was for a colder-than-usual spring and warmer-than-usual summer. Based on this, the buyer took a chance and discounted only some types of the shorts 25 percent. The weather prediction came true, resulting in fewer sales of shorts in spring; however, all the remaining shorts were sold in the summer at full price. This action resulted in $50,000 more profit to Mark's. Also, because the forecast called for warmer summer in Western Canada, 8,000 additional shorts were diverted to the Western Canada stores, and subsequently were all sold.

In another example, winter was predicted to be less severe. This resulted in Mark's buying more removable-liner jackets and fewer fixed-liner jackets. Planalytics also provides how much more or less a product will sell during a season; for example, 20 percent more demand for cotton fleece.

Sources: Inforem User's Manual; J.K. Speer, "Rain or Shine, Mark's Work Wearhouse Has the Right Stuff: Thanks to Weather-based Business Intelligence from Planalytics, the Scramble Factor at Mark's Work Wearhouse Has Been Drastically Reduced," *Apparel* 48(2) Oct 2006, 20–22.

---

predictor variables
Variables that can be used to predict values of the variable of interest.

The essence of associative models is the development of an equation that summarizes the effects of **predictor variables** on the variable of interest. The primary method of analysis is **regression**.

Simple Linear Regression

regression Technique for fitting a line to a set of points.

The simplest and most widely used form of regression involves a linear relationship between two variables. A plot of the values might appear like that in Figure 3-7. The objective in linear regression is to obtain an equation of a straight line that minimizes the sum of squared vertical deviations of data points (x, y) from the line. This **least squares line** has the equation

least squares line Minimizes the sum of the squared deviations around the line.

$$\hat{y} = a + bx \tag{3-8}$$

where

$\hat{y}$ = Predicted (dependent) variable

x = Predictor (independent) variable

b = Slope of the line

a = Value of $\hat{y}$ when $x = 0$ (i.e., the height of the line at the y intercept)

Figure 3-7

A straight line is fitted to a set of points, each a pair (x, y).

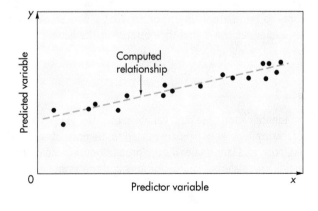

(*Note:* It is conventional to represent values of the predicted variable on the y axis and values of the predictor variable on the x axis.) Figure 3-8 illustrates the linear regression equation.

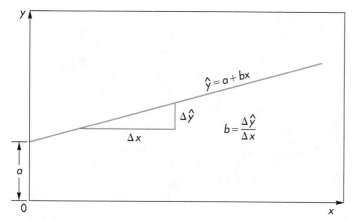

Figure 3-8

Equation of a straight line.

The line intersects the y axis where $\hat{y} = a$. The slope of the line $= b$.

The coefficients a and b of the line are computed using these two equations:

$$b = \frac{n\left(\sum xy\right) - \left(\sum x\right)\left(\sum y\right)}{n\left(\sum x^2\right) - \left(\sum x\right)^2} \tag{3-9}$$

$$a = \frac{\sum y - b\sum x}{n} \text{ or } \bar{y} - b\bar{x} \tag{3-10}$$

where

$\quad n\ =$ Number of paired observations
$\quad (x, y) =$ the symbols showing a pair of observations

Healthy Hamburgers has a chain of 12 stores. Revenue and profit for the stores are given below. Obtain a regression line for the data, and predict profit for a store with revenue of $10 million.

Example 10

Revenue, x	Profit, y
(in millions of dollars)	
7	.15
2	.10
6	.13
4	.15
14	.25
15	.27
16	.24
12	.20
14	.27
20	.44
15	.34
7	.17

First, plot the data and decide if a linear model is reasonable (i.e., do the points seem to scatter around a straight line? Figure 3-9 suggests they do). Next, compute the quantities Σx, Σy, Σxy, and Σx^2 and substitute into the (3-9) and (3-10) equations to find:

SOLUTION

$$b = \frac{b\left(\sum xy\right) - \left(\sum x\right)\left(\sum y\right)}{n\left(\sum x^2\right) - \left(\sum x\right)^2} = \frac{12(35.29) - 132(2.71)}{12(1{,}796) - 132(132)} = .01593$$

$$a = \frac{\sum y - b\left(\sum x\right)}{n} = \frac{2.71 - 0.01593(132)}{12} = .0506$$

Figure 3-9 ▶

*A linear model seems reasonable
for Example 10.*

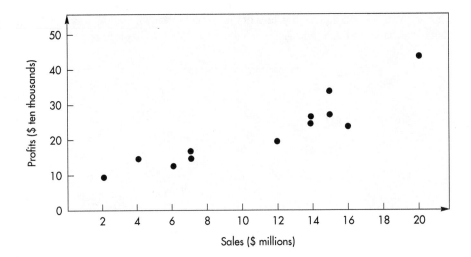

Thus, the regression equation is: $\hat{y} = .0506 + .01593x$. For revenue of $x = 10$ (i.e., $10 million), estimated profit is: $\hat{y} = .0506 + .01593(10) = .2099$, or $209,900. (It may appear strange that substituting $x = 0$ into the equation produces a predicted profit of $50,600 because it seems to suggest that profit will occur with no sales. However, the value of $x = 0$ is *outside the range of observed values*. The regression line should be used only for the range of values from which it was developed; the relationship may be nonlinear outside that range. The purpose of the *a* value is simply to establish the height of the line where it crosses the *y* axis.)

The Excel template of this problem on Connect is shown in Table 3-2. The symbol *r* represents correlation between *x* and *y*, and will be described next. The regression coefficients *b* and *a* can also be directly obtained in Excel using "=slope(RangeY,RangeX)" and "=intercept(RangeY,RangeX)" functions, respectively, where RangeY is the range of Excel cells containing the *y* values and RangeX is the range of Excel cells containing the *x* values.

Table 3-2 ▼

Excel template for Example 10.

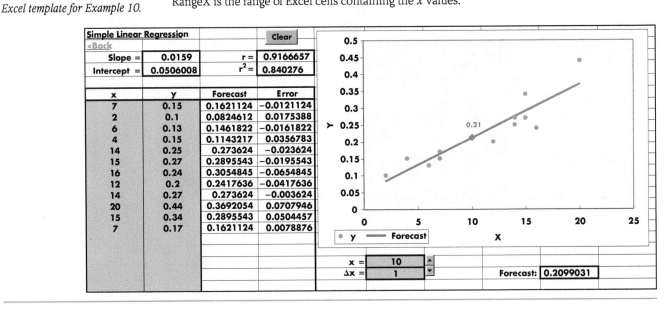

Correlation Coefficient

correlation coefficient A measure of the strength of relationship between two variables.

Correlation coefficient measures the strength of relationship between two variables. Correlation coefficient can range from -1.00 to $+1.00$. A correlation coefficient of $+1.00$ indicates that changes in one variable are always matched by changes in the other variable in the same direction; a correlation coefficient of -1.00 indicates that increases in one variable are matched by decreases in the other variable; and a correlation coefficient close to zero indicates little *linear* relationship between two variables. If a causal model is to be used to forecast the demand for an item (y), it is important that the relationship between x and y variables is strong. The correlation coefficient between two variables can be computed using the equation:

$$r = \frac{n\left(\sum xy\right) - \left(\sum x\right)\left(\sum y\right)}{\sqrt{n\left(\sum x^2\right) - \left(\sum x\right)^2} \cdot \sqrt{n\left(\sum y^2\right) - \left(\sum y\right)^2}}$$ (3-11)

The square of the correlation coefficient, r^2, provides a measure of the proportion of variability in the values of y that is "explained" by the independent variable. The possible values of r^2 range from 0 to 1.00. The closer r^2 is to 1.00, the greater the proportion of explained variation. A high value of r^2, say .80 or more, would indicate that the independent variable is a good predictor of values of the dependent variable. A low value, say .25 or less, would indicate a poor predictor, and a value between .25 and .80 would indicate a moderate predictor.

The correlation coefficient can be obtained in Excel using "=CORREL(RangeY,RangeX)" function, where RangeY is the range of Excel cells containing the y values and RangeX is the range of Excel cells containing the x values. Similarly, r^2 can be obtained in Excel using "=RSQ(RangeY,RangeX)" function.

Monthly sales of LCD television sets in a store and the unemployment rate in the region are shown below for 11 months. Determine if unemployment levels can be used to predict demand for LCD TVs and, if so, derive the correlation coefficient and the predictive equation.

◄ Example 11

Month	1	2	3	4	5	6	7	8	9	10	11
Units sold (y)	20	41	17	35	25	31	38	50	15	19	14
Unemployment % (x)	7.2	4.0	7.3	5.5	6.8	6.0	5.4	3.6	8.4	7.0	9.0

1. Plot the data to see if a linear model seems reasonable. In this case, a linear model seems somewhat appropriate.

SOLUTION

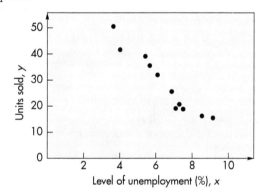

2. Compute the correlation coefficient:

$$r = \frac{11(1{,}750.8) - 70.2(305)}{\sqrt{11(476.3) - (70.2)^2} \cdot \sqrt{11(9{,}907) - (305)^2}} = -.966$$

This is a high negative correlation, indicating a strong downward-sloping linear relationship.

3. Compute the regression line:

$$b = \frac{11(1{,}750.8) - 70.2(305)}{11(476.4) - 70.2(70.2)} = -6.91$$

$$a = \frac{305 - (-6{,}9145)(70.2)}{11} = 71.85$$

$$y = 71.85 - 6.91x$$

Note that the equation pertains only to unemployment levels in the range 3.6 to 9.0 percent, because sample observations cover only that range.

Multiple Regression

Simple linear regression may prove inadequate to handle certain problems because more than one predictor variable is needed. Models that involve more than one predictor require the use of multiple regression. While this is beyond the scope of this text, you should be aware that it is often used. The computations lend themselves more to computers than to hand calculation. It is necessary to weigh the additional cost and effort against potential improvements in accuracy of predictions.

Accuracy and Control of Forecasting Process

Accuracy and control of forecasting process are vital aspects of forecasting. Forecasting accuracy is the degree of correctness of the forecasts generated by the forecasting process. The large number of factors usually influencing the demand for a product or spare part, and random variations, makes it almost impossible to correctly predict future values of demand on a regular basis. Consequently, it is important to include the extent to which the forecast might deviate from the actual value. This will allow the forecast user to better prepare for probable values of demand, provided that this deviation is not too large (i.e., the forecasting process is accurate enough).

Accurate forecasts are necessary for the success of daily activities of every organization. Forecasts are the basis for an organization's schedules, and unless the forecasts are accurate enough, schedules will be generated that may provide for too few or too many resources, too little or too much output, the wrong output, or the wrong timing of output, all of which can lead to additional costs, dissatisfied customers, and headaches for managers.

forecast error Difference between the actual value and the forecast value for a given period.

A related concept is control of forecasting process. Assuming that a forecasting process was initially accurate enough, it is important to monitor forecast errors through time to ensure that the errors remain within reasonable bounds (i.e., forecasting process remains accurate enough). If they are not, it will be necessary to take corrective action. Both accuracy and control of forecasting process requires measurement of forecast errors. **Forecast error** is the difference between the value that actually occurs and the value that was forecasted for a given time period. Hence, Forecast error = Actual value − Forecast value:

mean absolute deviation (MAD) The average of absolute value of forecast errors.

$$e_t = A_t - F_t \tag{3-12}$$

mean squared error (MSE) The average of square of forecast errors.

Positive errors result when the forecast is too low relative to the actual value, whereas negative errors result when the forecast is too high relative to the actual value. For example, if actual demand for a month is 100 units and forecast demand was 90 units, the forecast was too low; the forecast error is $100 - 90 = +10$.

Accuracy of Forecasting Process

mean absolute percent error (MAPE) The average absolute percent forecast error.

Accuracy (or better, inaccuracy) of the forecasting process is measured using three alternative forecast-error summaries: **mean absolute deviation (MAD)**, **mean squared error (MSE)**, and **mean absolute percent error (MAPE)**. MAD is the average absolute forecast error, MSE

OM in ACTION

NIKE

Nike CEO Philip Knight launches a blistering attack on i2 Technologies for implementation issues relating to a demand forecasting application. The forecasting application did not perform as expected, resulting in severe shortages of some popular shoe models and excess stock of slow-selling models. Nike choose to work with software vendor i2 as part of a $400 million overhaul designed to streamline communications and collaborate forecasting with their upstream suppliers and downstream retail stores.

The software failed to meet expectations "both in performance and functionality," a Nike spokesperson said. Some orders were placed twice, once by the old system and once by the new system. In addition, the application consistently failed to submit new orders for new shoe models, forcing Nike to expedite the production of those models at the last minute and ship them by airfreight. Nike's stock dropped nearly 20 percent on the news.

Source: http://www.informationweek.com/i2-says-you-too-nike-/d/d-id/1010113.

is the average of squared forecast errors, and MAPE is the average absolute percent forecast error. The formulas used to compute MAD, MSE, and MAPE are[3]:

$$MAD = \frac{\sum |Actual - Forecast|}{n} \tag{3-13}$$

$$MSE = \frac{\sum (Actual - Forecast)^2}{n} \tag{3-14}$$

$$MAPE = \frac{\sum \left[\frac{|Actual - Forecast|}{Actual} \right] \times 100}{n} \tag{3-15}$$

where n is the number of periods. MAD and MSE are similar to the standard deviation and variance of the forecast error, respectively. Example 12 illustrates the calculation of MAD, MSE, and MAPE.

Calculate MAD, MSE, and MAPE for the following data.

◀ **Example 12**

Period	Actual	Forecast	Forecast Error	$(A-F)$ |Error|	Forecast Error^2	$\frac{\|Error\|}{Actual} \times 100$
1	217	215	2	2	4	.92%
2	213	216	−3	3	9	1.41
3	216	215	1	1	1	.46
4	210	214	−4	4	16	1.90
5	213	211	2	2	4	.94
6	219	214	5	5	25	2.28
7	216	217	−1	1	1	.46
8	212	216	−4	4	16	1.89
			−2	22	76	10.26%

Using the numbers shown in the above table,

SOLUTION

$$MAD = \frac{\sum |e|}{n} = \frac{22}{8} = 2.75$$

$$MSE = \frac{\sum e^2}{n} = \frac{76}{8} = 9.5$$

$$MAPE = \frac{\sum \left[\frac{|e|}{Actual} \times 100 \right]}{n} = \frac{10.26\%}{8} = 1.28\%$$

From a computational standpoint, the difference between these three measures is that MAD weighs all errors equally, MSE weighs errors according to their *squared* values, and MAPE weighs errors relative to their actual values.

Because MAD and MSE depend on the scale of data, it is not meaningful to compare the MAD or MSE of two different time series variables. However, we can compare the accuracy of two different forecasting techniques for the same time series variable: A lower value for MAD or MSE implies a more accurate forecasting technique. For an example, see Solved Problem 7.

MAPE can be used to measure forecasting accuracy irrespective of the specific time series data used. For example, the accuracy of the forecasting process resulting in the forecasts given in Example 12 is $100 - MAPE = 100 - 1.28 = 98.72\%$, a very accurate forecasting process. In

---

[3] The absolute value, represented by the two vertical lines in formula 3-13, ignores minus signs; all data are treated as positive values. For example, −2 becomes +2.

bias The sum of forecast errors.

practice, accuracy above 70 percent is considered satisfactory. A related concept to forecasting accuracy is the sum of forecast errors, sometimes called **bias**. A persistently positive bias implies that forecasts frequently underestimate the actual values, and a persistently negative bias implies that forecasts frequently overestimate the actual values. Bias occurs because either demand pattern has changed or the way forecasts are determined is flawed. For example, if forecasts are based on salespersons' opinions, the way their budget is determined tends to influence their forecasts: for new products they tend to underestimate the demand and for declining products they tend to overestimate the demand.[4]

The above statements about MAD, MSE, and MAPE assume negligible bias. If bias is substantial, it will reduce the accuracy of the forecasting process. For Example 12, bias = −2, which is very small relative to the scale of demand (over 210). It is important to reduce the bias in order to improve the accuracy of the forecasting process.

Controlling the Forecasting Process

It is necessary to monitor forecast errors to ensure that the forecasting process is performing adequately and remains accurate enough. If not, corrective action should be taken.

Monitoring forecast errors is usually accomplished by either control chart or tracking signal.

control chart for forecast errors A time series plot of forecast errors that has limits for individual forecast errors.

Control Chart. A **control chart for forecast errors** is a time series plot of forecast errors where they are compared to two predetermined values, or *control limits*. Forecast errors that fall outside either control limits signal that corrective action is needed.

Also, corrective action is needed if there is strong evidence against the following two assumptions:

1. Forecast errors are randomly distributed around a mean of zero (i.e., there is no bias).

2. The distribution of forecast errors is normal. See Figure 3-10.

The control limits are usually chosen as a multiple of the standard deviation of forecast errors. The square root of MSE is used in practice as an estimate of the standard deviation of forecast errors.[5] That is,

$$s = \sqrt{\text{MSE}} \tag{3-16}$$

Recall from your statistics course that for a normal distribution, approximately 95 percent of the values (forecast errors in this case) fall within limits of $0 \pm 2s$ (i.e., 0 ± 2 standard deviations), and approximately 99.7 percent of the values fall within $\pm 3s$ of zero. Hence, if the forecasting process is "in control," 99.7 percent or 95 percent of the forecast errors should fall within the control limits, depending on whether $3s$ or $2s$ control limits are used.

Figure 3-10 ▶

Conceptual representation of a control chart.

4 H. Petersen, "Integrating the Forecasting Process with the Supply Chain: Bayer Healthcare's Journey," *Journal of Business Forecasting Methods & Systems* 22(4), Winter 2003/2004, pp. 11–16.

5 The actual value could be computed as $s = \sqrt{\dfrac{\Sigma(e - \bar{e})^2}{n - 1}}$ (where e = forecast error and $\bar{e}$ = sample average of forecast errors).

Monthly sales of leather jackets at a store for the past 24 months, and forecasts and forecast errors for those months, are shown below. Determine if the forecasting technique is satisfactory using a control chart with 2s limits. Use data from the first eight months to develop the control chart, then evaluate the remaining data with the control chart.

◀ Example 13

Month	A (Sales)	F (Forecast)	A−F (Error)
1	47	43	4
2	51	44	7
3	54	50	4
4	55	51	4
5	49	54	−5
6	46	48	−2
7	38	46	−8
8	32	44	−12
9	25	35	−10
10	24	26	−2
11	30	25	5
12	35	32	3
13	44	34	10
14	57	50	7
15	60	51	9
16	55	54	1
17	51	55	−4
18	48	51	−3
19	42	50	−8
20	30	43	−13
21	28	38	−10
22	25	27	−2
23	35	27	8
24	38	32	6
			−11

SOLUTION

1. Make sure that the average forecast error is approximately zero:

$$\text{Average error} = \frac{\sum \text{errors}}{n} = \frac{-11}{24} = -0.46 \sim 0 \text{ relative to magnitude of sales.}$$

2. Compute the standard deviation of forecast errors using the first eight months:

$$s = \sqrt{\text{MSE}} = \sqrt{\frac{\sum e^2}{n}}$$

$$= \sqrt{\frac{\sum 4^2 + 7^2 + 4^2 + 4^2 + (-5)^2 + (-2)^2 + (-8)^2 + (-12)^2}{8}} = 6.46$$

3. Determine 2s control limits:

$$0 \pm 2s = 0 \pm 2(6.46) = -12.92 \text{ to } +12.92$$

4. **i.** Check that all forecast errors are within the control limits. Month 20's forecast error (−13) is just below the lower control limit (−12.92).

   ii. Check for nonrandom patterns. Note the runs of positive and negative errors in the following plot. This suggests nonrandomness (and that a better forecasting technique is possible). (We present more on control charts in Chapter 10.)

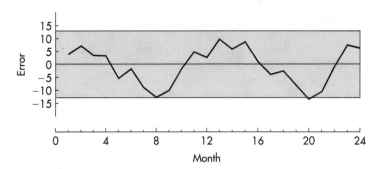

tracking signal A measure used to control the forecasting process: sum of forecast errors divided by mean absolute forecast error.

Tracking Signal. An alternative measure to control the forecasting performance is a **tracking signal**:

$$TS = \frac{\sum e}{MAD}.$$

When TS values exceed 4 in absolute value,[6] the analyst should study the model and make changes. For example, reset the initial values to eliminate the bias (the top of TS ratio), change parameters such as smoothing constant α to make the forecasting technique more responsive, use a different forecasting technique, etc.

LO8 Choosing a Forecasting Technique

Many different kinds of forecasting techniques are available, and no single technique works best in every situation. When selecting a technique for a given situation, the manager or analyst must take a number of factors into consideration.

The two most important factors are *cost* and *accuracy*. Cost is affected by the preparation time and complexity. Questions to ask are: How much money is budgeted for generating the forecast? What are the possible costs of errors, and what are the benefits that might accrue from an accurate forecast? Generally speaking, the higher the accuracy, the higher the cost, so it is important to weigh cost–accuracy trade-offs carefully. The best forecast is not necessarily the most accurate or the least costly; rather, it is some combination of accuracy and cost deemed best by the management. Other factors to consider in selecting a forecasting technique include the availability of historical data, the forecasting horizon, and pattern of data.

Some techniques are more suited to long-term forecasts while others work best for the shorter term. For example, moving average and exponential smoothing are essentially short-term techniques, since they produce forecasts for the *next* period. Regression trend models can be used to project over much longer time periods. If there is a strong and stable cause-and-effect relationship, then causal regression models could be used. Also, if the objective of forecasting is to understand what drives sales, then regression should be used. Several of the judgmental techniques are well suited for long-term forecasting because they do not require historical data. The Delphi method and executive opinion methods are often used for long-term planning. New products and services lack historical data, so forecasts for them must be based on subjective estimates. Table 3-3 provides a guide for selecting an appropriate forecasting method. Table 3-4 provides additional perspectives on forecasts in terms of the forecasting horizon.

In some instances, a manager might use more than one forecasting technique to obtain independent forecasts. If the different techniques produced approximately the same predictions, that would give increased confidence in the results; disagreement among the forecasts would indicate that additional analysis may be needed. The chosen forecasting technique should be tested before use to ascertain the level of accuracy.

The Institute of Business Forecasting and Planning (http://www.IBF.org) surveyed over 5,000 companies about their forecasting practices. Time series techniques are popular (61 percent use them),

---

[6] G.W. Plossl and O.W. Wight. *Production and Inventory Control.* Upper Saddle River, NJ: Prentice Hall, 1967.

especially moving average (15 percent), exponential smoothing (15 percent), and linear trend (21 percent). Also used are regression (16 percent) and surveys (7 percent).[7]

▼ Table 3-3

A guide to selecting an appropriate forecasting method.

Forecasting Method	Amount of Historical Data	Data Pattern	Forecasting Horizon	Preparation time	Complexity
Simple exponential smoothing	5 to 10 observations	Data should be stationary	Short	Short	Little sophistication
Trend-adjusted exponential smoothing	10 to 15 observations	Trend	Short to medium	Short	Moderate sophistication
Regression trend models	10 to 20	Trend	Short, medium, long	Short	Moderate sophistication
Seasonal	Enough to see 2 peaks and troughs	Seasonal patterns	Medium	Short to moderate	Moderate sophistication
Causal regression models	10 observations per independent variable	Can handle complex patterns	Medium or long	Long	Considerable sophistication

Source: J. Holton Wilson and D. Allison-Koerber, "Combining Subjective and Objective Forecasts Improves Results," *Journal of Business Forecasting Methods & Systems*, 11(3) Fall 1992, p. 4.

Factor	Short Term	Medium Term	Long Term
1. Frequency	Daily, weekly	Monthly, quarterly	Annual
2. Level of . . . . aggregation	Item	Product family	Total output
3. Type of . . . . model	Smoothing . . . . Trend Regression	Trend and . . . . Seasonal Regression	Managerial Judgment, Trend Regression
4. Degree of . . . . management involvement	Low	Moderate	High
5. Cost per forecast	Low	Moderate	High

◄ Table 3-4

Forecast perspectives, by forecasting horizon.

Source: C.L. Jain, "Benchmarking Forecasting Models," *Journal of Business Forecasting Methods & Systems*, Fall 2002, pp. 18–20, 30.

Using Forecast Information

A manager can take a *reactive* or a *proactive* approach to a forecast. A reactive approach views forecasts as probable descriptions of future demand, and a manager reacts to meet that demand (e.g., adjusts production rates, inventories, the workforce). Conversely, a proactive approach seeks to actively influence demand (e.g., by means of advertising, pricing, or goods/service changes).

Generally speaking, a proactive approach requires either a causal model (e.g., regression) or a subjective assessment of the influence on demand. It is possible that a manager might use two forecasts: one to predict what will happen under the status quo and a second one based on a "what-if" approach.

---

[7] C.L. Jain, "Benchmarking Forecasting Models," *Journal of Business Forecasting Methods & Systems* 21(3), Fall 2002, pp. 18–20, 30.

Computers in Forecasting

Computers play an important role in preparing forecasts based on quantitative data. Their use allows managers to develop and revise forecasts quickly and without the burden of manual calculations. There is a wide range of software packages available for forecasting.[8]

 OM in *ACTION*

Gazing at the Crystal Ball

Ram Reddy

Disregarding Demand Forecasting Technologies During Tough Economic Times Can Be a Costly Mistake

It's no secret that the IT sector has felt the brunt of the economic downturn. Caught up in the general disillusionment with IT has been demand forecasting (DF) technologies. Many companies blame DF technologies for supply chain problems such as excess inventory. Pinning the blame on and discontinuing DF technologies is the equivalent of throwing out the baby with the bathwater. The DF misunderstanding stems from the fact that, despite sophisticated mathematical models and underlying technologies, the output from these systems is, at best, an educated guess about the future.

A forecast from these systems is only as good as the assumptions and data used to build the forecast. Even the best forecast fails when an unexpected event—such as a recession—clobbers the underlying assumptions. However, this doesn't imply that DF technologies aren't delivering the goods. But, unfortunately, many DF and supply chain technology implementations have recently fallen victim to this mindset. DF is part science and part art (or intuition)—having the potential to significantly impact a company's bottom line. In this column, you'll find an overview of how DF is supposed to work and contrast that with how most companies actually practice it. I'll conclude with suggestions on how to avoid common mistakes implementing and using this particular class of technologies.

The Need for DF Systems

DF is crucial to minimizing working capital and associated expenses and extracting maximum value from a company's capital investments in property, plant, and equipment (PPE). It takes a manufacturing company a lot of lead time to assemble and stage the raw materials and components to manufacture a given number of products per day. The manufacturing company, in turn, generates its sales forecast numbers using data from a variety of sources such as distribution channels, factory outlets, value-added resellers, historical sales data, and general macroeconomic data. Manufacturing companies can't operate without a demand forecast because they won't know the quantities of finished goods to produce. The manufacturing company wants to make sure all or much of its finished product moves off the store shelves or dealer lots as quickly as possible. Unsold products represent millions of dollars tied up in inventory.

The flip side of this equation is the millions of dollars invested in PPE to manufacture the finished products. The company and its supporting supply chain must utilize as close to 100 percent of its PPE investments. Some manufacturing plants make products in lots of 100 or 1,000. Generally, it's cost prohibitive to have production runs of one unit. So how do you extract maximum value from your investments and avoid having money tied up in unsold inventory?

DF and supply chain management (SCM) technologies try to solve this problem by generating a production plan to meet forecasted demand and extract maximum value from PPE, while reducing the amount of capital tied up in inventory. Usually, the demand forecast is pretty close to the actual outcomes, but there are times when demand forecasts don't match the outcomes. In addition to unforeseen economic events, a new product introduction may be a stellar success or an abysmal failure. In the case of a phenomenal success, the manufacturing plant may not be able to meet demand for its product.

Consider the case of the Chrysler PT Cruiser. It succeeded way beyond the demand forecast's projections. Should it have started with manufacturing capacity to fulfill the runaway demand? Absolutely not. Given the additional millions of dollars of investment in PPE necessary to add that capacity, it would've backfired if the PT Cruiser had been a flop. The value provided by DF and supporting SCM technologies in this instance was the ability to add capacity to meet the amended forecast based on actual events. Demand forecasts can and do frequently miss their targets. The point to underscore here is that the underlying DF and supporting SCM technologies are critical to a company's ability to react and respond in a coordinated manner when market conditions change.

The manufacturing company and its supply chain are able to benefit from sharing information about the changed market conditions and responding to them in a coordinated manner. Despite best practices embedded in DF and SCM technologies to support this manner of collaboration, it plays out differently in the real world.

How It Works in Real Life—Worst Practices

A company prepares its forecast by taking into account data about past sales, feedback from distribution channels, qualitative assessments from field sales managers, and macroeconomic data. DF and SCM technologies take these inputs and add existing capacities within the company and across the supply chain to generate a production plan for optimum financial performance.

There's been incredible pressure on executives of publicly traded companies to keep up stock prices. This pressure, among other reasons, may cause manufacturing company executives to make bold projections to external financial analysts (or Wall

---

[8] For a survey, see F. Elikai et al., "A Review of 52 Forecasting Software Packages," *The Journal of Business Forecasting Methods & Systems*, Summer 2002, 21(2), pp. 19–27.

Street) about future sales without using the demand forecast generated from the bottom up. When the company realizes this disparity between the initial projection and the forecast, the forecast is changed to reflect the projections made by the company's officers, negating its accuracy.

The company arbitrarily sets sales targets for various regions to meet Wall Street numbers that are totally out of sync with input provided by the regional sales managers for the DF process. Even though the regional sales managers' input may have a qualitative element (art), they tend to be more accurate, given their proximity to the customers in the region. Unfortunately, the arbitrary sales targets make their way back to the supply chain, and the result is often excessive inventory build-up starting at the distribution channels to the upstream suppliers.

Seeing the inventory pile up, the manufacturing company may decide to shut down a production line. This action affects upstream suppliers who had procured raw materials and components to meet the executive-mandated production numbers, which may cause them to treat any future forecasted numbers with suspicion. Most cost efficiencies that could be obtained through planned procurement of raw materials and components go out the window. It's very likely that the companies try to blame DF and SCM technologies for failing to provide a responsive and efficient supply chain, even though the fault may lie in the company's misuse of the technologies and not the technologies themselves.

Guarding against the Extremes

Earlier in this column, I said that DF is part art or intuition and part science. The art/intuition part comes in when subject-matter experts (SMEs) make educated estimates about future sales. These SMEs could range from distribution outlet owners to sales and marketing gurus and economists. Their intuition is typically combined with data (such as historical sales figures) to generate the forecast for the next quarter or year. During a recession, the SMEs tend to get overly pessimistic. The demand forecasts generated from this mindset lead to inventory shortages when the economy recovers. Similarly, during an economic expansion, the SMEs tend to have an overly rosy picture of the future. This optimism leads to inventory gluts when the economy starts to slow down. In both instances, blaming and invalidating DF and SCM technologies is counterproductive in the long run.

It's very rare that a demand forecast and the actual outcome match 100 percent. If it's close enough to avoid lost sales or create an excess inventory situation, it's deemed a success. DF and supporting SCM technologies are supposed to form a closed loop with actual sales at the cash register providing a feedback mechanism. This feedback is especially essential during economic upturns or downturns. It provides the necessary information to a company and its supply chain to react in a coordinated and efficient manner.

Don't let the current disillusionment with DF and SCM technologies impede the decision-making process within your company. The intelligent enterprise needs these technologies to effectively utilize its capital resources and efficiently produce to meet its sales forecasts.

Ram Reddy is the author of *Supply Chains to Virtual Integration* (McGraw-Hill, 2001). He is the president of Tactica Consulting Group, a technology and business strategy consulting company.

Questions

1. What is DF and why is it important?

2. Why might a company executive make bold predictions about future demand to Wall Street analysts?

3. How might an executive's comments to Wall Street analysts affect demand forecasts, and what are the consequences of doing so?

Source: Ram Reddy, "Gazing at the Crystal Ball," *Intelligent Enterprise*, June 13, 2002. Copyright © 2002 Pention Media, Inc. Used with permission.

Summary

- Forecasts are vital inputs for the design and operation of the productive systems because they help managers anticipate the future.

- Forecasting horizons are classified into long, medium, and short term.

- Forecasting techniques can be classified as judgmental or quantitative.

- Judgmental methods rely on judgment, experience, and expertise of executives, sales staff, experts, or consumers to formulate forecasts.

- The judgmental methods include executive opinions, sales force estimates, consumer surveys, historical analogies, and expert opinions.

- Quantitative techniques use precise numerical calculations to develop forecasts.

- Two major quantitative approaches are described: time series and associative (causal) techniques.

- The time series techniques rely strictly on the examination of historical data; predictions are made by projecting past patterns of a variable into the future, which include averaging techniques (moving average and exponential smoothing), linear trend, and time series decomposition for seasonal data.

- Associative techniques such as regression attempt to explicitly identify influencing factors and to incorporate that information into equations that can be used for predictive purposes.

- Measures of forecast accuracy include Mean Absolute Deviation (MAD), Mean Squared

Error (MSE), and Mean Absolute Percent Error (MAPE).

- Control of forecasts involves deciding whether a forecast is performing adequately, using, for example, a control chart.

- When selecting a forecasting technique, a manager must choose a technique that will serve the intended purpose at an acceptable level of cost and accuracy.

Table 3-5 lists the formulas used in the forecasting techniques and in the methods of measuring their accuracy.

Table 3-5 ▶	Technique	Formula	Definitions
Summary of formulas.	Naïve forecast for stable data	$F_t = A_{t-1}$	F = Forecast A = Actual data t = Index of time period
	Moving average forecast	$F = \dfrac{\sum_{i=1}^{n} A_i}{n}$	n = Number of periods
	Exponential smoothing forecast	$F_t = F_{t-1} + \alpha(A_{t-1} - F_{t-1})$	α = Smoothing constant
	Linear trend forecast	$\hat{y} = a + bt$ where $b = \dfrac{n\sum ty - \sum t \sum y}{n\sum t^2 - (\sum t)^2}$ $a = \dfrac{\sum y - b\sum t}{n}$ or $\bar{y} - bt$	a = Intercept b = Slope y = Demand value $\hat{y}$ = Trend line value t = Index of time period
	Trend-adjusted exponential smoothing forecast	$\text{TAF}_{t+1} = S_t + T_t$ where $S_t = \text{TAF}_t + \alpha(A_t - \text{TAF}_t)$ $T_t = T_{t-1} + \beta(S_t - S_{t-1} - T_{t-1})$	TAF_{t+1} = Trend-adjusted forecast for next period $(t+1)$ S_t = Smoothed series at the end of current period (t) T_t = Smoothed trend at the end of current period (t) β = Smoothing constant for trend
	Linear regression forecast	$\hat{y} = a + bx$ where $b = \dfrac{n(\sum xy) - (\sum x)(\sum y)}{n(\sum x^2) - (\sum x)^2}$ $a = \dfrac{\sum y - b\sum x}{n}$ or $\bar{y} - b\bar{x}$	x = Predictor (independent) variable
	MAD	$\text{MAD} = \dfrac{\sum_{n}|e|}{n}$	MAD = Mean absolute deviation e = Forecast error = $A - F$
	MSE	$\text{MSE} = \dfrac{\sum_{n}e^2}{n}$	MSE = Mean squared error
	MAPE	$\text{MAPE} = \dfrac{\sum\left[\dfrac{|e|}{\text{Actual}} \times 100\right]}{n}$	MAPE = Mean absolute percent error
	Control limits	$\text{UCL} = 0 + z\sqrt{\text{MSE}}$ $\text{LCL} = 0 - z\sqrt{\text{MSE}}$	$\sqrt{\text{MSE}}$ = standard deviation z = Number of standard deviations; 2 and 3 are typical values
	Tracking signal	$\text{TS} = \dfrac{\sum e}{\text{MAD}}$	

Key Terms

adaptive (or variable response)
   exponential smoothing
associative models
bias
centred moving average (CMA)
control chart for forecast errors
correlation coefficient
cycles
Delphi method
demand forecast
exponential smoothing
forecast error

forecasting horizon
irregular variations
judgmental methods
least squares line
level (average)
linear trend equation
mean absolute deviation (MAD)
mean absolute percent error (MAPE)
mean squared error (MSE)
moving average
naïve forecast
predictor variables

random variations
regression
seasonal relatives
seasonal variations
seasonality
time series
time series models
tracking signal
trend
trend-adjusted exponential smoothing
weighted moving average

Solved Problems

Problem 1

Forecasts based on averages. Given the following data:

Period	Number of Complaints
1	60
2	65
3	55
4	58
5	64

Prepare a forecast using each of these approaches:

a. The appropriate naïve approach.

b. A three-period moving average.

c. A weighted average using weights of .50 (most recent), .30, and .20.

d. Exponential smoothing with a smoothing constant of .40.

Solution

a. This time series is stable. Therefore, the most recent value of the series can be used as the next forecast: 64.

b. $MA_3 = \dfrac{55 + 58 + 64}{3} = 59$

c. $F_6 = .50(64) + .30(58) + .20(55) = 60.4$

d.

Period	Number of Complaints	Forecast	Calculations
1	60		[The actual value of series in
2	65	60	Period 1 is used as the forecast for
			period 2]
3	55	62	$60 + .40(65 - 60) = 62$
4	58	59.2	$62 + .40(55 - 62) = 59.2$
5	64	58.72	$59.2 + .40(58 - 59.2) = 58.72$
6		60.83	$58.72 + .40(64 - 58.72) = 60.83$

You can also obtain the exponential smoothing forecasts using the Excel template on Connect:

Problem 2

Using *seasonal relatives*. An orchard ships boxed fruit regionally. Using the following information, forecast shipments for the first four months of next year.

Month	Seasonal Relative	Month	Seasonal Relative
Jan.	1.2	Jul.	.8
Feb.	1.3	Aug.	.6
Mar.	1.3	Sep.	.7
Apr.	1.1	Oct.	1.0
May	.8	Nov.	1.1
Jun.	.7	Dec.	1.4

The monthly trend forecast equation is estimated to be:

$$y_t = 402 + 3t$$

where

$t = 0$ corresponds to January of two years ago

y_t = trend value (no. of boxes of fruits to ship) in month t

Solution

a. Determine trend amounts for the first four months of next year: January, $t = 24$; February, $t = 25$; etc. Thus,

$$Y_{Jan} = 402 + 3(24) = 474$$

$$Y_{Feb} = 402 + 3(25) = 477$$

$$Y_{Mar} = 402 + 3(26) = 480$$

$$Y_{Apr} = 402 + 3(27) = 483$$

b. Multiply each monthly trend by the corresponding seasonal relative for that month.

Month	Seasonal Relative	Forecast
Jan.	1.2	474(1.2) = 568.8
Feb.	1.3	477(1.3) = 620.1
Mar.	1.3	480(1.3) = 624.0
Apr.	1.1	483(1.1) = 531.3

Problem 3

Linear trend line. Plot the following data on a graph, and verify visually that a linear trend line is appropriate. Develop a linear trend equation. Then use the equation to predict the next two values of the series.

Solution

Period	Demand
1	44
2	52
3	50
4	54
5	55
6	55
7	60
8	56
9	62

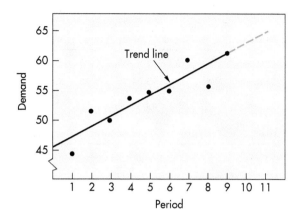

A time series plot of the data indicates that a linear trend line is appropriate:

Period, t	Demand, y	ty	t^2
1	44	44	1
2	52	104	4
3	50	150	9
4	54	216	16
5	55	275	25
6	55	330	36
7	60	420	49
8	56	448	64
9	62	558	81
45	488	2,545	285

$$b = \frac{n \sum ty - \sum t \sum y}{n \sum t^2 - (\sum t)^2} = \frac{9(2{,}545) - 45(488)}{9(285) - 45(45)} = 1.75$$

$$a = \frac{\sum y - b \sum t}{n} = \frac{488 - 1.75(45)}{9} = 45.47$$

Thus, the trend equation is $y_t = 45.47 + 1.75t$. The next two forecasts are:

$$y_{10} = 45.47 + 1.75(10) = 62.97$$
$$y_{11} = 45.47 + 1.75(11) = 64.72$$

You can also use the Excel template on *Connect* to obtain the regression coefficients and plot. Simply replace the existing data in the template with your data.

Problem 4

Calculating seasonal relatives. Obtain estimates of quarterly relatives for these data:

Year:	1				2				3				4
Quarter:	1	2	3	4	1	2	3	4	1	2	3	4	1
Demand:	14	18	35	46	28	36	60	71	45	54	84	88	58

Solution

Year	Quarter	Demand	CMA$_4$	CMA$_2$	Demand/CMA$_2$
1.......	1	14			
	2	18			
			28.25		
	3	35		30.00	1.17
			31.75		
	4	46		34.00	1.35
			36.25		
2	1	28		39.38	.71
			42.50		
	2	36		45.63	.79
			48.75		
	3	60		50.88	1.18
			53.00		
	4	71		55.25	1.29
			57.50		
3	1	45		60.50	.74
			63.50		
	2	54		65.63	.82
			67.75		
	3	84		69.38	1.21
			71.00		
	4	88			
4	1	58			

	Quarter			
	1	**2**	**3**	**4**
			1.17	1.35
	.71	.79	1.18	1.29
	.74	.82	1.21	___
	.145	.161	3.56	2.64
Average for the quarter:	.725	.805	1.187	1.320

The sum of these relatives is 4.037. Multiplying each by 4.00/4.037 will scale the relatives, making their total equal 4.00. The resulting relatives are quarter 1, 0.718; quarter 2, .798; quarter 3, 1.176; quarter 4, 1.308.

Problem 5

Casual regression analysis. A large retailer has developed a graph that displays the effect of advertising expenditures on sales volume. Using the graph, determine an equation of the form $\hat{y} = a + bx$ that describes this relationship.

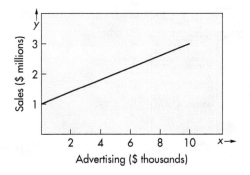

Solution

The linear equation has the form $\hat{y} = a + bx$, where a is the value of $\hat{y}$ when $x = 0$ (i.e., where the line intersects the y axis) and b is the slope of the line (the amount by which $\hat{y}$ changes for a one-unit change in x).

Accordingly, $a = 1$ and considering the points $(x = 0, y = 1)$ and $(x = 10, y = 3)$, $b = (3 - 1)/(10 - 0) = .2$, so $\hat{y} = a + bx$ becomes $\hat{y} = 1 + .2x$. [*Note:* $(3 - 1)$ is the change in y, and $(10 - 0)$ is the change in x.]

Problem 6

Causal regression analysis. The owner of a small hardware store has noted a weekly sales pattern for door locks that seems to move in parallel with the number of break-ins reported each week in the newspaper. The data are:

Sales:	46	18	20	22	27	34	14	37	30
Break-ins:	9	3	3	5	4	7	2	6	4

a. Plot the data to determine which type of equation, linear or nonlinear, is appropriate.

b. Obtain a linear regression equation for the data.

c. Estimate sales if the number of break-ins in a week is five.

Solution

a.

Number of break-ins

The graph supports a linear relationship.

b. The computations for a straight line regression equation are:

x	y	xy	x²
9	46	414	81
3	18	54	9
3	20	60	9
5	22	110	25
4	27	108	16
7	34	238	49
2	14	28	4
6	37	222	36
4	30	120	16
43	248	1,354	245

$$b = \frac{n\left(\sum xy\right) - \left(\sum x\right)\left(\sum y\right)}{n\left(\sum x^2\right) - \left(\sum x\right)^2} = \frac{9(1,354) - 43(248)}{9(245) - 43(43)} = 4.275$$

$$a = \frac{\sum y - b\left(\sum x\right)}{n} = \frac{248 - 4.275(43)}{9} = 7.129$$

Hence, the equation is: $\hat{y} = 7.129 + 4.275x$.

You can also obtain the regression coefficients using the appropriate Excel template on *Connect*. Simply replace the existing data for x and y with your data. *Note:* Be careful to enter the values for the variable you want to predict as y values. In this problem, the objective is to predict sales, so the sales values are entered in the y column.

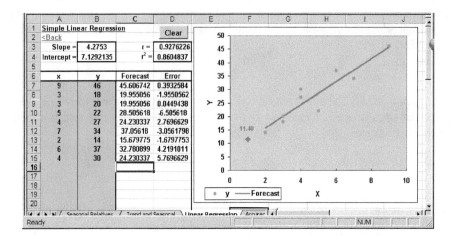

For $x = 5$, $\hat{y} = 7.129 + 4.275(5) = 28.50$ units.

Problem 7

Accuracy and control of forecasting process. The manager of a large manufacturer of industrial pumps must choose between two alternative forecasting techniques to forecast the demand for its top-selling pump. Both techniques have been used to prepare forecasts for a six-month period. Using MAD as a criterion, which technique produces more accurate forecasts?

Month	Demand	Forecast	
		Technique 1	Technique 2
1........	492	488	495
2........	470	484	482
3........	485	480	478
4........	493	490	488
5........	498	497	492
6........	492	493	493

Solution

Check that each forecast has an average error (= sum of errors/6) of approximately zero (see computations that follow.)

Month	Demand	Technique 1	e	|e|	Technique 2	e	|e|
1......	492	488	4	4	495	−3	3
2......	470	484	−14	14	482	−12	12
3......	485	480	5	5	478	7	7
4......	493	490	3	3	488	5	5
5......	498	497	1	1	492	6	6
6......	492	493	−1	1	493	−1	1
			−2	28		+2	34

$$\text{MAD}_1 = \frac{\sum |e|}{n} = \frac{28}{6} = 4.67$$

$$\text{MAD}_2 = \frac{\sum |e|}{n} = \frac{34}{6} = 5.67$$

Technique 1 produces more accurate forecasts because its MAD is smaller.

Problem 8

Control chart. Given the following demand data for a product, prepare a naïve forecast for periods 2 through 10. Then determine each forecast error, and use those values to obtain $2s$ control limits. If demand in the next two periods turns out to be 125 and 130 units, can you conclude that the forecasting process is not in control?

Period:	1	2	3	4	5	6	7	8	9	10
Demand:	118	117	120	119	126	122	117	123	121	124

Solution

For a naïve forecast, each period's demand becomes the forecast for the next period. Hence, the forecasts and forecast errors are:

Period	Demand	Forecast	Error	Error²
1	118	—	—	—
2	117	118	−1	1
3	120	117	3	9
4	119	120	−1	1
5	126	119	7	49
6	122	126	−4	16
7	117	122	−5	25
8	123	117	6	36
9	121	123	−2	4
10	124	121	3	9
			+6	150

The average forecast error ($+6/9$) is fairly small relative to size of demand (over 110).

$$s = \sqrt{\frac{\sum \text{error}^2}{n}} = \sqrt{\frac{150}{9}} = 4.08 \ (n = \text{Number of errors})$$

The control limits are $\pm 2 \,(4.08) = \pm 8.16$.

The forecast for period 11 is 124. Demand turned out to be 125, for a forecast error of $125 - 124 = +1$. This is within the limits of ± 8.16. The next demand turned out to be 130 and the naïve forecast is 125 (based on the period 11 demand of 125), the forecast error is $+5$. Again, this is within the limits, so you cannot conclude that the forecasting technique is not in control. With more values–at least five or six–you could plot the forecast errors as a time series plot in a control chart to see whether you could detect any patterns suggesting the presence of nonrandomness or non-normality.

Discussion and Review Questions

Note: An asterisk indicates that a question or problem may be more challenging.

1. What are the differences between quantitative and judgmental approaches to forecasting? What are the advantages and disadvantages of each approach? **LO1**

2. Name and explain, if not obvious, one feature common to all forecasts. **LO1**

3. Name one element of a good forecast and, if not obvious, explain why it is important. **LO1**

4. What are the three forecasting horizons? For each forecasting horizon, name one operations management decision that needs the forecast. **LO1**

5. Briefly describe the steps of forecasting process. **LO1**

*6. How can *shipments* to a customer differ from *demand* by the customer? **LO1**

7. Explain how flexibility in production systems relates to the forecasting horizon and accuracy. **LO1**

8. Pick one judgmental method and describe it.

9. What is a time series? **LO3**

10. Generally, how do time series models forecast?

11. How does the naïve method forecast a seasonal time series such as sales dollars during every hour of a particular day in a fast-food restaurant? **LO3**

12. Describe the moving average and exponential smoothing techniques, and explain why they are not suitable for seasonal or trend forecasting. **LO3**

13. What advantages does exponential smoothing have over moving average? **LO3**

14. How does the number of periods in a moving average affect the responsiveness of the forecast? **LO3**

15. How does the size of smoothing constant in exponential smoothing affect the responsiveness of the forecast? **LO3**

16. How is regression used in forecasting linear trend? **LO4**

*17. Explain the equation for an exponential trend. **LO4**

*18. Explain the three formulas used in trend-adjusted exponential smoothing. **LO4**

19. What is a seasonal relative? Give a numerical example and interpret it. **LO5**

20. Describe the centred moving average method and explain how it eliminates seasonality from a time series. **LO5**

21. Describe how seasonal relatives are determined using the centred moving average method. **LO5**

22. List the steps of time series decomposition for a seasonal time series with trend. **LO5**

23. Describe how the causal (associative) regression model is used for forecasting. **LO6**

24. What is the correlation coefficient and how it is used in associative regression model? What does it mean if correlation coefficient is negative? **LO6**

25. What is forecasting accuracy and how is it measured? **LO7**

26. Define and contrast MAD, MSE, and MAPE. **LO7**

27. Define control chart for forecast errors. What is the purpose of establishing control limits for forecast errors? **LO7**

*28. What factors would you consider in deciding whether to use a wide or narrow range of acceptable variation in a control chart? **LO7**

29. What is the tracking signal? Contrast it with the control chart. **LO7**

*30. Explain how control chart and tracking signal can be used to monitor bias. **LO7**

31. Contrast the reactive and proactive approaches to forecasting. Give an example of an organization or situation in which each type is used. **LO8**

*32. Choose a forecasting technique appropriate for predicting: **LO8**
    a. Demand for Mother's Day greeting cards.
    b. Popularity of a new television series.
    c. Demand for vacations on the moon.
    d. Demand for toothpastes in a particular supermarket.

33. List the specific weaknesses of each of these approaches to developing a forecast: **LO2**
    a. Consumer surveys.
    b. Saleforce composite.
    c. Committee of managers or executives.

Taking Stock

1. Explain the trade-off between cost and accuracy in a forecasting system. **LO8**

2. Who needs to be involved in preparing forecasts? **LO1**

3. How has technology had an impact on forecasting? **LO8**

*4. Forecasts are sometimes manipulated by managers to accomplish goals such as higher budget, capacity increases, etc. Also, sales people may underestimate the demand in order to beat it to receive a bonus, or they may overestimate it to keep their job. How can a company combat these unethical behaviours?[9] **LO2**

Critical Thinking Exercise

1. It has been said that forecasting using a time series exponential smoothing is like driving a car by looking in the rearview mirror. What are the conditions that would have to exist for driving a car that are analogous to the assumptions made when using exponential smoothing? **LO3**

2. When a new business is started, or a patent idea needs funding, venture capitalists or investment bankers will want to see a business plan that includes forecast information related to a profit and loss statement. What type of forecasting information do you suppose would be required? **LO1**

---

[9] A. Michail, "How to Identify and Correct Politically Motivated Forecasts," *Journal of Business Forecasting Methods & Systems* 23(4), Winter 2004/2005, pp. 3–9.

Experiential Learning Exercises

***1.** Obtain next-day temperature forecasts (daily highs) in your town/city for three days (you can visit http://www.theweathernetwork.com, choose your city, and use the Short Term Forecast in the afternoon of the same day and next day, in the middle of the Web page). Compare the accuracy of the next-day forecasts with naïve forecasts. Interpret your result. **LO7**

***2.** Gather data on 1-, 2-, and 3-day temperature forecasts (daily highs) and actual highs in your town/city for 4 days and compare the accuracy of each 1-, 2-, and 3-day temperature forecast (you can visit http://www.theweathernetwork.com, choose your city,

and use the Long Term Forecast highs in the bottom of the Web page). Interpret your results. **LO7**

***3.** Pick your favourite stock on the Toronto Stock Exchange and choose a forecasting method to forecast its next-day closing price. Repeat this for each of the next three days. (*Hint:* Go to http://www.tmx.com, click on Symbol Lookup at top left, find out the symbol for your company, then enter it under Get Quote . . . on the top left, and click Go. You can also get past prices (to choose and fine-tune your forecasting method) by clicking the Price History tab.) Are you satisfied with the results? Explain why you feel the forecasting method you chose worked or didn't work. **LO8**

Internet Exercise

Go to the Institute of Business Forecasting and Planning Web site (http://www.IBF.org) and look into jobs in forecasting (click on "Forecasting Jobs" on the top and "Search Job Listings" on the right). Select a job in Canada and briefly summarize it. You will have to fill in some information about yourself (i.e., register with IBF) to access the job description. **LO1**

Problems

1. A commercial bakery has recorded sales (in dozens) for three products during the last 15 workdays: **LO3**

Workday	Blueberry Muffins	Cinnamon Buns	Cupcakes
1	30	18	45
2	34	17	26
3	32	19	27
4	34	19	23
5	35	22	22
6	30	23	48
7	34	23	29
8	36	25	20
9	29	24	14
10	31	26	18
11	35	27	47
12	31	28	26
13	37	29	27
14	34	31	24
15	33	33	22

a. Plot the three time series variables to determine their pattern.

b. Forecast workday 16 sales for each of the products using an appropriate naïve method.

c. If you could use a more sophisticated method than naïve, what technique would you use for each variable?

2. A can opener manufacturer has had monthly sales for a seven-month period as follows: **LO3 & 4**

Month	Sales (000 units)
Feb	19
Mar	18
Apr	15
May	20
Jun	18
Jul	22
Aug	20

a. Plot the data.

b. Forecast September's sales volume using each of the following:

  i. A linear trend equation. (Use of Excel's Trendline, with display Equation on chart option, is recommended).

  ii. A four-month moving average.

  iii. Exponential smoothing with a smoothing constant .10, assuming a March forecast of 19(000).

iv. The naïve approach.

v. A weighted average using .50 for August, .30 for July, and .20 for June.

c. Which method seems *least* appropriate? Why?

d. What does use of the term *sales* rather than *demand* presume?

3. A dry cleaner uses exponential smoothing to forecast equipment usage as a percentage of capacity (i.e., utilization) at its main plant. August usage was forecast to be 88 percent of capacity, whereas actual usage turned out to be 89.6 percent of capacity. A smoothing constant of .2 is used. **LO3**

a. Prepare a forecast for September.

b. Assuming actual September usage of 92 percent, prepare a forecast for October's usage.

4. An electrical contractor's records during the last five weeks indicate the following number of job requests: **LO3**

Week:	1	2	3	4	5
Requests:	20	22	18	21	22

Predict the number of requests for week 6 using each of these methods:

a. Naïve.

b. Four-week moving average.

c. Exponential smoothing with $\alpha = .30$.

5. Freight car loadings during an 18-week period at a port are: **LO4**

Week	Number	Week	Number	Week	Number
1	220	7	350	13	460
2	245	8	360	14	475
3	280	9	400	15	500
4	275	10	380	16	510
5	300	11	420	17	525
6	310	12	450	18	541

a. Compute a linear trend line for freight car loadings. (Use of Excel's Trendline is recommended. Make sure to select the display equation option).

b. Use the trend equation to predict loadings for weeks 19 and 20.

c. The manager intends to install new equipment when the volume reaches 700 loadings per week. Assuming the current trend continues, the loading volume will reach that level in approximately what week?

6. Suppose it is the beginning of 2008 and you are trying to assist the forecaster in Case New Holland, an international agricultural and construction equipment manufacturer, forecast total agricultural equipment industry sales in Canada for the year. You have accessed

Statistics Canada's CANSIM 2 database and found the agricultural equipment manufacturing industry's GDP (in 2002 constant prices) in series v41881336. The data between 2000 and 2007 are as follows: **LO3**

Year	Agricultural Equipment Manufacturing Industry's GDP (in billion 2002$)
2000	9.8
2001	10.3
2002	11.4
2003	9.8
2004	10.5
2005	10.0
2006	9.4
2007	9.8

a. Plot the time series data.

b. Identify its patterns and suggest a forecasting technique.

7. a. Develop a linear trend equation for the following data on demand for white bread loaves at a bakery (use of Excel's Trendline, with display Equation on chart option, is recommended), and use it to forecast demand on day 16. **LO4**

Day	Loafs	Day	Loafs	Day	Loafs
1	200	6	232	11	281
2	214	7	248	12	275
3	211	8	250	13	280
4	228	9	253	14	288
5	235	10	267	15	310

b. The variations around the linear trend line seem to have above- and below-the-line runs. Therefore, use trend-adjusted exponential smoothing with $\alpha = .3$ and $\beta = .2$ to model the bread demand. Use the first four days to estimate the initial smoothed series (use the average of the first four days) and smoothed trend (use the increase from day 1 to day 4 divided by 3). Start forecasting day 5. What is the forecast for day 16?

*8. The agronomist in charge of canola seed production for a major seed-producing and marketing company is wondering if the forecast for production of seed #1234 for 2008, made by the head office, is a little too low. The sales of seed #1234, in thousand tonnes, for the past eight years are shown below. The company regularly improves its seeds, and has recently introduced a new seed. Given the life-cycle decline in the sales of #1234, the head office's 2008 forecast sales for #1234 is 10 percent lower than 2007 sales. Fit an appropriate model to the data and forecast sales of #1234 in 2008. Do you agree with the head office's forecast? Explain. **LO3 & 4**

Year	#1234 sales
2000	0.1
2001	2.1
2002	2.8
2003	3.1
2004	3.9
2005	3.7
2006	3.5
2007	3.4
2008	

9. After plotting the following demand data, a manager has concluded that a trend-adjusted exponential smoothing model is appropriate to predict future demand. Use period 1 to 4 to estimate the initial smoothed series (use the average of the first four periods) and smoothed trend (use the increase from day 1 to day 4 divided by 3). Use $\alpha = .5$ and $\beta = .4$ to develop forecasts for periods 5 through 10. **LO4**

Period, t	A_t Actual
1	210
2	224
3	229
4	240
5	255
6	265
7	272
8	285
9	294
10	

10. A manager of a store that sells and installs hot tubs wants to prepare a forecast for the number of hot tubs demanded during January, February, and March of next year. Her forecasts are a combination of trend and seasonality. She uses the following equation to estimate the trend component of monthly demand: $y_t = 70 + 6t$, where $t = 0$ in June of last year. Seasonal relatives are 1.10 for January, 1.02 for February, and .95 for March. What demands should she forecast? **LO5**

11. A gift shop in a tourist centre is open only on weekends (Friday, Saturday, and Sunday). The owner–manager hopes to improve scheduling of part-time employees by determining seasonal relatives for each of these days. Data on recent activity at the store (sales transactions per day) are shown in the following table: **LO5**

			Week			
	1	2	3	4	5	6
Friday	149	154	152	150	159	163
Saturday	250	255	260	268	273	276
Sunday	166	162	171	173	176	183

a. Develop seasonal relatives for each day using the centred moving average method.

b. Deseasonalize the data, fit an appropriate model to the deseasonalized data, project three days ahead, and reseasonalize the projections to forecast the sales transactions for each day, Friday to Sunday, of next week.

12. The manager of a fashionable restaurant open Wednesday through Saturday says that the restaurant does about 35 percent of its business on Friday night, 30 percent on Saturday night, and 20 percent on Thursday night. What are the seasonal relatives for each day? **LO5**

13. Coal shipments from a mine for the past 17 weeks are: **LO3 & 4**

Week	Tonnes Shipped	Week	Tonnes Shipped
1	405	10	440
2	410	11	446
3	420	12	451
4	415	13	455
5	412	14	464
6	420	15	466
7	424	16	474
8	433	17	476
9	438		

a. Plot the data as time series, determine the pattern, and explain why an averaging technique would not be appropriate in this case.

b. Use an appropriate technique to develop a forecast for week 18.

14. a. Calculate daily seasonal relatives for the number of customers served at a restaurant, given the following data. (*Hint:* Use a seven-day centred moving average.) **LO5**

b. Deseasonalize the data, fit an appropriate model to the deseasonalized data, project it 7 days ahead, and reseasonalize the projections to forecast daily demand next week.

Day	Number Served	Day	Number Served
1	80	15	84
2	75	16	77
3	78	17	83
4	95	18	96
5	130	19	135
6	136	20	140
7	40	21	37
8	82	22	87
9	77	23	82
10	80	24	98
11	94	25	103
12	125	26	144
13	135	27	144
14	42	28	48

*15. Echlin Inc. is an after-market supplier of automotive spare parts.[10] A part is usually made specifically for a particular model of a car. In order to forecast the demand for a part, Echlin tries to use the following process: (a) determine the total number of new vehicles using this part sold each year, (b) determine the replacement probability by age for the first replacement, second replacement, and so on of the part for current and future years, (c) calculate the total number of replacement units for each year, (d) break this down into original equipment manufacturer market and after-market manufacturer market, (e) calculate Echlin's annual share using its market share, and, finally (f) break down the annual forecast into quarterly and monthly sales forecasts using seasonal relatives.

Consider a specific part. Echlin makes brake callipers for a particular model of a car, first introduced in 1986. Suppose it is now the end of 1992 and using steps *a* to *e* above, Echlin has forecasted its own sales of this calliper for 1993. **LO5**

Year	Echlin's Sales of Callipers
1990	10,444
1991	10,319
1992	8,477
1993	6,334 (forecast)

Echlin also has quarterly sales of these callipers for the past three years.

Quarter	1990	1991	1992
Q_1	2,370	2,641	2,281
Q_2	2,058	2,198	1,814
Q_3	2,778	2,518	2,127
Q_4	3,238	2,962	2,255
Total	10,444	10,319	8,477

a. Use the 1990–92 quarterly data above to determine the quarterly seasonal relatives.

b. Use your answer to part *a* and 1993 forecast sales (6,334 units) to forecast quarterly sales for 1993.

c. Deseasonalize the data, fit an appropriate model to the deseasonalized data, project it four quarters ahead, and reseasonalize the projections to forecast quarterly demand in 1993. Contrast your results with part *b*.

16. A pharmacist has been monitoring sales of a certain over-the-counter (i.e., no prescription is needed) pain reliever. Daily sales during the last 15 days were: **LO4**

Day:	1	2	3	4	5	6	7	8	9
Number sold:	36	38	42	44	48	49	50	49	52

Day:	10	11	12	13	14	15
Number sold:	48	52	55	54	56	57

a. If you learn that on some days the store ran out of this pain reliever, would that knowledge cause you any concern regarding the use of sales data for forecasting demand? Explain.

b. Assume that there were no stock-outs. Plot the data. Is the linear trend model appropriate for this item? Explain.

c. Using trend-adjusted exponential smoothing with initial smoothed series and trend determined from days 1 to 8 and $\alpha = \beta = .3$, develop forecasts for days 9 through 16.

17. New-car sales of a dealer during the past year are shown in the following table, along with monthly seasonal relatives. **LO5**

Month	Units Sold	Seasonal Relative	Month	Units Sold	Seasonal Relative
Jan	640	0.80	Jul	765	0.90
Feb	648	0.80	Aug	805	1.15
Mar	630	0.70	Sept	840	1.20
Apr	761	0.94	Oct	828	1.20
May	735	0.89	Nov	840	1.21
Jun	850	1.00	Dec	800	1.21

a. Plot the data. Does there seem to be a trend?

b. Deseasonalize the new car sales.

c. Plot the deseasonalized data on the same graph as the original data. Comment on the two plots.

18. The following data shows a small tool and die shop's quarterly sales (in $000s) for the current year. What sales would you predict for the first quarter of next year? Quarterly seasonal relatives are $Q_1 = 1.10$, $Q_2 = .99$, $Q_3 = .90$, and $Q_4 = 1.01$. (*Hint*: First deseasonalize the data, then observe the trend and project it ahead one quarter, and finally reseasonalize.) **LO5**

Quarter	1	2	3	4
Sales	88	99	108	141

19. A farming cooperative's manager wants to forecast quarterly grain shipments for each quarter of next year (Year 6), based on the data shown below (quantities are in metric tonnes): **LO5**

---

[10] See J.A.G. Krupp, "Forecasting for the Automotive Aftermarket," *Journal of Business Forecasting Methods & Systems* 12(4), Winter 1993–94, pp. 8–12.

	Quarter			
Year	1	2	3	4
1	200	250	210	340
2	210	252	212	360
3	215	260	220	358
4	225	272	233	372
5	232	284	240	381

a. Determine quarterly seasonal relatives using the centred moving average method.

b. Deseasonalize the data, fit an appropriate model to the deseasonalized data, extend it four quarters, and finally reseasonalize the projections.

*20. Federated Cooperatives Limited (FCL) is the largest wholesaler of grocery, hardware, and agricultural supplies in Western Canada, and operates warehouses in Saskatoon, Edmonton, Calgary, and Winnipeg. In the Calgary warehouse, a particular golf club is carried in stock. The demand for this golf club during each month of the period 2003–05 is listed below (note that FCL uses weekly time buckets, but for simplicity we have combined these into monthly data): **LO5**

Month	2003	2004	2005
Jan	0	2	3
Feb	52	8	20
Mar	29	44	12
Apr	49	74	31
May	47	75	61
Jun	58	87	28
Jul	0	145	107
Aug	64	11	57
Sep	3	24	21
Oct	17	9	10
Nov	10	5	0
Dec	1	6	1

a. Determine the monthly relatives using the 12-period centred moving average method.

b. Deseasonalize the data, fit an appropriate model to the deseasonalized data, project it 12 months ahead, and reseasonalize the projections to forecast monthly sales for 2006. (These forecasts will be used to plan purchases of the golf club from the manufacturer.)

21. The following data are quarterly sales of natural gas in Saskatchewan by SaskEnergy (in peta joules ≈ 1 billion cubic feet) from Q1 of 2005 to Q3 of 2009.[11] **LO5**

Year	Q1	Q2	Q3	Q4
2005	49	24	18	37
2006	42	20	20	43
2007	48	24	20	40
2008	51	25	19	43
2009	51	24	15	

a. Compute the seasonal relative for each quarter using the centred moving average method.

b. Deseasonalize the data, fit an appropriate model to the deseasonalized data, extend the model four quarters, and reseasonalize these in order to forecast the sales of natural gas by SaskEnergy from Q4 2009 to Q3 2010.

*22. For planning production in the medium term, vehicle manufacturers need to forecast the demand for new motor vehicle sales. The following data are the number (in thousands) of Honda Ridgeline trucks manufactured by Honda during each quarter, starting from first quarter of 2005 (when Ridgeline was introduced) until the 3rd quarter of 2008.[12] Assume that all Ridgelines produced in a quarter were sold in the same quarter. **LO5**

Year	Q1	Q2	Q3	Q4
2005	11.5	19.2	17.4	12.7
2006	11.9	15.1	17.4	12.1
2007	10.6	19.1	13.9	11.5
2008	10.2	6.2	5.6	

a. Compute the seasonal relative for each quarter using the centred moving average method.

b. Deseasonalize the data, fit an appropriate model to the deseasonalized data, extend the model four quarters, and reseasonalize these in order to forecast the sales of Ridgeline trucks in the 4th quarter of 2008, and 1st, 2nd, and 3rd quarters of 2009.

*23. Mountain Aquaculture and Producers Association (MA&PA) is a small trout producers' cooperative in West Virginia.[13] Its main product is boned, head-removed trout sold to local stores. One of the problems MA&PA is facing is that the demand for its products is seasonal (see the sales in pounds of boned, head-removed trout from Q1 1997 to Q3 2000 below). The manager would like to plan production better. **LO5**

Year	Q1	Q2	Q3	Q4
1997	664	1,338	1,170	1,069
1998	422	1,098	1,939	843
1999	803	1,430	1,206	724
2000	698	1,076	1,149	

[11] http://www.saskenergy.com/about_saskenergy

[12] CANSIM series V429850230.

[13] R.M. Fincham. A Break-even Analysis of Trout Processing in West Virginia: A Case Study Approach, M.S. thesis, West Virginia University, 2001.

a. Compute the seasonal relative for each quarter using the centred moving average method.

b. Deseasonalize the data, fit an appropriate model to the deseasonalized data, extend the model four quarters, and reseasonalize these in order to forecast the sales of boned, head-removed trout from the 4th quarter of 2000 to 3rd quarter of 2001.

24. The manager of a seafood restaurant wants to establish a price on shrimp dinners. Experimenting with prices produced the following data: LO6

Average Number Sold per Day, y	Price, x	Average Number Sold per Day, y	Price, x
200	$6.00	155	$8.25
190	6.50	156	8.50
188	6.75	148	8.75
180	7.00	140	9.00
170	7.25	133	9.25
162	7.50		
160	8.00		

a. Plot the data as a scatter plot, determine the regression equation, and plot the regression line on the same graph as data. (You may use Excel's "=slope(RangeY,RangeX)" and "=intercept(RangeY, RangeX)" to obtain the regression coefficients b and a, respectively, where RangeY is the range of Excel cells containing the y values and RangeX is the range of Excel cells containing the x values. Alternatively, use Trendline in the Layout menu.)

b. Determine the correlation coefficient and interpret it. (You may use Excel's "=CORREL (RangeY,RangeX)" to determine r).

25. The following data were collected during a study of consumer buying patterns. LO6

Observation	X	Y	Observation	X	Y
1	15	74	8	18	78
2	25	80	9	14	70
3	40	84	10	15	72
4	32	81	11	22	85
5	51	96	12	24	88
6	47	95			
7	30	83			

a. Plot the data as a scatter plot.

b. Obtain a linear regression line for the data. (You may use Excel's "=slope(RangeY,RangeX)" and "=intercept(RangeY,RangeX, where RangeY is the range of Excel cells containing the y values and RangeX is the range of Excel cells containing the

x values)" to obtain the regression coefficients b and a, respectively. Alternatively, use Trendline in the Layout menu.)

c. What percentage of the variation is explained by the regression line? (You may use Excel's "=RSQ(RangeY,RangeX)" to obtain r^2).

d. Use the equation determined in part b to predict the value of y for $x = 41$.

26. A lawn and garden centre intends to use sales of lawn fertilizer to predict lawn mower sales. The store manager wishes to determine the relationship between fertilizer and mower sales. The pertinent data are: LO6

Period	Fertilizer Sales (tonnes)	Number of Mowers Sold	Period	Fertilizer Sales (tonnes)	Number of Mowers Sold
1	1.6	10	8	1.3	7
2	1.3	8	9	1.7	10
3	1.8	11	10	1.2	6
4	2.0	12	11	1.9	11
5	2.2	12	12	1.4	8
6	1.6	9	13	1.7	10
7	1.5	8			

a. Determine the correlation between the two variables. Does it appear that a relationship between these variables will yield good predictions? Explain. (You may use Excel's "=CORREL (RangeY,RangeX)" to determine r, where RangeY is the range of Excel cells containing the y values and RangeX is the range of Excel cells containing the x values. You also need R², RSQ(RangeY,RangeX)).

b. Obtain a linear regression line for the data. (You may use Excel's "=slope(RangeY,RangeX)" and "=intercept(RangeY,RangeX)" to obtain the regression coefficients b and a, respectively. Alternatively, use Trendline in the Layout menu.)

c. Predict lawn mower sales, given fertilizer sales of 2 tonnes.

27. Columbia Gas Company of Ohio distributes natural gas to residential, business, and industrial customers in Ohio.[14] In order to secure enough gas supply, Columbia Gas forecasts daily demand for the next five days using regression. It has identified the average daily temperature as the most important explanatory variable for daily demand for natural gas. The regression is estimated using daily data from the past two years. For brevity, we consider only a subset of this period as follows. LO6

a. Plot the average temperature and demand data for the past 10 days. Does there appear to be a linear relationship?

[14] Based on A.H. Catron, "Daily Demand Forecasting at Columbia Gas," *Journal of Business Forecasting* 19(2) Summer 2000, 10–15.

b. Estimate the regression coefficients. (You may use Excel's "=slope(RangeY,RangeX)" and "=intercept(RangeY,RangeX)" to obtain the regression coefficients b and a, respectively, where RangeY is the range of Excel cells containing the y values and RangeX is the range of Excel cells containing the x values.).

c. If the average temperature tomorrow is expected to be 54 degrees Fahrenheit, what is the forecast for demand for natural gas tomorrow?

Day	Avg. Temp (F)	Demand (thousand dekatherm)
−10	33	1005
−9	46	501
−8	41	612
−7	47	499
−6	37	692
−5	36	709
−4	32	951
−3	34	1053
−2	38	746
−1	43	458

28. An analyst must decide between two different forecasting techniques for weekly sales of inline skates: a linear trend equation and the naïve approach. The linear trend equation is $y_t = 124 + 2t$, and it was developed using data from periods 1 through 10. Based on data for periods 11 through 19 as shown below, which of these two methods has greater accuracy? (You can use any one of the three measures of forecast errors). **LO7**

t	Units Sold	t	Units Sold
11	147	16	152
12	148	17	155
13	151	18	157
14	145	19	160
15	155		

29. Two different forecasting techniques were used to forecast demand for cases of bottled water in a store. Actual demand and the two sets of forecasts for seven periods are as follows: **LO7**

		Forecast Demand	
Period	Demand	F1	F2
1	68	66	66
2	75	68	68
3	70	72	70
4	74	71	72
5	69	72	74
6	72	70	76
7	80	71	78

a. Calculate the MAD for each set of forecasts. Which technique appears to be more accurate?

b. Calculate the MSE for each set of forecasts. Which technique appears to be more accurate?

c. Calculate the MAPE for each set of forecasts. Which technique appears to be more accurate?

d. Do all three measures of forecast errors provide the same conclusion (i.e., are they consistent) in this case? Do you expect consistent results for every case? Explain.

e. In practice, *either* MAD, MSE, or MAPE would be employed to compute a measure of forecast errors. What factors might lead a manager to favour one?

30. Two independent set of forecasts based on judgment and experience have been prepared each month for the past 10 months. The forecasts and actual demand are as follows: **LO7**

Month	Demand	Forecast 1	Forecast 2
1	770	771	769
2	789	785	787
3	794	790	792
4	780	784	798
5	768	770	774
6	772	768	770
7	760	761	759
8	775	771	775
9	786	784	788
10	790	788	788

a. Calculate the MSE, MAD, and MAPE for each forecast. Does one forecast seem superior? Explain.

b. Do all three measures of forecast errors provide the same conclusion (i.e., are they consistent) in this case? Do you expect consistent results in every case? Explain.

c. Calculate $2s$ control limits for each forecast and determine if each forecasting process is in control. Explain.

31. The classified department of a monthly magazine has used a combination of quantitative and judgmental methods to forecast sales of advertising space. The forecast errors over an 18-month period are as follows: **LO7**

Month	Forecast Error	Month	Forecast Error
1	−8	10	−4
2	−2	11	1
3	4	12	6
4	7	13	8
5	9	14	4
6	5	15	1
7	0	16	−2
8	−3	17	−4
9	−4	18	−8

a. Using the first half of the data (Months 1 to 9), construct a control chart with $2s$ limits.

b. Plot the last nine forecast errors on the control chart. Is the forecasting process in control? Are the forecast errors random? Explain.

32. A textbook publishing company has compiled data on total annual sales of its business textbooks for the preceding eight years: **LO4 & 7**

Year:	1	2	3	4	5	6	7	8
Sales (000):	40.2	44.5	48.0	52.3	55.8	57.1	62.4	69.0

a. Plot the data and fit an appropriate model to it. Forecast the preceding eight years, and determine the forecast errors. Finally, construct a $2s$ control chart.

b. Using the model, forecast textbook sales for each of the next five years.

c. Suppose actual sales for the next five years turn out as follows:

Year:	9	10	11	12	13
Sales (000):	73.7	77.2	82.1	87.8	90.6

Calculate the forecast errors for years 9 to 13. Is the forecasting process in control? Explain.

33. A manager has just received an evaluation from an analyst on two potential forecasting methods. The analyst is indifferent between the two methods, saying that they should be equally accurate and in control. The demand and the forecasts using the two methods for nine periods follow: **LO7**

Period:	1	2	3	4	5	6	7	8	9
Demand:	37	39	37	39	45	49	47	49	51
Method 1:	36	38	40	42	46	46	46	48	52
Method 2:	36	37	38	38	41	52	47	48	52

a. Calculate the MSE for each method and compare the two methods.

b. Construct a $2s$ control chart for each method and interpret them. Do you agree with the analyst? Explain.

*34. Consider the usage of item #14-46-506: 4 ft. Supersaver fluorescent lamps in Sterling Pulp Chemicals (now part of ERCO Worldwide) in the first 10 months of 2008.

Month	2008
Jan	10
Feb	10
Mar	66
Apr	32
May	34
June	18
July	24
Aug	9
Sep	14
Oct	48

Fit a model to the data using each of the following techniques and forecast the November usage in each case. Also, plot the two moving average forecasts and the actual, the two exponential smoothing forecasts and the actual, and the linear trend and the actual (three graphs altogether). **LO3 & 4**

a. Three-month moving average.

b. Five-month moving average.

c. Exponential smoothing with smoothing constant = 0.1.

d. Exponential smoothing with smoothing constant = 0.3.

e. Linear trend (regression).

f. Just by observing the plots, which of the above techniques would you use to forecast the usage of fluorescent lamps and why? (*Hint:* The plot overall closest to actual demand will be most accurate).

g. Alternatively, compute the MAD for each forecasting technique and determine the most accurate technique.

*35. Consider the total production (and sales) of ice cream in Canada (in millions of litres) for the period 1995 until 2007 (from left to right)[15]:

341, 331, 317, 315, 321, 278, 298, 311, 302, 302, 335, 320, 285

Fit a model to ice cream production data using each of the following techniques and forecast the 2008 production in each case. Also, plot the two moving average forecasts and the actual, the two exponential smoothing forecasts and the actual, and the linear trend and the actual (three graphs altogether). **LO3 & 4**

a. Two-year moving average.

b. Four-year moving average.

c. Exponential smoothing with smoothing constant = 0.2.

d. Exponential smoothing with smoothing constant = 0.4.

e. Linear trend (regression).

f. Just by observing the plots, which of the above techniques would you use to forecast the ice cream production and why? (*Hint:* The plot overall closest to actual demand will be most accurate).

g. Alternatively, compute the MAD for each forecasting technique and determine the most accurate technique.

---

[15] CANSIM 2 database series v108517.

*36. The number of Toyota Corollas produced in the Cambridge, Ontario, plant during each month of January 2008 to December 2009 period was as follows[16]:

Month	No. Produced	Month	No. Produced
2008–01	4,959	2009–01	6,733
2008–02	8,463	2009–02	1,006
2008–03	11,706	2009–03	9,328
2008–04	9,907	2009–04	9,072
2008–05	9,354	2009–05	8,738
2008–06	11,297	2009–06	12,259
2008–07	8,905	2009–07	9,519
2008–08	12,249	2009–08	12,113
2008–09	19,160	2009–09	14,044
2008–10	14,264	2009–10	16,650
2008–11	13,687	2009–11	16,912
2008–12	8,657	2009–12	13,851

Assume that the cars are sold in the same month they are produced. Identify an appropriate forecasting technique, briefly state the reason(s) you chose it, and forecast Corolla demand in January 2010. **LO3, 4, 5, 7 & 8**

37. A cosmetics manufacturer's marketing department has developed a linear tread equation that can be used to predict annual sales of its popular hand cream. **LO4**

$$\hat{y}_t = 80 + 15t$$

where $\hat{y}_t$ = Annual sales (000 bottles) and t is the index of time periods

a. Are annual sales increasing or decreasing? By how much?

b. Predict annual sales for year 6 using the equation.

38. Long-Life Insurance has developed a linear model that is used to determine the amount of term life insurance a family of four should have, based on the current age of the head of the household. The equation is: **LO4**

$$y = 850 - 0.1x$$

where y = Insurance needed ($000) and x = Current age of head of household

a. Plot the relationship on a graph.

b. Use the equation to determine the amount of term life insurance to recommend for a family of four if the head of the household is 30 years old.

MINI-CASE   http://www.acadianbakers.com

Acadian Bakers

Acadian Bakers is a small sweets bakery in Houston, Texas. One of its products is a croissant. Acadian bakes the croissants from frozen croissants that it buys. For the sake of quality, the company don't want to store its frozen goods for more than one week. For orders of more than 576 cases, the delivery is free (saving $15 per order). A case contains 144 frozen croissants. Acadian has collected its total weekly sales for croissants (in cases) for the last 10 weeks. Management believes that the sales of croissants are increasing. Determine if and when Acadian can take advantage of the quantity discount.

Week	Sales
1	461
2	450
3	463
4	458
5	476
6	492
7	482
8	491
9	488
10	488

connect   **LEARNSMART**   **SMARTBOOK™**

For more information on the resources available from McGraw-Hill Ryerson, go to www.mheducation.ca/he/solutions.

---

[16] CANSIM 2 series v42190663.

CHAPTER 4
Product Design

Learning Objectives

After completing this chapter, you should be able to:

LO1 Describe the product design process.

LO2 Name some sources of ideas for new or revised designs.

LO3 Discuss key issues in product design.

LO4 Discuss special considerations for service design.

LO5 Describe and perform quality function deployment (QFD).

Satisfying customers begins with product (good and service) design. Moreover, decisions made in this area impact operations and organizations' overall success.

Similarly, production process design and capacity planning impact the ability of the production system to perform and satisfy customers, in addition to affecting cost of production. Process design and layout are closely related. Layout decisions involve the arrangement of the workplace, which affects the flow of work through the system. Facility layout is an important part of most services.

Work design focuses on the human element in production systems. Increasingly, managers are realizing that workers are a valuable asset and can contribute greatly to the organization's success.

The location decision influences operating costs, transportation costs, labour availability, and access to markets.

Design decisions have strategic significance for organizations. Many of these decisions are made jointly with the CEO and top managers of other functional areas of the organization.

Saskatoon, Saskatchewan–based Draganfly Innovations Inc. is busy designing the next generation of unmanned aerial vehicles (UAVs). Commonly known as drones, UAVs have a host of potential military and civilian applications. For instance, the Saskatoon Royal Canadian Mounted Police have been using UAVs like the Draganflyer X4ES system since 2011 in support at crime scenes, and for traffic accident reconstruction, tactical support, and search and rescue.

Careful design decisions made by Draganfly engineers ensure that their drones excel at providing fast and reliable situational awareness wherever needed. Available four-engine and six-engine designs provide the power that Draganfly drones need to field a wide range of payload options. When on-site, the drones help provide law enforcement with situational awareness and the capability to take aerial surveillance video and shoot high-resolution photos.

Source: http://www.rcmp-grc.gc.ca/sk/news-nouvelle/video-gallery/video-pages/search-rescue-eng.htm.

The essence of any business organization is the goods and services it offers, and every aspect of the organization and its supply chain are structured around those goods and services. There is an obvious link between the *design* of those goods and services and the *success* of the organization. Hence, organizations have a strategic interest in product and service design. Product or service design should be closely tied to an organization's strategy. It is a major factor in cost, quality, time-to-market, customer satisfaction, and competitive advantage. Consequently, marketing, finance, operations, accounting, IT, and HR need to be involved. Demand forecasts and projected costs are important, as is the expected impact on the supply chain. It is significant to note that an important cause of operations failures can be traced to faulty design. Designs that have not been well thought out, or incorrectly implemented, or instructions for assembly or usage that are wrong or unclear, can be the cause of product and service failures, leading to lawsuits, injuries and deaths, product recalls, and damaged reputations. The quality of the product is mainly, perhaps as much as 80 percent, determined during the design. Hence, organizations have a vital stake in achieving good product design.

Product design involves the determination of the form and function of the product. Business organizations select the products they want to offer based on their expected profit contribution. In most cases, products are redesigned to invigorate their demand and to take advantage of new technology.

product design Determining the form and function of the product.

The much anticipated Boeing 787 Dreamliner aircraft resumed flights after being grounded for more than three months for a battery defect. Aviation safety depends on well-maintained equipment and an expert flight crew who can handle emergencies as they come up.

In this chapter you will find many insights into good and service design. Among the topics covered are the steps involved in product design or redesign; sources of ideas for design or redesign; some design issues; service design; and quality function deployment, a method for translating the "voice of customers" into design attributes.

Product design—or redesign—should be closely tied to an organization's strategy. It is a major factor in customer satisfaction and competitive advantage.

 Product Design Process

Successful organizations use four elements to rapidly create new goods and services and bring them to consumers. The product approval committee consists of top management and oversees and directs the design/development activities. It is responsible for authorizing new products, reviewing their progress at phase (or stage) review points, allocating resources across different projects, and ensuring consistency between company strategy and design/development projects.

Core teams are cross-functional teams empowered to plan and lead the design/development projects from idea to commercialization. This involves resolving issues and conflicts, making trade-off decisions, and directing other support staff. Every function involved in the design/development should be represented in the core team, but the team should not be large (maximum of eight members) in order to be effective. It is important to clearly define every core member's role and responsibility, and those of the functional managers, to ensure that the core team is empowered. The limits of authority of the core team should be defined. Many core teams also include a legal and regulatory member.

Phase reviews (or stage-gates) are milestones during a new product design/development project when the progress of the core team is reviewed by the product approval committee. The decision will be to approve, cancel, or redirect the project. Reviews help top management acquire better understanding of the project, guide the project, and force closure of issues arising during each phase of the project. Phase reviews result in recognizing the problems and making necessary changes earlier, reducing the cost of changes and time to market. Cost of changes tends to multiply with each phase—changing a sketch is a lot easier than changing a prototype, and changing a prototype is a lot easier than changing the first production unit. This is called the "escalator effect."[1]

---

[1] See, for example, B. Huthwaite and G. Spence, "The Power of Cost Measurement in New Product Development," *National Productivity Review*, Summer 1989, 8(3), pp. 239–248.

The structured development process is the use of project management techniques. It involves breaking each phase (stage) into steps and each step into activities, determining their precedence relationships, scheduling, and execution and control. The steps are most critical and are planned and managed by the core team. An activity relates to one functional area and is planned and managed by the core team member from that function. Activities may be broken down into day-to-day tasks. It is important that the amount of structure is just right: too much structure results in bureaucracy and too little structure results in ineffective design/development process.

The usual phases (stages) for product design, and a brief description for each, are:

1. Idea generation and preliminary assessment (or scoping): Ideas can come from customers' feedback, research and development staff, suppliers, and competitors. Preliminary assessment involves market, technical, and financial evaluation.

2. Building a business case: Determine what customers want ("voice of the customer"), determine the nature of product and assess its technical feasibility, establish product goals and objectives (performance, price, quality, quantity, launch date, etc.), plan the nature of the production process (determine the inputs, process objectives, and production process in general), and perform a complete financial analysis.

3. Development of product and process: Translate the "voice of the customer" into technical (physical) product specifications, such as product size, features, and so on. As part of this, several concepts (sketch of product) are developed. Each concept represents a slightly different product form and/or function, and its components. Choose one concept and complete the design. Build product prototypes, test, and revise the design if necessary. Design the production/service delivery process: develop a few process concepts (sketches), evaluate them and choose one concept and complete the design, build a prototype of the process and evaluate it, and revise the process if necessary. Determine the machines and equipment, plant layout, and work centre designs.

4. Testing and validation: Perform external testing, finalize the product and process specifications, and buy the machines and equipment and start trial runs.

5. Launch.

A core team usually consists of a product manager, product designers (usually stylists, also called industrial designers, and engineers), and manufacturing/operations representatives. The team is expanded during each phase of design with marketing representatives (at the start and at the end), accountants (to establish cost goals), process engineers (for process design, tooling/equipment), quality control, and purchasing and supplier representatives (component design and manufacturing).

This team-based approach of simultaneously designing the product and process is called *concurrent engineering*. In contrast, in the past, because of time pressure and the "silo" mentality, each functional area performed its part of design in isolation and "threw" the work "over the wall" to the next department in design. The order was (1) marketing, (2) product design/engineering, (3) manufacturing, and (4) purchasing. This frequently resulted in late launches and costly design revisions. Concurrent engineering is further discussed later in the chapter. The new product design/development process is illustrated in Figure 4-1 (the stage-gate model).

In the stage-gate model, *Scoping* involves preliminary market, financial, and technical assessment; *Building Business Case* involves determining customer requirements, competitive analysis, detailed financial and technical analysis, product definition, and operations assessment; *Development*

▼ **Figure 4-1**

The stage-gate model of the new product design and development process.

Source: Stage-Gate® © Product Development Institute Inc. http://www.prod-dev.com/stage-gate.php.

involves further developing the product concept, making and testing prototypes, and operations process development; and *Testing and Validation* involves further in-house testing and customer trials, acquisition of production equipment, and operations trials.

Sources of Ideas for New or Redesigned Products

Ideas for new or redesigned goods and services can come from a wide range of sources, both from within the organization and from outside it: front-line employees, the suppliers and purchasing function, customers and sales/marketing functions, competitors (through reverse engineering), and the research and development (R&D) function.

Front-line employees—those who make the goods or deliver services to customers—have seen the problems in manufacturing/assembly operations or service delivery system caused by faulty design of the parts and products. Their feedback could improve the redesigned product. Suppliers of materials and parts/components and their contact within the organization, the purchasing agents, can be a rich source of ideas about the design/redesign of purchased items. Customers and their contacts within the organization, the customer service and marketing/sales employees, are aware of problems with products. Similarly, product failures and warranty claims indicate where improvements are needed. Marketing employees are often sources of ideas based on their studies of markets, buying patterns, and familiarity with demographics. Also, marketing can help craft a vision of what customers are likely to want in the future. Customers may submit suggestions for improvements of existing products or need for new products, or they may be queried through the use of surveys or focus groups.

One of the strongest motivators for new and improved products and services is competitors' products and services. By studying a competitor's products or services and how the competitor operates (pricing policies, return policies, warranties, location strategies, etc.), an organization can glean many ideas. Beyond that, some companies purchase a competitor's product and dismantle it to discover what it is composed of and how the components work, searching for ways to improve their own product. This is called **reverse engineering**. The following are some examples of reverse engineering. Xerox, despite inventing the copy machine, came under competitive pressure from cheaper Japanese copiers such as Toshiba in 1980s. Xerox tore down the competitors' copiers and learned their secrets. When IBM created its personal computer in 1980s, the only component that was not publicly available was the ROM-Bios chip. It did not take its competitors, such as Compaq, too long to produce a similar chip and make IBM clones. Ford Motor Company used reverse engineering in developing its highly successful Taurus model: it examined competitors' automobiles, searching for best-in-class components (e.g., best hood release, best dashboard display, best door handle). Sometimes reverse engineering can enable a company to "leapfrog" the competition by developing an even better product. Suppliers are still another source of ideas, and with increased emphasis on supply chains and supplier partnerships, suppliers are becoming an important source of ideas.

reverse engineering Dismantling and inspecting a competitor's product to discover what it is composed of and how the components work, searching for own-product improvements.

This 3.66 litre space-efficient square plastic twist and pour paint container with a hollow handle on one side, a snap-in pour spout, and a twist-off lid, is a significant innovation in paint packaging. Dutch Boy is a brand of Sherwin-Williams group.

Research is another source of ideas for new or improved products and services. **Research and development (R&D)** refers to organized efforts that are directed toward increasing scientific

research and development (R&D) Organized efforts that are directed toward increasing scientific knowledge and product or process innovation.

knowledge and product or process innovation. Most of the advances in semiconductors, medicine, communications, and space technology can be attributed to R&D efforts at colleges and universities, research foundations, government agencies, and private enterprises.

R&D efforts may involve basic research, applied research, or development.

Basic research has the objective of advancing the state of knowledge about a subject without any near-term expectation of commercial applications.

Applied research has the objective of achieving commercial applications.

Development converts the results of applied research into useful commercial applications.

Basic research, because it does not lead to near-term commercial applications, is generally underwritten by the government and large corporations. Conversely, applied research and development, because of the potential for commercial applications, appeals to a wide spectrum of business organizations.

The benefits of successful R&D can be tremendous. Some research leads to patents, with the potential of licensing and royalties. However, many discoveries are not patentable, or companies don't wish to divulge details of their ideas so they avoid the patent route. Even so, the first organization to bring a new product or service to the market generally stands to profit from it before the others can catch up. Early products may be priced higher because a temporary monopoly exists until competitors bring out their versions.

The costs of R&D can be high. Large companies in the automotive (such as Magna International), computer (such as IBM Canada), communications (such as BCE), aerospace (such as Bombardier Inc.), and pharmaceutical/biotech (such as Apotex) industries spend a lot of money on R&D. For a list of Canada's top 100 R&D spenders, see http://www.researchinfosource.com/pdf/2013Top%20100%20R&D.pdf. For a list of top 100 R&D spenders worldwide, see http://www.spectrum.ieee.org/images/dec07/images/12.RDchart.pdf. Hewlett-Packard is considered one of the most innovative companies in the world. In a study of innovative projects in HP, it was discovered that having skilled and helpful people who work well together, and management support, as well as using a systematic product design process (to provide discipline and focus) are the required ingredients for a high degree of innovation.[2]

R&D also contributes to a company by developing the prototypes, testing the prototypes in engineering labs, and improving the products' reliability.

It is interesting to note that some companies are now shifting from a focus primarily on *products* to a more balanced approach that explores both product and *process* R&D. Also, there is increasing recognition that technologies often go through life cycles, the same way that many products do. This can impact R&D efforts on two fronts. Sustained economic growth requires constant attention to competitive factors over a life cycle, and it also requires planning to be able to participate in the next-generation technology.

The following OM in Action box illustrates some market-related sources of ideas for product design.

 OM in *ACTION*

Searching for New Product Ideas

What is the best way to find new product ideas? Consider the following approaches that have shown success in the past:

1. Listening to the Market Complaints

Many companies have made their products successful by listening to consumer complaints about products already on the market. Complaints about the inadequacies of two-ply tissues inspired Kimberly-Clark to create three-ply Cold Care Tissues, and Gillette found it could satisfy customers with complaints about white residue from its deodorants by creating the Clear Stick.

An equivalent complaint about lipstick smearing on coffee cups and shirt collars resulted in Lancome's transfer-resistant Rouge Idole lipsticks.

---

[2] R. Rivas and D.H. Gobeli, "Accelerating Innovation at Hewlett-Packard," *Research Technology–Management* 48(1), January/February 2005, pp. 32–39.

2. Gaps in the Market

3M used focus groups to create its Pop-up Tape Dispenser—it noticed consumers were one hand short of being able to hold wrapping paper, scissors, and tape when wrapping gifts. The new patented creation fit like a wristwatch, precutting tape strips and otherwise giving gift-wrappers a hand up. Black & Decker introduced its cordless DeWalt power tools for professionals who needed powerful equipment (such as drills) and could get this only from corded tools. The Black & Decker Snakelite twistable flashlight allows for hands-free use during repairs in tight-fitting spaces such as bathrooms or furnaces.

John Deere Co.'s "Gator" is an inexpensive, six-wheel, off-road all-terrain utility vehicle suitable for transporting everything from personnel and equipment to farming debris to wounded soldiers from the battlefield. The Gator simply doesn't have any direct competitors.

3. Exploring Niche Markets

For drivers who have been dropped by their insurance carriers because they are considered risky, Kingsway Financial Services Company of Mississauga, Ontario, provides an unparalleled service: offering car insurance to drivers like these, Kingsway has seen its annual revenue rocket from less than $20 million to more than $92 billion in a mere 10 years.

Coleman, traditionally a manufacturer of camping gear, found a lucrative niche in the market when it produced smoke detectors with large "broom button" alarm testers. Using a broom handle to shut off nuisance alarms triggered by burnt toast appealed especially to the elderly and gave Coleman a 40 percent market share as a result.

4. Using New Technology

Many new products have found that they could attract the attention of the market by exploiting a new science or art, whether it is a once-a-month pill to rid cats and dogs of fleas (Novartis), or frosted windows that clear with the flip of a switch (3M). Research in Motion (RIM) founders managed to use their capability with pagers to invent BlackBerry, a portable e-mail communicator, in the late 1990s at the peak of the high-tech boom.

5. Creating New Market Space

Westjet started by targeting a new market, the "friends and relatives" visitors who normally drive to visit. Sony Walkman created the new market of personal portable stereo market for joggers and commuters. Starbucks emphasizes the emotional value of drinking coffee by providing a chic "caffeine-induced oasis." Body Shop did the reverse by selling natural ingredients and healthy living instead of glamour and beauty.

Question

Can you name some more examples of the above sources of product ideas?

Sources: Adapted from Allan J. Magrath, "Mining for New Product Successes," *Business Quarterly* 62(2), Winter 1997, pp. 64–68; "The Edison Best New Product Awards," *Marketing News* 31(6), March 17, 1997, pp. E4–E12; W.C. Kim & R. Mauborgne, "Creating New Market Space," *Harvard Business Review* 77(1), January/February 1999, pp. 83–93.

Key Issues in Product Design

L03

Designers must take into account issues such as product life cycle, standardization, mass customization, product reliability, robust design, legal and ethical issues, design for environment, concurrent engineering of product and production process, computer-aided design, design for manufacturing and assembly, and component commonality. These topics are discussed in this section. We begin with life cycles.

life cycle Incubation, growth, maturity, saturation, and decline.

Life Cycle

The decision to design a new substitute product or to redesign an existing product, and its timing, depends on the nature and length of the product's life cycle. Most products go through a **life cycle**: incubation, growth, maturity, saturation, and decline.

Incubation. When an item is introduced, it may be treated as a curiosity. Demand is generally low because potential buyers are not yet familiar with the item. Many potential buyers recognize that all of the bugs have probably not been worked out and that the price may drop after the introductory period. Production methods are generally designed for low volumes.

Growth. With the passage of time, design improvements usually create a more reliable and less costly product. Demand then grows for these reasons and because of increasing awareness of the product. Higher production volume will involve automated production methods and contribute to lower costs.

Maturity. There are few, if any, design changes, and demand levels off.

Saturation. Saturation leads to a decline in demand.

OXO Good Grips Corn Stripper is an example of a product filling a need in the market.

Decline. In decline, companies attempt to prolong the useful life of a product by improving its reliability, reducing costs of producing it (and, hence, the price), redesigning it, or introducing a new substitute product. These stages are illustrated in Figure 4-2.

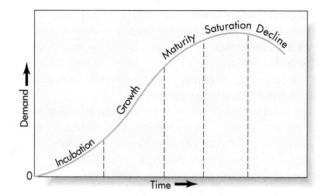

Most products exhibits a life cycle over time.

Consider the portable computer data storage products in various stages of the life cycle: Memory keys are in the growth stage, DVDs are in the saturation stage, and CDs are in the decline stage.

Some products do not exhibit life cycles: wooden pencils; paper clips; nails; knives, forks, and spoons; drinking glasses; and similar items. However, most new products do.

Services, too, experience life cycles. For example, in banking, using tellers is in saturation stage, using ABMs is in its maturity, and Internet banking is in its growth stage.

Wide variations exist in the amount of time a particular product takes to pass through a given phase of its life cycle: some pass through various stages in a relatively short period; others take considerably longer. Often it is a matter of the basic *need* for the item and the *rate of technological change*. Some toys, novelty items, personal computers, and style items have a life cycle of less than one year, whereas other items, such as clothes washers and dryers, may last for decades before yielding to technological change.

Standardization

Standardization refers to the extent to which there is absence of variety in a part or product, that is, having limited types, sizes, and colours. Standardized products are made in large quantities of identical items; paper, gasoline, and 2 percent milk are examples. Standardized service implies that every customer or item processed receives essentially the same service. An automatic car wash is a good example; each car, regardless of how clean or dirty it is, receives the same service.

standardization Extent to which there is absence of variety in a part or product.

Large-volume production and purchase of only a few types of standardized parts would reduce costs due to economies of scale. For example, auto manufacturers have standardized key components of their automobiles across similar product lines; components such as brakes, electrical systems, and other "under-the-skin" parts would be the same. By reducing variety, they save time and money while increasing quality and reliability in their products.

Another benefit of standardization is reduced time and cost to train employees. Similarly, inventory, purchasing, and accounting activities become much more routine. WestJet's using only Boeing 737 airplanes is an example, where costs of training the pilots and maintenance workers, and inventory of spare parts, are reduced.

Lack of standardization can at times lead to serious difficulties and competitive struggles, particularly when systems are incompatible. For example, lack of standardization in computer software and operating systems (Apple versus IBM) has presented users with hard choices because of the difficulty in switching from one system to the other.

Standardization also has disadvantages. A major one relates to the reduction in variety. This can limit the range of customers to whom a product appeals. Another disadvantage is that a manufacturer may lock in obsolescence and resist modification of a part.

Design for Mass Customization

Companies like standardization because it enables them to produce high volumes of relatively low-cost products, albeit products with little variety. Customers, on the other hand, typically prefer more variety, although they like the low cost. The question for producers is how to resolve these issues without (1) losing the benefits of standardization and (2) incurring the problems that are often linked to variety. The answer, at least for some companies, is **mass customization**, a strategy of producing standardized goods or services but incorporating some degree of customization in the final product. Several tactics make this possible. One is *delayed differentiation*, and another is *modular design*.

mass customization
Producing basically standardized goods or services but incorporating some degree of customization.

Delayed differentiation is a *postponement* tactic: the process of producing but not quite completing a product until customer preferences or specifications are known. In case of goods, almost-finished units might be held in inventory until customer orders are received, at which time customized features are incorporated according to customer requests. For example, furniture makers can produce dining room sets but not apply stain, allowing customers a choice of stains. Once the choice is made, the stain can be applied in a relatively short time. Another example is HP printers, made in Singapore, for the European market. By postponing country-specific customization, e.g., labels, packaging, and manuals, and doing this in its distribution centre in Stuttgart, HP saved 25 percent in total costs of manufacturing, shipping, and inventory costs. Finally, manufacturers of men's clothing produce dress pants that have legs that are unfinished, allowing the customers to choose the exact length.

delayed differentiation
Producing, but not quite completing, a product until customer preferences are known.

Modular design is grouping of parts into modules that are easily interchanged or replaced. The product is composed of a number of modules or components instead of a collection of individual parts. One familiar example of modular design is computers with modular components that can be replaced if they become defective. By arranging modules in different configurations, different computer capabilities can be obtained. This is the major reason that Dell Computers can assemble and have custom-ordered computers delivered to its Internet customers in a matter of days. For mass customization, modular design enables producers to quickly assemble modules to achieve a customized configuration for an individual customer, avoiding the long customer wait that would occur if individual parts had to be assembled.

modular design Parts are grouped into modules that are easily replaced or interchanged. The product is composed of a number of modules or components instead of a collection of individual parts.

Another advantage of modular design is that failures are often easier to diagnose and remedy because modules can be tested individually. Other advantages include simpler purchasing, inventory control, and assembly operations.

The main disadvantage of modular design is the inability to disassemble some modules in order to replace a faulty part; the entire module must be scrapped—usually at a higher cost.

For an example of modular design, see the "Magna Powertrain's Engine Module" OM in Action.

A relatively new way of mass customization uses computer technology. For example, Amazon.com uses a software program that analyzes a customer's browsing history and suggests other books that people with similar interests have bought.

Reliability

Reliability is a measure of the ability of a product, a part, or an entire system to perform its intended function under normal conditions.

reliability The ability of a product, part, or system to perform its intended function under normal conditions.

The term **failure** is used to describe a situation in which an item does not perform as intended. This includes not only instances in which the item does not function at all, but also instances in which the item's performance is substandard or it functions in a way not intended. For example, a smoke alarm might fail to respond to the presence of smoke (not operate at all), it might sound an alarm that is too faint to provide an adequate warning (substandard performance), or it might sound an alarm even though no smoke is present (unintended response).

failure Situation in which a product, part, or system does not perform as intended.

OM in *ACTION* http://www.magna.com/capabilities/powertrain-systems

Magna Powertrain's Engine Module

Automakers are increasingly looking to reduce the number of parts under the hood by moving to larger and more sophisticated engine modules. Magna Powertrain's front-engine cover module is one of the most advanced and value-added engine modules. The module incorporates a wide range of components, including the front engine cover, water pump, oil pump, idler, tensioner, pulleys, and fasteners. Magna Powertrain provides vehicle manufacturers with one-stop shopping in terms of concept design, development, prototyping, testing, and manufacturing, as well as complete program management. The module provides significant reductions in assembly time, which in turn results in cost savings.

New products are tested to find their breaking points. If this is low, the reliability of the product must be improved. For example, laptop and notebook computers need to be tough enough to absorb unintentional drops, and trucks, cars, and motorcycles need to endure bumps in the roads for many years. For more on reliability, see the supplement to Chapter 4.

Robust Design

Some products will function as designed only within a narrow range of conditions, while others will perform over a much broader range of conditions. The latter have **robust design**. Consider a pair of fine leather boots—obviously not made for trekking through mud or snow. Now consider a pair of heavy rubber boots—just the thing for mud or snow—as well as other conditions. The rubber boots have a design that is more *robust* than the fine leather boots.

The more robust a product, the less likely it is to fail due to a change in the environment in which it is used or in which it is performed. Hence, the more designers can build robustness into the product, the better it should hold up, resulting in a higher level of customer satisfaction.

robust design Design that can function over a broad range of conditions.

Taguchi's Approach. Japanese engineer Genichi Taguchi's approach is based on robust design. His premise is that it is often easier to design a product that is insensitive to environmental factors, either in manufacturing or in use, than to control the environmental factors.

The central feature of Taguchi's approach—and the feature used most often by North American companies—is *parameter design*. This involves determining the specification settings for the product that will result in robust design in terms of manufacturing variations, product deterioration, and conditions during use.

The Taguchi approach modifies the conventional statistical methods of experimental design. Consider this example. Suppose a company intends to use 11 chemicals in a new product. There are two suppliers for these chemicals, and the chemical concentrations vary slightly between the two suppliers. Classical design of experiments would require $2^{11} = 2,048$ test runs to determine which combination of chemicals would be optimum. Taguchi's approach would involve testing only 12 combinations.[3]

Legal and Ethical Issues

Designers must be careful to take into account a wide array of legal and ethical considerations. Organizations have been faced with many government (federal, provincial, municipal) acts and regulations, administered by government agencies and boards designed to regulate their activities. Among the more familiar ones are the *Food and Drug Acts* (Health Canada), the *Canadian Environmental Protection Act* (Environment Canada), the *Motor Vehicle Safety Act* (Transport Canada), and the *Hazardous Products Act* (Industry Canada). Bans or regulations on materials such as saccharin, CFC, phosphate, and asbestos have sent designers scurrying back to their drawing boards to find alternative designs acceptable to both government regulators and customers. Similarly, automobile pollution standards and safety features, such as seat belts, air bags, safety glass, and energy-absorbing bumpers and frames, have had a substantial impact on automotive design. Much attention also has been directed toward toy design to remove sharp edges, small pieces that can cause choking, and toxic materials. In construction, government (municipal) regulations require access to public buildings for persons with disabilities, and standards for insulation, electrical wiring, plumbing, and fire protection.

Designers should not infringe on patents, trademarks, and copyright of competitors. If the product is not significantly different from a patented/copyrighted product in functional and operational characteristics or appearance (if this results in undeserved benefit), the company can be sued.[4]

Product liability can be a strong incentive for design improvements.

Product liability means that a manufacturer is liable for any injuries or damages caused by a faulty product because of poor workmanship or design.

Ethical issues often arise in the design of products. Designers are often under pressure to speed up the design process and to cut costs. These pressures often require them to make trade-off decisions, many of which involve ethical considerations. One example is, should a software company

product liability A manufacturer is liable for any injuries or damages caused by a faulty product.

---

[3] See for example, http://controls.engin.umich.edu/wiki/index.php?title=Design_of_experiments_via_-taguchi_methods:_orthogonal_arrays&printable=yes (accessed April 19, 2010).
[4] See, for example, W.M. Fitzpatrick and S.A. DiLullo, "Attack of the Clones: Reverse Engineering, R&D, and the Law," *Competition Forum*, 2006, 4(2), pp. 501–514.

release a product as scheduled when it struggles with bugs in the software, or wait until most of the bugs have been removed?

Design for Environment

Design for Environment (DFE) is an umbrella term describing techniques used to incorporate environmental concerns, including the three Rs of reduce, reuse, and recycle, into product design. The most common DFE practices include:

- Design for energy efficiency of product and energy used in manufacturing.
- Design for hazardous material minimization, including emissions and wastes in manufacturing.
- Design for biodegradable disposal, including packaging.
- Design for reuse, including packaging.
- Design for disassembly and remanufacture.
- Design for recycling, including packaging.

OM in *ACTION*

Xerox Diverts 2 Billion Pounds of Waste from Landfills Through Green Initiatives

By recycling yet one more 5-pound toner cartridge from a Xerox multifunction system, Xerox Corporation announced today it has surpassed a major sustainability milestone by diverting billions of pounds of electronic waste from landfills around the world through waste-free initiatives that create sustainability benefits for the company and its customers.

Launched in 1991, long before sustainability was on most companies' radar screens, Xerox's environmental program achieved waste avoidance in two areas: reuse and recycling in imaging supplies and product take-back, and recycling and parts reuse. In addition, Xerox integrates innovative environmental priorities into manufacturing operations to add to its recycling efforts.

"Xerox's experience with reuse, recycling and remanufacturing has not only kept waste out of landfills, but saved the company billions of dollars as it did so," said Patricia Calkins, Xerox vice president, environment, health and safety. "If that amount of waste were loaded into garbage trucks, it would fill more than 160,000 trucks, stretching more than 1,000 miles, from Seattle to the Mexican border. We believe sustainability is an integral part of developing products, serving customers and posting profits."

Source: Xerox Press Release, November 9, 2007.

OM in *ACTION*

Some Applications of Design for Environment

Through its "Considered Index," Nike has started to measure its products' impact on the environment, including use of solvents as cleaners and primers, wastes in cutting materials, and impact of materials manufacture and end-of-life. It uses some products that contain recycled materials. For example, recycled polyester contains recycled plastic drink bottles, clothing scraps, uniforms, etc. Nike also uses organic cotton in all its apparel. It also has stopped using PVC in its products.

Patagonia is a high-end environmentally conscious outdoor/sports garments, shoes, and luggage company in Los Angeles. Patagonia designs its products and has them made by various manufacturers throughout the world but is intimately involved in the supply chain starting with sourcing of raw materials. Patagonia's products use organic cotton, recycled polyester, and little glue.

Xerox is a leader in design for the environment. Its printer cartridges are designed for refurbish. Customers are given a prepaid package to facilitate the return of empty cartridges. In addition, Xerox has a take-back program for old copiers. The copiers are designed for easy disassembly. If a copier can be remanufactured, faulty components are replaced. Good components are put through a test called "Signature Analysis" to ensure that they perform as well as new components. If a copier cannot be refurbished, it will be used as a source for components/parts. Parts are coded to facilitate recycling. Parts are cleaned using CO_2 blasts instead of solvents. Only a small percentage of a copier will be wasted. Xerox has invented small "cartridge free" solid-ink sticks to replace cartridges. Finally, Xerox factories are energy efficient, and produce minimal waste and emissions by recycling, and burning byproducts and wastes.

Sources: http://www.nikebiz.com/responsibility/considered_design/index.html; http://www.patagonia.com/web/us/footprint/index.jsp; http://www.xerox.com/about-xerox/environment/enca.html.

OM in *ACTION*

Kraft Foods' Recipe for Sustainability

The threat of global warming and the desire to protect the environment has many companies embracing sustainability initiatives. And they are finding that, in many instances, there are cost savings in doing so. Among them is the Kraft Foods company, whose well-known brands include Cool Whip, Philadelphia Cream Cheese, DiGiorno pizza, Oscar Mayer, Oreo cookies, and Kraft cheeses and salad dressings. Kraft is the world's second largest food company with 100,000 employees and annual revenues of $42 billion. The company is a member of the Dow Jones Sustainability Index and the Ethibel Sustainability Index.

The company has set some ambitious goals that it wants to achieve:

- Reduce plant energy usage by 15 percent.
- Reduce plant energy-related carbon dioxide emissions by 15 percent.
- Reduce plant water consumption by 15 percent.
- Reduce plant waste by 15 percent.
- Eliminate 150 million pounds of packaging material from the supply chain.

Some of Kraft's successes have come from redesigned packaging. The goal is ambitious. It will require more efficient packaging and a reduction in the amount of packaging material used. Kraft believes that the greatest opportunity to reduce the environmental impact of a package is early in the design phase. Its packaging designers worldwide critically consider the amount of packaging used, how much postconsumer material can be used, how much energy is used to create the packaging materials, how much CO_2 is generated as the materials are created and formed, and how well the package fits the product physically. According to Kraft's press releases, examples and benefits of recent packaging redesigns include:

- DiGiorno and California Pizza Kitchen pizzas: Using slimmer cartons that allow shipment of two extra pizza boxes per case and 14 percent more pizzas per pallet. This leads to a savings of approximately 1.4 million pounds of packaging per year, and the ability to load more pizzas on each truck

Kraft Natural Cheese new packaging zipper eliminates more than 1 million pounds of packaging per year.

means there are fewer trucks on the road and less fuel consumed.

- Oscar Mayer Deli Creations: Using 30 percent less paperboard than the previous design results in 1.2 million fewer pounds of packaging going to landfills.
- Kraft salad dressing: Using 19 percent less plastic per bottle translates to 3 million fewer pounds annually. Additionally, the new design allows more bottles to be shipped per truckload, leading to an increase in transportation efficiency of 18 percent.

The company is also working to help the environment, reduce water pollution/soil erosion, and support biodiversity. Considering these successes, Kraft's recipe for sustainability is one that other companies should emulate.

We will expand on some of these. **Remanufacturing** refers to refurbishing used products by replacing worn-out or defective components, and reselling the products. This can be done by the original manufacturer, or another company. Among products that have remanufactured components are automobiles, printers, copiers, cameras, computers, and telephones.

Designing products so that they can be taken apart more easily is **design for disassembly**, which includes using fewer parts and less material; using snap-fits and fewer screws, nuts, and bolts; and using no glue. It also means accessible screws and bolts, and requiring only common hand tools to disassemble.

Recycling means recovering materials for future use. This applies not only to manufactured parts but also to materials used during production, such as lubricants and solvents. Reclaimed

remanufacturing
Refurbishing used products by replacing worn-out or defective components.

design for disassembly
Design so that used products can be easily taken apart.

recycling Recovering materials for future use.

metal or plastic parts may be melted down and used to make different products. Recycling requires using materials that can be recycled, e.g., thermoset plastics vs. thermoplastics, not adding fillers in plastics, and identifying the material on the part.

Concurrent Engineering

concurrent engineering
Bringing engineering design, manufacturing engineers, and staff from marketing, manufacturing, and purchasing together early in the design phase.

To achieve a smoother transition from product design to production, and to decrease product development time, many companies are using *simultaneous development*, or concurrent engineering. In its narrowest sense, **concurrent engineering** means bringing design and manufacturing engineers together early in the design phase to simultaneously develop the product and the processes for creating the product. More recently, this concept has been enlarged to participative design/engineering, which includes manufacturing, marketing, and purchasing personnel in a cross-functional team. In addition, the views of suppliers and customers are frequently sought. The purpose is to achieve product designs that reflect customer wants as well as manufacturing capabilities.

Traditionally, designers developed a new product without any input from manufacturing, and then turned over the design to manufacturing, which would then have to develop a process for making the new product. This "throw-over-the-wall" approach created tremendous challenges for manufacturing, generating numerous conflicts and greatly increasing the time needed to successfully produce a new product. It also contributed to an "us vs. them" mentality.

For these and similar reasons, the simultaneous development approach has great appeal. Among the key advantages of this approach are the following:

1. Manufacturing engineers and personnel are able to identify production capabilities and capacities. Very often, there is some latitude in design in terms of selecting suitable materials and processes. Knowledge of production capabilities can help in this selection. In addition, cost and quality considerations can be greatly influenced by design, and conflicts during production can be greatly reduced.

2. There are early opportunities for design or procurement of critical machines or components, some of which might have long lead times. This can result in a major shortening of the product development process, which could be a key competitive advantage.

3. The technical feasibility of a particular design or a portion of a design can be assessed early on. Again, this can avoid serious problems during production.

4. The emphasis can be on *problem* resolution instead of *conflict* resolution.

However, despite the advantages of concurrent engineering, a number of potential difficulties exist in this co-development approach. Two key ones are the following:

1. Long-standing boundaries between design and manufacturing can be difficult to overcome. Simply bringing a group of people together and thinking that they will be able to work together effectively is probably naive.

2. There must be extra communication and flexibility if the process is to work, and these can be difficult to achieve.

Hence, managers should plan to devote special attention if this approach is to work.

Computer-aided Design (CAD)

computer-aided design (CAD) Product design using computer graphics.

Computer-aided design (CAD) uses computer graphics for product design. The designer can modify an existing design or create a new one on a display unit by means of a light pen, a keyboard, a joystick, or a mouse. Once the design is entered into the computer, the designer can manoeuvre it on the screen as if it was a three-dimensional object: it can be rotated to provide the designer with different perspectives, it can be split apart to give the designer a view of the inside, and a portion of it can be enlarged for closer examination. The designer can obtain a printed version of the completed design and file it electronically, making it accessible to people in the firm who need this information (e.g., marketing, operations).

An architect is using an iPad CAD (computer-aided design) application to model a 3D layout design of a new house.

A growing number of products are being designed in this way, including transformers, automobile parts, aircraft parts, integrated circuits, and electric motors.

A major benefit of CAD is the increased productivity of designers. No longer is it necessary to laboriously prepare manual drawings of products or parts and revise them repeatedly to correct errors or incorporate revisions. A rough estimate is that CAD increases the productivity of designers from 3 to 10 times. A second major benefit of CAD is the creation of a database for manufacturing that can supply needed information on product geometry and dimensions, tolerances, material specifications, and so on. It should be noted, however, that CAD needs this database to function and that this entails a considerable amount of effort.

Some CAD systems allow the designer to perform engineering and cost analysis on proposed designs. For instance, the computer can determine the weight and volume of a part and do stress analysis as well. When there are a number of alternative designs, the computer can quickly go through the possibilities and identify the best one, given the designer's criteria. For a tour

---

 OM in *ACTION*

CAD and 3D Printing Push Medical Boundaries

Image printing off a fully functional human kidney or heart with a simple click of a mouse. This may sound like something out of a science fiction novel, but medical researchers have already taken the initial steps to producing transplantable organs using 3D printers. As a matter of fact, researchers have already produced prosthetic limbs and even a human ear. Ultimately, the goal is to create human organs for a particular patient using his own cells. It is hoped this will solve a serious rejection problem where the body produces an immune response to attack the newly transplanted organ. Successful implementation of this technology could extend human life by numerous years—if not decades.

A 3D printer works in the same way a standard inkjet printer does, with a cartridge that deposits successive layers of material in different shapes. Each printed layer is only a fraction of the width of a single human hair and corresponds to a cross-section read from a CAD model.

Source: http://www.cbc.ca/strombo/technology-1/printed-on-the-body-3d-printers-create-bones-organs.html.

of capabilities of the SolidWorks 3D CAD software, see http://www.solidworks.com/sw/products/simulation/finite-element-analysis.htm. CAD that includes finite element analysis (FEA) capability can greatly shorten the time to market of new products. It enables developers to perform simulations that aid in the design, analysis, and commercialization of new products. Designers in industries such as aeronautics, biomechanics, and automotives use FEA.

Design for Manufacturing and Assembly

Designers need to clearly understand the capabilities of the production function (e.g., equipment, skills, types of materials, and technologies). This will help in choosing designs that match capabilities. When opportunities and capabilities do not match, management must consider the potential for expanding or changing capabilities to take advantage of those opportunities.

Manufacturability is a key concern for manufactured goods: ease of fabrication and/or assembly is important for cost, productivity, and quality.

The term **design for manufacturing (DFM)** is used to indicate the designing of products that are compatible with manufacturing capabilities. A related concept is **design for assembly (DFA)**. Design for assembly focuses on reducing the number of parts in an assembly, as well as on the assembly methods and sequence that will be employed.

design for manufacturing (DFM) Takes into account the organization's manufacturing capabilities when designing a product.

design for assembly (DFA) Focuses on reducing the number of parts in a product and on assembly methods and sequence.

Component Commonality

Companies can realize significant benefits when a component can be used in multiple products. For example, car manufacturers use the same chassis (platform) and internal components, such as engines and transmissions, on several models. In addition to the savings in design time, companies reap benefits through standard training for assembly and installation, increased opportunities for savings by buying in bulk from suppliers, and commonality of parts for repair, which reduces the inventory dealers and auto parts stores must carry, as well as the training needed by technicians. Computer software often comprises a number of modules that are commonly used for similar applications, thereby saving the time and cost to write the code for major portions of the software. Tool manufacturers use a design that allows tool users to attach different power tools to a common power source.

ervice

Hewlett-Packard's Design-for-Supply-Chain program includes a simple quantitative decision-making tool for designers to make commonality trade-off decisions.[5] The trade-off is between annual holding cost saved by using commonality versus extra cost of manufacturing to provide commonality. An example of a unique part is a power adapter that works with 110V electricity (for North America), and another that works with 220V electricity (for Europe). If commonality is used, the universal power adapter will work with either 110 or 220V electricity. To make the decision whether a universal power adapter will be cheaper in terms of both manufacturing and after-sale service, an analysis similar to the following is used: Based on number of products sold that need this adapter (e.g., 10,000), number of service locations throughout the world (e.g., 400), and annual failure rate of the adapter (e.g., 1 percent), it follows that average annual demand for this power adapter in a service location will be 10,000(.01)/400 = .25 unit. Given replenishment lead time of 4 days (from the supplier or other locations), average demand during lead time is only .25(4)/365 = .003 unit. Therefore, to provide, for example, a four-hour service response, keeping one unit of this adapter in stock at each service location is more than sufficient. Now, if one universal adapter is kept in stock instead of two unique adapters, there will be a saving of one unit at each service location. If each adapter costs $100 and annual holding cost rate is 20 percent of unit cost, the savings in the annual holding cost will be (400)(1)($100)(.20) = $8,000. If the extra cost of manufacturing a universal adapter (relative to a unique adapter) is $.50 per unit, annual additional cost will be $.50 × 10,000 = $5,000. Because $5,000 < $8,000, using the universal adapter is cheaper than using two unique adapters.

---

[5] J. Amaral and B. Cargille, "How "Rough-cut" Analysis Smoothes HP's Supply Chain," *Supply Chain Management Review* 9(6), September 2005, pp. 38–45.

BlackBerry Limited

BlackBerry Limited of Waterloo, Ontario, is a successful Canadian high-tech company that at one time dominated the North American smartphone market with a market share in excess of 50 percent, even though it has only one product, the BlackBerry wireless handheld device. The continuous improvement of the technology of pagers for more than 15 years paid off in 1999 when BlackBerry Limited decided to convert its two-way pager to work with e-mail programs.

The market accepted BlackBerry as the best device of its kind, resulting in ever-increasing sales. One distinguishing feature of BlackBerry is that as it receives or sends e-mails, it automatically updates the e-mail program on the desktop using data communication lines. This eliminates the duplication of using the e-mail program. Similarly, the BlackBerry automatically updates the personal calendar on the desktop.

The competition in this market segment is fierce, with most products converging to handle e-mail, voice, and video. BlackBerry was also modified in 2002 to work like a phone, and, more recently, to have a colour display and touch screen.

Given the stiff competition, BlackBerry Limited is "protecting" itself by licensing its excellent wireless e-mail software to its competitors. This strategic move (i.e., if you can't beat them, join them) seems to be paying off. BlackBerry Limited handles the subscription of its customers to a wireless telecommunication service.

BlackBerry Limited had revenues of more than $11 billion and more than 7,000 employees in 2014.

Differences in Designing Services

Most of this chapter so far also applies to service design. However, there are some key differences between goods and services that warrant special consideration for service design:

1. Goods are generally tangible; services are intangible. Consequently, service design often includes secondary factors such as peace of mind, ambiance, and convenience. Another consequence of this is that it is hard to sketch a service. A new service must rely on faith and trust of customers; thus, the importance of image.

2. In many instances, services are created and delivered at the same time. For example, if a bus company makes changes to the bus schedule, or the bus routes, or the types of buses used, those changes will not be hidden to the riders. Obviously, this service redesign could not be done realistically without considering the *process* for delivering the service. In such instances, there is less latitude in finding and correcting errors *before* the customer has a chance to discover them. Consequently, training, process design, and customer relations are particularly important; hence, the increased role of operations. Quality is measured by measuring customer satisfaction.

3. Most services involve some degree of customization (variety). Because of this, there will be variability in length of service. When there is little or no contact, service can be much more standardized, whereas high contact provides the opportunity to tailor the service to the precise needs of individual customers. For example, see Figure 4-3, which shows different types of clothes retailing.

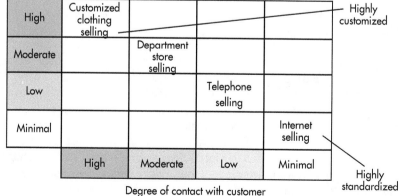

Figure 4-3

The relationship between service variability and customer contact in retail clothes selling.

4. Services have lower barriers to entry and exit. Even in capital-intensive services such as air travel, introducing a new service, e.g., a new type of ticket with new restrictions on its use, is relatively easy because it uses the current resources of the airline. The disadvantage of this is that the company cannot easily measure the cost of introducing the service because of the shared resources. Too many similar services will no doubt increase the complexity and cost of operations. This places pressure on service design to be innovative but selective. Because of its relative ease of introduction, many new services are copies of competitors' services.

5. Location is often important to service design, with convenience as a major factor. Hence, design of services and choice of location are often closely linked.

To illustrate service design process further, let's look at service design process in the financial sector.

The Service Design Process in the Financial Sector

The financial services sector is one of the largest service sectors in Canada and introduces most new services. In a survey of 82 North American financial institutions (banks, insurance, trust, leasing, reinsurance, and mutual fund companies), it was discovered that some financial institutions do not perform some of the activities given in the product design process. In particular, few do "detailed market study/market research" and "precommercialization business analysis." The reason for this is that most new services offered by a company are copies of successful services offered by a competitor or the company itself.

In comparing high and low performers, it was found that the difference is "better idea screening," "preliminary market assessment," "market research," "service development," and "postlaunch review."

Service Design Guidelines

A number of simple but highly effective rules are often used to guide the design of services:

1. Have a single, unifying theme, such as convenience or speed. This will help personnel work together rather than at cross-purposes.

2. Ensure that the service delivery system has the capability to handle any expected variability in service requirements.

3. Include design features and checks to ensure that service will be reliable and will provide consistently high quality.

4. Design the service delivery system to be user-friendly. This is especially true for self-service systems.

Quality Function Deployment

quality function deployment (QFD) A structured approach that integrates the "voice of the customer" into product design.

Quality function deployment (QFD) is a structured approach for integrating the "voice of the customer" into product design. The purpose is to ensure that customer requirements are factored into every aspect of the process. Listening to and understanding the customer is the central feature of QFD. Customer requirements often take the form of a general statement such as "It should be easy to adjust the cutting height of the lawn mower." Once the customer requirements are known, they must be translated into measurable technical terms. For example, a statement about changing the height of the lawn mower may be translated into the characteristics of mechanism used to accomplish that, e.g., tightness of the spring that controls the mechanism. For manufacturing purposes, these must be related to the materials, dimensions, and equipment used for processing.

The structure of QFD is based on a set of matrices. The main matrix relates customer requirements (what) to their corresponding technical requirements (how). This matrix is illustrated in Figure 4-4. The matrix provides a structure for data collection. Technical requirements are measurable physical and functional characteristics of the product. Additional features are usually added to the basic matrix to broaden the scope of analysis. Typical additional features include competitive

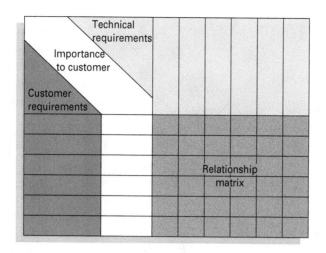

Figure 4-4

An example of the house of quality: the main QFD matrix.

Source: Ernst and Young Consulting Group, *Total Quality* (Homewood, IL: Dow-Jones Irwin, 1991), p. 121. Reprinted by permission.

evaluation of customer requirements, a correlation matrix for technical requirements (this can reveal conflicting technical requirements), and target values (product specs) for technical requirements. The matrix is often referred to as the *house of quality* because of its house-like appearance. This concept is illustrated in Figure 4-5.

Figure 4-5

The house of quality.

An example of a house of quality is shown in Figure 4-6. The data relate to a commercial printer (customer) and the company that produces the paper rolls. At first glance, the display appears complex. It contains a considerable amount of information for product and process planning. Therefore, let's break it up into separate parts and consider them one at a time. To start, a key part is the list of customer requirements on the left side of the figure. Next, note the technical requirements, listed vertically near the top. The key relationships and their degree of importance are shown in the centre of the figure. The circle with a dot inside it indicates the strongest relationship; that is, it denotes the most important technical requirement(s) for satisfying the customer requirement (see the lower right-hand side for relationship weights). Now look at the "customer requirements importance" weights that are shown next to each customer requirement (3 is most important). Designers will take into account the importance values and the strength of correlation in determining where to focus the greatest effort.

Next, consider the correlation matrix at the top of the "house." Of special interest is the strong negative correlation between "paper thickness" and "roll roundness." Designers will have to find some way to overcome that or make a trade-off decision.

Figure 4-6

An example of the house of quality for paper rolls used by a commercial printer.

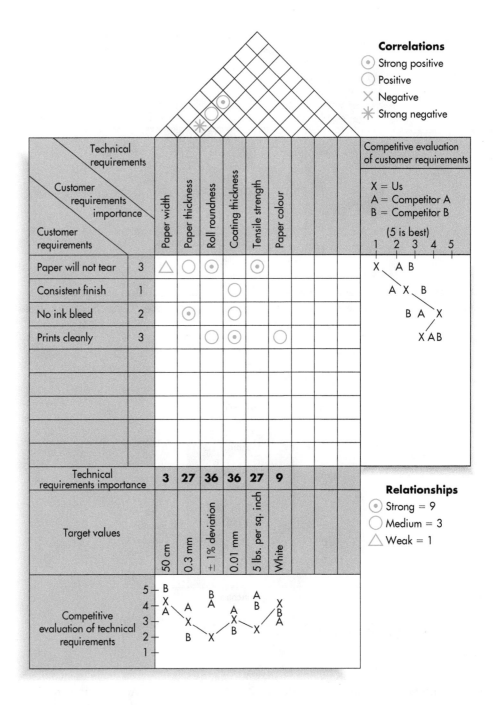

On the right side of the figure is the competitive evaluation of customer requirements, comparing the paper roll manufacturing company's performance on the customer requirements with each of its two key competitors (A and B). For example, the company (X) is worst on the first customer requirement and best on the third customer requirement. A line connects the X performances. Ideally, design will cause all of the Xs to be in the highest positions.

Across the bottom of Figure 4-6 are technical requirements importance weights, target values, and competitive evaluations of technical requirements, which can be interpreted in a manner similar to that of the competitive evaluation of customer requirements (note the line connecting the Xs). The target values typically contain technical specifications that are the result of the design process.

A technical value (or specification) may have a norm (midpoint) and a tolerance (±). A tolerance is established to (a) make the fabrication and/or assembly of the product easier and (b) enable the product to perform its function with minimum adjustment. Usually, these two objectives are in conflict. Too-tight a tolerance can ensure functional requirements, but is not cost-effective. Too-loose a tolerance can reduce fabrication and assembly costs, but requires frequent rework to maintain the product's performance. Technical requirements importance weights are the sums of values assigned to the relationships multiplied by customer requirements importance. For example, the 3 in the first column is the product of the importance to the customer, 3, and the weak (Δ) relationship, 1. These help designers focus on important technical requirements. In this example, the first technical requirement has the lowest importance while the next four technical requirements all have high importance.

The house of quality approach involves a sequence of "houses," beginning with house of quality (Figures 4-5 and 4-6), which determines the product design characteristics and target values (House 1), which in turn leads to specific component design characteristics and target values (House 2), which in turn leads to production process design characteristics and target values for each component (House 3), and finally, a quality plan for each production process (House 4). This sequence is illustrated in Figure 4-7. The construction of House 2 to House 4 is basically similar to construction of House 1, but the details are beyond the scope of this textbook.

"A QFD Snapshot" OM in Action contains another example of house of quality.

▼ **Figure 4-7**

The house of quality sequence.

OM in *ACTION*

 A QFD Snapshot 🌐 ⑤ervice

How a pencilmaker sharpened up its product by listening to "the voice of the customer" through quality function deployment.

Devised by Japan's Professor Yoji Akao, QFD has been winning adherents since it was transplanted to North America in the late 1980s. In this example of how it works, Writesharp Inc. is imaginary, but the technique in the accompanying diagram is real.

First, Writesharp's customers were surveyed to determine what they value in a pencil and how they rate the leading brands. Each wish list item was correlated with a pencil's physical and functional characteristics. Reverse engineering–tearing down a competitors' product to see what makes it tick–produced the competitive evaluation of technical requirements.

An analysis of the matrix quickly revealed that the improvement with the biggest potential was "point lasts" (see competitive evaluation of customer requirements). This is largely correlated with "Time between sharpenings" and "Lead dust." It was determined that these characteristics could be improved by using a better-quality lead. An interdepartmental team was assigned the task of evaluating new lead formulations that would last longer and generate less dust. The lead-formulation team organized its work with a similar matrix, segmented to show the physical and functional contributions of the ingredients in pencil lead. This revealed that the binder, or glue, used in forming the lead was the key variable. Tests found a polymer that dramatically reduced dusting by retaining more moisture and also wore down more slowly. While this binder was more expensive, better production controls promised to reduce waste enough to trim total per-pencil manufacturing costs by 1¢.

Source: Reprinted from October 25, 1991, issue of *BusinessWeek* by special permission, copyright © 1991 by The McGraw-Hill Companies, Inc.

Summary

- The design process involves market/competitor analysis, goal setting (product, performance, cost, quality), quality function deployment, concept design, product specification, and building and testing prototypes.
- The idea for a new or a redesigned product can come from customers, employees, suppliers, competitors, and the research and development department.
- The stage of life cycle of a product influences the nature of its redesign.
- Using standard parts and common modules saves operating costs, but it is possible to provide some mass customization by allowing customers options on modules and postponement.
- The reliability of well-designed products has to be extensively tested and improved.

- It may be cheaper to design robust products that perform consistently in varied production and use conditions.
- It is faster and less costly for the product team to perform both product and process designs concurrently.
- CAD has helped reduce the design time significantly. It is cheaper overall to design products that have fewer parts and are easier to manufacture and assemble.
- Services need to deal with customer presence and involvement, and the inherent variability in service requirements.
- QFD is a multifunctional process for product design that starts with the "voice of the customer" and ends with its translation into product characteristics.

Key Terms

computer-aided design (CAD)
concurrent engineering
delayed differentiation
design for assembly (DFA)
design for disassembly
design for manufacturing (DFM)
failure

life cycle
mass customization
modular design
product design
product liability
quality function deployment (QFD)
recycling

reliability
remanufacturing
research and development (R&D)
reverse engineering
robust design
standardization

Discussion and Review Questions

Note: An asterisk indicates that a question or problem may be more challenging.

1. What are some of the factors that cause organizations to redesign their products? **LO1**

2. What are the stages (phases) of the product design process? **LO1**

3. What is CAD? Describe some of the ways a product designer can use it. **LO3**

4. What is standardization? Give an example. Name some of the main advantages and disadvantages of standardization. **LO3**

5. What is modular design? Give an example. What are its main advantages and disadvantages? **LO3**

6. Explain the terms *design for manufacturing* and *design for assembly*, give an example of each, and briefly explain why they are important. **LO3**

7. What is concurrent engineering and what are some of the competitive advantages of concurrent engineering? **LO3**

8. What is the *stage-gate or phase-review* model? What are the stages? **LO1**

9. What is meant by the term *life cycle*? Give an example. Why would this be a consideration in product design? **LO3**

10. Name some ways the R&D department of a company contributes to produce design. **LO2**

11. What is *mass customization*? What is *delayed differentiation*? Give an example. **LO3**

12. Name two factors that make service design different from goods design. **LO4**

13. Explain the term *robust design*. Give an example. **LO3**

14. Explain what *quality function deployment* is, briefly how it is done, and what its objective is. **LO5**

15. What is reverse engineering? Give an example. Do you feel it is unethical? **LO2**

16. Name a service organization and describe the basic service(s) it provides. **LO4**

17. Contrast applied research and basic research. **LO2**

Taking Stock

1. Describe some of the trade-offs that are encountered in product design. **LO5**

2. Who needs to be involved in the design of products? Explain. **LO1**

3. How has technology had an impact on product design? **LO2 & 3**

4. Is designing products that are not refurbishable or recyclable, such as computers and electronics that end up in city garbage dumps, unethical? Discuss. **LO3**

Critical Thinking Exercise

Think of a new or revised good or service that you would like to see on the market. Discuss the implications of designing and producing that product relative to legal, profitability, competitiveness, design, and production issues. **LO3**

Experiential Learning Exercise

Visit http://www.baddesigns.com/examples.html and read about some bad designs. Describe one example from your own experience. **LO1 & 5**

Internet Exercises

1. Go to http://bits.me.berkeley.edu/develop and write a brief summary of important design elements in the design of the Boeing 777. **LO3**

2. Watch the video at http://solutions.3m.com/wps/portal/3M/en_WW/History/3M/Company/century-innovation. List two innovative products that 3M has invented. **LO1**

Problems

1. Prepare a table similar to Figure 4-3 and place each of these banking transactions in the appropriate cell of the table: **LO4**

   a. Make a cash withdrawal from an automated banking machine (ABM).
   b. Make a savings deposit using a teller.
   c. Open an account.
   d. Apply for a mortgage loan.

2. Prepare a table similar to Figure 4-3. Then place each of these transactions in the appropriate cell of the table: **LO4**

   a. Buy stamps from a postal clerk.
   b. Mail a package that involves checking different rates.
   c. Send money using Western Union.

3. a. Refer to Figure 4-6. What two technical requirements have the highest impact on the customer requirement "Paper will not tear"? Explain why. **LO5**

   b. The following table presents technical requirements and customer requirements for the output of a laser printer. First, decide if any of the technical requirements relate to each customer requirement. Decide which technical requirement, if any, has the greatest impact on that customer requirement. **LO5**

Customer Requirements	TECHNICAL REQUIREMENTS		
	Type of Paper	Internal Paper Feed	Print Element
Paper doesn't wrinkle			
Prints clearly			
Easy to use			

4. Prepare a house of quality for chocolate chip cookies made in a bakery. List what you believe are the three most important customer requirements and the three most relevant technical requirements. Next, indicate by a check-mark which customer requirements and which technical requirements are related. Finally, determine the target values. No need to fill in the other parts of the house. **L05**

5. Determine a house of quality for a ballpoint pen. In the house of quality, fill in three customer requirements. Determine one technical requirement for each customer requirement and fill it in. Relate the pair by a checkmark, and determine a reasonable target value for each technical requirement and fill it in. **L05**

*6. In 2002 Wilson Sporting Goods wanted to enter the market for youth baseball batting helmets with a durable, strong, stylish youth batting helmet with improved ventilation and a quick and simple adjustment feature for a one-size-fits-all youth batting helmet. Wilson commissioned the product design firm Designconcepts to design and develop the helmet. Designconcepts's sketch for the adjustment mechanism of helmet is shown below.[6] The finished helmet is now marketed as Cat Osterman's Signature Series.

For each of the five customer requirements given above, find a measurable technical requirement and enter both in a house of quality. Relate them by placing a checkmark at their intersection. Also fill in the target value (specification) for each technical requirement. **L05**

*7. In 2004 Calor (T-Fal), a member of Groupe SEB of France, the world's largest kitchen products and small appliances manufacturer, commissioned the product design firm of SeymourPowel to redesign its midline steam iron (http://www.seymourpowell.com/casestudies/view/25). The market for irons was in a slump and Calor wanted to reinvigorate the market. Like its predecessor, Avantis, Aquaspeed was desired to be attractive, easy to handle and ergonomic, and light, but had two additional requirements: (a) a larger hole and less-messy process for filling water in the reservoir, and (b) more stability to reduce chance of toppling off the ironing board. Avantis, like other irons, had a small water hole in the front part of the handle. The result of the redesign, Aquaspeed, is shown below (front and back views)[7]: In a house of quality, fill in five customer requirements. Determine one technical requirement for each customer requirement and fill it in. Relate the pair by a checkmark, and determine a reasonable target value for each technical requirement and fill it in. **L05**

*8. In the mid-2000s, DeWalt, a Black and Decker brand, saw the need by carpenters and do-it-yourselfers for a cordless battery-operated nailer.[8] At that time, the only automatic nailers in the market were pneumatic ones that were cumbersome because of the need for a compressor and a hose. DeWalt consulted and observed carpenters at work and determined the following customer requirements: speed, run time (length of time until the battery needs recharging), power (nail penetration), ease of loading nails, ergonomics (size, weight, and balance), being able to see the nail going in, and being able to work in tight spots. One of the eight related nailers in the designed family is shown on the next page. In a house of quality, fill in five customer requirements. Determine one technical requirement for each customer requirement and fill it in. Relate the pair by a checkmark, and determine a reasonable target value for each technical requirement and fill it in. **L05**

---

[6] D. Franchino, "Delivering Success Through Design: Reinventing the Batting Helmet," *Design Management Review* 18(1), Winter 2007, pp. 22–27.

[7] D. Powell, "Innovation in Practice: The Calor Aquaspeed Iron," *Design Management Review* 16(1), Winter 2005, pp. 26–32.

[8] J. Watson, "Building the Perfect Product: The Story of DeWalt Cordless Nailer," *Design Management Review* 17(1), Winter 2006, pp. 21–27.

*9. Puritan-Bennett is a manufacturer of medical test equipment.[9] In the early 1990s, its PB900A spirometer (equipment to measure lung capacity) was rapidly losing market share to a competitor's product, which was simpler and half its price. Puritan-Bennett decided to use Quality Function Deployment to redesign PB900A. It surveyed its customers (pulmonologists, allergists, and nurses) to identify customer needs. A total of 26 customer needs were identified. Puritan-Bennett's product design team translated these into 56 design attributes (technical requirements). Here, we will consider a small subset of the customer needs. The following customer needs were most important (importance is in brackets): product is affordable (150), provides accurate readings (100), eliminates technician (administrator) variability (140), is easy to operate (130), and is sanitary (108). Prepare a house of quality with five customer requirements. Determine one technical requirement for each customer requirement and fill it in. Relate the pair by a checkmark. Determine a reasonable target value for each technical characteristic and fill it in. **LO5**

*10. Ford and other automakers regularly use a house of quality to translate the voice of customers (customer requirements) into design characteristics (technical requirements) in areas such as rust prevention (body durability) and car door design.[10] Some of the most important customer requirements for a car door are the following: easy to close, stays open on a hill, easy to open, does not leak in rain, and doesn't allow road noise in. In a house of quality, fill in these five customer requirements. Determine one technical requirement for each customer requirement and fill it in. Relate the pair by a checkmark, and determine a reasonable target value for each technical requirement and fill it in. **LO5**

  MINI-CASE   http://www.harveys.ca

Open Wide and Say "Ultra"

In fourth place behind McDonald's, A&W, and Burger King, Harvey's, the Canadian quick-service hamburger chain with more than 340 restaurants, needed a new idea in the mid-1990s. Harvey's is part of Cara Operations Ltd., the airline food-services company that also owns the Swiss Chalet chain of restaurants, approximately 100 Air Terminal Restaurants, and Summit Food Services Distributors. Harvey's had had new ideas before (open grill and fresh vegetables, for one), but these had become old hat by 1995. Gabe Tsampalieros, Cara's new president, who was a major franchisee with 60 Harvey's and Swiss Chalet restaurants, started working on the idea in October 1995, and by the following month the mission was clear: "Create Canada's best-selling hamburger." Tsampalieros and Harvey's vice-president planned the launch of the new burger for May 1996.

Harvey's began polling burger lovers across Canada in January 1996, first by telephone and later in focus groups of 8 to 12 people. While the tradition of burgers had so far led to flattened-out, Frisbee-like burgers that hung over the edges of the buns (giving customers the impression that they were getting more for their money), feedback from the market produced another idea: go thicker, juicier, chewier, and tastier. To bring this simple idea to life, Harvey's brought in chef Michael Bonacini, whose upscale Toronto restaurants had been a big hit.

Bonacini's challenge was not only to produce a tasty burger, but also to produce a burger that could handily survive the fast-food process (mechanically produced, frozen for weeks, and shipped around the country). Bonacini produced 12 "taste profiles"—from the bland to the bizarre—and introduced them to the Harvey's executives at a suburban Harvey's training centre. This would be the first in a long series of tasting exercises. (Bonacini thinks he ate 275 bite-sized burgers in a four-month period.)

Each of Harvey's executives tasted a portion of the 12 unlabelled patties and ranked it for "mouth feel," taste, linger, fill factor, and bite. Exotic offerings (Cajun, Oriental, falafel, and so forth) were rejected, leaving three simply seasoned burgers on the short list.

McCormick Canada Inc., Harvey's spice supplier, was employed to determine the final proportions of seasonings and secret ingredients to replicate the taste of Bonacini's samples in a way that could survive the fast-food process. "They [the meat packagers] would give us a 500-pound batch—that's 2,000 burgers—and we would taste them a couple of days after they had been mixed. Then we would also taste them at one-, two-, three-, and four-week intervals to see how the flavours

(continued)

---

9 J.R. Hauser, "How Puritan-Bennett Used the House of Quality," *Sloan Management Review* 34(3) Spring 1993, pp. 61–70.
10 J.R. Hauser and D. Clausing, "The House of Quality," *Harvard Business Review*, May–June 1988, pp. 63–73.

would change," said Bonacini. McCormick's food technologists varied the seasonings by slight amounts with different results, and each change was followed by testing. For two months, all of Harvey's head-office workers gathered before breakfast to test the newest batches; it became clear that the May launch date was unrealistic, so they bumped back the launch to mid-September.

Though missing deadlines is rarely advisable, in this case it was fortuitous. On May 9, exactly one week before the original launch date, McDonald's introduced the Arch Deluxe with the most aggressive marketing campaign yet seen from McDonald's.

As the burger making neared completion, Harvey's turned its attention to choosing a name for the new burger. The company considered several (the Ultimate, the Canadian, the Big Burger, the One and Only), but settled wisely on the Ultra, a bilingual name. The company chose a foil packaging for better heat retention (and because the traditional box would appear larger than the burger itself), and reinitiated the advertising campaign, promoting a $1.88 price. Testing the burger in Calgary, Sudbury, and Quebec, Harvey's found customer reaction to be very positive ("It's more like a home-made burger," "It has a steak-like bite"), but went through five more adjustments to the amounts and mixing time of the ingredients.

On September 16, 1996, Ultra was launched and resulted in record sales, transaction counts, and restaurant visits. With over a million sold in the first two weeks, the Ultra resulted in more than 85 percent of Harvey's sales.

Since then, Harvey's has introduced other types of hamburgers such as bacon and cheese, veggie burger, and Big Harv Angus, as well as a chicken sandwich.

Big Harv, introduced in 2003, was an attempt to buck the trend of low-fat, low-calorie burgers offered by the other fast-food restaurants. It had double the calories and fat of the Original burger. Big Harv targeted male customers craving thick home-made barbequed burgers.

Cara has expanded its full-service restaurant offerings by purchasing the Kelsey's chain and the Second Cup chain. In 2004, Cara bought back its outstanding shares and became a private company. In 2006, Cara sold Second Cup to Gabe Tsampalieros's new company, Dinecorp Hospitality.

Questions

1. Identify the steps of the product design process used by Harvey's. (Specifically, consider market analysis, concept development, prototype development, and (external) testing and validation).

2. Did Harvey's use any other concepts discussed in the chapter?

3. Prepare a house of quality for Ultra's design. Fill in four customer requirements. For each customer requirement, determine a technical requirement and relate the pair using a checkmark. For each technical requirement, determine a reasonable target value.

Sources: Adapted from P. Roy, "Open Wide and Say 'Ultra' (Harvey's Had a Brilliant Idea About Burgers)," *Canadian Business* 69(12), December 1996, pp. 26–30; "Stay Hungry: Gabe Tsampalieros Knows the Food Business from the Kitchen Floor Up (Will That Be Enough for Cara?)," *Canadian Business* 69(11), September 1996, pp. 104–110; Cara Operations Annual Reports, 1999–2003, http://www.cara.com.

To access "Reliability," the supplement to Chapter 4, please visit Connect.

CHAPTER 5
Strategic Capacity Planning

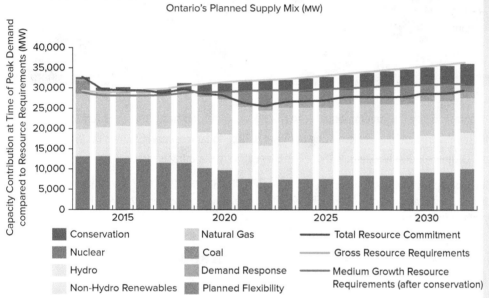

Ontario's Planned Supply Mix (MW)

Legend:
- Conservation
- Nuclear
- Hydro
- Non-Hydro Renewables
- Natural Gas
- Coal
- Demand Response
- Planned Flexibility
- Total Resource Commitment
- Gross Resource Requirements
- Medium Growth Resource Requirements (after conservation)

Y-axis: Capacity Contribution at Time of Peak Demand compared to Resource Requirements (MW)

Source: Achieving Balance: Ontario's Long-Term Energy Plan. Figure 18, p. 42. (c) Queen's Printer for Ontario, 2013. Published by the Ministry of Energy, Toronto, Ontario.

Learning Objectives

After completing this chapter, you should be able to:

LO1 Define capacity, explain the importance of long-term capacity, know how to measure capacity and understand two related performance measures, and describe factors influencing effective capacity.

LO2 Describe the strategic capacity planning process in organizations, know long-term demand patterns and calculate capacity requirements, and discuss major considerations for developing capacity alternatives.

LO3 Describe the break-even analysis approach for evaluating capacity alternatives, and use it to solve problems.

Strategic capacity planning involves long-term demand forecasting and supply planning. One of the most critical services is electricity. Planning electricity is particularly challenging because it is not enough that total electricity generated equals total electricity demand in a year or even a month. Supply should equal demand during every second. This means that the installed capacity should meet peak demand. But, peak demand is hard to predict (both in terms of size and timing) and peak capacity is rarely used throughout the year. Ontario Power Authority (OPA) is the agency responsible for long-term electricity capacity planning in Ontario. Since its creation in 2004, OPA has restructured Ontario's electricity supply away from coal dependency and toward less polluting sources (such as natural gas) and renewables (such as wind and solar). The journey has not been smooth. First, the demand stopped growing because the 2008 recession reduced manufacturing activities, thus reducing the need for early investments. Then, the decisions for locating two gas-powered plants in Mississauga and Oakville were taken without consulting the local communities, which resulted in public outcry ("not in my backyard"), followed by reversal of the decision by the government (due to re-election scare) and hasty and weak renegotiation with the contracted builders (resulting in over a billion-dollar loss), and finally hiding some of the facts. Despite all this, few dispute that electricity capacity planning is vital.

Sources: http://www.powerauthority.on.ca/sites/default/files/planning/LTEP_2013_English_WEB. pdf; http://www.auditor.on.ca/en/reports_en/mississaugapower_en.pdf; http://www.auditor.on.ca/en/reports_en/oakville_en.pdf.

 Capacity, Measures, Efficiency, Utilization, and Effective Capacity

capacity The upper limit on the workload that an operating unit can handle. Capacity is usually measured as maximum production rate or throughput. Alternatively, a major input is used, e.g., size.

Capacity is the upper limit on the workload that an operating unit can handle. An operating unit might be a plant, department, machine, store, or worker.

Capacity is usually measured as maximum production rate or throughput; e.g., the maximum number of motorcycles who can be assembled in a particular plant per shift, or the maximum number of customers that can be served in a particular restaurant per day. If output is hard to measure, a major input can be used, e.g., size (ft²) or number of seats in a particular restaurant.

Capacity decisions have different time frames: long term, medium term, or short term. Long term usually refers to one to five years into the future. We need to make long-term capacity decisions such as determining the plant size and major machines and equipment. Medium-term usually refers to next 12 months, and medium-term capacity decisions include determining the nature and level of the workforce, which in turn determines the aggregate operations plan. Short term relates to the next few days and weeks, usually up to 12 weeks ahead, and short-term capacity decisions include determining the nature and level of staffing and work shifts, which in turn determines the production schedule of products or capacity of service.

If production or service delivery is to be outsourced, then there is usually no need to create the capacity in-house. Outsourcing has been increasingly used by many organizations to reduce costs, gain flexibility (for variable demand), and take advantage of suppliers' expertise (quality). For example, Canadian toy company Spin Master usually outsources the production of its toys to China. The downside is reduced control. It is also possible to outsource part(s) of a good/service or a segment of production/service process. For example, many restaurants buy prepared/partially cooked frozen/vacuum-packed food ingredients. **Strategic capacity planning** is the systematic determination of facility and major machine/equipment requirements to meet long-term demand for goods and services.

strategic capacity planning Systematic determination of facility and major machine/equipment requirements to meet long-term demand for goods and services.

In this chapter, we study mainly long-term capacity planning, while deferring medium-term capacity decisions to Chapter 13 and short-term capacity decisions to Chapter 16 and Chapter 18. Note that a capacity decision usually has a location dimension. For example, suppose a long term–care facility needs to increase its number of beds. It can expand its current facility, open up another facility somewhere else to supplement the current facility, or close the current facility and open up a larger facility somewhere else. Note that services should be located close to their customers because location convenience is part of the service. Location decisions are covered in Chapter 8.

The Importance of Long-Term Capacity

For a number of reasons, long-term capacity decisions are among the most fundamental of all design decisions that managers must make. These include:

1. Capacity has a real impact on the ability of the organization to meet future demand for products; capacity essentially limits the rate of output (throughput) possible. Having capacity to satisfy demand allows a company to exploit opportunities. When Microsoft introduced its new Xbox in late 2005, there were insufficient supplies, resulting in lost sales and unhappy customers. And shortages of flu vaccine in some years due to production problems have affected capacity, limiting the availability of the vaccine.

2. Capacity affects operating costs. Ideally, capacity and demand requirements should be matched. A production level exceeding capacity is costlier, requiring overtime, expediting deliveries, lost sales, etc.

3. Capacity is usually a major determinant of initial capital cost. Typically, the greater the capacity of a productive unit, the greater its capital cost.

4. Capacity involves long-term commitment of resources and, once they are committed, it may be difficult to modify them without incurring major costs.

5. Capacity can affect competitiveness. If a company has excess capacity, or can quickly add capacity, that fact may serve as a barrier to entry of other companies. Then, capacity can affect delivery speed, which can be a competitive advantage.

6. Capacity affects ease of management; having appropriate capacity makes management easier than when capacity is mismatched.

7. Globalization has increased the importance and the complexity of capacity decisions. Far-flung supply chains and distant markets add to the uncertainty about capacity needs.

8. Because capacity decisions often involve substantial financial and other resources, it is necessary to plan for them far in advance. For example, it may take years for a new crude oil refinery to be constructed and become operational. This increases the risk that the designated amount of capacity will not match actual demand when the capacity becomes available.

Measuring Capacity and Two Related Performance Measures

In selecting a measure of capacity, it is better to choose one that does not require updating. Dollar amounts are often a poor measure of capacity (e.g., a restaurant may have capacity of $1 million of sales a year) because price changes over time necessitate updating of that measure.

Where only one product is involved, the capacity of the productive unit is expressed in terms of that item. However, when multiple products are involved, as is often the case, using a simple measure of capacity based on units of output can be misleading. For example, an appliance manufacturer may produce a combination of refrigerators and freezers. Becasue their resource usage and cost are different, it would not make sense to simply state the capacity in units of appliance. One possible solution is to state capacities in terms of each product. Thus, the company may be able to produce 100 refrigerators per day *or* 160 freezers per day. Sometimes this approach is helpful, sometimes not. For instance, if an organization has many different products, it may not be practical to list all of the relevant capacities. A better way is to choose a major product, and represent each other product in equivalent units of the major product (more in Chapter 13). Alternatively, one can use the *availability of a major input* as capacity. Thus, a hospital has a certain number of beds, a job shop has a number of labour hours available per week, and a bus has a certain number of seats.

Table 5-1 ▶		

Some examples of commonly used measures of capacity.

Business	Inputs	Outputs
Auto manufacturing		Number of cars per shift
Steel mill		Tonnes of steel per day
Oil refinery	Barrels of crude oil used per day	Barrels of gasoline produced per day
Farming	Number of acres	Bushels of grain per acre per year, litres of milk per day
Restaurant	Number of tables, number of seats	Number of meals served per day
Theatre	Number of seats	Number of tickets sold per day
Retailer	Floor space, sales per square foot	Revenue generated per day

A simple method for estimating the throughput capacity of a productive unit from its size is to divide the size by the average time a product spends in the productive unit (this is called Little's formula):

 Throughput capacity = size/avg cycle time

For example, if a reactor in a steel mill has size of 28 tonnes and iron ore needs to spend 15 minutes in the reactor, then throughput capacity of the reactor = 28/0.25 hour = 112 tonnes per hour.

No single measure of capacity will be appropriate in every situation. Rather, the measure of capacity must be tailored to the situation. Table 5-1 provides some examples of commonly used measures of capacity.

There are two definitions of capacity:

1. **Design capacity**: the maximum output rate under ideal conditions.
2. **Effective capacity**: the maximum output rate that can be sustained given work breaks, scheduling difficulties and expected delays, machine/equipment maintenance, etc. (also known as standard output rate).

Effective capacity is less than design capacity owing to realities of changing product mix, periodic maintenance of machines/equipment, lunch and coffee breaks, problems in scheduling and balancing operations, and similar circumstances. Actual output rate cannot exceed effective capacity and is often less because of machine/equipment breakdowns, absenteeism, shortages of materials, and quality problems, as well as other factors that are outside the control of the operations manager.

Two measures of operating unit performance are commonly used: efficiency and utilization. **Efficiency** is the ratio of actual output rate to effective capacity. **Utilization** is the ratio of uptime to available time.

design capacity
The maximum output rate under ideal conditions.

effective capacity
The maximum output rate that can be sustained given work breaks, product mix, scheduling difficulties and expected delays, machine/equipment maintenance, etc. (also known as standard output rate).

efficiency The ratio of actual output rate to effective capacity.

utilization The ratio of uptime to available time.

$$\text{Efficiency} = \frac{\text{Actual output rate}}{\text{Effective capacity}} \qquad (5\text{-}1)$$

$$\text{Utilization} = \frac{\text{Uptime}}{\text{Available time}} \qquad (5\text{-}2)$$

Example 1 ▶

Minco produces silica and magnesia (http://www.mincoitc.com). To process silica, eight furnaces are used. Each furnace has 2,200 pounds/hour capacity. Minco works 24 hours a day, 5 days a week. During a typical week, total preventive maintenance is 65 hours and total other downtime is 39 hours. Effective capacity is 1,700,000 pounds and actual production is 1,600,000 pounds per week. Calculate the design capacity, utilization, and efficiency of silica furnaces.

SOLUTION

Available hours per week = 8(24)(5) = 960

Design capacity per week = 2,200(960) = 2,112,000 pounds

Productive hours per week = 960 − 65 − 39 = 856

Utilization = uptime hours/available hours = 856/960 = 0.89 or 89%

Efficiency = actual output rate/effective capacity = 1,600,000/1,700,000 = 0.94 or 94%

Note: Effective capacity = 1,700,000 < utilization × design capacity = .89(2,112,000) = 1,879,680

Both efficiency and utilization are normally less than 100 percent. As utilization approaches 100 percent, cycle time (or wait time in the system) increases disproportionately (this will be shown in Chapter 18 on Waiting-Line Analysis). This drastically increases the number of jobs/people waiting, and if there is limited space for waiting, will actually reduce the throughput rate (capacity). For an example of a case where utilization has sometimes reached 100 percent, see the "Utilization in Canadian Hospitals" OM in Action. For capacity measure and utilization used by airlines, see the "Airline Capacity" OM in Action. For an application of utilization, see "Cisco's IT Network Capacity Planning" OM in Action later in the chapter.

Increasing both efficiency and utilization are important for an organization. Increasing efficiency, e.g., by improving quality, material availability, and maintenance, reduces costs and thus increases profits. Increasing utilization, e.g., by increasing machine uptime, usually increases

OM in *ACTION*

Utilization in Canadian Hospitals

Until the early 1990s, the Canadian health care system was the envy of the world. Then came a recession and federal government deficits, which were passed to provinces in the form of drastic cuts in social services transfer payments. In turn, provinces cut hospital budgets. The number of hospital beds in Canada dropped by over 32 percent from 176,000 in 1989 to fewer than 120,000 in 2002. The bed reductions were followed by hospital closures and amalgamations. For example, Calgary General Hospital was demolished in 1998. As a result, there is little slack in the system now, especially during the peak flu season. For example, in Alberta utilization rate rose from 70 percent to 95 percent by 2008.

Most hospitals in Canada are examples of operations where utilization has reached 100 percent some days. The Royal Columbian Hospital in Vancouver is an example. In peak season, the emergency room fills because there are no beds in the hospital to move patients to. The average stay in the emergency room increases up to three days from the customary two hours. Another example is Campbell River Hospital on Vancouver Island where during some days in October 2008, 83 patients crowded the 59-bed hospital, forcing cancellation of two cancer surgeries. The same story holds for most other hospitals such as the Foothills Hospital in Calgary, Pasqua and Regina General Hospitals, York Central and Sunnybrook Health Sciences Centre of Toronto, Ottawa Hospital, and the Queen Elizabeth II Health Sciences Centre of Halifax.

As a result, nurses, physicians, and other health care providers are stressed, and some people requiring emergency care are dying. Examples include a heart attack victim in Weyburn, Saskatchewan; an asthmatic teenager in Toronto; and

a construction worker who fell six stories in Mississauga. In all these cases, the ambulance was turned away by the hospitals because the emergency rooms were completely full. Furthermore, patients are waiting excessively long for most nonemergency surgeries, which can result in death. For example, three women have died waiting for urinary tract surgery in Alberta.

Sources: http://www.cbc.ca/health/story/2007/01/26/hospitals-emerg.html; Hospital Trends in Canada, Canadian Institute for Health Information 2005, http://secure.cihi.ca/cihiweb/dispPage.jsp?cw_page=AR_1215_E; http://www.cbc.ca/health/story/2008/10/29/bc-hospital-surgeries-cancelled-campbell-river.html?ref=rss; http://www.canada.com/topics/news/national/story.html?id=496f0573-e309-403a-8c3d-0768ccb7a372; http://en.wikipedia.org/wiki/Calgary_General_Hospital; R.M. Gerst, "Full House," *ASQ Six Sigma Forum Magazine*, May 2013, 12(3), 8–13.

OM in *ACTION*

Airline Capacity

Capacity in the airline industry is measured by Available Seat Miles (the sum over all planes of the number of their seats multiplied by the number of miles each normally flies per year). The capacity utilization is measured by Passenger Load Factor, which is the average percentage of seats occupied. Air Canada, with approximately 351 planes and 1,520 flights per day, had

approximately 67.3 billion Available Seat Miles and Passenger Load Factor of 82.7 percent in 2012. A related measure is Revenue Passenger Miles, which is Passenger Load Factor multiplied by Available Seat Miles. In 2012, Air Canada's Revenue Passenger Miles was = 67.3 × 0.827 = 55.65 billion.

Source: Air Canada's Annual Report, 2012, http://www.aircanada.com/en/about/investor/documents/2012_ar.pdf.

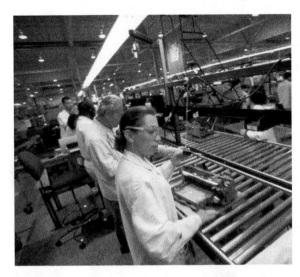

In only 48 hours Solectron in San Jose, California, can build to order, ship, and install a complex computer system. Suppliers hold inventory until it is pulled, thereby increasing manufacturing flexibility.

Making a violin requires precision and skill from an artisan. Capacity is highly limited when items are specialized and produced one at a time.

profit (if there is demand for more units). Further, because effective capacity acts as a lid on actual output, increasing effective capacity should also increase the profit. The following are a list of factors that influence effective capacity.

Factors Influencing Effective Capacity

Many aspects of design have an impact on effective capacity. The same is true for many planning and operating decisions.

Facilities and Machines. The design of facilities, including floor space and layout, directly influence effective capacity. Layout of the work area often determines how smoothly work can be performed, and environmental factors such as heating, cooling, lighting, and ventilation also play a significant role. Further, machine and equipment speed and their state directly influence capacity, which means their maintenance is important.

Product Mix. When items are similar, the ability of the system to produce those items is much greater than when successive items differ. There is less need for product change-over and machine/equipment setup. Thus, a restaurant that offers a limited menu can usually prepare and serve meals at a faster rate than a restaurant with an extensive menu. The more uniform the output, the more opportunities there are for standardization of machines, methods, and materials, which leads to greater effective capacity.

Workers. The tasks that make up a job, the variety of activities involved, and the training, skill, and experience required to perform a job all have an impact on the potential output. In addition, employee motivation has a very basic relationship to effective capacity, as do absenteeism and labour turnover.

Planning and Operational Factors. Scheduling problems may occur when there are differences in equipment capabilities or differences in job requirements. Effective capacity may be constrained by a bottleneck operation, inventory decisions, late deliveries from suppliers, acceptability of purchased materials and parts, and quality control procedures.

External Factors. Product standards, especially minimum quality and performance standards, can restrict management's options for increasing effective capacity. Also, pollution standards on products and equipment often reduce effective capacity, as does paperwork required by government regulatory agencies. A similar effect occurs when a union contract limits the type of work an employee may do.

For an equipment/machine, a composite measure is Overall Equipment Effectiveness (OEE):

$$OEE = Efficiency \times Utilization \times proportion\ of\ good\ quality\ items\ produced$$

(see e.g., http://en.wikipedia.org/wiki/Overall_equipment_effectiveness).

Strategic Capacity Planning Process in Organizations

Capacity decisions in organizations are usually part of the annual strategic planning process. They directly influence capital budgeting. The steps taken are as follows:

1. Forecast demand for products one to five years, or more, ahead.
2. Calculate capacity requirements to meet the forecasts.
3. Measure capacity now, and decide if and how to bridge the gap in capacity in the future.
    a. Generate technically feasible alternatives varying in nature (plant, machines/equipment, subcontract, lease), size, location, price changes, etc.
    b. Evaluate each alternative economically.
        i. Initial investment? Annual revenues? Annual operating expenses? Life of investment?
        ii. Method of evaluation: Break-even analysis, payback period, or net present value.
    c. Consider noneconomic aspects too, e.g., ease of use, reliability, etc.
    d. Choose the best alternative and implement it.

In the rest of this chapter, we will briefly describe Steps 1 and 2, provide some considerations for performing Step 3a, and describe use of breakeven analysis for Step 3b.

 OM in ACTION

Cisco's IT Network Capacity Planning

Cisco has over 140 offices in North America, each with staff who use their computers to do their work. The offices are connected to Internet (and hence together) using wide area network (WAN) lines with various bandwidths. The capacity or bandwidth initially chosen for each office (in megabits per second [Mbps]) was based on the number of employees (headcount) using the office. To increase the reliability of the system, a secondary circuit is usually made available.

Headcount	Primary WAN Bandwidth	Secondary WAN Bandwidth
1–10	1.5 Mbps	None
11–40	1.5 Mbps	1.5 Mbps
41–100	3 Mbps	3 Mbps
101–150	4.5 Mbps	4.5 Mbps
151–200	6 Mbps	6 Mbps
201–500	45 Mbps	6 Mbps
501 +	155 Mbps	45 Mbps

However, the increasing use of applications and database synchronization and backup, including the use of voice over Internet telephony (VoIP) and video on-demand, soon created congestion during some periods of the day, reducing productivity. Cisco uses the following utilization thresholds as triggers for watching and adding capacity to the WAN bandwidth of an office. These depend on whether there is a same-size backup line, or half-capacity line, or no backup.

Primary/ Backup WAN Bandwidth	*Percentage Utilization (Watch/Analyze)	**Percentage Utilization (Upgrade)
*** 100/100	60%	80%
**** 100/50	40%	50%
***** 50/50	40%	50%

*15-minute average threshold exceeded 10 percent or more during local business hours (monthly)

**15-minute average threshold exceeded or equalled 20 percent of local business hours (monthly)

***Primary circuit handles 100 percent of the traffic until failure, when the backup takes over

****Primary circuit handles 100 percent of the traffic until failure, when the backup takes over with 50 percent of the capacity of the primary

*****Primary and backup circuits load-share until a failure occurs

For example, for a 100/100 office (same size backup line), if utilization exceeds 60 percent during more than 10 percent of the business day, the utilization is watched and analyzed, whereas if utilization exceeds 80 percent during more than 20 percent of the business day, the capacity planning team puts a request to the networks operations for increased capacity. The analysis requires that the reason for traffic is legitimate. For example, backups can be done overnight and personal recreational use of Internet during busy times is discouraged. The WAN bandwidth utilization is monitored by Cisco's Netflow software, which is installed in its routers. Of course, the user performance expectations (quality of service) is balanced against capital budget as bandwidths are expensive.

Source: http://www.cisco.com/web/about/ciscoitatwork/downloads/ciscoitatwork/pdf/Cisco_IT_Case_Study_Capacity_Planning.pdf.

Forecasting Long-Term Demand

Figure 5-1 illustrates some basic long-term demand patterns. In addition to basic patterns, there are more complex patterns, such as a combination of cycles and trends.

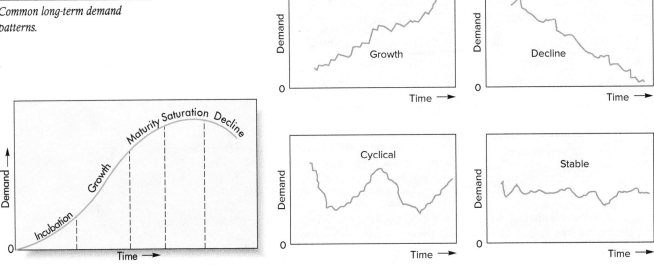

Figure 5-1

Common long-term demand patterns.

When trends are identified, the fundamental issues are (1) how long the trend might persist and (2) the slope of trend. If a cycle is identified, interest focuses on (1) the approximate length of the cycle, and (2) the amplitude of the cycle (i.e., deviation from average).

Long-term forecasting techniques include judgmental and regression. For details, please refer back to Chapter 3.

For two examples where technology changed a trend unexpectedly, see the "Capacity in the Aluminum Industry" and "Alberta Oil Sands" OM in Actions.

The link between marketing and operations is crucial. Through customer contacts and demographic analysis, marketing can supply vital information to operations.

Calculating Capacity Requirements

We will illustrate this by an example for determining the number of machines needed to make some products. Another method of determining capacity requirements in a health care setting is given in "Long-Term Care Capacity Planning" OM in Action.

OM in ACTION

Capacity in the Aluminum Industry

Making capacity decisions is hard. Consider the aluminum industry. In the 1970s and 1980s, aluminum can sales were growing at over 10 percent per year. This occurred when aluminum pop cans grabbed market share from glass bottles as containers used to hold soft drinks. Companies such as Alcan and Alcoa saw no end to the market growth for aluminum cans. Therefore, they invested heavily in mills to make rolled sheets of aluminum from which pop cans are made. But in the early 1990s, market growth stopped because PET (Poly-ethylene Terephthalate) plastic bottles grabbed market share from aluminum cans. In 2000s, the strong, seemingly never-ending, demand for aluminum by China (with 9 percent annual growth rate) and its inadequate future electricity supply to process

aluminum, resulted in takeover frenzy within major Western aluminum companies looking for available production capacity. For example, Alcan warded off Alcoa's takeover bid only to accept the $38 billion takeover bid of Rio Tinto, a large British/Australian mining company, in late 2007. However, this turned out to be a big mistake as the recession of 2008 depressed the Chinese market for aluminum imports, resulting in the selloff and $25 billion write-off of aluminum assets of Rio Tinto Alcan.

Source: M. Brooks, President, Alcan Rolled Products, "Insights on the Global Aluminum Industry," December 5, 2003; S. Silcoff, "Chinese Aluminum Demand Triggered Alcan Takeover," *CanWest News*, October 26, 2007, p. 1. J.W. Miller, Digging Out of a $38 Billion Hole, *Wall Street Journal*, February 12, 2013.

OM in *ACTION*

Alberta Oil Sands

The Alberta oil sands is a huge deposit (estimated as over 160 billion barrels) of oil-covered sands north of Edmonton. To recover the oil, ore has to be boiled in water. Then the heavy oil can be further processed to produce usable petroleum products such as gasoline. As the price of crude oil climbed over $30 per barrel in the 1970s, processing oil sands became economical. Many oil companies such as Suncor, Imperial Oil (Exxon), Canadian Natural Resources, Shell, and Cenovas have invested billions of dollars in processing plants in the oil sands (over $30 billion per year currently). Total current production is approximately 1.5 million barrels per day (b/d) but is expected to reach 4 million b/d in a decade or two. Until the recession of 2008, the investments were for both initial processing and also for upgrading. The upgraded oil is called synthetic crude oil (syncrude), which is a light crude oil. However, many companies delayed construction of upgraders because of the recession. In the meantime, the production of light oil from fracking in the United States (e.g., from the Bakken formation in North Dakota and Montana) has really taken off, creating excess supply of light crude oil (called tight oil) inland in the United States. This has reduced the gap between price of syncrude and price of heavy oil-sands oil. Many refineries can simply add a coker and upgrade heavy oil, making the need for upgraders redundant. As a result, upgrading in Alberta has become uneconomical, leading to billions of dollars of write-off. For example, Suncor has abandoned its half-finished voyageur upgrader at a total cost of $3.5 billion. The only two upgraders in Canada are the NewGrade Energy upgrader in the Coop Regina Complex and the Husky Lloydminster upgrader, which were built in the late 1980s and early 1990s.

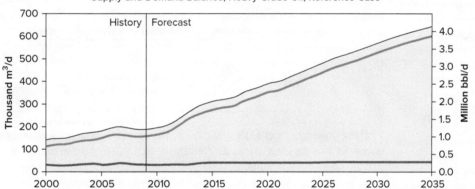

Supply and Demand Balance, Heavy Crude Oil, Reference Case

Another related booming industry involves transportation of oil from Alberta to the markets (or ports). This is economically and safely done using oil pipelines. Three major companies have pipelines and are expanding their capacities: TransCanada Pipelines, Enbridge, and Kinder Morgan Canada. TransCanada has recently built the Keystone Pipeline to the central United States and the Gulf of Mexico, and is trying to add another line called Keystone XL. Also, TransCanada has been approached by Irving family of New Brunswick to use its Mainline gas line to Montreal and build a pipeline from Montreal to St. John (this is called Energy East Pipeline). Enbridge has applied to the National Energy Board (NEB) for permission to build the twin Northern Gateway pipeline from Alberta to Kitimat, British Columbia. One pipe is for importing dilutant and the other is for exporting heavy oil mixed with dilutant (to make it easier to flow in the pipeline). Kinder Morgan Canada has applied to NEB to double its capacity of the Trans Mountain pipeline from Edmonton to Burnaby.

Sources: http://www.energy.alberta.ca/oilsands/791.asp; https://www.neb-one.gc.ca/clf-nsi/archives/rnrgynfmtn/nrgyrprt/nrgyftr/2011/nrgsppldmndprjctn2035-eng.pdf; http://www.theglobeandmail.com/globe-investor/suncor-cancels-voyageur-project-takes-hit-to-profit/article10453855; https://www.neb-one.gc.ca/clf-nsi/archives/rnrgynfmtn/nrgyrprt/trnsprttn/trnsprttnssssmnt2009/trnsprttnssssmnt2009-eng.pdf; http://thechronicleherald.ca/business/207244-company-lower-prices-expected-on-oil-from-syncrude-oilsands-mine; and http://business.financialpost.com/2014/03/27/keystone-oil-pipeline-energy-east-irving/?_lsa=b01d-afdb.

OM in *ACTION*

Long-Term Care Capacity Planning

As baby boomers approach old age, the percentage of the population over 65 increases from approximately 15 percent to 25 percent. This will cause a significant increase in demand for long-term care (LTC) provided by nursing homes. Thus, provincial governments and regional health authorities (RHA), being responsible for provision of health care in Canada, are concerned about LTC capacity issues. The most common measure of demand for LTC is number of beds per 1,000 population age 75+. This number varies among RHAs but averages around 100 beds

per 1000 people over 75 years old. However, many patients needing LTC are younger than 75, and it is a fact that there is a shortage of beds, resulting in many patients needing alternative levels of care and taking beds in hospitals. Using the above ratio is simple but will underestimate the demand for LTC, which will result in very long waits for LTC in the near future.

Sources: http://www.cfhi-fcass.ca/sf-docs/default-source/planning-for-the-aging-population-files/10-15-10-Carriere.pdf?sfvrsn=0; http://www4.hrsdc.gc.ca/.3ndic.1t.4r@-eng.jsp?iid=33; http://www.longwoods.com/content/22881.

Example 2 ▶

A department works one eight-hour shift, 250 days a year. Three new products with the following annual demands are to be produced in the department. There is no excess capacity, so the department needs to buy new machines. Fortunately, there is a type of machine that can produce all three products. The expected processing times per unit are also given below. How many machines are needed?

Product	Annual Demand	Standard Processing Time per Unit (Hr)	Processing Time Needed (Hr)
#1	400	5.0	2,000
#2	300	8.0	2,400
#3	700	2.0	1,400
			5,800

SOLUTION

Working one eight-hour shift, 250 days a year provides an annual capacity of $8 \times 250 = 2,000$ hours per year for each machine. We can see that three of these machines would be needed to handle the required volume:

$$\frac{5,800}{2,000 \text{ hours/machine}} = 2.90 \text{ machines (round up to 3)}$$

The size of the facility can be determined by summing the area required for machines, inventory, handling material, and the offices required.

Major Considerations for Developing Capacity Alternatives

1. Design Flexibility into System. The long-term nature of capacity decisions and the risks inherent in long-term forecasts suggest potential benefits from designing flexible systems. For example, provision for future expansion in the original design of a structure frequently can be obtained at a small price compared to what it would cost to remodel an existing structure that did not have such a provision. Hence, if future expansion of a restaurant seems likely, water lines, power hookups, and waste disposal lines can be put in place initially so that if expansion becomes a reality, modification to the existing structure can be minimized. Similarly, a new golf course may start as a nine-hole operation, but if provision is made for future expansion by obtaining options on adjacent land, it may progress to a larger (18-hole) course.

2. Differentiate Between New and Mature Products. Mature products tend to be more predictable in terms of capacity requirements, and they may have predictable life spans. This means less risk of choosing an incorrect capacity and length of life for the investment. New products tend to carry higher risk because of the uncertainty often associated with predicting the quantity and duration of demand. These uncertainties are due to unknown and changing reaction of customers, evolving technologies, and uncertain competitors reactions. Flexibility and starting small is more important in this case.

3. Take a "Big Picture" Approach to Capacity Changes. When developing capacity alternatives, it is important to consider how parts of the system interrelate. For example, when making a decision to increase the number of rooms in a motel, one should also take into account probable increased demands for parking, entertainment and food, and housekeeping. This is sometimes called *capacity balance*. Capacity *imbalance* results in *bottlenecks*, which restrict the capacity of the whole system (see Figure 5-2 and Example 3). To increase the capacity of the system, the capacity of the bottleneck operation should be increased.

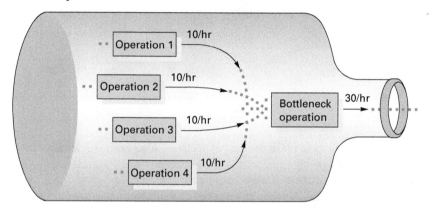

◀ **Figure 5-2**

Bottleneck operation.

The first product created by toy company Spin Master, now the third largest toy manufacturer in North America, was Earth Buddy, a grass head.[1] Spin Master was hoping to produce and sell 8,000 Earth Buddies for Mother's Day and had one week to produce them. The Earth Buddy assembly consisted of the following operations: A: fill grass seeds and sawdust in a nylon stocking (average time 90 seconds), B: form ears and nose using elastic bands (average time 48 seconds), C: stick on the eyeglass and eyes (average time 24 seconds; eyeglasses were formed off line), and D: paint the mouth (average time 15 seconds). Finally, Earth Buddies are left to dry overnight and then packed. There are 6 workers doing A, 3 doing B, 2 doing C, and 1 doing D. There is enough space for inventory between operations so that they can work fairly independently. Determine the bottleneck operation and capacity of the "line" for a 40-hour week. Is the line balanced? Can Spin Master meet its production goal?

◀ **Example 3**

SOLUTION

	Fill	Form	Eyes	Paint
Time per unit per worker (sec)	90	48	24	15
No. of units per minute per worker	60/90 = 2/3	60/48 = 1.25	60/24 = 2.5	60/15 = 4
Number of workers	6	3	2	1
Capacity per minute	6(2/3) = 4	3(1.25) = 3.75	2(2.5) = 5	4(1) = 4
Capacity per hour	4(60) = 240	3.75(60) = 225	5(60) = 300	4(60) = 240
		Bottleneck		

Line capacity = 225 units per hour. Yes, the line is fairly balanced because capacity per hour for the operations are all close.

Productive hours required to make 8,000 units = 8,000/225 = 35.6 hours.

Yes, Spin Master should be able to meet its target production goal of 8,000 units provided employees work approximately 36 hours (excluding breaks).

4. Choose Capacity Timing and Increments. Consider whether capacity is to be installed before, during, or after demand occurs. If before, it is called leading strategy and if after, lagging strategy (see Figure 5-3). Most organizations plan to have capacity available just before demand occurs because construction of capacity takes a long time. Leading competitors is more risky, but it has greater potential for rewards. If cost of capacity excess and cost of capacity shortage can be

---

[1] "Company, About Us, Video Biography," http://www.spinmaster.com.

Figure 5-3

Leading and lagging capacity strategies.

estimated, they can be used to make the timing decision. Also, consider whether incremental small expansions or a single big expansion is more appropriate. Using small expansions is less risky because it allows adjustment of the capacity based on demand changes over time, but it is usually more expensive overall. If goods are involved, any short-term mismatch between capacity and demand can be bridged by carrying inventory.

5. Prepare to Deal with Capacity "Chunks." Capacity increases are often acquired in fairly large chunks rather than smooth increments, making it difficult to achieve a match between desired capacity and actual capacity. For instance, the desired capacity of a certain Air Canada Jazz route may be 75 seats, but aircrafts available (Bombardier CRJ 700 NextGen and 900 Next-Gen) have 70 and 88 seats, respectively. One CRJ 700 would cause capacity to be five seats short of what is needed, but one CRJ 900 would result in an excess capacity of 13 seats. Most airlines would choose the larger aircraft in this case, because cost of shortage (lost profit) is usually larger than cost of excess capacity. This decision becomes more difficult when demand has a trend or cycle.

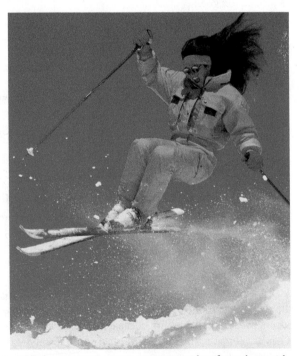

Capacity requirements are affected by seasonal variations. One approach to smooth out capacity requirements is to identify products with complementary seasonal demand pattern such as water skis and snow skis.

6. Attempt to Smooth Out Capacity Requirements. Unevenness in capacity requirements can create certain problems. For instance, during periods of inclement weather, public transportation ridership tends to increase substantially relative to periods of pleasant weather. If capacity is set slightly above normal demand, the system tends to alternate between underutilization and overutilization. Again, the best capacity basically depends on expected cost of shortage vs. expected cost of excess capacity. If the service is critical, spare capacity should be available or be arranged for peak periods. Another solution in some cases such as electricity generation is demand management, i.e., persuading some customers to shift their demand from peak periods to off-peak periods by differential pricing.

Seasonal variations are generally easier to cope with than random variations (e.g., due to weather) because they are *predictable*. One possible solution to seasonal demand is to identify products or services that have complementary demand patterns. For instance, demand for water skis and snow skis complement each other. (More in Chapter 13.)

7. Use Capacity Cushion. When demand is variable, capacity is usually chosen above the average (forecast) demand. The excess of capacity over the average demand is called **capacity cushion** or safety capacity. The size of capacity cushion again depends on the tradeoff between cost of capacity shortage and cost of capacity excess. See Figure 5-4, where a Normal (bell-shaped) demand distribution is assumed. For vital services such as electricity, the chosen capacity should be larger than normal *peak* demand, i.e., there should be a large (positive) capacity cushion because customers cannot wait too long for critical services (e.g., electricity to heat the home in cold winters). For an application of this and some other capacity considerations, see the "Capacity Planning for Electricity Generation" OM in Action.

> **capacity cushion** The excess of capacity over the average demand.

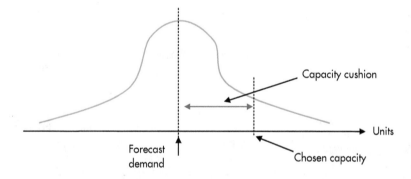

◀ **Figure 5-4**

Capacity cushion.

8. Identify the Optimal Operating Level. Production units typically have an ideal or optimal level of operation in terms of average unit cost of output. At the **optimal operating level**, average cost per unit is the lowest for that production unit; larger or smaller rates of output will result in a higher unit cost, i.e., the average cost curve is "u" shaped.

> **optimal operating level** The level of production that has the lowest average unit cost.

The explanation for the shape of the cost curve is that at low levels of output, the investment costs of facility and machines/equipment must be absorbed (paid for) by very few units. Hence, the cost per unit is high. As output is increased, there are more units to absorb the "fixed" cost of facility and machines/equipment, so unit cost decreases. However, beyond a certain point, unit cost will start to rise. Reasons for this include worker fatigue; equipment breakdown; the loss of flexibility, which leaves less of a margin for error; and, generally, greater difficulty in coordinating operations.

Both optimal operating level and the amount of the minimum average unit cost tend to be a function of size of the operating unit. As the size of a plant increases, the optimal operating level increases and the minimum average cost per unit decreases. Thus, larger plants tend to have a larger optimal operating level and lower average cost per unit than smaller plants. Figure 5-5 illustrates this point, called **economies of scale**. However, beyond a size, the plant will be too large, expensive, and complex to manage. This is called diseconomies of scale.

> **economies of scale** The economic conditions that favour larger plants and machines/equipment by causing minimum average unit cost to decrease as size increases.

In choosing the capacity of an operating unit, management must take these relationships into account along with the availability of financial and other resources and forecasts of demand.

Figure 5-5

Average cost per unit and optimal operating level are functions of size of a production unit (graph shows economies of scale).

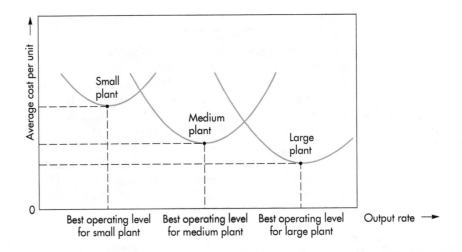

OM in *ACTION*

Capacity Planning for Electricity Generation

Electricity generation is a service operation because electricity cannot be stored in large amounts. The closest to inventoried electricity is having a water reservoir upstream from a dam equipped with electricity-generating turbines. Because voltage must be close (within ± 3 volts) to 110v (or else machines and equipment will not work), automatic fuses/relays will disconnect power (causing a blackout) if supply is not equal to demand. Therefore, to avoid blackouts, supply must equal demand at all times. This requires not only precise monitoring of demand and coordination of supply but also having enough capacity available at all times.

Electricity demand has seasonality and is also variable. Demand is at its highest during hot summer days (when air conditioners are used) and cold winter days (when room and car block heaters are used). Peak usage usually occurs between 4 p.m. and 8 p.m. when people return home, plug in their car, start cooking, possibly use the washing machine, and watch TV. In addition, the peak demand can be abnormal/extreme, e.g., the hottest day in a summer could be the hottest in 30 years.

The electricity supply can also be variable due to unexpected problems in generation and transmission (e.g., a hurricane can topple trees on transmission lines, ripping them). In addition, the generating plants require downtime for maintenance.

Therefore, to avoid much of the blackouts, the available capacity must not be much smaller than the extreme peak demand. The target for reserve capacity (or capacity cushion) is usually chosen so that the length of blackout is at most two hours per year. However, there are ways to avoid blackouts

altogether, e.g., (1) use demand response programs that, through differential pricing, encourage large consumers to shift their demand to off-peak times and (2) buy electricity from a neighbouring province/state.

Most provinces have one power company (e.g., SaskPower, a Crown corporation) or there is a central government-appointed authority to regulate and coordinate power generation and distribution (e.g., Ontario Power Authority/Independent Electricity System Operator IESO/Hydro One). The reason for this is that generating plants and transmission/distribution lines require significant investment, service to remote communities has to be subsidized, and reliable service is expected by all consumers (imagine no electricity, and hence no heating, in −40 degree temperature).

In the early and middle part of the last century, provinces invested heavily in power generation and transmission/distribution capacities. For example, many hydro dams, coal-powered power plants, and nuclear power plants were built. Unfortunately, during the latter part of last century there was little new investment, letting capacity drop (due to closing of aging plants) while peak demand kept increasing due to population growth. For example, Ontario had 30 gigawatts of capacity and extreme-weather peak demand of 22 gigawatts in 1997, but in 2001 capacity was down to 27 gigawatts and extreme-weather peak demand was up to 25 gigawatts. Fortunately, the trend in capacity decrease has been reversed recently due to refurbishment of the nuclear plants and building of several natural gas–fired plants with turbines, and the trend in demand increase has been reversed due to the recession.

Source: http://www.ieso.ca/Pages/Power-Data/default.aspx

 ## Evaluating Alternatives

An organization needs to evaluate alternatives for future capacity from a number of different perspectives. Most obvious are economic considerations: Will an alternative be economically feasible? How much will it cost? What will operating and maintenance costs be? What will the revenue be? What will its useful life be? Other considerations include, Will it be compatible with present personnel and operations? What is the personal preference of managers?

Less obvious, but nonetheless important, is possible negative public opinion. Any option that could disrupt lives and property (noise, traffic, pollution) is bound to generate hostile reactions. Construction of new facilities may necessitate moving personnel to a new location. Embracing a new technology may mean retraining some people and terminating some jobs. Relocation can cause unfavourable reactions, particularly if a town is about to lose a major employer.

A number of techniques are useful for evaluating capacity alternatives from an economic standpoint. Some of the more common are break-even analysis, payback period, and net present value. Break-even analysis is described in this chapter.

Break-even Analysis

Break-even analysis focuses on the relationship between costs, revenue, and volume (i.e., quantity) of output. The purpose of break-even analysis is to determine the quantity at which the initial investment starts to make a profit. Another name for break-even analysis is cost-volume-profit analysis.

Use of break-even analysis requires identification of all costs related to the production of a given product. These costs are then classified as fixed or variable costs. *Fixed costs* tend to remain constant regardless of quantity of output. Examples include facility lease (or amortized land and building) cost, property tax, machine/equipment cost, heating and cooling expenses, and certain administrative costs such as supervisors' salaries. *Variable costs* vary directly with quantity of output. The major components of variable costs are generally materials and labour costs. We will assume that variable cost per unit remains the same regardless of quantity of output.

Table 5-2 summarizes the symbols used in the break-even analysis formulas. All amounts, except v and R, have a unit of time such as a month or a year. These have been mainly omitted in this section due to simplicity.

FC = Fixed cost

VC = Total variable cost

v = Variable cost per unit

TC = Total cost

TR = Total revenue

R = Revenue per unit (i.e., price)

Q = Quantity or volume of output

Q_{BEP} = Break-even quantity

P = Profit

Break-even analysis symbols.

The total cost associated with a given quantity of output is equal to the sum of the fixed cost and the variable cost per unit times quantity:

$$TC = FC + VC \tag{5-3}$$
$$VC = Q \times v \tag{5-4}$$

Figure 5-6a shows the relationship between quantity of output and fixed cost, total variable cost, and total (fixed plus variable) cost.

Revenue per unit, like variable cost per unit, is assumed to be the same regardless of quantity of output. Assuming that all output can be sold, total revenue will have a linear relationship to output, as illustrated in Figure 5-6b. The total revenue associated with a given quantity of output, Q, is:

$$TR = R \times Q \tag{5-5}$$

Figure 5-6c describes the relationship between profit, which is the difference between total revenue and total cost, and quantity of output. The quantity at which total cost and total revenue are equal is referred to as the **break-even point (BEP)**. When quantity is less than the break-even point, there is a loss; when quantity is greater than the break-even point, there is a profit. The greater the deviation from this point, the greater the profit or loss. Total profit can be calculated using the formula:

break-even point (BEP) The quantity of output at which total cost and total revenue are equal.

(a) Fixed, variable, and total costs

(b) Total revenue increases linearly with output

(c) Profit = $TR - TC$

Figure 5-6 ▲

Break-even relationships.

$$P = TR - TC = R \times Q - (FC + v \times Q)$$

Factorizing Q, we have

$$P = Q(R - v) - FC \qquad (5\text{-}6)$$

Solving for Q, the required quantity needed to generate a specified profit P is:

$$Q = \frac{P + FC}{R - v} \qquad (5\text{-}7)$$

A special case of this is the quantity of output needed for total revenue to equal total cost, i.e., when profit $P = 0$. This is the break-even point:

$$Q_{BEP} = \frac{FC}{R - v} \qquad (5\text{-}8)$$

If demand is expected to be greater than the break-even point, then we conclude that it is a good capacity investment decision (i.e., will make a profit). Otherwise, it is not (i.e., will make a loss).

Example 4 ▶

The management of a large bakery is contemplating making pies, which will require leasing a new equipment for a monthly cost of $6,000. Variable cost will be $2.00 per pie and retail price will be $7.00 each.

   a. How many pies must be sold per month in order to break even?

   b. What would the profit (loss) be if 1,000 pies are made and sold in a month?

   c. How many pies must be sold to realize a profit of $4,000 per month?

   d. If demand is expected to be 1,500 pies per month, is this a good investment?

SOLUTION

$FC = \$6,000$ per month, $v = \$2$ per pie, $R = \$7$ per pie

   a. $Q_{BEP} = \dfrac{FC}{R - v} = \dfrac{\$6,000}{\$7 - \$2} = 1{,}200$ pies/month

   b. For $Q = 1{,}000$, $P = Q(R - v) - FC = 1{,}000\,(\$7 - \$2) - \$6{,}000 = -\$1{,}000$ (i.e., loss of $1,000)

   c. $P = \$4{,}000$; solve for Q using formula 5-7:

$$Q = \frac{\$4{,}000 + \$6{,}000}{\$7 - \$2} = 2{,}000 \text{ pies}$$

   d. Because $1{,}500 > 1{,}200 = Q_{BEP}$, this is a good investment.

Break-even analysis can also be used for (1) make-or-buy decisions, and (2) deciding between two or more capacity alternatives (cost-vs.-cost analysis). See Figure 5-7.

(a) Make-or-buy analysis   (b) Cost-vs.-cost analysis

The make-or-buy decision involves deciding whether to buy a machine (fixed cost) and make the product in-house (variable cost) or to buy the product (variable cost with no fixed cost). See Figure 5-7a. Let v_m = per unit variable cost of make and v_b = per unit variable cost of buy (i.e., purchase price). Then, the indifference point will be:

$$Q = FC/(v_b - v_m)$$

(5-9)

The cost-vs.-cost decision involves two (or more) "make" options: machine A vs. machine B. Each machine will have a fixed cost and a variable cost. See Figure 5-7b. Let FC_A and v_A be fixed cost and unit variable cost of machine A, and FC_B and v_B be fixed cost and unit variable cost of machine B. Then, the indifference point will be:

$$Q = (FC_A - FC_B)/(v_B - v_A)$$

(5-10)

Break-even Problem with Step Fixed Cost

Capacity alternatives may involve *step costs,* which are costs that increase stepwise as range of output increases. For example, a company may have the option of purchasing one, two, or three machines. Each additional machine increases the fixed cost, although perhaps not equally. (See Figure 5-8a.) In this case *multiple break-even quantities* may occur, possibly one for each range. This is illustrated in Figure 5-8b, where there is a break-even point in the second and another in the third range. In order to decide how many machines to purchase, a manager must compare forecast demand to the break-even points and choose the most appropriate number of machines, as Example 5 shows.

(a) Step fixed costs and variable costs   (b) Multiple break-even points

A manager has the option of purchasing one, two, or three machines. Fixed costs and range of output are as follows:

Number of Machines	Total Annual Fixed Cost	Corresponding Range of Output
1	$ 9,600	0 to 300
2	$ 15,000	301 to 600
3	$20,000	601 to 900

Variable cost is $10 per unit, and revenue is $40 per unit.

a. Determine the break-even point (if any) for each range.

b. For any value of annual demand between 0 and 900 units, determine how many machines the manager should purchase.

SOLUTION

a. Calculate the break-even point for each range using the formula $Q_{BEP} = FC/(R - v)$.

For one machine

$$Q_{BEP} = \frac{\$9,600}{\$40/unit - \$10/unit} = 320 \text{ units } [\text{not in the range, so there is no } BEP]$$

For two machines $Q_{BEP} = \dfrac{\$15,000}{\$40/unit - \$10/unit} = 500$ units

For three machines $Q_{BEP} = \dfrac{\$20,000}{\$40/unit - \$10/unit} = 666.67$ units

b. For demand ≤ 499 → use 0 machine (because the first feasible break-even point is 500 units)

For 500 ≤ demand ≤ 600 → use 2 machines

For 601 ≤ demand ≤ 766 → Do not use 3 machines, but use 2 machines and produce 600 units because profit(600) = 600($40 − $10) − $15,000 = $3,000 > profit(Q), 601 ≤ Q ≤ 766. For example, Profit(766) = 766($40 − $10) − 20,000 = $2,980.

For 767 ≤ demand ≤ 900 → use 3 machines

Break-even Point in Dollars

Suppose the decision maker wishes to know the BEP in dollars, $Q_{BEP\$}$, i.e., how much should the sales revenue $Q \times R$ be before the initial investment starts to make a profit. $Q_{BEP\$}$ can easily be determined from $Q_{BEP} = FC/(R - v)$. Simply multiply both sides by R and simplify the right-hand side:

$$Q_{BEP\$} = R \times Q_{BEP} = R(FC)/(R - v) = FC/(1 - v/R)$$

For Example 4, $Q_{BEP\$} = \$6,000/(1 - 2/7) = \$8,400$

The advantage of $Q_{BEP\$}$ is where the investment can produce more than one type of output. In this case,

$$Q_{BEP\$} = \frac{FC}{\sum\left[\left(1 - \dfrac{v_i}{R_i}\right)W_i\right]}$$

Where index i represents product i and W_i = proportion of revenue due to product i.

Example 6 ▶

The management of the bakery in Example 4 thinks that they can use the new equipment to also make quiche. Quiche will have variable cost of $3 and will sell for $10 each. The management estimates that pies and quiche will bring approximately the same amount of revenue. Recall that leasing the equipment will cost $6,000 per month, and that the variable cost of a pie is $2.00 and its sales price is $7.00 each. Calculate the break-even point in dollars.

SOLUTION

$$Q_{BEP\$} = \frac{FC}{\sum\left[\left(1 - \dfrac{v_i}{R_i}\right)W_i\right]} = \frac{6,000}{\left(1 - \dfrac{2}{7}\right)0.5 + \left(1 - \dfrac{3}{10}\right)0.5} = \$8,484.85$$

As with any quantitative tool, it is important to verify that the assumptions on which the break-even analysis is based are reasonably satisfied for a particular situation. Note that revenue per unit or variable cost per unit is not always constant. Also, break-even analysis requires that fixed and variable costs are separated, and this is sometimes exceedingly difficult to accomplish.

Payback is a crude but widely used method that focuses on the length of time it will take for an investment to return its original cost. For example, an investment with an original cost of $6,000 and a monthly net cash flow of $1,000 has a payback period of six months.

Summary

- Design capacity is the theoretical maximum output rate, but effective capacity is limited by work break hours, maintenance, etc. Efficiency is the ratio of actual output rate to effective capacity, and utilization is the proportion of the time the system is operating.

- A variety of factors can influence effective capacity. These include facility design and layout, human factors, product factors, equipment maintenance, scheduling problems, and quality considerations.

- Capacity planning is the process of determining alternatives to meet long-term forecast of demand.

- Development of capacity alternatives is enhanced by considering the life cycle of the product, designing systems with flexible capacity, timing the capacity plan before demand occurs, taking a systems approach to planning, recognizing that capacity increments are often acquired in chunks, practising demand management and complementary products, using capacity cushion, and choosing the right capacity and optimal operating level.

- In evaluating capacity alternatives, a manager must consider both quantitative and qualitative aspects. Quantitative analysis usually reflects economic factors, and qualitative considerations include intangibles such as operational fit and personal preferences of managers.

- Break-even analysis determines that quantity beyond which profit will be attained.

Key Terms

break-even point (BEP)
capacity
capacity cushion
design capacity

economies of scale
effective capacity
efficiency
optimal operating level

strategic capacity planning
utilization

Solved Problems

Problem 1

A manager must decide whether to make or buy a certain item used in the production of its vending machines. Cost and demand estimates are as follows:

	Make	Buy
Annual fixed cost	$150,000	0
Variable cost/unit	$60	$80
Annual demand (units)	12,000	12,000

a. Given these numbers, should the company buy or make this item?

b. There is a possibility that demand could change in the future. At what quantity would the manager be indifferent between making and buying?

Solution

a. Determine the annual cost of each alternative:

Total cost = Fixed cost + Quantity × Variable cost

Make: $150,000 + 12,000\ (\$60) = \$870,000$

Buy: $0 + 12,000\ (\$80) = \$960,000$

Because the annual cost of making the item is less than the annual cost of buying it, the manager should make the item.

b. To determine the quantity at which the two choices would be equivalent, set the two total costs equal to each other, and solve for quantity: $TC_{make} = TC_{buy}$. Thus, $\$150,000 + Q(\$60) = 0 + Q(\$80)$. Solving for Q, we get $Q = 7,500$ units. Alternatively, one can use formula 5-9: $BEP = FC/(v_b - v_m) = \$150,000/(\$80 - \$60) = 7,500$ units. Therefore, at 7,500 units a year, the manager would be indifferent between making and buying. For lower demand the choice would be to buy, and for higher demand the choice would be to make.

Problem 2

A toy company wants to make electric turtles. The line will have a monthly fixed cost of $42,000 and variable costs of $3 per turtle. Turtles would sell for $7 each. Prepare a table that shows total revenue, total variable cost, fixed cost, total cost, and profit for monthly demands of 10,000, 12,000, and 15,000 units. In what range do you expect the break-even point to lie? Calculate the break-even point.

Solution

Revenue $= \$7$ per unit

Variable cost $= \$3$ per unit

Fixed cost $= \$42,000$ per month

Profit $= Q(R - v) - FC$

Total cost $= FC + v \times Q$

Demand	Total Revenue	Total VC	Fixed Cost	Total Cost	Profit
10,000	$70,000	$30,000	$42,000	$72,000	$(2,000)
12,000	84,000	36,000	42,000	78,000	6,000
15,000	105,000	45,000	42,000	87,000	18,000

The break-even point would lie between 10,000 and 12,000 units per month (look at the Profits).

$$Q_{BEP} = \frac{FC}{R - v} = \frac{\$42,000}{\$7 - \$3} = 10,500 \text{ units per month}$$

Problem 3

Refer to Problem 2. Develop an equation that can be used to calculate monthly profit for any quantity. Use that equation to determine profit when quantity equals 22,000 units per month.

Solution

$$\text{Profit} = Q(R - v) - FC = Q(\$7 - \$3) - \$42,000 = \$4Q - \$42,000$$

$$\text{For } Q = 22,000, \text{ profit is } \$4(22,000) - \$42,000 = \$46,000$$

Problem 4

A manager must decide which type of machine to buy, Type A or Type B, and how many of each. Type A machine costs $15,000 each, and Type B machine costs $11,000 each. The machines are operated 8 hours a day, 250 days a year. The variable cost of using either machine is negligible.

Either machine can be used to perform two types of chemical analysis, C1 and C2, but the processing times will be different. Annual quantities (i.e., number of analyses) and processing times are shown in the following table. The goal is to minimize total purchase cost but meet annual requirements within the available hours.

Analysis Type	Annual Quantity	Processing Time per Analysis (hr) A	B
C1	1,200	1	2
C2	900	3	2

Solution

Total processing time (annual quantity × processing time per analysis) needed by type of equipment are:

Analysis Type	A	B
C1	1,200	2,400
C2	2,700	1,800
Total	3,900	4,200 hrs

Total processing time available per machine is 8 hours/day × 250 days/year = 2,000 hours per year. Hence, one machine can handle 2,000 hours of analysis, two machines can handle 4,000 hours, etc.

Given the total processing requirements, two Type A machines would be needed for a total cost of 2 × $15,000 = $30,000, or three Type B machines would be needed for a total cost of 3 × $11,000 = $33,000. Thus, two machines of Type A would have lower cost than three Type B machines.

Problem 5

Question: What is the capacity (attainable output) of this system where the product is made on two parallel lines (1-2-3 and 4-5-6) that join for finishing in operation 7?

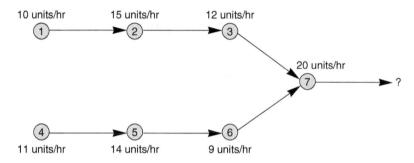

Solution

The attainable output of each portion of the system is equal to the output of the slowest operation. So the output of the upper portion is 10 units per hour and the output of the lower portion is 9 units per hour. Together the two portions can produce 10 + 9 = 19 units per hour. Although operation #7 can handle 20 units per hour, only 19 units per hour come from the two previous portions of the system, so the system output can be only 19 units per hour.

Discussion and Review Questions

Note: An asterisk indicates that a question or problem may be more challenging.

1. What is capacity? Give an example. **LO1**

2. How do long-term, medium-term, and short-term capacity decisions differ? **LO1**

3. Why is the long-term capacity decision important? Give three reasons. **LO1**

4. Contrast design capacity and effective capacity. **LO1**

5. Propose measures of capacity for a hospital and for an airline. In what way are the measures similar and different? **LO1**

6. Contrast efficiency and utilization. **LO1**

7. What is capacity planning and how is it done? **LO1 & 2**

8. How can long-term capacity requirements be determined? **LO2**

9. Give one example of building flexibility into system capacity. **LO2**

10. What is a bottleneck operation? Name two places/operations in an airport that are usually bottlenecks. **LO2**

11. What is meant by the term capacity "chunks"? Give an example. What are leading and lagging strategies for timing capacity increases? Should essential services such as utilities use the leading or lagging strategy? Explain. **LO2**

12. What are economies of scale? Give an example. Is there a limit to it? Explain. **LO2**

13. How do electrical utilities meet abnormal peak demand? Name three ways. **LO2**

14. What influences effective capacity? **LO1**

15. What is the optimal operating level for a machine and why is it usually less than its design capacity? **LO2**

16. What is capacity cushion? Give an example of an industry sector that should have capacity cushion. **LO2**

17. Discuss how capacity planning for essential services such as utilities differs from capacity planning for other services. **LO2**

*18. When Air Canada emerged from bankruptcy protection in 2004, its top management decided to replace some of its older planes with new ones. In particular, several relatively small Embraer and Bombardier planes (with fewer than 90 seats) and several large Boeing 777 and 787 (with more than 200 seats) were ordered. These are much more fuel efficient than the planes they replace. However, Air Canada operations are still not as low cost as WestJet's. An Available Seat Mile costs Air Canada approximately 17¢ whereas it costs WestJet approximately 14¢. Recall that WestJet is nonunionized, runs only one type of plane (Boeing 737, which seats 119–166 passengers), and is financially stronger (see the WestJet case at the end of Chapter 2). Discuss the pros and cons of Air Canada's decision. **LO1 & 2**

19. What is break-even analysis and how is it used? **LO3**

Taking Stock

1. What are two major trade-offs in capacity planning? **LO2**

2. Who needs to be involved in capacity planning? **LO1**

3. In what ways has technology had an impact on capacity planning? **LO2**

4. When Air Canada went into bankruptcy in 2003/2004, a new holding company, ACE, was formed with the goal of breaking up various business units of Air Canada such as the Aeroplan customer loyalty plan, the maintenance department, and the regional subsidiary airline Jazz. ACE managed to achieve its goals against the opposition of Air Canada employees, especially its pilots. What was left of Air Canada was practically worthless. Is what has happened to Air Canada unethical? Explain. **LO2**

Critical Thinking Exercise

An agricultural machinery manufacturer can potentially make eight units per day. Its effective capacity, however, is four units per day, and its actual output is three units per day. The manager would like to increase the output per day. Which of the following factors would you recommend that the manager investigate first: quality problems, absenteeism, or scheduling and balancing? Explain your reasoning. **LO1**

Experiential Learning Exercises

1. Estimate the hourly capacity of the following two service systems by obtaining their processing times. **LO2**

   a. An automatic car wash.
   b. A cashier in a supermarket, a teller in a bank, or a similar service operation.

   Obtain the processing times for approximately six customers.

2. How confident are you of your estimate for part *1a* and for part 1b? Explain.

Internet Exercises

1. Go to the following websites related to Airbus A380, the biggest passenger plane ever built (525 passengers or more on 2 floors, with a range of 15,700 km, and a wingspan of 80 metres): http://www.airbus.com/aircraftfamilies/passengeraircraft/a380family/whos-flying-the-a380; http://centreforaviation.com/analysis/where-the-airbus-a380-will-fly-next-59245. **LO2**

   Pick an airline flying A380, and try to explain its choice on a route.

2. The proposed TransCanada Pipelines' Keystone XL will have a diameter of 36 inches and the crude oil in it will have a velocity of 6.3 km/h (based on the number and power of the pump stations planned). It is claimed that it will be able to transport 830,000 barrels of oil per day. You are wondering if this is right. Calculate the flow rate or capacity of the pipeline (in barrels per day) using:

   a. Geometry. *Hint:* First, calculate how many barrels fit in a 6.3 km long pipe, where volume of a pipe with diameter d and length L is $(d/2)^2 \pi L$. *Note:* 18 inches = 0.4572 metre; 1 cubic metre = 8.3864 barrels.
   b. http://www.1728.org/flowrate.htm (to check your answer in part *a*).

Problems

1. a. Calculate the utilization and efficiency in each of these situations: **LO1**

    i. A bank loan officer processes an average of seven loans per day. She works an eight-hour shift, but takes 1 hour off for lunch break. The effective capacity is eight loans per day.

    ii. A furnace repair team services an average of four furnaces a day. The team is idle an average of two hours in an eight-hour shift. The effective capacity is five furnaces a day.

  b. Would you say that systems with higher efficiency will have higher utilization than other systems? Explain.

2. In a job shop, effective capacity is only 50 percent of design capacity, and actual output is 80 percent of effective capacity. What design capacity would be needed to achieve an actual output of eight jobs per week? **LO1**

3. A producer of pottery is considering the addition of a new factory to absorb the backlog of demand that now exists. The primary location being considered will have fixed cost of $10,000 per month and variable cost of $1 per unit produced. Each item is sold to retailers at a price that averages $2. **LO3**

  a. What quantity per month is required in order to break even?

  b. What profit would be realized on a monthly quantity of 20,000 units?

  c. What quantity is needed to obtain a profit of $16,000 per month?

  d. What quantity is needed to provide revenue of $23,000 per month?

  e. Plot the total cost and total revenue lines against quantity per month.

4. A small company intends to increase the capacity of its bottleneck operation by adding a new machine. Two alternatives, A and B, have been identified, and the associated costs and revenues have been estimated. Annual fixed costs would be $40,000 for A and $30,000 for B; variable costs per unit would be $10 for A and $12 for B; and revenue per unit would be $15 for A and $16 for B. **LO3**

  a. Determine each alternative's break-even point.

  b. At what quantity would the two alternatives yield the same profit?

  c. If expected annual demand is 12,000 units, which alternative would yield higher profit?

5. The selling price for a type of felt-tip pen is $1 per pen. Fixed cost of the operation is $25,000 per month and variable cost is 50 cents per pen. **LO3**

  a. Find the break-even quantity.

  b. How many pens must be sold to obtain a monthly profit of $15,000?

  c. What is the BEP$?

  d. Another type of marker with the following characteristics can also be produced by the machine: selling price = $2 each, variable cost = $0.75 each, and proportion of revenue = 30%. Calculate the BEP$.

6. Natalie is considering the purchase of a cell phone service plan. There are two service plans to choose from. Plan A has a monthly charge of $20 plus $0.45 a minute for daytime calls and unlimited evening/night/weekend calls. Plan B has a flat rate of $50 with 200 daytime minutes of calls allowed per month and a cost of $0.40 per daytime minute beyond that, and unlimited evening/night/weekend calls. **LO3**

  a. Determine the total charge under each plan for this case: 120 minutes of daytime calls a month.

  b. Prepare a graph that shows total monthly cost for each plan vs. daytime call minutes.

  c. Over what range of daytime call minutes will each plan be optimal?

7. A company plans to begin production of a new small appliance. The manager must decide whether to purchase the motor for the appliance from a vendor at $7 each or to produce them in-house. Either of two processes could be used for in-house production; one would have an annual fixed cost of $160,000 and a variable cost of $5 per unit, and the other would have an annual fixed cost of $190,000 and a variable cost of $4 per unit. Determine the range of annual quantity for which each of the alternatives would be best. **LO3**

8. A manager is trying to decide whether to purchase a certain part or to have it produced internally. Internal production could use either of two processes. One would entail a variable cost of $16 per unit and an annual fixed cost of $200,000; the other would entail a variable cost of $14 per unit and an annual fixed cost of $240,000. Three vendors are willing to provide the part. Vendor A has a price of $20 per unit for any annual quantity up to 30,000 units. Vendor B has a price of $22 per unit if demand is 1,000 units or less, but $18 per unit (for all units) if demand is greater. Vendor C offers a price of $21 per unit for the first 1,000 units, and $19 per unit for additional units. **LO3**

  a. If the manager anticipates an annual demand of 10,000 units, which alternative would be best from a cost standpoint? For 60,000 units, which alternative would be best?

  b. Determine the range for which each alternative is best. Are there any alternatives that are never best? If so, which ones?

9. A company manufactures a product using two identical machines. Each machine has a design capacity of 250 units per day and an effective capacity of 230 units per day. At present, actual output averages 200 units per machine, but the manager estimates that productivity improvements soon will increase output to 225 units per day. Annual demand for the product is currently 50,000 units, but it is expected that within two years annual demand will triple. How many machines should the company plan to have to satisfy the forecasted demand? Assume 240 workdays per year. **LO2**

10. A manager must decide which type of machine to buy, A, B, or C. Machine fixed costs are: **LO2**

Machine	Cost/Year
A	$40,000
B	$30,000
C	$80,000

The company makes four products. Product demand forecasts and unit processing times on each machine are as follows:

Product	Annual Demand	Processing Time Per Unit (Minutes)		
		A	B	C
1	16,000	3	4	2
2	12,000	4	4	3
3	6,000	5	6	4
4	30,000	2	2	1

a. How many machines of each type would be needed in order to meet annual demand for all the products? Based on annual fixed costs, which type of machine and how many will cost least to satisfy the demand? Machines operate 10 hours a day, 250 days a year.

b. Consider this additional information: The machines differ in terms of hourly operating costs: The A machines have an hourly operating cost of $10 each, B machines have an hourly operating cost of $11 each, and C machines have an hourly operating cost of $12 each. Which alternative machine should be selected, and how many would be necessary to minimize total cost while satisfying processing requirements?

11. A manager must decide how many machines of a certain type to purchase. Each machine can process 100 customers per day. One machine will result in a fixed cost of $2,000 per day, while two machines will result in a fixed cost of $3,800 per day. Variable costs will be $20 per customer, and revenue will be $45 per customer. **LO3**

a. Determine the break-even points for one machine and two machines.

b. If estimated demand is 90 to 120 customers per day, how many machines should be purchased?

12. The manager of a car wash must decide whether to have one or two wash lines. One line will have a fixed cost of $4,000 a month, and two lines will have a fixed cost of $7,000 a month. Each line would be able to process 15 cars an hour. Variable cost will be $1 per car, and revenue will be $3 per car. The manager projects average demand of between 14 and 18 cars an hour. Assume extra demand for one line will be lost. Would you recommend one or two lines? The car wash will be open 300 hours a month. **LO3**

13. The total demand for polypropylene, a type of plastic, in North America is approximately 11 billion pounds. H. Patrick Jack, VP of Fina Oil & Chemical Co., predicts (based on the previous 10 years) that total demand will grow anywhere between 5 and 8 percent annually. The total capacity is currently 12.3 billion pounds. In addition, a total of 4.5 billion pounds of new capacity is under construction by eight companies in eight locations and will be ready for production within the next four years. Would total capacity be enough to meet expected demand four years from now?[2] **LO2**

14. A parts manufacturer plans to replace its existing facility with a new one. The management is considering two possible capacities for the new facility: 200,000 or 250,000 units per year. The 200,000-unit plant would have an annual fixed cost of $4.0 million and a per unit production cost of $20. The 250,000-unit plant would have an annual fixed cost of $6 million and a per unit cost of $15. The parts will be sold for an average price of $60 per unit. **LO3**

a. Calculate the break-even point for each capacity alternative.

b. Suppose that the company projects its sales to be 220,000 units per year. Which alternative would you recommend? *Hint:* Calculate the annual profit in each case.

15. The fixed cost of running a gift store (wages, rent, etc.) in a particular mall is $250,000 per year.[3] The gross margin (i.e., sales − cost of goods sold or alternatively revenue − variable cost) is 45 percent of sales. Assuming that the store is open 364 days a year, **LO3**

a. What are the minimum daily sales dollars to break even?

b. If the owner's profit target is 10 percent of sales, what are the minimum daily sales dollars?

c. If the owner's profit target is $100,000 per year, what are the minimum daily sales dollars?

---

[2] D. Richards, "Polypropylene Capacity Soars But All of It May Be Needed," *Chemical Market Reporter* 251(12), March 24, 1997, pp. 7, 9.

[3] G. Cunningham, "Breakeven Analysis Key to Profits: The Next Century Promises More Stress and Retail Unpredictability," *Gifts & Tablewares* 25(1), January 2000, p. 58.

*16. One of the first Internet-based groceries home-delivery businesses was Homegrocer.com. In 1998, Mike Donald, president of Concord Sales, one of the largest food brokers in B.C., and two partners thought of starting such a business in Vancouver. However, they had to move it to Seattle in order to get financing from the U.S. financiers. Mike thought that because Microsoft and Boeing are located in Seattle, the proportion of households with Internet would be high. After raising approximately $4 million and using it to lease a large warehouse, purchase 10 trucks, set up the web page and software, and advertise, Homegrocer.com had fewer than 1,000 regular customers. Mike estimated that an average regular customer purchased 3 times a month and bought approximately $75 each time (below $75, Homegrocer.com charged a delivery fee of $10). The gross margin (i.e., sales — cost of goods sold or alternatively revenue — variable cost) was around 20 percent, and total monthly labour and overhead costs were approximately $300,000. **LO3**

 a. How many regular customers did Homegrocer.com need in 1998 to break even?

Despite the slow initial business, Homegrocer.com persevered and even expanded into Portland, Oregon. In the frenzy of the dot.com era in 1999, private investors, including Amazon.com, invested approximately $100 million in Homegrocer.com. Homegrocer.com used the money to further expand, trying to compete with Webvan, a California-based competitor. At the beginning of 2000, Homegrocer.com raised over $250 million by issuing shares to the public, and kept on expanding to more cities in the United States. However, its share prices started to decline due to increasing losses. In mid-2000, Webvan bought Homegrocer.com for over $1 billion. Webvan itself went bankrupt in 2001.

 b. Why would a startup company want to expand so fast? Why did most Internet grocery businesses fail?[4]

*17. A few years ago, the Toronto plant of a multinational soup producer was in competition with its U.S. sister plant to supply the Northeastern U.S. market. However, its cost of production was not competitive. One source of its cost disadvantage was the tin cans. The Toronto plant bought its tin cans for approximately $6.00 per case of 48 cans, whereas the U.S. plant made its own cans at the cost of $5.00 (in Canadian dollars) per case. The manager estimated that installing an automatic can line would cost $2.0 million for building expansion and $12 million for equipment. The can line would have a variable production cost of $5.50 per case. **LO3**

 a. Assuming a useful life of 10 years, no salvage value, and straight-line depreciation, calculate the annual fixed cost of the canning line.

 b. Calculate the annual break-even quantity between buying and making the cans in-house.

 c. Draw a graph of the annual cost of buying and annual cost of making (try to make it to scale), and determine which option is better if the annual requirement of the Toronto plant was 5 million cases of cans.

18. Suppose your friend is thinking of opening a new restaurant, and she hopes that she will have around 20 groups of (on average) 4 customers on a typical busy evening. Each meal will take around 1.5 hours and it is expected that on average a table will be used twice in an evening. Each table and its surroundings will require 4 square metres of space. **LO2**

 a. Calculate the required seating area.

 b. If each meal will take an average of 12 minutes to cook on a heating element, and each stove will have 4 elements, how many stoves would the restaurant require? Assume that all 10 "tables" could come at the same time and that the kitchen should be able to cook the meal for them during their first hour of visit.

*19. Corner Tavern is a small-town bar that sells only bottled beer. The average price of a bottle of beer at the tavern is $3.00 and the average cost of a bottle of beer to the tavern is $1.00. The tavern is open every night. One bartender and two to three waitresses are on duty each night. The fixed costs (salaries, rent, tax, utilities, etc.) total $260,000 per year. **LO3**

 a. The owner wishes to know how many bottles of beer the tavern must sell during the year to start making profit.

 b. What is the revenue at the break-even quantity found in part *a*?

 c. Draw the annual revenue and total annual cost vs. the number of bottles of beer sold per year. Make sure that the *y*-axis is to scale. Identify the important points on the graph.

 d. Using the graph in part *c*, answer the following question: If Corner Tavern sells 140,000 bottles of beer a year, would it make a profit? Explain.

 e. The owner thinks $50,000 is a reasonable annual profit. How many bottles of beer should the tavern sell to make $50,000 profit?

 f. An available option is to open the tavern earlier on the weekends. The attraction would be a discount of $0.50 off the regular price. The extra salaries of waitresses and bartender for the whole year are estimated to be $30,000. How many extra bottles of beer must the tavern sell in order to break-even in this option?

[4] J. Schreiner, "Net Grocer Debuts with Little Fanfare, Big Backers . . ." *National Post*, March 11, 2000, p. C03; J. Greenwood, "Canadians Break Bread with Amazon Online Grocery Store," *National Post*, May 19, 1999, p. C01.

*20. A small brewery reuses its own empty bottles, but it does not have a bottle-cleaning machine. The empty bottles are collected from liquor stores and bars, and brought back to the brewery. Once enough empty bottles accumulate, they are trucked to a cleaning facility and clean bottles are brought back. The cleaning facility charges 10 cents to wash a bottle, and cost of trucking is 2 cents per bottle. Management is thinking of buying an automated bottle-cleaning machine. The machine costs $1 million and has a useful life of 10 years. The machine will be used only when enough empty bottles accumulate. The operating cost of the machine is expected to be $108 per hour, washing 60 bottles per minute. **LO3**

   a. How many bottles per year would have equal total annual cost of doing the cleaning in-house vs. outsourcing the cleaning? Use straight-line depreciation.

   b. What is the total annual cost at the quantity found in part a?

   c. Draw the two total annual costs vs. the quantity of bottles per year. Make sure that the y-axis is to scale. If the brewery is expected to have 1 million bottles per year to wash, which decision is less costly?

21. The following diagram shows a four-step process that begins with Operation 1 and ends with Operation 4. The rates shown in each box represent the effective capacity of that operation. **LO2**

   a. Determine the capacity of this process.

   b. Which of the following three actions would yield the greatest increase in process capacity? (i) increase the capacity of Operation 1 by 15 percent; (ii) increase the capacity of Operation 2 by 10 percent; or (iii) increase the capacity of Operation 3 by 10 percent.

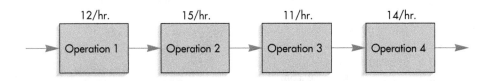

22. The mine hoist at a Mosaic Potash mine and mill in Saskatchewan had the following performance measures during a month. Determine the utilization of the hoist. **LO1**

   Total available time = 24 hours a day × 30 days × 60 minutes per hour = 43,200 minutes

   Scheduled hoist downtime (due to planned maintenance) = 5,820 minutes

   Unscheduled hoist downtime (due to breakdown) = 1,530 minutes

   Idle time due to upstream (mine) delays (mine bin empty) = 2,817 minutes

   Idle time due to downstream (mill) delays (mill bin full) = 4,578 minutes

   Source: R. Chadha, "Hoist Help," *Quality Progress*, February 2014, 47(2), 34–39.

23. Given the following diagram, **LO2**

   a. What is the capacity of this process?

   b. If the capacity of one operation could be increased in order to increase the output of the process, which operation should it be, and what amount of increase? *Note:* The upper line and lower line both produce the same product.

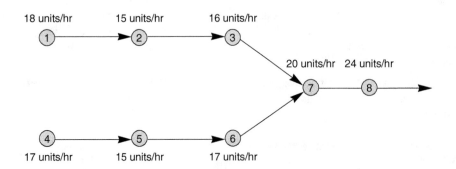

24. Find the capacity of this process:

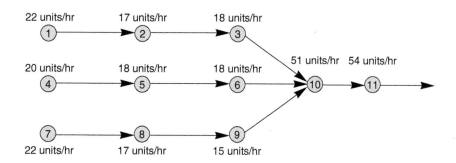

25. The following diagram describes a service process where customers go through either of two parallel three steps and then merge into a single line for two final steps. Capacities of each step are shown on the diagram. **LO2**

a. What is the current capacity of the entire process?

b. If you could increase the capacity of only one operation through process improvement efforts, which operation would you select, how much additional capacity would you strive for, and what would be the resulting capacity of the process?

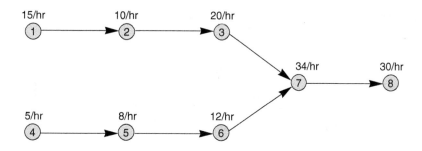

26. A new piece of equipment will cost $12,000 and will result in a reduced operation cost of $1,500 per year. What will the payback time be in years? **LO3**

27. A new machine will cost $18,000, but results in savings of $2,400 per year. What will be the payback time in years? **LO3**

28. Remodelling an office will cost $25,000 and will generate savings of $3,000 the first year, $4,000 the second year, and $5,000 per year thereafter. How long will it take to recoup the initial cost of remodelling? **LO3**

29. Mountain Aquaculture and Producers Association (MA&PA) is a small trout producers' cooperative in West Virginia. Its main product is boned, head-removed trout sold to local stores. Unfortunately, the cooperative has not made any profit since it was started in 1992 and has to rely on donations and government grants. The manager is interested to know under what circumstances would MA&PA make a profit. The building was built in 1992 for $49,000, and the processing equipment cost $37,500. The utilities cost $6,800 per year, and the building tax is $1,100 per year. A pound of whole trout

cost $1.40, and the yield is 60 percent (i.e., to make 1 pound of processed trout, 1.67 pound of whole trout is needed). It takes a worker 12 minutes to produce one pound of processed trout. The wage rate, including benefits, is $7.80 per hour. The total cost of processing supplies, advertising, and delivery is $1 per pound of processed trout. The processed trout is sold for $6.00 per pound. Use straight-line depreciation and life of 20 years for the building and 10 years for the processing equipment. **LO3**

a. Calculate the total annual fixed cost.

b. Calculate the variable cost per pound of processed trout.

c. Calculate the break-even quantity for the number of pounds of processed trout sold per year.

d. What is the minimum amount of processed trout that the cooperative must sell per year in order to make any profit?

Source: R. M. Fincham. A Break-even Analysis of Trout Processing in West Virginia: A Case Study Approach, M.S. thesis, West Virginia University, 2001.

W. C. Wood

W. C. Wood was the largest freezer manufacturer in Canada. It had two plants in Guelph, one in the United States, and another in Mexico. In the early 2000s, some appliance manufacturers, such as Whirlpool, had converted from using cardboard box packaging to using plastic stretch wrap with corner padding (called clear-view packaging). The VP of manufacturing was wondering whether to also convert. The damage warranty rate for cardboard box (1 to 3 percent depending on the type of freezer) was expected to remain the same with clear-view packaging. For simplicity, we consider only one of the Guelph plants with one line. Whereas a cardboard box required two workers to box an appliance, the clear-view packaging would be automated. Labour and material costs would be reduced by $0.50 and $1.50 per unit, respectively. However, electricity costs would increase by

$10,000 per year. The stretch wrap equipment by MSK Covertech cost $130,000. The fitting of corner posts on each freezer required another machine, which cost $140,000. In addition, all lift truck arms had to be converted to clamp type at a total cost of $30,000.

a. What is the total variable cost saving per freezer?
b. What is the total investment cost per year if all pieces of equipment are expected to last 10 years (use straight-line depreciation)?
c. How many freezers per year should the Guelph plant produce in order to break-even in the clear-view packaging conversion?

Source: http://www.hp.com/hpinfo/newsroom/press_kits/2008/ipgconference/images/clear-view-packaging-horizontal.jpg; http://www.tradekorea.com/product-detail/P00290675/Bale_clamp.html

Shoes for Moos

Jim Wells, the owner of a farm supply store in Elmira, Ontario, was thinking of introducing a new product: shoes for cows with foot (hoof) infection (rot). Jim had been approached by several farmers asking for it. He studied the market and found nothing durable and effective at the $40–$100 per shoe range. There are over 13 million dairy cows in North America, and approximately 2 percent of them develop foot infection annually (beef cows are slaughtered when this happens). Jim designed the shoe and approached Kaufman Footwear in Kitchener to make some prototypes. Next, he gave the prototypes to his farmer friends to test. After one year of design improvements, Jim was wondering whether to go ahead with marketing of the shoe. The cost of the mould

to be used by the shoe factory was $10,000, and the mould was expected to last 5 years (use straight-line depreciation). The cost of Jim's time promoting the shoe, including attending farm shows, was approximately $10,000 per year. The cost of shoe inventory and space in Jim's store was estimated to be $1,000 per year. The shoe factory wanted $20 per shoe with a minimum order size of 100 shoes. Jim was thinking of pricing a shoe at $40.

a. How many shoes per year must Jim sell to break even?
b. What is the annual cost at the BEP found in part *a*?
c. If Jim could sell 2,000 shoes per year, should he go ahead with this venture? Why?

Source: http://www.youtube.com/watch?v=VlqAQf4j7qI

CHAPTER 5
Decision Analysis

Learning Objectives

After completing this supplement, you should be able to:

LO1 Describe the decision analysis process and influence diagrams, model a single-stage decision problem as a decision table, and use the expected value approach to solve it.

LO2 Construct a decision tree and use it to analyze a multistage problem, understand and construct a risk profile chart and illustrate how a decision tree can be entered in and solved by a popular software, DPL.

LO3 Calculate expected value of perfect information (EVPI) and calculate expected value of sample (imperfect) information (EVSI) using Bayes rule.

LO4 Conduct sensitivity analysis to probability changes in a simple decision problem and understand sensitivity to input changes and a tornado chart.

LO5 Describe how risk aversion can be modelled by a utility function, and how multiple objectives can be handled.

L01 Introduction

Decision analysis is a scientific and structured method for making important difficult decisions. It was promoted in the 1960s by Professor Ron Howard of Stanford University. Decision analysis involves modelling the decision problem (alternatives, random variables, consequences/outcomes and their value) and then determining the best decision alternative that, for example, maximizes the expected value.

Decision analysis is suitable for a range of complex decisions, especially when uncertainties (i.e., random variables) are present. Among them are capacity planning, capital project selection, new product development, and medical treatment.

Decisions that lend themselves to the decision analysis approach tend to be characterized by the following elements:

1. There is at least one random variable with a set of possible values (called states of nature) that will have a bearing on the result of the decision.

2. There is a decision with a list of alternatives for the decision maker to choose from.

3. There is an outcome/consequence with a known payoff (or value) for each decision alternative under each state of nature.

Specifically, the process displayed in the chart on the left should be used:

The steps are expanded as follows. Identify the scope of decision, the decision maker(s), the decision analyst/team, the process of modelling and information gathering, and the problem. An objective may be monetary such as profit or net present value or nonmonetary such as quality-adjusted life expectancy. An objective has to be clear and measurable. Then, a list of possible *alternatives* for the decision(s) are developed using brainstorming and other creative methods in order to achieve the objective(s).

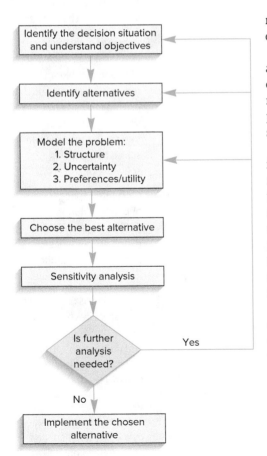

Next, random variables influencing the outcomes/payoffs are identified and the relationship between them and decision(s) and payoffs (i.e., the structure of the model of the problem) are determined using an influence diagram and a decision tree.

Then, states of nature for each random variable (e.g., low demand, medium, and high) are identified. Usually discrete random variables with a small number of states of nature are used. The *likelihood* of each state of nature has to be estimated by interviewing an expert (possibly the decision maker). This is called probability encoding. A random variable has to be clearly defined to avoid confusion of the expert. The interview should be structured to reduce experts' biases.

Next, the *payoff* (or value) associated with the outcome of each state of nature for each alternative has to be calculated. Feasibility and pros and cons of each alternative, given each state of nature, are reflected in the payoff. When values are small, the decision maker can be assumed to be risk-neutral and the payoffs are used directly to determine the best decision(s) alternative. However, for large payoffs, especially when a large loss is possible, empirical studies have shown that most people are risk averse, i.e., need to be paid to take a gamble. In this case, the utility to the decision maker of each payoff has to be measured and used to determine the alternative(s) with the best expected utility. The risk-averse utility is usually approximated by an exponential function. Utilities are described in the last section.

Then, the best alternative is determined, e.g., using the expected values. If the decision maker is risk-averse, expected utility is used. If there is more than one objective, all of them (e.g., a weighted average) are used to select the best alternative. We will focus on the single-objective case until the last section. In addition, usually the probability distribution of payoff of the best alternative (called the risk profile) is also determined in order to display the variation of the payoff if the best alternative is chosen.

Next, sensitivity of the best alternative to probabilities of random variables may be determined, i.e., as the probability of a state of nature changes, would the best alternative change? If the best alternative is sensitive to small changes in probabilities of a random variable, more information may be gathered (if the value of information is more than its cost) in order to reduce the uncertainty. In addition, the sensitivities of the best alternative to possible changes in "deterministic" inputs such as price and cost are determined and displayed as a tornado chart. An input that influences the payoff of best alternative greatly should be estimated more accurately. After a major change in data, the model should be re-solved.

In the final step, the analyst/team presents the best alternative and the reasons behind it (payoff, risk, etc.) to the decision maker(s). If accepted, the team will be involved in the implementation of the decision (e.g., proceeding with the development of a drug or exploration of an oil well).

A structured approach to decision making is important because the intuitive quick approach does not usually result in the best decision. The reasons for this are as follows:

- What is suggested first to the decision maker influences the decision (this is called anchoring).
- Most people choose to do nothing (i.e., they prefer the status quo).
- There is a tendency to waste good money after bad in order to avoid admission of having made a bad decision (this is called a sunk cost trap).
- People tend to decide intuitively and then look for confirming evidence.
- People are risk averse when a random variable (gamble) is posed in terms of gains but risk seeking when it is posed in terms of avoiding a loss, even though the two gambles are equivalent (this is called a framing trap).
- People are overconfident in estimating a random variable (i.e., they choose a small estimation range), and base their estimate on a dramatic unusual past event that they recall.

Chevron managers, like those in other oil and gas exploration companies, have to decide which prospects to explore and whether to partner with other companies. These decisions have costly consequences and have to be made under uncertainty (amount of hydrocarbon deposit, if any, is unknown). Chevron requires a structured approach to decision making. Decision analysis was introduced to Chevron employees more than 20 years ago and its use in making capital investment decisions valued over $50 million has become mandatory during the last 10 years. Chevron has approximately 100 decision analysts who are required to be certified and who assist project managers to make decisions. Projects go through peer review and feedback. There is an annual best-practice-sharing meeting of the analysts. It is generally agreed that the use of decision analysis and Chevron's culture are the main contributors to its great success.

Sources: http://decisionprofessionals.squarespace.com/storage/docs/SDP_Chevron_30Nov2010.pdf; http://www.youtube.com/chevron#p/u/12/JRCxZA6ay3M

Influence Diagrams

An influence diagram graphically represents the decision problem. The following example represents the decision of whether or not to introduce a new product. A random variable is represented by a blue circle (called a chance node), a decision is represented by a cream rectangle (called a decision node), and a payoff is represented by a green rounded square (called a payoff node). Actually, Profit is the direct payoff, and Revenue and Total Cost are the indirect payoffs (called calculation nodes in brown ovals) that determine the direct payoff. An arrow into a chance node affects its probability distribution, into a decision node determines its sequence and the information known before this decision is made, and into a payoff node determines its value (using a formula). Naturally, the nonexistence of an arrow indicates lack of influence.

Constructing and validating an influence diagram improves communication and consensus building at the beginning of the decision modelling process. Unfortunately, there is no procedure or guideline for drawing an influence diagram. Also, the context of every decision is different. Furthermore, not all the information needed to make a decision(s) is displayed in an influence diagram. For example, the following example does not show the decision alternatives and the states of nature of each random variable. Therefore, a decision tree (described later) is drawn based on the influence diagram and used to determine the best alternative(s). A decision tree is more structured than an influence diagram.

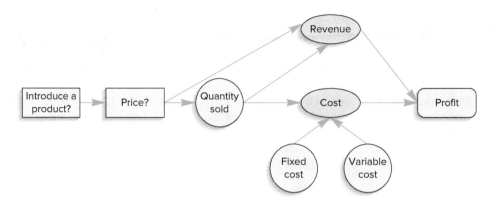

Source: Adapted from K. Chelst, "Can't See the Forest Because of the Decision Trees: A Critique of Decision Analysis in Survey Texts," *Interfaces* 28, 2, pp. 80–98.

Decision Tables

payoff table Table showing the payoff for each alternative under each state of nature of a one random-variable problem.

The data for a one random-variable problem can be summarized in a **payoff table**, which shows the payoff for each alternative under each state of nature of the random variable. These tables are helpful in choosing among alternatives because they facilitate comparison of alternatives. Consider the following payoff table, which illustrates a capacity planning problem.

| | (Future) Demand | | |
Alternatives	Low	Moderate	High
Small facility	$10*	$10	$10
Medium facility	7	12	12
Large facility	(4)	2	16

*Net present value (in $ millions).

The payoffs, in the body of the table, are net present values, which represent equivalent current dollar values of estimated future income less costs. This is a convenient measure because it places all alternatives on a comparable basis. If a small facility is built, the payoff will be $10 million for all three possible states of nature. For a medium facility, low demand will have net present value of $7 million, whereas both moderate and high demand will have net present values of $12 million. A large facility will have loss of $4 million if demand is low, net present value of $2 million if demand is moderate, and net present value of $16 million if demand is high.

The problem for the decision maker is to select one of the alternatives, taking the payoffs into account. In order to do so, the decision analyst needs to determine the probability of occurrence of each state of nature (unless one of the alternatives dominates the rest, i.e., would have the highest payoff under each state of nature). Because the states of nature for a random variable should be mutually exclusive and collectively exhaustive, these probabilities must add up to 1.00. As mentioned earlier, these probabilities are usually subjective opinions of experts. The decision analyst interviewing an expert should be careful not to ask leading questions and should be aware of psychological biases such as overconfidence or intentional underestimation by marketing/sales managers (to make meeting these goals easier). For more information on obtaining subjective probabilities, see "M. W. Merkhofer, Quantifying Judgmental Uncertainty: Methodology, Experiences, and Insights," *IEEE Transactions on Systems, Man, and Cybernetics*, 17, 5, 741–751.

Given the probabilities for each state of nature, as mentioned earlier a widely used approach is to use the *expected value (also called expected monetary value EMV)*. The expected value is calculated for each alternative, and the one with the highest expected value is selected. The expected value for an alternative is the sum over the states of nature of the payoff multiplied by probability of each state of nature.

Using the expected values, identify the best alternative for the following payoff table, given these probabilities for future demand: low = 0.30, moderate = 0.50, and high = 0.20.

◀ **Example 1**

	(Future) Demand		
Alternatives	**Low**	**Moderate**	**High**
Small facility	$10*	$10	$10
Medium facility	7	12	12
Large facility	(4)	2	16

*Net present value (in $ millions).

Calculate the expected value of each alternative by multiplying the probability of occurrence of each state of nature by the payoff of the alternative for that state of nature and summing them:

SOLUTION

$$EV_{small} = 0.30(\$10) + 0.50(\$10) + 0.20(\$10) = \$10$$
$$EV_{medium} = 0.30(\$7) + 0.50(\$12) + 0.20(\$12) = \$10.5$$
$$EV_{large} = 0.30(-\$4) + 0.50(\$2) + 0.20(\$16) = \$3$$

Hence, choose the medium facility because it has the highest expected net present value.

As mentioned earlier, expected value is appropriate when a decision maker is neither risk averse nor risk seeking, but is risk neutral. Note that the expected-value amount (e.g., $10.5 million in Example 1) is not an actual payoff but an expected or average amount that would be achieved if a large number of identical decisions were to be made. If the decision maker is risk averse, then he tends to consider the downside risk of payoff. For a risk-averse decision maker, the minimum payoff, if the medium facility is built, $7 million, may still be acceptable. If it is not, he may seek more accurate information about demand or choose to build a small facility that has a higher minimum payoff ($10 million). As mentioned earlier, a formal approach to deal with risk-averse decision makers is to use utilities (see the last section).

More complex decision problems will have more than one decision variable (e.g., a multistage decision problem) and/or more than one random variable. In this case, the decision problem cannot be represented by a table. Instead, decision trees are used to graphically model and solve the decision problem.

Decision Trees

A **decision tree** is a graphical representation of the decisions, random variables and their probabilities, and the payoffs. The nodes in a decision tree are arranged according to their occurrence. The term gets its name from the treelike appearance of the diagram (see Figure 5S-1). Decision trees are particularly useful for analyzing situations that involve *sequential* or multistage decisions. For instance, a manager may initially decide to build a small facility but she has to allow for the possibility that demand may be higher than anticipated. In this case, the manager may plan to make a subsequent decision on whether to expand or build an additional facility.

A decision tree is composed of a number of *nodes* that have *branches* emanating from them (see Figure 5S-1). Nodes represent points in time. Square nodes denote decision points, and circular nodes denote chance events (random variables). Read the tree from left to right. Branches leaving decision nodes represent alternatives (the decision maker can choose the preferred branch); branches leaving chance events represent the states of nature (the decision maker has no control over these). A branch from node i to node j means that node i has already occurred and the information about the decision or state of nature determined at node i is available at node j.

After a decision tree has been drawn and necessary data collected, it is evaluated from *right to left*; that is, it is "rolled" or "folded" back. For each decision, choose the alternative that will yield the greatest (expected) payoff. For each chance node, calculate the expected value of the payoffs of its states of nature. Continue folding back until the best alternative for all decisions is determined.

decision tree A graphical representation of the decisions, random variables and their probabilities, and payoffs.

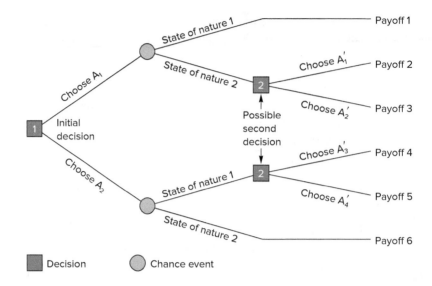

Example 2 ▶

A manager must decide the size of a video arcade to construct. The manager has narrowed the choices to two: large or small. Information has been collected on payoffs, and the following decision tree has been constructed. Determine which alternative (build small or large) should be chosen in order to maximize the expected value.

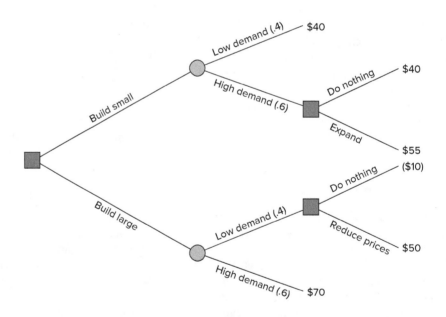

SOLUTION

The dollar amounts at the branch ends (on the right) indicate the estimated payoffs if a particular sequence of decision alternatives and states of nature occurs. For example, if the initial decision is to build a small facility and it turns out that demand is low, the payoff will be $40 (thousand). Similarly, if a small facility is built, and demand turns out high, and a later decision is made to expand, the payoff will be $55. A payoff in parentheses indicates a loss.

The figures in parentheses on branches leaving the chance nodes indicate the probabilities of those states of nature. Hence, the probability of low demand is 0.4, and the probability of high demand is 0.6. Note that these two probabilities add up to 1.0. Also note that the initial decision has to be made before demand is known and the second decision is made after demand is known. The probabilities, in general, are conditional on the decision alternative feeding into the chance node. However, in this case demand is assumed to be independent of the first decision.

Solve the tree from right to left:

1. Determine which alternative would be selected for each possible second decision. For a small facility with high demand, there are two choices: *do nothing*, or *expand*. Because *expand* has higher payoff ($55 > $40), you would choose it. You can either replace this second decision with a payoff of $55 and reduce the tree, or block the dominated alternative (do nothing) by placing a double slash through it. Similarly, for a large facility with low demand, there are two choices: *do nothing* or *reduce prices*. You would choose *reduce prices* because it has the higher payoff ($50 > −$10), so either replace this second decision by its payoff of $50 and reduce the tree, or place a double slash on the other branch (do nothing). We have chosen the former here:

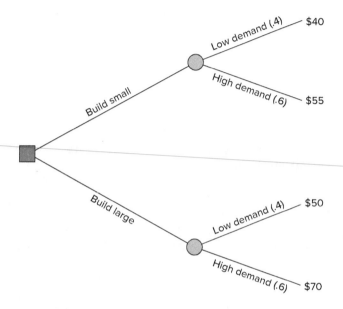

2. Now, continue with the rollback using the above reduced tree. Determine the product of the state of nature probabilities and their respective payoffs:

Chance node after Build small
 Low demand 0.4($40) = $16
 High demand 0.6($55) = $33
Chance node after Build large
 Low demand 0.4($50) = $20
 High demand 0.6($70) = $42
Therefore, the expected values of these chance nodes are:
 Chance node after Build small: $16 + $33 = $49
 Chance node after Build large: $20 + $42 = $62
Replace these chance nodes with their expected value:

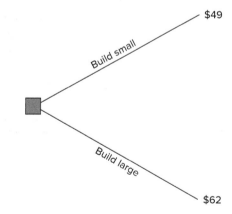

3. Continue with rollback. Clearly, the choice for the first decision should be to build a large facility because it has higher expected value than the small facility ($62 > $49).

Risk Profile

Because the decision maker is usually concerned with the downside risk of payoff, the probability distribution of the payoff of the best alternative is of interest to the decision maker. This is called the **risk profile**.

risk profile The probability distribution of payoff of the best alternative.

To determine the risk profile of the best alternative, the probability of each payoff that can be reached from the best alternative has to be determined. If there is more than one state of nature on the path from the best alternative to the payoff, their probabilities should be multiplied. Then, probabilities of the same payoff should be added. If there is only one random variable, the risk profile is simply the probability distribution of the random variable and its payoffs. For Example 2, the risk profile for Build large is displayed below:

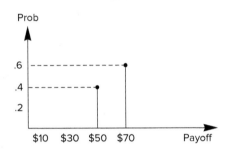

In this case the minimum payoff ($50) of Build large is larger than the minimum payoff of Build small ($40), therefore, Build large is better both in terms of average value and risk. In fact, if the cumulative probability distribution (CPD) of both large and small alternatives are drawn on the same chart, the CPD of large will be to the right of CPD of Small (this is called stochastic or probabilistic dominance), implying that any person, with any form of utility, will prefer Build large.

The above problem was entered in the popular decision analysis software DPL from Syncopation Software (http://www.syncopation.com) and solved. The process is described below.

How to Use DPL Software

Download a free trial version of DPL8 Professional from http://www.syncopation.com/dpl-8-professional-trial and install it. Click the File tab and then New. In the DPL's window, the top pane is for the influence diagram and the bottom pane is for the decision tree (however, you can split the view vertically in which case the influence diagram will be on the left). First add a decision node to the top (or left) pane: in the Model tab, click Add (top left), click the Decision icon (yellow rectangle), drag it to the centre of the top (or left) pane, click, then change the name of the node and the alternatives as follows:

Repeat this for the two versions of the second decision (we need two of these because the alternatives coming out of them have different names). Call them "React to high demand" and "React to low demand". Now, do the same for the demand node (called Discrete Chance, a green oval), change its name, and delete the nominal outcome as follows (we need only two states of nature, not three):

Continuing with Demand node definition, click Data (top left) and enter the probabilities as follows:

Now, drag the Build decision node to the bottom (or right) pane, double-click on it, click "asymmetric," and click OK. Drag the demand chance node from the top (or left) pane and drop it on the blue triangle attached to the end of the "Small" branch. Repeat this for the blue triangle at the end of the "Large" branch. Double-click on each of these chance nodes and specify asymmetric. Drag the "React to high demand" node from the top (or left) pane and drop it at the end of High outcome branch of the top demand node. Drag the "React to low demand" node from the top (or left) pane and drop it at the end of Low outcome branch of bottom demand node. Double-click on each of these decision nodes and specify asymmetric. Double-click each branch ending in a payoff and enter the payoff in front of Objective Function in the pink area. For example:

Now you have finished entering the decision model in DPL, and the panes should look as follows if you changed the view to "Vertical Split":

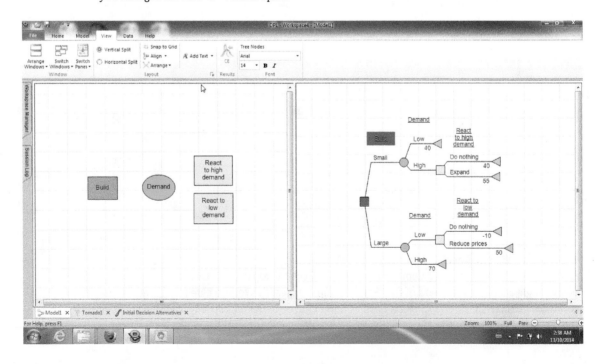

Click the Home tab, then "Decision Analysis," and finally "Fast Sequence Evaluation." The expected value solution of Example 2 in DPL is determined (called Policy Tree) and is as follows. Note that the optimal alternatives are shown with thick lines and the top nonoptimal part of tree is not shown.

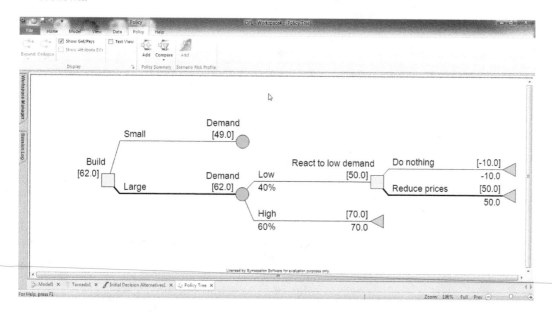

Value of Information

LO3

In certain situations, it is possible to know with more certainty which state of nature of a random variable will actually occur in the future and hence be able to make a better decision. For instance, the choice of location for a restaurant may weigh heavily on whether a new highway will be constructed nearby. A decision maker may have probabilities for this random variable; however, it may be possible to delay a decision until it is more clear which state of nature will occur. This might involve taking an option to buy the land. If the state of nature is favourable, the option can be exercised; if it is unfavourable, the option can be allowed to expire. The question to consider is whether the cost of the option will be less than the expected gain due to delaying the decision. Possible ways of obtaining information about a random variable depend on the random variable. Information about consumer preferences might come from market research, and information about technical potential of a product could come from product testing. If the information is perfect (i.e., it is 100 percent accurate and will pinpoint the state of nature of the random variable), then the expected gain in payoff is called the *expected value of perfect information*, or EVPI.

Expected value of perfect information (EVPI) is the difference between the expected payoff with perfect information (under certainty) and the expected payoff without the information (under risk).

> **expected value of perfect information (EVPI)** The difference between the expected payoff with perfect information and the expected payoff without the information.

$$\begin{matrix} \text{Expected value of} \\ \text{perfect information} \end{matrix} = \begin{matrix} \text{Expected payoff} \\ \text{under certainty} \end{matrix} - \begin{matrix} \text{Expected payoff} \\ \text{under risk} \end{matrix} \qquad (5S\text{-}1)$$

Using the information from Example 1, determine the expected value of perfect information using Formula 5S-1.

◄ Example 3

First, calculate the expected payoff under certainty. To do this, identify the best payoff under each state of nature. Then combine these by weighting each payoff by the probability of that state of nature and adding the amounts. Thus, the best payoff under low demand is $10, the best payoff under moderate demand is $12, and the best payoff under high demand is $16. The expected payoff under certainty is, then:

SOLUTION

$$0.30(\$10) + 0.50(\$12) + 0.20(\$16) = \$12.2$$

	(Future) Demand		
Alternatives	Low	Moderate	High
Small facility	$10*	$10	$10
Medium facility	7	12	12
Large facility	(4)	2	16

*Net present value (in $ millions).

The expected payoff under risk, as calculated in Example 1, is $10.5. The EVPI is the difference between these:

$$EVPI = \$12.2 - \$10.5 = \$1.7$$

EVPI indicates the upper limit on the amount the decision maker should be willing to spend to obtain information. Thus, if the cost exceeds EVPI, the decision maker would be better off not to spend additional money and simply go with the alternative that has the highest expected payoff.

In most cases, the information that can be obtained about a random variable is not perfect. In these cases, a statistical result called Bayes rule can be used to update the (prior) probability distribution of the states of nature of a random variable. The difference between the expected payoff with imperfect (sample) information and the expected payoff without sample information (i.e., under risk) is called the **expected value of sample information (EVSI)**.

expected value of sample information (EVSI) The difference between the expected payoff with sample (imperfect) information and the expected payoff without sample information (i.e., under risk).

Bayes Rule. Let A be an "information" event, and let B_1 and B_2 be mutually exclusive and exhaustive states of nature. Let $P(B_1)$ and $P(B_2)$ be the prior probabilities of the states of nature, and $P(A \mid B_1)$ and $P(A \mid B_2)$ be the likelihood of observing A given B_1 and B_2, respectively (i.e., the conditional probabilities). Then, the posterior probabilities $P(B_1 \mid A)$ and $P(B_2 \mid A)$ are:

$$P(B_1 \mid A) = (P(A \mid B_1)P(B_1))/(P(A \mid B_1)P(B_1) + P(A \mid B_2)P(B_2))$$

$$P(B_2 \mid A) = 1 - P(B_1 \mid A)$$

Note: $P(A) = P(A \mid B_1) P(B_1) + P(A \mid B_2) P(B_2)$.

Example 4 ▶

A manager is considering random drug testing of his employees. However, the test is not 100 percent accurate. The conditional probabilities are as follows: If a person uses drugs, then the test will be positive 93 percent of the time, whereas if he is not, the test will be negative 97 percent of the time. Suppose that 5 percent of the employees are drug users.

a. What are the posterior probabilities, i.e., the probabilities that a drug user and a nonuser are correctly identified after drug testing?

b. If the cost of not identifying (and dismissing) a drug user is $1,000, cost of falsely accusing a nonuser is $200, and other costs are zero, what is the maximum the manager should be willing to pay for a drug test, i.e., EVSI?

SOLUTION

a. Consider a random employee. Let B_1 = the event that he is a drug user, B_2 = the event that he is not a drug user. We have $P(B_1) = .05$ and hence $P(B_2) = 1 - .05 = .95$. Let $A+ =$ the event that test result is positive. We have $P(A + \mid B_1) = .93$ and $P(A + \mid B_2) = 1 - .97 = .03$. Then,

$$P(B_1 \mid A+) = (.93(.05))/(.93(.05) + .03(.95)) = .62$$

$$P(B_2 \mid A+) = 1 - .62 = .38.$$

Also, $P(A+) = P(A + \mid B_1)P(B_1) + P(A + \mid B_2)P(B_2) = .93(.05) + .03(.95) = .075,$

And $P(A-) = 1 - P(A+) = 1 - .075 = .925$

Note the relatively low (62 percent) probability that a drug user will be identified and a relatively high (38 percent) probability that a nonuser will be implicated.

Similarly $P(A - | B_1) = 1 - .93 = .07$ and $P(A - | B_2) = .97$, and

$P(B_1 | A-) = (.07(.05))/(.07(.05) + .97(.95)) = .0038$ and

$P(B_2 | A-) = 1 - .0038 = .9962$.

Note that if the drug test is negative, the probability that the employee tested is a nonuser is very high (.9962).

b. EVSI can be determined from the following decision tree. Note that negative payoffs are costs and the probabilities obtained in part *a* are used for outcomes related to drug testing. For example, the probability that an employee is a drug user, given a positive test result, is .62.

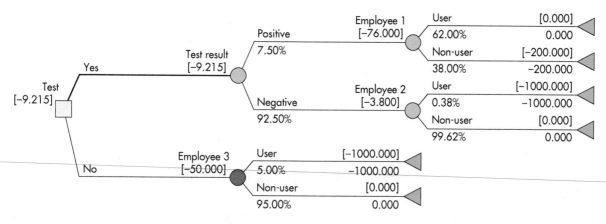

The maximum that the manager should pay for a drug test for an employee (i.e., EVSI) is $50 - $9.215 = $40.785.

Sensitivity Analysis

Generally speaking, both the payoffs (and its components such as price and cost) and the probabilities in a decision problem are estimated values. Consequently, it can be useful for the decision maker to have some indication of how sensitive the choice of an alternative is to changes in one or more of these values. Unfortunately, it is impossible to consider all possible combinations of every change in a typical problem. Nevertheless, we will consider two types of sensitivity: (1) sensitivity to probability in a small problem, and (2) sensitivity to a "deterministic" input (a component of a payoff).

Sensitivity to Probability

Sensitivity to probability provides the range of probability over which an alternative has the best expected payoff. The approach illustrated here is useful when there are two states of nature. It involves constructing a graph and then using algebra to determine the range of probabilities for which a given alternative is best. In effect, the graph provides a visual indication of the range of probability over which various alternatives are optimal, and the algebra provides exact values of the endpoints of the ranges. Example 5 illustrates the procedure.

sensitivity to probability Determining the range of probability for which an alternative has the best expected payoff.

Given the following payoff table, determine the range of probability for state of nature #2, P_2, for which each alternative is optimal using the expected values.

◀ **Example 5**

		State of Nature	
		#1	**#2**
	A	4	12
Alternative	B	16	2
	C	12	8

First, plot the expected payoff of each alternative relative to P_2. To do this, plot the #1 payoff on the left side of the following graph and the #2 payoff on the right side. For instance, for alternative A, plot 4 on the left side of the graph and 12 on the right side. Then, connect these two points with a straight line. The three alternatives are plotted on the graph as shown below.

The graph shows the range of values of P_2 over which each alternative is optimal. Thus, for low values of P_2 (and thus high values of P_1, since $P_1 + P_2 = 1.0$), alternative B will have the highest expected value; for intermediate values of P_2 alternative C is best; and for higher values of P_2 alternative A is best.

To find exact values of the ranges, determine where the lines intersect. Note that at the intersections, the two alternatives represented by the lines would be equivalent in terms of expected value; hence, the decision maker would be indifferent between the two at that point. To determine the intersections, you must obtain the equation of each line. Because these are straight lines, they have the form $y = a + bx$, where a is the y-intercept value at the left axis, b is the slope of the line, and x is P_2. Slope is defined as the change in y for a one-unit change in x. In this case, the distance between the two vertical axes is 1.0. Consequently, the slope of each line is equal to the right-hand value minus the left-hand value. The slopes and equations are:

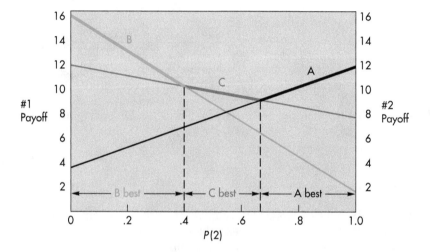

	#1	#2	Slope	Equation
A	4	12	$12 - 4 = +8$	$4 + 8\,P_2$
B	16	2	$2 - 16 = -14$	$16 - 14\,P_2$
C	12	8	$8 - 12 = -4$	$12 - 4\,P_2$

From the graph, we can see that alternative B is best from the point $P_2 = 0$ to the point where the alternative B line intersects the alternative C line. To find that point, solve for the value of P_2 at their intersection. This requires setting the two equations equal to each other and solving for P_2. Thus,

$$16 - 14\,P_2 = 12 - 4\,P_2$$

Rearranging terms yields

$$4 = 10\,P_2$$

Solving yields $P_2 = .40$. Thus, alternative B is best from $P_2 = 0$ up to $P_2 = .40$. Alternatives B and C are equivalent at $P_2 = .40$.

Alternative C is best from that point until its line intersects alternative A's line. To find that intersection, set those two equations equal and solve for P_2. Thus,

$$4 + 8\,P_2 = 12 - 4\,P_2$$

Rearranging terms results in

$$12\,P_2 = 8$$

Solving yields $P_2 = .67$. Thus, alternative C is best from $P_2 > .40$ up to $P_2 = .67$, where alternatives A and C are equivalent. For values of P_2 greater than .67 up to $P_2 = 1.0$, alternative A is best.

Note: If a problem calls for ranges with respect to P_1, you could find the P_2 ranges as above, and then subtract each P_2 from 1.00 (e.g., .40 becomes .60, and .67 becomes .33).

Sensitivity to Input

An input has a deterministic "nominal" value that is initially estimated as such. Inputs (e.g., price, cost) are components of payoffs. However, the nominal value is probably not exact and a range from low to high can be determined for its value. It would be difficult to vary all inputs simultaneously to see their effect on the best alternative. So, this perturbation is usually done one input at a time, leaving the other inputs at their nominal value. The resulting range of payoff for the best alternative as a result of varying each input is displayed in the tornado chart.

Tornado Chart. A tornado chart is a horizontal bar chart, named as such because the more important inputs, those that affect the best alternative's payoff most and hence have a longer bar, are placed on the top, making the chart look like a tornado. An influential input, especially one with large downside payoff, should in fact be considered a random variable and its values and probabilities properly estimated (i.e., more information should be collected). In fact some analysts start with a deterministic model of decision problem, then find the influential inputs using the tornado chart, next treat these inputs as random variables, and re-solve until the tornado chart does not show any more influential inputs.

◀ Example 6

Reconsider Example 2, the video arcade problem. Suppose the payoff (profit) is calculated as follows: revenue − cost. Revenue is number of customers times revenue per customer. Cost is amortized building cost plus operating costs. The nominal values are as follows: High demand = 30,000 per year, low demand = 15,000 per year, revenue per customer = $5, reduced-price revenue per customer = $4.5, increased demand as a result of reduced prices = 28,889, and cost per year of Build large = $80,000. Using the nominal values, the payoff (profit per year) for Build large and high demand is 30,000($5) − $80,000 = $70,000, and for low demand/reduced prices/increased demand is 28,889($4.5) − $80,000 = $50,000. These are what were given in Example 2.

Now, the analyst would like to investigate the sensitivity of Build large alternative and its expected payoff (recall it was $62,000 in Example 2) to the values of some of these inputs to payoff calculation. The experts are asked for a range of values for each input and the following are their answers [low, high]: High demand = [25,000, 35,000], Increased demand as a result of reduced prices = [15,000, 30,000], cost per year of Build large = [$70,000, $90,000]. Determine and draw the tornado chart.

SOLUTION

The low and high of expected payoff for each of these input ranges, while keeping the other inputs at their nominal value, are as follows:

High demand:

Build large and High demand payoff = [25,000($5) − $80,000, 35,000($5) − $80,000] = [$45,000, $95,000]

Expected payoff of Build large = [.4($50,000) + .6($45,000), .4($50,000) + .6($95,000)] = [$47,000, $77,000]

Increased demand as a result of reduced prices:

Build large and Low (but increased as a result of reduced prices) demand payoff
= [15,000($4.5) − $80,000, 30,000($4.5) − $80,000] = [−$12,500, $55,000]

Expected payoff of Build large
= [.4(−$12,500) + .6($70,000), .4($55,000) + .6($70,000)] = [$37,000, $64,000]

Cost per year:

Build large and High demand payoff = [30,000($5) − $90,000, 30,000($5) − $70,000] = [$60,000, $80,000]

Build large and Low (but increased as a result of reduced prices) demand payoff

= [28,889($4.5) − $90,000, 28,889($4.5) − $70,000] = [$40,000, $60,000]

Expected payoff of Build large = [.4($40,000) + .6($60,000), .4($60,000) + .6($80,000)] = [$52,000, $72,000]

The ranges of expected payoff for changes in the above inputs are $30,000, $27,000, and $20,000, respectively, by chance in decreasing order of size. Therefore, the tornado chart is as follows:

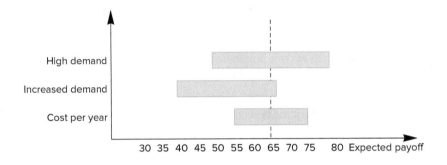

Even though "Increased demand as a result of reduced prices" is not at the top of the tornado chart, its expected downside payoff may be of concern to the decision maker. Perhaps this can be further investigated and made into a random variable.

 OM in ACTION

Oglethorpe Power

Oglethorpe Power is an electric generation and distribution cooperative supplying 20 percent of the electricity used in Georgia. Most of the remaining demand for electricity in Georgia is supplied by Georgia Power Co. Oglethorpe and Georgia Power jointly own most of the power transmission lines in Georgia, and supply their excess electricity to Florida.

Some years ago, Florida Power and Light (FPL) indicated to Oglethorpe that the organization was interested in the construction of another major transmission line between Florida and Georgia. Oglethorpe invited the consulting company Applied Decision Analysis Inc. to assist it in making a decision.

A team was formed to investigate the decision variables, random variables, and their payoffs. Brainstorming resulted in an influence diagram and identification of the three decision variables (alternatives): line (joint with Georgia Power, alone, or no line), nature of control (Oglethorpe, or FPL), and whether to upgrade the associated facilities (joint with Georgia Power, alone, or no upgrade). Five random variables (states of nature) were identified: construction cost (low, medium, or high), competitive situation in Florida (good, fair, or bad), Florida demand (low, medium, or high), Oglethorpe's share of demand (very low, low, medium, high, or very high), and future spot price for electricity (low, medium, or high). The payoffs were measured in terms of net present value.

The team estimated the probability of the states of nature for each random variable with the help of the planning staff ("experts") within Oglethorpe and the payoff for each combination of decision alternatives and states of nature. Using the DPL software, the alternative (in brackets) for each decision variable with highest expected value was line (alone), control (Oglethorpe), and upgrade (no). Then, the risk profile (the distribution of NPV) of this solution was determined by DPL. Because this showed considerable possible negative NPV, the team identified the random variable that affected the downside risk (and for which further information could be gathered): the competitive situation in Florida. The next step was to collect further information on this random variable (the value of this information was computed to be very high) in order to reduce the range of values for the payoff. The team also performed sensitivity analysis of all the inputs (e.g., the discount rate) and found that the optimal decisions [line (alone), control (Oglethorpe), and upgrade (no)] are fairly robust. The team presented all its findings to top management (including the risk profile of joint line and no line), who started negotiating with FPL.

Applied Decision Analysis, Inc. is now part of PricewaterhouseCoopers.

Source: A. Borison, "Oglethorpe Power Corporation Decides about Investing in a Major Transmission System," *Interfaces* (25)2, pp. 25–36.

Modelling Preferences/Utilities

Previously we have indicated that using expected payoff may not quite reflect the preference and attitude-towards-risk of the decision maker. A formal approach to include preferences is to use utilities. A utility is a quantification of a person's value for various payoffs. Empirical studies have identified that most people are risk averse (this is the reason most people buy insurance). A common risk-averse utility function is the exponential function:

$$U(x) = 1 - e^{-x/R}$$

where x is the payoff and R is the risk tolerance. A wealthier person or larger organization has a larger R. R is that payoff such that the decision maker is indifferent between zero payoff and a gamble with 50-50 chance of receiving R dollars or losing R/2 dollars. For example, exponential utility with R = $100,000 is as follows:

Exponential Utility with Risk Tolerance R = $100,000

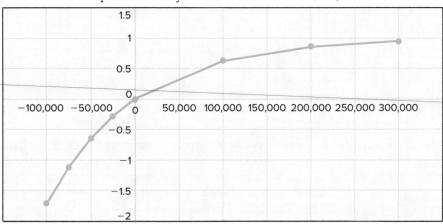

Consider the video arcade problem of Example 2, but suppose that the decision maker has exponential utility with risk tolerance R = $100,000. How would the answer change?

◀ **Example 7**

We first need to translate the dollar payoffs into utils (the unit of utility). Specifically, U($40,000) = .33, U($55,000) = .42, U(−$10,000) = −.105, U($50,000) = .39, and U($70,000) = .5. Using these in the problem as payoffs would present the following decision tree:

SOLUTION

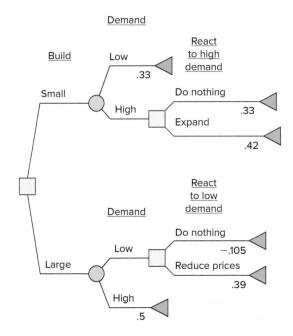

The alternative that maximizes the expected utility is still Build large (note that DPL rounds the utils to one decimal digit):

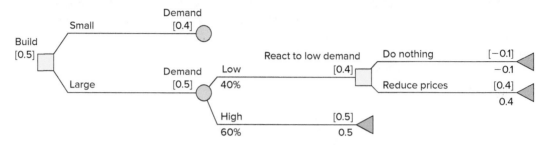

More exactly, the utility of Build large is $.4(.39) + .6(.5) = .456$.

As utils don't have an intuitive interpretation, a util is frequently translated back into dollars. This is called its certainty equivalent. The equation $U(x) = 1 - e^{-x/R}$ is used in reverse to do so: $1 - U(x) = e^{-x/R}$; take natural log of both sides: $-x/R = \ln(1 - U(x))$ or

$$x = -R \ln(1 - U(x))$$

For Example 7, the certainty equivalent to $U(x) = .456$ is $x = -\$100,000 \ln(1 - .456) = \$60,881$. Note that this is only a little smaller than the expected payoff of $62,000. The difference is called risk premium. In this case, risk premium is $\$62,000 - \$60,881 = \$1,119$.

Multiple Objectives

Multi-objective decisions occur when not all of the consequences/outcomes can be quantified into one measure (usually dollars). These cases mostly occur for government agencies whose objectives are not limited to dollars, but also include public safety and environmental steward-ship. For example, B.C. Hydro studied its strategic values and determined that they consist of economic, environmental, health & safety, and service quality.[1]

If the objectives can be measured, but not in one unit, it may be possible to compose a weighted sum of the scores of each consequence/outcome and use that as "payoff." For example, if a consequence/outcome has $10 million economic cost and results in 5,000 hectares of lost forest, its payoff may be measured as $10(.395) + 5000(.0025)(.25) = 3.95 + 3.125 = 7.075$, where .395 and .25 are weights of economic and environment objectives, respectively, and .0025 is the scale used for a hectare lost (in million dollars; in effect a hectare is worth $2,500).

If the objectives cannot be measured but weights for the objectives can be determined, then consequences for each objective have to be subjectively scored by the decision maker and a weighted score for each consequence determined (similar to factor rating method). If weights of objectives cannot be determined, an overall subjective score for each consequence has to be determined (similar to a utility) and used in decision tree evaluation.

Summary

- Decision analysis is a formal approach to decision making. It involves identifying the decision alternatives, chance events (random variables) and their probabilities, and payoffs. A visual tool useful for modelling the decision problem is an influence diagram. A simple decision problem can be represented as a decision table. A common evaluation method uses the expected values.

- Complex decision problems are modelled as a decision tree. In addition to using the expected values to determine the best alternative, the probability distribution of payoff for the best alternative is determined and displayed (called the risk profile). Downside risk of payoff is a concern and may be reduced by gathering more information. A popular decision analysis software is DPL.

[1] R.L. Keeney and T.L. McDaniels, Value-focused Thinking about Strategic Decisions at BC Hydro, *Interfaces*, 22, 6, 94–109.

- Information can be used to reduce the variability of the important random variables. Two concepts that can be used in deciding whether or not to buy information are expected value of perfect information (EVPI) and expected value of sample information (EVSI). EVSI uses Bayes rule to determine conditional probabilities.

- Graphical sensitivity analysis can be used for simple problems to determine the effect of variability of probabilities assigned to states of nature on the best alternative (called sensitivity to probability). Also, sensitivity of expected

payoff of best alternative to a fixed input (used to determine payoffs) can be determined. These are plotted in the tornado chart (most important input on the top).

- Utilities are used to measure the preference of a decision maker when risk is involved. Most people are risk-averse. A common utility form is the exponential function. Certainty equivalent is a sure payoff that has the same utility as a gamble. Multiple objectives occur when it is hard to measure consequences in one unit. It requires that the decision maker scores each outcome's objectives (similar to utilities).

Key Terms

decision tree
expected value of perfect information
 (EVPI)

expected value of sample information (EVSI)
payoff table
risk profile

sensitivity
sensitivity analysis
sensitivity to probability

Solved Problems

The following solved problems 1–4 refer to this payoff (profits) table:

		New Bridge Built	No New Bridge
Alternative capacity for new store	A	1	14
	B	2	10
	C	4	6

where A = small, B = medium, and C = large.

Problem 1

Using graphical sensitivity to probability, determine the probability for "No New Bridge" state of nature for which each alternative would be optimal.

Solution

Plot a straight line for each alternative. Do this by plotting the payoff for "new bridge built" on the left axis and the payoff for "no new bridge" on the right axis, and then connecting the two points with a straight line. Each line represents the expected profit for an alternative for the entire range of probability of "no new bridge." Because the lines represent expected profit, the line that is highest for a given value of *P*(no new bridge) is optimal. Thus, from the graph, you can see that for low values of this probability, alternative C is best, and for higher values, alternative A is best (alternative B is never the highest line, so it is never optimal, i.e., it is dominated).

   The dividing line between the ranges where alternatives *C* and *A* are optimal occurs where the two lines intersect. To find that probability, first formulate the equation for each line. To do this, let the intersection with the left axis be the *y* intercept; the slope equals the right-side payoff minus the left-side payoff. Thus, for C you have $4 + (6 - 4)P$, which is $4 + 2P$. For A, $1 + (14 - 1)P$, which is $1 + 13P$. Setting these two equal to each other, you can solve for *P*:

$$4 + 2P = 1 + 13P$$

   Solving, $P = 3/11 = .27$. Therefore, the ranges for *P*(no new bridge) for each alternative to be best are:

   A: $.27 \leq P \leq 1.00$

   B: never optimal

   C: $0 \leq P \leq .27$

Problem 2

Using the probabilities of .60 for a new bridge and .40 for no new bridge,

   a. Calculate the expected value of each alternative, and identify the alternative that would be selected using expected values.
   b. Construct a decision tree for the problem showing expected values.

Solution

   a. A: $.60(1) + .40(14) = 6.20$ [best]
   B: $.60(2) + .40(10) = 5.20$
   C: $.60(4) + .40(6) = 4.80$

   b.

Expected
values

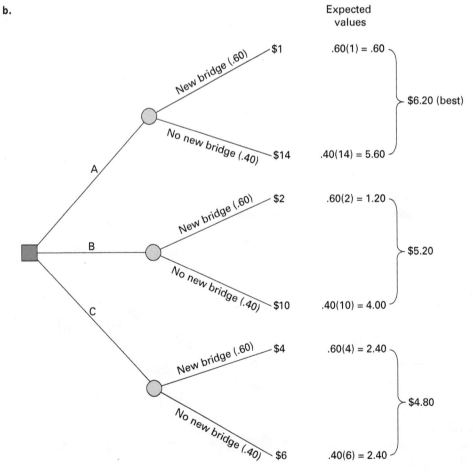

Problem 3

Calculate the EVPI using the data from the previous problem.

Solution

Using Formula 5S-1, the EVPI is the expected payoff under certainty minus the expected payoff under risk (i.e., the maximum expected value). The expected payoff under certainty involves multiplying the best payoff in each column by the column probability and then summing those amounts. The best payoff in the first column is 4, and the best in the second column is 14. Thus,

Expected payoff under certainty $= .60(4) + .40(14) = 8.00$

The maximum expected value is 6.20 from the previous problem. Therefore,

EVPI $= 8.00 - 6.20 = 1.80$

Problem 4

Suppose that the values in the payoff table represent *costs* instead of profits.

a. Using sensitivity to probability, determine the range of P(no new bridge) for which each alternative would be optimal.
b. If P(new bridge) $= .60$ and P(no new bridge) $= .40$, find the alternative to minimize expected cost.

Solution

a. The graph is identical to that shown in Solved Problem 1. However, the lines now represent expected *costs*, so the best alternative for a given value of P(no new bridge) is the *lowest* line. Hence, for very low values of P(no new bridge), A is best; for intermediate values, B is best; and for high values, C is best. You can set the equations of A and B, and B and C, equal to each other in order to determine the values of P(no new bridge) at their intersections.

Thus,

$A = B$: $1 + 13P = 2 + 8P$, solving, $P = 1/5 = .20$
$B = C$: $2 + 8P = 4 + 2P$, solving, $P = 2/6 = .33$

Hence, the ranges are:

A best: $0 \le P \le .20$
B best: $.20 \le P \le .33$
C best: $.33 \le P \le 1.00$

b. Expected value calculations are the same whether the values represent costs or profits. Hence, the expected payoffs for costs are the same as the expected payoffs for profits that were calculated in Solved Problem 1. However, now you want the alternative that has the *lowest* expected payoff rather than the one with the highest payoff. Consequently, alternative C is the best because its expected payoff (4.8) is the lowest of the three (6.2, 5.2, 4.8).

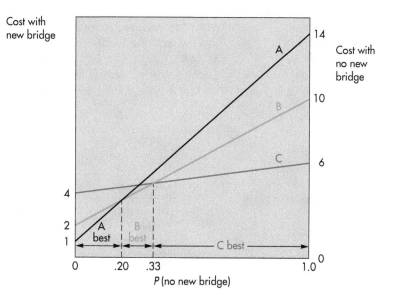

Problem 5

A diagnostic test of a certain disease has 95 percent sensitivity (i.e., probability that the test will be positive for a patient with the disease) and 96 percent specificity (i.e., probability that the test will be negative for a healthy person). Only 1 percent of the population has the disease in question. If the diagnostic test reports that a person chosen at random tests positive, what is the conditional probability that the person does, in fact, have the disease?

Solution

$P(+\text{test} \mid \text{disease}) = .95$

$P(-\text{test} \mid \text{no disease}) = .96$

$P(\text{disease}) = .01$

$P(\text{disease} \mid + \text{test}) = ?$

Bayes rule:

$P(\text{disease} \mid + \text{test})$

$= (P(+test|disease)P(disease))/(P(+test|disease)P(disease) + P(+test|no\ disease)P(no\ disease))$

$= \dfrac{.95(.01)}{.95(.01) + (1 - .96)(1 - .01)} = 0.1935$

or 19.35 percent, a small probability.

Discussion and Review Questions

Note: An asterisk indicates that a question or problem may be more challenging.

1. What is decision analysis? **LO1**

2. When should decision analysis be used? **LO1**

3. Why is decision analysis important? **LO1**

4. Under what circumstances is using expected value appropriate? When isn't it appropriate? **LO1**

5. When using expected values, suppose there is a tie between two alternatives. How should the decision maker make the decision? **LO2**

6. What is the difference between a decision tree and an influence diagram? When should each be used? **LO1 & 2**

7. What is a risk profile? **LO2**

8. Will expected value of perfect information be always greater than or equal to expected value of sample information? Briefly explain. **LO3**

9. What is sensitivity analysis, and how can it be useful to a decision maker? **LO4**

10. What is a tornado chart? **LO4**

11. What is utility? **LO5**

Internet Exercises

1. Read http://www.decisionprofessionals.com/storage/docs/Beccue%20-%20Transforming%20Culture%20of%20Startegic%20DM%20for%20Biotech%20Organization.pdf and http://daag.net/uploads/3/0/4/4/3044791/sprint_daag_2012.pdf, and summarize how decision analysis is being used in Baxter. **LO1–4**

2. Visit http://gunston.gmu.edu/healthscience/730/IntroductionToDecisionAnalysis.asp?E=0#Organization_of_the_Book, browse through the "Introduction to Decision Analysis" section, find out why some decisions are hard to make, and list them. **LO1**

Problems

1. A small building contractor has recently experienced two successive years in which work opportunities exceeded the firm's capacity. The contractor must now make a decision on capacity for next year. Estimated profit for each alternative under each of the two possible states of nature for next year's demand is shown to the right. **LO1–3**

| | Next Year's Demand | |
Alternative	Low	High
Do nothing	$50*	$60
Expand	20	80
Subcontract	40	70

*Profit in $ thousands.

Suppose after a certain amount of discussion, the contractor is able to subjectively assess the probabilities of low and high demand as: $P(low) = .3$ and $P(high) = .7$.

a. Determine the expected profit of each alternative. Which alternative is best?

b. Analyze the problem using a decision tree. Show the expected profit of each alternative on the tree.

c. Calculate the expected value of perfect information. How could the contractor use this knowledge?

2. Refer to Problem 1. Construct a graph that will enable you to perform sensitivity to probability on the problem. Over what range of $P(high)$ would each of the alternatives be best? **LO4**

3. A company that plans to expand its product line must decide whether to build a small or a large facility to produce the new products. If it builds a small facility and demand is low, the net present value after deducting for building costs will be $400,000; If demand is high, the company can either maintain the small facility or

expand it. Expansion would have a net present value of $450,000, and maintaining the small facility would have a net present value of $350,000. **LO2–5**

If a large facility is built and demand is high, the estimated net present value is $800,000; If demand turns out to be low, the net present value will be −$10,000.

The probability that demand will be high is estimated to be .60, and the probability of low demand is estimated to be .40.

a. Analyze this decision problem using a decision tree.

b. Draw the risk profile (for the better alternative).

c. Calculate the EVPI. How could this information be used?

d. Determine the range of $P(demand\ low)$ over which each alternative would be better.

e. Use an exponential utility with risk tolerance R = $300,000 to evaluate this problem.

4. Determine the course of action that has the highest expected payoff for the decision tree below. **LO2**

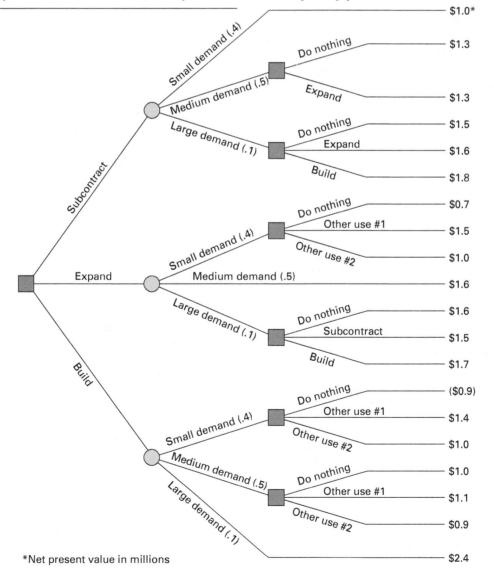

*Net present value in millions

5. The lease of an amusement park is about to expire. Management must decide whether to renew the lease for another 10 years or to relocate near the site of a proposed resort. The town planning board is currently debating the merits of granting approval to the resort. A consultant has estimated the net present value of amusement park's two alternatives under each state of nature as shown below. **LO1–3**

Options	Resort Approved	Resort Rejected
Renew (current location)	$3,000,000	$4,000,000
Relocate near resort	$5,000,000	$2,000,000

Suppose that the management of the amusement park has decided that there is a 75 percent probability that the resort's application will be approved.

a. If the management uses expected values, which alternative should it choose?
b. Represent this problem in the form of a decision tree and solve it.
c. If the management has been offered the option of a temporary lease while the town planning board considers the resort's application, would you advise the management to sign the lease? The temporary lease will cost $200,000.

6. Construct a graph that can be used for sensitivity to probability of the preceding problem. **LO4**

a. How sensitive is the solution to the problem in terms of the probability estimate of 0.75?
b. Suppose that, after consulting with a member of the town planning board, management decides that the estimate of resort approval should be 0.60. How sensitive is the solution to this revised estimate? Explain.
c. Suppose that management is confident of all the estimated payoffs except for $5 million. If the probability of resort approval is .60, for what range of payoff for relocate/approved will the relocate alternative remain optimal?

7. A company must decide whether to construct a small, medium, or large plant. A consultant's report indicates a 0.20 probability that demand will be low and a 0.80 probability that demand will be high.

If the company builds a small facility and demand turns out to be low, the net present value will be $42 million; if demand turns out to be high, the company can either subcontract some production and realize the net present value of $43 million or expand for a net present value of $48 million.

The company could build a medium-size facility: if demand turns out to be low, its net present value is estimated at $22 million; if demand turns out to be high, the company could do nothing and realize a net present value of $46 million, or it could expand and realize a net present value of $50 million.

If the company builds a large facility and demand is low, the net present value will be −$20 million, whereas high demand will result in a net present value of $72 million. **LO2–4**

a. Analyze this problem using a decision tree. What is the best alternative?
b. Calculate the EVPI and interpret it.
c. Perform graphical sensitivity to P(high).

8. A manager must decide how many machines of a certain type to buy. The machines will be used to manufacture a new gear for which there is increased demand. The manager has narrowed the decision to two alternatives: buy one machine or buy two machines. If only one machine is purchased and demand is more than it can handle, a second machine can be purchased at a later time. However, the cost per machine would be lower if the two machines were purchased at the same time.

The estimated probability of low demand is 0.30, and the estimated probability of high demand is 0.70.

The net present value associated with the purchase of two machines initially is $75,000 if demand is low and $130,000 if demand is high.

The net present value for one machine and low demand is $90,000; if demand is high, there are three options: one option is to do nothing, which would have a net present value of $90,000; a second option is to subcontract some production, which would have a net present value of $110,000; the third option is to purchase a second machine, which would have a net present value of $100,000.

How many machines should the manager purchase initially? Use a decision tree to analyze this problem. **LO2**

9. Determine the course of action that has the highest expected value for the following decision tree. **LO2**

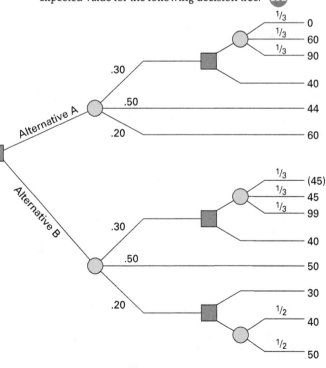

10. The director of social services of a province has learned that a new act has mandated additional information requirements. This will place an additional burden on the agency. The director has identified three alternatives to handle the increased workload. One alternative is to reassign present staff, the second is to hire and train two new workers, and the third is to redesign current practice so that workers can readily collect the information with little additional effort. An unknown factor is the caseload for the coming year when the new data will be collected on a trial basis. The estimated costs for various options and caseloads are shown in the following table: **LO1–3**

	Caseload		
	Moderate	High	Very High
Reassign staff	$50*	60	85
New staff	60	60	60
Redesign data collection	40	50	90

*Cost in $ thousands.

The director has decided that reasonable caseload probabilities are 0.10 for moderate, 0.30 for high, and 0.60 for very high.

a. Which alternative will yield minimum expected cost?

b. Construct a decision tree for this problem and solve it.

c. Determine the expected value of perfect information.

d. Suppose the director has the option of hiring an additional worker if one worker is hired initially and the caseload turns out to be high or very high. Under that plan, the cost if demand is moderate will be $40(000), the cost if demand is high will be $70(000), and the cost if demand is very high will also be $70(000). Construct a decision tree that shows this additional alternative and determine which alternative will minimize expected cost.

11. A manager has compiled estimated profits for various capacity alternatives but is reluctant to assign probabilities to the states of nature. The payoff table is: **LO4**

		State of Nature	
		#1	#2
	A	$20*	140
Alternative	B	120	80
	C	100	40

*In $ thousands.

a. Plot the expected profit lines on a graph as a function of P(#2).

b. Is there any alternative that would never be appropriate?

c. For what range of P(#2) would alternative A be the best choice?

d. For what range of P(#1) would alternative A be the best choice?

12. Repeat all parts of Problem 11, assuming the values in the payoff table are estimated *costs* and the goal is to minimize expected cost. **LO4**

13. Consider the following payoff table of estimated NPV for four alternatives: **LO4**

		State of Nature 1	State of Nature 2
	#1	$10*	−2
Alternative	#2	8	3
	#3	5	5
	#4	0	7

*In $ thousands.

Relative to the probability of state of nature 2, determine the range of probability for which each of the alternatives would maximize the expected NPV.

14. Given the following payoff table: **LO4**

		State of Nature	
		#1	#2
	A	$120*	20
Alternative	B	60	40
	C	10	110
	D	90	90

*In $ thousands.

a. Determine the range of P(#2) for which each alternative would be best, treating the payoffs as profits.

b. Answer part a, treating the payoffs as costs.

15. A law firm is representing a company that is being sued by a customer. The decision is whether to go through litigation or settle the case out of court. The cost of losing the case is estimated to be $1 million, whereas the cost of settling the case is $200,000. Winning the case in court would result in no loss. What is the minimum chance of winning for which the company should contest the case? **LO1 & 4**

16. An 18-year-old youth has just arrived at a hospital complaining of abdominal pain. The medical findings are consistent with appendicitis but not totally typical of appendicitis. The lab and X-ray test results are not clear. The surgeon is wondering whether to operate or wait 12 hours (in case it is not appendicitis). In this case, if the pain does not recede, then it must be appendicitis and the surgeon will operate. The probability that it is appendicitis is 56 percent using past experience with similar cases. Also, from similar cases, the probability that the appendicitis will perforate during the 12 hours of wait is 6 percent. The payoffs are measured in terms of death rate. The death rate of operating when appendicitis is present is 0.09 percent; it is 0.04 percent when appendicitis is not present. The death rate of operating a perforated appendicitis is 0.64 percent. Draw the

decision tree and determine the best course of action in this case.[2] **LO2**

17. An oil company has some land that may contain oil.[3] The oil reserve and its probability (based on experience in the area) are: **LO1 & 4**

Oil reserve (in 1,000 barrels)	500	200	50	0
Probability	.1	.15	.25	.50

The company has to decide whether to drill for oil or lease the land to a rancher. Cost of drilling will be $500,000 if it is a dry well or $750,000 if it is oil-producing. The profit per barrel will be $45. The revenue for leasing the land to the rancher will be $3,000,000.

a. Determine the best decision for the oil company.

b. If cost of drilling a dry well can range between $400,000 and $600,000, cost of drilling an oil-producing well can range between $600,000 and $900,000, and profit per barrel can range between $30 and $60, draw the tornado chart.

18. The board of governors of Santa Clara University is contemplating mandatory testing of its student athletes.[4] The test is not 100 percent accurate. The conditional probabilities are as follows: If an athlete uses drugs, then the test will be positive 94 percent of the time, whereas if he does not (i.e., he is a nonuser), the test will be negative 98 percent of the time. Suppose the board suspects that 4 percent of the athletes use drugs. **LO2 & 3**

a. Calculate the posterior probabilities (i.e., probability of correct identification after a drug test).

b. If a test costs $50, the cost of not identifying (and barring) a drug user is $1,000, the cost of falsely accusing a nonuser is $100, and other costs are zero, should the university test any athlete? Draw and use a decision tree.

19. An electric utility is trying to decide whether to replace the PCB transformer in a generating station with a new and safer one.[5] To evaluate this decision, the utility needs information about the likelihood of an incident, such as a fire, the cost of such an incident, and the cost of replacing the transformer. Suppose that the total cost of replacement is $75,000. If the transformer is replaced, there is virtually no chance of a fire. However, if the current transformer is retained, the probability of a fire is assessed to be 0.0025. If a fire occurs, then the clean-up cost could be high ($80 million) or low ($5 million). The probability of a high clean-up cost, given that a fire occurs, is assessed to be 0.2. **LO2 & 4**

a. Should the company replace the transformer?

b. Perform sensitivity analysis to the probability of a fire. Does the optimal decision from part *a* remain optimal for a wide range of values for this probability?

20. A 59 year-old executive has just completed his annual physical exam.[6] The exam included a test on a sample of his stool. The purpose of this test is to screen for cancer of the large intestine (colon cancer). The test looks for small amounts of blood in the stool. The executive is informed that the test showed presence of blood in his stool. The executive is quite anxious. The likelihood of any 59-year-old man having colon cancer is 1 in 1,000. The test detects 85 percent of cases of colon cancer, but 2 percent of patients without cancer have a small amount of blood in their stool. What is the probability that the executive has colon cancer? **LO3**

21. An offshore underwater structure has tested positive for oil by two exploratory wells drilled near the crest of the structure.[7] Management is now trying to determine whether it is wise to make a definite commitment to begin building a platform, and, if so, what size, or to defer the decision to allow for the drilling of an additional exploratory well. The principal uncertainty is the size of the field. If the structure is nearly filled with oil, the area of the field will be about 15 square miles and it would require installation of a large platform costing $50 million. If the structure is only partially filled with oil, the area will be much smaller and the field could be depleted with fewer wells and a smaller platform costing $30 million. Based on the subjective judgment of company's geologists, the likelihood of the structure being completely filled is 0.4 (i.e., field is large). If a small platform is built and the field turns out to be large, a second small platform will have to be built at the same cost. If another exploratory well is drilled along the flanks of the structure, there is a 10 percent chance that the result will be erroneous. However, management will base its platform size decision on the result of the exploratory well. The exploratory well will cost $2 million. **LO2 & 3**

a. Calculate the posterior probabilities given that the exploratory well indicates a small field.

b. Which decision has the lowest expected cost? Draw the decision tree.

---

[2] R. Clarke, "The Application of Decision Analysis to Clinical Medicine," *Interfaces* 17(2), pp. 27–34.

[3] F. S. Hillier and G. J. Lieberman, *Operations Research*, 2nd ed, San Francisco: Holden-Day, p. 598.

[4] C. D. Feinstein, "Deciding Whether to Test Student Athletes for Drug Use," *Interfaces* 20(3), pp. 80–87.

[5] W. E. Balson et al, "Using Decision Analysis and Risk Analysis to Manage Utility Environmental Risk," *Interfaces* 22(6), pp. 126–139.

[6] P. H. Hill et al, *Making Decisions*, Massachusetts: Addison-Wesley, p. 170.

[7] P. D. Newendorp, *Decision Analysis for Petroleum Exploration*, Tulsa, Oklahoma: PennWell Publishing, p. 524.

22. The management of a printed circuit boards (PCB) manufacturer is concerned about the significant number of bad (defective) PCBs that are being shipped to the company's customers.[8] The quality control procedure for the PCBs is as follows: each PCB is sent to a testing station where it is tested using an electronic instrument; those that pass are shipped to the customers; those that fail are retested; those that pass the second test are shipped to the customers; those that fail the second time are retested again; those that pass the third test are shipped to customers, and those that fail the third time are discarded. A consultant is brought in to examine the situation. She studied 1,136 PCBs. Of these, 1,087 passed the quality test at the first attempt. The 49 that failed were retested, and 37 passed. The remaining PCBs all failed the third time and were discarded. The consultant asked for retesting of the 37 that passed the second time. After several tests, it was discovered that 16 were defective. Also, the consultant asked for retesting of those that passed the first time. A sample of 200 was retested several times and it was discovered that 7 were defective. **L03**

    a. Calculate the probability of a good (nondefective) PCB passing the test the first time and the probability of a bad (defective) PCB failing the test the first time. Also, calculate the proportion of PCBs that are good (nondefective) and the proportion that are bad (defective).

    b. Propose a testing procedure that improves the quality of PCBs sent to the customers.

23. Decision analysis can be used to identify best decisions for a baseball manager. For example, suppose the team has a player on first base and no outs. Most managers choose to bunt, unless the batter has a particularly high batting average. Suppose the batter's average is not high and the manager has the following statistics for the average number of runs his team scored in the inning given a particular base occupied and a particular number of outs: **L02**

Expected no. of runs		Bases occupied	
Outs	None	First	Second
0	0.46	0.81	1.19
1	0.24	0.50	0.67
2	0.10	0.22	0.30

    a. Explain why, in general, bunting with a player on first base and no outs does not maximize the expected number of runs scored in the inning. Assume that the batter will be thrown out at first base.

    b. When, in general, would bunting with a player on first base and no outs be a good decision?

    c. Assume there is a player on first base and no outs. What probability of stealing second base makes it a good decision?

24. Worker's Compensation Board of B.C. receives claims from injured workers for support.[9] Some of the claims convert from short-term disability (STD) to long-term disability (LTD), which costs a lot more. So early detection of these cases helps reduce the costs. A study was done to find out a way to classify the claims into high risk (of conversion) and low risk (of conversion). The factors identified were the age of worker and the number of days a worker is on STD. These vary by type of injury. Focusing on sprains and strains, threshold days for STD, given age of worker, were determined based on costs and historical data. Given the determined classification rule, the data (number of claims for a specific period) was classified as follows: **L03**

	Claim Converts	Does Not Convert
Classified as high risk	3,580	13,396
Classified as low risk	1,479	140,645

    a. If a worker is classified as high risk, what is the probability that his/her claim converts?

    b. If a worker is classified as low risk, what is the probability that his/her claim does not convert?

25. The fecal occult blood test examines stool sample for blood.[10] It is used to test for colon and rectal cancer. A study found that out of 15,000 people over 50 years old tested, 10 percent were found to have blood in their stool. These 10 percent underwent further testing including colonoscopy. Only 2.5 percent of those had cancer. Also, 5 out of 1,000 who tested negative in the fecal blood test did eventually develop cancer. What is the sensitivity (i.e., probability of positive result given cancer) and specificity (i.e., probability of negative result given no cancer) of fecal blood test? **L03**

26. A physician has to decide whether to treat a 15-year old with sore throat, suspected of streptococcal, with antibiotics.[11] Failure to treat strep may lead to rheumatic heart disease RHD (which leads to early death). However, taking antibiotics may lead to allergic reaction (anaphylaxis) leading to death. Probability of anaphylaxis

[8] P. C. Bell, *Management Science/Operations Research: A Strategic Perspective*, Cincinnati: South-Western College Publishing, p. 90.

[9] E. Urbanovich et al, Early Detection of High-risk Claims at the Worker's Compensation Board of British Columbia, *Interfaces*, 33(4), 15–26.

[10] R.T. Clemen and T. Reilly, *Making Hard Decisions*, 2nd edition, Duxbury (Brooks/Cole), Pacific Grove, California, 2001, pp. 288–289.

[11] R.F. Nease, JR and D.K. Owens, Use of Influence Diagrams to Structure Medical Decisions, *Medical Decision Making*, 17, 263–275.

is .0003. If strep is present and there is no treatment, probability of RHD is .0063, but if there is treatment, probability of RHD is .0013. The physician estimates the probability of strep as 0.6. The physician uses quality-adjusted life expectancy (QALE) as payoff and estimates QALEs as follows: death due to anaphylaxis = 0 year, early death due to RHD = 25 years, no RHD or no strep = 60 years. Should antibiotics be prescribed? **LO3**

27. A drilling prospect has 15 percent chance of success in which case it is estimated that 6 billion cubic feet (BCF) of natural gas can be recovered.[12] No drilling has a payoff of 0. Dry hole has payoff of −$725,000. If successful, the company can decide to not drill further in which case the payoff will be $2,450,000. Otherwise, a second well can be drilled that will have a 60 percent chance of increasing the total find to 35 BCF of natural gas for a payoff of $26,500,000. If the second hole is dry, the payoff will be $485,000. **LO3 & 5**

    a. Using expected values, determine the best alternatives.
    b. Assuming exponential utility with risk tolerance of $16,667,000, what are the best alternatives? Determine the certainty equivalent.

 MINI-CASE

Southern Company

Fleet managers have a large pool of cars and trucks to maintain.[13] One approach to the vehicle maintenance is to use periodic oil analysis: the oil from the engine and transmission are subjected periodically to a test. These tests can sometimes signal an impending failure (for example, iron particles in the oil), and preventive maintenance is then performed (at a relatively low cost), eliminating the risk of failure (failure would result in a relatively high cost). However, oil analysis costs money and it is not perfect—it can indicate that a unit is defective when in fact it is not, and it can indicate that a unit is nondefective when in fact it is. As a possible substitute for oil analysis, the company could simply change the oil periodically, thereby reducing the probability of failure. The fleet manager for the Southern Company, an electrical utility based in

Atlanta (parent of Georgia Power and Light), has four alternatives: (1) do nothing, (2) use oil analysis only, (3) replace oil only, or (4) replace oil and do oil analysis. For option (1) the probability of failure is 0.1, and the cost of failure is $1,200. For option (2), the probability of failure remains at 0.1. If the unit is about to fail, the oil analysis will indicate this with probability 0.7; if the unit is not about to fail, the oil analysis will indicate this with probability 0.8. The oil analysis itself costs $20, and if it indicates that failure is about to occur, the oil will be changed at the cost of $14.80 and preventive maintenance will be performed. The cost of preventive maintenance to restore a unit that is about to fail is $500, whereas the cost of maintenance for a unit that is not about to fail is $250. For options (3) and (4), probability of failure decreases from 0.1 to 0.04. Analyze this decision problem.

 MINI-CASE

ICI Canada

ICI's Canadian subsidiary (now part of AkzoNobel) discovered a new, but un-patentable, application for a chemical agent to reduce pulp-mill water pollution.[14] However, everything was quite uncertain, and the management was trying to decide whether to go ahead with its R&D or abandon the product. The following questions indicate the primary risks:

- Would market tests confirm that there is a significant market for the product and could the company develop a new process for making this product—that is, is it technically feasible?

- After a production process is developed, would the company's board sanction production on a commercial scale?

- Would the venture turn out to be commercially successful?

The management team assumed that each of these questions had a yes or no answer. The probabilities of yes answers are shown to the right. The plus-or-minus values indicate management's uncertainty about the true probabilities.

Significant market and technical feasibility (P_1)	0.36 ± 0.09
Board sanctions plant (P_2)	0.8 ± 0.2
Commercial success (P_3)	0.8 ± 0.2

The primary economic factors and their expense/gain (in million dollars) were the following:

- The marketing development cost to determine whether there is a significant market and research expenses to identify a new production process for the product (C1): $1 ± 25%

- The process development costs, including pre-sanction engineering & commercial development (C2): $3.5 ± 25%

- The commercial development costs after the board's sanction (C3): $1.0 ± 25%

- The venture value (net present value) if successful (R): $25 ± 50%

The plus-or-minus values indicate management's considerable uncertainty about the values. Should management go ahead with R&D for this product? How can this question be fully answered?

---

[12] M.R. Walls, et al, Decision Analysis of Exploration Opportunities in the Onshore US at Phillips Petroleum Company, *Interfaces* 25, 6, 39–56.
[13] J. M. Mellichamp, "The Southern Company Uses a Probability Model for Cost Justification of Oil Sample Analysis," *Interfaces* 23(3), pp. 118–124.
[14] S. W. Hess, "Swinging on the Branch of a Tree: Project Selection Applications," *Interfaces* 23(6), pp. 5–12.

CHAPTER 6
Process Design and Facility Layout

Learning Objectives

After completing this chapter, you should be able to:

LO1 Describe the basic process types and which to select.

LO2 Explain production and service technologies.

LO3 Describe steps of process design and draw process flow diagrams.

LO4 Describe the basic plant/facility layout types.

LO5 Solve simple assembly-line balancing problems.

LO6 Develop simple process (functional) layouts.

Lavergne Groupe of Montreal is a relatively small plastics recycler, but its influence in plastics recycling has been enormous. Founder Jean Luc Lavergne started research on recycling PET (Polyethylene Terephthalate) pop plastic bottles in 1984. After decades of experiments, Lavergne has developed a unique plastics recycling expertise. So much so that in 2000 HP partnered with Lavergne to recycle the PET plastics in its inkjet cartridges. However, to get the quality of recycled PET to a level that allows HP to reuse recycled PET in its injection moulding machines to build new inkjet cartridges took more than a decade of experiments. Finally, in 2011, full recycling of PET plastics in HP inkjet cartridges started taking place. Through its recycling program called HP Planet Partners, HP receives a good portion of its inkjet cartridges back after use from consumers. In its Nashville recycling plant, inkjet cartridges are disassembled, and the plastics are shredded and shipped to Lavergne's Montreal plant. Each day a large container of shredded plastics (approximately 30,000 pounds) arrives. There, the HP shredded plastic is mixed with a larger amount of shredded PET made out of recycled pop bottles and some additives in a large V-shape blender for more than three hours. Then the mixture goes through a hot extruder, which creates spaghetti-like strands at 575°F. The strands are cooled with water, chopped, treated, packed, and shipped back to Nashville. Of course, details of the recycling process are secret. HP has produced over 1 billion new ink cartridges using Lavergne's recycled PET. Lavergne is an example of a successful company that has used its process design not only to profit but also to help the environment.

Sources: http://www.youtube.com/watch?v=5WMAORbFMtE; http://www.canadianmanufacturing.com/sustainability/canadian-innovation-changes-way-hp-recycles-plastic-products-101312; http://www.hp.com/hpinfo/globalcitizenship/environment/pdf/idc223180HPsupplies.pdf.

(L01) Introduction and Process Types

Product design, strategic capacity planning, process and layout design, and location are among the most important decisions managers must make, because they have long-term consequences for the organization.

Processes convert inputs into outputs; they are at the core of operations management. But the impact of processes goes beyond operations management: they affect the entire organization and its ability to achieve its mission. So process choices have strategic significance.

Process design and facility layout (i.e., the arrangement of the workplace) are closely tied, and for that reason these two topics are presented in a single chapter.

process design Determining the form and function of how goods or services are produced, i.e., the sequence of operations.

Process design determines the form and function of how production of goods or services is to occur, i.e., the sequence of operations. It has major implications for layout of facilities, equipment, and design of work/jobs. Process design or redesign occurs as a matter of course when new products are being designed or existing products are redesigned. However, process redesign also occurs due to technological changes in equipment and material, and methods/quality improvement.

make or buy Decide whether to make a part or product in-house or to buy it or a segment of production process from another company.

The very first step in process design is to consider whether to **make or buy** some or all of a product or a segment of the production process. If a decision is made to buy a part/product or a segment of the production process, this eliminates the need to produce the part/product or perform that segment of production process inhouse.

Make-or-buy decisions, also called insourcing/outsourcing, are often strategic, based on existing or desired core capabilities. Other factors include available capacity, quality, whether demand is steady or temporary, the secrecy of technology, and cost.

The first part of this chapter covers basic process types, technology/automation, and process design, whereas the second part is devoted to types of layout, assembly-line balancing, and designing process (functional) layouts.

job shop A process type used when a low quantity of high-variety customized goods or services is needed.

Every production process is different because the choice of operations depends on the material used and the product's shape, size, quantity, and variety. However, there are certain similarities between processes based on quantity and variety of the products that are produced by the process, and the flexibility of the process. This enables us to classify processes into four basic types: job shop, batch, repetitive (assembly line), and continuous. Projects are discussed in Chapter 17.

Job Shop

A **job shop** process is used when a low quantity of high-variety customized goods or services will be needed. The process is *intermittent*; work shifts from one small job to the next, each with somewhat different requirements. High flexibility of equipment and skilled workers are important characteristics of a job shop. A manufacturing example of a job shop is the process used by a custom spring maker that is able to produce one-of-a-kind springs. A service example is the process used in the surgery department of a hospital that is able to perform a variety of procedures.

The managerial challenge in a job shop is to schedule the jobs so that the due dates are met and the resources are utilized as much as possible.

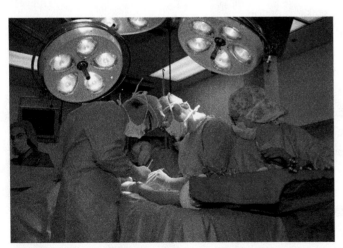

A job shop process: A hospital medical team performs a diagnostic procedure involving a cardiac catheterization.

◀ **Example 1**

Hi-Bek Precision Spring Company is a small job shop located in the centre of Hamilton, Ontario. Owned and operated by R.J. Hick, Hi-Bek fills a niche market, making custom springs for a variety of distributors and manufacturers, such as the springs in Jolly Jumper® baby exercisers, Delta Faucet products, and Frost fences. Each spring requires a unique design.

Many of Hi-Bek's customers specify the design of the spring they need, sending a blueprint or a sample of the spring with their request, which includes (1) number of pieces desired (varying anywhere from 50 to 500,000 units); (2) type of material required, gauge of wire, any finishing required, etc.; and (3) the date by which the order is required.

All of these factors are taken into consideration by Hick, who personally quotes on all orders. Naturally, it is easier for Hick to quote on jobs that Hi-Bek has done before. The quoted price is based on cost of raw material, time required to run the job, and the delivery dates (rush orders command higher margins).

After a quote has been accepted by a customer, the job order is sent to the shop floor. The shop operates from 7:30 a.m. to 5:00 p.m., Monday to Friday, employing between six and nine workers depending on the demand. Hick handles prioritization of orders and scheduling of machines and personnel along with the shop foreman. Production on a given job begins with the setup of the appropriate machine. Coiling machines can be custom configured for specific jobs, allowing for alterations to the gauge (thickness) and type of wire, the circumference and length of the spring, the number of coils in the spring, and the length of the spring ends. As well, the machine can be set to wind springs at varying speeds, depending on the level of quality required. Depending on the complexity of the product, a job being run in the machine may or may not require the full-time attention of an operator, and the time required for quality checking by the operator and foreman will vary accordingly. The setup of the job will cost the customer between $140 and $300, depending on complexity, and the skilled labour required to set up the job will cost $35 to $40 per hour. As well, customers are charged a "burden rate"–essentially a cost per hour for use of the machine during setup–of about $12 per hour. Finally, customers are charged for the operator's time to process the job, anywhere from $18 to $40 per hour.

Some jobs are quite simple, and springs are transported directly from the coiling machine to the oven on large metal racks where the steel is heated to temper it, giving the spring its tension (or its bounce, in the case of compression springs). Different springs require different temperatures (from 120°C for phosphor bronze–a low grade of wire–to 315°C for stainless steel), and a different length of time in the oven. The oven must also be scheduled for use for each individual job.

In the simplest jobs, after cooling, the springs can be packaged and arranged for shipping. In most cases, however, there are additional steps both before and after firing in the furnace.

Before firing, some springs require precision adjustments for their custom usage. The coiled springs are transported from the coiling machine to the precision-adjustment area of the shop in metal pails or large plastic drums, depending on the size of the job. An extension spring (the kind you stretch) or a torsion spring (the kind you twist) may require particularly crafted ends to suit its use. Each of these adjustments is done by hand, using a grinder or a press set for the specific job. Like the coiling machine, each press requires a certain amount of setup time and time for a shop worker to actually make the adjustments, all of which is factored into the price of the order. In the case of a press, a customer will be billed the same $140 to $300 per hour for setup though the customer is typically charged less for the labour required in the actual adjustment ($18 to $20 per hour) and the burden rate for the press (about $2 per hour).

Following the furnace, springs may undergo grinding or finishing, for either practical or aesthetic reasons. In some cases, springs are electroplated with zinc. This is a complex process involving electricity and acid or alkaline solutions, and for this reason is outsourced. Depending on the needs of the job, it may be outsourced to a company as near as Cambridge, Ontario (60 km away), or as far as Buffalo, NY (more than 100 km away). In other cases, springs are coated with oil or painted with "Black Japan" (a coating of linseed oil and Gilsonite varnish) for durability, depending on their eventual use. Unlike electroplating, these operations can be done in-house at a competitive rate.

Finally, the product is packaged and readied to be shipped. This, too, can take a good deal of time (10,000 springs can take a half day or more to pack).

The illustration below shows the layout diagram of the shop and the production process for three types of springs. The colours and icons correspond to the departments of the shop.

Job A is the type of compression spring used inside a ballpoint pen. Here, after setting up the coiling machine, the springs are wound, then heat-treated in the furnace and shipped to the customer.

Job B is a typical machine spring, which undergoes the same basic steps as the ballpoint pen spring, but has its ends ground and is coated with oil in the finishing stage to add durability to the spring before shipping.

Job C is Jolly Jumper® springs. In this case, the coiling machine requires a special setup, because the Jolly Jumper® springs require tapered ends. After this, each spring must be precision adjusted to give it an especially looped end. It is heat treated, but before shipping is sent to an outside company to be electroplated. The springs then return to Hi-Bek and are shipped to the customer.

Batch

batch process A type of process used when a moderate quantity and variety of goods or services is desired.

Batch process is used when a moderate quantity and variety of goods or services is desired. The equipment need not be as flexible as in a job shop, but process is still intermittent. The skill level of workers doesn't need to be as high as in a job shop because there is less variety in the jobs. Manufacturing examples of batch process include the process used by small bakeries that make bread, cakes, or cookies in batches; large restaurants that make batches of dishes and desserts; breweries; and clothing manufacturers. Service examples include movie theatres that show a movie to a group (batch) of people, and airlines that carry a planeload (batch) of people from airport to airport.

The managerial challenge in a batch process is scheduling batches in order to meet planned production and demand while utilizing the resources at a high level. Capacity issues and technology management are more important than in job shops.

A batch process: Menu items are prepared in batches, in the kitchen of a large restaurant.

Great Western Brewing Company (GWB) was formed in 1989 when Molson decided to close its Saskatoon brewery. Its employees bought the plant and reopened it as a private company. GWB produces lager, light, Pilsner, Pilsner Light, and six other specialty beers, and packages them in glass and plastic bottles, cans, and kegs.

◀ **Example 2**

The main ingredient in beer is malt, which is partially sprouted barley. Other ingredients are grains such as corn or wheat, and hops, which produces its bitter taste.

The production process for beer can be divided into four stages: brewing, fermentation, finishing, and packaging. Brewing starts with mixing ground malt and water in the mash mixer and heating it to 150°F. Then, the mash (solid) and the wort (malt sugar liquid) are separated (by filtering) in the lauter tun. Next, the wort is boiled in the brew kettle for approximately 1.5 hours while hops are added. Hops and other solids are separated from wort (by centrifuge) in the hot liquor tank. Then, the brew is aerated and cooled in the cold liquor tank. So far, the process has taken approximately five hours. The batch size in the brewing part of the process is approximately 20,000 litres.

Fermentation starts in one of the many fermenters where yeast is added. Yeast converts the wort sugar into alcohol and carbon dioxide (CO_2). Fermentation is complete in nine days and the fermented beer is now cooled and pumped into one of many primary aging tanks. The yeast, which settled in the fermenter, is recovered and reused in subsequent batches.

Finishing involves cold aging (about 0°C) of the beer for a minimum of one week in a primary aging tank and then filtering and recooling it in a secondary aging tank where it rests a further week. The beer is then ready to be filtered and cooled again and pumped to a bright beer (packing) tank where it is now ready to be packaged. CO_2 that has been collected during fermentation is injected into the beer each time it is moved, to ensure a specific level of CO_2 in the final product.

The bottles used are empty bottles collected from liquor stores. They are washed, machine inspected, filled with beer, and crowned. Then they move slowly through a pasteurizer, and are labelled, packed, and palletized (approximately 100 cases per pallet). The canning process is similar but uses only new cans, which do not require washing or labelling. GWB's packaging capacity is 360 bottles and 480 cans per minute. Overall capacity of GWB is 45 million litres of beer per year.

Different types of beer differ in terms of taste, colour, and alcohol content. These are influenced by the ingredients, temperature, and length of each step of the process, yeast, hops, separation, and filtration. The chemistry of brewing is very complex and is still not fully understood. The equipment is specialized, with all beer following the same processing route. The remotely activated pumps and gauges are controlled by a central control room. Changeover from one type of beer to another requires washing the tanks, which takes approximately half an hour. The process flow diagram and plant floor plan (layout) are displayed below.

The brew kettle.

The lauter tun.

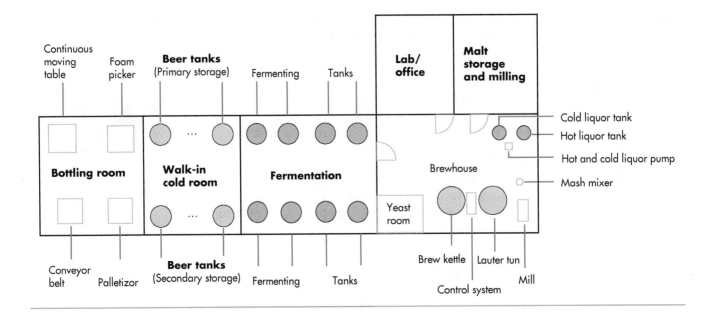

Repetitive

repetitive process A type of process used when higher quantities of more standardized goods or services are needed.

production line A sequence of machines/workstations that perform operations on a part/product.

assembly line A production line where parts are added to a product sequentially.

When higher quantities of more standardized goods or services are needed, **repetitive process** is used. The standardized output means only slight flexibility of equipment is needed. Skill of workers is generally low. Examples of this type of process include a **production line** and an **assembly line**. A production line is a sequence of machines/workstations that perform operations on a part/product. An assembly line is a production line where parts are added to a product sequentially.

A repetitive process: Motorcycles on an assembly line with parts added in a sequential order.

The line can be either machine-paced (same speed) or worker-paced (variable speed). Familiar products made by this type of process include automobiles, trucks, motor cycles, television sets, and computers. Examples of repetitive service include automatic carwashes, cafeteria lines, and ticket collectors at sports events and concerts.

The managerial challenges in a production/assembly line are capacity balance, technology management, quality, and materials management.

Example 3 ▶ Paccar Trucks builds some of its high-end Kenworth and Peterbilt medium and heavy-duty trucks at its 360,000 ft² assembly plant in Sainte-Therese, Quebec. A truck has two major subassemblies: chassis and cab. The chassis is made up of the bottom frame, the engine and power train, wheels, etc. The Quebec plant receives its engines from Paccar's U.S. engine plants and Paccar buys the other major components from its suppliers. The cab and hood are purchased already fabricated. The Quebec plant paints them and stores them in a buffer area on the second floor. This is to let the paint dry and because it is more efficient to use a batch process for painting (i.e., a large number of the same colour cabs and hoods are painted one after another). Sixty hoods and 30 cabs can be stored in the buffer area. Typically, a cab and hood are painted two to five days before they are used.

Four out of every five trucks are white. However, the different interior, motor, chassis length, and brand result in approximately 40 different products. In addition, several options are available. Paccar constantly introduces new models offering better technologies such as no-idle solution (to provide heating or cooling to the sleeper cabin while the truck engine is turned off) and hybrid engines (built by Eaton Corp of Cleveland). The equipment is specialized but flexible. Most material handling is by overhead conveyors. Workers appreciate this in the frame shop where heavy (1–2.5 tonnes) and long (6–13 metres) beams are assembled. The overhead conveyors also save floor space.

The parts and components are received just-in-time and delivered straight to the point of use. There are 31 receiving docks near the points of use. The two subassembly lines (chassis and cab) join in the middle of the left side of the plant and the truck is hauled to the final assembly and test area on the right. Capacity of the plant is 40 trucks per eight-hour shift, which means that, at capacity, every 12 minutes a truck moves up one workstation. The Quebec plant periodically changes its employment level to match its production with North American demand for its trucks. In recent years, 60 to 70 trucks have been assembled per day during two shifts.

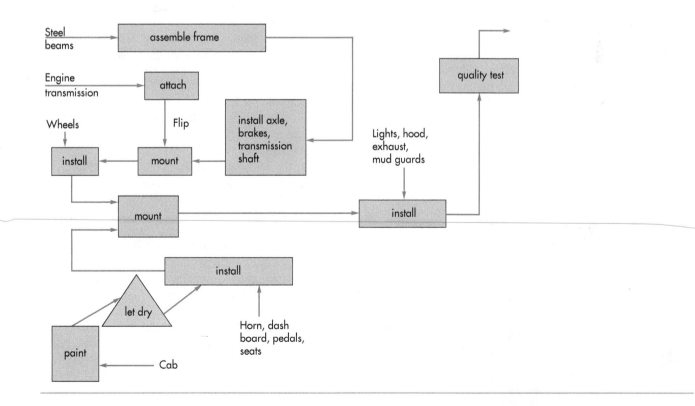

Continuous

continuous process Used when a high volume of highly standardized output is required.

When a very high volume of highly standardized output is desired, a **continuous process** is used. There is almost no variety in output and, hence, no need for equipment flexibility. As in repetitive process, workers are generally low skilled (except for maintenance technicians). Product is usually also continuous, i.e., it cannot be counted. Examples of products made using continuous process include gasoline, steel, paper, sugar, flour, and salt. Continuous services include utilities and the Internet.

A continuous process: An oil refinery performs a continuous process, mixing and separating crude oil into gasoline, fuel oil, chemicals, and many other products.

The managerial challenges in a continuous process are the same as in a repetitive process, but because of faster speed of production, greater care is required for automated control of the flow, and start and stop of production are more challenging.

Example 4 ▶

The "mingler."

Vacuum vessels used for recrystallization.

The Redpath Sugar Refinery is located on the Toronto waterfront. The refinery runs 24 hours a day, 7 days a week.

Sugar cane is grown on large plantations in the tropics and processed in huge mills close to the field by crushing the cane stalks and extracting the juice (sap). Boiling the juice crystallizes it into "raw sugar," which is purchased by Redpath Sugar and shipped to Toronto in large cargo ships.

Raw sugar is brought to the refinery in loads of 25,000 tonnes (the limit of ships passing through the St. Lawrence Seaway) and unloaded by dockside cranes and then transferred by conveyor belt to the refinery's raw sugar shed. This building has a capacity of 65,000 tonnes and has a floor the size of two football fields. This is necessary because the seaway closes in the winter and raw sugar must be brought in and stored before then to ensure continuous production year-round.

Although the raw sugar is of a relatively high quality, it still contains a residue of original cane-trash, ash, waxes, as well as any additional solids or other impurities that might have contaminated the cargo during transportation. Refining is designed to remove all of these unwanted elements and to leave only pure sucrose at the end.

The process commences with the transfer of the raw sugar into the refinery building, where it is weighed and fed into a mixing trough called a "mingler." Blended together with a solution of molasses and warm water, the resultant slurry ("magma") is spun at high speed in one of a set of oversized washing machines ("affination centrifugals"). The spun-off syrup is recycled, while the crystal ("washed raw sugar") is melted and dissolved in hot water to produce a syrup ("raw liquor"), which is then passed through a sequence of filters to remove the impurities.

Starting with a simple mechanical sieve ("strainer") that removes the larger visible solids, the liquor passes through a "carbonation" and "sweetland" system, whereby chalk (calcium carbonate) encapsulates the remaining solids, making them larger so that they can be removed by fine cloth filters in the sweetland presses. The final filtration, to remove the undesirable yellow colouration in the liquor, is done by the use of absorption in large tanks filled with commercial resin and carbon-based filtration agents, similar to those used in municipal water purification systems. The end result of this series of filtrations is a clear, colourless syrup ("fine liquor") consisting of nothing but sucrose and water.

The fine liquor is now recrystallized by boiling it for an hour under vacuum. The resultant "white massecuite" (a combination of recrystallized sucrose, uncrystallized sucrose syrup, and water) is spun in the "white sugar centrifugals" to separate the liquid from the crystals. While the syrups are recycled to create additional crystals, the crystals of pure white sucrose are dried in large rotary driers ("granulators") to reduce their moisture content to less than .03 percent.

The granular sugar is either packaged in a range of weights or sold in larger "bulk" loads and shipped out in road or rail tanker loads (of up to 100 tonnes) for further use in a variety of industrial and commercial applications.

The Redpath Sugar Refinery in Toronto, Ontario.

Process Flow Diagram

Table 6-1 provides an overview of major characteristics of the four types of production process. Note that by the nature of the market, higher variety implies smaller demand for each variation, and lower variety implies larger demand for each variation.

▼ **Table 6-1**

Major characteristics of the four types of production process.

	Job Shop	Batch	Repetitive/Assembly	Continuous
Product variety	Customized	Semi-standardized	Standardized	Highly standardized
Quantity/Volume	Low	Low-moderate	High	Very high
Equipment flexibility	Very high	Moderate	Low	Very low
Equipment technology	General purpose (adjustable)	──────────────→		Special
Scale of equipment	Many small units	──────────────→		One large unit
Equipment arranged by	Function	──────────────→		Product need
Linking of process steps	Loose	──────────────→		Tight
Flexibility	High	──────────────→		Low
Operation of equipment	Intermittent (stop & go)	──────────────→		Continuous
Worker skill level	High	──────────────→		Low
Flow pattern	Jumbled	──────────────→		Linear
Fixed cost	Low	──────────────→		High
Variable cost	High	──────────────→		Low
Challenge	Scheduling	──────────────→		Capacity, technology
Inventory	Mostly work-in-process	──────────────→		Mostly raw material
Notion of capacity	Vague	──────────────→		Clear

The ideal is to have production process capabilities such as equipment flexibility, linkages (loose vs. automated and tight), and flow (jumbled vs. one dominant) match product requirements such as product variety and quantity/volume. This relationship is displayed as the shaded main diagonal of the product-process matrix of Figure 6-1.

Failure to match product requirements and production process characteristics can result in inefficiencies and higher costs than are necessary, perhaps creating a competitive disadvantage. For example, using a batch process when there is only one product is usually inefficient because the process does not use enough automation. On the other hand, when there are many products produced on a continuous or repetitive process, the frequent product switches will result in long changeover times, which are nonproductive.

Another consideration is that products often go through a *life cycle* that begins with low quantity and increases as the product becomes better known. When that happens, a manager must know when to shift from one type of production process (e.g., job shop) to the next (e.g., batch).

The processes discussed above do not always exist in their "pure" forms. It is not unusual to find hybrid processes—processes that have elements of other process types embedded in them.

Another point is that processes that produce high-quantity products specialize in these products. This concept is called "focused factory." Recently, however, some companies have managed to handle high quantity and high variety on the same process, e.g., the "made-for you" system of McDonald's or Dell Computer's mass customization.

Within each production process, many individual operations are performed. The choice of operations used in a process depends on nature, shape, size, quantity, variety, and other competitive attributes of the products to be produced by the process. Examples of types of materials include metal, plastic, glass, wood, food ingredients, and yarn. Examples of shape include round, square, and with cavity. Examples of operations include forming (e.g., casting, forging), reshaping (e.g., drilling, cutting, bending, cold-drawing), and assembly (e.g., welding, bolting, gluing).

 Technology

technology Applications of scientific discoveries to the development and improvement of goods and services and/or the processes that produce or provide them.

Technology refers to applications of scientific discoveries to the development and improvement of goods and services and/or the processes that produce or provide them. It can involve factors such as knowledge, materials, methods, and equipment. Technological innovation refers to the discovery and development of new or improved goods, services, or processes for producing or providing them.

Process technology and information technology can have a major impact on costs, productivity, and competitiveness (include speed of delivery). *Process technology* includes methods, procedures, and equipment used to produce goods and provide services. Examples include robotics and automation on the factory floor. *Information technology (IT)* is the science and use of computers and other electronic equipment to store, process, and send information. This includes software such as Enterprise Resource Planning (ERP), the use of bar codes to identify and track goods, data transmission, the Internet, e-mail, and more.

To properly integrate technology into an organization, it is essential to understand what the technology will and won't do. Also, there are economic considerations (initial cost, space, cash flow, maintenance, consultants), integration considerations (cost, time, resources), and human considerations (training, safety, job loss).

Automation

Automation is using machinery/equipment with sensing and control devices that enable it to operate automatically. If a company decides to automate, the next question is by how much. Automation can range from factories that are completely automated to a single automated operation.

Automation offers a number of advantages over human labour. It has low variability, whereas it is difficult for a human to perform a task in exactly the same way, rapidly and on a repetitive basis. In a production setting, variability is detrimental to quality and to meeting schedules. Moreover, automated machines do not get bored or distracted or injured, nor do they go on strike, ask for higher wages, or file labour grievances. Still another advantage of automation is reduction of variable costs. In order for automated processing to be an option, job-processing requirements must be *standardized* (i.e., have very little or no variety).

Both manufacturing and service organizations are increasing their use of automation as a way to reduce costs, increase productivity, and improve quality and consistency.

Automation is frequently touted as a strategy necessary for competitiveness. For example, in steel-making, a "mini" mill, controlled by an integrated computer system, produces an uninterrupted hot band of steel using scrap metal and electrical charge. Mini-mills have a substantial productivity advantage over foundries, which use iron ore in blast furnaces. An example of a mini-mill is the Direct Strip Production Complex of Algoma Steel in Sault Ste. Marie, Ontario. Another example of using automation for competitiveness is the gigantic automated paper-making machines that automatically sense the thickness of paper and adjust to run at speeds of more than 60 km per hour.

However, automation also has certain disadvantages and limitations compared to human labour. To begin with, it can have high initial cost. In addition, automation is much less flexible than human labour. Once a process has been automated, it is hard to change it.

automation Using machinery/equipment with sensing and control devices that enable it to operate automatically.

http://www.essarsteelalgoma.com/facilities/dspc

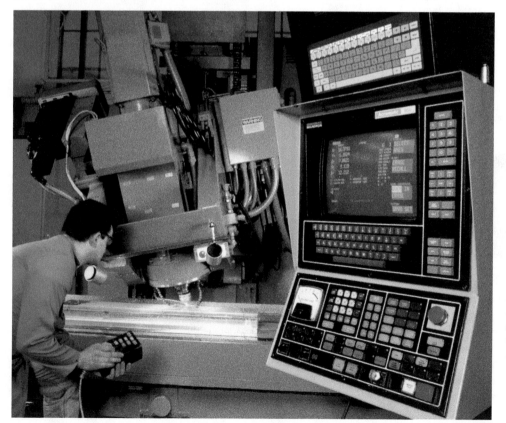

Computer numerical control (CNC) refers to a computer that reads instructions and drives a machine. CNC machines are controlled directly from files created by computer-aided manufacturing (CAM) software. With increased automation of manufacturing processes with CNC machining, considerable improvements in consistency and quality have been achieved. CNC automation reduces the frequency of errors and provides operators with time to perform additional tasks. The intelligence of CNC controllers has dramatically increased production. Some machines might even make 1,000 parts on a weekend with no operator, checking each part with lasers and sensors.

Management must carefully examine whether to automate and the degree to automate, so that they clearly understand all the ramifications. Also, much thought and careful planning are necessary to successfully integrate automation into a production process. Otherwise, it can lead to major problems. Moreover, automation has important implications not only for cost and flexibility, but also for the fit with overall strategic priorities. If the decision is made to automate, care must be taken to remove waste from the system prior to automating, to avoid building the waste into the automated system.

Generally speaking, there are three kinds of automation: fixed, programmable, and flexible.

Fixed automation is the most rigid of the three types. The concept was perfected by the Ford Motor Company in the early 1900s, and it has been the cornerstone of mass production in the auto industry. It uses high-cost, specialized equipment for a fixed sequence of operations. Low unit cost and high volume are its primary advantages; minimal variety and the high cost of making major changes in either product or process are its primary limitations.

Programmable automation involves the use of high-cost, flexible equipment controlled by a computer program that provides both the sequence of operations and specific details about each operation. Changing the process is as easy (or difficult) as changing the computer program. This type of automation has the capability of economically producing a fairly wide variety of low-quantity products in small batches. Numerically controlled (N/C) machines and some robots are examples of programmable automation.

numerically controlled (N/C) machines Machines that perform operations by following mathematical processing instructions.

Numerically controlled (N/C) machines are programmed to follow a sequence of processing instructions based on mathematical relationships that tell the machine the details of the operations to be performed. The instructions are stored on a device such as a computer disk, magnetic tape, or microprocessor. Individual machines may have their own computer; this is referred to as *computer numerical control* (*CNC*). Or one computer may control a number of N/C machines, which is referred to as *direct numerical control* (*DNC*). The computer can directly use the dimensions of the item from the CAD software to accelerate machine programming. This is part of computer-aided manufacturing (CAM) which is using software to control machines.

N/C machines are best used in cases where part geometry is complex, close tolerances are required, mistakes are costly, and there is the possibility of frequent changes in the design. The main limitations of N/C machines are the higher skill levels needed to program the machines and their high initial cost.

robot A machine consisting of a mechanical arm, a power supply, and a controller.

A **robot** consists of three parts: a mechanical arm, a power supply, and a controller. Unlike movie versions of robots, which vaguely resemble human beings, industrial robots are much less glamorous and much less mobile; most robots are stationary except for their movable arms.

Robots can handle a wide variety of tasks including welding, assembly (mainly surface mounting for circuit boards), loading to and unloading from machines, painting, and testing. They relieve humans from heavy, dirty, and unsafe work and often eliminate drudgery.

Some uses of robots are fairly simple, others are much more complex. At the lowest level are robots that follow a fixed set of instructions. Next are programmable robots, which can repeat a set of movements after being led through the sequence. These robots "play back" a mechanical sequence much as a camcorder plays back a visual sequence. At the next level up are robots that follow instructions from a computer. At the top are robots that can recognize objects and make simple decisions. Robots can be powered pneumatically (by air), hydraulically (by fluids), or electrically.

Aliment Putter's Sainte-Sophie, Quebec, plant uses this Motoman palletizing robot to arrange its cases of pickle jars into pallets (which can then be moved efficiently by forklifts). Before installing the robot, the palletizing step was a bottleneck in the process. Also, the heavy cases were difficult to handle manually.[1]

Flexible automation evolved from programmable automation. It uses equipment that is more customized than that of programmable automation. A key difference between the two is that flexible automation requires significantly less changeover time. This permits almost continuous operation of equipment *and* product variety without the need to produce in batches.

In practice, flexible automation is used in several different formats. A *machining centre* is a machine capable of performing a variety of machining operations such as milling, turning, and drilling on parts. The machine is numerically controlled.

---

[1] http://www.motoman.com/casestudies/acs-081.php.

Redline CNC

Redline CNC is a small (7,000 ft²) machine shop in Surrey, B.C. To program its complex CNCs, Redline bought GibbsCAM software, which translates the CAD data for each part into machine instructions for tool paths. The CAM software is especially useful as Redline has started to use its CNCs unattended during nights. There is an automatic pallet changer on a track that loads and unloads the CNCs (see image on the right).

A **flexible manufacturing system (FMS)** is a group of machining centres, controlled by a computer, with automatic material handling, robots or other automated equipment. They can produce a variety of *similar* products. A FMS may have from three or four to more than a dozen machines. They are designed to handle intermittent processing requirements with some of the benefits of automation and some of the flexibility of individual, or stand-alone, machines (e.g., N/C machines). A FMS offers reduced labour costs and more consistent quality compared with more traditional manufacturing methods, lower capital investment and higher flexibility than fixed automation, and relatively quick changeover time. A FMS appeals to managers who hope to achieve both the flexibility of job shop and the productivity of repetitive process.

A FMS also has some limitations. One is that this type of system can handle a relatively narrow range of part variety, so it must be used for a family of similar parts requiring similar machining. Also, a FMS requires longer planning and development times than more conventional processing equipment because of its increased complexity and cost. Furthermore, companies sometimes prefer a gradual approach to automation, but FMS represents a sizable chunk of technology.

The suitability of these systems to a production environment primarily depends on the variety and quantity of products. See Figure 6-2.

Computer-integrated manufacturing (CIM) is a system that uses an integrating computer system to link a broad range of manufacturing and other activities, including engineering,

flexible manufacturing system (FMS) A group of machining centres controlled by a computer, with automatic material handling, robots or other automated equipment.

computer-integrated manufacturing (CIM) A system for linking a broad range of manufacturing and other activities through an integrating computer system.

◀ Figure 6-2

Applicability of automated process technology based on product quantity and variety.

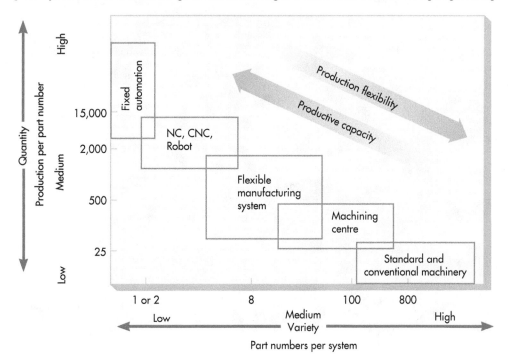

design, and production planning and control. More encompassing CIM systems can link order taking, scheduling, purchasing, inventory control, shop control, and distribution to manufacturing. In effect, a CIM system integrates information from other areas of an organization with manufacturing. The overall goal of using CIM is to link various parts of an organization to achieve rapid response to customer orders and/or product changes, to allow rapid production, and to reduce *indirect* labour costs.

Service Automation. Automated services are becoming increasingly important. Examples include ATMs, online banking, online journals and databases, electronic airplane tickets, self-service store checkout, automated toll payments, automatic meter reading, and automated package sorting and mail processing,

From self check-in at the airport to depositing a cheque from anywhere, automation speeds up service and reduces the need to stand in line.

McDonald's in Europe has started to replace human order takers with touch-screen kiosks. Kiosks also benefit customers by speeding up order taking process and reducing waiting time. Kiosks have actually increased sales by an average of $1 over face-to-face purchases. Managers explain this by the kiosk's ability to prompt customers for more purchases by showing pictures of products they might want to buy.

Process Design

LO3

Process design involves determining the form and function of how production of goods or services is to occur. It involves identifying the operations and their sequence, resources, and controls directly needed in the production of goods or rendering of services.

There are other activities needed in operating an organization (besides the creation of goods and services) that should also be designed as processes, such as marketing, new product development, supply management, and order fulfillment. These are referred to as "business" processes. Our focus here is the production or service process design.

We assume that this is a new production process for a new product. More often, production processes are only redesigned and this is done by either automating one part of the process or replacing a machine with a newer one. In this case, only some of the following steps need to be performed.

Methodology for Production Process Design

Production process design is part of the product design methodology of Chapter 4, and, as such, was briefly mentioned there. Here, we will expand it.

Given the product quantity, variety, cost, quality, delivery speed (lead time), and product specifications (nature, shape, size, components, and how they fit together),

1. **Define the production process** (performed in "Build business case" stage of the Stage-gate model—Figure 4-1)

   - Determine how completed the input materials should be. These are make-or-buy decisions.

   - Set production process objectives:

     - Capacity (or production speed), flexibility

     - Type of process (job shop, batch, repetitive, continuous)

     - Cost (fixed, variable), process quality capability

     - Technology/extent of automation, production start date

   - Determine the nature of process in general.

2. **Production process development** (performed in "Development" stage of the Stage-gate model—Figure 4-1)

   2.1 Conceptualize the design

   This answers the question: How do you get from inputs (materials) to output? That is, what is the sequence of major operations needed?

   - Develop a few alternative process concepts (sketches). Two approaches can be used:

     - Incremental: do one step at a time from start to end.

     - Hierarchical (top down): break the whole job into two operations, then divide each into suboperations, etc., until the desired level of detail is reached.

   - Usually a *process flow diagram* is used to show the operations and the movement of material between the operations.

   - Evaluate each alternative process concept.

   2.2 Make an embodiment of the design

   - Choose one process concept and complete the design.

   - Build a prototype process (can use computer modelling) and test it. This is called a pilot plant.

     - Determine the resources (machines, equipment, and labour) needed, in general.

     - Estimate the costs, quality, etc., and compare with the objectives.

   - Refine the process and re-evaluate it.

   2.3 Create a detailed design

   - Finalize the process specifications.

     - Determine the specific machines, equipment (their capacities and make), and labour.

– Design the plant layout.

– Design the work centres.

3. **Buy the machines and equipment, recruit workers, and start trial runs** (performed in "Testing and validation" stage of the Stage-gate model—Figure 4-1)

process flow diagram
Shows the operations and movement of material between the operations.

Drawing a **process flow diagram** starts with identifying the boundaries of the process (inputs and outputs) and the level of detail required. The incremental approach involves following the flow of material (or customer, in services) through the transformation process, and identifying the operations and resources (machines, labour, and their capabilities) required and their sequence. Experience with a similar process is useful. For technical products, expertise of process/manufacturing engineers is required.

As an example, the process flow diagram for making a cheeseburger at McDonald's is as follows:

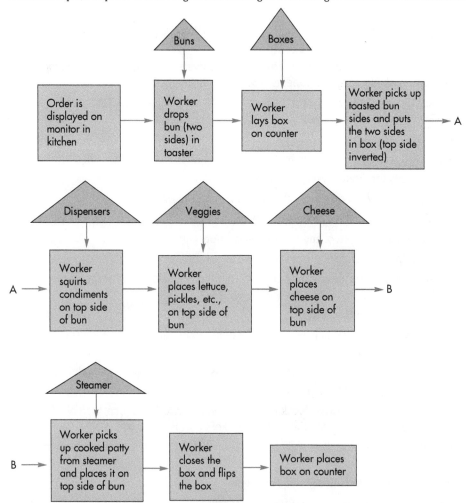

Note that storage is shown by a triangle and an operation is shown by a rectangle. Also note that flows (arrows) are usually from left to right. If there is a need to show the information flows, they could be shown as dashed arrows. In practice, time (or capacity) and cost of each operation is estimated and displayed in its box. A similar tool is value stream mapping (Chapter 15) which focuses on delay reduction.

The following two examples illustrate the basics of process design.

Example 5

A company wants to diversify into mass-production of bread loaves. It requires a process flow diagram.

SOLUTION

We start with the recipe for making a loaf of bread:

1. Mix flour, salt, yeast, and water to obtain dough.

2. Knead the dough.

3. Shape the dough into a ball, put in a pan, and leave to rise.

4. Bake in oven.

5. Let bread cool and remove from pan.

Because of the large quantity of flour needed (and the economy of quantity buying), a raw material storage room (or silo) will be used. Because mixing large quantities of ingredients by hand is difficult, a mixing machine is required. The same reason applies to kneading. As it happens, a machine exists that does both mixing and kneading. To automate the shaping, the easiest method is to dump the big lump of dough into a hopper that cuts and drops small pieces of dough in bread pans, which are then transported on a conveyor belt for a while to let bread rise and then into an open-ended oven (like an automated carwash). Next, the pans are transported on a conveyor belt for a while to cool down. Finally, bread loaves are taken out of the pans, sliced, and bagged.

The following process flow diagram is a good first step:

Suppose you wish to design a production process to make simple oak tables. The input material is oak planks approximately 2 inches thick by 6 inches wide by 6 feet long. The tables will have square tops with dimensions of 1 inch thick by 3 feet each side. Each of the four legs for the table should be round with a radius of 1 inch and length of 3 feet. All parts are sanded and varnished before assembly. The legs are attached to the top using brackets. The low production quantity implies batch production. Design a production process to manufacture the tables by drawing a process flow diagram. Identify the machines used for each operation. *Hints:* Saw a plank in half thickness and glue the resulting boards side-by-side to form part of table top. To make the legs, saw the planks into 2-inch wide segments and then use a lathe to make them round.

◀ **Example 6**

SOLUTION

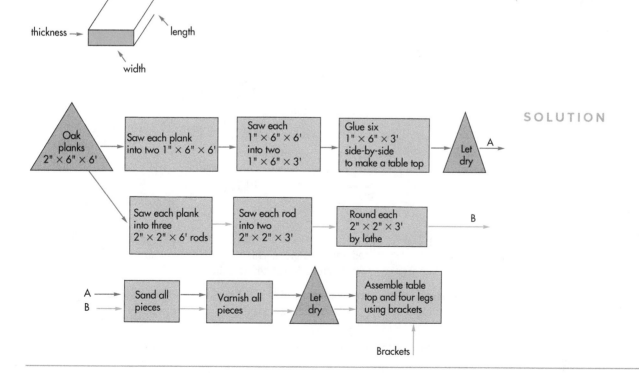

Service Process Design

Service process design is similar to manufacturing process design except that instead of material, the flow of the customer or something belonging to the customer should be followed. If the customer is not present, service process is very similar to manufacturing process, e.g., cheque processing. If the customer is present, a range of service delivery processes exist based on degree of customization and interaction allowed or required. The higher customization/choices provided, the more flexible/extensive the service delivery process and server involvement need to be. This requires higher skills but costs more money. Production efficiency goes down but sales opportunity goes up. For example, getting a mortgage requires customization and involvement from a mortgage officer, and costs more to the bank than using ATM for cash withdrawal. However, there is more sales opportunity for the bank during mortgage application, e.g., the loan officer can entice the borrower to also get a line of credit or the bank's credit card. The self-service nature of ATM reduces costs to the bank but service variety has to be limited.

The service positioning can easily be changed by varying the choices and degree of customization and involvement of customers at any step of the service. For example, a restaurant can require reservations or not; serve complimentary hot bread or not; take orders at the table or give customers an iPad to place their own order; increase or decrease the number of appetizers, entrees, desserts, and/or drinks; and allow credit card payments or not.

Service Blueprinting. The process flow diagramming for services is called service blueprinting. It is beneficial to the service provider to distinguish operations seen by the customer and those hidden from customers. These are separated by the line of visibility on the service blueprint. Also, services are especially vulnerable to quality and delivery problems because the customer is usually present during service delivery and there is little time to fix any problems then. That is why there is a need to identify potential failure points and incorporate features that minimize the chance of failure. Figure 6-3 shows a blueprint for a shoeshine stand in an airport.

Figure 6-3

Blueprint for a corner shoeshine.

Source: G. L. Shostack, Designing Services that Deliver," *Harvard Business Review* 62(1), Jan–Feb 1984, p. 135. Copyright © 1983 by the President and Fellows of Harvard College. All rights reserved.

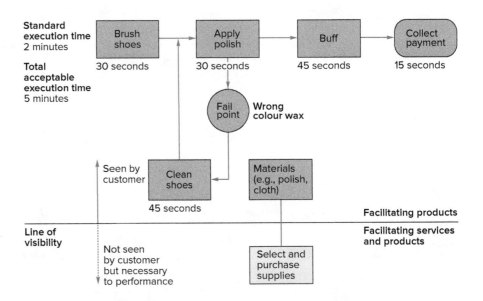

Customer Perception in Service Process Design. Another difference with manufacturing is that a service is usually varied and intangible. This raises the customer perception issue. Some suggestions to improve customer perception in services are:

- Do not raise customer expectations too high in the beginning. This is because customers compare their expectation and the actual service they receive in order to judge the quality of service.

- End the service positively because customers remember the end more.

- If the service is pleasurable, divide it into segments. For example, two short rides in an amusement park may be better than one long ride.

- If the service is painful, combine the segments. For example, cleaning teeth in a one-hour session may be better than two half-hour sessions.

- Let customers control part or all of the process. For example, self-services such as ATMs are preferred by most people. In this case, it is important to make the process user-friendly.

- Communicate the evidence of quality to customers.

Types of Layout

Layout is the location of departments, work centres, or equipment in the facility/factory/plant. A good layout facilitates flow of work, whereas a bad one results in congestion.

This section describes the main types of layout designs and the models used to obtain good layout designs.

The need for layout planning arises both in designing new facilities and in redesigning existing facilities. The most common reasons for redesign of layouts include inefficient operations (e.g., excessive material handling/delay), changes in the design of products, changes in the quantity or mix of products, and changes in methods or equipment.

There are generally two types of layout—product (line) layout (for repetitive and continuous processes) and process (functional) layout (for job shop and batch processes).

Product (Line) Layout

In **product layout** production resources are arranged linearly according to the progressive steps by which a product is made. Product layout is used to achieve a smooth and rapid flow of large quantities of goods or customers through the process. This is made possible by highly standardized goods or services that allow highly standardized, continual production. The work is divided into a series of standardized tasks, permitting specialization of both labour and equipment. Because only one or few very similar items are involved, it is feasible to arrange an entire layout to correspond to the production requirements of the product. For instance, if a portion of a manufacturing process requires the sequence of cutting, sanding, and painting, the appropriate pieces of equipment would be arranged in that sequence. And because each item follows the same sequence of operations, it is often possible to utilize fixed-path material-handling equipment such as conveyors to transport items between operations. The resulting arrangement forms a line like the one in Figure 6-4. In manufacturing environments, a line refers to a production line or an assembly line, depending on the type of activity involved. In services, the term *line* may or may not be used. It is common to refer to a cafeteria line as such but not a car wash, although from a conceptual standpoint the two are nearly identical. Figure 6-5 illustrates the layout of a typical cafeteria line. Examples of this type of layout are less common in services because service requirements usually exhibit too much variability to make standardization

product layout Arrangement of production resources linearly according to the progressive steps by which a product is made.

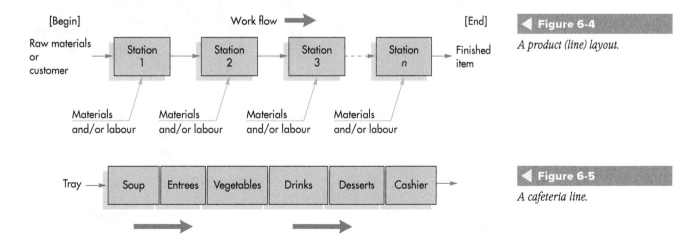

Figure 6-4

A product (line) layout.

Figure 6-5

A cafeteria line.

feasible. Without high standardization, many of the benefits of a repetitive process are lost. When lines are used, certain compromises must be made. For instance, an automatic car wash provides equal treatment to all cars—the same amount of soap, water, and scrubbing—even though cars may differ considerably in cleaning needs. As a result, very dirty cars may not come out completely clean, and relatively clean cars go through the same system with considerable waste of soap, water, and energy.

Product layouts achieve a high degree of labour and equipment utilization, which tends to offset their high equipment cost. Because items move quickly from operation to operation, the amount of work-in-process is often minimal. Consequently, operations are so closely tied to each other that the entire system is highly vulnerable to being shut down because of mechanical failure or absenteeism. *Preventive maintenance*—periodic inspection and replacement of worn parts or those with high failure rates—reduces the probability of breakdowns during the operation. Of course, no amount of preventive maintenance can completely eliminate failures, so management must take measures to provide quick repair. These include maintaining an inventory of spare parts and having repair personnel available to quickly restore equipment to normal operation.

Advantages of product layout include low-cost production and simplified accounting, purchasing, and inventory control.

Disadvantages of product layout include higher equipment cost; dull, repetitive jobs; repetitive stress injuries; and inflexibility in response to changes in the quantity of output or in product mix.

A Ford assembly line.

Process (Functional) Layout

process layout Arrangement of production resources according to similarity of function.

In **process layout** production resources are arranged according to similarity of function. This method of production processes items that have a variety of production requirements. The variety of jobs requires frequent adjustments to equipment. This causes a discontinuous work flow, which is referred to as *intermittent processing*. A manufacturing example of a process layout is a *machine shop*, which has separate departments for milling, grinding, drilling, and so on. Items that require these operations are moved in lots or batches to the departments in a sequence that varies from job to job. Consequently, variable-path material-handling equipment (forklift trucks, skids on wheels, tote boxes, etc.) is needed.

The use of *general-purpose equipment* provides the flexibility necessary to handle a wide range of production requirements. Workers who operate the equipment are usually skilled. Figure 6-6 illustrates the departmental arrangement typical of a process layout.

Process layouts are quite common in services. Examples include various departments of a hospital, a grocery store, and an auto repair shop. For instance, a hospital has emergency rooms, X-ray rooms, surgery rooms, etc.

Because equipment in a process layout is arranged by type rather than by production sequence, the system is much less vulnerable to shutdown caused by mechanical failure or absenteeism. In manufacturing systems, especially, idle equipment is usually available to replace machines that are temporarily out of service. Moreover, because items are often processed in lots, there is considerably less interdependence between successive operations than with a product layout. Maintenance costs tend to be lower because the equipment is less specialized than that of product layout, and the grouping of machinery permits repair personnel to become skilled in handling that type of equipment. Machine similarity reduces the necessary investment in spare parts. On the negative side, routing and scheduling must be done on a continual basis to accommodate the variety of production requirements typically imposed on these systems. Material handling is inefficient, and unit handling costs are generally much higher than in product layout. In-process inventories can be substantial due to batch processing. Furthermore, it is not uncommon for such systems to have equipment utilization rates under 50 percent because of routing and scheduling complexities related to the variety of production requirements being handled.

Cellular Layout

A **cellular layout** is a type of layout in which different machines are arranged in a *cell* that can process items with similar processing requirements, called *part family*. A cell is a small version of a product layout. A cell may have no conveyorized movement of parts between machines, or may have a conveyor (automatic transfer). Figure 6-7 compares a typical functional (process) layout and a cellular layout. Observe that in the cellular layout, machines are arranged to handle all of the operations necessary for a group (family) of similar parts. Thus, all parts in the same family follow the same route, although minor variations (e.g., skipping an operation) are possible. In contrast, the functional (process) layout involves multiple paths for these parts.

A cell is usually U-shaped (see Figure 6-8). A U-shaped line permits increased communication among workers on the line, thus facilitating teamwork. Also, flexibility in work assignments is increased because workers can handle not only adjacent stations but also stations on opposite sides of the line.

There are numerous benefits of cells. These include faster processing time, less material handling, less work-in-process inventory, and reduced setup times.

Grouping of similar items is known as **group technology** and involves identifying items with similarities in either design or manufacturing characteristics, and grouping them into part families. Design characteristics include size, shape, material, features (holes, slots, notches, grooves), and function; manufacturing characteristics involve the type/sequence of operations and tolerance (precision) required. Figure 6-9 illustrates a group of parts with similar characteristics.

Once similar items have been identified, items can be classified according to their families, and a system can be developed that facilitates retrieval of these codes from the database for purposes of design and manufacturing. For instance, a designer can use the system to determine if there is an existing part similar or identical to the one that needs to be designed. It may happen that an existing part, with some modification, is

▼ **Figure 6-6**

Process (functional) layout.

Dept. A	Dept. C	Dept. E
Dept. B	Dept. D	Dept. F

cellular layout Layout in which different machines are arranged in a cell that can process items that have similar processing requirements.

group technology Grouping items with similar design or manufacturing characteristics into part families.

Standard Aero provides a variety of maintenance, repair, and overhaul services to the aviation industry, including repair of gas turbine engines. It has over 4,000 employees and a dozen major locations in Winnipeg, the United States, Europe, Australia, and Asia. In the 1990s, among other things, Standard Aero reorganized its repair facilities into a cellular layout. Instead of a job shop layout where similar machines are bunched together, Standard Aero segmented the repair process and also grouped similar parts into same cells. Each cell is operated by a self-managed team whose performance is measured and displayed in front of the cell. Standard Aero has become so proficient at conversion into cellular layout that it started a division that sells this service to other engine repair facilities. In 2007, Standard Aero was purchased by Dubai Aerospace Enterprises.

Figure 6-7

Comparison of functional (process) and cellular layouts.

Figure 6-8

A U-shaped cell.

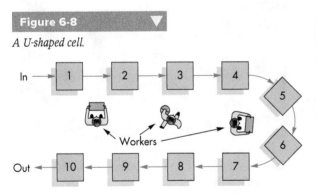

satisfactory. This greatly enhances the productivity of design. Similarly, planning the manufacturing of a new part can include matching it with one of the part families in existence, thereby alleviating much of the burden of specific processing details.

The conversion to group technology is often a major undertaking; it is a time-consuming job that involves the analysis of a considerable amount of data. Three primary methods for accomplishing this are visual inspection, examination of design and production data, and production flow sequence and routing analysis. For an example of a cellular layout, see the photo and caption of Standard Aero (on the previous page).

Some variations/combinations of line and cellular layouts are possible. For example, see Figure 6-10. The decision between line layout and cellular layout depends on room (line requires larger space), lot size (larger lots favour line), nature of workforce (temporary workers do better with simpler shorter tasks of a line), required flexibility (cells are better for dissimilar products of various lot sizes), and budget (line requires roller or belt conveyors).

Warehouse Layout

The design of a warehouse is based on a different set of factors than the design of factories. Items requiring cold storage are stored together in freezers and coolers. Other items that are ordered frequently and in large amounts should be placed near the shipping area. Any correlation between items is also significant (e.g., item A is usually ordered with item B), suggesting that placing those two items close together would reduce the cost and time of order *picking* (retrieving).

◀ **Figure 6-9**

A group of parts with similar characteristics.

Main assembly line

Sub-assembly lines

m/c2

m/c3

cell open

m/c1   m/c4

Single line, Single side

Single line, Double side

U-shaped open, Single side (typical for cells)

U-shaped open, Single side

Multiple lines, Single side

▲ **Figure 6-10**

Some variations/combinations of line and cellular layouts.

Retail Layout

The objectives of manufacturing layouts are cost minimization and product flow. However, with retail layouts such as department stores, supermarkets, and specialty stores, the primary objective is to influence sales, i.e., maximize revenues. Some large retail chains use standard layouts for all of their stores.

Office Layout

Office layouts underwent a transformation as the flow of paperwork was replaced with electronic communication. That means that there is less need to place office workers in a layout that optimizes the physical transfer of information or paperwork. A new trend is to create an image of openness; office walls are giving way to low-rise partitions.

Restaurant Layout

There are many different types of restaurants, ranging from fast food to full service. Many belong to chains, and some of those are franchises. That type of restaurant typically adheres to a floor plan established by the company. Independent restaurants and bars have their own floor plans. Some have what could be considered very good designs, while others do not. The most important element is process workflow. Food and non-food products should transition easily through the process from storage, preparation, and cooking, to the customer.

Hospital Layout

Key elements of hospital layout design are patient care and safety, with easy access to critical resources such as X-ray, CAT scan, and MRI equipment.

Layout Design Steps

The following steps are used in manufacturing layout design. Other layout designs follow similar steps.

- Determine the location of receiving and shipping.
- For "product layout," fit the process flow diagram onto a sketch of the factory floor, starting from receiving and ending in shipping. Determine the approximate location of each part of the process.
- For "process layout," determine the expected work flow between each pair of departments, and place the two departments with the highest workflows closest to each other. Continue until all departments are located.
- Keep special requirements of machines in mind (e.g., a heavy press needs a strong foundation, the paint department needs a clean environment).
- Allow space for machines, in-feeds, out-feeds, workers, and carts/forklifts.
- Keep rearranging the plan using feedback from workers until you find what works best.
- On the factory floor, paint an outline of machines, in-feed and out-feed spaces.
- Walk through the normal sequence of activities.
- Install the electricity and other lines, and move the machines in.

Assembly-Line Balancing

Assembly lines range from fairly short, with just a few operations, to long lines that have a large number of operations. Automobile assembly lines are examples of long lines. Figure 6-11 illustrates the assembly chart for a typical automobile.

Many of the benefits of a product (line) layout relate to the ability to divide the required work into a series of tasks (e.g., "assemble parts C and D") that can be performed quickly and routinely by low-skilled workers or specialized equipment. The durations of these tasks typically range from a few seconds to a few minutes. Most time requirements are so brief that it would be impractical to assign only one task to each worker. For one thing, most workers would quickly become bored by the limited job scope. For another, the number of workers required to complete even a simple product would be enormous. Instead, tasks are usually grouped into manageable bundles and assigned to workstations staffed by one or two operators.

line balancing Assigning tasks to workstations in such a way that the work stations have approximately equal time requirements.

Assigning tasks to workstations in such a way that the workstations have approximately equal time requirements is referred to as **line balancing**. This minimizes the idle time along the line and results in high utilization of labour and equipment. Idle time occurs if time requirements are not equal among workstations. Workstations with less work are capable of producing at higher rates than others. These "fast" workstations will experience periodic waits for the output from slower workstations or to avoid build-ups of work in downstream workstations. Unbalanced lines are undesirable in terms of inefficient utilization of labour and equipment and because they may create morale problems at the slower workstations for workers who must work continuously.

The major obstacle to attaining a perfectly balanced line is the difficulty of forming task bundles that have the same duration. One cause of this is that it may not be feasible to combine certain activities into the same bundle, either because of differences in skill or equipment requirements or because the activities are not compatible (e.g., risk of contamination of paint from grinding). Another cause of difficulty is that differences among task lengths cannot always be overcome by grouping the tasks. A third cause of an inability to perfectly balance a line is that the technological sequence may prohibit otherwise desirable task combinations. Consider a series of three operations that have

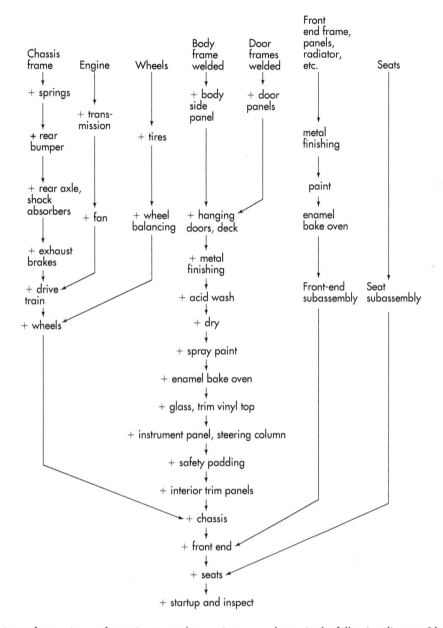

◀ **Figure 6-11**

Assembly chart for a typical automobile.

durations of two minutes, four minutes, and two minutes, as shown in the following diagram. Ideally, the first and third operations could be combined at one workstation and have a total time equal to that of the second operation. However, it may not be possible to combine the first and third operations. In the case of an automatic car wash, scrubbing and drying operations could not realistically be combined at the same workstation due to the need to rinse cars between the two operations.

Usually, each workstation has one worker who handles all of the tasks at that workstation, although an option is to have two workers at a single workstation. For purposes of illustration, however, all of the examples and problems in this chapter have workstations with one worker.

A manager could decide to use anywhere from one to five workstations to handle five tasks. With one workstation, all tasks would be done at that workstation; with five workstations, one task would be assigned to each workstation. If two, three, or four workstations are used, some or all of the workstations will have multiple tasks assigned to them. How does a manager decide how many workstations to use?

cycle time The maximum time allowed at each workstation to complete its set of tasks on a unit.

The primary determinant is the line's **cycle time** (also called **takt time**). The line's cycle time (cycle time for short) is the *maximum* time allowed at each workstation to perform its assigned tasks before the unit moves on. The cycle time also establishes the output rate of a line. For instance, if the cycle time is two minutes, units will come off the end of the line at the rate of one every two minutes.

As a general rule, the cycle time is determined by the desired output rate. We can calculate the cycle time using:

$$CT = \frac{OT}{D} \tag{6-1}$$

where

CT = Cycle time

OT = Operating time per day

D = Desired output per day (i.e., demand)

For example, suppose that the desired output rate is 480 units per day, and the line will operate for eight hours per day (480 minutes). Using Formula 6-1, the necessary cycle time is

$$\frac{480 \text{ minutes per day}}{480 \text{ units per day}} = 1.0 \text{ minute per unit}$$

The number of workstations that will be needed is a function of the cycle time, the sum of task times, and our ability to combine tasks into workstations. We can determine the *theoretical minimum* number of workstations necessary, given a cycle time, as follows:

$$N_{min} = \frac{\sum t}{CT} \tag{6-2}$$

where

N_{min} = Theoretical minimum number of workstations

$\sum t$ = Sum of task times

Given cycle time of 1 minute per unit, if sum of task times is 2.5 minutes, the minimum number of workstations required to achieve this goal is:

$$N_{min} = \frac{2.5 \text{ minutes per unit}}{1 \text{ minute per unit per workstation}} = 2.5 \text{ workstations}$$

Because 2.5 workstations is not feasible, it is necessary to *round up* (because 2.5 is the minimum) to three workstations. Thus, the actual number of workstations used will equal or exceed three, depending on how successfully the tasks can be grouped into work bundles.

precedence network A diagram that shows the tasks and their precedence requirements.

A very useful tool in line balancing is a **precedence network**. Figure 6-12 illustrates a simple precedence network. It visually portrays the tasks that are to be performed along with the *precedence* requirements; that is, the *order* in which tasks may be performed. The network is read from left to right, so the initial task(s) are on the left and the final task is on the right. In terms of precedence relationship, we can see from the diagram, for example, that the only requirement to begin task *b* is that task *a* must be finished. However, in order to begin task *d*, tasks *b* and *c* must *both* be finished.

Now let's see how a line is balanced. This involves assigning tasks to workstations. Generally, no technique is available that guarantees an optimal set of assignments. Instead, managers employ *heuristic (intuitive) rules*, which provide good sets of assignments. A number of line-balancing heuristics are in use, three of which are described here for purposes of illustration:

1. Assign the task with the longest time.

2. Assign the task with the most followers.

3. Assign the task with the largest positional weight (= sum of task's time plus the time of all the following tasks).

Figure 6-12 ▼

A simple precedence network.

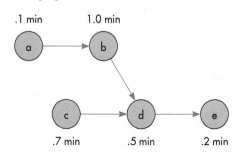

The following tasks are all tasks that you would encounter by following all paths (in the direction of arrows) from the task in question through the precedence network.

The general procedure used in line balancing is described in Table 6-2.

◀ **Table 6-2**

Line balancing procedure.

1. Identify the cycle time and determine the minimum number of workstations.

2. Make assignments to workstations in order, beginning with workstation 1. Tasks are assigned to workstations moving from left to right through the precedence network. Start each workstation with time left = cycle time.

3. Before each assignment, use the following criteria to determine which tasks are (a) eligible and (b) will fit:

   a. All its preceding tasks in the precedence network have been assigned.

   b. The task time does not exceed the time left at the workstation.

   If no eligible tasks will fit, set idle time = time left and move on to the next workstation.

4. Assign tasks (and break ties) using one of these heuristic rules:

   a. Assign the task with the longest time.

   b. Assign the task with the most followers.

   c. Assign the task with the largest positional weight.

5. After each task assignment, update the time left at the workstation by subtracting the time of assigned task from time left.

6. Continue until all tasks have been assigned to workstations. Calculate total idle time.

Assign the tasks shown in Figure 6-12 to workstations using a cycle time of 1.0 minute. Use the heuristic rule "Assign the task with the most followers."

◀ **Example 7**

SOLUTION

Workstation	Time Left	Eligible	Will Fit	Task (time)	Idle Time
1	1.0	a, c	a, c*	a (.1)	
	.9	b, c	c	c (.7)	
	.2	b			.2
2	1.0	b	b	b (1.0)	
	.0	d	–		.0
3	1.0	d	d	d (.5)	
	.5	e	e	e (.2)	
	.3	–	–		.3
					.5

*Task a was assigned because it has more followers (three, vs. two for task c).

Comment: The initial "Time Left" for each workstation is equal to the cycle time. For a task to be eligible, tasks preceding it on the precedence network must have been assigned, and for it to fit, the task's time must not exceed the workstation's time left.

Two widely used measures of effectiveness of the set of assignments are:

percentage idle time one hundred times sum of idle times per unit divided by actual number of workstations times cycle time.

1. The **percentage idle time** of the line. This is sometimes referred to as the *balance delay*. It can be calculated as follows:

$$\text{Percentage idle time} = \frac{\text{Sum of idle times per unit}}{N_{\text{actual}} \times \text{cycle time}} \times 100 \qquad (6\text{-}3)$$

where N_{actual} = Actual number of workstations.
For the preceding example, the value is:

$$\text{Percentage idle time} = \frac{.5}{3 \times 1.0} \times 100 = 16.7\%$$

2. The *efficiency* of the line. This is calculated as follows:

$$\text{Efficiency} = 100 - \text{percentage idle time} \qquad (6\text{-}4)$$

In the preceding example, efficiency = 100% − 16.7% = 83.3%

Example 8 ▶

Suppose we were to design an assembly line for assembling the oak accessory table shown in the following photos. Assume the top and legs come as subassemblies and that both leg assemblies need to be screwed to the top before leg braces (cross-bars) can be assembled. The steps of assembly and their estimated times are:

Task	Time (seconds)
a. Place top subassembly upside down on the work surface.	4
b. Place a leg subassembly over the top subassembly as shown in the left-hand photo, insert a screw in the predrilled hole, align, and drive the screw in.	20
c. Insert another screw in the other predrilled hole and drive the screw in.	13
d. Place another leg subassembly over the other side of the top subassembly, insert a screw in the predrilled hole, align, and drive the screw in.	20
e. Insert another screw in the other predrilled hole and drive the screw in.	13
f. Place a leg brace between two leg subassemblies as shown in the right-hand photo, insert a screw in the predrilled hole, align, and drive the screw in.	20
g. Insert another screw in the other side's predrilled hole and drive the screw in.	13
h. Place another leg brace between two leg subassemblies on the other side, insert a screw in the predrilled hole, align, and drive the screw in.	20
i. Insert another screw in the other side's predrilled hole and drive the screw in.	13
j. Tighten all screws.	32

1. Draw the precedence network.
2. Assuming that we need to assemble one table per minute, assign the tasks to workstations using the "assign the task with the most followers" heuristic rule, breaking a tie with the

"assign the task with the longest time" heuristic rule. If there is a further tie, break it randomly (i.e., you can choose any one of the tasks tied).

1. Drawing the precedence network is not difficult. Begin (from the left) with the activity(ies) with no predecessor(s). Then place the immediate followers and draw arrows to them. Note that an activity may require completion of two or more activities. For example, to be able to start f or h (installing a leg brace), both leg assemblies should be already installed (c and e). That is why there are two arrows into f and h from c and e.

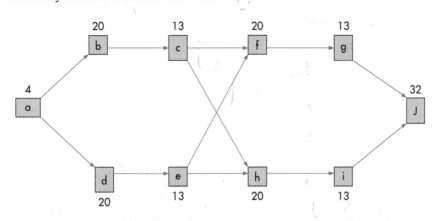

2.

WS	Time Left	Eligible	Will Fit	Assign (time)	Idle Time
1	60s	a	a	a(4)	
	56	b, d	b, d*	b(20)	
	36	c, d	c, d**	d(20)	
	16	c, e	c, e***	c(13)	
	3	e	—	—	3
2	60s	e	e	e(13)	
	47	f, h	f, h****	f(20)	
	27	g, h	g, h*****	h(20)	
	7	g, i	—	—	7
3	60s	g, i	g, i******	g(13)	
	47	I	i	i(13)	
	34	J	j	j(32)	
	2	—	—	—	2
					12s

*b is assigned randomly—both b and d have 6 followers and their time is tied at 20s also.

**d is assigned because it has 6 followers, more than 5 followers of c.

***c is assigned randomly—both c and e have 5 followers and their time is tied at 13s also.

****f is assigned randomly—both f and h have 2 followers and their time is tied at 20s also.

*****h is assigned because it has 2 followers, more than 1 follower of g.

******g is assigned randomly—both g and i have 1 follower and their time is tied at 13s also.

If the last workstation has a large idle time and the desired output rate is flexible, it might be worthwhile to increase the cycle time slightly and see if the number of workstations can be reduced by 1, thus saving significant labour cost.

Variable Task Times

Although it is convenient to treat assembly operations as if their time will be the same in each repetition, it is more realistic to assume that task times will be variable. The reasons for the variations are numerous, including worker fatigue, boredom, material shortages, defects, mechanical problems, and product differences.

The following example shows the effect of variation in task times. If three workstations each take 3 minutes to perform their tasks, then the capacity of the line will be 20 units per hour, with percentage idle time = 0 (see case (a) in the following figure). However, if each workstation's time ranges from 2 to 4 minutes uniformly, assuming that there is no room for inventory between the workstations, it can be shown using simulation that the capacity of the line drops to 17.4 units per hour, with percentage idle time = 13 percent (see case (b) in the figure below). Note that the average workstation time is still 3 minutes; however, workstations 1 and 2 are blocked if their successor workstation takes longer and workstations 2 and 3 are starved if their predecessor workstation takes longer.

			1 unit/3 min
Workstation 1	Workstation 2	Workstation 3	20 units/hr
3 min/unit	3 min/unit	3 min/unit	0 percent idle time

(a) Nonrandom production line

			1 unit/3.45 min
Workstation 1	Workstation 2	Workstation 3	17.4 units/hr
.5 prob.	.5 prob.	.5 prob.	13 percent idle time
2–4 min/unit	2–4 min/unit	2–4 min/unit	

(b) Line with random processing times

Solutions to the variable task times include:

- Reducing the variability, e.g., by designing the work better, by using high-quality material, and by doing preventive maintenance.
- Using buffer inventory between workstations.
- Leaving some idle time in workstations that have variable time.
- *Cross-training* workers so that when a bottleneck occurs, the worker with temporarily-increased idle time can assist another worker who is temporarily overburdened.

Treatment of Bottlenecks

Several solutions are used. First, one or more tasks in the bottleneck workstation can be automated or made easier using equipment such as a tool balancer. Secondly, if bottleneck occurs because of only some products, the tasks for these products can be done offline or online by a special crew of "floaters." The third approach is to use *parallel workstations*. Parallel workstations increase the work flow and provide flexibility.

Consider the following example. A job has four tasks; task times are 1 minute, 1 minute, 2 minutes, and 1 minute. Assume each task is assigned to a different workstation and there are no buffer inventories between the workstations. The cycle time for the line will be 2 minutes per unit and the output rate will be 30 units per hour:

$$\frac{60 \text{ minutes per hour}}{2 \text{ minutes per unit}} = 30 \text{ units per hour}$$

Bottleneck

| 1 min | 30/hr | 1 min | 30/hr | 2 min | 30/hr | 1 min | → 30/hr |

Using parallel workstations for the third task would result in a cycle time of 1 minute per unit because the output rate at the parallel workstations would total 60 units per hour, and this allows an output rate for the line of 60 units per hour:

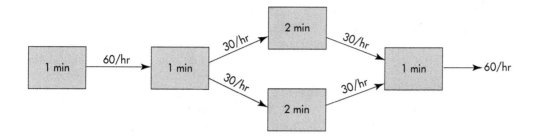

Designing Process (Functional) Layouts

The main issue in design of process layouts is the relative positioning of the departments involved. As illustrated in Figure 6-13, departments must be assigned to locations on the facility floor. The challenge is to develop a reasonably good layout. Some departments may benefit from having adjacent locations, whereas others should be separated. For example, a lab with delicate equipment should not be located near a department with strong vibrations. Conversely, two departments that share some of the same equipment would benefit from being close together.

The ideal situation is to first develop a layout and then design the physical structure (building) around it, thus permitting maximum flexibility in design. This procedure is commonly followed when new facilities are constructed. Nonetheless, many layouts must be developed in existing structures where the shape of floor, the dimensions of the building, location of entrances and elevators, reinforced flooring, and other similar factors must be carefully weighed in designing the layout. Note that multilevel structures pose special problems for layout planners.

Customers or materials in a process layout may require different operations and different sequences of operations, which causes them to follow different paths through the facility. Because transportation costs or time can be significant, one of the major objectives in process layout design is to minimize total transportation cost, distance, or time.

Minimizing Total Transportation Cost or Distance

We require the following information:

1. A list of departments or work centres, their approximate dimensions, and the dimensions of the building that will house the departments.
2. Current and forecast future work flows between the various departments.
3. The distance between centres of locations and the cost per unit of distance to move loads between locations.
4. A list of any special considerations (e.g., operations that must be close to each other or operations that must be separated).

It can be helpful to summarize the necessary data in *from-to charts* like those in Tables 6-3 and 6-4. Table 6-3 displays the distance between centres of each pair of locations, and Table 6-4 displays current or forecast work flow between each pair of departments. For instance, the distance chart reveals that a trip from the centre of location A to the centre of location B will involve a distance of 20 metres. Oddly enough, the length of a trip between centres of two locations may differ depending on the *direction* of the trip, due to one-way routes, elevation, or other factors. To simplify the discussion, we assume the same distance between centres of any two locations regardless of direction. However, it is not realistic to assume that interdepartmental work flows are equal—there is no reason to suspect that department 1 will send as much work to department 2 as department 2 sends to 1. For example, several departments may send goods to the packaging department, but packaging may send goods only to the shipping department.

▼ **Figure 6-13**

Departments must be assigned to locations on facility floor.

Locations			Departments to be assigned
A	B	C	1
D	E	F	2
			3
			4
			5
			6

▼ **Table 6-3**

Distance between centres of locations (metres).

		Location		
From	**To**	**A**	**B**	**C**
A		–	20	40
B		20	–	30
C		40	30	–

▼ **Table 6-4**

From-to departmental work flow (loads per day).

		Department		
From	**To**	**1**	**2**	**3**
1		–	10	80
2		20	–	30
3		90	70	–

Transportation costs can also be summarized in from-to charts, but we shall avoid that complexity, assuming instead that costs are a direct, linear function of distance.

In practice, there are a large number of possible assignments. For example, there are more than 87 billion different ways that 14 departments can be assigned to 14 locations. This makes finding an optimal solution difficult. Often planners must rely on heuristic rules to obtain a good, but not necessarily optimal, solution. A reasonable rule is to locate departments with relatively high interdepartmental work flow as close together as possible.

Heuristic

1. Assign the pair of departments with the greatest interdepartmental work flow to locations whose centres are closest to each other, keeping the future assignments in mind.

2. Then pick the pair with second highest work flow and assign them to two available locations whose centres are the next two closest, keeping their relationship with those already assigned and future assignments in mind.

3. Continue until all departments have been assigned.

Example 9 ▶ Assign the three departments shown in Table 6-4 to locations A, B, and C, which are separated by the distances shown in Table 6-3, in such a way that total transportation cost is minimized. Assume that the cost per metre to move any load is $1. Note that distances between centres of departments are independent of direction of flow (i.e., the distance from-to chart is symmetrical).

SOLUTION

Sum the work flow between every pair of departments in each direction and sort the pairs of departments by the total work flow:

Department Pair	Work Flow	
3–1	90	} 170
1–3	80	
3–2	70	} 100
2–3	30	
2–1	20	} 30
1–2	10	

You can see that departments 1 and 3 have the highest interdepartmental work flow. Also note that centres of locations A and B are the closest. Thus, it seems reasonable to consider assigning departments 1 and 3 to locations A and B, although it is not yet obvious which department should be assigned to which location. Further inspection of the work flow list reveals that departments 2 and 3 have higher interdepartmental work flow than departments 1 and 2, so departments 2 and 3 should be located more closely than departments 1 and 2. Hence, it would seem reasonable to place department 3 between departments 1 and 2. The resulting assignments might appear as in Figure 6-14.

Because the cost per metre to move any load is $1, you can compute the total daily transportation cost for this assignment by multiplying each department's number of loads by the distance between their centres, and summing those quantities:

Department	Number of Loads to:	Location	Distance between Centres:	Loads × Distance
1.........	2: 10	A..........	C: 40	10 × 40 = 400
	3: 80		B: 20	80 × 20 = 1,600
2.........	1: 20	C..........	A: 40	20 × 40 = 800
	3: 30		B: 30	30 × 30 = 900
3.........	1: 90	B..........	A: 20	90 × 20 = 1,800
	2: 70		C: 30	70 × 30 = 2,100
				7,600

At $1 per load metre, the cost for this plan is $7,600 per day.

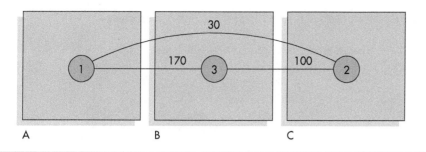

◀ Figure 6-14

Interdepartmental work flows for Example 9.

Closeness Ratings

The preceding approach suffers from the limitation of focusing on only one objective (i.e., the total transportation cost), but many situations involve multiple criteria. Richard Muther developed a more general approach to the problem, which allows for subjective input from managers to indicate the relative importance of closeness or remoteness of each department pair.[2] That information is then summarized in a grid like that shown in Figure 6-15. The letters represent the importance of closeness for each department pair, with A being absolutely necessary, E being very important, and X representing an undesirable pairing. Thus, in the grid below it is "absolutely necessary" to locate departments 1 and 2 close to each other because there is an A at the intersection of those departments on the grid. On the other hand, departments 1 and 4 should not be close together because their intersection has an X. In practice, the letters on the grid are often accompanied by numbers that indicate the reason for each closeness rating: they are omitted here to simplify the illustration. Muther suggests the following reasons for closeness/remoteness:

1. Use same equipment or facilities.
2. Share the same personnel.
3. Sequence of work flow.
4. Ease of communication.
5. Unsafe or unpleasant conditions.
6. Similar work performed.

Muther suggests that closeness ratings in the grid be first used to draw a relationship graph, using the A and X ratings, but keeping E ratings in mind. Then this graph is fitted onto the floor drawing. Example 10 illustrates this heuristic.

◀ Figure 6-15

A simplified Muther grid.

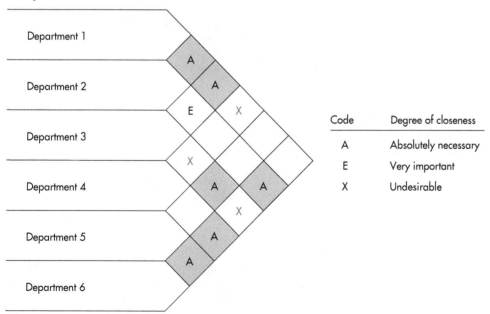

Code	Degree of closeness
A	Absolutely necessary
E	Very important
X	Undesirable

[2] Richard Muther and John Wheeler, "Simplified Systematic Layout Planning," *Factory* 120, nos. 8, 9, and 10 (August, September, October, 1962) pp. 68–77, 111–19, 101–13.

▶ Assign the six departments in Figure 6-15 to a 2 × 3 set of locations.

SOLUTION

Prepare a list of A and X ratings by referring to the grid in Figure 6-15:

A	X
1–2	1–4
1–3	3–4
2–6	3–6
3–5	
4–6	
5–6	

Next, form a cluster of A links, beginning with the department that appears most frequently in the A list (in this case, department 6):

Take the remaining departments in order of number of appearance in the A list, and add them to the above main cluster, rearranging the cluster as necessary. Form separate clusters for departments that do not link with the main cluster. In this case, all departments link with the main cluster.

Next, graphically portray the Xs as "separation" cluster(s):

Finally, fit the As cluster into a 2 × 3 arrangement, keeping X separations in mind:

1	2	6
3	5	4

Note that alternative solutions are possible. For this solution, the E rating has also been satisfied, even though no attempt was made to explicitly consider it. Naturally, not every problem will yield the same results, so it may be necessary to do some additional adjusting to see if improvements can be made, keeping in mind that the A and X assignments deserve the greatest consideration.

Note that departments may be considered close not only when they touch side to side, but also when they touch corner to corner. However, side-by-side departments are closer.

Computer Software

The difficulty and significant time required to accurately draw and visualize factory equipment and flows and to analyze the production process has led to the development of a number of computer software programs. One example is the Plant Design & Optimization module of the Tecnomatix software of Siemens. This family (FactoryCAD, FactoryFlow, and Plant Simulation) provides icons for graphical display, calculates total material flow distances, uses several heuristics to determine a good layout, performs simulation of material flow, and provides 3-D walk-through.

Another software is Factory Design module of Autodesk, which does similar visualization and analysis to the Siemens software. In particular, it has icons for equipment that easily snap together and unsnap, facilitates new equipment drawing, allows easy 2D (AutoCAD) to 3D (Inventor) conversion, and helps identify interferences (e.g., a pillar blocking product movement).

Atomic Energy of Canada Limited uses Siemens' Robcad (Robot CAD) and Solid Edge (CAD) to digitally model reactors and simulate human and robot operations that it services in order to speed up the service. This modelling is now done in one day vs. weeks it used to take.

Magna Steyr, the Austrian subsidiary of Magna International, produces BMW X3 for BMW in its plant in Graz. BMW also commissioned Magna Steyr to produce MINI Countryman on the same line. In order to model the inclusion of MINI on the line, the staff used Siemens Tecnomatix software to digitally model the robotics part of bodyshell manufacturing. The objective was to shorten the production line planning and diminish downtime. First, they made a 3D scan of the robots on the factory floor. These were loaded in Tecnomatix. Then, the welding requirements of MINI were loaded in the software. The result was surprisingly good: the software used as much as 95 percent of current robots for MINI.

http://www.plm.automation.siemens.com/en_us/products/tecnomatix/plant_design/index.shtml; http://www.autodesk.com/suites/factory-design-suite/overview.

Summary

- Production process design involves determining the form and function of the production process, i.e., the activities, their sequence, and resources and controls used to make the product.

- Process types include job shop, batch, repetitive, and continuous flow. Job shop is used for many low-quantity customized products, batch process is used for few medium-quantity standard products that are produced in batches, and repetitive and continuous processes are used for one or two high-quantity/volume standard products.

- The product-process matrix relates the product quantity and variety to the process type and its flexibility.

- Automation is used to reduce the production costs and improve quality and speed. Examples include numerically controlled machines.

- Process design involves finding a sequence of operations to produce the good or service, testing it, and finalizing it by determining the machines and plant layout. A process flow diagram is used to display the sequence of operations.

- Facility layout design is used to determine the location of the machines and departments on the facility floor. Product layouts are geared to

high-volume standardized items. Workers and equipment are arranged according to the technological sequence required by the product. Emphasis in design is on work flow through the system, and specialized processing and handling equipment is used.

- Process layouts group similar activities into departments or work centres. They can handle a wide range of processing requirements. However, the variety of processing requirements necessitates continual routing and scheduling. The rate of output is generally much lower than that of product layouts.

- Cellular layouts use a cell that processes a group of similar products or parts using different machines arranged in a "U" shape.

- The main effort in product layout design is assembly-line balancing, which focuses on dividing the work required to produce a product into tasks and bundling them so that they are as nearly equal as possible in terms of time. The goal is to achieve high utilization of labour and equipment.

- In process layout design, efforts focus on the relative positioning of departments to minimize total transportation cost or to meet other requirements concerning the closeness of certain department pairs.

Key Terms

assembly line
automation
batch process
cellular layout

computer-integrated manufacturing (CIM)
continuous process
cycle time

flexible manufacturing system (FMS)
group technology
job shop

line balancing

make or buy

numerically controlled (N/C)
   machines

percentage idle time

precedence network

process design

process flow diagram

process layout

product layout

production line

repetitive process

robot

Solved Problems

Problem 1

The tasks shown in the following precedence network are to be assigned to workstations with the intent of minimizing percentage idle time. Management desires an output rate of 275 units per day. Assume 440 minutes are available per day.

  a. Determine the appropriate cycle time.

  b. What is the minimum number of workstations possible?

  c. Assign the tasks using the "assign the task with the largest positional weight" heuristic rule.

  d. Calculate efficiency.

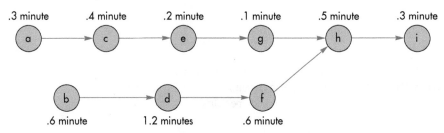

Solution

  a. $CT = \dfrac{\text{Operating time}}{\text{Desired output}} = \dfrac{440 \text{ minutes per day}}{275 \text{ units per day}} = 1.6$ minutes per unit per workstation

  b. $N_{\min} = \dfrac{\sum t}{\text{Cycle time}} = \dfrac{4.2 \text{ minutes per unit}}{1.6 \text{ minutes per unit per workstation}}$

        $= 2.625$, round up to 3 workstations

  c. Add positional weights (task time plus the sum of all the following times) to the diagram. Start at the right end and work backward:

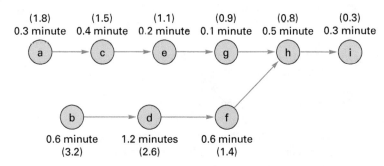

Workstation	Time Left*	Eligible	Will Fit	Assign Task (time)	Idle Time
1	1.6	a, b	a, b	b(.6)	
	1.0	a, d	a	a(.3)	
	.7	c, d	c	c(.4)	
	.3	e, d	e	e(.2)	
	.1	g, d	g	g(.1)	

(continued)

Workstation	Time Left*	Eligible	Will Fit	Assign Task (time)	Idle Time
	.0	d	—	—	.0
2	1.6	d	d	d(1.2)	
	.4	f	—	—	.4
3	1.6	f	f	f(.6)	
	1.0	h	h	h(.5)	
	.5	i	i	i(.3)	
	.2	—	—	—	.2
					.6

* The initial time for each workstation is the cycle time calculated in part *a*.

The resulting assignments are shown below.

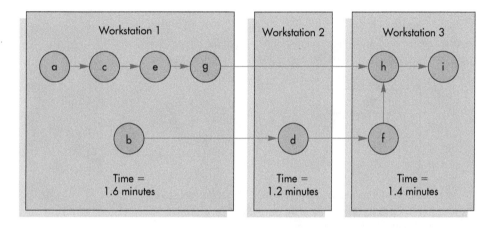

Time = 1.6 minutes	Time = 1.2 minutes	Time = 1.4 minutes

d. Efficiency $= 100\% -$ Percent idle time $= 100\% - \dfrac{0.6 \text{ min.}}{3 \times 1.6 \text{ min.}}100 = 87.5\%$.

Problem 2

Assign nine automobile service departments to bays in a 3 × 3 floor grid so that the closeness ratings in the following Muther grid are satisfied. Only A and X ratings are shown. The location of department 4 must be in the middle right-hand side of the floor grid.

Department 1
Department 2
Department 3
Department 4
Department 5
Department 6
Department 7
Department 8
Department 9

Solution

Department 1 has most A ratings, making it the centre position in the cluster. After connecting all the other departments with A rating to Department 1 and adding the other A ratings, we get the cluster on the right:

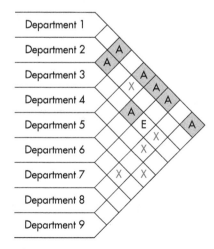

Next, we can identify the clusters of departmental pairings that should be avoided:

The departments in each X cluster should be spaced around the perimeter of the grid. Placing the A cluster on the floor plan with dept 1 in the centre room and arbitrarily starting with dept 6 in top right room, we get:

Now, using the X clusters, it follows that we should move dept 5 and 7 one room to the right and place dept 8 in the bottom left room, so that dept 5 is not close to dept 9 and dept 8 is not close to dept 4. The following final floor plan results:

2	3	6
9	1	4
8	7	5

Problem 3

Five departments, 1 to 5, are to be assigned to locations B–F in the grid below. For technical reasons, department 6 must be assigned to location A. Transportation cost is $2 per metre. The objective is to minimize total transportation cost. Information on from-to departmental work flows and distances between centres of locations is shown in the following tables. Use the heuristic given in the section "Minimizing Total Transportation Cost or Distance." Calculate total transportation cost.

Distance between Centres of Locations (metres)

From	To	A	B	C	D	E	F
A		—	50	100	50	80	130
B			—	50	90	40	70
C				—	140	60	50
D					—	50	120
E						—	50
F							—

From-To Departmental Workflows (number of trips per day)

From	To	1	2	3	4	5	6
1		—	90	25	23	11	18
2		35	—	8	5	10	16
3		37	2	—	1	0	7
4		41	12	1	—	4	0
5		14	16	0	9	—	3
6		32	38	13	2	2	—

A Dept. 6	B	C
D	E	F

Solution

First, determine the total interdepartmental work flows (e.g., for 1–2 the flow is $90 + 35 = 125$) because the distances are symmetric. Then, arrange them from high to low.

Pair of Dept.	Workflow
1–2	125
1–4	64
1–3	62
2–6	54
1–6	50
2–5	26
1–5	25
3–6	20
2–4	17
4–5	13
2–3	10
5–6	5
3–4	2
4–6	2
3–5	0

From this, we can see that departments 1 and 2 have the greatest interdepartmental work flow, so they should be closest, perhaps at B and E (which have the smallest between-centres distance). However, since work flow between 2 and 6 is larger than between 1 and 6, place department 1 in location E and department 2 in location B. Next, work flow between 1 and 4 is highest. The work flow between 4 and 6 is low, suggesting that they need not be close. Therefore, place department 4 in F. Next, work flow between 1 and 3 is highest. Hence, place department 3 in location D. Finally, department 5 has to be placed at location C.

A Dept. 6	B Dept. 2	C Dept. 5
D Dept. 3	E Dept. 1	F Dept. 4

Total cost:

Pair of Dept.	b Distance	c Workflow	(b × c × $2) Cost	Pair of Dept.	b Distance	c Workflow	(b × c × $2) Cost
1–2	(B–E) 40	125	$10,000	2–6	(A–B) 50	54	5,400
1–3	(D–E) 50	62	6,200	3–4	(F–D) 120	2	480
1–4	(F–E) 50	64	6,400	3–5	(D–C) 140	0	0
1–5	(E–C) 60	25	3,000	3–6	(A–D) 50	20	2,000
1–6	(A–E) 80	50	8,000	4–5	(C–F) 50	13	1,300
2–3	(B–D) 90	10	1,800	4–6	(A–F) 130	2	520
2–4	(B–F) 70	17	2,380	5–6	(A–C) 100	5	1,000
2–5	(B–C) 50	26	2,600				$51,080

Discussion and Review Questions

Note: An asterisk indicates that a question or problem may be more challenging.

1. Define process design and describe its importance. **LO1**

2. Briefly describe the four basic process types and give a manufacturing example for each that is not described in the chapter. **LO1**

3. Give a service example for each of the four basic process types. **LO1**

4. Briefly discuss the advantages and disadvantages of automation. **LO2**

5. Briefly describe computer-aided approaches to production. **LO2**

6. What is a numerically controlled machine? **LO2**

7. What is the product-process matrix? What is its purpose? **LO1**

8. Describe the method for process design. **LO3**

9. What is a process flow diagram? **LO3**

10. What are the differences between goods and service process design? **LO3**

11. Describe the general approach for layout design. **LO4**

12. Relate process and product layout to process types. **LO4**

13. What are the main advantages of a product layout? The main disadvantages? **LO4**

14. What are the main advantages of a process layout? The main disadvantages? **LO4**

15. Why are routing and scheduling continual problems in process layouts? **LO4**

16. Compare machine/equipment maintenance strategies in product and process layouts. **LO4**

17. Briefly outline the impact that job operations sequence has on each of the layout types. **LO4**

18. A city transportation planning committee must decide whether to begin a long-term project to build a subway system or to upgrade the present bus service. Suppose you are an expert in fixed-path and variable-path material-handling equipment, and the committee seeks your counsel on this matter. What are the advantages and limitations of the subway and bus systems? **LO4**

19. Why are product layouts atypical in service environments? **LO4**

20. According to a study, it costs more than three times the original purchase price in parts and labour to replace a totally wrecked automobile. Explain the reasons for this large discrepancy. **LO1 & 4**

21. How can a layout help or hinder productivity? **LO4**

22. What is a cellular layout? What are its main benefits and limitations? **LO4**

23. What is group technology? **LO4**

24. What is the goal of line balancing? What happens if a line is unbalanced? **LO5**

25. Explain the consequences of task time variability on line balancing. **LO5**

26. What is the main objective of process layout? **LO6**

Taking Stock

1. Name a major trade-off in (a) process design and (b) layout design. **LO3 & 5**

2. Who needs to be involved in process design? Layout design? **LO3 & 4**

3. In what ways does technology have an impact on process design? Layout design? **LO2 & 6**

4. Use of efficient production processes in raising animals for meat has resulted in factory farms where animals (pigs, hens, etc.) are kept in confinement at high stocking density. For example, female pigs are impregnated and kept in gestation crates (2 feet by 7 feet) for the whole 4 months of pregnancy. This process is repeated after the delivery. Many people consider this practice unethical. In fact, it has been banned in Europe. Smithfield Foods, the largest U.S. pork producer, under pressure from McDonald's, has decided to stop the use of gestation crates in its 187 pig nurseries.[3] Where in the process design methodology should this kind of ethical issue be considered? **LO3**

---

[3] M. Kaufman, "Largest Pork Processor to Phase out Crates," *Washington Post*, January 26, 2007, p. A06.

Critical Thinking Exercises

1. When would automation be feasible? Name one or two of the most important factors and briefly explain their importance. **LO2**

2. Layout decisions affect a wide range of facilities, from factories, grocery stores, offices, department stores, and warehouses, to malls, parking lots and garages, and kitchens.

Layout is also important in the design of some products such as the interiors of automobiles and the arrangement of components inside computers and other electronic devices. Select three different items from above lists, or other similar items, and explain for each the one or two key considerations for layout design. **LO4**

Experiential Learning Exercises

1. Visit a supermarket and identify an area of the store that has the characteristics of each of these process types: job shop, batch, repetitive, and continuous. **LO1**

2. Compare the layout of a supermarket to the layout of a convenience store. Explain the differences you observe. **LO4**

3. Design an assembly line for preparing a turkey sub (lettuce, tomato, mayo, and turkey). Use about six workstations. Begin with cutting the bun open, and end with cutting the sub in half. Estimate the time needed in seconds for each workstation. **LO3**

4. Draw the layout of two gas stations you know and compare the two. Which is better? **LO4**

5. Buy a few copies of a Lego game such as a racer (8119), and form a team of at least two.

a. Disassemble the car and familiarize yourself with the pieces.

b. Assemble the car according to the instructions sheet (in the box) a few times until you learn how to do it from memory.

c. Assign tasks to individual members, and make an assembly line.

d. Run the assembly line until all cars of your group are assembled, while timing the total time.

e. Discuss various ways of reducing your time without causing quality problems.

f. Disassemble all cars.

g. Implement your improvement, run the line again, and time it.

h. Summarize what you learned from this exercise.

Internet Exercises

1. Visit the Web page (or view the video) of one of the following companies and draw its process flow diagram: **LO3**

- AirBoss of America http://www.airbossofamerica.com/tour
- Lego http://www.youtube.com/watch?v=wnRRDIFNxoM
- Potash Corp http://minetour.potashcorp.com
- Guildcrest Homes http://www.guildcrest.com/index.php/gallery/factory-tour
- Dofasco http://www.dofasco.ca/HOW_Steel_Is_Made/html/index.html

2. Visit http://manufacturing.stanford.edu, click on "How Everyday Things Are Made," choose a product from the left column (e.g., airplane, motorcycle, cars, jelly beans, bottles, wool, denim), click on it, watch the video, and draw the process flow diagram. **LO3**

Problems

1. An assembly line with 17 tasks is to be balanced. The longest task is 2.4 minutes, and the total time for all tasks is 18 minutes. The line will operate for 450 minutes per day. **LO5**

a. What is the minimum number of workstations needed if the output rate is to be 180 units per day?

b. What cycle time will provide an output rate of 125 units per day?

c. What output will result if the cycle time is (i) 9 minutes? (ii) 15 minutes?

2. A manager wants to assign tasks to workstations to achieve an hourly output rate of 33 units. Assume that the shop works 60 minutes per hour (i.e., no breaks). **LO5**

a. Assign the tasks shown in the following precedence network (times are on the nodes and are in minutes) to workstations using the following heuristic rules: (i) "Assign the task with the most followers." (ii) Tiebreaker: "Assign the task with the longest time."

b. What is the efficiency?

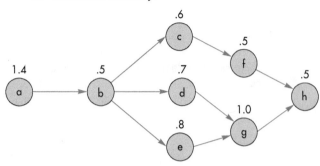

3. A manager wants to assign tasks to workstations in order to achieve an hourly output rate of four units. The department uses a working time of 56 minutes per hour. **LO5**

a. Assign the tasks shown in the following precedence network (times are on the nodes and are in minutes) to workstations using the following heuristic rules: (i) "Assign the task with the largest positional weight." (ii) Tiebreaker: "Assign the task with the longest time." If a tie still exists, choose randomly.

b. What is the efficiency?

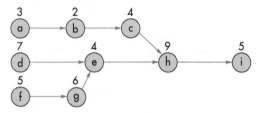

4. A large manufacturer of pencil sharpeners is planning to add a new sharpener, and you have been asked to balance the assembly line, given the following task times and precedence relationships. Assume that cycle time is 1.3 minutes per unit. **LO5**

Task	Duration (minutes)	Immediate Follower
a	.2	b
b	.4	d
c	.3	d
d	1.3	g
e	.1	f
f	.8	g
g	.3	h
h	1.2	—

a. Do each of the following:
i. Draw the precedence network.
ii. Assign the tasks to workstations using the heuristic rule "Assign the task with the most followers." Break ties using the heuristic rule "Assign the task with the longest time."
iii. Determine the percentage idle time.
iv. Calculate the rate of output that could be expected for this line assuming a 420-minute working day.

b. Answer these questions:
i. What is the shortest cycle time that will permit the use of only two workstations? Identify the tasks you would assign to each workstation.
ii. Determine the percentage idle time that would result if two workstations were used.
iii. What is the daily output under this arrangement?

5. As part of a major plant renovation project, the industrial engineering department has been asked to balance a revised assembly line to achieve an output rate of 240 units per eight-hour day. Task times and precedence relationships are as follows: **LO5**

Task	Duration (minutes)	Precedes Task
a	.2	b
b	.4	d
c	.2	d
d	.4	g
e	1.2	f
f	1.2	g
g	1.0	—

Do each of the following:

a. Draw the precedence network.
b. Determine the required cycle time.
c. Determine the minimum number of workstations needed.
d. Assign the tasks to workstations using the heuristic rule "Assign the task with the most followers." Use the heuristic rule "Assign the task with the longest time" as a tiebreaker. If a tie still exists, choose randomly.
e. Calculate the percentage idle time for the assignments in part *d*.

6. Twelve tasks, with times and precedence requirements as shown in the following table, are to be assigned to workstations using a cycle time of 1.5 minutes. Heuristic rule "Assign the task with the most followers" will be tried. The tiebreaker will be the heuristic rule "Assign the task with the longest time." **LO5**

Task	Duration (minutes)	Follows Task	Task	Duration (minutes)	Follows Task
a	.1	—	g	.4	f
b	.2	a	h	.1	g
c	.9	b	i	.2	h
d	.6	c	j	.7	i
e	.1	—	k	.3	j
f	.2	d, e	l	.2	k

a. Draw the precedence network.
b. Assign tasks to workstations.
c. Calculate the percentage idle time.

7. For the following tasks: **LO5**

   a. Develop the precedence network.
   b. Determine the cycle time (in seconds) for a desired output rate of 500 units in a seven-hour day.
   c. Determine the minimum number of workstations for output rate of 500 units per day.
   d. Balance the line using the "Assign the task with the most followers" heuristic rule. Break ties with "Assign the task with the longest time" heuristic rule. Use a cycle time of 50 seconds.
   e. Calculate the percentage idle time for the line.

Task	Task Time (seconds)	Immediate Predecessors
A	45	—
B	11	A
C	9	B
D	50	—
E	26	D
F	11	E
G	12	C
H	10	C
I	9	F, G, H
J	10	I
	193	

8. A shop works a 400-minute day. The manager of the shop wants an output rate of 200 units per day for the assembly line that has the tasks shown in the following table. Do the following: **LO5**

   a. Construct the precedence network and calculate the cycle time.
   b. Assign tasks according to "Assign the task with the most followers" rule. In the case of a tie, use "Assign the task with the longest time" heuristic rule.
   c. Calculate the balance delay.

Task	Immediately Precedes Task(s)	Task Time	Task	Immediately Precedes Task(s)	Task Time
a	b, c, d	.5	g	h	.4
b	e	1.4	h	k	.3
c	e	1.2	i	j	.5
d	f	.7	j	k	.8
e	g, j	.5	k	m	.9
f	i	1.0	m	—	.3

9. Arrange six departments into a 2 × 3 floor grid so that these conditions are satisfied: 1 is close to 2; 5 is close to 2, 4, and 6; and 3 is not close to 1 or 2. **LO6**

10. Using the information given in the preceding problem, develop a Muther grid using the letters A and X.

Leave any pair of combinations not mentioned blank. **LO6**

11. Using the information in the following Muther grid, determine the department locations on the following floor plan. Note that departments 1 and 7 must be in the locations shown. **LO6**

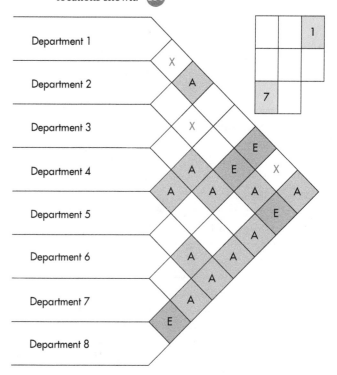

12. Arrange the eight departments shown in the following Muther grid into a 2 × 4 floor plan. *Note:* Department 2 must be in the location shown. **LO6**

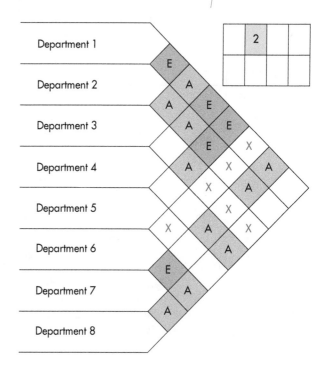

13. Arrange nine departments into a 3 × 3 floor grid so that they satisfy the conditions shown in the following Muther grid. Place department 5 in the lower left corner of the 3 × 3 floor grid. **LO6**

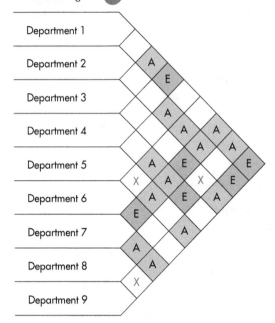

14. Determine the placement of departments on the following floor plan that will minimize total transportation cost using the data in the following tables. Assume that reverse distances are the same. Use a cost of $1 per trip metre. Use the heuristic in the section "Minimizing Total Transportation Cost or Distance." **LO6**

Location A	Location B	Location C
	Location D	

Distance between Centres of Locations (metres)

From	To	A	B	C	D
A		—	40	80	70
B			—	40	50
C				—	60
D					—

Number of Trips per Day From–To Departments

From	To	1	2	3	4
1		—	10	20	30
2			—	40	40
3				—	25
4		50	50	30	—

15. Eight work centres must be arranged in an L-shaped building. The locations of work centres 1 and 3 have already been assigned as shown in the following diagram. Assuming that transportation costs are $1 per load per metre, develop a suitable layout that minimizes total transportation cost using the information given below. (Assume the reverse distances are the same.) Use the heuristic in the section "Minimizing Total Transportation Cost or Distance." **LO6**

A 1	B	
C	D	E 3
F	G	H

Distance (metres)

From	To	A	B	C	D	E	F	G	H
A		—	40	40	60	120	80	100	110
B			—	60	40	60	140	120	130
C				—	45	85	40	70	90
D					—	40	50	40	45
E						—	90	50	40
F							—	40	60
G								—	40
H									—

Loads per Day

From	To	1	2	3	4	5	6	7	8
1		—	10	5	90	365	135	125	0
2		0	—	140	10	0	35	0	120
3		0	220	—	110	10	0	0	200
4		0	110	240	—	10	0	0	170
5		5	40	100	180	—	10	40	10
6		0	80	40	70	0	—	10	20
7		0	45	20	50	0	40	—	20
8		0	0	0	20	0	0	0	—

16. Develop a process layout that will minimize the total distance travelled by patients at a medical clinic, using the following information. Assume a distance of 35 feet between the reception area and each other location A to F. Assume that the reverse distances are the same. Use the floor plan shown below. Use the heuristic in the section "Minimizing Total Transportation Cost or Distance." **LO6**

Distance between Centres of Locations (feet)

From	To	A	B	C	D	E	F
A		—	20	60	80	120	160
B			—	40	60	80	120
C				—	40	60	80
D					—	40	60
E						—	40
F							—

Trips From–To Departments (per day)

From \ To	1	2	3	4	5	6	Reception
Reception	10	10	200	20	0	100	—
1	—	0	0	80	20	40	10
2	0	—	0	0	0	20	40
3	40	0	—	10	190	10	10
4	30	50	0	—	10	70	0
5	60	40	60	30	—	20	10
6	10	100	0	20	0	—	30

17. Ten labs should be assigned to the circular floor plan shown below. Recalling a similar layout's congestion in the halls, the new lab manager has requested an assignment that will minimize traffic between offices, but movement in the hall is restricted to a counterclockwise route. Develop a suitable layout using the following information. Assign Lab 1 to Location A, Lab 2 to Location I, and Lab 8 to Location E. **LO6**

Number of Trips per Day From–To Labs

From \ To	1	2	3	4	5	6	7	8	9	10
1	—	40	1	20	20	4	0	2	6	5
2	0	—	2	15	25	10	2	12	13	6
3	50	35	—	10	13	4	0	4	7	1
4	6	1	8	—	0	14	10	20	22	11
5	3	2	7	35	—	22	5	9	19	10
6	5	5	10	0	2	—	15	0	1	20
7	20	16	50	4	9	2	—	1	3	0
8	10	6	14	2	4	44	13	—	1	25
9	5	5	18	1	2	40	30	42	—	32
10	30	30	35	20	15	5	40	10	15	—

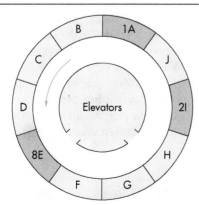

18. For the process of conducting a bank transaction using a teller in your bank, draw a process flow diagram (i.e.,

service blueprint). Start when customer arrives at the bank. Fail-safe this process. No need for line-of-visibility or activity times. **LO3**

19. Draw a process flow diagram for customer service/eating in a full-service restaurant. Start when a customer arrives at the restaurant. **LO3**

20. Draw a process flow diagram for preparing a personal income tax return. **LO3**

21. Draw a process flow diagram for mass producing potato chips. Start with trucks bringing potatoes to the plant. *Hint:* First imagine how this can be done at home at small scale and then try to covert the process to large-scale mass production. **LO3**

22. Draw a process flow diagram for batch production of bagels, as done by for example, Great Canadian Bagel Company. *Hint:* First imagine how this can be done at home (it is similar to making bread) and then try to covert the process to batch production at a store. **LO3**

23. a. A pencil is made from a graphite rod and wooden body (plus a metal band and eraser at one end). Given the graphite rod, come up with two different ways (concepts) of manufacturing a pencil (ignore the metal band and eraser). **LO3**

    b. Draw a process flow diagram for mass producing a pencil. You may use the photos and descriptions from http://www.generalpencil.com/how-a-pencil-is-made.html.

24. Draw a process flow diagram for making yarn (thread) from fleece (sheep wool). Use approximately four major steps. You may use http://www.blackberry-ridge.com/prosdscr.htm as a source.

25. a. Chocolate is toasted, ground (and heated), refined, and moulded seeds of cocoa beans. Draw a process flow diagram (approximately five operations) for making chocolate from cocoa beans at home. State what equipment (if any) you plan to use for each operation. **LO3**

    b. View the video at https://www.hersheys.com/ads-and-videos/how-we-make-chocolate.aspx and draw the process flow diagram for mass producing milk chocolate with almond (approximately eight operations).

26. Paper is made from wood pulp. Wood pulp is made from wood chips by either cooking it with chemicals (called Kraft pulp) or grinding the wood chips into its fibres (called Thermo-mechanical pulp). Pulp is cleaned and possibly bleached before papermaking. If one were to make paper at home, the following process could be used: **LO3**

    "The pulp is poured into a large tub and the fibres are suspended in the water. A framed screen is dipped into the water and is lifted to the surface, catching the fibres onto the screen. The screen can either be left in the sun to dry, or be pressed, smoothed and then dried."[4]

Design a continuous process for mass producing paper. Assume pulp has already been made. Draw the process flow diagram.

27. Audio Innovations of Stillwater, Oklahoma, makes car speaker cabinets and enclosures. Before 2001, it made 12,000 cabinets per month using 130 workers and a labour-intensive process. Then it was purchased by Rockford Corp of Arizona, which increased its capacity and productivity. **L03**

Before the change the process was as follows: 5/8 inch–thick Medium Density Fiberboard (MDF) was cut into individual sides of the cabinet using a beam saw (a circular saw on a table guided by beams). Then, for each piece a router was used to machine the slanted edges. Next, to cover the four sides a strip of carpet was cut, and the four sides were glued to the strip. Then, the strip ends were glued together. Finally, the front and back pieces were glued.

The process change involved both the nature of operations and their automation. A machine (called a laminator) was bought to glue carpet to the whole sheet of MDF. Then, the carpeted board is cut into a piece the size of the four sides using the beam saw. A computerized grooving line was purchased to make three V-grooves where the piece will be folded to form the sides of the box. After this, a worker glued the strip ends together. Finally, the front and back pieces were glued.

As a result of the change, the company can make 20,000 cabinets per month using the same number of workers.

1. Draw the process flow diagram before the change.
2. Draw the process flow diagram after the change.
3. Determine the productivity before and after the change.[5]

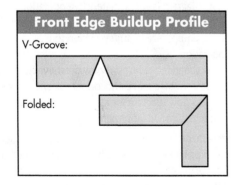

28. Draw a process flow diagram for packing six 227-gram cartons of baby cereal into cardboard cases. Assume that filled cartons arrive from the manufacturing process on a conveyor, collapsed cases are on a close-by cart, and packed cases are put on a conveyor to palletizing area.[6] **L03**

29. The tasks performed in a cafeteria to serve a customer and the average service times are as follows: **L05**

Tasks	Service Time per Customer (seconds)
Serve vegetables	25
Serve entrée	30
Serve soup	20
Serve dessert	15
Serve drink	10
Collect money	60

The only precedence relationship is that "collect money" has to be last. The current layout performs these tasks in the sequence given; each task is performed by one worker except that only one worker serves both dessert and drink.

a. i. Draw the precedence network.
   ii. What is the maximum number of customers who can be served per hour (capacity) using the current layout?
   iii. Assuming that capacity in part *ii* equals desired output, what are the cycle time and minimum number of workstations (workers) needed?
   iv. Suppose that capacity has to be increased. Where can the sixth worker be employed, assuming that equipment is not a constraint?
   v. How can we keep the same number of workers (five) but change the process in order to increase the capacity?

b. Using cycle time = 35 seconds and "Assign the task with the longest time" heuristic rule, balance the assembly line, and calculate the percentage idle time.

30. Suppose you need to assemble 67 Quickline Guest tables in one hour (see the photos on the next page). The assembly activities and their standard times are listed below. Using common sense, draw a precedence network and calculate the cycle time. Then, perform assembly-line balancing using "Assign the task with the longest time" heuristic rule, breaking ties using "Assign the task with the most followers" heuristic rule. Any further ties can be broken randomly. **L05**

---

[4] http://www.hqpapermaker.com/paper-history

[5] L. Ohm, "Automation Boosts Production 65 Percent," *FDM—The Magazine of Woodworking Production Management*, August 2003, 75(12), pp. 48–54.

[6] An automated case packer can be seen at http://www.trinamics.com/616sl.html and its use in H. J. Heinz is described in J. Mans, "Servos Increase Case-packing Efficiency," *Packaging Digest*, 43(7), July 2006, pp. 26–29.

Activity	Standard Time (seconds)
A. Lay the top face down on a clean surface.	10
B_1. Attach a mounting bracket to a corner of the top using three screws.	35
C_1. Add a compression ring on the bracket.	5
D_1. Slide one end of a leg over the compression ring and turn it so that the hole is aligned with the Allen screw.	10
E_1. Tighten the screw with Allen wrench.	15
B_2. Attach another mounting bracket to another corner of top using three screws.	35
C_2. Add another compression ring.	5
D_2. Slide one end of another leg over the compression ring and turn it.	10
E_2. Tighten with Allen wrench.	15
B_3. Attach another mounting bracket to another corner of top using three screws.	35
C_3 Add another compression ring.	5
D_3. Slide end of another leg over the compression ring and turn it.	10
E_3. Tighten with Allen wrench.	15
B_4. Attach another mounting bracket to another corner of top using three screws.	35
C_4. Add another compression ring.	5
D_4. Slide end of another leg over the compression ring and turn it.	10
E_4. Tighten with Allen wrench.	15
F. Turn the table over on its legs.	30

Sheet metal screws

Compression ring

Camar mounting plate

Black Camar Leg

6 mm Allen Wrench

Mounting Plate

31. Consider the Scoot & Go Rider shown on the next page, made by the Processed Plastic Company (PPC). Suppose that PPC has received a rush order from Walmart for 8,800 units to be shipped in five days. **LO5**

   a. Assuming 16 hour workdays, calculate the cycle time.

   b. Start with the body on the table, and assume all parts are within reach. Also assume that the steering wheel subassembly has already been made. Using common sense, draw a precedence network for the following activities, which are required to assemble a Scoot & Go Rider.

Activity	Standard time (seconds)
a. Insert the steering wheel subassembly in the body.	7
b. Hammer the front (short) axle into a pal nut (using the pal nut tool).	10
c. Slide a wheel in the component resulting from b.	5
d. Pass component resulting from c through the steering shaft hole.	5
e. Slide a wheel into component resulting from d.	4
f. Hammer the component resulting from e into a pal nut (using the pal nut tool).	12
g. Hammer the rear (long) axle into a pal nut (using the pal nut tool).	10
h. Slide a wheel in the component resulting from g.	6
i. Pass component resulting from h through the body's rear axle holes.	7
j. Slide a wheel into component resulting from i.	4
k. Hammer the component resulting from j into a pal nut (using the pal nut tool).	13
l. Place walker bar on the body and attach using one screw.	15
m. Insert another screw into walker bar to attach it to the body.	11
n. Insert another screw into walker bar to attach it to the body.	11
o. Insert another screw into walker bar to attach it to the body.	11
p. Perform final quality check and box it.	30

c. If the cycle time is 33 seconds, what is the minimum number of workstations needed?

d. Perform assembly-line balancing using 33 seconds cycle time, the standard times, and the precedence network from part b. Use "Assign the task with the longest time" heuristic rule, breaking ties using "Assign the task with the most followers" heuristic rule. Any further ties can be broken arbitrarily.

#17300/#17360
Go & Scoot Rider™/MC
A Tim Mee Toy by
Processed Plastic Co.
1001 Aucutt Road
Montgomery, IL 60538

PARTS LIST		
#	DESCRIPTION	QTY
A	BODY	1
B	WALKER BAR	1
C	WHEEL	4
D	PAL NUT	4
E	PAL NUT TOOL	2
F	SHORT AXLE	1
G	LONG AXLE	1
H	3/4" SCREW	4

Note: Pal nut tools (E) are used for assembly, then discarded.

32. Consider the Playskool Storage Studio on the next page. We wish to design an assembly line to assemble several units. The assembly tasks and their standard times (in seconds) are as follows. **L05**

Tasks	Standard Time (seconds)
a. Place the Toy Chest (A), with the Lid/ Art Board (F) already attached, on the conveyor.	8
b_1. Slide one Side Support (B) in the holes on one side of top of Toy Chest.	9
b_2. Slide the other Side Support (B) in the holes on the other side of top of Toy Chest.	9
c_1. Attach one Bin Support (C) to Side Supports in the front using 2 pins (D).	20
c_2. Attach another Bin Support (C) to Side Supports in the front using 2 pins.	20
d. Insert 4 pins in the Brace (G).	15
e_1. Place one Bin Support (C) in the back on Side Supports.	8
e_2. Place another Bin Support (C) in the back on Side Supports.	8
f. Attach the Brace (with pins) to the Bin and Side Supports in the back.	40
g_1. Place a Storage Bin (E) on the Bin Supports.	7
g_2. Place another Storage Bin on the Bin Supports.	7
g_3. Place another Storage Bin on the Bin Supports.	7
g_4. Place another Storage Bin on the Bin Supports.	7
g_5. Place another Storage Bin on the Bin Supports.	7
g_6. Place another Storage Bin on the Bin Supports	7

The parts are to be assembled according to the following precedence network:

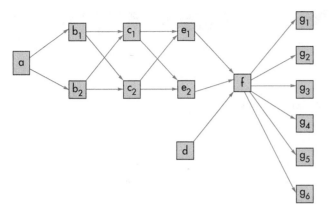

a. Calculate the cycle time if 75 units per hour are to be assembled.
b. What is the minimum number of workstations?
c. Using your answer to part *a*, perform assembly-line balancing using "Assign the task with the longest time" heuristic rule, breaking any ties using "Assign the task with the most followers" rule. If there is still a tie, break it randomly.

PLAYSKOOL® **Storage Studio**™ TM/MC

33. To assemble the plastic chair (shown below) using an assembly line, the following activities with estimated standard times are required. **L05**

Activity	Standard Time (seconds)
A Place left side inside up on the work area	5 seconds
B Tap back in	8
C Tap seat in	13
D Tap bottom rung in	7
E Tap bottom rack in	9
F Align all slots and tap right side in	15

a. Draw a precedence network for this assembly.
b. If the desired output rate of the assembly line is 120 chairs per hour, what is the minimum number of workstations required?
c. Using a cycle time of 30 seconds per chair, and "Assign the task with the longest time" heuristic rule, design the assembly line (i.e., balance the line).

34. A large centralized food production (i.e., kitchen) facility is to be constructed for 29 hospitals. A small consulting firm has been contracted to design the facility. The firm has determined that the production process should be decomposed into the following departments and desired area for each, in addition to departments given on the following layout diagram (which has 200 ft by 150 ft floor space). Using common sense, determine the location of the unassigned departments on the layout:

Department	Desired Area (ft²)
Vegetable fridges	2,700
Dry storeroom and dairy fridges	2,300
Poultry and meat freezers	1,500
Cook-chill area	3,800
Finished products coolers and fridges	2,800

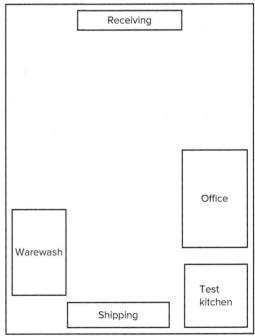

School Chairs

School chairs are usually made of plastic and metal, costing anywhere from $30 to $100 each. You wish to evaluate the idea of manufacturing wooden chairs for sale to schools, churches, etc. You have found the following design for a chair.

Most wooden chairs are made of hardwoods such as oak, maple, cherry, or cedar. Suppose that cedar is the cheapest where you live. The dimensions of the parts of the chair are as follows:

Item	Number	Dimension (inches) (thickness, width, length)
Back post	2	2 × 2 × 36
Front post	2	2 × 2 × 18
Crossbar	10	1 × 1 × 14
Rails	3	2 × 1 × 14
Seat	1	1 × 16 × 16

The most economical size of cedar lumber is 2" × 4" × 8" (i.e., 2 inches thick by 4 inches wide by 8 feet long). Therefore, you intend to buy only this size.

Questions

1. Calculate the number of this lumber you will need per chair.

2. Determine the operations needed to make the chair and draw a process flow diagram. Note that the crossbars and rails have a tenon (a small round tip) on each end that will go in the mortise (the hole) of the posts. These have to be made. Also, the seat's corners have to be cut to allow for the posts.

Source: Based on H. Quesada and R. Gazo, "Development of a Manufacturing System for Construction of School Furniture," *Forest Products Journal* 53(9), September 2003, pp. 47–54.

The Double-D Cell

Sometimes converting an assembly line into two or more cells will actually reduce the staffing requirements. Such was the case in the hardware (mechanical parts) subassembly of recliners in the Franklin Corp. plant.

The Initial Subassembly Frames (ISF) were assembled by four workers. Then, the ISFs were stored in the ISF queue until they were needed by the circular line, at which time a material handler mounted ISFs on wheeled tables, which were secured to the outer ring of the line with rollers (see the sketch and photo below on the left). Five workers worked inside the ring. The cycle time in the ring was approximately 30 seconds, but there was a total of 35 seconds of idle time per subassembly assembled in the ring. There were four types of subassemblies but they were similar.

In order to improve the efficiency of the circular line, the Double-D layout was proposed (see the sketch and photo below on the right).

Questions

1. What are the advantages of the Double-D cells over the circular line?

2. Suppose that the task times of the five workstations in the ring were 30, 25, 20, 20, and 20 seconds, respectively. Explain how four workers, two in each D, can produce the same output as the five workers in the ring.

Source: http://fwrc.msstate.edu/pubs/doubled.pdf.

Q   MINI-CASE

Lego Car

On the right is the precedence network for assembling the Lego Racer (8119). For example, the black rectangle (19) can be attached only after the yellow rectangle (12) and the two sides (2 and 3) are attached. Note that in order to reduce the size of problem (and possibly make assembly easier), items 5–9 and 13–16 are subassemblies. Answer the following questions.

a. We wish to assemble 240 cars in one hour. What should be the cycle time (in seconds)?

b. The following are the standard times (in seconds) of attaching each piece to its immediate predecessor(s). (*Note:* For items 5–9 and 13–16, the time includes time of assembling the subassemblies. *Note:* Time of the 1st piece is for reaching and grasping it). What is the theoretical minimum number of workstations needed if cycle time = 15 seconds?

Precedence Network:

(continued)

Task	1	2	3	4	5	6	7	8	9	10	11	12	13	14	15	16	17	18	19	20	21	22
Time	1	1	1	1	3	3	2	2	5	1	1	1	2	2	3	7	1	1	1	1	1	1

c. Pick an appropriate heuristic and cycle time of 15 seconds, and perform assembly line balancing.

To access "Linear Programming," the supplement to Chapter 6, please visit Connect.

connect **LEARNSMART** **SMARTBOOK**

For more information on the resources available from McGraw-Hill Ryerson, go to www.mheducation.ca/he/solutions.

CHAPTER 6
Linear Programming

Learning Objectives

After completing this supplement, you should be able to:

LO1 Formulate a linear programming model from the description of a problem.

LO2 Solve two-variable linear programming problems using the graphical solution method.

LO3 Solve linear programming problems using Excel's Solver.

LO4 Do sensitivity analysis on the solution of a linear programming problem.

Introduction and Linear Programming Model

Linear programming is a powerful quantitative tool used to obtain optimal solutions to problems that involve requirements or limitations for resources, such as available material, budget, labour, and machine time. These problems are referred to as *constrained optimization* problems. Linear programming has been successful in optimizing numerous decision-making problems including:

- Determining optimal blends of animal feed and gasoline ingredients.
- Developing optimal production schedules.
- Identifying the optimal mix of products to produce in a factory.

Linear programming (LP) techniques consist of a sequence of steps that will lead to an optimal solution to linear-constrained problems, if an optimum exists. There are a number of different linear programming techniques; some are special-purpose (i.e., used to find solutions for specific types of problems) and others are more general in scope. This supplement covers the two general-purpose solution techniques: graphical linear programming and computer solutions. Graphical linear programming provides a visual portrayal of many of the important concepts of linear programming. However, it is limited to problems with only two variables. In practice, computers are used to obtain solutions for problems, some of which involve a large number of variables.

A linear programming model is a mathematical representation of a constrained optimization problem. Four components provide the structure of a linear programming model:

1. Decision variables.
2. Objective.
3. Constraints.
4. Parameters.

decision variables Choices in terms of amounts of either inputs or outputs.

Decision variables represent choices in terms of amounts of either inputs to use or outputs to produce. Each unknown quantity is assigned a decision variable (e.g., x_1, x_2).

A linear programming model requires a single goal or *objective*. An objective is either maximized and minimized. A maximized objective might involve profit, revenue, etc. Conversely, a minimized objective might involve cost, time, or distance. The **objective function** is a mathematical expression involving the decision variables representing the objective, e.g., profit, cost.

objective function A mathematical expression involving the decision variables that represent the objective, e.g., profit, cost.

constraints Represent the requirements or limitations that restrict the available choices.

Constraints represent the requirements or limitations that restrict the choices available. The three types of constraints are less than or equal to ($\leq$), greater than or equal to ($\geq$), and simply equal to ($=$). A $\leq$ constraint implies an upper limit on the amount of some resource (e.g., machine hours, labour hours, material) available for use. A $\geq$ constraint specifies a minimum that must be achieved in the final solution (e.g., the product must contain at least 50 percent real orange juice). The $=$ constraint is more restrictive in the sense that it specifies *exactly* what a mathematical expression of decision variables should equal (e.g., make 200 units of product A). A linear programming model can consist of one or more constraints. The constraints of a given problem define the set of all feasible combinations of values of decision variables; this set is referred to as the **feasible solution space**. A linear programming solution technique is designed to search the feasible solution space for the combination of values of decision variables that will yield an optimum (i.e., best possible value) in terms of the objective function.

feasible solution space The set of all feasible combinations of values of decision variables as defined by the constraints.

parameters Coefficients of decision variables in the objective function and constraints.

In a linear programming model, symbols (e.g., x_1, x_2) represent the decision variables and numerical values, called **parameters**, represent their coefficients in the objective function and constraints. The parameters are input to the model and have fixed values.

Example 1 illustrates the components of a linear programming model.

First, the model lists and defines the decision variables. In this case, they are quantities of three different products that might be produced.

Decision variables	x_1 = Quantity of product 1 to produce	
	x_2 = Quantity of product 2 to produce	
	x_3 = Quantity of product 3 to produce	
Maximize	$5x_1 + 8x_2 + 4x_3$ (profit)	(Objective function)
Subject to		
Labour	$2x_1 + 4x_2 + 8x_3 \leq 250$ hours	(Constraints)
Material	$7x_1 + 6x_2 + 5x_3 \leq 100$ kg	
Product 1	$x_1 \qquad\qquad \geq 10$ units	
	$x_1, x_2, x_3 \geq 0$	(Non-negativity constraints)

◀ **Example 1**

Next, the model states the objective function. It includes every decision variable in the model and the profit contribution (per unit) of each decision variable. Thus, product 1 has a profit of $5 per unit. The profit from product 1 for a given solution x_1 will be 5 times the value of x_1; the total profit from all products will be the sum of the individual product profits. Thus, if $x_1 = 10$, $x_2 = 0$, and $x_3 = 6$, the value of the objective function would be:

$$5(10) + 8(0) + 4(6) = 74$$

The objective function is followed by a list (in no particular order) of four constraints. Each constraint has a right-side value (e.g., the labour constraint has a right-side value of 250) that indicates the amount of the constraint and a relation sign that indicates whether that amount is a maximum ($\leq$), a minimum ($\geq$), or an equality ($=$). The left side of each constraint consists of the variables and a coefficient for each variable that indicates how much of the right-side quantity *one unit* of the decision variable represents. For instance, for the labour constraint, one unit of product 1 will require two hours of labour. The sum of the values on the left side of each constraint represents the amount of that constraint used by a solution. Thus, if $x_1 = 10$, $x_2 = 0$, and $x_3 = 6$, the amount of labour used would be:

$$2(10) + 4(0) + 8(6) = 68 \text{ hours}$$

Because this amount does not exceed the quantity on the right-hand side of the constraint, it is *feasible* for the labour constraint.

Note that the third constraint refers to only a single variable; x_1 must be at least 10 units. X_1's coefficient is, in effect, 1, although that is not shown.

Finally, there are the non-negativity constraints. These are listed on a single line but they reflect the condition that no decision variable is allowed to have a negative value.

In order for a linear programming model to be used effectively, certain *assumptions* must be satisfied. These are:

1. *Linearity:* The impact of decision variables is linear in constraints and in the objective function.

2. *Divisibility:* Noninteger values of decision variables are acceptable.

3. *Certainty:* Values of parameters are known and are constant.

4. *Non-negativity:* Negative values of decision variables are unacceptable.

Model Formulation

An understanding of the components of linear programming models is necessary for model formulation. This helps provide organization to the process of assembling information about a problem into a model.

Naturally, it is important to obtain valid information on what constraints are appropriate, as well as on what values of the parameters are appropriate. If this is not done, the usefulness of the model will be questionable. Consequently, in some instances, considerable effort must be expended to obtain that information.

In formulating a model, use the format illustrated in Example 1. Begin by identifying the decision variables. Very often, decision variables are "the quantity of" something, such as x_1 = the quantity of product 1. Generally, decision variables have profits, costs, times, or a similar measure of value associated with them. Knowing this can help you identify the decision variables in a problem.

Constraints are restrictions or requirements on one or more decision variables, and they refer to available amounts of resources such as labour, material, or machine time, or to minimal requirements, such as "Make at least 10 units of product 1." It can be helpful to give a name to each constraint, such as "labour" or "material 1." Let's consider some of the different kinds of constraints you will encounter

1. *A ratio.* For example, "the ratio of x_1 to x_2 must be at least 3 to 2." To formulate this requirement, begin by setting up the ratio:

$$\frac{x_1}{x_2} \geq \frac{3}{2}$$

But this is not a linear constraint. Cross-multiply to obtain:

$$2x_1 \geq 3x_2$$

Although this is a linear constraint, it is not yet in the standard form: all variables in a constraint must be on the left side of the inequality (or equality) sign, leaving only a constant on the right side. To achieve this, we must subtract the variable amount that is on the right side from both sides. That yields:

$$2x_1 - 3x_2 \geq 0$$

Note that the direction of the inequality remains the same.

2. *A percentage.* For example, "x_1 cannot be more than 20 percent of the mix." Suppose that the mix consists of variables x_1, x_2, and x_3. In mathematical terms, this constraint would be:

$$x_1 \leq .20(x_1 + x_2 + x_3)$$

Again, all variables must appear on the left side of the constraint. To accomplish that, we can expand the right side and then subtract the result from both sides. Thus,

$$x_1 \leq .20x_1 + .20x_2 + .20x_3$$

Subtracting yields:

$$.80x_1 - .20x_2 - .20x_3 \leq 0$$

Example 2 ▶

A small company that assembles computers is about to start production of two new types of personal computers. Each type will require assembly time, inspection time, and storage space. The amounts of each of these resources that can be devoted to the production of these computers are limited. The manager of the firm would like to determine the quantity of each computer to produce in order to maximize the profit generated by sales of these computers. In order to develop a suitable model of the problem, the manager has met with the design and manufacturing personnel. As a result of those meetings, the manager has obtained the following information:

	Type 1	Type 2
Profit per unit	$60	$50
Assembly time per unit	4 hours	10 hours
Inspection time per unit	2 hours	1 hour
Storage space per unit	3 cubic feet	3 cubic feet

The manager also has acquired information on the availability of company resources. These daily amounts are:

Resource	Amount Available Per Day
Assembly time	100 worker hours
Inspection time	22 worker hours
Storage space	39 cubic feet

The manager met with the firm's marketing manager and learned that demand for the computers was such that whatever combination of these two types of computers is produced, all of the output can be sold at the determined prices.

In terms of meeting the assumptions, it would appear that the relationships are *linear*: The contribution to profit per unit of each type of computer and the time and storage space per unit of each type of computer is the same regardless of the quantity produced. Therefore, the total impact of each type of computer on the profit and each constraint is a linear function of the quantity of that variable. There may be a question of *divisibility* because, presumably, only whole units of computers will be produced. However, because this is a recurring process (i.e., the computers will be produced daily, a noninteger solution such as 3.5 computers per day will result in 7 computers every other day), this does not seem to pose a problem. Regarding the question of *certainty*, the manager could be questioned to determine whether the values shown for assembly times, etc., are known with certainty. Later in this chapter supplement, under "Sensitivity Analysis," the effect of uncertainty in parameters is studied.

Because we have concluded that linear programming is appropriate, let us now turn our attention to constructing a linear programming model of the problem. First, we must define the decision variables. The decision variables are the quantity of each type of computer to produce. Thus,

x_1 = quantity of type 1 computer to produce per day

x_2 = quantity of type 2 computer to produce per day

Next, we can formulate the objective function. The profit per unit of type 1 computer is listed as $60, and the profit per unit of type 2 is $50. So the objective function is

Maximize $Z = 60x_1 + 50x_2$

where Z is the value of the objective function, given values of x_1 and x_2. (In practice, the objective function is often written without the Z.)

Now, we formulate the constraints. There are three resources with limited availability: assembly time, inspection time, and storage space. The fact that availability is limited means that these constraints will all be $\leq$ constraints. Suppose we begin with the assembly constraint. Type 1 computer requires 4 hours of assembly time per unit, whereas type 2 computer requires 10 hours of assembly time per unit. Therefore, with a limit of 100 hours available per day, the assembly constraint is:

$4x_1 + 10x_2 \leq 100$ hours

Similarly, each unit of type 1 computer requires 2 hours of inspection time, and each unit of type 2 computer requires 1 hour of inspection time. With 22 hours available per day, the inspection constraint is:

$2x_1 + 1x_2 \leq 22$ hours

(*Note:* The coefficient 1 for x_2 need not be shown. Thus, an alternative form for this constraint is: $2x_1 + x_2 \leq 22$.) The storage constraint is determined in a similar manner:

$3x_1 + 3x_2 \leq 39$ cubic feet

The non-negativity constraints are:

$x_1, x_2 \geq 0$

In summary, the mathematical model of the computer problem is:

x_1 = quantity of type 1 computer to produce per day
x_2 = quantity of type 2 computer to produce per day

Maximize	$60x_1 + 50x_2$
Subject to	
Assembly	$4x_1 + 10x_2 \leq 100$ hours
Inspection	$2x_1 + 1x_2 \leq 22$ hours
Storage	$3x_1 + 3x_2 \leq 39$ cubic feet
	$x_1, x_2 \geq 0$

Once you have formulated a model, the next task is to solve it (i.e., find the best feasible solution). The following sections describe two approaches to problem solution: graphical solution method and computer solutions.

Graphical Solution Method

graphical solution Solution method that involves drawing the feasible solution space and contours of the objective function on paper, and finding the optimal solution by observation. This method applies to only two-variable linear programs.

The **graphical solution** method plots the constraints on a graph and identifies an area that satisfies all of the constraints. The area is referred to as feasible solution space. Next, the objective function is plotted and used to identify the optimal point in the feasible solution space. The coordinates of the point can sometimes be read directly from the graph, although generally an algebraic determination of the coordinates of the point is necessary. This method applies to only two-variable linear programs.

Consider the linear programming model described in Example 2 above.

Plotting the Constraints and Determining the Feasible Solution Space

Begin by drawing x_1 as x-axis and x_2 as y-axis on a coordinate system. Then, represent the non-negativity constraints as the top-right quadrant, as in Figure 6S-1.

Figure 6S-1

Graph showing the non-negativity constraints.

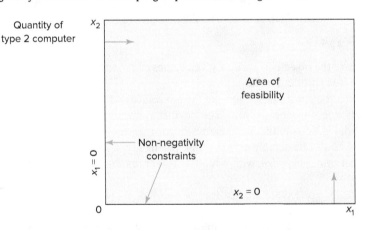

An equality constraint is represented by a straight line on the coordinate system that is simple to draw (see steps 2 and 3 below). The procedure for representing an inequality constraint is more involved:

1. Replace the inequality sign with an equal sign. This transforms the constraint into an equation that is represented by a straight line. Plot this line according to steps 2 and 3 below.

2. Determine where the line intersects each axis.

    a. To find where it crosses the x_2 axis, set x_1 equal to zero and solve the equation for the value of x_2.

    b. To find where it crosses the x_1 axis, set x_2 equal to zero and solve the equation for the value of x_1.

3. Mark these intersections on the axes, and connect them with a straight line. (*Note:* If a constraint has only one variable, it will be a vertical line if the variable is x_1, or a horizontal line if the variable is x_2.)

4. Indicate by shading (or by an arrow) whether the inequality is greater than or less than. (A general rule to determine which side of the line satisfies the inequality is to pick a point that is not on the line, such as the origin (0,0), plug it in the left side of the constraint and see whether the left side is greater than or less than the constraint's right-hand-side RHS.)

5. Repeat steps 1–4 for each constraint.

Consider the assembly time constraint:

$$4x_1 + 10x_2 \leq 100$$

Removing the inequality portion of the constraint produces this equation:

$$4x_1 + 10x_2 = 100$$

Next, identify the points where the line representing the above equation intersects each axis, as step 2 describes. Thus, with $x_2 = 0$, we find

$$4x_1 + 10(0) = 100$$

Solving, we find that $4x_1 = 100$, so $x_1 = 25$. Similarly, we can solve the equation for x_2 when $x_1 = 0$:

$$4(0) + 10x_2 = 100$$

Solving for x_2, we find $x_2 = 10$.

Thus, we have two points: ($x_1 = 0$, $x_2 = 10$), and ($x_1 = 25$, $x_2 = 0$). We can now add this line to our graph of the non-negativity constraints by connecting these two points (see Figure 6S-2).

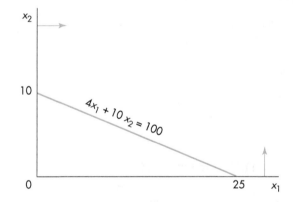

◀ **Figure 6S-2**

Plot of the first constraint (assembly time) as an equation.

Next, we must determine which side of the line represents points that are less than 100. To do this, we can select a test point that is not on the line, and substitute the x_1 and x_2 values of that point into the left side of the equation of the line. If the result is less than 100, this tells us that all points on that side of the line are less than the value of the line (e.g., 100). Conversely, if the result is greater than 100, this indicates that the other side of the line (relative to the point chosen) represents the set of points that will yield values that are less than 100. A relatively simple test point to use is the origin (i.e., $x_1 = 0$, $x_2 = 0$). Substituting these values into the left side of the equation yields:

$$4(0) + 10(0) = 0$$

Obviously 0 is less than 100. Hence, the side of the line containing the origin represents the "less than" area (i.e., the feasible region for the first constraint).

The feasible region for this constraint and the non-negativity constraints then becomes the shaded portion shown in Figure 6S-3.

For the sake of illustration, suppose we try one other point, say $x_1 = 10$, $x_2 = 10$. Substituting these values into the assembly equation yields:

$$4(10) + 10(10) = 140$$

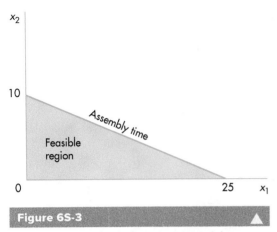

Figure 6S-3

The feasible region for the first constraint and the non-negativity constraints.

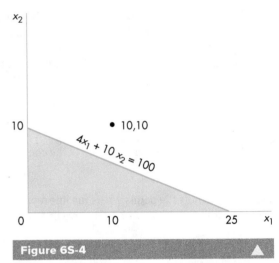

Figure 6S-4

The point (10, 10) is above the constraint line.

Clearly this is greater than 100. Therefore, all points on this side of the line are greater than 100 (see Figure 6S-4).

Continuing with the problem, we add the two remaining constraints to the graph. For the inspection constraint:

1. Convert the constraint into an equation by replacing the inequality sign with an equality sign:

   $2x_1 + 1x_2 \leq 22$ becomes $2x_1 + 1x_2 = 22$

2. Set x_1 equal to zero and solve for x_2:

   $2(0) + 1x_2 = 22$

   Solving, we find $x_2 = 22$. Thus, the line will intersect the x_2 axis at 22.

3. Next, set x_2 equal to zero and solve for x_1:

   $2x_1 + 1(0) = 22$

   Solving, we find $x_1 = 11$. Thus, the other end of the line will intersect the x_1 axis at 11.

4. Add the line to the graph and determine the side of the line that represents the constraint (see Figure 6S-5). Note that the area of feasibility for the inspection constraint is also below the line. However, the area feasible to both inspection and assembly constraints is the intersection of the area feasible to assembly and the area feasible to inspection.

The storage constraint is handled in the same manner:

1. Convert it into equality:

   $3x_1 + 3x_2 = 39$

2. Set x_1 equal to zero and solve for x_2:

   $3(0) + 3x_2 = 39$

   Solving, we find $x_2 = 13$. Thus, $x_2 = 13$ when $x_1 = 0$.

3. Set x_2 equal to zero and solve for x_1:

   $3x_1 + 3(0) = 39$

   Solving, we find $x_1 = 13$. Thus, $x_1 = 13$ when $x_2 = 0$.

4. Add the line to the graph and determine the side of the line that represents the constraint (again it is below the line because of $\leq$ constraint) (see Figure 6S-6).

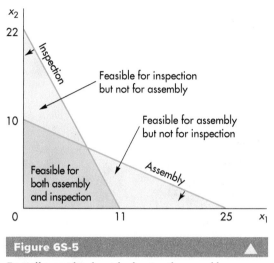

Figure 6S-5 ▲

Partially completed graph, showing the assembly, inspection, and non-negativity constraints.

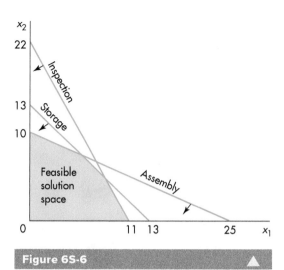

Figure 6S-6 ▲

Completed graph of the computer problem showing all the constraints and the feasible solution space.

The feasible solution space is the set of all points that satisfies *all* constraints. The shaded area shown in Figure 6S-6 is the feasible solution space for our problem.

The next step is to determine which point in the feasible solution space will produce the optimal value of the objective function. This determination is made by plotting objective function contours.

Plotting Objective Function Lines and Determining the Optimal Point

Plotting an objective function line involves the same logic as plotting a constraint line: determine where the line intersects each axis. But the objective function is not an equation. We can get around this by simply setting it equal to some number. Any number will do, although one that is evenly divisible by both coefficients is desirable.

Recall that the objective function for the computer problem is $60x_1 + 50x_2$. Suppose we decide to set the objective function equal to 300. That is,

$$60x_1 + 50x_2 = 300$$

We can now plot the line on our graph. As before, we can determine the x_1 and x_2 intercepts of the line by setting one of the two variables equal to zero and solving for the other, and then reversing the process. Thus, with $x_1 = 0$, we have:

$$60(0) + 50x_2 = 300$$

Solving, we find $x_2 = 6$. Similarly, with $x_2 = 0$, we have:

$$60x_1 + 50(0) = 300$$

Solving, we find $x_1 = 5$. This line is plotted in Figure 6S-7.

The $300 profit line is an *isoprofit* line; every point on the line (i.e., every combination of x_1 and x_2 that lies on the line) will provide a profit of $300. We can see from the graph that many combinations are both on the $300 profit line and are within the feasible solution space. In fact, considering noninteger as well as integer solutions, the possibilities are infinite.

Suppose we now consider another profit line, say the $600 line. To do this, we set the objective function equal to this amount. Thus,

$$60x_1 + 50x_2 = 600$$

Solving for the x_1 and x_2 intercepts yields these two points:

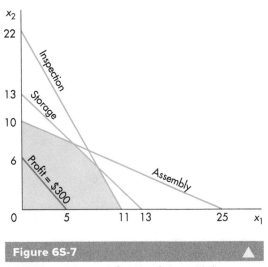

Computer problem with $300 profit line added.

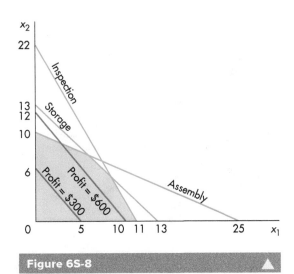

Computer problem with profit lines of $300 and $600.

x_1 intercept	x_2 intercept
$x_1 = 10$	$x_1 = 0$
$x_2 = 0$	$x_2 = 12$

This line is plotted in Figure 6S-8, along with the previous $300 line for purpose of comparison.

Two things are evident in Figure 6S-8 regarding the profit lines. One is that the $600 line is *farther* from the origin than the $300 line; the other is that the two lines are *parallel*. The lines are parallel because they both have the same slope. The slope is not affected by the right side of the equation. Rather, it is determined solely by the coefficients 60 and 50. Regardless of the number we select for the value of the objective function, the resulting line will be parallel to these two lines. Moreover, if the number is greater than 600, the line will be even farther away from the origin than the $600 line. If the number is less than 300, the line will be closer to the origin than the $300 line. And if the number is between 300 and 600, the line will fall between the $300 and $600 lines. This knowledge will help us in determining the optimal solution.

Consider a third line, one with the profit equal to $900. Figure 6S-9 shows that line along with the previous two profit lines. As expected, it is parallel to the other two, and even farther away from the origin. However, the line does not touch the feasible solution space at all. Consequently, there is no feasible combination of x_1 and x_2 that will yield that amount of profit. Evidently, the maximum possible profit is an amount between $600 and $900.

We could continue to select profit lines in this manner, and eventually, determine an amount that would yield the greatest feasible profit. However, there is a much simpler alternative. We can plot just one profit line, say the $300 line. We know that all other profit lines will be parallel to it. Consequently, by moving this one line parallel to itself we can represent other profit lines. We also know that as we move away from the origin, the profits get larger. What we want to know is how far the line can be moved out from the origin and still be touching the feasible solution space, and the values of the decision variables at that point (i.e., the optimal solution). Locate this point on the graph by placing a ruler along the $300 line (or any other convenient line) and sliding it away from the origin, being careful to keep it parallel to the line. This approach is illustrated in Figure 6S-10.

Once we have determined where the optimal solution is in the feasible solution space, we must determine the values of the decision variables at that point. Note that the optimal solution is at the intersection of the inspection boundary line and the storage boundary line (see Figure 6S-10). In other words, the optimal combination of x_1 and x_2 must satisfy both boundary (equality) conditions. We can determine those values by solving the two equations *simultaneously*. The equations are:

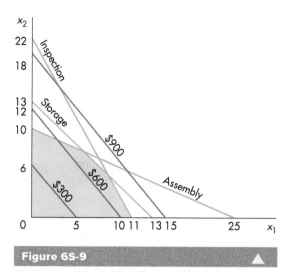

Figure 6S-9

Computer problem with profit lines of $300, $600, and $900.

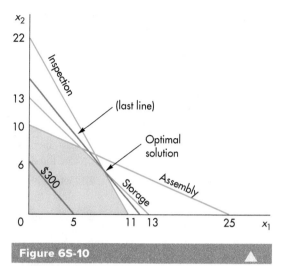

Figure 6S-10

Finding the optimal solution to the computer problem.

Inspection $2x_1 + 1x_2 = 22$

Storage $3x_1 + 3x_2 = 39$

The idea behind solving two *simultaneous equations* is to algebraically eliminate one of the unknown variables (i.e., to obtain an equation with a single unknown). This can be accomplished by multiplying the coefficients of one of the equations by a fixed amount and then adding (or subtracting) the modified equation from the other. (Occasionally, it is easier to multiply each equation by a fixed amount.) For example, we can eliminate x_2 by multiplying the inspection equation by 3 and then subtracting the storage equation from the modified inspection equation. Thus,

$3(2x_1 + 1x_2 = 22)$ becomes $6x_1 + 3x_2 = 66$

Subtracting the storage equation from this produces:

$$\begin{array}{r} 6x_1 + 3x_2 = 66 \\ -(3x_1 + 3x_2 = 39) \\ \hline 3x_1 + 0x_2 = 27 \end{array}$$

Solving the resulting equation yields $x_1 = 9$. The value of x_2 can be found by substituting $x_1 = 9$ into either of the original equations or the modified inspection equation. Suppose we use the original inspection equation. We have:

$2(9) + 1x_2 = 22$

Solving, we find $x_2 = 4$.

Hence, the optimal solution to the computer problem is to produce 9 units of type 1 computers and 4 units of type 2 computers per day. We can substitute these values into the objective function to find the optimal profit:

$\$60(9) + \$50(4) = \$740$

Hence, the last profit line—the one that would last touch the feasible solution space as we moved away from the origin parallel to the $300 profit line—would be the line where profit is $740.

In this problem, the optimal values for both decision variables are integers. This will not always be the case for the optimal solution to the linear programming model; one or both of the decision variables may turn out to be noninteger. In some situations noninteger values would be of little consequence. This would be true if the decision variables were measured on a continuous scale, such as the amount of fuel oil needed or if the profit contribution per unit was small, as with the number of nails or ball bearings to make. In some cases, the answer can simply be rounded down (maximization problems) or up (minimization problems) with very little impact on the objective function. Here, we assume that noninteger answers are acceptable as such.

Let's review the procedure for finding the optimal solution using the graphical solution method:

1. Draw the x_1 and x_2 axes.

2. Graph the constraints. Identify the feasible solution space.

3. Set the objective function equal to some number so that it crosses the feasible solution space. Plot the line. Slide it in parallel in the direction of increasing objective function until just before the line leaves the feasible solution space. This point is the optimal solution.

4. Determine which two constraints intersect there. Solve their equations simultaneously to obtain the values of the decision variables at the optimum.

5. Substitute the values obtained in the previous step into the objective function to determine the value of the objective function at the optimum.

Redundant Constraints

redundant constraint A constraint that does not form a unique boundary of the feasible solution space.

In some cases, a constraint does not form a unique boundary of the feasible solution space. Such a constraint is called a **redundant constraint**. Two such constraints ($x_2 \leq 25$ and $2x_1 + 3x_2 \leq 60$) are illustrated in Figure 6S-11. Note that a constraint is redundant if its removal would not alter the feasible solution space.

Figure 6S-11 ▶

Examples of redundant constraints.

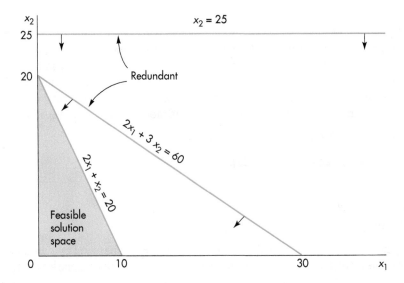

When a problem has a redundant constraint, at least one of the other constraints in the problem is more restrictive than the redundant constraint.

Solutions and Corner Points

The feasible solution space is a polygon, a convex shape with straight-line sides (convex means that any point between two feasible points is also feasible). Moreover, the solution to any problem will be at one of the corner points (intersections of constraints) of the polygon (except if there are multiple optimal solutions; described below). It is possible to determine the coordinates of each corner point of the feasible solution space, and use those values to compute the value of the objective function at those points. Comparing the values of the objective function at the corner points and identifying the best one (e.g., the maximum value) is another way to identify the optimal solution. For problems that have more than two decision variables, a variation of this approach (called Simplex method) is used to find the optimal solution.

In some instances, the objective function lines will be *parallel* to one of the constraint lines that form the *boundary of the feasible solution space*. When this happens, *every* combination of x_1

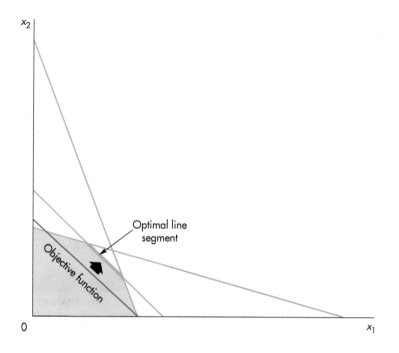

Some LP problems have multiple optimal solutions.

and x_2 on the segment of the constraint line that touches the feasible solution space represents an optimal solution. Hence, there are **multiple optimal solutions** to the problem. Figure 6S-12 illustrates an objective function line that is parallel to a constraint line.

Minimization

Graphical solution method for minimization problems is quite similar to maximization problems. There are, however, two important differences. One is that at least one of the constraints will be of the $\geq$ variety. This causes the feasible solution space to be away from the origin. The other difference is that the optimal corner point is the one closest to the origin. We find the optimal corner point by sliding the objective function line (which is an *isocost* line) *toward* the origin instead of away from it.

multiple optimal solutions When the objective function line is parallel to a constraint line that forms a boundary of the feasible solution space, all points on that boundary are optimal.

Solve the following problem using graphical solution method.

◀ **Example 3**

Minimize	$Z = 8x_1 + 12x_2$
Subject to	$5x_1 + 2x_2 \geq 20$
	$4x_1 + 3x_2 \geq 24$
	$x_2 \geq 2$
	$x_1, x_2 \geq 0$

1. Plot the constraints (shown in Figure 6S-13).

    a. Change constraints to equalities.

    b. For each constraint, set $x_1 = 0$ and solve for x_2, then set $x_2 = 0$ and solve for x_1.

    c. Graph each constraint. Note that $x_2 = 2$ is a horizontal line parallel to the x_1 axis and 2 units above it.

2. Shade the feasible solution space (see Figure 6S-13).

3. Plot the objective function.

    a. Select a value for the objective function that causes it to cross the feasible solution space. Try $8 \times 12 = 96$.

    b. Graph the line $8x_1 + 12x_2 = 96$ (see Figure 6S-14).

SOLUTION

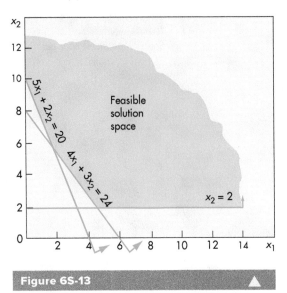

Figure 6S-13 ▲

The constraints define the feasible solution space for Example 3.

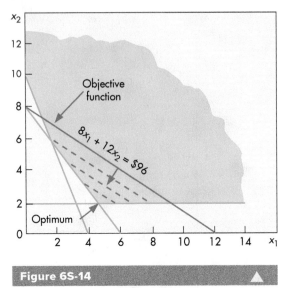

Figure 6S-14 ▲

The optimum is the last point the objective function touches as it is moved toward the origin (Example 3).

4. Slide the objective function toward the origin, being careful to keep it parallel to the original line.
5. The optimum (last feasible point) is shown in Figure 6S-14. The x_2 coordinate ($x_2 = 2$) can be determined by inspection of the graph. Note that the optimal point is at the intersection of the line $x_2 = 2$ and the line $4x_1 + 3x_2 = 24$. Substituting the value of $x_2 = 2$ into this equation will yield the value of x_1 at the intersection:

$$4x_1 + 3(2) = 24 \rightarrow x_1 = 4.5$$

Thus, the optimum is $x_1 = 4.5$ and $x_2 = 2$.

6. Calculate the optimal objective value:

$$8x_1 + 12x_2 = 8(4.5) + 12(2) = 60$$

Slack and Surplus

binding constraint A constraint that forms the optimal corner point of the feasible solution space.

surplus When the optimal values of decision variables are substituted into the left side of a ≥ constraint, surplus is the amount the left side exceeds the right side.

slack When the optimal values of decision variables are substituted into the left side of a ≤ constraint, slack is the amount the left side is less than the right side.

If a constraint forms the optimal corner point of the feasible solution space, it is called a **binding constraint**. A binding constraint limits the value of the objective function; if the constraint could be relaxed, an improved solution would be possible. For constraints that are not binding, making them less restrictive will have no impact on the optimal solution.

If the optimal values of the decision variables are substituted into the left side of a binding constraint, the resulting value will exactly equal the right-side value of the constraint. However, this is different for a nonbinding constraint. If the left side is greater than the right side, we say that there is **surplus**; if the left side is smaller than the right side, we say that there is **slack**. Slack can occur only in a ≤ constraint; it is the amount by which the left side is less than the right side when the optimal values of the decision variables are substituted into the left side. And surplus can occur only in a ≥ constraint; it is the amount by which the left side exceeds the right side of the constraint when the optimal values of the decision variables are substituted into the left side.

For example, suppose the optimal values for a problem are $x_1 = 10$ and $x_2 = 20$. If one of the constraints is:

$$3x_1 + 2x_2 \leq 100,$$

substituting the optimal values into the left side yields:

$$3(10) + 2(20) = 70$$

Because the constraint is $\leq$, the difference between the values of 100 and 70 (i.e., 30) is the slack. Suppose the optimal values had been $x_1 = 20$ and $x_2 = 20$. Substituting these values into the left side of the constraint would yield $3(20) + 2(20) = 100$. Because the left side equals the right side, this is a binding constraint; slack is equal to zero.

Now consider the constraint:

$$4x_1 + x_2 \geq 50$$

Suppose the optimal values are $x_1 = 10$ and $x_2 = 15$; substituting these into the left side yields:

$$4(10) + 15 = 55$$

Because this is a $\geq$ constraint, the difference between 55 and 50 (i.e., 5) is the *surplus*. If the optimal values had been $x_1 = 12$ and $x_2 = 2$, substitution would result in the left side of 50. Hence, the constraint would be a binding constraint, and there would be no surplus (i.e., surplus would be zero).

Computer Solutions

L03

For linear programming problems with more than two decision variables, graphical solution methods cannot be used. Instead, a linear programming (LP) software must be used. There are various LP software available that can solve very large problems with thousands of variables and thousands of constraints (e.g., CPLEX). Here we will be using a software that comes as an Add-in to Excel, thus making it widely available. It is called Solver.

We will use the computer problem of Example 2 to illustrate, using Excel's Solver. We repeat its linear programming formulation here for ease of reference.

Maximize $\quad 60x_1 + 50x_2 \qquad$ where x_1 = the number of type 1 computers

$\qquad\qquad\qquad\qquad\qquad\qquad\qquad x_2$ = the number of type 2 computers

Subject to

Assembly	$4x_1 + 10x_2 \leq 100$ hours
Inspection	$2x_1 + 1x_2 \leq 22$ hours
Storage	$3x_1 + 3x_2 \leq 39$ cubic feet
	$x_1, x_2 \geq 0$

To use Solver:

1. First, enter the problem in an Excel worksheet, as shown in Figure 6S-15. What is not obvious from the figure is the need to enter a formula for each cell where there is a zero (Solver automatically inserts the zero after you input the formula). The formulas are for the value of the objective function and the constraints. Before you enter the formulas, designate the cells where you want the optimal values of x_1 and x_2 to appear (highlighted in yellow). Here, cells B4 and C4 are used for decision variables. To enter a formula, click on the cell that the formula will belong to, and then enter the formula, starting with an equal sign. We want the optimal value of the objective function to appear in cell D5. Therefore, in D5, enter the formula:

= SUMPRODUCT(B4:C4;,B5:C5)

This is equivalent to = B4*B5 + C4*C5, but will be easier to use for larger problems.

The constraint formulas, in cells D7, D8, and D9, are

for D7: = SUMPRODUCT(B4:C4,B7:C7)

for D8: = SUMPRODUCT(B4:C4,B8:C8)

for D9: = SUMPRODUCT(B4:C4,B9:C9)

Excel worksheet for the computer problem.

2. Now, click on Data on the top of the worksheet, and in that menu, click on Solver (on the top right). If Solver is not there, you will need to add it in (In Excel 2013, click File, then Options, next Add-ins; then click Go . . . in the bottom; a small window opens; check Solver add-in, and finally click OK). The Solver Parameters menu will appear (Figure 6S-16 is the filled-in version). Begin by

Figure 6S-16

Solver Parameters menu for the computer problem (filled in).

entering the coordinate of the objective (profit) function in front of Set Objective. Alternatively, you can click and then use the mouse (cursor) to select the cell. In this case, Solver will put $ signs in front of the row number and column label (D5).

Click on the radio button for Max if it isn't already highlighted. The By Changing Variable Cells are the cells where you want the optimal values of the decision variables to appear. Here, they are cells B4 and C4. We indicate this by the range B4:C4 (Solver will add the $ signs).

Next, add the constraints by clicking on Add. When the "Add Constraint" menu appears, enter the cell that contains the formula for the left side of the first constraint under "Cell Reference," next select the appropriate inequality sign in the middle, and then enter the cell that has the right-side amount under the "Constraint." After you have entered the first constraint, click on Add again, and then enter the next constraint. (Note that constraints can be entered in any order.) After the last constraint, click OK rather than Add in the Constraints window, and you will return to the Solver menu. Check "Make Unconstrained Variables Non-Negative," if it is not checked already. Select Simplex LP under "Select a Solving Method:" (this is for linear programs; Solver can also solve other optimization problems). Finally, click Solve.

3. The Solver Results menu will then appear, indicating that a solution has been found, or that an error has occurred. If there has been an error, go back to the Solver Parameters menu and try to find the source of the error. For example, check to see that your constraints refer to the correct changing cells, and that the inequality directions are correct. Make the corrections and click on Solve. Assuming everything is correct, in the Reports box, highlight both Answer and Sensitivity (by clicking on them), and then click on OK.

4. Solver will incorporate the optimal values of the decision variables and the objective function on your worksheet (see Figure 6S-17). We can see that the optimal values are Type 1 = 9 units and Type 2 = 4 units, and the total profit is 740. The Answer Report will also show the optimal values of the Objective Cell and Variable Cells (middle part of Figure 6S-18), and some information on the constraints (lower part of Figure 6S-18). Of particular interest here is the indication of which constraints have slack and how much slack. We can see that the constraint entered in cell D7 (Assembly) has a slack of 24, and that the constraints entered in cells D8 (Inspection) and D9 (Storage) have slack of zero, indicating that they are binding constraints.

◄ Figure 6S-17

Excel worksheet solution to the computer problem.

Figure 6S-18

Answer report for the computer problem.

Sensitivity Analysis

sensitivity analysis
Assessing the impact of potential changes of the parameters (numerical values) of an LP model on its optimal solution.

Sensitivity analysis involves assessing the impact of potential changes of the parameters (the numerical values) of a linear programming model on its optimal solution. Such changes may occur due to forces beyond a manager's control or a manager may be contemplating making the changes, say, to increase profits or reduce costs. Also, if a parameter is originally only roughly estimated, the sensitivity analysis will show if its value has a significant effect on the optimal solution. If so, further effort should be exerted to obtain a more accurate estimate.

There are three types of parameters:

1. Objective function coefficients.
2. Right-side values of constraints.
3. Left-side coefficients.

We will consider the first two types of parameters here (changes to left-side constraint coefficients are difficult to study). We begin with changes to objective function coefficients.

Objective Function Coefficient Changes

A change in the value of an objective function coefficient can cause a change in the optimal solution. In the graphical solution method, this means a change to another corner point of the feasible solution space. However, there is a *range of values for which the optimal values of the decision variables will not change*. For example, in the computer problem, if the profit on type 1 computers increased from $60 per unit to, say, $65 per unit, the optimal solution would still be to produce 9 units of Type 1 and 4 units of Type 2 computers. Similarly, if the profit per unit on type 1 computers decreased from $60 to, say, $55 per unit, producing 9 of Type 1 and 4 units of Type 2 would still be optimal. These sorts of changes are not uncommon; they may be the result of things such as price changes in raw materials, price discounts, cost reductions in production, and so on. Obviously, when a change does occur in the value of an objective function coefficient, it can be helpful for a manager to know if that change will affect the optimal values of the decision variables. The manager can quickly determine this by referring to that coefficient's **range of optimality**, which is the range of values of an objective function coefficient over which the optimal values of the decision variables will not change.

range of optimality Range of values for an objective function coefficient over which the optimal solution values of the decision variables remain the same.

Using the Graphical Solution Method. The range of optimality for Type 1 coefficient in the computer problem is 50 to 100. This is so because this corner point of the feasible solution space will remain optimal as long as the slope of the objective function line (60/50) stays within the slope of the constraint lines that are binding at the optimal solution. For the Computer example, the binding constraints are the Inspection (with slope of 2/1) and Storage (with slope of 3/3) (see Figure 6S-10). Note that currently we have $3/3 < 60/50 < 2/1$. Let $C_1 =$ coefficient of Type 1 computer in the objective function. Note that if C_1 is changed, to hold the same relationships, i.e., $3/3 < C_1/50 < 2/1$, we should have $50 \le C_1 \le 100$. If C_1 exceeds 100, the optimal solution will move to the neighbour corner point $x_1 = 11, x_2 = 0$, and if C_1 goes below 50, the optimal solution will move to the neighbour corner point, which is the intersection of the Inspection and Assembly constraint lines ($x_1 = 7.5, x_2 = 7$).

Instead, suppose the coefficient of Type 2 computers were to change. Its range of optimality is 30 to 60. This is so because of a similar argument as above. Let $C_2 =$ coefficient of Type 2 computer in the objective function. If C_2 is changed, to hold the relationships between the slope of the objective function and the slope of the binding constraints, we should have $3/3 < 60/C_2 < 2/1$, or $30 \le C_2 \le 60$.

In summary, as long as the value of the change doesn't take an objective coefficient outside this range, 9 and 4 will still be the optimal values. Note, however, even for changes that are *within* the range of optimality, the optimal value of the objective coefficients *will* change. If the Type 1 coefficient increased from $60 to $61, and 9 units of Type 1 is still optimum, profit would increase by $9: 9 units times $1 per unit. Thus, for a change that is within the range of optimality, a revised value of the objective function must be determined.

Now, let's see how we can determine the range of optimality using Excel's Solver.

Using Solver. The range of optimality of the objective coefficients can be determined from the Sensitivity Report (see Figure 6S-19). It shows the value of the objective coefficients that was used in the problem for each type of computer (i.e., 60 and 50), and the allowable increase and allowable decrease for each coefficient. By subtracting the allowable decrease from the original value of the coefficient, and adding the allowable increase to the original value of the coefficient, we can obtain the range of optimality for each coefficient. Thus, for Type 1:

$60 - 10 = 50$ and $60 + 40 = 100$

Hence, the optimality range for the Type 1 coefficient is 50 to 100. For Type 2:

$50 - 20 = 30$ and $50 + 10 = 60$

Hence, the optimality range for the Type 2 coefficient is 30 to 60.

Range for Simultaneous Objective Coefficient Changes. To determine if simultaneous changes to two or more objective coefficients will result in a change to the optimal solution, divide each coefficient's change by the allowable change, given by its range of optimality, in the same

Sensitivity report for the computer problem.

direction. Thus, if the change is a decrease, divide that amount by the allowable decrease. Treat all resulting fractions as positive. Sum the fractions. If the sum does not exceed 1.00, then simultaneous changes are within the range of optimality and will not result in any change to the optimal values of the decision variables. For example, suppose the objective coefficient of Type 1 computers was $75 (instead of $60) and the objective coefficient of Type 2 computers was $40 (instead of $50). Recall the upper limit of range of optimality of Type 1 objective coefficient was $100 and the lower limit of range of optimality of Type 2 objective coefficient was $30. Then $|(75 - 60)/(100 - 60)| + |(40 - 50)/(30 - 50)| = .375 + .5 < 1 \rightarrow$ no change in the optimal solution. However, if the objective coefficient of Type 1 computers was $85, we will have $|(85 - 60)/(100 - 60)| + |(40 - 50)/(30 - 50)| = .625 + .5 > 1 \rightarrow$ change in the optimal solution (to $x_1 = 11$, $x_2 = 0$).

Changes in the Right-Hand-Side (RHS) Value of a Constraint

shadow price Amount by which the value of the objective function would change as a result of a one-unit change in the RHS value of a constraint.

In considering right-hand-side changes, it is important to know if a particular constraint is binding at an optimal solution. Recall that a constraint is binding if substituting the optimal values of the decision variables into the left side of the constraint results in a value that is equal to the RHS value. In other words, that constraint stops the objective function from achieving a better value (e.g., a greater profit or a lower cost). Each constraint has a corresponding **shadow price**, which is the amount by which the value of the objective function would change if there were a one-unit change in the RHS value of that constraint. If a constraint is nonbinding, its shadow price is zero, meaning that increasing or decreasing its RHS value by one unit will have no impact on the value of the objective function. Nonbinding constraints have either slack (if the constraint is ≤) or surplus (if the constraint is ≥). Suppose a constraint has 10 units of slack at the optimal solution, which means 10 units that are unused. If we were to increase or decrease the constraint's RHS value by one unit, the only effect would be to increase or decrease its slack by one unit. But there is no profit associated with slack, so the value of the objective function wouldn't change. On the other hand, if the change is to the RHS value of a binding constraint, this will cause the optimal values of the decision variables to change, and hence cause the value of the objective function to change. For example, in the computer problem, the inspection constraint is a binding constraint and has a shadow price of 10 (this can be derived using Figure 6S-10; if the RHS of Inspection is changed from 22 to 23, the optimal solution will change to $x_1 = 10$, $x_2 = 3$, and the objective function value will change to 60(10) + 50(3) = 750, $10 more than the current objective value of 740. Similarly, if there was one hour less of inspection time, total profit would decrease by $10).

In general, multiplying the amount of change in the RHS value of a constraint by the constraint's shadow price will indicate the change's impact on the optimal value of the objective function. However, this is true only over a limited range called the **range of feasibility**. In this range, the value of the shadow price remains constant. Hence, as long as a change in the RHS value of a constraint is within its range of feasibility, the shadow price will remain the same, and one can readily determine the impact on the objective function. However, if a change goes beyond the range of feasibility, a new solution and shadow prices would have to be determined.

range of feasibility Range of values for its RHS of a constraint over which its shadow price remains the same.

Let's see how to determine the range of feasibility from Excel Solver.

Using Solver. In the Sensitivity Report there is a table in the bottom labelled "Constraints" (see Figure 6S-19). The table shows the shadow price for each constraint, its RHS value, and the allowable increase and allowable decrease. Adding the allowable increase to the RHS value and subtracting the allowable decrease from the RHS value will produce the range of feasibility for that constraint. For example, for the inspection constraint the range of feasibility would be:

$$22 + 4 = 26; 22 - 4 = 18$$

Hence, the range of feasibility for Inspection is 18 to 26 hours. Similarly, for the storage constraint, the range of feasibility is:

$$39 - 6 = 33 \text{ to } 39 + 4.5 = 43.5$$

The range of feasibility for the assembly constraint is a little different; the assembly constraint is nonbinding (note the shadow price of 0) while the other two are binding (note their nonzero shadow prices). The assembly constraint has a slack of 24 (the difference between its RHS value of 100 and its final value of 76). With its slack of 24, its RHS value could decrease by as much as 24 (to 76) before it would become binding. Conversely, increasing its right-hand side value will produce only more slack. Thus, no amount of increase in the RHS value of Storage will make it binding, so there is no upper limit on its allowable increase. Solver indicates this by the large value $(1E + 30)$ shown for the allowable increase. So Storage's range of feasibility has a lower limit of 76 and no upper limit.

Range for Simultaneous RHS Changes. If there are changes to more than one constraint's RHS value, analyze these in the same way as simultaneous changes to the objective function coefficients. That is, if the change is an increase, divide that amount by that constraint's allowable increase; if the change is a decrease, divide the decrease by the allowable decrease. Treat all resulting fractions as positive. Sum the fractions. As long as the sum does not exceed 1.00, the shadow prices won't change. For example, suppose the RHS of Inspection changed to 20 (instead of 22) and the RHS of Storage changed to 41 (instead of 39). Then $|(20 - 22)/(18 - 22)| + |(41 - 39)/(43.5 - 39)| = .5 + .44 < 1 \rightarrow$ no change in the shadow prices. However, if the RHS of Storage changes to 42, we will have $|(20 - 22)/(18 - 22)| + |(42 - 39)/(43.5 - 39)| = .5 + .67 > 1 \rightarrow$ change in the shadow prices.

Table 6S-1 summarizes the impacts of changes that fall within either the range of optimality or the range of feasibility.

CHANGES TO OBJECTIVE FUNCTION COEFFICIENTS THAT ARE WITHIN THE RANGE OF OPTIMALITY	
Component	**Result**
Values of decision variables	No change
Value of objective function	Will change
CHANGES TO RHS VALUES OF CONSTRAINTS THAT ARE WITHIN THE RANGE OF FEASIBILITY	
Component	**Result**
Value of shadow price	No change
Values of decision variables	Will change
Value of objective function	Will change

◀ **Table 6S-1**

Summary of the impact of changes within their respective ranges.

Key Terms

binding constraint

constraints

decision variables

feasible solution space

graphical solution

multiple optimal solutions

objective function

parameters

range of feasibility

range of optimality

redundant constraint

sensitivity analysis

shadow price

slack

surplus

Solved Problems

Problem 1

A construction firm specializes in building and selling single-family homes. The firm offers two basic types of houses, model A house and model B. Model A houses require 4,000 labour hours, 2 tonnes of stone, and 2,000 board feet of lumber. Model B houses require 10,000 labour hours, 3 tonnes of stone, and 2,000 board feet of lumber. Due to long lead times for ordering supplies and the scarcity of skilled and semiskilled workers in the area, the firm will be forced to rely on its present resources for the upcoming building season. It has 400,000 hours of labour, 150 tonnes of stone, and 200,000 board feet of lumber. What mix of Model A and B houses should the firm construct if Model A yields a profit of $10,000 per unit and Model B house yields a profit of $20,000 per unit? Assume that the firm will be able to sell all the units it builds.

Solution

a. Formulate the objective function and constraints:

Maximize $Z = 10{,}000A + 20{,}000B$

Subject to

Labour	$4{,}000A + 10{,}000B \leq 400{,}000$ labour hours
Stone	$2A + 3B \leq 150$ tonnes
Lumber	$2{,}000A + 2{,}000B \leq 200{,}000$ board feet
	$A, B \geq 0$

b. Graph the constraints and objective function, and identify the optimum corner point (see graph below). Note that the lumber constraint is *redundant*: it does not form a boundary of the feasible solution space.

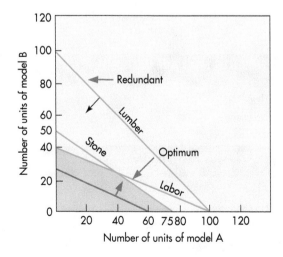

c. Determine the optimal quantities of models A and B, and calculate the resulting profit. Because the optimal point is at the intersection of the stone and labour constraints, solve those two equations for their common point:

$$\text{Labour } 4{,}000A + 10{,}000B = 400{,}000$$

$$\frac{-2{,}000 \times (\text{Stone } 2A + 3B = 150)}{4{,}000B = 100{,}000}$$

$$B = 25$$

Substitute $B = 25$ in one of the equations, and solve for A:

$$2A + 3(25) = 150A = 37.5$$

$$Z = 10{,}000(37.5) + 20{,}000(25) = \$875{,}000$$

Problem 2

This LP model was solved by Excel's Solver:

Maximize $15x_1 + 20x_2 + 14x_3$ where x_1 = quantity of product 1

x_2 = quantity of product 2

x_3 = quantity of product 3

Subject to

Labour $5x_1 + 6x_2 + 4x_3 \leq 210$ hours

Material $10x_1 + 8x_2 + 5x_3 \leq 200$ kg

Machine $4x_1 + 2x_2 + 5x_3 \leq 170$ minutes

$$x_1, x_2, x_3 \geq 0$$

The following Sensitivity Report was obtained.

Variable Cells

Cell	Name	Final Value	Reduced Cost	Objective Coefficient	Allowable Increase	Allowable Decrease
B4	Variables Prod 1	0	−10.6	15	10.6	1E + 30
C4	Variables Prod 2	5	0	20	2.4	10.6
D4	Variables Prod 3	32	0	14	36	1.5

Constraints

Cell	Name	Final Value	Shadow Price	Constraint R.H. Side	Allowable Increase	Allowable Decrease
E7	Labour	158	0	210	1E + 30	52
E8	Material	200	2.4	200	70.90909091	30
E9	Machine	170	0.4	170	30	120

a. By how much would the profit per unit of product 1 have to increase in order for it to have a positive value?

b. If the profit per unit of product 2 increased by $2 to $22, would the optimal production quantities of products 2 and 3 change? Would the optimal value of the objective function change?

c. If the available amount of labour decreased by 12 hours, would that cause a change in the optimal values of the decision variables or the optimal value of the objective function?

d. If the available amount of material increased by 10 kg to 210 kg, how would that affect the optimal value of the objective function?

e. If profit per unit on product 2 increased by $1 and profit per unit on product 3 decreased by $.50, would these be within the range of simultaneous changes? Would the values of the decision variables change? What would be the change in the value of the objective function?

Solution

a. Note that the Final (i.e., optimal) Value of Product 1 is 0. The amount of increase in profit of product 1 would have to equal the Allowable Increase of $10.60.

b. No, because the change would be within its Allowable Increase of $2.4 (i.e., the range of optimality), Yes, the objective function value would increase by an amount equal to the optimal quantity of product 2 times its increased unit profit. Hence, it would increase by 5($2) = $10.

c. No, labour has a slack of 52 hours. Consequently, the only effect would be to decrease the slack to 40 hours.

d. The change is within the range of feasibility because $10 < 70.91 =$ Allowable Increase in Material. The objective function value will increase by the amount of change multiplied by material's shadow price of $2.40. Hence, the objective function value would increase by 10($2.40) = $24.00.

e. To determine if the changes are within the range for simultaneous changes, we first calculate the ratio of the amount of each change to the maximum allowable change *in the same direction.* For product 2, it is $1/$2.40 = .417; for product 3, it is −$.50/−$1.50 = .333. Next, we calculate the sum of these ratios: .417 + .333 = .750. Because this does not exceed 1.00, we conclude that these changes are within the allowable range of optimality. This means that the optimal values of the decision variables will not change. We can calculate the change to the value of the objective function by multiplying each product's optimal quantity by its changed profit per unit: 5($1) + 32(−$.50) = −$11. Hence, with these changes, the value of the objective function would decrease by $11.

Problem 3

MHK manufactures appliances. The production planner needs to submit a production plan for next year. The aggregate forecasts of demand for MHK appliances are as follows: Q1: 14,800, Q2: 26,400, Q3: 35,000, and Q4: 19,200 units. The initial inventory is zero. It costs MHK $24 per appliance to hold it in inventory for a quarter. The regular workforce is 160 workers and cannot be changed. The annual output per worker is approximately 480 appliances. A worker costs $15 per hour (including fringe benefits) and works 480 hours a quarter. MHK can hire temp workers to work during a second shift (a maximum of 160 temp workers can be used). The hiring cost, including training, is estimated to be $1,800 each, and layoff cost is $1,200 each. Temp wage rate and productivity are the same as permanent workers. Back-order cost is $150 per unit per quarter. Assume all unmet demand not met during a quarter is back-ordered; however, there should be no back orders at the end of the fourth quarter. Ending inventory can be zero. The objective is to minimize total labour, hire and lay off, inventory, and back-order costs. Formulate this problem as a linear program in Excel and solve it using Excel's Solver.

Solution

The output of 160 regular workers is 160 × (480 units per year/4 quarters in a year) = 19,200 units per quarter. The labour cost per unit is $15 × (480 hours per quarter/120 units per quarter) = $60. We introduce variables to represent the numbers of new hires and layoffs of temp workers during each quarter. From these, the number of temp workers employed during each quarter is determined, which in turn determines the number of units of product produced each quarter by temp workers. The total permanent and temp production minus forecast demand determines "Output − Forecast." We also introduce variables to represent the ending inventory and back-orders at the end of each quarter. The constraints are non-negativity for all variables and number of temp workers during each quarter, and equations to set beginning inventory + (output − forecast) − previous quarter's back order equal to ending inventory − back-order for each quarter. The latter constraints and the fact that both ending inventory and back order cost money would force at most one of ending inventory and back order to be positive and equal to beginning inventory + (output − forecast) − previous quarter's back order. Choose Simplex LP and make sure "Make Unconstrained variables Non-negative" is checked. The optimal solution is given below. The optimal number of temp workers 77.5 can be rounded up to 78.

Quarter		1	2	3	4	Total
Forecast		14,800	26,400	35,000	19,200	95,400
Output						
Perm.		19,200	19,200	19,200	19,200	76,800
Temp. hired (workers)		0.0	77.5	0.0	0.0	
Temp. laid-off (workers)		0.0	0.0	0.0	77.5	
Temp. (workers)	0	0.0	77.5	77.5	0.0	155
Temp. (units)		0	9,300	9,300	0	
Output Forecast		4,400	2,100	−6,500	0	0
Inventory						
Beginning		0	4,400	6,500	0	
Ending		4,400	6,500	0	0	
Back order		0	0	0	0	
Ending inv − back-order		4,400	6,500	0	0	
Beg inv + output-forecast						
− previous back order		4,400	6,500	0	0	
Average inv		2,200	5,450	3,250	0	10,900
Costs						
Perm. /unit @	60	1,152,000	1,152,000	1,152,000	1,152,000	4,608,000
Temp. /unit @	60	0	558,000	558,000	0	1,116,000
Hire /person @	$1,800	0	139,500	0	0	139,500
Lay off /person @	$1,200	0	0	0	93,000	93,000
Inventory /unit @	24	52,800	130,800	78,000	0	261600
Back order /unit @	150	0	0	0	0	0
Total		1,204,800	1,980,300	1,788,000	1,245,000	$6,218,100

Discussion and Review Questions

1. What is linear programming? Why is it important? When should it be used? **LO1**

2. What is a linear programming model? Briefly describe each of its four components. **LO1**

3. What is meant by the term *feasible solution space?* What are its characteristics? **LO1 & 2**

4. What is the standard form of a constraint? **LO1**

5. What is an isocost line? An isoprofit line? **LO2**

6. What does sliding an objective function line toward the origin represent? Away from the origin? **LO2**

7. Explain the terms (a) *redundant constraint* and (b) *multiple optimal solutions.* **LO2**

8. What is meant by (a) surplus (b) slack? **LO2**

9. Briefly explain these terms: **LO4**
   a. Sensitivity analysis.
   b. Shadow price.
   c. Range of feasibility.
   d. Range of optimality.
   e. Range for simultaneous changes.

Problems

1. Solve these problems using the graphical solution method and answer the questions that follow. Use simultaneous equations to determine the optimal values of the decision variables. **LO2**

   a. Maximize $Z = 4x_1 + 3x_2$

      Subject to

Material	$6x_1 + 4x_2 \leq 48$ kg
Labour	$4x_1 + 8x_2 \leq 80$ hr
	$x_1, x_2 \geq 0$

   b. Maximize $Z = 2x_1 + 10x_2$

      Subject to

R	$10x_1 + 4x_2 \geq 40$
S	$1x_1 + 6x_2 \geq 24$
T	$1x_1 + 2x_2 \leq 14$
	$x_1, x_2 \geq 0$

   c. Maximize $Z = 6A + 3B$ (revenue)

Subject to

Material	$20A + 6B \leq 600$ kg
Machinery	$25A + 20B \leq 1,000$ hr
Labour	$20A + 30B \leq 1,200$ hr

$$A, B \geq 0$$

i. What are the optimal values of the decision variables and Z?

ii. Do any constraints have slack? If yes, which one(s) and how much slack does each have?

iii. Do any constraints have surplus? If yes, which one(s) and how much surplus does each have?

iv. Are any constraints redundant? If yes, which one(s)? Explain briefly.

2. Solve these problems using the graphical solution method and then answer the questions that follow. Use simultaneous equations to determine the optimal values of the decision variables. **LO2**

a. Minimize $Z = 1.80S + 2.20T$

Subject to

Potassium	$5S + 8T \geq 200$ grams
Carbohydrate	$15S + 6T \geq 240$ grams
Protein	$4S + 12T \geq 180$ grams
T	$T \geq 10$ grams

$$S, T \geq 0$$

b. Minimize $Z = 2x_1 + 3x_2$

Subject to

D	$4x_1 + 2x_2 \geq 20$
E	$2x_1 + 6x_2 \geq 18$
F	$1x_1 + 2x_2 \leq 12$

$$x_{1, x_2} \geq 0$$

i. What are the optimal values of the decision variables and Z?

ii. Do any constraints have slack? If yes, which one(s) and how much slack does each have?

iii. Do any constraints have surplus? If yes, which one(s) and how much surplus does each have?

iv. Are any constraints redundant? If yes, which one(s)? Explain briefly.

3. An appliance manufacturer produces two models of microwave ovens: H and W. Both models require fabrication and assembly work; each H uses four hours of fabrication and two hours of assembly, and each W uses two hours of fabrication and six hours of assembly. There are 600 fabrication worker hours available this week and 480 worker hours of assembly. Each H contributes $40 to profit and each W contributes $30 to profit. Formulate this problem as a linear program and use the graphical solution method to determine the quantities of H and W that will maximize total profit. **LO1 & 2**

4. A small grocery store is preparing for the holiday season. The owner must decide how many bags of deluxe mix and how many bags of standard mix of Peanut/Raisin to prepare. The deluxe mix has $2/_3$ pound (lb) raisins and $1/_3$ lb peanuts, and the standard mix has $1/_2$ lb raisins and $1/_2$ lb peanuts per bag. The store has 90 lb of raisins and 60 lb of peanuts to work with. **LO1 & 2**

Peanuts cost $.60 per lb and raisins cost $1.50 per lb. The deluxe mix will sell for $2.90 per bag, and the standard mix will sell for $2.55 per bag. The owner estimates that no more than 110 bags of any type of mix can be sold. Formulate this problem as a linear program in order to maximize total profit and use the graphical solution method to solve it.

5. A retired couple supplement their income by making pie crusts, which they sell to a local grocery store. During the month of September, they produce regular and sweet crusts. The regular crusts are sold for $1.20 per unit, and the sweet crusts are sold for $1.50 per unit. The couple is able to sell all of the crusts they produce. Flour and sugar are purchased once each month. For the month of September, they have 1,200 cups of sugar and 2,100 cups of flour. Each regular crust requires $1^1/_2$ cups of sugar and 3 cups of flour, and each sweet crust requires 2 cups of sugar and 3 cups of flour. **LO1 & 2**

a. Formulate an LP model to determine the number of regular and sweet crusts that will maximize revenues if the couple working together can make a crust of either type in six minutes. They plan to work no more than 60 hours.

b. Solve this problem using graphical solution method. Determine the optimal solution, and the amounts of sugar, flour, and time that will be unused.

6. Solve each of these LP problems by Excel's Solver.

a. Maximize $4x_1 + 2x_2 + 5x_3$

Subject to

$$1x_1 + 2x_2 + 1x_3 \leq 25$$
$$1x_1 + 4x_2 + 2x_3 \leq 40$$
$$3x_1 + 3x_2 + 1x_3 \leq 30$$
$$x_1, x_2, x_3 \geq 0$$

b. Maximize $10x_1 + 6x_2 + 3x_3$

Subject to

$$1x_1 + 1x_2 + 2x_3 \leq 25$$
$$2x_1 + 1x_2 + 4x_3 \leq 40$$
$$1x_1 + 2x_2 + 3x_3 \leq 40$$
$$x_1, x_2, x_3 \geq 0$$

7. For Problem 6a, determine the following:

a. The range of feasibility for each constraint's RHS.

b. The range of optimality for the coefficients in the objective function.

8. For Problem 6*b*: (LO4)

   a. Find the range of feasibility for each constraint's RHS, and interpret your answers.

   b. Determine the range of optimality for each coefficient in the objective function and interpret your results.

9. A small company makes three similar products, which all follow the same three-step process, consisting of milling, inspection, and drilling. Product A requires 12 minutes of milling, 5 minutes for inspection, and 10 minutes of drilling per unit; product B requires 10 minutes of milling, 4 minutes for inspection, and 8 minutes of drilling per unit; and product C requires 8 minutes of milling, 4 minutes for inspection, and 16 minutes of drilling. The company has 20 hours available during the next period for milling, 15 hours for inspection, and 24 hours for drilling. Product A contributes $2.40 per unit to profit, B contributes $2.50 per unit, and C contributes $3.00 per unit. Formulate an LP to determine the mix of products in order to maximize total contribution to profits for the period. Solve it using Excel's Solver. Then, find the range of optimality for the profit coefficient of each variable. (LO1, 3 & 4)

10. A company makes four juice products using orange, grapefruit, and pineapple juices. (LO1 & 3)

Product	Price/Litre
Orange juice	$1.00
Grapefruit juice	.90
Pineapple juice	.80
All-in-One	1.10

The All-in-One juice has equal parts of orange, grapefruit, and pineapple juice. Each product is produced in a one-litre size container. On hand are 1,600 litres of orange juice, 1,200 litres of grapefruit juice, and 800 litres of pineapple juice. The cost per litre is $0.50 for orange juice, $0.40 for grapefruit juice, and $0.35 for pineapple juice. In addition, the manager wants grapefruit juice containers to be no more than 30 percent of all containers produced. She also wants the ratio of the number of containers of orange juice to the number of containers of pineapple juice to be at least 7 to 5. Formulate a linear programming model to determine how many containers of each product to produce to maximize total profit, and solve it using Excel's Solver.

11. A wood products manufacturer uses idle time at the end of each week to make goods for stock. Currently, two products are produced for stock: a chopping board and a knife holder. Both items require three operations: cutting, gluing, and finishing. The manager has collected the following data on these products: (LO1 & 2)

		Time per Unit (Minutes)		
Item	Profit/Unit	Cutting	Gluing	Finishing
Chopping board	$2	1.4	5	12
Knife holder	$6	0.8	13	3

The manager has also determined that 56 minutes are available for cutting, 650 minutes for gluing, and 360 minutes for finishing.

   a. Formulate this problem as an LP and solve it using the graphical solution method.

   b. Which resources are not completely used by your optimal solution? How much of each resource is unused?

12. The manager of the deli section of a grocery store has just learned that she has 112 kg of mayonnaise, of which 70 kg is approaching its expiration date and must be used. To use up the mayonnaise, the manager has decided to prepare two items: a ham spread and a deli spread. Each container of ham spread will require 1.4 kg of mayonnaise, and each container of the deli spread will require 1.0 kg of mayonnaise. The manager has received an order for 10 containers of ham spread and 8 containers of the deli spread. In addition, the manager has decided to have at least 10 more containers of each spread available for sale. Both spreads will cost $3 per container to make, but ham spread sells for $5 per container and deli spread sells for $7 per container. (LO1 & 2)

   a. Formulate an LP that will minimize total cost. Solve it using the graphical solution method.

   b. Formulate an LP that will maximize total profit. Solve it using the graphical solution method.

13. A manager wants to know how many units of each product to produce on a daily basis in order to achieve the highest contribution to profit. Production requirements for the products are shown in the following table. (LO1 & 3)

Product	Material 1 (kg)	Material 2 (kg)	Labour (hours)
A	2	3	3.2
B	1	5	1.5
C	6	—	2.0

Material 1 costs $5 per kg, material 2 costs $4 per kg, and labour costs $10 an hour. Product A sells for $80 a unit, product B sells for $90 a unit, and product C sells for $70 a unit. Available resources each day are 200 kg of material 1; 300 kg of material 2; and 150 hours of labour.

   The manager must satisfy certain output requirements: The output of product A should not be more than one-third of the total number of units produced; the ratio of units of product A to units of product B should be 3 to 2;

and there is a standing order for 5 units of product A each day. Formulate a linear programming model for this problem, and then solve it using Excel's Solver.

14. A chocolate maker has contracted to operate a small candy counter in a fashionable store. To start with, the selection of offerings will be intentionally limited. The counter will offer a regular mix of candy made up of equal parts of cashew, raisin, caramel, and chocolate, and a deluxe mix that is one-half cashew and one-half chocolates which will be sold in one-pound boxes. In addition, the candy counter will offer individual one-pound boxes of cashew, raisin, caramel, and chocolate. **LO1 & 3**

A major attraction of the candy counter is that all candies are made fresh at the counter. However, storage space for supplies and ingredients is limited. Bins are available that can hold the amounts shown in the following table:

Ingredient	Capacity (pounds)
Cashews	120
Raisins	200
Caramels	100
Chocolates	160

In order to present a good image and to encourage purchases, the counter will make at least 20 boxes of each type of product each day. Any leftover boxes at the end of the day will be given to a nearby nursing home for goodwill. The profit per box for various items has been determined as follows:

Item	Profit per Box
Regular	$.80
Deluxe	.90
Cashews	.70
Raisins	.60
Caramels	.50
Chocolates	.75

a. Formulate an LP model in order to maximize total profit.
b. Solve it using Excel's Solver.

15. Given the following linear programming model, solve it using Excel's Solver, and then answer the questions that follow. **LO4**

Maximize $12x_1 + 18x_2 + 15x_3$
where x_1 = the quantity of product 1 to make etc.

Subject to

Machine	$5x_1 + 4x_2 + 3x_3 \leq 160$ minutes
Labour	$4x_1 + 10x_2 + 4x_3 \leq 288$ hours
Material	$2x_1 + 2x_2 + 4x_3 \leq 200$ kg
Product 2	$x_2 \leq 16$ units

$x_1, x_2, x_3 \geq 0$

a. Are any constraints binding? If so, which one(s)?
b. If the profit on product 3 was changed to $22 a unit, what would be the optimal values of the decision variables? The objective function? Explain.
c. If the profit on product 1 was changed to $22 a unit, what would be the optimal values of the decision variables? The objective function? Explain.
d. If 10 hours less of labour time was available, what would be the optimal values of the decision variables? The objective function? Explain.
e. If the manager decided that up to 20 units of product 2 could be produced (instead of 16), how much additional profit would be generated?
f. If profit per unit on each product increased by $1, would the optimal values of the decision variables change? Explain. What would be the optimal value of the objective function?

16. A garden supplies store prepares various grades of pine bark for mulch: nuggets (x_1), mini-nuggets (x_2), and chips (x_3). The process requires pine bark, machine time, labour time, and storage space. The following LP model has been developed. **LO4**

Maximize $9x_1 + 9x_2 + 6x_3$ (profit)

Subject to

Bark	$5x_1 + 6x_2 + 3x_3 \leq 600$ kg
Machine	$2x_1 + 4x_2 + 5x_3 \leq 660$ minutes
Labour	$2x_1 + 4x_2 + 3x_3 \leq 480$ hours
Storage	$1x_1 + 1x_2 + 1x_3 \leq 150$ bags

$x_1, x_2, x_3 \geq 0$

a. What is the shadow price of a kilogram of bark? Over what range is it appropriate?
b. What is the maximum price the store should pay for additional pine bark?
c. What is the shadow price of labour? Over what range is it in effect?
d. The manager obtained additional machine time through better scheduling. How much additional machine time can be effectively used for this operation? Why?
e. If the manager can obtain *either* additional bark *or* additional storage space, which one should she choose, and how much?
f. If a change in the chip operation increased the profit on chips from $6 per bag to $7 per bag, would the optimal quantities change? Would the value of the objective function change? If so, what would be the new value(s)?
g. If profits on chips increased to $7 per bag and profits on nuggets decreased by $.60 per bag, would the optimal quantities change? Would the value of the objective function change? If so, what would be the new value(s)?
h. If the amount of bark available decreased by 15 kg, machine time available decreased by 27 minutes, and storage capacity increased by 5 bags, would this

fall in the range of feasibility for simultaneous changes? If so, what would be the value of the objective function?

17. Linear programming has been used for determining a hospital or a ward's mix of nursing staff.[1] Consider a ward of Fairbanks Memorial Hospital in Alaska. The hospital uses registered nurses (RN), licensed practical nurses (LPN), and nursing assistants (NA). The wage rates per hour are $21, $13, and $11, respectively. The total patient care hours required in a 24-hour period is estimated to be 150 hours. The hourly capability coefficients (efficiencies) are 1.0, .90, and .75, respectively, i.e., 1 hour of work of an RN satisfies 1 hour of the demand, 1 hour work of an LPN satisfies only .9 hour of the demand, and 1 hour work of a NA satisfies only .75 hour of demand. RNs are qualified to do 100 percent, LPNs up to 85 percent, and NAs up to 50 percent of all tasks. Hospital policy is that at least 50 percent of the staff is RNs. The number of LPNs and NAs to employ per day is limited to six. Each RN, LPN, or NA works eight hours per day. Formulate a linear program to decide the number of RN, LPN, and NA to employ per day in order to minimize total wages subject to the constraints given above. Solve it using Excel's Solver. **LO1 & 3**

18. Formulate Example 4 of Chapter 13, Aggregate Operations Planning and Master Scheduling, as a linear program in Excel and solve it using Excel's Solver. There is no need to consider the use of overtime. **LO1 & 3**

*19. A composite wall has 100 m^2 area and consists of three layers: plaster, fibreglass, and plywood.[2] The thermal resistance of the wall should be at least 1.59 degrees Celsius per watt. Plaster should be between 2 and 10 cm thick. Fibreglass should be between 1 and 5 cm thick. Plywood should be between 1 and 10 cm thick. The thermal resistance and cost of the material are given in the table below. Formulate a linear program to determine the thickness of each layer in order to minimize the total cost of the wall subject to meeting the minimum thermal resistance and minimum/maximum thickness of each layer. Solve it using Excel's Solver. **LO1 & 3**

Material	Thermal Resistance (degrees Celsius per Watt per metre)	Cost ($/m^3)
Plaster	3.57	300
Fiberglass	25	1,000
Plywood	7.69	200

20. A small oil refinery must decide how to mix the ingredients to produce gasoline in order to minimize total ingredient cost subject to meeting demand for gasoline, not exceeding the supply of each ingredient, and meeting minimum octane number and volatility index, and maximum vapour pressure of the gasoline.[3] The data are: **LO1 & 3**

Ingredient	Availability (barrels)	Octane Number	Vapour Pressure	Volatility Index	Cost ($/barrel)
Butane	1,700	120	60	105	52
Light naphtha	1,000	84.5	18	30	64
Heavy naphtha	2,300	73	4	12	83
Catalytic naphtha	6,200	96	6.4	15	102
Catalytic reformate	4,000	99	2.5	3	110

Gasoline Requirements

Demand (barrels)	Minimum Octane Number	Maximum Vapour Pressure	Minimum Volatility Index
10,000	95	11	18

Formulate this problem as a linear program and solve it using Excel's Solver.

*21. The manager of an injection moulding shop is interested in using aggregate planning to determine the shop's production and inventory levels during each of the next 17 months.[4] The shop uses 8 moulding machines to produce approximately 150 different products, employing 15–25 workers. Because of the variety of products, standard (production) hour is used to measure production and demand. The demands (in hundred standard hours) for the next 17 months are 18, 24, 34, 30, 34, 29, 29, 20, 21, 22, 24, 19, 25, 25, 34, 33, and 37. Each worker provides 126 standard hours per month. Currently, 18 workers are employed. Hiring cost is estimated at $470 per worker and layoff cost is estimated at $400 per worker. Labour cost is $13.50 per standard hour and overtime labour cost is $23.50 per standard hour. End-of-the-month inventories are desired to be close to the following levels (in hundreds of standard hours) for each of the next 17 months: 51, 62, 62, 67, 65, 59, 48, 48, 47, 49, 44, 51, 53, 64, 67, 73, and 75. The current inventory

[1] S. K. Bordoloi and E. J. Weatherby, "Managerial Implications of Calculating Optimum Nurse Staffing in Medical Units," *Health Care Management Review* 24(4), Fall 1999, pp. 35–44.
[2] Based on C. Onwubiko, *Introduction to Engineering Design Optimization*, New Jersey: Prentice Hall, 2000, p. 76.
[3] Based on N. J. Driebeek, *Applied Linear Programming*, Massachusetts: Addison-Wesley, 1969, p. 28.
[4] N. K. Kwak and S. A. DeLurgio, "Optimal Production Scheduling and Inventory Control Under Non-stationary Demands," pp. 116–131, in *Studies in Linear Programming*, H. M. Salkin and J. Saha, Editors, Amsterdam: North-Holland Publishing, 1975.

level is 5,400 standard hours. If there is excess inventory above the desired inventory amount, $.80 per standard hour per month is charged as carrying cost, and if there is "shortage" below the desired inventory amount, $3.60 per standard hour per month is charged as shortage cost. The maximum number of workers cannot exceed 25. Formulate this problem as a linear program in Excel and solve it using Excel's Solver. **LO1 & 3**

22. In an analysis of a cattle feedlot, the following data about cattle feed, their nutrients, and minimum daily requirements for fattening two-year-old cattle with average weight of 900 pounds were collected.[5] **LO1 & 3**

Formulat a linear program to determine the amount of each ingredient to feed a two-year-old cow per day in order to minimize the total feedstuff cost subject to meeting the minimum daily requirements. Solve it using Excel's Solver.

*23. The management of a tomato canning company has to decide the quantity of its products: (whole tomato, tomato juice, and tomato paste cans), to make from the contracted tomatoes that are expected soon. The tomatoes will have two grades: A and B; 600,000 pounds of grade A and 2,400,000 pounds of grade B are expected. The purchase cost will be $.56 per pound of grade A and $.31 per pound of grade B. The products are sold in cases of 6 cans. A case of whole tomato cans sells for $4.00, a case of tomato juice cans sells for $4.50, and a case of tomato paste cans sells for $3.80. The maximum demand for tomato juice is 200,000 cases and for tomato paste is 300,000 cases (demand for whole tomato cans has no limit). A case of whole tomato cans is made of 4.5 pounds of tomatoes, a case of juice cans is made of 5 pounds of tomatoes, and a case of tomato paste cans is made of 6 pounds of tomatoes. The grades of tomatoes have been quantified on a nine-point standard scale as follows: Grade A is 9 whereas Grade

Feedstuff/ Units	Calcium %	Phosphorous %	Total Dry Matter %	Digestible Protein %	Total Digestible Nutrients %	Net Energy (Therms/100 pound)	Carotene (mg/pound)
Alfalfa	1.47	.24	90.5	10.5	50.3	40.6	8.2
Corn silage	.1	.06	27.4	1.2	18.1	18.1	5.8
Sorghum Silage	.08	.04	25.3	.8	15.2	12.2	3.3
Grain corn	.02	.28	87	6.8	82	82	1.3
Grain sorghum	0	0	89.1	8.8	80	77.9	0
Wheat	.04	.39	89.5	11.1	80	80	.04
Cottonseed meal	.24	.89	92.2	32.2	69.1	69.1	.1
Minimum Daily Requirement	.044 pound	.044 pound	20.7 pound	1.53 pound	15 pound	14 Therms	50 mg

The costs of feedstuff (cents/pound) are as follows:

Alfalfa	7.2
Corn silage	9.5
Sorghum Silage	10
Grain corn	8.6
Grain sorghum	7.2
Wheat	10.8
Cottonseed meal	20

---

[5] S. Ashour and C. Anderson, "Linear Programming Analysis of a Cattle Feedlot," p. 191, in *Studies in Linear Programming*, H. M. Salkin and J. Saha, Editors, Amsterdam: North-Holland Publishing, 1975.

B is 5. The minimum standard of whole tomato cans is 8 and of juice cans is 6. **LO1 & 4**

a. Formulate the above problem as a linear program in order to maximize the total profit contribution, and solve it using Excel's Solver.

b. i. What is the most profitable product? Why?

   ii. There is an option to buy additional Grade A tomatoes from a different supplier. Should the management buy more Grade A tomatoes at $.85 per pound? If so, how much should be purchased? In what product should the additional Grade A tomatoes be used? (*Hint:* Use Solver's Sensitivity Report)

24. The number of employees required to work at the French fries station of a McDonald's restaurant on a given Saturday is as follows.[6] **LO1 & 3**

Period	FF Staff Required
11–noon	1
noon–1 p.m.	2
1–2 p.m.	2
2–3 p.m.	1
3–4 p.m.	1
4–5 p.m.	1
5–6 p.m.	1

For simplicity, assume shifts are 3, 5, or 7 hours long, and can start at the beginning of each hour starting at 11 a.m. but have to end by 6 p.m.. The objective is to minimize total staff hours used plus the number of shifts (staff) used. Formulate a linear program in Excel to model this shift scheduling problem, and solve it using Excel's Solver.

25. A small refinery wants to optimize the blending of the inputs to gasoline production.[7] The inputs, their daily availability (in litres), and some of their important characteristics are shown below: **LO1 & 3**

Inputs	Availability	Octane Rating	Reid Vapour Pressure
Reformate	15,572	98.9	7.66
Fluid Catalytic Cracker Gasoline (FCCG)	15,434	93.2	9.78
Isomerate	6,709	86.1	29.62

The output requirements are as follows:

	Demand (daily litres)	Octane Rating (min)	Reid Vapour Pressure (max)
Regular gas	≥ 25,000	≥ 90	≤ 21.18
Premium gas	≥ 10,000	≥ 96	≤ 21.18

At most, 38 percent of each type of gasoline can consist of FCCG. Regular gasoline sells for $1.20 per litre and premium gasoline sells for $1.4 per litre.

a. Formulate a linear program to maximize daily revenue subject to the constraints given above. Solve it using Excel's Solver.

b. Is all FCCG used? Why not?

26. A farmer has two distant pieces of land and would like to grow wheat and canola on them. Because of differing soil conditions, there are differences in average yield and cost of growing on the two lands. The yields and costs are: **LO1 & 3**

	Land 1	Land 2
Canola yield/acre	30 bushels	35 bushels
Cost/acre of canola	$220	$250
Wheat yield/acre	45 bushels	40 bushels
Cost/acre of wheat	$200	$180

Each land is 100 acres. The farmer has $45,000 budget to pay for the costs (before receiving any revenues). Selling price of a bushel of canola is $14 and a bushel of wheat is $7. Formulate a linear program to maximize the total profit for the farmer, and solve it using Excel's Solver.

27. One of the products of Edwards Lifesciences (EL) is artificial heart valves made from the heart valves of pigs.[8] Different sizes of valves are required. However, the size of a pig's heart valve cannot be ascertained before the heart is purchased and opened. Therefore, EL has a mismatch problem: shortages of some sizes and excess of others. A program was established to document the size distribution of valves supplied by each supplier, and purchases were made from those suppliers with the needed sizes. Linear programming was used to determine the set of the suppliers that collectively satisfied EL's demand. Suppose EL purchases pig valves from three suppliers. The cost and size mix of the valves purchased from each supplier are given in the table below. Each

---

[6] M. Hojati and A. S. Patil, "An Integer Linear Programming-based Heuristic for Scheduling Heterogeneous Part-time Service Employees," *European Journal of Operational Research*, 209 (2011), pp. 37–50.

[7] Based on K. Magoulas et al, "Instructions Are Given for Building Gasoline-blending LP," *Oils and Gas Journal*, 86(27), July 1988, pp. 32–37.

[8] S. S. Hilal and W. Erikson, "Matching Supplies to Save Lives: Linear Programming the Production of Heart Valves," *Interfaces*, 11(6), Dec. 1981, pp. 48–56.

month EL places one order with each supplier. Suppose next month, 250 large, 300 medium, and 100 small valves are needed. Formulate an LP that can be used to minimize the cost of acquiring the needed valves, and use Excel's Solver to solve it. **LO1 & 3**

Supplier	Cost Per Valve ($)	Percent Large	Percent Medium	Percent Small
1	10	30	50	20
2	14	10	60	30
3	12	20	55	25

*28. A Connecticut hospital employs 31 full-time orderlies.[9] Each orderly works five days per week. The demand for orderlies fluctuates with the day of the week, so the number required each day depends on which day of the week it is: Saturday, 20; Sunday, 18; Monday, 18; Tuesday, 30; Wednesday, 20; Thursday, 31; Friday, 15. The hospital wants to schedule the orderlies in order to minimize the number of orderlies whose days off are not consecutive. Formulate a linear program that will accomplish this goal, and solve it using Excel's Solver. *Hint:* Define a variable for staff having days off on each consecutive pair of days, and orderlies having days off on each day and another (nonspecific) consecutive day. **LO1 & 3**

*29. A small manufacturer currently has an inventory of 120 20-ft rods, 160 15-ft rods, and 40 8-ft rods.[10] For production next week, the manufacturer needs at least 200 10-ft rods and 250 6-ft rods. Each 20-ft rod is worth $10, each 15-ft rod is worth $8, and each 8-ft rod is worth $5. Each cut costs $1. The manufacturer has the option to buy each 10-ft rod for $6 and each 6-ft rod for $4. Formulate a linear program to minimize the total cost of meeting the demand, and solve it using Excel's Solver. **LO1 & 3**

30. The manager of a shipyard is wondering what type of business to accept in order to maximize its total profit over next year. The possible jobs include ship repair and new ship construction. The maximum number of ship repairs is 30 and of new ship construction is 2. The profits are $0.5 million for each ship repair and $7 million for each new ship. Each repair requires 60,000 hours of labour and each new ship requires 1.35 million hours of labour. The shipyard has a maximum of 3 million hours of labour available next year. Each repair requires 10 days in the dock and each new ship requires 140 days in the dock. The shipyard has a maximum of 350 dock days. Formulate a linear programming model to determine the number of each job to accept in order to maximize total profit subject to the above capacity constraints. Solve it using the graphical solution method. **LO1 & 2**

MINI-CASE

Airline Fuel Management

Linear programming has been used for airline fuel management. Given a sequence of flight legs, the problem is to determine the number of kilograms of jet fuel to buy in each stop in order to minimize the total purchase cost subject to restrictions on tank capacity, maximum take-off weight, and safety stock of fuel at the end of each leg. The problem is complicated by the fact that the weight of jet fuel itself causes more fuel burn-off. Consider the following small problem for the flight sequence of an A310-200 of Middle East Airlines.

The jet has just landed in Beirut with 8,000 kg of fuel on board. The next leg is to Kuwait. The average flight time to Kuwait is 2.54 hours. The fuel burn-off has been shown to be approximately a linear function of the duration of flight multiplied by the take-off weight of the airplane. On this leg, the fuel burn-off in kilograms is expected to equal .0258(duration × weight) + 4,254, where weight = deadweight of 81,522 kg + payload of 19,478 kg + weight of fuel on board, which includes the initial fuel plus any fuel uplifted in Beirut (to be determined). The tank capacity is 44,000 kg, and the maximum take-off weight is 138,600 kg. The safety stock of fuel at the end of this leg is 7,508 kg. The price of jet fuel in Beirut is $.7615 per gallon (a gallon of jet fuel weighs 3.1 kg). The price of jet fuel in Kuwait is $.7454 per gallon.

The return leg from Kuwait to Beirut is expected to take 2.79 hours. The fuel burn-off in kilograms is expected to equal .0277(duration × weight) + 4,083. The payload will be approximately 8,278 kg. The safety fuel for this leg is 6,250 kg.

The next leg is from Beirut to Copenhagen and is expected to take 4.25 hours. The fuel burn-off in kilograms is expected to equal .02575(duration × weight) + 5,775. The payload will be

[9] M. Rothstein, "Hospital Manpower Shift Scheduling by Mathematical Programming," *Health Services Research* 8(1), 1973, pp. 60–66.

[10] Based on H. A. Eiselt and C-L Sandblom, *Linear Programming and its Applications*, Berlin: Springer-Verlag, 2007, p. 77.

approximately 17,378 kg. The safety fuel for this leg is 5,450 kg. The price of jet fuel in Copenhagen is $.682 per gallon.

The return leg from Copenhagen to Beirut is expected to take 3.83 hours. The fuel burn-off in kilograms is expected to equal .02872(duration × weight) + 3,757. The payload will be approximately 19,678 kg. The safety fuel for this leg is 6,122 kg.

The next leg is from Beirut to Jeddah and is expected to take 2.46 hours. The fuel burn-off in kilograms is expected to equal .0254(duration × weight) + 4,009. The payload will be approximately 21,878 kg. The safety fuel for this leg is 10,263 kg. The price of jet fuel in Jeddah is $.7696 per gallon.

The return leg from Jeddah to Beirut is expected to take 2.37 hours. The fuel burn-off in kilograms is expected to equal .0252(duration × weight) + 4,084. The payload will be approximately 2,778 kg. The safety fuel for this leg is 6,085 kg.

a. Formulate this problem as a linear program.

b. Solve it using Excel's Solver. Are the results what you expect? Is there a direct way to determine the optimal solution without using linear programming?

Source: P. P. Zouein et al., "A Multiple Period Capacitated Inventory Model for Airline Fuel Management: A Case Study," *Journal of Operational Research Society* 53, 2002, pp. 379–386.

 MINI-CASE

Son Ltd.

Son Ltd. manufactures a variety of chemical products used by photoprocessors. Son was recently bought out by a conglomerate, and managers of the two organizations have been working together to improve the efficiency of Son's operations. Managers have been asked to adhere to weekly operating budgets and to develop operating plans using quantitative methods whenever possible. The manager of one department has been given a weekly operating budget of $11,980 for production of three chemical products, which for convenience shall be referred to as Q, R, and W. The budget is intended to pay for direct labour and materials. Processing requirements for the three products, on a per-unit basis, are shown in the table below.

The company has a contractual obligation for 85 units of product R per week.

Material A costs $4 per kg, as does material B. Labour costs $8 an hour.

Product Q sells for $122 a unit, product R sells for $115 a unit, and product W sells for $76 a unit.

The manager is considering a number of different proposals regarding the quantity of each product to produce. The manager is primarily interested in maximizing total profit contribution.

Moreover, the manager wants to know how much labour will be needed, as well as the amount of each material to purchase.

Questions

Prepare a report that addresses the following issues:

1. The optimal quantities of products and the necessary quantities of labour and materials.

2. One proposal is to make equal amounts of the products. What amount of each will maximize contribution, and what quantities of labour and materials will be needed? How much less will total profit contribution be if this proposal is adopted?

3. How would you formulate the constraint for material A if it was determined that there is a 5 percent waste factor for material A?

Product	Labour (hours)	Material A (kg)	Material B (kg)
Q	5	2	1
R	4	2	–
W	2	1/2	2

CHAPTER 7
Work/Job Design and Measurement

Learning Objectives

After completing this chapter, you should be able to:

LO1 Briefly describe efficiency and behavioural approaches to work/job design.

LO2 Explain the purpose of work methods analysis and describe how it is performed.

LO3 Discuss the impact of working conditions on work/job design.

LO4 Describe time-study methods and perform calculations.

LO5 Describe various compensation methods.

UPS is the largest parcel delivery company in the world. Since its beginning early last century, UPS founder J. E. Casey and subsequent executives have emphasized a disciplined/structured approach to running UPS. A large part of this is the standard work methods that all UPS employees are expected to follow. There are more than 340 procedures/methods such as the 12-step "unloading" procedure, starting from parking the delivery truck until the driver steps off with the parcel (see the footnote). This task and each of its steps/elements have been thoroughly studied and there is a standard time for it. For example, the 12-step "unloading" should take 15.5 seconds for 1 package from a shelf, 25.1 seconds for 1 package from the floor, 29.6 seconds for 3 packages from a shelf, and 65.5 seconds for 5 packages from the rear door. There is even a hands-on UPS school called Integrad (http://www.youtube.com/watch?v=cTuqgr8vd7o) that teaches future drivers (in a five-day course) the safe way to drive, get off the truck (three points of contact: hold the handrail), lift and lower parcels, walk at a brisk pace, and the standard way to use the delivery truck and the hand-held device (called a delivery information acquisition device). There is also training for how to slip and fall safely. Clearly, using the best work design (including work methods and standard times) has increased the productivity/profitability of UPS.[1]

Work/Job Design

L01

This chapter covers work/job design, the last step in process design. Work/job design is determining its content and method, as well as the work environment/conditions. It also includes work/job measurement which is establishing standard time for the work/job. We will also cover types of compensation, i.e., how to pay employees for their work/job.

Work/job design is one of the oldest activities in operations management and was the main focus of scientific management (later called industrial engineering) of Frederick Taylor at the beginning of the last century. **Work/job design** involves specifying the content (what) and method (how) of a work/job. A work/job consists of a set of tasks (e.g., a UPS parcel delivery driver's work/job involves the task of carrying a parcel from the truck to a customer's residence). Scientific management breaks this task into a sequence of elements (e.g., pick up the parcel) and each element into a sequence of motions (e.g., reach for the parcel). The objective of work/job design is to assign the required organizational tasks to employees so that long-term productivity/profitability of the organization is maximized.

work/job design Specifying the content and method of the work or job.

The factors that affect work/job design and the implications of various alternatives are often so complex that a person without a good background in work/job design is likely to overlook important aspects of it. Ideally, everyone affected by work/job (re)design should be consulted. Both physical (strength, energy, and precision and speed of movements) and mental requirements (info processing speed and accuracy) are usually important factors in work/job (re)design.

Current practice in work/job (re)design is affected by two basic approaches. One is *efficiency* (which is a refinement of scientific management and emphasizes a systematic, logical approach to labour cost reduction); the other is *behavioural*, which emphasizes satisfaction of wants and needs of workers as a motivator for increased productivity.

The behavioural approach emerged during the 1950s and includes initiatives such as job enlargement, enrichment, rotation, and teams. It is noteworthy that specialization is a primary issue of disagreement between the efficiency and behavioural approaches.

Efficiency Approach

The efficiency approach includes specialization, work methods analysis, and time standards. We will discuss specialization here, and cover work methods analysis and time standards later in the chapter.

Specialization focuses work/jobs to a narrow scope. Examples range from assembly-line jobs to medical specialties. For instance, an assembly-line worker could be installing windshields the whole shift (i.e., hundreds of them, same task repeated every minute). College/university professors often specialize in teaching certain courses, some auto mechanics specialize in transmission repair, and some bakers specialize in wedding cakes. The main rationale for specialization is the ability to concentrate one's efforts and thereby become proficient at that type of work.

specialization Focusing the work/job to a narrow scope.

Unfortunately, some of these jobs, e.g., assembly-line jobs, can be monotonous and boring. The advantages and disadvantages of assembly-line specialization for a company and a worker are summarized in Table 7-1.

---

[1] 1. Shift into the lowest gear. 2. Turn the ignition off and engage the parking brake. 3. Release the seatbelt with your left hand. 4. Open the door. 5. Place key on ring finger. 6. Select package without stepping through door (if possible). 7. Only select packages from selection area. 8. Close the door. 9. Pick up the DIAD (Delivery Information Acquisition Device). 10. Fasten DIAD to clip. 11. Look before stepping into the street. 12. Hold on to the handrail and exit truck. Source: http://www.archive.fortune.com/magazines/fortune/fortune_archive/2007/11/12/101008310/index.htm

Advantages	
For a company:	For a worker:
1. Simplified training	1. Low education and skill requirements
2. High productivity	2. Minimum responsibilities
3. Relatively low-wage costs	3. Little mental effort needed
Disadvantages	
For a company:	For a worker:
1. Difficult to motivate	1. Monotonous/boring work
2. Worker dissatisfaction, possibly resulting in absenteeism, high turnover, disruptive tactics	2. Limited opportunities for advancement
	3. Little control over work
	4. Little opportunity for self-fulfillment

The seriousness of the problems with assembly-line specialization resulted in the creation of behavioural approach.

Behavioural Approach

People work for a variety of reasons (in addition to monetary compensation). These include socialization, self-actualization, status, and a sense of purpose and accomplishment. Awareness of these factors can help management develop a motivational framework that encourages workers to respond in a positive manner to the goals of the organization.

Another factor that influences motivation, productivity, and employee–management relations is *trust*. In an ideal work environment, there is a high level of trust between workers and managers. When managers trust employees, there is a greater tendency to give employees added responsibilities. When employees trust management, they are more likely to respond positively and be loyal to the organization.

New management approaches such as Total Quality Management (TQM) are based on behavioural approaches such as employee involvement (deciding how work is done and can be improved) and quality at the source (being able to stop the line if worker observes a quality issue).

Various names are used for the behavioural approach including quality of work life, employee empowerment, and the sociotechnical approach. The behavioural approach includes job enlargement, job rotation, job enrichment, and self-directed teams.

job enlargement Giving a worker a larger portion of the total activity.

Job enlargement means giving a worker a larger portion of the total activity of making the good or providing the service. This is referred to as *horizontal loading* because additional tasks are on the same level of skill and responsibility as the original job. The goal is to make the work/job more interesting by increasing the variety of skills required and by letting the worker make a more recognizable contribution to the overall output. For example, an assembly-line worker's work/job might be expanded so that he/she is responsible for a longer *sequence* of tasks. Two examples of job enlargement from the City of Winnipeg are the elimination of the distinction between welders and blacksmiths, and combining the jobs of a vehicle-frame straightener and a painter as body repairman.

job rotation Workers periodically exchange jobs.

Job rotation means having workers periodically exchange jobs. A company can use this approach to avoid having one or a few employees stuck in monotonous/repetitive jobs. Job rotation allows workers to broaden their learning experience and enables them to fill in for others in the event of sickness or absenteeism. Also, repetitive motion injuries may be avoided by periodically doing a different type of physical work. An example of job rotation is a Honda assembly-line worker who rotates with his team mates every hour.

job enrichment Increasing employee responsibility for planning, execution, and control of job.

Job enrichment involves an increase in the level of employee responsibility for planning, execution, and control of the job. It is sometimes referred to as *vertical loading*. An example of this is an operator who is also responsible for the maintenance, setup, and quality control of the machine/process he/she uses. An example of job enrichment from Shell refinery in east Montreal is that the job of operator now includes minor maintenance; completing time sheets; planning rotation, overtime, and vacation/shut down; writing operations and training manuals; training; and participating in reliability groups.

A **self-directed team**, sometimes referred to as a self-managed or *autonomous team*, is a group of employees who perform the same function, e.g., the milling operation in a plant. They are empowered to make decisions involving their work as a group, e.g., membership, work assignment, pace of work, training, and quality. The underlying concept is that the workers, who are close to their work and have the best knowledge of it, are better suited than management to make the most effective decisions involving their work. Moreover, they tend to work harder to ensure that the desired results are achieved. For these teams to function properly, team members must be trained in new skills, including communication, problem solving, and leadership. Self-directed teams have a number of benefits. One is that fewer managers/supervisors are necessary, and their role is changed from command and control to team leader and coach. Other benefits include higher quality, productivity, and worker satisfaction. However, middle managers/supervisors often feel threatened as teams assume more of their traditional functions. See the "Ralston Foods" OM in Action for an example and more details.

Other new initiatives include flexible work hours and flexible work location (see, for example, http://hrcouncil.ca/hr-toolkit/workplaces-flexible.cfm).

self-directed team A group of employees who perform the same function and are empowered to make certain decisions and changes in their work.

Role of Unions

Labour unions can affect all aspects of work/job design and how work is accomplished. In approximately 30 percent of organizations (more public than private), labour unions represent employees in negotiating labour contracts (collective agreements) and their execution. A collective agreement determines the wages, benefits (health care, vacation, pension, etc.), security of jobs/limits to outsourcing and hiring temporary workers, hiring/layoff/promotion/seniority, safety standards/working conditions, work rules, job classification, scheduling, and grievance procedures. A cooperative working relationship between management and unions can lead to higher productivity and reduced labour strikes.

Examples of labour unions include Unifor (created from a recent merger of Canadian AutoWorkers Union and Communications, Energy and Paperworks Union of Canada); United Steelworkers, which also represents some mining, forestry, and rubber company workers; Teamsters Canada, which represents truck drivers and also rail company workers; International Association of Machinists & Aerospace Workers; United Food & Commercial Workers Canada; Construction & Specialty Workers Union; National Union of Public and General Employees; Bakery, Confectionery, Tobacco Workers and Grain Millers Union; and International Union of Operating Engineers.

 OM in ACTION   http://www.ralstonfoods.com

Ralston Foods

Ralston Foods makes private-brand breakfast cereals, e.g., for IGA. Ralston follows a team-based work management approach in its plants. The operating work groups are maintenance, milling, extrusion, flaking, packing, warehousing, and logistics. The support work groups are human resources, accounting, engineering services, and tech services. Each group consists of 8–50 members. Groups larger than 10 are further divided into teams. All groups are either autonomous or semi-autonomous, and have a self-appointed group leader. Each group decides its own interviewing, hiring, work assignments, schedules, job rotation, performance appraisals, discipline, termination, cost control, quality, safety, continuous improvement, food safety, purchased services, capital projects,

communications, counselling, customer relations, security, and temperature management. The management also works as a group, acting both as enforcer and facilitator, and is involved in activities such as communication of business trends, production scheduling and prioritization, cost/budget management, benefits and wage adjustments, mass meetings, and support for programs for continuous improvement, safety, counselling/discipline, substance abuse, and employee assistance. The participatory management has resulted in achieving the goals on productivity, cost reduction, and quality, while keeping employees happy. Ralston Foods is now part of ConAgra Foods.

Source: D. R. Kibbe and J. Casner-Lotto, "Ralston Foods–from Greenfield to Maturity in a Team-based Plant," *Journal of Organizational Excellence*, 21(3), pp. 57–67.

Methods Analysis

methods analysis Breaks down the job into a sequence of tasks/elements/motions and improves it.

Methods analysis, also known as work methods analysis, methods engineering, or operations analysis, breaks down the job into a sequence of tasks/elements/motions and tries to make it more efficient.

If methods analysis is done for an existing job, the analyst should observe the job as it is currently being performed by the worker in the workplace, ask several questions, and then devise improvements. For a new job, the analyst must rely on the method being used for similar jobs.

The basic procedure in methods analysis is:

1. Identify the job to be studied. A candidate job has high labour content, is done frequently, is unsafe/tiring/unpleasant/noisy, causes quality problems, and/or is a bottleneck.

2. Gather all pertinent facts about worker (age, gender, size, motivation, satisfaction, education, fitness, protective equipment), tasks (how parts flow in/out, what happens, motions, fixtures, automation, tools, layout, awkward motions, lifting, fatigue, sensory input, cycle time, standard time), workplace (light, glare, noise, heat, vibration), and administrative factors (wage incentive, job rotation/team, enlargement, enrichment, training, policy).

3. Document and analyze the present method, and discuss the job/facts with the worker and supervisor.

4. Question the present method and propose a new method.

Analyzing and questioning the method and proposing a new method requires careful thought about the what, why, when, where, and who of the job. Some questions to ask include:

Can a task/element/motion be eliminated? Combined with another?

Can the sequence of tasks/elements/motions be changed? Can it be done elsewhere?

Are tolerances necessary? Can cheaper material be substituted?

Can material handling equipment be improved? Can distance moved be reduced?

Can setup time be reduced? Can fixtures and tools be improved?

Can any delay, storage, or inspection be eliminated?

Can the part be redesigned for easy manufacturing/assembly?

Are working conditions satisfactory? Is the work area arranged well?

Can worker motions be improved? Can work be made more ergonomic?

Does the worker have the right skill level?

Can technology assist in the method improvement?

Documenting, analyzing, and improving methods is facilitated by the use of various charts, such as *a flow process chart* and *a worker–machine process chart.*

flow process chart Chart used to examine the sequence of steps/tasks/element by focusing on movements of the worker or flow of material.

A **flow process chart** is used to review and examine the sequence of steps/tasks/elements by focusing on the movements of the worker or the flow of material. Each step/task/element is categorized as one of operation, movement, inspection, delay, and storage. Examples of an operation include driving a nail in, mixing, or using a computer. Delay means waiting to be processed (hours) whereas storage is a much longer wait (days). Flow process chart is helpful in identifying the nonproductive steps of the process (e.g., delays, distances travelled). Figure 7-1 illustrates a flow process chart for "Requisition of petty cash" in a company. The petty cash is used for minor expenses such as buying a hand tool or stationery. For this example, after considering the amount of work involved in petty cash requisition, a solution may be to issue a corporate credit card (with a certain limit) to the department heads.

worker–machine process chart Used to determine portions of a work cycle during which a worker and his/her machine are busy or idle.

A **worker–machine process chart**, also known as a man and machine chart, is helpful in visualizing the portions of a work cycle during which the worker and his/her machine are busy or idle. The analyst can easily see when the worker and machine are working independently and when their work overlaps or is interdependent. One use of this type of chart is to determine how many machines the operator can manage.

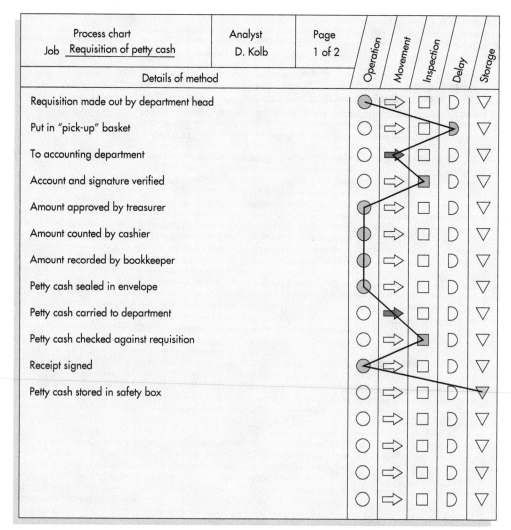

◀ Figure 7-1

Example of a flow process chart.

Source: Elias M. Awad, *Systems Analysis and Design*, 4th ed. (Burr Ridge, IL: Richard D. Irwin), p. 113. © by Richard D. Irwin, Inc. Reprinted by permission of the McGraw-Hill Companies Inc.

Figure 7-2 presents an example of a worker–machine process chart where the worker/operator runs two machines in a staggered way (times are in hours). As evident, it is hard to improve the synchronization of the work—each machine is used approximately .0096/.0134 = 0.72 or 72 percent of the time and the worker is used 100 percent of the time.

Motion Study

Motion study is the systematic study of the human motions used to perform a task/element. The purpose is to eliminate unnecessary motions and to identify the best sequence of motions for maximum efficiency. Hence, motion study can be an important tool for methods analysis and productivity improvement. Present practice evolved from the work of Frank Gilbreth, who originated the concept in the bricklaying trade in the early 20th century. Through the use of motion study, Gilbreth increased the number of bricks laid per hour by a factor of 3. Usually, motion study is performed in conjunction with (but before) time study (described later).

There are a number of different techniques/tools that motion-study analysts can use to develop efficient procedures. The most popular techniques/tools are:

1. Motion economy principles.

2. Analysis of a task/element into motions.

3. Slow-motion video study.

4. Simo or two hand process chart.

motion study Systematic study of the human motions used to perform a task/element.

Figure 7-2 ▶

Example of a worker–machine process chart.

Worker and Machine Process Chart

Subject Charted Milling slot in regulator clamp   **Chart No.** 807
Drawing No. J-1492   **Part No.** J-1492-1   **Chart of Method** Proposed
Chart Begins Loading mchs. for milling   **Charted by** C.A. Anderson
Chart Ends Unloading milled clamps   **Date** 8-27   **Sheet** 1 **of** 1

Element description	Operator	B.&S. Hor. Mill *Machine 1*	B.&S. Hor. Mill *Machine 2*
Stop machine #1	.0004		
Return table mch. #1 5 inches	.0010	Unloading .0024	
Loosen vise remove part and lay aside (mch. #1)	.0010		Mill slot .0040
Pickup part and tighten vise mch. #1	.0018	Loading .0032	
Start machine #1	.0004		
Advance table and engage feed mch. #1	.0010		Idle
Walk to machine #2	.0011	Mill slot .0040	
Stop machine #2	.0004		
Return table mch. #2 5 inches	.0010		Unloading .0024
Loosen vise remove part and lay aside (mch. #2)	.0010		
Pick up part and tighten vise mch. #2	.0080		Loading .0032
Start machine #2	.0004		
Advance table and engage feed mch. #2	.0010	Idle	
Walk to machine #1	.0011		
Idle man time per cycle	.0000	Idle hours machine #1	.0038
Working man time per cycle	.0134	Productive hours mch. #1	.0096
Man-hours per cycle	.0134	Machine #1 cycle time	.0134

Idle hours machine #2	.0038
Productive hours mch. #2	.0096
Machine #2 cycle time	.0134

motion economy principles Guidelines for designing motion-efficient work procedures.

Gilbreth's work laid the foundation for the development of **motion economy principles**, which are guidelines for designing motion-efficient work procedures. The guidelines are divided into three categories: use of arms and body, arrangement of the workplace, and design of tools and equipment. Table 7-2 lists some examples of the principles.

A list of some common motions includes reach, grasp, move, and disengage. Breaking the task/element into motions enables motion analysis and also easy timing of the motion. Describing a job/task using motions often takes a substantial amount of work. However, for short, repetitive tasks, motion analysis may be justified.

slow motion study Use of motion pictures and slow motion to study motions that otherwise would be too rapid to analyze.

Frank Gilbreth and his wife, Lillian, an industrial psychologist, were also responsible for introducing motion pictures for studying motions, called **slow motion study**. This approach is applied not only in industry but also in some other areas such as sports. Use of camera and slow-motion replay enables analysts to study motions that would otherwise be too rapid to see. In addition, the resulting films provide a permanent record that can be referred to not only for training workers and analysts but also for settling disputes involving standard times.

simo chart A chart that shows the motions performed by each hand, side-by-side, over time.

Motion-study analysts may use a two-hand process chart or **simo chart** (see Figure 7-3a) to study the motions performed by each hand, side-by-side, through time. Here, the methods analyst studies a trim/blanking task on a hand-operated press with an accompanying die. He/she breaks

A. The use of arms and body:

  1. Both hands should begin and end their activity simultaneously and should not be idle at the same instant, except during frequent but short rest periods.

  2. The motions made by the hands should be minimal and symmetrical.

  3. Momentum should assist workers wherever possible and should be minimized if it must be overcome by muscular effort.

  4. Continuous natural curved motions are preferable to straight-line motions involving sudden and sharp changes in direction.

  5. Strength requirements should be much less than the maximum available. Avoid lifting heavy objects. Use slow movements for maximum muscle strength.

  6. Eliminate bend and rise, as well as awkward positions, and make the tasks easier to reduce fatigue.

  7. Eliminate eye travel and avoid losing eye focus.

B. The arrangement of the workplace:

  1. Fixed locations for all tools and material should be provided to permit the best sequence and to eliminate or reduce search and selection.

  2. Gravity bins and drop delivery should reduce reach and move times; wherever possible, ejectors should remove finished parts automatically.

  3. All materials and tools should be located within easy reach.

  4. Provide a chair or stool if possible.

C. The design of tools and equipment:

  1. Where possible, power tools should replace hand tools.

  2. All levers, handles, wheels, and other control devices should be readily accessible to the operator and designed to give the best possible mechanical advantage and to utilize the strongest available muscle group.

  3. Parts should be held in position by fixtures.

◀ Table 7-2

Examples of motion economy principles.

Source: Adapted from Benjamin W. Niebel, *Motion and Time Study*, 8th ed. (Burr Ridge, IL: Richard D. Irwin, Inc.), pp. 206–207. Reprinted with permission of the McGraw-Hill Companies Inc.

the task down into a right- and left-hand process chart (aligned through time). A review of the process charts shows that delays are occurring because the motions of the right and left hand are not balanced: the left hand is waiting while the right hand raises the handle of the press, again while the right hand removes the part from the die, and again when the right hand regains control of the press handle. If the operator did not have to remove the finished piece from the die, he/she would be freed from the action of regrasping the press handle. The improved method is shown in Figure 7-3b. A fixture was developed to lift the part clear from the die while the press is being raised and eject it through the back of the press by an air blast. Simo charts are invaluable in studying operations such as data entry, sewing, surgical and dental procedures, and certain fabrication and assembly operations.

Working Conditions

Working conditions are important for work/job design. In many instances, government standards and regulations apply. Physical factors such as temperature and humidity, ventilation, illumination, noise and vibration, work hours, work breaks, safety, ergonomics, and workers' well-being and a healthy workplace can have significant impacts on worker performance in terms of productivity and quality of output.

http://www.hrsdc.gc.ca/eng/labour/health_safety/index.shtml

Government Regulation of Workplace. The creation of factories in the 19th century was the start of increasing worker health and safety problems. To address these, the government passed worker protection acts that required guards on the machines, fire safety, boiler and elevator inspection, sanitation, ventilation, and adequate heating and lighting. The Canadian Labour Code of

Figure 7-3 ▶

A simo or two-hand process chart.

Source: B. W. Niebel, *Motion and Time Study*, 5th ed. (Homewood, IL: Richard D. Irwin). © 1976. Figure 7.15, p. 201 and Figure 7.16, p. 202. Reprinted by permission.

a. Right- and left-hand analysis of a blanking operation

The Airfelt Mfg. Corp.
Right and Left Hand Analysis

Operation _Blank supporting strip on hand arbor press_
Part No. _P-1107-7_   Dwg. No. _PB-1107_   Date _1-12-_
Drawn By _W. Eitele_   Dept. _13_   Plant _Bellefonte_   Sheet _1_ of _1_

Sketch

RAW MATERIAL — PRESS — DISPOSAL GRAVITY CHUTE

OPERATOR

Left Hand	Symbols		Right Hand	
1. Pick up part from hopper			Pull press handle down	1.
Reach for part	Re	H	Hold handle	
Grasp part	G	H	Hold handle	
Move part adjacent to die	M	M	Move press handle down	
2. Wait for right hand			Raise press handle up	2.
Unavoidable delay	UD	M	Move press handle up	
Unavoidable delay	UD	RI	Release press handle	
3. Wait for right hand			Get part from die	3.
Unavoidable delay	UD	Re	Reach for part in die	
Unavoidable delay	UD	G	Grasp part	
4. Place part in die			Drop part in chute	4.
Move part to die	M	M	Move part to chute	
Position part in die	P	RI	Release part	
Release part	RI	UD	Wait for left hand	
5. Wait for right hand			Get press handle	5.
Unavoidable delay	UD	Re	Reach for handle	
Unavoidable delay	UD	G	Grasp handle	

b. Right- and left-hand analysis of a blanking operation in which avoidable delays have been omitted

The Airfelt Mfg. Corp.
Right and Left Hand Analysis

Operation _Blank supporting strip on hand arbor press_
Part No. _P-1107-7_   Dwg. No. _PB-1107_   Date _1-12-_
Drawn By _W. Eitele_   Dept. _13_   Plant _Bellefonte_   Sheet _1_ of _1_

Sketch

RAW MATERIAL — PART AIR EJECTED TO GRAVITY CHUTE

OPERATOR

Left Hand	Symbols		Right Hand	
1. Get part from hopper			Pull press handle down	1.
Reach for part	RE	H	Hold handle	
Grasp part	G			
Move part to die	M	M	Move press handle down	
2. Place part in die				2.
Move part to die	M	M	Raise press handle up	
Position part	P	M	Move handle up	
Release part	RI	H	Hold handle	

1966 included safety as well as other work standards such as minimum wage and a 40-hour work week. In 1978, the Labour Code was amended to give three rights to workers: (a) to refuse dangerous work, (b) to participate in improving safety and health problems (through joint management/labour committees), and (c) to know about hazards in the workplace (See http://laws-lois.justice.gc.ca/eng/acts/L-2/ for details of the Labour Code). In 1988, the right to know about hazards in the workplace was shaped into the requirement for a Workplace Hazardous Materials Information System (WHMIS), which mandates proper labelling of hazardous material and making the material safety data sheets available.

Temperature and Humidity. Many operations need to be performed in high temperatures, such as in an iron foundry, and some others need to be performed in low temperatures, such as in a slaughterhouse. Although human beings can function under a fairly wide range of temperatures, work performance tends to be adversely affected if temperatures are outside a very narrow *comfort band*. That comfort band depends on how strenuous the work is; the more strenuous the work, the smaller the comfort range.

For most work activities, the comfort band is about 10°C to 21°C at a relative humidity of between 30 to 80 percent. Productivity drops sharply below 0°C and above 30°C and at relative humidity close to 100 percent. Solutions range from selection of suitable clothing to space heating or cooling devices.

Ventilation. Some factories (such as lumber mills and grinding operations) create large amount of dust; some others (such as pulp and paper mills) generate gases and foul odours. These are unhealthy and unpleasant. Large fans and air-conditioning equipment are commonly used to exchange and recondition the air.

Illumination. The amount of light required depends largely on the type of work being performed; the more detailed the work, the higher the level of illumination needed for adequate performance. Other important considerations are the amount of glare and contrast.

Sometimes natural daylight can be used as a source of illumination. It is not only free, but also provides some psychological benefits. Workers in windowless factories may feel cut off from the outside world and experience various psychological problems. On the downside, the inability to control natural light (e.g., cloudy days) can result in dramatic changes in light intensity.

Noise and Vibrations. Noise is caused by the movement and vibrations of machines or equipment. Noise can be annoying or distracting, leading to errors and accidents. It can also damage or impair hearing if it is loud enough. Figure 7-4 illustrates loudness level of some typical sounds.

Successful sound control begins with measurement of the offending sounds. In a new operation, selection and placement of equipment can eliminate or reduce many potential problems. In the case of existing equipment, it may be possible to redesign or substitute equipment. In some instances, the source of noise can be isolated from other work areas. If that isn't feasible, acoustical walls and ceilings that deflect sound waves may prove useful. Sometimes the only solution is to provide earplugs or earmuffs for those in the immediate vicinity.

Vibrations can be a factor in work/job design even without a noise component. Vibrations can come from tools, machines, vehicles, air-conditioning systems, pumps, and other sources.

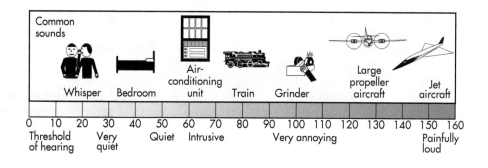

◄ Figure 7-4

Decibel values of typical sounds (db).

Source: From Benjamin W. Niebel, *Motion and Time Study*, 8th ed. Copyright © 1988 Richard D. Irwin, Inc. Used by permission of McGraw-Hill Companies, Inc., p. 248.

Corrective measures include padding, stabilizers, shock absorbers, cushioning, and rubber mountings.

Work Hours. Reasonable (and sometimes flexible) work hours can provide a sense of freedom and control over one's work. This is useful in situations where the emphasis is on completing work on a timely basis and meeting performance objectives rather than being "on duty" for a given time interval, as is the case for most retail and manufacturing operations. Shift work (working nights) is required for mostly services such as health care. Though necessary, it can cause medical and social problems.

Work Breaks. The frequency, length, and timing of work breaks (i.e., rests) can have a significant impact on both productivity and quality of output. Efficiency generally declines as the day wears on, but breaks for lunch and rest can cause an upward shift in efficiency.

An important variable in the rate of decline of efficiency and potential effects of work breaks is the amount of physical and/or mental requirements of the job. Steelworkers, for instance, may need rest breaks of 15 minutes per hour due to the strenuous nature of their jobs. In fact, one of Taylor's experiments showed that for men carrying 92-pound pig-irons up a ramp, maximum output was quadrupled when the workers rested 58 percent of the time. For 40-pound pig-irons, optimal rest was 48 percent of the time. People working at computer monitors also need periodic breaks, and students need study breaks.

Safety. Worker safety is one of the most important issues in work/job design and needs constant attention from management and employees. Workers cannot be motivated if they feel they are in physical danger.

From an employer standpoint, accidents are undesirable because they are expensive (insurance and compensation) and are bad publicity.

The two basic causes of accidents are worker carelessness and unsafe conditions. Carelessness includes unsafe acts. Examples include failure to use protective equipment, overriding safety controls (e.g., taping control buttons down), disregarding safety procedures, improper use of tools and equipment, and failure to use reasonable caution in danger zones.

Unsafe conditions include unprotected pulleys, chains, material-handling equipment, machinery, and so on. Also, poorly lit or slippery walkways, stairs, and loading docks constitute hazards. So do toxic wastes, gases and vapours, and radiation. Having faulty or inadequate equipment such as a two-person suspended platform used by five workers is also an unsafe work condition.

Protection against hazards involves use of proper equipment and lighting, clearly marked danger zones, use of protective equipment (hardhats, goggles, earmuffs, gloves, steel-toe shoes, and clothing), safety devices (machine guards, dual-control switches that require an operator to use both hands), emergency equipment (emergency showers, fire extinguishers, fire escapes), and thorough instruction and training in safety procedures and use of regular and emergency equipment. Housekeeping (clean floors, open aisles, waste removal) is another important safety factor. Management must enforce safety procedures and use of safety equipment.

The enactment of Occupational Health and Safety regulations emphasizes the importance of safety in work/job design. It provides specific safety regulations with inspectors to see that they are adhered to. Inspections are carried out both at random and to investigate complaints of unsafe conditions. The officials are empowered to issue warnings, to impose fines, and even to order shutdown for unsafe conditions.

A more effective way to deal with management of safety issues is to incorporate it into the company's management planning and control activities, just as product quality is managed. A safety management system based on the guidelines of BSI OHSAS 18000 can be used. This is similar to ISO 9001 (for quality systems) and ISO 14001 (for environment systems).

The OHSAS 18000 requires that health and safety activities be planned.[2] This process requires that, after an annual risk assessment, realistic objectives and targets be set and that the roles,

---

[2] J. J. Janssen, "OHSAS 18001: Another @#$%& Standard?" *OH&S Canada* 18(1), January/February 2002, p. 58.

The most common ergonomic risk factors are awkward postures; excessive force for lifting, pushing, pulling, and gripping; and repetition involving the same group of muscles. On the left, the worker was using a pistol grip driver in a vertical application, which was placing her in a poor shoulder posture. She was experiencing increasing pain in her right shoulder. On the right, by using a hanged palm-grip driver, the worker is now in a good shoulder posture.

responsibilities, and timelines necessary to achieve the targets be clearly communicated to—and understood by—all those involved in achieving them. Operational controls (procedures) and emergency plans must be developed and documented for those risks found to be intolerable. Employees must be trained. Performance and compliance with system requirements must be measured in order to ensure that they are controlled. Any incident, accident, or other nonconformance within the system needs to be investigated at a level appropriate to its impact on the system. The resulting corrective and preventive action developed from this process ensures that the standards of practice are complied with and are adequate. Finally, senior management must periodically review the system (e.g., internal or external audits every six months) to ensure that it is meeting the objectives stated in its policy and that it is effectively implemented. Improvements in the overall system are identified and implemented through the planning process.

Ergonomics. **Ergonomics** involves fitting the job to the worker's capability and size by removing awkward reaching and bending, forceful gripping of tools, heavy lifting, and endless

ergonomics Fitting the job to the worker's capability and size.

 OM in *ACTION*   http://www.nexgenergo.com

NexGen Ergonomics

NexGen Ergonomics is a well-known Canadian company, located in Montreal, involved in production or reselling (under distribution agreement) of software and products used in ergonomics. The products include a virtual mannequin that can be dimensioned according to average or extreme sizes of a male or female body, to be used in testing CAD drawings of products that directly interact with a human body. Also, NexGen sells force/pressure and motion sensors and measurement products (see the photo on the right), video analysis software, and many types of medical and safety equipment.

OM in *ACTION*

Supermarket Meat Department

The workers in a supermarket's meat department cut, package, and wrap the meat in a cold environment (10°C). Cutting involves bringing a large box of meat from cold storage, cutting it into big pieces, removing the fat, and slicing/grinding the pieces (see the sketch on the left).

Awkward body positions and required forceful movements can cause repetitive motion injuries in neck and shoulders.

Low room and meat temperatures affect dexterity and increase the required effort. Also, lifting heavy boxes and prolonged standing on a hard floor can cause back and leg issues.

Ergonomic solutions (besides job rotation with meat packing and meat wrapping workers) include use of adjustable tables (see the sketch in the middle), wearing meat cutters' gloves, using proper knives (see the sketch below), and using antifatigue mats.

repetition of motions. Ergonomics prevents common workplace injuries such as back injuries and repetitive motion injuries. Workers vary in their physical dimensions and capabilities, and some activities, when continually repeated, result in strains in muscles and joints (called *musculoskeletal injuries*, *repetitive motion injuries*, or *cumulative trauma disorders*). Most ergonomic problems are unintentional mistakes that develop because no one had the knowledge or the time to design the work properly.

Components of a comfortable workstation.

Ergonomic problems can also occur in the office. A common problem in using the computer mouse is that it is usually placed beside the keyboard. This results in the need for constant reaching and stretching of the arm, which can result in long-term joint problems. A solution is using a rotating platform for the mouse so that it can be moved closer to the body. The arm should be at a right angle close to the body and the wrist should not be bent. Another common problem is bad sitting posture. An ergonomic chair that can be adjusted for the user's body dimensions should be used. The back of the user should be completely supported (with a slight angle). An angled foot rest provide support for legs. The display monitor should be just below the horizontal eyesight so that there is no need for slouching. It should be approximately 60 to 80 cm from the eyes. Because monitors emit light, one should look away from the screen every few minutes for a few seconds (preferably at distant objects). If a document is being read, it, not the monitor, should be lit using a lamp. Also, because monitors act like mirrors, their angle should be adjusted to avoid glare. For more information on ergonomics, see the Canadian Centre for Occupational Health and Safety website at http://www.ccohs.ca.

An industrial application of ergonomics is described in the "Supermarket Meat Department" and some ergonomics products are mentioned in the "NexGen Ergonomics" OM in Action.

Workers' Well-being and a Healthy Workplace

Many organizations are realizing that productivity of their employees depends on their general health and well-being. The National Quality Institute (now called Excellence Canada), in cooperation with Health Canada, developed the Healthy Workplace award in 1998 to recognize companies that have a holistic system for a healthy workplace, including physical, mental, safety, personal, and social aspects. The criteria include four "drivers" of a healthy workplace: leadership role (having a policy and management being involved in healthy workplace program); planning process (needs assessment, setting goals, designing programs); fostering worker involvement (to use the programs); and process management (collecting and using feedback). The outcomes—the results of a healthy workplace program such as reduction in absenteeism, turnover, and accident rates—should be measured and compared with goals. The program can affect the physical environment (safety, cleanliness, protective equipment, ergonomics, lighting, air quality, noise, wheelchair accessibility, etc.), health practices (assistance to give up smoking and alcohol abuse, promoting healthy nutrition in the cafeteria, a fitness facility, etc.), and social environment (developing self-respect and a sense of belonging and control over work, protection against harassment and workplace violence, coping with stress, fairness in job assignment and evaluation, reasonable pace of work, flexible hours, benefits plan, etc.). For an application of Healthy Workplace, see the "North York General Hospital's Healthy Workplace" OM in Action. For an overview of Excellence Canada's Healthy Workplace Checkup, see http://www.excellence. ca/en/knowledge-centre/products-and-tools/healthy-workplace-checkup.

Members of the occupational health, safety, and wellness team of North York General Hospital.

OM in ACTION   http://www.nygh.on.ca/Default.aspx?cid=1983&lang=1

North York General Hospital's Healthy Workplace

North York General Hospital (NYGH) is affiliated with the University of Toronto and has over 5,000 staff, physicians, and volunteers located across three sites.

NYGH takes health and safety of staff, physicians and volunteers very seriously. Not only does the hospital have an Occupational Health, Safety and Wellness department, it also has a culture-changing People Plan as part of the human resource strategy. The 2012 employee engagement survey showed a 9 percent increase in engagement by staff and 32 percent increase by physicians.

Programs available include physical fitness (e.g., onsite gym and yoga class), partnerships with YMCA and GoodLife Fitness, regular blood pressure checks, smoking cessation assistance, employee assistance program, and regular ergonomic assessments. NYGH's priority is the health and safety of patients and staff. For example, a $400,000 investment in overhead ceiling lifts was made to make it safer for staff to transfer immobile patients.

NYGH has won the Ontario Hospital Association's Quality Healthcare Workplace Award (Gold Level) four years in a row and was a recipient of the Excellence Canada's (formerly known as National Quality Institute) Healthy Workplace Award.

Source: http://www.nygh.on.ca/Default.aspx?cid=2137&lang=1; http://www.youtube.com/watch?v=x9-IW5SNnes.

Time Study

time study Determining how long it should take to do a task. Also called work measurement.

Time study or work measurement is determining the *length of time* it should take to complete a task. Task times are vital inputs for personnel planning, estimating labour costs, assembly-line balancing, and designing incentive systems.

A **standard time** is the amount of time it should take a qualified worker to complete a specified task, working at a sustainable rate, and using given methods, tools and equipment, raw materials, and workplace arrangement. Whenever a standard time is developed for a task, it is essential to provide a complete description of the parameters of the task because the actual time to do the task is sensitive to all of these factors; changes in any one of the factors can materially affect the time requirement. For instance, changes in product design or changes brought about by a methods analysis should trigger a new time study to update the standard time. As a practical matter, though, minor changes do not justify the expense of restudying the task. Consequently, the standard time for many tasks may be slightly inaccurate. Periodic time studies may be used to update the standard times.

standard time The amount of time it should take a qualified worker to complete a specified task, working at a sustainable rate, and using given methods, tools and equipment, raw materials, and workplace arrangement.

Organizations develop standard times in a number of ways. The most commonly used methods are:

1. Stopwatch time study.
2. Predetermined time standards.
3. Work sampling.

Stopwatch Time Study

stopwatch time study Development of a standard time based on timing one worker over a number of cycles.

Stopwatch time study is used to develop a standard time for a job based on timing one worker over a number of cycles. The standard time is then applied to the work of all others in the organization who perform the same task. The basic steps in a stopwatch time study are:

1. Define the task to be studied, and inform the worker who will be studied.
2. Determine the number of cycles to observe.
3. Time the task, and rate the worker's performance.
4. Calculate the standard time, allowing for rest periods.

People work for a variety of reasons besides compensation. The work environment at Google makes it an appealing place to work. Google provides its employees a number of perks, including massage rooms, a music room, cafeteria, arcade games, and other benefits. The office in Dublin is the technology hub in Europe.

The analyst who studies the task should be thoroughly familiar with it because it is not unusual for workers to attempt to include extra motions during the study in the hope of gaining a time standard that allows more time per piece. Furthermore, the analyst will need to check that the task is being performed efficiently (i.e., a methods analysis should first be performed on the job) before setting the standard time.

In most instances, an analyst will break all but very short tasks down into elements and obtain times for each element. There are several reasons for this: One is that some elements are not performed in every cycle and the breakdown enables the analyst to get a better perspective on them. Another is that the worker's proficiency may not be the same for all elements of the task. A third reason is to build a file of element times that can be used to set times for other tasks.

Workers sometimes feel uneasy about being studied and fear changes that might result. The analyst should make an attempt to discuss these things with the worker prior to the study to reduce such fears and to enlist the cooperation of the worker.

The number of cycles that must be timed is a function of three things: (1) the variability of observed times, (2) the desired accuracy (maximum acceptable error proportion), and (3) the desired level of confidence for the estimated task time. Very often the desired accuracy is expressed as a percentage of the mean of the observed times. For example, the goal of a stopwatch time study may be to achieve an estimate that is within 10 percent of the actual mean. The sample size needed to achieve this goal can be determined using:

$$n = \left(\frac{zs}{a\bar{x}}\right)^2$$

(7-1)

where

$z =$ Number of Normal standard deviations needed for the desired confidence

$s =$ Sample standard deviation

$a =$ Maximum acceptable error proportion ($=$ percentage/100)

$\bar{x} =$ Sample mean

$n =$ Number of observations ($=$ sample size)

Typical values of z used are:[3]

Desired Confidence (%)	z Value
90	1.65
95	1.96
95.5	2.00
98	2.33
99	2.58

Of course, the value of z for any desired confidence can be obtained from the Normal table in Appendix B, Table A, working backward (first divide the desired confidence by 200). For example, if a 97 percent confidence is required, then $97/200 = .485$, which relates to $z = 2.17$ in the table.

To make a preliminary estimate of sample size, it is typical to take a small number of observations (i.e., 10 to 20) and calculate values of $\bar{x}$ and s to use in the formula for n. Toward the end of the study, the analyst may want to recalculate n using revised estimates of $\bar{x}$ and s based on the increased data available.

---

[3] Theoretically, a t rather than a z value should be used because the population standard deviation is unknown. However, the use of z is simpler and provides reasonable results when the number of observations is 30 or more, as it generally is. In practice, z is used almost exclusively.

An alternate formula used when the desired accuracy is stated as an *amount* (e.g., within one minute of the true mean) instead of a proportion is:

$$n = \left(\frac{zs}{e}\right)^2 \tag{7-2}$$

where

e = Accuracy amount or maximum acceptable error amount

Example 1 ▶

An industrial engineer wants to estimate the time required to perform a certain task. A preliminary study yielded a mean of 6.4 minutes and a standard deviation of 2.1 minutes for the task. The desired confidence is 95 percent. How many observations will she need (including those already taken) if the maximum acceptable error is:

a. ±10 percent of the sample mean?

b. .5 minute?

SOLUTION

a. $s = 2.1$ minutes $\qquad z = 1.96$ for 95% confidence
$\bar{x} = 6.4$ minutes $\qquad a = .10$

$$n = \left(\frac{zs}{a\bar{x}}\right)^2 = \left(\frac{1.96(2.1)}{.10(6.4)}\right)^2 = 41.36 \text{ (round up to 42)}$$

b. $e = .5, \quad n = \left(\frac{zs}{e}\right)^2 = \left(\frac{1.96(2.1)}{.5}\right)^2 = 67.77 \text{ (round up to 68)}$

Development of a standard time actually involves calculation of three times: *observed time (OT)*, *normal time (NT)*, and *standard time (ST)*.

Observed Time. The observed time is simply the average of the recorded times. Thus,

$$OT = \frac{\sum x_i}{n} \tag{7-3}$$

where

OT = Observed time

$\sum x_i$ = Sum of recorded times

n = Number of observations

Note: If an element does not occur during each cycle, its average time should be determined separately.

Normal Time. The normal time is the observed time adjusted for the worker's performance. It is calculated by multiplying the observed time by a *performance rating*. That is,

$$NT = OT \times PR \tag{7-4}$$

where

NT = Normal time

PR = Performance rating

This assumes that a single performance rating has been determined for the entire task. If ratings are made on a element-by-element basis, the normal time is obtained by multiplying each element's average time by its performance rating and then summing those values:

$$NT = \sum (\bar{x}_j \times PR_j) \tag{7-5}$$

where

$\bar{x}_j$ = Average time for element j

PR_j = Performance rating for element j

The reason for including this adjustment factor is that the worker being observed may be working at a rate different from a "normal" rate, either to deliberately slow the pace or because his or her natural abilities differ from the norm. For this reason, the analyst assigns a performance rating to adjust the observed times to a "normal" pace. A normal performance rating is 1.00. A performance rating of .9 indicates a pace that is 90 percent of normal, whereas a rating of 1.05 indicates a pace that is slightly faster than normal. For long tasks, each element may be rated; for short tasks, a single rating may be made for an entire cycle.

When assessing performance, the analyst must compare the observed performance to her concept of normal. Obviously, there is room for debate about what constitutes normal performance, and performance ratings are sometimes the source of considerable conflict between labour unions and management. Although no one has been able to suggest a way around these subjective evaluations, sufficient training and periodic *recalibration* of analysts using training films can provide a high degree of consistency in the ratings of different analysts.

Standard Time. Normal time is the length of time a worker should take to perform a task if there are no delays or rest breaks. It does not take into account factors such as personal needs (getting a drink of water or going to the washroom), unavoidable delays (machine adjustments and repairs, talking to a supervisor, waiting for materials), or rest breaks to recover from fatigue. The standard time for a task is the normal time multiplied by an *allowance* for these factors.

$$ST = NT \times AF \tag{7-6}$$

where

ST = Standard time

AF = Allowance factor

Allowance can be based on either task time or time worked (e.g., a workday). If allowance is based on the *task time*, the allowance factor must be calculated using the formula

$$AF_{task} = 1 + A, A = \text{Allowance proportion based on task time} \tag{7-7}$$

This is used when different tasks have different allowances. If allowances are based on the proportion of the time worked (i.e., the *workday*), the appropriate formula is

$$AF_{day} = \frac{1}{1 - A}, A = \text{Allowance proportion based on workday} \tag{7-8}$$

This is used when tasks are the same or similar and have the same allowance factor.

Time-Study Observation Sheet. Usually a standard form is used to record the observations in a stopwatch time study. (Alternatively a handheld device with time study software and internal stopwatch can be used). In the following example, the task is attaching 2 feet by 3 feet chart sheets together. The task has been decomposed into four elements (the left column). Under each element in parentheses is the event that signifies the end of the element. For example, grasping the stapler signifies the end of element 1 and the start of element 2. Focusing on these events makes measuring the times easier. Also note that to the right of each element are two rows. The top row is the individual time of the element in each of the 10 cycles, whereas the bottom row is the cumulative times. For example, for element 2 in cycle 1, the cumulative time is .23 minute. The individual time for this element is therefore $.23 - .07 = .16$ minute, where .07 was the (cumulative) time at the end of element 1 in cycle 1. The cumulative time steadily advances as more cycles are timed. However, the minute digit of the cumulative time has been omitted in order to save recording time. For example, the cumulative time for element 4 in cycle 2 is actually 1.09, but only .09 is shown. It is clearly easier, faster, and more accurate to record the cumulative times first, and then calculate the individual times after the completion of the study.

Time Study Observation Sheet														
Identification of operation				ASSEMBLE 24" × 36" CHART BLANKS							Date 10/9			
Began Timing: 9:26 Ended Timing: 9:32		Operator 109				Approval				Observer				

Task description and Breakpoint		Cycles										Summary			
		1 .00	2	3	4	5	6	7	8	9	10	ΣT	T	PR	NT
1	Fold over end (grasp stapler)	.07	.07	.05	.07	.09	.06	.05	.08	.08	.06	.68	.07	.90	.06
		.07	.61	.14	.67	.24	.78	.33	.88	.47	.09				
2	Staple five times (drop stapler)	.16	.14	.14	.15	.16	.16	.14	.17	.14	.15	1.51	.15	1.05	.16
		.23	.75	.28	.82	.40	.94	.47	.05	.61	.24				
3	Bend and insert wire (drop pliers)	.22	.25	.22	.25	.23	.23	.21	.26	.25	.24	2.36	.24	1.00	.24
		.45	.00	.50	.07	.63	.17	.68	.31	.86	.48				
4	Dispose of finished chart (touch next sheet)	.09	.09	.10	.08	.09	.11	.12	.08	.17	.08	1.01	.10	.90	.09
		.54	.09	.60	.15	.72	.28	.80	.39	.03	.56			.55 normal minute for cycle	
5															
6															
10															

Normal cycle time _.55_ + Allowance (.55 × .143) or .08 = Std. time _.63 min/pc._

Source: Adapted from R. B. Chase et al., *Operations Management for Competitive Advantage*, 10th ed. (Boston: McGraw-Hill, 2004). Reprinted with permission of The McGraw-Hill Companies, Inc.

Example 2 ▶ Calculate the allowance factor for these two cases:

a. The allowance is 20 percent of *task* time.

b. The allowance is 20 percent of *work* time.
$A = .20$

SOLUTION

a. $\text{AF}_{\text{task}} = 1 + A = 1.20$, or 120%

b. $\text{AF}_{\text{day}} = \dfrac{1}{1 - A} = \dfrac{1}{1 - .20} = 1.25$, or 125%

Table 7-3 displays some typical allowances. In practice, the allowance may be based on the judgment of the analyst, work sampling (described later in the chapter), or negotiations between labour unions and management.

Example 3 ▶ A time study of an assembly task yielded the following observations for a task for which the analyst gave a performance rating of 1.13. Using an allowance of 20 percent of task time, determine the standard time for this task.

i Observation	Time, x (minutes)
1	1.12
2	1.12
3	1.16
4	1.12
5	1.15
6	1.18
7	1.14
8	1.14
9	1.19
Total	10.35

$n = 9, PR = 1.13, A = .20$

a. $OT = \dfrac{\Sigma x_i}{n} = \dfrac{10.35}{9} = 1.15$ minutes.

b. $NT = OT \times PR = 1.15(1.13) = 1.30$ minutes.

c. $ST = NT \times (1 + A) = 1.30(1.20) = 1.56$ minutes.

Note: If an abnormally short time has been recorded, it typically would be assumed to be an observation error and thus discarded. If one of the observations in Example 3 had been .10, it would have been discarded. However, if an abnormally *long* time has been recorded, the analyst would want to investigate that observation to determine whether some irregularly occurring aspect of the task (e.g., retrieving a dropped tool or part) exists, which should legitimately be factored into the task time.

Despite the obvious benefits that can be derived from stopwatch time study, some limitations also must be mentioned. One limitation is the fact that only those tasks that can be observed can be studied. This eliminates most managerial and creative tasks, because these tasks involve mental aspects. Also, the cost of the study rules out its use for irregular operations and infrequently occurring tasks. Finally, it disrupts the normal work routine, and workers resent it.

▼ **Table 7-3**

Allowance percentages for different working conditions recommended by the International Labour Organization, a UN agency.

	Percent			Percent
A. Constant allowances for work breaks:		**4.** Bad light:		
1. Personal	5	**a.** Well below		2
2. Basic fatigue	4	**b.** Very inadequate		5
B. Variable allowances:		**5.** Atmospheric conditions (heat and humidity, cold)—variable		0–10
1. Standing	2			
2. Abnormal position		**6.** Close attention required:		
a. Awkward (bending)	2	**a.** Fine or exacting		2
b. Very awkward (lying, stretching)	7	**b.** Very fine or very exacting		5
3. Use of force or muscular energy (lifting, pulling, or pushing):		**7.** Noise level:		
Weight lifted (in pounds):		**a.** Intermittent—loud		2
5	0	**b.** Intermittent—very loud		5
10	1	**c.** High-pitched—loud		5
15	2	**8.** Mental strain:		
20	3	**a.** Fairly complex process		1
25	4	**b.** Complex or wide span of attention		4
30	5	**c.** Very complex		8
35	7	**9.** Monotony:		
40	9	**a.** Medium		1
45	11	**b.** High		4
50	13	**10.** Tediousness:		
60	17	**a.** Tedious		2
70	22	**b.** Very Tedious		5

Source: A. Freivalds, *Niebel's Methods, Standards, and Work Design,* 13th ed., Table 11.9, p. 466. © 2014 Reprinted with permission of the McGraw-Hill Companies Inc.

Bombardier

Bombardier Aerospace's de Havilland plant in Toronto tried the AutoMOST software package from H.B. Maynard and Co. in order to become more efficient in its sheet metal, machining, and assembly operations. AutoMOST uses the MOST (Maynard Operation Sequence Technique) time study method, a newer and simpler version of MTM (see below). A Maynard consultant and five de Havilland methods engineers used some frame and ribs subassembly work centres as test areas for using Auto-MOST. After getting the cooperation of the workers' union (Canadian Auto Workers union, now part of Unifor), they introduced the project and its goals to the work centres' operators. Then, they identified the work elements performed in each work centre and improved the work methods to make them more efficient. They included elements such as locating inputs, verifying inputs, and deburring drilled holes as standard practices. The motions and their difficulty index were entered in AutoMOST, which generated standard times for various operations. The project took about four months. Both the employees and the company were satisfied with the results. Later on, de

Havilland methods engineers, having learned how to use Auto-MOST, continued expanding the use of time study to other work centres.

Source: http://www.hbmaynard.com/ClientArticles/dehavilland.asp

Predetermined Time Standards

predetermined time standards Published data based on extensive research on element/motion times.

Predetermined time standards are published data based on extensive research on element/motion times.

A commonly used set of tables is *methods-time measurement* (MTM), which was developed in the late 1940s by the Methods Engineering Council. To use this approach, the analyst must divide the task into elements and each element into its basic motions (e.g., reach, grasp, move, turn, disengage), measure the distances involved, rate the difficulty of the motion (e.g., into three types of move: against stop; to approximate location; and to exact location), and then refer to the appropriate table of data to obtain the time for that motion. The time for an element is obtained by adding the times for all of the motions. Times of the motions are measured in Time Measurement Unit (TMU); one TMU equals .036 second. One minute of work may cover a few motions; a typical task may involve several tens or more of these motions. The analyst needs a considerable amount of skill to adequately analyze the operation and develop realistic time estimates. Table 7-4 presents the MTM table for "move" to give an idea of the kind of information the MTM tables provide.

For example, suppose that a motion is to move a tape measure that is in your hand 12 inches to the end of a plank of lumber that is on the table in front of you. This is a Case B move: move object to approximate location. It is not an Exact move (Case C) because there are many possible locations at the end of the plank. The table says that this move should take 13.4 TMUs or approximately .5 second.

The weight allowances on the right of the table are for moving heavier objects. In this case, the formula for calculating the predetermined time is:

Predetermined time = static constant + dynamic factor × time from the left of table.

For example, suppose a hammer weighing 3 pounds is to be moved 12 inches (to strike a nail). Because 2.5 < 3 < 7.5, the second category on the right of the table applies. Hence,

Predetermined time = 2.2 + 1.06 × 13.4 = 16.4 TMUs or .6 seconds.

Time (TMU)					Weight Allowance			
Distance Moved (inches)	A	B	C	Hand in Motion B	Weight (pounds) up to:	Dynamic Factor	Static Constant TMU	Case and Description
¾ or less	2.0	2.0	2.0	1.7				
1	2.5	2.9	3.4	2.3	2.5	1.00	0	
2	3.6	4.6	5.2	2.9	7.5	1.06	2.2	**A. Move object to other hand or against stop.**
3	4.9	5.7	6.7	3.6				
4	6.1	6.9	8.0	4.3	12.5	1.11	3.9	
5	7.3	8.0	9.2	5.0				
6	8.1	8.9	10.3	5.7	17.5	1.17	5.6	
7	8.9	9.7	11.1	6.5				
8	9.7	10.6	11.8	7.2	22.5	1.22	7.4	
9	10.5	11.5	12.7	7.9				
10	11.3	12.2	13.5	8.6	27.5	1.28	9.1	**B. Move object to approximate or indefinite location.**
12	12.9	13.4	15.2	10.0				
14	14.4	14.6	16.9	11.4	32.5	1.33	10.8	
16	16.0	15.8	18.7	12.8				
18	17.6	17.0	20.4	14.2	37.5	1.39	12.5	
20	19.2	18.2	22.1	15.6				
22	20.8	19.4	23.8	17.0	42.5	1.44	14.3	**C. Move object to exact location.**
24	22.4	20.6	25.5	18.4				
26	24.0	21.8	27.3	19.8	47.5	1.50	16.0	
28	25.5	23.1	29.0	21.2				
30	27.1	24.3	30.7	22.7				

Source: MTM Association for Standards and Research. Copyrighted by the MTM Association for Standards and Research. No reprint permission without written consent from MTM Association, 1111 E. Touhy Ave., Des Plaines, IL 60018.

▲ Table 7-4

The MTM table for "move."

A high level of skill is required to generate a predetermined time. Analysts take training or certification courses to develop the necessary skills to do this kind of work.

There are many MTM tables. There is a table for reach, move, turn, apply pressure, grasp, position, release, disengage, eye travel and eye focus, and body, leg, and foot motions. Each table has various values depending on the distance, difficulty (e.g., reach to fixed location or to variable location, etc.), whether the hand was in motion before or not, weight carried, degree turned, and size of object. Obviously, using the MTM tables is very time consuming and requires many years of experience.

We will instead use the Simplified MTM Table (see Table 7-5), which contains approximate values for most motions.

◄ Example 4

Suppose a carpenter needs a 2-foot-long piece out of a 2" × 4" × 8" plank of lumber that is located on his work table in front of him. First he needs to mark the 2-foot location from one end of the lumber. His retractable measurement tape is in one of his pockets, and his pencil is in the other pocket. After marking the lumber, both tape and pencil should be returned to the respective pockets. Decompose this marking element into motions and determine a standard time for marking the wood using Table 7-5. We assume a right-handed person (i.e., mark with the right hand).

Table 7-5 ▶

The simplified methods-time-measurement (MTM) table.

METHODS-TIME MEASUREMENT APPLICATION DATA

SIMPLIFIED DATA
(All times on this Simplified Data Table include 15% allowance)

HAND AND ARM MOTIONS	BODY, LEG, AND EYE MOTIONS
REACH or MOVE TMU 1″...................................... 2 2″...................................... 4 3″ to 12″ 4 + length of motion over 12″ 3 + length of motion (For TYPE 2 REACHES AND MOVES use length of motion only)	TMU Simple foot motion .... 10 Foot motion with pressure ...... 20 Leg motion............................ 10 Side step case 1 .... 20 Side step case 2 40
POSITION Fit Symmetrical Other Loose 10 15 Close 20 25 Exact 50 55	Turn body case 1 .... 20 Turn body case 2 .... 45 Eye time 10
TURN—APPLY PRESSURE TURN............................ 6 APPLY PRESSURE............ 20	Bend, stoop or kneel on one knee .... 35 Arise...................................... 35 Kneel on both knees .... 80 Arise...................................... 90
GRASP Simple .... 2 Regrasp or Transfer .... 6 Complex 10	Sit .... 40 Stand 50
DISENGAGE Loose .... 5 Close .... 10 Exact 30	Walk per pace.................... 17
	1 TMU = .00001 hour = .0006 minute = .036 second

Source: Harold Maynard, *Industrial Engineering Handbook,* 2nd ed. (New York: McGraw-Hill, 1963). Reprinted with permission of the McGraw-Hill Companies, Inc.

SOLUTION

Motion	Standard Time (TMU)
Reach for the measuring tape in pocket using the left hand (assume 12 inches)	4 + 12 = 16
Grasp (simple)	2
Move it to the end of the lumber (assume 12 inches)	4 + 12 = 16
Reach and grasp the end of the tape with the right hand (assume 12 inches)	(4 + 12) + 2 = 18
Position the end of the tape on the end of lumber (assume loose, symmetrical)	10
Move the measuring tape left across the lumber and locate (eye time) the two-foot mark	(3 + 24) + 10 = 37
Disengage the right hand, reach, and grasp pencil in the other pocket (assume 12 inches; assume complex grasp)	5 + (4 + 12) + 10 = 31
Move it close to the location of two-foot mark on the tape (assume 12 inches)	4 + 12 = 16
Position the pencil exactly and mark the location of two-foot mark (move 1 inch)	50 + 2 = 52
Put the pencil back into the pocket, disengage, and return hand	(4 + 12) + 5 + (4 + 12) = 37
Move the tape up 1 inch and wait until it retracts into its case (assume 1 second = 28 TMU retracting time)	2 + 28 = 30
Put the tape back into the pocket, disengage, and return hand	(4 + 12) + 5 + (4 + 12) = 37
	302 TMUs
	or 10.9 seconds

Maynard Operation Sequence Technique (MOST). MOST is a newer and simpler version of MTM that is used widely (http://www.hbmaynard.com). For an application see the "Bombardier" OM in Action. The elements (sequence of motions) are categorized into only three sequences: General Move, Controlled Move, and Tool Use.

General Move (GM) consists of get, put, and return. Get consists of (horizontal) action distance (A), (vertical) body motion (B), and gain control (G). Put consists of A, B, and placement (P). Return is just A. So, GM is ABGABPA.

Controlled Move (CM) consists of get, move/actuate, and return. Get is A, B, G. Move/actuate consists of controlled move (M), process time (X), and alignment (I). Return is A. So, CM is ABGMXIA.

Tool Use (TU) consists of get tool, put tool in place, use tool, put tool aside, and return. Get tool is A, B, G. Put tool in place is A, B, P. Use tool is fasten (F)/loosen (L), cut (C), surface treat (S), measure (M), record (R), or think (T). Put tool aside is A, B, P. Return is A. So, TU is ABGABP*ABPA, where * is F, L, C, S, M, R, or T.

The predetermined times for MOST, depending on distance, difficulty, etc., are given in the following tables.

BasicMOST® System		General Move			ABGABPA
Index × 10	A Action Distance	B Body Motion	G Gain Control	P Placement	Index × 10
0	≤ 2 in. (5 cm)			Pickup Toss	0
1	Within Reach		G R A S P Light Object Light Objects Simo	P U T Lay Aside Loose Fit	1
3	1–2 Steps	Sit or Stand Bend and Arise 50% occ.	G Light Objects Non-Simo E Heavy or Bulky T Blind or Obstructed Disengage Interlocked Collect	P Loose Fit Blind or L Obstructed A Adjustments C Light Pressure E Double Placement	3
6	3–4 Steps	Bend and Arise		P O S Care or Precision I Heavy Pressure T Blind or Obstructed I Intermediate Moves O N	6
10	5–7 Steps	Sit or Stand with Adjustments			10
16	8–10 Steps	Stand and Bend Bend and Sit Climb On or Off Through Door			16

General Move data card.

Source: Figure 3.1, from K. B. Zandin, *MOST Work Measurement Systems,* 3e, Taylor & Francis, Boca Raton, 2003, p. 34.

BasicMOST® System		Controlled Move					A B G M X I A

Index × 10	M Move controlled		X Process Time			I Alignment	Index × 10
	Push/Pull/Turn	Crank	Seconds	Minutes	Hours		
1	≤ 12 in. (30 cm) Button Switch Knob		.5 Sec.	.01 Min.	.0001 Hr.	1 Point	1
3	> 12 in. (30 cm) Resistance Seat or Unseat High Control 2 Stages ≤ 24 in. (60 cm) Total	1 Rev.	1.5 Sec.	.02 Min.	.0004 Hr.	2 Points ≤ 4 in. (10 cm)	3
6	2 Stages > 24 in. (60 cm) Total 1–2 Steps	2–3 Rev.	2.5 Sec.	.04 Min.	.0007 Hr.	2 Points > 4 in. (10 cm)	6
10	3–4 Stages 3–5 Steps	4–6 Rev.	4.5 Sec.	.07 Min.	.0012 Hr.		10
16	6–9 Steps	7–11 Rev.	7.0 Sec.	.11 Min.	.0019 Hr.	Precision	16

Controlled Move data card.
Source: Figure 3.10, from K. B. Zandin, *MOST Work Measurement Systems,* 3e, Taylor & Francis, Boca Raton, 2003, p. 55.

BasicMOST® System			Tool Use								A B G A B P * A B P A

Index x 10	Finger Action		Wrist Action			Arm Action					Power Tool	Index x 10
	Spins	Turns	Strokes	Cranks	Taps	Turns		Strokes	Cranks	Strikes	Screw Diam.	
	Fingers, Screwdriver	Hand, Screwdriver, Ratchet, T-Wrench	Wrench	Wrench, Ratchet	Hand, Hammer	Ratchet	T-Wrench, 2-Hands	Wrench	Wrench, Ratchet	Hammer	Power Wrench	
1	1	–	–	–	1	–	–	–	–	–	–	1
3	2	1	1	1	3	1	–	1	–	1	1/4 in. (6 mm)	3
6	3	3	2	3	6	2	1	–	1	3	1 in. (25 mm)	6
10	8	5	3	5	10	4	–	2	2	5		10
16	16	9	5	8	16	6	3	3	3	8		16
24	25	13	8	11	23	9	6	4	5	12		24
32	35	17	10	15	30	12	8	6	6	16		32
42	47	23	13	20	39	15	11	8	8	21		42
54	61	29	17	25	50	20	15	10	11	27		54

Tool Use data card for Fasten or Loosen. Values are read up to and including.
Source: Figure 3.20, from K. B. Zandin, *MOST Work Measurement Systems,* 3e, Taylor & Francis, Boca Raton, 2003, p. 76.

Index x10	Cutoff (Pliers / Wire)	Secure (Pliers)	Cut (Scissors / Cuts)	Slice (Knife / Slices)	Air-Clean (Nozzle / sq. ft. (0.1 m²))	Brush-Clean (Brush / sq. ft. (0.1 m²))	Wipe (Cloth / sq. ft. (0.1 m²))	Measure (Measuring Tool)	Write Digits (Pencil/Pen)	Write Words	Mark (Marker / Digits)	Inspect (Eyes/Fingers / Points)	Read (Digits, Single Words)	Read (Text of Words)	Index x10
1		Grip	1	—	—	—	—		1	—	Check Mark	1	1	3	1
3	Soft		2	1	—	—	1/2		2	—	1 Scribe Line	3	3	8 (Gauge)	3
6	Medium	Twist From Loop	4	—	1 Spot Cavity	1	—		4	1	2	5 Feel for Heat	6	15 Scale Value Date or Time	6
10	Hard		7	3	—	—	1	Profile Gauge	6	—	3	9 Feel for Defect	12	24 Vernier Scale	10
16		Secure Cotter Pin	11	4	3	2	2	Fixed Scale Caliper ≤ 12 in. (30 cm)	9	12 (Signature or Date)	5	14		38 Table Value	16
24			15	6	4	—	—	Feeler Gauge	13	3	7	19		54	24
32			20	9	7	5	5	Steel Tape ≤ 6 ft. (2 m) Depth Micrometer	18	4	10	26		72	32
42			27	11	10	7	7	OD-Micrometer ≤ 4 in. (10 cm)	23	5	13	34		94	42
54			33					ID-Micrometer ≤ 4 in. (10 cm)	29	7	16	42		119	54

Tool Use data card for Cut, Surface Treat, Measure, Record and Think. Values are read up to and including.
Source: Figure 3.21, from K. B. Zandin, *MOST Work Measurement Systems*, 3e, Taylor & Francis, Boca Raton, 2003, p. 77.

Consider the same activity (measuring and marking a two-foot piece of a plank) as in Example 4. Determine the standard time using MOST.

◀ Example 5

SOLUTION

Activity	Operation Sequence	Time (TMU)
Get and put tape on the end of lumber (GM)	$A_1B_0G_1A_1B_0P_1A_0$	4 × 10
Grab end of tape and position (GM)	$A_1B_0G_1A_0B_0P_1A_0$	3 × 10
Move tape to left 2 feet (CM)	$A_0B_0G_0M_3X_0I_0A_0$	3 × 10
Pencil use (TU)	$A_1B_0G_1A_1B_0P_6R_1A_1B_0P_1A_1$	13 × 10
Let tape retract (CM)	$A_0B_0G_0M_1X_3I_0A_0$	4 × 10
Put tape back (GM)	$A_0B_0G_0A_1B_0P_1A_1$	3 × 10
		300 TMUs
		or 10.8 seconds

GM = General Move, CM = Controlled Move, and TU = Tool Use

Note: Time is the sum of the subscripts of the sequence multiplied by 10. For example, for the first sequence, time is $(1 + 0 + 1 + 1 + 0 + 1 + 0) \times 10 = 40$ TMUs.

Work Sampling

work sampling Technique for estimating the proportion of time that a worker spends on each activity/task or is idle.

Work sampling is a technique for estimating the proportion of time that a worker spends on each activity/task or is idle.

Unlike time study, work sampling does not require timing an activity/task, nor does it even involve continuous observation of the activity. Instead, an observer makes brief observations of a worker at random intervals and simply notes the nature of the activity/task. For example, a secretary may be typing, filing, talking on the telephone, and so on; and a carpenter may be carrying supplies, taking measurements, cutting wood, and so on. The resulting data are *counts* of the number of times each activity or idle time was observed.

Although work sampling is occasionally used to set standard times, its primary use is for analysis of nonrepetitive jobs. In a nonrepetitive job, such as secretarial work or maintenance, it may be important to establish the percentage of time an employee is doing a particular activity/task or is idle. Work sampling can also be an important tool in developing the job description.

Work sampling estimates include some degree of error. Hence, it is important to treat work sampling estimates as *approximations* of the actual proportion of time devoted to a given activity/task. The goal of work sampling is to obtain an estimate of the proportion that provides a specified confidence of not differing from the true value by more than a specified error proportion. For example, we may desire an estimate of the idle time that will provide a 95 percent confidence of being within 4 percent of the actual percentage. Hence, work sampling is designed to produce a value, $\hat{p}$, which estimates the true proportion, p, within some acceptable error proportion, a: $\hat{p} \pm a$. The variability associated with sample estimates of p tends to be approximately Normal for large sample sizes.

The amount of acceptable error proportion is a function of the sample size, the desired level of confidence, and sample proportion. For large samples, the acceptable error proportion a can be calculated using the formula

$$a = z\sqrt{\frac{\hat{p}(1 - \hat{p})}{n}} \tag{7-9}$$

where

$z =$ Number of standard deviations needed to achieve the desired confidence

$\hat{p} =$ Sample proportion (the number of occurrences divided by the sample size)

$n =$ Sample size

$a =$ Maximum acceptable error proportion

In most instances, management will specify the desired confidence level and amount of acceptable error proportion, and the analyst will be required to determine a sample size sufficient to obtain these results. The appropriate value for n can be determined by solving formula 7-9 for n, which yields

$$n = \left(\frac{z}{a}\right)^2 \hat{p}(1 - \hat{p}) \tag{7-10}$$

Example 6 ▶

The manager of a small supermarket wants to estimate the proportion of the time the stock clerks spend placing price stickers on merchandise. The manager wants a 98 percent confidence that the resulting estimate will be within 5 percent of the true value. What sample size should she use?

SOLUTION

$a = .05$, $z = 2.33$ (for 98% confidence), $\hat{p}$ is unknown

When no sample estimate of p is available, a preliminary estimate of sample size can be obtained using $\hat{p} = .50$. After 20 or so observations, a new estimate of $\hat{p}$ can be obtained from those observations and a revised value of n calculated using the new $\hat{p}$. It would be prudent to recalculate the value of n at two or three points during the study to obtain a better indication of the necessary sample size. Thus, the initial estimate of n is:

$$n = \left(\frac{2.33}{.05}\right)^2 (.50)(1 - .50) = 542.89, \ \text{or } 543 \text{ observations}$$

Suppose that, in the first 20 observations, stock clerks were found to be placing price stickers twice, making $\hat{p} = 2/20 = .10$. The revised estimate of n at that point would be:

$$n = \left(\frac{2.33}{.05}\right)^2 (.10)(1 - .10) = 195.44, \ \text{or } 196$$

Suppose a second check is made after a total of 100 observations, and $\hat{p} = .11$ at this point (including the initial 20 observations). Recalculating n yields:

$$n = \left(\frac{2.33}{.05}\right)^2 (.11)(.89) = 212.60, \ \text{or } 213$$

The overall procedure consists of the following steps:

1. Clearly identify the worker to be studied.

2. Notify the worker of the purpose of the study to avoid arousing suspicion.

3. Calculate an initial estimate of sample size using a preliminary estimate of p, if available (e.g., from analyst's experience or past data). Otherwise, use $\hat{p} = .50$.

4. Develop a random observation schedule.

5. Begin taking observations. Recalculate the required sample size several times during the study.

6. Determine the estimated proportion of time spent on the specified activity.

Observations must be spread out over a period of time so that a true indication of variability is obtained.

Determination of a random observation schedule involves the use of a random number table (see Table 7.6), which consists of *unordered sequences* of numbers (i.e., random). Any number of digits can be read as one number. The digits are in groups of four for convenience only. The basic idea is to obtain numbers from the table and to convert each one so that it corresponds to an observation time. There are a number of ways to accomplish this. In the approach used here, we will obtain three sets of numbers from the table for each observation: the first set will correspond to the *day*, the second to the *hour*, and the third to the *minute* when the observation is to be made. The number of digits necessary for any set will relate to the number of days in the study, the number of hours per day, and minutes per hour. For instance, if the study covers 47 days, a two-digit

	1	2	3	4	5	6	
1	6912	7264	2801	8901	4627	8387	
2	3491	1192	0575	7547	2093	4617	
3	4715	2486	2776	2664	3856	0064	
4	1632	1546	1950	1844	1123	1908	
5	8510	7209	0938	2376	0120	4237	
6	3950	1328	7343	6083	2108	2044	
7	7871	7752	0521	8511	3956	3957	
8	2716	1396	7354	0249	7728	8818	
9	2935	8259	9912	3761	4028	9207	
10	8533	9957	9585	1039	2159	2438	
11	0508	1640	2768	4666	9530	3352	
12	2951	0131	4359	3095	4421	3018	

◀ **Table 7-6**

Portion of a random number table.

number will be needed to generate random days; if the activity is performed for eight hours per day, a one-digit number will be needed for hours. Of course, since each hour has 60 minutes, a two-digit number will be needed for minutes. A study requiring observations over a seven-day period in an office that works nine hours per day needs one-digit numbers for days, one-digit numbers for hours, and two-digit numbers for minutes.

Suppose that three observations will be made in the last case (i.e., seven days, nine hours, 60 minutes). We might begin by determining the days on which observations will be made, then the hours, and finally the minutes. Let's begin with the first row in the random number table and read across (from left to right): The first number is 6, which indicates day 6. The second number is 9. Since it exceeds the number of days in the study, it is simply ignored. The third number is 1, indicating day 1, and the next is 2, indicating day 2. Hence, observations will be made on days 6, 1, and 2. Next we determine the hours. Suppose we read the second row of column 1, again obtaining one-digit numbers. We find 3 (= 3rd hour), 4 (= 4th hour), and 9 (= 9th hour). Moving to the next row and reading two-digit numbers (from left to right), we find 47 (= 47th minute), 15 (= 15th minute), and 24 (= 24th minute). Combining these results yields the following:

Day	Hour	Minute
6	3	47
1	4	15
2	9	24

This means that on day 6 of the study an observation is to be made during the 47th minute of the 3rd hour; on day 1, during the 15th minute of the 4th hour; and on day 2, during the 24th minute of the 9th hour. For simplicity, these times can be put in chronological order by day. Thus,

Day	Hour	Minute
1	4	15
2	9	24
6	3	47

A complete schedule of observations might appear as follows, after all numbers have been arranged in chronological order, assuming 10 observations per day for two days:

DAY 1

Observation	Time	Busy(✓)	Idle (✓)
1	8:15		
2	9:24		
3	9:02		
4	9:31		
5	9:48		
6	10:05		
7	10:20		
8	11:02		
9	1:13		
10	3:55		

DAY 2

Observation	Time	Busy(✓)	Idle (✓)
1	8:04		
2	9:15		
3	9:24		
4	9:35		
5	10:12		
6	10:27		
7	10:38		
8	10:58		
9	11:50		
10	1:14		

The general procedure for using a random number table is to read the numbers in some sequence (across rows, down or up columns), discarding any that fall outside the study period.

It is possible to have work sampling self-administered, provided that the employees are motivated to cooperate and see no negative consequences from the study. In this case, observations during random times is not necessary–the employee can record the start time of each activity during the period of study. For an application of self-administered work sampling, see the "Scotiabank Work Sampling" OM in Action.

Scotiabank's Work Sampling

TimeCorder® Time Tracking System is a calculator-like device that keeps track of activity times of an employee. It is self-administered: when the employee starts a new activity, he/she pushes the associated code in the TimeCorder. After two or more weeks, the device is returned to Pace Productivity Inc. in Toronto and an anonymous report is issued to the employer. Scotiabank used the TimeCorder to find out what percentage of the time its personal banking officers actually spent selling. This was discovered to be only 29 percent. The rest of the time was spent on administrative duties, such as documenting calls and reviewing reports, and servicing, planning, and sales management. After centralizing some administrative work and performing some training, the TimeCorder was used again. This time it showed that selling percentage went up to 37 percent of the employees' time.

Source: http://www.paceproductivity.com/results.htm.

Compensation

It is important for organizations to develop suitable monetary compensation plans for their employees. If wages are too low, organizations may find it difficult to attract and hold competent workers. If wages are too high, the increased costs may result in lower profits, or may force the organization to increase its prices, which might adversely affect demand for the organization's products.

Organizations use two basic approaches for compensating employees: time-based pay and output-based pay. **Time-based pay**, also known as hourly pay, compensates the employee for the time he/she works. Salary also represent a form of time-based pay. **Output-based pay**, also known as piece rate, compensates employees according to the amount of output they produce, thereby tying pay directly to performance. Commissions also represent a form of output-based pay.

Time-based pay is more widely used than output-based pay, particularly for office and managerial employees, but also for blue-collar workers. One reason for this is that calculation of compensation is straightforward. Also, employees often prefer time-based pay because the pay is steady and they know how much compensation they will receive for each pay period. In addition, employees may resent the pressures of the output-based pay.

Another reason for using time-based pay is that many jobs do not lend themselves to the use of piece rate. In some cases, it may be difficult or impossible to measure output. For example, jobs that require creative or mental work cannot be easily measured on an output basis. Other jobs may include irregular activities or have so many different forms of output that measuring output and determining pay are fairly complex. Finally, *quality* considerations may be as important as *quantity* considerations. In health care, for example, emphasis is placed on both the quality of patient care and the number of patients processed.

On the other hand, situations exist where piece rate is desirable. Piece rate rewards workers for their output, causing some workers to produce more than they might under time-based pay. Note that only acceptable-quality output should be counted.

In the past, piece rate pay was fairly popular. Now minimum-wage legislation makes it somewhat impractical. Even so, many of the compensation plans currently in use represent variations of the piece rate pay. They typically incorporate a base rate that serves as a floor: workers are guaranteed that amount as a minimum, regardless of output. The base rate is tied to an output standard. If the worker produces more than the standard output, he/she will receive a *bonus*. This is an example of incentive plan, as is skills/knowledge-based pay.

Skills/Knowledge-based Pay. Organizations are increasingly setting up bonus plans to reward workers who undergo training to increase their skill/knowledge. This is referred to as a **skills/knowledge-based pay**. A skills/knowledge-based pay has three dimensions: *horizontal skills* reflect the variety of tasks the worker is capable of performing; *vertical skills* reflect managerial tasks the worker is capable of; and *depth skills* reflect quality and productivity results.

An example of a skills/knowledge-based pay is used in the Molson Breweries (Montreal) plant, where a multiskill premium of $4 per day is paid to client service truck drivers and a $0.50 per

time-based pay
Compensation based on length of time an employee works.

output-based pay
Compensation based on amount of output an employee produces.

skills/knowledge-based pay Rewarding workers who undergo training to increase their skills/knowledge.

hour premium is paid to multiskilled brewing operations employees. The team leaders in warehouse, shipping, and garage operations receive a team leader premium of $15 per week.[4]

Group Bonus Plans. A variety of group bonus/incentive plans, which stress sharing of output/profit/productivity gains among employees, are in use. Some focus exclusively on output (called group incentive), while others reward employees for output and for reductions in costs (called gain sharing), or increases in profit (called profit sharing).

Summary

- Work/job design involves determining content of work as well as methods analysis, working conditions, time study, and compensation.

- In the past, job design tended to focus on efficiency, but now there is an increasing use of the behavioural approach. This includes job enlargement, rotation, enrichment, and teamwork.

- Analysts often use methods analysis and motion-study techniques to make the job/task/element (a component of a task) more efficient. Charts such as flow process chart, worker–machine chart, and simo chart are used to document how work is done.

- Working conditions such as temperature, illumination, and work breaks affect productivity and health and safety of workers.

Ergonomics, i.e., fitting the job to the worker's capabilities, is also important.

- Time study is concerned with determining the time needed to complete a task (i.e., its standard time). Commonly used approaches include stopwatch time study and predetermined time standards. A related technique is work sampling, which is used to estimate the proportion of time a worker spends on a certain aspect of the job. Table 7-7 provides a summary of the formulas used in time study and work sampling.

- Time-based (hourly, salaried) pay is most common. Output-based (piece rate, commission) pay is used in some industries. Group bonus plans, such as profit sharing, and skills/knowledge-based pay are becoming more common.

Table 7-7

Summary of formulas.

Time Study		Work Sampling	
A. Sample size		A. Maximum acceptable error proportion	
$n = \left(\dfrac{zs}{a\bar{x}}\right)^2$	(7-1)	$a = z\sqrt{\dfrac{\hat{p}(1-\hat{p})}{n}}$	(7-9)
$n = \left(\dfrac{zs}{e}\right)^2$	(7-2)	B. Sample size	
B. Observed time		$n = \left(\dfrac{z}{a}\right)^2 \hat{p}(1-\hat{p})$	(7-10)
$OT = \dfrac{\sum x_i}{n}$	(7-3)	**Symbols:**	
		a = Maximum acceptable error proportion	
C. Normal time		A = Allowance proportion	
$NT = OT \times PR$	(7-4)	e = Maximum acceptable error amount	
$NT = \sum(\bar{x}_i \times PR_i)$	(7-5)	n = Number of observations needed	
D. Standard time		NT = Normal time	
$ST = NT \times AF$	(7-6)	OT = Observed time	
		PR = Performance rating	
E. Allowance factor		$\hat{p}$ = Sample proportion	
$AF_{task} = 1 + A$	(7-7)	s = Standard deviation of observed times	
$AF_{day} = \dfrac{1}{1 - A}$	(7-8)	ST = Standard time	
		x_i = Time for ith observation ($i = 1, 2, 3, \ldots, n$)	
		z = No. of standard deviations needed to achieve desired confidence	

---

[4] S. Payette, "What's New in Workplace Innovations?" *Workplace Gazette* 3(1), 2000, pp. 110–119.

Key Terms

flow process chart
job enlargement
job enrichment
job rotation
methods analysis
motion economy principles
motion study

output-based (piece rate) pay
predetermined time standards
self-directed teams
simo chart
skills/knowledge bonus plan
slow motion study
specialization

standard time
stopwatch time study
time-based pay
time study
work sampling
worker–machine process chart
work/job design

Solved Problems

Problem 1

A time-study analyst timed an assembly operation for 30 cycles, and then computed the average time per cycle, which was 18.75 minutes. The analyst assigned a performance rating of 0.96 to the operator, and decided that an appropriate allowance was 15 percent. Assume that the allowance factor is based on the *workday*. Determine the observed time (OT), the normal time (NT), and the standard time (ST).

Solution

$OT = 18.75$ minutes, $PR = .96$, $A = .15$

$NT = OT \times PR = 18.75$ minutes $\times .96 = 18$ minutes

$AF = \dfrac{1}{1 - A} = \dfrac{1}{1 - .15} = 1.176$

$ST = NT \times AF = 18 \times 1.176 = 21.17$ minutes

Problem 2

A time-study analyst wants to estimate the number of observations that will be needed to achieve a specified maximum error, with a confidence of 95.5 percent. A preliminary study yielded a mean of 5.2 minutes and a standard deviation of 1.1 minutes for the job. Determine the number of observations needed for these two cases:

a. A maximum acceptable error of ±6% of the sample mean.

b. A maximum acceptable error of .40 minute.

Solution

a. $\bar{x} = 5.2$ minutes $z = 2.00$ for 95.5% confidence

$s = 1.1$ minutes $a = .06$

$n = \left(\dfrac{zs}{a\bar{x}}\right) = \left(\dfrac{2.00(1.1)}{.06(5.2)}\right)^2 = 49.72$ (round up to 50 observations)

b. $e = .40$

$n = \left(\dfrac{zs}{e}\right)^2 = \left(\dfrac{2.00(1.1)}{.40}\right)^2 = 30.25$ (round up to 31 observations)

Problem 3

Work sampling. An analyst has been asked to prepare an estimate of the proportion of time that a lathe operator spends adjusting the machine, with a 90 percent confidence level. Based on previous experience, the analyst believes the proportion will be approximately 30 percent.

a. If the analyst uses a sample size of 400 observations, what is the maximum possible error percentage that will be associated with the estimate?

b. What sample size would the analyst need in order to have maximum error proportion of no more than ±5 percent?

Solution

a. $\hat{p} = .30$, $z = 1.65$ (for 90-percent confidence), $n = 400$

$$a = z\sqrt{\frac{\hat{p}(1-\hat{p})}{n}} = 1.65\sqrt{\frac{.3(.7)}{400}} = .038 \text{ or } 3.8\%$$

b. $a = .05$, $n = \left(\frac{z}{a}\right)^2 \hat{p}(1-\hat{p}) = \left(\frac{1.65}{.05}\right)^2(.3)(.7) = 228.69$, or 229

Problem 4

A supervisor timed a hotel maid performing the four main tasks necessary to clean a room. These times (in minutes) for five rooms and the performance rating of the maid for each task are given below. Assuming a 10 percent allowance factor based on task time, calculate the standard time for cleaning a room.

Task	Performance Rating	Room 1	2	3	4	5
Replenishing the mini-bar	100	2	2.5	1.5	1	2
Making the bed	90	2.5	3	4	3	2.5
Vacuuming the floor	110	3	4	2.5	3	2.5
Cleaning the bathroom	80	4	4.5	3.5	4	6

Solution

$A = .1$, $AF = 1 + A = 1.1$

Task	Performance Rating *PR*	Observations X_i (min. per cycle) 1	2	3	4	5	$OT = (X_1 + \ldots + X_5)/5$	$NT = OT(PR)$	$ST = NT(AF)$
1	100%	2.0	2.5	1.5	1.0	2.0	1.80	1.8	1.98
2	90%	2.5	3.0	4.0	3.0	2.5	3.00	2.7	2.97
3	110%	3.0	4.0	2.5	3.0	2.5	3.00	3.3	3.63
4	80%	4.0	4.5	3.5	4.0	6.0	4.40	3.52	3.87
								Job Standard Time:	12.45

Discussion and Review Questions

1. What is job design and why is it important? **LO1**

2. What are some of the main advantages and disadvantages of specialization from a company's perspective? From a worker's perspective? **LO1**

3. Contrast the meanings of the terms *job enlargement* and *job enrichment*. **LO1**

4. What is the purpose of behavioural approach to job design? **LO1**

5. What is a self-directed work team? What are some potential benefits of using these teams? **LO1**

6. Some Japanese companies have a policy of rotating their managers among different managerial jobs. In contrast, North American managers are more likely to specialize in a certain area (e.g., finance or operations). Discuss the advantages and disadvantages of each of these approaches. Which one do you prefer? Why? **LO1**

7. Name some reasons methods analysis is needed. How is methods analysis linked to productivity improvements? **LO2**

8. How are tools such as a flow process chart and a worker–machine process chart useful? **LO2**

9. What are the motion economy principles? **LO2**

10. What is a standard time? What does it assume?

11. What are the main uses of standard time?

12. Could problems with determining performance rating be avoided by studying a group of workers and averaging their times? Explain briefly.

13. If an average worker could be identified, what advantage would there be in using that person for a stopwatch time study? What are some reasons an average worker might not be studied?

14. What are the main limitations of stopwatch time study? **LO4**

15. Comment on the following. "At any given instant, the standard times for many tasks will not be strictly correct." **LO4**
    a. Why is this so?
    b. Does this mean that those standard times are useless? Explain.

16. Why do workers sometimes resent time studies? **LO4**

17. What is work sampling? How does it differ from time study? **LO4**

18. What are the key advantages and disadvantages of: **LO5**
    a. Time-based pay? (i) for management and (ii) workers?
    b. Output-based pay? (i) for management and (ii) workers?

19. Explain the skills/knowledge-based pay.

20. The temperature in the meat department of a grocery store is usually kept about 10–11°C. The activities include cutting, packing, and wrapping the meat. Explain how the workers could cope with this low temperature. **LO3**

21. Why should a company care about the health and safety of its workers? Is it possible to operate profitably without this concern? Give an example of a company that cares about its workers and another that doesn't. **LO3**

22. What is ergonomics? Give an example.

23. What is a healthy workplace? Give an example.

Taking Stock

1. What are the trade-offs in each of the following situations?
   a. Using self-directed work teams exclusively instead of a more conventional approach with occasional use of teams. **LO1**
   b. Deciding how often to update standard times due to minor changes in work methods. **LO4**

2. Who uses the results of time study in an organization? **LO4**

3. In what ways does technology have an impact on job design? **LO1, 3 & 4**

4. In Canada, the health and safety of workers are protected by the Occupational Health and Safety Act of each province, which is enforced by the ministry (or department) of Labour of the province. The website http://www.labour.gov.on.ca/english/news/courtbulletins.php describes recent court cases brought under the OHSA in Ontario. As it can be seen from reading some of the cases, the employer is responsible for any accident; for example, a mechanic's hand being pulled between rollers of a conveyor while greasing it from underneath, an explosion inside a tank due to methane gas when a welder started work in it, or a load of steel bars falling on a delivery driver helping a forklift driver to unload it. In addition, lack of procedures, training, and warning signs also make the employer responsible for any injuries to the worker. An employee not wearing a hard hat, or low light that can cause a fall, is grounds to fine the company. Moreover, a supervisor can personally be fined if he did not inform an employee of the right procedure or training. Do you think that the Occupational Health and Safety Act is now being unfair to companies and supervisors? Discuss. **LO3**

Critical Thinking Exercise

Can work design be of strategic importance to a company? Explain and give examples. **LO1 & 5**

Experiential Learning Exercises

1. Select one of the following tasks and prepare a worker–machine process chart that displays the elements and their estimated times: **LO2**
   a. Visit an ATM and make a withdrawal.
   b. Visit a gas station and fill up.

2. Develop a standard time for the task of preparing a ham and cheese sandwich: **LO4**
   a. List the steps (elements) required to prepare the sandwich.
   b. Observe the task for several repetitions and make improvements if necessary.
   c. Time each element for several repetitions.
   d. Assign a performance rating to the overall task.
   e. Develop the standard time.

Internet Exercises

1. Go to the Association of Canadian Ergonomists website (http://www.ace-ergocanada.ca) and identify the types of activities ergonomists undertake. **LO3**

2. Go to http://www.ergoweb.com/casestudies to find an interesting ergonomics case study and summarize it. **LO3**

3. Visit https://www.osha.gov/dts/osta/oshasoft/index.html, choose an industry e-tool, then choose an application area/task, and identify a safety or ergonomic lesson for work design in that industry. **LO3**

4. Visit http://www.youtube.com/watch?v=S9D2hmOtRio and describe how Ford's ergonomics staff help its job design.

5. Visit http://www.nqi.ca/en/awards/2012-cae-recipients/2012-cae-profiles/2012-caeprofile-lii and describe Lassonde Industries' healthy workplace.

6. Visit http://www.hbmaynard.com/CaseStudies/2004/SevenEleven07-22-04.asp and describe what H. B. Maynard and Co. did for 7-Eleven.

Problems

1. An analyst has timed a metal-cutting task for 50 cycles. The average time per cycle was 10.40 minutes, and the standard deviation was 1.20 minutes for a worker with a performance rating of 125 percent. Assume an allowance of 16 percent of task time. Calculate the standard time for this task. **LO4**

2. A task was timed for 60 cycles. It took an average of 1.2 minutes per cycle. The performance rating was 95 percent, and workday allowance is 10 percent. Determine each of the following: **LO4**

   a. Observed time.
   b. Normal time.
   c. Standard time.

3. A time study was conducted on a task that consists of four elements. The observations and performance ratings for six cycles are shown in the following table. **LO4**

		Observations (minutes per cycle)					
Element	Performance Rating	1	2	3	4	5	6
1	90%	.44	.50	.43	.45	.48	.46
2	85	1.50	1.54	1.47	1.51	1.49	1.52
3	110	.84	.89	.77	.83	.85	.80
4	100	1.10	1.14	1.08	1.20	1.16	1.26

   a. Calculate the average time for each element.
   b. Calculate the normal time for each element.
   c. Assuming an allowance factor of 15 percent of workday, calculate the standard time for this task.

4. Given these observations (in minutes) for four elements of a task, determine the observed time (*OT*) for each element. *Note:* The second element occurs only in every other cycle. **LO4**

	Cycle					
Element	1	2	3	4	5	6
1	4.1	4.0	4.2	4.1	4.1	4.1
2	—	1.5	—	1.6	—	1.4
3	3.2	3.2	3.3	3.2	3.3	3.3
4	2.7	2.8	2.7	2.8	2.8	2.8

5. Given these observations (in minutes) for five elements of a task, determine the observed time (*OT*) for each element. *Note:* Some of the elements occur only periodically. Also, using a performance rating of 90 percent for each element and allowance of 15 percent of task time, calculate the standard time for the task. Why does your answer overestimate the task time? How can a better task time-estimate be derived? **LO4**

	Cycle					
Element	1	2	3	4	5	6
1	2.1	2.0	2.2	2.1	2.1	—
2	—	1.1	—	1.0	—	1.2
3	3.4	3.5	3.3	3.5	3.4	3.3
4	4.0	—	—	4.2	—	—
5	1.4	1.4	1.5	1.5	1.5	1.4

6. Using Table 7-3, develop an allowance percentage for a task that requires the worker to lift a weight of 10 pounds while (1) standing, (2) in light that is well below recommended standards, and (3) with intermittent loud noises occurring. The monotony for this task is high. Include a personal allowance of 5 percent and a basic fatigue allowance of 4 percent. **LO4**

7. A worker–machine operation was found to involve 3.3 minutes of machine time per cycle. In the course of 40 cycles of a stopwatch time study, the worker's time

loading and unloading the machine averaged 1.9 minutes per cycle, and the worker was given a rating of 120 percent. Assuming an allowance factor of 12 percent of task time, determine the standard time for this operation (including the machine time). **LO4**

8. A recently negotiated union contract allows workers in a shipping department a total of 24 minutes for rest, 10 minutes for personal time, and 14 minutes for delays for each four-hour shift worked. A time-study analyst observed a task in the shipping department that is performed continuously and found an average time of 6.0 minutes per cycle for a worker she rated at 95 percent. What standard time is applicable for that task? **LO4**

9. The following data were obtained by observing three elements of a financial manager's task. **LO4**

   a. Using the data and an allowance of 10 percent of task time, determine a standard time for the task.
   b. Determine the number of observations that would be required to estimate the mean time for the first element within 4 percent of the true value with a confidence of 98 percent.
   c. How many observations would be needed to estimate the mean time for element C to within 0.10 minutes of its actual value with a confidence of 90 percent?

		Observations (minutes per cycle)				
Element	Performance Rating	1	2	3	4	5
A	90%	1.40	1.42	1.39	1.38	1.41
B	120	2.10	2.05	2.00	1.85	1.80
C	110	1.60	1.40	1.50	1.45	1.55

10. The data in the following table represent time-study observations for a woodworking operation/task. **LO4**

    a. Based on the observations, determine the standard time for the operation, assuming an allowance of 20 percent of task times.

b. How many observations would be needed to estimate the mean time for element 1 within 1 percent of its true value with a 95.5 percent confidence?
c. How many observations would be needed to estimate the mean time for element 1 within .01 minute of its true value with a 95.5 percent confidence?

		Observations (minutes per cycle)					
Element	Performance Rating	1	2	3	4	5	6
1	110%	1.20	1.17	1.16	1.22	1.24	1.15
2	115	.83	.87	.78	.82	.85	1.32*
3	105	.58	.53	.52	.59	.60	.54

*Unusual delay, disregard time.

11. How many observations should a stopwatch time-study analyst plan for in an operation that has a standard deviation of 1.5 minutes per piece if the goal is to estimate the mean time per piece to within .4 minute with a confidence of 95.5 percent? **LO4**

12. How many work cycles should be timed to estimate the average cycle time to within 2 percent of the sample mean with a confidence of 99 percent if a pilot study yielded these times (in minutes): 5.2, 5.5, 5.8, 5.3, 5.5, and 5.1? **LO4**

13. In an initial survey designed to estimate the percentage of time air-express cargo loaders are idle, an analyst found that loaders were idle in 6 of the 50 observations. **LO4**

    a. What is the estimated percentage of idle time?
    b. Based on the initial results, approximately how many observations would you require to estimate the actual percentage of idle time to within 4 percent with a confidence of 95 percent?

14. An analyst made the following observations about whether customer service representatives were busy (B) or idle (I): **LO4**

    a. What is the percentage of idle time?
    b. Given these results, how many observations would be needed to estimate the actual percentage of idle time to within 6 percent with a confidence of 90 percent?

Observation	1	2	3	4	5	6	7	8	9	10	11	12	13	14	15	16	17	18	19	20
Busy or idle	B	B	I	B	I	B	B	B	I	B	B	B	B	I	B	B	B	B	B	I

15. A job in an insurance office involves telephone conversations with policy holders. The office manager estimates that about half of the employee's time is spent on the telephone. How many observations are needed in a work sampling study to estimate that time percentage to within 4 percent and have a confidence of 95 percent? **LO4**

16. A hospital administrator thinks that the X-ray equipment is only in use about 20 percent of the time. What number of observations in a work sampling study would be needed to estimate the true percentage of time to within 5 percent with a confidence of 98 percent? **LO4**

17. Design a schedule of work sampling observations in which eight observations are made during one

eight-hour day (use 0:00 to 7:59). Using Table 7.6, read the *last digit* going down column 4 for hours (e.g., 1 7 4 4 6. . .), and read across row 3 from left to right in sets of two for minutes (e.g., 47 15 24 86. . .). Arrange the times chronologically. **LO4**

18. The manager of a large office intends to conduct a work sampling of the time the staff spends on the telephone. The observations will be taken over a period of 50 work-days. The office is open five days a week for eight hours a day (use 0:00 to 7:59). Although the study will consist of 200 random observations, in this problem you will be asked to determine times for 11 observations. Use random numbers from Table 7.6. **LO4**

   a. Determine times for 11 observations. For days, read sets of two-digit numbers going across row 4 from left to right (e.g., 16 32 15 46 . . .), and do the same in row 5.

   b. For hours, read one-digit numbers going *down,* using the first digit of column 1 (e.g., 6 3 4 1 . . . then column 2).

   c. For minutes, read two-digit numbers going *up* column 4 using the first two digits (e.g., 30 46 10 . . .), and then repeat for the second two digits going *up* column 4 (e.g., 95 66 39 . . .).

   d. Arrange the combinations chronologically by day, hour, and minute.

   e. Assume March 1 is a Monday and that there are no holidays in March, April, or May.

   Convert your observation days to dates in March, April, and May.

19. A work sampling study is to be conducted on rush-hour traffic (4:00 p.m. to 6:59 p.m.) five days per week. The study will encompass 40 days. Determine the day, hour, and minute for 10 observations using the following procedure and Table 7.6: **LO4**

   a. Read two-digit numbers going *down* the first two digits of column 5 (e.g., 46 20 38 . . .), and then down the second two digits of that column (e.g., 27 93 56 . . .) for days.

   b. For hours, read one-digit numbers going from left to right across row 1 and then across row 2. (Read only 4s, 5s, and 6s.)

   c. For minutes, read two-digit numbers going *down* column 6, first using the *last* two digits (e.g., 87 17 64. . .) those numbers, repeat using the first two digits of that column (e.g., 83 46 00 19. . .).

   Arrange your times chronologically by day, then hour, and then minute.

20. The killing and disassembly of a hog in a slaughter plant is very labour intensive, because the tasks cannot easily be automated. This is because each hog is slightly different and the carcasses cannot in general be held in place in a consistent way in order to automate the work. To achieve the target production (which is high in order to make a profit), tasks need to be very specialized. For example, one task is called "snatching guts." Suppose you are helping the industrial engineer to determine the standard time for this task. The videotape of five cycles revealed the following task times (in seconds): 14, 13, 13, 12, and 14. Assume a performance rating of .90 and allowance of 15 percent of task time. Calculate the standard time for this task.[5] **LO4**

21. The following two activities are commonly used to train stopwatch time-study observers to get a feel for an average performance rating, i.e., performance rating of 1.0. **LO4**

   a. Walk at 3 miles per hour (= 80 metres per minute = 1.34 metres per second).

   b. Deal a deck of 52 cards into 4 equal piles one foot apart (make a square) in .5 minute.

   Choose one of these and time yourself trying to achieve these times. If you are too slow, repeat the exercise faster until you reach these speeds. Do you believe that these times are sustainable? Explain.

22. We wish to time installing new shingles on our house. To start, we will try to time driving one nail into a shingle. Assume that the shingle is already in place. You have squatted on your roof facing the shingle. The hammer is on the roof next to the shingle. Nails are in your pocket. **LO4**

   a. Use the Simplified MTM technique (Table 7-5) to determine the time of driving one nail into the shingle.

   b. Use MOST.

23. Using the simplified MTM times given in Table 7-5 and the "Made for You" McDonald's video (available as a streaming video from http://bevideos.mhhe.com/business/video_library/0072917776/swf/Clip_08.html), estimate the time it should take a McDonald's employee to:

   a. Pick up a bun from the rack and drop its two sides into the toaster (the 9:19th–9:22nd minutes of the video). **LO4**

   b. Squirt the second condiment on the bun, side step, and place small pieces of the first vegetable on the bun. Start from just after the first condiment dispenser is put back in its place and end just after the first vegetable pieces are placed on the bun (the 9:42nd–9:48th minutes of the video).

   If you have access to the nonstreaming video (Volume 08, OM McGraw-Hill video Library), you can slow down the speed of video play by choosing "Full screen" in view menu, then right-clicking and setting play speed to Slow.

---

[5] Based on J.S. Moore and A. Garg, "Participatory Ergonomics in a Red Meat Packing Plant, Part II: Case Studies," *American Industrial Hygiene Association Journal* 58(7), July 1997, pp. 498–508.

24. In the bottle-recycling department of Labatt's Brewery in St. Johns, Newfoundland, the "throw on" task involves lifting cases of empty bottles from a pallet and throwing them on a conveyor.[6] A case weighs approximately 6 kg. "Throw on" sometimes involves reaching up above shoulder-height or bending and lifting elements (see the two sketches below). Each "throw on" takes between two and five seconds, and the pallet is unloaded in about three minutes. Even though the workers rotate out of this task every half hour, there is still a chance of repetitive motion injuries and lower back pain. Propose an ergonomic solution for this problem. **LO3**

25. In the assembly operation of Mother Hubbard's Kitchens in Dartmouth, Nova Scotia, the worker holds the tool with his operating hand and the piece of cabinet with the other hand (see the three sketches below), and the work requires reaching and bending, exerting force from shoulder, and awkward positions for arms and body.[7] There is a chance of repetitive motion injuries and shoulder and lower back pain. Propose an ergonomic solution for this problem. **LO3**

26. In the Buttered Sole line of Burin's Secondary Processing plant of Fishery Products International (later High Liner), in Newfoundland, the "spreading" operation involved spreading the sole on the conveyor belt.[8] The job involved standing in a stooped position and reaching. Propose an ergonomic solution for this problem. **LO3**

---

[6] Canadian Centre for Occupational Health and Safety. "Bottle Recycling Department of a Brewery," http://www.ccohs.ca/oshanswers/occup_workplace/brewery.html.

[7] Canadian Centre for Occupational Health and Safety. "Cabinet Manufacturing," http://www.ccohs.ca/oshanswers/occup_workplace/cab_manu.html.

[8] Canadian Centre for Occupational Health and Safety. "Fish Processing," http://www.ccohs.ca/oshanswers/occup_workplace/fish_pro.html.

Earthwise Pallet Recyclers

Earthwise Pallet Recyclers (EPR) is a small business refurbishing damaged wood pallets in Saskatoon. Gary Wurst founded EPR in 1996 after he saw so many unwanted damaged pallets lying around in contruction sites. He started collecting them, fixing them, and selling them at a low price ($3–$5 each) to local manufacturers and distributors that use pallets. Currently he has about 12 employees, including approximately 4 "nailers." The company takes in approximately 2,800 pallets each week and produces approximately 2,000 refurbished pallets. The difference are pallets that are dismantled and their pieces are used in other pallets. Each nailer produces approximately 130 refurbished pallets per day (8-hour shift). Gary would like to see this number to increase to 160 pallets per day. Nailer responsibilities include assessing a damaged pallet (called a core), taking damaged boards off, nailing replacement boards in, and repairing the frame using a scab (a piece of 2" × 4" with a notch cut out of it) or block (a piece of 2" × 4").

A more detailed list of elements and time measurements (in seconds) for five cycles of a nailer fixing a pallet are given below. Also given is a layout diagram of EPR shop. Occasionally a nailer runs out of good boards and has to walk to the Chop Saw workstation or other good-board bins to retrieve good boards. Part of the problem is that there are different sizes of pallets so nailers need different sizes of good boards. Nailers are also responsible for moving both the core stacks and the finished stacks to and from their workstation, and moving bad core stacks to the dismantler. They use a manual pallet jack to do so. Each leg takes approximately two minutes. There are only two pallet jacks in the shop. Cores and fixed pallet stacks are transported in and out of the shop using a forklift. Estimate the processing time of a pallet and make suggestions to Gary to increase EPR's productivity.

Building a pallet (times in seconds)	1	2	3	4	5
Pick pallet from Cores pile (in workstation) and put on nail table	8	9	9	7	10
Assess pallet: if bad, put it aside; if good, proceed	6	7	4	14	8
Hit nails down with hammer	2	5	6	4	3
Rip off broken boards with crowbar	8	12	10	5	8
Remove broken boards by hand	6	11	8	12	11
Throw broken boards in garbage bin (on the left)	1	2	2	2	1
Grab good boards from good-board bin (on the right)	11	10	48	25	21
Place good boards on pallet	8	5	3	17	3
Nail good boards in with nail gun	3	7	10	6	6
Place block/scab in	3	10	9	8	3
Hammer in block/scab	6	4	31	3	9
Flip pallet	2	2	10	4	2
Hit nails down with hammer	7	11	20	15	5
Rip off broken boards with crowbar	9	6	13	14	8
Remove broken boards by hand	11	14	9	18	13
Throw broken boards in garbage bin	1	1	1	2	2
Grab good boards from good-board bin	48	6	5	4	3
Place good boards on pallet	13	3	10	5	7
Nail good boards in with nail gun	17	6	10	8	6
Move pallet to finished pallet pile (in workstation)	9	9	8	8	8

Source: Joy-Anne Caswell, "Earthwise Pallet Recyclers" (term paper), December 2004, COMM 205: Introduction to Operations Management.

To access "Learning Curves," the supplement to Chapter 7, please
visit Connect.

For more information on the resources available from McGraw-Hill Ryerson, go to www.mheducation.ca/he/solutions.

CHAPTER 8
Location Planning and Analysis

Within the last few years, we have seen a proliferation of red-light cameras at busy intersections in many cities throughout Canada. The reason local and provincial governments have continued to support their use is because red-light cameras appear to be very effective at preventing accidents. For instance, a recent study of the benefits of red-light cameras in British Columbia has revealed a 14 percent reduction in collisions resulting in injuries. Considering the resounding success of red-light cameras in reducing the frequency and severity of accidents, it was decided that their use should be further expanded. The following are some of the factors that were considered to be critical for deciding the locations of new red-light cameras.

- *Potential for improvement.* This is the difference between the total number of observed collisions and what is considered to be the normal frequency of collisions at any particular intersection. Clearly, the higher the number of recorded collisions at any intersection, the more dangerous it is, and the larger the potential for improvement.

- *Severity of collisions.* The overall goal of any red-light camera program is to mitigate the severity of life-threatening collisions. Consequently, it is important to identify intersections with the most severe collisions. To help identify the most dangerous intersections, a collisions severity index was created by simply weighing collision frequency with collision severity. In British Columbia, the collision weights are 100 for collisions with a fatality, 10 for an injury, and 1 for property damage.

- *High proportion of collision types.* Evidence shows that red-light cameras are best for reducing 90-degree, "T-bone" type collisions; side-impact collisions; and head-on collisions. Intersections with a high proportion of these collision types are given more weight.

- *Low proportion of collision types.* The literature suggests that red-light cameras can actually increase the likelihood of rear-end type collisions. Consequently, the identification of those intersections with a low proportion of such collisions types are recommended as good candidate locations.

The procedure for finding the best location to place a red light camera is the same as the procedure for choosing a location for a facility, which is the topic of this chapter.

Source: Paul de Leur and Mark Milner, "Site Selection Process and Methodology for Deployment of Intersection Safety Cameras in British Columbia, Canada," *Transportation Research Record: Journal of the Transportation Research Board*, March 2012, Vol. 2265, pp. 129–136.

Importance of Location

New companies obviously need a plant or store/office in which to make or provide their new goods or services. Existing organizations may also need to make location decisions for a variety of reasons. Companies such as banks, fast-food chains, supermarkets, and retail stores view location as part of their marketing strategy and look for locations that will help them expand their markets. Basically, the location decisions in those cases reflect the *addition* of new locations to an existing system. A similar situation occurs when an organization experiences a growth in demand for its products or services that cannot be satisfied by expansion at an existing location. The addition of a new location to complement an existing system is often a realistic alternative.

Some companies face location decisions because of depletion of their basic input. For example, fishing and logging operations are often forced to relocate due to the exhaustion of fish and forests at a given location. Mining and petroleum operations face the same sort of situation.

For other companies, a shift in market causes them to consider relocation, or the cost of doing business at a particular location reaches a point where other locations begin to look more attractive. Another reason may be centralizing dispersed locations to gain economies of scale.

There are several reasons that location decisions are an important part of production or service systems design. First, they entail a long-term commitment that makes mistakes difficult to overcome. Second, location decisions impact investment requirements, operating costs, and revenues. Third, a poor choice of location might result in a shortage of qualified labour, inadequate supplies of raw materials, or some similar condition that is detrimental to operations.

Because, by its nature, a location decision is usually based on many factors, no single location may be significantly better than the others. There may be numerous acceptable locations from which to choose, as shown by the wide variety of locations in which successful organizations can be found.

Location factors can depend on where a business is in the *supply chain*. For instance, at the retail end of a chain, site selection tends to focus more on accessibility, consumer demographics (population, age distribution, average income), traffic patterns, and local customs. Businesses at the beginning of a supply chain, if they are involved in supplying raw materials, are often located near the source of the raw materials. Businesses in the middle of a chain may locate near suppliers or near their customers, depending on a variety of circumstances. For example, businesses involved in storing and distributing goods often choose a central location to minimize distribution costs. However, Web-based and phone-based businesses are much less dependent on location decisions; they can exist just about anywhere.

Call Centres Flock to Ontario

At one time or another, every organization needs to decide where to locate a new facility. The best location clearly depends on the organization's particular needs. If you are a manufacturer, you may want a location that has easy access to resources and distribution networks. If you are a retailer, you should be mainly interested in obtaining access to customers with disposable income. For the particular case of call centres, the important factors are operating costs, labour skills, and government incentives.

With access to modern technology, a call centre can be built anywhere in the world. So, where should you locate yours? Many organizations are finding Ontario to be an ideal location. Why do call centres want to locate in Ontario? First, locating in Ontario can save companies up to 15 percent on their bottom line compared to similar locations in the United States. Second, Ontario has access to a highly educated and bilingual workforce where close to 60 percent of the population has some postsecondary education. Third, Ontario offers employers generous training subsidies in the form of a tax credit in the amount of $5,000 per year. These factors combine to make Ontario one of the world's premier destinations for call centres.

Source: H. Sheff, "Labor Guides the Site Selection Process—When You're Opening a New Call Center, the Key to Finding a Place Is the People," *Call Center*, June 2007, 20.6, p. 22.

Location Decision Process

The way an organization approaches location decisions often depends on its size and the nature and scope of its operations. New or small organizations tend to adopt a rather informal approach to location decisions. New companies typically locate in a certain area simply because the owner lives there. Similarly, managers of small companies often want to keep operations in their backyard, so they tend to focus almost exclusively on local alternatives. Large established companies, particularly those that already operate in more than one location, tend to take a more formal approach. Moreover, they usually consider a wider range of geographic locations. The discussion here pertains mainly to a formal approach to location decisions.

Whether a company chooses to use a location/site selection consultant or assign the project to someone in-house, the basic steps to a successful location decision will be similar:

1. Identify important search parameters and factors, such as location of markets or raw materials. The factors will differ depending on the type of facility.
2. Gather information on appropriate sites (e.g., through telephone and Internet inquiries, reading literature, etc.).
3. Eliminate some to obtain a shortlist of three or four sites.
4. Visit the shortlisted sites, meeting with local authorities and real estate agents.
5. Evaluate the alternatives and make a selection.

Typically, the process will take six months to a year.

 ## Factors That Affect Location Decisions

Many factors influence location decisions. However, often one or a few factors are so important that they dominate the decision. For example, in manufacturing, the potentially dominating factors may include availability of abundant energy and proximity to raw materials (e.g., aluminum production needs large amounts of electricity). Cost of transportation to market can be a major factor (e.g., most soft drinks are produced in local bottling plants). In service organizations, possible dominating factors are market related. For example, car rental agencies locate in airports and downtowns where their customers are.

This section contains a description of regional/country factors, community and site factors, and advantages of Canadian locations for foreign companies.

Regional/Country Factors

The primary regional factors involve raw materials, markets, and labour considerations.

Location of Raw Materials. Companies locate near or at the source of their raw materials for three primary reasons: necessity, perishability, and transportation costs. Mining operations, farming, forestry, and fishing fall under *necessity*. Obviously, such operations must locate close to the raw materials. Companies involved in canning or freezing of fresh fruit and vegetables, processing of dairy and meat products, and so on must consider *perishability* when considering location. *Transportation costs* are important in industries where processing eliminates much of the bulk connected with a raw material, making it much less expensive to transport after processing. Examples include potash, lumber, and pulp and paper production. Being close to raw materials is the reason many forest-products companies such as Catalyst Paper and Canfor have plants in British Columbia. Many petrochemical plants are located in Alberta, many farms are located in the prairies, and many fish-processing plants are located in the Atlantic provinces. Transportation costs are often the reason that companies locate near their major customers. Moreover, regional warehouses are used by supermarkets and other retail operations to supply multiple outlets, so often the choice of new locations and additional warehouses reflects the locations of existing warehouses or retail outlets.

A worker inspects cans of Coca-Cola on the production line at a plant in the Middle East. Coke production overseas expands markets and serves local customers.

Location of Markets. Retailers and service providers are usually found near the centre of the markets they serve. Examples include fast-food restaurants, gas stations, and supermarkets. Quite often their products and those of their competitors are so similar that they rely on convenience to attract customers. Hence, these businesses seek locations with high population densities or traffic. This is also true for banks, drugstores, and convenience stores. Other factors include distribution costs or the perishability of a finished product.

ervice

Competitive pressure on retail operations can be extremely high. In some cases, the market served by a particular location may be too small to justify two competitors (e.g., one burger franchise per block), so the search for potential locations tends to concentrate on locations without competitors. The opposite also might be true; it could be desirable to locate near competitors. Large department stores often locate near each other, and small stores like to locate in shopping centres that have large department stores as anchors. The large stores attract large numbers of shoppers who become potential customers in the smaller stores or in the other large stores.

Some companies must locate close to their markets because of the perishability of their products. Examples include bakeries, flower shops, and fresh seafood stores. For other types of companies, distribution (transportation) costs are the main factor in closeness to market (for example, sand and gravel retailers and bottling plants). Another example is regional warehouses used by

In Canada, High Liner Foods uses eight deep-sea trawlers to fish around Nova Scotia and Newfoundland. Its two primary processing plants are nearby in Lunenburg, Nova Scotia, and Burin, Newfoundland.

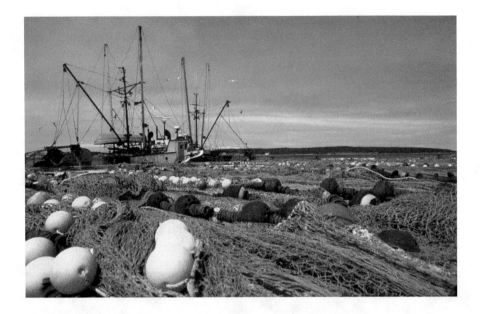

supermarkets and other retail operations to supply multiple outlets. Still other companies require close customer contact, so they too tend to locate within the area they expect to serve. Typical examples are custom tailor shops, home remodellers, home repair services, rug cleaners, lawn and garden services, and component suppliers to just-in-time manufacturers.

Location of many government services should be near the centre of the markets they are designed to serve. Police and emergency health care locations are frequently selected on the basis of client needs. For instance, police patrols often concentrate on high-crime areas, and emergency health care facilities are usually found in central locations to provide ready access from all directions.

Labour Factors. Primary labour considerations are availability of workers, the wage rates and labour productivity, attitudes toward work, and whether unions are a potential problem. Large plants usually locate in or near population centres. Some companies target regions with high unemployment in order to tap the large pool of unemployed workers.

Labour costs are very important for labour-intensive companies and they can differ significantly across regions.[1] Labour rates are related to the cost of living, which also varies across regions. Internationally, Canadian average hourly compensation is close to the United States, lower than many European countries, but higher than Mexico and Asian countries (see http://www.bls.gov/news.release/ichcc.t02.htm). See "Dell's Short-lived Call Centres in Canada" OM in Action as an example of influence of the labour in location decisions.

Skills of potential employees may be a factor, although some companies prefer to train new employees rather than rely solely on previous experience. Increasing specialization in many industries makes this possibility even more likely than in the past. Although most companies concentrate on the supply of blue-collar workers, some companies are more interested in scientific and technical people as potential employees, and they look for areas with high concentrations of those types of workers.

Worker attitudes toward turnover, absenteeism, and similar factors may differ among potential locations—workers in large urban centres may exhibit different attitudes than workers in small towns or rural areas. Furthermore, worker attitudes in different parts of the country or in different countries may be markedly different.

Other Factors. Electric power sometimes plays a role in location decisions. For instance, many aluminum smelting plants are located in Quebec because they use a large amount of electricity, which is inexpensive in Quebec. The same is true for British Columbia.

---

[1] See CANSIM's "Labour Force Survey Estimates" Table #282-0074 for wage rates in each province.

Dell's Short-lived Call Centres in Canada

Before 2004, Dell Computers used to outsource its North American customer service to India. However, some customers were not happy with the excessive waits; being passed to other representatives, sometimes in other countries; and not having their problems resolved. In the 2004, Dell opened a call centre in Edmonton, and later one in Ottawa, employing approximately 500 people in each location. Dell was so impressed with the performance of its educated and bilingual labour force in Ottawa that it acquired the neighbouring building (about 150,000 ft²) and added another 1,200 people in 2007. However, the recession forced Dell to cut its workforce by 10 percent worldwide. Unfortunately, Dell decided to close both its Edmonton and Ottawa call centres. The strong Canadian dollar seems to have been a factor.

Sources: J. Lyne, "Growing by Degrees: 1200 More Call Centre Jobs Coming to Ottawa," *Site Selection*, November 20, 2006; http://www.itworldcanada.com/article/cutbacks-at-dell-canada-span-edmonton-to-ottawa/01879; http://www.cbc.ca/news/business/dell-closing-ottawa-area-call-centre-at-cost-of-1-100-jobs-1.726470

Also, both business and personal taxes in some provinces can reduce or enhance a province's attractiveness to companies seeking new locations. Provinces such as Alberta and Quebec have used lower taxes to attract companies. Federal and provincial governments give tax incentives to encourage more research and development, manufacturing, and investment. For examples, see the "Some Examples of Subsidies" OM in Action.

Land and building costs are also usually significant and can differ across regions. The presence of unions usually results in higher wages and less flexible work rules. Therefore, many companies prefer to locate in regions where unions are not strong.

Some Examples of Subsidies

An example of a company obtaining a large subsidy is GM of Canada when it invested $2.5 billion to renovate its Oshawa assembly complex in 2005. GM received $235 million from the federal and Ontario governments. Subsidies have been a fact of life in the auto industry, with southern U.S. states being the prime example of securing auto investment by this means. More recently, with the downturn in economy and sharp drop in auto sales, GM has laid off several thousand employees, despite receiving a huge bailout of several billion dollars.

Another example of government subsidy is a US$40 million grant by the Government of Ontario to Linamar, Canada's second largest auto-parts manufacturer, to build a R&D/training centre and five to six parts/components manufacturing plants in Guelph, costing a total of approximately $1 billion. Linamar, which started in the garage of its founder, Frank Hasenfratz, in Guelph, has 50 parts/components manufacturing plants in 8 countries employing over 10,000 workers, most of which are located in Guelph itself. For this last expansion decision, Linamar was looking to Michigan; however, the Ontario Government subsidy enticed Linamar to invest more in Guelph.

In 2005, Bombardier decided to assemble its new C-series mid-size (110–130 seat) planes in Mirabel, a Montreal suburb, close to its main plant and headquarters. However, the rising Canadian dollar forced it to reconsider the location decision. In particular, Bombardier considered Kansas City, the location of its subsidiary, Lear Jets. The decision criteria included accessibility to an international airport, financial considerations and tax benefits, and access to a trained labour pool. After two years of studies and receiving US$350 million from the federal government and $117 million from the Québec government, Bombardier decided that Mirabel is the best location for the C series after all. The wings of the C series, however, will be made by Short Brothers, the subsidiary of Bombardier in Belfast, Northern Ireland.

Sources: http://www.siteselection.com/ssinsider/bbdeal/bd050307.htm; http://www.siteselection.com/ssinsider/bbdeal/bd060615.htm; http://www.siteselection.com/features/2008/sep/Quebec.

OM in *ACTION*

Bravado Designs

Bravado Designs is a Toronto-based maternity undergarment manufacturer that sells its products worldwide. When in the mid-2000s the Canadian dollar was soaring against the U.S. dollar, Bravado saw its cost of manufacturing (when converted into U.S. dollars) soar and its profits disappear. At the suggestion of one of its staff, Bravado looked and found a Mexican manufacturer of lingerie in Toluca, one hour from Mexico City. The plant was making lingerie for Victoria's Secret, but had excess capacity.

Bravado outsourced some of its products to this contractor. As a result, manufacturing costs dropped by 30 percent immediately. Bravado staff visits the contractor plant once every two weeks and are happy with its quality. The advantage of Mexico over China is that the Mexican plant is able to produce in small quantities (as small as 4,000 units per month), is closer to Toronto for visiting, and its products can be sold in North America tariff-free.

Source: J. White Bardwell, "Say Hola! to Mexico," *PROFIT*, November 2007, 26(5), pp. 69–70.

Foreign Locations. Some Canadian companies are attracted to foreign locations to exploit their natural resources. Others view foreign locations as a way to expand their markets. Many developing countries offer an abundant supply of cheap labour. For example, many North American companies have plants in China.

A company contemplating a foreign location must carefully weigh the potential benefits against the potential problems. A major factor is the stability of a country's government and its attitude toward foreign companies. Some of the problems of a foreign location can be caused by language and cultural differences. One factor that has negatively impacted the bottom line of some Canadian companies operating plants in foreign countries is the level of corruption (i.e., abuse of entrusted power for private gain). Transparency International, a nonprofit international organization based in Germany, annually publishes a Corruption Perception Index for over 170 countries.[2] Canada is one of the least corrupt countries.

Further, it can be much harder to coordinate the activities of foreign locations with domestic locations. The "Bravado Designs" OM in Action provides an example of a foreign location decision.

Community/Site-related Considerations

Usually workers live close to their place of work. Blue-collar workers tend not to relocate to find a job. Therefore, companies ensure that there are sufficient numbers of potential applicants living near a site. If there are other large employers in the vicinity, then the pool of available workers will be smaller. Large employers usually locate in or around a big city for this reason. Companies employing office workers, engineers, lab researchers, and specialized trades need the services of a college, university, or technical institution in the community. White-collar employees may relocate, but they usually require a higher quality of life.

From a company standpoint, a number of factors determine the desirability of a community as a place for its workers and managers to live. They include facilities for education, shopping, recreation, transportation, entertainment, and medical services.

Many communities actively try to attract new businesses because they are viewed as potential sources of future tax revenues and new job opportunities. Communities offer tax abatements, low-cost loans, and grants for worker training. However, communities do not, as a rule, want companies that will create pollution problems or otherwise lessen the quality of life in the community. Examples of this include community resistance to airport expansion, changes in zoning, construction of nuclear facilities, "factory farms," and highway construction.

For heavy industries, it is important to be close to a railway line, just at the outskirt of a city or town, usually on a green-field site (i.e., on a vacant out-of-town lot). Light industries usually need to be close to highways. Offices may want to be close to airports. Call and data centres need to be close to major telephone and data transmission lines.

---

[2] http://www.transparency.org/cpi2013/results.

OM in *ACTION*

Toyota in Woodstock

In the mid-2000s, Toyota was looking for a location to build its RAV4 in North America. After considering several locations, Toyota decided on Woodstock, 40 km from Cambridge, the location of Toyota's existing Canadian plant. Toyota was looking for a green-field location close to one of its existing plants in order to share some of the management and workers, and reduce duplication of facilities. The reasons for choosing Woodstock are

as follows: the Cambridge plant was at half the capacity of Toyota's Kentucky plant (therefore, it has room to grow); the federal and Ontario governments provided $100 million in grants; the local government assisted in purchasing the 1,000 acre land from 20 farmers; the site is just off Highway 401 and is connected to both CN and CP rail lines; and there is sufficient labour force in the Woodstock area. The $650 million plant opened in 2008.

Source: http://www.siteselection.com/issues/2005/sept/p524/pg02.htm.

Land and building prices may differ significantly across cities/communities. See http://www.colliers.com/Default.aspx (Canada Locations, click city of your choice, then Market Reports) for commercial real estate prices in major cities in Canada.

The primary considerations related to sites are land and access. Usually a company first estimates the size of land and building required. In many cases, both vacant buildings and undeveloped sites are considered. Other site-related factors include room for future expansion, utility and sewer capacities, and sufficient parking space for employees and customers. In addition, for many companies, access roads for trucks or rail spurs are important.

Industrial parks may be worthy alternatives for companies involved in light manufacturing or assembly, warehouse operations, and customer-service facilities. Typically, the land is already developed—power, water, and sewer hookups have been attended to, and zoning restrictions do not require special attention.

For an example of community/site-related factors, see the "Toyota in Woodstock" OM in Action.

Service and Retail Locations

Services and retailers are typically governed by somewhat different considerations than manufacturers in making location decisions. For one thing, proximity to raw materials is not a factor. Customer access is sometimes a prime consideration, as it is with banks and supermarkets, but not a consideration in others, such as call centres, catalogue sales, and online services. Manufacturers tend to be cost focused, and concerned with labour, energy, and material costs and availability, as well as distribution costs. Services and retailers tend to be profit or revenue focused, concerned with demographics such as age, income, and education; population/drawing area; competition; traffic volume/patterns; and customer access/parking.

Retail and service organizations typically place traffic volume and convenience high on the list of important factors. Generally, retail businesses prefer locations that are near other retailers (although not necessarily competitors) because of the higher traffic volumes and convenience to customers. Thus, restaurants and specialty stores often locate in and around malls, benefiting from the high traffic.

Medical services are often located near hospitals for patients' convenience. Doctors' offices may be located near hospitals, or grouped in other, centralized areas with other doctors' offices.

OM in *ACTION*

Liquor Store Location

In a study of survival of Alberta liquor stores since privatization in 1993, it was discovered that location, among other factors such as population of trade area and age of the store, is an important determinant of a liquor store's survival. Those liquor stores located near a grocery store had an almost 100 percent

chance of survival. The next best location was in shopping centres. Locating in a downtown area or near pubs did not help with survival.

Source: A. Eckert and D.S. West, "Firm Survival and Chain Growth in a Privatized Retail Liquor Store Industry," *Review of Industrial Organization*, February 2008, 32(1), pp. 1–18.

Good transportation and/or parking facilities can be vital to retail establishments. Downtown areas have a competitive disadvantage in attracting shoppers compared to malls because malls offer ample free parking and proximity to residential areas.

Competitors' locations can be important. In some cases, services and retailers will want to locate near competitors to benefit from the concentration of potential customers. Mall stores and auto dealers are good examples. In other cases, it is important *not* to be near a competitor (e.g., another franchise operation of the same fast-food chain).

Among the questions that should be considered to make a location decision for a multifacility service or retail company are the following:

1. How can sales, market share, and profit be optimized for the entire set of locations? Solutions might include some combination of upgrading facilities, expanding some sites, adding new outlets, and closing or changing the locations of some outlets.

2. What are the potential sales to be realized from each potential solution?

3. Where should outlets be located to maximize market share, sales, and profits without negatively impacting other outlets? This can be a key cause of friction between the operator of a franchise store and the franchising company.

4. What probable effects would there be on market share, sales, and profits if a competitor located nearby?

For an example of retail location, see the "Liquor Store Location" OM in Action.

Why Should Foreign Companies Locate in Canada?

Foreign companies locate plants in Canada to shorten delivery time and reduce delivery costs to markets in Canada and the United States, as well as to exploit Canadian natural resources and use Canadian skilled labour. We have already seen some examples of these companies in previous OM in Actions (Dell computers, and Toyota). Notable Canadian natural resources are energy (oil, gas, electricity), forestry (lumber, newsprint, pulp), and minerals (nickel, copper, zinc, aluminum, gold, diamond, potash, uranium).

Canadian workers are educated, basic health care is free, and the country is politically stable. Canada is generally safe and secure, energy costs are low, and governments provide R&D tax incentives. Canada has good phone and Internet infrastructure. According to a recent study by KPMG,[3] Canada is one of the cheapest of nine major industrialized countries in which to operate a plant. According to country competitiveness rankings (based on a survey of executives' opinions in each country) by World Economic Forum (a nonprofit organization), Canada ranks 14th in the world.[4]

Many companies, mainly from the United States, have set up plants in Canada over the last century, thus helping to industrialize Canada. One industry greatly benefiting Canada is the auto industry. The Big Three U.S. automakers, Toyota, and Honda have several assembly and component plants in Canada, mainly in Southern Ontario.

OM in ACTION

Microsoft Canada

In 2007 Microsoft decided to open a software development centre in Vancouver, employing 200–300 people initially. Other foreign Microsoft software development centres are in the U.K., India, China, Ireland, Denmark, and Israel. The main reason for locating the new centre outside the United States was that Microsoft was not able to convince the U.S. legislature to grant enough H1B visas

for Microsoft to bring foreign programmers to work in the United States. Canada was chosen because it has a liberal immigration legislation for high-tech workers, and Vancouver was chosen because it is very close to Microsoft's headquarters near Seattle.

Source: Microsoft Cites US Immigration Restrictions as Primary Reason Behind Decision to Open Vancouver Software Development Centre," *Research Money*, July 23, 2007, 21(12), p. 4.

---

[3] http://www.competitivealternatives.com/highlights/international.aspx.
[4] http://www3.weforum.org/docs/GCR2013-14/GCR_Rankings_2013-14.pdf.

Canadian Competitiveness

KPMG has recently released a study on the relative cost of doing business and other competitiveness factors in 14 developed and developing countries across the Americas, Europe, and Asia. The key cost factors being considered include labour, facility, utilities, transportation, and taxes. Numerous noncost factors that influence global competitiveness such as labour availability and skills, infrastructure, regulatory environment, and cost of living have also been considered. The final analysis shows that Canada is one of the most competitive locations in which to conduct business in the world and is more competitive than the United States in many major industries. Specifically, Canada has a cost advantage of 10.7 percent in the field of research and development, a 8.3 percent cost advantage in services, and a 3.5 percent cost advantage in manufacturing as compared to the United States.

Source: KPMG, *Competitive Alternatives KPMG's Guide to International Business Location Costs, 2012,* http://www.competitivealternatives.com/reports/2012_compalt_report_vol1_en.pdf.

Every province has something to offer. For example, Quebec has been promoting the development of its high-tech industries (which include e-commerce, multimedia, and biotech firms) for decades. It gives a 40 percent income tax credit for employee salaries of high-tech firms, and also a 40 percent tax credit on specialized machinery. This entices innovative companies to locate in Quebec and to take more risk in developing high-tech products.

The "Microsoft Canada" OM in Action provides another example of foreign companies setting up facilities in Canada.

Evaluating Location Alternatives

LO3

A number of techniques are helpful in evaluating location alternatives. They include locational break-even analysis, transportation method, factor rating, and the centre of gravity method to determine trade areas.

Locational Break-even Analysis

Locational break-even analysis identifies the least (fixed and variable) cost location choice based on quantity to be produced. The analysis can be done numerically or graphically. The graphical approach will be demonstrated here because it enhances understanding of the concept and indicates the ranges over which one of the alternatives is superior to the others.

The procedure for locational break-even analysis involves these steps:

1. Determine the fixed and variable costs associated with each location alternative.

2. Plot the total-cost lines for all location alternatives on the same graph.

3. Determine which location will have the lowest total cost for the expected level of output.

This method assumes that fixed and variable costs are constant for the range of probable output, and only one product is involved.

The total cost for each location is represented mathematically as:

$$\text{Total cost} = FC + v \times Q \tag{8-1}$$

where

FC = Fixed cost

v = Variable cost per unit

Q = Quantity of output

Fixed and variable costs for four potential plant locations are shown below:

locational break-even analysis Identifies the least (fixed and variable) cost location choice based on quantity to be produced.

◄ **Example 1**

Location	Fixed Cost per Year	Variable Cost per Unit
A	$250,000	$11
B	100,000	30
C	150,000	20
D	200,000	35

a. Plot the total-cost lines for these locations on a single graph.

b. Identify the range of output for which each alternative is superior (i.e., has the lowest total cost).

c. If the expected output at the selected location is 8,000 units per year, which location would provide the lowest total cost?

SOLUTION

a. To plot the total-cost lines, select an output that is approximately equal to the expected output level (e.g., 10,000 units per year). Calculate the total cost for each location at that level:

	Fixed Cost +	Variable Cost =	Total Cost
A ...	$250,000 +	$11(10,000) =	$360,000
B ...	100,000 +	30(10,000) =	400,000
C ...	150,000 +	20(10,000) =	350,000
D ...	200,000 +	35(10,000) =	550,000

Plot each location's fixed cost (at output = 0) as a point and the total cost at 10,000 units as another point; and connect the two points with a straight line. (See the graph.)

b. The *approximate* ranges for which the various alternatives will yield the lowest total cost are shown on the graph. Note that location D is never superior. The *exact* ranges can be determined by finding the output level at which lines B and C and lines C and A cross. To do this, set their total cost equations equal and solve for Q, the break-even output level. Thus, for B and C:

$$\text{(B)} \qquad\qquad\qquad \text{(C)}$$
$$\$100,000 + \$30Q = \$150,000 + \$20Q$$

Solving, you find $Q = 5,000$ units per year.

For C and A:

$$\text{(C)} \qquad\qquad\qquad \text{(A)}$$
$$\$150,000 + \$20Q = \$250,000 + \$11Q$$

Solving, $Q = 11,111$ units per year.

c. From the graph you can see that for 8,000 units per year, location C provides the lowest total cost.

Similar analysis can be performed using profit instead of total cost. Note that if the selling price and demand is the same across the sites, then the answer will be the same as when using total cost.

For a profit analysis, calculate the total profit for each location:

$$\text{Total profit} = Q(R - v) - FC \qquad\qquad (8\text{-}2)$$

where

R = Revenue per unit

Solved Problem 2 at the end of the chapter illustrates profit analysis.

Where the expected level of output is close to the middle of the range over which one alternative is superior, the choice is readily apparent. If the expected level of output is very close to the edge of a range, it means that the two alternatives will yield comparable annual costs, so management would be indifferent in choosing between the two *in terms of total cost*. However, it is important to recognize that, in most situations, other factors besides production cost must also be considered (such as transportation cost and availability of labour).

Transportation Method

Transportation costs sometimes play an important role in location decisions. These stem from the movement of raw materials and finished goods. When there is only one facility, the company can include the transportation cost in the locational break-even analysis by incorporating the transportation cost per unit into the variable cost per unit.

When there is more than one facility, the company should use the *transportation method* of linear programming. This is a special-purpose algorithm used to determine the shipments in order to minimize total transportation cost subject to meeting the demands and not exceeding the capacities of facilities.

Various models can be run, each adding one of the potential sites to the set of existing facilities. The site resulting in minimum total transportation cost will be chosen. See the chapter supplement for further description of the transportation model.

Factor Rating

A typical location decision involves both qualitative and quantitative factors, which tend to vary from situation to situation depending on the needs of each organization.

Factor rating involves scoring the factors (both quantitative and qualitative) and determining the weighted score for each location, and choosing the location with highest weighted score.

The following procedure is used in factor rating:

1. Determine which factors are relevant (e.g., location of market, labour supply, parking facilities, revenue potential).

2. Assign a weight to each factor that indicates its relative importance compared with all other factors. Typically, weights sum to 1.00.

3. Decide on a common scale for all factor scores (e.g., 0 to 100).

4. Score all factors for each location.

5. Multiply the factor weight by the score for each factor, and sum the results for each location.

6. Choose the location that has the highest composite score.

This procedure is illustrated by the next example.

factor rating Involves scoring the factors (both quantitative and qualitative) and determining the weighted score for each location, and choosing the location with the highest weighted score.

A retailer intends to open another store in the same city. The table below contains information on two potential sites. Which is the better alternative?

◀ **Example 2**

SOLUTION

Factor	Weight	Scores (Out of 100) Alt. 1	Alt. 2	Weighted Scores Alternative 1	Alternative 2
Lease cost	.10	100	60	.10(100) = 10.0	.10(60) = 6.0
Renovation cost	.05	80	80	.05(80) = 4.0	.05(80) = 4.0
Traffic volume	.40	70	90	.40(70) = 28.0	.40(90) = 36.0
Operating cost	.10	86	92	.10(86) = 8.6	.10(92) = 9.2
Distance from existing store	.20	40	70	.20(40) = 8.0	.20(70) = 14.0
Size	.15	80	90	.15(80) = 12.0	.15(90) = 13.5
	1.00			70.6	82.7

Alternative 2 is better because it has higher composite score.

In some cases, managers may prefer to establish minimum *thresholds* for composite scores. If an alternative fails to meet that minimum, they can reject it without further consideration. If none of the alternatives meets the minimum, this means that additional alternatives must be identified.

Centre of Gravity Method

centre of gravity method Method for locating a distribution centre/warehouse that minimizes total distribution cost.

Centre of gravity method determines the location of a distribution centre/warehouse that will minimize total distribution cost. It treats distribution cost as a linear function of the distance and the quantity shipped.

The method uses a map that shows the locations of destinations (demand points). The map must be accurate and drawn to scale. A coordinate system is overlaid on the map to determine relative locations. The location of the (0,0) point of the coordinate system, and its scale, are unimportant. Once the coordinate system is in place, you can determine the coordinates of each destination. (See Figure 8-1a and b.)

Figure 8-1 ▶

Centre of gravity method.

If distance is rectilinear (i.e., travel is east-west and north-south only), then we can decompose the problem into x-axis and y-axis problems and solve them independently. We assume that distance is rectilinear.

If the quantities to be transported to every destination are *equal*, you can obtain the coordinates of the centre of gravity (i.e., the location of the distribution centre/warehouse) by finding the average of the x coordinates and the average of the y coordinates (see Figure 8-1c).

These averages can be easily determined using the following formulas:

$$\bar{x} = \frac{\sum x_i}{n}$$

$$\bar{y} = \frac{\sum y_i}{n}$$

(8-3)

where

$x_i = x$ coordinate of destination i

$y_i = y$ coordinate of destination i

$n = $ number of destinations

When the number of units to be transported is not the same for all destinations, which is usually the case, a *weighted average* must be used to determine the centre of gravity, with the weights being the *quantities* to be transported.

The appropriate formulas in this case are:

$$\bar{x} = \frac{\sum x_i Q_i}{\sum Q_i}$$

$$\bar{y} = \frac{\sum y_i Q_i}{\sum Q_i}$$

(8-4)

where

$Q_i = $ Quantity to be transported to destination i

Determine the coordinates of the centre of gravity for the problem that is depicted in Figure 8-1a. Assume that the shipments from the centre of gravity to each of the four destinations will be equal quantities.

◀ **Example 3**

The coordinates of the destinations can be obtained from Figure 8-1b:

SOLUTION

Destination	x,	y
D1	2,	2
D2	3,	5
D3	5,	4
D4	8,	5
	18,	16

$$\bar{x} = \frac{\sum x_i}{n} = \frac{18}{4} = 4.5 \qquad \bar{y} = \frac{\sum y_i}{n} = \frac{16}{4} = 4$$

Hence, the centre of gravity is at (4.5, 4), which places it just west of destination D3 (see Figure 8-1c).

Suppose that the shipments for the problem depicted in Figure 8-1a are not all equal, but instead are the following:

◀ **Example 4**

Destination	x, y	Weekly Quantity
D1	2, 2	800
D2	3, 5	900
D3	5, 4	200
D4	8, 5	100
		2,000

Determine the centre of gravity in this case.

SOLUTION

Because the quantities to be shipped differ among destinations, you must use the weighted average formulas.

$$\bar{x} = \frac{\sum x_i Q_i}{\sum Q_i} = \frac{2(800) + 3(900) + 5(200) + 8(100)}{2,000} = \frac{6,100}{2,000} = 3.05 \text{ [round to 3]}$$

$$\bar{y} = \frac{\sum y_i Q_i}{\sum Q_i} = \frac{2(800) + 5(900) + 4(200) + 5(100)}{2,000} = \frac{7,400}{2,000} = 3.7$$

Hence, the coordinates of the centre of gravity are approximately (3, 3.7). This would place it south of destination D2.

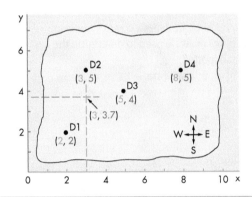

Location Analysis Software

geographic information system (GIS) A computer-based tool for collecting, storing, retrieving, and displaying location-dependent demographic data on maps.

Two types of software are used in location analysis: geographic information system and modelling/optimization. **Geographic information system (GIS)** is a computer-based tool for collecting, storing, retrieving, and displaying location-dependent demographic data on maps. A GIS relies on an integrated system of computer hardware, software, data, and trained personnel to make available a wide range of geographically referenced information. The data might involve age, incomes, type of employment, type of housing, or other similar data deemed useful for the decision at hand. The intuitive graphical maps facilitate communication of facts and hence decision making. Companies providing GIS software and services are MapInfo (now part of Pitney Bowes) and ESRI. For some applications involving MapInfo and ESRI software, see the "GIS Case Studies" OM in Action. Internet mapping programs used to obtain travel directions are an example of a GIS.

Many countries have an abundance of GIS data that can be accessed. For location analysis, a GIS makes it relatively easy to obtain detailed information on factors such as population density,

 OM in *ACTION*

GIS Case Studies

Cara

When Cara Operations purchased five more restaurant chains in the beginning of the 2000s (in addition to Harvey's and Swiss Chalet), the director of market planning in the real estate department needed assistance to keep up. Cara purchased MapInfo's site selection software AnySite. The software provides not only electronic maps of trade areas but also demographic information such as the number of people and their spending habits for eating out. Cara also uses a plug-in software called Site Matcher that assists in matching a new trade area with a similar one that already has an existing restaurant in it. MapInfo has reduced the analysis time per site from half a day down to one hour.

Source: http://resource.mapinfo.com/static/files/document/1086796426697/Cara.5.7.pdf.

Levi Strauss

In 2004, Levi Strauss decided to maximize its distribution by also selling its jeans in specialty stores such as workwear and western apparel outfitters. In order to not impact the sales of its existing retailers, Levi Strauss purchased BusinessMAP and Business Analyst Online services from ESRI. For each existing retailer, the software determines a 1-, 3-, and 5-mile ring (or square if driving distance is used) around the retailer (similar to Voronoi polygons). Any new potential retailer is also geocoded, and if it is too close to an existing retailer, it will not be approved.

Source: http://www.esri.com/library/casestudies/levistrauss.pdf.

age, incomes, ethnicity, traffic patterns, competitor locations, educational institutions, shopping centres, crime statistics, transportation resources, utilities, recreational facilities, maps and images, and a wealth of other information associated with a given location. Local governments use a GIS to organize, analyze, plan, and communicate information about community resources. And job seekers can use GISs for their searches.

Here are some of the ways businesses use GISs:

- Logistics companies use GIS data to plan fleet activities such as routes and schedules based on the locations of their customers.

- Publishers of magazines and newspapers use GISs to analyze circulation and attract advertisers.

- Real estate companies rely heavily on GISs to make maps available online to prospective home and business buyers.

- Banks use GISs to help decide where to locate branch banks and to understand the composition and needs of different market segments.

- Insurance companies use GISs to determine premiums based on population distribution, crime figures, and likelihood of natural disasters such as flooding in various locations, and to manage risk.

- Retailers are able to link information about sales, customers, and demographics to geographic locations in planning locations. They also use GISs to develop marketing strategies and for customer mapping, site selection, sales projections, promotions, and other store portfolio management applications.

- Utility companies use GISs to balance supply and demand, and to identify problem areas.

- Emergency services use GISs to allocate resources to locations to provide adequate coverage where they are needed.

A geographic information system (GIS) is a tool that can be used for location planning. This graphic of New York State combines information from different databases to answer demographic questions about the state. This information also can be broken down into smaller units, such as counties.

Modelling/optimization software packages are also available for location analysis. Many packages employ linear programming or a variation called mixed integer programming algorithms. In addition, some software packages use heuristic approaches to obtain reasonable solutions to location problems. One company producing modelling/optimization location software is MicroAnalytics.

MicroAnalytics OptiSite uses the transportation model to determine the optimal use and allocation of suppliers, warehouses, and customer demand points, as well as optimal location of plants and warehouses. Other software from Micro-Analytics includes Bustops and TruckStops used for optimal routing (http://www.bestroutes.com).

Summary

- Location decisions confront both new and existing organizations.

- Growth, market shifts, depletion of raw materials, and the introduction of new products are among the reasons organizations are concerned with location decisions.

- The importance of location decisions is underscored by the long-term commitment necessary and by their impact on costs.

- A common approach to location analysis is to first identify a country or region that seems to satisfy overall needs and then identify a number of community/site alternatives for more in-depth analysis.

- The major influences on location decisions are location of raw materials, labour supply,

- market considerations, and community/site-related factors.

- Most retailers decide on a site far from locations of their other stores and the competitors' stores, taking potential sales into account.

- Foreign locations may be attractive in terms of labour cost, abundance of raw material, or potential markets for a company's products.

- Canada is one of the best locations for a foreign plant/facility, because it is close to the U.S. market, has an educated labour force, and has abundant natural resources.

- A variety of methods are used to evaluate location alternatives. Those described in the chapter include locational break-even analysis, factor rating, and the centre of gravity method.

Key Terms

centre of gravity method
factor rating

geographic information system (GIS)
locational break-even analysis

Solved Problems

Problem 1

Locational Break-even Cost-vs.-Cost Analysis. A manufacturer that sells its products in Saskatchewan is looking for a production location there. There are three potential locations: Saskatoon, Regina, and Yorkton. Saskatoon would involve a fixed cost of $4,000 per month and a variable cost of $4 per unit; Regina would involve a fixed cost of $3,500 per month and a variable cost of $5 per unit; and Yorkton would involve a fixed cost of $5,000 per month and a variable cost of $6 per unit. Use of the Saskatoon location would decrease the manufacturer's distribution costs by $19,000 per month, Regina by $22,000 per month, and Yorkton by $18,000 per month. Which location would result in the lowest total cost to distribute 800 units per month in Saskatchewan?

Solution

Given: Quantity = 800 units per month

	FC per Month	Variable Cost per Unit, v	Decrease in Distribution Cost per Month
Saskatoon	$4,000	$4	$19,000
Regina	3,500	5	22,000
Yorkton	5,000	6	18,000

Monthly total cost = $FC + VC$ − Decrease in distribution cost

Saskatoon: $4,000 + $4 per unit × 800 units − $19,000 = −$11,800

Regina: 3,500 + 5 per unit × 800 units − 22,000 = −14,500

Yorkton: 5,000 + 6 per unit × 800 units − 18,000 = −8,200

Hence, Regina would have the lowest total cost.

Problem 2

Locational Break-even Profit-vs.-Profit Analysis. A manufacturer is about to lose its lease, so it must move to another location. Two locations are currently under consideration. Fixed costs would be $8,000 per month at location A and $9,400 per month at location B. Variable costs are expected to be $5 per unit at location A and $4 per unit at location B. Monthly demand has been steady at 8,800 units for the last several years and is not expected to deviate from that amount in the foreseeable future. The product sells for $6 per unit. Determine which location would yield higher profit under these conditions.

Solution

Profit = $Q(R - v) - FC$

Location	Q	R	v	$Q(R-v)$	FC	Monthly Profit
A	8,800	$6	$5	$8,800	$8,000	$ 800
B	8,800	$6	$4	$17,600	$9,400	$8,200

Hence, location B is expected to yield higher monthly profit.

Problem 3

Factor rating. Determine which location, A or B, has a higher composite score given the following information:

Factor	Weight	Score A	Score B
Labour cost	.50	20	40
Material cost	.30	10	30
Supplier base	.20	50	10
	1.00		

Solution

Multiplying the weights with the location scores and adding, we can see that location B has higher composite score:

Factor	Weight	Score A	Score B	Weighted Scores A	Weighted Scores B
Labour cost[1]	.50	20	40	.50(20) = 10	.50(40) = 20
Material cost[1]	.30	10	30	.30(10) = 3	.30(30) = 9
Supplier base[2]	.20	50	10	.20(50) = 10	.20(10) = 2
	1.00			23	31

[1] Lower gets a higher score.
[2] Higher gets a higher score.

Problem 4

Centre of gravity. Determine the centre of gravity location for these destinations:

Destination	(x,y) Coordinate	Weekly Quantity
D1	3,5	20
D2	6,8	10
D3	2,7	15
D4	4,5	15
		60

Solution

Because the weekly quantities are not all equal, we must use the formulas in formula 8-4.

$$\bar{x} = \frac{\sum xQ}{\sum Q} = \frac{3(20) + 6(10) + 2(15) + 4(15)}{60} = \frac{210}{60} = 3.5$$

$$\bar{y} = \frac{\sum yQ}{\sum Q} = \frac{5(20) + 8(10) + 7(15) + 5(15)}{60} = \frac{360}{60} = 6.0$$

Hence, the centre of gravity has the coordinates $x = 3.5$ and $y = 6.0$

Discussion and Review Questions

1. In what ways can the location decision have an impact on the production system? **LO1**

2. Respond to this statement: "The importance of the location decision is often vastly overrated; the fact that virtually every type of business is located in every region of the country means that there should be no problem in finding a suitable location." **LO1**

3. Outline the general approach for developing location alternatives. **LO1**

4. What regional/country factors influence location decisions? **LO2**

5. What community/site-related factors influence location decisions? **LO2**

6. How are manufacturing and service location decisions similar? Different? **LO2**

7. What are the potential benefits of locating in foreign countries? Potential drawbacks? **LO2**

8. What is the factor rating method, and how does it work? **LO3**

9. What are the basic assumptions in locational break-even analysis? **LO3**

10. What is the centre-of-gravity method, and when should it be used? **LO3**

11. The problem of finding a hub for an airline or for a package delivery service such as FedEx (for which Memphis is the hub) can be modelled and solved by the centre-of-gravity method. Explain how. **LO3**

12. Crude oil in Canada that was first explored near Sarnia, Ontario, is long gone by now. Still, Sarnia is known as the Chemical Capital of Canada, having 16 chemical and 3 major oil refineries. Explain what advantage Sarnia has relative to locations in Alberta that are closer to oil and petrochemical feedstock production. **LO2**

13. Determine the main factors that might be used for locating each of the following facilities:
   a. hospital.
   b. chemical factory.
   c. fire station.
   d. high-end hotel.
   e. motel. **LO2**

Taking Stock

1. What trade-offs are involved in deciding to have a single large centrally located facility instead of several smaller dispersed facilities? **LO2**

2. Who needs to be involved in facility location decisions? **LO1**

3. Name two ways that technology has had an impact on location decisions. **LO3**

4. Governments compete with each other to attract businesses to create jobs in their jurisdictions. There is no doubt that some of these have helped keep jobs in Canada. However, some people argue that subsidies are not in the long-term interest of taxpayers. For example, between 1982 and 2005, Pratt & Whitney Canada, the largest recipient of government subsidies, received over $1.5 billion in low-interest loans. However, they have repaid only a small percentage of the loans and at the same time are laying off thousands of employees.[5] Also, there have been abuses. For example, Morgan Stanley received tax credits from the Government of Quebec for opening a 300-employee software development centre in Montreal although 200 of the employees were working for a contractor, Compuware, in Montreal, and simply transferred from Compuware to Morgan Stanley. Another example is Videotron, which created a subsidiary and transferred 100 of its employees to it (without physically moving them) to take advantage of Quebec tax credits.[6] Are government subsidies appropriate? Discuss. **LO2**

Critical Thinking Exercise

The owner of a franchised fast-food restaurant has exclusive rights to operate in a city. The owner currently has a single outlet, which has proved to be very popular and there are often waiting lines of customers. The owner is therefore considering opening one or more other restaurants in the area. What are the key factors that the owner should investigate before making a final decision? **LO2 & 3**

Experiential Learning Exercise

Identify a nearby location that has seen several businesses fail. Visit the location and try to determine the reasons for failures. Alternatively, visit a new business in your area and determine why it located there. **LO2 & 3**

---

[5] http://www.taxpayer.com/news-releases/more-tax-dollars-for-these-welfare-bums.
[6] D. MacPherson, "Quebec Gives Money to Company for Existing Jobs," *The Gazette*, May 8, 2008, p. A21.

Internet Exercises

1. Visit http://www.pbinsight.com/support/education/ video-tutorials/product/mapinfo-professional. View the MapInfo Professional multimedia tour and briefly summarize what MapInfo software does. **LO3**

2. Visit http://www.SiteSelection.com, type "Canada" in the search box on the top right, and press Enter. Find an article about a location decision involving Canada. Identify the company and the major factors it used to find a suitable site. **LO2**

Problems

1. A newly formed company must decide on a plant location. There are two alternatives under consideration: locate near the major raw materials or locate near the major customers. Locating near the raw materials will result in lower fixed and variable costs than locating near the market, but the owners believe that there would be a loss in sales volume because customers tend to favour local suppliers. Revenue per unit will be $180 in either case. Using the following information, determine which location would produce greater profit. **LO3**

	Near Raw Materials	Near Customers
Annual fixed costs ($ millions)	$1.2	$1.4
Variable cost per unit	$36	$47
Expected annual demand (units) . . .	8,000	12,000

2. The owner of a sandwich shop hopes to add one new outlet. She has studied three locations. Each would have the same labour and materials costs (food, serving containers, napkins, etc.) of $1.76 per sandwich. Sandwiches sell for $2.65 each in all locations. Rent and equipment costs would be $5,000 per month for location A, $5,500 per month for location B, and $5,800 per month for location C. **LO3**
   a. Determine the quantity necessary at each location to realize a monthly profit of $10,000.
   b. If expected sales at locations A, B, and C are 21,000, 22,000, and 23,000 sandwiches per month, respectively, which location would yield the greatest profit?

3. A manufacturer of industrial machines wants to move to a larger plant, and has identified two alternatives. Location A has annual fixed cost of $800,000 and variable cost of $14,000 per unit; location B has annual fixed cost of $920,000 and variable cost of $12,000 per unit. **LO3**
   a. At what quantity of output would the two locations have the same total cost?
   b. For what range of output would location A be superior? For what range would B be superior (i.e., have lower total annual cost)?

4. A company that produces pleasure boats has decided to expand one of its lines. The current facility is insufficient to handle the increased workload, so the company is considering three alternatives, A (new location), B (subcontract), or C (expand existing facility).

   Alternative A would involve substantial fixed cost but relatively low variable cost: fixed cost would be $250,000 per year and variable cost would be $500 per boat. Subcontracting would involve a cost per boat of $2,500, and expansion would require an annual fixed cost of $50,000 and a variable cost of $1,000 per boat. **LO3**
   a. Find the range of output for each alternative that would yield the lowest total cost.
   b. Which alternative would yield the lowest total cost for an expected annual quantity of 150 boats?
   c. What other factors might be considered in choosing between expansion and subcontracting?

5. Rework Problem 4b using this additional information: Expansion would result in an increase of $70,000 per year, subcontracting would result in an increase of $25,000 per year, and adding a new location would result in an increase of $40,000 per year in transportation costs. **LO3**

6. A company that has recently experienced growth is seeking to lease a small plant in Winnipeg, Montreal, or Toronto. Prepare an economic analysis of the three locations given the following information: annual cost for building, equipment, and administration would be $40,000 for Winnipeg, $60,000 for Montreal, and $100,000 for Toronto. Labour and materials are expected to be $8 per unit in Toronto, $4 per unit in Winnipeg, and $5 per unit in Montreal. The Montreal location would increase total transportation cost by $50,000 per year, the Winnipeg location by $60,000 per year, and the Toronto location by $25,000 per year. Expected annual quantity is 10,000 units. **LO3**

7. A retired auto mechanic hopes to open a rustproofing shop. Customers would be local dealers. Two locations are being considered, one in the centre of the city and one in the outskirts. The central city location would involve fixed monthly cost of $7,000 and labour, materials, and transportation costs of $30 per car. The outskirt location would have fixed monthly costs of $4,700 and labour, materials, and transportation costs of $40 per car. Price at either location will be $90 per car. **LO3**

a. Which location will yield the greatest profit if monthly demand is (i) 200 cars? (ii) 250 cars?

b. At what quantity of cars will the two sites yield the same monthly profit?

8. For each of the four types of organizations shown below, rate the importance of each factor given in the left column in terms of making location decisions using L = low importance, M = moderate importance, and H = high importance. **LO2**

Factor	Local Bank	Steel Mill	Grocery Warehouse	Public School
Convenience for customers	____	____	____	____
Attractiveness of building	____	____	____	____
Proximity to raw materials	____	____	____	____
Large amounts of power	____	____	____	____
Labour cost and availability	____	____	____	____
Transportation cost	____	____	____	____
Construction cost	____	____	____	____

9. Using the following factor ratings (100 points is the maximum), determine which location for a clothing store, A, B, or C, should be chosen. **LO3**

		Location		
Factor	Weight	A	B	C
Convenience of access ..	.15	80	70	60
Parking facility	.20	72	76	92
Frontage	.18	88	90	90
Shopper traffic	.27	94	86	80
Operating cost	.10	98	90	82
Neighbourhood	.10	96	85	75
	1.00			

10. A manager has received an analysis of several cities being considered for a new office complex. The data (10 points is the maximum) are: **LO3**

	Location		
Factor	A	B	C
Business services	9	5	5
Community services . . .	7	6	7
Construction cost	5	6	5
Cost of living	4	7	8
Personal taxes	5	5	4
Commuting ease	6	7	8

a. If the manager weighs the factors equally, how would the locations compare?

b. If business services and construction cost are given weights that are double the weights of the other factors, how would the locations compare?

11. A toy manufacturer distributes its toys from five distribution centres (DCs) throughout the country. A new plant is to be built for a new line of toys. The monthly quantities to be shipped to each DC are approximately the same. A coordinate system has been established and the coordinates of each DC have been determined as shown below. Determine the optimal coordinates of the plant. **LO3**

Location	(x,y)
A	3,7
B	8,2
C	4,6
D	4,1
E	6,4

12. A clothing manufacturer produces women's clothes at four locations. A coordinate system has been determined for these four locations as shown below. The location of a central warehouse for rolls of cloth must now be determined. Weekly quantities to be shipped to each location are shown below. Determine the coordinates of the location that will minimize total transportation cost. **LO3**

Location	(x,y)	Weekly Quantity
A	5,8	15
B	6,9	20
C	3,9	25
D	9,4	30

13. A company that handles hazardous waste wants to open up a central disposal centre. The objective is to minimize the total shipping cost to the disposal centre from five receiving stations it operates. Given the locations of the receiving stations and the volumes to be shipped daily below, determine the location of the disposal centre. **LO3**

Location of Receiving Station, (x, y)	Volume, Tonnes per Day
10, 4	26
4, 1	9
4, 7	25
2, 6	30
8, 7	40

14. Determine the centre of gravity of the destinations shown on the following map. Monthly shipments will be the quantities listed below. **LO3**

Destination	Quantity
D1	900
D2	300
D3	700
D4	600
D5	800

Acadian Bakers

Acadian Bakers is a small but well-known bakery, making and selling cakes and croissants in Houston. Its major customers, their locations on a coordinate system, and their weekly purchases are listed below.

Acadian's coordinates are (27, 36). Is Acadian centrally located to serve its customers?

Customer	Coordinates		Weekly Purchases ($)
	X	Y	
B. Catering	22	31	80
B. Bar & Grill	38	38	70
H's	38	36	90
H Club	38	37	120
H.C. Club	30	33	90
J's Hideaway	−10	12	60
M's	38	36	140
M. Club	−10	44	140
N.M.	47	33	300
K.S. Catering	33	33	50

Stone Consolidated

In 1990, Stone Consolidated (now part of AbitibiBowater) decided to develop new landfills for six of its seven mills in eastern Canada. Three of its mills in the St. Maurice Valley area of Quebec were closely situated: the Laurentide mill in Grand-Mere produced uncoated ground-wood papers; the Belgo mill in Shawinigan (10 km south) produced newsprint and de-inked pulp; and the Wayagamack mill in Trois-Rivières (40 km further south) produced Kraft specialty paper. Given their proximity, Stone Consolidated began a search for a landfill site that could hold the combined waste generated by these three mills.

Stone Consolidated forecasted its total waste output over the next 25 years. It was calculated that the required landfill would need to take up a 58-hectare area.

Stone Consolidated began its search in a 45 × 60 km area containing the three mills, identifying all parcels of land that were at least 58 hectares and satisfied the Quebec Ministry of Environment's landfill guidelines; 175 potential sites were found. This number was reduced by consulting zoning restrictions affecting each of the potential sites, excluding sites within or close to residential and commercial areas as well as those in agricultural areas, which would have required zoning modification and a public hearing at the Quebec Commission for the Protection of Agricultural Territories. Still further sites were excluded for political reasons, being in municipalities that had negative histories with landfills. Of

the original 175 potential sites, 67 were still viable after this initial exclusion phase.

To further exclude sites, Stone Consolidated consulted available geological and geotechnical reports and aerial photographs. Sites predominantly of water-bearing sand and those with shallow bedrock were thus excluded because of risks of groundwater contamination and the costs of implementing measures in line with environmental protection. After this second exclusion phase, six potential sites remained.

Each of these six sites was subjected to tests to confirm viable subsoil conditions. No unexpected conditions were uncovered, so a decision table containing nine criteria was prepared to help select the optimum site: topography, road access, visual impact, weighted average distance to mills, geology and soil condition, groundwater, surface water, actual or potential land use, and population density. Each criterion was assigned a weight varying between 3 and 8. For each evaluation criterion, a specific site was rated as follows:

– Favourable = 4

– Acceptable = 2

– Marginally acceptable = 1

The numerical ranking system is explained in Table 1. The scores of each of the six potential sites are shown in Table 2.

(continued)

Table 1
Numerical ranking system.

Criteria	Weighting	Favourable Factor (4)	Acceptable (2)	Marginally Acceptable (1)
Topography	5	Natural relief and slopes favourable to development	Acceptable relief and slopes—not seriously complicated for development	Abrupt relief—difficult or complicated development
Road access	6	Provincial highways bordered by few or no houses	Road network through areas with few houses	Road network through high-density population areas
Visual impact	3	Site not readily noticeable by passersby	Site could be readily noticeable to passersby; visual screening measures may be required	Site readily noticeable to passersby; screening measures necessary
Weighted avg. distance to mills	3	Average distance less than 15 km	Average distance less than 20 km	Average distance more than 20 km
Geology and soils	7	Low permeable soils	Moderately permeable soils	Permeable soils
Groundwater	8	Favourable depth to groundwater	Probably acceptable depth to groundwater	Potentially unacceptable depth to groundwater
Surface water	6	Drainage network a fair distance from the site	Drainage network at minimal distance from the site	Drainage network to be altered
Actual or potential land use	8	Forestry or industrial zoning—few or no houses	Adjacent to agricultural zoning	Site close to residential area
Population density	6	Minimal residential development	Scattered residential development	Moderate to dense residential development

Table 2
Site evaluation matrix.

Criteria	Weight	St-Georges-de-Champlain	Ste-Geneviere	St-Barnabe	St-Mathieu	St-Gerard	Grandes-Piles
Topography	5	4	4	4	1	2	1
Road access	6	4	2	1	1	1	4
Visual impact	3	4	2	2	4	1	4
Weighted avg. distance to mills	3	4	1	2	2	4	2
Geology and soils	7	4	2	1	1	2	2
Groundwater	8	4	2	2	2	2	4
Surface water	6	1	2	2	4	2	2
Actual or potential land use	8	4	4	1	4	1	2
Population density	6	4	2	1	2	1	2

Question
Calculate the total weighted score for each site. Which one is the best?

Source: Based on F. Villeneuve, D. Dallaire, and V.G. Fournier, "Site Location and Open Communications Are the Keys to a Successful Landfill Permitting: How One Company Handled Its Expansion Needs," *Pulp & Paper Canada* 99(2), February 1998, pp. 29–31ff.

WhiteWater West Industries

Whitewater West Industries was founded by Geoff Chutter in the early 1980s. An accountant working in Vancouver, Geoff got interested in waterslides in 1980 while visiting his uncle in Kelowna who had done consulting on a waterslide in a local park. Geoff quit his job, bought 18 acres of land in Penticton, 60 km south of Kelowna, and built his own water park. More interested in creative aspects of design, he sold his water park in 1983 and bought half-ownership of a Kelowna fibreglass factory. Slides are made by manually spraying melted fibreglass and resin on moulds.

Whitewater West entered the wave pool business in 1987 through a technology agreement with a Scottish company. Due to this and various other design and manufacturing innovations, Whitewater West kept growing. Most of its sales were international and products were trucked to Vancouver and shipped from there. Whitewater moved its headquarters to Richmond, B.C., and expanded its design and engineering staff.

In 1995, the Kelowna plant was getting too small for Whitewater West's sales volume. Geoff needed a larger factory. He had to decide its location: in or near Kelowna or near its headquarters in Richmond? List the advantages and disadvantages of each alternative location and recommend one.

Sources: http://www.whitewaterwest.com; http://www.formashape. com; C. Clark, "He Turns Water into Fun," *CA Magazine*, January 1993, 126(1), pp. 6–7; R. McQueen, "Canada's 50 Best Managed Companies: Whitewater West Industries Ltd," *Financial Post*, December 13, 1997, p. 48.

Palliser Furniture

Palliser Furniture is the largest furniture manufacturer in Canada, but it grew out of the basement of its founder, A.A. DeFehr, who made simple wood products in Winnipeg in the 1940s. It grew steadily until 1963 when it moved to a 40 acre site in McLeod Industrial Park in northeast Winnipeg, the location of most of its current plants. Palliser's revenue was approximately $50 million and it employed approximately 800 workers in 1963.

The growth was steady but the furniture market in Canada was limited. In 1968, Palliser bought a bankrupt furniture upholsterer in Airdrie, north of Calgary, and started selling in the United States. However, it did not have much success there. In 1981, Palliser opened a furniture factory in Fargo, North Dakota, near Winnipeg, to make selling in the United States easier. In 1985, seeing the surge of cheap imports from Asia, Palliser got into wholesale trade by creating the World Trade division, which bought furniture from the Far East and sold it to North American furniture retailers.

Later, Palliser opened a particle board plant on its site in Winnipeg, becoming more vertically integrated in order to control quality and costs. In 1991, Palliser bought a bankrupt North Carolina furniture plant. Then, seeing the attractive prices for leather sofas and chairs, it started making more leather furniture. It also started a line of furniture for

children's bedrooms, called Logic. Palliser had grown to 1,800 employees and $200 million revenue. After NAFTA, in 1994, Palliser took advantage of free trade with the United States by doubling its sales and employees. It also built a plant in Mexico to reduce its costs and to get closer to the southern U.S. market for leather furniture. Mexico was chosen over a plant in China because Palliser chose to follow the customization and fast (2–4 weeks) delivery strategies, knowing that the transport time from China would be 6–8 weeks for its competitors, even though labour cost would be cheaper there. Also, because of NAFTA, there would be no duties for goods produced in Mexico.

In 2001, Palliser introduced a line of trendy furniture for youth, called EQ3, and got into retailing furniture. Later, the rising Canadian dollar and cheap imports from China put pressure on solid wood furniture businesses, forcing Palliser to differentiate itself by making veneer products on machine-driven processes in Canada, but buying labour-intensive traditional wood products from the Far East. To reduce costs, Palliser built more factories in Mexico, and shifted more of the production of leather furniture from Winnipeg to Mexico. Currently it has 4 factories in Mexico employing approximately 1,400 employees and 4 factories in Canada employing approximately 2,800 employees.

(continued)

Question

How has Palliser competed internationally? How have its location strategies helped it?

Sources: J. Rusen, "From Humble Beginnings . . .," *Manitoba Business*, September 1988, 10(7), Sec. 1, p. 6; J.E. Watson, "Entrepreneur of the Year," *Manitoba Business*, May 1, 2000, 22(4), p. 7; M.J. Knell, "Palliser to Shift some Leather Mfg. to Mexico," *Furniture Today*, April 4, 2005 (http://www.furnituretoday.com/article/28738-Palliser_to_shift_some_leather_mfg_to_Mexico.php); M.J. Knell, "Palliser Restructures into Five Operating Companies," *Furniture Today*, August 10, 2006 (http://www.furnituretoday.com/article/36914-Palliser_restructures_into_five_operating_companies.php?q=Palliser).

CHAPTER 8
The Transportation Model

Learning Objectives

After completing this supplement, you should be able to:

LO1 Describe the transportation problem, set it up as a transportation model, and solve it using Excel's Solver.

LO2 Describe assignment and transshipment problems, and solve them using Excel's Solver.

Transportation Problem, Model, and Solution

The transportation problem involves finding the lowest-cost plan for distributing goods from multiple sources that supply the goods to multiple destinations that demand the goods. For instance, a company might have three factories (supply), all of which are capable of producing identical units of the same product, and four warehouses (demand) that stock those products, as depicted in Figure 8S-1. The *transportation model* can be used to represent the structure and data of the transportation problem to determine how to allocate the supplies available from the factories to the warehouses in such a way that total transportation cost is minimized. Usually, analysis of the problem will produce a shipping plan that pertains to a certain period of time (day, week, month), although once the plan is established it will generally not change unless one or more of the parameters of the problem (supply, demand, unit transportation cost) changes.

Although Figure 8S-1 illustrates the nature of the transportation problem, in real life managers must often deal with allocation problems that are considerably larger in scope. A beer maker may have four or five breweries and hundreds or even thousands of distributors, and an automobile manufacturer may have eight assembly plants scattered throughout North America and thousands of dealers that must be supplied with those cars. In such cases, the ability to identify the optimal distribution plan makes the transportation model very important.

Transportation Model

The supply points can be factories, warehouses, or any other place from which goods are sent. Destinations can be warehouses, retail stores, or other points that receive goods. The information needed to use the model consists of the following:

1. A list of the sources and each one's capacity or supply quantity per period.
2. A list of the destinations and each one's demand per period.
3. The unit cost of transporting items from each source to each destination.

This information is arranged in a *transportation table* (see Table 8S-1), where S_i = supply of Source i, $i = 1, \ldots, 3$, D_j = demand of Destination j, $j = A, B, C, D$, ΣS_i = total supply, ΣD_j = total demand, and C_{ij} = cost to transport 1 unit of the product from Source i to Destination j.

Figure 8S-1 ▶

The transportation problem involves determining a minimum-cost plan for transporting a product from multiple sources to multiple destinations.

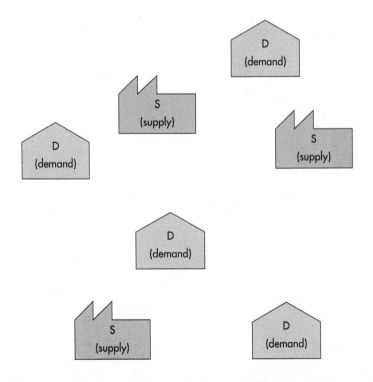

Table 8S-1

A transportation table (symbols represent the parameters).

The first thing to do in transportation modelling is to collect or estimate values of the input parameters.

A company makes a product in three factories and distributes them to four warehouses. The transportation cost (dollar per unit), and supply and demand (in units per week) are shown in Table 8S-2. Note that total supply = total demand. If this was not the case, an extra ("dummy") origin or destination with zero unit transportation costs should be added to the table. If a route (cell) is not possible, a large unit transportation cost, e.g., $999, can be used for it.

Example 1

Table 8S-2

The transportation table for Example 1.

The output from the transportation model is the optimal quantity of product to be transported on each source–destination route and may be displayed inside the cells of the transportation table (see Table 8S-3), where x_{ij} = units to transport from Factory i, $i = 1, \ldots, 3$, to Warehouse j, $j = $ A, B, C, D.

Table 8S-3

The transportation table for Example 1 with quantity symbols added.

Use of the transportation model implies that certain assumptions are satisfied. The major ones are:

1. The items to be transported are homogeneous (i.e., they are the same regardless of their source or destination).

2. Transportation cost per unit C_{ij} is the same regardless of the number of units transported.

3. There is only one route or mode of transportation being used between each source and each destination.

Linear Programming Formulation. The transportation model is a special case of linear programming model. The decision variables for the transportation model are the quantities to be transported x_{ij}. The objective function consists of the sum of cell costs C_{ij} times decision variables x_{ij}. In most cases, the capacity of each source cannot be exceeded, but the demand at each destination must be met. For example, the transportation problem of Example 1 can be formulated as a linear programming model as follows:

Minimize $4x_{1A} + 7x_{1B} + 7x_{1C} + 1x_{1D} + 12x_{2A} + 3x_{2B} + 8x_{2C} + 8x_{2D} + 8x_{3A} + 10x_{3B}$
$$+ 16x_{3C} + 5x_{3D}$$

Subject to:

Supply (rows) $\quad x_{1A} + x_{1B} + x_{1C} + x_{1D} \leq 100$

$$x_{2A} + x_{2B} + x_{2C} + x_{2D} \leq 200$$

$$x_{3A} + x_{3B} + x_{3C} + x_{3D} \leq 150$$

Demand (columns) $\quad x_{1A} + x_{2A} + x_{3A} = \quad 80$

$$x_{1B} + x_{2B} + x_{3B} = \quad 90$$

$$x_{1C} + x_{2C} + x_{3C} = 120$$

$$x_{1D} + x_{2D} + x_{3D} = 160$$

If total supply is less than total demand, the problem will be infeasible. To avoid this, add an extra (dummy) row (source) with supply equal to the difference between demand and supply to restore feasibility. Since there is no such supply, no units will actually be shipped, and unit-shipping costs for each dummy cell are $0. Units in the dummy row in the final solution indicate the destinations that will not receive all the units they desire and the amount of the shortage for each.

Compact Formulation and Solution. We can represent the linear programming model of a transportation problem in a more compact form in Excel. Figure 8S-2 illustrates the compact Excel formulation of Example 1. The Input Table at the top shows the unit transportation costs, supplies, and demands, whereas the Solutions Table at the bottom shows the decision variables—the quantities to transport (in yellow), Row Totals (i.e., sum of units sent out of each source), Column Totals (i.e., sum of units received in each destination), and Total Cost (i.e., sum product of the unit transportation costs and decision variables).

Solver is shown on the top right if the Data menu item is clicked. Then, clicking on Solver will open the Solver Parameters window. Enter the coordinates of Total Cost in front of Set Objective, click in the radio button before Min, enter the range of decision variables after "By Changing Variable Cells," and enter the constraints (Column Total = Demand and Row Total ≤ Supply). See Figure 8S-3. Note that there is no need to enter each supply or each demand constraint individually. Also note that "Simplex LP" should be chosen as the Solving Method.

The optimal solution to the problem (Example 1) is given in Figure 8S-4.

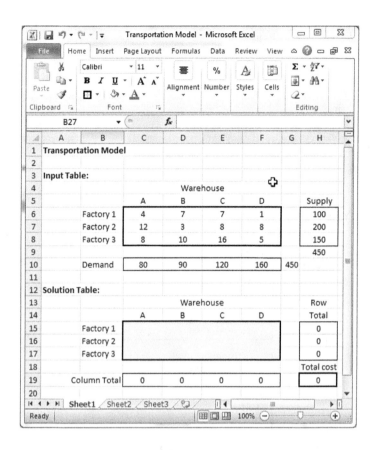

► **Figure 8S-2**

Compact Excel Formulation of Example 1.

► **Figure 8S-3**

Solver parameters for the problem given in Figure 8S-2.

Figure 8S-4 ▶

Optimal solution to the problem given in Figure 8S-2.

Assignment and Transshipment Problems

Some of the other uses of the transportation model include aggregate operations planning (illustrated in Chapter 13), assignment of resources to jobs, transshipment problems, and location decisions.

Assignment Problem

When there are multiple units of a resource that are slightly different in terms of capability and jobs requiring one unit of the resource, the assignment of units to jobs can be done by the transportation method. The only change is to use 1 for each demand and supply quantity.

Example 2 ▶

The coach of a university swimming team needs to choose swimmers for the 200-metre medley men's relay team (four swimmers, each swimming 50 metres of one of the four strokes). Since most of the best swimmers are very fast in more than one stroke, it is not clear which swimmer should be assigned to each of the four strokes. The five fastest swimmers and their best times (in seconds) in each of the strokes (for 50 metres) are:

	Backstroke	Breaststroke	Butterfly	Freestyle
Aaron	37.7	43.4	33.3	29.2
Anton	32.9	33.1	28.5	26.4
Branden	33.8	42.2	38.9	29.6
Chris	37	34.7	30.4	28.5
Eric	35.4	41.8	33.6	31.1

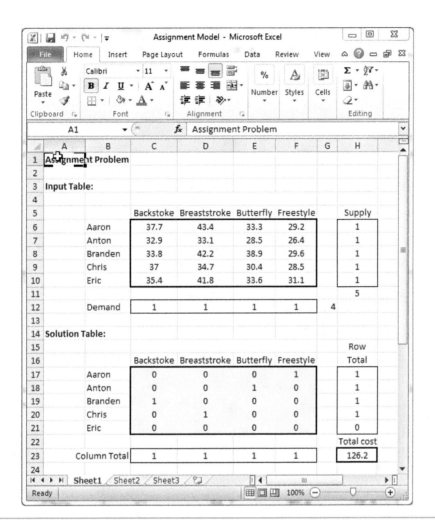

Transshipment Problems

Transshipment problems, in addition to sources, have major distribution centres (transshipment points) that in turn redistribute to smaller market destinations. A transshipment problem can be formulated as a linear program in a manner similar to the transportation model. However, a transshipment point does not have a fixed supply or demand quantity—instead, we should equate (balance) the total input into it to total output out of it.

An agricultural cooperative that buys wheat from the surrounding farms is faced with deciding to which of two mills to send its recently purchased 50,000 bushels.[1] From the mills, the ground flour is to be sent to three local markets. As well as deciding how much wheat to send to each mill, the cooperative must instruct each mill as to which market(s) to deliver the flour to. The transportation and milling costs are shown below along with demand for flour in each of the markets. *Note:* A bushel of flour is defined as the amount of flour resulting from milling a bushel of wheat. Formulate this transshipment problem as a linear program and solve it using Solver.

Transportation costs ($/bushel):

From:	To:	Mill 1	Mill 2
	Cooperative	.62	.66

From:	To:	Market 1	Market 2	Market 3
	Mill 1	.36	.44	.54
	Mill 2	.50	.46	.38

[1] R. D. Shapiro, *Optimization Models for Planning and Allocation: Text and Cases in Mathematical Programming*, New York: Wiley, 1984, p. 25.

Milling cost ($/bushel):

Mill 1	Mill 2
.26	.32

Demand (bushels):

	Market 1	Market 2	Market 3
	10,000	15,000	25,000

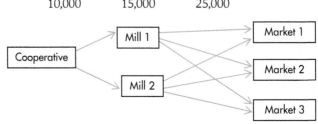

SOLUTION

x_1 = amount of wheat to send from the Cooperative to Mill 1 (in bushels)
x_2 = amount of wheat to send from the Cooperative to Mill 2 (in bushels)
x_3 = amount of flour to send from Mill 1 to Market 1 (in bushels)
x_4 = amount of flour to send from Mill 1 to Market 2 (in bushels)
x_5 = amount of flour to send from Mill 1 to Market 3 (in bushels)
x_6 = amount of flour to send from Mill 2 to Market 1 (in bushels)
x_7 = amount of flour to send from Mill 2 to Market 2 (in bushels)
x_8 = amount of flour to send from Mill 2 to Market 3 (in bushels)

Minimize $(.62 + .26)\,x_1 + (.66 + .32)\,x_2 + .36\,x_3 + .44\,x_4 + .54\,x_5 + .50\,x_6 + .46\,x_7 + .38\,x_8$

Subject to:

Cooperative	$x_1 + x_2$		$\leq 50{,}000$
Mill 1 balance	$x_1 \quad -x_3 - x_4 - x_5$		$= 0$
Mill 2 balance	$x_2 \quad -x_6 - x_7 - x_8$		$= 0$
Market 1	$x_3 \quad +x_6$		$= 10{,}000$
Market 2	$x_4 \quad +x_7$		$= 15{,}000$
Market 3	$x_5 \quad +x_8$		$= 25{,}000$

$$x_1, x_2, x_3, x_4, x_5, x_6, x_7, x_8 \geq 0$$

Note that the milling cost was added to the transportation cost from the Cooperative to each mill. The optimal solution obtained by Solver is as follows:

OM in *ACTION*

Some Applications of the Transportation Model

Armstrong World Industries

Armstrong is a major producer of flooring and ceiling material.[2] Armstrong operates a complex supply chain: 35 plants across 9 countries supplying multiple distribution centres and many customers. Armstrong's modelling team helped management improve their decision making in the supply chain with IBM ILOG LogicNet Plus XE, a network design software. Management has taken significant transportation, warehousing, and manufacturing costs out of the supply chain, added capacity in growing markets in a timely manner, removed capacity in shrinking markets, and responded when major customers restructured their supply chain.

Horoz Lojistik

Horoz Lojistik is a logistics services provider in Turkey.[3] Horoz used AIMMS (a linear programming model building software) to optimize the distribution (transportation and storage) of fertilizer in Turkey for one of its customers. Fertilizers are either manufactured locally or imported into Turkish

harbours, where they are then destined for the final client. There are 3 manufacturing facilities, 17 possible harbour locations for imports, 14 stocking locations (local warehouses), 22 commodity types, and 80 major client destinations. A mathematical model was developed using clients' data (production, demand, etc.) and Horoz's data (capacities, costs, and route and harbour options). The solution was analyzed, and sensitivity analysis was carried out on it. Multiple scenarios were tested for potential changes in the distribution network. Addition of new facilities or routes was assessed. The result was annual cost savings of US$400,000.

Royal Mail

Royal Mail operates the UK's largest road vehicle fleet of 40,000 vehicles as well as overnight rail and air networks, moving some 81 million items a day. The road fleet includes vehicles for national distribution network (4,100 large vehicles and trailers) and fleet for local delivery and collection.[4] In 2004, Royal Mail selected PlanOp, Jeppesen's logistics optimization software, to assist in reviewing and rationalizing its postal transport network. PlanOp helped develop a new distribution network for Royal Mail that reduced the operating costs by £41 million per annum.

Location Decisions

The transportation model can be used to compare location alternatives in terms of their impact on the total distribution cost. The procedure involves working through a separate problem for each location being considered and then comparing the resulting total costs.

If other costs, such as production costs, differ among locations, these can easily be included in the analysis, provided they can be determined on a per-unit basis. For each factory, just add the unit production cost to the unit transportation cost of factory-demand point pairs.

The above procedure can be automated by formulating the problem as a variation of linear programing called mixed integer linear programming. The resulting formulation is called location-allocation model.

Discussion and Review Questions

1. What information do you need to use the transportation model? **LO1**

2. What is linear about the objective function in a transportation problem? **LO1**

3. How is the transportation model useful in location decisions? How does use of the transportation model in location decisions differ from its use as a tool to develop an optimal distribution plan for a given set of sources and destinations? **LO2**

4. How are total costs determined for a given distribution plan? **LO1**

---

[2] http://www-03.ibm.com/software/businesscasestudies/us/en/corp?synkey=X826929F74440G60.
[3] http://www.aimms.com/case-studies/optimizing-nationwide-distribution-network-horoz-lojistik.
[4] http://www.jeppesen.com/documents/land/Royal-Mail-network-redesign.pdf.

Problems

1. Formulate the following linear program as a compact transportation model in Excel and solve it using Excel's Solver. **LO1**

Minimize $8x_{11} + 2x_{12} + 5x_{13} + 2x_{21} + x_{22} + 3x_{23}$
$$+ 7x_{31} + 2x_{32} + 6x_{33}$$

Subject to $x_{11} + x_{12} + x_{13} \leq 90$
$$x_{21} + x_{22} + x_{23} \leq 105$$
$$x_{31} + x_{32} + x_{33} \leq 105$$
$$x_{11} + x_{21} + x_{31} = 150$$
$$x_{12} + x_{22} + x_{32} = 75$$
$$x_{13} + x_{23} + x_{33} = 75$$

All variable ≥ 0

2. A toy manufacturer wants to open a third shop/warehouse that will supply three retail outlets. The new shop/warehouse can supply 500 units of backyard playsets per week. Two locations are being studied, N1 and N2. Unit transportation costs for location N1 to stores A, B, and C are $6, $8, and $7, respectively; for location N2, unit transportation costs are $10, $6, and $4, respectively. The existing network's data are shown in the following table. Which location would result in lower total transportation cost? Assume that unit production costs are the same in N1 and N2. **LO2**

	Store			Capacity/wk
	A	B	C	
Shop/Warehouse 1	8	3	7	500
Shop/Warehouse 2	5	10	9	400
Demand/wk	400	600	350	

3. A large firm is contemplating construction of a new manufacturing facility. The two leading locations are Hamilton and Thunder Bay. The new factory would have a supply capacity of 160 units per week. Unit transportation cost from each potential location and existing manufacturing facilities locations 1, 2, and 3 to markets A, B, and C are shown in the following tables. Determine which new location would provide lower total transportation cost. **LO2**

From Hamilton To	Transport Cost per Unit	From Thunder Bay To	Transport Cost per Unit
A	$18	A	$7
B	8	B	17
C	13	C	13

	A	B	C	Supply/wk
1	10	14	10	210
2	12	17	20	140
3	11	11	12	150
				500
Demand/wk	220	220	220	660

4. A large retailer is planning to open a new store (the retailer currently has stores A and B). Three locations are currently under consideration: South Coast Plaza (SCP), Fashion Island (FI), and Laguna Hills (LH). Unit transportation costs from warehouses 1, 2, and 3 to the new locations and unit transportation costs, demands, and supplies from the warehouses to the existing stores are shown below. Each of the new store locations has a demand potential of 300 units per week. Which new store location would yield the lowest total transportation cost for the distribution network? **LO2**

		To	
From Warehouse	SCP	FI	LH
1	$4	$7	$5
2	11	6	5
3	5	5	6

	Store		Supply/wk
Warehouse	A	B	
1	15	9	660
2	10	7	340
3	14	18	200
			1200
Demand/wk	400	500	900

5. A petroleum company has two refineries in NE and SW United States from which it supplies gasoline to three markets.[5] The supplies and demands of premium gasoline and unit transportation cost from each refinery (S_1 and S_2) to each market (D_1, D_2, and D_3) are given below. Formulate this problem as a transportation model in Excel and solve it using Excel's Solver. **LO1**

	Proposed Volumes (in 1,000 barrels/day)
NE refinery (S_1)	30.70
SW refinery (S_2)	28.06
NE market (D_1)	29.38
SE market (D_2)	8.81
SW market (D_3)	20.57

[5] J. S. Aronofsky et al, *Managerial Planning with Linear Programming in Process Industry Operations*, New York: Wiley, 1978, p. 168.

Unit Transportation Cost ($/barrel)

$S_1 \rightarrow D_1$	1.4
$S_1 \rightarrow D_2$	2.8
$S_1 \rightarrow D_3$	3.5
$S_2 \rightarrow D_1$	3.2
$S_2 \rightarrow D_2$	2.4
$S_2 \rightarrow D_3$	1.2

6. An oil company has three oil fields and five refineries.[6] The availabilities and requirements (in million barrels per week), and unit transportation costs (in $ per barrel) are given below: **LO1**

Oil field	R1	R2	R3	R4	R5	Availability
OF1	5	3	3	3	7	4
OF2	5	4	4	2	1	6
OF3	5	4	2	6	2	7
Requirements	2	2	3	4	4	

Refineries (spans R1–R5 header)

Formulate this problem as a transportation model in Excel and solve it using Excel's Solver.

7. A construction company has to move 4 large cranes from 4 old construction sites to 4 new construction sites.[7] The distances (in km) between the old and new sites are: **LO2**

	N1	N2	N3	N4
O1	25	30	17	43
O2	20	23	45	30
O3	42	32	18	26
O4	17	21	40	50

Determine a plan for moving the cranes that will minimize the total distance involved in the move.

8. A rent-a-car company has to fulfill the excess demand for cars in 4 different cities: 2 cars in City A, 3 in City B, 5 in City C, and 7 in City D. The company has excess supply of cars in 3 cities: 6 cars in City E, 1 in City F, and 10 in City G. The distances between the cities (in 100 km) are: **LO2**

	A	B	C	D
E	7	11	3	2
F	7	6	10	1
G	9	15	8	5

What is the optimal distribution policy that minimizes total travelling distance?

9. The association responsible for central power transmission in Norway would like to determine the usage of each independent electric power generator (subscriber) of the common power network.[8] Each subscriber may have power generators in various locations and may sell its power to various customers. Suppose a subscriber has three sources (power generators in three locations) and four major customers. The supply and demand, and the distances of sources and destinations are given below. Determine the minimum total km-megawatt needed to supply the demands. The association agrees that this minimum is an acceptable measure of the usage of the network by this subscriber. The usage of the common network is then multiplied by a fee for each km-megawatt to determine the charge to the subscriber. **LO1**

Supply (1000 megawatt):	Source 1	Source 2	Source 3
	35	50	40

Demand (1,000 megawatt):	Cust 1	Cust 2	Cust 3	Cust 4
	45	20	30	30

Distances (100 km):

	Cust 1	Cust 2	Cust 3	Cust 4
Source 1	8	6	10	9
Source 2	9	12	13	7
Source 3	14	9	16	5

10. The school board in Monroe County of Indiana must choose the bus companies to drive their students during next academic year.[9] Six companies have bid on eight bus routes (some bid on only some bus routes). The bids (in $1,000) are as follows: **LO2**

Company	Route 1	Route 2	Route 3	Route 4	Route 5	Route 6	Route 7	Route 8
1		8.2	7.8	5.4		3.9		
2	7.8	8.2		6.3		3.3	4.9	
3		4.8			4.4	5.6	3.6	
4			8	5	6.8		6.7	4.2
5	7.2	6.4		3.9	6.4	2.8		3
6	7	5.8	7.5	4.5	5.6		6	4.2

a. If the school board wishes to limit the number of bus routes awarded to any company to 2, determine the awards.

[6] S. P. Bradley et al., *Applied Mathematical Programming*, Massachusetts: Addison-Wesley, 1977, p. 359.
[7] A. J. Hughes and D. E. Grawiog, *Linear Programming: An Emphasis on Decision Making*, Massachusetts: Addison-Wesley, 1973, p. 350.
[8] O. Aarvik and P. Randolph, "The Application of Linear Programming to the Determination of Transmission Line Fees in an Electric Power Network," *Interfaces*, 6(1), November 1975, pp. 47–49.
[9] W. L. Winston and S. C. Albright, *Practical Management Science*, 2nd Ed, California: Duxbury, 2001, p. 225.

b. If there is no limit on the maximum number of bus routes a company can receive, what would be the awards? *Hint:* You can determine this visually from the bids.

*11. The Austin-based out-of-state Auditors of State of Texas were to be relocated out of Texas.[10] This move was due to the high cost of frequent trips that the auditors took in order to audit the out-of-state companies that did business in Texas. The audits were to make sure that the companies paid sales, franchise, and fuel taxes. Five locations were considered. The fixed annual cost of having an office in each location is given below. Also, the companies to be visited have been grouped into five regions, with the demand for audit represented as number of trips to the companies in that region per year (each trip lasted approximately two weeks); see below. Finally, the data for typical airfare from each potential office location to a city in each region is given below. The maximum number of audit trips out of each office is limited to 375 (in order to limit the number of auditors in each office to 15). **LO2**

a. Determine the optimal locations of offices by using the transportation model for each possible set of potential office locations.

b. Determine the optimal locations of offices by using the location-allocation formulation of the transportation model as follows: Define a binary variable for each potential location, for each row calculate the Row Total $\times$ Binary variables $-$ 999 $\times$ Binary variable, add sum of Fixed cost $\times$ Binary variable to the objective function cell; in the Solver Parameters window, include binary variables as variables, add constraints defining binary variables, and add constraints Row Total $\times$ Binary variable $-$ 999 $\times$ Binary variable $\leq$ 0. A binary variable is a variable that can assume only values 0 or 1. The last set of constraints will force the binary variable for a location to be 1 if any quantities are sent out from it.

Fixed annual cost (in $1000):	LA	Tulsa	Chicago	Atlanta	New York
	160	80	140	70	200

Demand for audits/year:	West (W)	South-central (SC)	Midwest (MW)	South (S)	Northeast (NE)
	460	230	230	270	310

Typical air fare between potential office locations and a city in each region:

	W (Portland)	SC (Denver)	MW (Minot)	S (Miami)	NE (Pittsburgh)
LA	$360	210	435	373	349
Tulsa	406	290	584	412	361
Chicago	441	313	518	234	224
Atlanta	537	293	537	477	278
New York	518	349	530	275	125

*12. The crude oil to be exploited from under Elk Hills Naval field in California must be awarded to the highest bidders.[11] A smaller version of the problem is as follows. There are two shipping points, A and B, each with an expected production of 10,000 barrels of crude oil per day. There are two bidders: Company C's bid for crude oil at shipping point A offers a bonus of $1/barrel over the highest price offered for similar grade crude oil produced from nongovernment fields in the area. Company D's bid for shipping point A crude oil offers a $0.90/barrel bonus. Company C's bid for shipping point B crude oil has a $2/barrel bonus and Company D's bid for shipping point B crude oil has a $1.5/barrel bonus. According to legislation, no bidder should receive more than 75 percent of the total crude oil exploited. In addition, Company D cannot handle more than 12,000 barrels per day. **LO1 & 2**

a. Formulate this problem as a Transportation model but *maximize* the total bonus received by the government.

b. Because of fixed costs involved, both companies have requested a minimum quantity of 5,000 barrels per day for any shipping point sales awarded to them (i.e., if x_{ij} . 0 then it must be $\geq$ 5,000). Represent this in your formulation of part *a*, and re-solve the problem. *Hint:* You need to introduce a binary variable for each shipment quantity and compute the (Shipment quantity $-$ 10,000 $\times$ Binary variable) and (Shipment quantity $-$ 5,000 $\times$ Binary variable), and in the Solver Parameters window, include the binary variables as variables, and add binary variables, (Shipment quantity $-$ 10,000 $\times$ Binary variable $\leq$ 0) and (Shipment quantity $-$ 5,000 $\times$ Binary variable $\geq$ 0) as constraints.

13. Sinofert's urea (a nitrogen compound) distribution in China is not profitable. The management is trying to find a more efficient production and distribution plan. The following data is for a reduced version of the problem. Formulate this problem as a transportation model in

[10] J. A. Fitzsimmons and L. A. Allen, "A Warehouse Location Model Helps Texas Comptroller Select Out-of-State Audit Offices," *Interfaces*, 13(5), 1983, pp. 40–46.
[11] B. L. Jackson and J. M. Brown, "Using LP for Crude Oil Sales at Elk Hills: A Case Study," *Interfaces*, 10(3), 1980, pp. 65–69.

Excel and solve it using Excel's Solver. *Hint:* Add the unit manufacturing cost of each plant to each unit transport cost out of the plant.

Plants	Manuf. Cost (yuans/ton)	Capacity (tons/yr)
Sinofert Pingyuan	1,700	980,000
Jiansu Linggu	1,750	1,000,000
Shandong Ruixing	1,700	1,000,000
Shanxi Fengxi	1,650	900,000

	Transport Cost (yuans/ton)				
Plants	Shandong	Jiansu	Guandong	Anhui	Jianxi
Sinofert Pingyuan	58	67	164	69	114
Jiansu Linggu	77	44	117	43	65
Shandong Ruixing	61	65	161	65	107
Shanxi Fengxi	50	56	126	53	88

Customer	Shandong	Jiansu	Guandong	Anhui	Jianxi
Demand (tons/yr)	500,000	450,000	230,000	230,000	270,000

MINI-CASE

NewPage's Wickliffe Kentucky Paper Mill

Every day large rolls of paper have to be distributed from New-Page's Wickliffe paper mill to its North American customers.[12] First the load planner consolidates less-than truckloads and splits larger-than truckloads into two or more truckloads. Then, the transportation planner assigns the truckloads to available carriers (some contracted). A small version of the problem is as follows. There are 32 truckloads that have to be delivered to 12 destinations (some trucks need to stop on the way and drop off 1 to 3 loads). There are 33 trucks available (one will not be used) with specific number of trucks from each of the 6 carriers. All carriers have a minimum charge per truckload and stop-off charge (if any). Some carriers should receive a minimum number of truckloads according to their contract. These data, including the distance to the destinations and transport cost ($ per truckload per mile) for each destination/carrier pair are given in the following table. What is the least-cost assignment of truckloads to carriers that will meet the above requirements?

						Carrier					
Destination	State	Truckloads	Stops	Miles	A	B	C	D	E	F
Atlanta	GA	4	0	612	—	.88	1.15	.87	.95	1.05
Everett	MA	1	3	612	—	1.18	1.27	1.39	1.35	1.28
Ephrata	PA	3	0	190	—	3.42	1.73	1.71	1.82	2
Riverview	MI	5	0	383	.79	1.01	1.25	.96	.95	1.11
Carson	CA	1	2	3,063	—	.8	.87	—	1	—
Chamblee	GA	1	0	429	—	1.23	1.1	1.22	1.33	1.47
Roseville	MN	1	3	600	1.24	1.13	1.89	1.32	1.41	1.41
Hanover	PA	1	0	136	—	4.78	2.23	2.39	2.26	2.57
Sparks	NV	2	0	2,439	—	1.45	—	1.2	—	—
Parsippany	NJ	1	1	355	—	1.62	1.36	1.39	1.03	1.76
Effingham	IL	5	0	570	.87	.87	1.25	.87	.9	1.31
Kearny	NJ	7	0	324	—	2.01	1.54	1.53	1.28	1.95
		Minimum charge per truckload			350	400	350	300	350	300
		Stop-off charge			50	75	50	35	50	50
		Available trucks			4	8	7	7	3	4
		Commitment (per contract)			1	7	6	0	0	4

---

[12] W. L. Winston and S. C. Albright, *Practical Management Science*, 2nd Ed, California: Duxbury, 2001, pp. 271–273.

Part 4

CHAPTER 9
Management of Quality

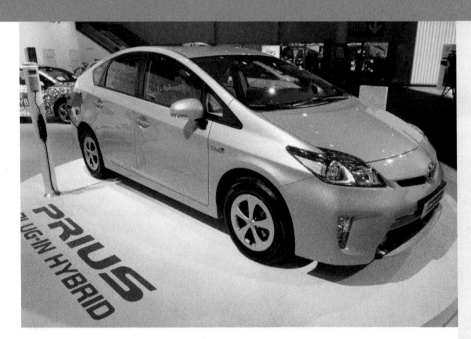

The topics in this part relate to quality. There are two chapters: Chapter 9, Management of Quality, introduces quality concepts, quality awards and quality certificates such as ISO 9001 and ISO 14000, HACCP, and Canada Awards for Excellence, and quality tools. Chapter 10 explains statistical quality control.

Learning Objectives

After completing this chapter, you should be able to:

LO1 Define the term *quality*, describe evolution of quality management, discuss dimensions and determinants of quality, describe various costs associated with quality, and discuss philosophies of quality gurus.

LO2 Discuss quality certifications.

LO3 Describe HACCP and apply it.

LO4 Describe Canada Awards for Excellence (CAE) and Total Quality Management (TQM), and apply them.

LO5 Give an overview of problem solving and process improvement, and describe and use various quality tools.

On February 12, 2014, Toyota Canada issued another recall of the 13,791 Toyota Prius vehicles, with model years 2010–2014 that were in operation around the country. This brings the worldwide total number of recalled hybrid Prius vehicles to nearly 1.9 million. The latest problem is related to faulty software used to control the hybrid drive system. Toyota states the current software settings can result in higher than normal thermal stress on certain transistors, which can cause the vehicle stability control, antilock brakes, and traction control functions to intermittently turn off. In some cases, the hybrid system may even shut down, causing the car to completely lose power while being driven.

Up until now, Toyota has been considered by many to be one of the most reputable automobile manufacturers in the world. Toyota cars and trucks were seen as some of the best-built, safest, and most reliable vehicles on the road. Since its founding in 1937, the company has helped to redefine the phrase "Made in Japan" as a synonym for quality. Toyota's resounding success has helped to propel the company to become the largest and most profitable automobile manufacturer in history. However, a series of serious recalls beginning in 2009 has brought the company to the "verge of death," according to Toyota CEO Akio Toyoda. The Japanese automaker suffered through numerous quality problems involving poorly designed floor mats, unreliable brakes, and accelerator pedals that do not disengage when released. Executives were accused of deliberately hiding quality problems and of putting profits before public safety. Toyota has since been forced to pay millions in fines and more than C$1.3 billion to settle hundreds of lawsuits alleging personal injury or wrongful death stemming from these quality problems.

What exactly is quality and why is it important? This is the topic of the current chapter.

Recall Timeline:

August 28, 2009
The beginning of Toyota's recall troubles can be traced back to a frantic 911 call from veteran police officer Mark Saylor, his wife, daughter, and brother-in-law, while their Lexus ES350 careened out of control on the highway. He reported that the brakes on the vehicle had failed and the gas pedal had become stuck in the fully depressed position, causing the engine to accelerate unabated to speeds far exceeding 190 kph. Unable to keep the vehicle in control, Mr. Saylor collided with another vehicle on the road and crashed into a ravine, instantly killing all four passengers onboard. This tragic event sent shockwaves around the world.

November 2, 2009
Toyota issues a major recall of floor mats affecting 3.8 million vehicles shortly after authorities release a detailed incident report regarding the "runaway Lexus." The report revealed the cause of the accident to be incorrectly installed floor mats. Rubber all-weather floor mats designed for the Lexus RX400h was incorrectly installed in the Saylor's car by the Lexus dealer who loaned them the car. In addition, the oversized mats were not properly secured using the provided retaining clips, causing the driver's side mat to rise up and become stuck over the accelerator pedal. Evidence gathered during the investigation showed the accelerator pedal still bonded onto the SUV floor mat.

January 21, 2010
Toyota issues a second major recall in response to complaints regarding "sticky" accelerators pedals in cars without floor mats. In its announcement, Toyota stated that faulty pedals can become worn, resulting in a pedal that is harder to depress, slower to return, or in the worst case, becomes stuck in a depressed position. More than 2 million vehicles were affected by the recall worldwide. Immediately following the announcement, sales of recalled models were suspended for several weeks.

February 8, 2010
Less than one month after the later, Toyota issues a third major recall for hybrid antilock brake software. The recall was made in response to complaints of delayed braking response, which can lead to increased stopping distance. Toyota was able to fix the "short delay" braking problem via a software update for the ABS system.

Sources: http://www.ctvnews.ca/autos/toyota-recall-includes-prius-rav4-tacoma-rx350-in-canada-1.1682158#ixzz2to6ang2z (accessed February 12, 2014); http://en.wikipedia.org/wiki/2009%E2%80%9311_Toyota_vehicle_recalls (accessed February 12, 2014).

Importance of Quality

quality The ability of a good or service to consistently meet or exceed customer expectations.

Broadly defined, **quality** refers to the ability of a good or service to consistently meet or exceed customer expectations. Prior to the increased level of Japanese competition in the North American marketplace in the 1980s, quality was not uppermost in the minds of management. They tended to focus on quantity, cost, and productivity rather than on quality. It wasn't that quality was *unimportant*, it just wasn't *very* important.

Partly because of this thinking, foreign companies, many of them Japanese, captured a significant share of the North American market. In the automotive sector, leading Japanese manufacturers Toyota and Honda became major players in the North American market.

Many North American companies changed their views about quality after that. Stung by the success of foreign competitors, they embraced quality in a big way. They hired consultants, sent their people (including top executives) to seminars, and initiated a vast array of quality improvement programs. These companies clearly recognized the importance of quality and the fact that quality isn't something that is tacked on as a special feature, but is an *integral part* of a good or service. In the 1990s, North American automakers began to close the quality gap.

Evolution of Quality Management

Prior to the Industrial Revolution, skilled craftsmen performed all stages of production. Pride of workmanship and reputation often provided the motivation to see that a job was done right. Lengthy guild apprenticeships caused this attitude to carry over to new workers. Moreover, one person or a small group of people were responsible for an entire product.

quality control Monitoring, testing, and correcting quality problems after they occur.

Division of labour accompanied the Industrial Revolution; each worker was then responsible for only a small portion of each product. Consequently, pride of workmanship became less meaningful. However, producing to specifications (e.g., product dimensions) became more important because of requirements for interchangeable parts. The responsibility for **quality control** (monitoring, testing, and correcting quality problems after they occur) shifted to the foremen and full-time quality inspectors. In many instances, 100 percent inspection was performed at the end of the production line.

quality assurance Providing confidence that a product's quality will be good by preventing defects before they occur.

During the 1950s, the quality movement started to evolve into **quality assurance** (providing confidence that a product's quality will be good), which aims to prevent defects before they occur rather than finding them after they occur. Operators were given more responsibility for quality during the production process.

Various quality gurus such as Deming, Juran, Feigenbaum, and Crosby contributed to the evolution of quality assurance.

In the 1970s, NASA and the Pillsbury company created a quality management system to assure and control food safety. Later, the International Organization of Standards created the ISO 9000 set of standards for a quality management system.

continuous improvement Never-ending improvements to key processes as part of total quality management.

The evolution of quality took a dramatic shift from quality control and assurance to a strategic management approach to quality in the 1980s, called total quality management (TQM). This approach places greater emphasis on customer satisfaction, and it involves all levels of management as well as workers (all functions of the organization) in a continuing effort to increase quality (called **continuous improvement**, never-ending improvements to key processes as part of TQM).

Recently, some companies are pursuing a problem solving/process improvement approach called Six Sigma, which uses sophisticated statistical tools.

Dimensions of Quality

The term *quality* is used in a variety of ways. Sometimes it refers to the characteristics of material or grade of a product, such as "Canada Choice" or "grade A" eggs. At other times, it refers to workmanship, or performance, or reliability, or special features such as "waterproof" or "subtle aroma." We first describe product quality and then service quality.

The implication in these various connotations of quality is that customers value certain aspects of a good or service, and therefore associate those aspects with the quality that they perceive a good or service has.

Quality of Goods. The aspects or **dimensions of quality of goods** include:[1]

Performance—main characteristics or function of the product.

Aesthetics—appearance, feel, smell, taste.

Special features—extra characteristics or secondary functions.

Conformance—how well a product corresponds to design specifications.

Reliability—consistency of performance over time (not failing for certain length of time).

Durability—long life.

Perceived quality—subjective evaluation of quality (e.g., reputation, image).

Serviceability—handling of complaints or repairs.

These dimensions are illustrated by the examples of quality dimensions for a car in Table 9-1. In a broader sense, the term *fitness for use* is used to define quality. This means quality is whatever customer expects in the product, including things such as on-time delivery.

dimensions of quality of goods Performance, aesthetics, special features, conformance, reliability, durability, perceived quality, and serviceability.

Dimension	Example
1. Performance	Everything works, ride, handling, leg room
2. Aesthetics	Interior design, soft touch, fit and finish, grade of materials used
3. Special features	
Convenience	Placement of gauges and controls
High tech	GPS, DVD player
Safety	Antilock brakes, airbags
4. Conformance	Car matches manufacturer's specifications
5. Reliability	No breakdowns in the first 5 years
6. Durability	Long life, resistance to rust and corrosion
7. Perceived quality	Top-rated car, e.g., Cadillac
8. Serviceability	Warranty, handling of complaints, maintenance

◀ **Table 9-1**

Examples of quality dimensions for a car.

Service Quality. The dimensions of quality of goods above don't adequately describe service quality. Instead, service quality is often described using the following dimensions:[2]

Tangibles—the physical appearance of facility, equipment, personnel, and communication materials.

Convenience—the availability and accessibility of the service.

Reliability—the ability to perform a service dependably, consistently, and accurately for a certain length of time.

Responsiveness—the willingness of the service provider to help customers in unusual situations and to deal with problems.

Time—the speed with which service is delivered.

Assurance—the knowledge exhibited by personnel and their ability to convey trust and confidence.

Courtesy—the way customers are treated by employees.

Consistency—the ability to provide the same level of good quality repeatedly.

Table 9-2 illustrates the dimensions of service quality for car repair.

---

[1] Adapted from David Garvin, "Competing on the Eight Dimensions of Quality," *Harvard Business Review* 65, no. 6 (1987).

[2] Adapted from Valerie A. Zeithhaml, A. Parasuraman, and Leonard L. Berry, *Delivering Quality Service and Balancing Customer Expectations*, New York: The Free Press, 1990; and J. R. Evans and W. M. Lindsey, *The Management and Control of Quality*, 3rd ed., St. Paul, MN: West Publishing, 1996.

Table 9-2 ▶

Examples of service quality dimensions for car repair.

Dimension	Examples
1. Tangibles	Clean facilities and neat personnel
2. Convenience	Convenient location of repair shop and open evenings and weekends
3. Reliability	Problem fixed right every time
4. Responsiveness	Willing and able to answer questions
5. Time	Reasonable wait time
6. Assurance	Staff knowledgeable about the repair
7. Courtesy	Friendly and courteous treatment of customers by staff
8. Consistency	Was the service quality good, and was it consistent with previous visits?

We have already seen the dimensions of product quality in the quality function deployment (described in Chapter 4). They are the types of customer requirements in the house of quality.

Customers evaluate a good or service's quality relative to their expectation. If the quality, as perceived by a customer, is higher than expected, he will be delighted; if it is the same, the customer is satisfied, but if it is less, he will be dissatisfied.

Determinants of Quality

A product's quality is determined during:

1. Product design.
2. Process design.
3. Production.

The product design phase is the starting point for the level of quality eventually achieved. Product design involves decisions about the characteristics and specifications of a product such as size, shape, and material. Note that quality is what the customers require. Quality function deployment (house of quality in Chapter 4) should be used to translate the customer requirements into technical attributes of the product and their target values (specifications). For example, in creating a new burger, the customer requirement of "juicy" can be translated into "moisture content of a burger" with target value of "1 millilitre."

During process design, technical (product) characteristics should be translated into process characteristics and specifications. For example, "moisture content = 1 ml" can be translated into "use a grill capable of maintaining 350 ± 10 degrees Fahrenheit" (which will be used for 8 minutes (4 minutes per side) to grill a meat patty). The ± 10 is the tolerance allowed.

conformance to design specifications during production The degree to which produced goods or services conform to the specifications of the designers.

During production, **conformance to design specifications** refers to the degree to which the produced goods or services conform to (i.e., *achieve*) the specifications of the designers. This is affected by factors such as documentation of processes and procedures, the skills and training of operators, the stability and monitoring of processes, taking corrective actions (e.g., through problem solving) when necessary, communication and meeting of staff, record keeping and verification (audits), and having good quality suppliers.

OM in *ACTION*

The Sounds of Quality

Consumers often associate quiet operation as a sign of product quality, and they are willing to pay extra to get it. Such is the case with clothes washers, dishwashers, air conditioners, shredders, and automobiles. In the case of automobiles, designers know that buyers associate a quiet ride with quality, so doors, hood, windshield and exhaust systems have extra soundproofing and sealing to keep noise out. Designers also know that buyers value safety, and that buyers associate safety with how solid a car door sounds when it is closed, so designers have given extra attention to those sorts of details. Likewise, cell phone manufacturers give careful attention to ring tones and other sounds emitted by their products, as do manufacturers of other electronic gadgets.

Source: Based on David Kiley, "Fine-Tuning a Brand's Signature Sound," *BusinessWeek*, August 13, 2007.

OM in ACTION

Diversicare

Achieving customer and employee satisfaction in the retirement and nursing home industry is not an easy task. Diversicare, based in Mississauga, Ontario, operates 7 long-term-care and 20 retirement homes across Canada. Some of these are owned by Diversicare and the others are managed by Diversicare, some with staff from another company. As a result, there were huge discrepancies in services offered across its facilities and a lot of staff turnover, which was quite disruptive. In 1993, a committee of Diversicare employees met to identify how to improve the quality of operations. The result was the "Continuous Quality Improvement" (CQI) initiative, designed to encourage employees to achieve excellence in quality of care.

CQI required four crucial elements:

1. *Key indicators*: Continual measuring and monitoring of specific health care issues to ensure the effectiveness of programs and services.

2. *Human resources*: Training of management and staff, and development of management systems to achieve optimal use of human resources.

3. *Commitment*: Active encouragement of individual initiatives to implement improvements in the quality of care.

4. *Empowerment*: Empowering caregivers to review existing mechanisms and to make recommendations to improve the quality of life for residents.

CQI involved focus on not only the customers, but also on the processes. In order to achieve their quality goals, a common mission and vision was created. The company focused its quality initiative on improving customer satisfaction and employee recruitment, development, and reward. For example, Diversicare looked at recruitment, selection, and retention processes. Each home identified the best workers and set up a "talent team." The talent teams took a central role in recruitment and selection, and mentored the new staff. Management took a cheerleader role, encouraging staff to participate in the CQI program.

CQI had 16 key indicators that measured a host of employee and resident concerns such as safety (e.g., falls, bedsores, work injuries). The company also added eight quality of life indicators, including a "key wish" for residents. Diversicare constantly looks for ways to improve these indicators. Initiatives from all levels within the organization are celebrated and shared through an annual CQI conference, which promotes the exchange of best practices within the organization. Diversicare won a 2001 Canada Award for Excellence Quality Trophy, and a 2012 Order of Excellence (reaffirming its maintenance of quality excellence).

Sources: Recipient Profiles, http://www.excellence.ca/en/awards/2012-cae-recipients/2012-cae-profiles/2012-caeprofile-dcms and http://www.diversicare.ca/corporate.shtml (accessed September 3, 2014).

Benefits of Good Quality

Business organizations with good quality tend to be more profitable compared to those with poor quality because profitability is driven by both the quality of product design and conformance to design specifications. Improved quality of design will help the organization differentiate its product from competitors and enhance its reputation for quality, allowing the organization to charge premium prices and increase market share. On the other hand, improved conformance to design specifications leads to lower manufacturing and warranty expenses. Put succinctly, good quality is important because: "No quality, no sales. No quality, high warranty costs. No sales and high costs, no profit."

Costs of Quality

To show the importance of dealing with quality issues and to manage quality, one must estimate the various costs associated with quality. Those costs can be classified into four categories:

Internal failure costs.

External failure costs.

Appraisal (detection) costs.

Prevention costs.

Failure costs are incurred by defective parts or products. **Internal failures** are those discovered during production; **external failures** are those discovered after delivery to the customer.

Internal failures occur for a variety of reasons, including defective material from vendors, incorrect machine settings, faulty equipment, incorrect methods, incorrect processing, and faulty or improper material handling procedures. The costs of internal failures include lost production time, scrap and rework, possible equipment damage, and possible employee injury.

failure costs Costs caused by defective parts or products.

internal failures Failures discovered during production.

external failures Failures discovered after delivery to the customer.

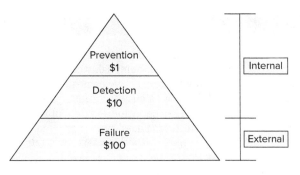

appraisal (detection) costs Costs of inspection and testing.

prevention costs Costs of preventing defects from occurring.

External failures are defective products that go undetected by the producer. Resulting costs include warranty work, handling of complaints, replacements, liability/litigation, payments to customers or discounts used to offset the inferior quality, loss of customer goodwill, and opportunity costs related to lost sales.

Appraisal (detection) costs relate to inspection, testing, and other activities intended to uncover defective products. They include the cost of inspectors, testing, test equipment, and labs.

Prevention costs relate to attempts to prevent defects from occurring. They include costs such as quality planning and administration, working with vendors, standard operating procedures, and training.

Internal and external failure costs represent costs related to poor quality, whereas (some) appraisal and prevention costs represent investments for achieving good quality. It is generally accepted that spending $1 on prevention may save as much as $10 on detection and as much as $100 on fixing failures.

Hidden Costs of Quality. When managers think about the costs of quality, those categories that typically come to mind are the most visible ones, such as the costs associated with buying high quality materials, investing in employee training, and paying for inspections. However, this is just the tip of the iceberg. When managers attempt to cut costs by choosing lower quality materials, reducing employee training, or reducing inspections, the hidden costs of poor quality become larger. The use of lower quality materials is known to cause more product defects and lower production yields, which may require employees to put in extra hours to rework those defects. Since new employees are not sufficiently trained, senior employees may need to spend more of their time dealing with dissatisfied customers. If products are not sufficiently inspected, more defects are likely to be passed onto customers, which results in costly returns and loss of future business. Other examples of hidden costs include equipment downtime due to lack of preventive maintenance, injuries, accidents, product recalls, field service costs, late fees, and extra warranty expenses caused by mistakes. For every dollar that is cut from the tip of the iceberg, much more would need to be spent on the bottom of the iceberg. This is why quality is actually free, when one considers the hidden costs of poor quality.

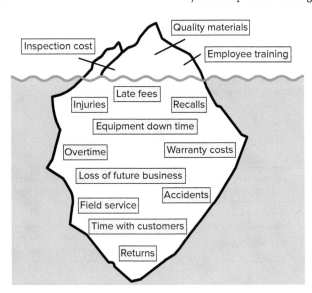

Failure Costs Increase Over Time

The closer a defective product gets to the customer, the more expensive the cost of the defect. Preventing the defect at the design stage is the cheapest way to produce a quality product. If the defect is found during production, it will be more expensive to fix. The cost is greater because the product may need to be reworked, which means extra labour, or the product may need to be scrapped, which means the raw materials would be wasted. If the defect is found during testing, the entire production batch may need to be reworked or scrapped, which is even more expensive. Have you ever sent an email with an attachment, but forgot to include the attachment? It would have taken only a minute or two to look over the email and make sure everything was correct. However, you did not so, now you have to write another follow-up email, which is a waste of time. If the defect reaches the customer, even more expenses would need to be incurred to pay for repairs in the field. Consequently, an ounce of prevention is really worth a pound of cure.

British Petroleum

On the evening of April 20, 2010, British Petroleum's Deepwater Horizon offshore oil platform was drilling an exploratory well at a record depth of more than 4,000 metres below the ocean surface. At approximately 9:50 p.m., the protective cement barrier around the well suddenly failed, allowing high-pressure methane gas to rise up onto the oil platform. The escaped gas ignited and began a chain reaction that culminated in a series of catastrophic explosions. Eleven men tragically lost their lives that evening, and an unprecedented amount of oil began to pour into the Gulf of Mexico.

Immediately after the oil was released underwater, it rose to the surface of the ocean as a foamy mousse. As the oily mousse approached shorelines, it began to engulf sensitive aquatic ecosystems such as coral reefs, oyster beds, marshes, and mangrove stands that lay in its path. Within hours, hundreds of oil-coated birds, dolphins, sea turtles and other marine animals, some of which are endangered, began to wash ashore. Over the next 87 days, nearly five million barrels of oil were discharged into the Gulf of Mexico, affecting more than 10,000 kilometres of pristine coastline in Texas, Louisiana, Mississippi, Alabama and Florida, resulting in the largest and most devastating oil spill in history.

On September 14, 2011, the United States government issued a detailed report placing responsibility for the oil spill on British Petroleum and its partners, oil rig operator Transocean and contractor Halliburton. The report attributes the central cause of the blowout to the failure of the cement barrier around the well, which allowed the pent-up gas and oil to gush out of the oil platform. BP and its partners failed to perform the cement job in accordance with industry-accepted standards. In addition, they attempted to work faster and more cheaply by cancelling an independent diagnostic test used to test the strength of the cement. The test would have detected the problems with the cement seal at a cost of only C\$140,000. In sharp contrast to this modest sum, BP had to ultimately pay out more than C\$46 billion in fines, costs to restore the damaged shoreline, and settlements to compensate the millions of people who lived and worked in the region. The tragic loss of life and the subsequent pollution of the Gulf of Mexico were the results of poor management decisions, based on a lack of understanding of the costs of poor quality.

Source: http://docs.lib.noaa.gov/noaa_documents/DWH_IR/reports/dwhfinal.pdf (accessed February 12, 2014).

Quality Gurus

A core of quality experts has shaped modern quality practices. Among the most famous are Deming, Juran, Feigenbaum, and Crosby. Together, they have had a tremendous impact on the management of quality, and the way companies operate.

W. Edwards Deming.   A statistics professor at New York University in the 1940s, Deming went to Japan after the Second World War to assist the Japanese in improving their quality and productivity. His contributions were so much appreciated that an annual quality prize, the Deming Prize, was established in his name in 1951.

Although the Japanese revered Deming, he was largely unknown to business leaders in North America. In fact, he worked with the Japanese for almost 30 years before North American companies turned their attention to Deming, embraced his philosophy, and requested his assistance in setting up quality improvement programs.

Deming compiled a list of 14 points he believed were the prescription needed to achieve quality in an organization (see Table 9-3). His message is basically that the cause of inefficiency and poor quality is the *system*, not the employees. Deming felt that it was *management's responsibility* to correct the system to achieve the desired results. Deming stressed the need to reduce variation in output, which can be accomplished by distinguishing between *special causes* of variation (i.e., correctable) and *common causes* of variation (i.e., random). This is the foundation of statistical process control (SPC), covered in the next chapter. Deming also promoted the plan-do-study-act (PDSA) cycle of problem solving (covered later in this chapter).

Deming believed that workers want to create and learn, but that management unintentionally often does things such as establishing rating systems that rob workers of their internal motivation. He believed that management's greatest challenge in achieving quality was in motivating workers to contribute their collective efforts to achieve a common goal.[3]

---

[3] For a three-part video about Deming, see http://www.youtube.com/watch?v=GHvnIm9UEoQ, http://www.youtube.com/watch?v=mKFGj8sK5R8, and http://www.youtube.com/watch?v=6WeTaLRb-Bs.

Table 9-3 ▶
Deming's 14 points.

1. Create constancy of purpose toward improvement of goods and services with a plan to become competitive and to stay in business. Decide to whom top management is responsible.
2. Adopt the new philosophy. We are in a new economic age. We can no longer live with commonly accepted levels of delays, mistakes, defective materials, and defective workmanship.
3. Cease dependence on mass inspection. Require instead statistical evidence that quality is built in. (*Prevent* defects rather than *detect* defects.)
4. End the practice of awarding business on the basis of price tag. Instead, depend on meaningful measures of quality along with price. Eliminate suppliers that cannot qualify with statistical evidence of quality.
5. Find problems. It is management's job to work continually on the system (design, incoming materials, composition of material, maintenance, improvement of machines, training, supervision, retraining).
6. Institute modern methods of training on the job.
7. The responsibility of foremen must be changed from sheer numbers to quality . . . [which] will automatically improve productivity. Management must prepare to take immediate action on reports from foremen concerning quality barriers such as inherent defects, machines not maintained, poor tools, and fuzzy operational definitions.
8. Drive out fear so that everyone may work effectively for the company.
9. Break down barriers between departments. People in research, design, sales, and production must work as a team to foresee problems of production that may be encountered with various materials and specifications.
10. Eliminate numerical goals, posters, and slogans for the work force, asking for new levels of productivity without providing methods.
11. Eliminate work standards that prescribe numerical quotas.
12. Remove barriers that stand between the hourly worker and his right to pride of workmanship.
13. Institute a vigorous program of education and retraining.
14. Create a structure in top management that will push every day on the above 13 points.

Source: Deming, W. Edwards, *Out of Crisis*, pages 23–24: 14 Points, © 2000 Massachusetts Institute of Technology, by permission of The MIT Press.

Joseph M. Juran. Juran, like Deming, taught Japanese manufacturers how to improve the quality of their goods, and he, too, can be regarded as a major force in Japan's success in quality. He made his first trip to Japan a few years after the publication, in 1951, of his *Quality Control Handbook*.

Juran viewed quality as fitness-for-use. He also believed that roughly 80 percent of quality defects are controllable; thus, management has the responsibility to correct this deficiency. He described quality management in terms of a *trilogy* consisting of quality planning, quality control, and quality improvement. According to Juran, quality planning is necessary to establish processes *capable* of meeting quality standards; quality control is necessary in order to know when corrective action is needed; and quality improvement will help to find better ways of doing things. A key element of Juran's philosophy is the commitment of management to continuous improvement.

Juran is credited as one of the first to measure the cost of quality, and he demonstrated the potential for increased profits that would result if costs of poor quality could be reduced.

Armand Feigenbaum. Feigenbaum was General Electric's top expert on quality. He recognized that quality was not only a collection of tools and techniques, but also a "total field." He saw that when improvements were made in a process, other areas of the company also achieved improvements. Feigenbaum's understanding of systems theory led him to create an environment in which people could learn from each other's successes, and his leadership and open work environment led to cross-functional teamwork. Also, he introduced the concept of **quality at the source**, meaning that every worker is responsible for his own work. For example, a worker can stop the assembly line if there is a defect.

http://www.juran.com

quality at the source Every employee is responsible for his own work.

Philip B. Crosby. Crosby worked at Martin Marietta Company in the 1960s. While he was there, he developed the concept of *zero defects* and popularized the phrase "Do it right the first time." He stressed prevention and argued against the idea that "there will always be some level of defectives."

In accordance with the concept of **zero defects**, Crosby believed that any level of defects is too high, and that management must install programs that help the organization move toward zero defects. Among some of his key points are the following:[4]

zero defects The philosophy that any level of defects is too high.

1. Top management must demonstrate its commitment to quality and its willingness to give support to achieve good quality.

2. Management must be persistent in efforts to achieve good quality.

3. Management must spell out clearly what it wants in terms of quality and what workers must do to achieve that.

4. Make it (or do it) right the first time.

 OM in *ACTION*   http://www.deltahotels.com

Delta Hotels

With more than 7,000 employees and 38 hotels distributed across Canada, Delta is one of the nation's top hotel chains. Delta Hotels is a subsidiary of Fairmont Hotels & Resorts.

The company has continued to develop and improve procedures for hotels' daily operations. These are based on Excellence Canada's Criteria for Canada Awards for Excellence.

Delta Hotels trains internal assessors to conduct individual hotel assessments and develop a quality improvement plan. Every two years, a hotel will undergo an initial three-day assessment and a subsequent five-day assessment to ensure that ongoing quality measures are incorporated into the hotel's culture and all aspects of operations. External assessors are also invited, ensuring that assessments meet the professional standards of Excellence Canada. According to the senior vice president (people and quality), "Our goal is to ensure a seamless approach to quality, so that it is part of our culture." Assessments, their frequency, and their outcome are listed in the table below.

From their first days, employees are told that they are key to the hotel's success and that their opinions matter. Trust between management and employees has developed to the extent that an employee can walk in her manager's office and say, "I think this really needs to be changed" or "This is what I need in order to get my job done." Employees receive an additional week's pay if they participate in a certain number of training hours per year.

Delta internally delivers over 40 programs on topics ranging from conflict resolution to valuing leadership.

There are also annual reviews of each employee's performance.

There is an employee assistance program (to deal with personal problems). The return-to-work program offers a modified workload, flexible hours, and personal days off.

Delta has also created management development reviews, including 360° feedback, that examine specific managerial competencies such as flexibility, ability to handle stress, ability to work with a team, and interpersonal sensitivity. The results, including employee satisfaction, are tied to managers' bonuses.

Employee satisfaction and professional development have risen dramatically. Employee accomplishments are recognized during regular "town hall" meetings.

Problem-solving teams regularly monitor processes for improvement opportunities. One result of these improvements is Delta's "one-minute check-in guarantee" for Delta Privilege members. Delta's power-to-please program empowers employees to have control over a customer's experience.

As a result of all these initiatives and improvements, Delta has realized improved results in guest satisfaction and won a Canada Award for Excellence Quality Trophy in 2000, Healthy Workplace Gold Trophy in 2004, and Order of Excellence in Quality (renewing the Quality Trophy) in 2007.

Sources: "Canada Awards for Excellence," *Canadian Business*, December 11, 2000, pp. 93–96, http://www.excellence.ca/en/awards/All_CAE_Recipients_Alpha (accessed 2007); http://www.deltahotels.com.

Assessment	Frequency	Outcome
Quality business assessment (QBA)	Once in 24 months	Quality improvement plan (QIP)
Employee opinion survey (EOS)	Once in 12 months	People action plan (PAP)
Minimum standard checklist	Once in 24 months	People resources plan
Benefits/pension/compensation reports	Once a month at each hotel and corporate office	Security/wellness plan

---

[4] Philip Crosby, *Quality without Tears: The Art of Hassle-Free Management*, New York: McGraw-Hill, 1984.

Unlike the other gurus, Crosby maintained that achieving quality can be relatively easy. Crosby's quality-is-free concept is based on the following: costs of poor quality are much greater than traditionally recognized and these costs are so great that rather than viewing quality efforts as costs, organizations should view them as a way to reduce costs, because the improvements generated by quality efforts will more than pay for themselves.

Table 9-4 provides a summary of the important contributions of the gurus to modern quality management.

Table 9-4	Contributor	Key Contributions
A summary of key contributions to quality management.	Deming	**14** points; special versus common causes of variation, SPC, PDSA cycle
	Juran	Quality is fitness-for-use; quality trilogy
	Feigenbaum	Quality is a total field; quality at the source
	Crosby	Quality is free; zero defects

LO2 Quality Certifications

The purpose of the International Organization for Standardization (ISO) is to promote worldwide standards that will improve operating efficiency and productivity, and reduce costs. The ISO is composed of the national standards bodies of over 100 countries. The Canadian representative body is the Standards Council of Canada. The work of the ISO is conducted by some 180 technical committees. Two of the most well-known certifications are ISO 9001 and ISO 14000, which relate to an organization's processes rather than its products and services.

 OM in *ACTION*

Holland College, PEI

Holland College is a large community college with campuses in seven towns in PEI. Holland College offers both competency-based (career-oriented) diploma/certificate programs and continuing education. It considers its products to be the programs it offers. Its primary customers are the students while its secondary customers are the future employers of the students. Holland College is one of the few colleges/universities in Canada that is ISO 9001 certified.

The quality management system (QMS) set up by Holland College includes quality policies (e.g., involve industry/business leaders in development and evaluation of the programs) and quality objectives (e.g., more than 80 percent of students should recommend their program to someone they know). QMS also includes a quality manual that delineates how Holland College provides and manages its resources, and designs, delivers, controls, and improves its programs. This is done by setting up several processes for its major activities. The processes and other information/instructions are described in a set of procedures. A procedure has the following sections: purpose, scope, related procedures, documents/definitions/responsibilities, and sections that describe guidelines and instructions, possibly including a process flow diagram.

Adequate funding is provided for resources such as staff and faculty, and buildings and equipment (e.g., computers and audiovisuals). There is a procedure for recruiting qualified staff/faculty based on education, training, skills, and experience. There are several procedures for appraisal and training of employees to improve their services to the students and to maintain the relevance and appeal of the programs. Computers are periodically replaced with new ones.

To design and deliver its programs and services, and to deal with its customers (the students), Holland College has several processes: Marketing and recruitment, admissions and registration, student exit and graduation, career counselling/accommodation/disability services, design and development of programs and curriculum, delivery of programs and courses, purchasing of equipment, and library/bookstore/computer services/student-finance services. These processes are provided under controlled conditions. Some of the procedures used to control some of the above processes include using course outlines, taking attendance, assessing students, using transcripts, dealing with student misconduct, and equipment maintenance and repair.

The programs are measured, analyzed, and improved by getting feedback from students and employers. Instructors and managers continuously review the performance of their programs and take corrective action. The executive committee annually reviews the programs' performance against the objectives and prescribes action plans to improve them.

For a list of links to Holland College QMS, visit https://sam.hollandcollege.com/AngelUploads/Content/Quality_Management_System/_assoc/3BD141D6699D44C593DF73C5A236438F/QMS-Welcome.pdf.

Sources: http://www.hollandc.pe.ca/quality (accessed 2012); http://sam.hollandcollege.com/AngelUploads/Content/Quality_Management_System/_assoc/9F99DA3D6BED484E8C5DBA903BBDB366/HC_Quality_Manual.pdf (accessed September 3, 2014).

ISO 9001

ISO 9001 is the international standard for a quality management system. This standard is critical for companies doing business internationally, particularly in Europe. A company wanting to be certified must document its processes and procedures, and undergo an external on-site assessment by accredited auditors. The process often takes 12 to 18 months. With certification comes registration in an ISO directory that companies seeking suppliers can refer to. They are generally given preference over unregistered companies. Approximately one million companies are registered worldwide; almost half of them are located in Europe, but China has the most numbers (see http://www.iso.org/iso/iso-survey2010.pdf).

The ISO 9001 review process involves considerable self-appraisal, resulting in problem identification and improvement. Registered companies face an ongoing series of audits, and they must be re-registered every three years. A graphical representation of major ISO 9001 activities and their interaction is shown below.

ISO 9001 The international standard for a quality management system, critical to international business.

http://www.iso.org

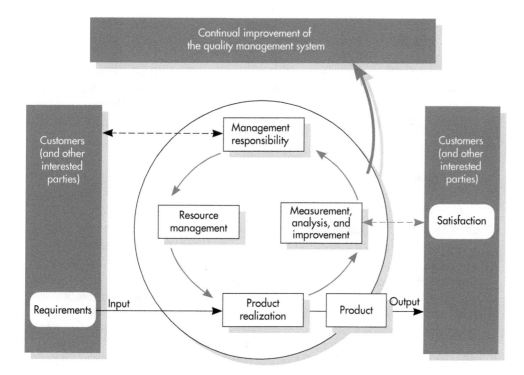

There are usually three types of documents created for ISO 9001: a quality manual, a procedures manual, and detailed work instructions and other supporting documents. The procedures manual includes all critical processes of the organization, and for each process a description (in general terms) of how it is to be done (using a process flow diagram) and what to do if there is a problem.

ISO 14000

ISO 14000 is a family of standards related to environmental management that was introduced by the International Organizations for Standardization in 1996. ISO 14000 concerns what an organization does to minimize harmful effects to the environment caused by its operations. The standards for certification bear upon three major areas:

ISO 14000 A set of international standards for assessing a company's environmental performance.

- Management systems—System development and integration of environmental responsibilities into business planning.

- Operations—Consumption of natural resources and energy.

- Environmental systems—Measuring, assessing, and managing emissions, effluents, and other waste streams.

Hazard Analysis Critical Control Point (HACCP)

HACCP A quality management system designed for food processors.

HACCP is a quality management system, similar to ISO 9001, designed for food processors, especially meat, poultry, and fish processors. It originated with the Pillsbury company when it had to design and manufacture food for the NASA space missions in the 1970s. HACCP is mandatory for fish processors in Canada and is becoming mandatory for meat and poultry processors. Meat exporters to other countries, such as the United States and Japan, need to have HACCP certification too. HACCP is enforced by the Canadian Food Inspection Agency (CFIA). Other food-related industries such as dairies, fruit and vegetable processors, and egg producers are also encouraged to implement HACCP.

HACCP deals with food safety, in particular, biological, chemical, and physical hazards.[5] HACCP is implemented by a multidisciplinary team, including a food biologist and sanitation expert in addition to representatives from production, engineering, quality assurance, etc. As in ISO 9001, top management's commitment is essential.

First, the HACCP team inspects various construction and/or sanitary aspects of the plant, equipment, and personnel. For example, the land should have good drainage and water source, and no garbage or odours. The building should have easy-to-clean walls, floors, and ceilings; sloped floors to drains; screened windows; close-fitting doors; self-closing washroom doors; good ventilation; and be pest proof.

If there is any shortcoming, corrective action is undertaken. Also, the team ensures that there is a regular system of work instructions, inspection, and prevention in place for the building, equipment, and personnel. Guidelines and standard operating procedures (SOP) are provided by the CFIA and other government agencies. Further, there should be a procedure for product recall, i.e., a product coding system and records.

The following product and process background information is required:

1. Describe the product, source of raw material, product characteristics, ingredients, packaging, how the product is used, shelf life, where the product will be sold, labelling instructions, and distribution control.

2. Draw the process flow diagram and number the steps of the process. Also, draw the plant layout diagram, identifying each operation by its number and showing the material flows by arrows.

3. Identify all the Regulatory Action Points (RAP), i.e., points in the process where safety control is mandated by the government. These usually include the receiving point(s) of raw material(s) and the shipping point of the products, but may also include other critical points such as where thawing of fish and the labelling of fish cans take place. SOPs are provided for most of these activities, specifying parameters such as time and temperature. If there is no SOP for a RAP, the company needs to define one. The RAP plan specifies the control measures (such as SOPs), the inspection (detection) procedures (what, how, frequency, and who), and corrective actions.

There are three main HACCP steps:

1. Perform Hazard Analysis:
   - For each ingredient/processing step, identify potential hazard(s). To do this, one can use the reference database of CFIA; books on microbiology, food processing, and plant sanitation; Health Canada reports on illnesses, recalls, and complaints; and scientific papers. Hazards are classified into biological, chemical, and physical.
   - Determine if the potential hazard is significant and provide justification.
   - Provide preventive measures for significant hazards in process design (e.g., include pasteurization operation).

2. Determine the Critical Control Points (CCPs):
   - For every ingredient/processing step with one or more significant hazard(s), if there will not be a subsequent step that would eliminate the hazard, then this step is a CCP. The receiving point of raw material, the closing point of the cans, and the sterilization point are typical CCPs.

---

[5] http://www.inspection.gc.ca/english/fssa/polstrat/haccp/haccpe.shtml; http://www.omafra.gov.on.ca/english/food/foodsafety/processors/haccp.htm.

Canadian Quality Milk (CQM)

Modern consumers expect the food they eat to be safe and nutritious. To this end, the Dairy Farmers of Canada developed the Canadian Quality Milk (CQM) program, which is based on the HACCP (Hazard Analysis Critical Control Points) approach, to ensure that the quality of their milk will satisfy even the highest of expectations. CQM is a food safety program that is designed to help dairy producers reduce or even eliminate food safety hazards on their farms. The program is recognized by the Canadian Food Inspection Agency as being technically sound, and is now mandatory in almost all Canadian provinces.

The successful implementation of the CQM program requires three main steps:

1. Identification of all *hazards to* food safety:
   - Potential hazards on a dairy farm could be chemical, biological or physical in nature. For example, livestock medication and pesticide residues are chemical threats. Biological threats include harmful bacteria and parasites. Physical threats include sediment, dust, hair and flies in raw milk. Food hazards must be identified before proceeding to the next step.

2. Specifying *Critical Control Points* in the production process:
   - This includes any step in the production process at which control can be applied and food hazards can be reduced or eliminated. For example, the locations where milking takes place and the storage of milk are typical CCPs.

3. Monitoring of CCPs and performing *corrective actions* when measurements are outside acceptable limits.
   - Corrective actions outline the steps that are needed to correct a problem. One potential problem could be trace amounts of growth hormones found in milk. Growth hormones such as recombinant bovine somatotropin (rBST) are used in the United States to increase milk production and to stimulate growth of body mass in cows. Canada has much stricter regulations on the use of hormones and antibiotics. rBST is not allowed in Canada and any test recognized by the provincial regulatory authority that gives a positive result for the hormone indicates the dairy producer needs to be investigated.
   - All Canadian milk is rigorously tested for antibiotics prior to it being accepted at a milk processing plant. Cows that are administered antibiotics must have their milk discarded until there is no longer any trace of antibiotics. If any traces of antibiotics are found, the milk must be discarded.

Milk may have a high bacteria count if not properly cooled or stored. The temperature of milk must be monitored at all times during storage. Any abnormal temperature fluctuations outside accepted limits indicate the milk must be discarded.

Sources: http://www.dairyfarmers.ca/content/download/886/6983/version/3/file/CQM+Reference+Manual-Jun2010.pdf (accessed September 3, 2014).

3. Establish the HACCP Plan:
   - For each CCP/significant hazard, determine a control/preventive measure, the critical limits, the monitoring procedure (what, how, frequency, and who), the corrective action and records, and the verification procedures.

The product description is chunk-style tuna, canned in small cans, sealed at the bottom and top, packaged in brine (salt water) or oil, ready-to-eat, with a five-year shelf life, and sold in retail stores.

◄ **Example 1**

The company buys the cans, with the bottom already sealed to the wall, but separate can tops. For simplicity, we assume that the tuna is canned fresh (If the tuna is frozen, it has to be thawed first). The process briefly is as follows: after receiving, the fish's head and tail are cut off, and racks of fish are precooked in order to make skinning and deboning easier. Then, the automated canning line cuts the fish into chunks, fits a chunk in a can, adds ingredients, and vacuum-seals the top. Next, baskets of fish cans are sterilized and cooked further in pressurized steam rooms, washed, dried, and individually weighed and labelled.

Government regulations require that the tuna not be tainted or decomposed (i.e., should be safe and wholesome), and the can should be accurately labelled with a product code (including the date canned). In addition to sanitation and hygiene at the plant, equipment, and operator levels, HACCP requirements can be satisfied by the following Critical Control Points and quality control/assurance plans:

Critical Control Point	Quality Assurance Plan	Quality Control Plan
Receiving	Vessel records of cooling	Visual inspection and tests for toxins (60 fish per lot)
Precooking	Standard operating procedures (SOP), cooking time and temperature	

Critical Control Point	Quality Assurance Plan	Quality Control Plan
Cans and Tops	Manufacturing record of material and SOP	Visual inspection
Close cans		Visual (every half hour) and teardown tests (every four hours) for seams
Pasteurize	SOP, temperature, time, pressure	
Wash with chlorine		Test residual chlorine in water
Label		Inspect continuously for accuracy

Canada Awards for Excellence (CAE) and Total Quality Management (TQM)

Canada Awards for Excellence recognize outstanding quality achievement by Canadian organizations, administered annually by the Excellence Canada, an independent not-for-profit organization. Excellence Canada investigated the workings of successful organizations and developed a set of criteria for business excellence. The criteria also provide a comprehensive, practical, and well-tested framework for continuous improvement. The six main categories of the criteria are displayed below. Note that quality is embedded in strategic management of the organization, i.e, all functions of the organization are engaged in quality management.

Excellence Canada
Framework for Organizational Excellence

In recent years, to make the implementation of the quality management system easier for organizations, Excellence Canada has divided the implementation into four stages or levels (called Progressive Excellence Program; see the following figure): Level 1: Foundation, Level 2: Transformation, Level 3: Role Model, and Level 4: World Class.

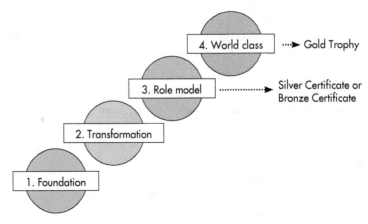

For each level, Excellence Canada provides the requirements to certify in that level (minor differences are made between private and public organizations, education, and hospitals).

Level 1 CAE certification requires developing a mission statement, defining customers, planning training in management principles and practices, and performing an assessment of the above activities.

Level 2 CAE certification involves strategic planning; identifying customer needs; human resource planning; identifying, documenting, and improving key processes; and supplier/partner planning. These activities start after an initial gap analysis and internal/external assessment using questionnaires, used to determine an improvement plan, and end with review of improvement results.

At Level 3 CAE certification, the organization demonstrates shared commitment; performs periodic planning, sets priorities, and communicates performance; measures customer satisfaction and receives feedback; involves employees in health and safety, provides training and measures its effectiveness, and measures employee satisfaction; analyzes, improves, and documents processes, involves customers and suppliers and benchmarks process management; and shares information with suppliers and involves them in new product design. Also, all activities are continuously improved. These activities start after an initial gap analysis and internal/external assessment using questionnaires, used to determine an improvement plan, and end with review of improvement results.

Level 4 CAE requirements build on the other levels, and the organization demonstrates that it has achieved good to excellent overall results and at least three years of positive trends from the improvement efforts.[6]

Since 1989, the awards have honoured more than 50 Canadian organizations for outstanding quality achievement. For three examples, see the "Toronto East General Hospital" OM in Action below, and "Diversicare" and "Delta Hotels" OM in Actions earlier in the chapter.

Total Quality Management

Total quality management (TQM) is an approach to quality management that involves everyone in an organization in quality management and a continual effort to improve quality and customer satisfaction. There are three key features in TQM. One is a never-ending push to improve quality, which is referred to as *continuous improvement*; the second is the *involvement of everyone* in the organization in quality management; and the third is the goal of ever-increasing *customer satisfaction*.

We can describe the TQM approach as follows:

1. Find out what customers want. This might involve the use of surveys, focus groups, interviews, or some other technique that integrates the customer's voice in the decision-making process.

2. Design a product that will meet (or exceed) what customers want.

3. Design processes that facilitate doing the job right the first time (called "quality at the source"). Determine where mistakes are likely to occur and try to prevent them (called **Poka-yoke (fail-safeing)**, i.e., incorporating process design elements that prevent mistakes). Involve and empower the workers in quality management. When mistakes do occur, find out why, and implement corrective actions so that they are less likely to occur again.

4. Keep track of results (TQM is data driven), and use them to guide improvement in the system. Never stop trying to improve (called "continuous improvement").

5. Extend these concepts to suppliers/partners.

Many companies have successfully implemented TQM. Management must be totally committed and involved by becoming educated in quality, setting and enforcing improvement goals, providing resources, and reviewing progress. If it isn't, TQM will become just another fad that quickly dies and fades away. The above five steps should remind you of the criteria for Canada Awards for Excellence, described earlier.

It would be incorrect to think of TQM as merely a collection of techniques. Rather, TQM reflects a whole new attitude toward quality. It is about the *culture* of an organization. To truly reap the benefits of TQM, the culture of an organization must change.

Table 9-5 illustrates the differences between cultures of a TQM organization and a more traditional organization.

total quality management (TQM) An approach to quality management that involves everyone in an organization in quality management and continual effort to improve quality and customer satisfaction.

Poka-yoke (fail-safeing) Incorporating process design elements that prevent mistakes.

---

[6] See http://www.for.gov.bc.ca/hfp/frep/qmgmt/index.htm for an example of applications and assessments for Levels 1 to 3 of CAE requirements by the Forest and Range Evaluation Program (FREP) of BC.

Toronto East General Hospital

Toronto East General Hospital (TEGH), with 515 beds, is one of the full-service teaching hospitals serving Toronto, and one of two hospitals in Canada that have passed Level 4 certification of Excellence Canada. TEGH received a gold trophy for quality and healthy workplace in 2008 and a silver trophy for mental health at work in 2013. TEGH defines its vision, mission, values, success factors, and priorities and performance measures (indicators) during its strategic planning process, which is performed every three years (led by the board of directors/top management). These are determined after collecting data on patient needs, Toronto health district priorities (to coordinate services with other Toronto hospitals), and Ontario health priorities.

Both strategic plans and annual reviews are shown on the TEGH Web site for patients and employees to see. The performance measures are compared with other Toronto and Ontario hospitals as benchmarks. For those measures that require improvement, action plans are determined by top management, and each action plan is assigned to a corporate support manager. Also, there are funds for departments/programs to apply for projects.

TEGH has commissioned a demographic study of its catchment area and is familiar with its patients. It performs surveys of its patients' satisfaction with quality of care they received, performs post-discharge phone calls, collects testimonials from its satisfied patients, and has a community advisory council.

TEGH has designed and documented many processes and procedures, e.g., patient flow (to reduce patient stay), continuity of care (to reduce the time until patient is transferred to the right place for care), patient preparation for various tests or surgeries, research study funding, "Good catch" program for staff to identify errors or safety risks before they occur, and standards for service delivery, appearance, etc.

Annually, TEGH provides care for nearly 20,000 inpatients, 200,000 outpatient visits, delivers nearly 3,200 babies, and handles more than 70,000 emergency visits. TEGH has no difficulty recruiting physicians (it has approximately 400) and nursing staff (it has approximately 2,500). Also, TEGH has approximately 500 volunteers. TEGH has introduced a violence prevention program and has enhanced its wellness facilities and programs. It offers a foundation of leadership program for both its physicians and nurses (so far more than 350 have taken the course). It offers a 2.5 year onsite program for its nurses to get a bachelor's degree from Ryerson University. TEGH has also increased its online training programs. Employee and physician satisfaction scores are annually determined by sampling staff. TEGH has partnered with North York General Hospital and Sunnybrook Health Science Centre to perform thoracic (spine) surgery on their patients, and with University of Toronto Medical School to train residents and supervise student projects, etc.

Sources: Retrieved 2014. http://www.excellence.ca/en/awards/2013-cae-recipients/2013-cae-profiles/2013-caeprofile-tegh; http://www.tegh.on.ca/bins/doc.aspx?id=7828; http://www.tegh.on.ca/bins/doc.asp?rdc_id=5234.

Table 9-5 ▶

Comparing the cultures of TQM and traditional organizations.

Aspect	Traditional	TQM
Overall mission	Maximize return on investment	Meet or exceed customer expectations
Objectives	Emphasis on short term	Balance of long term and short term
Management	Not always open; sometimes inconsistent objectives	Open; encourages employee input; consistent objectives
Role of manager	Issue orders; enforce	Coach, remove barriers, build trust
Customer requirements	Not highest priority; may be unclear	Highest priority; important to identify and understand
Problems	Assign blame; punish	Identify and resolve
Problem solving	Not systematic; individuals	Systematic; teams
Improvement	Erratic	Continuous
Supplier relations	Adversarial	Partners
Jobs	Narrow, specialized; much individual effort	Broad, more general; much team effort
Focus	Product-oriented	Process-oriented

Problem Solving and Continuous Improvement

L05

Problem solving is one of the basic activities in quality improvement. In order to be successful, problem-solving efforts should follow a standard approach. Table 9-6 describes the basic steps and quality tools (explained later) used in the problem-solving process. This methodology, when used in continuous quality improvement, is called the plan-do-study-act cycle.

Step 1 Define the problem.

Give problem definition careful consideration. Quality tools include benchmarking.

Step 2 Collect data.

The solution must be based on facts. Quality tools include check sheet, scatter diagram, histogram, run chart, and control chart.

Step 3 Analyze the problem.

Find the root cause. Quality tools include Pareto chart, cause-and-effect diagram, design of experiments, and analysis of variance.

Step 4 Generate potential solutions.

Tools include brainstorming, interviewing, and surveying.

Step 5 Choose a solution and implement it.

Keep everyone informed.

Step 6 Monitor the solution to see if it accomplishes the goal.

If not, modify the solution, or return to Step 1. Quality tools include control chart and run chart.

Table 9-6

Basic steps in problem solving and quality tools used.

Plan-Do-Study-Act Cycle

The **plan-do-study-act (PDSA) cycle**, also referred to as the *Deming cycle*, is the problem-solving and quality improvement methodology used in continuous improvement. The cycle is illustrated in Figure 9-1. Representing the cycle with a circle underscores the continuing nature of its use in the continuous improvement.

plan-do-study-act (PDSA) cycle The problem-solving and quality improvement methodology used in the continuous improvement.

Figure 9-1

The PDSA cycle.

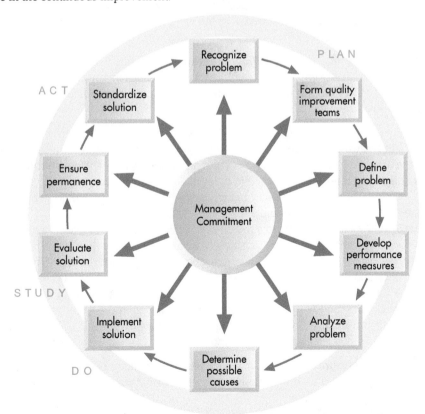

There are four basic steps in the PDSA cycle:

Plan. Begin by studying the current problem (or opportunity for quality improvement). Document the problem. Then collect data. Next, analyze the data and develop a plan for improvement. Specify measures for evaluating the plan.

Do. Implement the plan, on a small scale if possible. Document any changes made during this phase. Collect data systematically for evaluation.

Study. Evaluate the data collected during the *do* phase. Check how closely the results match the original goals of the *plan* phase.

Act. If the results are acceptable, *standardize* the new solution and communicate it to all people associated with the problem. Implement training for the new solution. If the results are unacceptable, revise the plan and repeat the cycle or cease the project.

Six Sigma

Six Sigma A more sophisticated statistical approach to problem solving and quality improvement than used in the PDSA cycle of the continuous improvement.

Six Sigma is a more sophisticated statistical approach to problem solving and quality improvement than used in the PDSA cycle of the continuous improvement. The problem-solving and quality improvement methodology in Six Sigma has five steps: define, measure, analyze, improve, and control (DMAIC). In Six Sigma the best employees are trained to become full-time change agents, called black belts, who act like internal consultants with considerable power and resources at their disposal. Consequently, Six Sigma projects are more coordinated than the improvement projects of TQM/Continuous Improvement. Each project chosen should significantly increase the value for customers, shareholders, or employees. In a narrower sense, Six Sigma refers to having very capable and precise processes that make only three or four defects per million parts produced. Companies such as Motorola, GE, Allied Signal, Boeing, and American Express have implemented Six Sigma projects successfully.[7] There will be more on Six Sigma in Chapter 10.

Basic Quality Tools

An organization can use a number of quality tools for problem solving and quality improvement. The tools aid in data collection and interpretation, and provide the basis for decision making.

The first seven tools are often referred to as the *seven basic quality tools*. Figure 9-2 provides a quick overview of the seven tools.

process flow diagram A diagram of the steps in a process.

Process Flow Diagram. A **process flow diagram** is a diagram of the steps in a process. As a problem-solving or quality improvement tool, a process flow diagram can help investigators identify possible points in a process where problems or opportunities for improvement occur. Process flow diagrams were described in Chapter 6.

check sheet A sheet of paper that provides a format for recording and organizing data in a way that facilitates collection and analysis.

Check Sheets. A **check sheet** is a sheet of paper that provides a format for recording and organizing data in a way that facilitates collection and analysis. Check sheets are designed on the basis of what the users are attempting to learn by collecting data. Many different formats can be used for a check sheet and there are many different types of check sheets. One frequently used form of check sheet deals with types of defects and when they occur, another with location of defects. These are illustrated in Figures 9-3 and 9-4.

Figure 9-3 shows tallies that denote the types of defects in a product's labels and the time of day each occurred. Problems with missing labels tend to occur early in the day and smeared print tends to occur late in the day, whereas off-centre labels are found throughout the day. Identifying types of defects and when they occur can help in pinpointing causes of the defects.

Figure 9-4 makes it easy to see where defects on a product are occurring. In this case, defects seem to be occurring on the tips of the thumb and first finger, in the finger valleys (especially between the thumb and first finger), and in the centre of the gloves. Again, this may help determine why the defects occur and lead to a solution.

histogram A chart of the frequency distribution of observed values.

Histograms. A **histogram** is a chart of the frequency distribution of observed values. Among other things, one can see if the distribution is symmetrical, what the range of values is, and if there

---

[7] T. Pyzdek, *The Six Sigma Handbook*, 2nd ed., New York: McGraw-Hill, 2003.

Process flow diagram

A diagram of the steps in a process

Check sheet

Defect	Day			
	1	2	3	4
A	///		////	/
B	//	/	//	///
C	/	////	//	////

A tool for organizing and collecting data; a tally of problems or other events by category

Histogram

A chart that shows an empirical frequency distribution

Pareto chart

A chart that arranges categories from highest to lowest frequency of occurrence

Scatter diagram

A graph that shows the degree and direction of the relationship between two variables

Control chart

A line plot of time-ordered values of a sample statistic (e.g., sample mean) with control limits

Cause-and-effect diagram

A diagram used to organize (categorize) the (possible) cause of a problem; also known as a fishbone diagram

Figure 9-2

The seven basic quality tools.

Day	Time	Type of Defect					
		Missing label	Off-centre	Smeared print	Loose or folded	Other	
M	8–9	IIII	II				6
	9–10		III				3
	10–11	I	III	I			5
	11–12		I		I	I (Torn)	3
	1–2		I				1
	2–3		II	III	I		6
	3–4		II	IIIII			8
Total		5	14	10	2	1	32

Figure 9-3

An example of a check sheet identifying the type and time of defect occurring in a product's labels.

are any unusual values. Figure 9-5 illustrates a histogram for repair times of a machine. Note the two peaks. A possible cause might be that there are two types of breakdowns, those requiring minor repairs and others requiring major repairs.

Pareto Analysis. **Pareto analysis** is a technique for focusing attention on the most important problem (or opportunity for improvement). The Pareto concept is that relatively few factors account for a large percentage of the total problems (e.g., complaints, defects), thus making these few factors important. More specifically, the Pareto concept states that approximately 80 percent of the problems are from 20 percent of the types of problems. For instance, 80 percent of machine

Pareto analysis Technique for focusing attention on the most important problem (or opportunity for improvement).

Figure 9-4 ▶

A check sheet that identifies the location of defects on a rubber glove.

x = Location of a defect

Figure 9-5 ▶

A histogram of a machine's repair times.

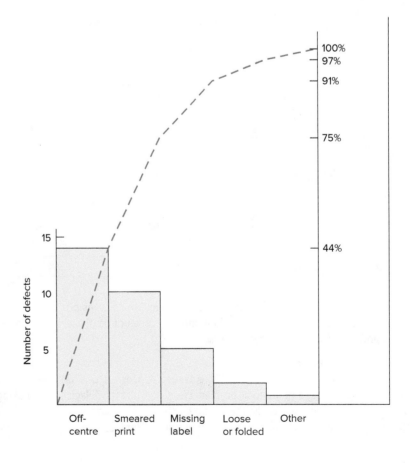

breakdowns are from 20 percent of the types of breakdowns, and 80 percent of the product defects are from 20 percent of the types of defects. The idea is to focus on resolving the most important problems, leaving the less important.

Often, it is useful to prepare a chart that shows the number of occurrences by category (type), arranged in order of frequency. Figure 9-6 illustrates such a chart corresponding to the check sheet

Figure 9-6 ▶

A Pareto chart based on data in Figure 9-3.

shown in Figure 9-3. The dominance of off-centre labels becomes apparent. Presumably, the manager and employees would first focus on trying to resolve this problem. Once they accomplish that, they could address the remaining defects in a similar fashion; "smeared print" would be the next major category to be resolved, and so on. Additional check sheets would be used to collect data to verify that the defects in these categories have been eliminated or greatly reduced. Hence, in later Pareto diagrams, categories such as "off-centre" may still appear but would be much less prominent.

Sometimes each defect type has a different consequence, and the company may assign different weights to each. Then, the weighted value (weight × frequency) will be used in the Pareto analysis. For example, an overnight package delivery company such as FedEx has a lower number of lost packages than number of abandoned calls to its call centres due to busy operators, but the lost package error is much more serious and should be dealt with first.

Scatter Diagrams. A **scatter diagram** is a plot of pairs of observations of two variables and can show the correlation between the two variables. A correlation may point to a cause of a problem. Figure 9-7 shows an example of a scatter diagram. In this particular diagram, there is a *positive* (upward-sloping) relationship between the humidity and the number of errors per hour. High values of humidity result in high numbers of errors. On the other hand, a *negative* (downward-sloping) relationship would mean that when values of one variable are high, values of the other variable are low.

The higher the correlation between the two variables, the less scatter in the points; the points will tend to line up. Conversely, if there were little or no relationship between two variables, the points would be completely scattered. In Figure 9-7, the correlation between humidity and errors seems high, because the points appear to scatter closely along an imaginary line.

scatter diagram A plot of pairs of observations of two variables that can show the correlation between the two variables.

Control Charts. A **control chart** is a line plot of time-ordered values of a sample statistic with control limits. It can be used to monitor a process to see if the process output is stable. It can help detect the presence of *assignable* or *correctable* causes of variation. Figure 9-8 illustrates a control chart. Note that the variations for this control chart seem random, with no assignable causes. Control charts can also indicate when a problem occurred and thus give insight into what caused the problem. Control charts are described in detail in Chapter 10.

control chart A line plot of time-ordered values of a sample statistic with control limits.

Cause-and-Effect Diagrams. A **cause-and-effect diagram** or *fishbone* or *Ishikawa diagram* is a diagram used to organize (categorize) the (possible) causes of a problem (the effect). Usually 4Ms—machine (and equipment), method, manpower, and materials—are used as categories. Often this tool is used in the brainstorming sessions to organize the ideas generated.

An example of a cause-and-effect diagram is shown in Figure 9-9. Each of the factors listed in the diagram is a potential source of ticket defects. Note that related factors are bunched up; for example, maintenance frequency and tension adjustment of the printer. Some factors are more

cause-and-effect diagram A diagram used to organize (categorize) the (possible) causes of a problem (the effect); also called a fishbone diagram.

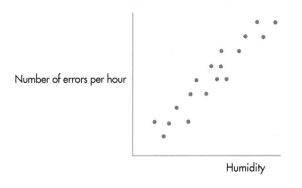

▲ **Figure 9-7**

A scatter diagram.

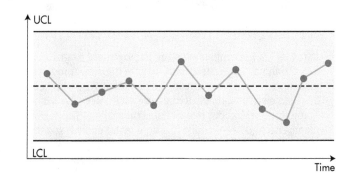

▲ **Figure 9-8**

A control chart.

Figure 9-9

Cause-and-effect diagram for ticket defects.

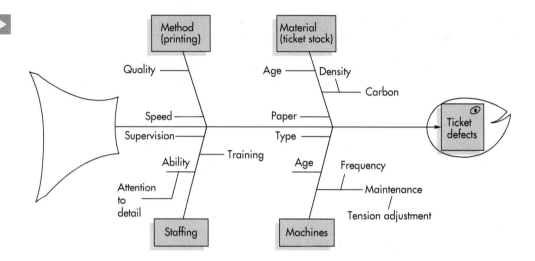

likely causes than others. If the cause is still not obvious at this point, additional investigation into the *root cause* may be necessary, involving a more in-depth data collection and analysis. For an application of the cause-and-effect diagram, see the "Kentucky Fried Chicken" OM in Action.

In addition to the seven basic quality tools above, another useful tool is the run chart.

run chart A time plot that can be used to track the values of a variable over time.

Run Charts. A **run chart** is a time plot that can be used to track the values of a variable over time. This can aid in identifying trends or other patterns that may be occurring. Figure 9-10 provides an example of a run chart showing a decreasing trend in accident frequency over time.

Figure 9-10

A run chart.

OM in *ACTION*

Kentucky Fried Chicken (KFC)

In the 1990s, KFC implemented an improvement program in its four Oklahoma City restaurants to reduce the drive-through service times, which were considered excessive. KFC bought and installed electronic timers to measure wait times. The window "hang time" was about two minutes on average. The regional manager set goals to reduce this time by 10 percent at a time. When the window hang time exceeded the goal, a buzzer would go off and the employee had to write down the reason for the delay in a "blocker log."

The more frequent causes were identified and solutions were sought for them by the improvement team. For example,

sufficient working headsets and spare batteries were provided, layout was changed to reduce the distance employees walked, and rarely ordered items were discontinued and variety of desserts was reduced. This process of continued improvement was continued for about a year (several more solutions were implemented such as pricing items so that they cost whole dollars after tax) until the average hang time was reduced to one minute.

Source: U.M. Apte and C.C. Reynolds, "Quality Management at Kentucky Fried Chicken," *Interfaces* 25(3), May/June 1995, pp. 6–21.

Methods for Generating Ideas and Reaching Consensus

Some additional tools that are useful for generating ideas in problem solving/quality improvement are brainstorming, quality circles, interviewing, benchmarking, and the 5W2H approach.

Brainstorming. **Brainstorming** is a technique for generating a free flow of ideas on finding causes and solutions, and implementing the solutions in a group of people. In successful brainstorming, criticism is absent, no single member is allowed to dominate sessions, and all ideas are welcomed.

brainstorming Technique for generating a free flow of ideas on finding causes and solutions, and implementing the solutions in a group of people.

Quality Circle. A **quality circle** is a group of workers, usually in the same department, who meet to discuss ways of improving the products and processes. Quality circles are not only a valuable source of worker input, but also can motivate workers by demonstrating management interest in worker ideas. Quality circles are usually less structured and more informal than teams involved in continuous improvement, but in some organizations quality circles have evolved into continuous improvement teams. Perhaps a major distinction between quality circles and teams is the amount of authority given to the teams. Typically, quality circles have had very little authority to implement any but minor changes; continuous improvement teams are sometimes given a great deal of authority. Consequently, continuous improvement teams have the added motivation generated by empowerment.

quality circle A group of workers who meet to discuss ways of improving the products or processes.

Interviewing. Another technique that an improvement team can use to collect information about a problem (or opportunity for improvement) is interviewing. Internal problems may require interviewing employees; external problems may require interviewing customers and suppliers.

Benchmarking. **Benchmarking** is the process of measuring an organization's performance against the best in the same or another industry. Its purpose is to establish a standard against which performance is judged, and to possibly learn how to improve. Once a benchmark has been identified, the goal is to meet or exceed that standard through improvements.

benchmarking Process of measuring an organization's performance against the best in the same or another industry.

Selecting an industry leader provides insight into what competitors are doing; however, competitors may be reluctant to share this information. Selecting organizations that are world leaders in other industries is another alternative. For example, Xerox uses many benchmarks: for employee involvement, Procter & Gamble; for quality process, Florida Power & Light and Toyota; for high-volume production, Kodak and Canon; for bill collection, American Express; for research and development, AT&T and Hewlett-Packard; for order filling and distribution, L.L. Bean and Hershey Foods; and for daily scheduling, Cummins Engine. For an example of benchmarking, see the "Benchmarking the Student Residence Application Process at Carleton University" OM in Action.

OM in ACTION

Benchmarking the Student Residence Application Process at Carleton University

The Office of Quality Initiatives at Carleton University uses benchmarking to improve various university processes. One such project was the students residence application process. Three-quarters of rooms were reserved for new students who indicated such a need in their entrance application form. When they received conditional acceptance in February, they also received a form for residence. However, they had until June to apply. Other students could also apply but were put on a waiting list. All applicants were assigned to residences in July in a batch operation. However, reassignment of rooms continued until the end of August. This resulted in a 3–4 percent vacancy rate at the beginning of September. Benchmarking involved studying the process used by other Canadian universities. The information was collected from their Web pages and by making phone calls (interviewing). Eventually, the process used at McGill University was chosen. This involved bringing the deadline for application for residence by new students from June to March. Students were assigned a room then. Other students were assigned as they applied after that. Also, an online application form was created to make the process easier. The new process resulted in a vacancy rate of less than 1 percent at the beginning of September.

Sources: M.J. Armstrong, "Benchmarking Goes to School," *Quality Progress*, May 2007, 40(5), pp. 54–58; http://www.carleton.ca/qualityinitiatives.

5W2H approach A method of asking questions about a problem that begin with *what, why, where, when, who, how,* and *how much.*

The 5W2H Approach. Asking questions about the problem (or opportunity for improvement) can lead to important insights about the cause of the problem, as well as potential ways to improve it. One method is called the **5W2H** (5 "w" words and 2 "h" words) **approach**, which asks questions about a problem that begin with *what, why, where, when, who, how,* and *how much.*

Sometimes posing the questions in a negative way may help. For example, in addition to asking, "Where is the defect on the object?" also ask, "Where else could the defect have been on the object, but isn't?" In addition to asking, "When did the defect occur?" also ask, "When else could the defect have occurred, but didn't?"

Reaching Consensus. The team approach works best when it reaches decisions based on consensus. This may be achieved using one or more of the following methods:

1. *List reduction* is applied to a list of possible solutions. Its purpose is to clarify items and, in the *process*, reduce the list of items by posing questions about affordability, feasibility, and likelihood of solving the problem (or improving the quality).

2. A *balance sheet* approach lists the pros and cons of each item and focuses discussion on important issues.

3. *Paired comparisons* is a process by which each item on a list is compared with every other item, two at a time. For each pair, team members select the preferred item. This approach forces a choice between items. It works best when the list of items is small—say, five or fewer.

Summary

- Quality has evolved from artisan's workmanship to quality control inspectors, to quality assurance and prevention of defects, and finally to incorporation of quality in the company strategy as total quality management.
- Quality is defined according to various dimensions such as performance, esthetics, reliability, and durability.
- Quality is determined during product design, process design, and production.
- Costs of quality include external and internal failure, detection, and prevention costs. Modern quality management is directed at preventing mistakes (i.e., quality assurance) rather than finding them after they occur (i.e., quality control).
- The chapter includes a description of the key contributors (gurus) to quality management: Deming, Juran, Feigenbaum, and Crosby.
- ISO 9001 is a standard for quality management system, which is made up of elements such as a quality manual and procedures; management responsibility; resource management; product realization and measurement; analysis; and improvement.
- Hazard Analysis Critical Control Point (HACCP) is also a quality management system (QMS), but its focus is on food safety. It involves finding control points for hazards and setting up quality assurance and control plans at each control point.
- The Canada Awards for Excellence (CAE) are given annually to organizations that have shown great achievement in quality management. Its criteria involve areas of leadership, planning, customer focus, people focus, process management, and supplier/partner focus. The Progressive Excellence Program has divided the implementation of the QMS efforts into four levels to make it easier to achieve. CAE requirements lead to total quality management.
- Total quality management (TQM) is a never-ending pursuit of higher quality that involves everyone in an organization. The driving force is customer satisfaction; a key activity is continuous improvement. Training of managers and workers in quality concepts, tools, and procedures is an important aspect of the approach. Improvement teams are an integral part of TQM/continuous improvement. A major activity is problem solving. The methodology used is the plan-do-study-act (PDSA) or the Deming cycle.
- The seven basic quality tools used in problem solving and quality improvement include check sheet, histogram, cause-and-effect diagram, and control and run charts.

Key Terms

5W2H approach

appraisal (detection) costs

benchmarking

brainstorming

cause-and-effect diagram

check sheet

conformance to design specifications
    during production

continuous improvement

control chart

dimensions of quality of goods

external failures

failure costs

HACCP

histogram

internal failures

ISO 9001

ISO 14000

Pareto analysis

plan-do-study-act (PDSA) cycle

Poka-yoke (fail-safeing)

prevention costs

process flow diagram

quality

quality assurance

quality at the source

quality circle

quality control

run chart

scatter diagram

Six Sigma

total quality management (TQM)

zero defects

Solved Problems

Problem 1

The Royal Canadian Mounted Police issued the following traffic tickets on a winter's weekend in Saskatoon. Make a check sheet and a Pareto diagram for the types of infraction tickets were issued for. If the RMCP wants to reduce the number of traffic infractions, what type of traffic infraction should the department focus on?

Ticket Number	Infraction	Ticket Number	Infraction
1	Excessive speed	11	Expired licence
2	Expired licence	12	DUI
3	Improper turn	13	Improper turn
4	Excessive speed	14	DUI
5	DUI	15	Excessive speed
6	DUI	16	DUI
7	Excessive speed	17	DUI
8	DUI	18	DUI
9	Improper turn	19	Excessive speed
10	DUI	20	DUI

Solution

Check sheet (list the types of infractions, tally, summarize frequencies):

Infraction	Tally	Frequency
Excessive speed	〢〢/	5
Expired licence	//	2
Improper turn	///	3
Driving under influence (DUI)	〢〢/ 〢〢/	10

Pareto diagram (array infractions from highest frequency to lowest):

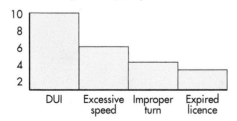

The police department should focus on reducing driving under influence (DUI). It is 50 percent of all traffic infractions.

Problem 2

A friend of yours has told you that no matter how much she studies, she does badly in exams. Help her set up a cause-and-effect diagram for her problem.

Solution

The "effect" is "does not do well in exams." The possible causes can be categorized as in 4M's: machine, method, manpower, and material. Some of the causes under each category are:

Machine: Does not know how to use computer/Internet/library effectively to study
Method: Does not know how to study effectively; does not spend enough time studying
Manpower: Does not have the right background (e.g., lacks math skills); has problem memorizing things
Material: Does not know what is important to study (types of questions in the exam); does not have the textbook and study guide

Discussion and Review Questions

1. List and briefly explain the dimensions of goods and service quality. **LO1**

2. Explain the terms *conformance to design specifications during production.* **LO1**

3. Contrast quality assurance, control, and improvement. **LO1**

4. Use the dimensions of quality to describe typical characteristics of these goods and services: **LO1**
   a. A television set
   b. A restaurant meal (a good)
   c. A restaurant meal (a service)
   d. Painting a house

5. Describe the cost of quality, and its categories. Give an example for each category for a fast-food restaurant. **LO1**

6. Describe the evolution of quality management. **LO1**

7. Select one of the quality gurus and briefly describe his contributions to quality management. **LO1**

8. What is ISO 9001, and why is it important for global businesses to have ISO 9001 certification? **LO2**

9. Briefly summarize the elements of ISO 9001. **LO2**

10. Describe HACCP. **LO3**

11. Briefly describe the criteria for the Canada Awards for Excellence. **LO4**

12. What are the key elements of TQM? **LO4**

13. Briefly describe each of the seven basic quality tools. **LO5**

14. Briefly explain each of these tools: **LO5**
    a. Brainstorming.
    b. Benchmarking.
    c. Run chart.

15. Explain each of these methods: **LO5**
    a. The plan-do-study-act (PDSA) cycle
    b. The 5W2H approach

16. List the steps of problem solving. **LO5**

17. Is there a specific set and sequence of basic quality tools used in problem solving/continuous improvement? **LO5**

18. Contrast ISO 9001, ISO 14000, HACCP, and CAE. **LO2, 3, & 4**

19. What is ISO 14000 and why is it more important now than ever? **LO2**

Taking Stock

1. What trade-offs are involved in deciding how much to spend on quality improvement? **LO1**

2. According to TQM, who needs to be involved in quality management? **LO4**

3. Name one way that technology has had an impact on quality management. **LO1–5**

4. Determine the CAE requirements that necessitate ethical behaviour. Describe why ethics is important in TQM. **LO4**

Critical Thinking Exercise

Consider an auto assembly operation. What kinds of quality problems can arise during assembly? Name one or two. How can each be fixed? Prevented? **LO1 & 5**

Experiential Learning Exercise

Identify a bad-quality good or service you recently bought. Describe the quality problem and suggest how it could have been avoided.   **LO1 & 5**

Internet Exercises

1. Visit http://www.theacsi.org, select two companies that you are familiar with, and look up their customer satisfaction indices. Do the indices agree with your knowledge of the quality of the products of the two companies? Explain.   **LO1**

2. Visit http://www.isto.ch/index_1.htm, click on "On-line Trial Exam," then on "Free sample exam (ISO 9000)" and take the test.   **LO3**

3. Visit http://www.youtube.com/watch?v=VTOxYFt1yT8 for a video on the Toyota recall.

Problems

1. Make a check sheet and then a Pareto chart for the following car service repair shop data.   **LO5**

Ticket No.	Work	Ticket No.	Work	Ticket No.	Work
1	Tires	11	Brakes	21	Lube & oil
2	Lube & oil	12	Lube & oil	22	Brakes
3	Tires	13	Battery	23	Transmission
4	Battery	14	Lube & oil	24	Brakes
5	Lube & oil	15	Lube & oil	25	Lube & oil
6	Lube & oil	16	Tires	26	Battery
7	Lube & oil	17	Lube & oil	27	Lube & oil
8	Brakes	18	Brakes	28	Battery
9	Lube & oil	19	Tires	29	Brakes
10	Tires	20	Brakes	30	Tires

2. An air-conditioning repair department manager has compiled data on the primary reason for 41 service calls during the previous week, as shown. Using the data, make a check sheet for the problem types for each customer type, and then construct a Pareto chart for each type of customer.   **LO5**

Job Number	Problem/ Customer Type	Job Number	Problem/ Customer Type	Job Number	Problem/ Customer Type
301	F/R	315	F/C	329	O/C
302	O/R	316	O/C	330	N/R
303	N/C	317	W/C	331	N/R
304	N/R	318	N/R	332	W/R
305	W/C	319	O/C	333	O/R
306	N/R	320	F/R	334	O/C
307	F/R	321	F/R	335	N/R
308	N/C	322	O/R	336	W/R
309	W/R	323	F/R	337	O/C
310	N/R	324	N/C	338	O/R
311	N/R	325	F/R	339	F/R
312	F/C	326	O/R	340	N/R
313	N/R	327	W/C	341	O/C
314	W/C	328	O/C		

Key: Problem type:
  N = Noisy
  F = Equipment failure
  W = Runs warm
  O = Odour
Customer type:
  C = Commercial customer
  R = Residential customer

3. Prepare a run chart for the number of defective computer monitors produced in a plant shown below. Workers are given a 15-minute break at 10:15 a.m. and 3:15 p.m., and a lunch break at noon. What can you conclude?   **LO5**

Interval Start Time	Number of Defects	Interval Start Time	Number of Defects	Interval Start Time	Number of Defects
8:00	1	10:45	0	2:15	0
8:15	0	11:00	0	2:30	2
8:30	0	11:15	0	2:45	2
8:45	1	11:30	1	3:00	3
9:00	0	11:45	3	3:30	0
9:15	1	1:00	1	3:45	1
9:30	1	1:15	0	4:00	0
9:45	2	1:30	0	4:15	0
10:00	3	1:45	1	4:30	1
10:30	1	2:00	1	4:45	3

4. Prepare a run chart for the following 911 call data. Use five-minute intervals (i.e., count the calls received in each five-minute interval. Use intervals of 0–4, 5–9, etc.). *Note:* Two or more calls may occur in the same minute; there were three operators on duty this night. What can you conclude from the run chart?   **LO5**

Call	Time	Call	Time	Call	Time
1	1:03	5	1:12	9	1:28
2	1:06	6	1:17	10	1:29
3	1:09	7	1:21	11	1:31
4	1:11	8	1:27	12	1:36

(continued)

Call	Time	Call	Time	Call	Time
13	1:39	23	1:56	33	2:08
14	1:42	24	2:00	34	2:08
15	1:43	25	2:00	35	2:11
16	1:44	26	2:01	36	2:12
17	1:47	27	2:02	37	2:12
18	1:48	28	2:03	38	2:13
19	1:50	29	2:03	39	2:14
20	1:52	30	2:04	40	2:14
21	1:53	31	2:06	41	2:16
22	1:56	32	2:07	42	2:19

5. Suppose that a table lamp fails to light when turned on. Prepare a cause-and-effect diagram to analyze possible causes. Use categories such as lamp, cord, etc. **LO5**

6. Prepare a cause-and-effect diagram to analyze why a machine has produced a defective part. **LO5**

7. Prepare a scatter diagram for each of the following pairs of variables and then express in words the apparent relationship between the two variables. Put the first variable on the horizontal axis and the second variable on the vertical axis. **LO5**

a.
Age	24	30	22	25	33	27	36	58	37	47	54	28	42	55
Days absent	6	5	7	6	4	5	4	1	3	2	2	5	3	1

b.
Temperature (°C)	18	17	22	19	28	14	24	30	25	18	26
Error rate		1	2	0	0	3	3	1	5	2	1	3

8. The Royal Canadian Mounted Police has responded to a vehicle accident along a stretch of highway. Prepare a cause-and-effect diagram for this accident. Use categories such as vehicle, driver, weather, etc. **LO5**

9. Suppose you are going to have a prescription filled at a local pharmacy. Referring to the dimensions of service quality, for each dimension, give an example of how you would judge the quality of the service. **LO1**

10. Prepare a HACCP analysis for burgers made in a fast-food restaurant such as McDonald's. **LO3**

11. Consider the processing of Northern (cold water) shrimp. They are caught off the East and West coast,

beheaded at sea and frozen or iced, and then further processed on shore. Consider a processing that results in cooked, peeled, and frozen small shrimps. Government regulations require that product not be tainted (rancid; bad taste and odour) or unsafe, or decomposed (rotten), and the bag/box should be accurately weighed and labelled with a product code (including place and date of processing). A process flow diagram for processing shrimp is given on the layout diagram below. Identify hazards/defects, and determine a Critical Control Point and a quality assurance/control plan for each hazard/defect.[8] **LO3**

8 http://www.inspection.gc.ca/english/anima/fispoi/qmp/files/cookshrp.doc (accessed 2006).

MINI-CASE

North Shore University Hospital

North Shore University Hospital in New York has initiated some improvement projects in order to accommodate the increasing number of patients. One project involved reducing the turnaround time of patient-discharge-to-bed-ready process, displayed below.

The process seemed to take many hours with significant variations. To study this process, the times between pairs of consecutive steps of the process for 195 patient discharges were computed and plotted (see distributions below). For example, Discharge-bed tracking system (step 1 to step 2) took from 200 to 850 minutes.

> Discharge time entered by clerical support associate and patient receives discharge instructions
>
> Time discharge entered into bed tracking system by patient care associate/support care associate who walks the patient out
>
> Time environmental services enters "in progress" in bed tracking system
>
> Time environmental services enters "clean" in bed tracking system
>
> Time admission RN is notified of clean/ready bed

Identify which part(s) of the process could be targeted for time reduction and suggest some solutions.

Source: A. Pellicone and M. Martocci, "Faster Turnaround Time," *Quality Progress*, March 2006, 39(3), pp. 31–36. Copyright © 1993–2014 American Society for Quality. All rights reserved. Reprinted with permission. http://asq.org. No further distribution allowed without permission.

MINI-CASE

Chick-n-Gravy Dinner Line

The operations manager of a company that produces frozen dinners had received numerous complaints from supermarkets about the company's Chick-n-Gravy dinners. The manager asked her assistant, Ann, to investigate the matter and to report her recommendations.

Ann's first task was to determine what problems were generating the complaints. The majority of complaints centred on five defects: underfilled packages, a missing item, spilled/mixed items, unacceptable taste, and improperly sealed packages.

Next, she took 800 samples of dinners from the two production lines and examined each sample, making note of any defects that she found. A summary of those results is shown in the table below.

What should Ann recommend to her boss?

				Defect Observed			
Date	Time	Line	Underfilled	Missing Item	Spilled/Mixed	Unacceptable Taste	Improperly Sealed
5/12	0900	1		√√	√	√√√	
5/12	1330	2			√√		√√
5/13	1000	2				√	√√√
5/13	1345	1	√√		√√		
5/13	1530	2		√√	√√√		√
5/14	0830	1		√√√		√√√	
5/14	1100	2	√√		√	√√	
5/14	1400	1			√		√

(continued)

				Defect Observed			
Date	Time	Line	Underfilled	Missing Item	Spilled/Mixed	Unacceptable Taste	Improperly Sealed
5/15	1030	1		√√√		√√√√√	
5/15	1145	2			√	√√	
5/15	1500	1	√		√		
5/16	0845	2				√√	√√
5/16	1030	1		√√√	√	√√√	
5/16	1400	1					
5/16	1545	2	√	√√√√√	√	√	√√

MINI-CASE

Tip Top Markets

Tip Top Markets is a regional chain of supermarkets. On July 28, Karen Martin, manager of one of the stores, was disturbed by the large number of recent complaints from customers at her store, particularly on Tuesdays, so she obtained complaint records from the store's customer service desk for the last three Tuesdays. These are shown below.

Analyze the data and make a recommendation to Karen.

July 13

wrong price on spaghetti	overcharged
water on floor	out of brown rice
store looked messy	out of mushrooms
store too warm	overcharged
checkout lines too long	checkout wait too long
cashier not friendly	shopping cart broken
out of feta cheese	couldn't find Aspirin
overcharged	out of brown lunch bags
out of Saran Wrap	out of straws
out of Haagen-Dazs Bars	

July 20

out of low-salt pickles	out of large eggs
checkout lines too slow	out of cran-apple juice
broken glass on floor	out of pretzels
lost keys	out of apricot jam

wrong price on sale item	telephone out of order
overcharged on corn	out of cocktail sauce
wrong price on baby food	water on floor
out of 500-mL Tide	out of frozen onion rings
out of green tea	out of frozen squash
checkout lines too long	out of powdered sugar
out of romaine lettuce	out of nonfat peanut butter

July 27

out of dill pickles	open milk carton found in fridge
reported accident in parking lot	
wrong price on cran-apple juice	store too warm
out of carrot juice	oatmeal spilled in bulk section
out of licorice sticks	telephone out of order
out of chocolate milk	out of soap
out of Lava Bars	water on floor
windows dirty	out of glazed doughnuts
out of iceberg lettuce	out of baby carrots
store decorations are dated	spaghetti sauce on floor
out of St. John's wort	out of Skippy crunchy peanut butter
out of vanilla soy milk	out of butter

Staples' Extended-Service Warranty Process

Ron bought a Toshiba laptop with a two-year extended warranty from Staples Store number 52 in Saskatoon on November 8, 2007. The laptop developed a problem in January 2009: a broken wire in the AC power supply. In the beginning of February 2009, Ron went to Store 52 with his power supply and showed the staff the problem. They said that he should call the Toronto service centre to get a claim number. Ron called the Toronto service centre and explained the problem. After about 10 minutes he received a repair number. He found out that he has to also turn in the laptop even though the problem was only with the power supply. On February 11, 2009, Ron took his laptop and power supply, in the original box, to Store 52. It took the employee about 20–25 minutes to issue a Repair Depot Technician Service Request (he had difficulty completing the form on the computer). Ron waited until March 23, when he went to Store 52 around 1 p.m. He told the employee that it had been more than six weeks since he turned in his laptop and power supply, and he was wondering what had happened. First, the employee brushed off Ron's question by saying that repairs may take two to six weeks. Ron pointed out that it had been more than six weeks and the repair was a simple replacement of a common power supply. Reluctantly, the employee tried to pull up the service request on the computer. He had

trouble locating it. After five minutes, he found the service request, which appeared to be cancelled. The employee couldn't explain what happened and said that Ron should return and talk to Dylan after 4 p.m. Unfortunately, Ron didn't have time to do that. The next day, he went to Store 52 around 7 p.m., and asked for Dylan. The manager, Jen, said that Dylan wasn't working then. Ron asked Jen if she could help. She couldn't find the service request on her computer, so she checked in her office in the back. After 10 minutes, she returned and said that the laptop had been shipped last Friday from Winnipeg and should arrive soon. On April 3, Ron received a phone call from Store 52 saying that the laptop had arrived. Ron went there the next day. An employee gave him his laptop and power supply. Ron pointed out that he had also turned in the box (which contained some installation CDs, manuals, etc.). She read the Service Request form and said that she didn't think that was correct. Ron left the store with his laptop and power supply. On April 9, Ron received a phone call from Store 52 saying that his laptop box was there to be picked up.

Questions

1. State the quality problems incurred during the extended service warranty process described above.

2. For each quality problem, determine a quality assurance plan that could have prevented it in the first place.

CHAPTER 10
Statistical Quality Control

Learning Objectives

After completing this chapter, you should be able to:

LO1 List and briefly explain the elements of the statistical process control planning process.

LO2 Explain how control charts are designed and the concepts that underlie their use, and solve problems that involve control chart design and use.

LO3 Assess process capability, and solve problems involving process capability.

LO4 Describe Six Sigma quality and design of experiments.

A recent report released by the Canadian Institute for Health Information estimates that preventable medical errors kill up to 24,000 Canadians each year. In addition, patients spend more than 1 million extra days in hospital being treated for complications relating to their care. One of the most common types of preventable medical errors relates to medication. One in nine adults reported receiving an incorrect dose or type of medication. Health care is a complex environment where even small errors can maim or kill. Consequently, it is critical for hospitals to find the root causes of these medical errors and then determine how to prevent them from reoccurring.

To address this issue, some hospitals are now using bar codes. With bar code technology, a nurse scans each patient's wristband as well as the medications to be given. This allows nurses who administer drugs to check to make sure the drug, dosage, and timing are all appropriate. If the bar codes on the patient and medication do not match, the nurse will be given a warning. Such innovations hold great promise for reducing the frequency of medication errors.

Source: Health Care in Canada 2004 booklet, Canadian Institute for Health Information, https://secure.cihi.ca/free_products/hcic2004_e.pdf (accessed April 5, 2014).

Statistical Quality Control

LO1

The best companies emphasize *designing quality into the process (e.g., by undertaking continuous improvement and Six Sigma quality projects), thereby greatly reducing the need for inspection.* The least progressive companies rely heavily on receiving and shipping inspections. As you might expect, different business organizations are in different stages of this evolutionary process. Inspection alone is generally not sufficient to achieve a reasonable level of quality. Most companies occupy a middle ground that involves some inspection and a great deal of process control. The most progressive have achieved an inherent level of quality so that they can avoid any inspection/test and process control. That is the ultimate goal.

Statistical quality control uses statistical techniques and sampling in monitoring and testing of quality of goods and services.

statistical quality control Use of statistical techniques and sampling in monitoring and testing of quality of goods and services.

The part of statistical quality control that relies primarily on inspection of previously produced items is referred to as *acceptance sampling.* This is described in the chapter supplement, which can be accessed on Connect. The part of statistical quality control that occurs during production are referred to as statistical process control, and we examine this in this chapter (see Figures 10-1 for phases of statistical quality control in a company and 10-2 for location of use of acceptance sampling and statistical process control within production).

Statistical quality control is important because it provides an economical way to evaluate the quality of products and meet the expectations of the customers.

Inspection is an appraisal activity that compares the quality of a good or service to a standard. Inspection is a vital but often unappreciated aspect of quality control. Although for well-designed processes little inspection is necessary, inspection cannot be completely eliminated. To determine whether a process is functioning as intended or to verify that a batch or lot of raw materials or final products does not contain more than a specified percentage of defective goods, it is necessary to physically examine at least some of the items in question.

inspection Appraisal of a good or service against a standard.

Statistical Process Control Planning Process

Effective statistical process control requires the following planning steps:

1. Define the quality characteristics important to customers, and how each is measured.

2. For each characteristic,

   a. Determine a quality control point.

   b. Plan how inspection is to be done, how much to inspect, and whether centralized or on-site.

   c. Plan the corrective action.

◀ **Figure 10-1**

Phases of statistical quality control/improvement in a company.

◀ **Figure 10-2**

Location of use of an acceptance sampling and statistical process control within production.

Food and beverage companies use Omron Electronics' fibre optic sensors to monitor processes and to perform quality inspections such as checking beverage content and caps.

Define the Quality Characteristics. The first step is to define, in sufficient detail, what is to be controlled. It is not enough, for example, to simply refer to a painted surface. The paint can have a number of important characteristics such as its colour, gloss, thickness, and resistance to fading or chipping. Different characteristics may require different approaches for control purposes. Only those characteristics that can be measured are candidates for control. Thus, it is important to consider how measurement will be accomplished. There must be a standard that can be used to evaluate the measurement. This relates to the level of quality being sought.

A Toyota technician prepares to remove the accelerator assembly in a recalled Toyota Avalon.

Determine a Quality Control Point. Many operations have numerous possible inspection points. Because each inspection adds to the cost of a product, it is important to restrict inspection efforts to the points where they can do the most good. In manufacturing, some of the typical inspection points are:

1. *At the beginning of the process.* There is little sense in paying for goods that do not meet quality standards and in spending time and effort on material that is bad to begin with.

2. *At the end of the process.* Customer satisfaction and company's image are at stake here, and repairing or replacing products in the field is usually much more costly than doing it at the factory.

3. *At the operation where a characteristic of interest to customers is first determined.* In particular, before a costly, irreversible, or covering (e.g., painting) operation.

The HACCP system described in the previous chapter also provides some guidelines for determining the quality control points.

In the service sector, inspection points include where personnel and customer interface (e.g., service counter) and the parts of the facility that customer sees. Table 10-1 illustrates some examples of inspection points and quality characteristics inspected in some businesses.

How Inspection Is to Be Done. This is usually technical and needs engineering knowledge. For example, to test clarity of beer, a white light is shined through it and its dispersion is measured.

How Much to Inspect. The amount of inspection can range from no inspection whatsoever to inspection of each item. Low-cost, high-volume items such as paper clips, nails, and pencils often require little inspection because (1) the cost associated with passing defective items is quite low and (2) the processes that produce these items are usually highly reliable, so that defects are rare. Conversely, items that have large costs associated with passing defective products often require more intensive inspection. Thus, critical components of a vehicle are closely scrutinized because of the risk to human safety and the high cost of failure. In high-volume systems, automated inspection is one option that may be employed.

The majority of quality control applications lie somewhere between the two extremes. Most require some inspection, but it is neither possible nor economically feasible to examine every product. The cost of inspection and resulting interruptions of a process (if inspection is not automated) typically outweigh the benefits of 100 percent inspection. However, the cost of letting undetected defects slip through is sufficiently high that inspection cannot be completely ignored. The amount of inspection needed is governed by the costs of inspection and the expected cost of passing defective items.

Type of Business	Inspection Points	Quality Characteristics
Fast food	Service counter	Appearance, friendliness of server, waiting time
	Eating area	Cleanliness
	Building and grounds	Appearance, safety hazards
	Kitchen	Cleanliness, quality of food, temperature and time of food storage, temperature and time of cooking, health regulations, and hygiene
Supermarket	Cashiers	Accuracy, courtesy, waiting time, productivity
	Aisles and stockrooms	Clutter
	Shelf stock	Availability, rotation of perishables, appearance
	Shopping carts	Good working condition, availability, theft/vandalism
	Building and parking lot	Appearance, safety, good lighting
Brewery	Hot/cold liquor tanks	Bitterness
	Filtering	Clarity
	Fermentation tank	Alcohol content

◄ Table 10-1

Examples of inspection points and quality characteristics in some businesses.

As illustrated in Figure 10-3, if inspection activities increase, inspection costs increase, but the cost of passing defectives decreases. The goal is to minimize the sum of these two costs. In other words, it may not pay to attempt to catch every defect, particularly if the cost of inspection exceeds the penalties associated with letting some defects get through.

As a rule of thumb, operations with a high proportion of human involvement necessitate more inspection than mechanical operations, which tend to be more reliable. The frequency of inspection depends largely on the rate at which a process may go out of control. A stable process will require only infrequent checks, whereas an unstable one or one that has recently given trouble will require more frequent checks. Likewise, many small lots will require more samples than a few large lots because it is important to obtain sample data from each lot. For high-volume, repetitive operations, computerized automatic inspections at critical points in a process are cost effective.

Centralized versus On-site Inspection. Some situations require that inspections be performed on site. For example, inspecting the hull of a ship for cracks requires inspectors to visit the ship. If the test is simple enough (e.g., measuring dimensions), it can be done by a handheld

Figure 10-3 ▶

The amount of inspection is optimal when the sum of the costs of inspection and passing defectives is minimized.

A Mattel technician in China does a pulling test with a Dora the Explorer doll in the name of product safety. Mattel has 10 labs in 6 countries and has set up strict requirements for vendors because of safety recalls.

caliper or micrometer. Alternatively, automated inspection, e.g., using a vision system or laser gauge, can be installed on the machine (which can perform 100 percent inspection). At other times, specialized tests need to be performed and can best be performed in a lab (e.g., medical tests, analyzing food and water samples, testing metals for hardness or paper for tensile strength and tear resistance, running viscosity tests on lubricants, and measuring dimensions that require large expensive coordinate measuring machines).

The central issue in the decision concerning on-site or lab inspections is whether the advantages of specialized lab tests are worth the time and interruption needed to obtain the results. Specialized equipment, skilled quality control inspectors, and a more favourable test environment (less noise, vibrations, and dust) offer strong arguments for using a lab. More companies are now relying on self-inspections by operators on-site. See the "Harley-Davidson" OM in Action later in the chapter for an example of on-site inspection.

Plan the Corrective Action. When a process is judged out of control for an important characteristic, the process should be stopped and corrective action must be taken. This involves uncovering the cause (e.g., worn-out tool bits, or failure to follow specified procedures) and correcting it. Also, any potentially off-specification (i.e., defective) parts or products should be tested, and if defective, should be either reworked or scrapped. To ensure that corrective action is effective, the output of a process must be monitored for a sufficient period of time to verify that the problem has been eliminated.

Statistical Process Control Charts

Statistical process control (SPC) is concerned with statistical evaluation of the product in the production process. To do SPC, the operator takes periodic samples from the process and compares them with predetermined limits. If the sample results fall outside the limits, the operator stops the process and takes corrective action. If the sample results fall within the limits, the operator allows the process to continue.

statistical process control (SPC) Statistical evaluation of the product in the production process.

Types of Variations

All processes that produce a good or service exhibit a certain amount of "natural" variation in their output. The variations are created by the combined influences of countless minor factors, each one so unimportant that even if it could be identified and eliminated, the decrease in process variability would be negligible. In effect, this variability is inherent in the process. It is often referred to as a *chance* or **random variation**. In Deming's terms, this is referred to as *common variability* of the process. The amount of random variation differs from process to process. For instance, older machines generally exhibit a higher degree of random variation than newer machines, partly because of worn parts and partly because new machines may incorporate design improvements that lessen the variability in their output.

random variation Natural variation in the output of a process, created by countless minor factors.

A second kind of variability in process output is nonrandom and is called **assignable variation**. In Deming's terms, this is referred to as *special variation*. Unlike random variation, the main sources of assignable variation can usually be identified (assigned to a specific cause) and eliminated. Excessive tool wear, equipment that needs adjustment, defective materials, and human errors (e.g., failure to follow correct procedures) are typical sources of assignable variation.

assignable variation Nonrandom variability in process output; a variation whose cause can be identified.

The main task in SPC is to distinguish assignable from random variation. Taking a sample of two or more observations and calculating a sample statistic such as sample mean makes the task easier. This is because random variations are reduced in sample statistics.

Sampling and Sampling Distributions

In statistical process control, periodic samples of process output are taken and sample statistics, such as sample means or the number of occurrences of a certain type of outcome, are determined. The sample statistics can be used to judge randomness of process variations. The sample statistics exhibit variation, just as processes do. The variability of a sample statistic is described by its *sampling distribution*, which is the theoretical distribution of the values of the statistic for all possible samples of a given size from the process. Consider the process for filling bottles with soft drink. If the amount of soft drink in a large number of bottles is measured accurately, we would discover slight differences among the bottles. If these amounts were arranged on a graph, the frequency distribution would reflect the *process variability*. The values would be clustered close to the process average (e.g., 2 litres), but some of the values would vary somewhat from the mean.

If we take *samples* of three bottles at a time and compute, for example, the *mean* amount of soft drink in each sample, we would discover that these values also vary, just as the *individual* values varied. However, the distribution of the sample mean is more concentrated around process mean (2 litres) than the distribution of process. Figure 10-4 illustrates a sampling distribution and a process distribution (i.e., individual bottles).

The sampling distribution of the sample mean exhibits less variability (i.e., it is less spread out) than the process distribution. This reflects the *averaging* that occurs in computing the sample means: high and low values in samples tend to offset each other, resulting in less variability among sample means than among individual values. Note that both distributions have the same mean. Finally, note that the sampling distribution is approximately *Normal*. This is true even if the process distribution is not normal.

central limit theorem The distribution of sample averages tends to be normal regardless of the shape of the process distribution.

In the case of sample means, the **central limit theorem** states that as the sample size increases, the distribution of sample averages approaches a normal distribution regardless of the shape of the sampled population. This tends to be the case even for fairly small sample sizes. For other sample statistics, the normal distribution serves as a reasonable approximation to the shape of the actual sampling distribution.

Figure 10-5 illustrates what happens to the shape of the sampling distribution relative to the sample size. The larger the sample size, the narrower the sampling distribution. This means that the likelihood that a sample statistic is close to the true value in the population is higher for large samples than for small samples.

A sampling distribution serves as the theoretical basis for distinguishing between random and assignable variation of a sampling statistic. Very simply, limits are selected within which most values of a sample statistic should fall if its variations are random. The limits are stated in terms of number of standard deviations from the distribution mean. Typical limits are ±2 standard

Figure 10-4 ▶

The sampling distribution of the sample mean, for a given sample size, has less variability than the process.

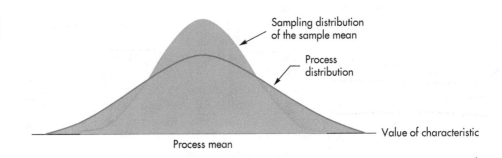

Figure 10-5 ▶

The larger the sample size, the narrower the sampling distribution.

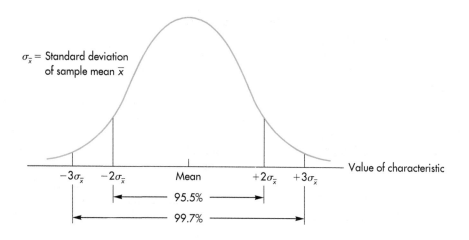

$\sigma_{\bar{x}}$ = Standard deviation of sample mean $\bar{x}$

Figure 10-6

Percentage of values under the curve within given ranges in a Normal sampling distribution of the sample mean.

deviations or ±3 standard deviations. Figure 10-6 illustrates these possible limits and the probability that a sample statistic would fall within those limits if only random variations are present. Conversely, if the value of a sample statistic falls outside those limits, there is only a small probability ($1 - 0.9974 = 0.0026$ for ± 3 limits, and $1 - 0.9544 = 0.0456$ for ± 2 limits) that the value reflects random variation. Instead, we can conclude that the process most likely has shifted, and hence there is an assignable cause.

Control Charts

An important tool in statistical process control is the control chart, which was developed by Walter Shewhart. A **control chart** is a *time-ordered* plot of a sample statistic, with limits. It is used to distinguish between random and assignable variation (or equivalently no shift and a shift in the process). It has upper and lower limits, called control limits. A control chart is illustrated in Figure 10-7. The purpose of a control chart is to monitor process output to see if it is random. A necessary (but not sufficient) condition for a process to be deemed "in control," or stable, is for all the data points to fall between the upper and lower control limits. Conversely, a data point that falls outside either limit would be taken as evidence that the process most likely has shifted, and hence there is an assignable cause, therefore, not "in control." If that happens, the process would be halted to find and correct the cause of the nonrandom variation. The essence of statistical process control is to assure that the output of a process is random so that *future output* will be random.

The basis for a control chart is the sampling distributions, which essentially describes random variability. There is, however, one minor difficulty relating to the use of a normal sampling distribution. The theoretical distribution extends in either direction to *infinity*. Therefore, *any* value is theoretically possible, even one that is a considerable distance from the mean of the distribution. However, as mentioned before, we know that 99.7 percent of the values will fall within

control chart A time-ordered plot of a sample statistic with limits.

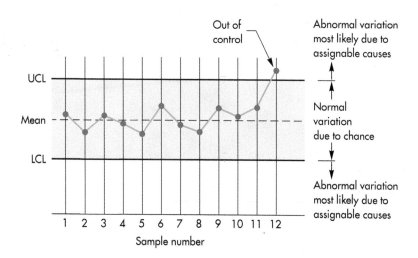

Figure 10-7

The components of a sample mean control chart.

±3 standard deviations of the mean of the distribution. Therefore, we could decide to set the limits at ±3 standard deviations from the mean, and conclude that any value that was farther away from the mean than these limits reflects a shift in the process, and hence an assignable variation.

control limits The dividing lines between random and assignable deviations from the mean of the distribution.

In effect, these limits are called **control limits**. Figure 10-8 illustrates how control limits for a sample mean control chart are based on the sampling distribution of the sample mean.

Control charts have two limits that separate random and assignable variations. The larger value is the *upper control limit* (UCL), and the smaller value is the *lower control limit* (LCL). A sample statistic that falls between these two limits suggests random variation (i.e., no process shift) while a value outside or on either limit suggests assignable variation (i.e., the deviation from the long-standing known process mean is so large that the process must have shifted).

Note that the control limits are not directly related to specification limits. Control limits are based on the characteristic of the process, whereas the specification limits are based on the desired characteristic of the product. The process is capable if the process values fall within the specification limits. However, control limits are for sample statistics, so they should fall well within the specification limits. This will be further explained in the "Process Capability" section later in the chapter.

It is important to recognize that because any control limits will leave some area in the *tails* of the distribution, there is a small probability that a sample statistic value will fall outside the limits *even though only random variations are present* (i.e., there is no process shift). For example, if ±2 Sigma (standard deviation) limits are used, they would include 95.5 percent of the values. Consequently, the complement of that number (100 percent − 95.5 percent = 4.5 percent) would not be included. That percentage (or *probability*) is sometimes referred to as the probability of a **Type I error**, where the "error" is concluding that a process has shifted (i.e., an assignable variation is present) when it has not (i.e., only random variation is present). This is also referred to as *alpha* risk, where alpha (α) is the sum of the probabilities in the two tails. Figure 10-9 illustrates this concept.

Type I error Concluding that a process has shifted (i.e., an assignable variation is present) when it has not (i.e., only random variation is present).

Type II error Concluding that a process has not shifted (i.e., only random variation is present) when it has (i.e., an assignable variation is present).

Using wider limits (e.g., ±3 Sigma limits) reduces the probability of a Type I error because it decreases the area in the tails of the distribution. However, wider limits make it more difficult to detect assignable variations (i.e., a shift in the process) *if* they are present. For example, the process might shift (an assignable cause of variation) enough to be detected by Two Sigma limits, but not enough to be readily apparent using Three Sigma limits. That could lead to a second kind of error, known as a **Type II error**, which is concluding that a process has not shifted (i.e., only random variation is present) when it has (i.e., an assignable variation is present). In theory, the costs of making each error should be balanced by their probabilities. However, in practice, Two Sigma

Figure 10-8 ▶

Control limits are based on the sampling distribution of the sample mean.

Figure 10-9 ▶

The probability of a Type I error.

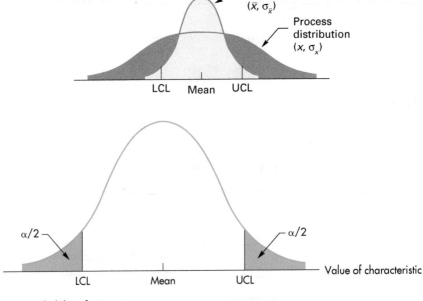

α = Probability of a Type I error

		And the conclusion is that it is:	
		In Control	Out of Control
If a process is actually:	In control	No error	Type I error (producer's risk)
	Out of control	Type II error (consumer's risk)	No error

◀ **Table 10-2**

Type I and Type II errors.

limits and Three Sigma limits are commonly used without specifically referring to the probability of a Type II error.

Table 10-2 illustrates how Type I and Type II errors occur.

Each sample is represented by a single value (e.g., the sample mean) on a control chart. Moreover, each value is compared to the extremes of the sampling distribution (the control limits) to judge if it is within the acceptable range. Figure 10-10 illustrates this concept.

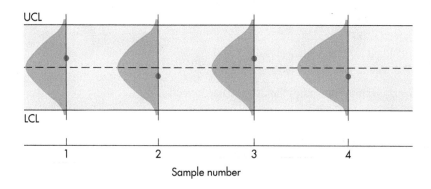

◀ **Figure 10-10**

Each sample mean (a red dot) is compared to the control limits.

What is the probability x will be within $+/-1.5$ from the mean of a standard normal distribution?

◀ **Example 1**

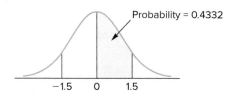

To find the area under the curve between -1.5 and 1.5, we look up 1.5 from Appendix B, Table A. Since Table A shows the areas from 0 to 1.5, in order to find the probability x will be within $+/-1.5$, we need to double the value listed under the table, which gives us $0.4332 \times 2 = 0.8664$. (See above figure).

Designing Control Charts. The following steps are usually taken to design control charts:

1. Determine a sample size n (usually between 2 and 20). The choice of n depends on the cost of inspection versus the expected cost of Type II error. The larger n is, the smaller the probability of Type II error.

2. Obtain 20 to 25 samples of size n. Compute the appropriate sample statistic for each sample (e.g., sample mean).

3. Establish preliminary control limits using appropriate formulas (given in following sections), and graph them.

4. Plot the sample statistic values on the control chart, and note whether any points fall outside the control limits.

5. If you find no points outside control limits, assume that there is no assignable cause and therefore the process is stable and in control (other cases showing instability will be illustrated at the end of this section). If not, investigate and correct assignable causes of variation; then repeat the process from step 2 on.

Sample Mean and Range Control Charts

sample mean ($\bar{x}$) control chart
The control chart for sample mean, used to monitor the process mean.

The **sample mean control ($\bar{x}$) chart**, sometimes referred to as an $\bar{x}$ chart, is used to monitor the process mean. The centre line used in an $\bar{x}$ chart represents the process mean. This is estimated by taking a few samples, computing their mean, and then averaging these means. These samples are used to ensure that the process is stable and in control. It can be shown that the average of means is the mean of all the observations in the samples, and hence is called the grand mean. The control limits can be determined in two ways. The choice depends on what information is available.

The first approach to calculate the control limits is to use the standard deviation of the process, σ.

$$\text{Upper Control Limit (UCL}_{\bar{x}}) = \bar{\bar{x}} + z\sigma_{\bar{x}}$$

$$\text{Lower Control Limit (LCL}_{\bar{x}}) = \bar{\bar{x}} - z\sigma_{\bar{x}}$$

(10-1)

where

$\sigma_{\bar{x}}$ = Standard deviation of the sampling distribution of the sample mean = $\sigma/\sqrt{n}$
σ = Process standard deviation
n = Sample size
z = Standard Normal deviate (usually $z = 3$)
$\bar{\bar{x}}$ = Average of sample means = grand mean

The following example illustrates the use of these formulas.

Example 2 ▶

A quality inspector took five samples, each with four observations, of the length of a part (in cm). She computed the mean of each sample (see table below).

a. Use the following data to obtain Three Sigma (i.e., $z = 3$) control limits for sample mean. Is the process in control?

b. If a new sample has values 12.10, 12.19, 12.12, and 12.14, using the sample mean control chart in part a, has the process mean changed (i.e., is there an assignable variation)?

It is known from previous experience that the standard deviation of the process is .02 cm.

		Sample				
		1	**2**	**3**	**4**	**5**
	1	12.11	12.15	12.09	12.12	12.09
	2	12.10	12.12	12.09	12.10	12.14
Observation	**3**	12.11	12.10	12.11	12.08	12.13
	4	12.08	12.11	12.15	12.10	12.12
	$\bar{x}$	12.10	12.12	12.11	12.10	12.12

SOLUTION

a. $\bar{\bar{x}} = \dfrac{12.10 + 12.12 + 12.11 + 12.10 + 12.12}{5} = 12.11$ cm

Using formula 10-1, with $z = 3$, $n = 4$ observations per sample, and $\sigma = .02$, we find:

$$\text{UCL}_{\bar{x}}: 12.11 + 3\left(\frac{.02}{\sqrt{4}}\right) = 12.14$$

$$\text{LCL}_{\bar{x}}: 12.11 - 3\left(\frac{.02}{\sqrt{4}}\right) = 12.08$$

Because all 5 sample means fall between the control limits (12.08 and 12.14), the process is in control.

b. $\bar{x}_6 = \dfrac{12.10 + 12.19 + 12.12 + 12.14}{4} = 12.1375$ cm

Because $12.08 < 12.1375 < 12.14$, the process mean has not changed (i.e., there is only random variation).

Note: The fact that some of the *individual* measurements fall outside the control limits (e.g., the first observation in Sample 2, the last observation in Sample 3, and the second observation in Sample 6) is irrelevant. You can see why by referring back to Figure 10-8: *individual* values are represented by the process distribution, a large portion of which lies outside the control limits for the sample *mean*.

A second approach to calculate the control limits is to use the sample *range* (i.e., maximum value − minimum value in the sample) as a measure of process variability (instead of σ). The appropriate formulas for sample mean control limits in this case are:

$$\text{UCL}_{\bar{x}} = \bar{\bar{x}} + A_2\bar{R}$$
$$\text{LCL}_{\bar{x}} = \bar{\bar{x}} - A_2\bar{R}$$

(10-2)

where

A_2 can be obtained from Table 10-3
$\bar{R}$ = Average of sample ranges of a few samples

		Factors for *R*-Charts	
Number of Observations in Sample, n	**Factor for** $\bar{x}$ **Charts,** A_2	**Lower Control Limit,** D_3	**Upper Control Limit,** D_4
2	1.88	0	3.27
3	1.02	0	2.57
4	0.73	0	2.28
5	0.58	0	2.11
6	0.48	0	2.00
7	0.42	0.08	1.92
8	0.37	0.14	1.86
9	0.34	0.18	1.82
10	0.31	0.22	1.78
11	0.29	0.26	1.74
12	0.27	0.28	1.72
13	0.25	0.31	1.69
14	0.24	0.33	1.67
15	0.22	0.35	1.65
16	0.21	0.36	1.64
17	0.20	0.38	1.62
18	0.19	0.39	1.61
19	0.19	0.40	1.60
20	0.18	0.41	1.59

◄ **Table 10-3**

Factors for Three Sigma control limits for $\bar{x}$- and R-charts.

Source: Adapted from Eugene Grant and Richard Leavenworth, *Statistical Quality Control,* 4th ed. (New York: McGraw-Hill, 1972), p. 645.

Twenty samples of $n = 8$ have been taken of the weight of a part. The average of sample ranges for the 20 samples is .016 kg, and the average of sample means is 3 kg. Determine Three Sigma control limits for sample mean of this process.

◄ **Example 3**

SOLUTION

$\bar{\bar{x}} = 3, \quad \bar{R} = .016, \quad A_2 = .37 \quad \text{for} \quad n = 8 \text{ (from Table 10-3)}$

$\text{UCL}_{\bar{x}} = \bar{\bar{x}} + A_2\bar{R} = 3 + .37(.016) = 3.006 \text{ kg}$

$\text{UCL}_{\bar{x}} = \bar{\bar{x}} - A_2\bar{R} = 3 - .37(.016) = 2.994 \text{ kg}$

---

sample range (R) control chart The control chart for sample range, used to monitor process dispersion or spread.

Sample Range Control Chart. The **sample range (R) control chart** is used to monitor process dispersion or spread. Although the underlying sampling distribution is not Normal, the concept for design and use of sample range control chart is much the same as that for $\bar{x}$ chart. Control limits for sample range control chart are found using these formulas:

$$\begin{Vmatrix} \text{UCL}_R = D_4\bar{R} \\ \text{LCL}_R = D_3\bar{R} \end{Vmatrix}$$

(10-3)

where values of D_3 and D_4 are obtained from Table 10-3.

Example 4 ▶

Twenty-five samples of $n = 10$ observations have been taken from a milling process. The average of sample ranges is .01 centimetre. Determine upper and lower control limits for the sample range.

SOLUTION

$\bar{R} = .01 \text{ cm}, \quad n = 10$

From Table 10-3, for $n = 10, \quad D_4 = 1.78$ and $D_3 = .22$

$\text{UCL}_R = 1.78(.01) = .0178 \text{ cm}$

$\text{LCL}_R = .22(.01) = .0022 \text{ cm}$

In Example 4, a sample range of .0178 centimetre or more would suggest that the process variability has increased. A sample range of .0022 cm or less would imply that the process variability has decreased. In the former case, this means that the process is producing too much variation; we would want to investigate this in order to remove the assignable cause of variation. In the latter case, even though decreased variability is desirable, we would want to determine what is causing it: Perhaps an improved method has been used, in which case we would want to identify it.

If the standard deviation of process σ is not known but the average of sample ranges $\bar{R}$ is known, then σ can be estimated from $\bar{R}$ as follows: Equate the two UCLs in formulas 10-1 and 10-2, substitute 3 for z, and simplify:

$$\bar{\bar{X}} + 3\sigma_{\bar{x}} \approx \bar{\bar{X}} + A_2\bar{R}$$

$$3\sigma_{\bar{x}} \approx A_2\bar{R}$$

$$3\frac{\sigma}{\sqrt{n}} \approx A_2\bar{R}$$

(10-4)

$$\sigma \approx \frac{\sqrt{n}}{3}A_2\bar{R}$$

Why Use Both Sample Mean and Sample Range Control Charts? Sample mean and sample range control charts provide different perspectives on a process. Sample mean control charts are sensitive to shifts in the process mean, whereas sample range control charts are sensitive to changes in process dispersion or spread. Because of this difference in perspective, both charts must be used to monitor a process. The logic of using both is readily apparent from Figure 10-11. In Figure 10-11a, the sample mean control chart picks up the shift in the process mean, but because the dispersion is not changing, the sample range control chart fails to indicate a problem. Conversely, in Figure 10-11b, a change in process dispersion is not detected by the sample mean control chart, but is detected by the sample range control chart. Thus, use of both control charts provides more information than either chart alone.

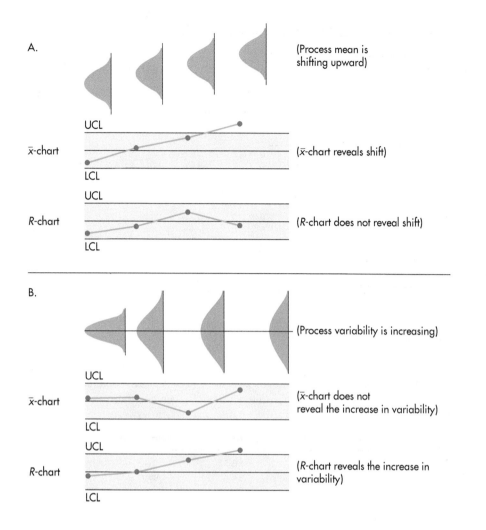

◄ **Figure 10-11**

Sample mean and sample range control charts used together complement each other.

Individual Unit and Moving Range Control Charts

When the rate of production is low, testing is expensive, or there is no reason to expect additional information by taking more observations, only one unit (i.e., $n = 1$) is used for inspection. In this case, the sample mean control chart reduces to **individual unit (X) control chart**, and its control limits can be determined by:

$$\begin{aligned} \text{UCL}_x &= \overline{X} + z\sigma \\ \text{LCL}_x &= \overline{X} - z\sigma \end{aligned} \tag{10-5}$$

individual unit (X) control chart Control chart for individual unit, used to monitor single observations ($n = 1$).

where $\overline{X}$ is the mean of a few individual observations (that estimates the process mean), σ is the process standard deviation, and z is the standard Normal deviate. It is important to note that the above formulas assume a Normal process distribution.

The "sample" range cannot be calculated in the usual way in this case because there is only one observation in each sample. Instead, the differences between consecutive observations, called moving range (MR), are calculated and used in the **moving range (MR) control chart** to control the dispersion or spread. We can still use the formula for the sample range control limits (10-3) but determine D_4 and D_3 from Table 10-3 using $n = 2$. Thus, the control limits for the moving range control chart are:

$$\begin{aligned} \text{UCL}_{\text{MR}} &= 3.27\overline{R} \\ \text{LCL}_{\text{MR}} &= 0\overline{R} = 0 \end{aligned} \tag{10-6}$$

moving range (MR) control chart Control chart for moving range, i.e., the difference between consecutive observations, used to monitor the dispersion or spread when $n = 1$.

where $\overline{R}$ is the average of the moving ranges (the absolute value of the difference between two consecutive observations). It is important to note that consecutive moving range values are not independent and that this fact has to be considered when analyzing the moving range control chart.

▶ The following data are the (Brinell) hardness measures of 10 individual steel screws produced by a screw machine.

    a. Determine the Three Sigma control limits for the X-chart and the moving range control chart. Is the process in control?

Sample Number	Hardness
1	36.3
2	28.6
3	32.5
4	38.7
5	35.4
6	27.3
7	37.2
8	36.4
9	38.3
10	30.5

    b. If the 11th observation is 38.7, using the control charts in part a, is the process still in control?

SOLUTION

    a. We have to compute the average and standard deviation of the individual observations (estimate of process standard deviation). Also, we need to calculate the difference of consecutive observations (absolute value) to obtain the moving ranges, and then average these to get $\bar{R}$. These are displayed below:

Sample Number	Hardness	Moving Range
1	36.3	—
2	28.6	7.7
3	32.5	3.9
4	38.7	6.2
5	35.4	3.3
6	27.3	8.1
7	37.2	9.9
8	36.4	0.8
9	38.3	1.9
10	30.5	7.8
Average =	34.12	5.51
Std dev =	4.11	

The control limits for X-chart are:

$$\text{UCL}_x = \bar{X} + z\sigma = 34.12 + 3(4.11) = 46.45$$
$$\text{LCL}_x = \bar{X} - z\sigma = 34.12 - 3(4.11) = 21.79$$

The control limits for moving range control chart are:

$$\text{UCL}_{\text{MR}} = 3.27(5.51) = 18.02$$
$$\text{LCL}_{\text{MR}} = 0$$

    All 10 hardness values fall within the X-chart control limits and all nine moving range values fall within the moving range control limits. Therefore, the process is in control.

    b. $21.79 < 38.7 < 46.45$, therefore the 11th observation is within its control limits. The new moving range $= 38.7 - 30.5 = 8.2$. Because $0 < 8.2 < 18.02$, the new moving range is also within its control limits. Therefore, the process is still in control.

Note that if formula 10-4 were used to estimate σ from $\overline{R}$ in the above example instead of calculating it directly, we would have obtained:

$$\sigma \approx \frac{\sqrt{n}}{3} A_2 \overline{R} = \frac{\sqrt{2}}{3}(1.88)(5.51) = 4.88$$

The relatively large discrepancy between 4.88 and 4.11 (estimate of σ derived directly from samples) is due to the fact that the data are not distributed Normally, as evident from the histogram below (note that formula 10-4 assumes that process distribution is Normal).

Control Charts for Attributes

Control charts for attributes are used when the process characteristic is *counted* rather than measured, i.e., when an item in a sample is either defective or not. There are two types of attribute control charts, one for the fraction of defective items in a sample (*p*-chart) and one for the number of defects per unit (*c*-chart). A *p-chart* is appropriate when the data consist of two categories of items. For instance, if glass bottles are inspected for chipping and cracking, both the good bottles and the defective ones can be counted. However, one can count the number of accidents that occur during a given period of time but not the number of accidents that did not occur. Similarly, one can count the number of scratches on a polished surface, the number of bacteria present in a water sample, and the number of crimes committed during the month of August, but one cannot count the number of nonoccurrences. In such cases, a *c-chart* is appropriate. See Table 10-4.

◀ Table 10-4

Use a p-chart or c-chart?

The following tips should help you select the type of control chart, a *p*-chart or a c-chart, that is appropriate for a particular application:

Use a *p*-chart:	Use a *c*-chart:
1. When observations can be placed into one of *two* categories. Examples include items (observations) that can be classified as a. Good or bad. b. Pass or fail. c. Operate or don't operate. 2. When the data consist of multiple samples of *n* observations each (e.g., 15 samples of *n* = 20 observations each).	When only the number of occurrences per unit of measure can be counted; nonoccurrences cannot be counted. Examples of occurrences and units of measure include a. Scratches, chips, dents, or errors per item. b. Cracks or faults per unit of distance (e.g., metres, miles). c. Breaks or tears, per unit of area (e.g., square yard, square metre). d. Bacteria or pollutants per unit of volume (e.g., gallon, cubic foot, cubic yard). e. Calls, complaints, failures, equipment breakdowns, or crimes per unit of time (e.g., hour, day, month, year).

p-chart Control chart for sample proportion of defectives, used to monitor the proportion of defective items generated by a process.

p-Chart. The **p-chart** is the control chart for the sample proportion of defectives, and is used to monitor the proportion of defective items generated by the process. The theoretical basis for a p-chart is the Binomial distribution, although for large sample sizes the Normal distribution provides a good approximation to it. Conceptually, a p-chart is constructed and used in much the same way as an $\bar{x}$-chart.

The centre line on a p-chart is the average proportion of defectives in the population, p. The standard deviation of the sampling distribution of the sample proportion, when p is known, is

$$\sigma_p = \sqrt{\frac{p(1-p)}{n}}$$

Control limits for p-chart are calculated using the formulas

$$UCL_p = p + z\sigma_p$$
$$LCL_p = p - z\sigma_p$$

(10-7)

If p is unknown, it can be estimated from a few samples. That estimate, $\bar{p}$, replaces p in the preceding formulas, as illustrated in the following example.

Note: Because formula 10-7 is an approximation, sometimes LCL_p will be negative. In this case, zero should be used as the lower control limit.

Example 6 ▶

A quality inspector counted the number of defective parts a prototype machine made in samples of 100 taken every hour during a 20-hour period.

a. Using the following data, construct a Three Sigma control chart for the sample proportion of defectives.

b. Is the machine producing a stable proportion of defectives?

Sample	Number of Defectives	Sample	Number of Defectives
1	4	11	8
2	10	12	12
3	12	13	9
4	3	14	10
5	9	15	21
6	11	16	10
7	10	17	8
8	22	18	12
9	13	19	10
10	10	20	16
			220

SOLUTION

a. $\bar{p} = \dfrac{\text{Total number of defectives}}{\text{Total number of observations}} = \dfrac{220}{20(100)} = .11$

$$\hat{\sigma}_p = \sqrt{\frac{\bar{p}(1-\bar{p})}{n}} = \sqrt{\frac{.11(1-.11)}{100}} = .03$$

Control limits are:

$$UCL_p = \bar{p} + z(\hat{\sigma}_p) = .11 + 3(.03) = .20$$

$$LCL_p = \bar{p} - z(\hat{\sigma}_p) = .11 - 3(.03) = .02$$

b. Plotting the control limits and the sample proportion of defectives, you can see that the process is not in control: sample 8 ($^{22}/_{100} = .22$) and sample 15 ($^{21}/_{100} = .21$) are above the upper control limit. Therefore, the machine operation should be investigated for assignable causes and, after corrective action, new data should be collected and new p-control limits should be calculated.

c-Chart. When the goal is to control the number of *occurrences* of defects *per unit product*, a **c-chart** (the control chart for the sample number of defects per unit product) is used. A unit might be an automobile, a hotel room, a typed page, or a roll of carpet. In this case, there is no sample size, only occurrences may be counted: the nonoccurrences cannot be. The underlying sampling distribution is the Poisson distribution. Use of the Poisson distribution assumes that defects occur over some *continuous* region and that the probability of more than one defect at any particular spot is negligible. The mean number of defects per unit product is c and the standard deviation is $\sqrt{c}$. For practical reasons, the Normal approximation to the Poisson is used. The control limits are:

$$UCL_c = c + z\sqrt{c}$$
$$LCL_c = c - z\sqrt{c}$$

(10-8)

c-chart Control chart for sample number of defects per unit product, used to monitor the number of defects per unit product.

If the value of c is unknown, as is generally the case, the average of number of defects per unit product from a few samples, $\bar{c}$, is used in place of c, i.e., $\bar{c}$ = total number of defects ÷ total number of samples.
When the lower control limit is negative, it is set to zero.

Rolls of coiled wire are monitored using a c-chart. Eighteen rolls have been examined, and the number of defects per roll has been recorded in the following table.

◀ **Example 7**

a. Is the process in control? Plot the values on a c-chart using three standard deviation control limits.

b. Suppose a new roll has seven defects. Using the c-chart of part a, is the process still in control?

Sample	Number of Defectives	Sample	Number of Defectives
1.	3	10	1
2	2	11.	3
3	4	12	4
4	5	13	2
5	1	14	4
6	2	15	2
7	4	16	1
8	1	17	3
9	2	18	1
			45

SOLUTION

a. $\bar{c} = 45/18 = 2.5$

$$\text{UCL}_c = \bar{c} + 3\sqrt{\bar{c}} = 2.5 + 3\sqrt{2.5} = 7.24$$

$$\text{LCL}_c = \bar{c} - 3\sqrt{\bar{c}} = 2.5 - 3\sqrt{2.5} = \rightarrow 0$$

As shown in the *c*-chart below, the process is in control.

b. Because $0 < 7 < 7.24$, the process is still in control.

Using Control Charts

So far we have used the rule that a process should be investigated when a sample statistic falls outside the control limits. There are other cases when a process should be investigated. These relate to nonrandom patterns in the control chart plots. These are shown in Figure 10-12.

In some instances, a manager can choose between using a $\bar{x}$-chart and a *p*-chart. If she is monitoring the diameter of a drive shaft, either the diameter could be measured and a $\bar{x}$-chart used for

Figure 10-12 ▶

Some examples of nonrandom patterns in control chart plots.

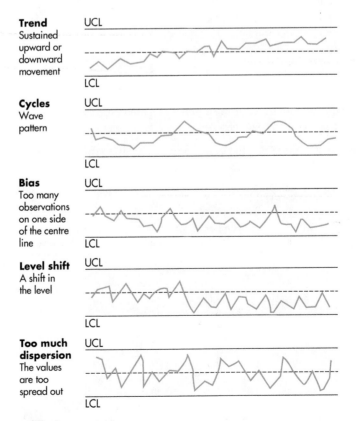

Trend
Sustained upward or downward movement

Cycles
Wave pattern

Bias
Too many observations on one side of the centre line

Level shift
A shift in the level

Too much dispersion
The values are too spread out

control, or the shafts could be inspected using a *go, no-go gauge*—which simply indicates whether a particular shaft is within specification or not, without giving its exact dimensions—and a *p*-chart could be used. Measurement is more costly and time consuming per unit than a yes–no inspection using a go, no-go gauge, but because measurement supplies more information than merely counting items as good or bad, one needs a much smaller sample size for a $\bar{x}$-chart than a *p*-chart. Hence, a manager must weigh the time and cost of sampling against the information provided.

Process Capability

Once the stability of a process has been established (i.e., no nonrandom variations are present), it is necessary to determine if the process is capable of producing output that is within an acceptable range. The variability of a process becomes the focal point of the analysis. Three terms relate to the process capability: design specification, control limits, and process variability. Each term represents a slightly different aspect of variability, so it is important to differentiate these terms.

Design specification, established by engineering design or customer requirements, is a range of values in which a product must fall in order to be acceptable.

Control limits are statistical limits that reflect the extent to which *sample statistics* such as mean and range can vary due to randomness alone.

Process variability is the actual variability in a process for a product.

Control limits and process variability are directly related: control limits are based on sampling distribution variability, and sampling distribution variability is a function of process variability. On the other hand, there is no direct link between design specification and either control limits or process variability. The output of a process may or may not conform to design specification, even though the process may be statistically in control. That is why it is also necessary to take into account the *capability* of a process. The term **process capability** refers to the ability of a process to meet the design specification. Measuring this capability is called capability analysis.

Capability Analysis

Capability analysis determines whether the process output falls within the design specification. If it is within the design specification for all its output, then the process is said to be "capable." If it is not, the process is said to be incapable and the manager must decide how to correct the situation.

Consider the three cases illustrated in Figure 10-13. In case A, process output and design specification are well matched, so that nearly all of the process output can be expected to meet the design specification. In case B, 100 percent of the output is within the design specification limits. In case C, however, the design specification is tighter than what the process is capable of, so a few percentages of the output fail to meet the design specification.

In instances such as case C in Figure 10-13, a manager might consider a range of possible solutions: (1) redesign the process or reduce its variability by, for example, performing experiments to find the best settings for the controllable factors; (2) use an alternative process that can achieve the desired accuracy; (3) retain the current process but attempt to eliminate unacceptable output using 100 percent inspection; and (4) examine the design specification to see whether it could be relaxed without adversely affecting customer satisfaction.

Process variability is typically measured as the interval ±3 standard deviations from the process mean. To determine whether the process is capable, compare this ±3 standard deviations value to the acceptable range of variation (i.e., design specification range or width), assuming that the process mean is centred at the midpoint of design specification. For example, suppose that the ideal length of time to perform a service is 10 minutes, and an acceptable range of variation around this time is ±1 minute. If the process has a standard deviation of .5 minute, it would not be capable because ±3 standard deviations would be ±1.5 minutes, which exceeds ±1 minute.

design specification A range of acceptable values established by engineering design or customer requirements.

process variability Actual variability in a process for a product.

process capability The ability of a process to meet the design specification.

Lower design specification Upper design specification	Lower design specification Upper design specification	Lower design specification Upper design specification
A. Process output matches design specification	B. Process output is well within design specification	C. Some process output is outside design specification

Figure 10-13

Process output and design specification may or may not match.

An alternative way is to compare six standard deviations of the process with the design specification width (upper design specification − lower design specification). For the above example, 6 sigma of the process is 6(.5) = 3 minutes, and the design specification width is 2(1) = 2 minutes.

Example 8 ▶

A manager has the option of using any one of three machines, A, B, or C, for making a part. The machines and their standard deviations of outputs (in millimetres) are listed below. Determine which machines are capable if the design specification for the part's length is between 101.00 mm and 101.60 mm.

Machine	Standard Deviation (mm)
A	.10
B	.08
C	.13

SOLUTION

Determine the output variability of each machine (i.e., 6 standard deviations) and compare that value to the specification width of .60 mm (= 101.60 − 101.00).

Machine	Standard Deviation (mm)	Machine Variability = 6σ
A	.10	.60
B	.08	.48
C	.13	.78

We can see that both machine A and machine B are capable of producing output that is within the specification (assuming they can be centred at the midpoint of the design specification 101.30) but that machine C is not, because its variability of .78 exceeds the design specification width of .60. See Figure 10-13 for a visual portrayal of these results.

C_p

To express the capability of a machine or process, some companies use the ratio of the design specification width to the process width (= 6 sigma). This can be calculated using the following formula:

$$\text{Process capability ratio, } C_p = \frac{\text{Design specification width}}{\text{Process width}}$$

$$= \frac{\text{Upper design specification} - \text{Lower design specification}}{6\sigma} \tag{10-9}$$

OM in *ACTION* http://www.harley-davidson.com

Harley-Davidson

Harley-Davidson implemented a PC–based networked statistical process control system in two of its power-train plants. Harley controls approximately 500 critical dimensions such as bore diameter, hole location, flatness, and surface finish of motorcycle parts. Upgrading from paper control charts, Harley installed more than 60 personal computers in strategic locations throughout both plants and connected the on-site coordinate measuring machines and other gauges into the network. As soon as an operator completes a measurement, an updated control chart is displayed on the monitor. If the process is out of control but the part's characteristic is still within tolerance, a yellow status flag is shown. If it is outside the specification limits, a red flag is displayed.

Whenever a process goes out of control, or a part is produced outside specification limits, a dialogue box pops up and the operator is prompted to enter an assignable cause. In many cases the cause of the problem is readily apparent to the operator and is immediately fixed. If the operator can't find the cause of the problem, he contacts the workgroup quality adviser. If additional assistance is needed, then a manufacturing engineer is brought in.

OM in *ACTION*

Imperial Bondware

Imperial Bondware of Kenton, Ohio, makes paper cups for hot and cold drinks. It has 62 large automated machines, each making cups starting from rolls of printed paperboard strip. The dimensions (rim diameter, rim thickness, and cup height) are important because the cups have to work flawlessly in automated drink machines (i.e., they must be released from the stack just before a drink is poured). Before automating the data gathering and analysis, Imperial Bondware used to take four hours just to print the quality control charts. After installing automated laser gauges and Zontec's Synergy software, the manager can access the performance of each machine quickly. Of particular interest is the process capability of each machine. Two examples of the charts used by Imperial Bondware to control rim diameters produced by a cup-making machine are shown. The individual unit chart (without showing the control limits but showing the design specification limits) is displayed on the top, and a process distribution with the design specification limits is shown at the bottom. This particular machine makes cups that have diameters 97.7 percent within specification.

Question

Using the information given in the charts, can you verify that $C_p = 0.875$ and $C_{pk} = 0.6656$?

Source: K. Aldred, "Paper Cup Manufacturer Slashes Report Time," *IIE Solutions* 30(8), August 1998, pp. 44–45. Reprinted with permission of the Institute of Industrial Engineers, 3577 Parkway Lane, Suite 200, Norcross, GA, 720-449-0461.

Calculate the process capability index for each machine in Example 8.

◀ Example 9

The design specification width in Example 8 was .60 mm. Hence, to determine the capability index for each machine, divide .60 by the process width (i.e., 6 standard deviations) of each machine. The results are:

SOLUTION

Machine	Standard Deviation (mm)	Machine Capability	C_p
A	.10	.60	.60/.60 = 1.00
B	.08	.48	.60/.48 = 1.25
C	.13	.78	.60/.78 = 0.77

Using the capability ratio, you can see that for a process to be capable, it must have a capability ratio of at least 1.00. A ratio of 1.00 implies that 99.74 percent of the output of a process can be expected to be within the design specification limits, hence only 0.26 percent, or 2,600 parts per million, fall outside the design specification. Moreover, the greater the process capability ratio, the greater the probability that the output of a machine or process will fall within design specification.

C_{pk}

If a process is not centred between design specification limits, or if there is no design specification limit on one side, a slightly different measure is used to calculate its capability. This ratio is represented by the symbol C_{pk}. It is calculated by finding the difference between each of the specification limits and the process mean, dividing that difference by three standard deviations of the process, and identifying the smaller ratio. Thus, C_{pk} is equal to the *smaller* of:

$$\frac{\text{Upper design specification} - \text{Process mean}}{3\sigma} \qquad (10\text{-}10)$$

and

$$\frac{\text{Process mean} - \text{Lower design specification}}{3\sigma}$$

Example 10

A process's output has a mean of 9.20 kg and a standard deviation of .30 kg. The lower design specification is 8.00 kg and the upper design specification is 10.00 kg. Calculate the C_{pk}.

1. Calculate the ratio for the lower design specification:

$$\frac{\text{Process mean} - \text{Lower design specification}}{3\sigma} = \frac{9.20 - 8.00}{3(.30)} = \frac{1.20}{.90} = 1.33$$

2. Calculate the ratio for the upper design specification:

$$\frac{\text{Upper design specification} - \text{Process mean}}{3\sigma} = \frac{10.00 - 9.20}{3(.30)} = \frac{.80}{.90} = .89$$

The smaller of the two ratios is .89, so this is the C_{pk}. Because the C_{pk} is less than 1.00, the process is *not* capable. Note that if C_p had been used, it would have given the false impression that the process was capable:

$$C_p = \frac{\text{Upper design Specification} - \text{Lower design specification}}{6\sigma} = \frac{10.00 - 8.00}{6(.30)} = \frac{2.00}{1.80} = 1.11 > 1.00$$

See the "Imperial Bondware" OM in Action for an application of process capability analysis.

LO4 Six Sigma Quality

Six Sigma quality A more advanced version of problem solving/continuous improvement. It also refers to the goal of achieving process variability so small that the half-width of design specification equals six standard deviations of the process.

Six Sigma quality is a more advanced version of problem solving/continuous improvement that was discussed in the previous chapter. It also refers to the goal of achieving process variability so small that the half-width of design specification equals six standard deviations of the process. That means that the process capability ratio equals 2.00, resulting in an extremely small probability (.00034 percent, or 3.4 units per million) of getting any output outside design specification. This is illustrated in Figure 10-14.[1]

The differences of Six Sigma quality and continuous improvement are:[2]

	Six Sigma Quality	Continuous Improvement
Objective	Product and process perfection	Product and process improvement
Tools	Statistical, e.g., design of experiments and analysis of variance	Simple data analysis, e.g., Pareto chart, cause-and-effect diagram
Methodology	Define, measure, analyze, improve, control (DMAIC)	Plan, do, study, act (PDSA)
Team leader	Black belt	Champion
Training	Long/formal	Short/informal
Culture change	Usually enforced	Sometimes enforced
Project time frame	Months/years	Days/weeks

---

[1] Actually 3.4 defects per million corresponds to 4.5σ. The other 1.5σ is to allow process mean to be off-centre by up to 1.5σ.

[2] "Baldrige, Six Sigma, & ISO: Understanding Your Options," http://www.nist.gov/baldrige/publications/upload/Issue_Sheet_SS.pdf, Summer 2002; J. Bossert et al., "Your Opinion: Are Six Sigma and Lean Manufacturing Really Different?," *ASQ Six Sigma Forum Magazine* 2(1), November 2002, pp. 38–43.

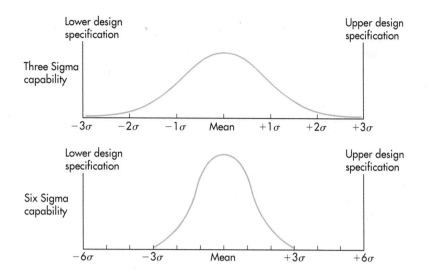

Figure 10-14

Three Sigma versus Six Sigma capability. (Blue curves show the process output; note x-axis scales are different in the two charts.)

The Six Sigma improvement methodology DMAIC involves:

Define	Determine the customers and critical-to-quality procedures
Measure	Identify and measure the quality problem, determine the baseline Sigma, and identify possible influencing factors
Analyze	Test the influencing factors and identify the vital few
Improve	Select the solution method, prove its effectiveness, and implement it
Control	Develop a process control plan

Example 11

The North Shore-Long Island Jewish Health System[3] consists of several hospitals and nursing homes around New York City. A central lab performs blood tests for the health system as well as for other private clinics. The Six Sigma consultants are housed in the Center for Learning and Innovation of the health system. Although the health system has a very large and capable Quality Management Department, the Six Sigma group decided to remain separate. The Six Sigma group focuses on chronic issues that cannot be solved easily and uses systematic statistical and change management techniques.

One project the Six Sigma group worked on in 2002/2003 was the labelling of test specimens in the central lab. The tests are done by automated machines, so most errors occur before the test. The critical-to-quality procedures for labelling are (a) receiving the requisition of blood test and specimen, (b) entering patient information into the computer, (c) delivering the specimen to the automated machines, (d) obtaining results, and (e) sending the results to the requisitioner.

The Six Sigma team consisted of some members of the Six Sigma group, lab management, and representatives from Compliance, Quality, and Marketing. The objective was to reduce the errors and missing data. The data accompanying the specimens were patient name, social security number, date of birth, gender, physician's name, name of test, and a code name for the diagnosis.

The percentage of errors and omissions was 5 percent. The major problem was identified to be omission of the code name for diagnosis. The solution was rather simple: a pocket guide to the diagnosis code for the requisioners. This reduced the error and omission rate to 0.7 percent.

To further reduce labelling errors and omissions, the next common error (approximately 50 percent of remaining errors or omissions) was identified as the social security number. A pattern was easily found: most of these errors originated from units that used a special set of codes (called addressograph) which presented the information in a confusing way. Again, an easy solution was discovered: peel off the bar code at the bottom of patient's chart and attach it to the requisition.

---

[3] N.B. Riebling et al., "Toward Error Free Lab Work," *ASQ Six Sigma Forum Magazine* 4(1), 2004, pp. 23–29.

The team also performed a benchmarking study of the productivity of the labelling staff (accessioners). A labeller prepared an average of 17 labels per hour, whereas the industry norm was 20. Although some workers were faster than the others, there was no statistically significant difference in their productivity. The team decided to look at the method of labelling. A meeting of all staff was called. Their opinion was that there was quite a bit of walking and moving involved and sometimes it was confusing to find the right machines for the particular test needed for a specimen. Solutions suggested were (a) provide a colour-coded book of tests and machines that perform each, (b) put up same colour signs over machines, and (c) employ a runner to move the batch of specimens to the machines. The team decided to try these and also to create a position of lead labeller who would take 20 requisitions/specimen per hour to each labeller and answer any questions they might have.

An experiment was designed to measure the influence of (a) using barcodes, (b) expertise of individual labellers (accessioners), and (c) the new work process (called distribution) on the productivity of labellers. This is done by collecting data under various levels of the factors above. The results are shown in the figure below.

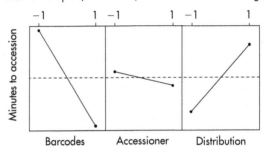

Main effects plot (data means) for minutes to accessioning

As can be seen, the use of barcodes (barcodes = 1) and the new work process (distribution = −1) reduces minutes to accession, i.e., increases productivity. Finally, the individual unit and moving range control charts were constructed to monitor the productivity of each labeller. Productivity has been improving and has exceeded 20 labels per hour per accessioner.

Design of Experiments

design of experiments
Performing experiments by changing levels of factors to measure their influence on output and identifying best levels for each factor.

Design of experiments involves performing experiments by changing levels of factors to measure their influence on output and identifying best levels for each factor. However, if this is done by changing the level of one factor at a time, while keeping the levels of other factors constant, an extremely large number of experiments will be required.

Factorial design suggests a more concise set of experiments by changing the level of more than one factor at a time. For example, suppose we have three factors, each having two levels. Then, if we change one factor's level at a time, in order to determine the best levels for each factor, we will need $2^3 = 8$ different experiments. However, factorial design suggests that, in this case, the following four experiments are adequate (the body of the table shows the level of each factor; this is called fractional factorial design):[4]

	Experiment			
Factor	(i)	(ii)	(iii)	(iv)
A	1	1	2	2
B	1	2	1	2
C	1	2	2	1

[4] G.S. Peace, *Taguchi Methods,* Reading, Massachusetts: Addison-Wesley, 1993.

Runs	2	3	4	5	6	7	8	9
4	2^2	2^{2-1}_{III}						
8		2^3	2^{4-1}_{IV}	2^{5-2}_{III}	2^{6-3}_{III}	2^{7-4}_{III}		
16			2^4	2^{5-1}_{V}	2^{6-2}_{IV}	2^{7-3}_{IV}	2^{8-4}_{IV}	2^{9-5}_{III}
32				2^5	2^{6-1}_{VI}	2^{7-2}_{IV}	2^{8-3}_{IV}	2^{9-4}_{IV}
64					2^6	2^{7-1}_{VII}	2^{8-2}_{V}	2^{9-3}_{IV}
128						2^7	2^{8-1}_{VIII}	2^{9-2}_{VI}
256							2^8	2^{9-1}_{IX}
512								2^9

In general, the number of experiments (runs) one needs to perform, given the number of factors (at 2 levels), are given below, where white (and one black) cells are for full factorial experiments (which can also identify interaction between factors) and other colours show progressively more restrictive analyses (green, yellow, and red, respectively) whose results may be less reliable. For example, a full factorial experiment with 4 factors (at 2 levels) requires 16 experiments (runs).

◀ **Example 12**

In the early 1990s, Navistar's Indianapolis engine plant had a problem with the flatness of its cylinder heads (the top part of the engines). The specification width was a lot smaller than process variability, rendering the process incapable. The final machining operation shaved a small amount of metal from the top of cylinder heads. The variation in the flatness resulting from this operation needed to be reduced. Possible factors were thought to be:

a. Feed rate for broach that shaved the metal.

b. The thickness of metal removed.

c. The pressure of clamp holding the cylinder head down.

For each factor, two levels were determined:

a. (1 = 80 feet/minute, 2 = 120 feet/minute)

b. (1 = .020 inch, 2 = .0028 inch)

c. (1 = 600 pounds, 2 = 500 pounds)

Four experiments were used (see the design given above). Each experiment (i) to (iv) was repeated six times in order to improve the accuracy of the results. For example, in the first experiment, all factors were set to level 1. For each cylinder head produced, the height of 32 points on its flat surface was measured and the difference between the maximum height and the minimum height was calculated. This high-low difference was averaged over the six pieces produced using the same experiment. The results are:

	Experiment			
	(i)	(ii)	(iii)	(iv)
Average high-low difference (in 1/10,000 inch):	33.32	45.93	25.88	27.17

From these results, the influence of each level of each factor can be determined. For example, Factor 1, level 1 was used in experiments (i) and (ii). Therefore, its average high-low difference is $(33.32 + 45.93)/2 = 39.63$. The other results were calculated in a similar manner:

Factor	Level 1	Level 2
a	39.63	26.53
b	29.60	36.55
c	30.25	35.90

It can be shown that the levels of all three factors have significant influence on average high-low difference. Therefore, to reduce the variation in cylinder head flatness, this operation should use Level 2 of factor a (i.e., 120 feet/minute tool speed), Level 1 of Factor b (i.e., remove .020 inch metal), and Level 1 of Factor c (i.e., use 600 pounds of clamp pressure). This will reduce the variation in flatness as much as possible.

Source: Based on R.W. Schmenner, *Production/Operations Management*, 5th ed. (New York: MacMillan, 1993, pp. 118–119).

Summary

- Statistical process control focuses on detecting departures from stability in a process. Control charts are commonly used for this.
- There are two types of variations: random and assignable.
- Sample mean ($\bar{x}$) control charts are used to monitor the process mean.
- Sample range control charts are used to monitor process dispersion or spread.
- Individual unit X control charts are used to monitor single observations ($n = 1$).
- Moving range control charts are used to monitor the dispersion or spread between the difference between consecutive observations.
- p-charts are used to monitor the proportion of defective items generate by a process.
- c-charts are used to monitor the number of defects per unit product.
- Process capability analysis is used to determine if the output of a process will satisfy design specification.
- Six Sigma quality is the approach that improves process capability to very high levels (3.4 defects per million).
- Design of experiments is a major tool in Six Sigma quality. Factorial design provides an efficient method for design of experiments.
- Figure 10-15 can be used to choose the right control chart.
- Table 10-5 provides a summary of the formulas.

Figure 10-15 ▶

Choosing the right control chart.

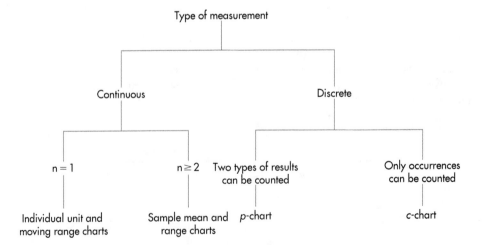

Control Charts		
Name	**Symbol**	**Control Limits**
Sample mean	$\bar{x}$	$\bar{\bar{x}} \pm z\dfrac{\sigma}{\sqrt{n}}$ or $\bar{\bar{x}} \pm A_2\bar{R}$
Sample range	R	$\text{UCL} = D_4\bar{R},\ \text{LCL} = D_3\bar{R}$
Sample proportion of defectives	P	$\bar{p} \pm z\sqrt{\dfrac{\bar{p}(1-\bar{p})}{n}}$
Sample number of defects	C	$\bar{c} \pm z\sqrt{\bar{c}}$

Process Capability		
Name	**Symbol**	**Formula**
Capability index for a centred process	C_p	$\dfrac{\text{Design specification width}}{6\sigma \text{ of process}}$
Capability index for a noncentred process	C_{pk}	Smaller of $\begin{cases} \dfrac{\text{Process mean} - \text{Lower design specification}}{3\sigma} \\ \dfrac{\text{Upper design specification} - \text{process mean}}{3\sigma} \end{cases}$

◀ **Table 10-5**

Summary of formulas.

Key Terms

assignable variation
c-chart
central limit theorem
control chart
control limits
design of experiments
design specification

individual unit (X) control chart
inspection
moving range (MR) control chart
p-chart
process capability
process variability
random variation

sample mean ($\bar{x}$) control chart
sample range (R) control chart
Six Sigma quality
statistical process control (SPC)
statistical quality control
Type I error
Type II error

Solved Problems

Problem 1

Process distribution and sampling distribution. An industrial process makes 3 feet plastic pipes with an average inside diameter of 1 inch and a standard deviation of .05 inch.

a. If you randomly select one piece of pipe, what is the probability that its inside diameter will exceed 1.02 inches, assuming that the process distribution is Normal?

b. If you select a random sample of 25 pieces of pipes, what is the probability that the sample mean will exceed 1.02 inches?

$\mu = 1.00,\ \sigma = .05$

Solution

a. $z = \dfrac{x - \mu}{\sigma} = \dfrac{1.02 - 1.00}{.05} = .4$

Using Appendix B, Table A, $P(z > .4) = .5000 - .1554 = .3446$.

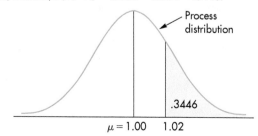

$\mu = 1.00 \quad 1.02$

b. $z = \dfrac{\bar{x} - \mu}{\sigma/\sqrt{n}} = \dfrac{1.02 - 1.00}{.05/\sqrt{25}} = 2.00$

Using Appendix B, Table A, $P(z > 2.00) = .5000 - .4772 = .0228.$

Sampling distribution of the sample mean

.0228

$\mu = 1.00$ 1.02

Problem 2

Control charts for sample mean and range. Processing new accounts at a bank is intended to average 10 minutes each. Five samples of four observations each have been taken. Use the sample data below in conjunction with Table 10-3 to construct upper and lower control limits for both sample mean and sample range control charts. Do the results suggest that the process is in control?

	Sample 1	Sample 2	Sample 3	Sample 4	Sample 5
	10.2	10.3	9.7	9.9	9.8
	9.9	9.8	9.9	10.3	10.2
	9.8	9.9	9.9	10.1	10.3
	10.1	10.4	10.1	10.5	9.7
Totals	40.0	40.4	39.6	40.8	40.0

Solution

a. Determine the mean and range of each sample.

$$\bar{x} = \frac{\sum x}{n}, \quad \text{Range} = \text{Largest} - \text{Smallest}$$

Sample	Mean	Range
1	40.0/4 = 10.0	10.2 − 9.8 = .4
2	40.4/4 = 10.1	10.4 − 9.8 = .6
3	39.6/4 = 9.9	10.1 − 9.7 = .4
4	40.8/4 = 10.2	10.5 − 9.9 = .6
5	40.0/4 = 10.0	10.3 − 9.7 = .6

b. Calculate the average sample mean and average sample range:

$$\bar{\bar{X}} = \frac{10.0 + 10.1 + 9.9 + 10.2 + 10.0}{5} = \frac{50.2}{5} = 10.04$$

$$\bar{R} = \frac{.4 + .6 + .4 + .6 + .6}{5} = \frac{2.6}{5} = .52$$

Note that one can use Excel to compute these quantities. For average, "= average(cells)" should be used where "cells" is the coordinates of cells where data are located. For example, if data are in cells A2 to A5, then use "= average(A2:A5)." Similarly, for range, "max(A2:A5) − min(A2:A5)" should be used.

c. Obtain factors A_2, D_4, and D_3 from Table 10-3 for $n = 4$: $A_2 = .73, D_4 = 2.28, D_3 = 0.$

d. Calculate upper and lower limits:

$$\text{UCL}_{\bar{x}} = \bar{\bar{x}} + A_2\bar{R} = 10.04 + .73(.52) = 10.42$$
$$\text{LCL}_{\bar{x}} = \bar{\bar{x}} - A_2\bar{R} = 10.04 - .73(.52) = 9.66$$

$$UCL_R = D_4\overline{R} = 2.28(.52) = 1.19$$
$$LCL_R = D_3\overline{R} = 0(.52) = 0$$

e. Plot sample means and ranges on their respective control charts, or otherwise verify that points are within limits.

All sample means (10.0, 10.1, 9.9, 10.2, 10.0) are larger that LCL of $\overline{X}$ (9.66) and smaller than UCL of $\overline{X}$ (10.42). Similarly, all sample ranges (.4, .6, .4, .6, .6) are larger than LCL of R(0) and smaller than UCL of R(1.19). Hence, the process is in control.

Problem 3

Type I error (alpha risk). After several investigations of points outside control limits revealed nothing, a manager began to wonder about the probability of the Type I error for the control limits used, which were based on $z = 1.90$.

a. Determine the alpha risk for this value of z.
b. What z would provide an alpha risk of about 2 percent?

Solution

a. Using Appendix B, Table A, we find that the area under the curve between $z = 0$ and $z = +1.90$ is .4713. Therefore, the area (probability) of values within 1.90 to +1.90 is 2(.4713) = .9426, and the area beyond these values is $1 - .9426 = .0574$. Hence, the alpha risk is 5.74 percent.

b. Because half of the risk lies in each tail, the area under the curve between $z = 0$ and the value of z you are looking for is .49. The closest value is .4901 for $z = 2.33$. Thus, control limits based on $z = 2.33$ provide an alpha risk of about 2 percent.

Problem 4

p-chart and c-chart. Using the appropriate control chart, determine Two Sigma control limits for each case:

a. An inspector found an average of 3.9 scratches in the exterior paint of each of the automobiles being prepared for shipment to dealers.
b. Before shipping lawn mowers to dealers, an inspector attempts to start each mower and notes the ones that do not start on the first try. The lot size is 100 mowers, and an average of 4 did not start on the first try based on a few samples (4 percent).

Solution

The choice between these two types of control charts relates to whether *two* types of results can be counted (*p*-chart) or whether *only occurrences* can be counted (*c*-chart).

a. The inspector can count only the scratches that occurred, not the ones that did not occur. Consequently, a *c*-chart is appropriate. The sample average is 3.9 scratches per car. Two Sigma control limits are found using the formulas:

$$UCL = \overline{c} + z\sqrt{\overline{c}}$$
$$LCL = \overline{c} - z\sqrt{\overline{c}}$$

where $\overline{c} = 3.9$ and $z = 2$. Thus,

$$UCL = 3.9 + 2\sqrt{3.9} = 7.85 \text{ scratches}$$
$$LCL = 3.9 - 2\sqrt{3.9} = -.05, \text{ So the lower limit is 0 scratches}$$

b. The inspector can count both the lawn mowers that started and those that did not start. Consequently, a *p*-chart is appropriate. Two Sigma control limits can be calculated using the following:

$$UCL = \overline{p} + z\sqrt{\frac{\overline{p}(1 - \overline{p})}{n}}$$

$$LCL = \overline{p} - z\sqrt{\frac{\overline{p}(1 - \overline{p})}{n}}$$

where:

$$\bar{p} = .04$$

$$n = 100$$

$$z = 2$$

Thus,

$$UCL = .04 + 2\sqrt{\frac{.04(.96)}{100}} = .079$$

$$LCL = .04 - 2\sqrt{\frac{.04(.96)}{100}} = .001$$

Problem 5

Determine if these three processes are capable:

Process	Mean	Standard Deviation	Lower Spec	Upper Spec
1	7.5	.10	7.0	8.0
2	4.6	.12	4.3	4.9
3	6.0	.14	5.5	6.7

Solution

Notice that the means of the first two processes are exactly in the centre of the upper and lower specs. Hence, the C_p index (Formula 10-9) is appropriate. However, the third process is not centred, so C_{pk} (Formula 10-10) is appropriate.

For processes 1 and 2: $C_p = \dfrac{\text{Upper spec} - \text{Lower spec}}{6\sigma}$

In order to be capable, C_p must be at least 1.0.

Process 1: $C_p = \dfrac{8.0 - 7.0}{6(.10)} = 1.67$ (capable)

Process 2: $C_p = \dfrac{4.9 - 4.3}{6(.12)} = 0.83$ (not capable)

For Process 3, C_{pk} must be at least 1.0. It is the lesser of these two:

$$\frac{\text{Upper spec} - \text{Mean}}{3\sigma} = \frac{6.7 - 6.0}{3(.14)} = 1.67$$

$$\frac{\text{Mean} - \text{Lower spec}}{3\sigma} = \frac{6.0 - 5.5}{3(.14)} = 1.19$$

Minimum $\{1.67, 1.19\} = 1.19 > 1.0 \rightarrow$ capable.

Discussion and Review Questions

1. What is statistical quality control and why is it important?

2. List the steps in the statistical process control planning process. **LO1**

3. Answer these questions about inspection: **LO1**

   a. What level of inspection is optimal?

   b. What are the main considerations in choosing between centralized inspection and on-site inspection?

   c. What points are potential candidates for inspection?

4. What are the key concepts that underlie the construction and interpretation of control charts? **LO2**

5. What is the purpose of a control chart? **LO2**

6. Classify each of the following as either a Type I or a Type II error: **LO2**

   a. Putting an innocent person in jail.

   b. Releasing a guilty person from jail.

7. Why is order of observation important in control charts?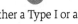

8. What are the steps for designing a control chart? **LO2**

9. Briefly explain the purpose of each of these control charts: **LO2**

    a. $\bar{x}$
    b. R
    c. Individual unit
    d. Moving range
    e. p
    f. c

10. Why are $\bar{x}$ and R charts used together? **LO2**

11. If all the observations are within control limits, does that guarantee that the process variation contains only randomness? **LO2**

12. Identify a process in a bank and one in a retail store that control charts can be used to monitor. **LO2**

13. Define and contrast control limits and design specification limits. **LO3**

14. A customer has recently tightened the design specification for a part your company supplies. The design specification is now much tighter than the machine being used for the job is capable of. Briefly identify alternatives you might consider to resolve this problem. **LO3**

15. Define and contrast C_p and C_{pk}. **LO3**

16. Can the value of C_{pk} exceed the value of C_p for the same process and specification limits? Explain. **LO3**

17. A process can be capable but out of control. Another process can be in control but incapable. Explain. **LO2 & 3**

18. What is Six Sigma quality and how does it differ from continuous improvement's PDSA? **LO4**

19. What is design of experiments and why is it useful for Six Sigma quality? **LO4**

Taking Stock

1. What trade-offs are involved in each of these decisions?

    a. Deciding whether to use Two Sigma or Three Sigma control limits. **LO2**
    b. Choosing between a large sample size and a smaller sample size. **LO1**

2. Who needs to be involved in statistical process control (SPC)? **LO1**

3. Name two ways that technology has had an impact on SPC. **LO1**

4. What kind of ethical issues arise in SPC when the operators are put in charge of quality control at their own workstations? How can these concerns be addressed? Explain. **LO1**

Critical Thinking Exercise

Analysis of the output of a process has suggested that the variability was nonrandom on several occasions recently. However, each time the investigation has not revealed any assignable causes. What are some of the possible explanations for not finding any causes? What should the manager do? **LO2**

Experiential Learning Exercise

Obtain approximately 10 small bags of M&M candies (multicoloured), or similar candies. Arrange the unopened bags in a single row, and treat each bag as a sample from an ongoing process, in the order you have placed them. Treat the yellow candies (or another colour that is the fewest in number in each bag) as defects. **LO1, 2, & 3**

a. List the four or five steps needed to obtain sample information for each bag, beginning with opening the bag.
b. Determine the upper and lower control limits for the sample proportion of defectives using Three Sigma control limits. *Note:* the number of candies in each bag may not be exactly the same. You can ignore that.
c. Is the process variation random? Explain how you reached your conclusion.

Internet Exercises

1. Visit http://jobs.isixsigma.com, choose a job announcement related to Six Sigma quality, and describe the job description. **LO4**

2. Visit http://www.qualitymag.com, find the case study from the current issue (under Departments on the lower right side) and summarize it. **LO1**

3. Visit http://www.statease.com/pubs/breaddoe.pdf and summarize the design of experiment to determine the ingredients for bread. **LO4**

Problems

1. Design specification for a motor housing states that it should weigh between 24 and 25 kg. The process that produces the housing yields a mean of 24.5 kg and a standard deviation of .2 kg. The distribution of output is Normal. **LO2 & 4**
   a. What percentage of housing will not meet the design specification?
   b. Within what values should 95.44 percent of sample means of this process fall if samples of $n = 16$ are taken?

2. An automatic filling machine is used to fill 2-litre bottles of cola. The machine's output is known to be approximately Normal with a mean of 2.0 litres and a standard deviation of .01 litre. Output is monitored using means of samples of five observations. **LO2**
   a. Determine the upper and lower control limits that will include roughly 95.5 percent of the sample means.
   b. If the means for 6 samples are 2.005, 2.001, 1.998, 2.002, 1.995, and 1.999, is the process in control?

3. Process time at a workstation is monitored using sample mean and range control charts. Six samples of $n = 10$ observations have been obtained and the sample means and ranges computed (in minutes): **LO2**

Sample	Mean	Range
1	3.06	.42
2	3.15	.50
3	3.11	.41
4	3.13	.46
5	3.06	.46
6	3.09	.45

   a. Using the factors in Table 10-3, determine the upper and lower limits for sample mean and range control charts.
   b. Is the process in control?

4. Six samples of five observations each have been taken of 80 kg concrete slabs produced by a machine, and the results are displayed below. **LO2**

   a. Using factors from Table 10-3, determine the upper and lower control limits for sample mean and range, and decide if the process is in control.
   b. A new sample results in the following slab weights: 81.0, 81.0, 80.8, 80.6, and 80.5. Use the control limits determined in part a to decide if the process is still in control.

			Sample		
1	**2**	**3**	**4**	**5**	**6**
79.2	80.5	79.6	78.9	80.5	79.7
78.8	78.7	79.4	79.4	79.6	80.6
80.0	81.0	80.4	79.7	80.4	80.5
78.4	80.4	80.3	79.4	80.8	80.0
81.0	80.1	80.8	80.6	78.8	81.1

5. In a refinery, the octane rating of gasoline produced is measured by taking one observation from each batch. Twenty observations follow. **LO2**
   a. Construct Three Sigma control charts for the individual unit and moving range. Is the process in control?[5]
   b. A new batch has an octane rating of 94.0. Using the control charts in part a, is the process still in control?

Observation Number	Octane Rating	Observation Number	Octane Rating
1	89.2	11	85.4
2	86.5	12	91.6
3	88.4	13	87.7
4	91.8	14	85.0
5	90.3	15	91.5
6	87.5	16	90.3
7	92.6	17	85.6
8	87.0	18	90.9
9	89.8	19	82.1
10	92.2	20	85.8

---

[5] Adapted from Amitava Mitra, *Fundamentals of Quality Control and Improvement*, 2nd ed., Englewood Cliffs, NJ: Prentice Hall, 1998.

6. Using four samples of 200 credit card statements each, an auditor found the following number of erroneous statements in each sample: **LO2**

	Sample			
	1	**2**	**3**	**4**
Number of errors	4	2	5	9

a. Determine the proportion of defectives in each sample.
b. If the true proportion of defectives for this process is unknown, what is your best estimate of it?
c. What is your estimate of the mean and standard deviation of the sampling distribution of the sample proportion of defectives for samples of 200?
d. What control limits would give an alpha risk of .03 for this process?
e. What alpha risk would control limits of .047 and .003 provide?
f. Using control limits of .047 and .003, is the process in control?
g. Suppose that the long-term proportion of defectives of the process is known to be 2 percent. What are the values of the mean and standard deviation of the sampling distribution?
h. Construct a p-control chart for the process, assuming a proportion of defectives of 2 percent, and Two Sigma control limits. Is the process in control?

7. A medical facility does MRIs for sports injuries. Occasionally a test yields inconclusive results and must be repeated. Using the following 13 sample results for the number of retests in $n = 200$ observations each, construct a control chart for the proportion of retests using Two Sigma limits. Is the process in control? **LO2**

	Sample												
	1	**2**	**3**	**4**	**5**	**6**	**7**	**8**	**9**	**10**	**11**	**12**	**13**
Number of retests	1	2	2	0	2	1	2	0	2	7	3	2	1

8. The operations manager of a large manufacturer received a certain number of complaints during the last two weeks. **LO2**
a. Construct a control chart with Three Sigma limits for the number of complaints received each day using the following data. Is the process in control?
b. If 16 complaints are received today (day 15), using the control chart of part a, is there a change in the average number of complaints per day?

	Day													
	1	**2**	**3**	**4**	**5**	**6**	**7**	**8**	**9**	**10**	**11**	**12**	**13**	**14**
Number of complaints	4	10	14	8	9	6	5	12	13	7	6	4	2	10

9. a. Construct a control chart with Three Sigma limits for the number of scratches per 6m × 2m stainless steel sheet based on the following data. Is the process in control? **LO2**
b. If a new sheet has five defects, using the control chart of part a, has the process changed?

	Observation													
	1	**2**	**3**	**4**	**5**	**6**	**7**	**8**	**9**	**10**	**11**	**12**	**13**	**14**
Number of scratches	2	3	1	0	1	3	2	0	2	1	3	1	2	0

10. After a number of complaints about its directory assistance, a telephone company examined samples of calls to determine the frequency of wrong numbers given to callers. Each sample consisted of 100 calls. The manager stated that the error rate is about 4 percent. Construct a control chart using 95 percent limits and using $\bar{p} = .04$. Is the process in control? Is the manager's assertion about the error rate correct? Explain. **LO2**

	Observation															
	1	**2**	**3**	**4**	**5**	**6**	**7**	**8**	**9**	**10**	**11**	**12**	**13**	**14**	**15**	**16**
Number of errors	5	3	5	7	4	6	8	4	5	9	3	4	5	6	6	7

11. Specification for the diameter of a metal shaft is much wider than the machine used to make the shafts is capable of. Consequently, the decision has been made to allow the cutting tool to wear a certain amount before replacement. The tool wears at the rate of .004 centimetre per metal shaft produced. The process has a natural variation, σ, of .01 centimetre and is Normally distributed. Specification for the diameter of the metal shafts is 15.0 to 15.2 centimetres. How many shafts can the process turn out before tool replacement becomes necessary (i.e., before the process makes an out-of-spec shaft)? (See diagram below.) **LO3**

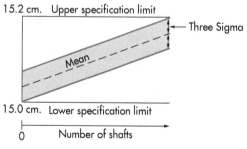

12. Design specification for the concrete slabs in Problem 4 is between 78 and 81 kg.
a. Based on the data given in Problem 4, is the specification being met? **LO3**
b. Estimate the process standard deviation from the average range in Problem 4 using formula 10-4. Then calculate the C_p. Is the process capable? Compare with your answer to part a.

13. The time needed for performing a machining operation is to be investigated. Historically, the process has had a standard deviation equal to .146 minute. The means (in minutes) of 39 samples of $n = 6$ are: **L02**

Sample	Mean	Sample	Mean	Sample	Mean
1	3.86	14	3.81	27	3.81
2	3.90	15	3.83	28	3.86
3	3.83	16	3.86	29	3.98
4	3.81	17	3.82	30	3.96
5	3.84	18	3.86	31	3.88
6	3.83	19	3.84	32	3.76
7	3.87	20	3.87	33	3.83
8	3.88	21	3.84	34	3.77
9	3.84	22	3.82	35	3.86
10	3.80	23	3.89	36	3.80
11	3.88	24	3.86	37	3.84
12	3.86	25	3.88	38	3.79
13	3.88	26	3.90	39	3.85

Construct an $\bar{x}$-chart for this process with Two Sigma limits. Is the process in control?

14. A company has just negotiated a contract to produce a part for another company. In the process of manufacturing the part, the inside diameter of successive parts becomes smaller and smaller as the cutting tool wears. However, the specification is so wide relative to machine capability that it is possible to set the diameter initially at a large value and let the process run for a while before replacing the cutting tool. **L03**

The inside diameter decreases at an average rate of .001 cm per part, and the process has a standard deviation of .01 cm and the variability is approximately Normally distributed. After how many parts must the tool be replaced if the design specification is between 3 cm and 3.5 cm, and the initial setting is 3 standard deviations below the upper design specification?

15. Refer to Solved Problem 2. Suppose that the design specification is between 9.65 and 10.35 minutes. Based on the data given in the Solved Problem 2, does it appear that the design specification is being met? If not, what should one do? **L03**

16. A technician in a quick oil change shop had the following service times (in minutes) for 20 randomly selected cars: **L02**

	Sample		
1	**2**	**3**	**4**
4.5	4.6	4.5	4.7
4.2	4.5	4.6	4.6
4.2	4.4	4.4	4.8
4.3	4.7	4.4	4.5
4.3	4.3	4.6	4.9

a. Determine the mean of each sample.
b. Estimate the mean and standard deviation of the process.
c. Estimate the mean and standard deviation of the sampling distribution of the sample mean.
d. What would Three Sigma control limits for the sample mean be? What alpha risk would they provide?
e. What alpha risk would control limits of 4.14 and 4.86 for the sample mean provide?
f. Using the control limits of 4.14 and 4.86, are any sample means beyond these control limits? If so, which one(s)?
g. Construct the control charts for sample mean and sample range using Table 10-3. Are any sample means and ranges beyond the control limits? If so, which one(s)?
h. Explain why the control limits are different for sample mean in parts d and g.
i. If the process has a known mean of 4.4 and a known standard deviation of .18, what would Three Sigma control limits be for a sample mean chart? Are any sample means beyond the control limits? If so, which one(s)?

17. A process screens a certain type of potash granules resulting in a mean diameter of .03 cm and a standard deviation of .003 cm. The allowable variation in granule diameter is from .02 to .04 cm. **L03**
a. Calculate the capability ratio C_p for the process.
b. Is the process capable?

18. Given the following list of machines, the standard deviation for their output, and specification half-width for the job that may be processed on that machine, using C_p determine which machines are capable of performing the given jobs. **L03**

Machine	Standard Deviation (cm)	Job Half-Width Specification (6 cm)
001	.02	.05
002	.04	.07
003	.10	.18
004	.05	.15
005	.01	.04

19. Suppose your manager presents you with the following information about machines that could be used for a job, and wants your recommendation on which one to choose. The design specification width is .48 mm. Calculate the C_p index for each machine, and explain what additional information you will need to make a choice. **L03**

Machine	Cost per Unit ($)	Standard Deviation (mm)
A	20	.079
B	12	.080
C	11	.084
D	10	.081

20. Each of the processes listed below is noncentred with respect to the design specification. Calculate the C_{pk} index for each, and decide if the process is capable. **LO3**

Process	Process Mean	Process Standard Deviation	Lower Design Specification	Upper Design Specification
H	15.0	.32	14.1	16.0
K	33.0	1.00	30.0	36.5
T	18.5	.50	16.5	20.1

*21. As part of an insurance company's training program, participants learn how to conduct a fast but effective analysis of clients' insurability. The goal is to have participants achieve a time less than 45 minutes. There is no minimum time, but the quality of assessment should be acceptable. Test results for three participants were Armand, a mean of 38 minutes and a standard deviation of 3 minutes; Jerry, a mean of 37 minutes and a standard deviation of 2.5 minutes; and Melissa, a mean of 37.5 minutes and a standard deviation of 2.5 minutes.

Which of the participants would you judge to be capable? Explain. **LO3**

*22. The following data (in ohms) are the resistance of resistors made on an automated machine. The mean and range of each sample are given in the right two columns, and the mean of sample means and the mean of sample ranges are given below these. **LO2**

a. Develop sample mean and sample range control charts for resistance of resistors using the first 10 samples. Is the process in control?

b. Use the control charts developed in part *a* to decide if the 11th sample (also given below) indicates an out-of-control situation.

Resistance of Resistors (in Ohms)

Sample	Obs 1	Obs 2	Obs 3	Obs 4	Mean	Range
1	1,010	991	985	986	993.00	25
2	995	996	1,009	994	998.50	15
3	990	1,003	1,015	1,008	1,004.00	25
4	1,015	1,020	1,009	998	1,010.50	22
5	1,013	1,019	1,005	993	1,007.50	26
6	994	1,001	994	1,005	998.50	11
7	989	992	982	1,020	995.75	38
8	1,001	986	996	996	994.75	15
9	1,006	989	1,005	1,007	1,001.75	18
10	992	1,007	1,006	979	996.00	28
					1,000.03	22.30
11	996	1,006	997	989		

*23. Essex Corp. of St. Louis is a small manufacturer of parts for Boeing's Aircraft and Missile Systems. In the late 1990s, Essex was trying to establish a SPC program. Part number 528003-N was typical. The following samples[6] of two were observed for a critical dimension of the part (in inches). The lower specification, nominal, and upper specification values were .4160, .4185, .4210 inches, respectively. **LO2**

a. Is the process capable?

b. Construct sample mean and sample range control charts. Is the process in control?

Sample

1	2	3	4	5	6	7	8	9	10
.4190	.4190	.4180	.4180	.4175	.4180	.4175	.4173	.4183	.4185
.4190	.4185	.4180	.4179	.4175	.4179	.4175	.4176	.4184	.4185

*24. When Polaroid reduced the number of quality inspectors and increased operator responsibility for statistical process control in its R2 plant (which made instant film cartridges with 10 films in each) in Waltham, Massachusetts, in 1985, it encountered an unexpected result.[7] Instead of quality improving, it actually got worse. To identify the problem, Bud Rolfs, quality control manager, asked an operator from each shift to sample six observations of the critical characteristics of the product and report these to him. One important characteristic of instant films is the pod weight. A pod is a small capsule at the end of each film that contains chemicals. When the film is pulled out, the pod bursts and releases the chemicals that will develop the film. Too much chemical overdevelops the film and too little underdevelops it. **LO2**

a. Use the following three samples of six observations each (in grams) from the first day of the data collection period to develop a sample mean and sample range control chart for the pod weight. Is the process in control?

b. The first sample from the second day is 2.841, 2.802, 2.802, 2.806, 2.807, and 2.807. Is the process still in control?

Sample	Shift	1	2	3	4	5	6	Average
1	A	2.800	2.799	2.760	2.802	2.805	2.803	2.795
2	B	2.750	2.820	2.850	2.740	2.850	2.790	2.800
3	C	2.768	2.807	2.807	2.804	2.804	2.803	2.799

*25. A small manufacturer of metal ring seals for aircraft engines has been asked by its major customer to implement SPC. One major type of ring requires cutting a one-eighth inch wide slot using a milling machine. The following six samples of five observations each, taken

---

[6] Data retrieved from S.K. Vermani, "SPC Modified with Percent Tolerance Pre-control Charts," *Quality Progress* 33(10), October 2000, pp. 43–48.

[7] Process Control at Polaroid (A), 1987, HBS case: 9-693-047.

every half hour, are the width of the slots (in inch) made by the milling machine on the rings. **LO2**

1	2	3	4	5	6
0.1261	0.1259	0.1239	0.1225	0.1259	0.1255
0.1253	0.1263	0.1265	0.1249	0.1243	0.1273
0.1245	0.1247	0.126	0.1265	0.1242	0.1245
0.1249	0.124	0.1257	0.1248	0.1257	0.1268
0.1248	0.1251	0.1243	0.1256	0.1251	0.1263

a. Set up the sample mean and range control charts for this operation. Is the process in control?

b. The seventh sample contains the following values: 0.124, 0.1252, 0.1295, 0.1262, and 0.1275. Using the control charts from part *a*, is the process still in control?

*26. The management of a dried milk manufacturer wanted to evaluate the process capability of its packaging lines. A can line was studied for weight of filled cans. The specification is 974 grams plus or minus 14 grams (including the weight of the can itself). Thirty-five samples of six cans were weighed, and sample mean and range were calculated. The process was in control. The grand mean was 975.7 grams and process standard deviation was 4.7581 grams. **LO3**

a. Calculate the C_p and C_{pk} ratios. Is the filling line capable?

b. After changing the wearable parts of the line, including the piston cylinders, 46 samples of 6 cans were weighed. The grand mean was 976.19 grams and process standard deviation was 2.891 grams. Calculate the new values of C_p and C_{pk} ratios. Has the filling line become capable?

*27. Suppose a process capability study was conducted on a punch-press operation. One of the characteristics of interest is the width of the slot having a specification of 0.4040 ±0.007 inch. Twenty-five samples of five pieces were obtained during a shift, and the sample means and ranges are plotted below. Determine if the process is capable of meeting the specification.[8] **LO3**

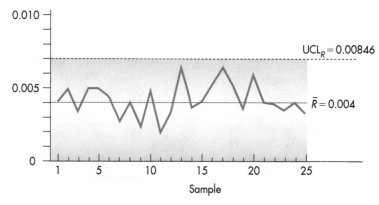

Sample

*28. Royal North Shore Hospital, a 650-bed teaching hospital in Sidney, Australia, uses control charts for quality management.[9] One control chart used shows the number of outpatients waiting more than 30 days for elective surgery (see below). Because the number was increasing (see the plot to the left of *X* up to 3 months before *X*), the hospital appointed a waiting list coordinator (3 months before *X*) who helped reduce the number (see the plot between 3 months before *X* and *Y*), and later reduced further by reducing the holidays for elective

[8] J. Heinricks and M.M.K. Fleming, "Quality Statistical Process Control at Cherry Textron," *Industrial Management*, May/June 1991, 33(3), pp. 7–10.

surgery from six weeks to three weeks during Christmas (see the plot to the right of Y). The control limit lines are 3 standard deviations of the values during each of the 3

subperiods from their centre lines. Determine what type of control chart this is. **L02**

Number of outpatients waiting more than 30 days for elective surgery

July '96 to April '00

*29. Lexington, Kentucky's Shriners Hospital for children is a small hospital specializing in orthopedics.[10] The chief of staff uses various control charts to monitor the performance of the physicians such as the number of patient days a specific doctor works in a month. For example, see the two charts below for Doctor X. Determine

(a) what type of chart the left chart below is and (b) verify the upper control limit for the chart on the right. *Note:* The upper control limit of the left chart is 3 standard deviation of all the values shown (Jan 02–July 03) from its centre line (the average). **L02**

*30. A design of experiments was conducted to study the effect of various factors on the yield and taste of microwave popcorn.[11] The factors and their settings were as follows: **L04**

Table 1   Factors and Levels

Factor	Low (−1)	High (+1)
Price	Generic	Brand
Time	4 min.	6 min.
Power	Medium	High
Preheat	No	Yes
Elevate	No	Yes

Preheat involves heating water in the microwave for 1 minute prior to popcorn. Elevate means put a plate or something similar under the popcorn bag to raise the bag.

Fractional factorial design was used to obtain two responses: (a) Bullets = weight of nonpopped pop corns, in ounces; and (b) taste (a score between 1 and 10, 10 = best).

[9] H. E. Ganley and J. Moxey, "Making Informed Decisions in the Face of Uncertainty," *Quality Progress*, October 2000, 33(10), pp. 76–78.
[10] D. E. Lighter and C. M. Tylkowski, "Case Study: Using Control Charts to Track Physician Productivity," *Physician Executive*, September/October 2004, 30(5), pp. 53–57.
[11] http://www.statease.com/pubs/popcorn.pdf.

A	B	C	D	E	Bullets	Taste
−1	−1	−1	−1	1	1.5	7.5
1	−1	−1	−1	−1	1.4	8.0
−1	1	−1	−1	−1	1.9	9.0
1	1	−1	−1	1	0.6	6.5
−1	−1	1	−1	−1	1.8	7.0
1	−1	1	−1	1	0.3	7.5
−1	1	1	−1	1	0.2	2.5
1	1	1	−1	−1	0.9	1.0
−1	−1	−1	1	−1	1.7	7.0
1	−1	−1	1	1	0.8	6.0
−1	1	−1	1	1	0.6	4.5
1	1	−1	1	−1	0.9	4.0
−1	−1	1	1	1	0.6	9.0
1	−1	1	1	−1	1.3	7.5
−1	1	1	1	−1	Missing	—
1	1	1	1	1	Missing	—

The last two experiments were botched and produced no results.

Determine the influence of each level of each factor on each response and prescribe the best levels for each response (Bullets to be minimized and Taste to be maximized).

*31. Stat-Ease Inc, the producer of a Design of Experiments software, performed an experiment a few years ago to identify the factors that were important in increasing the response rate of engineers to Stat-Ease workshop announcements. The factors and their levels were:[12]

Factor A: Number of colours (two vs. four)
Factor B: Postcard size (4" × 6" vs. 5.5" × 8.5")
Factor C: Paper stock (index vs. heavyweight)

Stat-Ease made eight types of its announcement postcard and sent each type to 1/8 of this mailing list of engineers. The levels of each type and number of fax responses received were:

Version	Factor A Number of Colours	Factor B Postcard Size	Factor C Postcard Thickness	Response
1	2-colour (−)	4" × 6" (−)	Index (−)	34
2	4-colour (+)	4" × 6" (−)	Index (−)	18
3	2-colour (−)	5.5" × 8.5" (+)	Index (−)	44
4	4-colour (+)	5.5" × 8.5" (+)	Index (−)	26
5	2-colour (−)	4" × 6" (−)	Heavyweight (+)	26
6	4-colour (+)	4" × 6" (−)	Heavyweight (+)	17
7	2-colour (−)	5.5" × 8.5" (+)	Heavyweight (+)	29
8	4-colour (+)	5.5" × 8.5" (+)	Heavyweight (+)	21

Determine the influence of each level of each factor on the response and prescribe the best levels for each factor. What do you recommend Stat-Ease should do? **LO4**

*32. A chocolate manufacturer makes a variety of chocolate products including large chocolate bars (340 grams) and boxes of six smaller chocolate bars (170 grams in total). **LO3**

a. Specification for a large bar is 330 grams to 350 grams. What is the largest standard deviation (in grams) that the machine that fills the bar moulds can have and still be considered capable if its average fill is 340 grams?

b. The machine that fills the bar moulds for the smaller bars has a standard deviation of .80 grams. The filling machine is set to deliver an average of 28.5 grams per bar. Specification for the 6-bar box is 160 to 180 grams. Is the process capable? *Hint:* The variance of the box's weight is equal to six times the variance of each smaller bar's weight.

c. What is the lowest setting (in grams) for the smaller-bar filling machine that will leave the process for the 6-bar box capable?

33. An appliance manufacturer wants to contract with a repair shop to handle authorized repairs in Indianapolis. The company has set an acceptable range of repair time of 50 minutes to 90 minutes. Two firms have submitted bids for the work. In test trials, one firm had a mean repair time of 74 minutes with a standard deviation of 4.0 minutes and the other firm had a mean repair time of 72 minutes with a standard deviation of 5.1 minutes. Which firm would you choose? Why? **LO2**

34. Boxes of 50 small packages of M & M milk chocolate candies, produced by Mars, should weigh 625 grams. Therefore, Mars has to ensure that there are enough candies in each package. Suppose two packages of M&Ms were sampled every hour from the packaging machine during a 6-hour period and the number of candies in each package was: **LO2**

			Sample			
	1	2	3	4	5	6
	14	15	15	16	13	14
	15	16	15	15	15	15

a. Calculate the sample mean and sample range for each sample.

b. Calculate the average of sample means and sample ranges.

c. Calculate the control limits for sample mean and sample range control charts.

___
[12] http://www.statease.com/pubs/marketingvoodoo.pdf.

d. Was the process in control? Why?

e. Suppose that the above control limits were then used to control the process. The next day, two packages were sampled and they contained 17 and 14 candies, respectively. Was the packaging machine still in control? Why?

MINI-CASE

Cereal Manufacturer

The plant manager of a cereal manufacturer is wondering if the company could save some cereal by slightly lowering the cereal content of each box. Studying a major product, a 454 gram (net weight) ready-to-eat cereal, he discovers that four boxes are routinely taken from the filling machine every 10 minutes and weighed. Data for approximately 2.5 hours of inspection are shown below.

Questions

1. Is the process in control?

2. Determine what weight the filler head is likely set to.

3. If the *Weights and Measures Act* dictates that the tolerance for weight of a product of approximately 454 grams is 2 grams, what is the probability that an inspector will find a legally defined underweight box (i.e., weighing less than 452 grams)?

4. Has the filler head been set too conservatively? Discuss.

Samples

1	2	3	4	5	6	7	8	9	10	11	12	13	14	15
455.5	456.0	456.0	452.5	456.0	452.0	457.5	454.5	456.0	453.0	455.0	458.0	457.5	458.0	460.0
460.0	455.5	453.0	455.0	456.0	455.0	455.5	453.0	454.0	455.0	457.5	456.0	456.5	453.0	455.5
456.5	456.0	454.0	453.0	455.0	453.0	457.0	453.0	453.0	456.0	456.5	454.5	453.0	456.5	454.5
456.5	456.0	455.0	455.0	454.5	456.0	452.0	458.0	455.0	456.5	456.5	454.0	455.5	456.0	457.0

MINI-CASE   http://company.ingersollrand.com/aboutus/Pages/default.aspx

Quality Control at Ingersoll-Rand

The Ingersoll-Rand plant in Davidson, North Carolina, assembles air compressors for air tools. A few years ago it installed a SPC software that collects critical information about the quality of its air compressors. This made tracking of the percentage of defectives (for each compressor type, components in each compressor, and parts of each component) much easier. Note that percentage defective is just 100 times proportion defective. It also made it possible to monitor these percentages using *p*-charts (sample percentage defective control charts). Using the previous month's percentage defective *p*, Ingersoll-Rand monitored the percentage of defective compressors that it made on each day; if this number was larger than two standard deviations above *p*, Ingersoll-Rand would try to identify the cause of the most frequent defect and find a solution for it. For example, the portable line showed an increased percentage of defectives on January 6. First, the 69 defects were classified according to defect types (see Figure 1): air leaks (30), motors (15), pumps (3), pressure switch (14), cosmetic (2), miscellaneous (3), and bad check valve (2). Given that each of these defects had a control chart in the software, Ingersoll-Rand found out that air leaks' percentage defective

was more than two standard deviations above its previous month's percentage defective (3 percent). Then, the company classified the 30 air leak defects by location of air leak (see Figure 2): tanks weld (5), manifold (12), discharge elbow (1), discharge tube (11), and drain valve (1). Using the control charts for each of these, manifold percentage defective was more than two standard deviations above its previous month's percentage defective (0.7 percent). Having identified the most frequent defect source (air leak from manifold), Ingersoll-Rand contacted the manifold manufacturer and provided this information. The manufacturer found the root cause and fixed the problem. Use of SPC in Ingersoll-Rand facilities continues.

Questions

1. Verify that the percentage of defective portable compressors produced on January 6 was more than twice its standard deviation above the expected proportion (*Hint:* use $\bar{p} = 8\%$ and $n = 578$).

2. Do the same for air leaks (*Hint:* use $\bar{p} = 3\%$ and $n = 578$).

3. Do the same for manifolds (*Hint:* use $\bar{p} = .7\%$ and $n = 578$).

Sources: P. J. Cooper and N. Demos, "Losses Cut 76 Percent with Control Chart System," *Quality* 30(4), April 1991, pp. 22–24. Reprinted with permission from *Quality Magazine.*

(continued)

p̄%	Defect	4	5	6	7	11	12
3.0	Air leaks	4	6	30	8	17	3
2.6	Motors	4	3	15	6	9	8
.4	Pumps		1	3	1	1	1
.1	Sheaves				1		
.3	Pressure switch	2	3	14			5
.2	Cosmetic			2	1		
1.0	Misc.	2	2	3			
.4	Bad check valve		1	2			2
8.0	Total defects	12	16	69	16	28	19
	Total produced	247	367	578	120	453	531
	% Defect	4.9	4.5	11.9	13.3	6.2	3.6

Figure 1

Portable Line

p̄%	Defect	4	5	6	7	11	12
.5	Tanks weld	1	1	5		1	1
.1	Insp. plugs						
.7	Manifold	1	3	12	4	3	1
	Pressure switch				1	10	
.5	Check valve				1		1
.1	Discharge elbow			1			
.1	Nylon tube						
.7	Discharge tube	1	2	11		1	
.1	Drain valve	1		1			
.3	Other				2	2	
3.0	Total defects	4	6	30	8	17	3
	Total produced	247	367	578	120	453	531
	% Defect	1.6	1.6	5.2	6.7	3.8	.6

Figure 2

Air Leaks

To access "Acceptance Sampling," the supplement to Chapter 10,
please visit Connect.

CHAPTER 11
Supply Chain Management

Supply chain management refers to the collaboration of companies, and coordination of their activities, that make up a supply or value chain, starting from raw material and ending with the consumers, linking across supplier–customer companies.

Learning Objectives

After completing this chapter, you should be able to:

LO1 Explain what a supply chain is; discuss the need for managing supply chains; identify strategic and tactical/operational supply chain activities; describe quick response and other similar initiatives, distribution requirement planning, global supply chains, and technologies used in supply chain management; and outline the key steps in creating an effective supply chain, including Collaborative Planning, Forecasting, and Replenishment (CPFR) and performance metrics.

LO2 Explain the purchasing function in organizations, e-commerce, and supplier management and partnership.

LO3 Describe what logistics is, know how to select a transportation mode and solve problems, and discuss third-party logistics and reverse logistics.

Grower Direct is a major flower importer and retail franchise chain in Canada. It is a privately held company started by Skip Kerr in 1986 in Edmonton (http://www.growerdirect.com/our-people). Most Grower Direct flowers, as well as those of other North American flower distributors, are imported from Columbia and Ecuador. The North American flower industry has made long-term arrangement with the flower farmers there to supply flowers as needed in North America, especially to meet the peak demand days of Mothers' Day and Valentine's Day. Planted rose bushes flower after six to eight months and thereafter for approximately nine years. The blooming of rose flowers are curtailed during low season by "pinching" the buds. The harvest is so well timed that flowers arrive just before peak-demand days. The transport takes about one week. How are the roses kept fresh during the transport? They are cooled to just above freezing (approximately 1 degree Celsius) just after cutting and processing (immersing in citric acid, removing some foliage and thorns, grading by type, colour, length, and head size, bundling in bunches of 25, and hydration for 6 to 24 hours) and kept dormant at that temperature throughout the long journey. All modes of transport are refrigerated. The flower boxes are air lifted to Miami International Airport and go through U.S. customs in 24 hours (each box is X-rayed). Those for Grower Direct are picked up and transported to a Grower Direct facility in Miami and packed in refrigerated trucks destined for each region of Canada. The trucks are driven by a team of two drivers who drive in shifts. The trucks are pre-cleared and pass through Canada Customs (a.k.a. Canada Border Services Agency) in a matter of minutes, and are in flower shop coolers approximately four to six days after they are cut. Given their life of three weeks, they will last another two weeks.

Sources: http://www.growerdirect.com/a-cut-flowers-journey; http://www.supplychain247.com/article/the_logistics_of_delivering_fresh_roses_in_time_for_valentines_day/c.h._robinson.

 Introduction to Supply Chain Management

supply chain Sequence of organizations—their facilities and activities—that are involved in producing and delivering a product.

A **supply chain** is the sequence of organizations—their facilities and activities—that are involved in producing and delivering a product. The sequence begins with suppliers of raw materials and extends all the way to the final customer (the consumer). Facilities include factories, warehouses/distribution centres, and retail outlets. Activities include forecasting, product design, scheduling, purchasing, transportation, inventory management/warehousing, production, distribution/delivery, and customer service. There are two kinds of movement in these systems: the physical movement of material (generally toward the end of the chain, the consumer) and the exchange of information and money (mainly toward the beginning of the chain, the source of material).

The term *chain* in supply chain signifies the importance of a close relationship and integration between a supplier and a customer such as a manufacturer and a retailer. This term was first used approximately three decades ago when automatic replenishment systems were introduced between Procter & Gamble and its retail-chain customers.

Every organization is part of at least one supply chain, and many are part of multiple supply chains. Figure 11-1a illustrates a typical supply chain for a product. Figure 11-1b is the supply chain for Wavefarer Board Shorts by Patagonia, a Los Angeles-based clothing designer and distributor. Note that all Patagonia's manufacturing activities are outsourced to Far East companies (this is called offshoring). In Chapter 1, Figure 1-7, a typical supply chain for bread was displayed.

Supply chains are sometimes referred to as value chains, a term that reflects the concept that value is added as goods progress through the chain. Supply or value chains typically comprise separate organizations, rather than just a single organization. However, the objective of a supply chain is that these organizations integrate their activities so that the supply chain acts as one.

supply chain management Collaboration of supply-chain companies and coordination of their activities so that market demand is met as efficiently and effectively as possible.

Supply chain management is collaboration of supply-chain companies and coordination of their activities so that market demand is met as efficiently and effectively as possible.

The same competitive attributes that were given for the products of a company in Chapter 2 are important for supply chains: price, timeliness, quality, variety, and service. Therefore, supply chains should be efficient (reduce costs) and effective (meet timeliness and quality requirements). See "Some Examples of Supply Chain Goals and How They Are Achieved" OM in Action for other desirable characteristics of supply chains.

a.

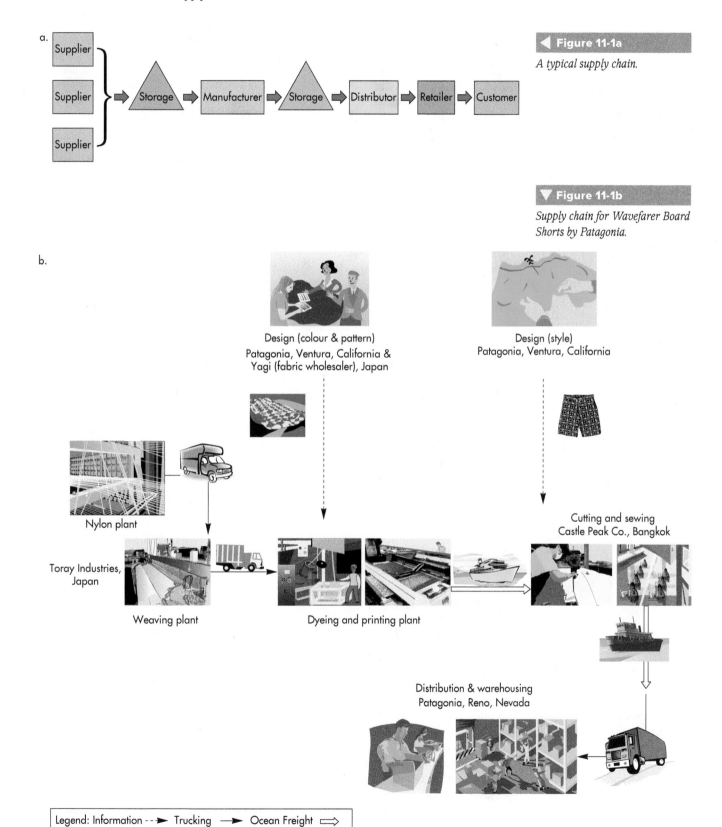

◀ **Figure 11-1a**

A typical supply chain.

▼ **Figure 11-1b**

Supply chain for Wavefarer Board Shorts by Patagonia.

b.

Design (colour & pattern)
Patagonia, Ventura, California &
Yagi (fabric wholesaler), Japan

Design (style)
Patagonia, Ventura, California

Nylon plant

Toray Industries,
Japan

Weaving plant

Dyeing and printing plant

Cutting and sewing
Castle Peak Co., Bangkok

Distribution & warehousing
Patagonia, Reno, Nevada

Legend: Information - - ▶   Trucking ——▶   Ocean Freight ⇨

OM in ACTION

Some Examples of Supply Chain Goals and How They Are Achieved

In addition to being efficient and fast, a supply chain should be agile (i.e., react quickly to sudden changes in supply or demand), adaptable (i.e., change its structure over time as markets change), and align its members' interests. As an example of agility, Dell Computers continually changes the price of some of the components on its website so that the components that are abundant are demanded more and those in short supply are demanded less. As an example of adaptability, Gap Inc. has adapted the supply chains of its

three brands (Gap, Old Navy, and Banana Republic) to their competitive attributes (speed and variety, cost, and quality, respectively). This is done by choosing the country-location of their suppliers. Gaps suppliers are in Central America, Old Navy's suppliers are in China, and Banana Republic's suppliers are in Italy. As an example of interest alignment, R.R. Donnelly, the largest book printer in the world, is sharing the cost savings suggested by its paper and ink suppliers with them. These encourages the suppliers to make cost-saving suggestions.

Source: H. L. Lee, "The Triple-A Supply Chain," *Harvard Business Review*, October 2004, pp. 102–112.

The Need for Supply Chain Management

In the past, most organizations did little to manage their supply chains. Instead, they tended to concentrate on their own operations (silo mentality). However, a number of factors have made it desirable for organizations to actively manage their supply chains. The major factors are:

1. *Increasing competition.* During the last three decades, many organizations have adopted practices such as Just-In-Time (JIT) and lean. As a result, they have cut much of the excess costs out of their operations. Opportunity now lies largely with their suppliers and customers.

outsourcing Buying goods or services instead of producing or providing them in-house (called in-sourcing).

2. *Increasing outsourcing.* Organizations are increasing **outsourcing** by buying goods or services instead of producing or providing them in-house (called in-sourcing). As companies are reducing their costs and increasing their product quality, they are focusing on their core activities and subcontracting the others.

3. *Increasing globalization.* Globalization has extended the physical length of supply chains, and the quantity of materials and products being transported.

4. *Increasing e-commerce.* Increasing e-commerce has resulted in more Internet purchasing, which requires more and faster package delivery services.

5. *The need to manage orders and inventories across the supply chain.* Inventories play a major role in the success or failure of a supply chain, so it is important to coordinate inventory levels throughout a supply chain. Shortages can severely disrupt timely production or sales, while excess inventories add unnecessary holding costs. It would not be unusual to find inventory shortages in some parts of a supply chain and excess inventories in the other parts of the same supply chain.

bullwhip effect Demand/order variability gets progressively larger the further back in a supply chain the company is.

The **bullwhip effect** or demand/order amplification is the phenomenon in which the demand/order variability gets progressively larger the further up in the supply chain the company is. While the demand at a retail store for a particular product is usually fairly stable, the orders of the retailer from wholesaler/distributor are more variable. These variations are even more magnified in the orders of wholesaler/distributor from the manufacturer. Clearly, the bullwhip effect causes inefficiencies at the wholesaler/distributor and manufacturer, such as excess inventory holding cost and overtime, and shortage cost and lower customer service. This phenomenon was discovered by Jay Forrester at MIT many decades ago, where a business simulation game called Beer Distribution game was created to illustrate its existence. A typical result from playing this game is displayed in Figure 11-2.

▲ **Figure 11-2**

Typical results from playing the Beer Distribution Game (http://www.beergame.org) showing the Bull Whip effect. The supply chain consists of three stages: a brewery, a wholesaler, and a retailer. Consumer demand is 5 cases per week for the first 4 weeks and then is raised to 10 units per week (known only to the retailer). Each stage starts with 20 cases of inventory. Each stage plays once a week, receiving a shipment from its supplier (if its supplier had inventory), shipping to its customer (if it has inventory), receiving an order from its customer, and then placing an order to its supplier. There is 2 weeks of lag from issuing an order until receiving it. There is 1 week of lag in receiving an order. The cost of carrying inventory is $0.5 per case per week and cost of shortage is $1 per case per week. The game is played for 20 weeks. As can be observed, all stages are interdependent, and shipment lag makes decision making difficult. As the Wholesaler develops a shortage in week 9, it places a larger order (17 cases) which causes a bigger shortage at Brewery (10 cases), which causes Brewery to order 30 cases next week.

The major cause of the bullwhip effect is slow and/or erratic reaction to a change in demand/order due to lack of end-of-line demand visibility, long lead times, inexperience, and lack of understanding of the impact of one's action on supplier. Other causes are manufacturer price discounts that lead to surges in demand, and gaming by retailers when there is a shortage by inflating their orders in anticipation of receiving only a portion of them.

 OM in ACTION

Nikon's North American Supply Chain

Nikon manufactures most of its cameras in the Far East. Because of a short product life cycle and high value, Nikon uses air cargo to transport its cameras to North America. Many retail chains require customization of packaging or a kit, e.g., camera, lens, batteries, and a charger. Until recently, after the air cargo arrived from Asia in Los Angeles, the shipment was sent to a contract kitter near LA that took days or weeks to do its job. Then, the shipment was

received back, and half was distributed by trucks and the other half put on a plane to New York City. Now, Nikon has a contract with UPS, which transports the shipment from Asia directly to its hub in Louisville, Kentucky, and performs kitting in its facility there. Then it distributes the shipments in North America. UPS also provides customs brokerage service, advance shipping notice, and real-time tracking to Nikon. This integrated supply chain has reduced the total delivery time to 2–3 days.

Source: R. Morton, "Keeping the Supply Chain in Focus," *Logistics Today,* 48(7), Jul 2007, pp. 12–15.

Effective supply chain management is a prerequisite for success in the marketplace, as demonstrated by companies such as P&G, Walmart, Apple, Amazon.com, Best Buy, HP, Cisco, Sony, and Campbell Soup. Also, package delivery companies such as UPS, FedEx, and Purolator have expanded their services to include warehousing, light assembly, and distribution. For an example, see "Nikon's North American Supply Chain" OM in Action.

Supply Chain Management Activities

Strategic (Design) Activities. Strategic decisions have long-term impacts on a supply chain. First, goals and competitive characteristics such as quality, cost, variety (flexibility), timeliness (speed), customer service, and fill rate (i.e., percentage of demand filled from stock on hand) should be agreed upon by the members of the supply chain. Then, products are designed/redesigned with these competitive characteristics in mind. Next, supply chains are designed/redesigned for these products, goals, and competitive characteristics. This involves determining the number, location, capacity, products to produce, and process types of the facilities. Information systems should also be able to communicate seamlessly. Determining the best supply chain network (i.e., the location and capacity of the facilities) is usually performed using linear-programming-based optimization (see supplements to Chapter 6

OM in ACTION

Kodak's Service Parts Supply Chain Redesign

Kodak makes a variety of products including digital cameras, photo printers, photo kiosks, and radiography equipment for hospitals. Kodak has hundreds of field engineers (FE) dispersed throughout North America who repair Kodak equipment. Some of the inventory of spare parts used in repairs is in the central warehouse in Rochester. The rest are in the

trunks of the cars that the FEs use. Until recently, the proportion of inventory split between the central warehouse and the trunks of the FEs was 50–50. A study team was set up to reduce the supply chain costs. The team discovered that 50 percent of the items in the FEs' trunks were expensive items costing more than $700 (mostly refurbishables), but they accounted for only 5 percent of the demand. The process used for refurbishing a part after an equipment repair is shown in the diagram below.

Kodak's old way of supplying parts

The FE would send the repairable expensive part to the central warehouse, which then would send it to a repair vender for repair. The total time averaged 15 days. To redesign this process, the study team decided to pool trunk inventories of the FEs who were located near one another and set up Forward Stock Locations (FSL). The team determined these locations with the help of the Prophet (optimization) software of Baxter Planning Systems. Kodak contracted with UPS to perform the delivery from the closest FSL to the location of repair or the FE when the need arises (FEs don't carry expensive slow-moving parts in their trunk anymore). Also, an FE now sends the old part directly to the repair vendor, saving Kodak 10 days of inventory. The new supply chain reduced the inventory carrying costs by more than 50 percent. The new process is shown in the following diagram. The consolidation in the FSLs is an example of risk pooling.

Source: M. Brienzi and S. Kekre, "How Kodak Transformed Its Service Parts Supply Chain," *Supply Chain Management Review* 9(7), Oct 2005, pp. 25–32.

The new way of supplying parts

- Field engineer is not allowed to carry expensive slow-moving parts.
- Repairable parts are tracked closely.
- Field engineer needs to identify parts requirements before the site visit.

and 8). For smaller problems, heuristics such as "locate a supplier factory close to customer's manufacturing factory" or "locate a regional DC close to major retail customers" is used. For an example of redesign of a supply chain, see the "Kodak's Service Parts Supply Chain Redesign" OM in Action.

Note that determining the extent of vertical integration (i.e., the ownership of a segment of supply chain) is also a strategic decision. Recently, instead of ownership, companies are outsourcing noncore parts of the supply chains, and customer–supplier partnerships are becoming more widespread.

Tactical (Planning)/Operational Activities. The important tactical/operational activities in supply chains relate to production planning and control, including forecasting, purchasing/ordering, transportation of material, inventory control/warehousing, scheduling of production and distribution/deliveries, and customer service. Questions such as "should a product be manufactured at this plant, today or later, or shipped from another location, today or later?" should be answered. Supply chain management involves getting agreement on decisions that affect other members of the supply chain or even jointly making decisions and performing the above activities. We will discuss some of these in the rest of this chapter.

Inventory in a Supply Chain. An important tactical/operational decision is where in a supply chain the inventory should be held. Two general rules apply to this decision:

1. The value of inventory increases as materials move down the supply chain toward the consumers, but the response (or lead) time to consumer demand decreases. Management must strike a balance between additional carrying cost (due to increased value) and better customer service (shorter lead time) to determine the location of inventory in the supply chain.

2. The nature of inventory becomes more specific (thus it loses flexibility of use) as inventory moves down the supply chain. This reduces **risk pooling**: holding (safety) stocks in one central location rather than in multiple regional locations closer to customers. Risk pooling can provide better availability to customers, because the variations in demands in various regional locations typically cancel each other out for the central location.

risk pooling Holding (safety) stocks in one central location rather than in multiple locations.

However, it is possible to achieve both risk pooling and hold inventory closer to customers by **delayed differentiation/postponement**, i.e., waiting until late in the process to add differentiating features to standard components and products. For example, in the paint industry, manufacturers send only white base paint to retail stores where a small amount of colour paint is mixed into white to create the customer's desired colours when demanded.

delayed differentiation/ postponement Waiting until late in the process to add differentiating features to standard components and products.

Some companies have started to use inventory optimization software that determines the optimal location of inventory based on the agreed-upon lead times and costs of carrying inventory. If a facility in the supply chain can replenish its own inventory and produce within the agreed-upon lead time, then it does not have to hold any inventory; otherwise, it has to keep either finished goods or raw material inventory. See e.g., http://www.logility.com/solutions/inventory-optimization/voyager-inventory-optimization.

Warehousing/Transportation in a Supply Chain. Besides storage of goods, a warehouse/ distribution centre (DC) is used for consolidating (combining) shipments of customers' orders, deconsolidating (break bulk) shipments of suppliers' products, and cross-docking. Consolidating shipments means collecting the incoming shipments from various geographic areas headed toward another geographic area and combining them into a larger shipment in order to take advantage of economies of scale in transportation. Deconsolidating shipments is the opposite: splitting a large incoming shipment into smaller shipments that are headed to different customers. There will be more on warehousing in the next chapter and more on transportation at the end of this chapter as part of logistics.

In **cross-docking**, goods arriving at a warehouse/DC from a supplier are directly loaded onto outbound trucks, thereby avoiding warehouse/DC storage. Walmart initiated cross-docking to reduce inventory holding costs and delivery lead times.

cross-docking Loading goods arriving at a warehouse/DC from a supplier directly onto outbound trucks, thereby avoiding warehouse/DC storage.

Efficient Replenishment Methods

Just-In-Time (JIT) replenishment started in the auto industry in the 1980s, and for an automobile manufacturer it means that parts/components are received in small lots and frequently, only a few hours before they will be used. At about the same time, JIT replenishment was modified and applied to apparel/textile and wholesale/retail sectors under the name "quick response."

Quick response (QR) involves making sales information available to vendors. The purpose is to create a JIT replenishment system that is automated and keyed to consumer buying patterns, as opposed to periodic orders by retailers. Another name for quick response is *continuous product replenishment*. QR results in frequent small-lot shipments.

quick response (QR) Just-in-time replenishment system used in retailing where orders are based on actual sales, not periodic orders by retailers.

Quick response has several benefits. Among them are reduced dependency on forecasts and the ability to achieve a closer match between supply and demand, which results in savings in inventory holding and shortage costs. For two applications, see the "Sears Canada's QR" OM in Action and "Nygard" OM in Action later in the chapter.

Efficient consumer response (ECR), initiated by Procter & Gamble, is an expanded version of quick response, used in the grocery industry. In addition to continuous product replenishment, ECR includes further collaboration on forecasting, planning of store assortments, promotions, and product introductions. ECR is continued by Collaborative Planning, Forecasting, and Replenishment (CPFR) which is described later in the chapter.

efficient consumer response (ECR) An expanded version of quick response, used in the grocery industry, which includes further collaboration.

Sears Canada's QR

Sears Canada, with 118 department stores, 48 Home Stores (furniture and appliance stores), 1,446 catalogue pickup locations, 11 outlet stores, 4 specialty appliance and mattress stores, and 234 Sears Hometown Deal Stores (franchises in small towns) is one of the largest retailers in Canada. A few years ago the chain began an initiative to redesign its merchandise procurement processes for big-ticket items such as large appliances, seeking to streamline activities from purchase to delivery to payment.

In simplifying, the company went from 37 distinct procurement methods to four; from many distribution methods to total flow-through (the name sometimes used for quick response); and from 31 ways to pay to one.

Other changes included using more negotiations, cross-docking, advance shipping notices (ASNs), and electronic fund transfer.

For example, under the old approach there were large monthly shipments of large appliances from suppliers to Sears's warehouses, from which customer orders were filled. This required a large, expensive inventory, high storage costs, and extensive handling with the commensurately higher possibility of damage.

Now, when a customer in a store decides to buy a Whirlpool dishwasher, for example, the sales associate connects online to Whirlpool via a store terminal to confirm the availability of the item. The associate then places the order (via EDI) and commits to a firm delivery date.

Whirlpool then sends an ASN and ships the next day using SLH Transport, the trucking subsidiary of Sears Canada. The product is cross-docked at a Sears warehouse (likely Vaughan National Logistics Center NLC) and put on an outbound truck. Nearly 100 big-ticket suppliers, including Whirlpool, GE, Panasonic, and LG have been converted to the new approach.

Results included $65 million in inventory takeout and an 11 percent improvement in the customer fill rate.

ASNs have become a vital part of the overall supply chain visibility, with the top 700 suppliers—representing 85 percent of all purchases—regularly issuing ASN.

Gone with this new approach are attempts by Sears Canada to forecast customer demand. Instead, the chain agrees to provide its suppliers with its sales information and its promotional marketing plans. The suppliers then must agree to decrease lead time and be responsive to actual demand by replacing what is sold.

Sources: C. Gruske, "Counting on the Warehouse," *Materials Management and Distribution*, 58(6), October 2013, 14–15; http://www.mmdonline.com/features/video-sears-calgary-nlc-tour; "Sears Canada on Forecasts: Let the Manufacturer Do It," *Chain Store Age* 71(8) pp. 44–46.

Vendor-managed inventory (VMI) is a related, though not necessarily fast, replenishment method where the vendor's sales/account manager periodically visits the buyer's premise (or uses electronic means), counts the inventories of her company on the buyer's shelves (or in the computer database), and has them replenished to the previously agreed-upon levels. VMI has been used by soft drink companies supplying convenience stores, electrical distributors supplying small maintenance warehouses, etc.

vendor-managed inventory (VMI) An agreement in which the supplier has access to the customer's inventory and is responsible for maintaining the inventory levels required by the customer.

Distribution Requirements Planning

Distribution requirements planning (DRP) is a system for synchronizing replenishment schedules across the supply chain. It is especially useful in multi-echelon distribution networks (hierarchical levels of factory, regional warehouses/DCs, and retail stores). It uses a concept similar to material requirements planning (see Chapter 14) for distribution. Starting with forecast demand at the end of the distribution network (retail stores), DRP works backward through the network to obtain time-phased replenishment schedules for moving goods from the factory through each level of the distribution network. Note that DRP is a push system (it produces and ships based on demand forecasts and plans) whereas quick response is a pull system (it produces and ships based on actual demand).

distribution requirements planning (DRP) Starts with the forecast demand at the end of the distribution network (retail stores), and works backward through the network to obtain time-phased replenishment schedules for moving goods from the factory through each level of the distribution network.

Global Supply Chains

As international trade barriers fall, more companies are expanding their global operations. This is presenting tremendous opportunities and opening up previously untapped markets for raw materials, goods, and services. The ability to export to other countries, as opposed to making the product there, has allowed multinational companies to centralize the production of families of their products in one location. Also, increasing e-commerce has resulted in increasing global package deliveries.

Supply chain disruptions can reduce revenue and threaten production and distribution. A risk from accidents is shown here with containers falling from the deck of a damaged cargo ship after a collision between two cargo ships.

Managing a global supply chain that may have far-flung customers and/or suppliers magnifies some of the challenges of managing a domestic supply chain. Obviously, distances and lead times increase as the supply chain becomes longer. In addition, there is the possibility of having to deal with different languages, cultures, and currencies; additional modes of transportation (resulting in additional shipment changing hands); intermediaries such as freight forwarders (consolidators of small shipments e.g., http://www.tslnz.com/index.htm) and customs brokers; and risk of damage, disruption, and terrorism.

Canada's most significant trading partner by far is the United States, and bulk goods are transported between these two nations mainly by rail whereas other goods are transported by truck. Most overseas trade involves ocean transport and is mainly through the port of Vancouver. However, perishable, lightweight, and expensive goods are transported by air cargo. For an example, see the Grower Direct opening vignette.

Supply Chain Management Information System

Data and information are used in supply chains for transaction processing (execution), including visibility (tracking of shipments), making planning/design decisions, and collaboration (an example of collaboration in forecasting CPFR will appear later in the chapter). It is said that information "replaces" inventory. This means that an organization can reduce the inventory it carries if it has relevant, accurate, and timely information.

To be cost effective, an information system should be based on open systems concept (i.e., nonproprietary) and use the Internet (for communication). Relevant accurate data should be collected and data should be synchronized (i.e., be updated without delay across the supply chain).

Information technology (IT) comprises tools that are used to gather (e.g., for tracking), access, analyze (for decision making), and share information (for linking the supply chain). IT includes computers (hardware and software) and communication devices. IT enables supply chain processes/activities to be performed cheaper, faster, and more accurately. IT automates flow of information.

Supply chain planning software can be classified into strategic (e.g., network design optimization), tactical (e.g., production planning such as sales and operation planning explained in Chapter 13, and distribution planning), and operational (e.g., forecasting/demand management, production scheduling, transport planning).

Supply chain execution software includes order taking, purchasing/replenishment/order fulfillment, Warehouse Management System (WMS; see Chapter 12), Transport Management System (TMS; selecting carriers, vehicle routing, dispatch, visibility/tracking, etc.).

A more general type of software is enterprise resource planning (ERP) or enterprise software, which was originally focused on managing and coordinating all the resources and functions of an organization from a shared database (more in Chapter 14).

Initially, supply chain management software produced by companies such as Manugistics and i2 Technologies (both now part of JDA) had to work with the ERP software of an organization to be able to function seamlessly. Through acquisition, general business modules/software were added to their suite, thus getting closer to an ERP.

At the same time, ERP software producers such as SAP and Oracle added supply chain modules to their ERPs to make them more suitable for supply chain management. These modules usually facilitate interaction with suppliers (called Supplier Relationship Management SRM) and with customers (called Customer Relationship Management CRM).

Supply chain software tends to change over time. A new application is event management software that monitors the supply chain for out-of-tolerance (exception) events, e.g., delay of shipment, and notifies the relevant person. This software is related to visibility and tracking.

The use of tracking can be observed in online shopping where the parcel delivery or trucking company assigns a unique number/bar code to a shipment and makes it available to the customer who can monitor the status of shipment as it flows in the supply chain. The carrier uses bar code readers to update the status of the shipment (more on bar codes in the next chapter). A more sophisticated approach is to use Radio Frequency Identification (RFID) which reads the identity of the item electronically rather than by scanning required for a bar code.

A recent trend in software purchase option is to use a Software as a Service (SaaS) which involves using the Internet to access the computer of an application service provider that maintains the customer's data. The advantage of SaaS is that it requires no initial investment and the service can usually be terminated with a month's notice.

One technical difficulty in supply chain information systems is data standardization, which allows easier interconnectivity and economies of scale. The computer languages used for this purpose include Electronic Data Interchange (EDI) for electronic communication and, more recently, Extensible Mark-up Language (XML) used for designing Web pages.

Another technical difficulty in supply chain information systems is application integration, i.e., the ability of supply chain member information systems to easily communicate with each other's application software. Efforts in this regard include developing Service-oriented architecture (SOA) such as Microsoft.NET and Java.

Electronic Data Interchange. **Electronic data interchange (EDI)** is direct, computer-to-computer transmission of inter-organizational transactions and information, including purchase orders, sales data, advance shipping notices, invoices, engineering drawings, and more. Among the reasons companies use EDI (see e.g., the "QLogitek" OM in Action later in the chapter) are:

- Reduction in clerical labour (no need for receiving and entering data manually).
- Reduction of paperwork.
- Increased accuracy (avoids re-entry of data, thus reducing errors).
- Increased speed.

In most JIT systems, EDI is used to signal a replenishment to the supplier. There are many applications of EDI in retailing involving electronic communication between retailers and vendors. Walmart has a satellite network for EDI that allows its retail store point-of-sale data to be downloaded every night to its main database, which vendors can also access through RetailLink. This enables the vendors to manage their own inventory; Walmart saves money and fill rates are up. For more information, see the "Walmart" OM in Action.

RFID. **Radio frequency identification (RFID)** is a technology that uses radio waves to identify objects such as goods in a supply chain. This is done through the use of an RFID tag that is attached to an object. The tag has an integrated circuit chip and an antenna that emits information to network-connected RFID readers using radio waves. The illustration on the next page shows a RFID tag. It looks like a label, although the centre of the middle layer contains a microchip surrounded by a thin metal object, which acts as antenna.

There are two kinds of RFID tags: (1) Active tags have a battery and emit radio waves by themselves; hence they have a longer range (perhaps up to 50 metres or so) but are more

electronic data interchange (EDI) The direct transmission of inter-organizational transactions and information, computer-to-computer, including purchase orders, sales data, advance shipping notices, invoices, and engineering drawings.

radio frequency identification (RFID) A technology that uses radio waves to identify objects such as goods in a supply chain.

OM in *ACTION*

Walmart

Walmart uses a satellite to transmit store point-of-sale and other data (shelf space and local sales decisions captured by handheld devices from store staff) to Walmart's computers in Bentonville, Arkansas, several times a day. There are three supply chains: (1) Some suppliers (of mainly soft lines such as apparel, footwear, etc.) have access to the POS data through RetailLink and perform vendor-managed inventory and replenish the stores directly.

(2) Other suppliers receive orders from Walmart and ship to the distribution centres, which cross-dock most items to the retail stores. (3) Walmart replenishes fast-moving items in the stores according to its POS data from inventory kept in the distribution centres. See the following diagram for Walmart Canada.

Sources: http://www.youtube.com/watch?v=SUe-tSabKag; F.A. Kuglin, *Customer-centered Supply Chain Management*. New York: AMACOM (American Management Association), 1998, p. 175.

expensive; (2) passive tags do not have a battery but work by responding to electromagnetic waves emitted by the RFID reader; hence have a shorter range (perhaps up to 5 metres or so).

RFID tags can be attached to pallets, cases, or individual items. They provide unique identification, enabling businesses to identify, track, monitor, or locate practically any object in the supply chain that is within the range of a tag reader. These tags are similar to bar codes, but have the advantage of conveying much more information and they do not require the line-of-sight reading that bar codes require. And unlike bar codes, which must be scanned individually and usually manually, multiple RFID tags can be read simultaneously and automatically. Furthermore, an RFID tag provides more precise information than a bar code: RFID tags contain detailed information on each object, whereas bar codes convey only an object's classification, such as its stock keeping unit (SKU).

RFID eliminates the need for manual counting and bar-code scanning of goods at receiving docks, in warehouses, and on retail shelves. This eliminates errors and greatly speeds up the process.

The costs involved in setting up an RFID system include the cost of the tags themselves as well as the cost of programming and fixing individual tags to the objects, the cost of readers, and the cost of hardware and software to transmit and analyze the data generated. Other than the cost (currently a passive RFID tag costs approximately 10 cents), the downside of RFIDs is that the radio waves are affected by the nature of some objects (e.g., liquid and metal objects interfere with the proper working of the RFID tags).

Creating an Effective Supply Chain

Successful supply chain management requires forming close relationships, effective communication and coordination of activities, supply chain visibility and information sharing, event management capability, and performance metrics.

Forming Close Relationships. It is important for the members of a supply chain to form close relationships (even partnerships). This requires trust, willingness to cooperate, sharing similar goals, and confidence that they will take actions that are mutually beneficial. See the "Aligning Incentives" OM in Action for an example of how economic incentives of supply chain members can be aligned.

Effective Communication and Coordination of Activities. Effective supply chains require close and regular communication among members at all levels in order to coordinate activities for effective operations. This requires integrated information systems and standardized ways and means of communicating among members. One example is collaborative planning, forecasting, and replenishment (CPFR), explained later.

Supply Chain Visibility and Information Sharing. **Supply chain visibility** means that a member can connect to any part of the supply chain to access data in real time on forecasts and sales data, inventory levels, shipment status, impending shortages, and other problems that could impact the timely flow of products through the chain. Thus, instead of each organization in a supply chain making plans based on forecast of demand of its immediate customer, by sharing data on end-customer sales on a real-time basis, each organization in the supply chain can develop plans that contribute to synchronization across the supply chain.

supply chain visibility A member can connect to any part of the supply chain to access data in real time.

Event Management Capability. **Event management** is the ability to detect and respond to unplanned events such as delayed shipment or a warehouse running low on a certain item.

event management The ability to detect and respond to unplanned events.

Performance Metrics. Performance metrics are necessary to confirm that the supply chain is functioning as expected, or that there are problems that must be addressed. A variety of measures can be used. These are presented later in this section.

OM in *ACTION*

Aligning Incentives

For the members of a supply chain to have economic incentive to work together for the good of all members of the supply chain, the risks, costs, and rewards of doing business should be divided fairly.

To illustrate, suppose a newspaper vendor buys newspapers from a printer for 80 cents each and sells them for $1 each. Also, suppose that it costs the printer 45 cents to print a newspaper, demand for the vendor's newspapers is uniform between 100 and 200 copies per day, and that any unsold newspapers have no value at the end of the day. In the next chapter on inventory management, we will model this problem as the single-period model and provide a formula for its optimal solution. In this case, the optimal solution for the vendor is to buy 120 copies. It can be shown that this would result in an expected daily profit of $21.92 for the vendor and $42 for the printer (a total of $63.92

profit). Note that in this case the vendor is bearing all the risk of demand variability.

Now, if both agree that the printer sells each paper to the vendor at cost (45 cents each) and shares in the revenue (e.g., 35 percent printer, 65 percent vendor), it can be shown that the optimal solution will be 131 copies, with expected daily profit of $23.01 for the vendor and $44.13 for the printer (a total of $67.14 profit). In this case, vendor and printer will be sharing the risk of demand variability.

Better still, if the printer agrees to buy back any unsold papers for 60 cents each, it can be shown that the optimal solution will be 150 copies, with expected daily profit of $24.95 for the vendor and $49.34 for the printer (a total of $74.29 profit). In this case also, vendor and printer will be sharing the risk of demand variability.

Source: V. G. Narayanan and A. Raman, "Aligning Incentives in Supply Chains," *Harvard Business Review*, November 2004, pp. 94–102.

Steps in Creating an Effective Supply Chain

Creation of an effective supply chain entails several key steps:

1. Develop strategic objectives. These will guide the process.

2. Integrate and coordinate activities inside the organization. This requires (a) overcoming barriers caused by functional thinking that lead to attempts to optimize a subset of a system rather than the system as a whole, and (b) sharing data and coordinating activities.

3. Coordinate activities with suppliers and with customers. This involves addressing supply and demand issues.

4. Coordinate planning and execution across the supply chain. This requires a system for sharing data across the supply chain, allowing access to data to those who engage in operations to which it will be useful.

5. Consider the possibility of forming *strategic supplier/customer partnerships*. A **strategic supplier/customer partnership** occurs when a buyer and a supplier agree to collaborate so that each may realize a strategic benefit. There are different degrees of partnership. A basic version occurs when a supplier agrees to hold inventory for a customer, thereby reducing the customer's cost of holding the inventory in exchange for the customer agreeing to a long-term commitment, thereby relieving the supplier of the costs of continually looking for new customers, negotiating prices and services, and so on. It is important that the number of partners in a supply chain be small and the number of chains a company belongs to be limited so that working relationships and trust can be established.

strategic supplier/customer partnership A buyer and a supplier agree to collaborate so that each may realize a strategic benefit.

Collaborative Planning, Forecasting, and Replenishment (CPFR)

CPFR is the latest effort to increase the effectiveness and efficiency of supply chains. It moves efficient consumer response one step further by establishing a process for communicating and agreeing on forecasts and orders between the manufacturer and the customer (the distributor/retail chain). For collaborative forecasting, a two-step process is usually used. In the first step, the retailer/distributor collects POS data, forecasts sales, and electronically shares them with the manufacturer, which compares the sales forecasts with capacity. If there will be any significant shortfall (called "exception"), the manufacturer tries to resolve the difference. If this is not possible, the manufacturer contacts the retailer/distributor (usually by making a phone call), and the two try to reconcile the difference. After the two agree on sales forecast, the second step involves the order forecast (which considers the sales forecasts and the inventories, etc.). A similar process to step 1 is used to create the order forecast.

For more details, see the diagram in http://www.copilotes.eu/images/CPFR_1.gif. Companies such as Best Buy, Sony, Motorola, HP, and Whirlpool regularly use CPFR with their major distributor/retailer customers. For an application of CPFR, see "Whirlpool's CPFR" OM in Action.

CPFR A process for communicating and agreeing on forecasts and orders between the manufacturer and the customer (distributor/retailer).

Performance Metrics

The following attributes/metrics are commonly used to measure performance of a supply chain (note their similarity with the competitive attributes of Chapter 2):

1. Cost (unit cost, inventory turnover, logistics costs).

2. Variety/flexibility (speed of production and product changes).

3. Delivery (lead time, percentage of on-time delivery).

4. Customer service (item fill rate).

inventory turnover The rate at which inventory (material) goes through the supply chain.

item fill rate Percentage of demand for an item filled from stocks on hand.

Inventory turnover refers to the rate at which inventory (material) goes through the supply chain. Faster is better: The quicker materials pass through the supply chain, the lower inventory costs will be, and the quicker products will be delivered to the customer. **Item fill rate** is the percentage of demand for an item filled from stocks on hand.

A similar set of performance attributes/metrics has been proposed by the Supply Chain Council (now part of APICS), a not-for-profit association of organizations and consultants interested in supply

Whirlpool's CPFR

In 2002 Whirlpool's Logistics Department was reorganized into the Supply Chain Department so it could improve its customer service performance. As part of that, Whirlpool tested CPFR with two of its major customers (retail chains). Even though there was informal collaboration before, the lack of a shared-files database and a predetermined collaboration schedule (specific hourly and daily plan in a weekly cycle) meant that the process of forecast reconciliation was not effective. After getting internal and external buy-in, the project manager formed two separate CPFR teams, one for each customer, and prepared a training manual on CPFR.

The teams included Whirlpool's demand managers dealing with each customer, some production planners, deployment planners (responsible for inventory levels in Whirlpool's regional distribution centres), and marketing forecast managers (who generated top-down forecasts based on industry trends and market shares). The customers each also formed a team including inventory managers/planners, buyers, and information system staff. One team chose i² Technologies' Supply Chain Collaborator (now called JDA Collaborative Supply Execution), while the other used another software used by the customer with another supplier.

The CPFR process actually affected Whirlpool's internal forecasting and planning process. Instead of monthly sales and operations planning, Whirlpool executives review the weekly sales and order forecasts generated jointly with the customer. Sales and Marketing are alerted about short-supply and excess-supply stock keeping units (SKUs) in order to shape the demand.

After only a few months, the sales forecast inaccuracy significantly decreased (Mean Absolute Percentage Error for SKUs at store-level decreased from an average of 69 percent to 44 percent). Also, CPFR has given better understanding of Whirlpool-customer problems. The improvement process continues.

Source: N. Sagar, "CPFR at Whirlpool Corporation: Two Heads and an Exception Engine," *Journal of Business Forecasting Methods & Systems* 22(4), Winter 2003/2004, pp. 3–10.

chain management. The metrics are part of the Supply Chain Operations Reference (SCOR) model and the top-level attributes/metrics are shown in Table 11-1 (for more details see https://supply-chain.org/f/SCOR-Overview-Web.pdf). The SCOR model reflects an effort to standardize measurement of supply chain performance. Perfect order fulfillment is the percentage of orders on time, complete, and with accurate invoice. Cost of Goods Sold (COGS) is the material, direct labour, and indirect labour costs. Cash-to-cash cycle time is the number of days of working capital tied up in the supply chain. It is calculated by adding the number of days of inventory on hand to number of days of receivables (sales) outstanding and subtracting the number of days of payables outstanding.

Attribute	Metric
Reliability	Perfect order fulfillment
Responsiveness	Lead time
Agility	Upside flexibility/adaptability
Costs	Supply chain management cost
	COGS
Assets management	Cash-to-cash cycle time
	Return on fixed assets
	Return on inventory

◀ **Table 11-1**

Supply Chain Operations Reference (SCOR) model 10.0: attributes and top-level metrics.

Purchasing

The purchasing department/services is responsible for buying the raw materials, manufacturing parts, supplies and spare parts, machines and equipment, and services needed to produce a good or provide a service. Purchasing is a major part of supply chain management. You can get some idea of the importance of purchasing when you consider that most of the cost of many finished goods comes from purchased parts and materials. Furthermore, all goods sold by retailers and wholesalers have to be purchased first (retail/wholesale buying also requires merchandising skills). Nonetheless, the importance of purchasing is more than just the cost of goods purchased; other important factors include the *quality* of goods and services, and *timing* of deliveries of goods or services, both of which can have a significant impact on operations. Also, purchasing plays the central role in forming partnerships.

OM in ACTION

QLogitek

QLogitek is a B2B-EDI supply chain solutions provider in Toronto. QLogitek's set of 9 supply chain software programs are mainly used as SaaS (Software-as-a-Service), and are based on Microsoft's BizTalk Server Platform. The service allows a company to connect with its suppliers over the Internet using QLogitek's servers, instead of directly. Over 20,000 companies in 170 countries use the service. Over 80,000 users made 3.7 billion transactions last year.

HMV (Canada) used QLogitek's SaaS Supplier Order Management, which allowed HMV's approximately 113 stores to send purchase orders to and receive invoices from its small suppliers. The larger suppliers and all the stores use EDI directly.

Hudson's Bay Company used QLogitek's Inbound Management SaaS to receive advance shipping notices and invoices from its small suppliers. QLogitek was acquired by Smart Employee Benefits, a Toronto employee-benefits software company.

Source: http://www.qlogitek.com/company.

The company

Figure 11-3

Purchasing's interfaces.

The basic goal of purchasing is to develop and implement purchasing plans for goods and services that support the business plan. Among the duties of a buyer (the professional who does the purchasing) are identifying sources of supply, negotiating contracts, maintaining a database of suppliers, obtaining goods and services that meet operations' requirements in a timely and cost-efficient manner, managing suppliers, establishing partnerships, and acting as liaison between suppliers and various internal departments/functions.

Purchasing is taking on increased importance as organizations place greater emphasis on supply chain management, quality improvement, JIT, and outsourcing.

Purchasing's Interfaces. Purchasing interfaces with a number of other functional areas within an organization, as well as with outside suppliers (see Figure 11-3).

The *operations* department constitutes the main source of requests for purchased materials (manufacturing parts and operating supplies). Another user of purchasing services is the *maintenance* department, which requires spare parts and repair supplies. New machines and equipment are requisitioned by manufacturing engineers.

Accounting is responsible for handling payments to suppliers.

Design engineering requests new material/parts.

Receiving staff check incoming shipments and receive them, and material handling staff move the goods to their destination (the requisitioner).

OM in ACTION

Nygard

Nygard International is the largest women's fashion clothing company in Canada (with estimated revenue of over $1 billion). Its design facilities are in Winnipeg (also its headquarters) and New York City (its new U.S. HQ); its production facilities are mainly in southeast Asia now (its last Winnipeg sewing shop closed in 2008); its sales offices are in Winnipeg, Toronto, and New York; and it has large distribution (service) centres in Winnipeg (155,000 ft²), Vaughan, Ontario (300,000 ft²), and Los Angeles, California (800,000 ft²). Nygard also has over 200 stores in Canada. Founder Peter J. Nygard is a visionary in the apparel industry and the use of technology. Starting in the 1980s, Nygard computerized all its operations including design

and production activities using CAD, computerized cutting, planning/control, and receiving and shipping. All the programming, equivalent to a full-blown ERP software, was done in-house. In the mid-1990s, Nygard turned his attention to the supply chain. He asked his major customers, such as Hudson's Bay Company, to let an EDI software be installed on their computer system so that when an item was sold at a store, this information was immediately relayed to Nygard. Nygard guaranteed 24-hour response time, from the time of receiving an order to shipment (any item short was shipped the following day free). This quick response/continuous replenishment system was and is revolutionary in the apparel industry, where the usual lead time is at least two weeks. Nygard's system also has EDI connection to its major suppliers of fabric, zippers, buttons, etc. Nygard spent over $66 million on its information technology in the 1980s and 1990s, and $10 million per year since then.

In the mid-2000s, Nygard partnered with Dillard's, Inc., a major U.S. clothing retail chain, to implement CPFR. This involved both merchandise planning/forecasting and replenishment. The IT applications in the two companies had to be integrated to enable this (synchronized data). Results were positive in all test stores. One of the largest stores experienced a 40 percent sales increase while carrying 20 percent less inventory. Time from replenishment order to goods-on-selling floor was cut from 16 to 7 days.

Sources: http://corporate.nygard.com/scf/News.aspx?id=7984&terms= Quick%20Response; http://corporate.nygard.com/scf/News.aspx?id= 10986&terms=quick%20response; http://corporate.nygard.com/scf/News. aspx?id=7964&terms=Quick%20Response; http://corporate.nygard.com/scf/ News2007.aspx?id=12286.

Make-or-Buy and Insourcing-Outsourcing Decisions. A make-or-buy decision applies when a company can both produce and purchase a part. The question is whether to manufacture the part or buy it from a supplier. Some companies buy most of parts they need. For example, personal computer manufacturers buy most of their parts from suppliers and merely assemble the computers. So do automobile manufacturers. Note that custom parts are usually designed by the buying company and only its manufacturing is contracted out.

Insourcing is bringing the performance of a major business function (e.g., IT, HR, manufacturing) in-house, whereas outsourcing is paying a supplier to perform it.

Organizations may buy/outsource for a variety of reasons: a supplier may have lower cost (due to economies of scale, etc.), more expertise and knowledge, or patent; demand may be temporary or seasonal; or the company may not have idle capacity. Buying/outsourcing carries some risk: reduction in control and expertise. Strategic considerations may outweigh other factors: organizations should make/in source those parts or processes that are or should be their core competencies, i.e., long-term organizational capabilities that help the organization to compete.

In some cases, a company might do both: make a portion of the quantity needed in-house and pay a supplier make the rest. The benefits include maintaining expertise and flexibility, and hedging against loss of a supplier or higher prices.

The following simple example (Example 1) illustrates how one might compare the costs of make versus buy of a part.

Analyze the following data to determine the total annual cost of make and buy for a part.

◀ **Example 1**

	Make	**Buy**
Expected annual quantity	20,000 units	20,000 units
Variable cost per unit	$5.00	$6.00
Annual fixed costs	$30,000	

SOLUTION

Total annual cost = Fixed cost + Variable cost per unit × Estimated annual quantity

Make : $30,000 + $5 × 20,000 = $130,000

Buy : $0 + $6 × 20,000 = $120,000

In this instance, buying would save $10,000 a year. This information should be combined with information on other relevant factors to decide which alternative, make or buy, would be better.

Purchasing Cycle. The **purchasing cycle** is a series of steps that begins with a purchase requisition from within the organization and ends with paying the supplier. The main steps in the purchasing cycle are:

purchasing cycle A series of steps that begins with a request for purchase and ends with paying the supplier.

1. *Purchasing receives a purchase requisition.* The purchase requisition includes (a) a general description of the item desired, (b) the quantity and quality necessary, and (c) desired delivery date.

2. *Purchasing selects a product/supplier.* The buyer must identify suppliers that have the capability of supplying the desired good/service. If there is no approved supplier(s), Google can be

used to search for a source. Potential suppliers may be prequalified (by e.g., testing a proto-type part made by them) and then asked to quote a price. If the order is not well defined, potential suppliers are asked to submit a proposal saying how they will meet the need.

3. *Purchasing decides how the good or service is purchased.* High value customized manufacturing parts are negotiated using long-term contracts/partnership. Low-value standard items such as supplies (e.g., stationery) are purchased by blanket purchase (or standing) orders. This involves annual negotiation of prices for a total annual purchase dollar, with deliveries subject to operating units' direct request throughout the year. Many companies have EDI connection with their suppliers. Electronic purchasing is referred to as e-procurement. Low value one-time purchases should be handled directly between the operating unit and the supplier using corporate credit cards.

4. *Monitoring orders (and expediting).* Routine follow-up, especially those with lengthy lead times, allows the buyer to prevent delays.

5. *Receiving shipments.* Receiving staff must check the incoming shipment against the purchase order and notify purchasing and accounting departments by preparing a receiving report. If the quality of the incoming shipment is in doubt, quality control staff must inspect the shipment. If the goods are not satisfactory, the supplier should be notified without delay.

6. *Paying the supplier.* Upon receipt of shipment, accounts payable must pay the invoice. If a discount is given for early payment, this should be taken advantage of.

value analysis Examination of the function and design of a part/product in an effort to reduce its cost.

Value Analysis. **Value analysis** refers to the examination of the *function* and design of a part/product in an effort to reduce its cost. Typical questions that are asked are included in Table 11-2.

A team is formed with representatives from design engineering, manufacturing, and cost accounting to work with purchasing to conduct the value analysis.

Determining Prices. Prices are determined in one of three ways: published price list, competitive bidding, and negotiation.

Standard items that are bought infrequently and/or in small quantities are purchased at a fixed market price (published price list). Large orders of standard items receive a price break (due to quantity discount). To do so, buyer should get at least two to three quotes or use *competitive bidding.* The buyer calls (in the informal version) or sends written requests (in the formal version) for bids to potential suppliers, asking them to quote a price. Large government purchases of goods or services are usually made through formal competitive bidding. Usually, the lowest quote or bid wins the contract. Commodities have volatile prices and could be purchased ahead of the need to hedge against price increase. Future prices provided by futures markets could be used to forecast future prices.

Price negotiation is used for customized goods or services, or when only few potential sources exist. A take-it-or-leave-it approach or one that capitalizes on the weaknesses of the supplier will have detrimental effects later. The most reasonable approach is one of give and take (referred to as win-win).

Table 11-2 ▶	1. Select a part/product that has a high annual dollar value.
The value analysis process and questions.	2. Identify the basic function of the item (in a verb–noun form, e.g., a bolt "joins things.")
	3. Obtain answers to these kinds of questions:
	a. Can the function be performed in another way?
	b. Could another material or part be used instead?
	c. Can specifications be made less stringent?
	d. Can two or more parts of the item be combined?
	e. Can a different manufacturing process be used?
	f. Do suppliers have suggestions for improvement?
	g. Can packaging be made less costly?
	4. Evaluate the answers obtained, and make a recommendation.

Centralized versus Decentralized Purchasing. **Centralized purchasing** means that purchasing is handled by a central purchasing department. **Decentralized purchasing** means that individual departments or separate locations handle their own purchasing requirements.

The purchasing department may be able to obtain lower prices than decentralized units if the higher volume created by combining orders enables the company to take advantage of quantity discounts offered on large orders. It may also be able to obtain better service and closer attention from suppliers. In addition, centralized purchasing enables companies to assign certain categories of items to specialist buyers who tend to become more efficient and skilled. For an application of purchasing centralization, see "Teck" OM in Action.

Decentralized purchasing has the advantage of awareness of differing "local" needs and being better able to respond to those needs. Where locations are widely scattered, decentralized purchasing may be able to save on transportation costs by buying locally.

Some organizations manage to take advantage of both centralization and decentralization by permitting individual units to buy certain items while other items are bought centrally. For example, small orders and rush orders are handled locally or by departments, while centralized purchasing is used for high-volume, high-value items/commodities or corporate services such as payroll, personnel, information systems, legal, etc.

Spend Analysis. Many organizations fail to collect accurate and useful purchasing data. This is because (1) different codes may be used to describe the same supplier or item in different plants,

centralized purchasing
Purchasing is handled by a central purchasing department.

decentralized purchasing
Individual departments or separate locations handle their own purchasing requirements.

OM in *ACTION*   http://www.teck.com

Teck

Teck is a copper and zinc mining company based in Vancouver, but has expanded into oil and coal mining recently. Teck's mines are in B.C., Alberta, the United States, Chile, and Peru. When, in 2008, Teck bought six coal mines in B.C., the spare parts inventory management of the six mines were run independently using six independent software programs not connected to the legacy mainframe in Vancouver. To be able to

coordinate purchasing and buy spare parts as a group, Teck's information system department oversaw the purchase and installation of Microsoft Dynamics, a tier 2 ERP software. Now, there is a centralized database that can be accessed by each mine and the head office. Purchase orders are accumulated over the six mines and inventory is controlled more efficiently.

Source: http://www.microsoft.com/en-ca/dynamics/customer-success-stories-detail.aspx?casestudyid=4000008850.

OM in *ACTION*

Mountain Equipment Co-op

Mountain Equipment Co-op (MEC) was established in 1971 by six mountaineers in Vancouver who wanted to have quality mountain climbing equipment available for sale in Canada. It is a consumers' co-op and its profits are distributed to its members based on their purchases. Lifetime membership is only $5 and there are over 3 million members. MEC now has stores in 18 Canadian cities and over $321 million revenue. MEC designs and manufactures approximately 60 percent of the items it sells. Other items are purchased from high-quality manufacturers. MEC has a strong sustainability policy for environment and ethical sourcing. The environmental efforts involve using greener material (e.g., PVC-free, organic cotton, recycled polyester), green buildings, waste reduction (e.g., no hang tags, poly bags, paper), and using greener logistics (intermodal instead of truck for shipping from Vancouver to the East, no overseas air cargo). MEC is a member of 1% For the Planet and donates 1 percent of its

gross sales to environmental causes. The ethical sourcing policy is the MEC Supplier Code of Conduct, which requires suppliers to have respect for the environment and the health and safety of their workers. It requires that a supplier not employ children under 16 or forced labour such as prisoners. The supplier should not abuse its workers, prevent unions, or force its workers to work more than 48 hours regular time and 12 hours overtime per week. Workers should have at least one in seven days off and should be paid fairly. Workplace health and safety norms should be followed such as use of earplugs and dust masks. There should be no discrimination or harassment. New potential suppliers and current suppliers (every 1.5 years) are audited by an MEC team or external auditors. This entails a one-day visit. MEC publishes the identity of its supplier-manufacturers, called the Factory List, which contains approximately 80 names, mostly in China and other southeast Asian countries.

Source: http://www.mec.ca.

(2) there may not be an easy way to relate and aggregate similar items using their stock codes and description (no product classes or types are defined), (3) relationships between suppliers may have been missed. (*Note:* expenditure with all subsidiaries of a company should be aggregated when negotiating quantity discounts). These problems can be rectified by undertaking spend analysis.

spend analysis Collecting, cleansing, classifying, and analyzing expenditure data with the purpose of reducing procurement costs, improving efficiency, and monitoring compliance with purchasing policies.

Spend analysis involves collecting, cleansing (i.e, amending or removing data that is incorrect, incomplete, improperly formatted, or duplicated), classifying, and analyzing (e.g., using charts) expenditure data with the purpose of reducing procurement costs, improving efficiency, and monitoring compliance with purchasing policies. Spend analysis can provide answers to questions such as What was bought? From which suppliers? What is the total expenditure on a part? How much is the total expenditure with a supplier?

It is important that deficiencies of data collection and/or purchasing practice be fixed (e.g., using a spend analysis software) so that the need for spend analysis in future is diminished. For example, maverick buying (users buying from nonapproved suppliers) should be minimized. Companies have realized up to 5 percent reduction in their total expenditure by performing spend analysis.[1]

Ethics in Purchasing. Ethical behaviour is particularly important in purchasing where buyers are authorized to spend significant amounts of the organization's funds and also may be tempted to use their position for personal gain. Furthermore, salespeople are often eager to make a sale and may resort to unethical behaviour such as giving gifts to buyers.

Companies often expect ethical behaviour from their suppliers. An organization known for its ethical purchasing is Mountain Equipment Co-op (see the OM in Action).

E-Commerce

e-commerce The use of computers and Internet to conduct buying and selling.

E-commerce refers to the use of computers and Internet to conduct buying and selling. E-commerce involves business to business (B2B) and business to consumer (B2C) commerce. Table 11-3 lists some of the numerous advantages of e-commerce.

Table 11-3 ▶
Advantages of e-commerce.

Companies have a global presence and customers have global choices and easy access to information.

Companies can improve competitiveness and quality of service by allowing access to their services any time.

Companies can analyze the interest in various products based on the number of hits and requests for information.

Companies can collect detailed information about clients' choices, which enables mass customization and personalized products. An example is the purchase of Dell Computers over the Web, where the buyer specifies the final configuration.

Supply chain response times are shortened. The biggest impact is on products that can be delivered directly on the Web, such as software.

The roles of the intermediary and sometimes the traditional retailer or service provider are reduced or eliminated entirely in a process called *disintermediation*. This process reduces costs and adds alternative purchasing options.

Substantial cost savings and price reductions related to the reduction of transaction costs can be realized. Companies that provide purchasing and support through the Web can save significant personnel costs.

E-commerce allows the creation of virtual companies that distribute only through the Web, thus reducing costs. Amazon.com and other etailers can afford to sell for a lower price because they do not need to maintain retail stores.

The playing field is levelled for small companies, which lack significant resources to invest in infrastructure and marketing.

---

[1] http://www.supplychainbrain.com/content/index.php?id=5032&cHash=081010&tx_ttnews[tt_news]=1406.

There are two essential features of e-commerce businesses: the website, and order fulfillment. Companies may invest considerable time and effort in front-end design (the website, its visual appeal and ease and speed of product search), but the back end (order fulfillment) is at least as important. **Order fulfillment** involves order processing, scheduling, inventory management, warehousing, packaging, billing, and delivery.

Order fulfillment and its lead time varies by the nature of work required. For items made ahead and kept in stock (make-to-stock), fulfillment simply involves assigning the order to the nearest distribution centre (DC), whereas for make-to-order, the order has to be scheduled for production first. For assemble-to-order items, components have already been made and only final assembly has to be scheduled. Finally, for engineer-to-order items, the item needs to be designed first according to customer's specification.

In the early days of Internet selling, many organizations thought that they could avoid bearing the costs of holding inventories by acting solely as intermediaries, having their suppliers ship directly to their customers. But this approach failed as sales increased because suppliers ran out of certain items. Industry giants such as Amazon.com built large warehouses so they could maintain greater control over their inventories.

Traditional retailers (called "brick-and-mortar") have now added online shopping (now called "click and mortar" or "bricks and clicks"), e.g., Walmart.ca, FutureShop.ca. These use the Web in a different way, offering low-volume, slow-moving items online. This complements their in-store products. They fulfill online orders from their regular distribution centres (DCs) (if total online dollars is small) or have dedicated DCs for online orders (if total online dollars is large). Also, instead of parcel delivery, the goods are made available in the nearest store for the consumer to pick up (the goods are prepared for the consumer at a DC or at the store). To facilitate B2B e-commerce, some e-marketplaces or exchanges have been created. See Table 11-4 for some examples. An important industry-led nonprofit organization is GS1 Canada, which is trying to advance e-commerce by standardizing communication between trading partners and improving data accuracy. GS1 was the founder of bar codes many decades ago and controls the assignment of bar codes in Canada.

order fulfillment Involves order processing, scheduling, inventory management, warehousing, packaging, billing, and delivery.

Type	Description	Website
Buyer-initiated Exchanges		
CareNet Services Inc.	Has over 450 hospitals using EDI for ordering and receiving invoices from more than 95 health care vendors.	http://www.carenet.ca
Avendra	Set up by Marriott and Hyatt; buys for about 5,000 hotels, resorts, and restaurants from 800 suppliers.	http://www.avendra.com
Seller-initiated Exchange		
Global Healthcare Exchange	Set up by a few large pharmaceutical and medical/surgical equipment suppliers. Over 4,100 health care providers and 400 manufacturers in North America use GHX.	http://www.ghx.com/ghxcanada/canada.aspx

◀ **Table 11-4**

Examples of e-exchanges.

Supplier Management and Partnership

Reliable and trustworthy suppliers are a vital link in an effective supply chain. Timely deliveries of high-quality goods or services contribute to effective operations. A buyer functions as an "external operations manager," working with suppliers to coordinate the supplier's operations and the buyer's needs.

Choosing Suppliers. In many respects, choosing a supplier involves taking into account many of the same factors associated with making a major purchase (e.g., a car). A person considers price, quality, availability of product or timely delivery, the supplier's reputation, past experience with

Table 11-5 ▶	Factor	Typical Questions
Factors and typical questions to ask when selecting a product/supplier.	**Quality**	Is the supplier technically capable of achieving the desired quality?
		What procedures does the supplier have for quality control?
	Flexibility	How flexible is the supplier in handling changes in delivery schedules, quantity, and product or service?
	Location	Is the supplier nearby?
	Price	Are prices reasonable?
	Financial Stability and Reputation	What is the reputation of the supplier? Is the supplier financially stable?
	Lead time	What lead time can the supplier provide?
		What policies does the supplier have for keeping items in stock? Is the supplier reliable?
	Other customers	Is the supplier heavily dependent on other major customers, causing a risk of giving priority to their needs over ours?
	Service after sale	How much after-sale support does the supplier provide?

the supplier, and service after sale. The factors a company takes into account when it selects a product/supplier and typical questions to ask are outlined in Table 11-5.

Because different factors are important for different organizations, purchasing must decide, with the help of the requisitioner, the importance of each factor (i.e., how much weight to give to each factor), and then rate potential products/suppliers according to how well they can be expected to perform against this list. This process is called **supplier analysis**. The information required can be obtained from the potential supplier, its current customers (reference), and business intelligence vendors such as Dun & Bradstreet. If the potential supplier was used before, its performance should be evaluated and used in decision making.

supplier analysis Evaluating a supplier in terms of factors such as price, quality, delivery, and service.

Supplier Relationship. In the past, many organizations regarded their suppliers as adversaries. One lesson learned from the Japanese manufacturers is that numerous benefits derive from a good supplier relationship, including supplier flexibility in terms of accepting changes in delivery schedule, quality, and quantity. Moreover, suppliers can often help identify improvements in the design of an item (value analysis). In fact, they can be involved in the design of new products (called *early supplier involvement*).

Many Japanese companies rely on only one or two suppliers to handle their needs for an item. The advantages of single-sourcing/partnership include lower number of orders, deliveries, and invoices, and being able to work with the supplier to reduce lead time, improve quality, and reduce the price.

Supplier Partnership. More and more organizations are seeking to establish partnerships with their suppliers. This implies fewer suppliers, longer-term relationships, sharing of information (sales date, forecasts, problems), and cooperation in planning.

Supplier partnerships are required for initiatives such as JIT, quick response, VMI, and CPFR, where both sides need to invest time and money in a long-term relationship.

Professor D.M. Lambert has developed a partnership model that has been used dozens of times.[2] The partnership model is as follows. After the number of suppliers is reduced, those that provide key materials/services and with whom a company does a lot of business are approached for partnership discussion. Top executives and managers from functional areas from each company are invited to a retreat, facilitated by a third-party consultant.

---

[2] D.M. Lambert and A.M. Knemeyer, "We're in This Together," *Harvard Business Review*, December 2004, pp. 114–122.

OfficeMax Grand & Toy

Grand & Toy Company is one of the largest office supplies distributors in Canada. It carries approximately 6,000 stock-keeping units in its eight regional distribution centres. It had 75 retail locations but recently has been closing them to focus on online order-taking and delivery. Grand & Toy provides EDI service to its customers using its own wide area network, computers, and an ERP software. It also allows its customers to order over the Internet (using its OrderPoint system), where they can use Grand & Toy's electronic catalogue. Grand & Toy also keeps records of customer purchase quantities and allows them to access this data, in effect providing inventory record keeping for its customers. Grand & Toy provides next-day delivery in major cities, and has an in-stock rate of 98 percent. Grand & Toy also helps organizations develop EDI connections with their other suppliers. In return the customer organization agrees to use Grand & Toy as the sole source for its office product needs for a certain number of years. This is an example of supplier partnership. In 1996, Grand & Toy was purchased by Boise Cascade, which later changed its name to OfficeMax. More recently, OfficeMax merged with Office Depot, and Grand & Toy's name has been changed to OfficeMax.

Source: https://www.officemaxcanada.com/en/sites/core/aboutUs_corporateProfile.aspx.

Cargill Value-added Meats—Canada

Cargill Value Added Meats–Canada (CVAM-Canada) supplies McDonald's Canada with beef and chicken. The relationship is exclusive, i.e., CVAM-Canada is the only beef and chicken supplier to McDonald's Canada and McDonald's Canada is the only customer of CVAM-Canada. This relationship started in January 2002 for chicken. The London, Ontario, chicken processing facility employs approximately 900 people and processes 80,000 chickens each day. The hatchery in Jarvis, Ontario, has 70 employees and, on average, produces 150,000 chicks per day. The beef partnership started in September 2004. The beef patty-processing facility is in Spruce Grove, Alberta, employs approximately 120 people, and produces approximately 1.5 million pounds of beef patties each week.

CVAM-Canada's annual business planning process is conducted together with McDonald's Canada. The output from this process is used to form CVAM-Canada's three-year strategic plan. Annual and monthly meetings are conducted with McDonald's Canada to review the strategic-plan progress and customer needs and expectations. A formal supplier performance review is conducted jointly every two years. The tight approach to determine current and future customer needs and expectations ensures daily interactions between CVAM-Canada and McDonald's Canada. As a result, CVAM-Canada has won four supplier excellence awards from McDonald's Canada, and the Spruce Grove facility has won a food safety award for its complaint reductions and food safety.

Source: http://www.excellence.ca/en/awards/2011-cae-recipients/2011-cae-profiles/2011-caeprofiles-cvam.

During 1.5 days, each company's managers first determine the key reasons they should get into partnership (e.g., cost reduction, customer service enhancement, etc.), provide a metric and target for each reason, and then share these with the other company's managers. There should be frank discussions to clarify the issues. These key expectations are called partnership drivers.

Next, if both sides agree that partnership will likely meet their expectations, they proceed to identify the so-called facilitators. These include compatibility of cultures and management philosophy, and other factors that influence the ease of coordination of activities required for partnership.

Then, if coordination appears to be reasonably easy, based on the level of expectation of benefits of partnership (i.e., attainment of partnership drivers), the intended partnership can be classified as Type I (low benefits), Type II (moderate benefits), or Type III (high benefits).

Finally, based on the type of intended partnership, both sides have to identify the extent of cooperation in planning, control, communication, and risk/reward sharing, and implement activities to achieve this. For example, joint planning can range from ad hoc (sharing plans for a project) to regularly scheduled meetings (joint planning for key processes); performance measures can range from separate (but shared) to joint (i.e., joint performance); communication can range from ad hoc (one way) to linked electronic communication system (two ways); short-term loss tolerance can range from low to high; and desire to help the other party gain financially can range from limited to high. For two examples of partnership, see "OfficeMax Grand & Toy" and "Cargill Value-added Meats–Canada" OM in Actions.

LO3 Logistics

logistics The movement and warehousing of materials/products and information.

Logistics refers to the transport and warehousing of both incoming materials/parts and outgoing distribution of products. It also includes the use of information to control the activities. In the past, inbound logistics was controlled by purchasing/manufacturing and outbound logistics was controlled by marketing/sales. However, more and more organizations are integrating these two to reduce costs. Logistics management is a major part of supply chain management.

Logistics costs (mainly transportation and warehousing/inventory holding cost) in Canada usually range between 3 and 8 percent of a product's sales price: pharmaceutical/chemicals have the highest and petroleum/motor vehicles have the lowest logistics costs relative to their sales price.

We will cover inventory control/warehousing/material handling in the next chapter.

traffic management Involved in planning and overseeing the delivery of incoming and outgoing goods.

Traffic management is involved in Transport planning and overseeing transport execution and control (the delivery of incoming and outgoing goods). This function handles schedules and decisions on delivery methods and times, taking into account costs of various alternatives, government regulations, the needs of the organization relative to quantities and timing, and external factors such as potential delivery delays or disruptions (e.g., highway construction, truckers' strikes).

Transport Planning

Given the quantity and speed-of-delivery requirements of the expected shipments, an organization has to make the following decisions:

- Decide whether to outsource the transportation.
- Select mode of transportation.
- Select carrier.
- Negotiate the transport rates.

If the quantity to be shipped is small and shipment is infrequent, a common carrier (for hire) can be used as the transport need arises. However, most manufacturers have ongoing transportation needs. They can either employ professionals or outsource the transportation (or even logistics) function to a third-party logistics (3PL) service provider. Similarly, they can purchase (or lease) and manage their own trucks (private fleet) or contract with transport companies (contract carrier).

3PL. A 3PL service provider is a logistics service management company. It can own its own transport equipment (trucks, planes, ships) or it can be only a logistics management company. So, a third-party logistics company can employ a transport company (the second party). Many transport companies also provide 3PL services, as do package delivery companies such as UPS (its 3PL service division is called UPS Supply Chain Services). One possible reason for outsourcing logistics is a desire to concentrate on the core business. Employing a company that specializes in logistics provides other benefits such as a well-developed logistics information system, experienced logistics personnel, customs clearance facilities, foreign locations, and the ability to provide lower transportation rates.

modes of transportation The equipment used for delivery, including pipelines, ships, trains, trucks, and airplanes.

Modes of Transportation. The equipment used for delivery includes pipelines, ships, trains, trucks, and airplanes. The order of modes given above is from least costly to most costly and from slowest to fastest. The most common delivery method inland is trucking (which is most flexible), followed by railways, which are used for bulk transport of heavy goods over long distances. Ocean freight is used for bulk transport of goods or ocean containers (20 or 40 feet long) on oceans. Some cargo ships are used on the Great Lakes, and pipelines transport crude oil and natural gas. Air cargo is used for expensive, light, urgent products. Some logistics companies use a combination of these modes. For example, parcel delivery companies such as UPS use air and trucks. The use of intermodal transport of large containers (e.g., truck → train → truck) is increasing (the container is put on the back of a flat-bed truck, transported to a rail station, trans-loaded on a flat-bed rail car, transported to the destination rail station, and trans-loaded back on another flat-bed truck).

The trucking industry in North America is very efficient. There are many trucking companies including small one-person owner-operator. Trucking service is categorized into Truckload (TL), when approximately 15,000 pounds or more is shipped, and Less-Than-Truckload (LTL) when between 150 and 15,000 pounds is shipped. Less than 150 pounds is small package and is shipped by package delivery companies. In TL, the whole truck is hired and a direct delivery can be made, whereas LTL involves several pickups and deliveries in order to increase the utilization of the capacity of the truck. Trucking companies are moving toward offering both TL and LTL, and package delivery companies are increasing their maximum shipment weight (e.g., FedEx has now a ground freight service).

CN and CP are the main rail carriers in Canada. Because they are a natural monopoly, they are regulated by the federal government. Because laying new rail track is very expensive, their capacity is fixed. Because there are not enough pipelines out of Alberta, Saskatchewan, and North Dakota, oil companies have started using crude oil railcars to ship their oil to refineries/ports. This has caused delays for other users of rail such as grain exporters and farmers.

Most air cargo is transported by passenger airlines (in the cargo hold).

In terms of delivery reliability, the order from most to least reliable is air cargo, trucking, railway, and ocean freight (same order as speed because the longer the trip, the more likely there will be delays). Because of low delivery reliability, until recently JIT manufacturers have been hesitant to use ocean freight for their inbound logistics from Southeast Asia.

Selecting a Transportation Mode. Mode selection factors include pickup/delivery accessibility, transit time, reliability, product safety (including theft), product characteristics (weight, size, fragility, temperature sensitivity, and perishability), value (low-value product needs low-cost mode), and freight cost. For some shipments, one or more of the above factors dictates a particular mode of transport. However, companies sometimes must make a choice between rapid (but more expensive) delivery such as overnight or second-day air and slower (but less expensive) alternatives such as using a truck. The decision in such cases often focuses on the total transportation and in-transit inventory holding cost of each alternative. An important assumption is that the buyer takes ownership at the supplier's location and pays for delivery, which is the case in some purchases. Initially, we make the assumption that the two alternative modes of transportation are equally reliable; hence they require the same level of safety stock; safety stocks are extra inventory kept when supply and/or demand are variable.

The in-transit inventory holding cost incurred by an alternative is calculated as:

$$\text{In-transit holding cost} = \frac{H(d)}{365} \tag{11-1}$$

where H = annual holding cost of items being transported

d = duration of transport (in days)

Total delivery cost = transportation (freight) cost + in-transit holding cost

$$= \text{transportation (freight) cost} + \frac{H(d)}{365}$$

Determine which delivery alternative, one day or three days, is best when the holding cost of the item is $1,000 per year, the one-day delivery transportation cost is $40, and the three-day delivery transportation cost is:

◀ Example 2

a. $35   **b.** $30

H = $1,000 per year

SOLUTION

Total cost of 1-day delivery = $40 + $1,000(1/365)

= $42.74

Total cost of 3-day delivery

a. $= \$35 + \$1,000(3/365)$

$\qquad = \$43.22 > \$42.74$

Therefore, 1-day delivery is cheaper.

b. $= \$30 + \$1,000(3/365)$

$\qquad = \$38.22 < \$42.74$

Therefore, 3-day delivery is cheaper.

When the modes of transportation are different (e.g., air vs. ocean freight), the unequal reliability of these modes requires different levels of safety stocks. Therefore, the cost of holding safety stocks at the destination should also be included in the total cost of a mode.

| Example 3 ▶ | Consider a part that is to be transported from China to Europe. The annual demand for the part is 23,000 units. Price is $210 per unit. Annual holding cost rate is 20 percent of unit price. There are two transportation options. |

Air cargo: Takes 7 days (door to door) and costs $52 per unit.
Ocean freight: Takes 35 days and cost $10 per unit.

Because of variability of transportation time and demand, 2 weeks of demand will be kept at destination as safety stock [(2/52)(23,000) units] if air cargo is used. On the other hand, 8 weeks of demand will be kept at destination as safety stock if ocean freight is used. Assume that order quantity will be the same in either case. Calculate the total annual freight, in-transit holding, and safety stock costs for each mode, and choose the cheaper mode.

SOLUTION

Annual costs:

Air

Freight $= \$52(23,000)$ $\qquad\qquad = \$1,196,000$
In-transit holding $= 23,000(\$210)(.20)(7/365) =$ $\qquad 18,526.03$
Safety stock $= (2/52)(23,000)(\$210 + \$52)(.20) =$ $\qquad 46,353.85$
$\qquad\qquad\qquad\qquad\qquad\qquad\qquad\qquad\qquad \overline{\$1,260,879.88}$

Note: Cost of the part at the destination includes air transportation cost: $210 + $52.

Ocean

Freight $= \$10(23,000)$ $\qquad\qquad = \$230,000$
In-transit holding $= 23,000(\$210)(.20)(35/365) =$ $\quad 92,630.14$
Safety stock $= (8/52)(23,000)(\$210 + \$10)(.20) =$ $\quad 155,692.31$
$\qquad\qquad\qquad\qquad\qquad\qquad\qquad\qquad\qquad \overline{\$478,322.45}$

Note: Cost of the part at the destination includes ocean transportation cost: $210 + $10.
Ocean is much cheaper.[3]

Selecting a Carrier. Relevant capability and service quality factors include transit time average and variation, on-time pick-up and delivery, vehicle availability and capacity, technical/information system capability, geographic coverage, damage protection, billing accuracy, responsiveness to emergencies/problem resolution, financial stability, and whether the product can be delivered

---

[3] T. Miller, "The International Modal Decision (Part 1)," *Chilton's Distribution*, 90(11), pp. 82–92; T. Miller, "Air vs. Ocean: Two Critical Factors (Part 2)," *Chilton's Distribution*, 90(12), pp. 46–52.

direct (e.g., TL) or indirect (involving stops and transfers, e.g., LTL, rail). To be able to reduce costs and improve service, an organization should use only a limited number of carriers.

Negotiating a Transport Rate. If one is using a carrier regularly, it is advantageous to enter into a contract with the carrier in order to take advantage of price discounts. In doing so, some negotiation may be involved on transport cost (or freight rate). For this reason, one should be aware how the rate is determined.

To simplify rate determination, postal code of origin and destination is usually used. Rate increases with distance, almost linearly, by zone. Rate of a LTL common carrier for a given origin-destination pair is usually in $ per 100 pounds (= cwt). For a TL carrier, it is by $/mile, for a given truck capacity. For LTL, there are usually weight breaks reflecting economies of scale. For example, if weight is < 500 pounds, rate is $47.94/cwt, if weight is between 500 and 1000 pounds, rate is $38.35/cwt, etc.

For LTL, the characteristics of product, called its transportability, affect the rate. These include:

- Density
  - Weight/volume ratio
  - Lower density → higher rate
- Stowability
  - To allow compact packing (i.e., space utilization) e.g., an assembled bicycle is not very stowable (i.e., will waste space)
  - More stowable → lower rate
- Difficulty of handling
  - Need for repacking, re-palletizing, special equipment
  - More difficult → higher rate
- Liability
  - For loss, damage (e.g., fragile, perishable), theft
  - Is also a function of value of product
  - Higher liability → higher rate

For LTL, to simplify rate determination, products are grouped into classes of same transportability. The National Motor Freight Traffic Association has created the National Motor Freight Classification (NMFC) used in North America. There are 18 classes, from 50 to 500. Class 100 is average transportability class. Class 200 is twice harder. Class 50 is twice easier. Class 400 is four times harder. Note that packaging affects the class.

Product classes for railways are called Uniform Freight Classification (there are 31 classes). Rates for railways are called Commodity rates. Water carriers use weight or volume. Freight-all-kind rate is for a mixed shipment.

Transport Execution and Control

Transport execution and control involves load planning and consolidation, load tendering (= selecting carrier(s)), appointment scheduling, checking carriers' legal compliance (safety, etc.), having in-transit visibility and tracking, freight payment, and measuring performance of carrier.

Some buyers ask their suppliers to use a particular carrier based on their location and weight of shipment. This is sometimes contained in a Transportation Routing Guide, which may also have guidelines for packaging.

Bill of lading (BOL) is the transport contract. It provides all the information the carrier needs. It also specifies the carrier's liability for loss and damage. Furthermore, it acts as a receipt for when the carrier delivers the shipment to the buyer.

Carriers tend to use the shortest distance or time route between an origin and a destination. This is called route planning. A common technology used by truckers is PCMiler, which has a GPS and electronic maps.

Local delivery to drop off or load shipments also requires finding the shortest distance or time but the route starts and ends at a depot. There are also time window restrictions at various stops. This is called the vehicle routing problem.

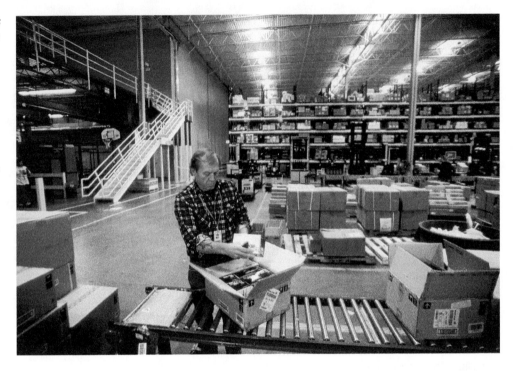

An Amazon.com employee inspects returned products at a distribution warehouse in Nevada. The returned goods are inspected for restocking if in pristine condition, forwarded to a repair centre if necessary, inventoried, and examined for potential product, process, or packaging improvements if they are defective.

Reverse Logistics

reverse logistics Backward flow of goods returned by consumers or retailers.

Reverse logistics is the backward flow of goods returned by consumers or retailers. Goods are returned because they are defective, unsold (excess inventory), or because customers simply changed their minds or don't know how to use them. Returns management includes processing returned goods, which generally involves sorting, examining/testing, restocking items that are in good condition, repairing defectives, reconditioning, recycling materials, and disposing of obsolete or hazardous materials. The goal of returns management is to recapture value in returned goods and to properly dispose of goods that cannot be resold.

gate keeping Screening returned goods at the point of entry into the system to prevent inappropriate acceptance of goods.

Two key elements of reverse logistics are gate keeping and avoidance. **Gate keeping** oversees the acceptance of returned goods with the intent of reducing the cost of returns by screening returns at the point of entry into the system and refusing to accept goods that should not be returned or goods that are returned to the wrong destination. **Avoidance** refers to preventing returns by dealing with their causes. It can involve product design and quality assurance issues. It may also involve careful monitoring of forecasts during promotional programs to avoid overestimating demand.

avoidance Preventing returns by dealing with their causes.

Summary

- A supply chain consists of the sequence of organizations—their facilities and activities—that are involved in producing a product, from the initial suppliers to the final consumer. Supply chain management (SCM) is collaboration of members and coordination of activities of the supply chain so that market demand is met as efficiently and effectively as possible.

- Supply chain management offers the benefits of lower operating costs, reduced inventories (e.g., by avoiding the bullwhip effect), better product availability, and customer satisfaction. The need for SCM has increased due to increased outsourcing (buying as opposed to making), globalization, and e-commerce.

- Activities in supply chain management can be classified as strategic (e.g., network design), and tactical/operational (e.g., production and distribution planning, inventory and transportation management, fulfillment).

- Retailers/wholesalers and manufacturers have initiated efficient replenishment systems with their suppliers under the names of *quick response, efficient consumer response (ECR), and vendor managed inventory (VMI)*.

- Global supply chains are long and have to deal with intermediaries, customs clearance, and shipment changing hands several times.

- Accurate and timely information is vital in supply chain management. Information is used for transaction processing as well as planning and collaboration. Internet is used for data communication. Planning software includes network design, production planning, and forecasting. Execution software includes order management, warehouse management system, transportation management system, and tracking/visibility software. ERP software programs have been adding supply chain management modules to their suite. Electronic data interchange is used for purchasing, order confirmation and payment, and arranging shipments. Radio frequency identification (RFID) is for fast identification of items.

- The key to an effective supply chain is to link companies, develop trust, align goals, share information, and measure performance. Collaborative planning, forecasting, and replenishment (CPFR) extends ECR further in forecasting by using a formal reconciliation process for forecasts and orders. The Supply Chain Operations Reference (SCOR) model is increasingly used for supply chain performance measurement.

- The purchasing function obtains materials, manufacturing parts, supplies and spare parts, equipment and machines, and services needed to produce a product. Purchasing selects suppliers, negotiates contracts, helps establish partnerships, and acts as liaison between suppliers and various internal departments. Organizations are outsourcing and buying more of their noncore services

and parts. The purchasing cycle starts with a purchase requisition and ends with paying the invoice. Value analysis is used to provide the basic function of a part/product at minimum cost. Prices for many products are determined using competitive bidding and negotiation. Multiplant organizations use a hybrid system where common material and services are centralized and small purchases are bought locally. Spend analysis examines the purchases in order to group them by item families and suppliers, so that price discounts can be obtained and purchases from unapproved suppliers are minimized. Ethics in purchasing is important because of the amount of money involved and because buyers may be enticed by salespeople to favour their company. Controlling ethical treatment of workers by overseas suppliers is part of ethical purchasing.

- E-commerce is the use of computers and the Internet to conduct buying and selling. The use of e-commerce is rapidly expanding and has resulted in increasing need for small-package delivery services. Fulfillment is the process of order taking, scheduling, warehousing, order picking and packing, and delivery.

- Price, quality, and timely delivery are important factors for a product purchase. These plus technical and managerial capability, flexibility, service, and financial stability are important for choosing a supplier.

- In many organizations there is a move to reduce the number of suppliers and to establish and maintain longer-term relationships with suppliers. Supplier partnership is the closest form of relationship where both buyer and supplier benefit by assisting each other. The Lambert partnership model provides a process for deciding if partnership between a buyer and a supplier is desirable and, if so, to what extent.

- Logistics involves the movement and warehousing of goods, material, and information in a supply chain. This includes incoming materials and outgoing goods. Transportation planning involves an outsourcing decision, selecting transport mode, choosing carrier, and negotiating freight rates. A third-party logistics (3PL) service provider is a logistics management company that oversees the logistics function of the buyer organization. Transport modes include pipeline, ships, trains, trucks, and airplanes. Truck load (TL) involves a full truck load and less-than-truck-load (LTL) is a portion of a truck's capacity.

- In selecting a shipping mode, the tradeoff is between a faster mode with higher freight cost and a slower mode that is cheaper in terms of freight cost but results in higher in-transit holding cost. Selecting a carrier is like purchasing any other service. Transport rate depends whether it is TL or LTL. TL for a given truck capacity is charged by miles, and LTL is charged by origin-destination distance,

weight, and transportability (density, stow-ability, difficulty of handling, and liability).

- Transport execution and control involves load planning and consolidation, load tendering, appointment scheduling, checking carriers' legal compliance, in-transit visibility and tracking, freight payment, and measuring performance of carrier.
- Reverse logistics is returns logistics and management. Gatekeeping and returns avoidance are important.

Key Terms

avoidance
bullwhip effect
centralized purchasing
CPFR
cross-docking
decentralized purchasing
delayed differentiation/postponement
distribution requirements planning
    (DRP)
e-commerce
efficient consumer response (ECR)
electronic data interchange (EDI)

event management
fill rate
gate keeping
inventory turnover
item fill rate
logistics
modes of transportation
order fulfillment
outsourcing
purchasing cycle
quick response (QR)
radio frequency identification (RFID)

reverse logistics
risk pooling
spend analysis
strategic supplier/customer partnership
supplier analysis
supply chain
supply chain management
supply chain visibility
traffic management
value analysis
vendor-managed inventory

Solved Problem

a. Determine which shipping alternative is best if the annual holding cost of an item is 25 percent of its unit price, and a single unit with a price of $6,000 is to be delivered, either by the two-day delivery at a cost of $400 or by the five-day delivery at a cost of $350.

b. At what unit price would the two-day delivery be less costly?

Solution

a. $H = .25(\$6,000) = \$1,500$ per year

Total two-day delivery cost $= \$400 + \$1,500(2/365)$

$= \$408.22$

Total five-day delivery cost $= \$350 + \$1,500(5/365)$

$= \$370.55 < \$408.22$

Hence, use the five-day delivery.

b. Let $p =$ unit price. Total 2-day delivery cost $= \$400 + .25p\,(2/365)$

Total 5-day delivery cost $= \$350 + .25p\,(5/365)$.

Set the two total costs equal: $\$400 + .25p\,(2/365) = \$350 + .25p\,(5/365)$

Or $50 = .25p\,(3/365)$ or $p = 50(365)/3(.25) = \$24,333.34$

Discussion and Review Questions

1. What is a supply chain? **LO1**
2. What is supply chain management? **LO1**
3. What factors have made it desirable to manage supply chains? What are some potential benefits of doing so? **LO1**
4. What is the bullwhip effect, and why does it occur? How can it be overcome? **LO1**
5. Explain how the need to reduce inventory holding costs would be a good reason to (re)design a supply chain, and give an example. **LO1**
6. What does supply chain design mean? **LO1**
7. What are the advantages and disadvantages of pushing inventory downstream closer to consumers? **LO1**
8. What is risk pooling? Delayed differentiation? **LO1**
9. Explain quick response, efficient consumer response, and vendor-managed inventory. **LO1**
10. What is cross-docking? **LO1**
11. Why is global supply chain management more challenging? **LO1**
12. Describe supply chain management information systems. **LO1**
13. What is RFID? What are its advantages and disadvantages for a company? **LO1**
14. What is EDI? What are its advantages and disadvantages for a company? **LO1**
15. What are the requirements for effective supply chain management? **LO1**
16. Name two supply chain performance metrics and explain them. **LO1**
17. What is CPFR? What are its advantages and disadvantages? **LO1**
18. Explain the importance of the purchasing function in organizations. **LO2**
19. Describe what a buyer (in an organization) does. Name at least five activities. **LO2**
20. Describe how purchasing interacts with two other functional areas of an organization. **LO2**
21. When should a company outsource the production of a part or performance of a service? Give an example. What are the disadvantages? **LO2**
22. How is price determined in B2B purchasing? Give an example for each way price is determined. **LO2**
23. Describe value analysis. **LO2**
24. Discuss centralization versus decentralization in purchasing. What are the advantages of each? **LO2**
25. What is spend analysis? Why is it necessary? **LO2**
26. What is e-commerce and what impact has it had on supply chain management? **LO2**
27. What are some of the advantages of e-commerce? **LO2**
28. What is fulfillment? **LO2**
29. Describe supplier analysis. What are the common factors used in selecting a supplier? **LO2**
30. Why are good supplier relations important? **LO2**
31. What are the advantages and disadvantages of a partnership to the buyer? To the supplier? **LO2**
32. Describe Lambert's partnership model. **LO2**
33. What is logistics? **LO3**
34. What is involved in transport planning? **LO3**
35. What is third-party logistics service? Give an example. **LO3**
36. What are the transportation modes? **LO3**
37. What is the trade-off in selecting a transportation mode? **LO3**
38. What is involved in transportation execution and control? **LO3**
39. What is reverse logistics? **LO3**

Taking Stock

1. What trade-offs are involved in sharing information with a supplier? With a customer? **LO1 & 2 & 3**
2. Who needs to be involved in supply chain management? **LO1 & 2 & 3**
3. Name two different ways that information system and technology has improved the ability to manage supply chains. **LO1**
4. Name one ethical issue related to a buyer's job, and explain it. **LO2**

Critical Thinking Exercises

1. Find and describe an example of RFID that you have seen in your daily life or work. **LO1**

2. For an item you recently bought (a) try to determine its supply chain, and (b) describe the criteria you used to select the product/supplier. **LO1 & 2**

Internet Exercises

1. Visit http://www.jda.com/real_results/case-studies.html, unde Solutions click a SCM topic, e.g., Network Design & Optimization; Supply Chain Planning; Transportation & Logistics Management; Visibility, Collaboration & Performance Management, click Search, choose a client company, read the case study and briefly describe how JDA software is helping the company. **LO1**

2. View http://www.youtube.com/watch?v=rqXIwjD3Cso and identify Pepsi's distribution channels.

3. View http://www.youtube.com/watch?v=KksQbzRMwvQ on LogicNet, a network design software, and summarize what it can do. **LO1**

4. Visit http://www.mobilcomm.com/downloads/motorola/case_studies/cs_amt.pdf and summarize how RFID is being used by Montreal Transit Authority. **LO1**

5. Visit http://www.rfidjournal.com/article/archive/4, choose a case study, and state how RFID is used. **LO1**

6. Visit http://www.sap.com/lob/scm/resources.html, click Customer Testimonial, choose a testimonial, and summarize it. **LO1**

7. Visit http://www.ops.fhwa.dot.gov/publications/fhwahop09035/video.htm, view the video "Keeping the Global Supply Chain Moving," and summarize it. **LO3**

8. Visit http://www.fisher.osu.edu/centers/scm, find and watch the video of Dr. Lambert's overview of his partnership framework, and summarize it. **LO2**

9. Visit http://www.nyk.com/english/index, watch the video NYK Group Profile, and summarize the supply chain/logistics services NYK Logistics performs for its customers. **LO3**

10. Visit http://www.purolator.com/en/resources-and-support/about-us/annual-review/2012/enabling-success.page? and view and summarize a customer video. **LO3**

11. View http://www.genco.com/Videos/new-trends-reverse-logistics.php and summarize the video "New Trends in Reverse Logistics" as seen by Genco, a 3PL service provider specializing in reverse logistics. **LO3**

12. BBC attached an RFID to a 40-foot ocean container and tracked it and its contents for a year in order to get a sample of global trade. Use http://news.bbc.co.uk/2/hi/in_depth/629/629/7600053.stm to identify each leg of the trip. *Hint:* Place the cursor on the blue discs to see the dates and follow the blue lines chronologically, shifting the map by pressing and holding the left mouse key. **LO3**

Problems

1. A manager must choose between two delivery alternatives: two-day freight and five-day freight. Using five-day freight would cost $135 less than using two-day freight for the shipment of 2,000 units. Another consideration is in-transit holding cost, which is $10 per unit per year. Assume 365 days per year. Which alternative would you recommend? Explain. **LO2**

2. a. Determine which delivery alternative would be most economical for 80 boxes of parts. Each box costs $200 and annual holding cost is 30 percent of cost. Assume 365 days per year. Freight costs are: **LO2**

Alternative	Freight Cost (for all 80 boxes)
Overnight	$300
Two-day	260
Six-day	180

b. For what range of unit cost for a box would each delivery alternative be least costly?

3. A manager must make a decision on delivery alternatives. There are two carriers, A and B. Both offer a two-day rate. In addition, A offers a three-day rate and a nine-day rate, and B offers a four-day rate and a seven-day rate. Three hundred boxes are to be delivered and the freight cost for the whole lot for each option is given below. Annual holding cost is 35 percent of unit cost, and each box has a cost of $140. Assume 365 days per year. Which delivery alternative would you recommend? **LO2**

Shipper A		Shipper B	
Option	Freight Cost	Option	Freight Cost
2 days	$500	2 days	$525
3 days	460	4 days	450
9 days	400	7 days	410

4. An appliance manufacturer has a plant near Toronto that receives small electric motors from a manufacturer located in Winnipeg. The demand for motors is 120,000 units per year. The cost of each motor is $120. The motors are purchased in lots of 3,000 units. The ownership of motors transfers to the appliance manufacturer in Winnipeg. The question is which mode of transportation, truck or train, the appliance manufacturer should use to bring the motors from Winnipeg to Toronto. The railroad company charges $2 per motor, and it takes approximately seven days by train. The trucking company charges $4 per motor, but it takes only three days. The appliance manufacturer will keep 1,000 units as safety stock if a truck is used and 3,000 units as safety stock if a train is used for transportation. Assume 365 days per year. If the holding cost rate is 25 percent of unit cost per year, which mode of transportation will minimize total transportation and in-transit and safety holding cost? *Hint:* The value of a motor in Toronto for calculating the safety stock holding cost is $120 plus cost of freight per unit. **LO2**

5. Pratt & Whitney, a major aircraft engine manufacturer, wants to re-evaluate the transportation mode it uses to send unfinished parts to its joint-venture facility in Chengdu, China.[4] Annual demand is 2,900 units. At present the company uses air freight. It takes approximately six days from Los Angeles to Chengdu (including pickup and delivery and customs delays). There are 20 parts in a lot, each weighing 30 kilograms. The air freight cost per part is $90. The pickup and delivery charges at origin and destination add up to $15 per part. The alternative is to use an ocean liner to ship the parts to Shanghai and from there to either use a truck or a train (a 2,000 km distance). The ocean freight for this lot size will cost $30 per part and will take 15 days. The truck from Shanghai to Chengdu will cost $20 per part and will take six days (including pickup and delivery and customs delays). Transportation by rail will cost $15 per part and will take 14 days (including pickup and delivery, customs, and transfer delays). In addition, for rail there is a $10 per part charge for pickup and delivery. The company's inventory holding cost rate is 12 percent per year, and the value of each part is $1,000. Assume 365 days per year. **LO2**

  Due to variability of lead times, at the destination, safety stocks of 60, 210, and 290 units will be kept if air, ship and truck, and ship and train are used, respectively. Determine the cheapest (total freight, delivery, and in-transit and safety holding cost) mode of transportation for these parts. *Hint:* The value of a part in Chengdu for calculating the safety-stock holding cost should include the freight cost.

6. A brick maker (BM) in Alberta mixes dry ink into its bricks to make them brown.

  BM's demand for dry ink is 60 tons per year. Currently, BM buys the dry ink from an import merchant that buys the ink from a East Coast U.S. manufacturer. The shipments arrive in lot size of 30 tons by rail. The current cost of dry ink is $C612.22 per ton, including rail transportation cost to BM's location. BM currently keeps 6 tons of dry ink as safety stock. BM's buyer has asked the import merchant to quote a price for truck deliveries in smaller lot sizes. The merchant has quoted C$567.78 per ton for a lot size of 20 tons.

  In the meantime, BM's buyer has contacted the manufacturer directly and asked if BM could purchase dry ink directly from the manufacturer. The answer was affirmative and the cost would be US$386.89 per ton (assume US$1 = C$1.05). A common carrier has quoted a price of C$2,600 to haul a full truckload of dry ink (20 tons) from the manufacturer to BM's location in Alberta. The trip will take 7 days.

  The holding cost rate for BM is 20 percent of unit cost per year. For truck deliveries, BM will hold only 2 tons of safety stocks. Assume 365 days per year. Which alternative has the lowest total annual purchase, transport, in-transit, safety stock, and average cycle stock holding cost? *Hint:* The value of a dry ink in Alberta for calculating the safety-stock and cycle stock holding cost of truck deliveries should include the freight cost. **LO2**

7. Given the following data, determine the total annual cost of making and of buying from each of vendor A and B. Estimated demand is 15,000 units a year. Which alternative is best? **LO1**

	Make	Vendor A	Vendor B
Variable cost per unit	$8	$11	$10
Annual fixed cost	$20,000	$ 0	$5,000 (annual charge)

8. Given the following data, determine the total annual cost of making with each of process A and B and of buying. Estimated demand is 10,000 units a year. Which alternative is best? **LO1**

	Make		Buy
	Process A	Process B	
Variable cost per unit	$50	$52	$51
Annual fixed cost	$40,000	$36,000	
Transportation cost per unit			$ 2

9. For the previous problem, suppose that the operations manager has said that it would be possible to achieve a

[4] Based on A. Z. Zeng and C. Rossetti, "Developing a Framework for Evaluating the Logistics Costs in Global Sourcing Processes," *International Journal of Physical Distribution & Logistics Management* 33(9/10), 2003, pp. 785–803.

10 percent reduction in the fixed cost of Process B and a 10 percent reduction in B's variable cost per unit. Would that be enough to change your answer if the estimated annual cost to achieve those savings was $8,000? Explain. **LO1**

10. Potash Corp, through Canpotex, has an order for 5,000 tons of potash from Sinofert, the largest fertilizer importer and distributor in China. How should this shipment be delivered (in terms of supply chain)? Draw the supply chain. *Hint:* You may find http://www.canpotex.com/what-we-do/logistics useful. **LO1**

11. All products sold at the Co-op retail stores in Western Canada are purchased and distributed by Federated Cooperatives Ltd (FCL). The produce buyer for FCL purchases 13 loads of Chiquita bananas per week (a load is the content of a 40 feet long ocean container). Also, 1 load per week is purchased from Dole. Chiquita bananas usually come from Guatemala in Central America on a Great White Fleet (Chiquita) ship in refrigerated containers. FCL receives the bananas from Chiquita's (refrigerated) warehouses in three different ports in the United States. (For the supply chain of bananas before getting to the port, you can view http://www.youtube.com/watch?v=SQ_gpZCvag). The bananas are destined for each of FCL's food warehouses in Calgary, Edmonton, Saskatoon, and Winnipeg. For the Calgary warehouse, FCL receives three loads per week from Hueneme (just north of Los Angeles) and 1 load per week from San Diego. For the Saskatoon warehouse, FCL receives four loads per week from Hueneme. For the Edmonton warehouse, FCL receives three to four loads per week from Hueneme. And for the Winnipeg warehouse FCL receives two loads per week from Freeport, Texas. A refrigerated company truck/trailer is sent down at regular intervals to pick up a load so that the ripening (ethylene) gas chambers in each DC are used evenly. Question: Is there a better way, in terms of supply chain management, to satisfy FCL's Chiquita banana demand? Briefly explain. **LO3**

 MINI-CASE http://www.clearwater.ca

Crusty Cargo

Clearwater Seafoods Limited Partnership of Bedford, Nova Scotia (N.S.), near Halifax, founded in 1976, is one of the largest harvesters, processors, and distributors of shellfish in the world. It has a combined total of 10 company-owned and joint venture–operated vessels that harvest off the coasts of the North Atlantic and Argentina. It also has two subsidiaries, one in Argentina harvesting scallops off the Argentinean continental shelf and one harvesting prawns off Newfoundland (NF) and selling them worldwide. Its processing facilities are Pierce Fisheries (in Lockeport, 200 km southwest of Halifax) which produces frozen scallops and lobster; a facility in St. Anthony, NF, which produces frozen shrimp, a facility in Grand Bank, NF, which produces clams; Highland Fisheries in Glace Bay, Nova Scotia, which produces snow crab; Arichat, Nova Scotia, which holds live lobsters in a dryland pound holding facility in the state of hibernation (8 million pounds per year go through Arichat), another live lobster holding facility in Bedford and a third (two 25,000 gallon salt-water tanks) in Louisville, Kentucky, for U.S. distribution. It also has cold storage facilities in the United Kingdom, France, and China, and ships globally out of Bedford.

The live lobsters are sold to many of the world's finest restaurants at short notice (24 hours)—over 30,000 pounds per week. Shipping live lobsters is a time-sensitive challenge. Clearwater ships live lobsters (in boxes) out of Halifax but this process was experiencing some difficulties because of delays due to paperwork mix-ups, technology interruptions, banning of gel

packs to chill the lobster in-transit after 9/11, and customs backlogs. A solution to this problem for shipping to the United States was to truck live lobsters (a 36-hour journey) once or twice a week from Bedford to Louisville (the U.S. air hub of UPS) on special reefer trucks, hold the lobsters in Louisville in cold water in salt-water tanks waiting for customer orders, and then courier them via UPS.

Question

What are the advantages and disadvantages of opening up Louisville holding tanks versus shipping live lobsters out of Bedford to the U.S.?

Source: http://www.clearwater.ca.

Summerwood

Summerwood is a high-end shed and gazebo manufacturer in Toronto (summerwood.com). The majority of Summerwood products are delivered to the customer in a kit (separate pieces of wood). Summerwood customers are located all over North America. The website has enough information for a potential buyer to choose the model and size of the structure she wants, and to order it online. The website has extensive information under "ordering" and "delivery" to make the fulfillment process clear to the buyer in order to reduce customer misunderstanding and disappointment. The fulfillment process is summarized in the following process flow diagram (for delivery to outside Southern Ontario). Summerwood uses various trucking companies to deliver its products throughout North America. Depending on the size of the structure, the kit could weigh anywhere from a few hundred pounds to 2,000 to 3,000 pounds. The LTL shipment is transported under "Standard Motor Freight," which is deliveries by semi-trailer truck that are offloaded by the buyer. Assistance with unloading can be arranged (for approximately $200) through local employment agencies but this has to be specified days before the delivery so that it can be arranged (the truck driver won't help with unloading). Even though the delivery process is clearly stated on the website, some customers are taken by surprise (unprepared) when the truck arrives. They complain that given the high cost of the product, the unloading should have been included and they assumed this. Management is wondering what else to do to prevent these types of customer complaints.

A possible solution may be to include unloading as part of the delivery, but at a higher delivery cost. FedEx Ground Freight (FXF) provides unloading service as the default. Summerwood management wishes to compare its current delivery rates with

FXF rate. As a sample, consider a small (5" × 7") shed. The current carrier is asking $750 for freight from Summerwood's shop in Toronto (postal code M1H 2W7) to the postal code S7N 5A7. The pre-cut unassembled shed wrapped on a skid weighs 740 pounds with dimensions 88" × 52" × 29". What is the FXF rate for this shipment?

Hint: You need to determine the transportability class of this shipment (http://shipfreight.van.fedex.com/ClassificationTool.aspx). Then, you can get the rate from https://www.fedex.com/ratefinder/standalone?method=goToFreight&from=Package: Enter From, To, no. of skid (1), Weight (in pounds), and Class, and press "Get—rates and transit times" in the bottom.

Source: http://www.summerwood.com.

CHAPTER 12
Inventory Management

The chapters in this part relate to the management of inventories, production planning, and scheduling—often key factors in the success or failure of operations management to achieve profit and/or cost objectives while satisfying customers. The basic issue is how to best manage resources to effectively match supply and demand.

Learning Objectives

After completing this chapter, you should be able to:

LO1 Define the term *inventory*, list major reasons for holding inventory, and discuss the objectives of inventory management.

LO2 List the main requirements for effective inventory management, and describe A-B-C classification and perform it.

LO3 Describe the basic economic order quantity model, the economic production quantity model, the quantity discount model, and the planned shortages model, and solve typical problems.

LO4 Describe how to determine the reorder point and solve typical problems.

LO5 Describe the fixed-interval model and solve typical problems.

LO6 Describe the single period model and solve typical problems.

LO7 Briefly discuss the multi-echelon inventory management.

A food/grocery, home and building supplies, animal feed, crop supplies, and petroleum and propane wholesaler and distributor such as Federated Co-operatives Ltd (FCL) moves and stores over 100,000 items. FCL also owns an oil refinery/upgrader in Regina and a fresh-produce wholesaler (TGP) in Edmonton. With revenue of almost $10 billion and 3,000 employees, FCL is the largest wholesaler in Canada (2013 revenue was larger than Ford Canada) and 48th largest company in Canada. FCL is owned by approximately 225 retail co-op associations in Western Canada that employ another 23,500 people. Beside group buying service and distribution, FCL provides its owner stores with centralized marketing (e.g., branding, advertising) and administrative services (e.g., IT, facility development). FCL has 4 DCs, 6 feed plants, 10 propane distribution facilities, a petroleum terminal near Calgary, 59 FCL-owned and 72 retail-member-owned bulk petroleum storage facilities, 1 FCL-owned and 379-retail-coop-owned gas bars, 225 semi-trailers, and 200 petroleum tankers. FCL competes with grocery chains such as Loblaw, hardware and lumber stores such as Home Depot, crop supply companies such as Glencore, and gas/diesel distributors such as Esso/Shell/Petro Canada. How has Federated Co-op remained competitive? One important factor is good inventory management.

Until 2011, the small but efficient Operations Research (OR) department in FCL managed Inforem, IBM's Inventory Forecasting and Replenishment Modules software, for decades. Run on a mainframe IBM computer, Inforem provided effective forecasting and inventory control service to over 30 FCL merchandise buyers located in the Saskatoon head office. Also, the small and efficient industrial engineering group helps manage the 4 FCL DCs in Calgary, Edmonton, Saskatoon, and Winnipeg. The OR group has also facilitated electronic ordering by the retail co-op stores and even provided them with space and shelf planning (planograms). Recently, FCL converted to JDA (Manugistics) demand forecasting and replenishment software and migrated away from the mainframe. FCL has always had good inventory turns (approximately 18, up to 60+ in produce) and customer service level (item fill rate of 96 to 98 percent in the DCs depending on the category of the item). The new JDA software has further improved FCL's inventory performance, especially in fresh produce/perishables with the following results: 1.2 percent increase in service level, 2.6 more inventory turns, and 14 percent less perishability cost.

Sources: https://www.coopconnection.ca/wps/portal/fclretail/FCLInternet/AboutUs; http://www.youtube.com/watch?v=500G-h2nPhk.

Good inventory management is important for the successful operation of most organizations, especially manufacturers and wholesaler/distributors/retailers that hold a lot of inventory. Operations, marketing, and finance have interests in good inventory management. Poor inventory management holds operations back and diminishes customer satisfaction, in addition to costing money.

This chapter describes inventory management of finished goods, some raw materials, supplies and spare parts, and wholesale/retail items. The demand for these items is unknown and has to be forecasted. For this reason, these items are said to have *independent demand.* Management of manufacturing parts and components will be described in chapters 14 and 15 on material requirements planning and just-in-time. Demand for manufacturing parts and components depends on the production schedule for the finished goods. For this reason, these items are said to have *dependent demand.* This chapter includes models for determining *how much* to order and *when* to order for independent-demand items. Emphasis is on inventory analysis.

Introduction

An **inventory** or stock is any material, part, or product sitting idle, not being used, usually in a warehouse or stockroom, and kept for use or sale in the future. Organizations typically store hundreds or even thousands of items in inventory, ranging from small things such as pencils, paper clips, screws, nuts, and bolts to large items such as equipment. An item kept in inventory is called a stock keeping unit (SKU). Naturally, many of the items a company holds in inventory relate to the kind of activities it engages in. Thus, manufacturers hold inventories of raw materials, purchased manufacturing parts and components, partially finished items (i.e., work-in-process [WIP]), and finished goods, as well as spare parts for machines, tools, and other supplies.

inventory An idle material, part, or product, usually in a warehouse or stockroom.

Work-in-process

Suppliers → Raw material/part → Work-in-process → Finished good → Customers

Work-in-process

Retail stores hold inventories of items, mostly on their shelves, for resale. Hospitals may stock drugs, surgical supplies, life-monitoring equipment, sheets and pillow cases, and more.

inventory management
Planning and controlling inventories.

Inventory management is concerned with planning and controlling inventories.

Importance of Inventory

A typical company probably has approximately half of its current assets in inventories (the other half are in receivables and cash). One widely used measure of business performance is *return on assets* (ROA), which is profit after tax divided by total assets. Because inventories may represent a significant portion of total assets in the balance sheet (also called statement of financial position), a reduction in inventories can result in a significant increase in ROA.

Inventory also influences the Income (or earnings) Statement through Cost of Goods Sold (COGS). COGS is the sum of material, direct labour, and indirect labour costs. Material cost is determined by the following equation: value of inventory at the start of the year + total cost of material purchase during the year − value of inventory at the end of the year. Thus, accounting is interested in value of inventory. Management also uses value of inventory for decision making. For example, if total value of finished goods (FGs) is high, management will reduce production and sell some of the FGs at a discount.

It is important that the value of inventory represent the true worth of inventory. Accountants use various methods of inventory valuation: first-in-first-out (FIFO), last-in-first-out (LIFO), and weighted average cost. If value of inventory gives a wrong impression about the quantity of inventory (in units), this can lead management to make wrong decisions. An example involved the CEO and CFO of SunOpta (http://www.sunopta.com), the Toronto-based natural and organic food producer. They thought that they had more strawberries (by weight) in inventory because the cost of growing strawberry was underestimated. Hence, they reduced the price of strawberry-based products. This error resulted in an unnecessary $11 million write-down. This caused a 30 percent SunOpta share price drop, which led to the executives' dismissal.[1]

The major source of revenue for retailers and wholesalers/distributors is the resale of merchandise (i.e., inventories). In fact, in terms of dollars, the inventory of goods held for resale is one of the largest assets of a merchandising business.

Service companies do not carry as many inventories, although they do carry inventories of supplies and equipment.

To understand why organizations have inventories at all, you need to be aware of the various functions (purposes) of inventory.

 Service ## Functions (Purposes) of Inventories

Inventories serve a number of functions. Among the most important are the following:

1. *To wait while being transported.* Raw materials and parts from suppliers, and finished goods from manufacturers heading to markets (being distributed) need to be transported. Depending on the mode of transportation, the freight could take up to a month to reach its destination. Items being transported are called *in-transit inventory.*

2. *To protect against stock-outs.* Delayed deliveries from suppliers and unexpected increases in customer demand increase the risk of stock-outs. Delays can occur because of weather conditions, supplier stock-outs, deliveries of wrong materials, quality problems, and so on. The risk of stock-out can be reduced by holding *safety stocks,* which are stocks in excess of average demand.

---

[1] S, Islam, "Strawberry Surprise," *Financial Post Magazine,* September 2008, p. 27.

3. *To take advantage of economic lot size and quantity discount.* To minimize purchasing, receiving, material handling, and accounts payable costs, an organization often buys in a quantity (called economic order quantity) that exceeds its immediate requirements. This necessitates storing some of the purchased goods for later use. Similarly, it is usually economical to produce in a large quantity (called economic production quantity). This results in consecutive orders occurring after some interval of time, called *order or replenishment cycle.* The resulting inventory is hence known as *cycle stock.* The ability to store extra goods also allows a company to take advantage of price discounts for larger orders.

4. *To smooth seasonal demand or production.* Manufacturers that experience seasonal patterns in demand (e.g., agricultural implements, breweries) often build up inventories during off-season to meet high requirements during peak season. Also, when supply is seasonal, such as in grain, fruit, and vegetable production, the producer may keep some of the products for later sales (possibly after freezing/canning). These inventories are aptly named *seasonal inventories.*

5. *To decouple operations.* Historically, manufacturers have used inventories as *buffers* between successive operations to maintain continuity of production that would otherwise be disrupted by events such as breakdowns of equipment and accidents that cause a portion of the operation to shut down temporarily. The *work-in-process buffers* permit other operations to continue temporarily while the problem is solved. WIP buffer is analogous to the water in a tank:

Workstation A → Supply rate → WIP level   → Demand rate → Workstation B

The average supply rate and the average demand rate should be equal, or else the tank will be empty or will overflow. The average WIP inventory (L), average time a unit spends waiting in the inventory/tank (W), and average supply (or demand) rate (λ) are related through Little's law: $L = \lambda W$.

6. *To hedge against price increases.* Occasionally a buyer is informed by her supplier that a substantial price increase is about to occur. Hence, she will purchase larger-than-normal amounts to avoid the price increase. This is called *anticipation inventory.*

Importance and Objectives of Inventory Management

Inadequate management of inventories can result in both understocking of some items and overstocking of the others. Understocking results in missed deliveries, lost sales, dissatisfied customers, and production stoppage; overstocking unnecessarily ties up funds that might be more productive elsewhere and also ties up storage space. Although overstocking may appear to be the lesser of the two evils, the price tag for excessive overstocking can be staggering. It is not unheard of for managers to discover that their company has a 10-year supply of some item. (No doubt they got a good deal on it!)

Inventory management has two main concerns. One is the *level of customer service (item availability or fill rate)*; that is, to have the right goods, in sufficient quantities, in the right place, at the right time. The other is the inventory costs: the *costs of ordering and holding inventories.*

The overall objective of inventory management is to achieve satisfactory levels of customer service while minimizing inventory costs. Toward this end, a buyer or inventory analyst must make two decisions for each item: the *timing* and *size* of orders (i.e., when to order and how much to order). The greater part of this chapter is devoted to models that can be applied to assist in making these decisions.

Managers have a number of measures of performance they can use to judge the effectiveness of their inventory management. The most obvious, of course, is customer satisfaction, which

OM in ACTION

SYSPRO

A good Enterprise Resource Planning (ERP) software for medium/small-size organizations is SYSPRO®. The first step in using the software is to define the inventory items. This is done by the Stock Codes program under Setup of the Inventory module. Each item will have a file (see the screenshot below). The typical information needed is Stock code, Warehouse to use, Part category (Bought out or Made-in), Product class (e.g., raw material), and Lead time (Days) or Batching rule (e.g., Lot-for-lot).

inventory turnover Ratio of annual cost of goods sold to average inventory investment.

they might measure by the in-stock percent or item *fill rate* (i.e., the percentage of demand filled from stocks on hand). Another measure is related to inventory costs: **inventory turnover** is the ratio of annual cost of goods sold (COGS) to average inventory investment. The inventory turnover ratio indicates how many times a year the inventory is sold or used. Generally, the higher the ratio the better, because that implies more efficient use of inventories. A benefit of this measure is that it can be used to compare companies in the *same* industry. For example, in the retail industry, supermarkets have high (over 15) inventory turnover (because most of their goods are perishable) whereas furniture stores have low inventory turnover (approximately 3–6)—see Figure 12-1.

Figure 12-1 ▶

Inventory turnover, by retail trade group (2008).

Source: Industry Canada. Based on data from Statistics Canada (Annual Retail Trade Survey), 2010. http://www.ic.gc.ca/eic/site/retra-comde.nsf/eng/qn00282.html?Open&pv=1.

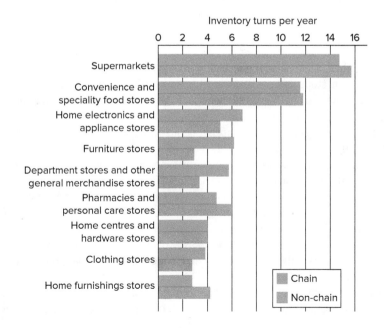

A related measure is *days of inventory* on hand, a number that indicates the expected number of days of sales or usage that can be supplied from existing inventory.

Reducing the Need for Inventories

Organizations can reduce the need for inventories without reducing customer service by addressing the reason for needing (or the function of) inventories:

Inventory Function	Ways to Reduce the Need for Inventory
In-transit	Locate companies in a supply chain as close to each other as possible
	Cross-dock or eliminate the DC (e.g., ask manufacturer to drop-ship direct to consumer)
Safety	Establish close long-term relationship with suppliers and customers
	Ensure high quality material
Cycle	Reduce the ordering/setup times
Seasonal	Develop sources of supply and demand that collectively extend seasons
WIP buffer	Reduce machine breakdown
	Train workers and accept idle time
Anticipation	Use forward/futures contracts

Requirements for Effective Inventory Management

L02

Inventory managers are required to perform the following activities:

1. Safely store and handle inventories.
2. Track inventories and use inventory control models.
3. Forecast demands and lead times.
4. Estimate inventory costs.
5. Perform A-B-C classification.

Let's take a closer look at each of these requirements.

Safely Storing and Handling Inventories

Most inventory items need to be protected from harsh outdoor environment such as rain and snow. Therefore, inventory is usually stored indoors, in a warehouse or stockroom. Depending on the nature of the item, racks, shelves, or bins may be used to hold it. Heavy items or fast-moving items are stored on the floor. Each location should have an address code. To save moving items long distances, warehouses usually use the vertical space, i.e., they have a very high ceiling (as high as three- or four-stories). Forklifts and high-reach industrial trucks are used to access the top locations.

A warehouse/stockroom should be uncluttered so that items can be stored and retrieved easily. Depending on the flow of items into and out of the warehouse/stockroom, the right level of automation should be used. Most warehouses use forklifts, which move cases/boxes of items piled on a pallet (an approximately 4 foot by 4 foot wood platform). Some use conveyors and some use carousels. A **warehouse management system** (WMS) is a computer software that controls the movement and storage of materials within a warehouse, and processes the associated transactions, including receiving, put-away, replenishment, picking, and shipping.

Basic warehouse activities can be described as follows: A shipment arrives on board a semi-trailer. A receiver drives the pallets out of the trailer using a forklift truck, identifies the associated purchase order, and receives each pallet by scanning the bar code of the product(s) (on the box(es)) and entering the quantity in WMS. WMS generates a bar-code label that provides

warehouse management system A computer software that controls the movement and storage of materials within a warehouse, and processes the associated transactions.

pallet tracking and also has the storage location address. Usually a large warehouse has two locations for each item: a bulk (reserve) rack location (usually high up) and an individual-item bin/shelf pick location (reachable by a person without equipment). After receiving, the pallets are left in a staging area for a put-away forklift driver to move to their bulk storage location. WMS is informed of the moves and updates the location of pallet. Later, as the pick location runs out of units of an item, WMS issues a replenishment order to move a box of the item from the bulk location to the pick location.

As customer orders arrive, they are assigned to a specific order picker. If the order contains various items, it may be divided and assigned to pickers who work in different zones of the warehouse. WMS assigns a box/tote/pallet bar code to the customer that is printed by the order picker and attached to the box/tote/pallet (if the order for an item is very large, a pallet from the bulk location will be retrieved). WMS then directs the picker to retrieve the order in the sequence that minimizes total distance travelled while picking heavy items first (so that they are in the bottom of box/tote/pallet). (Alternatively the customer order is printed on a sheet of paper and used for manual order picking). For material handling, carts-on-wheels are used in manual warehouses, whereas conveyors or pallet jacks are used in others. (It is also possible to automate both storage and picking by using Automated Storage and Retrieval Systems [ASRS].) Once at the picking location, the order picker scans the location bar code to confirm the location and product before picking the quantity requested. Once the WMS confirms a correct pick, it directs the picker to the next pick location until the order is filled. The order is then moved to a packing station where weight of the order is checked to make sure it is complete. Then, the box bar code is scanned and assigned to a specific carrier for shipment to the customer. For an application, see "The McGraw-Hill Ryerson Warehouse in Whitby, Ontario" Operations Tour at the end of this chapter. For an application of warehouse technology, see the "Groupe Leclerc" OM in Action later in the chapter.

The required warehouse capacity depends on yearly volume and frequency of inventory movements. For each item, the maximum space required at any time (including safety stock) should be determined. Also, the floor space needed for aisles and receiving/shipping, returns, etc. should be considered.

A warehouse is owned, rented, or leased (contracted). Ownership provides more control, but to be economical demand should be high and stable. Public (rented) warehousing is for short-term needs and requires no capital or personnel. Contract warehousing is offered by a 3PL service provider.

Food distributors require a warehouse that has cold rooms/zones for fresh produce and freezers for items such as ice cream. Some inventoried items are expensive, so access to the building should be controlled, and items that are prone to theft (e.g., small valuable items such as batteries and cigarettes) should be locked up in a secure area/room/zone. Also, because full pallets are heavy, racks in the warehouse can be high, and equipment such as forklifts and pallet jacks are large and fast moving, safety is an important issue in warehouse management.

A common problem in most warehouses/stockrooms is the existence of a considerable amount of obsolete items. These include parts for machines that no longer exist, wrong parts, excess material, used/old machines, etc. To be efficient, outdated items should be either sent back to the supplier or sold to a liquidator. Obsolete items are a drag on the company's assets and take space in the warehouse.

Tracking Inventories and Using Inventory Control Models

If inventories are not continually tracked, then they must be periodically reviewed and counted. Some small retailers that do not use a computer use this approach: a manager periodically checks the shelves and his records to determine the **inventory position** for each item, i.e., quantity on hand + on order − back-ordered. "On order" is a purchase order that has not arrived yet. A back-order is a shortage that the customer has accepted to wait for, i.e., it is a future inventory committed to a customer. Then, the manager estimates how much of the

inventory position Quantity on hand + on order − back-ordered.

OM in ACTION

Groupe Leclerc

Leclerc, based in Quebec City, manufactures cookies in three factories in Canada and two in the United States, employing 650 people. Leclerc products are distributed worldwide. Leclerc's facilities are one of the most automatic and efficient operations in the food industry. In addition to automated production lines, Leclerc's warehouses are also automated. Leclerc uses Swisslog Vectura pallet stacker cranes, Transbotics automatic guided forklifts, and automatic palletizers, so only two people run a large warehouse.

Sources: L. Klie, "Reaching New Heights," *Food Logistics*, Jul/Aug 2006, 88, pp. 29–31; http://www.leclercfoodsprivate.com/en/index.html.

item will be demanded prior to receipt of the next delivery (called the order up to level) and bases the order quantity on the difference between the two, i.e., order up to level − inventory position. This replenishment model is called **fixed-interval/order up to level model**. This model is also used when a computer keeps track of items continually. An advantage of this model is that items from the same supplier are ordered at the same time, which results in economies in ordering, shipping, receiving, and paying. A disadvantage is the possibility of stock-out between reviews.

Perpetual or continual tracking keeps track of removals from and additions to inventory on a continuous basis, so the system can provide information on the current inventory position for each item. Bank accounts are kept using this method, i.e., transactions such as deposits and withdrawals are instantly recorded and balance is determined continually. All modern inventory software keep track of inventories continually. For example, see the "SYSPRO" OM in Action earlier in the chapter.

Another common inventory control model is **fixed order quantity/reorder point model**. This model works only with perpetual tracking. When the inventory position drops down to or below a predetermined minimum (called the reorder point), a fixed quantity is ordered. Usually a computer keeps track of inventory for this model. An advantage of this model is that the probability or expected number of shortage can be controlled. Another advantage is that the order quantity is fixed; management can determine an optimal order quantity and use it for a while (provided that demand does not vary seasonally or have a trend). A disadvantage of this model is the added cost of individual ordering. This model is closely related to the popular Min/Max model: when inventory position drops to or below Min, an order equal to "Max − inventory position" is placed. Finding the optimal values for

fixed-interval/order up to level model Orders are placed at fixed time intervals to bring the inventory position up to the order up to level.

perpetual or continual tracking Keeps track of removals from and additions to inventory continuously, thus providing the current inventory position of each item.

fixed order quantity/reorder point model An order of a fixed size is placed when the inventory position drops to or below a minimum quantity called the *reorder point*.

Min and Max is a little more complex (it requires an iterative search procedure). Fortunately, we can approximate Min by ROP and Max by "ROP + EOQ" without a large cost penalty. This approximation slightly underestimates the optimal Min and Max.[2]

The above two models are appropriate if unused items can be carried over into subsequent periods. The single-period model is appropriate when items cannot be carried over, e.g., are perishable.

A simple implementation of the fixed order quantity/reorder point model that does not require perpetual inventory tracking is the **two bin system**. Items are withdrawn from the first bin until its contents are exhausted. It is then time to reorder. The second bin contains enough stock to satisfy expected demand until the order is filled plus safety stock. When the order arrives, the second bin is topped off and the remainder is placed in the first bin. Sometimes an order card is placed at the bottom of the first bin.

Most warehouses/stockrooms use laser scanners that read bar codes assigned to items, cases/boxes, pallets, etc. and the storage locations (racks, shelves, bins, etc.). A **bar code** is a unique number assigned to an item or a location, made of a group of vertical black and white bars that are read by a scanner. There are different types of bar codes. The standard grocery bar code is called Universal Product Code (UPC), has 12 digits, and is illustrated below (on the left). The zero on the left of the bar code identifies this as a regular grocery item, the next five numbers (36000) indicate the manufacturer, the next five numbers (29145) indicate the specific item, and the last digit (2) is a check-digit, used by the computer to check the validity of the first 11 digits that the scanner read. Each digit is made of 7 black or white bars. However, the colour of a bar depends on whether the digit is on the left of centre guard (L pattern) or on the right (R pattern). This is done so that a scanner can read the UPC from left to right or from right to left (and still get the same digits). Bar-code scanners have increased the speed and accuracy of transactions significantly.

two bin system Reorder when the first bin is empty; use the second bin until order arrives; top off the second bin and leave the rest in the first bin.

bar code A number assigned to an item or storage location, made of a group of vertical bars of different thickness that are readable by a scanner.

Digit	Left pattern	Right pattern	Widths
0	0001101	1110010	3211
1	0011001	1100110	2221
2	0010011	1101100	2122
3	0111101	1000010	1411
4	0100011	1011100	1132
5	0110001	1001110	1231
6	0101111	1010000	1114
7	0111011	1000100	1312
8	0110111	1001000	1213
9	0001011	1110100	3112

Forecasting Demands and Lead Times

Inventories are used to satisfy future demand requirements, so it is essential to have reliable estimates of the amount and timing of future demand. Also, it is essential to know the **purchase lead time**, the time it will take for purchase orders to be received. Similarly, manufacturing lead time is the time it will take for a batch of a part/product to be manufactured. In addition, managers need to know the extent to which demand and lead time might vary: the greater the potential variability, the greater the need for additional safety stock to reduce the risk of stock-out between deliveries. Thus, there is a crucial link between forecasting and inventory management.

purchase lead time Time interval between ordering and receiving the order.

---

[2] See, for example, E. A. Silver, D. F. Pyke, and R. Peterson. *Inventory Management and Production Planning and Scheduling*, 3rd Ed. New York: John Wiley and Sons, 1998, pp. 332–335).

Point-of-sale (POS) systems electronically record actual sales at the time and location of sale, which, after accumulation into daily or weekly or monthly sales for each stock keeping unit (S.K.U.), are used in forecasting.

Given the large number of SKUs of a typical organization, a simple time-series forecasting technique such as exponential smoothing (and its variants) is commonly used to forecast demand of SKUs.

Estimating Inventory Costs

Three basic costs, other than the purchase price, are associated with inventories: holding, order-ing, and shortage costs.

Holding or carrying cost relates to physically having items in storage. Costs include ware-housing costs (rent or building depreciation, labour, material-handling equipment depreciation, heating/cooling, light, etc.) and the opportunity cost associated with funds, which could be used elsewhere, tied up in inventory. Other holding costs include insurance, obsolescence, spoilage, pilferage, and breakage.

The significance of some of the components of holding cost depends on the type of item. Items that are easily concealed or are fairly expensive are prone to theft. Perishable items such as meat and dairy are subject to rapid spoilage. Computers and electronics, and their parts, are subject to rapid price devaluation (obsolescence).

Holding cost is stated in either of two ways: as a percentage of unit cost or as a dollar amount per unit. Typical annual holding cost rates range from 20 percent to 40 percent of the cost of an item. In other words, to hold a $100 item for one year could cost from $20 to $40.

Ordering cost, or acquisition cost, is the cost of placing an order (not including the purchase price), receiving it, and paying for it. This includes the time of purchasing/inventory control staff while determining how much is needed, periodically evaluating sources of supply, preparing pur-chase orders, and the fixed-cost portion of transportation, receiving, inspecting, and moving the goods to storage. It also includes the cost of time spent paying the invoice. Ordering cost is gener-ally expressed as a fixed dollar amount per order, regardless of order size.

When a company produces its own parts instead of ordering it from a supplier, the cost of machine setup is analogous to ordering cost; that is, it is expressed as a fixed charge per produc-tion run, regardless of the size of the run. Machine **setup** involves preparing the machine for the job by adjusting it, changing cutting tools, etc.

Shortage cost results when demand exceeds supply of inventory on hand. This cost can include the opportunity cost of not making a sale (i.e., unrealized profit), loss of customer goodwill, late charges, and expediting costs. Furthermore, if the shortage occurs in an item carried for internal use (e.g., to supply an assembly line), the cost of lost production or downtime is considered a shortage cost, which can easily run into hundreds of dollars a minute or more.

Performing A-B-C Classification

Items held in inventory are typically not of equal importance in terms of dollars invested, profit potential, sales or usage quantity, or shortage cost. For instance, a producer of electrical equipment might have electrical generators, coils of wire, and miscellaneous nuts and bolts among the items carried in inventory. It would be inefficient to devote equal attention to each of these items. Instead, a more reasonable approach would be to allocate control efforts according to the *relative importance* of various items in inventory.

The **A-B-C classification** groups inventory items into three classes according to some measure of importance, usually annual dollar value (i.e., cost per unit multiplied by annual usage or sales quantity), and then allocates inventory control efforts accordingly. The three classes are A (very important), B (moderately important), and C (least important). A items gen-erally account for about 15 to 20 percent of the items (SKUs, not counting multiple units of the same part/product) in inventory but about 70 to 80 percent of the annual *dollar value (ADV)*.

Cardinal Health Canada (CHC)

CHC is one of the two largest medical, surgical, and lab products distributors in Canada (the other is McKesson Canada). It offers over 80,000 items to its customers: hospitals, clinics, doctors' offices, nursing homes, clinical labs, etc. These items satisfy more than 85 percent of the customers' needs. The items include anything from bandages to operating tables. CHC has over 600 suppliers, such as 3M Canada, Procter & Gamble, and Kimberly-Clark.

CHC has a National Supply Centre (NSC), a 220,000 ft² warehouse/distribution centre, in Mississauga, Ontario, and 7 regional warehouse/distribution centres (DC), from Vancouver to St. John's. The regional DCs provide daily delivery service to customers. The NSC carries approximately 30,000 Stock Keeping Units (SKU). The rest are low-demand items (e.g., equipment) that are bought when necessary and are either cross-docked to the customer or directly shipped to the customer. Some of the SKUs are also inventoried in regional DCs (these are called national stocks) and others, used less frequently, are kept only in NSC (called central stocks).

The materials management team forecasts customer demand, monitors and improves supplier delivery performance, and controls the levels of inventory in each facility. Any low or high levels are investigated to identify their cause and the problem is solved with the cooperation of suppliers and/or customers. For example, the cause for a low inventory of an SKU may be an incorrect purchase order or a problem at a supplier. Using this method, CHC has reduced its inventories while increasing its fill rates.

Shipments from suppliers to the NSC are 30–35 full truckloads and 50–60 less than full truckloads per day. The NSC is divided in two parts: approximately 2,000 full case SKUs (A items) are kept on one side, and 28,000 other SKUs (B and C items) are kept on shelves on the other side. Radio frequency communication and bar code scanners are used for receiving, put away, replenishment, and order picking.

CHC has JIT or stockless inventory arrangement with its customers. This means that an order received by EDI from for example a ward of a hospital is delivered the next day directly to the ward, hence relieving the hospital of the need for a stockroom. CHC's Online ordering system (a B2B ecommerce portal) provides custom pricing and allows the use of a bar code scanner (the system is called OrderConnect) which makes ordering faster and easier. Also, rush deliveries are possible. The Advanced Customer Logistics team works with customers to improve the efficiency and effectiveness of the supply system, e.g., by performing product standardization. EDI is also used for communication within CHC and with its suppliers.

Sources: http://www.cardinalhealthcanada.com/en/pages/supply_chain. aspx; R. Robertson, "Saving Lives," *Materials Management and Distribution*, July/August 2003, 48(6), pp. 14–20.

At the other end of the scale, C items might account for about 50 to 60 percent of the SKUs but only about 5 to 10 percent of the ADV. These percentages vary from company to company, but in most instances a relatively small number of items will account for a large share of ADV, and these items should receive a greater share of inventory control efforts. For instance, A items should receive close attention through better forecasting, more frequent ordering, and better safety stock determination. The C items should receive only loose control (e.g., using a two-bin system, bulk orders), and the B items should have controls that lie between the two extremes.

Example 1 ▶ Classify the following inventory items as A, B, or C based on annual dollar value (ADV):

Item	Annual Demand ×	Unit Cost =	Annual Dollar Value (ADV)
1........	3,000	$10	$30,000
2........	9,000	3	27,000
3........	1,000	710	710,000
4........	2,500	250	625,000
5........	1,900	500	950,000
6........	400	200	80,000
7........	500	100	50,000
8........	1,000	4,300	4,300,000
9........	200	210	42,000
10........	5,000	720	3,600,000
11........	2,500	192	480,000
12........	1,000	35	35,000

Sort the rows by decreasing values of ADV and calculate the percentage of total ADV for each SKU:

Item	Annual Demand	×	Unit Cost	=	Annual Dollar Value (ADV)	% of Total ADV	
8........	1,000		$4,300		$4,300,000	39.3	} A
10........	5,000		720		3,600,000	32.9	
5........	1,900		500		950,000	8.7	} B
3........	1,000		710		710,000	6.5	
4........	2,500		250		625,000	5.7	
11........	2,500		192		480,000	4.4	
6........	400		200		80,000	.7	} C
7........	500		100		50,000	.5	
9........	200		210		42,000	.4	
12........	1,000		35		35,000	.3	
1........	3,000		10		30,000	.3	
2........	9,000		3		27,000	.3	
					$10,929,000	100.0	

Proceed down the list, adding percentage of total ADVs until you get close to 80 percent of total ADV. The first two items have 72.2 percent of total ADV and 2/12 = 17 percent of SKUs, so it seems reasonable to classify them as A items. (Also note the sharp drop in ADV from the second to third rows.) The next four items have moderate ADV (25.3 percent of total ADV and 4/12 = 33 percent of SKUs) and should be classified as B items. (Also note the sharp drop in ADV between the sixth and seventh rows.) The remainder are C items, based on their relatively low ADV (2.5 percent of total ADV and 6/12 = 50 percent of SKUs).

Although annual dollar value may be the primary factor in classifying inventory items, a manager may take other factors into account in making exceptions for certain items (e.g., changing the classification of a C item to A). Factors may include the risk of obsolescence, the consequence of a stock-out, the distance of a supplier, long lead time, and so on.

Managers use the A-B-C concept in many different settings to improve operations. For example, the A-B-C concept is sometimes used to guide **cycle counting**, which is counting the items in inventory on a cyclic schedule. The purpose of cycle counting is to (1) reduce discrepancies between inventory records and the actual quantities of inventory on hand, and (2) investigate the causes of inaccuracy and fix them. Accuracy is important because inaccurate records can lead to wrong inventory control decisions, which then lead to disruptions in production, poor customer service, or unnecessarily high inventory carrying cost.

cycle counting Counting the items in inventory on a cyclic schedule.

The key questions concerning cycle counting for management are:

1. How much accuracy is needed?
2. What kind of counting cycle should be used?
3. Who should do it?

APICS recommends the following guidelines for inventory record accuracy: ±0.2 percent for A items, ±1 percent for B items, and ±5 percent for C items. Therefore, A items should be counted more frequently than C items. For example, A items should be counted every month, B items quarterly, and C items annually.

http://www.apics.org

Some companies use regular stockroom personnel to do cycle counting during periods of slow activity, while others contract with outside companies to do it on a periodic basis. Use of an outside company provides an independent check on inventory and may reduce the risk of problems created by error-prone employees.

The "Cardinal Health Canada", see the OM in Action on the previous page, uses the A-B-C classification for locating items in their warehouse.

Fixed Order Quantity/Reorder Point Model: Determining the Economic Order Quantity

economic order quantity (EOQ) The order size that minimizes total inventory control cost.

In the fixed order quantity/reorder point model, the fixed quantity is ordered when the inventory position (amount on hand + on order − back-ordered) drops to or below the reorder point. For simplicity, we decompose the determination of the order quantity and the reorder point. Even though the formulas we will obtain will not necessarily give the optimal values, they generally give close-to-optimal values (the worst case cost penalty is approximately 12 percent.[3] The fixed quantity is usually the **economic order quantity (EOQ)**. EOQ is determined by minimizing the total annual inventory control cost. Four EOQ-related models are described here:

1. Basic economic order quantity.
2. Economic production quantity.
3. EOQ with quantity discounts.
4. EOQ with planned shortages.

Basic Economic Order Quantity (EOQ)

The basic EOQ model for an item will minimize the sum of annual costs of holding and ordering inventory. The annual purchase price is not included because it is assumed in the basic case that unit purchase price is unaffected by the order size.

The basic EOQ model is based on a number of assumptions. They are listed in Table 12-1.

Ordering, receiving, and usage occur in cycles. Figure 12-2 illustrates 2.5 order cycles. A cycle begins with receipt of a shipment of Q units, which are then used at a constant rate over time. When the quantity on hand is just sufficient to satisfy demand during a lead time, another purchase order for Q units is submitted to the supplier. Because it is assumed that both the demand rate and the lead time do not vary, the shipment will be received at the precise instant that the inventory on hand falls to zero. Thus, orders are timed to avoid both excess stock and stock-outs. Note that for simplicity, the profile is for inventory on hand, not inventory position. That is, the order quantity is not shown on the graph until it is actually received. The economic order quantity reflects a trade-off between total annual holding and total annual ordering costs: If the order size is relatively small, the average inventory will be low, resulting in low annual holding cost. However, a small order size will necessitate frequent orders, which will drive up annual ordering cost. Conversely, ordering large quantities at infrequent intervals can reduce annual ordering cost, but would result in higher average inventory levels and therefore increased annual holding cost. Figure 12-3 illustrates these two extremes.

Table 12-1 ▶

Assumptions of the basic EOQ model.

1. Only one item is involved.
2. Annual demand requirements are known.
3. Demand is spread evenly throughout the year so that the demand rate is reasonably constant.
4. Lead time does not vary and it is smaller than an order cycle.
5. Each order is received in a single delivery.
6. There are no quantity discounts. This includes the assumption that transportation cost per unit does not depend on order size.
7. Shortage is not allowed.

Thus, the ideal solution is an order size that is neither very large nor very small, but somewhere in between. The exact amount to order will depend on the relative magnitudes of holding and ordering costs.

---

[3] Y. S. Zheng, "On Properties of Stochastic Inventory Systems," *Management Science*, 38(10), 1992, 87–103.

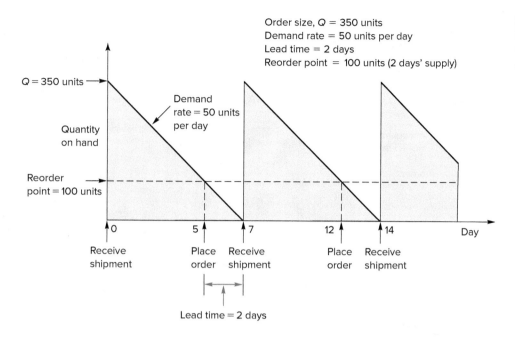

Order size, Q = 350 units
Demand rate = 50 units per day
Lead time = 2 days
Reorder point = 100 units (2 days' supply)

◀ Figure 12-2

Order cycles: profile of inventory on hand over time.

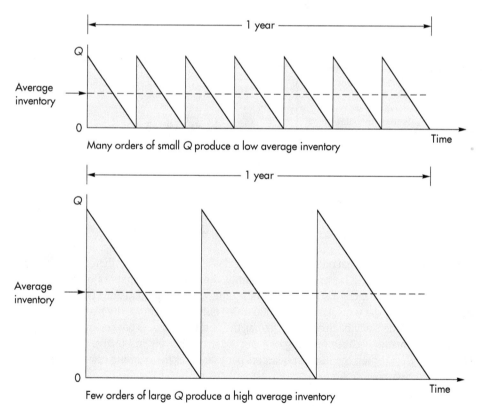

◀ Figure 12-3

Average inventory on hand and number of orders per year are inversely related: as one increases, the other decreases.

Annual holding cost is calculated by multiplying the average amount of inventory on hand by the cost to hold one unit for one year (even though any given unit would not be held for a year). The average inventory is simply half of the order quantity: The amount on hand decreases steadily from Q units to 0, for an average of (Q + 0)/2, or Q/2. Using the symbol H to represent the annual holding cost per unit, the *total annual holding cost* is:

$$\text{Annual holding cost} = \frac{Q}{2}H$$

where:

Q = Order quantity (units per order)

H = Holding (or carrying) cost per unit per year

Annual holding cost is thus a linear function of Q: it increases or decreases in direct proportion to changes in the order quantity Q, as Figure 12-4A illustrates.

A. Annual holding cost is linearly related to order quantity

B. Annual ordering cost is inversely and nonlinearly related to order quantity

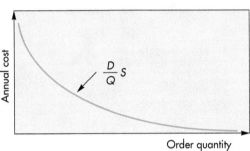

C. The total annual inventory cost curve is U-shaped, and at its minimum annual holding cost equals annual ordering cost

On the other hand, annual ordering cost will decrease as order quantity increases, because for a given annual demand, the larger the order quantity, the fewer the number of orders needed. For instance, if annual demand is 12,000 units and the order quantity is 1,000 units per order, there will be 12 orders during the year. But if Q = 2,000 units, only six orders will be needed; if Q = 3,000 units, only four orders will be needed. In general, the number of orders per year will be D/Q, where D = annual demand. Because ordering cost per order is relatively insensitive to order quantity, *annual ordering cost* equals the number of orders per year times the ordering cost per order:

$$\text{Annual ordering cost} = \frac{D}{Q}S$$

where:

D = Demand (units per year)

S = Ordering cost per order

Because the number of orders per year, D/Q, decreases as Q increases (but not at a constant rate), annual ordering cost is inversely and nonlinearly related to order quantity, as Figure 12-4b illustrates.

The total annual inventory cost of holding and ordering inventory, when Q units are ordered each time, is:

$$TC = \text{Annual holding cost} + \text{Annual ordering cost} = \frac{Q}{2}H + \frac{D}{Q}S \qquad (12\text{-}1)$$

Figure 12-4C reveals that the total-cost curve is U-shaped (i.e., a convex function, with one minimum) and that *it reaches its minimum at the quantity where annual holding and annual ordering costs are equal.* An expression for the optimal order quantity, Q_0, can be obtained using calculus.[4] The result is the formula:

$$EOQ = Q_0 = \sqrt{\frac{2DS}{H}} \qquad (12\text{-}2)$$

The minimum total cost is then found by substituting Q_0 for Q in Formula 12-1.
The length of an order cycle (i.e., the time between orders, if Q_0 is used) is:

$$\text{Length of order cycle (in years)} = \frac{Q_0}{D} \qquad (12\text{-}3)$$

A tire store expects to sell approximately 100 all-season tires of a certain make, model, and size next year. Annual holding cost is $16 per tire and ordering cost is $20 per order. The store operates 360 days a year and has enough storage space in the back.

 Example 2

a. What is the EOQ?

b. How many times per year would the store reorder if EOQ units are ordered each time?

c. What is the length of an order cycle if EOQ units are ordered each time?

d. What is the total annual inventory control cost if EOQ units are ordered each time?

SOLUTION

$D = 100$ tires per year

$H = \$16$ per unit per year

$S = \$20$ per order

a. $Q_0 = \sqrt{\dfrac{2DS}{H}} = \sqrt{\dfrac{2(100)(20)}{16}} = 15.8,$ round to 16 units

b. Number of orders per year: $D/Q_0 = \dfrac{100 \text{ tires/yr}}{16 \text{ tires each time}} = 6.25$ times per year

c. Length of order cycle: $Q_0/D = \dfrac{16 \text{ tires}}{100 \text{ tires/yr}} = .16$ year, which is $.16 \times 360$, or 57.6 workdays

or 2 months.

d. TC = Annual holding cost + Annual ordering cost

$= (Q_0/2)H + (D/Q_0)S$

$= (16/2)16 + (100/16)20$

$= \$128 + \$125$

$= \$253$

Note that the annual ordering and annual holding costs are almost equal at the EOQ, as illustrated in Figure 12-4c.

---

[4] We can find the minimum point of the total-cost curve by differentiating TC with respect to Q, setting the result equal to zero, and solving for Q. Thus,

$$\frac{d\text{TC}}{dQ} = \frac{dQ}{2}H + d(D/Q)S = H/2 - DS/Q^2$$

$$H/2 - DS/Q^2 = 0, \text{ so } Q^2 = \frac{2DS}{H} \text{ and } Q = \sqrt{\frac{2DS}{H}}$$

Note that the second derivative $\left(\dfrac{2DS}{Q^3}\right)$ is positive, which indicates a minimum has been obtained.

Holding cost is usually stated as a percentage i of the purchase price (or unit cost) of an item rather than as a dollar amount per unit H. However, as long as this percentage is converted into a dollar amount by multiplying it by unit cost R, the EOQ formula is still appropriate.

Example 3 ▶

A distributor of security monitors purchases 3,600 black-and-white monitors a year from the manufacturer at the cost of $65 each. Ordering cost is $30 per order and annual holding cost rate is 20 percent of the unit cost. Calculate the optimal order quantity and the total annual cost of ordering and holding the inventory.

SOLUTION

$D = 3,600$ monitors per year
$S = \$30$ per order
$i = $ holding cost rate per year $= 20\%$
$R = $ unit cost $= \$65$
$H = iR = .20(\$65) = \$13$

$$Q_0 = \sqrt{\frac{2DS}{H}} = \sqrt{\frac{2(3,600)(30)}{13}} = 128.9, \text{ round to } 129 \text{ monitors}$$

TC = Annual holding cost + Annual ordering cost
$$= (Q_0/2)H + (D/Q_0)S = (129/2)13 + (3,600/129)30 = \$838.50 + \$837.21 = \$1,675.71$$

Comment. Holding cost per unit per year and ordering cost per order are estimated rather than precisely determined from accounting records. Consequently, the EOQ value should be regarded as an approximate rather than an exact quantity. Thus, rounding the calculated value is perfectly acceptable; stating a value to several decimal places would tend to give an unrealistic impression of the precision involved. An obvious question is: How good is this "approximate" EOQ in terms of minimizing total annual inventory control cost? The answer is that the EOQ is fairly robust; the total cost curve is relatively flat near the EOQ, especially to the right of the EOQ. In other words, even if the approximate EOQ differs from the actual EOQ, total cost will not increase much (see Figure 12-5). Also note that annual demand D is usually estimated by multiplying next month's forecast of demand by 12 or next week's forecast

Figure 12-5 ▶

The total annual inventory cost curve is relatively flat near the EOQ.

of demand by 52. If there is seasonality in demand, a lot sizing technique, described in Chapter 14, will be more appropriate than EOQ. However, a simple solution commonly used is to determine the length of order cycle for EOQ and set the order quantity equal to the expected demand during that period. For example, for Example 2 above, order the forecast demand for the next 2 months.

Economic Production Quantity (EPQ)

The equivalent of EOQ in production is the Economic Production Quantity (EPQ). EPQ is used to determine the optimal production batch or lot size in a batch process.

The assumptions of the EPQ model are similar to those of the EOQ model, except that instead of shipments being received in a single delivery, units are received incrementally. Figure 12-6 illustrates how inventory on hand is affected by periodically producing a batch of a particular item that is received in storage and used incrementally.

During the production phase of the cycle, inventory builds up at a rate equal to the difference between production and usage rates. For example, if the daily production rate is 20 units and the daily usage rate is 5 units, inventory will build up at the rate of $20 - 5 = 15$ units per day. As long as production continues, the inventory will grow; when production ceases, the inventory will begin to decrease. Hence, the inventory on hand will be maximum, denoted by I_{max}, when production ceases. When the amount of inventory on hand is exhausted, production is resumed and the cycle repeats itself. It can be seen that the average inventory on hand is $.5I_{max}$.

Because the company makes the item itself, there is no ordering cost as such. Nonetheless, with every production run (batch), there is a setup cost–the cost to prepare the equipment for the job, such as cleaning, adjusting, and changing tools and fixtures. Setup costs are analogous to ordering costs because they are independent of the lot (run) quantity. They are treated in exactly the same way, and we use the same symbol, S, to denote setup cost per production run. The larger the run quantity, the fewer the number of runs needed per year and, hence, the lower the annual setup cost. The number of runs or batches per year is D/Q, and the annual setup cost is equal to the number of runs per year times the setup cost per run: $(D/Q)\,S$.

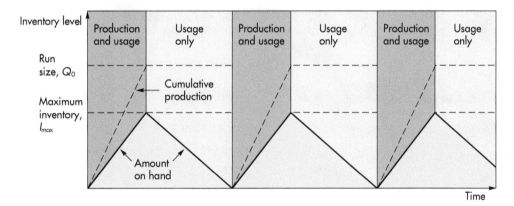

◀ **Figure 12-6**

Inventory on hand when a batch of an item is produced periodically.

Total annual inventory control cost is:

$$TC = \text{Annual holding cost} + \text{Annual setup cost} = \left(\frac{I_{max}}{2}\right)H + (D/Q)S \qquad (12\text{-}4)$$

where

$I_{max} =$ Maximum inventory
$Q =$ Production run quantity
$S =$ Setup cost per production run

To calculate I_{max}, let

$p =$ Production rate (e.g., units per day)
$d =$ Usage or demand rate (e.g., units per day)

The production run quantity Q is consumed at the rate of d during the entire cycle (= the time between the beginnings of two consecutive production runs). Therefore,

$$\text{Cycle length} = \frac{Q}{d} \qquad (12\text{-}5)$$

The production run quantity Q is produced at the rate of p during the production run (the production phase of the cycle). Therefore,

$$\text{Production run length} = \frac{Q}{p} \tag{12-6}$$

Therefore, the maximum inventory level I_{max} is

$$I_{max} = Q - d\left(\frac{Q}{p}\right) = \frac{Q}{p}(p - d) \tag{12-7}$$

Substituting (12-7) in (12-4), taking derivatives with respect to Q, setting it equal to zero, and solving for Q, will result in:

$$Q_0 = \sqrt{\frac{2DS}{H}}\sqrt{\frac{p}{p - d}} \tag{12-8}$$

Example 4 ▶

A toy manufacturer uses 48,000 rubber wheels per year for its popular dump truck series. The company can make its own wheels at a rate of 800 per day. The toy trucks are assembled uniformly over the entire year. Holding cost is $1 per wheel per year. Setup cost for a production run of wheels is $45. The company operates 240 days per year. Determine the:

a. Optimal production run quantity.

b. Minimum total annual cost for holding and setup.

c. Cycle length for the optimal production run quantity.

d. Production run length for the optimal production run quantity.

SOLUTION

$D = 48,000$ wheels per year
$S = \$45$ per production run
$H = \$1$ per wheel per year
$p = 800$ wheels per day
$d = 48,000$ wheels per 240 days, or 200 wheels per day

a. $Q_0 = \sqrt{\dfrac{2DS}{H}}\sqrt{\dfrac{p}{p-d}} = \sqrt{\dfrac{2(48,000)45}{1}}\sqrt{\dfrac{800}{800 - 200}} = 2,400$ wheels

b. $TC_{min} = \text{Annual holding cost} + \text{Annual setup cost} = \left(\dfrac{I_{max}}{2}\right)H + (D/Q_0)S$

Thus, you must first calculate I_{max}:

$$I_{max} = \frac{Q}{p}(p - d) = \frac{2,400}{800}(800 - 200) = 1,800 \text{ wheels}$$

$$TC_{min} = \frac{1,800}{2} \times \$1 + \frac{48,000}{2,400} \times \$45 = \$900 + \$900 = \$1,800$$

Note again the equality of the annual costs (in this example, setup and holding costs) at the EPQ.

c. Cycle length $= \dfrac{Q}{d} = \dfrac{2,400 \text{ wheels}}{200 \text{ wheels per day}} = 12$ days

Thus, a production run of wheels will be made every 12 days.

d. Production run length $= \dfrac{Q}{p} = \dfrac{2,400 \text{ wheels}}{800 \text{ wheels per day}} = 3$ days

Thus, each production run will take three days.

Note that in the above derivation, setup *time* is ignored. This is not a problem unless setup time is significant and the utilization of the operation is close to 100 percent due to making other products. In this case, there is no choice but to increase the production run quantity, which will result in fewer setups and setup times in a year, thus fitting in the limited time of the operation. However, inventory holding cost will increase.

EOQ with Quantity Discounts

Quantity discounts are price reductions for large orders, offered to customers to induce them to buy in large quantities. For example, a surgical supply company published the price list shown in Table 12-2 for boxes of extra-wide gauze strips. Note that the price per box decreases as order quantity increases. In this section, we consider the all-unit discount case where the price of every unit is the price per unit given for the order quantity. For example, if 60 gauze strips are purchased, the total cost will be 60($1.70) = $102. The alternate method, the "incremental discount" will charge $2.00 for the first 44, $1.70 for each unit above that up to the 69th unit, and $1.40 for each unit above that. For example, for an order of 60 units, 44($2.00) + 16($1.70) = $115.20 will be charged.

quantity discounts Price reductions for large orders.

Order Quantity	Price per Box
1 to 44	$2.00
45 to 69	1.70
70 or more	1.40

◄ Table 12-2

Price list for boxes of extra-wide gauze strips.

If quantity discounts are offered, the buyer must weigh the potential benefits of reduced purchase price and fewer orders that will result from buying in large quantities against the increase in holding cost caused by higher average inventory. The buyer's goal is to select that order quantity that will minimize total annual holding, ordering, *and* purchase cost:

$$\text{TC} = \frac{\text{Annual holding} + \text{Annual ordering} + \text{Annual purchase}}{\text{cost} \qquad\qquad \text{cost} \qquad\qquad \text{cost}} \tag{12-9}$$

$$\left(\frac{Q}{2}\right)H \quad + \quad \left(\frac{D}{Q}\right)S \quad + \quad RD$$

where

R = Unit price

Recall that in the basic EOQ model, determination of order quantity does not involve the purchase cost. The rationale for not including the purchase cost there is that under the assumption of no quantity discounts, annual purchase cost is not affected by the order quantity. A graph of total annual purchase cost versus order quantity would be a horizontal line. Hence, including purchase cost would merely raise the total cost curve (in Figure 12-4c) by the same amount (RD) at every point. That would not change the EOQ (see Figure 12-7).

When all-unit quantity discount is offered, there is a separate U-shaped total cost curve for each unit price. Again, including annual purchase price merely raises each curve by a constant amount. However, because the unit prices are all different, each curve is raised by a different amount: Smaller unit prices will raise the total cost curve less than larger unit prices. Note that no one curve applies to the entire range of quantities; each curve applies to only a *portion* of the range (see Figure 12-8). Hence, the applicable or *feasible* total cost is initially on the curve with the highest unit price and then drops down, curve by curve, at the *break quantities*. Note that from Table 12-2, the break quantities for gauze strips are at 45 and 70 boxes. The result is a total cost curve with *steps* at the break quantities. Even though each curve has a minimum, those points are not necessarily feasible. For example, the minimum point for the $1.40 curve in Figure 12-8 appears to be around 65 units. However, the price list shown in Table 12-2 indicates that an order size of 65 boxes will receive a unit price of $1.70. The actual total cost curve is denoted by the solid red

Figure 12-7 ▶

Adding annual purchase cost RD doesn't change the EOQ if there are no quantity discounts.

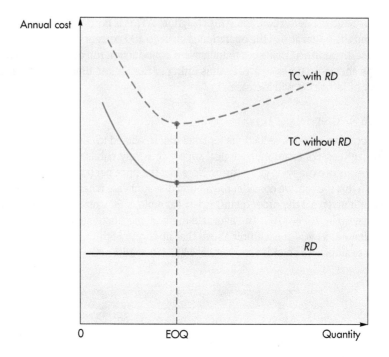

Figure 12-8 ▶

The total cost curve with all-unit quantity discount is composed of the solid red portion of the total cost curve for each unit price.

lines; only those price–quantity combinations are feasible. The objective of the quantity discount model is to identify an order quantity that will represent the lowest total cost for the solid lines.

Note that because holding cost is a percentage of price, lower prices will lead to lower holding cost, which results in larger EOQs. Thus, as price decreases, each curve's minimum point will be to the right of the previous curve's minimum point (see the dots in Figure 12-8).

We can determine the best purchase quantity with the following procedure:

1. Beginning with the lowest unit price, calculate the EOQ for each unit price until you find a feasible EOQ (i.e., until an EOQ falls in the quantity range for its unit price).

2. If the EOQ for the lowest unit price is feasible, it is the optimal order quantity. If not, compare the total cost at all the break quantities larger than the feasible EOQ with the total cost of the feasible EOQ. The quantity that yields the lowest total cost among these is optimum.

A casino uses 4,000 light bulbs a year. Light bulbs are priced as follows: 1 to 499, 90 cents each; 500 to 999, 85 cents each; and 1,000 or more, 80 cents each. It costs approximately $30 to prepare a purchase order, receive, and pay for it, and holding cost rate is 40 percent of purchase price per year. Determine the optimal order quantity and the total annual cost.

◀ **Example 5**

See Figure 12-9 for the graph of total annual cost:

SOLUTION

◀ **Figure 12-9**

Total annual cost for Example 5.

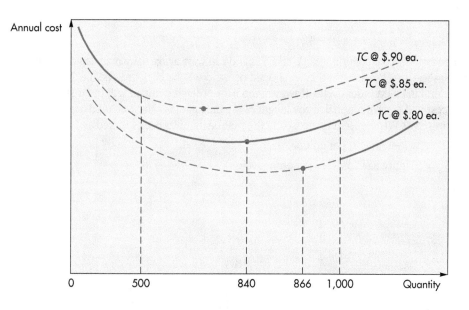

$D = 4,000$ light bulbs per year $S = \$30$ $H = .40R$ $R =$ unit price

Range	Unit Price R	H
1 to 499	$.90	.40(.90)=.36
500 to 999	$.85	.40(.85)=.34
1,000 or more	$.80	.40(.80)=.32

Find the EOQ for each price, starting with the lowest price, until you locate a feasible EOQ.

$$EOQ_{.80} = \sqrt{\frac{2DS}{H}} = \sqrt{\frac{2(4,000)30}{.32}} = 866 \text{ light bulbs}$$

Because an order size of 866 light bulbs is fewer than 1,000 units, 866 is not feasible for the unit price of $.80 per light bulb. Next, try $.85 per unit.

$$EOQ_{.85} = \sqrt{\frac{2(4,000)30}{.34}} = 840 \text{ light bulbs}$$

This EOQ is feasible; it falls in the $.85-per-light-bulb quantity range (500 to 999).

Now calculate the total cost for 840 order size, and compare it to the total cost of the break quantity larger than 840, i.e., 1,000 units.

$$TC = \text{Annual Holding cost} + \text{Annual Ordering cost} + \text{Annual Purchase cost}$$

$$= \left(\frac{Q}{2}\right)H + \left(\frac{D}{Q}\right)S + RD$$

$$TC_{840} = \frac{840}{2}(.34) + \frac{4,000}{840}(30) + .85(4,000) = \$3,686$$

$$TC_{1,000} = \frac{1,000}{2}(.32) + \frac{4,000}{1,000}(30) + .80(4,000) = \$3,480$$

Because $\$3,480 < \$3,686$, the minimum cost order quantity is 1,000 light bulbs.

Comment. Quantity discount may result from economies of scale in production as well as in transportation (a truckload is cheaper per unit weight of load than a less than truckload). In practice, it is also possible to get a discount for total dollars of all goods purchased during a year from a supplier.

EOQ with Planned Shortages

When holding cost per unit is large and demand can wait, a company may decide to intentionally allow shortages. We assume that all shorted demand will be back-ordered (i.e., all customers will wait until the next order cycle). However, the back-ordered demand will incur shortage cost, and this cost will be proportional to the length of the time a unit is back-ordered (similar to inventory holding cost). We represent this cost and the number of units back-ordered as:

B = back-order cost per unit per year

Q_b = quantity back-ordered per order cycle

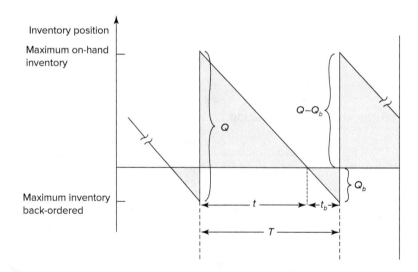

Figure 12-10

Inventory position for the EOQ with planned shortages model.

We also make the same assumptions as in the basic EOQ model, except that we allow shortages, which are all back-ordered. The inventory position in this case can be graphed as in Figure 12-10, where

T = length of an order cycle (in days)

t = time period (during an order cycle) when inventory position is non-negative

t_b = time period (during an order cycle) when inventory position is negative (i.e., back-order occurs).

When the next order arrives, the back-ordered demand is satisfied first, i.e., the inventory position just after an order arrival will be $Q - Q_b$. Let d = demand rate per day. Because $Q - Q_b$ units are used up at the rate of d units per day, then $Q - Q_b = d \times t$ or:

$t = \dfrac{Q - Q_b}{d}$. Similarly, $t_b = \dfrac{Q_b}{d}$ and $T = t + t_b = \dfrac{Q}{d}$. Hence,

$$\dfrac{t}{T} = \dfrac{\dfrac{Q - Q_b}{d}}{\dfrac{Q}{d}} = \dfrac{Q - Q_b}{Q} \text{ and } \dfrac{t_b}{T} = \dfrac{\dfrac{Q_b}{d}}{\dfrac{Q}{d}} = \dfrac{Q_b}{Q}$$

Therefore, average inventory on hand during the year is:

$$\dfrac{Q - Q_b}{2} \times \dfrac{t}{T} + 0\left(\dfrac{t_b}{T}\right) = \dfrac{(Q - Q_b)^2}{2Q},$$

and average level of back-orders during the year is:

$$\dfrac{Q_b}{2} \times \dfrac{t_b}{T} + 0\left(\dfrac{t}{T}\right) = \dfrac{Q_b^2}{2Q}$$

Finally, the total annual inventory control cost

TC = annual ordering cost + annual holding cost + annual back-order cost

$$= \left(\dfrac{D}{Q}\right)S + \left(\dfrac{(Q - Q_b)^2}{2Q}\right)H + \left(\dfrac{Q_b^2}{2Q}\right)B$$

Taking derivative of TC with respect to Q_b, setting it equal to zero, and solving for Q_b, we get:

$$Q_b = Q\left(\dfrac{H}{H + B}\right). \tag{12-10}$$

Taking derivative of TC with respect to Q, setting it equal to zero, multiplying it by $2Q^2$ and rearranging, we get:

$$-2DS + Q^2H - Q_b^2(H + B) = 0 \tag{12-11}$$

Substituting (12-10) in (12-11) and solving for Q, we get:

$$Q = \sqrt{\dfrac{2DS}{H}\left(\dfrac{H + B}{B}\right)} \tag{12-12}$$

Annual demand for a particular model of a refrigerator at an appliance store is 50 units. The holding cost per unit per year is \$200. The back-order cost per unit per year is estimated to be \$500. Ordering cost from the manufacturer is \$10 per order. Determine the optimal order quantity and the back-order quantity per order cycle.

◀ **Example 6**

SOLUTION

$D = 50$ units per year

$H = \$200$ per unit per year

$B = \$500$ per unit per year

$S = \$10$ per order

$$Q = \sqrt{\dfrac{2DS}{H}\left(\dfrac{H + B}{B}\right)} = \sqrt{\dfrac{2(50)(10)}{200}\left(\dfrac{200 + 500}{500}\right)} = 2.65, \text{ round to 3 units.}$$

$$Q_b = Q\left(\dfrac{H}{H + B}\right) = 3\left(\dfrac{200}{200 + 500}\right) = 0.86, \text{ round to 1.}$$

This has the following implication: Allow the inventory level to drop to zero. Then, when there is a customer demand (for a unit), place an order of three fridges from the manufacturer.

Fixed Order Quantity/Reorder Point Model: Determining the Reorder Point

reorder point (ROP) When the inventory position drops to or below this amount, the item should be reordered.

The **reorder point (ROP)** is that inventory position (= on hand + on order − back-ordered) at or below which an order should be issued.

If demand and purchase lead time are both constant, the reorder point is simply:

$$ROP = d \times LT \tag{12-13}$$

where

d = Demand rate (units per day or week or month)

LT = Lead time (in days or weeks or months)

Example 7 ▶

A patient takes two special tablets per day. The order is delivered to his home seven days after it is called in. At what point should the patient reorder?

SOLUTION

Usage = 2 tablets a day
Lead time = 7 days
ROP = Usage × Lead time
    = 2 tablets per day × 7 days = 14 tablets

Thus, the patient should reorder when 14 tablets are left.

Note: Demand and lead time must have the same time units.

When variability is present in demand and/or lead time, it creates the possibility that the actual demand during a lead time will exceed the expected demand during a lead time. Consequently, it becomes necessary to carry additional inventory, called **safety stock**, to reduce the risk of running out of inventory (a stock-out) or to reduce the number of units short. The reorder point then is increased by the amount of the safety stock:

safety stock Stock that is held in excess of expected demand due to variability of demand and/or lead time.

ROP = Expected demand during a lead time + Safety stock

For example, if the expected demand during a lead time is 100 units, and the desired amount of safety stock is 10 units, then the ROP would be 110 units.

Figure 12-11 illustrates how safety stock can reduce shortage or risk of stock-out during a lead time (LT). Note that for the fixed order quantity/ROP model, shortage or stock-out protection is needed only during lead times.

Figure 12-11 ▶

Safety stock reduces the risk of a stock-out or the number of units short during a lead time.

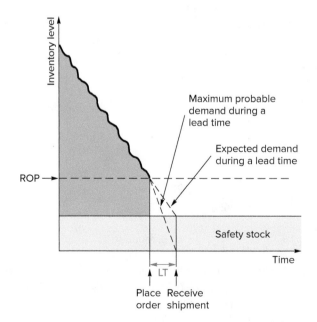

The amount of safety stock that is appropriate for an item depends on:

1. Demand and lead time variability.

2. The desired service level.

There are many ways to define the service level. We will focus on the following two:

1. Lead time service level.

2. Annual service level or fill rate.

Lead time service level, also known as cycle service level, is the probability that demand will not exceed inventory on hand during a lead time i.e., the probability of no stock-out during a cycle. It can be seen that lead time service level is also equal to fraction of cycles with no stock-out. **Annual service level** is the percentage of demand (during the year) filled from stocks on hand, i.e., fill rate.

In this chapter, we assume that management has a desired service level for a group of items. Alternatively, shortage cost can be used to determine the appropriated service level. We will use the shortage cost only in the last section of this chapter on Single Period Model.

The formula commonly used to determine the safety stock, in the presence of demand and/or lead time variability, assumes that demand during a lead time is Normally distributed:

$$\text{Safety stock} = z.\sigma_{dLT} \tag{12-14}$$

where

$z =$ Safety factor; number of standard deviations above the expected demand

$\sigma_{dLT} =$ Standard deviation of demand during a lead time

In the above formula, z is related to the service level. However, the exact nature of this relationship depends on the type of service level used: lead time or annual. First, we will describe it for the lead time service level.

ROP Using Lead Time Service Level

Given a desired lead time service level, the value of z can be determined directly from the (standard) Normal probability table, Appendix B, Table B (see Figure 12-12). Note that stock-out risk = 1 − lead time service level. For example, if the desired lead time service level is .95 or 95 percent, stock-out risk will be .05 or 5 percent. Also note that the smaller the desired stock-out risk, the greater the value of z.

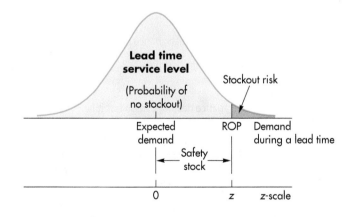

The manager of a hardware store has determined, from historical records, that demand for a given type and size of bagged cement during its lead time could be described by a Normal distribution that has a mean of 50 bags and a standard deviation of 5 bags. Answer these questions, assuming that the manager is willing to accept a stock-out risk of no more than 3 percent during a lead time:

lead time service level Probability that demand will not exceed inventory on hand during a lead time.

annual service level The percentage of annual demand filled (from stocks on hand), i.e., fill rate.

◀ **Figure 12-12**

Distribution of demand during a lead time, lead time service level, and ROP.

◀ **Example 8**

a. What value of z is appropriate?

b. How many bags of safety stock should be held?

c. What reorder point should be used?

SOLUTION

Expected demand during a lead time = 50 bags

$\sigma_{d\,LT} = 5$ bags

Stock-out risk = 3 percent

a. From Appendix B, Table B, using a service level of $1 - .03 = .97$, we obtain a value of $z = 1.88$.

b. Safety stock = $z\sigma_{d\,LT} = 1.88(5) = 9.40$ bags

c. ROP = Expected demand during a lead time + Safety stock = $50 + 9.40 = 59.40$ round to 59 bags

---

When data on demand during a lead time are not readily available, its mean and standard deviation are not directly available. Nevertheless, data are generally available on daily or weekly or monthly demand, and on the lengths of lead time. Using these data, a manager can determine whether demand and lead time are variable, and the related standard deviations. For these situations, one of the following formulas can be used:

If only demand is variable, then $\sigma_{dLT} = \sqrt{LT}\sigma_d$, and the reorder point is[5]

$$ROP = \bar{d}.LT + z\sqrt{LT}\sigma_d \qquad (12\text{-}15)$$

where

$\bar{d}$ = Average daily or weekly or monthly demand

σ_d = Standard deviation of daily or weekly or monthly demand

LT = Lead time in days or weeks or months

If both demand and lead time are variable, then[6]

$$\sigma_{dLT} = \sqrt{LT\sigma_d^2 + \bar{d}^2\sigma_{LT}^2}$$

and the reorder point is

$$ROP = \bar{d}\cdot\overline{LT} + z\sqrt{LT\sigma_d^2 + \bar{d}^2\sigma_{LT}^2} \qquad (12\text{-}16)$$

---

[5] If daily demand d_i are independent and have the same variance $\sigma_{d_i}^2$, then it can be shown, using elementary statistics, that $\text{Var}\left(\sum_{i=1}^{LT} d_i\right) = \left(\sum_{i=1}^{LT} \text{Var}(d_i)\right) = LT\,\text{Var}(d_i)$. Taking square root of both sides and substituting chapter notation, we get $\sigma_{dLT} = \sqrt{LT}\sigma_d$.

[6] The result follows from the well known variance decomposition formula:
Given two random variables X and Y,

$\text{Var } X = E_X X^2 - (E_X X)^2$, by the definition of the variance; E = Expectations
$\quad = E_Y(E_X(X^2|Y)) - E_Y(E_X(X|Y))^2$, conditioning on Y and then taking expectations with respect to Y
$\quad = E_Y(\text{Var}_X(X|Y) + E_X(X|Y)^2) - E_Y(E_X(X|Y))^2$, by the definition of the first term
$\quad = E_Y(\text{Var}_X(X|Y)) + E_Y(E_X(X|Y)^2) - E_Y(E_X(X|Y))^2$, expanding the first term
$\quad = E_Y(\text{Var}_X(X|Y)) + \text{Var}_Y(E_X(X|Y))$, by the definition of the second term

Now let $X = \sum_{i=1}^{LT} d_i$ and $Y = LT$. Then the variance decomposition formula becomes:

$$\text{Var}\left(\sum_{i=1}^{LT} d_i\right) = E_{LT}\left(\text{Var}\left(\sum_{i=1}^{LT} d_i|LT\right)\right) + \text{Var}_{LT}\left(E\left(\sum_{i=1}^{LT} d_i|LT\right)\right)$$

$\quad = E(LT)\text{Var}(d_i) + E(d_i)^2\text{Var}(LT)$, using elementary statistics
Taking square root of both sides and substituting chapter notation, we get $\sigma_{dLT} = \sqrt{LT\sigma_d^2 + \bar{d}^2\sigma_{LT}^2}$

Where $\overline{LT}$ = *Average* lead time, in days or weeks or months

σ_{LT} = Standard deviation of the lead time, in days or weeks or months

Note: Each of these models assumes that demand and lead time are *independent*.

◀ **Example 9**

A restaurant uses an average of 50 jars of a special sauce each week. Weekly usage of sauce has a standard deviation of 3 jars. The manager is willing to accept no more than a 10 percent risk of stock-out during a lead time, which is 2 weeks. Assume the distribution of usage is Normal.

  a. Which of the above formulas is appropriate for this situation? Why?

  b. Determine the value of z.

  c. Determine the ROP.

SOLUTION

$\overline{d}$ = 50 jars per week   LT = 2 weeks

σ_d = 3 jars per week   Acceptable stock-out risk = 10 percent, so lead time service level is .90

  a. Because only demand is variable (i.e., has a standard deviation), Formula 12-15 is appropriate.

  b. From Appendix B, Table B, using a service level of .90, we obtain $z = 1.28$.

  c. ROP = $\overline{d}.$LT + $z\sqrt{LT}\sigma_d$ = 50(2) + 1.28$\sqrt{2}$(3) = 100 + 5.43 = 105.43 round to 105 jars

◀ **Figure 12-13**

Composition of the demand during a lead time.

Comment. The logic of formula (12-15) may not be immediately obvious. The first part of the formula is the expected demand, which is the product of daily (or weekly or monthly) demand and the number of days (or weeks or months) of lead time. The second part of the formula is z times the standard deviation of demand during a lead time. Daily (or weekly or monthly) demand is assumed to be Normally distributed and has the same mean and standard deviation (see Figure 12-13). The standard deviation of demand for the entire lead time is found by summing the variances of daily (or weekly or monthly) demands and then taking the square root of that number. Note that, unlike variance, standard deviation is not additive. Hence, if lead time is e.g., four days, the variance of demand during a lead time will equal the sum of the four daily variances, which is $4\sigma_d^2$. The standard deviation of demand during a lead time will be the square root of this, which is $2\sigma_d$. In general, this becomes $\sqrt{LT}\sigma_d$ and, hence, the last part of Formula 12-15.

If daily demand is Normally distributed with a mean of 3 units and a standard deviation of 1 unit, and lead time is 2 days, then demand during a lead time will be Normally distributed with a mean of 6 units and a standard deviation of $\sqrt{1^2 + 1^2} = 1.41$ units (see the following charts where the charts on the left and in the middle are the distributions of day 1 and day 2 demands and the right chart is the distribution of the sum of day 1 and day 2 demands):

◀ **Example 10**

+ =

Also note that average demand is usually estimated using the forecast of demand, and standard deviation of demand is usually estimated using standard deviation of forecast error (i.e., square root of MSE or $1.25 \times$ MAD; refer to Chapter 3).

Finally, we assumed that there is a desired service level from which z, and then safety stock and ROP, are determined. An alternative method to determine the ROP is based on cost of overstocking and cost of shortage. This analysis is similar to the Single Period Model later in this chapter.

ROP Using Annual Service Level

Given a desired annual service level SL_{annual} (i.e., the percentage of demand filled directly from inventory on hand during the whole year; also known as the *item fill rate*), to find the required ROP a three-step procedure should be used:

1. Calculate $E(z) = \dfrac{Q(1 - SL_{annual})}{\sigma_{dLT}}$ (12-17)

Where $E(z)$ = Standardized expected number of units short during an order cycle.[7]

2. Take the $E(z)$ to Table 12-3 and determine the associated z value.

3. Use the z value in the following general ROP formula or a specific ROP formula (12-15) or (12-16):

ROP = expected demand during lead time + $z\sigma_{dLT}$

Example 11 ▶

An inventory item has order quantity $Q = 250$ units, expected demand during a lead time = 50 units, and standard deviation of demand during a lead time $\sigma_{dLT} = 16$ units. Determine the ROP if the desired annual service level is (a) 0.997, and (b) 0.98.

SOLUTION

a. $E(z) = \dfrac{Q(1 - SL_{annual})}{\sigma_{dLT}} = \dfrac{250(1 - .997)}{16} = 0.047$

From Table 12-3, $E(z) = 0.047$ falls between $E(z) = 0.048$ with $z = 1.28$ and $E(z) = 0.044$ with $z = 1.32$. Therefore, using interpolation, $z = 1.29$. Finally, ROP = $50 + 1.29(16) = 70.64$ round to 71 units.

b. $E(z) = \dfrac{Q(1 - SL_{annual})}{\sigma_{dLT}} = \dfrac{250(1 - .98)}{16} = 0.3125$

From Table 12-3, $E(z) = 0.3125$ falls between $E(z) = 0.324$ with $z = 0.16$ and $E(z) = 0.307$ with $z = 0.20$. Therefore, using interpolation, $z = 0.19$. Finally, ROP = $50 + 0.19(16) = 53.04$ round to 53 units.

---

[7] SL_{annual} = (expected number of units filled during a cycle)(number of cycles per year)/annual demand
    = (expected number of units filled during a cycle)(D/Q)/D
    = expected number of units filled during a cycle/Q
    = (Q – expected number of units short during a cycle)/Q, because average demand during an order cycle is Q. Multiplying both side by Q:
$Q(SL_{annual})$ = Q – expected number of units short during a cycle
Rewriting:
Expected number of units short during a cycle = $Q(1 - SL_{annual})$
(Standardized expected number of units short during a cycle)(σ_{dLT}) = $Q(1 - SL_{annual})$,
This follows from statistics. Using $E(z)$ notation,
$E(z)(\sigma_{dLT}) = Q(1 - SL_{annual})$

$E(z) = \dfrac{Q(1 - SL_{annual})}{\sigma_{dLT}}$

Lead time service levels and standardized expected numbers short during an order cycle for Normal distribution.

z	Lead Time Service Level	E(z)	z	Lead Time Service Level	E(z)	z	Lead Time Service Level	E(z)	z	Lead Time Service Level	E(z)
−2.40	.0082	2.403	−.80	.2119	.920	.80	.7881	.120	2.40	.9918	.003
−2.36	.0091	2.363	−.76	.2236	.889	.84	.7995	.112	2.44	.9927	.002
−2.32	.0102	2.323	−.72	.2358	.858	.88	.8106	.104	2.48	.9934	.002
−2.28	.0113	2.284	−.68	.2483	.828	.92	.8212	.097	2.52	.9941	.002
−2.24	.0125	2.244	−.64	.2611	.798	.96	.8315	.089	2.56	.9948	.002
−2.20	.0139	2.205	−.60	.2743	.769	1.00	.8413	.083	2.60	.9953	.001
−2.16	.0154	2.165	−.56	.2877	.740	1.04	.8508	.077	2.64	.9959	.001
−2.12	.0170	2.126	−.52	.3015	.712	1.08	.8599	.071	2.68	.9963	.001
−2.08	.0188	2.087	−.48	.3156	.684	1.12	.8686	.066	2.72	.9967	.001
−2.04	.0207	2.048	−.44	.3300	.657	1.16	.8770	.061	2.76	.9971	.001
−2.00	.0228	2.008	−.40	.3446	.630	1.20	.8849	.056	2.80	.9974	.0008
−1.96	.0250	1.969	−.36	.3594	.597	1.24	.8925	.052	2.84	.9977	.0007
−1.92	.0274	1.930	−.32	.3745	.576	1.28	.8997	.048	2.88	.9980	.0006
−1.88	.0301	1.892	−.28	.3897	.555	1.32	.9066	.044	2.92	.9982	.0005
−1.84	.0329	1.853	−.24	.4052	.530	1.36	.9131	.040	2.96	.9985	.0004
−1.80	.0359	1.814	−.20	.4207	.507	1.40	.9192	.037	3.00	.9987	.0004
−1.76	.0392	1.776	−.16	.4364	.484	1.44	.9251	.034	3.04	.9988	.0003
−1.72	.0427	1.737	−.12	.4522	.462	1.48	.9306	.031	3.08	.9990	.0003
−1.68	.0465	1.699	−.08	.4681	.440	1.52	.9357	.028	3.12	.9991	.0002
−1.64	.0505	1.661	−.04	.4840	.419	1.56	.9406	.026	3.16	.9992	.0002
−1.60	.0548	1.623	.00	.5000	.399	1.60	.9452	.023	3.20	.9993	.0002
−1.56	.0594	1.586	.04	.5160	.379	1.64	.9495	.021	3.24	.9994	.0001
−1.52	.0643	1.548	.08	.5319	.360	1.68	.9535	.019	3.28	.9995	.0001
−1.48	.0694	1.511	.12	.5478	.342	1.72	.9573	.017	3.32	.9995	.0001
−1.44	.0749	1.474	.16	.5636	.324	1.76	.9608	.016	3.36	.9996	.0001
−1.40	.0808	1.437	.20	.5793	.307	1.80	.9641	.014	3.40	.9997	.0001
−1.36	.0869	1.400	.24	.5948	.290	1.84	.9671	.013			
−1.32	.0934	1.364	.28	.6103	.275	1.88	.9699	.012			
−1.28	.1003	1.328	.32	.6255	.256	1.92	.9726	.010			
−1.24	.1075	1.292	.36	.6406	.237	1.96	.9750	.009			
−1.20	.1151	1.256	.40	.6554	.230	2.00	.9772	.008			
−1.16	.1230	1.221	.44	.6700	.217	2.04	.9793	.008			
−1.12	.1314	1.186	.48	.6844	.204	2.08	.9812	.007			
−1.08	.1401	1.151	.52	.6985	.192	2.12	.9830	.006			
−1.04	.1492	1.117	.56	.7123	.180	2.16	.9846	.005			
−1.00	.1587	1.083	.60	.7257	.169	2.20	.9861	.005			
−.96	.1685	1.049	.64	.7389	.158	2.24	.9875	.004			
−.92	.1788	1.017	.68	.7517	.148	2.28	.9887	.004			
−.88	.1894	.984	.72	.7642	.138	2.32	.9898	.003			
−.84	.2005	.952	.76	.7764	.129	2.36	.9909	.003			

Other Related Models

A commonly used variation of the fixed order quantity/reorder point or Min/Max model occurs when instead of instantaneous review, inventory position is reviewed periodically, e.g., every 3 days. Let RP = review period. To be safe in determining the ROP or Min, LT has to be increased by RP. Then, when demand is variable and LT is constant:

$$Min = \bar{d}(LT + RP) + z\sigma_d\sqrt{LT + RP} \text{ and}$$

$$Max = Min + EOQ.$$

Another variation is the Can-Order model. In this model, when an item's inventory position drops to or below its ROP, all related items (e.g., those bought from the same supplier) are investigated to see if their inventory position is at or below their can-order level. If so, they are ordered too (to bring their inventory level up to their Max).

LO5 Fixed-Interval/Order up to Level Model

The *fixed-interval/order up to level model* is used when orders are placed at fixed time intervals (e.g., weekly, twice a month, etc.), and inventory position is brought up to the order up to level. This model is widely used by wholesalers/distributors and retailers, where usually all items from the same supplier are ordered at the same time. The order size tends to vary from interval to interval depending on demand during the previous interval. This is quite different from the EOQ/ROP model in which the order size remains fixed from cycle to cycle while the length of the cycle may vary (shorter if demand is above average and longer if demand is below average).

Grouping orders for items from the same supplier can produce savings in ordering, shipping, receiving, and paying costs. Furthermore, some situations do not readily lend themselves to continuous monitoring of inventory positions. Many retail operations (e.g., small drugstores, small grocery stores) fall into this category. The alternative for them is to use fixed interval ordering, which requires only periodic checks of inventory positions.

Two decisions are needed to apply this model for a group of items from the same supplier: (1) the order interval, and (2) the order up to level for each item.

Determining the Order Interval

The order interval can be determined by minimizing total annual holding and ordering costs of all the SKUs received from a particular supplier. The complication is that there are two components to the ordering cost: the cost of issuing a purchase order and the cost of ordering each line item (SKU) in it. In the basic model, we assume that every SKU is ordered at every order time no matter how small its order quantity is. Later, we present the case where not every SKU is ordered at every order time (called Coordinated Periodic Review model).

Let

OI = order interval (in fraction of a year)

S = fixed ordering cost per purchase order

s = variable ordering cost per SKU included in the purchase order (line item)

For simplicity, we assume s is the same for every SKU

n = number of SKUs purchased from the supplier

R_j = unit cost of SKU$_j$, $j = 1, \ldots, n$

i = annual holding cost rate

D_j = annual demand of SKU$_j$, $j = 1, \ldots, n$

For each SKU$_j$ from this supplier, we will purchase enough to last until next order time, i.e., $Q_j = D_j \cdot OI$

$$\text{Total Annual Inventory Control Cost (TC)} = \sum\left(\frac{D_j \cdot OI}{2}\right)R_j \cdot i + (S + ns)\left(\frac{1}{OI}\right)$$

Taking derivative of TC with respect to OI, setting it equal to 0, and solving for OI, we get the optimal order interval:

$$OI^* = \sqrt{\frac{2(S + ns)}{i \sum D_j R_j}}$$

(12-18)

Three parts are purchased from the same supplier. The basic cost of placing an order for one of the SKUs is $1.50. The inclusion of each additional SKU costs $.50 more. The annual holding cost rate is 24 percent of unit cost. The annual demand (in units) and unit prices are given below. Assume that the buying company works 250 days a year. Calculate the optimal order interval.

◄ **Example 12**

SKU	Demand/Year	Price/Unit
1	12,000	.50
2	8,000	.30
3	700	.10

SOLUTION

$S = 1.50 - .50 = \$1.00$

$s = .50$

$i = .24$

$$OI^* = \sqrt{\frac{2(1.00 + 3(.50))}{.24(12{,}000 \times .50 + 8{,}000 \times .30 + 700 \times .10)}}$$

$= .0496 \text{ year} = 12.4 \text{ days}$

Round to 12 days

Determining the Order up to Levels

The order up to level for an item should be enough so that the item lasts until the next shipment arrives, i.e., after an order interval plus a lead time. This fact is illustrated in the bottom chart in Figure 12-14, which also contrasts the fixed-interval model with the fixed order quantity (EOQ/ROP) model. Note that the order quantity (the difference between order up to level and inventory position) for the fixed-interval model will vary from one order to another (depending on size of demand during the past interval). In the presence of demand and lead time variability, there is a need for safety stocks. The two models also differ in terms of safety stocks. The fixed-interval model must have stock-out protection until the *next* order arrives, but the fixed order quantity (EOQ/ROP) model needs protection only during this lead time. Therefore, the fixed-interval model necessitates a larger amount of safety stock for a given service level.

Therefore, order up to level or I_{max} can be determined by:

I_{max} = Expected demand during an order interval plus a lead time + safety stock   (12-19)

Like the fixed order quantity model, the fixed-interval model can have variations in demand and/or lead time. For the sake of simplicity and because it is the most frequently encountered situation, the discussion here will focus only on *variable demand* and *constant lead time case*. As in the fixed order quantity model, we assume that demand during an order interval and a lead time is Normally distributed.

Therefore, (12-19) becomes

$$I_{max} = \bar{d}(OI + LT) + z\sigma_d \sqrt{OI + LT}$$

(12-20)

where

$\bar{d}$ = *Average* daily or weekly or monthly demand
OI = Order interval (length of time between orders); in days or weeks or months
LT = Lead time in days or weeks or months

Figure 12-14 ▶

Comparison of the fixed quantity (EOQ/ROP) (on top) and the fixed-interval (on bottom) models.

z = Safety factor; number of standard deviations above the expected demand

σ_d = Standard deviation of daily or weekly or monthly demand

Note that I_{max} does not have to be recalculated at each order time if demand has no trend or seasonality. Also note that because the period of vulnerability covers the whole order interval, there is only one definition of service level for this model. Order quantity Q can be determined by:

$$Q = I_{max} - \text{inventory position}$$ (12-21)

Example 13 ▶

Given the following information for a SKU, determine its order up to level and amount to order (i.e., order quantity).

$\bar{d}$ = 30 units per day, Desired service level = 99 percent

σ_d = 3 units per day, Inventory position at reorder time = 71 units

LT = 2 days, OI = 7 days

SOLUTION

z = 2.33 for 99 percent service level (from Appendix B, Table B)

$$I_{max} = \bar{d}(\text{OI} + \text{LT}) + z\sigma_d\sqrt{\text{OI} + \text{LT}}$$

$$= 30(7 + 2) + 2.33(3)\sqrt{7 + 2} = 291 \text{ units}$$

Amount to order = I_{max} − inventory position = 291 − 71 = 220 units

Note that average demand is usually estimated using forecast of demand, and the standard deviation of demand is usually estimated using standard deviation of the forecast error (square root of MSE or 1.25 × MAD).

Coordinated Periodic Review Model

In the fixed-interval model, it might cost less to order some items every two, three, or more order intervals than ordering them at every interval, because their holding cost may be less than the line-item ordering cost. The coordinated periodic (or fixed-interval) review model accommodates this by determining a common order interval OI for reviewing every SKU and a multiple m_i of OI for ordering stock keeping unit i, SKU_i (this determines the order up to level for SKU_i).

After planning the model (i.e., determining OI and m_is), during operation and control of the model, at a review time the inventory position of each SKU is compared with its forecast demand for the next OI plus lead time plus safety stocks (just like ROP), and if inventory position is less, a quantity enough to bring the inventory position up to the SKU's order up to level is ordered. The order up to level for SKU_i should cover its forecast demand during the next m_i order intervals (OI) plus a lead time plus safety stocks only for the next OI + LT.

The determination of optimal values for OI and m_is is complicated. We will use a simple heuristic[8]:

1. Find the SKU with largest annual dollar value D_iR_i. Suppose, it is SKU_k. Let $m_k = 1$.

2. For every other SKU_p, calculate

$$m_j = \sqrt{\frac{s}{D_jR_jS + s} \frac{D_kR_k}{}}$$

(12-22)

   and round it to the nearest integer greater or equal to 1.

3. Calculate OI using:

$$OI^* = \sqrt{\frac{2\left(S + s\sum_{j=1}^{n}\frac{1}{m_j}\right)}{i\sum_{j=1}^{n}m_jD_jR_j}}$$

(12-23)

The rationale for this heuristic is that both purchase order cost (S) and line item ordering cost (s) are charged to the SKU_k because SKU_k will be ordered at every order interval. Then, m_j for other SKUs are determined using formula (12-22) relative to m_k. Finally, OI is calculated using formula (12-23), which is very similar to formula (12-18) but uses m_jD_j as the demand for SKU_j.

We use the same data as Example 12 in order to compare the coordinated periodic review model with the fixed-interval model. Recall that $S = \$1.00$, $s = 0.50$, and $i = 0.24$.

◀ **Example 14**

The annual demand and unit prices are repeated below. Calculate the m_js and OI.

SKU	Demand/Year (D_i)	Price/Unit (R_i)	D_iR_i
1	12,000	.50	$6,000
2	8,000	.30	$2,400
3	700	.10	$70

The SKU with largest D_iR_i is SKU_1. Therefore, $m_1 = 1$.

SOLUTION

$$m_2 = \sqrt{\frac{.5}{2,400}\frac{\$6,000}{1 + .5}} = .91 \text{ round to 1. Therefore, } m_2 = 1.$$

---

[8] E.A. Silver, D.F. Pyke, and R. Peterson. *Inventory Management and Production Planning and Scheduling*, 3rd ed. New York: John Wiley and Sons, 1998, pp. 426–429.

$$m_3 = \sqrt{\frac{.5}{70}\frac{\$6,000}{1 + .5}} = 5.35 \text{ round to 5. Therefore, } m_3 = 5.$$

$$OI^* = \sqrt{\frac{2(1.00 + .5(1 + 1 + .20))}{.24(1 \times 6,000 + 1 \times 2,400 + 5 \times 70)}}$$

$$= .0447 \text{ year} = 11.2 \text{ days (because the buyer works 250 days a year)}$$

Thus, OI is only slightly smaller than in Example 12, but the plan for SKU$_3$, because of its small annual dollar usage, is to order it every five order times.

Suppose LT and safety stocks are negligible. Demand for SKU$_3$ during the next 11 work days = 700(11)/250 = 30.8 units. Therefore, the order up to level for SKU$_3$ should be set to 5(30.8) = 154 units.

 ## The Single Period Model

single period model Model for ordering perishables and other items with limited useful lives.

The **single period model** (sometimes referred to as the *news-vender problem*) is used for ordering perishables (e.g., fresh fruits and vegetables, baked goods, seafood, cut flowers) and other items that have a limited useful life (e.g., newspapers, magazines, spare parts for specialized equipment). The *period* for a spare part is the life of the equipment, assuming that the part cannot be used for other equipment. What sets unsold or unused goods apart is that they are not typically carried over from one period to the next, at least not without penalty. Day-old baked goods, for instance, are often sold at reduced prices, leftover seafood may be discarded, and out-of-date magazines may be offered to used bookstores at bargain rates. There may even be some cost associated with disposal of leftover goods.

Analysis of single period model generally focuses on two costs: shortage and excess. Shortage cost may include a charge for loss of customer goodwill as well as the opportunity cost of lost sale, i.e., unrealized profit per unit. Usually the latter is used:

$$C_{\text{shortage}} = C_s = \text{Revenue per unit} - \text{Purchase cost per unit}$$

We assume $C_s \geq 0$. If a shortage or stock-out relates to an item used in production or to a spare part for a machine, then shortage cost is the cost of lost production.

excess cost Difference between purchase cost and salvage value of an item left at the end of the period.

Excess cost pertains to items left over at the end of the period. In effect, excess cost is the difference between purchase cost and salvage value. That is,

$$C_{\text{excess}} = C_e = \text{Purchase cost per unit} - \text{Salvage value per unit}$$

If there is a cost associated with disposal of excess items, then the salvage value will be negative and will therefore *increase* the excess cost per unit. On the other hand, if salvage value is larger than the purchase cost, then C_e will be negative. However, in this case, we must have $C_s + C_e > 0$, because salvage value per unit must be less than revenue per unit.

The goal of the single period model is to identify that order quantity, or stocking level, that will minimize the long-run (expected) total excess and shortage cost.

There are two general categories of problems that we will consider: those for which demand can be approximated by a continuous distribution (such as Uniform or Normal) and those for which demand can be approximated by a discrete distribution (say, historical frequencies or Poisson). The nature of item can indicate which type of model might be appropriate. For example, demand for liquids and items whose individual units are small but whose demand is large (such as muffins or newspapers) tends to vary over some *continuous scale*, thus lending itself to description by a continuous distribution. Demand for spare parts, expensive flowers, and computers is expressed in terms of the *number of units* demanded and lends itself to description by a discrete distribution.

Continuous Stocking Levels

The concept of identifying an optimal stocking level (i.e., order quantity) is perhaps easiest to visualize when demand is Uniform. Choosing the stocking level is similar to balancing a seesaw, but instead of a person on each end of the seesaw, we have the excess cost per unit (C_e) on one end of the seesaw and the shortage cost per unit (C_s) on the other. The seesaw represents the Uniform distribution. The optimal stocking level is analogous to the fulcrum of the seesaw; the stocking level equalizes the cost weights, as illustrated in Figure 12-15. If actual demand exceeds the balance point S_o, there is shortage; hence, C_s is on the right end of the seesaw. Similarly, if demand is less than S_o, there is excess, so C_e is on the left end of the seesaw. When $C_e = C_s$, the optimal stocking level will be halfway between the endpoints of the seesaw. If one cost is greater than the other, S_o will be closer to the larger cost.

The *service level* is the *probability* that demand will not exceed the stocking level. Calculation of the service level is the key to determining the optimal stocking level, S_o. It can be shown that in order to balance the seesaw on the fulcrum, service level should be chosen so that:

$$\text{Service level SL} = \frac{C_s}{C_s + C_e} \tag{12-24}$$

◀ **Figure 12-15**

The optimal stocking level (i.e., order quantity) balances unit shortage and excess costs.

Therefore, the optimal stocking level, S_o, is that point in the demand distribution that satisfies Probability (demand $< S_o$) = SL.

A cafeteria buys muffins daily. Demand varies Uniformly between 30 and 50 muffins per day. The cafeteria pays 20 cents per muffin and charges 80 cents per muffin. Unsold muffins are discarded at the end of the day. Find the optimal stocking level and the stock-out risk for that quantity.

◀ **Example 15**

SOLUTION

C_e = Cost per unit − Salvage value per unit
    = $.20 − $0
    = $.20 per unit

C_s = Revenue per unit − Cost per unit
    = $.80 − $.20
    = $.60 per unit

$$\text{SL} = \frac{C_s}{C_s + C_e} = \frac{\$.60}{\$.60 + \$.20} = .75$$

Thus, the optimal stocking level (i.e., order quantity) must satisfy 75 percent of demand. For the Uniform distribution, this will be at a point equal to the minimum demand plus 75 percent of the difference between maximum and minimum demands:

$S_o = 30 + .75(50 - 30) = 45$ muffins

The stock-out risk at stocking level of 45 muffins is $1.00 - 0.75 = 0.25$

A similar approach can be applied when demand is Normally distributed.

Example 16 ▶

Suppose the distribution of demand for muffins in the previous example was approximately Normal with a mean of 40 muffins per day and a standard deviation of 5 muffins per day. Find the optimal stocking level for the muffins.

Recall that $C_s = \$0.60$, $C_e = \$0.20$, and $SL = 0.75$

SOLUTION

This indicates that 75 percent of the area under the Normal curve must be to the left of the stocking level. Appendix B, Table B shows that a value of z between 0.67 and 0.68, say, 0.675, will satisfy this. Thus,

$S_o = 40 + 0.675(5) = 43.375$ or 43 muffins.

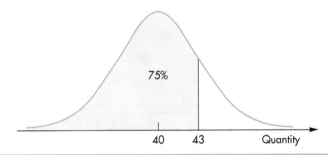

Discrete Stocking Levels

When stocking levels are discrete rather than continuous, the ratio $C_s/(C_s + C_e)$ usually does not coincide with the cumulative probability of a stocking level (e.g., the ratio may be *between* the cumulative probability of five and six units). The optimal stocking level in this case is the *higher level* (e.g., six units). In other words, choose the stocking level so that the cumulative probability equals or just *exceeds the ratio*. Figure 12-16 illustrates this concept.

Figure 12-16 ▶

The cumulative probability for optimal discrete stocking level must equal or just exceed the ratio $C_s/(C_s + C_e)$.

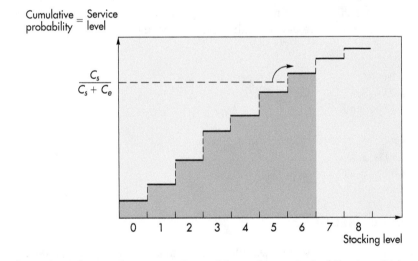

Example 17 ▶

Historical records on the use of a spare part for an old press (shown in the following table) are used to estimate usage for the spare part in a similar but new press. Stock-out cost involves downtime expenses and special ordering costs. These average $4,200 per unit short. The spare part costs $1,200 each, and an unused part has $400 salvage value. Determine the optimal stocking level for the spare part.

Number of Spares Used	Probability	Cumulative Probability
0.............................	.20	.20
1.............................	.40	.60
2.............................	.30	.90
3.............................	.10	1.00
4 or more..................	.00	
	1.00	

$$C_s = \$4,200, \ C_e = 1,200 - 400 = \$800, \ SL = \frac{C_s}{C_s + C_e} = \frac{\$4,200}{\$4,200 + \$800} = .84$$

The Cumulative Probability column indicates the fraction of time that demand was equal to or less than some amount. For example, demand ≤ one spare occurred 60 percent of the time, or demand ≤ two spares occurred 90 percent of the time. Go down the table until cumulative probabilities just exceed service level of 84 percent. This is .90, which relates to two spares.

The logic behind Formula 12-24 can be seen by solving Example 17 using a *decision table* approach. Table 12-4 illustrates this approach. The table enumerates the expected cost of each combination of stocking level and demand. For instance, if the stocking level is three, and demand turns out to be zero (see the blue-shaded cell), that would result in an excess of three units, at a cost of $800 each. The probability of a demand of zero units is 0.20, so the expected cost of that cell is 0.20(3)($800) = $480. Similarly, if no units are stocked and demand is two (see the yellow-shaded cell), the expected cost is the probability of demand being two (i.e., 0.30) multiplied by two units multiplied by the shortage cost per unit. Thus, the expected cost is .30(2)($4,200) = $2,520. For the cases in which the demand and stocking level are the same (the green-shaded cells), supply = demand, so there is neither a shortage nor an excess, and thus the cost is $0. The expected cost for each stocking level is the sum of the expected costs of each demand. For example, the expected cost of 0 stocking level is $0 + $1,680 + $2,520 + $1,260 = $5,400.

▼ **Table 12-4**

Expected cost for each possible outcome.

And the demand probabilities are

If the stocking level is	0 prob. = .20	1 prob. = .40	2 prob. = .30	3 prob. = .10	The expected cost will be
0	S = D $0	1 unit short .40(1) ($4,200) = $1,680	2 units short .30(2) ($4,200) = $2,520	3 units short .10(3) ($4,200) = $1,260	$5,460
1	1-unit excess .20(1) ($800) = $160	S = D $0	1 unit short .30(1) ($4,200) = $1,260	2 units short .10(2) ($4,200) = $840	$2,260
2	2-unit excess .20(2) ($800) = $320	1-unit excess .40(1) ($800) = $320	S = D $0	1 unit short .10(1) ($4,200) = $420	$1,060
3	3-unit excess .20(3) ($800) = $480	2-unit excess .40(2) ($800) = $640	1-unit excess .30(1) ($800) = $240	S = D $0	$1,360

The lowest expected cost is $1,060, which occurs for the stocking level of two units, which agrees with the SL ratio approach in Example 17.

Example 18 illustrates how to solve a problem when demand is Poisson distribution.

◀ **Example 18**

Demand for long-stemmed red roses at a small flower shop on a slow day can be approximated by a Poisson distribution that has a mean of four dozen roses. Profit on the roses is $3 per dozen. Leftover roses are marked down and sold the next day at a loss of $2 per dozen. What is the optimal stocking level?

Obtain the cumulative probabilities from the Poisson table (Appendix B, Table C) for a mean of 4.0:

$$C_s = \$3, \ C_e = \$2, \ SL = \frac{C_s}{C_s + C_e} = \frac{\$3}{\$3 + \$2} = .60$$

Demand (dozen)	Cumulative Probability
0	.018
1	.092
2	.238
3	.434
4	.629
5	.785
⋮	⋮

Compare the service level (ratio) to the cumulative probabilities. Go down the table until cumulative probability just exceeds SL = 0.60. This is 0.629, which relates to 4 dozen roses.

Multi-Echelon Inventory Management

Usually inventories of a product are kept at more than one location in the outbound-distribution supply chain, e.g., at the manufacturer's distribution centre (DC), at the retailer's warehouse, and at the retailer's store. Also, inventories of a part may be kept at various locations in the inbound supply chain, e.g., at the supplier, at various factories where it is modified, and at the assembly plant. The single location inventory models described so far can be used at each location, but because demands are dependent in a supply chain, this will be suboptimal, i.e., not minimum cost. Also, because of decentralized control, the total orders from the downstream facilities/operations may be overwhelming (all "customers" ordering at the same time).

Various methods are used for coordinated control of inventories in a supply chain:

- Multi-echelon control.
- Distribution requirements planning, including fair-share allocation.
- Inventory optimization.

Multi-Echelon Control

A distribution network is usually like a tree on its side (see Figure 12-17):

Figure 12-17 ▶

A frequently occuring multi-echelon supply channel.

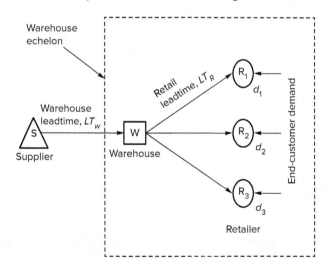

A warehouse echelon (level) is the warehouse and all the retailers it feeds into. In multi-echelon control, retailers transmit their point of sales (POS) data to the warehouse. Retailers may use their own inventory control model, e.g., fixed order quantity or fixed-interval model. The warehouse determines its inventory control model parameters using total POS data and its echelon lead time is equal to sum of lead time from supplier to warehouse (LT_W) and lead time of warehouse to a retailer (LT_R). Then, the warehouse uses its echelon inventory position, which is the total inventory in all retailers, warehouse, and en route to them minus any back-orders to end customers, in its inventory control model. In other words, the warehouse plans based on end-customer demand and supply.

Distribution Requirements Planning (DRP)

DRP determines time-phased replenishment schedules between a manufacturer's facility and DCs (or between a DC and retail stores). DRP is like MRP (see Chapter 14) but is for distribution planning, not material planning. For each SKU, DRP starts with forecast demand at DCs and works backward in time, offsetting for replenishment lead time. DRP requires:

- Forecast of demand at each DC (usually done by the DC itself).
- Current inventory on hand and on order.
- Order quantities/batch sizes.
- Lead times.

Note: The manufacturer may not be able to meet the orders because of capacity limitation (transportation may also be a limiting resource). Solutions include using overtime, outsourcing, and putting retailers on allocation.

Allocation here means that the retailers will not receive all their order quantity. A common allocation method is called fair share, which bases allocation on "actual sales – inventory on hand," and not order quantities (which may be inflated at the time of allocation). For an application of inventory management, including DRP, see the "Mark's Work Wearhouse" OM in Action.

Inventory Optimization

Inventory optimization determines the location and optimal level of inventory in the supply chain. It can be described as follows: given customer-promised LT, probability distribution of demand at each inventory location, cost of holding inventory in each location, processing time at each location, and transport times, determine committed LT (to the next location in supply chain) and amount of inventory to be kept at each location in order to minimize total inventory holding cost.

If a location does not hold inventory, its committed LT has to be met within its incoming raw-material LT + processing time. The fixed-interval inventory model is used at each stocking location. A special type of optimization method called dynamic programming is used to solve this problem.

 OM in *ACTION*   http://www.marks.com

Mark's Work Wearhouse

Mark's Work Wearhouse started as a work wear store in Calgary in 1977 but has expanded its merchandise to include casual, business, sports, and outdoor apparel for both men and women. It has now over 385 stores all over Canada, over 6,300 employees, and revenue of over $1 billion a year. This increased variety and expansion has put strain on its supply chain management's ability to forecast demand accurately and have the right merchandise in the right store at the right time.

Every region has different apparel needs. For example, in downtown Toronto, work wear is khaki pants and a golf shirt, but in the oil fields around Edmonton, guys will jump out of pickups covered head-to-foot in oil in search for new clothes. Mark's sells a lot more rainwear in Vancouver than in Saskatoon. Sizes also vary regionally. Mark's stores in British Columbia cater to a significant Asian population and smaller sizes are a steady part of the mix in the stores. In Gallic Quebec, customers tend to be of average stature, while in the prairie and mountain provinces, they "grow 'em big."

Therefore, Mark's needs a good forecasting, fulfillment, and merchandising software. In the 1990s Mark's was using Inforem, IBM's Inventory and Forecasting software which ran on an IBM mainframe computer. However, the forecasting module wasn't used effectively and Inforem didn't have the analytics and merchandising capabilities Mark's needs. Mark's was incurring significant costs for free delivery of out-of-stock merchandise to its customer's homes under Mark's Fastfind program. Since then, Mark's has bought and installed various software from JDA. These include JDA Demand, JDA Size Scaling, and JDA Fulfillment. JDA Demand is the forecasting

(continued)

module. JDA Size Scaling uses store-level data on sizes of apparel purchased to determine which size fits each store. It also determines what percentage of merchandise should be distributed at season-opening and what percentage should be kept in the Mark's distribution centres (DCs) for in-season replenishment. JDA Fulfillment is basically distribution requirements planning, i.e., using each store's weekly time-phased forecast for the coming season, it works backward and plans the distribution of apparel, the required inventory in Mark's DCs, and the required replenishments from Mark's suppliers.

The results are promising. The sales and customer satisfaction are up while inventories, logistics costs, store transfers, and excess store stocks are down.

Source: http://www.jda.com/realresultsmagazine/view-article. cfm?did=3096

Summary

- Inventory is any unused material, part, or product, usually stored in a warehouse.

- Inventories are important because holding them costs money, both for storage and the opportunity cost of money tied up in inventory. Management measures efficient use of inventory by inventory turnover ratio (= cost of goods sold / average inventory investment).

- Inventories serve different functions (or purposes), including meeting seasonal demand, decoupling operations, protection against stock-out (safety stocks), and allowing economic lot size or quantity discounts (cycle stocks).

- Successful inventory management requires keeping and handling them safely, a system to keep track of inventory position (= on hand + on order − back-ordered) and using inventory control models, accurate information about demand and lead times, realistic estimates of inventory costs, and a priority system for allocating control efforts (the A-B-C Classification).

- Three classes of models are described: fixed-order quantity (EOQ)/reorder point (ROP), fixed-interval/order up to level, and the single period models. The first two are appropriate if unused items can be carried over into subsequent periods.

- EOQ models address the question of how much to order. They include the basic EOQ, economic production quantity, quantity discounts, and planned shortages models.

- The ROP models address the question of when to order (in terms of inventory position) and are particularly helpful in dealing with situations that include variations in either demand or lead time. They involve service level and safety stock considerations. Two types of service level are lead time and annual (fill rate) service levels.

- When the time between orders is fixed, the fixed-interval model is useful. Coordinated periodic review is a more general model.

- Multi-echelon inventory management is management of inventory across various organization in a supply chain. Methods used are multi-echelon inventory control, DRP, and inventory optimization.

The formulas presented in this chapter are summarized in Table 12-5.

Table 12-5 ▼

Summary of inventory formulas.

Model	Formula		Symbols
1. Basic EOQ	$EOQ = Q_0 = \sqrt{\dfrac{2DS}{H}}$	(12-2)	Q_0 = Economic order quantity
	$TC = \dfrac{Q}{2}H + \dfrac{D}{Q}S$	(12-1)	D = Annual demand
			S = Ordering cost per order
			H = Annual holding cost per unit $= i \cdot R$
	Length of order cycle $= \dfrac{Q_0}{D}$	(12-3)	i = Annual holding cost rate
			R = Item unit cost (purchase price)

2. Economic production quantity

$$Q_0 = \sqrt{\frac{2DS}{H}}\sqrt{\frac{P}{p-d}} \qquad (12\text{-}8)$$

$$TC = \frac{I_{max}}{2}H + \frac{D}{Q}S \qquad (12\text{-}4)$$

$$\text{Cycle length} = \frac{Q}{d} \qquad (12\text{-}5)$$

$$\text{Production run length} = \frac{Q}{p} \qquad (12\text{-}6)$$

$$I_{max} = \frac{Q}{P}(p-d) \qquad (12\text{-}7)$$

$Q_0 =$ Optimal production run quantity

$P =$ Production rate

$d =$ Usage or demand rate

$I_{max} =$ Maximum inventory level

3. Quantity discounts

$$TC = \frac{Q}{2}H + \frac{D}{Q}S + RD \qquad (12\text{-}9)$$

4. Planned shortages

$$Q_b = Q\left(\frac{H}{H+B}\right) \qquad (12\text{-}10)$$

$$Q = \sqrt{\frac{2DS}{H}\left(\frac{H+B}{B}\right)} \qquad (12\text{-}12)$$

$Q_b =$ Quantity back-ordered in an order cycle

$B =$ Annual back-order cost per unit

5. Reorder point under:

   a. Constant demand and lead time $ROP = d(LT) \qquad (12\text{-}13)$

   b. Variable demand $ROP = \bar{d}(LT) + z\sqrt{LT}(\sigma_d) \qquad (12\text{-}15)$

   c. Variable lead time and demand $ROP = \bar{d}(\overline{LT}) + z\sqrt{\overline{LT}(\sigma_d^2) + \bar{d}^2(\sigma_{LT}^2)} \quad (12\text{-}16)$

$LT =$ Lead time

$\bar{d} =$ Average demand rate

$\sigma_d =$ Standard deviation of demand rate

$z =$ Standard Normal deviate

$\overline{LT} =$ Average lead time

$\sigma_{LT} =$ Standard deviation of lead time

6. Annual service level

$$E(z) = \frac{Q(1 - SL_{annual})}{\sigma_{dLT}} \qquad (12\text{-}17)$$

$E(z) =$ Standardized expected number short per order cycle

$\sigma_{dLT} =$ Standard deviation of demand during a lead time

$SL_{annual} =$ Annual service level (fill rate)

7. Fixed-interval

$$OI^* = \sqrt{\frac{2(S+ns)}{i\sum D_j R_j}} \qquad (12\text{-}18)$$

$OI =$ Order interval

$S =$ Group ordering cost (i.e., cost of a purchase order)

$s =$ Individual item ordering cost (i.e., cost of a line item in the purchase order)

$n =$ Number of SKUs ordered from same supplier

$D_j =$ Annual demand for SKU_j

$R_j =$ Unit cost of SKU_j

$$I_{max} = \bar{d}(OI + LT) + z\sigma_d\sqrt{OI + LT} \qquad (12\text{-}20)$$

$$Q = I_{max} - \text{inventory position} \qquad (12\text{-}21)$$

Inventory position = on hand + on order − back-ordered

8. Coordinated periodic review

$$m_j = \sqrt{\frac{s}{D_j R_j}\frac{D_k R_k}{S+s}} \qquad (12\text{-}22)$$

$$OI^* = \sqrt{\frac{2\left(S + s\sum_{j=1}^{n}\frac{1}{m_j}\right)}{i\sum_{j=1}^{n}m_j D_j R_j}} \qquad (12\text{-}23)$$

$m_j =$ Multiple of OI^* used for ordering SKU_j

$k =$ Index of the SKU with largest annual dollar value $D_j R_j$

9. Single period

$$SL = \frac{C_s}{C_s + C_e} \qquad (12\text{-}24)$$

$SL =$ Service level

$C_s =$ Shortage cost per unit

$C_e =$ Excess cost per unit

Key Terms

A-B-C classification

annual service level

bar code

cycle counting

economic order quantity (EOQ)

excess cost

fixed-interval/order up to level model

fixed order quantity/reorder point model

holding or carrying cost

inventory

inventory management

inventory position

inventory turnover

lead time service level

ordering cost

perpetual or continual tracking

point-of-sale (POS) system

purchase lead time

quantity discounts

reorder point (ROP)

safety stock

setup

shortage cost

single period model

two bin system

warehouse management system

Solved Problems

Problem 1

Basic EOQ. A small computer manufacturer uses 32,000 computer chips annually. The chips are used at a steady rate during the 240 days a year that the plant operates. Annual holding cost is 60 cents per chip, and ordering cost is $24 per order. Determine:

  a. The optimal (or economic) order quantity.

  b. The number of workdays in an order cycle.

Solution

$D = 32,000$ chips per year, $S = \$24$

$H = \$0.60$ per unit per year

  a. $Q_0 = \sqrt{\dfrac{2DS}{H}} = \sqrt{\dfrac{2(32,000)\$24}{\$.60}} = 1,600$ chips

  b. $\dfrac{Q_0}{D} = \dfrac{1,600 \text{ chips}}{32,000 \text{ chips/yr}} = \dfrac{1}{20} \text{ year} \times 240 \text{ days} = 12 \text{ workdays}$

Problem 2

Economic production quantity. A company is both a producer and a user of brass couplings. The company operates 220 days a year and uses the couplings at a steady rate of 50 per day. Couplings can be produced at a rate of 200 per day. Annual holding cost is $1 per coupling, and machine setup cost is $35 per production run.

  a. Determine the economic production quantity.

  b. How many production runs per year will there be?

  c. Calculate the maximum inventory level.

  d. Determine the length of the pure consumption portion of the cycle.

Solution

$D = 50$ units per day $\times$ 220 days per year $= 11,000$ units per year

$S = \$35$ per production run

$H = \$1$ per unit per year

$p = 200$ units per day

$d = 50$ units per day

  a. $Q_0 = \sqrt{\dfrac{2DS}{H}} \sqrt{\dfrac{p}{p-d}} = \sqrt{\dfrac{2(11,000)35}{1}} \sqrt{\dfrac{200}{200-50}} = 1,013$ units.

  b. Number of production runs per year: $D/Q_0 = 11,000/1,013 = 10.86$, or 11.

c. $I_{max} = \dfrac{Q_0}{p}(p - d) = \dfrac{1{,}013}{200}(200 - 50) = 759.75$ or 760 units.

d. Length of cycle $= \dfrac{Q_0}{d} = \dfrac{1{,}013 \text{ units}}{50 \text{ units per day}} = 20.26$ workdays

Length of production run $= \dfrac{Q_0}{p} = \dfrac{1{,}013 \text{ units}}{200 \text{ units per day}} = 5.06$ workdays

Length of pure consumption portion $=$ Length of cycle $-$ Length of production run

$= 20.26 - 5.06 = 15.20$ workdays

Problem 3

Quantity discounts. A small manufacturer uses roughly 3,400 kg of a chemical dye a year. Currently the company purchases 300 kg at a time and pays $3 per kg. The supplier has just announced that orders of 1,000 kg or more will be filled at the price of $2 per kg. The manufacturer incurs a cost of $100 each time it replenishes and uses the annual holding cost rate of 17 percent of the purchase price.

a. Determine the order quantity that will minimize the total cost.

b. If the supplier offered the discount at 1,500 kg instead of 1,000 kg, what order quantity would minimize total cost?

Solution

$D = 3{,}400$ kg per year, $S = \$100$, $H = .17R$

The quantity ranges are:

Range	Unit Price (per kg)
1 to 999	$3
1,000 +	$2

a. Calculate the EOQ for $2 per kg price:

$$Q_{\$2} = \sqrt{\dfrac{2DS}{H}} = \sqrt{\dfrac{2(3{,}400)100}{.17(2)}} = 1{,}414 \text{ kg}$$

Because this quantity falls in the $2 per kg quantity range, it is optimal.

b. If the discount is offered at 1,500 kg, the EOQ for the $2 per kg price is no longer feasible. Consequently, it becomes necessary to calculate the EOQ for $3 per kg and compare the total annual cost for that order quantity with the total annual cost of using the break quantity (i.e., 1,500).

$$Q_{\$3} = \sqrt{\dfrac{2DS}{H}} = \sqrt{\dfrac{2(3{,}400)100}{0.17(3)}} = 1{,}155 \text{ kg}$$

$$TC = \left(\dfrac{Q}{2}\right)H + \left(\dfrac{D}{Q}\right)S + RD$$

$$TC_{1{,}155} = \left(\dfrac{1{,}155}{2}\right)(.17)(3) + \left(\dfrac{3{,}400}{1{,}155}\right)100 + 3(3{,}400)$$

$$= \$294.53 + \$294.37 + \$10{,}200 = \$10{,}789$$

$$TC_{1{,}500} = \left(\dfrac{1{,}500}{2}\right)(.17)(2) + \left(\dfrac{3{,}400}{1{,}500}\right)100 + 2(3{,}400)$$

$$= \$255 + \$226.67 + \$6{,}800 = \$7{,}282$$

Because it would result in a lower total annual cost, 1,500 kg is the optimal order quantity (see the following figure).

Problem 4

ROP for variable demand and constant lead time. The housekeeping department of a hotel uses approximately 400 towels per day. The actual number tends to vary with the number of guests on any given night. Usage can be approximated by a Normal distribution that has a mean of 400 and a standard deviation of 9 towels per day. A linen service company washes the towels with a lead time of three days. If the hotel policy is to maintain a stock-out risk of 2 percent for towels, what is the minimum number of towels that must be on hand at reorder time (i.e., the ROP), and how much of that amount can be considered safety stock?

Solution

$\bar{d} = 400$ towels per day, $LT = 3$ days

$\sigma_d = 9$ towels per day, Stock-out risk = 2 percent, so lead time service level = 98 percent

From Appendix B, Table B, the z value that corresponds to an area under the Normal curve to the left of z of 98 percent is about 2.055.

$$ROP = \bar{d}\,LT + z\sqrt{LT}\sigma_d = 400(3) + 2.055\sqrt{3}(9)$$
$$= 1,200 + 32.03 = 1,232.03, \text{ or } 1,232 \text{ towels}$$

Safety stock is 32 towels.

Problem 5

ROP for variable demand and variable lead time. The hotel replaces broken and stolen drinking glasses at a rate of 25 per day. In the past, this quantity has tended to vary Normally and has a standard deviation of three drinking glasses per day. Drinking glasses are ordered from a distant supplier. Lead time is Normally distributed with an average of 10 days and a standard deviation of 2 days. What ROP should be used to achieve a lead time service level of 95 percent?

Solution

$\bar{d} = 25$ drinking glasses per day, $\overline{LT} = 10$ days
$\sigma_d = 3$ drinking glasses per day, $\sigma_{LT} = 2$ days

lead time SL = 95 percent, so $z = 1.645$ (from Appendix B, Table B)

$$ROP = \bar{d}\overline{LT} + z\sqrt{\overline{LT}\sigma_d^2 + \bar{d}^2\sigma_{LT}^2}$$
$$= 25(10) + 1.645\sqrt{10(3)^2 + (25)^2(2)^2} = 334 \text{ drinking glasses}$$

SL = 95%

250   334 drinking glasses

Problem 6

Annual service level. The manager of an office supplies store has decided to set an annual service level (or fill rate) of 96 percent for a certain model of telephone answering machine. The store sells approximately 300 of this model a year. Holding cost is $5 per unit annually, ordering cost is $25 per order, average demand during a lead time is 20, and standard deviation of demand during a lead time is 7. Calculate the ROP, assuming EOQ is used as the order quantity.

Solution

$SL_{annual} = 96$ percent $D = 300$ units $H = \$5$ $S = \$25$ $\mu_{dLT} = 20$ $\sigma_{dLT} = 7$

First, we need to calculate the EOQ:

$$Q = \sqrt{\frac{2DS}{H}} = \sqrt{\frac{2(300)(25)}{5}} = 54.77 \text{ (round to 55)}$$

$$E(z) = \frac{Q(1 - SL_{annual})}{\sigma_{dLT}} = \frac{55(1 - .96)}{7} = .314$$

Interpolation in Table 12-3 gives $z = 0.18$.

ROP $= 20 + 0.18(7) = 21.26$ round to 21 machines

Problem 7

Fixed-interval model. A lab orders a number of chemicals from the same supplier every 30 days. Lead time is five days. The assistant manager of the lab must determine how much of one of these chemicals to order. A check of stock revealed that eleven 25 mL jars are on hand and none are on order. Daily usage of the chemical is approximately Normal with a mean of 15.2 mL and a standard deviation of 1.6 mL. The desired service level for this chemical is 95 percent.

  a. What should be the amount of safety stock for the chemical?

  b. How many jars of the chemical should be ordered at this time?

Solution

$\bar{d} = 15.2$ mL per day, OI $= 30$ days, SL $= 95\%$ or $z = 1.645$

$\sigma_d = 1.6$ mL per day, LT $= 5$ days, Amount on hand $= 11$ jars $\times 25$ mL per jar $= 275$ mL

  a. Safety stock $= z\sigma_d\sqrt{OI + LT} = 1.645(1.6)\sqrt{30 + 5} = 15.57$ mL

  b. Amount to order $= I_{max} -$ Amount on hand

  $$I_{max} = \bar{d}(OI + LT) + z\sigma_d\sqrt{OI + LT}$$
  $$= 15.2(30 + 5) + 15.57 = 547.57 \text{ mL}$$

Amount to order $= 547.57 - 275 = 272.57$ mL

Convert this to number of jars:

$$\frac{272.57 \text{ mL}}{25 \text{ mL per jar}} = 10.90 \text{ or } 11 \text{ jars}$$

Problem 8

Single period model. A cable TV company uses a certain piece of equipment for which it carries two units of a spare part. The part costs $500 and has no salvage value. Part failures can be modelled by a Poisson distribution with a mean of two failures during the useful life of the equipment. Estimate the range of shortage cost per unit for which stocking two units of this spare part is optimal.

Solution

C_s is unknown $C_e = \$500$

The Poisson table (Appendix B, Table C) provides these values for a mean of 2.0:

Number of Failures	Cumulative Probability
0.........	0.135
1.........	0.406
2.........	0.677
3.........	0.857
4.........	0.947
5.........	0.983
⋮	⋮

For the optimal discrete stocking level, the service level must be rounded up. Hence, we know that the service level must have been between 0.407 and 0.677 in order to make two units the optimal stocking level. By setting the service level first equal to 0.407 and then to 0.677, we can establish bounds on the possible range of shortage cost.

$$\frac{C_s}{C_s + \$500} = .407, \text{so } C_s = .407(\$500 + C_s)$$

Solving, we find $C_s = \$343.17$.
Similarly,

$$\frac{C_s}{C_s + \$500} = .677, \text{so } C_s = .677(\$500 + C_s)$$

Solving, we find $C_s = \$1,047.99$. Hence, the range of shortage cost per unit is $\$343.17$ to $\$1,047.99$.

Discussion and Review Questions

1. What are the primary reasons for holding inventory? **LO1**

2. What are some ways that a company can reduce its needs for inventories? **LO1**

3. Why might it be inappropriate to use inventory turnover ratio to compare the inventory performance of companies in different industries? **LO1**

4. What are the requirements for effective inventory management? **LO2**

5. Define purchase lead time. What factors affect it? **LO2**

6. What benefits do bar codes have for inventory management? **LO2**

7. Briefly describe each of the costs associated with inventory. **LO2**

8. Describe briefly the A-B-C classification. **LO2**

9. How would you respond to the criticism that EOQ models tend to provide misleading results because values of S and H are, at best, educated guesses? **LO3**

10. Explain briefly how a higher holding cost can result in more frequent orders. **LO3**

11. Explain how a decrease in machine setup time can lead to a decrease in the average amount of work-in-process

inventory a company holds, and why that would be beneficial. **LO3**

12. How is the economic production quantity different from EOQ? **LO3**

13. Why would any company intentionally plan for shortage? Give an example. **LO3**

14. What is safety stock and what is its purpose? **LO4**

15. Under what circumstances should the amount of safety stock held be **LO4**
    a. Large?
    b. Small?
    c. Zero?

16. What is meant by the term *lead time service level*? Generally speaking, how is lead time service level related to the amount of safety stock held? **LO4**

17. What is annual service level and how is it related to z? **LO4**

18. What is the difference between fixed-interval/order up to level model and fixed order quantity/reorder point model? When would each be preferred?

19. What is the difference between fixed-interval/order up to level model and the coordinated periodic review model? When would each be preferred? **LO5**

20. What is the single period model, and under what circumstances is it appropriate? **LO6**

21. Can the optimal stocking level in the single period model ever be less than median (i.e., 50th percentile) demand? Explain briefly. **LO6**

22. Briefly describe the three methods used for multi-echelon inventory management. **LO7**

Taking Stock

1. What trade-offs are involved in each of these aspects of inventory management?
   a. Buying additional amounts to take advantage of quantity discounts.
   b. Conducting actual (physical) inventory counts once a quarter instead of once a year. **LO2**

2. Who needs to be involved in inventory decisions? **LO1 & 2**

3. How has technology aided inventory management? **LO2**

4. Employee theft of inventories can be a problem in a wholesaler/distributor/retailer warehouse. Name one thing a manager can do to combat this. **LO2**

Critical Thinking Exercises

1. To be competitive, many fast-food chains have begun to expand their menus to include a wider range of meals. Although contributing to competitiveness, this has added to the complexity of operations, including inventory management. Explain why. **LO2**

2. As a supermarket manager, how would you go about evaluating the criticality of an inventory shortage? **LO4**

Experiential Learning Exercises

1. Give three examples of inventory in your personal life. How do you manage them? **LO1**

2. Which inventory model would you use for each of the following activities? Which has the highest shortage cost? **LO3–6**

   a. Buying gasoline for your car.
   b. Buying groceries.
   c. Getting cash from your bank account.

3. How can the grocery store you use improve its inventory management? **LO2**

Internet Exercises

1. Visit RetailPro, the most popular retail software, find the Inventory Control and Management Capabilities of Retail Pro 9, watch the video, and summarize what it does for a retailer. **LO2** *Hint:* use http://www.retailpro.com/Solutions/RP9Capabilities.php?utm_source=solutions&utm_medium=retailpro9_capabilities&utm_campaign=solution_retailpro9_capabilities

2. Visit http://mhi.org/mediabank/general.asp, choose a category, click on "videos," pick a video and view it, and describe the equipment shown and its advantages. **LO2**

3. Answer the following questions about the "new" Montreal DC of Canadian Tire. You may find the following article useful http://www.mmh.com/images/site/MMH1011_SystemRptCanadianTire.pdf (also accessible from http://

www.mmh.com/article/super-sized_distribution) and the video http://www.youtube.com/watch?v=deE6pDBHlTc.

   a. What is the difference between conveyable and non-conveyable items? Give an example of each.
   b. What type of order picking system is used in the DC? Radio Frequency (RF), Light, Voice?
   c. What type of conveyor sorters are used in the DC?

4. Read http://img.en25.com/Web/DematicCorp/%7B3af4ab7f-7233-463e-88ab-d96299f6a4c5%7D_NA_CS-1017_UBC.pdf and describe how Dematics' Automatic Storage and Retrieval System is used by the UBC Library. **LO2**

5. Watch http://www.youtube.com/watch?v=4AcjAfWBVXg and summarize how SAP's SmartOps helped Celestica's supply chain inventory management.

Problems

1. a. Perform A-B-C classification on these items:

Item	Unit Cost	Annual Volume (00)
1	$100	25
2	80	30
3	15	60
4	50	10
5	11	70
6	60	85
7	10	60

   b. Find the EOQ given this information: $D = 4,500$ units/year, $S = \$36$, and $H = \$10$ per unit per year.

   c. Find the economic production quantity given this information.
$D = 18,000$ units/year, $S = \$100$, $H = \$40$ per unit per year, $p = 120$ units/day, and $d = 90$ units/day.

2. The manager of an automobile repair shop hopes to achieve a better allocation of inventory control efforts by adopting A-B-C classification. Given the monthly usages and unit costs in the following table, classify the items into the A, B, and C categories according to monthly dollar value. **LO2**

Item	Monthly Usage	Unit Cost
4021.......	50	$1,400
9402.......	300	12
4066.......	40	700
6500.......	150	20
9280.......	10	1,020
4050.......	80	140
6850.......	2,000	15
3010.......	400	20
4400.......	7,000	25
2307.......	1,958	14

3. The following table contains the monthly usage and unit costs for a random sample of 15 items from a list of 2,000 inventory items at a health care facility. **LO2**

Item	Unit Cost	Monthly Usage
K34	10	200
K35	25	600
K36	36	150
M10	16	25
M20	20	80
Z45	80	700
F14	20	300
F95	30	800
F99	20	60
D45	10	550
D48	12	90

Item	Unit Cost	Monthly Usage
D52	15	110
D57	40	120
N08	30	40
P05	16	500

   a. Develop an A-B-C classification for these items.

   b. How could the manager use this information?

   c. After reviewing your classification scheme, suppose that the manager decides to place item P05 into the A category. What are some possible explanations for this decision?

4. A large bakery buys flour in 25 kg bags. The bakery uses an average of 4,860 bags a year. Preparing an order, receiving the shipment, and paying the invoice costs $10 per order. Annual holding cost is $5 per flour bag. **LO3**

   a. Determine the economic order quantity.

   b. What is the average number of bags on hand (i.e., average cycle inventory) if EOQ is used?

   c. How many orders per year will there be if EOQ is used?

   d. Calculate the total annual cost of ordering and holding flour for EOQ.

   e. If ordering cost were to increase by 50 percent per order, by what percentage would the EOQ change?

5. A large law firm uses an average of 10 packages of copier paper a day. Each package contains 500 sheets. The firm operates 260 days a year. Holding cost for the paper is $1 per year per package, and ordering cost is $10 per order. **LO3**

   a. What order quantity would minimize total annual ordering and holding cost?

   b. Calculate the total annual inventory control cost using your order quantity from part *a*.

   c. Except for rounding, are annual ordering and holding costs equal at the EOQ?

   d. The office manager is currently using an order quantity of 100 packages. The partners of the firm expect the office to be managed in a cost-efficient manner. Would you recommend that the office manager use the optimal order quantity instead of 100 packages? Justify your answer.

6. A flower shop uses 250 clay pots a month. The pots are purchased for $2 each. Annual holding cost is estimated to be 30 percent of purchase cost, and ordering cost is $20 per order. The manager has been using an order quantity of 250 flower pots. **LO3**

   a. Calculate the EOQ.

   b. Calculate the EOQ's total annual inventory control cost.

   c. What additional annual inventory control cost is the shop incurring by using the current order quantity?

7. A fresh produce distributor uses 800 nonreturnable packing crates a month, which it purchases at a cost of $5 each. The manager has assigned an annual holding cost of 25 percent of the purchase price per crate. Ordering cost is $28 per order. Currently the manager orders 800 crates at a time. How much could the firm save annually in ordering and holding costs by using the EOQ? **LO3**

8. Demand for an item is projected to be 100 units per month. The monthly holding cost is $2 per unit, and it costs $55 to process an order. **LO3**

   a. Determine the EOQ.

   b. If the vendor is willing to offer the manager a discount of $10 *per order* for ordering in multiples of 50 units (e.g., 50, 100), would you advise the manager to take advantage of the offer? If so, what order quantity would you recommend?

   c. Alternatively, if the demand can wait at the cost of $5 per unit per month, what should the order quantity and the amount short per order cycle be?

9. A food processor uses approximately 27,000 glass jars a month. Because of storage limitations, a lot size of 4,000 jars has been used. Monthly holding cost is one cent per jar, and ordering cost is $20 per order. **LO3**

   a. What penalty is the company incurring by using its present order quantity?

   b. The manager would like to justify the present order quantity. One possibility is to simplify order processing to reduce the ordering cost. What ordering cost would enable the manager to justify the current order quantity?

10. A sausage factory can produce European wieners at a rate of 500 kg per day. It supplies wieners to local stores and restaurants at a steady rate of 100 kg per day. The cost to prepare the equipment for producing European wieners is $12. Annual holding cost is $4 per kg of wieners. The factory operates 300 days a year. Calculate: **LO3**

   a. The optimal production run quantity.

   b. The number of production runs per year.

   c. The length (in days) of a production run.

11. A chemical plant produces sodium bisulfate in 100 kg bags. Demand for this product is 20 tonnes per day. The capacity for producing this product is 50 tonnes per day. Setup cost is $400, and holding cost is $200 per tonne per year. The company operates 200 days a year. (*Note:* 1 tonne = 1,000 kg). **LO3**

   a. What is the optimal number of bags per production run?

   b. What would the average inventory level be for this lot size?

   c. Determine the approximate length of a production run, in days.

d. About how many production runs per year would there be?

e. How much could the company save annually in inventory control cost if the setup cost could be reduced to $200 per production run and the optimal production quantity is recalculated and used?

12. A company is about to begin production of a new product. The manager of a department that is asked to produce one of the components wants to know if there is enough machine time available. The machine will produce the item at a rate of 200 units a day. Eighty units will be used daily in assembling the final product. The company operates five days a week, 50 weeks a year. The manager estimates that it will take almost a full day to get the machine ready for a production run, at a cost of $300. Inventory holding cost will be $10 per unit per year. **LO3**

   a. What production run quantity should be used to minimize total annual setup and holding cost?

   b. What is the length of a production run (in days)?

   c. During production, at what rate will inventory build up?

   d. If the manager needs to run another job between runs of this job, and needs a minimum of 10 days per cycle of this job for the other job, will there be enough time?

13. A company manufactures hair dryers. It buys some of the components, but it makes the heating element, which it can produce at the rate of 800 per day. Hair dryers are assembled 250 days a year, at a rate of 300 per day. Because of the disparity between the production and usage rates, the heating elements are periodically produced in batches of 2,000 units. **LO3**

   a. Approximately how many batches of heating elements are produced annually?

   b. If production on a batch begins when there is no inventory of heating elements on hand, how much inventory will be on hand two days later?

   c. What will be the average level of inventory of the heating element, assuming each production cycle begins when there is no inventory on hand?

   d. The same equipment could also be used to make a component for another of the company's products. That job would require four days per cycle of the element. Setup time for making a batch of the heating elements is a half day. Is there enough time to do this job between production of batches of heating element? Explain.

14. A small mail-order company uses 18,000 boxes a year. Holding cost rate is 20 percent of unit cost per year, and ordering cost is $32 per order. The following quantity discounts are available. Determine: **LO3**

   a. The optimal order quantity.

   b. The number of orders per year.

Number of Boxes	Price per Box
1,000 to 1,999	$1.25
2,000 to 4,999	1.20
5,000 to 9,999	1.15
10,000 or more	1.10

15. A jewellery manufacturer buys semi-precious stones to make bracelets and rings. The supplier has quoted a price of $8 per stone for order quantities of 600 stones or more, $9 per stone for orders of 400 to 599 stones, and $10 per stone for smaller order quantities. The jewellery manufacturer operates 200 days per year. Usage rate is 25 stones per day, and ordering cost is $48 per order. **LO3 & 4**

a. If annual holding cost is 30 percent of unit cost, what is the optimal order quantity?

b. If lead time is six workdays, at what inventory level should the company reorder?

16. A manufacturer of exercise equipment purchases pulleys from a supplier who lists these prices: less than 1,000, $5 each; 1,000 to 3,999, $4.95 each; 4,000 to 5,999, $4.90 each; and 6,000 or more, $4.85 each. Ordering cost is $50 per order, annual holding cost is 20 percent of purchase cost, and annual usage is 4,900 pulleys. Determine the order quantity that will minimize total cost. **LO3**

17. The manager of a large electronics store wants to begin stocking a universal TV remote control device. Expected monthly demand is 800 units. The remote controls can be purchased from either supplier A or supplier B. Their price lists are as follows: **LO3**

Supplier A		Supplier B	
Quantity	Unit Price	Quantity	Unit Price
1–199	$14.00	1–149	$14.10
200–499	13.80	150–349	13.90
500+	13.60	350+	13.70

Ordering cost is $40 per order and annual holding cost is 25 percent of unit price. Which supplier should be used and what order quantity is optimal if the intent is to minimize total annual cost?

18. A manager just received a new price list for boxes from a supplier. It will now cost $1.00 a box for order quantities of 801 or more, $1.10 a box for 200 to 800, and $1.20 a box for smaller quantities. Ordering cost is $40 per order and holding cost rate is 40 percent of unit cost per year. The company uses 3,600 boxes a year. The manager has suggested a "round number" order quantity of 800 boxes. The manager's rationale is that total annual inventory cost is U-shaped and fairly flat at its minimum. Therefore, the difference in total annual cost between 800 and 801 units would be small anyway. How would you reply to the manager's suggestion? What order quantity would you recommend? **LO3**

19. A newspaper publisher uses roughly 800 metres of baling wire each day to secure bundles of newspapers. The paper is published Monday through Saturday. Lead time for purchase of wires is six workdays. The stock-out risk for various levels of safety stock is as follows: 1,500 metres, 0.10; 1,800 metres, 0.05; 2,100 metres, 0.02; and 2,400 metres, 0.01. What is the appropriate reorder point given that the company desires a lead time service level of 95 percent? **LO3**

20. Given the following information: **LO4**

Expected demand during a lead time = 300 units

Standard deviation of demand during a lead time = 30 units

Demand during a lead time is distributed Normally

a. Determine the safety stock needed to attain a 1 percent risk of stock-out during a lead time.

b. Would a stock-out risk of 2 percent require more or less safety stock? Explain.

21. Given the following information: **LO4**

Expected demand during a lead time = 600 kg

Standard deviation of demand during a lead time = 52 kg

Demand during a lead time is distributed Normally

Acceptable stock-out risk during a lead time = 4 percent

a. What amount of safety stock is appropriate?

b. At what level of inventory should this item be reordered?

22. Demand for vanilla ice cream at a small ice cream shop can be approximated by a Normal distribution with a mean of 21 litres per week and a standard deviation of 3.5 litres per week. The ice cream is purchased from an ice cream producer. The store manager desires a lead time service level of 90 percent. Lead time from the producer is two days. The store is open seven days a week. **LO4 & 5**

a. If the EOQ/ROP model is used for ordering the ice cream from the producer, what ROP would be consistent with the desired lead time service level?

b. If a fixed-interval model is used instead, what order quantity should be used if the order interval is 7 days and 8 litres are on hand and none are on order at the time of order?

c. Suppose that the manager is using the EOQ/ROP model described in part a. One day after placing an order with the producer, the manager receives a call from the producer saying that the order will be delayed because of problems at the producer's plant. The producer promises to have the order there in two days. After hanging up, the manager checks the inventory of vanilla ice cream and finds that 2 litres have been sold since the order was placed.

Assuming that the producer's promise is valid, what is the probability that the store will run out of vanilla ice cream before the shipment arrives?

23. The injection moulding department of a company uses an average of 30 litres of a special lubricant a day. The lubricant is replenished when the amount on hand is 170 litres. It takes four days for an order to be received. The current stock-out risk is 9 percent. What amount of safety stock would be needed if the acceptable risk of stock-out is to be reduced to 3 percent? **LO4**

24. A large electronics repair shop uses an average of 85 capacitors a day. The standard deviation is 5 units per day. The buyer follows this rule: Order when the amount on hand and on order drops to 625 units. Orders are delivered approximately six days after being placed. The delivery time is Normal with a mean of six days and a standard deviation of 1.10 days. What is the probability that the inventory of capacitors will be exhausted before the shipment is received? **LO4**

25. Demand for a particular tablet at an electronics store has recently surged, and the store manager must re-determine at what inventory level to replenish it. The manager wants a probability of at least 96 percent of not having a stock-out during a lead time. The manager expects demand to average a dozen units a day and to have a standard deviation of two units a day. Purchase lead time is variable, averaging four days with a standard deviation of one day. Assume demand during a lead time is Normal. At what inventory level (on hand + on order) should the manager reorder to achieve the desired service level probability? **LO4**

26. The manager of a car wash has received a revised price list from the vendor of the liquid soap, and a promise of a shorter lead time for deliveries. Formerly the lead time was four days, but now the vendor promises a reduction of 25 percent in that time (i.e., new lead time is 3 days). Annual usage of soap is 4,500 litres. The car wash is open 360 days a year. Assume that daily usage of soap is Normal, and that it has a standard deviation of two litres per day. The ordering cost is $10 per order and annual holding cost rate is 40 percent of unit cost. The revised price list is shown below. **LO3 & 4**

Quantity (litres)	Unit Price per litre
1–399	$2.00
400–799	1.80
800+	1.60

   a. What order quantity is optimal?
   b. What ROP is appropriate if the acceptable risk of a stock-out is 1.5 percent?

27. Experience suggests that usage of copy paper at a small copy centre can be approximated by a Normal distribution with a mean of five boxes per day and a standard

deviation of one-half box per day. Two days are required to fill an order for paper. Ordering cost is $10 per order, and annual holding cost is $10 per box. **LO3–5**

   a. Determine the economic order quantity, assuming 250 workdays a year.
   b. If the copy centre reorders when the paper on hand and on order is 12 boxes, calculate the risk of a stock-out during a lead time.
   c. If a fixed-interval of seven days, instead of the EOQ/ROP, is used for reordering, what shortage risk does the copy centre incur if it orders 36 boxes when the amount on hand is 12 boxes?

28. A bulk foods store sells unshelled peanuts by the kilo-gram. Historically, daily demand is Normally distrib-uted with a mean of 8 kg and a standard deviation of 1 kg. The purchase lead time from the supplier also appears to be Normally distributed with a mean of eight days and a standard deviation of one day. What ROP would provide stock-out risk of 10 percent during a lead time? **LO4**

29. A supermarket is open 360 days per year. Daily use of cash register tape averages 10 rolls, Normally distrib-uted, with a standard deviation of two rolls per day. The cost of ordering tapes is $10 per order, and holding cost is 40 cents per roll a year. Lead time is three days. **LO3 & 4**

   a. What is the EOQ?
   b. What ROP will provide a lead time service level of 96 percent?
   c. What ROP will provide an annual service level (i.e., fill rate) of 96 percent if order quantity = EOQ is used?

30. A car service shop uses 1,200 cases of oil a year. Order-ing cost is $20 per order, and annual holding cost is $3 per case. The shop owner has specified an *annual* service level of 99 percent. **LO3 & 4**

   a. What is the EOQ?
   b. What level of ROP is appropriate if demand during a lead time is Normally distributed with a mean of 80 cases and a standard deviation of 5 cases?

31. A small school bus depot operates 250 days a year. Daily demand for diesel fuel at the depot is Normal with an average of 250 litres and a standard deviation of 14 litres. Holding cost for the fuel is $.30 per litre per year, and ordering cost is $10 an order for more fuel. It takes one day to receive a delivery of diesel fuel. **LO3 & 4**

   a. Calculate the EOQ.
   b. Determine the ROP needed if the manager wants an annual service level of 99.5 percent.

32. A hospital reorders size 7 surgical gloves when the sup-ply on hand and on order falls to 18 units (pairs). Lead time for resupply is three days. Given the typical usage over the last 10 days below, what service level is achieved with the hospital's reorder policy? **LO4**

Day	1	2	3	4	5	6	7	8	9	10
Units	3	4	7	5	5	6	4	3	4	5

33. A drugstore uses the fixed-interval model for many of the items it stocks. The manager wants a service level of 0.98. Determine the order quantity for the following items if the order interval is 14 days and lead time is 2 days: **LO5**

Item	Average Daily Demand	Daily Standard Deviation	Quantity on Hand (none on order)
K033	60	5	420
K144	50	4	375
L700	8	2	160

34. A stockroom manager must set up inventory ordering procedures for two new items, P34 and P35. P34 can be ordered at any time, but P35 can be ordered only once every four weeks. The company operates 50 weeks a year, and the weekly usage rate for each item is Normally distributed. The manager has gathered the following information about the items: **LO3–5**

	Item P34	Item P35
Average weekly demand	60 units	70 units
Standard deviation	4 units per week	5 units per week
Unit cost	$15	$20
Annual holding cost rate	30%	30%
Ordering cost per order	$70	$30
Lead time	2 weeks	2 weeks
Acceptable stock-out risk	2.5%	2.5%

a. At what inventory level should the manager reorder P34?

b. Calculate the economic order quantity for P34.

c. Calculate the order quantity for P35 if 110 units are on hand at the time the order is placed.

35. Given the following list of items, **LO2 & 3**

a. Classify the items as A, B, or C.

b. Determine the economic order quantity for each item.

Item	Estimated Annual Demand	Ordering Cost	Holding Cost (%)	Unit Price
H4-010	20,000	$50	20	$2.50
H5-201	60,200	60	20	4.00
P6-400	9,800	80	30	28.50
P6-401	16,300	50	30	12.00
P7-100	6,250	50	30	9.00
P9-103	4,500	50	40	22.00
TS-300	21,000	40	25	45.00
TS-400	45,000	40	25	40.00
TS-041	800	40	25	20.00
V1-001	26,100	25	35	4.00

36. The distribution of demand (in dozens) for jelly doughnuts on Saturdays at a doughnut shop is shown in the following table. Determine the optimal number of doughnuts, in dozens, to make each Saturday morning if labour, materials, and overhead are estimated to cost $3.20 per dozen, doughnuts are sold for $4.80 per dozen, and leftover doughnuts at the end of each day are sold the next day at half price. What is the *resulting* service level? **LO6**

Demand (dozens)	Relative Frequency
19	.01
20	.05
21	.12
22	.18
23	.13
24	.14
25	.10
26	.11
27	.10
28	.04
29	.02

37. A public utility intends to buy a turbine as part of an expansion plan and must now decide on the number of spare parts to order. One part, X135, can be purchased for $100 each. Holding and disposal costs are estimated to be 145 percent of the purchase price over the life of the turbine. A stock-out is expected to cost $8,000 due to downtime, ordering, and "special purchase" factors. Historical records based on the performance of similar equipment operating under similar conditions suggest that demand for the spare part will tend to approximate a Poisson distribution with a mean of 3.2 units for the useful life of the turbine. **LO6**

a. What is the optimal number of units of this spare part to stock?

b. Stocking six spare parts would be the best strategy for what range of shortage cost per unit?

38. A fish store buys fresh tuna daily for $4.20 per kg and sells it for $5.70 per kg. At the end of each day, any remaining tuna is sold to a producer of cat food for $2.40 per kg. Daily demand for tuna at the fish store can be approximated by a Normal distribution with a mean of 80 kg and a standard deviation of 10 kg. What is the optimal stocking level? **LO6**

39. A small grocery store sells fresh produce, which it obtains from local farmers. During the strawberry season, demand for fresh strawberries at the store can be reasonably approximated using a Normal distribution with a mean of 40 litres per day and a standard deviation of 6 litres per day. Excess cost is 35 cents per litre. The grocer orders 49 litres per day. **LO6**

a. What is the implied cost of shortage per litre?

b. Why might this be a reasonable number?

40. Demand for Black Forest cake at the bakery of a supermarket can be approximated using a Poisson distribution with a mean of six per day. The manager estimates it costs $9 to prepare each cake. Fresh cakes sell for $12 each. Day-old cakes sell for $7 each. What stocking level is appropriate? **LO6**

41. A large burger restaurant buys ground beef at $3 per kg. The restaurant's policy is to use meat that is fresh daily. Any leftover meat at the end of each day is sold to the local zoo for $2 per kg. Eight burgers can be prepared from each kilogram of meat. Burgers sell for $2 each. Labour, overhead, meat, buns, and condiments altogether cost $1 per burger. Demand for ground beef is Normally distributed with a mean of 400 kg per day and a standard deviation of 50 kg per day. What daily order quantity for ground beef is optimal? **LO6**

42. The distribution of daily demand for carpet cleaning machines at a supermarket is shown in the following table. Machines are rented by the day only. Profit on a carpet cleaner is $10 per day. The store has four carpet cleaning machines. **LO6**

Demand	Frequency
0	.30
1	.20
2	.20
3	.15
4	.10
5	.05
	1.00

a. Assuming that the stocking decision is optimal, what is the implied range of excess cost per machine per day?
b. Your answer from part *a* has been presented to the manager, who protests that the amount is too low. Does this suggest an increase or a decrease in the number of carpet cleaning machines she stocks? Explain.

43. A manager wants to purchase a new piece of processing equipment and must decide on the number of a spare part to order with the new equipment. The spares cost $200 each, and any unused spares will have an expected salvage value of $50 each. The probability of usage of parts can be described by the following distribution: **LO6**

Number	0	1	2	3
Probability	.10	.50	.25	.15

If the part fails and a spare is not available, it will take two days to obtain a replacement and install it. The cost

for idle equipment is $400 per day. The spare is expected to cost the same in the future ($200 per unit). What quantity of spares should be stocked?

44. A Las Vegas bakery must decide how many wedding cakes to prepare for the upcoming weekend. Cakes cost $33 each to make and sell for $60 each. Unsold cakes are reduced to half-price on Monday, and typically one-third of those are sold. Any that remain are donated to a nearby senior centre. Analysis of recent demand resulted in the following probability distribution: **LO6**

Demand	0	1	2	3
Probability	.15	.35	.30	.20

How many cakes should be prepared?

45. Because there is a significant number of no-shows on a specific daily flight, the airline wants to intentionally overbook the flight. The number of no-shows can be described by a Normal distribution with a mean of 18 passengers and a standard deviation of 4.55 passengers. Profit per passenger is $99. If a passenger arrives but cannot board due to overbooking, the company policy is to provide a $200 coupon for any future flight on the airline. How many tickets should be overbooked to maximize expected profit? **LO6**

*46. The South Texas Center for Pediatric Care in San Antonio wants to reduce its inventory costs. The Centre carries vaccines (e.g., for whooping cough), noninjectable medical supplies (such as examining-table paper, alcohol swabs, tongue depressors), and office supplies (stationery, paper, and forms). Out of the 113 inventory items, seven vaccines account for approximately 70 percent of annual dollar value of $225,000. Approximately 210 whooping cough vaccines are needed per month. The office manager spends a total of approximately one half-hour finding out how much inventory of whooping cough vaccine is on hand and placing an order. She is paid approximately $17 an hour. The cost of capital for the centre is 8 percent per year, and the storage cost (including the use of freezers) is estimated to also be approximately 8 percent of item cost per year. A lot of 10 whooping cough vaccines costs an average of $160.[9] **LO3-5**

a. Calculate the EOQ for whooping cough vaccines.
b. Suppose that the purchase lead time is two days and daily demand for whooping cough vaccines is Normally distributed with a mean of seven vaccines and a standard deviation of two vaccines. Calculate the reorder point if lead time service level of 98 percent is desired.
c. Suppose that the office manager wants to make the replenishment of whooping cough vaccines easier for herself by ordering them every two weeks.

---

[9] D. M. Burns, M. J. Cote, and S. L. Tucker, "Inventory Analysis of a Pediatric Care Center," *Hospital Materiel Management Quarterly* 22(3), pp. 84–90.

i. Using the information in part *b*, what should the order up to level (I_{max}) be?

ii. Suppose that the Centre has 34 whooping cough vaccines on hand and none on order. What should the order quantity be, given your answer to part *i*?

47. The owner of a health food store has decided to intentionally allow shortage of a food supplement. The annual demand is 500 bottles, the ordering cost is $10 per order, and the holding cost is $1 per bottle per year. Cost of back-ordering one bottle is estimated to be $10 per bottle per year.

a. What should be the order quantity? **LO3**

b. How many bottles should be short per order cycle?

*48. Hallmark sells "personal expression" cards and gifts worldwide through either its own stores or other retailers. Most products are single runs. Unsold products are either discounted and sold to discount retailers, or are discarded.

A typical problem Hallmark faces is as follows: A Barbie Stationary Gift set, containing 16 notes, envelopes, and foil seals, is to be produced and marketed to celebrate the 55th year of Barbie. The price will be set at $12.99 per unit. The cost of production to Hallmark will be approximately $6 per unit. The product manager, based on previous sales of Barbie stationery products, estimates that demand and its probability for this product will be as follows:

Demand (in 1000s)	90	100	110	120	130
Probability	.1	.2	.4	.2	.1

Any units not sold through regular channels will be sold to discount retailers at $1 less than cost (i.e., $5 per unit). There is no penalty cost for being short. Determine the optimal order quantity for the Barbie Stationery Gift set.[10] **LO6**

*49. Teck (Cominco)[11] is a Canadian metal mining and processing company with new investments in coal and oil. The company has several warehouses in Western Canada that store thousands of parts and supplies for the machines and equipment used in its mines and operations. The stocks in the warehouses are controlled using computers in the Vancouver head office. For spare parts, the EOQ/ROP model is used.

The following data is the usage of specific spare part during a nine-month period:

Jan	Feb	Mar	Apr	May	Jun	Jul	Aug	Sep
2	5	10	4	12	0	8	16	4

Suppose that now is the end of September and the next reorder point is coming up. The forecast for October is

6.7 units. The part costs Teck $15/unit. Holding cost rate is 20 percent of unit cost per year. Ordering cost is $2/order (due to EDI connection with the supplier). Purchase lead time for this part is 20 days. Assume 30 days in a month. **LO3 & 4**

a. What should the EOQ be? *Hint:* Use the forecast for October × 12 to estimate next year's demand.

b. For how many days is the EOQ enough (i.e., what is order cycle for EOQ)?

c. Calculate the total annual inventory control cost of the EOQ.

d. Suppose now this part is ordered 7 at a time. How much more expensive is this?

e. Suppose there was no variability in demand or lead time. Determine the reorder point.

f. Suppose a 95 percent lead time service level is required. The standard deviation of monthly demand = 5.14 units. Determine the reorder point.

*50. Federated Cooperatives Limited (FCL) is the largest wholesaler/distributor of food and hardware in Western Canada. Until three years ago, for managing inventories FCL used the Inforem forecasting and inventory control software on its mainframe computer but has now switched to JDA (Manugistics) Demand and JDA (Manugistics) Order Optimization. FCL uses fixed-interval model to order products for its four warehouses. Many of the order review intervals are predetermined by vendors (weekly or biweekly). As an illustration, consider the ordering of Energizer batteries for the Calgary warehouse. The purchase lead time is approximately 15 days. For simplicity, suppose that there are only two types of Energizer batteries in the warehouse: Item #0378422CA, 6V Lantern battery with annual demand of 5,767 units and price of $3.85 each, and Item #0378539CA, 6V Lantern battery with annual demand of 603 units and price of $7.54 each. **LO5**

a. Suppose that the fixed cost of a purchase order for one SKU is $3.50 and the variable cost of each additional line item (SKU) is $0.50. Also, suppose that holding cost rate is 20 percent of unit cost per year. Determine the optimal order interval.

b. The forecast demand for Item #0378422CA is 138 units per week for the next few weeks and the standard deviation of demand is estimated to be 37 units per week. Currently there are 555 units on hand in the warehouse and none are on order. The service level for this SKU is desired to be 98.5 percent. Calculate the I_{max} (order up to level) for this battery, and determine the quantity to order.

---

[10] Based on F. H. Barron, "Payoff Matrices Pay off at Hallmark," *Interfaces* 15(4), pp. 20–25.
[11] K. B. Hustwick and J. W. Merkley, "Cominco's Computerized Inventory Control System," *Canadian Institute of Mining Bulletin*, 75(843), 136–141.

c. If the weekly demand forecast for Item #0378422CA for the next five weeks was in fact 144.2, 144.2, 133.1, 133.1, and 122 units, respectively (i.e., this item has seasonality), how would your answer to part b change? Assume that the standard deviation of demand remains at 37 units per week.

*51. Sterling Pulp Chemicals (ERCO) in Saskatoon produces chemicals for processing wood pulp, such as caustic soda. In its maintenance stockroom, it keeps all the spare parts for its equipment as well as supplies such as light bulbs. For inventory control, it uses the Min/Max model, which is basically the EOQ/ROP model. Every day, the inventory staff is supposed to use the computer system to identify those stocks that have reached their Min (ROP) level and to order those items. For illustration, consider the usage of item #14-46-506: four-foot supersaver fluorescent light bulbs in the first ten months of a year: 10, 10, 66, 32, 34, 18, 24, 9, 14, and 48. The forecast for November using Exponential Smoothing with $\alpha = .3$ is 27.48 units, and the standard deviation of monthly demand for these bulbs is 18.84 units. The lead time from the supplier, EECOL Electric, is 14 days, and the unit cost is $1.40. Holding cost rate for Sterling is estimated to be 20 percent of unit cost per year and ordering cost is $1 per order (because usually many items are ordered from the supplier together). Assume 30 days in a month. **LO3–5**

a. Calculate the EOQ for this item. (*Hint:* estimate $D =$ forecast for November $\times$ 12.)

b. For how many months is the EOQ enough (i.e., its order cycle)?

c. Calculate the total annual inventory control cost of the EOQ.

d. Now this part is ordered 30 units at a time. How much more costly is this?

e. Calculate the reorder point of these bulbs. Use a 97.5 percent lead time service level.

f. Given the noncriticality of this item, the new stockroom manager has suggested that it be reviewed only once a month. Calculate the Min and Max in this case. Use a 97.5 percent service level.

*52. The usage of Male Cord End (#14-20-391), purchased from EECOL Electric Ltd, by Sterling Pulp Chemicals (ERCO) during the June to October period of a year was 5, 1, 5, 9, and 8 units. Using Exponential Smoothing with $\alpha = .5$, the forecast usage for November is 7.25 units, and the standard deviation of monthly usage, using the above numbers, is 3.13 units. The price of one unit is $2.48. Suppose Sterling uses 20 percent as its holding cost rate per year, purchase lead time is approximately 14 days, and desired lead time service level is 97.5 percent. Assume 30 days in a month. **LO3–5**

a. If this item is ordered individually using the EOQ/ROP model, and ordering cost is $1 per order, calculate the EOQ and ROP for it.

b. If this item is ordered using Min/Max and it is reviewed only once a month, determine the Min and Max.

c. Suppose Sterling uses the fixed-interval model and orders the Eagle Male Cord Ends jointly with other SKUs supplied by EECOL Electric. For simplicity, assume that there is only one other SKU, item #14-20-390, Eagle Female Cord End. The forecast for usage of Eagle Female Cord End for November is 2.23 units. The price of a female cord end is $5.06. The ordering cost per purchase order for one SKU is $3 and for another line item is $.50.

   i. Calculate the optimal order interval.

   ii. If currently there are 13 units of Male Cord End on hand and none on order, how many should be ordered now?

*53. A franchisee of Fuddruckers, a hamburger restaurant chain, has signed a contract to supply food for a day-long music festival. Fuddruckers distinguishes itself from other hamburger restaurant chains with on-premise butcher shop and bakery. It is now the Wednesday before the Saturday festival. Approximately 5,000 tickets have been sold so far, and this number should increase because the weather forecast is that Saturday will be sunny. Based on previous experience, the manager believes that the eventual number of people who will attend the festival, and the associated probabilities, are: **LO6**

Numbers	6,000	7,000	8,000	9,000	10,000
Probability	.1	.2	.4	.2	.1

The manager expects that on average, each person will eat one meal during the seven-hour festival. She has decided to limit the menu to just two meals: one-third-pound burgers and quarter-pound hot dogs. She estimates, based on regular restaurant sales, that 60 percent of people will buy the burger and 40 percent will buy the hotdog. The cost of one burger will be $2.25 and it will sell for $5, whereas the hot dog will cost $1.34 and will sell for $4 each. Unused food has to be discarded, and there is no penalty for being short. The meat, hot dogs, buns, and vegetables need to be ordered today (three days before the festival so that the shipment will arrive on the day of the festival). Determine the optimal order quantities for burgers and hotdogs.[12] **LO6**

54. A distributor orders four products from a supplier. The fixed cost to place an order for one SKU is $23, and cost of each additional SKU added to the order is $3. The carrying cost rate is 24 percent per year. Purchase lead time is 1 week. Assume a 50-week year. The annual demand (units) and unit cost of the four SKUs are:

SKU	Annual demand	Unit cost
1	450	$8
2	2,000	12.50
3	200	3.52
4	3,000	33.30

The distributor wishes to use the coordinated periodic review model to plan ordering these SKUs. Calculate the multiples m_js and the optimal order interval OI*. **LO5**

*55. Schaan Healthcare Products is a distributor of medical/surgical products in Saskatchewan. Schaan has a warehouse in Saskatoon that carries thousands of items, one of which is item #345-5870, Micro-Touch Surgical Glove, size 7. The demand for this item (in cases) during a September to November period was 25, 57, and 50, respectively. Schaan's inventory manager uses a three-month moving average to forecast next month's demand for the items. The three-month moving average forecast for December's demand for size 7 gloves is 44 cases. Suppose that he uses the EOQ/ROP model to replenish this item. The surgical gloves are purchased from Ansell Limited in cases of 200 units at a cost of $120 per case. Using the three-month moving average forecast for December, ordering cost of $15 per order, inventory holding cost rate of 15 percent per year, and purchase lead time of two days, **LO3–5**

a. Calculate the EOQ for this item (rounded to a whole number).

b. Calculate the total annual holding and ordering cost if order quantity is 30 cases.

c. Using lead time service level of 96 percent and standard deviation of monthly demand of 16.82 cases, calculate the ROP (rounded to a whole number).

d. In fact, Schaan uses the fixed-interval model for replenishing this item. Calculate the order up to level (I_{max}) for this item (rounded to a whole number) if it is ordered every two weeks and the desired service level is 94 percent.

*56. A wholesale bottler and distributor of both imported and domestic alcoholic drinks purchases half its spirits in barrels, which it then blends and bottles (approximately 60 different types of spirit in up to 5 different bottle sizes). The most time-consuming activity is the changeover of the bottling line for a different bottle size. This takes one full day. Therefore, products that have the same bottle size are bottled one batch after another, saving the bottle-size changeover time (however, there is a smaller setup time for spirit, bottle, and label changeover). ROP of the 1-litre (L) bottles is set to one month of demand because they are usually bottled once a month. Each time, approximately 10 different spirits are run, one after another. The actual bottling time is negligible (only 2 days for all 10 spirits). Management wants the bottling batch size of each spirit to be equal to its EOQ. Note that because production rate is so much faster than the demand rate, we can use the EOQ formula instead of the Economic Production Quantity formula.

Suppose now is the beginning of June, and there is going to be a changeover to the 1-L bottles tomorrow. The on-hand inventory of the 1-L bottles of vodka is only 144 cases, whereas the demand forecast of this SKU in June is 312 cases. Assume that the demand has no trend or seasonality. The setup cost per bottle run for vodka is $73.23. The cost per case of vodka is $29.31. The carrying cost rate is 15 percent of unit cost per year. **LO3 & 4**

a. Calculate the optimal batch size (i.e., EOQ) for 1-L bottles of vodka.

b. After talking to the supervisor, it became clear that he does not use the EOQ to determine the batch size. Instead he produces enough 1-L bottles of a spirit so that this quantity plus any on-hand inventory is expected to last until the next production run for 1-L bottles, which is one month later. However, for items with uncertain demand such as vodka, he produces a quantity that, together with any on-hand inventory, is expected to meet two months of demand. Assuming that the standard deviation of monthly demand for vodka is 98 cases, what service level is the supervisor implicitly using?

*57. A high-end skiwear producer makes parkas for men, women, juniors, and preschoolers. For each "gender," there are tens of styles, and for each style approximately five colours and four sizes. This results in hundreds of parka SKUs for each "gender." This large variety plus the long lead time from design to distribution make the production planning of the skiwear producer very difficult. **LO6**

The design starts in February, concepts are finalized by May, prototypes are made by July, designs are finalized by September, first-half production quantity is determined and fabrics are ordered by November, fabrics are received and production starts by February of next year, retailers place their orders by March, shipments of products arrive from manufacturers in Asia by July, retailers receive their orders by August, sales pick up by December, and unsold goods are discounted by February of the third year.

It is now November and the VP of operations has to decide on the first-half production quantities. The buying committee has met and each of the six members forecasted the first-half demand for the parkas. For each parka, the VP has averaged these forecasts and calculated the standard deviation. To be more conservative, he has doubled the standard deviation.

As an illustration, a specific women's parka has average forecast value of 2,150 units and standard deviation of 807 units (after doubling). Assume a Normal distribution for the demand. Each parka will be sold for $173 to retailers. The unit cost will be approximately $130. If any parkas are left after January two years later, they will be sold at $115 each. Determine the best production quantity for this parka.

*58. A commercial laundromat products manufacturer wants to consolidate the purchase of all the cardboard boxes it needs for the detergents, bleaches, and fabric softeners it sells to laundromats. The total demand for all these boxes is 10,000 units per year (a unit = 1,000 packages). Assume that ordering cost is $50 per order and holding cost rate is 20 percent per year. Competitive bids have been solicited for this purchase. The following unit prices and the associated order quantity ranges are proposed by the most competitive bidder. If this bidder is chosen, what should the order quantity for the boxes? **LO3**

Order Quantity Range	Unit Price
1–500 units	$29.50
501–750	26.87
751–1500	24.77
1,501–2,000	23.93

59. Bike Friday is a small manufacturer of high-end folding travel bicycles. The bikes can be folded and carried in a Travelcase. The controller of Bike Friday is looking into ways to cut costs. The company purchases the Travelcases in lot sizes of 100, at a unit price of $65 plus $4.50 for shipping expense. A lot would last a little more than one month. The purchase lead time is six to eight weeks. The controller has discovered that if the company ordered a full truckload of 500 Travelcases at a time, the unit price will be $50 plus $2.50 for shipping

expense. However, Bike Friday would need a bigger storage space (350 square feet) which was not available in-house. Assuming that a nearby storage space could be leased for $400 a month, holding cost rate of 20 percent per unit per year, and ordering cost of $50 per order, determine if buying a truckload of Travelcases would have a lower total cost.[13] **LO3**

60. A grain elevator not only buys grains from nearby farmers but also sells them seeds and chemicals. But how much of each item will be sold in a given year is uncertain, making the decision on the purchase quantity difficult. Consider the ordering of a particular herbicide by a specific grain elevator manager. Each unit weighs 50 kg. The selling price is $56.93 per unit, and the purchase cost (including the transportation cost) is $45.54. Any excess herbicide after the growing season is transported to a warehouse at the cost of $1.09 per unit, and held over winter at the holding cost rate of 10 percent of unit cost per year (= 5% for half a year–approximate length of winter). It is estimated that 10 percent of shortage will be lost. The rest will incur $2.19 per unit in expediting cost from the supplier. The elevator manager estimates that the demand for this herbicide can take values 100, 400, and 1,500 units with probabilities of .1, .5, and .4, respectively. What is the best stocking level?[14] **LO6**

 MINI-CASE

Cameco Promotional Items

Audrey Blondeau is in charge of the promotional (gift) items of Cameco, one of the largest uranium producers in the World. Promotional items are items such as a mug or a T-shirt with a company logo on it. Located in Investor, Corporate, and Government Relations, Audrey receives requests for gift items from supervisors and employees of Cameco for special events and also from local charities for donation of gifts.

Audrey had no system in place for both receiving orders from the employees and for ordering the approximately 190 items her office carried. Most items are purchased from Impact Marketing (http://www.impactmarketing.ca) which will inscribe the company logo on the items. The reasons for carrying inventory are that the supplier requires a minimum order quantity, a setup charge (depending on the type of item), and a lead time of two weeks for producing an item. Large orders from supervisors,

(continued)

[13] G. A. Horsfall, "How to Leverage a Bad Inventory Situation," *Hospital Materiel Management Quarterly* 20(2), pp. 40–46; http://www.bikefriday.com.
[14] Based on D. J. Raby et al., "Inventory Management of Chemical Supplies at Alberta Wheat Pool," *Production and Inventory Management Journal* 32(1), pp. 1–6.

over the minimum, are passed directly to the supplier for production. The supplier needs artwork approval for new items. The donation requests have to be approved for a budget and are met mostly from slow-moving stocked items.

To improve efficiency, Audrey created a simple employee request form and reduced the number of items she carried to 40. She also added 11 new items to replace old models of popular items such as a mug, a bottle, and a bag. Audrey is also trying to make her job easier by establishing a fixed-interval system with order interval of two months for the promotional items. She has collected the demand (from Cameco employees) for the promotional items during the last few months and has estimated the average monthly demand for the next few months and the standard deviation of monthly demand for the items. First she is focusing on all-season items. Seasonal items such as golf balls and fleece vests will be replenished just before the season. Consider, for example, the following all-season items:

Item	Avg. monthly demand	Standard dev. of monthly demand	On hand	Min order quantity
Executive Sports Bag	12	4	0	25
Retro Stainless Steel Mug	15	2	4	60
Lava Pen	35	6	16	75
Heavyweight Brushed Cotton Cap	60	6	6	72

a. Calculate the order up to level and the order quantity for these items. Audrey thinks that a lead time service level of 70 percent is adequate as large orders are passed to the supplier and the requisitioner is willing to wait two weeks.

b. In case of the Heavyweight Brushed Cotton Cap, the supplier is offering the quantity discounts on the right. If carrying cost rate is 12 percent per year and set up cost is $50 per setup, how many units should Audrey order?

Quantity range	Unit price
72–143	$8.75
144–239	$7.95
240–575	$7.50

Source: Audrey Blondeau, "Cameco's Promotional Item System: Employee Ordering" (term paper), Dec. 2006. COMM 205.

MINI-CASE

Cameco Mine Supplies

Conor Shirley is a Materials Management (MM) intern in the Supply Chain Management department of Cameco, one of the largest uranium producers in the world. Cameco has three mines (Rabbit Lake, MacArthur River, and Cigar Lake) and a mill (Key Lake), all in Northern Saskatchewan. Each site has a warehouse containing supplies and spare parts. The data is maintained by the SAP software, which runs on a computer located in Cameco's head office in Saskatoon.

There are approximately 30,000 SKUs. Over 80 percent are bought from contracted suppliers. The inventory control module uses the Min/Max model. SAP checks the inventory position against the Min level every three days, and, if it is below, will automatically order enough stocks from contracted suppliers to bring inventory position up to the Max. A major initiative by the MM group is to reduce inventories by $10 million. This include re-adjusting the Min and Max levels to their optimal levels.

Conor has picked 4 SKUs from 2 plants to study. He is wondering if the Min/Max values have been set correctly. The item code, description, price, and lead time from the supplier are as follows:

Code	Description	Price	Lead time	Current Min	Current Max
20050008	Cable Hanger CAB826	$ 2.99	5 days	151	250
20073791	Grinding Wheel 5" ¼" 5/8" All Metal	$ 4.57	6	31	50
20126073	Pyrolon Coveralls XL Blue w/ HD Elastic	$ 8.05	8	4	75
20013742	Oil Pressure Gauge 2-1/2" 0-200 PSI	$44.75	14	1	3

Ordering cost per order is $10, holding cost rate per year is 20 percent, and lead time service level is 97.5 percent.

The monthly total usage for each item during 2013 were as follows:

Month	Cable Hanger	Grinding Wheel	Coveralls	Oil Pressure Gauge
Jan	0	44	3	0
Feb	150	57	1	0
Mar	75	61	0	0
Apr	100	28	0	0
May	0	102	26	0
Jun	0	53	0	0
Jul	100	97	26	0
Aug	75	27	25	0
Sep	0	27	66	0
Oct	0	74	9	0
Nov	0	31	0	0
Dec	0	25	2	0

Conor has noticed that the demand for Cable hanger and Coveralls is lumpy (there are many 0 usage months) and that Normal distribution may be inappropriate for determining the Min or ROP. Therefore, he has also collected dates and quantities of transactions for these two items:

Cable Hanger

Posting Date	Quantity
Feb 8	25
Feb 18	25
Feb 23	100
Mar 14	25
Mar 14	25
Mar 26	25
Apr 4	25
Apr 5	25
Apr 13	25
Apr 25	25
Jul 4	75
Jul 30	25
Aug 10	50
Aug 10	25

Coveralls

Posting Date	Quantity
Jan 6	2
Jan 21	1
Feb 14	1
May 19	1
May 23	25
Jul 6	2
Jul 7	10
Jul 10	14
Aug 17	25
Sep 1	2
Sep 2	2
Sep 2	2
Sep 3	6
Sep 8	50
Sep 18	2
Sep 23	2
Oct 1	9
Dec 7	2

OPERATIONS TOUR

The McGraw-Hill Ryerson Warehouse in Whitby, Ontario

The 85,000 ft² MHR warehouse in Whitby, Ontario, stores approximately 25,000 stock keeping units (SKUs). Approximately 80 percent of inventory is located in the bulk storage area. These are in full boxes on wooden pallets, located on approximately 7,000 racks. The racks have 5 levels, separated by very narrow aisles (see area A on the layout diagram and Photo 1). The remaining 20 percent of inventory is kept in the loose-book pick areas on easily accessible shelves within reach of order-pickers (areas B on the layout diagram).

(continued)

Photo 1: Bulk storage area (with manager Kathleen Ayow).

Photo 2: Loose-book pick area (with powered roller conveyor and shelves on both sides).

As shipments of books arrive from a book printer in the receiving/shipping staging area (area F on the layout diagram), they are entered in the computer system, which issues a rack location in the bulk storage area, and the lot is carried there by a lift truck. Full pallets are placed on first, fourth, and fifth levels of racking. Less than full pallets—up to 8 full boxes—are stored in the second- and third-level racks.

The loose-book pick areas are periodically replenished from the bulk storage area when the inventory of a SKU decreases and books are required to fulfill an order.

As a bookstore places an order, a packing list and a shipping label (see Photo 3) are printed. The shipping label contains a bar code and also indicates the type/size of box to be used, the pick locations, ISBN, and quantity. Once the right size of box is selected (one of eight sizes) in the dispatcher's work station, the shipping label is attached.

Photo 3: A packing list (to be inserted inside the box).

Photo 4: A bar code reader reads the shipping label on the box and diverts the box as necessary.

Using an RF (radio frequency) device, a picker scans the shipping label bar code, which directs her to the pick location. At the pick location, she picks the book and scans the check digit for verification. Then, she places the book in the box, and places the box on the powered roller conveyor (shown by two parallel lines to the right of areas B in the layout diagram). As the box moves on the conveyor, an optical character reader reads the label on the box and diverts the box to any other relevant loose-book pick aisles (Photo 4).

The conveyor continues to quality control (area C, Photo 5) where the box is scanned and checked by the weigh-in-motion scale for any "no-reads" (missed books). Here, a diverted box is checked for accuracy and the books are checked to ensure that they are in good saleable condition before shipping. If required, the box is then diverted to the pricing area (area D) where the list price is checked and the book is stickered. Then, the box continues to packing where it is packed and sealed (area E, Photo 6) and then to shipping (area F, Photo 7).

Photo 5: This is the quality control area where the boxes are checked for accuracy of item and quantity and to ensure books are in good saleable condition.

Photo 6: An employee fills a box with packing fillers made of recycled paper. Then the box is taped shut automatically.

(continued)

Photo 7: The shipping area (loose book shelves in the background).

If the order is large, full boxes containing the ordered books are picked up from the bulk storage area by a lift truck (see Photos 8 and 9), and the boxes are moved to the shipping staging area (area F on the layout diagram).

Photo 8: A Raymond turret truck is raised to pick up a pallet from a top rack

Photo 9: The truck driver retrieves a pallet of boxes of books for shipment.

The movement of each lift truck through the aisles is made safer and easier by an electronic guiding system (see Photo 10). The system electronically locks into a wire that runs along the centre of each aisle and keeps the truck centred as it moves (this prevents collision with the racks).

Photo 10: The electronic guiding system (the black box between the front wheels of the truck) and the wire embedded in the floor in front of it.

Area G on the layout diagram is for the returned books (also see Photo 11). Here, boxes are opened, and books are checked and then moved to their shelves in the loose-book pick area.

Photo 11: The returns work centre.

The warehouse can fill an order in one day and order-picking productivity is approximately 100 SKUs per hour on average.

CHAPTER 13

Aggregate Operations Planning and Master Scheduling

Learning Objectives

After completing this chapter, you should be able to:

LO1 Explain what sales and operations planning and aggregate operations planning are, and identify the variables and strategies used in aggregate production planning.

LO2 Prepare a good aggregate production plan.

LO3 Prepare a good aggregate service plan.

LO4 Explain what master production scheduling is and how it is performed.

The electronics retail chain Future Shop, like most other retailers, sees a sharp increase in the number of customers just before the Christmas holiday season. Naturally, Future Shop needs to meet this demand when it occurs. In order to be prepared, Future Shop buyers forecast the demand months ahead and arrange with their suppliers to bring the right products in the right quantity into their distribution centres and over 140 stores across Canada. In addition, the Human Resources department centrally plans the excess employees needed during this period. Like most other retailers, Future Shop hires seasonal/temporary staff during Christmas holiday season. These are mostly technically savvy students. The six-week-long holiday recruiting period starts in the end of September. Between 4,000 and 5,000 seasonal employees are hired (40 percent of regular workforce). Social media such as Facebook and Twitter are used to reach potential employees. Training is four days for nonsales and two weeks for sales employees. Former seasonal employees are preferred as they relearn their job faster. Occasionally, overtime work is used as well. Clearly, planning is crucial for Future Shop, as it is for other companies facing seasonal demand. This is particularly challenging for some manufacturers that also need to decide whether to produce ahead of peak season and carry inventory or not. This is the subject of this chapter.

Source: S. Klie, "Social Media, Training Help with Holiday Hires," *Canadian HR Reporter*, November 1, 2010, 23, 19, pages 1, 9.

Introduction to Planning

LO1

Organizations usually make capacity and production decisions on three levels: long term, intermediate term, and short term. Long-term decisions relate to products selection, facility size and location, major equipment decisions, and layout of facilities. These long-term decisions essentially define the capacity constraints within which intermediate planning must function. Intermediate decisions relate to general levels of employment, output, and inventories, which in turn define the boundaries within which short-term capacity and production decisions must be made. Short-term decisions involve master production scheduling (MPS): material requirements planning (MRP): and scheduling jobs, workers, and equipment. The three levels of capacity and production decisions are depicted in Figure 13-1. This chapter covers intermediate capacity and production decisions, as well as MPS. These decisions are usually made in the context of an activity called Sales and Operations Planning.

Sales and Operations Planning

sales and operations planning Process of integrating sales forecasts with operations plans.

Sales and operations planning (S&OP) is the process of integrating sales forecasts with operations plans. It is usually performed once a year with monthly updates (because near-term forecasts are more accurate). The information is at an aggregate (product family) level. The process must reconcile all supply, demand, and new-product plans at the aggregate level and tie them to the strategic plan. S&OP is for the intermediate term (usually the next 12 months), covering a horizon sufficient to plan for workforce and production changes. Figure 13-2 shows the hierarchy of production planning and the position of S&OP in it. This chapter covers the operations (or aggregate) planning and master scheduling. Material requirements planning will be covered in Chapter 14, and detailed planning/scheduling and execution systems in Chapter 16.

Figure 13-1

Overview of planning levels (chapter numbers are shown).

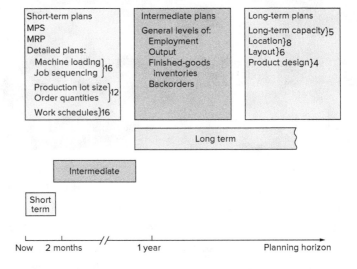

The process of updating S&OP begins with recording the sales, production, and inventory levels of the previous month, updating forecasts for the next 12 months or so, seeing if the necessary production changes are feasible, and providing a summary of information to top management for making decisions.

The monthly process used by the S&OP team of Ingersoll-Rand (a diversified industrial manufacturer of air conditioners, pumps, compressors, etc.) is as follows:

Demand planning

    Day 1: Prepare sales data; perform baseline forecasts

    Day 3: Gather field intelligence (salespeople info)

    Day 7: Regional managers review forecasts and possibly modify them

Supply planning

    Days 11–15: Review forecasts, compare with capacity, identify constraints, and develop countermeasures

Partnership meeting

> Day 16: Functional managers review and approve the forecasts, evaluate performance measures, analyze financial impact, work out some issues, and identify actions to balance demand & supply

Executive meeting

> Day 18: Understand and react to misalignments, resolve remaining issues, approve one set of numbers, authorize actions to achieve the forecast

Source: http://www.apics.org/industry-content-research/publications/apics-magazine/apics-magazine—landing-page—everyone/2013/09/09/s-op-step-by-step.

In the executive/top management meeting, the executives have time only to review a summary of sales, production, and inventory plans of a limited number (e.g., six to eight) families of products. An example of the summary information for a product family is shown in Figure 13-3. In Location A, the target file rate of 99 percent and finished goods inventory target of 10 days of supply are shown. Note that for make-to-stock products, the company needs to keep safety stocks of finished goods to meet demand variability. The level of finished goods inventory directly affects customer service level through fill rate.

Locations B and E show the old forecast sales for the past three months, and old and new (after update) forecasts for the next six months and the two quarters after that. Locations C and F show the operations plan and the actual production during the past three months, and the old and new (after update) production plan for the next six months and two quarters after that. Locations D and G show the inventory plan and the actual levels during the past three months, and the projected inventory levels resulting from the given forecasts and production plans (and the equivalent days of supply) during the next six months and two quarters after that. Also shown are fill rate performance during the past three months. Finally, in Locations H and J, any major demand and production issues are pointed out.

See the "Red Wing Shoes' Journey to S&OP" OM in Action for details of the transformation process Red Wing Shoes underwent to set up an effective S&OP process.

Aggregate operations planning is monthly planning for sum of all the products in the same family (produced in the same facility) for the next 12 months or so. It is particularly useful for organizations that experience seasonal fluctuations in demand. The goal of aggregate operations planning is to achieve a production plan that will satisfy total forecast demand at minimum cost. Planners must make decisions on employment levels and changes, production levels and changes, and the resulting inventory levels.

The Concept of Aggregation

In aggregate operations planning, planners focus on a group of similar products, or sometimes an entire product line. For example, planners in an ice cream plant would not concern themselves with flavours and brands of ice cream. Instead, planners would lump all tubs (containers) of the same size together and deal with them as though they were a single product, e.g., 2-litre tub of ice cream; hence, the term *aggregate*. If the products are very different, a typical product is chosen and all other products are represented in equivalent units of the chosen product. For example, if an ice cream line can make 2,000 11.4-litre tubs or 17,000 2-litre tubs per 8-hour shift, then an 11.4-litre tub is equivalent to 17,000/2,000 = 8.5 2-litre tubs.

Another example is space allocation in a department store. A manager might decide to allocate 40 percent of the available space in the clothing department to women's wear, 30 percent to juniors, and so on, without regard for what brand names will be offered or how much of juniors will be pants. The aggregate measure or equivalent unit might be racks of clothing.

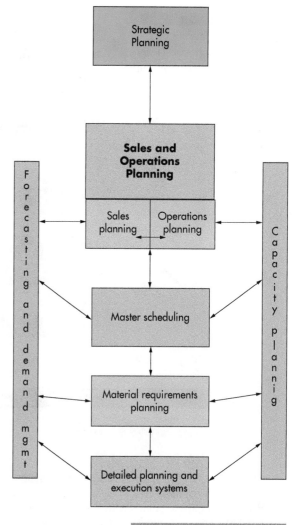

▲ **Figure 13-2**

Production planning hierarchy.

aggregate operations planning Monthly planning for sum of all the products in the same family (produced in the same facility) for the next 12 months or so.

Figure 13-3

An example of the summary information for a product family used in the top management S&OP meeting.

The ACME Widget Company — Sales & Operations plan for October 2015

Family: Medium Widgets (make-to-stock)
Target line fill: 99%
A
Unit of measure: 000 units
Target fin inv: 10 days

B Sales — History

Sales	J	A	S
Old forecast	200	200	200
New forecast			
New vs. old FCST			
Actual sales	222	195	227
Diff: month	22	−5	27
cum		17	44

E

	O	N	D	J	F	M	3rd 3 Mos	4th 3 Mos	Next 12 months	Latest call	Business plan
Old forecast	200	200	200	200	200	200	660	660	2,520	$25,540	$25,400
New forecast	210	210	210	210	210	210	690	690	2,640		
New vs. old FCST	10	10	10	10	10	10	30	30	120		

(Fiscal Year: Latest call / Business plan)

C Operations

Operations			
Old plan	200	200	200
New plan			
New vs. old plan			
Actual	200	205	199
Diff: month	0	5	−1
cum		5	4

F

	O	N	D	J	F	M	3rd 3 Mos	4th 3 Mos	Next 12 months
Old plan	210	210	200	200	200	220	660	660	2,540
New plan	210	220	220	220	220	220	690	690	
New vs. old plan		10	20	20	20		30	30	

D Inventory

Inventory			
Plan	100	100	100
Actual	78	88	60
Days supply	8	10	6
Line fill %	97%	98%	89%

G

	O	N	D	J	F	M	3rd 3 Mos	4th 3 Mos
Plan	60	70	80	90	100	110	110	110
Days supply	6	7	8	9	10	12	11	11

H Demand issues and assumptions
1. Forecast reflects launch of new designer widget line in 3rd qtr.
2. Asia forecasted to reach 2014 volume

J Supply issues
1. Xmas full plant shutdown rescheduled to staggered partials thru fall and winter

---

OM in ACTION

Red Wing Shoes' Journey to S&OP

Red Wing Shoes (RWS) is a private company founded over 100 years ago. It manufactures (in eight locations) and distributes (from six DCs) six brands of tough work boots and shoes (26,000 SKUs) and apparel (72,000 SKUs), globally. RWS is somewhat vertically integrated in that it has its own leather tannery, boot/shoe manufacturing plants, and few retail stores, but also has suppliers (especially for apparel) and mainly sells through other retailers such as Marks Work Wearhouse.

Before 2008, there was no integrated S&OP in RWS. A planner from the supply chain department and a representative of new product development collected and entered huge amount of data in Excel, and made a 12-month forecast for each SKU based on the previous-year's actual sales. The planner updated the forecasts monthly by taking the actual sales out of the forecasts, without talking to sales managers to identify the causes for forecast discrepancy. Data collection and entry in Excel were manual and required two weeks. The forecasts were not communicated to the manufacturing plants or suppliers, but instead work orders and purchase orders for immediate needs were issued. Huge amounts of excess inventory were stored in trailers, resulting in significant demurrage charges.

Then in 2008, RWS hired a process improvement manager. She embarked on creating an effective S&OP process. By 2009, she had involved 12 representatives of sales of each brand, product development, manufacturing, supply chain, and a senior executive. The meetings (once every two months) were long and looked at past performance rather than future plans. In 2010, she got the IT department to create the sales data spreadsheets automatically from RWS's ERP. This saved two weeks and prevented errors of data entry and worksheet setup. It also provided a longer history of sales. In 2011, she convinced senior management to create a demand planning department that is responsible for creation of sales forecasts. They communicate with brand managers, find the reasons for forecast discrepancies, oversee data collection and forecasting, and adjust forecasts. Also, the once-every-two-months long meeting was divided into smaller/shorter functional meetings every month: first, sales forecasts are generated, then they are approved by sales managers and next by the VP of Business Services, all in the first week of a month. Then the forecasts are transmitted to the supply chain (SC) department that checks their production/distribution feasibility; next, a consensus meeting between sales and SC occurs by the end of second week; and finally the executive review meeting (involving the president and all VPs) occurs by the third week. In 2012, a forecasting and replenishment software (Logility) was purchased and installed, reducing the forecasting work and improving the accuracy of forecasts. Staff were also trained in statistical techniques and the use of the software.

The results are a shorter and more effective S&OP process, better forecasts, forecast management by exception, shared forecasts and collaboration with manufacturing and suppliers, 27 percent reduction in inventory, 8–10 percent increase in customer fill rate, and 50 percent reduction in demurrage charges.

Source: http://www.scmr.com/plus/SCMR1405_F_RedWing.pdf.

For labour-intensive services, a common aggregate measure or equivalent unit is full-time equivalent (FTE) of workforce. For example, a half-time worker (working 20 hours a week) is counted as 0.5 FTE.

In each of these examples, an aggregate approach permits managers to make general decisions about intermediate-term capacity and production levels without having to deal with highly specific details.

Demand and Capacity Options

Management has a wide range of decision options at its disposal for sales and operations planning. These include demand-influencing actions such as changing prices, promotion, early orders, backorders, exporting, producing complementary products during off-season, and capacity-influencing actions such as hiring temporary workers, using overtime/idle time, hiring part-time workers, stockpiling inventories, and subcontracting.

Demand Options. The basic demand options, usually handled by marketing, are:

1. *Pricing.* Pricing differentials are commonly used to shift demand from peak periods to off-peak periods. For example, air fares are cheaper in the September to November period than in December.

2. *Promotion.* Advertising and other forms of promotion, such as displays, direct marketing, and extending the payment period, can sometimes be effective in shifting demand so that it conforms more closely to capacity.

3. Early orders. It might be possible to convince customers to place their order (may be an initial partial order) before the peak season.

4. *Backorders.* A company can shift demand to future periods by using backorders. That is, orders are taken in one period and deliveries promised for a later period. The success of this approach depends on how willing customers are to wait for delivery. Moreover, the costs associated with backorders include lost sales, annoyed or disappointed customers, and additional paperwork. Backorders can be thought of as negative inventory. Make-to-order companies carry an "inventory" of (back) orders as opposed to finished-goods inventory that is carried by make-to-stock companies. A form of backorder is the appointment system, which is an acceptable way to regulate demand in services such as health care.

5. *Exporting.* It might be possible to export excess production during the off-season to the Southern hemisphere, e.g., Australia or Brazil, where the temperature cycle is the reverse.

6. *Complementary products.* Manufacturers that experience seasonal demands for certain products (e.g., snow blowers) are sometimes able to develop a demand for a complementary product (e.g., lawn mowers) that makes use of their resources during the off-season. The same is true for air conditioners and heaters.

Capacity Options. The basic capacity options are:

1. *Hiring temporary workers.* Organizations may hire a limited number of temporary full-time workers (who work 40 hours a week). The nature of the operation determines the impact that changes in the workforce level will have on capacity. For instance, if a factory usually uses 10 of its 14 production lines, crews for additional lines (up to 4 lines) could be added on a temporary basis during peak season.

    Furthermore, a company can add or reduce the number of shifts. For example, instead of working 8 hours a day (i.e., one shift), a company can double its workforce on a temporary basis and operate in two shifts (i.e., work 16 hours a day) during peak season.

    Union contracts may restrict the number of temporary workers a company can hire. Also, hiring presumes an available supply of temporary workers. Another consideration is the skill level of workers. Highly skilled temporary workers are difficult to find.

    Hiring temporary workers entails certain costs. Hiring costs include screening, recruitment, and training costs to bring new temp workers "up to speed." And quality may suffer. Some savings may occur if workers who have recently worked for the organization are rehired.

Three Cases of Aggregate Plans

A Fridge Plant

This plant produces 3 brands of fridges in 15 sizes (models) and 3 colours. Summer months' sales are 20 percent higher than winter months, and there is a peak in November for Christmas sales. Monthly forecast sales for the next 12 months are aggregated at the brand level. There are two assembly lines that work one shift per workday. Holidays are two weeks in Christmas and two weeks in July. The company uses a chase demand strategy because fridges are large and expensive. The union has agreed that 25 percent of workforce can be temporary, on a three-month contract. A new hire needs two to three days of training. Overtime is used only for emergencies.

A Chocolate Plant

This plant produces Easter eggs and Christmas chocolate novelties (300 SKUs). Therefore, the periods before Easter and Christmas are the busy periods (Easter is busier). There are several chocolate tanks, moulding machines, and foiling/wrapping machines. Change of chocolate type is very time consuming (one to four shifts). The company produces chocolate for Christmas based on forecasts in May and June, and based on firm orders in July and August. Similarly, for Easter, initial production is in September to November based on forecasts, and in December to February based on firm orders. The

permanent employment is 120 to 140 workers (on two shifts but not all lines running). However, during the busiest months, October to January, up to 120 to 140 temporary workers on 4- to 50-week contracts are employed on a third shift. The training period is short. Overtime is used for new product trials and emergencies.

An Air Conditioner and Gas Heater Manufacturer

These products are highly seasonal. The company originally made air conditioners (ACs) but bought a gas-heater producer nearby to complement its production. Two of six AC assembly lines can switch from ACs to heaters. When needed, the company uses casual workers who need only three hours of training in the assembly area. Jobs are rotated daily in order to increase the flexibility of workers for reassignment to bottleneck operations. The plants are closed two weeks in Christmas, one week in April or June, and one week in September or October, depending on product demand. Forecast error is very high, so 1–2.5 months' worth of safety stocks are kept. Planners create rolling "rough-cut" monthly business plans for the next 12 months. Overtime is used as a last resort.

Source: G. Buxey, "Aggregate Planning for Seasonal Demand: Reconciling Theory with Practice," *International Journal of Operations & Production Management*, 25(11), pp. 1083–1100.

2. *Using overtime/idle time.* Overtime and idle time (i.e., nonproductive employment or slack time), usually of permanent workers, can be implemented easily and quickly. Organizations use idle time for training, performing maintenance, problem solving, and process improvement. Overtime (i.e., working longer than 40 hours a week) permits the employees to increase their earnings (overtime pay is usually 1.5 times the regular-time pay).

   On the other hand, overtime often results in lower productivity, poorer quality, more accidents, and increased payroll costs, and idle time results in less efficient use of resources. Overtime is usually used to meet unexpected demand.

3. *Hiring part-time workers.* In many instances, the use of part-time workers is a viable option—much depends on the nature of the work, training and skills needed, and union agreement. Part-time workers, such as high school students, typically work 20 hours a week or less, and usually do not receive fringe benefits such as dental insurance. Part-time workers are usually temporary.

4. *Stockpiling inventories.* The use of finished-goods inventories allows companies to produce goods in one period and sell them in a future period. Holding cost includes not only storage costs and the cost of money tied up in inventory, but also the cost of obsolescence, spoilage, and so on. Inventories can be built up during periods when production capacity exceeds demand and drawn down in periods when demand exceeds production capacity. This method is suitable for make-to-stock manufacturing.

5. *Subcontracting.* Subcontracting is asking another company to make the product or part of it. Subcontracting is like employing temporary workers but the work is done off-premise. Subcontracting may be cheaper than in-house production, however it has the disadvantages of outsourcing/buying: reduction in control and possibly quality issues. Conversely, in periods of excess capacity, an organization may subcontract in, that is, conduct work for another organization.

For three applications of demand and capacity options, see "Three Cases of Aggregate Plans" OM in Action.

Inputs to and Outputs from Aggregate Operations Planning

Effective aggregate operations planning requires good *information*. First, the production rates for various labour schemes (e.g., 40 hours a week regular time and 10 hours of overtime) must be known, and forecasts of demand must be available. Then planners must take into account company policies; for example, regarding changes in employment levels (e.g., some unions limit the number of temp workers). Costs of various variables should also be determined.

The output of aggregate planning is the level of production (output), which is determined from the level of employment, and in turn determines the amount of inventory at the end of each period. All these contribute to the total cost of the plan.

Table 13-1 lists the major inputs to and outputs from aggregate operations planning.

Inputs	Outputs
Resources	Total cost of the plan
Production rates (capacity) for various labour schemes	Projected levels of
Warehouse (inventory) capacity	Inventory
Demand forecasts	Output
Policy statements	Employment
Overtime (maximum)	
Maximum temporary/part-time workers	
Inventory levels (initial, safety stocks, desired ending)	
Costs	
Inventory holding	
Backorder	
Hiring	
Wage rates (permanent, temp, part time)	
Overtime	

◀ Table 13-1

Aggregate operation planning inputs and outputs.

Basic Aggregate Planning Strategies

In this section, we will concentrate on the capacity options.

A company might adopt one of the following aggregate planning strategies:

1. Maintain level output/workforce.
2. Change output to match demand period by period.
3. Use a combination.

Under the **level output/workforce strategy**, a steady rate of output and workforce is maintained while variations in forecast demand and changes in required safety stocks are met by using seasonal inventories. This strategy uses a fixed number of permanent workers that is equal to the average full-time worker requirements during the planning horizon (e.g., next 12 months) or longer. Level output/workforce strategy assumes that products have a long shelf life. This is true for some products such as durable goods, but not for others such as ice cream (which has a freezer life of three months).

Matching output to demand is **chase demand strategy**; the planned output for any period is equal to forecast of demand and changes in required safety stocks for that period. Chase demand strategy uses a smaller number of permanent workers and meets peak demand using a combination of part-time/temporary workers, subcontracting, and overtime.

A major advantage of chase demand strategy is that no inventories are carried, which can yield substantial savings for an organization. Service organizations that cannot regulate their demand have to use chase demand strategy. For an application of chase demand strategy, see the "Lands' End" OM in Action later in the chapter.

level output/workforce strategy Maintaining a steady rate of output and workforce while meeting variations in demand and changes in required safety stocks by inventories.

chase demand strategy Matching output to demand; the planned output for any period is set at the forecast of demand and required changes in safety stocks for that period.

Figure 13-4 illustrates the two strategies, using a seasonally varying demand pattern to highlight the differences in the two approaches.

A mixed strategy uses a combination of the decision variables, e.g., a company can have two levels of output, low in off-season and high in peak season, and also use overtime, temporary workers, and inventory buildup.

Choosing an Aggregate Planning Strategy. Whatever strategy a company is considering, two important factors are *company policy* and *costs*. Company policy may set constraints on the available options or the extent to which they can be used. For instance, company policy may require that no less than 70 percent of personnel (measured as full-time equivalent) should be permanent. Union agreements often impose restrictions. For example, a union contract may specify maximum numbers of weeks or months temporary workers can be used.

As a rule, aggregate planners seek to match supply and demand within the constraints imposed on them by policies or agreements and at minimum total cost. They usually evaluate alternative feasible aggregate plans in terms of their overall costs. In the next section, two techniques for aggregate production planning are described.

Techniques for Aggregate Production Planning

Two different approaches are used for determining the aggregate plan: trial-and-error and optimization. In practice, trail-and-error is used more frequently.

A general procedure for aggregate production planning consists of the following steps:

1. Determine product groups that can be aggregated (the fewer the better).
2. Determine the total demand forecast for each product group in each period of the planning horizon (e.g., next 12 months).
3. Identify a set of feasible labour schemes so that total production meets or exceeds the total demand and the required safety stocks for all product groups in each period. For example, use 1 shift (40 hours a week) during January–May and August–December and 2 shifts (80 hours a week) during June and July.
4. Determine the total labour and inventory holding cost of the plan obtained in Step 3, and repeat Steps 3 and 4 looking for a lower total cost.

If optimization is used, the software will automatically find the lowest total cost feasible plan, i.e., will perform Steps 3 and 4 repeatedly until the lowest-cost plan is obtained.

Trial-and-Error

Trial-and-error consists of developing simple tables/worksheets or graphs that enable managers to determine the production levels that meet projected demand requirements and safety stocks. The chief disadvantage of such techniques is that they do not necessarily result in the optimal (i.e., lowest total cost) aggregate plan.

Very often, graphs can be used to guide the development of alternative aggregate production plans. The obvious advantage of a graph is that it provides a visual portrayal of a production plan. Some planners prefer cumulative graphs while others prefer to see a period-by-period breakdown of a production plan (Figure 13-4 is an example of two period-by-period graphs). Figure 13-5A shows a cumulative graph for a production plan with level output (the slope of the dashed line represents the production rate) and seasonal inventory (the vertical difference between cumulative production and cumulative demand at any period) absorbing demand variations. Figure 13-5B is a cumulative graph used by Blue Bell (Wrangler) jeans (now part of VF Corp.) for a product line (e.g., men's corduroy jeans). Note that the cumulative demand is padded by safety stocks, seasonal inventory is called Build-up stock, and Target inventory is the sum of the two. The cumulative production line is chosen so that it meets the cumulative demand plus safety stock up to any month in the planning horizon. In this case, September of next year determines the slope of the cumulative production line, which is linear, indicating a level output/workforce strategy.

The three examples below illustrate the development and comparison of simple aggregate plans using tables/worksheets. In the first example, output/workforce is held level, with backorder

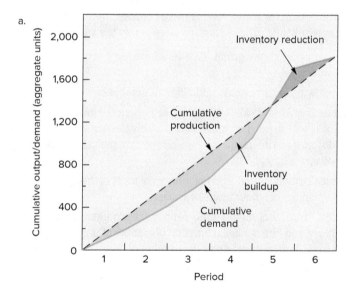

a.

Figure 13-5A

A cumulative graph for level output/workforce strategy.

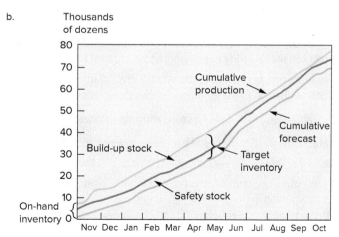

b.

Figure 13-5B

A cumulative graph for level output/workforce strategy used by Blue Bell (Wrangler).

Lands' End

Lands' End is a major phone/mail/Internet-order distributor of clothing and sewn goods located in the small town of Dodgeville, Wisconsin (population 4,000). Sales of Lands' End peak in November and December each year, much like other retailers, due to the holiday shopping season. Lands' End does 40 percent of its business during the fourth quarter. The number of inquiries received jumps from 40,000 a day to more than 100,000 on the busiest days. During the other three quarters, there is also some variation in sales. Lands' End employs customer sales workers (for orders), warehouse workers, and sewers who perform alterations. Lands' End employs approximately 3,500 permanent and 1,000 part-time workers year-round. How does the company meet its excess demand for labour hours during November and December? First, it employs approximately 2,000 more temporary full-time and part-time workers. The supply of part-time temporary workers

comes from high school, college, and university students who can work a six-hour shift after school (three times a week), and the supply of full-time temporary workers comes from some local cheese factories who end their busy season in October. Second, Lands' End encourages its workers to cross-train so that they can work in other jobs when they are needed (called job sharing). Third, employees can work extended schedules during November and December, up to 12 hours a day (the portion above eight hours is performed in a different department and is considered overtime). Approximately one-third of temporary workers return to work for Lands' End again the following year or later. A new hire receives six hours of orientation/training, but a rehire may receive only up to two hours of retraining.

Sources: J. J. Laabs, "Strategic Holiday Staffing at Lands' End," *Personnel Journal* 73(12), pp. 28ff; K. Haegele, "Gearing Up for the Holiday Rush," *Target Marketing* 23(6), pp. 44–48ff.

absorbing demand increases. In the second example, backorder is prevented by the use of overtime. The third example is similar, but uses temporary workers instead of overtime.

These and other examples and problems in this chapter are based on the following assumptions (unless otherwise stated). These assumptions simplify the analysis and calculations.

1. There is only one aggregate group. That is, all products can be represented in terms of an equivalent unit.

2. No allowance is made for holidays and different number of workdays in different months.

3. No allowance is made for safety stocks for each period. However, manufacturers can hold seasonal stocks and there is an initial and possibly desired end-of-planning-horizon inventory. In addition, backorders are allowed during any period but are cleared by the end of planning horizon.

4. We represent all production in terms of number of units of the aggregate measure (equivalent unit), not the number of labour hours or workers.

5. The total cost for each of regular time permanent production, overtime production, backorder, inventory, and hire is a linear function of number of units of the aggregate product; that is, it equals a constant unit cost times the number of units of the aggregate product.

6. The production of an equivalent unit can be associated to one worker in terms of hours it will take and labour cost. Hence, unit cost of labour (to make one equivalent unit) can be calculated using the wage rate and number of hours each equivalent unit will take a worker to make.

7. The hiring cost per unit is the hiring cost per worker divided by the number of equivalent units a worker can make during one period, and is charged to the first period of employment.

8. Inventory holding cost is charged to the average level of inventory held during a period, but backorder cost is charged to the amount of backorders carried to the next period.

The following relationships are used in calculating inventories in each period.

1. To determine the Ending inventory or backorder in any period i, first calculate X:

$$X = \text{Beginning inventory}_i + (\text{Output} - \text{Forecast})_i - \text{Backorder}_{i-1},$$

where Output is the sum of regular permanent, overtime, and part-time/temporary/subcontract production.

If $X \geq 0$, then Ending inventory$_i$ = X and Backorder$_i$ = 0; whereas if $X < 0$, then Ending inventory$_i$ = 0 and Backorder$_i$ = −X.

2. The average inventory for a period is equal to (Beginning inventory + Ending inventory)/2.

3. Beginning inventory$_i$ = Ending inventory$_{i-1}$

Planners for a company that makes garden tractors are about to prepare an aggregate production plan that will cover the next six months. They have assembled the following information for an aggregate unit:

◀ **Example 1**

Month	1	2	3	4	5	6	Total
Forecast demand	2,000	2,000	3,000	4,000	5,000	2,000	18,000

Permanent workforce = 140

Production per month = 2,800 units or 20 per worker

Initial inventory = 1,000 units

Desired ending inventory at the end of 6th month = 1,000 units

Costs

  Output (labour)

    Regular time permanent = $100 per tractor

    Overtime = $150 per tractor

    Temporary = $100 per tractor

  Hire cost = $500 per temporary worker or $25 (= $500/20 units) per unit (charged to the first month of employment); we have assumed that temp workers have the same productivity as permanent workers.

  Inventory = $10 per tractor per month (charged on the average inventory level)

  Backorder = $150 per tractor per month

They now want to evaluate a production plan that calls for level output/workforce (with the current level of permanent workforce, 140), using inventory to absorb the uneven forecast demand but allowing some backorder. They start with 1,000 units of inventory on hand in the first month and wish to end with the same amount. Prepare an aggregate production plan and determine its total cost.

The total regular-time output of permanent workers per month is 2,800 units. The filled worksheet for this level output/workforce strategy is shown below. The computations are explained after the worksheet.

SOLUTION

Month	1	2	3	4	5	6	Total
Forecast Demand	2,000	2,000	3,000	4,000	5,000	2,000	18,000
Output							
Regular permanent	2,800	2,800	2,800	2,800	2,800	2,800	16,800
Temporary	–	–	–	–	–	–	
Overtime	–	–	–	–	–	–	
Output − Forecast	800	800	−200	−1,200	−2,200	800	−1,200
Inventory							
Beginning	1,000	1,800	2,600	2,400	1,200	0	
Ending	1,800	2,600	2,400	1,200	0	0	
Average	1,400	2,200	2,500	1,800	600	0	8,500
Backorder	0	0	0	0	1,000	200	1,200
Costs							
Output (labour)							
Regular perm (at $100/unit)	$280,000	280,000	280,000	280,000	280,000	280,000	$1,680,000
Temporary (at $100/unit)	–	–	–	–	–	–	
Overtime (at $150/unit)	–	–	–	–	–	–	
Hire temporary (at $25/unit)	–	–	–	–	–	–	
Inventory (at $10/unit/month)	$14,000	22,000	25,000	18,000	6,000	0	$85,000
Backorder (at $150/unit/month)	$0	0	0	0	150,000	30,000	$180,000
Total cost	$294,000	302,000	305,000	298,000	436,000	310,000	$1,945,000

Starting with month 1, $(\text{Output} - \text{Forecast})_1 = 2{,}800 - 2{,}000 = 800$,

$$\begin{aligned}
X &= \text{Beginning inventory}_1 + (\text{Output} - \text{Forecast})_1 - \text{Backorder}_0 \\
&= 1{,}000 + 800 - 0 \\
&= 1{,}800.
\end{aligned}$$

Therefore, Ending inventory$_1$ = 1,800 and Backorder$_1$ = 0. Also,

$$\begin{aligned}
\text{Average inventory}_1 &= (\text{Beginning inventory}_1 + \text{Ending inventory}_1)/2 \\
&= (1{,}000 + 1{,}800)/2 \\
&= 1{,}400.
\end{aligned}$$

Then, Beginning inventory$_2$ = Ending inventory$_1$ = 1,800. Continue with the same formulas, but note that in month 5,

$$\begin{aligned}
X &= \text{Beginning inventory}_5 + (\text{Output} - \text{Forecast})_5 - \text{Backorder}_4 \\
&= 1{,}200 + (-2{,}200) - 0 = -1{,}000.
\end{aligned}$$

Therefore, Ending inventory$_5$ = 0 and Backorder$_5$ = $-(-1{,}000)$ = 1,000. Also, in month 6,

$$\begin{aligned}
X &= \text{Beginning inventory}_6 + (\text{Output} - \text{Forecast})_6 - \text{Backorder}_5 \\
&= 0 + 800 - 1{,}000 \\
&= -200.
\end{aligned}$$

Therefore, Ending inventory$_6$ = 0 and Backorder$_6$ = 200.

The costs were computed as follows. Regular permanent cost in each month equals 2,800 units × $100 per unit, or $280,000. Inventory holding cost equals average inventory × $10 per unit. Backorder cost is $150 per unit times the number of backorders. The total cost for this plan (either sum the row totals of costs or sum the column totals of costs) is $1,945,000.

Example 2 ▶

After reviewing the plan developed in the preceding example, planners noticed the large number of backorders in month 5 (1,000 units) and month 6 (200). Furthermore, the desired month-6 ending inventory of 1,000 units is not realized. Therefore, output has to increase by a total of 1,200 units during the planning horizon (the difference between total Forecast and total Regular permanent output, leaving the same amount of ending inventory as the initial inventory). The planners decided to investigate the use of overtime to make up for this shortage. It is the policy of the company that the maximum amount of overtime output per month be 400 units. Develop an aggregate production plan in this case and compare it to the previous plan.

SOLUTION

The 1,200 units to be produced during overtime must be scheduled on and before month 5 (when shortage or backorder starts to occur). Scheduling it earlier would increase inventory holding costs ($10/unit/month); scheduling it later would incur backorder cost ($150/unit/month), which is larger. That is why the maximum permitted overtime production should be used in months 3 to 5. The completed worksheet is given below.

Month	1	2	3	4	5	6	Total
Forecast	2,000	2,000	3,000	4,000	5,000	2,000	18,000
Output							
Regular permanent	2,800	2,800	2,800	2,800	2,800	2,800	16,800
Temporary	—	—	—	—	—	—	
Overtime	—	—	400	400	400	—	1,200
Output − Forecast	800	800	200	−800	−1,800	800	0
Inventory							
Beginning	1,000	1,800	2,600	2,800	2,000	200	
Ending	1,800	2,600	2,800	2,000	200	1,000	
Average	1,400	2,200	2,700	2,400	1,100	600	10,400
Backorder	0	0	0	0	0	0	0
Costs							
Output (labour)							
Regular perm (at $100/unit)	$280,000	280,000	280,000	280,000	280,000	280,000	$1,680,000
Temporary (at $100/unit)	0	0	0	0	0	0	0

(continued)

Month	1	2	3	4	5	6	Total
Overtime (at $150/unit)	—	—	60,000	60,000	60,000	—	180,000
Hire temporary (at $25/unit)	—	—	—	—	—	—	
Inventory (at $10/unit/month)	14,000	22,000	27,000	24,000	11,000	6,000	$104,000
Backorder (at $150/unit/month)	$0	0	0	0	0	0	0
Total cost	$294,000	302,000	367,000	364,000	351,000	286,000	$1,964,000

Note that, even though plan 2 has a larger total cost than plan 1, it produces 1,200 more units and leaves 1,000 units at the end of month 6.

Alternatively, the company can use temporary workers to meet the 1,200 units short. The unit cost of temporary-worker production ($100) is lower than unit cost of overtime production ($150), but there is a per unit hire cost of $25 for units produced during the first month of employment. Overall, using temporary workers is less costly than using overtime.

A third option is to use temporary workers during months of high demand. Suppose that temporary workers will be working during a second shift and enough of them are available. Develop an aggregate production plan in this case.

◀ Example 3

SOLUTION

Dividing the number of units needed (1,200) by the output rate of 20 per temporary worker, you find that 60 temporary worker-months are needed (e.g., 60 temporary workers for 1 month each, or 30 temporary workers for two months each, or 20 temporary workers for three months each, etc.).

Therefore, the planners tried each of the alternatives, i.e., hiring 60 temporary workers in month 5 on a one-month contract, or hiring 30 temporary workers in month 4 on a two-month contract, or hiring 20 temporary workers in month 3 on a three-month contract, and so on. The plan with the lowest total cost, including inventory carrying cost, hires temporary workers in month 4 on a two-month contract. Later, we will describe a trade-off analysis which can assist us in determining the cheapest alternative without actually completing the worksheet for each alternative. The completed worksheet for hiring 30 temporary workers in month 4 on a two-month contract is given below. Note that the hiring cost applies to only the first month of employment.

Month	1	2	3	4	5	6	Total
Forecast	2,000	2,000	3,000	4,000	5,000	2,000	18,000
Output							
Regular permanent	2,800	2,800	2,800	2,800	2,800	2,800	16,800
Temporary				600	600		1,200
Overtime	—	—	—	—	—	—	
Output Forecast	800	800	−200	−600	−1,600	800	0
Inventory							
Beginning	1,000	1,800	2,600	2,400	1,800	200	
Ending	1,800	2,600	2,400	1,800	200	1,000	
Average	1,400	2,200	2,500	2,100	1,000	600	9,800
Backorder	0	0	0	0	0	0	0
Costs							
Output (labour)							
Regular perm (at $100/unit)	$280,000	280,000	280,000	280,000	280,000	280,000	$1,680,000
Temporary (at $100/unit)				60,000	60,000		$120,000
Overtime (at $150/unit)	—	—	—	—	—	—	
Hire temporary (at $25/unit)	$0	0	0	15,000	0	0	$15,000
Inventory (at $10/unit/month)	$14,000	22,000	25,000	21,000	10,000	6,000	$98,000
Backorder (at $150/unit/month)	$0	0	0	0	0	0	0
Total cost	$294,000	302,000	305,000	376,000	350,000	286,000	$1,913,000

Overall, the total cost for this plan ($1,913,000) seems to be the lowest possible, i.e., this plan seems to be optimal.

Procedure for Trial-and-Error. From the three examples above, it is evident that one should follow the following steps to obtain a low-cost aggregate plan:

- Determine the production output by permanent workers (during regular time) for each period.
- Determine total units short if only permanent workers are used during regular-time, and the periods short.
- Determine the cheapest way (using the trade-off analysis, described below) to meet the units short in periods short, e.g.,
  - Hire temporary and/or part-time workers.
  - Use permanent workers during overtime.

Trade-off Analysis. It is possible to use the unit costs of labour, inventory, and backorder in trade-off analyses in order to make good production planning decisions, without having to recalculate the total plan cost. Let's look at some of the decisions we made in the above three examples. In Example 2, overtime should be used in the months when backorders will occur and, if more overtime production is needed, in the month(s) before them, not after, because backorder cost per unit ($150) is larger than inventory holding cost per unit ($10). Also, because holding inventory costs money, overtime should be used as close to the months with backorder as possible. Therefore, our decision to produce the maximum of 400 units in each of the 3rd, 4th, and 5th month during overtime.

Trade-off analysis would have been able to save us the trouble of even considering the second plan. This is because the cost of a unit made during overtime is $150, whereas the cost of a unit made by a temporary worker (employed say for one month) is less ($100 + hiring cost/number of units produced in a month = $100 + $500/20 = $125).

Another example is the question of how to use the temporary workers in the third plan. Consider, for example, employing 60 temporary workers for one month in month 5 versus 30 temporary workers for two months starting in month 4. As derived above, the cost of a unit produced by a temporary worker employed for one month is $125. However, the cost of a unit produced by a temporary worker employed for two months is in effect only $100 + $500/(20 × 2) = $112.50. However, because a unit needs to be carried in inventory for one month (from 4th to 5th month), its total unit cost is $112.50 + $10 = $122.50, which is still < $125. Therefore, using 30 temporary workers for two months starting in month 4 is cheaper than using 60 temporary workers for one month in month 5.

Now consider employing 20 temporary workers for three months starting month 2. The cost of a unit produced by a temporary worker employed for three months is in effect only $100 + $500/(20 × 3) = $108.33. However, because a unit needs to be carried in inventory for two months (from 3rd to 5th month), its total unit cost is $108.33 + 2(10) = 128.33, which is > $125. Therefore, using 20 temporary workers for three months starting in month 2 is more expensive than using 30 temporary workers for two months starting in month 3.

The following example further illustrates the trade-off analysis.

Example 4[1]

A food company makes puddings in a plant. It sells the puddings in cases (a case contains 48 pudding cups). The plant has 15 parallel production lines. The regular operating hours are 8 hours a day, 5 days a week, 13 weeks a quarter. Each line is automated but needs 6 workers to operate it and can produce 200 units of output (each unit = 1,000 cases) per quarter. Currently, only 11 production lines are used, for a total quarterly output of 2,200 units. The sales department has forecasted total demand for all flavours of puddings for the next five quarters as follows: 2,000, 2,200, 2,500, 2,700, and 2,200 units, respectively. Currently, there are no puddings, other than some safety stocks, in the warehouse. The company can increase production by hiring groups of six workers at a time, i.e., by opening one to four additional production lines. Hiring one worker costs approximately $2,000. Each worker is paid an average of $19.23 per hour. Overtime costs 1.5 times regular-time wage, and is limited to 20 percent of regular-time production in any quarter.

---

[1] Based on Bradford Manufacturing case in F. R. Jacobs, R. B. Chase, and N. J. Aquilano, *Operations & Supply Chain Management*, 12th ed. (New York: McGraw Hill/Irwin, 2009), pp. 541–542.

Holding inventory of a unit for a quarter will cost $50 (charged on the average level of inventory in the quarter). Backorder per unit per quarter is estimated to cost $200.

a. Determine all the relevant unit costs.

b. If the current number of workers is kept for the next five quarters, how many units will the company be short of at the end of Quarter 5?

c. Meet the forecast demands at minimum cost by

  i. Adding another production line.

  ii. Adding any number of production lines and/or using overtime.

You may use trade-off analysis to limit the number of plans considered.

SOLUTION

a. Labour cost per unit during regular time

  = Labour cost of one line for one quarter ÷ production of the line in the quarter

  = # of workers for the line × cost per worker per quarter ÷ 200

  = 6 × wage per hour × hours per quarter ÷ 200

  = 6 × \$19.23 × hours per day × days per week × weeks per quarter ÷ 200

  = 6 × \$19.23 × 8 × 5 × 13 ÷ 200

  = 299.99 round to \$300

Labour cost per unit during overtime

  = 1.5 × regular time cost

  = 1.5 × \$300 = \$450

Hiring cost per unit (charged to the first quarter employed)

  = Hiring cost per worker × number of workers per line ÷ production per line per quarter

  = \$2,000 × 6 ÷ 200

  = \$60

b. Number short at the end of Quarter 5

  = total demand forecasts − 5 × regular production per quarter

  = 11,600 − 5 (2,200)

  = 600 units

c. i. The 12th production line should work three quarters because the number short is 600 units (from part *b*) and the capacity of a line is 200 units per quarter. Note that the quarters with higher-than-average demand are Q3 and Q4. Therefore, the 12th production line should work during Q3 and Q4. It is evident that the 12th line should also work Q2 because holding a unit in inventory for two quarters (from Q2 to Q4) costs only 2 × \$50 = \$100 < \$200 = cost of backordering a unit from Q5 back to Q4. The completed worksheet is displayed below. Note that the output of the 12th production line is shown in the "Temporary" row.

Aggregate plan using an additional production line (Q2–Q4)

Quarter	1	2	3	4	5	Total
Forecast	2,000	2,200	2,500	2,700	2,200	11,600
Output						
Permanent	2,200	2,200	2,200	2,200	2,200	11,000
Temporary		200	200	200		600
Overtime						
Output—Forecast	200	200	−100	−300	0	0
Inventory						
Beginning	0	200	400	300	0	
Ending	200	400	300	0	0	
Average	100	300	350	150	0	900
Backorder	0	0	0	0	0	0

(continued)

Quarter	1	2	3	4	5	Total
Costs						
Permanent @ $300	660,000	660,000	660,000	660,000	660,000	3,300,000
Temporary @ $300	0	60,000	60,000	60,000	0	180,000
Overtime @ $450	0	0	0	0	0	0
Hire temporary/unit @ $60	0	12,000	0	0	0	12,000
Inventory @ $50	5,000	15,000	17,500	7,500	0	45,000
Backorder @ $200	0	0	0	0	0	0
Total	665,000	747,000	737,500	727,500	666,000	$3,537,000

ii. First we will show that using temporary workers is cheaper than using overtime:

Cost of a unit made by a temporary worker hired and laid off after one quarter = $300 + $60 = $360 < $450 = cost of a unit produced by a permanent worker during overtime.

Now, one way to reduce the total cost of the plan determined in part c_i above is to use two extra production lines during Q4. This will produce 400 units. To produce the remaining 200 units needed, it is clear that we need to start one of these two lines in Q3. As you can see in the worksheet below, the total cost in this case is lower than the plan in c_i.

Aggregate plan using two additional production lines (Q4 and Q3–Q4)

Quarter	1	2	3	4	5	Total
Forecast	2,000	2,200	2,500	2,700	2,200	11,600
Output						
Permanent	2,200	2,200	2,200	2,200	2,200	11,000
Temporary			200	400		600
Overtime						0
Output − Forecast	200	0	−100	−100	0	0
Inventory						
Beginning	0	200	200	100	0	
Ending	200	200	100	0	0	
Average	100	200	150	50	0	500
Backorder	0	0	0	0	0	0
Costs						
Permanent @ $300	660,000	660,000	660,000	660,000	660,000	3,300,000
Temporary @ $300	0	0	60,000	120,000	0	180,000
Overtime @ $450	0	0	0	0	0	0
Hire temporary/unit @ $60	0	0	12,000	12,000	0	24,000
Inventory @ $50	5,000	10,000	7,500	2,500	0	25000
Backorder @ $200	0	0	0	0	0	0
Total	665,000	670,000	739,500	794,500	672,000	$3,529,000

Note that producing 400 units in Q3 and 200 units in Q4 by extra lines will increase the total cost because 200 more units have to be carried in inventory from Q3 to Q4. Also, producing 600 units in Q3 and nothing in Q4 by the extra lines will increase the total cost because 400 more units have to be carried in inventory from Q3 to Q4, in addition to $60 extra hiring cost per unit. Finally, producing nothing in Q3 and 600 units in Q4 by the extra lines will increase the total cost because 100 units have to be backordered from Q4 to Q3, in addition to $60 extra hiring cost per unit. Therefore, the above plan (in the worksheet) is optimal.

Optimization

Linear Programming Model. A variable is assigned to each of the number of hires and the number of layoffs, amount of overtime, ending inventory, and backorder in each period (e.g., month). All other unknown quantities are represented in terms of these variables. The total cost formula, consisting of the unit costs times the variables, is the linear objective function. Each relationship is represented as a linear equation or inequality constraint. Once the model is entered in a linear programming software, after some iterations, the optimal solution (the lowest cost feasible solution) is found (if it exists). Excel has an add-on program, called Solver, which solves linear programs. See the supplement to Chapter 6 for more information on linear programming.

Transportation Model. When there are no hirings or layoffs, the problem can be formulated as a transportation model, which is even simpler to solve than a linear programming model. See the supplement to Chapter 8 for more information on the transportation model. In order to use this approach, planners must identify capacity (i.e., maximum supply) of regular time, overtime, and part-time/temp, and demand for each period, as well as related costs of production and inventory.

Table 13-2 shows the notation and format of a transportation table for aggregate production planning. There are n (e.g., 12) set of production rows and n consumption (demand) columns. There is also a row for the beginning inventory (at the top) and a column for unused capacity (on the right). The production quantities, to be determined by the software, will be in each cell. Unit costs are in the little squares in the top right corner of each cell. Note the systematic way that costs change as you move across a row from left to right. Regular cost, overtime cost, and part-time/ temporary costs are at their lowest when the output is consumed (i.e., delivered) in the same month as it is produced. If goods are produced in one month but carried over to later months (i.e., moving across a row to the right), holding costs are incurred at the rate of h per month. Conversely, with backorders, the unit cost increases as you move across a row to the left. For instance, if some goods are produced in month 3 to satisfy backorders from month 2, a unit backorder cost of b is incurred. Unused capacity is generally given a unit cost of 0. Finally, beginning inventory is given a unit cost of 0 if it is used to satisfy demand in month 1. However, if it is held over for use in later months, a holding cost of h per unit is added for each month.

Consumption Month

		Month 1	Month 2	Month 3	. . .	Month n	Unused capacity	Capacity
	Beginning inventory	0	h	$2h$	. . .	nh	0	I_0
1	Regular time	r	$r+h$	$r+2h$	. . .	$r+nh$	0	R_1
	Overtime	t	$t+h$	$t+2h$	. . .	$t+nh$	0	O_1
	Part-time/temp	s	$s+h$	$s+2h$	. . .	$s+nh$	0	S_1
2	Regular time	$r+b$	r	$r+h$	. . .	$r+(n-1)h$	0	R_2
	Overtime	$t+b$	t	$t+h$	. . .	$t+(n-1)h$	0	O_2
	Part-time/temp	$s+b$	s	$s+h$	. . .	$s+(n-1)h$	0	S_2
3	Regular time	$r+2b$	$r+b$	r	. . .	$r+(n-2)h$	0	R_3
	Overtime	$t+2b$	$t+b$	t	. . .	$t+(n-2)h$	0	O_3
	Part-time/temp	$s+2b$	$s+b$	s	. . .	$s+(n-2)h$	0	S_3
	:	:	:	:	. . .	:	:	:
	Demand							Total

(Left side labels: Month / Production Month)

Table 13-2

Transportation model and notation for aggregate production planning.

Example 5 illustrates the format and final solution of a transportation model of an aggregate production planning problem.

Example 5 ▶

Given the following information, formulate the aggregate production planning problem as a transportation table and solve it:

	Month		
	1	2	3
Demand forecast	550	700	750
Capacity (maximum)			
Regular	500	500	500
Overtime	50	50	50
Part time	120	120	100
Beginning inventory	100		

Costs	
Regular time	$60 per unit
Overtime	$80 per unit
Part time	$90 per unit
Inventory holding cost	$1 per unit per month
Backorder cost	$3 per unit per month

SOLUTION

The transportation table and an optimal solution (using Excel's Solver) for the above problem are shown in Table 13-3.

Thus, the demand of 550 units in period 1 will be met using 100 units from beginning inventory and 450 units obtained from regular-time output in month 1. The 700 units demanded in month 2 is met by 50 units produced during regular time, 50 units during overtime, and 30 units of part time in month 1 all carried to month 2; and 500 units produced during regular time, 50 units during overtime, and 20 units of part time in month 2. The 750 units demanded in month 3 is met by 100 units of part time in month 2 carried to month 3, and 500 units produced during regular time, 50 units during overtime, and 100 units of part time in month 3. The total cost for this solution is $100(0) + 450(60) + 50(61) + 50(81) + 30(91) + 500(60) + 50(80) + 20(90) + 100(91) + 500(60) + 50(80) + 100(90) + 90(0) = \$124{,}730$.

Table 13-3 ▶

Transportation table and optimal solution for Example 5.

Supply from		Month 1	Month 2	Month 3	Unused capacity	Total capacity available (supply)
Month	Beginning inventory	[0] 100	[1]	[2]	[0]	100
1	Regular time	[60] 450	[61] 50	[62]	[0]	500
	Overtime	[80]	[81] 50	[82]	[0]	50
	Part-time	[90]	[91] 30	[92]	[0] 90	120
2	Regular time	[63]	[60] 500	[61]	[0]	500
	Overtime	[83]	[80] 50	[81]	[0]	50
	Part-time	[93]	[90] 20	[91] 100	[0]	120
3	Regular time	[66]	[63]	[60] 500	[0]	500
	Overtime	[86]	[83]	[80] 50	[0]	50
	Part-time	[96]	[93]	[90] 100	[0]	100
Demand		550	700	750	90	2,090

OM in ACTION

Banner Good Samaritan Medical Center

Banner Good Samaritan Medical Center, a 662-bed hospital, was in a difficult budgetary situation. Its nursing budget was based on level workforce (approximately 1,000 FTEs) throughout the year. Because there was little allowance for seasonality, the staff had idle time (approximately 20 percent) during summer months and the hospital employed temporary nurses, hired from external nursing agencies, during winter months. Overtime was also used in winter at 1.5 times regular wage rate plus a premium of $7 per hour. These arrangements cost the hospital a great deal. In addition, the nurses were reluctant to serve as floats, to be traded between units when there was a short-term imbalance in nurse requirements between units. Finally, when these extra costs reached $10 million, a consultant was hired to assist the new senior administrator for nursing. Data were gathered on patient days during the year, and a time standard was set for the nursing hours required per patient day. Five levels of work for registered nurses (RNs) were established. Level 1

RNs, comprising the majority of RNs, work only in one unit (do not float). The number of RNs in Level 1 was based on annual patient days divided by 365. Level 2 RNs, also full time, work in three to four units that share similar skill requirements and are used to meet increases in patient numbers or acuity. Level 2 RNs were paid $.75 per hour more. Level 3 RNs work in many units and are primarily per diem employees. They are used to fill in when regular RNs are sick or if help is needed during winter. Level 4 RNs are part-time, filling in shifts of two hours' duration. Level 5 RNs comprise external agency nurses. Further efforts to reduce the permanent nurses' availability in the summer months were instituted in the form of career enhancement programs and voluntary leaves of absence. The new staffing system was very successful. The cost of external agency temporary nurses and overtime declined to $2 million, flexibility increased, patient care improved, and nurses were happier.

Sources: S. Hollabaugh and S. Kendrick, "Staffing: The Five-Level Pyramid," *Nursing Management* 29(2), pp. 34–36; http://www.bannerhealth.com/Locations/Arizona/Banner+Good+Samaritan+Medical+Center/_Banner+Good+Samaritan+Medical+Center+Home.htm.

Where backorders are not permitted, the cell costs for the backorders can be made prohibitively high so that no backorders will appear in the optimal solution.

Aggregate Services Planning

Aggregate planning for production and aggregate planning for services share many similarities, but there are some important differences:

1. *Services occur when they are rendered.* Unlike goods, services can't be inventoried or backordered. Consequently, it becomes important to match capacity and demand during any month or quarter (i.e., we need to use the chase demand strategy).

2. For labour-intensive services, it may be easier to measure the aggregate plan in terms of time (e.g., hours) or number of workers (FTE) instead of an aggregate measure of output. See the "Banner Good Samaritan Medical Center" OM in Action and Example 6.

The director of nursing of a hospital needs to plan the nursing levels for each quarter of next year. She has forecasted the average number of patients per day in each of the hospital wards throughout each quarter of next year. Then she multiplied these numbers by 90 days a quarter × 24 hours a day and divided the result by the number of patients to be assigned to each nurse in each ward (e.g., three patients per nurse in intensive care, etc.) to obtain the aggregate forecast for hours of nursing required in each quarter. Finally, these are converted into number of full-time equivalent (FTE) nurses needed each quarter by dividing them by 480 hours per quarter, and rounding them to the nearest integer. These numbers are displayed as Forecast (FTE) in the following table. There are currently 140 permanent nurses, each working 480 hours a quarter, and being paid an average of $14 an hour. Overtime is allowed up to 50 percent of regular permanent FTEs and is compensated at 1.5 times the regular wage rate. Temporary nurses are available but hospital policy dictates that the maximum number of temporary nurses be at most 20 percent of permanent nurses. Temporary nurses are paid an average of $17 per hour, but no overtime is permitted. The hiring cost is $480 per temporary nurse. Being a service, no inventory or shortage (backorder) is permitted.

a. Determine all the relevant costs per FTE and fill them in the table below.

b. Suppose one temporary nurse is hired for one quarter. Would this be cheaper than using a permanent nurse during overtime?

c. Determine the minimum total cost (feasible) aggregate service plan, and fill the whole table.

SOLUTION

Note: The unit of product here is FTE of nursing service.

a. Regular permanent wages = $14/hour × 480 = $6,720 per quarter; temporary nurse wages = $17/hour × 480 = $8,160 per quarter; overtime wages = 1.5 × 6,720 = $10,080 per FTE per quarter. Hiring cost per temporary FTE (charged to the first quarter hired) is $480.

b. Cost per FTE of temporary nurse kept for a quarter = hire cost per nurse + wages = $480 + $8,160 = $8,640 < $10,080 = cost per FTE of overtime. Yes, using temporary nurses is cheaper than using permanent nurses during overtime.

c. Given the result in part *b*, use up to the maximum number of temporary nurses in each quarter so that total output (FTE) equals forecast (recall we cannot have inventory or shortage). Maximum number of temporary nurses = 0.20 × 140 = 28 FTE in any quarter. If there is any more need for nurses, we have to use permanent nurses during overtime. In this case, no overtime is necessary. The following aggregate service plan has minimum total cost and is feasible. Note that the hiring cost applies only when the number of temporary nurses in a quarter is larger than in the previous quarter, and it equals $480 × the difference.

Quarter	1	2	3	4	Total
Forecast (FTE)	167	150	158	165	
Output (FTE)					
Reg. perm.	140	140	140	140	
Temporary	27	10	18	25	
Overtime					
Costs per FTE					
Reg. perm. @ $6,720	940,800	940,800	940,800	940,800	3,763,200
Temporary @ $8,160	220,320	81,600	146,880	204,000	652,800
Overtime @ $10,080	0	0	0	0	0
Hire temporary @ $480	12,960	0	3,840	3,360	20,160
					$4,436,160

Because service capacity is perishable (e.g., an empty seat on an airplane can't be saved for use on another flight), aggregate planners need to take this fact into account when deciding how to match supply and demand. **Yield management** is an approach that seeks to maximize revenue by using a strategy of variable pricing; prices are set relative to capacity availability. Thus, during periods of low demand, price discounts are offered to attract a wider population. Conversely, during peak periods, higher prices are posted to take advantage of limited supply. Users of yield management include airlines, hotels, and resorts.

yield management The application of variable pricing strategy to allocate capacity based on capacity availability.

 Master Production Scheduling

For the aggregate production plan to be translated into meaningful terms for production, it is necessary to *disaggregate* it. This involves breaking down the aggregate production plan into specific product's production schedule.

For example, suppose a lawn mower manufacturer's aggregate production plan is to produce 200 lawn mowers in January, 300 in February, and 400 in March. The company produces various models of lawn mowers. Obviously, there are some differences in the materials, parts, and operations

Aggregate plan	Month Planned output*	Jan.	Feb.	Mar.
		200	300	400

*Aggregate units

Figure 13-6

Example of disaggregating an aggregate plan.

Master production schedule	Month Planned output*	Jan.	Feb.	Mar.
	Model A	100	100	100
	Model B	75	150	200
	Model C	25	50	100
	Total	200	300	400

*Actual units—need to further disaggregrate into weekly planned output.
It is assumed that all products are equivalent.

Figure 13-6

Example of disaggregating an aggregate plan.

that each model requires. Hence, the 200, 300, and 400 aggregate lawn mowers must be broken down into specific numbers of mowers of each model prior to actually scheduling operations and planning inventory requirements.

The result of disaggregating the aggregate plan is **master production schedule (MPS)**, which shows the anticipated build schedule expressed in the quantity (lot size) and timing of each product for the next 12 weeks or so. It should be noted that, whereas the aggregate plan covers an interval of, say, 12 months (i.e., intermediate term), the MPS covers only a portion of this (i.e., the short term). In other words, only the first three months or so of the aggregate plan is disaggregated. Moreover, the MPS must be updated weekly. Figure 13-6 illustrates the concept of disaggregating the aggregate plan for the lawn mower manufacturer. The process of determining the MPS is called *master scheduling*.

An important issue in master scheduling is the setup time involved for product changeover. These are wasted times and reduce the effective capacity of the production process. If the chosen lot sizes are smaller than assumed in aggregating planning, there will be more setup times leading to the need for more labour hours than planned for in aggregate planning. On the other hand, large lot sizes result in excess inventories and lower customer fill rates. The objective of master scheduling is to minimize the total inventory holding and setup cost subject to meeting each product's anticipated demand while not exceeding the capacity determined in the aggregate plan.

Once a *tentative* MPS has been developed, a planner can do **rough-cut capacity planning (RCCP)**, which converts the MPS into requirements for key resources in order to test the feasibility of a proposed MPS. This means checking capacities of production and warehouse facilities, labour, and vendors to ensure that no gross deficiencies exist that will render the MPS unworkable. Example 7 illustrates MPS and RCCP.

Alternatively, master scheduling can be done using linear programming (LP) which will automatically find an optimal feasible MPS, thus sparing us the trial-and-error process of using RCCP. See e.g., the "Kellogg's" OM in Action later.

In the following section, we will show how one product's production schedule is determined in master scheduling.

master production schedule (MPS) The anticipated build schedule expressed in the quantity (lot size) and timing of each product for the next 12 weeks or so.

rough-cut capacity planning Converting the MPS into requirements for key resources in order to test the feasibility of a proposed master production schedule.

Suppose similar products (x, y, and z) have the following demand forecasts for Jan and Feb:

Example 7

	Jan	Feb
x:	100	100
y:	80	160
z:	20	40

The company uses chase demand strategy, i.e., aggregate Plan is 200 units for Jan and 300 units for Feb.

A possible Master Production Schedule is:

Week	Jan 1	2	3	4	Feb 5	6	7	8
x:	25	25	25	25	25	25	25	25
y:	20	20	20	20	40	40	40	40
z:	20				20		20	

Note: It is not economical to produce very small batches of products; so produce 20 units of z at a time.

To see if this MPS is feasible, RCCP can be used as follows. Suppose there is only one (bottleneck) key machine, setup time = 1 hour and run time = 0.5 hour per unit of any product x, y, z. Then the load on the machine in each week (in hours) will be:

Week	Jan 1	2	3	4	Feb 5	6	7	8 ...
x:	1 + 25/2	1 + 25/2	1 + 25/2	1 + 25/2	1 + 25/2	1 + 25/2	1 + 25/2	1 + 25/2
y:	1 + 20/2	1 + 20/2	1 + 20/2	1 + 20/2	1 + 40/2	1 + 40/2	1 + 40/2	1 + 40/2
z:	1 + 20/2				1 + 20/2		1 + 20/2	
Hrs req'd	35.5	24.5	24.5	24.5	45.5*	34.5	45.5*	34.5
Planned	40	40	40	40	40	40	40	40

* In Weeks 5 and 7 this machine will be overloaded. Possible solutions include: Use OT, change MPS (e.g., produce more z in Jan).

MPS Inputs

Master scheduling has three inputs for each product: the beginning inventory, which is the quantity on hand from the preceding week; demand forecasts for each week of the schedule (next 12 weeks or so); and customer orders, which are quantities already *committed* to customers. We assume that production cycle time is small and a production order issued for a week will be received in the same week. Also, negative inventory represents backorders.

The master scheduler should work closely with the demand planner to obtain the (committed) customer order and forecast information, and to cooperatively determine the MPS.

Consider the following example. A company that makes industrial pumps wants to prepare a master production schedule for June and July. Marketing has forecasted demand of 120 pumps for June and 160 pumps for July for its major product. These will be evenly distributed over the four weeks in each month: 30 per week in June and 40 per week in July, as illustrated in Figure 13-7.

Now, suppose that there are currently 64 pumps on hand, and that there are some customer orders that have been committed (booked) and must be filled (see Figure 13-8).

MPS Outputs

Master scheduling has three outputs for each week for each product: projected inventory (at the end of the week), planned production, and the resulting uncommitted planned inventory, which is referred to as **available-to-promise (ATP) inventory**. Knowledge of the uncommitted (ATP) inventory can enable the sales department to make realistic promises to customers about deliveries of new orders.

available-to-promise (ATP) inventory Uncommitted planned inventory.

Figure 13-7 ▶

Weekly forecast demand for the pumps.

Weeks

	June 1	2	3	4	July 5	6	7	8
Forecast	30	30	30	30	40	40	40	40

Beginning inventory	Weeks							
	June				July			
64	**1**	**2**	**3**	**4**	**5**	**6**	**7**	**8**
Forecast	30	30	30	30	40	40	40	40
Customer orders (committed)	33	20	10	4	2			

◀ Figure 13-8

The table for the pump showing forecast and (committed) customer orders for the next eight weeks, and the beginning inventory.

 OM in *ACTION*   http://www.kellogs.com

Kellogg's

Kellogg's uses linear programming to perform both aggregate planning and master production scheduling. The Kellogg Planning System (KPS) was written in-house to plan production/packaging and distribution of Kellogg's products (hundreds of SKUs including 80 cereals). The operational version of KPS plans the next 30 weeks of production/packaging (approximately 90 production and 180 packaging lines in five Kellogg's plants in North America and 15 subcontractor or co-packer plants) and distribution (seven distribution centres, DCs) for master scheduling. The linear program minimizes the production, inventory, and transportation costs subject to safety stocks (equal to two weeks of demand or four weeks of demand if the item is being promoted) and meeting the

demand at the DCs. The solution is used by the plant managers to schedule their production lines and by the logistics managers to schedule their inventories and transportation. The tactical version of KPS plans the next 18 months of production/packaging and distribution for aggregate planning. However, the products are not aggregated in the software, but the results are aggregated manually to determine plant budgets, inventory spaces required in distribution centres, etc. KPS also facilitates what-if questions. For example, production of a product over time or in different plants can be combined if its batch sizes are small.

Sources: G. Brown et al., "The Kellogg Company Optimizes Production, Inventory, and Distribution," *Interfaces* 31(6), pp. 1–15; orms.yonsei.ac.kr/Yonsei/.../4_Kellogg Planning System.ppt.

The first step for each product is to calculate the projected on-hand inventory (at the end of the week), one week at a time, until it falls below a specified limit (safety stock). In the above example, the specified limit is assumed to be zero. Hence, we will continue until the projected on-hand inventory (at the end of the week) becomes negative.

The projected on-hand inventory (at the end of the week) is calculated as follows:

$$\text{Projected on-hand inventory} = \text{Inventory from previous week} - \text{Current week's requirements} \qquad (13\text{-}1)$$

where we use the convention that current week's requirements is the *larger* of forecast and customer orders (committed).

For the first week, projected on-hand inventory (at the end of the week) equals beginning inventory minus the larger of forecast and customer orders. Because customer orders (33) is larger than the forecast (30), the customer orders amount is used. Thus, for the first week, we obtain:

Projected on-hand inventory (at the end of the week) = 64 − 33 = 31

Projected on-hand inventories for the first three weeks (i.e., until the projected on-hand becomes negative) are shown in Figure 13-9. When the projected on-hand inventory (at the end of the week) becomes negative, this is a signal that production will be needed to replenish inventory. Suppose that the economic production quantity is 70 pumps, and whenever production is called for, 70 pumps will be planned to be produced. (The determination of economic production quantity was described in Chapter 12.) Hence, the negative projected on-hand inventory at the end of third week will require production of 70 pumps in the third week, which will meet the projected shortfall of 29 pumps and leaves 41 (i.e., 70 − 29 = 41) pumps for future demand.

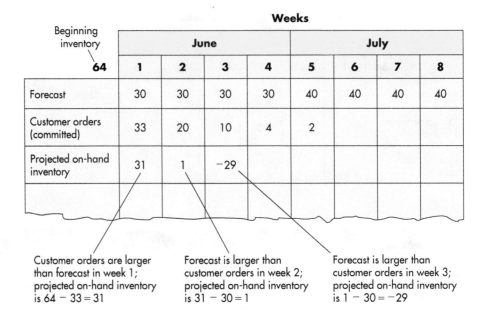

Figure 13-9

Projected on-hand inventory is calculated week by week until it becomes negative (assuming safety stocks = zero).

These calculations continue for the entire scheduling horizon. Every time projected on-hand inventory becomes negative, another production lot of 70 pumps is added to the table. Figure 13-10 illustrates the calculations. The result is planned production and updated projected on-hand inventories for each week (see Figure 13-11).

Figure 13-10

Determining the planned production and projected on-hand inventory.

Week	Inventory from Previous Week	Require-ments*	Net Inventory Before Planned Production		(70) Planned Production		Projected Inventory
1	64	33	31				31
2	31	30	1				1
3	1	30	−29	+	70	=	41
4	41	30	11				11
5	11	40	−29	+	70	=	41
6	41	40	1				1
7	1	40	−39	+	70	=	31
8	31	40	−9	+	70	=	61

* Requirements equals the larger of forecast and customer orders in each week.

Figure 13-11

Planned productions are added and projected on-hand inventories are updated.

		Weeks							
			June				**July**		
	64	1	2	3	4	5	6	7	8
Forecast		30	30	30	30	40	40	40	40
Customer orders (committed)		33	20	10	4	2			
Projected on-hand inventory		31	1	41	11	41	1	31	61
Planned production				70		70		70	70

It is now possible to determine the amount of inventory that is uncommitted and hence available to promise. Several methods are used in practice. The one we shall employ involves a "look-ahead" procedure: Sum customer orders week by week until (but not including) a week in which there is a planned production. For example, in the first week, this procedure results in summing customer orders of 33 (week 1) and 20 (week 2) and subtracting this from the beginning inventory of 64 pumps plus the planned production in week 1 (zero in this example). Thus, ATP for week 1 is:

$$64 + 0 - (33 + 20) = 11$$

This inventory is uncommitted and can be delivered in weeks 1 or 2. Note that the ATP quantity is calculated only for the first week and for any other week in which there is a positive planned production quantity. See Figure 13-12.

Weeks

	June				July			
64	**1**	**2**	**3**	**4**	**5**	**6**	**7**	**8**
Forecast	30	30	30	30	40	40	40	40
Customer orders (committed)	33	20	10	4	2			
Projected on-hand inventory	31	1	41	11	41	1	31	61
Planned production			70		70		70	70
Available-to-promise inventory (uncommitted)	11		56		68		70	70

Figure 13-12

The available-to-promise inventory quantities have been added to the table.

For weeks other than the first week, the beginning inventory drops out of the calculation, and ATP is the look-ahead customer orders subtracted from the planned production quantity in that week. Thus, for week 3, the customer orders (committed) amounts are $10 + 4 = 14$ and the ATP is $70 - 14 = 56$. For week 5, customer orders (committed) are 2 (future customer orders have not yet been booked), and the ATP is $70 - 2 = 68$. For weeks 7 and 8, there are no customer orders, so for the present all of the planned production amount is available to promise. As additional orders are booked, these would be entered in the table, and the ATP amounts would be updated to reflect those orders. The sales department can use the ATP amounts to quote realistic delivery dates to customers.

Stabilizing the MPS

Changes to a master production schedule (i.e., the set of planned productions for all the products) can be disruptive, particularly the near-future changes. Typically, the further out in the future a change is, the less it will cause problems.

The schedule horizon is often divided into three zones. The dividing lines between zones are referred to as **time fences**. The emergency zone (see Figure 13-13) is closest to present time. Changes in the emergency zone may affect commitment of key resources and therefore require top management approval. Changes to the trading zone can be approved at a middle management level and generally involve trading one product's planned production for another product's, as opposed to the emergency change that usually sacrifices something in the short term. In the planning zone, changes are managed without management approval, usually by the demand planner and master scheduler.

time fences Points in time that separate zones of a master production schedule.

Figure 13-13

An example of zones in an MPS.

MPS in Process Industries

Process industries use a raw material and process it into many products. Examples include food, beverage, chemical, and pharmaceutical industries. For example, in ice cream production, from a common base, e.g., a white mix of pasteurized/homogenized/cooled milk, various flavours of ice cream such as vanilla and chocolate are produced. In process industries, products are grouped in families based on the type of raw material used. For example, white mix and frozen yoghurt mix. Usually a large amount of a mix is produced and then a portion is used to produce a variety of products by adding various flavours/fruits. It turns out that a mix changeover/setup takes much more time and incurs much more cost than a flavour/fruit changeover/setup. Therefore, master scheduling in process industries is usually performed in two levels: first by family, then by SKUs within each family. That is, first families are scheduled, then within the time interval assigned to a family, individual members of the family are scheduled for production.

A similar approach is used in bottling beverages. It turns out that changeover of a bottle size takes a lot more time (e.g., an eight-hour shift) than changeover of the beverage type. Therefore, bottlers try to fill all products with the same bottle size one after the other, and then change to another bottle size.

For two examples of MPS in a process industry, see the "Scotsburn Dairy: The MPS Problem" and "Welch's" mini-cases.

Summary

- Sales and operations planning (S&OP) is the process of integrating sales forecasts with operations plans. This is usually done annually but updated monthly. A systematic calendar-driven process is used to forecast demand, to check against capacity limits, to reconcile the difference, and for review by top management.

- Aggregate operations planning establishes general levels of employment, output, and inventories for the next 12 months or so. In the spectrum of planning, it falls between the broad decisions of long-term strategic planning and short-term planning/scheduling.

- A basic requirement of aggregate planning is the aggregation of a category or family of products into an "equivalent" unit. This permits planners to consider overall levels of employment, output, and inventories without having to become involved with specific details that are better left to short-term planning.

- The planning variables include using overtime, part-time/temporary workers, subcontracting, and carrying inventory.

- Planning strategies range from level output/workforce to chase demand.

- Planners often use informal (trial-and-error) graphic and table/worksheet techniques to develop plans, although optimization techniques such as linear programming and transportation model are also used. Trade-off analysis, comparing marginal costs of various options, saves planning time.

- Services cannot use inventories and thus rely on chase demand strategy. They also usually use the amount of workforce (hours or FTE) as the equivalent unit.

- After the aggregate plan has been developed, it is disaggregated into specific product production plans. This leads to a master production schedule, which is the planned production quantities and their timing for all the products. Inputs to the master scheduling are on-hand inventory amounts, forecasts of demand, and committed orders. The outputs are planned productions, projected on-hand inventories, and uncommitted inventories (available-to-promise).

- Rough-cut capacity planning determines the load on the production process of an MPS, thus checking its feasibility.
- Time fences are used to reduce last-minute changes to an MPS. The near future is frozen unless an emergency occurs.

- Process industries first schedule families of products, and then individual products within each family's allotted time.

Key Terms

aggregate operations planning
available-to-promise (ATP) inventory
chase demand strategy

level output/workforce strategy
master production schedule (MPS)
rough-cut capacity planning

sales and operations planning
time fences
yield management

Solved Problems

Problem 1

A manager is attempting to put together an aggregate production plan for the coming nine months. She has obtained forecasts of aggregate demand for the planning horizon. The plan must deal with highly seasonal demand; demand is relatively high in months 3 and 4, and again in month 8, as can be seen below:

Month	1	2	3	4	5	6	7	8	9	Total
Forecast	190	230	260	280	210	170	160	260	180	1,940

The company has 20 permanent employees, each of whom can produce 10 units of output per month at a cost of $6 per unit. Inventory holding cost is $5 per unit per month, and backorder cost is $10 per unit per month. The manager is considering a plan that would involve hiring two people to start working in month 1, one on a temporary basis who would work until the end of month 5. The hiring of these two would cost $500. Beginning inventory is 0.

   a. What is the rationale for this plan?

   b. Determine the total cost of the plan, including production, inventory, and backorder costs.

Solution

   a. With the current workforce of 20 people each producing 10 units per month, regular capacity is $20 \times 10 \times 9 = 1,800$ units during the 9 months. That is 140 units less than total demand forecast. Adding one worker during the 9 months would increase regular capacity to $1,800 + 10 \times 9 = 1,890$ units. That would still be 50 units short, or just the amount one temporary worker could produce in five months. Since one of the two seasonal peaks is quite early, it would make sense to start the temporary worker right away to avoid some of the backorder cost.

   b. The worksheet for this strategy is as follows (here permanent and temp production are lumped together and hiring cost is accounted for separately):

Month	1	2	3	4	5	6	7	8	9	Total
Forecast	190	230	260	280	210	170	160	260	180	1,940
Output										
Regular	220	220	220	220	220	210	210	210	210	1,940
Overtime	—	—	—	—	—	—	—	—	—	—
Subcontract/part time	—	—	—	—	—	—	—	—	—	—
Output – Forecast	30	−10	−40	−60	10	40	50	−50	30	0

(continued)

Month	1	2	3	4	5	6	7	8	9	Total
Inventory										
Beginning	0	30	20	0	0	0	0	20	0	
Ending	30	20	0	0	0	0	20	0	0	
Average	15	25	10	0	0	0	10	10	0	70
Backorder	0	0	20	80	70	30	0	30	0	230
Costs per unit										
Output										
Regular @ $6	$1,320	1,320	1,320	1,320	1,320	1,260	1,260	1,260	1,260	$11,640
Overtime										
Subcontract/part time										
Inventory @ $5	$75	125	50	0	0	0	50	50	0	$350
Backorder @ $10	0	0	200	800	700	300	0	300	0	$2,300
Total	$1,395	1,445	1,570	2,120	2,020	1,560	1,310	1,610	1,260	$14,290

The total cost for this plan is $14,290 plus the $500 cost for two hirings, giving a total of $14,790. This plan is likely not the best (note the backorders in months 3-6 and 8). The manager would need to evaluate other plans before settling on the best.

You can also use the Excel template on *Connect* to obtain the solution:

Problem 2

A self-employed seamstress forecasts the following demand (in units) for her products for the next eight months:

Period	1	2	3	4	5	6	7	8	Total
Forecast	1,200	1,200	1,400	3,000	1,200	1,200	1,200	1,200	11,600

She wants to hire 2 temporary workers to handle the extra workload in month 4. The cost for hiring and training a temp worker is $50 per worker, and she plans to hire and train them at the end of month 3 for work in month 4. Develop an aggregate plan that uses steady output from the seamstress (1,200 units per month) with added output from the two temp workers (1,000 units per person per month) in month 4. The output rate for the temp workers is slightly less than that of the seamstress, so their cost per unit is higher. The cost per unit for seamstress is $4 per unit, while cost per unit for the temp workers is $5 per unit. Backorder cost is $1 per unit per month. Determine the total cost of the plan, including production, inventory, and backorder costs.

Solution

Period			1	2	3	4	5	6	7	8	Total
Forecast			1,200	1,200	1,400	3,000	1,200	1,200	1,200	1,200	11,600
Output											
Regular			1,200	1,200	1,200	1,200	1,200	1,200	1,200	1,200	9,600
Temp						2,000					2,000
Overtime											0
Subcontract											0
Output - Forecast			0	0	−200	200	0	0	0	0	0
Inventory											
Beginning			0	0	0	0	0	0	0	0	
Ending			0	0	0	0	0	0	0	0	
Average			0.0	0.0	0.0	0.0	0.0	0.0	0.0	0.0	0
Backorder			0	0	200	0	0	0	0	0	200
Costs:											
Regular	@	4	4,800	4,800	4,800	4,800	4,800	4,800	4,800	4,800	38,400
Temp	@	5	0	0	0	10,000	0	0	0	0	10,000
Overtime	@		0	0	0	0	0	0	0	0	0
Subcontract	@		0	0	0	0	0	0	0	0	0
Hire		.05			100						100
Inventory	@		0.0	0.0	0.0	0.0	0.0	0.0	0.0	0.0	0.0
Backorders	@	1	0	0	200	0	0	0	0	0	200
Total			4,800.0	4,800.0	5,100.0	14,800	4,800.0	4,800.0	4,800.0	4,800.0	48,700.0

Problem 3

Prepare an MPS table like that shown in Figure 13-12 for the following situation. The forecast for each of the next four weeks is 70 units. The starting inventory is zero. The MPS rule is to schedule production if the projected inventory on hand will be negative. The production lot size is 100 units. The following table shows customer (committed) orders.

Week	Customer Orders
1	80
2	50
3	30
4	10

Solution

Week	(A) Inventory from Previous Period	(B) Require-ments*	(C=B−A) Net Inventory before Planned Production	Planned Production	(Planned Production+C) Projected Inventory
1	0	80	−80	100	20
2	20	70	−50	100	50
3	50	70	−20	100	80
4	80	70	10	0	10

* Requirements equal the larger of forecast and customer orders in each week.

	Week			
Starting Inv. = 0	1	2	3	4
Forecast	70	70	70	70
Customer orders	80	50	30	10
Projected on-hand inventory	20	50	80	10
Planned production	100	100	100	
ATP	20	50	60	

Discussion and Review Questions

1. What is sales and operations planning? How is it done? **LO1**

2. What is aggregate operations planning? What is its purpose? **LO1**

3. Why is there a need for operations planning? **LO1**

4. What is an equivalent unit and why is it used? **LO1**

5. What are the most common decision variables for aggregate planning in a manufacturing setting? In a service setting? **LO1**

6. What options are available for changing the medium-term capacity of (a) a school, (b) an airline? **LO1**

7. Under what circumstances would a company use the following strategies? **LO1**

   a. Maintain level output/workforce and let inventories absorb fluctuations in demand.

   b. Vary the size of the workforce to correspond to predicted changes in demand requirements.

   c. Maintain a constant workforce, but vary hours worked (through overtime and idle time) to correspond to predicted demand requirements.

8. How does the trial-and-error table/worksheet approach for aggregate operations planning work? **LO2**

9. Give an example of a product with highly seasonal demand and discuss how its manufacturer meets the demand. **LO2**

10. What are the differences between aggregate planning for services and goods? **LO3**

11. What is master scheduling and how is it done? **LO4**

12. What is RCCP and why is it useful? **LO4**

13. What is ATP and how is it determined? **LO4**

14. What is a time fence and why is it useful? **LO4**

15. How is MPS for a process industry different? **LO4**

Taking Stock

1. What general trade-offs are involved in master scheduling for determining the length of emergency zone of the schedule? **LO4**

2. Who needs to interface with the master production schedule and why? **LO4**

3. How has technology had an impact on aggregate planning? **LO1 & 2**

4. Many companies are using temporary workers to meet their peak demand. Is this ethically wrong? Briefly discuss. **LO2 & 3**

Critical Thinking Exercise

Discuss disaggregating an aggregate service plan, and give an example of it in an organization such as a hospital. **LO3 & 4**

Experiential Learning Exercise

Aggregate planning in operations is like budgeting in finance/accounting. Prepare a personal budget for next year following the concept of aggregate planning. Forecast your need for money each quarter and identify the supply of money and its sources. Make sure supply (it could include student loan) meets the demand. **LO2 & 3**

Internet Exercises

1. Visit http://info.steelwedge.com/rs/steelwedge/images/sw_sony_case_study_2014.pdf, and summarize how Sony Entertainment is using Steelwedge's planning software. **LO1**

2. Visit http://www.kinaxis.com/Global/resources/case-studies/supply-chain-responsiveness-mtd-case-study-kinaxis.pdf, and summarize what RapidResponse is doing for MTD. **LO1**

3. Visit https://www.oliverwight-americas.com/system/files/public/clients/profiles/caterpillarna.pdf and oliverwight-americas.com/system/files/public/clients/profiles/caterpillarttt.pdf, and summarize how Caterpillar improved its planning. **LO1**

Problems

1. Calculate the total cost for each of the following aggregate plans using these unit costs: **LO2**

> Regular output = $40
> Overtime = $50
> Subcontract = $60
> Inventory per month = $10

a.

Month	Jan	Feb	Mar	Apr	May	Jun
Forecast	300	320	320	340	320	320
Output						
Regular	300	300	300	300	300	300
Overtime	20	20	20	20	20	20
Subcontract	0	0	0	0	0	0
Output–Forecast						
Inventory						
Beginning						
Ending						
Average						

b.

Month	Jul	Aug	Sep	Oct	Nov	Dec
Forecast	320	340	360	380	400	400
Output						
Regular	300	300	300	300	300	300
Overtime	20	20	20	20	30	30
Subcontract	20	30	40	40	60	70
Output–Forecast						
Inventory						
Beginning						
Ending						
Average						

c. (Refer to part *b*.) After complaints from some workers about working overtime every month during the first half of the year, the manager is now considering adding some temporary workers for the second half of the year, which would increase regular output to a steady 350 units a month, not using any overtime, and using subcontracting to make up the shortage. Determine the total cost of this plan.

2. A manager would like to know the total cost of a plan that meets the forecasts below using a steady regular production rate of 200 units a month, a maximum of 20 units per month of overtime, and subcontracting as needed to make up any shortages. The unit costs are: **LO2**

> Regular production = $35
> Overtime = $70
> Subcontracting = $80

Month	1	2	3	4	5	6
Forecast	230	200	240	240	250	240

3. Determine the total cost for the following plan given the following forecasts: **LO2**

Month	1	2	3	4	5	6
Forecast	380	400	420	440	460	480

Use steady regular output of 400 units per month, use overtime as needed for up to 40 units per month, and use subcontracting to make up any shortage. Unit costs are:

> Regular output = $25
> Overtime = $40
> Subcontract = $60
> Inventory per month = $15

4. a. Given the following forecasts and steady regular output of 550 every month, what total cost would result if overtime is limited to a maximum of 40 units a month, and subcontracting is limited to a maximum of 10 units a month? Unit costs are: **LO2**

> Regular output = $20
> Overtime = $30
> Subcontract = $25
> Inventory per month = $10
> Backorder per month = $18

Month	1	2	3	4	5	6
Forecast	540	540	570	590	600	580

b. Suppose backorders are not allowed. Modify your plan from part *a* to accommodate this as economically as possible. The limits on overtime and subcontracting remain the same. **LO2**

5. Refer to Example 3. Suppose that the new union contract limits the number of temporary workers in any month to 28 (i.e., 20 percent of permanent workers). Recall from Example 2 that up to 400 units can be produced during overtime per month. Using trade-off analysis and trial-and-error, find the minimum cost plan in this case. (*Hint:* Hire 10 temps for 3 months and 15 temps for 2 months starting in Month 3.) **LO2**

6. A manufacturer of heavy truck engines must develop a production plan, given the following demand forecasts for engine. The company currently has 13 workers and makes 130 engines per month. Regular labour cost is $500 per engine. The beginning inventory is zero. Overtime labour costs $750 per engine. Hiring cost is $3,000 per worker. Inventory holding cost is $50 per engine per month, and backorder cost is $250 per engine per month. Develop the minimum cost plan for this company. *Hint:* Start with level output/workforce plan, and use the trade-off analysis to show that changing this plan will only increase the total cost. **LO2**

Month	1	2	3	4	5	6	7	8	Total
Forecast	120	135	140	120	125	125	140	135	1,040

7. A fabric mill has developed the following forecasts (in hundred bolts of cloth). The mill has a normal capacity of 275 units (a unit = hundred bolts) per month, and employs 275 workers. Regular labour cost is $2,000 per unit and overtime labour cost is $3,000 per unit. Up to 50 units per month can be made during overtime. The beginning inventory is zero. Hiring cost is $1,500 per worker. The inventory holding cost is $1,000 per unit per month, and backorder cost is $5,000 per unit per month. **LO2**

   a. Develop a level output/workforce plan.
   b. Starting with your answer to part *a*, use the trade-off analysis to find the minimum cost plan.

Month	1	2	3	4	5	6	7	Total
Forecast	250	300	250	300	280	275	270	1,925

8. A small company produces recreational vehicles. The marketing manager has developed the following forecasts (in units): **LO2**

Month	Mar	Apr	May	Jun	Jul	Aug	Sep	Total
Forecast	50	44	55	60	60	40	50	359

   Use the following information:

Regular labour cost	$240 per unit
Overtime labour cost	$360 per unit
Regular capacity	40 units per month, using 5 workers
Overtime capacity	8 units per month
Holding cost	$30 per unit per month
Backorder cost	$100 per unit per month
Beginning inventory	0
Desired ending inventory	0
Hiring cost	$2,000 per worker

   Develop the minimum cost plan and compute its total cost. *Hint:* Hire 8 new workers and meet any shortages with overtime.

9. A small distiller produces whisky. The salesperson has developed the following forecasts for demand (in cases) for the next six months. **LO2**

Month	May	Jun	Jul	Aug	Sep	Oct
Forecast	4,000	4,800	5,600	7,200	6,400	5,000

Use the following information:

Regular labour cost	$20 per case
Regular labour capacity	5,000 cases per month using 50 workers
Overtime labour cost	$30 per case
Part time labour cost	$40 per case
Holding cost	$2 per case per month
Backorder cost	$10 per case per month
Beginning inventory	0

Develop the minimum cost plan using level output/workforce, supplemented with each of the following, and compute the total cost for each plan. Which plan has lower total cost?

   a. Use overtime (up to 1,000 cases per month). *Hint:* Use OT in a three-month period.
   b. Use a combination of overtime (500 cases per month maximum) and part-time labour (500 cases per month maximum). *Hint:* Use OT in a five-month period, supplemented with part-time production.

10. A company produces sofas. The manager wants to prepare a plan for the next six months using the following information: **LO2**

	MONTH					
	1	2	3	4	5	6
Forecast Demand	160	150	160	180	170	140

Cost Per Unit	
Regular time	$100
Overtime	$150
Part time	$120
Inventory, per month	$10
Backorder, per month	$50

There are 5 workers, each making 30 sofas a month. The maximum number of sofas produced during overtime is 30 per month. Part-time workers can handle a maximum of 20 units per month. Beginning inventory is zero. Develop a plan that minimizes total cost. No ending inventory or backorders are desired at the end of month 6.

11. Refer to Solved Problem 1. Start with 20 permanent workers. Prepare a minimum cost plan that may use some combination of hiring ($250 per worker), subcontracting ($8 per unit, maximum of 20 units per month, must use for at least three consecutive months), and overtime ($9 per unit, maximum of 25 units per month). The ending inventory in month 9 should be zero with no backorders at the end. Compute the total cost. *Hint:* Use max. OT and subcontracting in Months 2–4. **LO2**

12. A spring-water bottling company has recently expanded into flavoured water. The marketing manager is predicting an upturn in demand based on the new offerings and the

increased public awareness of the health benefits of drinking more water. She has prepared aggregate forecasts for the next six months (in truckloads): **L02**

Month	May	Jun	Jul	Aug	Sept	Oct	Total
Forecast	50	60	70	90	80	70	420

The production manager has gathered the following information:

Regular production cost	$1,000 per truckload
Regular production capacity	60 truckloads per month using 20 employees
Overtime production cost	$1,500 per truckload
Holding cost	$200 per truckload per month
Backorder cost	$5,000 per truckload per month
Beginning inventory	0

The regular production can be supplemented by up to 30 truckloads a month from overtime. Determine the plan that has the lowest total cost. *Hint:* Use overtime in August–October.

13. A niche bicycle manufacturer manufactures bicycles in two different sizes. David, the company's owner-manager, has just received the following forecasts for the next six months. **L02**

	16-inch	20-inch
Nov.	1,000 units	500 units
Dec.	900	500
Jan.	600	300
Feb.	700	500
Mar.	1,100	400
Apr.	1,100	600

a. Under what circumstances is it appropriate to develop just one plan rather than two (one for each size)?

b. Suppose forecasts for the two sizes are summed to obtain one forecast for each month. Currently David employs 27 full-time, highly skilled employees, each of whom can produce 50 bikes per month. Because skilled labour is in short supply in the area, David would like to keep them permanently. There is no inventory on hand at present, but David would like to have 300 units on hand at the end of April. A maximum of 200 bikes can be produced during overtime each month. Determine the minimum cost plan using these unit costs:

Regular	$50	Inventory	$2.00 per month
Overtime	$75	Backorder	$10.00 per month

Hint: Use overtime in November, December, and April.

14. A sports-goods manufacturer makes baseball and hockey gloves. Suppose now is the end of December and the manager wishes to plan production for the next three quarters. The forecasts for aggregate pairs of gloves are Q1: 9,400; Q2: 16,200; and Q3: 18,500. There are 26 permanent workers. Each works 480 hours a quarter and makes 1 pair of gloves per hour. The wage rate is $8 per hour, holding cost per unit per quarter is $1, and the backorder cost per unit per quarter is $10. The manager can hire full-time temporary workers at the cost of $960 per person. Temporary workers also receive $8 per hour and work 480 hours a quarter. Overtime by full-time workers is possible at 1.5 times the regular wage rate, up to a maximum of 20 percent of regular time production. Current inventory level is zero and there is no inventory expected at the end of the planning horizon. **L02**

a. If the 26 permanent workers are kept throughout the planning horizon, how many units will the company be short at the end?

b. Do tradeoff analysis to show that using temporary workers will be cheaper than using permanent workers during overtime.

c. Find the plan that minimizes total cost. *Hint:* Hire 7 temps for 2 quarters starting in Q2.

15. MR is a manufacturer of industrial fridges, freezers, and air conditioners. In December, the production planner needs to submit a production plan to the plant manager for the next year. The aggregate forecast for each quarter of next year is Q1: 14,800; Q2: 26,400; Q3: 35,000, and Q4: 19,200 units. The beginning inventory in January is 0, and the year-end inventory in December of next year can be 0. It costs MR $24 to hold an appliance in inventory for one quarter. Shortages are undesirable. Assume that all shortage will be backordered, and that backorder cost is $100 per unit per quarter. There are 160 permanent workers who produce 19,200 units per quarter. In busy quarters, workers can produce up to 9,600 additional units during overtime. Regular-time labour cost is $60 per unit appliance and overtime labour cost is $83 per unit. MR can hire up to 160 temporary workers for a second shift. Assume temporary workers have the same productivity and can produce up to 19,200 units per quarter. A unit produced by temporary workers also costs $60 in labour cost. However, there will be an extra hiring cost of $25 per unit during the first quarter of employment. **L02**

a. If permanent workers are used for the next four quarters during regular time, how many units will MR be short at the end of the year and in which quarters?

b. Meet units short by hiring temporary workers. Use trade-off analysis to choose the minimum cost plan in this case. *Hint:* Hire approximately 78 temps for 2 quarters starting in Q2.

c. Would using overtime (in addition to some temporary production) be less expensive? Use trade-off analysis to choose the overall minimum cost plan. *Hint:* Hire approximately 38 temps for 2 quarters starting in Q2, supplemented with overtime.

*16. MT makes small camping and snowmobile trailers. The demand for camping trailers occurs between January and June (mostly in April and May). MT makes camping trailers from January to June, shuts down in July and then makes snowmobile trailers from August to November. Suppose now is the end of December. For simplicity, we consider every two months as a period. The forecasts for camping trailers during each of the next three periods (six months) are:

Period 1	Period 2	Period 3
869	1,730	1,374

MT employs 40 permanent workers who are paid an average of $20 per hour (including fringe benefits) and work approximately 320 hours a period (2 months). They make approximately 1,000 camping trailers per period during regular time. They can also work up to 50 percent more as overtime (i.e., up to 12 hours a day vs. the regular 8 hours a day) and will be paid 1.5 times the regular wage rate. Alternatively, MT can hire *up to* 40 additional temporary workers to work during a second shift. Hiring cost is $3,000 per temporary worker. Assume temporary workers' wage rate and productivity are the same as permanent workers. Also assume that temporary workers work only during regular time (no overtime) and are kept for whole periods (i.e., for 2 months or 4 months). Inventory holding cost per camping trailer per period is $180, and is charged to average inventory level during each period. Currently there are no camping trailers on hand, and the desired inventory at the end of period 3 is zero (although a small positive number is also acceptable). MT wishes to meet the total demand, but shortage during a period (except last) is acceptable, in which case the shortage is assumed to be backordered at the cost of $600 per camping trailer per period. **LO2**

a. Calculate all the relevant unit costs.
b. Suppose MT uses permanent workers during regular time and overtime. Determine the minimum cost plan in this case. *Hint:* Use overtime in each period.
c. Suppose MT hires temporary workers, but decides not to use permanent workers during overtime (just regular time). Determine the minimum cost plan in this case. *Hint:* Hire 15 temps for two periods and 9 temps for 1 period starting in period 2.
d. Would overtime production by permanent workers and regular time production by temporary workers simultaneously result in a lower total cost? Do a

trade-off analysis. What is the overall minimum cost plan?

17. Mity-Lite (ML) is a manufacturer of folding and stackable chairs and folding tables for social events. The demand for ML's products is seasonal, peaking in spring and summer. Suppose it is December now, and the production manager needs to prepare the production plan for the next 12 months (for simplicity we use four quarters). Also for simplicity, we aggregate all products. The forecast during each of the next 4 quarters is:

Q1	Q2	Q3	Q4
141,330	242,550	217,866	129,900

ML currently employs 348 "permanent" workers. The workers are paid $10 per hour and work 480 hours a quarter. The workers can make approximately 167,040 units per quarter during regular time (10 hours a day, 4 days a week). (*Note:* This works out to 1 hour per unit per worker). They can also work up to 25 percent more as overtime (i.e., work 10 hours more on Fridays) and will be paid 1.5 times the regular wage rate. ML can hire up to 200 temporary workers for a second shift. The average hiring cost (searching, interviewing, and training) is estimated to be $480 per new employee. *Note:* Hiring cost is charged to each unit produced during the first quarter of employment. Temps are kept for one or two quarters. For simplicity, we assume that the productivity of a new temp worker is the same as a permanent worker. Also, a temp workers' wage rate is $10 per hour. The inventory holding cost rate per quarter is 3% of unit cost, and the unit cost is $90. There are no products on hand now, and the desired seasonal inventory at the end of the year is zero. (In reality, ML keeps the equivalent of two weeks of demand as safety stock; we can assume that these are kept separately). ML wishes to meet all demand, but shortage during any quarter (except last) is allowed, in which case assume that the shortage is backordered at the cost of $15 per unit per quarter.

a. Calculate all the relevant unit costs. Suppose ML uses permanent workers during regular time and nothing else. In the last quarter, ML will produce only what is needed and then will let workers go on vacation (i.e., they plan to produce 129,900 units). Determine the number of units short during each quarter.
b. Suppose ML hires temp workers to meet the shortages of part *a*. Determine when and how many temp workers should be used. *Hint:* Hire 104 temps for two quarters starting in Q2, and 2 temps for one quarter in quarter 3.
c. Using trade-off analysis, show why levelling (i.e., equalizing) the temp workers in Q2 and Q3 of the above solution is not cost-effective. (*Hint:* Show that

producing one more unit in Q2 and one less unit in Q3 by temp workers is not cost effective).

   d. Using trade-off analysis, show why using permanent workers during overtime in part b's solution is not cost-effective. (*Hint:* show that producing one more unit in Q3 during OT and one less unit in Q3 by temp workers is not cost-effective).

18. A small high-end swimwear manufacturer needs to plan for next year. Demand for swimwear (in units) follows a seasonal pattern: **LO2**

Quarter	Demand Forecast
1	2,000
2	9,000
3	9,000
4	4,000

Given the following information:

Permanent workforce	5 workers
Overtime capacity	Maximum = 50% of regular production
Production rate per worker	750 units/quarter (perm or temp)
Regular wage rate	$15 per hour (480 hours per quarter)
Overtime wage rate	$22.5 per hour (only for perm)
Temp hiring cost	$1,500 per worker (charged to first quarter of employment)
Holding cost	$1.50 per unit/quarter
Backorder cost	$30 per unit/quarter
Beginning inventory	0

   a. Determine the unit costs.
   b. Determine how many units the company will be short during each quarter if only permanent workers are used during regular time.
   c. Do a tradeoff analysis to determine if temp workers cost less than permanent workers during overtime.
   d. Find the lowest cost plan. *Hint:* Hire six temp workers for two quarters.

19. The manager of an injection moulding shop is interested in using aggregate planning to determine the shop's production levels during each of the next four quarters. The shop uses 8 moulding machines to produce approximately 150 different products, employing 18 permanent workers. Because of the variety of products, standard (production) hour is used to measure demand and production. The demand forecast (in hundred standard hours) for the next four quarters is 84, 90, 58, and 69, respectively. Each worker provides 126 standard hours per month. Up to 7 temp workers can be hired. Hiring cost is $870 per worker. Labour cost (permanent or temp) is $13.50 per standard hour and

overtime labour cost (by permanent workers) is $23.50 per standard hour. Maximum overtime production is 20 percent of regular time production by permanent workers. The current inventory level is 0. Inventory carrying cost is $2.40 per standard hour per quarter, and shortage cost is $10.80 per standard hour per quarter. Assume all shortages are backordered. **LO2**

   a. Show that total production standard hours by 18 permanent workers is 6,804 per quarter.
   b. Show that maximum total temp standard hours is 2,646 per quarter.
   c. Show that maximum total overtime standard hours is 1,361 per quarter.
   d. Show that hire cost per standard hour during the first quarter of work is $2.30.
   e. Calculate the Beginning & Ending inventories and Backorders for each quarter for the plan that only uses regular permanent standard hours.
   f. Using trade-off analysis, show that hiring temp workers will be cheaper than using permanent workers during overtime.
   g. Consider the following two temp options (in addition to permanent worker production): Plan A: 16(100) standard hours in Q1 and 22(00) in Q2; Plan B: 16(100) standard hours in Q1 and 21(00) in Q2. Using trade-off analysis, show why plan B is cheaper.

20. Refer to Example 5. Suppose that an increase in warehousing costs has increased the inventory holding cost to $2 per unit per month. All other costs and quantities remain the same. Determine a revised optimal solution to this transportation problem using Excel's Solver. **LO2**

21. Refer to Example 5. Suppose that regular-time capacity in month 3 will be reduced to 440 units to accommodate a companywide safety inspection of equipment. Using Excel's Solver, what will the additional cost of the optimal plan be as compared to the one shown in Example 5? Assume all input data are the same as Example 5 except for the regular-time capacity in month 3. **LO2**

22. Using Excel's Solver, solve the previous problem with an inventory holding cost of $2 per unit per month. **LO2**

23. Prepare an MPS table for the pumps of Figure 13-12 using the same inputs but change the MPS rule from "schedule production when the projected on-hand inventory would be negative without production" to "schedule production when the projected on-hand inventory would be less than 10 units without production." **LO4**

24. Update the MPS table shown in Figure 13-12 given these inputs: It is now the end of week 1; customer orders are 35 units for week 2, 16 for week 3, 11 for week 4, 8 for week 5, and 3 for week 6. Inventory on hand is now 33 units. Use the MPS rule of ordering production when

projected on-hand inventory would be negative without production. **LO4**

25. Prepare an MPS table like Figure 13-12 using the following information: The forecast for each week of an eight-week schedule is 50 units. The MPS rule is to schedule production if the projected on-hand inventory would be negative without it. Customer orders (committed) are:

Week	Customer Orders
1	52
2	35
3	20
4	12

Use a production lot size of 75 units and no beginning inventory. **LO4**

26. Verify the available-to-promise (ATP) quantities for each week of Solved Problem 3. **LO4**

27. Prepare an MPS table like Figure 13-12 for the following situation: The forecast is 80 units for each of the first two weeks and 60 units for each of the next three weeks. The starting inventory is 30 units. The company uses lot size of 150 units. Also, the desired safety stock is 20 units. Committed orders are:

Week	Customer Orders
1	82
2	80
3	60
4	40
5	20

Hint: If ATP in a week is negative, reduce the previous ATP by the same amount and make this ATP = 0. **LO4**

28. Minco Inc. is a small manufacturer of fused magnesia and silica.[2] Minco's continuous improvement efforts led to a capacity and production planning software. To prepare for the use of software, a spreadsheet was first used to determine the capacity requirements for the main equipment (the fusion furnaces) and the production schedule for the main products. A major product had the following forecast and committed orders (all in thousand pounds):

	January			February			
Week	2	3	4	1	2	3	4
Forecast	56	56	56	66	66	66	66
Committed order	44	0	18				

The initial inventory was 119,000 pounds and the minimum stock at the end of each week was to be 83,000 pounds. **LO4**

a. Calculate the Economic Production quantity if the annual demand is 3,000,000 pounds, setup cost is $350 per setup, inventory holding cost rate is 20 percent per year, unit cost is $2 per pound, demand rate is 500 pounds per hour, and production rate is 1,000 pounds per hour. *Hint:* Refer to Chapter 12.

b. If the EPQ = 100,000 pounds, prepare a production schedule for this product for the next seven weeks.

c. Determine the available-to-promise inventory for the next seven weeks.

*29. Owens Corning Fiberglas (OCF) makes several types, weights, and widths of Fiberglas mats from chopped strands of fibreglass for boat hulls on two production lines in a plant.[3]

Aggregate planning for OCF involves choosing a certain number of shifts (1 to 4, i.e., 40, 80, 120, or 160 hours of operation per week), depending on forecast demand. MPS is determined by optimization, minimizing product change-over, production, and inventory costs. Product change-over takes between 0.5 and 1 hour, and is sequence dependent, taking longest for fiberglass type change, and least for width change. Change-over cost includes loss of profit, direct labour, and mat waste.

For simplicity, we will consider only one production line and two products: light (3/4 ounce/ft^2, 76 inches wide), and heavy (1.5 ounces/ft^2, 76 inches wide) mats. The forecast for the next eight weeks for light mat is 110,000 pounds, and for heavy mat is 120,000 pounds. Given the aggregate plan, the line can make 370,000 pounds of light or 185,000 pounds of heavy mats during each of the next eight weeks. Instead of optimization we will use the Economic Production Quantity (EPQ) for each mat. **LO4**

a. If product change-over cost from heavy to light is $1,100 and from light to heavy is $1,500, holding cost rate is 12% per year, price of light mat is $0.75 per pound, price of heavy mat is $0.50 per pound, and demand occurs 50 weeks a year, calculate the EPQ for each product.

b. If there are 230,000 pounds of light and 240,000 pounds of heavy mats on hand, determine which product will run out first.

c. Using the above results and safety stocks of 110,000 pounds of light and 120,000 pounds of heavy mats,

---

[2] W. S. Beversluis and H. H. Jordan, "Using a Spreadsheet for Capacity Planning and Scheduling," *Production and Inventory Management Journal* 36(2), pp. 12–16.

[3] M. D. Oliff and E. E. Burch, "Multiproduct Production Scheduling at Owens-Corning Fiberglas," *Interfaces*, 15(5), pp. 25–34.

plan production of the two products so that neither product's projected on hand dips below its safety stock level and their production lot sizes are as close to their EPQ as possible. That is, if light mat will be short, interrupt the production of heavy mat (at the end of the week) and start making light mat.

30. Land's End is a phone/mail/Internet-order retailer of outdoor clothes and shoes. Like other retailers, Land's End's customer orders surge just before Christmas. Therefore, Land's End requires more employees just before Christmas. Jobs include customer sales and service, warehouse operations, and seamstressing. The Full time Equivalent (FTE) employee requirements for October to December of last year were as follows: October: 4,000 FTE, November: 6,600 FTE, and December: 7,100 FTE. Land's End employs 4,000 FTE employees throughout the year (3,500 full-time and 1,000 half-time). During November and December, Land's End can employ up to 1,000 additional full-time temp workers (idle workers from local cheese factories) and up to 1,000 half-time high school students. Also, Land's End can use up to 2,000 FTE of overtime per month using its permanent and year-round part-time workers (e.g., working 12-hour shifts instead of 8-hour shifts). Each FTE permanent employee receives $3,000 a month. Each FTE of overtime work receives $4,500 a month. Each FTE Temp employee also receives $3,000 a month, and each half-time student receives $1,500 per month. However, new employees require two to six hours of training. This is estimated to cost $300 on average, and is charged to the first month of employment. **L03**

a. Set up this problem as a planning problem and determine the minimum cost plan. Briefly state the trade-off analysis you used.

b. What factors, other than cost, should be considered? Explain.

31. Banner Good Samaritan Medical Center is a 662-bed hospital. Like other hospitals, the number of its patients increases in the winter. The full-time equivalent (FTE) nurse requirements for Q1 to Q4 of next year are forecasted to be Q1: 1,300 FTE; Q2: 1,000 FTE; Q3: 800 FTE; and Q4: 1,000 FTE. Banner Good Samaritan employs 1,000 FTE permanent nurses throughout the year. During peak season, it can employ up to 500 additional FTE temporary nurses from local temp agencies. Also, it can use up to 500 FTE of overtime (hours worked beyond an eight-hour shift in a day). Each FTE permanent nurse receives an average of $8,000 a quarter. Each FTE of overtime work receives $12,000 a quarter. Each FTE Temp receives $8,000 a quarter, but needs an average of $1,000 for training (charged to the first quarter of employment). **L03**

a. Set up this problem as a planning problem and determine the minimum cost plan. Briefly state the trade-off analysis you used. Calculate the total cost. *Note:* If demand is less than the number of permanent nurses in a quarter, the nurses will still be paid but the idle time will be used as paid holidays and/or for further training.

b. What factors, other than cost, should be considered? Explain.

 MINI-CASE

Scotsburn Dairy

Scotsburn Dairy's plant in Truro, Nova Scotia, makes over 300 types and sizes of ice cream and frozen yoghurt products. The process is in two stages. In the first stage, a type of mix such as premium white is made in one of the two large pasteurizing vats (with 5,400 and 7,500 litres capacities), homogenized, cooled, and stored in one of 8 storage tanks. In the second stage, the mix is fed into one of the three lines where

flavor(s)/fruit(s) are added and the mix is packaged in containers (tubs) of various sizes. All three lines feed into the spiral freezer and then the tubs are stored in the on-site warehouse. For simplicity, we assume that all the products can be aggregated and that the volume of the product determines its production speed and cost. The plant manager has received the following aggregate demand forecasts (in units, a unit = 10,000 litres) for the next 12 months: **L02**

Jan	Feb	Mar	Apr	May	Jun	Jul	Aug	Sep	Oct	Nov	Dec
140	160	190	180	180	220	240	210	170	170	160	130

A major consideration is product changeover time. These are significant as a mix is changed and as a tub size is changed. The manager estimates that out of 4.3 weeks per month, on average 1 week is spent for changeovers.

Although production speed of a line in the second stage varies by product (and not as a linear function of products' tub size), the spiral freezer's speed is based on volume of ice cream

going through it (10,000 litres per hour). For some products, the line is a bottleneck but for most products the spiral freezer is. For simplicity, we assume that the production capacity of the plant is determined by the capacity of the spiral freezer (1 unit or 10,000 litres per hour).

The plant manager uses the following labour schemes: 40 hours a week (1 shift; 10 hours a day for 4 days), 50 hours a

(continued)

week (40 + 10 hours of overtime on Fridays), and 80 hours a week (2 shifts; 10 hours a day for 4 days each).

The initial inventory is 210 units (i.e., 2,100,000 litres). The manager would like to have safety stocks at the end of each month equal to the next month's forecast demand. Also, the ending inventory next December should be at least 170 units.

Scotsburn has on-site warehouse space for 6,500 pallets of products. Each pallet's load differs by product size. For example, 550 2-litre tubs are placed on a pallet. For simplicity, we will use this as a measure of on-site warehouse capacity, i.e., 6500(550)(2) = 7,150,000 litres or 715 units.

The production cost of the 40-hour a week labour scheme (requiring 3 freezer operators, 9 freezer packers, 1 freezer bypass, 5 palletizer, 1 quality control lab supervisor, 1 lab technician, 2 wash-up staff, 4 mixers, 1 production supervisor, 1 maintenance manager, and 4 maintenance workers) is $78,408 per month. Overtime production cost is approximately 1.5 times regular

time production. A temp worker's production cost is approximately the same as a permanent worker's.

The average hiring cost of 32 temp workers required to run the plant is $500 each, charged to the first month of employment.

Value of a litre of product is $1, cost of capital is 11 percent per year, each pallet holds 1,100 litres, and warehousing cost is $20 per pallet per month. From these, inventory holding cost per unit (10,000 litres) per month is 0.11($1)(10,000)/12 + 20(10,000/1100) = $273. Shortage/backorder is highly undesirable. Assume a cost of $1,000 per unit per month backordered. Determine the minimum cost plan for Scotsburn Dairy. *Hint:* Use the second shift in May and June, supplemented by overtime in several months.

Sources: http://www.scotsburn.com/index.htm; Andrea Cameron, Production Scheduling and Inventory Management for an Ice Cream Manufacturer using Hierarchical Planning Models, M.Sc. thesis, Dalhousie University 2009.

MINI-CASE

Scotsburn Dairy: The MPS Problem

The Master Scheduling problem at Scotsburn is to determine the production quantity for the products during each week for the next 13 weeks subject to the limitation of production hours imposed by the aggregate plan. Because some products have "joint" setup, it is more efficient to group them as a family if possible. For example, some products are made from the same base mix (e.g., no sugar) and some use the same tub size (e.g., 2 litre). Changing base mix on a line requires washing all the equipment, and changing the tub size requires physical adjustment to the filling and packaging equipment. Either action requires approximately a half-hour, and changing base mix also results in approximately $300 of wasted mix. Exceptions include multiflavour products (e.g., Neapolitan ice cream) which require tight coordination of flavours and products containing a particular allergen (e.g., peanuts). In these cases, all sizes of these products should be included in their own family. Within a family, a flavour or fruit change requires approximately five minutes.

Scotsburn produces tens of families of ice cream and frozen yogurts on three lines. For simplicity, we assume two families, one line, and only three weeks. Suppose that the setup time for each family is 1 hour, cost of labour involved in changeover is $300 per hour, and cost of mix loss is $300. Holding cost rate is 30% per year, cost of 1 litre of ice cream is $1, and there are 50 work weeks per year.

The demand (in production hours) for each family per week (after adjusting for initial inventories and safety stocks) during the next three weeks are as follows:

Family	Week 1	Week 2	Week 3
F1	11	12	18
F2	13	16	24

The aggregate plan has specified 40-hour weeks (4 days of 10 hours each) during these 3 weeks. Determine the lot sizes of each family in each week in order to minimize total setup and holding cost subject to meeting the demand during the next three weeks within 40-hour weeks. Assume that a week's demand for a family cannot be split between two weeks.

MINI-CASE

Welch's

Welch's, a major producer of grape juice, packages a few families of the products on each line. In order to prepare the master production schedule, the planner first aggregates the demand and the required safety stock of each product in each family during the next four weeks. She also aggregates the initial inventory of each product to obtain the family initial inventory.

Then, given the production hours available during the regular time and overtime, the production rates and the setup time for each family, and some other cost data, she uses a linear programming software to determine the production quantity of each family during the next four weeks in order to minimize the total cost of holding inventory, setup time, and overtime, such that after satisfying the demand, the ending inventories each week are greater or equal to the safety stocks.

On a particular line, four families are packaged. One of the families has three products in it. The forecast demand (in 1,000 cases), the safety stock, and the beginning inventory for each product during the next four weeks are as follows:

Demand Forecast	Week 1	Week 2	Week 3	Week 4
Product 1	6.7	6.78	6.78	6.78
Product 2	.5	1.48	1.48	1.48
Product 3	2.0	1.88	1.88	1.88

Safety Stock	Week 1	Week 2	Week 3	Week 4
Product 1	17.99	19.03	17.12	16.73
Product 2	.93	.98	3.16	3.60
Product 3	3.02	3.16	5.72	6.23

Initial inventory	
Product 1	12.89
Product 2	2.66
Product 3	4.45

a. Calculate the aggregate forecast and aggregate safety stock for each week; and the aggregate initial inventory.

b. Using the result of part *a*, and available hours during regular time (80 hours per week) and overtime (36 hours per week), production rate of 1.14 hours per unit, setup time of eight hours, holding cost per unit per week of $150, setup cost of $400, and overtime cost of $212 per unit, and similar information about the other families, the linear programming software has determined the following quantities for this family for Weeks 1 to 4: 11.14, 14.00, 10.34, and 10.70 units. Determine the aggregate ending inventory in each week, and verify that they are greater or equal to aggregate safety stocks.

The aggregate production quantities are next disaggregated by also using linear programming for each family. Given the production rates and setup time for each product, and some other cost data, the linear programming software determines the production quantity for each product during the next four weeks in order to minimize the total cost of holding inventory and setup time and the deviation of total production quantity from that derived in the aggregate model for each week, such that after satisfying the demand, the ending inventories each week are greater or equal to the safety stocks.

c. Using the aggregate production quantities given in part *b*, production rates of 1.10, 1.21, and 1.12 hours per unit for products 1 to 3, respectively, setup time of 0.5 hour for each production run, holding cost per unit per week of $150, setup cost of $100 per product run, the linear programming software has determined the following quantities for each product for Weeks 1 to 4. Determine the ending inventories for each product in each week, and verify that they are greater or equal to the safety stocks.

Production	Week 1	Week 2	Week 3	Week 4
Product 1	12.44	7.24	5.43	5.77
Product 2	0	1.42	4.95	0
Product 3	1.69	5.34	0	5.00

Sources: Based on S. J. Allen and E. W. Schuster, "Practical Production Scheduling with Capacity Constraints and Dynamic Demand: Family Planning and Disaggregation," *Production and Inventory Management Journal* 35(4), pp. 15–21; http://www.welchs.com.

connect   LEARNSMART   SMARTBOOK

For more information on the resources available from McGraw-Hill Ryerson, go to www.mheducation.ca/he/solutions.

CHAPTER 14

Material Requirements Planning and Enterprise Resource Planning

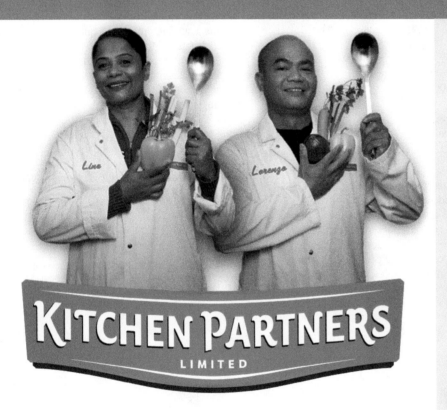

Learning Objectives

After completing this chapter, you should be able to:

LO1 Describe material requirements planning (MRP) and the conditions under which it is most appropriate.

LO2 Describe the inputs to MRP.

LO3 Describe the calculation of MRP, and solve typical problems.

LO4 Describe lot sizing methods, capacity requirements planning, and MRP II.

LO5 Describe enterprise resource planning (ERP).

Kitchen Partners Ltd (KPL) is a 90-employee food manufacturer in Edmonton. KPL makes around 100 custom private-label foods (soup, lasagna, cabbage roll, etc.) for retail chains such as Sobey's and Costco, and ground beef toppings for pizza and taco salad at Boston Pizza restaurants. KPL is growing fast (40 percent per year) and required a software to store all the recipes/bills of materials, perform MRP and MPS, trace ingredients and products, enable EDI (required by Costco), as well as print labels for pallets stored in the off-site warehouse. KPL chose Justfooderp software, which is based on Microsoft Dynamics but has additional programs for food manufacturers such as government-regulation compliance, quality management (HACCP), lot traceability and recall, recipe management, etc. The implementation team consisted of lead hands/supervisors from every area of business and VP of SCM of KPL. The team pushed data entry to shop floor and offsite warehouse, providing terminals for supervisors/employees. As a result of using the ERP, inventory accuracy is up and inventory-on-hand is down. Receiving dates for ingredients are entered in the software and tracked. Justfooderp suggests the ingredient lots to be used based on first-come-first-served rule.

Source: http://www.justfooderp.com/JustFoodERPRefresh/media/JustFoodERP/PDF/Case%20Study/ Kitchen-Partners-Ltd.pdf.

Introduction to MRP

This chapter describes MRP (material requirements planning) and ERP (enterprise resource planning). MRP is a planning and scheduling technique used to manage production or purchase of the components of assembled items. In this chapter, a component refers to a raw material, part, or subassembly. ERP or enterprise software is used to manage and coordinate all the resources, information, and functions of an organization from a shared database. ERP grew out of MRP software, and includes other business modules.

First we will show why production/purchase plans for components of products require a different treatment than production/purchase plans for finished goods, supplies, or spare parts.

Dependent Demand

When demand for items is derived from plans to make certain products—as it is with components used in producing a finished product—those items are said to have **dependent demand**. For example, the components that go into the production of a particular model of automobile have dependent demand because the amounts needed are a function of the number of cars that is planned to be produced. Conversely, demand for the *finished* cars is *independent*. The customer demand for cars is not known before it occurs and has to be forecasted.

Independent demand of most finished goods and supplies is fairly steady once allowances are made for seasonal variations, but dependent demands tend to be sporadic or "lumpy"; large quantities are used at specific points in time with little or no usage at other times. For example, a company that produces lawn and garden equipment might make a variety of products such as lawn mowers and small tractors, but these are usually made in batches. Suppose that the products are produced as follows—in one month, push mowers; in the next month, mulching mowers; and in the third month, tractors. Some components may be used in most of the items (e.g., nuts and bolts, screws). It makes sense to have a continual inventory of these parts because they are always needed. On the other hand, some parts might be used for only one product. Consequently, demand for those parts occurs only when that product is being produced, which might be once every few months; the rest of the time, demand is zero. Thus, demand is "lumpy." Because of these tendencies, independent-demand items must be carried on a continual basis, but dependent-demand items need only be stocked just prior to the time they will be needed in production. Moreover, the predictability of usage of dependent-demand items implies that there is little need for safety stock.

Figure 14-1 illustrates key differences between independent and dependent demand, and inventory levels resulting from using inventory control models of Chapter 12 vs. MRP. The inventory control models of Chapter 12 are used for purchasing or production of items with independent demand. In this chapter, we will use MRP for planning the purchasing or production of dependent-demand items.

Overview of MRP

Material requirements planning (MRP) is the activity that determines the plans for purchasing and production of dependent-demand components. The production plan for a specified number of each product during the next 12 weeks or so (i.e., MPS) is converted into the requirements for its components, working backward from the due date of the product, using lead times and inventories on hand and on order. This determines when and how much to order each component. Hence, requirements for end items generate requirements for lower-level items, so that ordering, fabrication, and subassembly of parts can be scheduled for timely completion of end items while inventory levels for parts are kept reasonably low. Thus, MPS leads into MRP (see Figure 14-2).

L01

dependent demand
Demand for components derived from the plan for production of finished goods.

material requirements planning (MRP) The activity that determines the plans for purchasing and production of dependent-demand components.

Figure 14-1

Comparison of independent and dependent demand, and inventory levels resulting from using inventory control models of Chapter 12 vs. MRP.

Figure 14-2

A material requirements plan indicates quantity and timing details needed to achieve the master schedule.

Historically, planning purchasing and production of components for assembled products suffered from two difficulties. One was the enormous task of setting up production schedules for products, keeping track of large numbers of components, and coping with plan changes. The other was a lack of differentiation between independent demand and dependent demand items. All too often, techniques designed for independent-demand items were used to handle dependent-demand items, which resulted in excess inventories.

Then, manufacturers began to recognize the importance of the distinction between independent- and dependent-demand items and to approach these two categories in different ways. Much of the burden of record keeping and determining material requirements in many companies has now

OM in ACTION

UView Ultraviolet Systems

UView Ultraviolet Systems, based in Mississauga, makes innovative auto repair equipment and supplies such as an air conditioner leak-detection system. It has over 100 patents, 100 employees, and a 60,000 ft² plant. UView installed INDUSTRIOS ERP from INDUSTRIOS Software of Oakville, Ontario, to improve its inventory accuracy and reduce its inventories. UView especially uses the inventory, MRP worksheet, forecasting, production control, ATP, EDI, and shipment workbench of INDUSTRIOS. UView accountants use the MRP worksheet in INDUSTRIOS Test Environment to test forecasts/production plans.

Source: http://www.industrios.com/upload/New_UView_Success_Story.pdf.

Figure 14-3

Overview of MRP system.

been transferred to computers. A great deal of the credit for publicizing MRP and educating potential users about MRP goes to Joseph Orlicky,[1] George Plossl, Oliver Wight, and APICS.

The primary inputs to MRP are bills of materials, which contain the breakdown of products; a master production schedule, which states how many finished products are desired and when; and inventory on hand and on order (open shop or purchase orders already issued and being executed) and lead times. Outputs from MRP include planned order releases, immediate order releases (= planned order releases next period) and various reports (e.g., exception or changes needed). Figure 14-3 provides an overview of an MRP system.

Applications of MRP are spread throughout this chapter.

MRP Inputs

An MRP system has three major sources of information: the master production schedule; bills of materials; and inventory on hand, open orders, and lead times. Let's consider each of these inputs.

Master Production Schedule

A **master production schedule (MPS)**, as described in the previous chapter, is the anticipated build schedule stating which end items are to be produced, when, and in what quantities for the next 12 weeks or so. Figure 14-4 illustrates a portion of an MPS that shows planned production for the end item X for the planning horizon. The schedule shows that 100 units of X should be available (e.g., for shipments to customers) at the *start* of week 4 and that another 150 units should be available at the *start* of week 8.

Recall that the quantities in an MPS are determined to satisfy customer orders and forecasts.

The MPS separates the planning horizon into a series of time periods or *time buckets*, which are expressed in weeks or days. However, the time buckets need not be of equal length. In fact, the near-term portion of an MPS may be in days, but later portions may be in weeks or months. Usually, plans for those more distant time periods are more tentative than near-term requirements.

master production schedule (MPS) The anticipated build schedule stating which end items are to be produced, when, and in what quantities for the next 12 weeks or so.

Week number

Item: X	1	2	3	4	5	6	7	8
Quantity				100				150

Figure 14-4

A portion of the master production schedule for the end item X.

---

[1] Orlicky is the author of *Material Requirements Planning* (New York: McGraw-Hill, 1975).

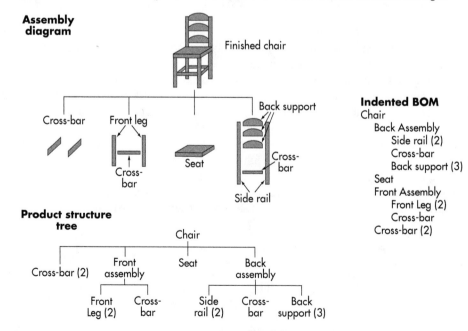

cumulative lead time The sum of the lead times that sequential phases of a process require, from ordering components to completion of final assembly.

It is important that the planning horizon be longer than the **cumulative lead time** necessary to produce the end items. This amounts to the sum of the lead times that sequential phases of the purchasing and production process require, as illustrated in Figure 14-5, where a total of nine weeks of lead time is needed from ordering components until final assembly is completed.

Some subassemblies are also included in the MPS if they are made to stock (and later used to assemble the final product to order).

Bills of Materials

bill of materials (BOM) A listing of all of the components (raw materials, parts, and subassemblies) needed to produce one unit of a product.

A **bill of materials (BOM)** is a listing of all of the components (subassemblies, parts, and raw material) that are needed to produce *one* unit of a finished product. Thus, each finished product has its own bill of materials.

A bill of materials is related to the assembly diagram and **product structure tree**, which provide a hierarchical diagram of the components needed to assemble a product. Figure 14-6 shows an assembly diagram for a chair, the associated product structure tree, and the indented BOM. The end item (in this case, the chair, the finished product) is shown at the top. Just beneath the end item are the back and front subassemblies that must be put together with two cross-bars and a seat to make up the end item; beneath each subassembly are the parts for it. Note that the numbers in the product structure tree refer to the quantity of a component needed to complete one unit of the parent at the next higher level. For example, three back supports are needed for one back assembly. One is not shown, e.g., 1 seat is needed. For the indented BOM, the subassemblies are indented one tab to the right, and the components of each subassembly are listed under it and indented one tab further to the right.

product structure tree A hierarchical diagram of the components needed to assemble a product.

SYSPRO

SYSPRO is a reasonably priced MRP/ERP software that is easy to use. Suppliers, work centres, all the components (raw materials/parts/subassemblies), products, and customers must be defined first. Then, the structure and routing (operations) of each product and its subassemblies must be defined. This involves listing each operation to be performed on the item and the components used in that operation. Using these structures and routings, customer orders or master production schedule, and inventories, SYSPRO determines the requirements plans. Below is the BOM for a simple table.

Let's consider the product structure tree shown in Figure 14-7. End item X is composed of two Bs and one C. Moreover, each B consists of three Ds and one E, and each D requires four Es. Similarly, each C is made up of two Es and two Fs. These *requirements* are listed by *level*, beginning with level 0 for the end item, then level 1 for the next level, and so on. The items at each level are children of the next level up and, as in a family tree, are *parents* of their respective children. For a software's use of BOM, see the "SYSPRO" OM in Action. Example 1 shows how a BOM can be used in MRP.

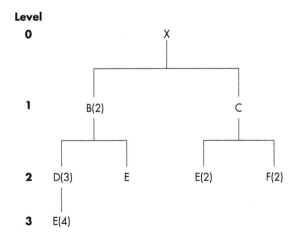

Figure 14-7

A product structure tree for end item X.

Example 1 ▶ Use the information presented in Figure 14-7 to do the following:

a. Determine the quantities of B, C, D, E, and F needed to assemble one X.

b. Determine the quantities of these components that will be required to assemble 10 Xs, taking into account the following inventories on hand (and none on order) of various components:

Component	On Hand
B	4
C	10
D	8
E	60
F	5

SOLUTION

a.

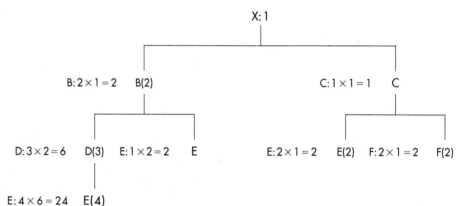

Thus, one X will require:

B:	2
C:	1
D:	6
E:	28 (Note that E occurs in three places, with requirements of 24 + 2 + 2 = 28)
F:	2

b.

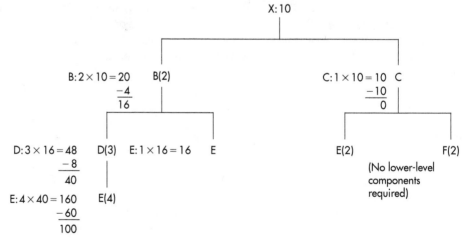

Thus, given the amounts of on-hand inventory, 10 Xs will require:

B:	16
C:	0
D:	40
E:	116 (= 100 + 16)
F:	0

OM in ACTION

Aqua Lung

When there are very similar end products with only minor differences such as different-colour trims, and if the final assembly can be postponed until late in production, then it is possible to simplify the planning process by combining similar end products into an artificial product with a BOM called a planning bill. For example, Aqua Lung, a manufacturer of scuba diving equipment and wet suits, used the planning bill shown to the right for its Spectrum wet suit.

Each suit required 2 yards of fabric. Roughly 75 percent of suits were black and 25 percent were blue. Therefore, in the planning bill 1.5 yards of black and 0.5 yard of blue fabric were specified.

Component	Description	Unit	Qty	Level
1-7001	Fabric, Black	Yard	1.5	1
1-7002	Fabric, Blue	Yard	.5	1
1-7500	Bind Tape, Black	Inch	300	1
1-7600	Bind Tape, Blue	Inch	100	1
1-1410	Velcro Hook, Black	Inch	33	1
1-1420	Velcro Hook, Blue	Inch	11	1
2-3510	Airway Assembly	Each	1	1
2-8-228	Tank Band Assembly	Each	1	1
1-2567	Foam Pad	Each	1	1
1-9001	Box, Spectrum	Each	1	1

Sources: G.H. French, "Linking Design, Marketing, and Shipping for Success: A Case Study in Integration," *Production and Inventory Management Journal*, 33(3), pp. 44–48; http://www.aqualung.com/us/gear/wetsuits.

Note that the amount on hand for each component is *netted out* (i.e., subtracted from the requirement) before determining the requirements of its children.

Determining net requirements is usually more complicated than Example 1 might suggest. The issue of *timing* is essential (i.e., when the components must be purchased or made) and must be included in the analysis.

Special Types of BOM. There are three special types of BOM.

A **planning bill**, also called a pseudo bill or a kit, is a combination of several BOMs (see e.g., the "Aqua Lung" OM in Action). While it does not relate to a real product, its use will result in the calculation of the right number of components to be purchased or produced. Planning bills are used to reduce the number of BOMs necessary for planning when the products have various options.

A **modular bill** is a type of planning bill that is arranged in product modules or options. Modular bills are used to reduce the number of BOMs when a product consists of many modules, each with a few options. For example, if there are 10 modules each with 2 options, the number of product configurations is $2^{10} = 1,024$, whereas there are only $10(2) = 20$ options. Thus, a company will use the 20 modular bills to plan the purchase or production of the modules and later will assemble the final products to order.

A **phantom bill**, also called a transient bill, is for an item that is usually not kept in inventory. However, it may be sometimes needed, e.g., a spare part or a work-in-process in an assembly line. A phantom item has zero lead time and special stock code so that it will not be regularly ordered. Use of a phantom bill makes planning easier.

planning bill Also called a pseudo bill or a kit, is a combination of several BOMs.

modular bill A type of planning bill that is arranged in product modules or options.

phantom bill Also called a transient bill, is for an item that is usually not kept in inventory.

Comment. It is important that the bill of materials accurately reflect the breakdown of a product, particularly since errors at one level will become magnified by the multiplication process used to determine quantity requirements of its components. As obvious as this might seem, many companies find themselves with incorrect bills of materials. This makes it impossible to effectively determine material requirements; moreover, the task of correcting these records can be complex and time consuming. Accurate records are a prerequisite for effective MRP.

Inventory On-hand, Open Orders, and Lead Times

Each item in stock (product, subassembly, part, or raw material) should have a separate description file that contains information about the item and, if purchased, the purchase lead time. Also, the quantity on hand (inventory balance) of each item should be updated continuously as transactions (receipts and issues) occur, and be used to net the requirements as in Example 1b.

Each fabricated or assembled item will have a configuration file that shows the operations necessary and the components used. Each operation will have a standard time for setup and per unit operation run time. Using these and the number of items to be produced, the total manufacturing lead time for a batch of the item is computed. Lead times will be used for timing orders.

Each open shop order and open purchase order (called scheduled receipt in MRP) has a quantity and due date and will be considered projected on-hand inventory on its due date (and used to net the requirements).

MRP Processing

MRP processing takes the end items' requirements specified by the MPS and "explodes" them into *time-phased* requirements for fabrication of parts or assembly of subassemblies, and purchase of purchased parts and raw materials using the bills of materials, offset by the lead times and netted for any inventory on hand or scheduled receipts (on order). You can see the time-phasing of requirements in the *assembly time chart* in Figure 14-8. For example, raw materials D, F, and I must be purchased at the start of week 2, part C at the start of week 4, and part H at the start of week 5 in order for 100 units of the end item to be made and be available for delivery at the start of week 12. The figure also shows the planned fabrication or assembly start times of manufactured items.

Figure 14-8

Assembly time chart showing material purchase points and production start times needed to meet scheduled delivery of 100 units of the end item at the start of week 12.

Lectronic is a small Mississauga, Ontario-based company with an innovative product: a radio-controlled golf caddy (http://www. kaddy.com). Lectronic has been using the full version (including the MRP module) of the Business System from Minotaur Software of Brampton.

Note that the length of horizontal lines represents the lead times. For example, the purchase lead time for raw material D is two weeks, and the manufacturing lead time for 100 units of part E has been computed to be two weeks. This is based on the speed of the operation(s) involved in fabricating part E.

The quantities that are generated by exploding the bills of materials are *gross requirements*; they do not take into account any inventory that is currently on hand or is due to be received (scheduled receipt). The materials that a company must actually acquire to meet the demand generated by the MPS are the *net requirements*.

The determination of the net requirements (*netting*) is the core of MRP processing. One accomplishes this by subtracting from gross requirements the sum of inventory on hand and any scheduled receipts, and then adding in safety stock requirements, if applicable:

$$\begin{array}{c} \text{Net} \\ \text{requirements in} \\ \text{period } t \end{array} = \begin{array}{c} \text{Gross} \\ \text{requirements} \\ \text{in period} \\ t \end{array} - \begin{array}{c} \text{Projected} \\ \text{inventory at} \\ \text{the start of} \\ \text{period } t \end{array} - \begin{array}{c} \text{Scheduled} \\ \text{receipt} \\ \text{in period } t \end{array} + \begin{array}{c} \text{Safety} \\ \text{stock} \\ \text{in period } t \end{array} \qquad (14\text{-}1)$$

If the formula gives a negative value, then there is no net requirement (i.e., it is 0). For simplicity, we will omit safety stock from the calculations in the examples and most problems. It is convenient to subtract the safety stock from inventory on hand and exclude it from MRP processing as if it was locked up in a stockroom. Net requirements are sometimes adjusted to include an allowance for scrap; but for simplicity, this too will not be included in the examples or most problems.

The timing and sizes of orders (i.e., materials ordered from suppliers or work ordered within the company) are determined by *planned-order releases*. The timing of the receipts of these quantities is indicated by *planned-order receipts*. Depending on ordering policy, the planned-order releases may have a minimum quantity, may be multiples of a specified quantity (e.g., 50 units), or may be equal to the quantity needed at that time (called lot-for-lot ordering). Example 2 will illustrate the difference between these ordering policies as well as the general concept of time-phasing material requirements in MRP. As you work through the example, you may find the following definitions helpful:

- **Gross requirement:** The demand for an item *during* a time period (a week or a day) without regard to the amount on hand or on order. For an end item, this is the production plan from the MPS; for a component, this is equal to the planned-order release of its immediate "parent" multiplied by the number of item used in one parent.

- **Scheduled receipt:** Open order scheduled to arrive from a vendor or shop floor in the *beginning* of a period.

- **Projected on-hand:** The amount of inventory that is expected to be on hand at the *beginning* of a time period: it equals the scheduled receipt this period plus any ending inventory expected from the last period.

- **Net requirement:** The actual amount needed in a time period.

- **Planned-order receipt:** The quantity planned to be received in the *beginning* of a period. Under lot-for-lot ordering, it will equal net requirement. Under lot-size ordering, it may exceed net requirement. We assume that any excess is added to available inventory in the beginning of the *next* time period.

- **Planned-order release:** The quantity planned to be released (i.e., ordered) in the beginning of a period. It equals planned-order receipt offset by the lead time. This amount generates gross requirement(s) at the next level down in the BOM. When an order is executed (i.e., the planned-order release of week 1 is released), it is removed from planned-order releases and receipts rows, and is entered in the scheduled receipts row, a lead-time period later.

These quantities are used in a time-phased plan in the following format. The column for period 0 is used to show beginning on-hand inventory.

Week or day number	0	1	2	3	4	5	6	7	8
Item:									
Gross requirements									
Scheduled receipts									
Projected on-hand									
Net requirements									
Planned-order receipts									
Planned-order releases									

gross requirement The demand for an item during a time period.

scheduled receipt Open order scheduled to arrive from a vendor or shop floor.

projected on-hand Expected amount of inventory that will be on hand at the beginning of a time period.

net requirement The actual amount needed in a time period.

planned-order receipt Quantity planned to be received in the beginning of a period.

planned-order release Quantity planned to be released (i.e., ordered) in the beginning of a period; that is, planned-order receipt offset by the lead time.

Example 2

A company that produces wood shutters has received two orders for a particular model of wood shutters: 100 units are due for delivery at the start of week 4 and 150 units are due for delivery at the start of week 8. Each shutter consists of two frames and four slatted wood sections. The wood sections are purchased, and the purchase lead time is one week. The frames are also purchased, and the purchase lead time is two weeks. Assembly of the shutters requires one week for lot sizes of 100 to 200 shutters. There will be a previously-arranged scheduled receipt of 70 wood sections from the vendor at the beginning of week 1. Currently, there is no on-hand inventory. Determine the size and timing of planned-order releases necessary to meet delivery requirements under each of these conditions:

Lot-for-lot ordering (i.e., order sizes are equal to net requirements).

Lot-size ordering with a minimum lot size of 320 units for frames and multiples of 70 units for wood sections.

SOLUTION

a. The production schedule for shutters is:

Week number:	1	2	3	4	5	6	7	8
Quantity:				100				150

b. Draw the product structure tree for a shutter:

c. Using *lot-for-lot ordering*, the MRP processing is shown in Figure 14-9.

At the start of week 4, the production schedule calls for 100 shutters to be ready for delivery and no shutters are projected to be on hand, so the net requirements are 100 shutters. Therefore, planned-order receipt for week 4 equals 100 shutters. Because shutter assembly for 100 units requires one week, this means a planned-order release at the start of week 3. Using the same logic, 150 shutters must be assembled during week 7 in order to be available for delivery at the start of week 8.

The planned-order release of 100 shutters at the start of week 3 means that 200 frames (gross requirement) must be available at that time. Because none are expected to be on hand, this generates net requirement of 200 frames and necessitates planned-order receipt of 200 frames by the start of week 3. With a two-week purchase lead time, this means that the company must order 200 frames at the start of week 1. Similarly, the planned-order release of 150 shutters at the start of week 7 generates gross and net requirements of 300 frames for week 7 as well as planned-order receipt for that time. The two-week purchase lead time means that the company must order frames at the start of week 5.

The planned-order release of 100 shutters at the start of week 3 also generates gross requirement of 400 wood sections at that time. However, because 70 wood sections are expected to be received (scheduled receipt) at the start of week 1 and will be on hand, net requirement is 400 − 70 = 330 for week 3. This means a planned-order receipt of 330 by the start of week 3. Since purchase lead time for wood sections is one week, the purchase order must be issued (planned-order release) at the beginning of week 2.

Similarly, the planned-order release of 150 shutters in week 7 generates gross requirement of 600 (150 × 4) wood sections at that time. Because no on-hand inventory of wood sections is projected for week 7, net requirement is also 600, and planned-order receipt is 600 units at the start of week 7. Again, the one-week purchase lead time means 600 sections should be purchased (planned-order release) at the start of week 6.

Production schedule for shutters:

◀ **Figure 14-9**

MRP tables with lot-for-lot ordering for Example 2.

d. Under lot-size ordering, the only difference is the possibility that planned receipts will exceed net requirements. The excess is recorded as projected on-hand inventory in the beginning of the following week. For example, in Figure 14-10, the minimum order size for frames is 320 units, but net requirement for week 3 is 200; thus, 320 units are ordered, resulting in an excess of 320 − 200 = 120 units, which become projected on-hand inventory in the start of next week. Similarly, net frame requirement is 300 − 120 = 180 units in week 7, thus 320 units are ordered, and the excess of 320 − 180 = 140 units becomes projected on-hand inventory in the start of week 8. The same thing happens with wood sections; the excess of planned-order receipts in weeks 3 and 7 is added to projected-on-hand in the start of weeks 4 and 8. Note that the order size for wood sections must be in *multiples* of 70; for week 3 it is 5 times 70 because 350 is the first multiple of 70 larger than 330, and for week 7 it is 9 times 70 because 630 is the first multiple of 70 larger than 580.

Figure 14-10 ▶

MRP tables with lot-size ordering for Example 2.

Production schedule for shutters:

Week number	Beg. Inv.	1	2	3	4	5	6	7	8
Quantity					100				150

Shutters
LT = 1 week
Lot size = lot-for-lot

	Beg. Inv.	1	2	3	4	5	6	7	8
Gross requirements					100				150
Scheduled receipts									
Projected on-hand									
Net requirements					100				150
Planned-order receipts					100				150
Planned-order releases				100				150	

times 2   times 2

Frames
LT = 2 weeks
Lot size = minimum of 320

	Beg. Inv.	1	2	3	4	5	6	7	8
Gross requirements					200				300
Scheduled receipts									
Projected on-hand					120	120	120	120	140
Net requirements					200				180
Planned-order receipts					320				320
Planned-order releases		320				320			

times 4   times 4

Wood sections
LT = 1 week
Lot size = multiples of 70

	Beg. Inv.	1	2	3	4	5	6	7	8
Gross requirements					400			600	
Scheduled receipts		70							
Projected on-hand	70	70	70	70	20	20	20	20	50
Net requirements					330			580	
Planned-order receipts					350			630	
Planned-order releases				350			630		

Example 2 is useful for describing some of the main features of MRP processing, but it understates the enormity of the task of keeping track of material requirements, especially in situations where the same subassemblies, parts, or raw materials are used in different products. Differences in timing of demands, revisions caused by late deliveries, high scrap rates, and cancelled orders all have an impact on processing.

Example 3 ▶

Consider the two product structure trees shown in Figure 14-11. Note that both products A and C have D as a component. Suppose we want to develop a material requirements plan for D given this additional information: the demand for A is 80 units at the start of week 4 and the demand for C is 50 units at the start of week 5; there is a beginning inventory of 110 units of D on hand, all items have manufacturing or purchase lead times of one week, and we order D using lot-for-lot ordering. The plan is shown in Figure 14-12. Note that the requirements for B and E are not shown because they are not a "parent" of D.

Figure 14-11 ▶

Two different products (A and C) having D as a component.

Production schedule

Week number		1	2	3	4	5	6
Quantity (A, C)					80	50	

◀ **Figure 14-12**

Material requirements plan for component D of Example 3.

A Assembly LT = 1	Beg. Inv.	1	2	3	4	5	6
Gross requirements					80		
Scheduled receipts							
Projected on-hand							
Net requirements					80		
Planned-order receipts					80		
Planned-order releases				80			

times
1

C Assembly LT = 1	Beg. Inv.	1	2	3	4	5	6
Gross requirements					50		
Scheduled receipts							
Projected on-hand							
Net requirements					50		
Planned-order receipts					50		
Planned-order releases					50		

times
2

D Purchase LT = 1	Beg. Inv.	1	2	3	4	5	6
Gross requirements				80	100		
Scheduled receipts							
Projected on-hand	110	110	110	110	30		
Net requirements					70		
Planned-order receipts					70		
Planned-order releases				70			

The term **pegging** denotes working the MRP processing in reverse; that is, identifying the immediate parent items that have generated a given set of requirements for an item such as D. Although this may appear simple enough, when multiple products are involved, it is more complex. Pegging enables managers to determine which items will be affected if an order for an item such as D is late.

The importance of the computer becomes evident when you consider that a typical company would have hundreds of end items for which it needs to develop material requirements plans, each with its own set of components. Inventories on hand and on order, planned order releases, and so on must all be updated as changes and rescheduling occur. Without the aid of a computer, the task would be hopeless.

pegging Identifying the immediate parent items that have generated a given set of requirements for an item.

Updating the System

A material requirements plan is not a static document. As time passes, some purchase/work orders will have been completed, and new purchase/work orders will have to be released. In addition, there may have been changes to purchase/work orders, such as changes in quantity, delays, missed deliveries of parts or raw materials, and so on. In addition, MPS may have changed and new customer order may have been received. Hence, a material requirements plan is a "living" document, one that changes over time. And what we refer to as Week 1 (i.e., the current week) is continually moving ahead; so what is now Week 2 will soon become Week 1. In a sense, requirements plans such as these have *a rolling horizon*, which means that plans are updated and revised so that they reflect the next set of weeks.

The two basic approaches used to update MRP tables are *regenerative* and *net change*. Regenerative MRP is run periodically; net-change MRP is continuously updated.

regenerative MRP
Recomputes all the MRP quantities periodically.

Regenerative MRP is essentially a batch-type approach. All inputs to MRP are updated (e.g., inventory on-hand, MPS, BOMs), the MRP quantities are blanked, and the MRP is processed again.

net-change MRP
Immediately updates only MRP tables affected by a change.

In **net-change MRP**, the requirements plan is modified to reflect changes as they occur. If some defective purchased parts had to be returned to a vendor, the manager can enter this information into the system as soon as it becomes known. Only the *changes* are "exploded" through the system, level by level; the entire plan would not be regenerated.

Regenerative MRP is best suited for fairly stable situations, whereas net-change MRP is best suited for situations that have frequent changes. The obvious disadvantage of regenerative MRP is the potential amount of lag between the time information becomes available and the time it can be incorporated into the material requirements plan. One way around this is to use a day as the time bucket (instead of a week) and rerun the MRP every night.

Processing costs are typically less using regenerative MRP; changes that occur in a given time period could ultimately cancel each other, thereby avoiding the need to modify and then remodify the plan.

Even a small change in requirements of an item at the top of the product structure tree can have large effects on items down the tree. This is referred to as MRP system *nervousness*. This is especially a problem if it results in changes in purchase or shop orders. MRP system nervousness is similar to the bullwhip effect in supply chains (see Chapter 11). As stated in Chapter 13, one solution to this problem is to freeze the master production schedule for the near future (e.g., next four weeks).

backflushing Exploding an end item's BOM to determine the quantities of the components that must have been used to make the item.

Backflushing is "exploding" an end item's BOM periodically to determine the quantities of the components that must have been used to make the item (and updating their inventory on-hand). This eliminates the need to collect detailed usage information on the production floor.

MRP Outputs

MRP systems have the ability to provide management with a fairly broad range of outputs, in addition to the MRP tables described previously. These are often classified as *primary reports*, which are the main reports, and *secondary reports*, which are optional outputs.

Primary Reports. Immediate order releases, planned-order releases, and changes (exceptions) are part of primary reports:

immediate order releases
Authorization for the execution of week 1 planned-order releases.

1. **Immediate order releases** authorize the execution of week 1 planned-order releases.
2. Planned order releases indicate the amount and timing of future purchase/work orders.
3. Changes to open orders: revisions to due dates and quantities, e.g., expedite, de-expedite, move forward, and move backward. For example, in Example 2, the software would indicate postponing the 70 unit Scheduled Receipt of Wood sections in Week 1 to Week 3.

Secondary Reports. Performance-control and demand history reports belong to secondary reports.

performance-control reports
Evaluation of system operation, including deviations from plans and cost information.

1. **Performance-control reports** evaluate system operation. They aid managers by measuring deviations from plans, including missed deliveries and stock-outs, and by providing information that can be used to assess cost performance.

2. **Demand history reports** are useful in forecasting future inventory requirements. They include net requirements and other data that can be used to forecast future component requirements.

demand history reports
Data useful for forecasting future component requirements.

The wide range of outputs generally permits users to tailor MRP to their particular needs.

Some Related Concepts

Safety Stock

Theoretically, inventory systems with dependent demand should not require safety stock below the end-item level. This is one of the main advantages of the MRP approach. Supposedly, safety stock is not needed because the manager can project the requirements once the MPS has been established. Practically, however, there may be exceptions. For example, a bottleneck process or one with varying scrap rates can cause shortages in downstream operations. Furthermore, shortages may occur if orders are late or fabrication or assembly times take longer than expected.

MRP systems deal with these problems in several ways. The manager's first step is to identify activities or operations that are subject to variability and to determine the extent of that variability. When lead times are variable, the concept of safety *time* instead of safety *stock* is often used. This results in scheduling orders for arrival or completion sufficiently ahead of the time they are needed in order to eliminate or substantially reduce the element of chance in waiting for those items. It is important in general to make sure that lead times are accurate. If safety stock is needed because of possible quality problems resulting in scrap, planned order release amounts can be increased by a percentage.

Lot Sizing

Determining a lot size to purchase or to produce an order is an important issue in inventory management for both independent- and dependent-demand items. This is called **lot sizing**. For independent-demand items, managers often use economic order quantity or economic production quantity. For dependent-demand systems, however, a wider variety of models is used to determine lot sizes, mainly because no single model has a clear advantage over the others. Some of the most popular models for lot sizing are described in this section.

A primary goal of inventory management for both independent- and dependent-demand items is to minimize the sum of annual ordering cost (or setup cost) and holding cost. With independent demand, the demand is frequently distributed uniformly throughout the year. However, demand tends to be much more lumpy for dependent demand, and the planning horizon is shorter (e.g., three months), so economic lot sizes are usually much more difficult to identify. See Figure 14-13 for an example of lumpy demand for a part.

Managers can usually realize economies by grouping consecutive orders. This would be the case if the additional cost incurred by holding the extra units until they are used lead to a savings in setup or ordering cost. This determination can be very complex at times for two reasons. First,

lot sizing Choosing a lot size for a purchase or production order.

	Period				
	1	2	3	4	5
Demand	70	50	1	80	4
Cumulative demand	70	120	121	201	205

▲ **Figure 14-13**

Lumpy demand for a part.

  OM in ACTION

Atlas Hydraulics

Atlas Hydraulics (AH) makes tubes and hoses for agriculture/forestry/construction equipment manufacturers in two plants in Canada and three plants in the United States. AH performs some of the operations (brazing, plating, and bending) in its main plant in Brantford, Ontario, and ships work-in-process to other plants. Scheduling and control of all operations in all plants are centralized in Brantford. AH uses Epicor's CMS (ERP for discrete manufacturers) to do so, especially the MRP module and the EDI. Before

Epicor, AH used Excel for planning, and back-flushed inventory of components as products were shipped, and was able to do only one physical inventory per year. Now, AH does cycle counting 220 days/year, which has improved its inventory accuracy from 90 percent to 98.8 percent. The software has also allowed AH to meet the customer-promised one-week lead time for hoses and six-week lead time for tubes, despite long-distance shipments.

Sources: http://www.epicor.com/MRCPR/Atlas-Hydraulics-CS-ENS.pdf; http://www.atlashyd.com.

combining the demands for some of the periods into a single order, particularly for middle-level or end items, has a cascading effect down through the product structure tree; that is, in order to achieve this grouping, you must also group items at lower levels in the tree and incorporate their setup and holding costs into the decision. Second, the uneven period demands and the relatively short planning horizon require continual recalculation and updating of lot sizes.

The choice of a lot-sizing technique must take into account the nature of demand (degree of uniformity), the relative importance of holding cost versus ordering (or setup) cost, and any other considerations that affect ordering. No single method is suited to all conditions.

Regardless of the lot-sizing method in use, there is always the possibility of adjustments in order sizes due to allowance for shrinkage or scrap, minimum and maximum order quantities established by management or supplier (e.g., do not order more than five months' supply), and operating or shipping constraints (e.g., 200 pieces per run or 12 dozen per shipment). Below are two of the more common lot sizing methods.

Fixed-Interval Ordering. This type of ordering provides coverage for some predetermined number of periods (e.g., two or three weeks). In some instances, the span is simply arbitrary; in other cases, a review of historical demand patterns may lead to a more rational designation of order interval. The rule can be modified when common sense suggests a better way. For example, take a look at the demand shown in Figure 14-13. Using two-period intervals, an order size of 120 units would cover the first two periods. However, the demand in period 3 is so small that it would make sense to combine it with the demand during the first two periods; that is, order 121 units for the first three periods.

Part-Period Method. This method provides a better way to determine the number of periods to order for at the same time. The part-period method, like the EOQ, attempts to balance setup (or ordering) and holding costs. The term *part period* refers to holding a part or parts over a number of periods. For instance, if 10 parts (or units) were held for two periods, this would be $10 \times 2 = 20$ part periods. The economic part period (EPP) can be calculated as the ratio of setup (or ordering) cost to the cost to hold a unit for one period. Thus, the formula for calculating the EPP is:

$$EPP = \frac{\text{Setup (or ordering) cost}}{\text{Unit holding cost per period}} \qquad (14\text{-}2)$$

To determine an order size that is consistent with the EPP, various order sizes equal to various cumulative demands are examined and each one's number of part periods is determined. The one that comes closest to the EPP is selected as the best lot size. Example 4 illustrates this approach.

Example 4 ▶

Use the part-period method to determine production run sizes for the following demands (i.e., net requirements) for a manufactured part:

		Period						
	1	**2**	**3**	**4**	**5**	**6**	**7**	**8**
Demand	60	40	20	2	30	—	70	50
Cumulative demand	60	100	120	122	152	152	222	272

Setup cost is $80 per production run for this item, and unit holding cost is $0.95 per period.

SOLUTION

1. First calculate the EPP: EPP = $80/$0.95 = 84.21, which rounds to 84 part periods. This is the target.

2. Next, try the cumulative lot sizes, beginning with 60, until the part periods approximate the EPP. The calculations of part periods on the next page indicate that 122 units should be ordered in period 1 to cover the demand for the first 4 periods. Repeat this process starting at period 5, which results in 100 units to be ordered in period 5 to cover periods 5 to 7. The next lot will be ordered in period 8, but there is insufficient information now to determine its size.

Period When Order Is Placed	Lot Size	Extra Inventory Carried	×	Periods Carried	=	Part Periods	Cumulative Part Periods
1	60	0		0		0	0
	100	40		1		40	40
	120	20		2		40	80
	122	2		3		6	86*
5	30	0		0		0	0
	100	70		2		140	140**
8	50	0		0		0	0

*Closer to 84 (than 80)
**Closer to 84 (than 0).

The part-period method worked well for the first lot size because the cumulative number of part periods is close to the EPP, but the effect of lumpy demand is apparent for the second lot size of 100 (140 part periods is not very close to 84 part periods).

Capacity Requirements Planning

Capacity requirements planning (CRP) is the process of determining and adjusting detailed capacity requirements of MRP. The inputs to CRP are planned-order releases of MRP for fabricated or assembled items, the current shop load, routing information, and job times. The output of CRP is load reports for each work centre.

An MPS and the resulting MRP may not be feasible given the capacities of the production process. It is often necessary to run the MPS and MRP through CRP in order to obtain a clearer picture of actual requirements, which can then be compared to available capacities. If it turns out that the MPS/MRP are not feasible, management can either increase the capacity of overloaded work centre(s) (e.g., through overtime) or revise the MPS/MRP. In the latter case, this may entail several revisions, each of which is run through the CRP system until a feasible plan is obtained. At that point, the MPS and MRP are *frozen*, at least for the near term, thus establishing a firm schedule and requirements plan.

Figure 14-14 presents an overview of the capacity requirements planning process. The process begins with a proposed or tentative master production schedule that must be tested for feasibility and possibly adjusted before it becomes permanent. The proposed schedule is processed using MRP to determine the material requirements. These are then translated into resource (i.e., capacity) requirements for items made in-house involving assembly or fabrication. This is often in the form of a series of **load reports** for each department or work centre, which compares known and expected future capacity requirements with capacity availability. Figure 14-15 illustrates the nature of a load report. It shows expected resource requirements for jobs currently being worked on and the future planned-order releases. Given this sort of information, the manager can more easily determine whether capacity is sufficient to satisfy these requirements. In the load report illustrated in Figure 14-15, planned-order releases in time period 4 will cause an overload. However, it may be possible to accommodate demand by shifting some orders to adjacent periods. In cases where capacity is insufficient, a manager may be able to increase capacity by scheduling overtime or transferring personnel from other areas if this is possible and economical, or revise the MPS/MRP.

If the master production schedule must be revised, this generally means that the manager must assign priorities to orders because some orders will be finished later than originally planned.

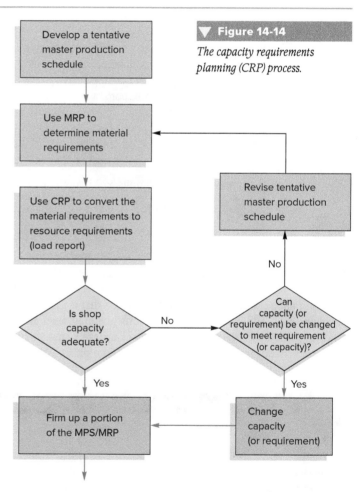

▼ **Figure 14-14**

The capacity requirements planning (CRP) process.

capacity requirements planning The process of determining and adjusting detailed capacity requirements of MRP.

load reports Department or work centre reports that compare known and expected future capacity requirements with capacity availability.

Figure 14-15 ▶

An example of a work centre or department's load report.

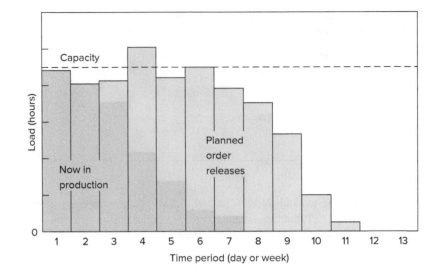

One note of caution is in order concerning the load reports. Often, the load reports are only approximations, and they may not give a true picture because the loading does not take into account queuing delays.

An important aspect of capacity requirements planning is the conversion of quantity requirements into time requirements. This is accomplished by multiplying each period's quantity requirements by standard time per unit plus a setup time per production run. For instance, if 10 units of product A are scheduled in the fabrication department and each unit has a standard time of 2 hours plus a set up time of 8 hours for the batch, then 10 units of A converts into:

10 units × 2 hours/unit + 8 = 28 hours

By the way, this is the manufacturing lead time for fabricating 10 units of A.

MRP II

manufacturing resource planning (MRP II) Expanded system for production planning and scheduling, involving sales and operations planning, MPS, MRP, CRP, and detailed scheduling.

Material requirements planning has been expanded into a broader system for planning and scheduling the resources of manufacturing companies. This expanded system is dubbed **MRP II** (two), which is also referred to as **manufacturing resource planning**. MRP II is a *closed-loop MRP*, which means that it involves the whole production planning process, starting with sales and operations planning; then MPS, MRP, and CRP; and finally detailed scheduling, with feedback going back up (see Figure 14-16).

See the "Caterpillar" OM in Action for an example of the MRP II implementation.

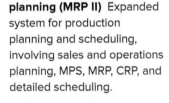 **OM in ACTION** http://www.cat.com

Caterpillar

Caterpillar's Construction Industry (Cat) division makes Bull-dozers. Cat went through a long labour strike that destroyed labour–management trust. The new chairman instituted a Common Values program to restore trust, mutual respect, and teamwork. After a few years, there were still too many emergencies and too much time spent searching for parts, and unreliable deliveries of parts to dealers. Also, manufacturing did not trust marketing's forecasts, which frequently overestimated the demand. So the division was mandated to certify for Oliver Wight International's Class A in Planning and Control. Oliver Wight was one of the originators of MRP, and established a certification program so that companies could learn to perform

effective production planning (called MRP II). To combat communication issues, Oliver Wight consultants served as change agents and independent observers. They instituted formal processes so that employees started meeting regularly and working together. The major initiative was Sales & Operations Planning (S&OP, see Chapter 13). Classes were conducted for middle managers and planners/schedulers on S&OP and developing valid schedules. Every operator was trained for two hours on inventory record and BOM accuracy. As a result, Cat's on-time delivery is now 98 percent, inventory of dealers is down, and use of overtime and expedited freight is down significantly.

Source: https://www.oliverwight-americas.com/system/files/public/clients/profiles/caterpillarttt.pdf.

Enterprise Resource Planning

ERP (enterprise resource planning) or enterprise software is used to manage and coordinate all the resources, information, and functions of an organization from a shared database. ERP involves *standardized* record keeping that will facilitate *information sharing.*

ERP became popular when enterprises were revamping their legacy mainframe computer systems in anticipation of possible year 2000 (Y2K) problems. Tier 1 ERPs at that time, such as SAP, PeopleSoft, J.D. Edwards, BAAN, and Oracle cost millions of dollars to buy and implement, and had a high annual maintenance fee. But top managers felt that they had no choice and jumped on the bandwagon. Because of their complexity, the implementation of most ERPs took many years. The complexity was due to the fact that the software had thousands of features/settings. For example, Tier 1 ERPs are multicurrency and multilanguage.

However, Tier 1 ERPs offered more capabilities than accounting software such as Great Plains and ACCPAC, which primarily kept track of transactions. Tier 1 ERPs included high-volume fast databases that could be connected to supplier systems, and modules to perform HR, manufacturing planning and control, materials management, customer relationship management (CRM), and e-commerce. They also provided industry-specific solutions and the ability to control work flow such as enforcing the authorization requirement for a high-dollar purchase by a buyer. See Table 14.1 for a brief description of common ERP software modules.

Now, many midmarket accounting software have expanded to become complete business systems, even including manufacturing modules. Microsoft has also entered this market by buying Great Plains, Navision, and Solomon accounting software, and even introduced its own ERP software called Axapta (now these software are called Microsoft Dynamics GP, Nav, Sl, and Ax, respectively).

The difference between Tier 1 ERPs and some Tier 2 ERPs has shrunk. At the same time, many companies have realized the high cost and complexity of Tier 1 ERPs. As a result, ERP companies such as SAP are providing mid-market products such as SAP Business One. Also, there has been significant consolidation. For example, PeopleSoft bought J.D. Edwards, then Oracle bought PeopleSoft, and Baan is now part of Infor. For a list of ERP vendors and news, see http://www.180systems.com/portals/erp. For some applications of ERP, see "Some SYSPRO Applications" OM in Action and other OM in Actions spread throughout the chapter.

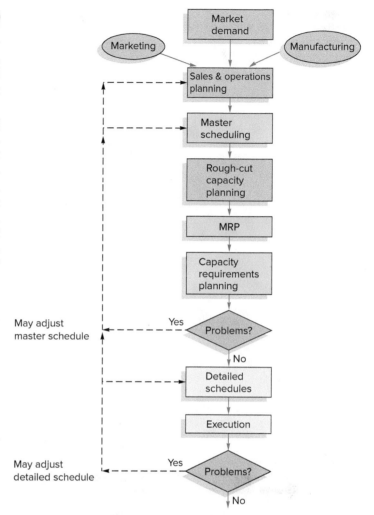

▲ **Figure 14-16**

An overview of MRP II process.

enterprise resource planning (ERP) Also known as enterprise software, it is used to manage and coordinate all the resources, information, and functions of an organization from a shared database.

ERP Definition and Solutions[2]

ERP attempts to integrate all departments and functions of a company onto a single computer system that can serve all those different departments' particular needs.

It's a tall order, building a single software program that serves the needs of the people in finance as well as it does the people in human resources and in the warehouse. Each of those departments typically has its own computer system, each optimized for the particular ways that the department

---

[2] Most of this section is based on C. Koch and T. Wailgum, "ERP Definition and Solutions," http://www.cio.com/article/40323/ERP_Definition_and_Solutions.

	Module	Brief Description
Table 14-1 *An overview of some ERP software modules*	Accounting/Finance	A central component of most ERP systems. It provides a range of financial capabilities, including general ledger, accounts payable, accounts receivable, payroll, income statements, and balance sheets.
	Marketing	Supports lead generation, target marketing, direct mail, and sales.
	Human Resources	Maintains a complete database of employee information such as date of hire, salary, contact information, performance evaluations, and other pertinent information.
	Purchasing	Facilitates vendor selection, price negotiation, issuing purchase orders, and receiving shipments.
	Production Planning	Integrates information on forecasts, orders, production capacity, on-hand inventory quantities, bills of materials, work in process, schedules, and production lead times.
	Inventory Management	Identifies inventory requirements, inventory availability, replenishment rules, and inventory tracking.
	Distribution	Contains information on third-party carriers, shipping and delivery schedules, delivery tracking.
	Sales	Information on orders, invoices, order tracking, and shipping.
	Supply Chain Management	Facilitates supplier and customer management, supply chain visibility, and event management.
	Customer Relationship Management	Contact information, buying behaviour, shipping preferences, contracts, payment terms, and credit history.

OM in *ACTION*   http://www.syspro.com

Some SYSPRO Applications

Hayward Gordon (http://www.haywardgordon.com)

Hayward Gordon (HG) designs, manufacturers, and distributes industrial pumps for mining, waste-water treatment, and other

process industries. It has a head office and 50,000 ft² plant in Halton Hills, Ontario, and sales offices in Montreal, Calgary, and Vancouver. HG has 78 employees and exports worldwide. In order to reduce costs, HG installed SYSPRO. Besides the Financials, HG uses the BOM, WIP, and Requirements Planning modules to plan and control production. SYSPRO also helps track operations/labour times on the shop floor. Furthermore, Microsoft's CRM is integrated in SYSPRO for order entry, credit check, etc.

Higginson Equipment (http://www.higginson.ca)

Higginson Equipment (HE), founded in 1945, is a Canadian cylinder manufacturer and distributor that has been providing products and services to thousands of customers across Canada from its 50-employee facility in Burlington, Ontario.

The company designs and manufactures hydraulic and pneumatic cylinders to National Fluid Power Association (NFPA) standards and custom specifications, and distributes more than 30 fluid power and industrial product lines.

In 2009, management decided to replace its 15-year old business software, which didn't have MRP. HE was using an Excel worksheet for each job and to calculate the product's dimensions. With the help of two grants, HE purchased SYSPRO, which automatically generates work orders from sales orders, stores BOMs and uses them in quotations, etc.

Since installing the MRP software, sales have more than doubled. The original office staff are still able to process all the orders and HE has had to add only manufacturing employees.

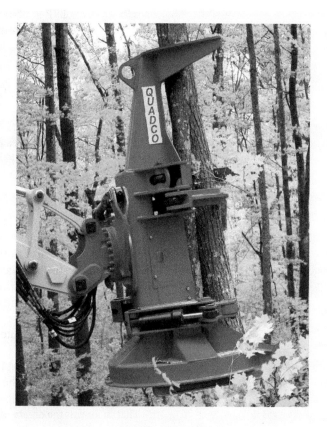

Quadco Equipment (http://www.quadco.com)

Quadco Equipment (QE) designs and manufactures configurable saw teeth heads for wood harvesting equipment in the forestry industry. It is based in St. Eustache, Quebec, with two parts and service facilities in Canada and two in the U.S. QE employs 200 employees and holds 40 patents. It has been using SYSPRO for over a decade. QE uses all the programs in SYSPRO but finds the Product Configurator especially useful. This program allows QE to easily create a new product structure from existing components. SYSPRO generates a sales order/price quote and a work order automatically. Another useful feature of SYSPRO is that all the product information is available in one screen.

Arctic Manufacturing (http://www.arcticmfg.com)

Arctic Manufacturing (AM) designs and manufactures log-hauling trailers. Its 35,000 ft² shop is located in Prince George, British Columbia. AM has been using SYSPRO for over two decades. It uses most SYSPRO modules, but especially finds the WIP module useful for tracking costs. AM also finds the customizable screens useful.

Sources: http://americas.sypro.com/resources/case_studies/ca/hayward_gordon_canada_syspro_case_study.pdf; http://www.syspro.com/resources/case_studies/ca/higginson_canada_syspro_case_study.pdf; http://www.syspro.com/resources/case_studies/ca/quadco_equipment_canada_syspro_case_study.pdf; http://www.syspro.com/resources/case_studies/ca/arcticmanufacturing_canada_syspro_case_study.pdf.

does its work. But ERP combines them all into a single, integrated software program that runs off a single database so that the various departments can more easily share information and communicate with each other, and also it reduces redundant data entry.

The integrated approach can have a tremendous payback if companies install the software correctly. Take a customer order, for example. Typically, when a customer places an order, that order begins a mostly paper-based journey from in-basket to in-basket around the company, often being keyed and rekeyed into different departments' computer systems along the way. All that lounging around in in-baskets causes delays and lost orders, and all the keying into different computer systems invites errors. Meanwhile, no one in the company truly knows what the status of the order is at any given point in time because there is no way for the finance department, for example, to get into the warehouse's computer system to see whether the item has been shipped.

How Can ERP Improve a Company's Business Performance? ERP automates the tasks involved in performing a business process—such as order fulfillment, which involves taking an order from a customer, making it, shipping it, and billing for it. With ERP, when a customer service representative takes an order from a customer, he or she has all the information necessary to complete the order (the customer's credit rating and order history, the company's MPS and inventory levels, and the shipping/trucking schedule). Everyone else in the company has access to the single database that holds the customer's new order. When one department finishes with the order, it is automatically routed using the ERP system to the next department. To find out where the order is at any time, one needs only to log on to the ERP system and track it down. Customers get their orders faster and with fewer mistakes than before. ERP can apply that same magic to the other major business processes, such as employee benefits or financial reporting.

That, at least, is the dream of ERP. The reality is much harsher. Let's go back to those in-baskets. That process may not have been efficient, but it was simple. Finance did its job, the warehouse did its job, and if anything went wrong outside the department's walls, it was somebody else's problem. Not anymore. With ERP, the customer service representatives are no longer just typists entering someone's name into a computer and hitting the Enter key. The ERP screen makes them business people. It flickers with the customer's credit rating from the finance department and the product inventory levels from the warehouse. Will the customer pay on time? Will we be able to ship the order on time? These are questions that customer service representatives have never had to answer before and they affect the customer and every other department in the company. But it's not just the customer service representatives who have to wake up. People in the warehouse who used to keep inventory in their heads or on scraps of paper now need to put that information online. If they don't, customer service will see low inventory levels on their screens and tell customers that their requested item is not in stock. Accountability, responsibility, and communication have never been tested like this before.

To do ERP right, the ways a company does business will need to change and the ways people do their jobs will need to change too. Real transformational ERP implementation usually runs between one and three years.

Will ERP Fit the Way a Company Does Business? It's critical for companies to figure out if their ways of doing business will fit within a standard ERP package before the cheques are signed and the implementation begins. The most common reason that companies walk away from multi-million dollar ERP projects is that they discover that the software does not support one of their important business processes. At that point there are two things they can do: They can change the business process to accommodate the software, which will mean deep changes in long-established ways of doing business and shaking up important people's roles and responsibilities. Or they can modify the software to fit the process, which will slow down the project, introduce dangerous bugs into the system, and make upgrading the software difficult.

What Does ERP Really Cost? The total cost of ownership of ERP, including hardware, software, professional services, and internal staff costs (for one to two years after installation, which is when the real costs of maintaining, upgrading, and optimizing the system are felt) usually ranges between $50,000 and a few million dollars, depending on the number of licences (seats) and the software.

The Hidden Costs of ERP ERP practitioners point to the following areas as most likely to result in budget overrun:

1. *Training.* Training expenses are high because workers almost invariably have to learn a new set of processes, not just a new software.

2. *Integration and testing.* A typical manufacturing company may have add-on applications for logistics, production planning, and bar coding. If this laundry list also includes customization of the core ERP package, expect the cost of integrating, testing, and maintaining the system to skyrocket.

3. *Data conversion.* It costs money to move corporate information, such as customer and supplier records, product design data and the like, from old systems to a new ERP system.

4. *Consultants.* When users fail to plan for disengagement, consulting fees run wild.

How Do You Configure ERP Software? The packages are built from database tables, thousands of them, that programmers and end users must set to match their business processes; each table has a decision "switch" that leads the software down one decision path or another. By presenting only one way for the company to do each task—say, run the payroll or close the books—a company's individual operating units and far-flung divisions are integrated under one system. But figuring out precisely how to set all the switches in the tables requires a deep understanding of the existing processes being used to operate the business. As the table settings are decided, these business processes are re-engineered ERP's way. Most ERP systems are preconfigured, allowing just hundreds—rather than thousands—of procedural settings to be made by the customer.

Summary

- Material requirements planning (MRP) is the activity that determines the ordering of dependent-demand items (i.e., components of assembled products).
- The planning process begins with a master production schedule.
- The end items are "exploded" using bills of materials, inventory on-hand and on order (scheduled receipts) are netted, and planned order releases are developed by offsetting for lead times. These show the quantity and timing for purchasing or producing components.
- Little safety stock is used in MRP. Instead, safety time (ordering earlier) is used.

- Various lot-sizing methods are used in MRP such as part-period method. However, the main approach is lot-for-lot ordering.
- Capacity requirements planning (CRP) uses the MRP shop order releases and standard operations times to determine the capacity requirements from each work centre.
- MRP II is a second-generation MRP that adds a broader scope to planning because it links sales and operations planning, MPS, MRP, CRP, and detailed scheduling.
- ERP systems build on these linkages even further by integrating all functions of business on a single common database.

Key Terms

backflushing
bill of materials (BOM)
capacity requirements planning
cumulative lead time
demand history reports

dependent demand
enterprise resource planning (ERP)
gross requirement
immediate order releases
load reports

lot sizing
manufacturing resource planning
   (MRP II)
master production schedule
material requirements planning (MRP)

modular bill
net requirement
net-change MRP
pegging
performance-control reports

phantom bill
planned-order receipt
planned-order release
planning bill
product structure tree

projected on-hand
regenerative MRP
scheduled receipt

Solved Problems

Problem 1

The following product structure tree shows the components needed to assemble one unit of product W. Determine the quantities of each component needed to assemble 100 units of W. *Note:* For the procedure when there are on-hand inventories, see Example 1.

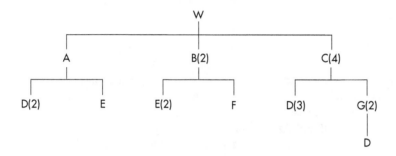

Solution

An easy way to calculate and keep track of component requirements is to first do it for one end item right on the tree, as shown by the subscripts in the following product structure tree.

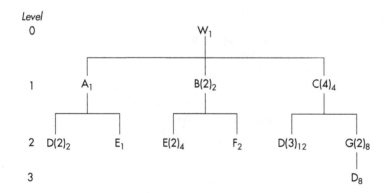

Summary:

Item	(1 W) Quantity	(100 W) Quantity
W	1	100
A	1	100
B	2	200
C	4	400
E	$5 = (1 + 4)$	500
F	2	200
G	8	800
D	$22 = (2 + 12 + 8)$	2,200

Problem 2

Material Requirements Plan Setup Guide

Twelve units of the end item End are needed at the beginning of week 6. Prepare a material requirements plan for component D given that there is a scheduled receipt of 10 units of subassembly A in week 3 plus the following information:

Item	End	A	B	C	D
Units on hand	2	6	4	32	15
Lead time (weeks)	1	2	1	2	2

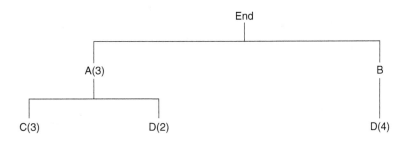

Steps

1. If a question asks for a material requirements plan for a component such as D in the product structure tree, circle all occurrences of that component so you will be sure to include them.

2. Label the spreadsheet sections, top to bottom, following the order shown in the product structure tree:

   Top section: End
   Next section: A
   Next section: B
   Last section: D

   (You don't need one for C because the problem asks for D, and C isn't needed for D.)

3. Add the LT (lead time) for the end item and each component next to the section labels.

4. Add any beginning inventory (on hand) for the end item and each component to their spreadsheet sections.

5. Place the desired end item quantity in the master schedule in the week it is needed, and in the gross requirements of the end item in that same week.

6. Complete the remainder of the plan.

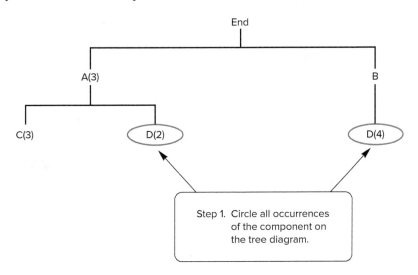

Step 1. Circle all occurrences of the component on the tree diagram.

Master	Week	1	2	3	4	5	6
Schedule	Quantity						

End	Beg. Inv.	1	2	3	4	5	6
Gross requirements							
Scheduled receipts							
Projected on hand							
Net requirements							
Planned-order receipts							
Planned-order releases							

A (3)	Beg. Inv.	1	2	3	4	5	6
Gross requirements							
Scheduled receipts							
Projected on hand							
Net requirements							
Planned-order receipts							
Planned-order releases							

B	Beg. Inv.	1	2	3	4	5	6
Gross requirements							
Scheduled receipts							
Projected on hand							
Net requirements							
Planned-order receipts							
Planned-order releases							

D(2) D(4)	Beg. Inv.	1	2	3	4	5	6
Gross requirements							
Scheduled receipts							
Projected on hand							
Net requirements							
Planned-order receipts							
Planned-order releases							

Step 2. Label spreadsheet sections in the order shown in the product structure tree.

Master	Week	1	2	3	4	5	6
Schedule	Quantity						

End LT = 1	Beg. Inv.	1	2	3	4	5	6
Gross requirements							
Scheduled receipts							
Projected on hand							
Net requirements							
Planned-order receipts							
Planned-order releases							

A (3) LT = 2	Beg. Inv.	1	2	3	4	5	6
Gross requirements							
Scheduled receipts							
Projected on hand							
Net requirements							
Planned-order receipts							
Planned-order releases							

Step 3. Add lead times.

B LT = 1	Beg. Inv.	1	2	3	4	5	6
Gross requirements							
Scheduled receipts							
Projected on hand							
Net requirements							
Planned-order receipts							
Planned-order releases							

D(2) D(4) LT = 2	Beg. Inv.	1	2	3	4	5	6
Gross requirements							
Scheduled receipts							
Projected on hand							
Net requirements							
Planned-order receipts							
Planned-order releases							

Master	Week	1	2	3	4	5	6
Schedule	Quantity						

End LT = 1	Beg. Inv.	1	2	3	4	5	6
Gross requirements							
Scheduled receipts							
Projected on hand	2						
Net requirements							
Planned-order receipts							
Planned-order releases							

A (3) LT = 2	Beg. Inv.	1	2	3	4	5	6
Gross requirements							
Scheduled receipts				10			
Projected on hand	6						
Net requirements							
Planned-order receipts							
Planned-order releases							

B LT = 1	Beg. Inv.	1	2	3	4	5	6
Gross requirements							
Scheduled receipts							
Projected on hand	4						
Net requirements							
Planned-order receipts							
Planned-order releases							

D(2) D(4) LT = 2	Beg. Inv.	1	2	3	4	5	6
Gross requirements							
Scheduled receipts							
Projected on hand	15						
Net requirements							
Planned-order receipts							
Planned-order releases							

Step 4. Enter specified beginning inventory and scheduled receipts quantities.

Master	Week	1	2	3	4	5	6
Schedule	Quantity						12

Step 5 . Enter the master schedule quantities and end item gross requirements in the specified week(s).

End LT = 1	Beg. Inv.	1	2	3	4	5	6
Gross requirements							12
Scheduled receipts							
Projected on hand	2						
Net requirements							
Planned-order receipts							
Planned-order releases							

A (3) LT = 2	Beg. Inv.	1	2	3	4	5	6
Gross requirements							
Scheduled receipts				10			
Projected on hand	6						
Net requirements							
Planned-order receipts							
Planned-order releases							

B LT = 1	Beg. Inv.	1	2	3	4	5	6
Gross requirements							
Scheduled receipts							
Projected on hand	4						
Net requirements							
Planned-order receipts							
Planned-order releases							

D(2) D(4) LT = 2	Beg. Inv.	1	2	3	4	5	6
Gross requirements							
Scheduled receipts							
Projected on hand	15						
Net requirements							
Planned-order receipts							
Planned-order releases							

Master	Week	1	2	3	4	5	6
Schedule	Quantity						12

End LT = 1	Beg. Inv.	1	2	3	4	5	6
Gross requirements							12
Scheduled receipts							
Projected on hand	2	2	2	2	2	2	2
Net requirements							10
Planned-order receipts							10
Planned-order releases						10	

Step 6. Complete the remainder of the plan, starting with the end item and working down, subtracting projected on hand from gross requirements to get net requirements. Planned order receipts = Net requirements, and all are in the same week. Planned order releases are always the same as planned order receipts, but earlier by lead time (one week in this case).

A (3) LT = 2	Beg. Inv.	1	2	3	4	5	6
Gross requirements						30	
Scheduled receipts				10			
Projected on hand	6	6	6	16	16	16	
Net requirements						14	
Planned-order receipts						14	
Planned-order releases				14			

Subassemblies A and B both come under End in the product structure tree, so their gross requirements are in the same column as the End item's planned-order releases (Week 5), using the multiples given in the product structure tree:
3 times 10 for A = 30
1 times 10 for B = 10

B LT = 1	Beg. Inv.	1	2	3	4	5	6
Gross requirements						10	
Scheduled receipts							
Projected on hand	4	4	4	4	4	4	
Net requirements						6	
Planned-order receipts						6	
Planned-order releases					6		

D(2) comes under A in the product structure tree, so its gross requirements are related to A's planned-order releases and in that same week:
2 times 14 = 28 in week 3

D(4) comes under B in the product structure tree, so its gross requirements are related to B's planned-order releases and in that same week:
4 times 6 = 24 in week 4

D(2) D(4) LT = 2	Beg. Inv.	1	2	3	4	5	6
Gross requirements				28	24		
Scheduled receipts							
Projected on hand	15	15	15	15	0		
Net requirements				13	24		
Planned-order receipts				13	24		
Planned-order releases		13	24				

Problem 3

The product structure tree for end item E follows. The manager wants to know the material requirements for the purchased part R that will be needed to complete 120 units of E by the start of week 5. Manufacturing lead times for items of this order are one week for level 0 and level 1 items, and purchase lead time is two weeks for level 2 items. There is a scheduled receipt of 60 units of M at the *end* of week 1 and 100 units of R at the *start* of week 1. Lot-for-lot ordering is used, and there are no inventories on-hand.

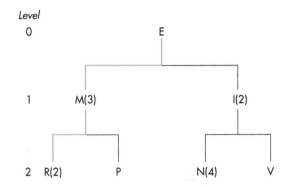

Solution

A partial assembly time chart that includes R and leads to completion of E by the start of week 5 looks like this:

The relevant MRP tables are shown on the next page. The table entries are arrived at as follows:

Production schedule for E: 120 units of E is to be available at the start of week 5.

Table for Item E: Gross requirement equals the quantity specified in the production schedule. Since there is no on-hand inventory, net requirement also equals 120 units. Using lot-for-lot ordering, 120 units must be scheduled to be available at the start of week 5. Because there is a one-week lead time for assembly of 120 units of Es, shop order will need to be released (i.e., work started) at the beginning of week 4.

Table for Item M: The *gross* requirement for M is three times the planned-order release for E (120 × 3 = 360), because each E requires three Ms. These must be available at the start of week 4. The net requirement is 60 units less due to the 60 units of scheduled receipt expected to be on hand at that time. Note that the 60 units expected at the end of week 1 are entered in week 2 because, according to our convention, scheduled receipts occur at the start of the week. Also note that according to our convention, the scheduled receipt goes into projected on-hand immediately. Hence, 360 − 60 = 300 additional units of M must be available at the start of week 4. With the one-week lead time, there must be a shop order release for 300 Ms at the start of week 3.

Table for Item R: Because each M requires two units of R, 600 Rs will be needed to assemble 300 units of M. However, 100 units of R will be on hand because of the scheduled receipt of 100 units at the start of week 1, so only 500 units of R need to be ordered. Because there is a purchase lead time of two weeks, 500 Rs must be ordered at the start of week 1.

Production schedule for E

Week number	Beg. Inv.	1	2	3	4	5
Quantity						120

Item: E LT=1 week						
Gross requirements						120
Scheduled receipts						
Projected on-hand						
Net requirements						120
Planned-order receipts						120
Planned-order releases					120	

Multiplied by 3
(see product structure tree)

Item: M LT=1 week						
Gross requirements					360	
Scheduled receipts			60			
Projected on-hand			60	60	60	
Net requirements					300	
Planned-order receipts					300	
Planned-order releases				300		

Multiplied by 2
(see product structure tree)

Item: R LT=2 weeks						
Gross requirements				600		
Scheduled receipts		100				
Projected on-hand		100	100	100		
Net requirements				500		
Planned-order receipts				500		
Planned-order releases		500				

Problem 4

Capacity requirements planning. Given the following planned-order releases and the production standard times for a component produced at a work centre, determine the labour hour requirements of the component each week. Are the planned-order releases feasible if capacity is 120 labour hours per week at the work centre?

Planned-order Releases:

Week	1	2	3	4
Quantity	200	300	100	150

Standard Times:

Processing	0.5 hour/unit
Machine setup	10 hours (assume one production run per week)

Solution

Convert the quantity requirements into labour requirements by multiplying the quantity requirements by the respective standard times and adding the setup time:

Week	1	2	3	4
Quantity	200	300	100	150
Processing hours	100	150	50	75
Machine setup hours	10	10	10	10
Total labour hours	110	160	60	85

Capacity in week 2 is insufficient because 160 labour hours required > 120 labour hours available.

Discussion and Review Questions

1. Contrast independent and dependent demand. **LO1**

2. What is MRP and when is it appropriate? **LO1**

3. How can the use of MRP contribute to profitability? **LO1**

4. Why should the planning horizon be at least as long as the cumulative lead time? **LO1**

5. What are planning and modular BOMs? **LO2**

6. Briefly define or explain each of these terms: **LO2 & 3**
   a. Master production schedule.
   b. Bill of materials.
   c. Manufacturing lead time.
   d. Gross requirement.
   e. Net requirement.

7. What is the difference between the determination of purchasing lead time and manufacturing lead time? **LO2**

8. Describe MRP processing. **LO3**

9. Contrast planned-order receipts and scheduled receipts. **LO3**

10. What is pegging and why is it used? **LO3**

11. Contrast net-change and regenerative MRPs. What is MRP system nervousness? **LO3**

12. What is backflushing and why is it used? **LO3**

13. What is safety time? **LO4**

14. What is CRP? What can the planner do if the capacity of a work centre will be exceeded? **LO4**

15. Briefly describe MRP II and indicate how it relates to MRP. **LO4**

16. What is lot sizing and what is its goal? **LO4**

17. Explain the part-period method. **LO4**

18. How does an ERP system differ from MRP II software? **LO5**

19. What are some unforeseen costs of the ERP implementation? **LO5**

Taking Stock

1. What trade-offs are involved in customizing an ERP software? **LO5**

2. Who in the organization needs to be involved in MRP? **LO2 & 3**

3. Why are each of the following considerations in an ERP software important? **LO5**
   a. Ease of use.
   b. Complete integration.
   c. Data reliability.

4. Why should future users of MRP, MRP II, or ERP software be involved in its selection and implementation? **LO4 & 5**

Critical Thinking Exercise

Suppose you work for a furniture manufacturer, one of whose products is the chair depicted in Figure 14-6. Finished goods inventory is held in a central warehouse in anticipation of customer orders. Finished goods are controlled using an EOQ-ROP model. The warehouse manager has suggested using the same model for controlling component inventories. Write him a brief memo outlining your opinion on doing that. **LO1**

Experiential Learning Exercise

Select an assembled item that you can disassemble and has several parts (e.g., a stapler, pencil sharpener, toy car or truck). Develop a product structure tree for the item. **LO2**

Internet Exercises

1. Choose one of the following applications of MRP/ERP and determine the benefit of using the software: **LO5**

   a. http://www.industrios.com, click Our Success Stories on the top, then scroll down approximately 29 applications and click Cam Tran.

   b. http://www.sixspartners.com/pdf/casestudy/Epicor-SixSPartnerCSA4ENS0713.pdf: CRS Electronics using Epicor.

   c. http://www.microsoft.com/en-ca/dynamics/customer-success-stories-detail.aspx?casestudyid=4000006948: Allan Candy Company using Microsoft Dynamics.

2. Read http://www.ism.ws/files/RichterAwards/IBMSupportDocs2012.pdf: IBM's supply chain MRP, and explain its benefit to IBM. **LO1**

Problems

1. a. Given the following product structure tree for product E, determine the quantity of each component required to assemble one unit of E. **LO2**

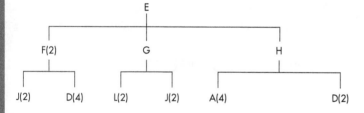

   b. Draw the product structure tree for a stapler using its indented BOM below:

Item
Stapler
Top assembly
Cover
Spring
Slide assembly
Slide
Spring
Base assembly
Base
Strike plate
Rubber pad (2)

2. The following table shows the components needed to assemble an end item, their manufacturing or purchase lead times for typical lot sizes, and amount on hand. The following product structure tree for the End Item shows the number of each component per its immediate parent. **LO2**

Item	End Item	B	C	D	E	F	G	H
LT (wk)	1	2	3	3	1	2	1	2
Amount on hand	0	10	10	25	12	30	5	0

   a. If 20 units of the End item are to be assembled, how many additional units of E are needed? (You don't need to develop the MRP tables to determine this.)

b. An order for the End item is scheduled to be shipped at the start of week 11. What is the latest week that production or purchase of the components of the order can be started and the order still be ready to ship on time? (You don't need to develop the MRP tables for this part either.)

3. The following table lists the components needed to assemble an end item, the manufacturing or purchase lead times (in weeks) for typical lot sizes, amount on hand, and the direct components of each item and, in brackets, the number of each component for each parent. **LO2 & 3**

Item	Lead Time	Amount on Hand	Direct Components
End item	1	—	L(2), C(1), K(3)
L	2	10	B(2), J(3)
C	3	15	G(2), B(2)
K	3	20	H(4), B(2)
B	2	30	
J	3	30	
G	3	5	
H	2	—	

a. Draw the product structure tree for the End item.

b. If 40 units of the End item are to be assembled, how many additional units of B are needed? (You don't need to develop the MRP tables.)

c. An order for 40 units of the End item is scheduled to be shipped at the start of week 8. What is the latest week that the components of the order can be started and the order still be ready to ship on time? (You don't need to develop the MRP tables.)

4. Eighty units of product E are needed at the beginning of week 6. Three cases (30 units per case) of J have been ordered and one case is scheduled to arrive in week 3, one in week 4, and one in week 5. *Note:* J must be ordered by the case, and B must be produced in multiples of 120 units. There are 60 units of B and 20 units of J on hand now. Manufacturing lead times are two weeks each for E and B, and purchase lead time is one week for J. **LO3**

a. Prepare the material requirements plan for component J.

b. Suppose that now is week 4 and the quantity of E needed in week 6 has changed from 80 to 70. The planned order releases through week 3 and scheduled receipts have all been executed as in part *a.* How many more (relative to part *a*) Bs and Js will be on hand in week 6?

5. a. One hundred twenty units of end item Z are needed at the beginning of week 7. Prepare a material requirements plan for component C. Take into account that on hand there are 40 units of Z, 70 units of A, 100 units of B, and 30 units of C. Also, there is a scheduled receipt of 20 units of component C in week 4. Lead times are two weeks for Z and B, and one week for the other components. Lot-for-lot ordering will be used for all items.

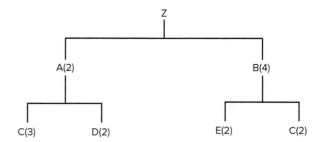

b. Ninety-five units of end item E are needed at the beginning of week 7. Prepare a material requirements plan *for component D*. Take into account that 5 units of E are currently on hand, as well as 50 units of B, 100 units of C, and 80 units of D. Also, 30 units of C have been outsourced and are expected to arrive in week 4. Lead times are two weeks for E and C, and one week for the other components. Assume lot-for-lot ordering except for D, where multiples of 40 must be used. **LO3**

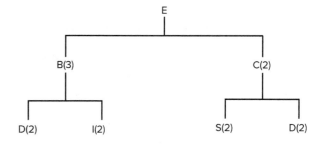

6. Product P is composed of three subassemblies: K, L, and W. Subassembly K is assembled using 3 Gs and 4 Hs; L is made of 2 Ms and 2 Ns; and W is made of 3 Zs.

On-hand inventories are 40 Gs and 200 Hs. Scheduled receipts are 10 Ks at the start of week 3 and 30 Ks at the start of week 6. **LO2 & 3**

One hundred Ps must be shipped at the start of week 6, and another 100 at the start of week 7. Manufacturing lead times are two weeks for subassemblies and purchase lead times are one week for the components. Final assembly of P requires one week for 100 units. Include an extra 10 percent scrap allowance in each planned order of G. The minimum order size for H is 200 units. For other items, use lot-for-lot ordering. Develop each of the following:

a. The product structure tree.
b. The material requirements plan for P, K, G, and H.

7. A table is assembled using three components, as shown in the following product structure tree. The company that makes the table wants to ship 100 units at the beginning of day 4, 150 units at the beginning of day 5, and 200 units at the beginning of day 7. Receipts of 100 wood sections are scheduled at the beginning of day 2. There are 120 legs on hand. An additional 10 percent of the order size on legs is added as scrap allowance. There are 60 braces on hand. Lead time (in days) for all items is a function of each order quantity and is shown below. Prepare the material requirements plan using lot-for-lot ordering. **LO3**

Order Quantity	Lead Time (days)
1–200	1
201–550	2
551–999	3

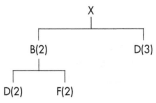

8. Eighty units of product X are needed at the beginning of week 6, and another 30 units are needed at the beginning of week 8. Prepare the material requirements plan for component D, B, and X. D can be ordered only in whole cases (50 units per case). One case of D is automatically received every other week, beginning in week 1 (i.e., week 1, 3, 5, 7). Also, there are 30 units of B and 20 units of D on hand now. Lead times for all items are a function of quantity: one week for up to 100 units, two weeks for 101 to 200 units, three weeks for 201 to 300 units, and four weeks for 301 or more units. **LO3**

9. A company sells three models of radar detector. It buys three basic units (E, F, and G) from a Japanese manufacturer and adds one, two, or four lights (component D) to further differentiate the models. D is bought from a domestic producer. **LO3**

Lead times are one week for all items except C, which is two weeks. There are ample supplies of the basic units (E, F, and G) on hand. There are also 10 units of B, 10 units of C, and 25 units of D on hand. Lot sizing rules are lot-for-lot ordering for all items except D, which must be ordered in multiples of 100 units. There is a scheduled receipt of 100 units of D at the start of week 1.

The production schedule calls for 40 units of A to be available at the start of week 4, 60 units of B at the start of week 5, and 30 units of C at the start of week 6. Prepare the material requirements plan for D and its parents.

10. Assume that you are the manager of a shop that assembles power tools. You have just received an order for 50 chain saws, which are to be shipped at the start of week 8. Pertinent information on the chain saw are: **LO2 & 3**

Item	Lead Time (weeks)	On Hand	Direct Components
Chain saw	2	15	A (2), B (1), C (3)
A	1	10	E (3), D (1)
B	2	5	D (2), F (3)
C	2	30	E (2), D (2)
D	1	20	
E	1	10	
F	2	30	

a. Draw the product structure tree for the chain saw and an assembly time chart for this order.
b. Develop the material requirements plan for component E and its parents using lot-for-lot ordering.
c. Suppose that capacity to produce part E is limited to a maximum of 100 units per week. Revise the planned-order releases for weeks 1–4 so that this maximum is not exceeded in any period, keeping in mind the objective of minimizing holding cost. The quantities need not be equal in every period. Note that the gross requirements for E will remain the same. However, quantities in some of the other rows will change. Determine the new values in those rows.

11. Assume that you are the manager of a robot manufacturer. You have just received an order for 40 units of an industrial robot, which is to be delivered at the start of week 7. Using the following information, determine how many units of part G to order and the timing of those orders, given that part G must be ordered in multiples of 80 units and all other components are ordered lot-for-lot. *Hint:* You just need tables for Robot, C, and G. **LO2 & 3**

Item	Lead Time (weeks)	On Hand	Direct Components
Robot	2	10	B, G, C(3)
B	1	5	E, F
C	1	20	G(2), H
E	2	4	—
F	3	8	—
G	2	15	—
H	1	10	—

12. Determine the material requirements plan for parts N and V and subassembly I as described in Solved Problem 3 (see figure there) for each of the following situations: **LO3**

   a. Assume that there are currently 100 Ns on hand and scheduled receipts of 40 Is and 10 Vs are expected at the beginning of week 3. Suppose that 120 Es are needed at the start of week 5.

   b. Assume on-hand and scheduled receipts are as in part *a*. Now suppose that 100 Es are needed at the start of week 5 and 50 at the start of week 7. Also, use multiples of these order sizes: N, 800; V, 200. Use lot-for-lot ordering for I and E.

   c. Using your answer to part *a*, update the MRP for I, N, and V, using the following additional information for each of these cases: (1) one week has elapsed (making it the start of week 2), and (2) three weeks have elapsed (making it the start of week 4). *Note:* Start your revised plans so that the updated time in each case is designated as week 1. The updated production schedule now has an order for 100 units of E in week 8 of case 1 and in week 6 of case 2 (i.e., week 9 under the former production schedule). Assume all orders are released and received as planned.

13. Information concerning the product structure, lead times, and quantities on hand for an electric golf cart is shown in the following table. Use this information to do each of the following: **LO2 & 3**

   a. Draw the product structure tree.
   b. Draw the assembly time chart.
   c. Develop the material requirements plan that will provide 200 golf carts at the start of week 8, assuming lot-for-lot ordering.

Parts List for Electric Golf Cart	Lead Time (for Typical Order Size)	Quantity on Hand
Electric golf cart	1	0
Top	1	40
Base	1	20
Top		
Supports (4)	1	200
Cover	1	0
Base		
Motor	2	300
Body	3	50
Seats (2)	2	120
Body		
Frame	1	35
Controls	1	0
Wheels (4)	1	240

14. Refer to Problem 13. Assume that unusually mild weather has caused a change in the quantity and timing of orders for golf carts. The revised plan calls for 100 golf carts at the start of week 6, 100 at the start of week 8, and 100 at the start of week 9. **LO3**

   a. Determine the timing and quantities of orders for Top and Base.

   b. Assume that equipment problems have reduced the manufacturer's capacity for assembling Bases to 50 units per week. Revise your material requirements plan for Base to reflect this, but still meet delivery dates.

15. A manufacturer buys a certain part in varying quantities throughout the year. Ordering cost is $11 per order, and holding cost is $0.14 per unit per month. Given the following demand (net requirements) for the part for the next eight months, determine the order sizes and timing of purchase orders using the part-period method. **LO4**

Month	Demand (units)
1	—
2	80
3	10
4	30
5	—
6	30
7	—
8	30

16. A company periodically produces a part that is a basic component of an assembled product. Each time the part is run, a fixed cost of $125 is incurred. The cost to hold one unit for a week is estimated to be $1.65. For the demand (net requirements) shown below, determine the

quantity and timing of production runs using the part-period method. **LO4**

Week	Demand (units)
1	40
2	20
3	100
4	20
5	—
6	20
7	80

17. A company that manufactures paving material for driveways and parking lots expects the following demand for its products for the next four months. **LO4**

Month number	1	2	3	4
Material (tonnes)	40	80	60	70

The company's machine standard time and available capacity are:

Machine standard time (hours per tonne)	3
Monthly production capacity (hours)	200

a. Determine the capacity requirement for each of the four months.

b. In which months do you foresee a problem? What options would you suggest to resolve any problems?

18. A company produces two products, A and B, that go through a three-step sequence of fabrication, assembly, and packaging. Processing requirements for the departments (hours per unit) are: **LO4**

Product	Fabrication	Assembly	Packaging
A	2	1.5	1
B	1	1	1.5

Department capacities are all 7 hours per day. The following production schedule is for the next three days:

Day	Mon	Tues	Wed
A	2	4	1
B	3	2	2

a. Develop, for each department and day, the capacity requirements for each product and the total load for each day. Ignore changeover time between A and B.

b. Evaluate the projected loads for each day. Is the schedule feasible? What do you suggest for balancing the load?

*19. The IT department has a problem. Its computer died just as it spit out the following information: Planned-order release for item J27 = 640 units in Week 2. The company has been able to reconstruct all the information it lost except the production schedule for the end item 565. The company is fortunate because J27 is used only in 565. Given the following product structure tree and the associated inventory on-hand, lot sizing, and lead-time information, determine what production schedule entry for item 565 was exploded into the material requirements plan that killed the computer. **LO3**

Part Number	On Hand	Lot Sizing	Lead Time
565	0	Lot-for-lot	1 week
X43	60	Multiples of 120	1 week
N78	0	Lot-for-lot	2 weeks
Y36	200	Lot-for-lot	1 week
J27	0	Lot-for-lot	2 weeks

20. Using the drawing of a pair of scissors below, do the following: **LO2 & 3**

a. Draw the product structure tree for the scissors.

b. Perform MRP for the scissors and all its components except the screw. Lead times are one day for buying each type of blade, assembling the blades with grips, and for final scissors assembly, but two days for buying each type of plastic grip. Six hundred pairs of scissors are needed on Day 6. *Note:* there are 200 straight blades, 350 bent blades, and 40 top blade assemblies on hand.

21. Develop the material requirements plan for component H of the end product A that has the following product structure tree. Lead times for A and each component except B are one week. The lead time for B is three weeks. Sixty units of A are needed at the start of week 8. There are currently 15 units of B and 130 units of E on hand, and 50 units of H are in production by a supplier and are scheduled to be received by the start of week 2. **LO3**

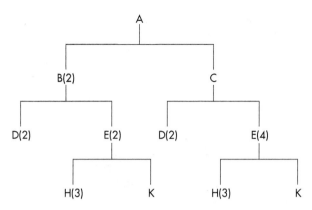

*22. Promotional Novelties manufactures a wide range of novelty items for its corporate customers. It has just received an order for 20,000 toy tractor-trailers that will be sold by a gas station chain as part of a holiday promotion. The order is to be shipped at the beginning of week 9. The product structure tree below shows various components of the tractor-trailers and the way it is assembled. **LO3**

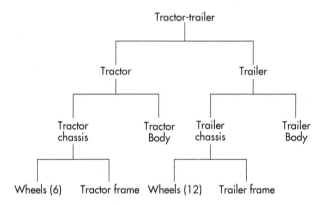

The company can complete final assembly of the tractor-trailers at the rate of 10,000 a week. Assembly time of Tractors and Trailers for this size order, in different departments, is one week each.

The tractors and trailers each have their own chassis departments that can produce chassis at the rate of 20,000 a week. Wheels are purchased from a supplier. Ordered wheels come in sets of 6,400. The lead time for delivery of wheels from the supplier is three weeks. Perform MRP for the wheels and its parents and answer the following questions:

a. How many wheels will the manager need to order?
b. When should the manager place the order?
c. How many wheels should the manager expect to have left over?

*23. A small furniture maker has just received an order to deliver 250 chairs at the beginning of week 6. The production/purchase planner needs to arrange for the assembly of subassemblies and purchase of parts required for the order. The product structure tree for the chair is displayed as follows. The chairs, leg

assemblies, and back assemblies are to be assembled by one worker each. During an eight-hour day, 25 chairs, 25 legs assemblies, and 50 back assemblies can be assembled. The company operates five days a week. The seats, spindles, tops, legs, and rails are purchased from another company. Purchase lead time for this size order for each part is one week. The company has some inventory of parts from previous productions: 40 seats, 100 rails, 150 legs, 30 tops, and 80 spindles. **LO3**

a. Calculate assembly lead times for chairs, leg assemblies, and back assemblies required for this order. Assume that an assembly will start only after the whole batch of its components is available.
b. Develop material requirements plan for this order. Use lot-for-lot ordering. What action should you take now?

*24. A furniture maker has received an order for 100 units of its kitchen table to be delivered in six work days. The table consists of 1 top and 4 legs, made from purchased lumber (2″ by 6″ by 6′). Each top is made from 1.5 units of lumber, and each leg is made from 1/6 unit of the lumber. Tops and legs can be made independently in two different workstations, and manufacturing time for 1 top is expected to be 12 minutes and for 1 leg 2 minutes. All 100 tops and 400 legs should be made before any tables are assembled, and final assembly of 1 table is expected to take 4 minutes. The shop works eight hours a day, Monday to Friday. Currently, the company has 20 units of lumber in stock, and purchase lead time for lumber is one work day. **LO2 & 3**

a. Calculate the manufacturing lead time for each operation (round up) and draw the product structure tree.
b. Perform material requirements planning for this order. What action should be taken now?
c. How would your answer for lumber change:
  i. If the safety stock for lumber is 20 units?
  ii. If lumber is purchased in batch size of 250 units?
  iii. If 250 units are scheduled to be received on the next work day?

*25. You need to plan the fabrication and assembly of an order of 40 side (accessory) tables (see Example 8 in Chapter 6) due in 6 work days. See the product structure tree on the next page. The raw material is 1 inch by

4 inches by 6 feet long planks of oak. The product structure tree below shows that one End Table is made of 1 Top Subassembly, 2 Leg Subassemblies, and 2 Cross Bars. One Top Subassembly is made from 1 plank of Oak, one Leg Subassembly is made from 0.5 plank of Oak, and one Cross Bar is made of 0.1 plank of Oak. The cutting and assembly time of one Top Subassembly is 20 minutes. The cutting and assembly time of one Leg Subassembly is 10 minutes. The cutting time to make one Cross Bar is 2 minutes. Finally, the final assembly of one End Table is 15 minutes. Assume that the shop works 8 hours a day, 5 days a week. The purchase lead time for oak is 1 work day. Assume that each operation is performed by a different worker in a different work centre and each batch is to be completed before it is moved to the next work centre. Assume lot-for-lot ordering for all items, except that oak is bought in batch of 150 planks. There are no inventories on hand or on order, except for 40 planks of oak on hand. Also, there are no safety stocks required, except 30 planks of oak. **LO2 & 3**

a. Determine each of the manufacturing lead times for this order (round up to whole days).

b. Develop the MRP tables. What action should you take now?

End Table

- Top Subassembly
  - Oak (1)
- Leg Subassembly (2)
  - Oak (0.5)
- Cross Bar (2)
  - Oak (0.1)

*26. Restaurants need to plan the purchase and production of their food ingredients and components based on the forecast of demand for each meal. Consider the following example for veal picante with linguini in a restaurant.[3] **LO2 & 3**

The forecasts for demand for veal picante with linguini during each of the next four days are Thursday, 6; Friday, 10; Saturday, 9; and Sunday, 8. The product structure tree of one veal picante with linguini is as follows: The chef assembles the dish from one serving of cooked linguini and one piece of grilled veal steak. The assistant chef makes the cooked linguini using approximately 100 grams of uncooked linguini (takes approximately 15 minutes). The chef grills the veal steak from a marinated piece of veal (takes approximately 17 minutes). Marinating of a raw veal steak needs to be done the day before (by assistant chef) using some picante sauce, lime juice, oil, salt, and pepper (takes approximately 5 minutes

but needs to rest in the fridge overnight). On hand, we have 1 kg of uncooked linguini, six marinated veal steaks and thirteen unmarinated veal steaks. All production lead times are negligible (zero day), except marinating veal steaks, which takes one day. All purchase lead times are one day. The restaurant orders uncooked linguini in 10 kg bags and unmarinated veal steaks in 20-piece boxes.

a. Draw the product structure tree for a veal picante with linguini.

b. Develop MRP tables for all items except picante sauce, lime juice, oil, salt, and pepper.

*27. Consider this magazine rack and its pieces shown below. The raw material is 1 inch by 6 inches by 6 feet long planks of oak lumber. The 6 rails and handle are made from one plank of lumber, but to make the 2 ends and bottom, first two planks have to be glued together side-by-side. **LO3**

Magazine rack

Pieces:
(Top: 2 end pieces and bottom piece; bottom: 6 rails and handle)

The product structure tree on the next page shows that one kit of 6 rails and a handle is made from one plank of lumber, and one kit of 2 ends and a bottom is made from one side-by-side glued piece of lumber, which, in turn, is made of 2 planks of lumber. The cutting time of one plank of lumber into one kit of 6 rails and a handle will be 5 minutes. The glue time of 2 planks of lumber will be 5 minutes (assume that the glue will dry overnight). The cutting and router time (for the grooves) of one side-by-side glued piece of lumber into one kit of 2 ends and a bottom will be 10 minutes. Finally, the assembly of one kit of 6 rails and a handle and one kit of 2 ends and a bottom will take 15 minutes. The shop works eight hours a day, five days a week. The purchase lead time for lumber is one work day. The shop has just sold 80 magazine racks to a customer to be delivered in 8 workdays. Assume that each operation is performed by a different operator and each batch should be completed before it is moved to the next operation.

a. Calculate the manufacturing lead time for each operation to make this order.

[3] Based on John G. Wacker, "Effective Planning and Cost Control for Restaurants: Making Resource Requirements Planning Work," *Production and Inventory Management Journal*, 26(1), pp. 55–70.

b. Complete MRP tables for each item. Suppose we currently have 100 planks of lumber in stock. Assume lot-for-lot ordering for all items except lumber, which is purchased in lots of 200 planks.

c. What action should we take now?

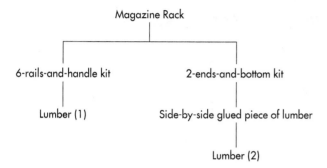

*28. Consider the chair described in Figure 14-6. Suppose that the chair is made by a small furniture manufacturer that has just received an order to deliver 100 chairs in 6 workdays. The production/purchase planner needs to arrange for the purchase of parts and their assembly. The chairs, front assemblies, and back assemblies are to be assembled by one worker each. During an 8-hour day, 100 front assemblies and 50 back assemblies can be assembled. After a batch of 100 front assemblies and 100 back assemblies are produced, the whole chair will be assembled at the rate of 50 per 8-hour day. The company works 5 days a week. The seats, front legs, cross bars, side rails, and back supports are purchased from another company. The purchase lead time for any order is one work day. The company has some inventory of parts from previous purchases: 100 front legs, 160 cross bars, 40 side rails, and 90 back supports. All items are purchased or assembled lot-for-lot, except cross bars, which are purchased in a lot size of 200. In anticipation for this order, an order of 100 seats has already been placed and is expected on the next workday. **LO3**

a. Calculate the assembly lead times for the chairs, front assemblies, and back assemblies required for this order.

b. Develop the material requirements plan for this order. What action should you take now?

*29. Consider the School Chairs Mini-Case at the end of Chapter 6. Suppose the seat is made in a seat-fabrication work centre, all other parts (posts, cross bars, rails) are made in a post-bar-rail work centre, and the chair is assembled in the chair-assembly work centre. Suppose that a chair takes 15 minutes to assemble and uses 1 seat and one kit of other parts (2 front posts, 2 back posts, 10 cross bars, and 3 rails). A seat takes 5 minutes to make from half a plank (a plank is 2" by 4" by 8"). Assume that glue will be dried overnight. A kit of other parts takes 10 minutes to make from 1 plank. Suppose each work centre is staffed by one worker who works

8 hours a day, 5 days a week (Mon–Fri), and that we promised 90 chairs to a school to be delivered in 7 workdays. **LO3**

a. Determine the manufacturing lead times (in day) for assembling 90 chairs, making 90 seats, and making 90 kits of other parts. Round up if a fraction of day is used.

b. There is no inventory on hand or on order, no safety stocks are needed, lot-for-lot ordering is used, and purchase lead time for lumber is one workday. Use MRP to determine when and how many units of lumber to purchase, seats to make, other parts to make, and chairs to assemble.

c. What action should be taken now?

d. If we have 35 planks on hand, how would your answer change?

e. If we have 35 planks on hand and we order lumber in batch size of 200 planks, how would your answer change?

30. DMD makes specialty bikes. The manager used to order enough bike parts for four months' worth of production, but parts were stacked all over the place, seriously reducing work space and hampering movement of workers. And no one knew exactly where anything was.

The manager heard about MRP, and wants to use it. DMD makes two types of bikes: Arrow and Dart. The manager wants to assemble 15 Arrows and 10 Darts each week from weeks 4 through 8. The product structure trees for the two bikes follow. **LO3**

He has collected the following information on lead times, inventory on hand, and lot-sizing methods (established by suppliers and/or DMD):

Item	Lead Time (weeks)	On Hand	Lot-Sizing Method
Arrow	2	5	Lot-for-lot
Dart	2	2	Lot-for-lot
X	1	5	Q = 25
W	2*	2	Multiples of 12
F	1	10	Multiples of 30
K	1	3	Lot-for-lot
Q	1	15	Q = 30
M	1	0	Lot-for-lot

*LT = 3 weeks for orders of 36 or more units.

Scheduled receipts are:

Week 1: 20 Arrows, 18 Ws
Week 2: 20 Darts, 15 Fs

Develop the material requirements plan for all the items.

Zurn

Zurn makes various plumbing products such as fixtures, faucets, drainage equipment, and valves (under Wilkins brand name). The plant manager is concerned with excessive amounts of inventory of parts in the plant. The materials manager (MM) has been tasked to identify if these inventories can be reduced. Zurn uses an accounting software, which also has an MRP module. The MM has chosen a popular and reliable pressure vacuum breaker valve (backflow preventer), Model 720A, to study.

Model 720A consists of various parts, most made in the plant but some bought from suppliers, both domestic and Asian. The BOM and assembly chart for 720A are displayed on the right.

Note that there is a repair kit for Model 720A (in the bottom of the BOM). This is used by some contractors to repair a faulty installed Model 720A and replaces only the internal parts of the pressure valve. The weekly forecast demand for 720A and repair kit for the next quarter (13 weeks) is fairly constant:

Item	720A	repair kit
Weekly demand (units)	1154	135

To save time, the MM has decided to look at the requirements plans for only the following components: body, plastic washer, and ball valves. In addition to Model 720A and repair kit, some of these components are used in other valves as well. The weekly forecast demand for these components for the next quarter (13 weeks) is fairly constant:

Item	body	plastic washer	ball valve
Weekly demand (units)	804*	2,265	12

* only weeks 9–13

MODEL 720A
WILKINS. a ZURN. company
Pressure Vacuum Breakers
1/2" to 1"

ITEM NO.	DESCRIPTION	PART NO.
1	CANOPY SCREW	721-11
2	CANOPY	721-3
3	BONNET	721-20
4	PLASTIC WASHER	721A-12
5	O-RING	WK-138N
6	LOAD NUT & GUIDE	721-90
7	LOAD WASHER	721-80
8	DISC UPPER	721A-34
9	POPPET	721-30
10	SPRING	721-33
11	SCREW	721-11A
12	LOWER DISC	721B-34
13	GUIDE SPIDER	721-31
14	NUT, HEX	721-9A
15	TEST COCK	18-860
16	BALL VALVE 1/2" TAP	12-850T
	BALL VALVE 3/4" TAP	34-850T
	BALL VALVE 1" TAP	1-850T
17	POPPET ASSEMBLY	721-300
18	SPIDER ASSEMBLY	721-310

REPAIR KITS

RK1-720A		REPAIR KIT MODEL 720A, 1/2", 3/4" & 1"
PART NO.	QTY.	DESCRIPTION
721A-12	1	PLASTIC WASHER
WK-138N	1	O-RING
721-33	1	SPRING
721-300	1	POPPET ASSEMBLY
721-310	1	SPIDER ASSEMBLY

71

Some more information about these five items are as follows:

Item	Lead time (weeks)	Safety stocks	Lot size	Currently On hand
Model 720A	0	0	L4L	8,600
Repair kit	1	360	L4L	434
Body	2	0	50,000	15,536
Plastic washer	5	9,000	55,000	16,680
Ball valve	8	0	10,300	9,387

a. Perform MRP for these 5 items for the next 13 weeks.
b. Determine if Zurn is carrying too much inventory. *Hint:* look at on-hand, safety stocks, and lot sizes.

CHAPTER 15
Just-in-Time and Lean Production

In the exciting world of Formula 1 racing, the difference between first place and second is often measured in fractions of a metre. At racing speeds in excess of 350 km/hour, one extra second spent in the pits represents well over 90 metres on the racetrack. Multiply this by an average of two to three stops each race, depending on the racetrack, and some simple arithmetic shows why it has become critically important for pit crews to try to absolutely minimize the time it takes to change a set of tires.

Using principles from lean production, Formula 1 pit crews have reduced the time required to completely change a set of four tires to under two seconds.* Compare this number to the time it took you to put on some winter tires for your car. How do these race cars get in and out of the pit so quickly? While the process may not be easy, the methods used are fairly simple to understand. The key is the conversion of activities that can be

_____

* 1.923 second record set in 2013.

done only when the race car is stopped into activities that can be done before the car is stopped. This allows the pit crew to prepare as much as possible and ensure that the least amount of time is wasted after the car is stopped. This and other concepts from lean production are the topic of this chapter.

Source: http://www.redbull.com/ca/en/motorsports/f1/stories/1331621211398/red-bull-racing-pitstop-record, retrieved April 10, 2014.

JIT and Lean Production

just-in-time (JIT) Production system in which processing and movement of parts/ modules/work-in-process occur just as they are needed, usually in small batches.

lean production JIT in a broad sense, is a philosophy of waste reduction and continuous improvement.

The term **just-in-time (JIT)** in a narrow sense, also called *little JIT*, refers to a production system in which both the movement of work-in-process (WIP) during production and deliveries of parts/ modules from suppliers are carefully timed so that at each step of the process, the next (usually small, ideally one-unit) batch arrives for processing just as the preceding batch is completed—thus the name, *just-in-time*. The result is a system with few idle items waiting to be processed (i.e., inventory) and a balanced, rapid flow.

In a broader sense, JIT, also called *big JIT*, is a philosophy of "waste" reduction, be it inventory or resources (such as workers, equipment, or floor space), and continuous improvement. In this sense, JIT is identical to **lean production**.

JIT, in the narrow sense, is sometimes contrasted with material requirements planning (MRP; see Chapter 14). MRP relies on a computer-based *component-scheduling* system (using daily or weekly time periods) to trigger and "push" production and deliveries through the process, whereas JIT relies on visual signals to trigger and "pull" production and deliveries (usually hourly) through the process. MRP controls the work centre capacities, whereas JIT controls the inventory (through *kanbans*).

The JIT/lean approach was developed at the Toyota Motor Company by Taiichi Ohno (who eventually became vice-president of manufacturing) and several of his colleagues. The development of JIT/lean in Japan was probably influenced by the fact that Japan is a crowded country with few natural resources. Not surprisingly, the Japanese are very sensitive to waste and inefficiency. They regard rework as waste and excess inventory as evil because it takes up space and ties up resources.

A stunning example of the potential of lean manufacturing was illustrated by the successful adoption of lean methods in the mid-1980s in a Fremont, California, auto plant. The plant was originally operated by General Motors (GM). However, GM closed the plant in 1982 because of its low productivity and high absenteeism. A few years later the plant was reopened as a joint venture of Toyota and GM, called NUMMI (New United Motor Manufacturing, Inc.). About 80 percent of the former plant workers were rehired, but the white-collar jobs were shifted from directing to supporting workers, and small teams were formed and trained to design, measure, and improve their performance. The result? By 1985 productivity and quality improved dramatically, exceeding all other GM plants, and absenteeism was negligible.

A few years later, more interest in lean production arose when *The Machine That Changed the World*, by Womack, Jones, and Roos, was published. Now JIT/lean is being promoted by some government programs, associations, and companies, and being used by most progressive organizations.

Just like the awards for quality, there is a prize for world-class lean systems, called the Shingo Prize. The principles and criteria for a lean system are given in the "Shingo Prize" OM in Action.

A slightly different representation of the JIT/lean principles and tools, which better match the chapters in this textbook, is given in Figure 15-1. Displayed are the goals and building blocks of JIT/lean systems. We will describe the goals and each of the building blocks (product design, process design, personnel/organization, and planning and control) in a separate section below. The chapter concludes with a section on implementation of JIT/lean.

◀ **Figure 15-1**

An overview of the goals and building blocks of JIT/lean systems.

The Goals of Lean Production

The ideal JIT/lean production system produces one piece at a time, defect-free, on demand, fast, without waste, in a safe production environment. This can be achieved by a balanced rapid flow.

A Balanced Rapid Flow.

A *balanced rapid flow* of a family of products is a smooth, even, swift flow of materials, information, or work through the steps of the production process. Here, "balanced" has the same interpretation as in the line balancing of Chapter 6, i.e., the workload should be distributed evenly among the workstations. This goal includes the elimination of unevenness (*mura* in Japanese) and overburden (i.e., using a resource in excess of its optimal operating rate; *muri* in Japanese). A balanced rapid flow can be achieved by the following four supporting goals.

Elimination of Disruptions. Disruptions upset the smooth flow of products through the production system and cause variability. Disruptions are caused by a variety of factors such as poor quality, equipment breakdowns, changes to the schedule/customer demand, and late deliveries of parts/components. All these sources of variability should be eliminated as much as possible.

System Flexibility. A *flexible system* is one that is robust enough to handle a mix of products and changes in the level of output, while still maintaining balance and throughput speed. Reduction of machine setup and lead time will increase system flexibility. Flexibility enables the system to meet changing demand.

Elimination of Waste. Waste (*muda* in Japanese) represents unproductive resources. Eliminating waste can free up resources and enhance production. In the JIT/lean system, wastes include:

a. Overproduction—excess inventory.

b. Unnecessary inventory—excess supplies and equipment.

c. Waiting—order waiting to be processed, requests for information awaiting answers.

d. Unnecessary transportation—inefficient routing.

e. Overprocessing—using a complex process instead of a simpler one; work that adds no value.

f. Inefficient work methods/excess motions—poor layout design, unnecessary steps, inadequate training.

g. Producing defective products—scrap and rework.

h. Underutilization of employee knowledge/skill—not tapping all of the mental and creative capabilities of workers.

The existence of these wastes is an indication that improvement is possible. For an implementation of JIT/lean system in a service, including examples of waste, see the "RBC" OM in Action.

Continuous Improvement. *Kaizen* (or *continuous improvement*) is continual work to improve the system. In operations, examples include reduce inventories, setup cost, and time; improve quality; increase the output rate; and generally cut waste and disruptions. But kaizen also applies to customer-related processes such as order taking, product development processes such as quality function deployment, supply-related processes such as issuing purchase orders, and support processes such as hiring.

Kaizen is based on the following tenets:

1. Improvement should be done gradually and continuously.

2. Everyone should be involved.

3. It does not require spending great sums of money on technology or consultants.

4. It can be applied anywhere.

5. It involves learning by doing, using scientific thinking.

6. *Kaizen* relies on direct observation and data collection.

One can think of *kaizen* as continuous problem solving (see Chapter 9). Thus, continuous improvement/problem solving becomes a way of life—a "culture" that must be assimilated into the thinking of everyone. It becomes a never-ending quest for improving processes as all members of the organization strive to improve the system. Improvements are made at the lowest possible level in the organization (usually front-line workers). Of particular importance are problems that interrupt the smooth flow of work. These must be dealt with quickly, usually by the employee with the help of his supervisor.

OM in *ACTION*   http://www.rbc.com/about-rbc.html

RBC

RBC (Royal Bank of Canada) started using lean and Six Sigma tools to reduce waste and defects, respectively, in 2003 but the projects were led by outside consultants who did not transfer the knowledge of the improvement process to RBC staff. In 2007, RBC started employing some master black belts and black belts who not only lead improvement projects but also train the staff on how to undertake improvement projects themselves. One project was to make the "skimming" fraud investigation more efficient. Skimming is using a counterfeit debit card. The team consisted of a master black belt, two fraud agents, and the manager of National Fraud Detection Group in the Enterprise Operations of RBC. The project was in the form of a *kaizen* event (or blitz), which took five days. On day 1, the current skimming fraud investigation process was mapped, and the process was examined for wastes (vs. value to client). On days 2 and 3, possible new processes were mapped and examined. On day 4, the chosen

process was implemented, and on day 5 its improvements were evaluated. Some of the waste reductions were (1) 20 percent reduction in unnecessary data entry, (2) elimination of e-mails to branches, (3) reduction in choices of general ledger accounts required for posting the transaction (from 30 to 2), (4) elimination of duplicate or fraudulent transaction checks, and (5) conversion of manual paper-based process to electronic filing process (saved walking to the shared printer, which had caused the agents to batch the cases). The electronic filing process has also cut manual searches, enabled catching of missed information (mandatory fields) earlier, and standardized the procedure. The waste reduction has reduced the investigation time from 3 days to 1 day, resulting in happier customers who get their refund faster. It also saved 2,500 hours of work, 14,000 e-mails, 1,000 km of walking, and 315,000 sheets of printed paper per year.

Source: "RBC Embeds Black Belts in a Bid to Get Lean," *Plant*, 2008, pp. 42–46.

The tools (or building blocks) used to achieve the above goals are classified into four classes: product design, process design, personnel and organizational elements, and planning and control. These tools follow.

Product Design

Product quality is crucial to JIT/lean systems because poor quality can create major disruptions. Quality must be designed into goods and services. QFD (Quality Function Deployment) should be used to capture the "voice" of customers and deploy it in the product design. This will create value for the customers. Concurrent engineering should be used to increase functional communications, reduce the need for engineering changes, and speed up the design process.

Products should be designed for easy manufacturing and assembly (DFM and DFA). This speeds up the operations. Value analysis may be used to identify the necessary functions of the product and to cut down product features not valued by the customers. For more information on these and other elements of product design that contribute to a JIT/lean system, see Chapter 4.

OM in ACTION

Shingo Prize

The Shingo Prize for Operational Excellence was established in 1988 to recognize the achievement of companies worldwide that are implementing JIT/lean systems. It is named after the Japanese guru lean manufacturing, Dr. Shigeo Shingo. The criteria currently used to judge a company are principle based. These are displayed in the following figure. The 10 guiding principles are the key concepts or foundations of the philoso-

phy of lean/JIT according to the Shingo Prize. Note that "Flow & Pull value" means shorten lead-time and match supply with demand. Four categories (or dimensions) of principles are shown, starting from the bottom: Cultural enablers, Continuous improvement, Enterprise alignment, and Results. Each category has some subcategories, and each is assessed based on how the company has progressed from basic use of tools and techniques, to systems thinking (involving all parts of the company), to

THE GUIDING PRINCIPLES

Results
Create Value
for the Customer

Enterprise Alignment
Create Constancy of Purpose
Think Systemically

Continuous Improvement
Focus on Process · Embrace Scientific Thinking
Flow & Pull Value · Assure Quality at the Source
Seek Perfection

Cultural Enablers
Lead with Humility
Respect Every Individual

Utah State University

(continued)

incorporating lean approach as part of work principles. Category 2 (i.e., Continuous Improvement) is assessed in each of the business process areas: customer relations, product development, operations, supply, and management (other functions of business). Some explanation and the maximum point for each subcategory are given in the table below.

	Max. Points
1. Cultural Enablers	250
Leadership	
People development	
Education, training & coaching	
Empowerment & involvement	
Environmental & safety systems	
2. Continuous Improvement	350
Customer relations	
(having a process for assessing voice of customer, order taking, invoicing, etc.)	
Product development	
(QFD, concurrent engineering, benchmarking, new markets, DFM and DFA, component standardization & modularity, value analysis, innovations, involvement of suppliers/customers, etc.)	
Operations	
(one-piece flow, demand pull, value stream mapping, total preventive maintenance, SMED, *poka-yoke*, visual systems, cellular layout, *Kaizen*, level loading, 5S, right-sized equipment/facilities, Six Sigma/SPC/design of experiments, tools for quality improvement, etc.)	
Supply	
(integration with suppliers, a process for making the linkage visible, transport and distribution alliances, respect for suppliers, commitment to supplier development)	

	Max. Points
Management	
(alignment and integration of other functions in support of production value stream, value stream mapping of other processes, use of JIT/lean/quality improvement tools in other processes)	
3. Enterprise Alignment	200
Enterprise thinking in a global environment (reporting of lean principles/policy, having common management/reporting system, using lean accounting, simple/visual information systems, etc.)	
Policy deployment	
(scientific thinking, planning process for policy deployment, alignment of objectives, constancy of purpose, etc.)	
4. Results	200
Quality	
(internal quality, quality to the customer, etc.)	
Delivery	
(lead time, on-time delivery, etc.)	
Cost/Productivity	
(labour productivity, asset productivity, inventory turns, etc.)	
Customer satisfaction	
(customer survey, etc.)	
Safety/Environment/Morale	
(employee survey, etc.)	

Source: http://www.shingoprize.org/files/ModelsGuidelines_v5.pdf, retrieved April 1, 2014.

 Process Design

A Balanced System

takt time The maximum time allowed at each workstation to complete its set of tasks on a unit. Also called cycle time.

In a balanced system, workload is distributed evenly among workstations (see line balancing in Chapter 6). Recall that the maximum time allowed at each workstation to complete its set of tasks on a unit is called cycle time or ***takt* time**. *Takt* time is changed periodically (e.g., daily) to meet changing demand.

Calculating cycle or takt time was covered briefly in Chapter 6. Here, we illustrate it in more detail. The procedure for obtaining the *takt* time is:

1. Determine the net time available per shift by subtracting any nonproductive time from total shift time.

2. If there is more than one shift per day, multiply the net time per shift by the number of shifts to obtain the net available time per day.

3. Calculate *takt* time by dividing the net available time by demand during the day.

Given the following information, calculate the *takt* time: Total time per shift is 480 minutes per day, and there are two shifts per day. There are two 20-minute rest breaks and a 30-minute lunch break per shift. Daily demand is 80 units.

◀ **Example 1**

1. Calculate net time available per shift:

SOLUTION

Total time	480 minutes
Rest breaks	−40 minutes
Lunch	−30 minutes
	410 minutes per shift

Calculate the net time available per day:

410 minutes per shift × 2 shifts/day = 820 minutes per day

2. Calculate the *takt* time:

$$Takt \text{ time} = \frac{\text{Net time available per day}}{\text{Daily demand}} = \frac{820 \text{ minutes per day}}{80 \text{ units per day}}$$

$$= 10.25 \text{ minutes per unit}$$

A Flexible System

Process design can increase *production flexibility* in a variety of ways. Table 15-1 lists some of the techniques used for this purpose.

◀ **Table 15-1**

Techniques for increasing production flexibility.

1. Reduce changeover (set up) time.

2. Cross-train workers so they can help others facing overcapacity.

3. Use many small machines rather than a few large machines.

4. Use safety stocks.

5. Keep some idle capacity.

Small Lot Sizes

In the JIT/lean system, the ideal lot size is one unit, a quantity that may not always be realistic owing to practical considerations requiring minimum lot sizes (e.g., machines that process multiple items simultaneously, and machines with very long setup times). Nevertheless, the objective is to reduce the lot size as much as possible. Small lot sizes in both the production process and deliveries from suppliers yield a number of benefits that enable JIT/lean systems to operate efficiently. First, with small lots moving through the system, work-in-process (WIP) inventory is considerably less than it is with large lots. This reduces holding cost, space requirement, and clutter in the workplace. Second, inspection and rework costs are less when problems with quality occur, because there are fewer items in a lot to inspect and rework.

Small lots also result in greater system flexibility. Batch systems typically produce a small variety of products. This usually means long production runs of each product, one after the other. Although this spreads the setup cost for a run over many items, it also results in long cycles over the entire range of products. For instance, suppose a company has three product models, A, B, and C. In a batch system, there would be a long run of model A (e.g., covering two or three days or more), then a long run of model B, followed by a long run of model C before the sequence would repeat. In contrast, a JIT/lean system, using small lots, would frequently shift from producing A to producing B and C. This enables JIT/lean systems to respond more quickly to changing customer demands. The contrast between small and large lot sizes is illustrated in Figure 15-2. A summary of the benefits of small lot sizes is presented in Table 15-2.

It is important to note that the use of small lot sizes is not in conflict with the EOQ approach; in JIT/lean, there is an emphasis on reducing the setup time (and hence cost), which reduces the optimal lot size.

Figure 15-2 ▶

Small-lot JIT/lean versus large-lot batch approaches.

Small-lot JIT/lean approach

AAA   BBBBBBB   CC   AAA   BBBBBBB   CC   AAA   BBBBBBB   CC   AAA   BBBBBBB   CC

Time ⟶

Large-lot batch approach

AAAAAAAAAAAA   BBBBBBBBBBBBBBBBBBBBBBBBBBBBBB   CCCCCCCCC   AAAAAAAAAAAA

Time ⟶

Table 15-2 ▶

Benefit of small lot sizes.

Reduced inventory, lower carrying costs

Less space required to store inventory

Less rework if defects occur

Less inventory to "work off" before implementing product improvements

Increased visibility of problems

Increased production flexibility

Increased ease of balancing operations

Setup Time Reduction

Small lots and changing product mixes require frequent machine setups. An example of a machine changeover or setup is putting a different fixture in a machine to hold a different part or putting in a different die in a press to "stamp" a different part. Another example of a machine changeover/setup is adjusting the heights of fillers and labellers on a beverage bottling line to fill different size bottles. Unless setups are quick and relatively inexpensive, the time and cost to accomplish them can be prohibitive. In JIT/lean systems, workers are often trained to do their own setups. Moreover, tools and methods are used to reduce setup time.

Multipurpose equipment or attachments can help reduce setup time. For instance, a machine with multiple spindles that can easily be rotated into place for different job requirements can drastically reduce changeover time. Moreover, *group technology* may be used to reduce setup cost and time. This is because parts that are similar in shape, materials, and so on require similar setups.

Another method for setup time reduction is to separate the internal setup activities (i.e., those that cannot be done off line in advance) from the external setup activities (i.e., those that can be done off line in advance), and to make as many setup activities as possible external; for example, bring the tools and fixtures to the machine before the setup, or preheat the injection mould. Yet another technique is to streamline the setup. For example, preset the desired settings (one-touch setting), use locator pins to prevent misalignment of a die on a press, reduce or eliminate tools, and make movements easier. Finally, train the operators and standardize the setup procedure.

single-minute exchange of die (SMED) A system for reducing changeover time.

Shigeo Shingo made a very significant contribution to lean operation with the development of what is called the **single-minute exchange of die (SMED)** system for reducing changeover time. It involves first categorizing changeover activities as either "internal" or "external" activities. Internal activities are those that can be done only while a machine is stopped (i.e., not running). Hence, they contribute to long changeover times. External activities are those that do not involve stopping the machine—they can be done before or after the changeover—hence, they do not affect changeover time. After activities have been categorized, a simple approach to achieving quick changeovers is to convert as many internal activities as possible to external activities and then streamline the remaining internal activities.

The potential benefits that can be achieved using the SMED system were impressively illustrated in 1982 at Toyota, when the changeover time for a machine was reduced from 100 minutes to 3 minutes! The principles of the SMED system can be applied to any changeover operation.

Setup tools and equipment and setup procedures must be simple and standardized. Multipurpose equipment or attachments can help to reduce setup time. For instance, a machine with multiple spindles that can easily be rotated into place for different job requirements can drastically reduce job changeover time. Moreover, group technology (described in Chapter 6) may be used to reduce setup cost and time by capitalizing on similarities in recurring operations. For instance, parts that are similar in shape, materials, and so on, may require very similar setups. Processing them in sequence on the same equipment can reduce the need to completely change a setup; only minor adjustment may be necessary.

Cellular Layout

Many JIT/lean systems have one or more *cells*. A cell contains the machines and tools needed to process a family of parts that have similar processing requirements (see Chapter 6). In essence, a cell is a highly specialized and efficient production centre.

Conversion to a cell requires:

- Determining a family of products.
- Mapping the current process for the family of products.
- Determining the operations required.
- Determining the capacity requirements.
- Rearranging the layout and bringing the necessary machines closer together, usually in U-shaped configuration.
- Determining the capacity of the cell.
- Upgrading the machines if the capacity is inadequate.
- Balancing the cell and determining labour requirements.
- Determining the WIP required between the machines/work stations in the cell.

The advantages of cells include faster throughput (i.e., shorter lead times), less material handling, reduced space requirement, and flexibility to increase/decrease the capacity by adding/subtracting workers. The disadvantages of cells are that the machines may not be fully utilized and bringing various machines close together may raise safety/ergonomic issues. For an example of a cell, see Figure 2 of the Mini-Case "Airline Manufacturing" at the end of this chapter.

 OM in *ACTION*   http://www.sconatrailers.com

Scona Trailer Manufacturing

Scona Trailer Manufacturing of Edmonton, part of McCoy Corp., manufactures large, heavy-duty trailers. In 2003, the demand for trailers was soaring but Scona could not keep up with demand. The new president of McCoy, Jim Rakievich, heard about JIT/lean manufacturing and with Scona plant manager, Giorgio Overeem, started to study it. Jim brought in a consultant and Giorgio enrolled in a course on JIT/lean manufacturing at the Northern Alberta Institute of Technology. In the summer of 2005 they introduced JIT/lean production to Scona, starting with one cell. JIT/lean tools used included value stream mapping, identifying nonvalue steps and eliminating these wastes, identifying the bottleneck and rearranging the flow to improve the throughput, and tidying up the shop floor (5S). Eventually, the whole plant (25,000 ft²) was converted into three to four cells. The capacity of plant has more than doubled. A trailer can now be produced in only 3 days (down from approximately 25 days before).

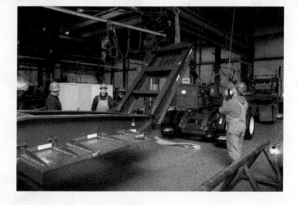

Source: K. Laudrum, "McCoy Gets Leaner and Doubles Productivity," *Plant*, March/April 2009, 4(2), p. 8.

poka-yoke Any mechanism that helps an equipment operator avoid mistakes. Its purpose is to eliminate product defects by preventing, correcting, or drawing attention to human errors as they occur.

autonomation Intelligent automation: if an abnormal situation arises, the machine automatically stops, preventing production of defective products.

jidoka Japanese term for quality at the source: avoid passing defective products to the following workstation, and stop and fix the problem.

andon A set of lights used at each workstation to signal problems or slowdowns.

Process Quality

Because of low inventories in JIT/lean systems, it is important to prevent defects from occurring; hence, the importance of a capable production process, SPC (Statistical Process Control including control charts) to control and stabilize the production process, Six Sigma to reduce its variability, and *poka-yoke* to mistake-proof it.

A **poka-yoke** is any mechanism that helps an equipment operator avoid mistakes. Its purpose is to eliminate product defects by preventing, correcting, or drawing attention to human errors as they occur. Examples of *poka-yoke* include an alarm that sounds if the weight of a package is too low (indicating missing components), an ABM signal if a card is left in the machine, and detectors at department stores that signal if a monitoring tag hasn't been removed from an item. Much of the credit for *poka-yoke* goes to Shigeo Shingo.

A related term is **autonomation** (note the extra syllable *no* in the middle of the word), meaning intelligent automation. It means that if an abnormal situation arises, the machine automatically stops, preventing production of defective products. Another related term is **jidoka**, meaning quality at the source: avoid passing defective products to the following workstation, and stop and fix the problem. Clearly, both *poka-yoke* and autonomation assist in *jidoka*.

Some companies use lights to signal problems; in Japan, this is called **andon**. Each workstation is equipped with a set of three lights. A green light means no problems, an amber light means a worker is falling a little bit behind, and a red light indicates a serious problem. The purpose of the light system is to enable supervisors to immediately see where problems are occurring.

Standardized Processes

Processes include customer-related processes such as invoicing, product development processes such as standardization and modularity, supply-related processes such as supplier qualification, and support processes such as capital budgeting. Here we will focus on the production

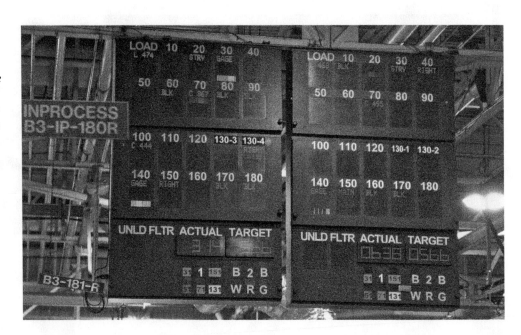

The Andon board in the GM Powertrain Engine facility is a visual communication tool. It advises employees of the real-time status of each machine within the manufacturing lines, enabling the production system to be run more effectively.

process. The Toyota Production System has rigid rules for work, interaction, work flow, and improvement process.[1]

The content, sequence, timing, and output of every employee's work are fully specified, even for nonrepetitive work such as training or shifting equipment. The worker learns her job primarily by doing it. While in training, the supervisor constantly monitors the worker, compares her performance to the standards, and asks questions to make the worker think and learn her job (e.g., how do you know if you are doing the job right, and what do you do if there is a problem?).

Every connection or link (i.e., people–work interaction) is standardized and specified: it shows the people involved, the form and quantity of product to be supplied, the way the request is made, and the time it should take to meet the request. For example, when a worker cannot do her job, she is supposed to immediately inform her supervisor, and the supervisor should be there promptly to help her (if not, a specified alternative person should be available). *Kanbans* and *andon* are examples of tools used to establish a direct link.

Every product or work flows along a simple, specified path (with no loops), not to the next available machine or workstation.

Improvement of all aspects of the work is done by the front-line person, with guidance and teaching of her supervisor, based on scientific method. That is, a hypothesis is formed to predict the outcome of a solution to a problem, and experiments are performed by the worker to see if the hypothesis can be rejected. This will enforce decision making based on data and facts, rather than guesses.

The advantage of these standardizations is that they provide consistency and repeatability, hence the system can be learned and constantly improved. If there was no standard way to, e.g., install a car seat, the variations across workers (and shifts) would confuse the results, making learning and improvement of the operation difficult.

Little Inventory

JIT/lean systems are designed to *minimize* inventory. Recall that in JIT/lean systems, inventory is a waste. Inventories are buffers that tend to cover up recurring problems that are never resolved, partly because they aren't obvious and partly because the presence of inventory makes them seem less serious. When a machine breaks down, it won't disrupt the system if there is sufficient inventory of the machine's output to feed into the next workstation. A better solution is to investigate the *causes* of machine breakdowns and focus on eliminating them. Similar situations occur with quality problems, unreliable vendors, and scheduling problems.

A useful analogy is a boat on a pond that has large, hidden rocks (see Figure 15-3). The rocks represent problems that can hinder production (the boat's movement). The water in the pond that covers the rocks is the inventory in the system. As the water level is lowered, the largest rocks are the first to appear. At that point, efforts are undertaken to remove these rocks from the water (resolve these problems). Once that has been accomplished, the lower water level (inventory) is adequate.

One way to minimize inventory of raw materials/purchase parts in a JIT/lean system is to have deliveries from suppliers go directly to the production floor, which eliminates the need to store

A   B   C

◀ Figure 15-3

Large rocks (problems) are hidden by a higher water level (inventory) in A. Lower water level (B) reveals the rocks. Once the large rocks are removed, the lower water level (inventory) is adequate (C).

---

[1] S. Spear and H. K. Bowen, "Decoding the DNA of the Toyota Production System," *Harvard Business Review,* September/October 1999, pp. 97–106.

OM in *ACTION* http://www.dana.com/wps/wcm/connect/DEXT2/dana/home

Dana

When Toyota decided to build a truck assembly plant in Princeton, Indiana, to make Tundra and Sequoia in the late-1990s, it chose Dana Corporation to build its truck frames. Dana built a 129,080 ft² plant employing about 300 people 73 miles away in Owensboro, Kentucky. To be as lean as possible, Dana makes the frames to the sequence of trucks planned in the Toyota Plant. There are 14 frame models, which are sequenced in batch sizes of one. Therefore, the Dana plant has to be very flexible: it takes a maximum of only three seconds to change over from one model to another in any work centre on the production line. The order information comes via Internet (EDI) from the Toyota plant and is displayed on every work centre. About nine hours later, after operations such as welding, machining, and painting, the frames are trucked to the Toyota plant in batches of 25, about one truck every half hour.

Source: T. Vinas, "In Sync with the Customer," *Industry Week* 252(10), October 2002, pp. 46–48.

incoming parts and materials. At the other end of the process, completed units are shipped out as soon as they are ready, which minimizes storage of finished goods. Coupled with small manufacturing lot sizes resulting in low work-in-process inventory, these features result in systems that operate with very little inventory.

 L05 ## Personnel/Organization

Workers as Assets. A fundamental tenet of JIT/lean is that *workers are assets* and should be respected. Well-trained and motivated workers with high morals are the heart of a JIT/lean system. Education, training, and coaching are essential to develop the workers, as is the promotion of their health and safety. They are given authority (empowered) to make decisions. Workers are expected to participate (be involved) in continuous improvement (*kaizen*). In return, their contribution is recognized and rewarded. Workers are *cross-trained* to perform several steps of a process and operate a variety of machines. This adds to system flexibility because workers are able to help one another when bottlenecks occur or when a coworker is absent.

Leadership. Top management should take leadership in conversion to JIT/lean because it involves culture change, i.e., the way workers do their job. Goals should be set to progress toward world-class JIT/lean status, their importance should be communicated to the employees to create constancy of purpose, and resources should be allocated so that progress toward JIT/lean is systematic. Employees should be both directed and encouraged to use tools and techniques of JIT/lean and incorporate its principles in their daily work. On the other hand, managers and supervisors are expected to be facilitators, not just order givers. JIT/lean encourages two-way communication between workers and managers. Leaders should lead with humility and seek input from everyone in the organization.

Non-Manufacturing Support. Clearly, support is needed from sales/marketing for product design, from accounting for product costing, from HR for hiring and training good employees, and from quality assurance and control for improving the quality of products and processes. Further, finance needs to provide the cash for faster but more flexible equipment, purchasing needs to identify qualified JIT/lean suppliers and maintain close relationship with them, and MIS needs to provide the information required to track performance measures and to provide data gathering/communication links. In addition, all these functions should reduce their own department's "wastes."

OM in *ACTION*   http://www.cglmfg.com

CGL Manufacturing

CGL Manufacturing is a machining, welding, and painting shop in Guelph, Ontario. It started in 1977 as a job shop with five employees. Later, through quality and service, CGL expanded, producing parts for heavy equipment manufacturers such as Raymond lift-trucks. In 2000, CGL had revenue of $10 million and employed approximately 100 workers, but a major customer unexpectedly demanded a 20 percent price cut. The general manager, David Deskur, knew that a major change in CGL had to occur. He attended a JIT/lean manufacturing seminar, was captivated, and acted as the JIT/lean champion. All staff were educated in JIT/lean tools such as value stream mapping, cellular layout, teamwork, and *kaizen*. The plant was reconfigured so that high-volume orders were made

in five cells. During the first year, the distance travelled by forklifts was reduced by 1,000 km, revenues were up by 50 percent, inventories were down by 30 percent, and lead times were down by 20 percent. David believes that the two most important keys to JIT/lean manufacturing are [to] (1) communicate its importance to all staff and (2) tie employee performance measures to their participation in continuous improvement projects. Now, CGL has 170 employees and $35 million in revenue. It has established partnerships with two suppliers: (1) Excel Steel of Cambridge, Ontario, which supplies CGL with sheet metal and (2) a company in China that supplies CGL with castings. CGL has become a role model for JIT/lean manufacturing.

Source: "Get Lean," *Plant*, 2008, pp. 55–64.

Planning and Control   L06

Level Loading

JIT/lean places a strong emphasis on achieving stable, level daily mixed-model schedule/sequence. This will result in *level capacity loading* (*heijunka* in Japanese).

When a company produces different products or models, it is desirable to produce in small lots (to minimize the work-in-process inventories and to maintain flexibility) and to spread out the production of different products or models throughout the day to achieve even smooth production. The ideal case would be to produce one unit of one product or model, then one unit of another, then one unit of another, and so on.

The simplest method for determining a *level mixed-model sequence* is as follows[2]:

a. Determine a "due time" for each unit of each product or model so that the units of the product or model are evenly distributed throughout the day.

b. Sequence the units of all products or models based on their "due times" (from smallest to largest).

The "due times," based on daily demand for each model, are as follows:

Daily Demand	Due Times (start of day = 0, end of day = 1)
1	1/2
2	1/4, 3/4
3	1/6, 3/6, 5/6
4	1/8, 3/8, 5/8, 7/8
5	1/10, 3/10, 5/10, 7/10, 9/10
6	1/12, 3/12, 5/12, 7/12, 9/12, 11/12
7	1/14, 3/14, 5/14, 7/14, 9/14, 11/14, 13/14
8	1/16, 3/16, 5/16, 7/16, 9/16, 11/16, 13/16, 15/16
⋮	

In general, if daily demand is n for a product or model, the due times will be:

$$\frac{1}{2n}, \frac{3}{2n}, \frac{5}{2n}, \cdots \frac{2n-1}{2n}.$$

---

[2] R. R. Inman and R. L. Bulfin, "Sequencing JIT Mixed-Model Assembly Lines," *Management Science* 37(7), July 1991, pp. 901–904.

Example 2 ▶

Determine a level mixed model sequence if daily demand for product A = 7, B = 16, and C = 5 units.

SOLUTION

The due times for each product are:

A: 1/14 = .071, 3/14 = .214, 5/14 = .357, 7/14 = .5, 9/14 = .643, 11/14 = .786, 13/14 = .929

B: 1/32 = .031, 3/32 = .094, 5/32 = .156, 7/32 = .219, 9/32 = .281, 11/32 = .344, 13/32 = .406, 15/32 = .469, 17/32 = .531, 19/32 = .594, 21/32 = .656, 23/32 = .719, 25/32 = .781, 27/32 = .844, 29/32 = .906, 31/32 = .969

C: 1/10 = .1, 3/10 = .3, 5/10 = .5, 7/10 = .7, 9/10 = .9

Now, sequence the due times from the smallest to the largest. The smallest due time is .031 for a B, so the first unit to produce is B. The next smallest due time is .071 for an A, so the second unit to produce is A, and so on. The level mixed model sequence is:

B-A-B-C-B-A-B-B-C-B-A-B-B-A-C-B-B-A-B-C-B-B-A-B-C-B-A-B

Pull System and *Kanban*

push system Based on MRP plan, a batch of items is made and pushed to the next work centre as it is completed.

pull system Based directly on customer demand, a work centre pulls items from the preceding work centre as they are needed.

The terms *push* and *pull* are used to describe two different approaches for making and moving items (raw material, parts, subassemblies, products) through a production process. In the traditional production environments that use MRP, a **push system** is used: A batch is started at a work centre according to the production plan derived from MRP. When the batch is finished at the work centre, the output is *pushed* to the next work centre or, in the case of the final operation, it is pushed on to the finished goods warehouse. Consequently, inventory will pile up at work centres. Conversely, in a **pull system**, control of moving the batch (preferably only one unit) rests with the following operation; each work centre *pulls* the output from the preceding work centre as it is needed; output of the final operation is pulled by customer demand. JIT/lean uses the pull system.

In a pull system, communication moves backward through the system from work centre to work centre. Each work centre communicates its need for more items to the preceding work centre. The batch moves "just in time" to the next operation; the flow is thereby coordinated, and the accumulation of excessive inventories between operations is avoided. Of course, some buffer inventory is usually allowed because operations are not instantaneous. When the buffer inventory decreases to a certain level (i.e., the reorder point), this signals the preceding work centre to produce enough output to replenish the buffer supply. The size of the buffer supply depends on the lead time. If the lead time is short, the buffer can be small. The communication between the two work centres can be done in a variety of ways, including a shout or a wave, but by far the most commonly used

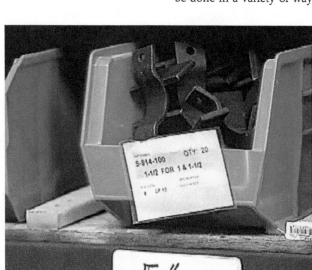

At TriState Industries, a kanban system is in effect to move work through the production system. Shown here, a kanban card provides the authorization to move or work on parts.

Special carts were designed that, when filled, act as a visual signal that they are ready to be moved to the next work cell. An empty cart indicates that it is time to produce, in order to refill the cart.

method is the use of **kanban** cards. *Kanban* is Japanese for "signal" or "visual card." When a worker needs a batch of an item from the preceding work centre, she uses a *kanban* card. In effect, the *kanban* card is the *authorization* to make the batch. No item can be made without one of these cards.

The system works this way: A *kanban* card is affixed to each container. When a work centre needs to replenish its supply of a batch of an item, a worker goes to the area where these items are stored and withdraws one container of the item. Each container holds a predetermined quantity. The worker removes the *kanban* card from the container and posts it in a designated spot where it will be clearly visible to the operator of the producing work centre (e.g., a *kanban* board), and the worker moves the container to the using work centre. The posted *kanban* is later picked up by the operator of the producing work centre and another batch of the item is made. Usually because of significant setup time and the desire for high utilization of the producing work centre, a few *kanbans* are first accumulated before production is triggered. Similar withdrawals and replenishments—all controlled by *kanbans*—occur all the way up and down the line from vendors to finished-goods warehouse. Each item will have kanbans between each pair of supplying-using work centres. If supervisors decide the system is too loose because inventories are building up, they may decide to withdraw some *kanbans*. Conversely, if the system seems too tight, they may introduce additional *kanbans*. It is apparent that the number of *kanban* cards in use is an important variable. One can calculate the ideal number of *kanban* cards for each item, between each pair of supplying-using work centres, by this formula:

> **kanban** Card that communicates demand for a batch of an item to the preceding work centre.

$$N = \frac{DT(1 + X)}{C} \tag{15-1}$$

where

N = Total number of *kanbans* (1 *kanban* per container)

D = Average usage rate of using work centre

T = Average lead time for replenishment of one container (includes wait before production, setup, production, and transport times)

X = Policy variable set by the management that represents the safety stocks (as a proportion of average usage during lead time T)

C = Capacity of a standard container

Note that D and T must use the same time unit (e.g., hour, day). The concept underlying the above formula is the same as the concept underlying the reorder point in the EOQ $-$ ROP inventory model (see Chapter 12): ROP $=$ DT(1 $+$ X) $=$ average demand during a lead time plus safety stock, where safety stock is a proportion X of the average demand during a lead time.

Usage at a work centre is 300 units of a specific part per day, and a standard container holds 25 units. It takes an average of 0.12 day from the time a *kanban* card is posted until the full container is received by the using work centre. Calculate the number of *kanban* cards needed for this part between these two work centres, if $X = 0.20$.

◀ **Example 3**

SOLUTION

N = ?

D = 300 units per day

T = 0.12 day

C = 25 units per container

X = 0.20

$$N = \frac{300(.12)(1 + .20)}{25} = 1.728 \text{ round to 2 containers}$$

Note: Rounding up will cause the system to be looser, and rounding down will cause it to be tighter. Usually, rounding up is used.

Other forms of signal include empty squares on the floor, empty carts or containers, and empty shelves/racks. For an application, see the "Waterville TG" OM in Action.

Waterville TG

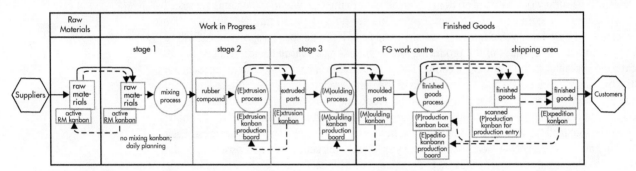

Figure 1

Waterville TG (WTG), of Quebec, designs and manufactures insulation for doors, hoods, and trunks of cars from various types of rubber. Waterville TG is part of Toyoda Gosei Co. Ltd., a division of Toyota Motor Company. WTG has close to 385 different models of insulations designed for almost all types of automobiles. The raw material is synthetic powder rubber. The production process is four stages: mixing, extrusion, moulding, and finishing. WTG uses *kanbans* for pulling material through most of the production process, as shown in Figure 1.

There are raw material (RM) *kanbans*, WIP extrusion (E) and moulding (M) *kanbans*, finished-goods production (P) *kanbans*, and shipping or expedition (E) *kanbans*. An example of a RM *kanban* is shown in Figure 2:

Figure 2

The use of bar codes on a *kanban* is unusual. WTG uses the computer and bar codes to keep track of inventories and changes the number of active *kanbans* as demand varies. The bar codes make this easier. The card itself is printed on plain white paper and inserted in a protective clear plastic pouch that in turn is placed in a self-adhesive pouch. This pouch is then attached to a container. Soon after a full container is moved to

its point of use, the *kanban* is detached and moved back to the originating area. The punched hole in the top left corner is used to hang the card on the *kanban* boards.

Figure 3 shows an example of a WIP E *kanban*. A zip-top seal was added to the pouch for easier maintenance. After trying out several versions of this card, WTG found that *kanban* maintenance was easier when cards included only information that changed little or not at all over time.

At the finished-goods level, two cards are used instead of one to allow some excess production (relative to shipment). These *kanbans* are similar to the WIP *kanbans*.

Source: S. Chausse, S. Landry, F. Pasin, and S. Fortier, "Anatomy of a Kanban: A Case Study," *Production and Inventory Management Journal* 41(4), Fourth Quarter 2000, pp. 11–16.

Close Supplier Relationship

JIT/lean companies typically have *close relationships with their suppliers*, which are expected to provide frequent small deliveries of high-quality goods on time. Buyers work with suppliers to help them achieve the desired quality and on-time delivery. The ultimate goal of the buyer is to be able to *certify* a supplier as a reliable producer of high-quality goods, and hence remove the need for inspection of the goods purchased from them.

In effect, the supplier becomes part of an extended JIT/lean system that integrates the facilities of buyer and supplier as part of the value chain. Integration is easier when a supplier is dedicated to only one or few buyers.

Because of the need for frequent small deliveries, many buyers attempt to find local suppliers to shorten the lead time for deliveries and to reduce the lead-time variability. An added advantage of having suppliers nearby is quick response when problems arise. Of course, EDI with the supplier is a must.

Ford is taking a page out of Toyota's JIT/lean book at its Chicago plant that opened in 2004 by having some of its suppliers locate very close to its assembly plant. Ford leased production facilities on its 155 acres land to approximately 10 key suppliers. Suppliers' parts and modules feed directly into Ford's assembly line, carefully coordinated to match the sequence of vehicles Ford is producing, which can range from small cars to SUVs. Not only are suppliers nearby in case problems arise, but also the shortened travel distance and lead times yield tremendous savings in the in-transit inventories of parts and modules.

JIT/lean companies employ a tiered approach for suppliers: They use relatively few first-tier suppliers that work directly with the company and supply major subassemblies. The first-tier suppliers are responsible for dealing with their own suppliers (the second-tier suppliers) that provide parts for the subassemblies, thereby relieving the final buyer from dealing with a large number of suppliers.

The automotive industry provides a good example of this situation. Suppose a certain car model has an electric seat. The seat and its motor together might entail 250 separate parts. A traditional automobile manufacturer might use more than 30 suppliers for the electric seat, but a JIT/lean auto manufacturer will use a single (first-tier) supplier that has the responsibility for the entire seat unit. The auto manufacturer will provide some specification for the overall unit, but leave the details of the motor, springs, and so on, to the supplier. The first-tier supplier, in turn, might subcontract the motor to a second-tier supplier, the track to another second-tier supplier, and the cushions and fabric to another. The second-tier suppliers might subcontract some of their work to third-tier suppliers, and so on. Each tier has to deal with only those just above it and just below it. Suppliers on each level are encouraged to work with each other, and they are motivated to do so because that increases the probability that the resulting item (the seat) will meet or exceed the final buyer's expectations. Figure 15-4 illustrates the difference between the traditional and tiered (JIT/lean) supplier networks.

▼ **Figure 15-4**

Traditional supplier network compared to supplier tiers used in JIT/lean.

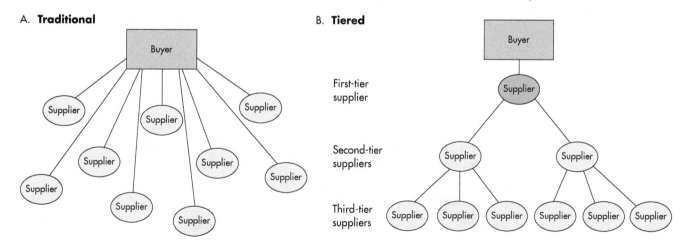

A. **Traditional**

B. **Tiered**

Plains Fabrication & Supply

Plains Fabrication & Supply (PF&S) is a metal shop in Calgary that makes custom industrial heaters, separators, and pressure vessels. It started with 16 people in 1988 and now employs 150 workers and has $20 million revenue. Low profit margin (4 percent) and an old plant brought PF&S to a crossroads in 2005: either it had to become more efficient or had to close down. It decided the former and got help from a provincial government program called Productivity Alberta, which provided JIT/lean manufacturing guidance at a low price. After a four-hour assessment, all employees were put through a four-hour workshop on

JIT/lean manufacturing. One area of the shop, the small vessels area, was chosen for lean improvement. The improvements included use of visual and shadow boards, *kanban* cards and shelves, and cleaning and organizing the shop floor. After 12 months, the amount of inventory on the shop floor was reduced by 75 percent and lead time was reduced from 44 days to 5 days.

Sources: http://www.albertacanada.com/productivity/lean/plainsfabrication.html, accessed August 30, 2009; C. Lynds, "Making the Most of Time and Space," *Plant*, October 18, 2008, 67(10), p. 20; http://www.productivityalberta.ca/articles/187/plains-speaking.

A very close cooperation with suppliers, called JIT II, has been used by Bose Corporation, the manufacturer of luxury audio equipment, in which a supplier representative is located in Bose's facility and performs the functions of Bose's buyer. This reduces lead times. For another application, see the "Dana" OM in Action.

Preventive Maintenance and Housekeeping

Because JIT/lean systems have very little work-in-process inventory, equipment breakdowns can be extremely disruptive. To minimize downtime, JIT/lean companies use **preventive maintenance** programs, which emphasize maintaining equipment in good operating condition and replacing parts that have a tendency to fail before they do fail.

Even with preventive maintenance, occasional equipment failures will occur. Companies must be prepared for this, so they can quickly return equipment back to working order. This may mean maintaining supplies of critical spare parts and making other provisions for emergency situations, perhaps maintaining a small team of repair people or training workers to do certain repairs themselves.

Housekeeping involves keeping the workplace clean, because it facilitates discovery of problems. For example, clean floors will show oil leaks from a machine, which could result in a worker slipping, a safety hazard. Housekeeping also involves keeping the workplace free of anything that is not needed for production, because it takes up space and may cause disruption to the work flow. These and other principles of housekeeping are included in the *5S principles*:

- *Sort:* remove all objects that do not need to be in the workstation or area.
- *Set in order:* tidy up the objects needed and organize them such that they can be seen and therefore found quickly. For example, use a peg or shadow board for hand tools.
- *Shine:* clean the workstation completely and eliminate all signs of dust or grime on the floor, machines, and equipment.
- *Standardize:* Set standards in cleanliness and organization, and audit the area for compliance.
- *Sustain:* train workers to perform housekeeping and continuously improve on the standards; make 5S part of the work culture.

For an application, see the "Plains Fabrication & Supply" OM in Action.

JIT/lean systems have been described in the preceding pages. Table 15-3 provides a brief overview of JIT/lean vs. traditional production systems. The next section lists JIT/lean implementation steps and an implementation tool called value stream mapping.

preventive maintenance Keeping equipment in good operating condition and replacing parts that have a tendency to fail before they do fail.

housekeeping Keeping the workplace clean and free of unnecessary things.

http://www.lmsi.ca/5s.htm

LO7 Implementing JIT/Lean

The discussion of lean systems has focused on manufacturing simply because that is where it was developed, and where it has been used most often. It is important to recognize that the full spectrum of lean benefits are more difficult to achieve in service operations. Nonetheless,

Factor	Traditional	JIT/lean
Inventory	Much, to offset late deliveries, etc.	Minimal necessary to operate
Deliveries	Few, large	Many, small
Lot sizes	Large	Small
Setups, runs	Few, long runs	Many, short runs
Vendors	Adversaries	Partners
Workers	Replaceable	Assets

◀ **Table 15-3**

Comparison of JIT/lean and traditional production systems.

services can and do benefit from many lean concepts. When just-in-time is used in the context of services, the focus is often on the time needed to perform a service—because speed is often an important order winner for services. Some services do have inventories of some sort, so inventory reduction is another aspect of lean that can apply to services. Examples of speedy delivery ("available when requested") are Domino's Pizza, FedEx and Express Mail, fast-food restaurants, and emergency services. Other examples include just-in-time publishing and work cells at fast-food restaurants.

In addition to speed, lean services emphasize consistent, high-quality, standard work methods; flexible workers; and close supplier relationships.

Process improvement and problem solving can contribute to streamlining a system, resulting in increased customer satisfaction and higher productivity. The following are the ways lean benefits can be achieved in services:

- *Eliminate disruptions:* For example, try to avoid having workers who are servicing customers also answer telephones.

- *Make the system flexible:* This can cause problems unless approached carefully. Often, it is desirable to standardize work because that can yield high productivity. On the other hand, being able to deal with variety in task requirements can be a competitive advantage. One approach might be to train workers so that they can handle more variety. Another might be to assign work according to specialties, with certain workers handling different types of work according to their specialty.

- *Reduce setup times and processing times:* Have frequently used tools and spare parts readily available. Additionally, for service calls, try to estimate what parts and supplies might be needed so they will be on hand, and avoid carrying huge inventories.

- *Eliminate waste:* This includes errors and duplicate work. Keep the emphasis on quality and uniform service.

- *Minimize work-in-process:* Example include orders waiting to be processed, calls waiting to be answered, packages waiting to be delivered, trucks waiting to be unloaded or loaded, and applications waiting to be processed.

- *Simplify the process:* This works especially when customers are part of the system (self-service systems including retail operations, ATMs and vending machines, service stations, etc.)

JIT service can be a major competitive advantage for companies that can achieve it. An important key to JIT service is the ability to provide service when it is needed. That requires flexibility on the part of the provider, which generally means short setup times, and it requires clear communication on the part of the requester. If a requester can determine when it will need a particular service, a JIT server can schedule deliveries to correspond to those needs, eliminating the need for continual requests, and reducing the need for provider flexibility—and therefore probably reducing the cost of the JIT service.

Although lean concepts are applicable to service organizations, the challenge of implementing lean in service is that there are still relatively few lean service applications that service companies can reference to see how to apply the underlying lean principles. Consequently, it can be difficult to build a strong commitment among workers to achieve a lean service system.

Lean Services

Reasons for implementing JIT/lean include not making enough profit, not meeting delivery deadlines, and not having enough capacity. JIT/lean implementation usually follows the following steps. Management communicates JIT/lean's importance to the employees and obtains their cooperation. Usually an outside consultant is brought in as a facilitator. The employees go through a class on JIT/lean tools, techniques, and principles. Implementation is usually piecemeal. A product family is chosen. Usually the products are being produced in batches and excessive material handling is involved. A team of the operators is formed, the product flow is studied and drawn (called the value stream mapping), wastes are identified and eliminated, a cycle (*takt*) time is determined based on demand, and a new streamlined process is designed. This requires rearranging the equipment into a cellular layout, cross-training the operators, reducing setup times, standardizing the work, balancing the line, applying 5S principles, setting up a demand pull system and arranging *kanban* signals with suppliers, putting in *jidoka* (quality at the source) quality controls, implementing performance-based pay, and continuously improving the line. Then, JIT/lean production is expanded to other products and other business processes such as supplier selection, product design, sales process, and recruiting.

For two implementations of JIT/lean, see the "Scona Trailer Manufacturing" and "CGL Manufacturing" OM in Actions earlier in the chapter.

Value Stream Mapping

value stream mapping A visual tool to systematically examine the flow of materials and information.

Value stream mapping (VSM) is a visual tool to systematically examine the flow of materials and information involved in bringing a product or service to a consumer. The technique originated at Toyota, where it is referred to as "Material and Information Flow Mapping."

The map is a sketch of an entire process that typically ranges from incoming goods from suppliers to shipment of a product or delivery of a service to the customer. The map shows all processes in the value stream, from arrivals of supplies to the shipping of the product. The objective is to increase value to the customer, where value is typically defined in terms of quality, time, cost, or flexibility (e.g., rapid response or agility). Data collected during the mapping process might include times (e.g., cycle time, setup time, changeover time, touch time, lead time), distances travelled (e.g., by parts, workers, paperwork), mistakes (e.g., product defects, data entry errors), inefficient work methods (e.g., extra motions, excessive lifting or moving, repositioning), and waiting lines (e.g., workers waiting for parts or equipment repairs, orders waiting to be processed). Information flows are also included in the mapping process.

You can get a sense of value stream mapping from the following tips for developing an effective mapping of a value stream:

1. Map the value stream in person.
2. Begin with quick walk-through of the system from beginning to end to get a sense of the system.
3. Then do a more thorough walk-through following the actual pathway to collect current information on material or information flow.
4. Record elements of the system such as cycle times, scrap rates, amounts of inventory, downtimes, number of operators, distances between processes, and transfer times.

Value improvement for a product or a service embodies the five lean principles described earlier and repeated here. It begins by specifying value from the customer's standpoint. You can see where value stream mapping can help process improvement:

1. Specify value from the standpoint of the end customer.
2. Identify all the steps in the value stream and create a visual (map) of the value stream.
3. Eliminate steps that do not create value to create flow.
4. Use next-customer-in-the-process demand to pull from each preceding process as needed to control the flow.
5. Repeat this process as long as waste exists in the system.

Once a value stream map is completed, data analysis can uncover improvement opportunities by asking key questions, such as:

- Where are the process bottlenecks?
- Where do errors occur?
- Which processes have to deal with the most variation?
- Where does waste occur?

Summary

- Just-in-time (JIT), in a narrow sense, is a system of production in which processing and movement of parts/modules/work-in-process occur just as they are needed, usually in small batches. JIT systems require very little inventory because successive operations are closely coordinated. JIT in a broad sense, also called lean production, is a philosophy of eliminating wastes, especially setup, lead times, and inventories, and continuous improvement.
- The goals of JIT/lean are a balanced rapid flow, elimination of waste and disruption, a flexible system, and continuous improvement.
- The building blocks of a JIT/lean system are various tools and methods used in product design, process design, personnel and organization, and planning and control.
- Products should be simple to make and assemble (DFM and DFA). Concurrent engineering and QFD should be used to ensure a fast product design process and that the voice of the customer is reflected in the product's quality.
- A JIT/lean system is balanced. One unit is produced every *takt* (or cycle) time to meet the demand. It is flexible (e.g., changeover times are fast) to meet the mix of products and changes in demand.
- Small production lot sizes are used in order to reduce the WIP, increase flexibility, and facilitate defect detection. Setup times should be reduced to render small lot sizes economical. Product families are identified and produced in dedicated cells; this reduces material handling and manufacturing lead times. JIT/lean requires the highest quality parts because there is little safety stock. Through *jidoka* or quality at the source, a defective item isn't passed through; workers stop and fix the problem. Standardized work, interaction, and work flow are required in order to learn and improve a JIT/lean system. In addition to WIP, raw material and finished goods inventories should also be minimized.
- Workers should be respected and empowered in order to participate in continuous improvement (*kaizen*) and cross-trained in order to help with system flexibility. Top management should assign the necessary resources, communicate its importance, and direct the JIT conversion process. Other functions of business should support manufacturing to become lean, and they should also initiate waste reduction programs within their own departments.
- To reduce inventories, production of various products should be levelled. Level loads are achieved by mixed-model sequencing. Production is synchronized to demand by using *kanbans* to pull the minimum amount of parts and materials through the manufacturing process and from the suppliers. There is a need to integrate operations with the suppliers; hence, the number of suppliers should be reduced in order to establish close relationships and partnerships. Preventive maintenance is crucial for JIT/lean systems, because machine downtime may stop the whole plant's production. The 5S housekeeping method is also important because organized and clean workstations operate faster and help in discovering problems.
- A value stream map, which displays the process steps, and material and information flows are used in the production of a family of products.

Lean systems are designed to operate with fewer resources than traditional systems. Elements of lean operation include:

Smooth flow of work (the ultimate goal).

Elimination of waste.

Continuous improvement.

Elimination of anything that does not add value.

Simple systems that are easy to manage.

Use of product layouts that minimize time spent moving materials and parts.

Quality at the source: Each worker is responsible for the quality of his or her output.

Poka-yoke: fail-safe tools and methods to prevent mistakes.

Preventive maintenance to reduce the risk of equipment breakdown.

Good housekeeping: an orderly and clean workplace.

Setup time reduction.

Cross-trained workers.

A pull system.

There are seven types of waste:

Inventory.

Overproduction.

Waiting time.

Excess transportation.

Processing waste.

Inefficient work methods.

Product or service defects.

Key Terms

andon	*kanban*	push system
autonomation	lean production	single-minute exchange of die (SMED)
housekeeping	*poka-yoke*	*takt* time
jikoda	preventive maintenance	value stream mapping
just-in-time (JIT)	pull system	

Solved Problems

Problem 1

Determine the number of *kanbans* needed for a part in a workstation that uses 100 units of the part per hour if the time from posting a *kanban* until receiving a full container (wait, setup, fill, return) is 90 minutes and a standard container holds 84 units. A safety factor of 0.10 is currently being used.

Solution

$N = ?$

$D = 100$ units per hour

$T = 90$ minutes (1.5 hours)

$C = 84$ units

$X = .10$

$$N = \frac{D(T)(1 + X)}{C} = \frac{100(1.5)(1 + .10)}{84} = 1.96, \text{ round to 2 } \textit{kanbans.}$$

Problem 2

Determine a level mixed-model sequence for the following set of products and demand. The plant operates five days a week.

Product	Weekly Quantity
A	20
B	40
C	30
D	15

Solution

Convert weekly quantities to daily quantities:

Product	Daily Quantity = Weekly Quantity ÷ 5
A	20 ÷ 5 = 4
B	40 ÷ 5 = 8
C	30 ÷ 5 = 6
D	15 ÷ 5 = 3

The due times are:

A: $1/8 = .125, 3/8 = .375, 5/8 = .625, 7/8 = .875$

B: $1/16 = .0625, 3/16 = .1875, 5/16 = .3125, 7/16 = .4375, 9/16 = .5625, 11/16 = .6875, 13/16 = .8125, 15/16 = .9375$

C: $1/12 = .083, 3/12 = .25, 5/12 = .417, 7/12 = .583, 9/12 = .75, 11/12 = .917$

D: $1/6 = .167, 3/6 = .5, 5/6 = .83$

Sort the due times from the smallest to the largest. The smallest due time is .0625 for B, so the first unit in the sequence should be B. The next smallest due time is .083 for C, so the second unit in sequence to produce should be C, and so on:

B-C-A-D-B-C-B-A-C-B-D-B-C-A-B-C-B-D-A-C-B

Problem 3

Cars are to be assembled on a moving assembly line. Five hundred cars are required per day. Production time per day is eight hours minus a half-hour for lunch break. What is the *takt* time?

Solution

$8(60) = 480 - 30 = 450$ minutes per day

Takt time $= 450/500 = 0.9$ minute $= 54$ seconds

Discussion and Review Questions

1. Distinguish between little JIT and big JIT. **LO1**

2. Explain briefly how a JIT/lean system differs from an MRP-based system. **LO1**

3. What are the main benefits of JIT/lean? Name a company using JIT/lean, and describe how JIT/lean contributes to the company's competitive advantage. **LO1**

4. Contrast the principles of the Shingo prize with the goals of JIT/lean given in Figure 15-1. Why can't a Shingo Prize winner's production process be unbalanced and slow? Explain. **LO1**

5. **a.** What are the goals of JIT/lean system? **LO2**
   b. What are the eight wastes? **LO2**

6. What aspects of product design are important for JIT/lean? **LO3**

7. What are (a) *takt* time, (b) SMED, (c) *jidoka*, and (d) *poka-yoke*? **LO4**

8. What are the benefits of (a) small lot sizes, (b) standardized process, (c) low inventories? **LO4**

9. What is the role of workers in JIT/lean?

10. What is a *kanban*? **LO6**

11. Contrast push and pull systems of moving parts/modules/work-in-process through the production system. **LO6**

12. What is level mixed-model sequencing and why is it important? **LO6**

13. Briefly discuss supplier relations in JIT/lean in terms of the following issues: **LO6**
    a. Why are they important?
    b. How do they tend to differ from the more adversarial relations of the past?

14. What is 5S and why is it important? **LO6**

15. What is value stream mapping and why is it important?

Taking Stock

1. What trade-offs are involved in shifting from an MRP system to a JIT/lean system? **LO1**

2. Who in the company is affected by a decision to shift from an MRP system to a JIT/lean system? **LO7**

3. To what extent has technology had an impact on JIT/lean systems? **LO4 & 6**

4. A cellular layout contains various machines in close proximity to one another. What kind of health and safety issues can arise in a cell? Give an example. *Hint: see e.g., G. D. Brown and D. O'Rourke, "Lean Manufacturing Comes to China: A Case Study of its Impact on Workplace Health and Safety," International Journal of Occupational and Environmental Health*, 13(3), July/September 2007, pp. 249–257. **LO4**

Critical Thinking Exercises

1. What are the key enablers for successful implementation of JIT/lean? **LO7**

2. Is the service system of WestJet JIT/lean? (See the end of Chapter 2 for a Case on WestJet.) Explain. **LO3–6**

3. In what way is a *kanban* system similar to the EOQ-ROP system of Chapter 12? **LO6**

Experiential Learning Exercise

Visit a McDonald's restaurant and observe its production system. Is it using JIT/lean? Is the production schedule levelled? Is the system flexible (both in terms of equipment and workers)? Is there any visible waste? Does McDonald's use *kanbans*? Explain. **LO3–6**

Internet Exercises

1. Visit http://www.shingoprize.org/recognition/#recipients, choose a recent recipient of the Shingo prize, and briefly summarize its JIT/lean program. **LO1**

2. View http://www.youtube.com/watch?v=3mcMwlgUFjU &feature=related and summarize value stream mapping is. **LO7**

3. Visit http://totalqualitymanagement.wordpress.com/2008/10/28/lean-production-system, and compare the concepts of JIT/lean production system there with that given in the chapter. **LO1 & 2**

Problems

1. A manager wants to determine the number of *kanbans* to use in a new process for a part. The process will have a usage rate of 80 pieces of the part per hour. Because the process is new, the manager has assigned a safety factor of 1.0. Each container holds 45 pieces and a *kanban* will take an average of 75 minutes to complete a cycle. How many *kanbans* should be used? As the system improves, will more or fewer *kanbans* be required? Why? **LO6**

2. A JIT/lean system uses *kanban* cards to authorize production and movement of materials. In one portion of the system, a work centre uses an average of 100 pieces of a part per hour. The manager has assigned a safety factor of .50. Standard containers are designed to hold six dozen pieces each. The cycle time for a kanban is 105 minutes. How many *kanbans* are needed? **LO6**

3. A cell uses 90 kg of a certain material each day. The material is transported in vats that hold 54 kg each. Cycle time for a *kanban* is about two hours. The manager has assigned a safety factor of .50. The plant operates on an eight-hour day. How many *kanbans* are needed? **LO6**

4. Determine a level mixed-model sequence, given the following demand data: **LO6**

Product	Daily Quantity
A	1
B	2
C	3
D	4

5. Determine a level mixed-model sequence, given the following demand data: **LO6**

Product	Daily Quantity
A	2
B	12
C	4
D	5
E	9

6. Determine a level mixed-model sequence, given the following demand data: **LO6**

Product	Daily Quantity
F	9
G	8
H	5
K	6

7. Toyota decided to make its minivan, Sienna, in the same plant as Camry and Avalon. Suppose that during a half-hour period, 12 Camrys, 9 Avalons, and 6 Siennas are to be produced. Determine a level mixed-model sequence. **LO6**

8. The whirlpool factory in Oxford, Mississippi, makes built-in kitchen ovens.[3] In the 1990s, this plant re-engineered its processes to become JIT/lean. One of the parts of a particular oven, Part A, is processed by two 600 ton presses (in series), and then goes through a porcelain system to be coated. Finally, it is stored in the WIP storage location until it is used

600 TON PRESSES

→ PART FLOW – ► *KANBAN* FLOW

by the assembly lines. As a container of Part A is to be used, the *kanban* attached to it is taken to the press area and posted on the *kanban* post. Demand for Part A is 175 units per workday. A workday is 19 hours. The container size is 30 units. The setup time is 1 hour. Because of the large setup time, 5 *kanbans* are accumulated before production of A begins on the presses (approximately 16 hours of wait time). Production rate for A is 120 units per hour. The safety factor is 120 percent. Determine the number of *kanbans* required for Part A. **LO6**

9. Calculate the *takt* time for a system where the total time per shift is 480 minutes, there is one shift, and workers are given two 15-minute breaks and 45 minutes for lunch. Daily demand is 300 units. **LO4**

10. What *takt* time would match capacity and demand if demand is 120 units a day, there are two shifts of 480 minutes each, and workers are given three half-hour breaks during each shift, one of which is for lunch or dinner? **LO4**

11. Calculate the *takt* time for a service system that is intended to perform a standardized service. The system will have a total work time of 440 minutes per day, two 10-minute breaks, and an hour for lunch. The service system must process 90 jobs a day. **LO4**

*12. A motorcycle manufacturer produces three models: A, B, and C. This month's master production schedule, divided by 22 work days, has resulted in daily production targets of 54 As, 42 Bs, and 30 Cs. The company works one shift per day, and effective production time is seven hours per day. Determine a level mixed-model sequence. *Hint:* To reduce the size of the problem, divide each production target by their greatest common divisor. **LO6**

---

[3] Based on J. D. Hall et al., "An Optimizer for the Kanban Sizing Problem: A Spreadsheet Application for Whirlpool Corporation," *Production and Inventory Management Journal* 39(1), First Quarter, 1998, pp. 17–22.

MINI-CASE

Airline Manufacturing

Airline Manufacturing is a 275,000 ft², 100-employee wood component manufacturer supplying upholsterers (e.g., sofa manufacturers), and is located in Columbus, Mississippi. When Judy Dunaway took the helm of the company following her father in 2000, the company had used a batch production system for 40 years. However, the threat of competition led her to start JIT/lean manufacturing. High-run (quantity) products were identified and grouped together if their required sequences of operations were identical. The machines required for each group were located close together in a dedicated cell (flow line). As a result, the amount of WIP inventory has been cut by more than half, the number of material-handling carts has been reduced from 3,000 to 1,000, and the number of material handlers has been reduced by half. Also, manufacturing lead time is down from four weeks to less than a week.

A high-run product is part #146-3843. Consider the production of a 2,900-unit customer order. Before the layout change, batches of approximately 1,000 units were transported from the warehouse to the CNC Router, and from there batches of approximately 380 units were carried, when ready, from one machine to another by two workers using heavy carts. See the Batch Plant Layout diagram, Figure 1. These workers returned the empty carts to the originating machine. After the final operation, Dowel, the finished product was transported in batches of approximately 380 units to the Finished-Goods Warehouse using forklifts. The total worker-feet of movement using the forklifts (including the return to their origin) was approximately 5,300.

After the layout change, the only transport is by forklifts bringing in and taking out the product. The total worker-feet of movement using the forklifts has remained at approximately 5,300. However, the amount of machine-to-machine material handling has been greatly reduced because the machines are located close to each other. See the Cellular Layout, Figure 2. Due to elimination of delays waiting for material handling, the company can now make the 2,900-unit customer order in one day whereas it used to take six days.

Question

What are the benefits of the cellular layout to Airline Manufacturing?

Batch Plant Layout

Figure 1

Cellular Layout

Figure 2

Sources: W. Duane Motsenbocker et al., "Wood Furniture Components: Implementation of Flow-Line Technology Based on Lean Manufacturing Concepts," *Research Bulletin*, Forest and Wildlife Centre, Mississippi State University; http://www.airlinemfg.com/capabilities.html. Figures courtesy of Mississippi State University.

MINI-CASE

Level Operations

Level Operations is a small company that produces a variety of security devices and safes. The safes come in several different designs. Recently, a number of new customers have placed orders, and the production facility has been enlarged to accommodate the increased demand for the safes. The production manager is currently working on a production plan for the safes. She has obtained the following information from the marketing department on projected average daily demand for each model:

Model	Daily Quantity
A	4
B	3
C	10
D	12
E	5

Question

What might the production manager determine as the level mixed-model sequence for each day?

To access "Maintenance," the supplement to Chapter 15, please visit Connect.

For more information on the resources available from McGraw-Hill Ryerson, go to www.mheducation.ca/he/solutions.

CHAPTER 16
Job and Staff Scheduling

Sivaco, Marieville, Quebec, produces steel wires for bed and garage springs, rivets, and various types of cables to customer order. Sivaco is part of Heico Wire Group, which itself is part of Heico Companies, a $2 billion private conglomerate. The raw materials are spools of wires that are pickled (acid washed), possibly annealed (heat treated in ovens), cold drawn (pulled through an orifice to reduce their diameter in 40 nonidentical machines), galvanized (coated with zinc), and respooled. The assignment of the wire drawing machine for an order depends on setup time/cost, appropriateness and availability of machine, and due date of the job. Setup time/cost depends on the diameter of input to and output from drawing. Heat treatment in an oven is done in batches of spools based on the required temperature and duration (7–62 hours). Some jobs are simple and require only pickling and drawing, but others are complex requiring e.g., pickling, annealing, repickling, drawing, and galvanizing.

Until 2002, Sivaco used a simple home-grown program (integrated in its ERP) for scheduling jobs, but many complex production rules, known only to the experienced schedulers, were not included in it. Therefore, order promise dates were not accurate and the availability of raw material was not considered in the schedule, resulting in borrowing raw material from other orders. Then Sivaco purchased and installed Preactor 400, a popular scheduling software (now part of Siemens). Because wire drawing is the bottleneck operation for Sivaco, it is scheduled before the other operations. Much time was spent identifying and incorporating the complex production rules into Preactor. The scheduling engine creates dynamic clusters of jobs for the wire drawing operation based on hierarchal product similarities that minimizes sequence-dependent setup time/cost but also considers the appropriateness and availability of machines and the due dates of jobs. Also, a bin packing program has been written in Preactor to maximize the number of similar spools used in each oven. Scheduling time is now reduced from 1 hour to 5 minutes.

Source: http://www.preactor.com/Case-Study/Case-Studies/Sivaco#.U6zNDE18P5o.

Introduction to Scheduling

Job (or detailed) scheduling is establishing the starting and completion hour/date of operations for jobs or orders. It involves assignment of jobs to work centres and to machines within each work centre, sequencing the jobs in front of each work centre/machine, and specifying their start and end times.

A **work centre** is a production area consisting of one or more workers and machines with similar capabilities, which can be considered as one unit for purpose of scheduling.

In the production planning hierarchy, job scheduling is the final step before the actual output is produced (see the bottom box in Figure 13-2, called "Detailed planning and execution systems"). Many decisions have to be made long before job scheduling. They include strategic planning such as the capacity of the process and equipment, aggregate planning such as selection and training of workers, and master production scheduling (MPS) and material requirements planning (MRP). Consequently, job scheduling must be done within the constraints established by the above decisions, making it fairly narrow in scope and latitude.

Figure 16-1 depicts the location of job scheduling in JDA's Factory Planning and Scheduling, a popular software. It is called Production Scheduler. In this chapter, we will also cover **shop-floor control**, which relates to execution of the schedule and involves maintaining, communicating, and monitoring the status of material, orders, and process, and taking any necessary actions.

Recall that ordinary MRP does not take the load on the component work centres into account during its computation, and thus can result in overloaded machines. One has to perform capacity requirement planning to identify the capacity needs of MRP and accommodate them to make the MRP feasible. However, advanced planning and scheduling software have the ability to combine and automate these activities. For example, in Figure 16-1, the Factory Planner is the capacitated version of MRP (and MPS). So is Taylor Scheduler (see the "Beaver Plastics" OM in Action later).

MRP schedules the planned order releases backward, starting from the due date for the product. This is an example of **backward scheduling**. However, often scheduling begins from the start time of a job, and works forward into the future. This is called **forward scheduling**.

Staff scheduling involves determining the workdays, and start and end times on each workday, for each employee. This is covered in the last section of this chapter.

Job and staff scheduling are important because they affect customer-order completion dates and production costs through the utilization of resources.

Loading

Loading refers to the assignment of jobs to work centres and to various machines within each work centre. In cases where a job can be processed only by a specific line/machine, loading presents little difficulty, except for determining the time of the operation. However, a decision needs to be made when there are a number of work centres or machines within a work centre capable of

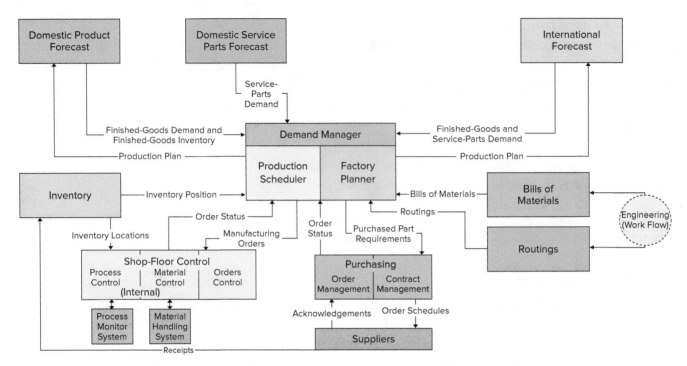

Demand Manager is used for forecasting demand, Factory Planner performs the function of MRP but keeps within production capacities, and Production Scheduler performs detailed scheduling, the topic of this chapter. This software is uses by hundreds of large companies such as 3M Canada.

Figure 16-1 ▲

JDA's Factory Planning and Scheduling system in a multinational company.

Source: http://www.jda.com/ solutions/factory-planning-scheduling-overview.

Gantt chart A visual aid for loading, scheduling, and control purposes.

load chart A Gantt chart that shows the loading and timing of jobs for each resource.

performing the required work. In such cases, the scheduler needs some way of assigning jobs to the work centres or machines within each work centre.

When making an assignment, managers often choose a work centre or machine that will minimize processing and setup costs, minimize idle time among work centres or machines, allow an operator to run two or more machines simultaneously, or is the least sophisticated work centre or machine that can do the job depending on the situation. The Assignment model later in this section will select the best assignment for a set of jobs.

Gantt Chart

A visual aid called **Gantt chart** is used for a variety of purposes related to loading, scheduling, and control. It derives its name from Henry Gantt, who pioneered its use for industrial scheduling in the early 1900s.

There are two types of Gantt chart: *load chart* and *schedule chart* (described later in the chapter).

Load Chart. A **load chart** depicts the loading and timing of jobs for each resource such as a machine or work centre. This chart is used in services as well. Two examples are illustrated in Figure 16-2, which shows scheduling courses to classrooms and scheduling patients (or surgeons) to a hospital's operating rooms. The purpose of a load chart is to organize and clarify the actual or intended use of resources over *time*. Time scale is represented horizontally, and resources are listed vertically. The use of the resources is reflected in the body of the chart.

Managers may use the load chart for trial-and-error schedule development. Thus, a tentative surgery schedule might reveal insufficient time allowance for a surgery that may take longer than expected. Use of the chart for classroom scheduling would help avoid assigning two different classes to the same room at the same time. Another example of a load chart is given in Figure 16-3. This chart indicates that work centre 3 is completely loaded for the entire week, work centre 4 will

Classroom schedule: Fall   Friday

Room	8	9	10	11	12	1	2	3	4	5
A100	Stat 1	Econ 101	Econ 102	Fin 201	Mar 210	Acct 212			Mar 410	
A105	Stat 2	Math 2a	Math 2b			Acct 210	CCE —— —— —— —— ——			
A110	Acct 340	Mgmt 250	Math 3		Mar 220					
A115	Mar 440		Mgmt 230				Fin 310	Acct 360		

City hospital, surgery schedule   Date: 5/8

Operating room — Hour

Operating room	7	8	9	10	11	12
A	Peters			Anderson		
B	Henderson					
C	Dun			Smith		

☐ Scheduled
☐ Idle
▨ Cleaning

Figure 16-2

Examples of load chart used for scheduling facilities in services.

OM in ACTION

Beaver Plastics

Beaver Plastics, based just outside Edmonton, makes polystyrene construction and packaging products such as egg cartons. The production process starts with polystyrene beads that are cured, and later fed into moulding machines. Large products may be cut using electric-heated wires. Some construction products such as insulated walls have reinforcement embedded in them. Beaver Plastics uses Taylor Scheduler to schedule the customer orders on its moulding machines and to also schedule the moulds. The schedule is updated every afternoon with new orders and order completions. The software is also used to help sales staff promise achievable due dates. Beaver Plastics also uses Taylor Scheduler to enable sharing of some of its expensive moulds among its plants, in Edmonton; Chilliwack, BC; and Mexico. Taylor Software is also based in Edmonton. Taylor Scheduler has the ability to use optimization (integer linear programming) to perform capacitated master scheduling and material requirements planning, thus ensuring that machine (and mould) capacities are not exceeded.

Sources: http://www.taylor.com/downloads/Beaver_Plastics.pdf; http://www.beaverplastics.com.

---

be available from Tuesday on, and the other two work centres have idle time scattered throughout the week. This information can help a manager rework loadings to better utilize the work centres. For instance, if all work centres perform the same kind of work, the manager might want to free one work centre for a long job or a rush order.

Dealing with Infinite Loading

Sometimes it is easier or advantageous to schedule jobs without capacity considerations. An example is MRP scheduling. This is called *infinite loading*. **Infinite loading** assigns jobs to work centres without regard to the available capacity of the work centres.

However, most scheduling is done by finite loading. **Finite loading** assigns jobs to work centres, taking into account the available capacities of work centres and the processing times of jobs, so that the capacities are not exceeded. Schedules based on finite loading may have to be updated

infinite loading Jobs are assigned to work centres without regard to the available capacity of the work centres.

finite loading Jobs are assigned to work centres, taking into account work centres' available capacities and jobs' processing times.

A.

Work center	Mon.	Tues.	Wed.	Thurs.	Fri.
1	Job 3			Job 4	
2		Job 3	Job 7		✕
3	Job 1	✕	Job 6		Job 7
4	Job 10				

▢ Processing

✕ Center not available (e.g., maintenance)

B.

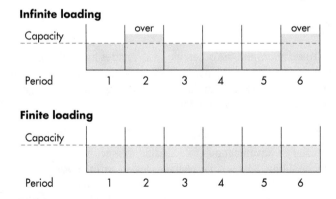

often, perhaps daily, due to processing delays at work centres, the addition of new jobs, and completion of current jobs. The following diagram contrasts finite vs. infinite loadings.

Infinite loading

Capacity

Period   1   2   3   4   5   6

Finite loading

Capacity

Period   1   2   3   4   5   6

With infinite loading, a manager needs to respond to overloaded work centres. Among the possible responses are shifting work to other periods, working overtime, or contracting out a portion of the work. Example 1 illustrates some of these responses.

OM in ACTION   http://www.plastiquemicron.com/en

Plastique Micron

Plastique Micron (PM), located in Sainte Claire near Quebec City, is a medium-sized plastic-bottles manufacturer, primarily for the pharmaceutical and cosmetic industry. PM has 29 plastic moulding machines that use the blow moulding method. Each machine melts polyethylene pellets (four types in various colours), forms hollow cylinders of plastic in the right size (called preforms; there are hundreds of sizes), places the preforms in moulds (there are hundreds and they can also be custom made), blows air into the neck of preforms to expand them into the shape of the inside of the moulds, cools the bottles, and finally ejects them. There are several types/models of blow moulding machines, with different capabilities and speeds, some requiring specific moulds.

Before 2006, a customer service/planner planned the production, all based on his knowledge of the machines that could produce a particular order and the moulds available. Other required information for scheduling, such as current load on machines, was not easily available, despite PM's having a computer system. A production schedule was determined and displayed on a board in the office on a daily basis. The production supervisors had to walk into the office several times a day to find out what they should produce on what machine using what mould. Consequently, customer order promises and follow-up were unsatisfactory and slow.

Then PM purchased Preactor 300 scheduling software (http://www.preactor.com/Products/Scheduling-Software/Preactor-300-FCS#.U6-lQE18Nv4). The implementation team (the planner, the IT person, and a consultant) started to define the machines and moulds, and their relationships. Because of the large varieties and lack of any previous documentation, this process is taking a long time and is ongoing. Preactor 300 has brought order and speed to the scheduling of jobs, thus improving customer service.

Source: http://www.preactor.com/Case-Study/Case-Studies/Plastique-Micron#.U6-ll018Nv4.

The work centre loads resulting from MRP for order #1, 100 units of a kitchen table due on Day 6 (see problem 24 of Chapter 14, p. 601), can graphically be represented by the following Gantt chart where a blue horizontal bar represents the duration of an operation. For example, Top Fab work centre is scheduled to produce table tops for this order during working hours (8 hours a day) of Days 2 to 4:

◀ **Example 1**

Order #1	Day 1	Day 2	Day 3	Day 4	Day 5	Day 6	Day 7
Top Fab		▬	▬	▬			
Leg Fab			▬	▬			
Table Assembly					▬		

Also, suppose order #2, 50 units of a different table due on Day 7, was also promised, with the following additional loads determined by MRP on the same work centres:

Order #2	Day 1	Day 2	Day 3	Day 4	Day 5	Day 6	Day 7
Top Fab				▮			
Leg Fab				▬			
Table Assembly					▬	▬	

Order #2 tables need less time for Top Fab but more time for Table Assembly. Note that order #2 needs only half a day in Top Fab, hence a red horizontal bar with half the length represents it. Capacity of work centres Top Fab and Leg Fab on Day 4 and Table Assembly on Day 5 are exceeded, because the total load (of both orders) exceeds 8 hours in each case. What can the scheduler do?

Many options are possible. Four are tried below. Choose the least expensive option.   SOLUTION

1. Move due date for order #2 to Day 8. This relieves the overload. However, order #2 will be 1 day late.

Order #1	Day 1	Day 2	Day 3	Day 4	Day 5	Day 6	Day 7
Top Fab		▬	▬	▬			
Leg Fab			▬	▬			
Table Assembly					▬		

Order #2	Day 1	Day 2	Day 3	Day 4	Day 5	Day 6	Day 7
Top Fab					▪		
Leg Fab					▬		
Table Assembly						▬	▬

2. Move Leg Fab for order #1 to Day 2 to Day 3, if possible, and increase capacity of Top Fab on Day 4 and Table Assembly on Day 5. Neither order will be late but this will cost more.

Order #1	Day 1	Day 2	Day 3	Day 4	Day 5	Day 6	Day 7
Top Fab		▬	▬	▬			
Leg Fab		▬	▬				
Table Assembly					▬		

Order #2	Day 1	Day 2	Day 3	Day 4	Day 5	Day 6	Day 7
Top Fab				▪			
Leg Fab				▬			
Table Assembly					▬	▬	

3. Schedule order #2 first (i.e., change the sequence of scheduling). Order #1 will be half a day late but work centres are utilized more in the near future.

Order #1	Day 1	Day 2	Day 3	Day 4	Day 5	Day 6	Day 7
Top Fab		▪	▬	▬	▪		
Leg Fab			▬	▬			
Table Assembly					▪	▪	

Order #2	Day 1	Day 2	Day 3	Day 4	Day 5	Day 6	Day 7
Top Fab		▪					
Leg Fab		▬					
Table Assembly			▬	▬			

4. Use solution 3 and Split Top Fab for order #1 (e.g., move 50 tops to Table Assembly when 50 tops are ready, and start Table Assembly. Move the other 50 tops later when they are ready.). Neither order will be late and work centres are utilized more in the near future.

Order #1	Day 1	Day 2	Day 3	Day 4	Day 5	Day 6	Day 7
Top Fab		▪	▬	▬	▪		
Leg Fab			▪	▬			
Table Assembly					▬		

Order #2	Day 1	Day 2	Day 3	Day 4	Day 5	Day 6	Day 7
Top Fab		▪					
Leg Fab		▬					
Table Assembly			▬	▬			

Assignment Method of Linear Programming

The **assignment model** is a special-purpose linear programming model that is useful in situations that call for assigning tasks/jobs or other work requirements to resources. Typical examples include assigning jobs to machines or workers, territories to salespeople, and repair jobs to repair crews. The idea is to obtain an optimum *matching* of tasks/jobs and resources. Commonly used criteria include costs, profits, efficiency, and performance.

Table 16.1 illustrates a typical problem, where four jobs are to be assigned to four workers. The problem is arranged in a format that facilitates evaluation of assignments. The numbers in the body of the table represent the value or cost associated with each job–worker combination. In this case, the numbers represent costs. Thus, it would cost $8 for worker A to do job 1, $6 for worker B to do job 1, and so on. If the problem involved minimizing the cost for job 1 alone, it would clearly be assigned to worker C, because that combination has the lowest cost. However, that assignment does not take into account the other jobs and their costs, which is important since the lowest-cost assignment for any one job may not be consistent with a minimum-cost assignment when all jobs are considered.

If there are to be n matches, there are $n!$ different possibilities. In this case, there are $4! = 24$ different matches. One approach is to investigate each match and select the one with the lowest cost. However, if there are 12 jobs, there would be 479 million different matches! A much simpler approach is to use a procedure called the **Hungarian method** to identify the lowest-cost solution.

To be able to use the Hungarian method, a one-for-one matching is required. Each job, for example, must be assigned to only one worker. It is also assumed that every worker is capable of handling every job, and that the costs or values associated with each assignment combination are known and fixed (i.e., not subject to variation). The number of rows and columns must be the same. Solved Problem 1 at the end of the chapter shows what to do if they aren't the same.

Once the relevant cost information has been acquired and arranged in tabular form, the basic procedure of the Hungarian method is as follows:

1. Subtract the smallest number in each row from every number in the row. This is called a *row reduction*. Enter the results in a new table.

2. Subtract the smallest number in each column of the new table from every number in the column. This is called a *column reduction*. Enter the results in another table.

3. Test whether an optimum assignment can be made. You do this by determining the *minimum* number of lines (horizontal or vertical) needed to cross out (cover) all zeros. If the number of lines equals the number of rows (or columns), an optimum assignment is possible. In that case, go to step 6. Otherwise go on to step 4.

4. If the number of lines is less than the number of rows, modify the table in this way:
   a. Subtract the smallest uncovered number from every uncovered number in the table.
   b. Add the smallest uncovered number to the numbers at the *intersections* of cross-out lines.
   c. Numbers crossed out, but not at intersections of cross-out lines, carry over to the next table.

5. Repeat steps 3 and 4 until an optimal table is obtained.

6. Make the assignments. Begin with rows or columns with only one zero. Use only one match for each row and each column. Eliminate both the row and the column after each match.

assignment model A linear programming model for optimal assignment of tasks/jobs to resources.

▼ Table 16-1

A typical assignment problem showing job costs for each job/worker combination.

		WORKER			
		A	B	C	D
	1	8	6	2	4
	2	6	7	11	10
Job	3	3	5	7	6
	4	5	10	12	9

Hungarian method A simple method of assigning jobs to resources by a one-for-one matching at lowest-cost.

Determine the optimum assignment of jobs to workers for the following data (from Table 16.1):

◄ **Example 2**

		WORKER				
		A	B	C	D	Row Minimum
	1	8	6	2	4	2
Job	2	6	7	11	10	6
	3	3	5	7	6	3
	4	5	10	12	9	5

a. Subtract the smallest number in each row from every number in the row, and enter the results in a new table. The result of this row reduction is:

		WORKER			
		A	B	C	D
Job	1	6	4	0	2
	2	0	1	5	4
	3	0	2	4	3
	4	0	5	7	4
Column Minimum		0	1	0	2

b. Subtract the smallest number in each column from every number in the column, and enter the results in a new table. The result of this column reduction is:

		WORKER			
		A	B	C	D
Job	1	6	3	0	0
	2	0	0	5	2
	3	0	1	4	1
	4	0	4	7	2

c. Determine the *minimum* number of lines needed to cross out all zeros. (Try to cross out as many zeros as possible when drawing lines.)

		WORKER			
		A	B	C	D
Job	1	6	3	0	0
	2	0	0	5	2
	3	0	1	4	1
	4	0	4	7	2

d. Since only three lines are needed to cross out all zeros and the table has four rows (or columns), this is not the optimum. Note that the smallest uncovered value is 1.

e. Subtract the smallest uncovered value from every uncovered number (that hasn't been crossed out), and add it to numbers that are at the intersections of covering lines. The results are as follows:

		WORKER			
		A	B	C	D
Job	1	7	3	0	0
	2	1	0	5	2
	3	0	0	3	0
	4	0	3	6	1

f. Determine the minimum number of lines needed to cross out all zeros. One way to cover all the zeros with a minimum number of lines is displayed below, where 4 lines are used. Since this number equals the number of rows (or columns), you can make the optimum assignment.

		WORKER			
		A	B	C	D
Job	1	7	3	0	0
	2	1	0	5	2
	3	0	0	3	0
	4	0	3	6	1

g. Make assignments: Start with rows and columns with only one zero. Match jobs with workers that have a zero cost.

			WORKER		
		A	B	C	D
Job	1	7	3	[0]	0
	2	1	[0]	5	2
	3	0	0	3	[0]
	4	[0]	3	6	1

Assignment	Cost
1-C	$2
3-D	6
2-B	7
4-A	5
	$20

The assignment problem can also be solved using an Excel template on CONNECT, as seen in Table 16.2. The ones in the solution matrix denote assignments (e.g., assign job 1 to Worker C), and the zeros denote no assignment for a worker and job combination.

Excel solution to Example 2.

Input Matrix:

		A	B	C	D	E	F	G	H	
Job	1	8	6	2	4					1
	2	6	7	11	10					1
	3	3	5	7	6					1
	4	5	10	12	9					1
	5									0
	6									0
	7									0
	8									0
		1	1	1	1	0	0	0	0	

Worker/Machine

Total Jobs = 4
Total Workers/Machines = 4

Do not change or delete unshaded cells.

Solution Matrix:

Worker/Machine

		A	B	C	D	E	F	G	H	
Job	1	0	0	1	0	0	0	0	0	1
	2	0	1	0	0	0	0	0	0	1
	3	0	0	0	1	0	0	0	0	1
	4	1	0	0	0	0	0	0	0	1
	5	0	0	0	0	0	0	0	0	0
	6	0	0	0	0	0	0	0	0	0
	7	0	0	0	0	0	0	0	0	0
	8	0	0	0	0	0	0	0	0	0
		1	1	1	1	0	0	0	0	

Total Cost = 20

As you can see, the process is relatively simple. The simplicity of the Hungarian method belies its usefulness when the assumptions are met. Not only does it provide a rational method for making assignments, it guarantees an optimal solution, often without the use of a computer, which is necessary only for fairly large problems. When profits instead of costs are involved, the profits can be converted to *relative costs* by subtracting every number in the table from the largest number and then proceeding as in a minimization problem.

It is worth knowing how to prevent undesirable assignments. For example, union rules may prohibit one person's assignment to a particular job, or a manager might wish to avoid assigning an unqualified person to a job. Whatever the reason, specific combinations can be avoided by assigning a relatively high cost to that combination. In the previous example, if we wish to avoid combination 1-A, assigning a cost of $50 to that combination will achieve the desired effect, because $50 is much greater than the other costs.

Sequencing

sequencing Determining the order in which jobs will be processed in a work centre or machine.

Although loading decisions determine the machines or work centres that will be used to process specific jobs, they do not necessarily indicate the *order* in which the jobs waiting there are to be processed. **Sequencing** is concerned with determining the order of processing the jobs on a machine or work centre.

If work centres or machines are lightly loaded, or if the jobs all require the same amount of processing time, have the same due date, and setup time/cost is sequence independent, sequencing presents no particular difficulties. Otherwise, the order of processing can be important in terms of work centre/machine utilization/costs and order due dates. In this section, we will examine some of the ways in which jobs are sequenced.

Priority Rules and Performance Measures

priority rules Simple heuristics used to select the order in which jobs will be processed.

Typically, a number of jobs will be waiting for processing. **Priority rules** or dispatching rules are simple heuristics used to select the order in which jobs will be processed. Some of the most common priority rules are listed in Table 16-3. The rules generally rest on the assumption that a job's setup time is *independent* of the processing sequence, and processing time for each job includes its setup time. Due dates may be the result of delivery times promised to customers, MRP planned order receipts, or warehouse replenishment due dates. They are subject to revision and must be kept current to give meaning to sequencing choices.

Performance Measures. The effectiveness of any given sequence is judged in terms of one or more *performance measures*. The most frequently used performance measures are:

- *Job flow time.* This is the length of the time a job is in a shop. It includes not only the actual setup and processing time but also any time waiting to be processed, and movement time between operations. The *average flow time* for a group of jobs is equal to the total flow time for the jobs divided by the number of jobs.

- *Job lateness.* This is the length of time the job completion time/date exceeds the time/date the job was due. We assign zero lateness to jobs that are early. The *average lateness* for a group of jobs is equal to the total jobs lateness divided by the number of jobs.

make-span Time needed to complete a group of jobs from the beginning of the first job to the end of the last job.

- *Make-span.* **Make-span** is the time needed to complete a *group* of jobs. It is the length of time between the start of the first job in the group and the end of the last job in the group.

- *Average WIP.* Jobs that are in the shop are considered to be work-in-process inventory. The average work-in-process for a group of jobs can be calculated using the following formula: Average WIP = Total flow time for the group/Make-span of the group.

Note that average WIP and average flow time are closely related. If a priority rule results in small average flow time, it will also result in small average WIP and vice versa.

Table 16-3 ▶

Common priority rules.

FCFS (first come, first served): Jobs are processed in the order in which they arrive at the machine/work centre.

SPT (shortest [imminent] processing time): Jobs are processed according to processing time at the machine/work centre, shortest job first.

SRPT (shortest remaining processing time): Jobs are processed according to smallest sum of the processing times at all the remaining required machines/work centres for this job.

EDD (earliest due date): Jobs are processed according to due date, earliest due date first.

MST (minimum slack time): Jobs are processed according to their slack time (i.e., time until due date minus remaining processing time), minimum first.

CR (critical ratio): Jobs are processed according to smallest ratio of time until due date to remaining processing time.

Rush: Emergency or preferred customers first.

OM in ACTION

GIRO

GIRO is a Montreal-based public-transport software producer. GIRO's HASTUS software is for public transport planning (routes and location of terminals and stops), analysis (run times and ridership data), scheduling (vehicles, drivers), operations (assigning drivers to runs, managing changes to schedule, collecting driver worktime data), and providing service information to customer.

GIRO's ACCES is for demand-responsive transport of disabled (paratransit). Paratransit doesn't follow set routes, unlike regular public transport. Another GIRO software is GeoRoute for mail and parcel distribution. GIRO's software is used all over the world. In Canada, applications of HASTUS include Montreal, Quebec City, Calgary, Edmonton, Ottawa, Winnipeg and Mississauga public transports, and applications of ACCES include Toronto, Montreal, and Calgary.

The horizontal axis is time of a day. For example, 4 means 4 am and 25 means 1 am. A block is a sequence of trips to be operated by a bus; it starts by the vehicle pulling out of the depot and ends by the vehicle returning to the depot (pull in). Several drivers can operate the same block; they will relieve each other at a given time and location along the route. This graph combines information about the vehicles (blocks) and the crew (duties, pieces). For a given block, the upper horizontal bar shows the duty pieces defined on the block, with the corresponding duty number indicated above it; the lower portion shows the trips. A run is a sequence of duty pieces for a driver. As part of crew scheduling, the vehicle blocks are "cut" so pieces can be combined into crew duties that can be operated by drivers according to collective agreement rules. The vehicle will operate its complete block, but several drivers will operate the vehicle throughout the day. The black numbers on each bar (e.g., 23, 34, 12 on Block 9-40 bar) are the piece start/end time, indicated by the minutes relative to the hour of the grid: 4:23, 6:34, 9:12.

Sources: http://www.giro.ca; http://www.giro.ca/en/references/success-stories/giro-acces-a-successful-integration.

Of the priority rules, the FCFS and rush are quite simple and need no explanation. The other rules and the performance measures above are illustrated in the following one-machine shop example.

Processing times (including setup times) and due dates for six jobs that arrived today and are waiting to be processed at the only machine in a shop are given below. Determine the sequence of jobs, the make-span, the average flow time, average days late, and average WIP in the shop for each of these priority rules:

◀ **Example 3**

a. SPT.   **b.** EDD.   **c.** MST.   **d.** CR.

Job	Processing Time (days)	Due Date (end of day)
A	2	7
B	8	16
C	4	4
D	10	17
E	5	15
F	12	18

SOLUTION

a. Using the shortest processing time (SPT) rule, the job sequence is A-C-E-B-D-F. So, rearrange the job processing time and due date columns so that jobs appear in the SPT order in the Job Sequence column. Also add Completion Time and Days Late columns. See the table below. The completion time column shows the *cumulative* processing times. For example, job C's completion time is 4 days after job A's completion time, i.e., $2 + 4 = 6$. Job A is not late because it is completed at the end of the second day, before its due date, the end of day 7, but Job C is late by 2 days because it is completed at the end of day 6, whereas its due date is the end of day 4. Summing the completion times gives the total flow time (108 days) and completion time of the last job, job F, is the make-span = 41 days. Note that for one-machine shops, make-span is the same no matter what priority rule is used. The resulting measures of performance are:

i. *Average flow time*: $108/6 = 18$ days.
ii. *Average days late*: $40/6 = 6.67$ days.
iii. *Average WIP*: $108/41 = 2.63$ jobs.

Job Sequence	(i) Processing Time	(ii) Completion Time	(iii) Due Date	(ii)–(iii) Days Late [0 if negative]
A	2	2	7	0
C	4	6	4	2
E	5	11	15	0
B	8	19	16	3
D	10	29	17	12
F	12	41	18	23
		108		40

b. Using the earliest due date (EDD) rule, the job sequence is C-A-E-B-D-F. Repeating the steps in part *a* results in the table below. The resulting measures of performance are:

i. *Average flow time*: $110/6 = 18.33$ days.
ii. *Average days late*: $38/6 = 6.33$ days.
iii. *Average WIP*: $110/41 = 2.68$ jobs.

Job Sequence	(i) Processing Time	(ii) Completion Time	(iii) Due Date	(ii)–(iii) Days Late [0 if negative]
C	4	4	4	0
A	2	6	7	0
E	5	11	15	0
B	8	19	16	3
D	10	29	17	12
F	12	41	18	23
		110		38

c. Using minimum slack time (due date − processing time) MST rule, the job sequence is C-A-F-D-B-E (see the slack times in the table below; e.g., slack time of Job C = $4 − 4 = 0$ and slack time of Job A = $7 − 2 = 5$; note the sequence is in increasing size of slack time). Doing the calculations results in the table below. The measures of performance are:

i. *Average flow time*: $133/6 = 22.17$ days.
ii. *Average days late*: $57/6 = 9.5$ days.
iii. *Average WIP*: $133/41 = 3.24$ jobs.

Job Sequence	(i) Slack Time	(ii) Processing Time	(iii) Completion Date	(iv) Due Date	(iii)–(iv) Days Late [0 if negative]
C	0	4	4	4	0
A	5	2	6	7	0
F	6	12	18	18	0
D	7	10	28	17	11
B	8	8	36	16	20
E	10	5	41	15	26
			133		57

d. Using the critical ratio (due date ÷ processing time) CR rule, the job sequence is C-F-D-B-E-A (see the critical ratios in the table below; e.g., CR for Job C is 4/4 = 1, and CR for Job F is 18/12 = 1.5; note the sequence is in increasing size of CR). Doing the calculations results in the following measures of performance:

i. *Average flow time:* 160/6 = 26.67 days.
ii. *Average days late:* 85/6 = 14.17 days.
iii. *Average WIP:* 160/41 = 3.90.

Job Sequence	(i) Critical Ratio	(ii) Processing Time	(iii) Completion Date	(iv) Due Date	(iii)–(iv) Days Late [0 if negative]
C	1.0	4	4	4	0
F	1.5	12	16	18	0
D	1.7	10	26	17	9
B	2.0	8	34	16	18
E	3.0	5	39	15	24
A	3.5	2	41	7	34
			160		85

The results of these four rules are summarized in Table 16-4. In this example, the SPT rule is the best according to average flow time and average WIP and a little worse than the EDD rule on average days late. The CR rule is the worst in every case. For a different set of processing time and due date numbers, the performance of priority rules may be a little different.

Rule	Average Flow Time (days)	Average Days Late	Average WIP
SPT	18.00	6.67	2.63
EDD	18.33	6.33	2.68
MST	22.17	9.5	3.24
CR	26.67	14.17	3.90

◀ **Table 16-4**

Comparison of performance measures of the four rules for Example 3.

Guidelines for Selecting a Priority Rule. The following results about priority rules apply for every one-machine shop: SPT is always superior in terms of minimizing average flow time and, hence, average WIP; if all jobs are late, then SPT will always minimize average days late as well; however, EDD always minimizes the maximum days late.

For multi-machine shops, the following statements about the priority rules can be made. The primary limitation of FCFS is that long jobs may delay the following jobs and machine idle times for downstream work centres will increase. However, for service systems in which customers are directly involved, FCFS is by far the dominant priority rule, mainly because of the inherent fairness, but also because of the difficulty to obtain realistic estimates of processing time for individual jobs. FCFS also has the advantage of simplicity.

Because SPT results in low average flow time, and because it often provides low average days late, it can result in high customer service levels. In addition, since it involves low average WIP in the shop, there tends to be less congestion in the shop. SPT also minimizes downstream idle times. However, due dates are often uppermost in managers' minds, so they may not use SPT or SRPT because it doesn't incorporate due dates. The major disadvantage of SPT is that it tends to make long jobs wait, perhaps for rather long times (especially if new, shorter jobs are continually added to the shop). Various modifications may be used in an effort to avoid this. For example, after waiting for a given time period, a long job is automatically moved to the head of the line.

EDD directly addresses due dates and usually results in low maximum days late. Although it has intuitive appeal, its main limitation is that it does not take processing time into account. One possible consequence is that it can result in a long job being processed first, resulting in other jobs waiting a long time, which adds to both in-process inventories and shop congestion.

MST and CR have intuitive appeal. Both use both the due dates and remaining processing times. Although they had the poorest results in Example 3 for all three measures, they usually do quite well.

Sequencing Jobs through Two Work Centres/Machines

Johnson's rule Technique for minimizing make-span for a group of jobs to be processed on two successive work centres/machines.

Johnson's rule is a technique that schedulers can use to minimize the make-span for a group of jobs to be processed on two successive work centres/machines (sometimes referred to as a two-machine flow shop).[1] It also minimizes the total idle time at the second work centre/machine. For the technique to work, several conditions must be satisfied:

1. Job time (setup and processing) must be known for each job at each work centre/machine.
2. Job times must be independent of the job sequence.
3. All jobs must follow the same two-step work sequence.
4. All units in a job must be completed at the first work centre/machine before the job is moved to the second work centre/machine, i.e., no job splitting.
5. There is adequate space for WIP before the second work centre/machine.

Determination of the optimal sequence involves these steps:

1. Determine the jobs and their times at each work centre/machine.
2. Select the job with the shortest time. If the shortest time is at the first work centre/machine, schedule that job first; if the time is at the second work centre/machine, schedule the job last. Break ties arbitrarily.
3. Eliminate the job and its times from further consideration.
4. Repeat steps 2 and 3, working toward the centre of the sequence, until all jobs have been sequenced.

Example 4 ▶

A group of six jobs is to be processed through a two work-centre flow shop. The first operation involves cleaning and the second involves painting. (a) Determine a sequence that will minimize the make-span for this group of jobs. (b) Determine the make-span, and the idle times on work centre 2. Processing times (including setups) are expected to be as follows:

	Processing Time (Hours)	
Job	Work Centre 1	Work Centre 2
A	5	5
B	4	3
C	8	9
D	2	7
E	6	8
F	12	15

SOLUTION

a. Select the job with the shortest processing time. It is job D, with a time of 2 hours. Since this time is at the first work centre, schedule job D first. Eliminate job D from further consideration. Job B has the next shortest processing time (3 hours). Since it is at the second work centre, schedule it last and eliminate job B from further consideration. We now have partially identified the sequence:

1st	2nd	3rd	4th	5th	6th
D					B

---

[1] S. M. Johnson, "Optimal Two- and Three-Stage Production with Setup Times Included," *Naval Research Quarterly* 1, 1, pp. 61–68.

The remaining jobs and their times are:

Job	1	2
A	5	5
C	8	9
E	6	8
F	12	15

Note that there is a tie for the shortest remaining time (5 hours): job A has the same time at each work centre. It makes no difference whether we place it toward the beginning or the end of the partially filled sequence. Suppose A is placed arbitrarily toward the end. Eliminate job A's times. We now have:

1st	2nd	3rd	4th	5th	6th
D				A	B

The shortest remaining time is 6 hours for job E at work centre 1. Thus, sequence that job toward the beginning of the partially filled sequence (after job D) and eliminate job E's times. Thus, the partially filled sequence is:

1st	2nd	3rd	4th	5th	6th
D	E			A	B

Job C has the shortest time of the remaining two jobs (8 hours). Since it is for the first work centre, place it third in the sequence. Finally, assign the remaining job (F) to the fourth position and the resulting sequence is:

1st	2nd	3rd	4th	5th	6th
D	E	C	F	A	B

b. One way to determine the make-span and idle times at work centre 2 is to construct a Gantt load chart:

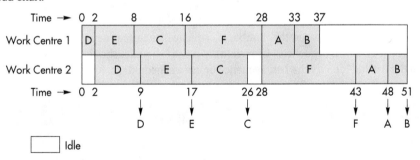

Note that work centre 2 has to wait until the end of the 2nd hour for job D, because job D has to first finish work centre 1 (a job can't be in two places at the same time, unless it can be split). Similarly, work centre 2, after completing job C at the end of the 26th hour, has to wait for job F because work centre 1 will not finish with job F until the end of the 28th hour. Thus, this group of jobs will take 51 hours to complete, i.e., make-span = 51 hours, and the second work centre will wait two hours for its first job and also wait two hours after finishing job C.

When significant idle time at the second work centre occurs, job splitting at the first work centre, just prior to the occurrence of idle time, may alleviate some of the problem and also shorten the make-span. The use of transfer batches (i.e., splitting jobs) is an important tool in the theory of constraints described later in the chapter. Solved Problem 5 at the end of this chapter illustrates the use of job splitting.

Sequencing Jobs When Setup Times Are Sequence-Dependent

The preceding discussion and examples assumed that machine setup times are independent of processing order, but in many instances that assumption is not true. Consequently, a manager may want to sequence jobs at a work centre or machine while taking these dependencies into account. The goal is usually to minimize total setup time.

Consider the following table which shows setup times based on job processing order. For example, if job A is followed by job B, the setup time for B will be 6 hours. Furthermore, if job C follows job B, it will have a setup time of 4 hours. If a job is done first, its setup time will be the amount shown in the Initial setup time column to the right of the job. Thus, if job A is done first, its setup time will be 3 hours.

		Initial setup time (hours)	Resulting following job setup time (hours) is		
			A	B	C
If the	A	3	—	6	2
preceding	B	2	1	—	4
Job is	C	2	5	3	—

The simplest way to determine which sequence will result in the smallest total setup time is to list each possible sequence and determine its total setup time. In general, the number of different alternatives is $n!$ (i.e., n factorial), where n is the number of jobs. Here, n is 3, so $n! = 3 \times 2 \times 1 = 6$. The six alternatives and their total setup times are:

Sequence	Setup Times Total
A-B-C	$3 + 6 + 4 = 13$
A-C-B	$3 + 2 + 3 = 8$
B-A-C	$2 + 1 + 2 = 5$ (smallest)
B-C-A	$2 + 4 + 5 = 11$
C-A-B	$2 + 5 + 6 = 13$
C-B-A	$2 + 3 + 1 = 6$

Hence, to minimize total setup time the scheduler would select sequence B-A-C.

This procedure is relatively simple to do manually when the number of jobs is small. However, as the number of jobs increases, the number of sequences increases exponentially. For example, six jobs would have 720 sequences. In such instances, a scheduler should employ a computer to generate the list and identify the best sequence or use a scheduling software.

OM in ACTION

Mattec MES

Mattec Manufacturing Execution System (MES), now part of Epicor, is a popular production control software used especially by plastic injection moulding plants. It collects shop floor status information (on machines and jobs) both automatically from machines and through in-shop communication equipment used by the operators. Data includes whether a machine is running or is down (and the reason for this), its speed and quality (SPC data), number of good parts produced for a job, and how many hours are left to complete the job. The data also includes number of times a particular tool or die is used, so that it can be replaced in time. Mattec MES can display real-time status of all machines, and detailed production information for each machine/job. The Mattec scheduler can automatically schedule jobs on the most efficient machine, assist in rescheduling jobs, and report tool conflicts. The real-time information is used by shop management to reduce scrap and improved quality, increase uptime (by performing corrective actions and preventive maintenance), and reduce cycle times. Canadian companies using Mattec MES include Canplas Industries of Barrie, Ontario, which makes plastic plumbing, ventilation, and vacuum fittings; Chrysler's die casting shop in Etobicoke, Ontario, that makes pistons, brackets, and housings; Lakeside Plastics of Oldcastle, Ontario, that makes thermoplastic trims for cars; and Starplex Scientific of Etobicoke, Ontario which makes plastic food, beverage, and drug containers.

Sources: http://www.epicor.com/Company/PressRoom/Pages/ SuccessStories.aspx; mattecsupport.com/products/phepm/page2.htm.

Shop-Floor Control

Shop-floor control or production activity control involves the execution of the job schedule; maintenance, communication, and monitoring of the status of material, orders, and process; and taking any necessary actions. Also, shop-floor control measures the efficiency and utilization of the workforce and machines.

Tools for shop-floor control include:

- *Daily dispatch list*: a list of jobs to be run in priority sequence for each work centre/machine. Dispatch list is also called work centre/machine schedule.
- *Anticipated delay report*: report issued by manufacturing and purchasing regarding late shop and purchase orders, causes of delay, actions taken, and new due dates.
- *Input/output control report*: a work-flow control report where amount of planned and actual inputs, and planned and actual outputs, for each work centre/machine is monitored. This is explained further below.
- *Schedule Gantt chart*: described below.

A Manufacturing Execution System (MES) usually helps generate the above list/reports/chart.

Schedule Gantt Chart

A manager often uses a **schedule Gantt chart** to monitor the progress of jobs. It is also called a job progress chart. The vertical axis on this type of Gantt chart shows the jobs or their components in progress, and the horizontal axis shows the time. The chart indicates which jobs or their components are on schedule and which are behind or ahead. A typical schedule chart is illustrated in Figure 16-4 for a service. It shows the current status of a landscaping job with planned and actual starting and finishing times for the five components of the job. The scheduled times are shown with red square brackets and actual times are shown with blue rectangles/horizontal bars. The chart indicates that approval of the drawings and the ordering of trees and shrubs were on schedule. The site preparation was a bit behind schedule. The trees were received earlier than expected, and planting started ahead of schedule and has already been completed. However, the shrubs have not yet been received. The chart indicates some slack between scheduled receipt of shrubs and shrub planting, so if the shrubs arrive by the end of the week, the schedule can still be met.

schedule Gantt chart A Gantt chart that shows the jobs or their components in progress and whether they are on schedule.

Component/Week	1	2	3	4	5	6	7
Drawings	[Approval]						
Site		[Preparation]					
Trees		[Order]		[Receive]	[Plant]		
Shrubs		[Order]		[Receive]		[Plant]	
Final Inspection							[Approval]

Scheduled   [   ]

Now

Actual progress

◀ Figure 16-4

Schedule Gantt chart for a landscaping job.

Input/Output Control

Input/output (I/O) control is a workflow control technique that involves managing the work inflows and outflows at each work centre/machine. Without I/O control, demand (i.e., work inflow) may exceed processing capacity, causing an overload at the work centre/machine. Conversely, work may arrive slower than the rate a work centre/machine can handle, leaving the work centre underutilized ("starved"). Ideally, a balance can be struck between the input and output rates, thereby achieving effective use of work centre/machine capacity without experiencing excessive queues or starvation at the work centre/machine. See Figure 16-5 for a water tank analogy.

input/output (I/O) control Managing work flow at each work centre/machine.

Figure 16-5 ▶

Input/output control for a work centre/machine is like control of the input and output valves of a water tank so that there will be enough water in the tank for continuous supply of water.

Input/output control is done by periodically generating planned inputs and outputs for each work centre/machine, comparing the actual inputs and outputs to them, and making changes if necessary. The planned inputs and outputs come from the capacity requirement planning system, which are then approved by manufacturing management. Comparing planned and actual inflow may indicate a problem with inflow, and comparing planned and actual outflow may indicate a problem with the work centre/machine production.

Figure 16-6 illustrates an input/output report for a work centre. A key portion of the report is the WIP waiting to be processed (in the bottom). The report highlights deviations from planned for both input and output. The deviations in each period are determined by subtracting "Planned" from "Actual." For example, in the first period, subtracting the planned input of 100 hours from the actual input of 120 hours produces a deviation of +20 hours. Similarly, in the first period, the planned and actual outputs are equal, producing a deviation of 0 hour. The WIP for each period is determined by subtracting the "Actual Output" from the "Actual Input" and adjusting the WIP from the previous period by that amount. For example, in the first period, actual input exceeds actual output by 10 hours. Hence, the current WIP of 40 hours is increased by 10 hours to 50 hours. It appears that the production controller planned inputs lower than outputs, therefore reducing the WIP to zero, which is not usually desirable.

Figure 16-6 ▶

An input/output report for a work centre.

		Period (week)					
		1	2	3	4	5	6
Input	Planned	100	100	90	90	90	90
	Actual	120	95	80	88	93	94
	Deviation	+20	−5	−10	−2	+3	+4
	Cum. dev.	+20	+15	+5	+3	+6	+10

		1	2	3	4	5	6
Output	Planned	110	110	100	100	100	95
	Actual	110	105	95	101	103	96
	Deviation	0	−5	−5	+1	+3	+1
	Cum. dev.	0	−5	−10	−9	−6	−5

WIP*	40	50	40	25	12	2	0

*Note: Figures represent standard hours of processing time.

Difficulty of Scheduling and Using the Bottleneck Operation

Why Scheduling Can Be Difficult

Scheduling can be difficult because the scheduler must deal with variability in setup times, processing times, interruptions, and changes in the set of jobs. Another reason is that, except for very small problems, there is no practical method for identifying the optimal schedule. Job shops where each job may need a different sequence of operations are especially hard to schedule. See the following example for an illustration.

There are one lathe, one milling, one grinding, and one vertical drill machine in a shop. Five jobs should be processed in the machine sequence given in the table below (from top down), with standard times given to the right of the machine name. For example, for job 1, first one hour of drill is required, then two hours of lathe, etc. The four machines are available starting tomorrow morning and there is no WIP in the shop. Also, the due hour of each job is at the end of tomorrow's shift, i.e., the end of hour 8. Hours 9 to 14 correspond to the first six hours of the day after tomorrow. Setup times are included in the operation times. It is possible to interrupt the processing of a job on a machine (without increasing its setup time), but no job splitting is permitted. Determine the schedule that meets the due hours.

◀ **Example 5**

	Job 1		Job 2		Job 3		Job 4		Job 5	
1.	Drill	1	Lathe	2	Grind	2	Drill	1	Mill	1
2.	Lathe	2	Mill	2	Drill	2	Grind	2	Drill	1
3.	Grind	1	Grind	1	Mill	2	Lathe	1	Lathe	1
4.	Mill	2	Drill	2	Lathe	2		—	Grind	2
Total (hours)		6		7		8		4		5

All five jobs have the same due hour, so EDD will not provide a specific sequence. The shortest remaining processing time (SRPT) rule results in the sequence 4-5-1-2-3. In the following table, first job 4 is scheduled all the way on all machines (this is called job-based loading), then job 5, etc:

SOLUTION

4-5-1-2-3	Hours													
	1	2	3	4	5	6	7	8	9	10	11	12	13	14
Lathe	2	2	5	4	1	1							3	3
Mill	5		2	2				1	1		3	3		
Grind	3	4	4	5	5	2	1	3						
Drill	4	5	1				2	2	3	3				

We observe that the above schedule results in job 3 being six hours late, and job 1 being one hour late. The minimum slack time (MST) rule results in the opposite sequence: 3-2-1-5-4, with the following schedule (using job-based loading):

3-2-1-5-4	Hours													
	1	2	3	4	5	6	7	8	9	10	11	12	13	14
Lathe	2	2	1	1	5		3	3			4			
Mill	5		2	2	3	3	1	1						
Grind	3	3			2	1	5	5	4	4				
Drill	1	5	3	3	4	2	2							

Even though the MST rule performs better than the SRPT rule, its schedule still results in job 4 being three hours late.

As you can see, scheduling in a job shop is very difficult. One needs to try various sequences and choose the best. The problem is that there are too many sequences. Note that we made many simplifying assumptions. In general, there is WIP in the shop, the processing time estimates may be inaccurate, a machine could break down, an operator may become ill, set up times may be sequence-dependent, and jobs could be split and transferred to the next operation in smaller batch sizes.

How to Reduce Scheduling Difficulty

- Set realistic due dates.
- Focus on the bottleneck operation: schedule the bottleneck operation first, and then schedule the non-bottleneck operations around the bottleneck operation. Don't interrupt the bottleneck operation. More on this in the theory of constraints next.
- For non-bottleneck operations, consider lot-splitting for large jobs, i.e., transfer a portion of the job after it is done in a work centre/machine to the next operation.
- Use a scheduling software.
- Use shop-floor control, and reschedule frequently, e.g., every day.

The Theory of Constraints

The theory of constraints (TOC), developed by Eli Goldratt in the 1980s and illustrated in his book *The Goal*,[2] focuses on the *bottleneck* operation. It is based on the following observation: Because the output of a process is limited by the output of the bottleneck operation, it is essential to schedule it first and then schedule the non-bottleneck operations in a way that minimizes the disruption to the bottleneck operation. Thus, idle times of non-bottleneck operations are not a factor in overall capacity of the system, as long as the bottleneck operation is used effectively. Note that TOC applies only when there is a permanent bottleneck operation. In many cases, bottleneck operation changes as product mix changes.

Theory of constraints uses the *drum-buffer-rope* conceptualization to manage the process. The "drum" is the master schedule; it sets the pace of the production of the bottleneck operation. The "buffer" refers to inventory just before the bottleneck operation. The "rope" represents the synchronizing of non-bottleneck operations feeding the bottleneck operation to ensure that these non-bottleneck operations produce the right quantities of products and at the right times. The goal is to avoid costly and time-consuming multiple setups at the bottleneck operation.

Theory of constraints also uses varying batch sizes at non-bottleneck operations to achieve the greatest output of the bottleneck operation. The term *process batch* denotes the production lot size for a job and *transfer batch* denotes a portion of the production lot that could be moved to the bottleneck operation. The "OFD" OM in Action is an application of drum-buffer-rope technique.

Staff Scheduling

Staff scheduling involves determining the workdays and the start and end times of work on each workday for each employee. Staff scheduling in a manufacturing company is usually easy: a typical company works 8 hours a day (e.g., 9 a.m. to 5 p.m.) and 5 days a week (Mon–Fri), a total of 40 hours a week (i.e., full-time employment) for all its employees. If it is very busy, a second shift (e.g., 5 p.m. to 1 a.m., Mon–Fri) will be instituted. Some processing companies such as pulp and paper mills operate continuously: 24 hours a day, 7 days a week. They use four sets of full-time shifts in a week, possibly rotating the shifts among employees so that everyone gets to work the unpopular night and weekend shifts.

---

[2] Eliyahu M. Goldratt and Jeff Cox, *The Goal: Excellence in Manufacturing* (New York: North River Press), 1984. For a summary of the book, see http://maaw.info/ArticleSummaries/ArtSumTheGoal.htm.

OM in *ACTION*   http://www.ofd.com

OFD (Oregon Freeze Dry)

OFD has three plants on a 35 acre site (with 300 workers) that freeze-dry vegetables, fruits, and meats by removing their water at low temperature and pressure. After freezing the product, in the low-pressure drying chambers the ice is evaporated without melting it into water first. Freeze-drying retains the flavour, and the natural structure of the food is regained by adding water at the time of consumption. Production begins with wet processing of products—a labour-intensive technique involving activities such as cooking or heating. The next step is freezing. This is a capital-intensive operation that uses one of the six very large freezers. The product is then processed through one of 32 dryers (low pressure chambers). The drying operation is also capital intensive and may take from 8 to 50 hours (depending on the product), although 14 to 20 hours is typical. The final step is dry processing—a labour-intensive step including activities such as blending, packaging, and boxing.

Before, the production was scheduled on a make-to-stock basis according to predetermined batch sizes and sequence. This resulted in large inventories of finished goods and WIP in the freezers, which increased the production lead times and caused the company to be slow in responding to customer orders that could not be satisfied from finished goods. In addition, it resulted in extensive costly overtime and disruptive expediting efforts. Meanwhile, the plants were overstocked with products for which there were no current orders.

Specifically, materials were released for processing according to production schedule, available wet-processing capacity, and available storage space for the accumulated WIP (in the freezers). The wet-processing schedule drove all other operations as in a push system. There were no formal schedules for

the freezers, dryers, or dry processing. Typically, about six to eight weeks' worth of demand for each product were processed. The highly variable product times created a "feast or famine" environment in the various operations in which periods of work overload were followed by periods in which there was nothing to do.

Then the company implemented the drum-buffer-rope technique. The capacity analysis clearly indicated that wet processing and dry processing were not constraints. The constraint (i.e., bottleneck) was drying. The dryer schedule was set based on market demand and dryer capacity. All other departments' schedules were subordinated to support the dryer schedule, which fully utilized dryer capacity. Specifically, materials were released to wet processing at the rate dictated by the dryer schedule (offset by lead times). See the above process flow diagram with the drum-buffer-rope illustration. As a result, the wet-processing department could not overproduce and cause excess WIP inventory in the freezers. Furthermore, having a set schedule at the dryers resulted in a predictable product flow to downstream operations at dry processing. The dryer schedule provided greater visibility to future work schedules in wet and dry processing and made the labour requirements in these departments smoother and predictable. Monitoring the buffer inventory in the freezers highlights when the system is having a problem.

Bank of dryers at OFD.

Source: M. Umble, et al., "Integrating Enterprise Resources Planning and Theory of Constraints: A Case Study," *Production and Inventory Management Journal* 42(2), pp. 43–48.

On the other hand, staff scheduling in services presents certain problems not generally encountered in manufacturing. This is due primarily to (1) the inability to store services, and (2) the random nature and timing of customer requests for service. For this reason, in this section we will focus on staff scheduling in services such as a restaurant or an airline. Employment can be full time (40 hours a week) or part time (e.g., 20 hours a week). Three staff scheduling problems are considered in this section:

a. Many services operate every day (i.e., seven days a week). However, employees usually work only five consecutive days and then receive two days off. The problem of determining the minimum number of full-time workers with five consecutive days of work and two consecutive days off that meet the daily staff requirements in a week is considered first.

b. Usually a service employee works during a given "shift" (i.e., a period with fixed start and end times). The problem of determining a set of shifts with minimum total duration that meet the hourly staff requirements in a day is considered next.

c. A complex staffing problem arises while scheduling an airline's pilots (and to a lesser degree flight attendants). Besides time, location also plays a role because a pilot has a home base and needs to get back to his/her home base after a few days. This problem is briefly considered last.

Scheduling Two Consecutive Days Off

First, based on forecast demand, the number of staff needed per day is determined. Note that we have assumed that the weekly demand for staff is fairly stable from week to week, but daily demand for staff vary. For example, the daily full-time kitchen-staff requirements in a week for a small restaurant are as follows:

OM in ACTION

Chyma

Chyma is a physician scheduling software and communication tool created by Dr. Reich of Sudbury, Ontario. Physicians work in various facilities and are assigned shifts or are on call after hours or in the weekend. Chyma, a Software as a Service,

communicates where each physician will be at any time to hospital administrators. Also, Chyma acts as a Web communication tool among physicians, which makes trading shifts/on-call duty much easier. Several Canadian hospitals use Chyma.

Source: http://www.chyma.net.

OM in ACTION

ClickSoftware

ClickSoftware's ClickSchedule and ClickExpress are field service workforce management software used by many field-service providers such as Bell Canada, Direct Energy (furnace and AC service and repair company in Ontario), Gas Metropolitan Plus (gas appliance service and repair company in Quebec), and Ledcor Technical Services (builds and services communication networks). The software assists in managing the whole field-service process, from receiving an order for service, scheduling it, assigning it to a qualified technician, and keeping track of location and time of technicians using GIS and Gantt chart. These companies have reported significant productivity gains due to using the software.

Sources: http://www.clicksoftware.com; http://www.youtube.com/watch?v=tEbXYgBQWxM.

OM in ACTION

Trapeze Group

Trapeze Group, based in Mississauga, provides transport management systems for Demand Responsive (DR) services such as para-transit and taxis, as well as for other applications. The computerized dispatching system works with in-vehicle GPS-enabled computers to automate the operations. The results are more efficient scheduling, routing, multicustomer rides, and reporting (e.g., a historical dashboard for each customer, on-time performance of vehicles). Trapeze systems are installed in many Canadian organizations, as well as internationally. Examples of Canadian organizations using Trapeze NOVUS-DR include one-vehicle Handy-Bus of Whitehorse, 30-vehicle Regina (Para) Transit, Toronto Circle of Care, 172-vehicle Edmonton DATS (Disabled Adult Transit Service), 25-vehicle Huron & Perth One Care (shared centralized service for 7 agencies), and 6-vehicle Kiwanis Transit of 3 towns north of Kitchener-Waterloo.

Applications of Trapeze IntelliFleet include 650-vehicle Checker (Yellow) Cabs and 75-vehicle Mayfair Taxis of Calgary, 470-vehicle Toronto Co-op Cabs, and Saskatoon's United Blueline. Taxis require in-vehicle credit card verification and taximeters that Trapeze in-taxi Ranger computers provide. IntelliFleet also includes IntelliClerk for driver account management. The automatic order taking displays the customer's name and address as she calls and the automatic dispatching identifies the closest available vehicle (which is centrally tracked using GPS). There is also an Interactive Voice Response (IVR) that is totally automated, bypassing a live dispatcher. All the automation has resulted in reduction of the time of order-taking and dispatching from 5 minutes to 30 seconds. IntelliFleet can

also call customers as the taxi is approaching or has arrived at the customer's location. Automated dispatching also results in fair trip distribution among drivers.

Source: http://www.trapezegroup.com.

OM in ACTION

InTime Solutions

InTime Solutions is a Vancouver software developer for law-enforcement employee scheduling. The InTime Scheduling Engine (ISE) integrates with time and attendance equipment, the organization's ERP Payroll program, and courts and subpoena databases. ISE is used by over 400 police departments in North America such as Calgary, Thunder Bay, and Saint John police services. ISE also has an Employee Self-service Web portal that allows employees to sign up for overtime shifts, request leave, swap shifts, etc. ISE also keeps track of overtime, the training and skill sets of employees, and equipment (assets such as rifle, laptop, and vehicle) assigned to each officer. ISE issues daily rosters, reports early/late employees, keeps work history, issues notification, and estimates cost of policing an event.

Source: http://www.intimesoft.com.

Day	Mon	Tue	Wed	Thu	Fri	Sat	Sun
Staff needed	2	4	3	4	6	5	5

A fairly simple but effective approach for determining the minimum number of workers needed (who work five consecutive days and then take two consecutive days off) is the following[3]:

1. Write "Worker 1" under "Staff needed" and repeat the daily staff needs for Worker 1 (see table below). Choose the first worker's workdays assignment such that the two consecutive days with the lowest maximum daily staff need are designated as his days off. Here Mon–Tue, Tue–Wed, and Wed–Thu all have a maximum of four staff needs. Among these three pairs, choose the one with minimum sum of staff needs: min (2 + 4, 4 + 3, 3 + 4) = 6. Therefore, Mon–Tue should be the two consecutive days off for worker 1. Circle those days. (*Note:* In case of a further tie, pick the pair whose previous day is not part of the pairs in the tie.)

Day	Mon	Tue	Wed	Thu	Fri	Sat	Sun
Staff needed	2	4	3	4	6	5	5
Worker 1	2	4	3	4	6	5	5

2. Write "Worker 2" under "Worker 1." Subtract one from each day's staff needs in the row of Worker 1, except for the circled days, and write them in front of worker 2. See the following table. These are the remaining staff needs. Assign worker 2's days off using the lowest maximum daily remaining staff needs of two consecutive days. Wed–Thu has the lowest maximum (3) of any consecutive pair of days of remaining staff needs in front of Worker 2. Circle those days.

Day	Mon	Tue	Wed	Thu	Fri	Sat	Sun
Staff needed	2	4	3	4	6	5	5
Worker 1	2	4	3	4	6	5	5
Worker 2	2	4	2	3	5	4	4

3. Write "Worker 3" under "Worker 2." Subtract one from each day's remaining needs, except for the circled days, and write them in front of worker 3 (see table below). Assign worker 3's days off using the lowest maximum remaining staff needs of two consecutive days. In this case, Mon–Tue, Tue–Wed, Wed–Thu, Sat–Sun, and Sun–Mon all have a maximum remaining staff needs of three employees. The sum of Mon–Tue and Sun–Mon is the smallest (1 + 3 = 4) among these five pairs. The day before Sun (i.e., Sat) is not part of these two tied pairs. Therefore, circle Sun–Mon as the third employee's days off, and repeat the preceding steps for each additional worker until all staffing needs have been met (see below). *Note:* Don't subtract from a value of zero.

Day	Mon	Tue	Wed	Thu	Fri	Sat	Sun
Staff needed	2	4	3	4	6	5	5
Worker 1	2	4	3	4	6	5	5
Worker 2	2	4	2	3	5	4	4
Worker 3	1	3	2	3	4	3	3
Worker 4	1	2	1	2	3	2	3
Worker 5	1	2	0	1	2	1	2
Worker 6	0	1	0	1	1	0	1
Worker 7	0	0	0	0	1	0	0
Number working:	4	5	5	5	6	5	5

To identify the days each worker is working, go across each worker's row to find the values that are not circled. Similarly, to find the workers who are assigned to work during any particular day,

---

[3] R. Tibrewala et al., "Optimal Scheduling of Two Consecutive Idle Periods," *Management Science* 19(1), pp. 71–75.

go down that day's column to find the values that are not circled. *Note:* Worker 6 is needed to work only three days, and worker 7 is needed only *one* day. Perhaps two part-time employees can be found to work these days.

Shift Scheduling

Many services have to meet uneven customer demand throughout a day. For example, restaurants have peak lunch and supper demands. To meet the peak demand but save on wages, short shifts, e.g., three to four hours long, staffed by part-time workers, are commonly used. A part-time worker works up to 5 days a week, and usually has limitations on his availability times.

Usually, the work schedule is determined for the following week. It involves the following steps:

1. Forecast the amount of work that needs to be done during each hour of next week.
2. Convert the work into the number of workers required during each hour.
3. Try to cover these requirements with a minimum number of shifts.
4. Assign the shifts to staff according to their skill, availability, and agreed-upon total weekly work hours. A common method is to sort staff by seniority.

For step 2, company standards may exist that specify labour hours required per sales dollar forecasted (This may also be called a manning chart).

We will focus on step 3 (called shift scheduling) and illustrate it with an example from McDonald's. We will focus on shifts for the part-time employees and leave out the scheduling of managers who are typically full-time and whose shift determination is straightforward. For example, for a McDonald's restaurant that is open 24 hours a day, a manager's shift could be one of: 6 a.m. → 2 p.m., noon → 8 p.m., 2 p.m. → 10 p.m., or 10 p.m. → 6 a.m., 5 days a week. Note that peak times are covered by more than one manager.

While we will perform shift scheduling manually, McDonald's Canada uses a sophisticated software called ESP by ThoughtWorks, a Toronto software company. ESP also performs Step 1: forecasting, Step 2: converting the forecasts using manning charts, and Step 4: assignment of employees to the derived shifts using a complex heuristic procedure (called simulated annealing). See the "ESP by ThoughtWorks Inc." OM in Action later in the chapter.

A McDonald's restaurant uses the following manning chart (positioning guide) for regular menu (we will focus on the 5 a.m. to 11 p.m. period):

◄ **Example 6**

Sales/Hour	Counter	Drive Thru	CSA	Assembly Board	Grill	French Fries
0–$162	1	1			1	
163–223	1	1		1	1	
224–338	1	2		1	1	
339–395	1	2		2	1	
396–492	2	2		2	1	
493–542	2	2		2	1	1
543–621	2	2		3	1	1
622–723	2	3		3	1	1
724–905	2	3	1	4	1	1
906–1,109	3	3	1	4	1	1
>1,110	3	3	1	5	1	1

The hourly forecast sales for a particular day, starting from 5 a.m. until 11 p.m. was:

5–6	6–7	7–8	8–9	9–10	10–11	11–noon	noon–1	1–2	2–3	3–4
$20	$90	$180	$320	$410	$410	$920	$1,260	$630	$420,	$360

4–5	5–6	6–7	7–8	8–9	9–10	10–11
$590	$1,040	$1,040	$810	$390	$340	$240.

    a. Determine the number of drive-thru (DT) staff required during each hour.

    b. Determine the shifts (three to eight hours long) using the following heuristic.

        1. Start from the opening hour:

          i. Determine the length of the shift: begin with a three-hour shift. Increase it by one hour if the number of staff required during this hour is not smaller than the maximum number of staff required so far on the shift. Continue. Stop if the shift is eight hours long.

          ii. Set the number of workers on this shift equal to 1 and reduce the number of staff required for each hour of this shift by 1. Repeat step (i) if the number of staff required (still not met) at the beginning of this shift is not zero.

        2. Move to the next hour with a positive number of staff required (still not met). Repeat Steps 1 (i) and 1 (ii), and continue until all the requirements (still not met) are 0.

    a. The number of DT staff required during each hour is determined based on the hour's forecast sales and the manning chart (see the following table, the second column from the left). For example, between 8 and 9 a.m., the forecast sales are \$320, which falls within the \$224–\$338 Forecast Sales range. Therefore, 2 DT employees are required then.

    b. Shifts $S_1, S_2, \ldots$ are created to meet or exceed these staff requirements. S_1's length is the maximum 8 hours because the number of DT staff required is not decreasing from 5 a.m. until 1 p.m. Set the number of DT staff on $S_1 = 1$, and calculate number of staff required, still not met, N_1:

$$N_1 = \text{original requirement} - 1, \quad \text{during any hour of } S_1$$
$$= \text{original requirement}, \qquad \text{during any other hour.}$$

Shift 2 (S_2) starts at 8 a.m. because that is the first hour when N_1 is positive. The length of S_2 is only 6 hours because N_1 starts decreasing after 2 p.m. Set the number of DT staff on $S_2 = 1$ and calculate the number of staff required, still not met, N_2:

$$N_2 = N_1 - 1, \text{ during any hour of } S_2$$
$$= N_1, \qquad \text{during any other hour.}$$

Shift 3 (S_3) starts at 11 a.m. because that is the first hour when N_2 is positive. The length of S_3 is 8 hours because N_2 does not decrease until 8 p.m. Set the number of DT staff on $S_3 = 1$ and calculate the number of staff required, still not met, N_3:

$$N_3 = N_2 - 1, \text{ during any hour of } S_3$$
$$= N_2, \qquad \text{during any other hour.}$$

Shift 4 (S_4) starts at 1 p.m. because that is the first hour when N_3 is positive. The length of S_4 is 7 hours because N_3 starts decreasing after 8 p.m. Set the number of DT staff on $S_4 = 1$ and calculate the number of staff required, still not met, N_4:

$$N_4 = N_3 - 1, \text{ during any hour of } S_4$$
$$= N_3, \qquad \text{during any other hour.}$$

Shift 5 (S_5) starts at 5 p.m. because that is the first hour when N_4 is positive. The length of S_5 is 6 hours because N_4 does not decrease and 11 p.m. is assumed to be the end of the operating time. Set the number of DT staff on $S_5 = 1$ and calculate the number of staff required, still not met, N_5:

$$N_5 = N_4 - 1, \text{ during any hour of } S_5$$
$$= N_4, \qquad \text{during any other hour.}$$

Shift 6 (S_6) starts at 7 p.m. because that is the first hour when N_5 is positive. The length of S_5 is 4 hours because N_5 does not decrease and 11 p.m. is assumed to be the end of the operating time. Set the number of DT staff on $S_6 = 1$ and calculate the number of staff required, still not met, N_6:

$N_6 = N_5 - 1$, during any hour of S_6

$\quad = N_5$,   during any other hour.

Because N_6 is all zeros, all staff requirements have been met. There is no need for another shift.

Time	Forecast Sales	DT Staff Required	S1 1	N1	S2 1	N2	S3 1	N3	S4 1	N4	S5 1	N5	S6 1	N6
5 am														
6	$20	1		0										
7	90	1		0										
8	180	1		0										
9	320	2		1										
10	410	2		1		0								
11	410	2		1		0								
Noon	920	3		2		1		0						
1 pm	1,260	3		2		1		0						
2	630	3		3		2		1		0				
3	420	2		2		2		1		0				
4	360	2		2		2		1		0				
5	590	2		2		2		1		0				
6	1,040	3		3		3		2		1		0		
7	1,040	3		3		3		2		1		0		
8	810	3		3		3		3		2		1		0
9	390	2		2		2		2		2		1		0
10	340	2		2		2		2		2		1		0
11	240	2		2		2		2		2		1		0

Airline Crew Scheduling

Airlines first schedule the flights for a period (e.g., for the next season) based on market demand, then assign their planes to the flight legs and schedule their maintenance, and finally schedule the crews. Crews are further divided into cabin (flight attendants) and cockpit (pilots and flight engineer). While cabin crew can be scheduled on any flight, cockpit crew is typically licensed for only one type/model of aircraft, so the problem can be decomposed by aircraft type/model for pilots. (Flight engineers are scheduled separately).

The scheduling of pilots (for a given type/model of aircraft) is divided into two steps: (1) determining good crew "pairings," typically one to seven days long, and (2) stringing the pairings together to form a bid line or roster for one month.

In Step 1, a "pairing" or rotation or trip is a sequence of scheduled flights, with short connection times (one to four hours) and overnight layovers, starting from an airline base and ending in the same city. A pairing has to satisfy government, airline, and union rules. For example, the maximum hours of flying per day is eight hours, unless there are long rest periods before and after the flight. A feasible set of pairings covers each flight scheduled during a month. The best set of feasible pairings is the one that minimizes pilot idle times and layover times and costs.

In Step 2, bid lines or rosters are generated, each consisting of a string of the best feasible pairings from Step 1. Bid lines are determined in order to maximize the utilization of crew while satisfying government, airline, and union rules, and presumed preferences of the pilots. An example of a rule for rosters is that in seven days there has to be a continuous rest period of at

ESP by ThoughtWorks Inc.

The Employee Scheduling Program (ESP) of ThoughtWorks Software Solutions, of Dundas, Ontario, is used by major fast-food chains such as McDonald's. ESP allows the restaurant manager to enter the information on:

- Each employee, including skill level and qualifications to work at one or more of the stations (e.g., front counter, assembly board, fries), hours and days available, and maximum hours in a day or in a week she can work.

- Staffing requirements for each station based on expected sales during each hour of next week (called *positioning guide* or *manning chart*).

- Any fixed shifts (e.g., specific hours for receiving material) as deemed necessary by the manager.

- Operating hours, shift lengths and their desirability during various times of the day, and preferences such as desired

average skill level for a station during a particular period, and fairness (giving part-time workers approximately equal number of hours in a week).

- Sales each hour of past weeks.

ESP will use the history of sales from the past few weeks or year to forecast next week's sales on an hourly basis (using the moving average method). Then, using the positioning guide, it will determine the number of staff (excluding the managers) required in each station. Next, using linear programming, ESP determines feasible shifts to cover the required staff every hour. Finally, ESP will assign the employees to the chosen shifts according to their availability, skill level, maximum hours and days, and fairness.

Source: http://www.thoughtworksinc.com.

Employee Scheduling in Hard Rock Café

Hard Rock Café has 175 locations (restaurants, hotels, and casinos) in 55 countries including one restaurant in Toronto. To schedule a particular restaurant's employees for each day of a particular week, the manager first obtains sales from the same day of last year, and then adjusts it based on major concerts in town. Even the occupancy rates of nearby hotels may be checked. From the forecast, she calculates the number of employees needed each day for kitchen, bar, host, and table service. Each week employees submit work request forms, including daily availability. This information, including the priority of employees (1 to 9 based on seniority and importance to the restaurant), are fed in the linear-programming-based employee scheduling software. The resulting employee schedules are posted. Shift trades are handled directly between employees.

Source: J. Heizer et al, *Operations Management*, Canadian Ed., Pearson, Toronto, 2014, p. 619.

least 24 hours. Also, there are rules for the maximum and minimum hours of flying per month, minimum number of days off, maximum number of trips, etc. Pilots seem to prefer long blocks of days off, crossing limited time zones, same-city layovers, long rest periods between night followed by day flying, etc.

The rosters are called bid lines because they are presented to pilots for bidding (choosing). If this is done by seniority (most common in North America) and bid lines are constructed according to the pilots' preferences, Step 2 is called a preferential bidding system.

Because of the rules, some of the pairings, called open or unassigned pairings, may not be included in any bid line. These should be limited to 1–5 percent of the pairings. The unassigned pairings, and those dropped by sick pilots, are given to backup or reserve pilots.

Two software companies that provide software for airline crew scheduling are AD OPT of Montreal (http://www.ad-opt.com) and Navtech Inc. of Waterloo (http://www.navtech.aero/airline_solutions/crew_planning.html).[4]

OM in *ACTION*

AltaLink Uses SAP's Multi-Resource Scheduling

AltaLink is Alberta's privately owned electric-power transmission company. It operates 12,000 km of power lines and poles, and 280 electrical substations through which it distributes electricity to customers. The service technicians are based in the major cities (Calgary, Edmonton, Red Deer, and Lethbridge). Even though AltaLink used SAP's Human Capital Management for personnel management and SAP's Enterprise Asset Management for substation management, the seven schedulers located in these cities used their own independent Excel-based systems to manage and schedule preventive maintenance of substations. To improve efficiency, AltaLink centralized maintenance management and installed SAP's Multiresource Scheduling module in Calgary. The resources include the technician and equipment such as cranes and scaffoldings. As a result, AltaLink could eliminate four scheduler jobs, and the remaining three schedulers are producing better schedules by combining the work orders for the same substations, thus saving technician times.

Source: http://www.sap.com/bin/sapcom/en_us/downloadasset.2013-09-sep-17-10.altalink-improving-service-delivery-through-improved-maintenance-scheduling-pdf.html.

[4] S. Yan and J-C Chang, "Airline Cockpit Crew Scheduling," *European Journal of Operational Research*, 136, pp. 501–511; B. Gopalakrishnan and E. L. Johnson, "Airline Crew Scheduling: State-of-the-Art," *Annals of Operations Research*, 140, pp. 305–337; A. I. Z. Harrah and J. T. Diamond, "The Problem of Generating Crew Bidlines," *Interfaces*, 27(4), pp. 49–64; H. Achour, et al., "An Exact Solution Approach for the Preferential Bidding System Problem in the Airline Industry," *Transportation Science*, 41(3), pp. 354–365.

Summary

- Job scheduling involves determining the timing (i.e., start and completion hour/date) of operations for jobs or orders. Staff scheduling involves determining the timing (i.e., start and end times) of work of staff, and the days they work.
- A major problem in job scheduling is assigning (loading) jobs to machines/work centres. Load Gantt chart is frequently employed to help managers visualize workloads on each machine/work centre.
- MRP uses infinite loading (i.e., workloads may exceed work centre/machine capacities), and the schedule has to be made feasible by either increasing the work centre/machine capacities or rescheduling.
- The Hungarian method for the Assignment Model assigns each job to a different machine in order to minimize total assignment time/cost of a group of jobs.
- An important activity in job scheduling is sequencing the jobs. Various priority rules can be used such as shortest processing time (SPT), earliest due date (EDD), and minimum slack time (MST).

- Job scheduling is usually difficult but it can be solved (i.e., the sequence that results in the minimum makespan can be found) for two work-centre/machine flow shop problems using Johnson's rule.
- Sometimes job setups are sequence-dependent.
- Shop-floor control involves execution of the job schedule, and maintenance, communication, and monitoring of the status of material, orders, and process, and taking any necessary actions.
- Schedule Gantt chart or job progress chart is useful for shop-floor control.
- Input/output control is used to monitor the work flows at work centres/machines.
- The theory of constraints focuses on the bottleneck operation to perform scheduling.
- Staff scheduling is a common problem in services. Determining two consecutive days off for full-time employees and daily shifts for part-time employees are common staff scheduling problems. Another common but complex staff scheduling problem is airline crew scheduling.

Key Terms

assignment model
backward scheduling
finite loading
forward scheduling
Gantt chart
Hungarian method
infinite loading

input/output (I/O) control
job (or detailed) scheduling
Johnson's rule
load chart
loading
make-span
priority rules

schedule Gantt chart
sequencing
shop-floor control
staff scheduling
work centre

Solved Problems

Problem 1

The assignment method. The following table contains information on the cost to run three jobs on four available machines. Determine an assignment plan that will minimize total cost.

		MACHINE			
		A	B	C	D
	1	12	16	14	10
Job	**2**	9	8	13	7
	3	15	12	9	11

Solution

In order to be able to use the assignment method, the numbers of jobs and machines must be equal. To remedy this situation, add a *dummy* job with costs of 0, and then solve as usual.

		MACHINE			
		A	B	C	D
	1	12	16	14	10
Job	2	9	8	13	7
	3	15	12	9	11
(dummy)	4	0	0	0	0

a. Subtract the smallest number from each row. The results are:

		MACHINE			
		A	B	C	D
	1	2	6	4	0
Job	2	2	1	6	0
	3	6	3	0	2
	4	0	0	0	0

b. Subtract the smallest number in each column. (Because of the dummy zeros in each column, the resulting table will be unchanged.)

c. Determine the minimum number of lines needed to cross out the zeros. One possible way is:

		MACHINE			
		A	B	C	D
	1	2	6	4	0
Job	2	2	1	6	0
	3	6	3	0	2
	4	0	0	0	0

d. Because the number of lines is less than the number of rows (or columns), modify the numbers.

   1. Subtract the smallest uncovered number (1) from each uncovered number.
   2. Add the smallest uncovered number to numbers at line intersections.

The result is

		MACHINE			
		A	B	C	D
	1	1	5	4	0
Job	2	1	0	6	0
	3	5	2	0	2
	4	0	0	1	1

e. Test for optimality:

		MACHINE			
		A	B	C	D
	1	1	5	4	0
Job	2	1	0	6	0
	3	5	2	0	2
	4	0	0	1	1

Because the minimum number of lines needed equals the number of rows (or columns), an optimum assignment can be made.

f. Assign jobs to machines. Start with rows 1 and 3, because they each have one zero, and columns A and C, also with one zero each. After each assignment, cross out all the numbers in that row *and* column. The result is:

		MACHINE			
		A	**B**	**C**	**D**
Job	**1**	1	5	4	0
	2	1	0	6	0
	3	5	2	0	2
	4	0	0	1	1

Notice that there is only one assignment in each row, and only one assignment in each column.

g. Compute total costs, referring to the original table:

1-D	$10
2-B	8
3-C	9
4-A	0
	$27

h. The implication of assignment 4-A is that machine A will not be assigned a job. It may remain idle or be used for another job.

Problem 2

Priority rules. Job times (including setup) and due hours are shown in the following table for five jobs waiting to be processed in a one-machine shop:

Job	Job Time (hours)	Due Hour
a............	12	15
b............	.6	24
c............	14	20
d............	.3	8
e............	.7	6

Determine the processing sequence that would result from each of these priority rules:

a. SPT.

b. EDD.

Solution

	a. SPT		b. EDD	
Job	**Job Time**	**Processing Order**	**Due Hour**	**Processing Order**
a	12	4	15	3
b	6	2	24	5
c	14	5	20	4
d	3	1	8	2
e	7	3	6	1

Problem 3

Priority rules. Using the job times and due hours from the Solved Problem 2 above, determine each of the following performance measures for FCFS sequence (a-b-c-d-e):

a. Make-span.

b. Average flow time.

c. Average hours late.

d. Average WIP.

Solution

Job	Job Time	Completion Time	Hour Due	Hours Late
a	12	12	15	0
b	6	18	24	0
c	14	32	20	12
d	3	35	8	27
e	7	42	6	36
Total		139		75

a. Make-span = 42 hours

b. Average flow time = $\dfrac{\text{Total completion time}}{\text{Number of jobs}} = \dfrac{139}{5} = 27.80$ hours

c. Average hours late = $\dfrac{\text{Total hours late}}{\text{Number of jobs}} = \dfrac{75}{5} = 15$ hours

d. Average WIP = $\dfrac{\text{Total completion time}}{\text{Makespan}} = \dfrac{139}{42} = 3.31$ jobs

Problem 4

Sequencing jobs through two work centres/machines. Use Johnson's rule to obtain the sequence that minimizes the make-span for the jobs shown below through work centre 1 and 2.

Job Times (hours)

Job	Work Centre 1	Work Centre 2
a	2.50	4.20
b	3.80	1.50
c	2.20	3.00
d	5.80	4.00
e	4.50	2.00

Solution

Identify the smallest time: job b (1.50 hours at work centre 2). Because the time is for work centre 2, sequence this job last, and eliminate job b times.

The next smallest time is job e (2.00 hours at work centre 2). Sequence job e next to last, and eliminate job e times.

Identify the smallest remaining job time: job c (2.20 hours at work centre 1). Because the time is for work centre 1, sequence job c first and eliminate job c times. At this point, we have: c, ___, ___, e, b.

The smallest time for remaining jobs is 2.50 hours for job a at work centre 1. Sequence this job after job c. The one remaining job (job d) fills the remaining slot. Thus, we have the sequence: c-a-d-e-b

Problem 5

For Solved Problem 4 above, determine what effect splitting jobs c, d, e, and b in work centre 1 would have on the idle time of work centre 2 and on the make-span. Assume that each job can be split into two equal parts.

Solution

The solution from the previous problem is shown in the following load Gantt chart. The chart below it shows reduced idle time at work centre 2 when splitting is used.

An inspection of these two charts reveals that make-span has decreased from 20.30 hours to 19.55 hours. In addition, the original idle time was 5.6 (= 2.2 + 1.1 + .5 + 1.8) hours. After splitting c, d, e, and b, idle time was reduced to 4.85 (= 1.1 + .6 + 1.1 + 2.05) hours, so some improvement

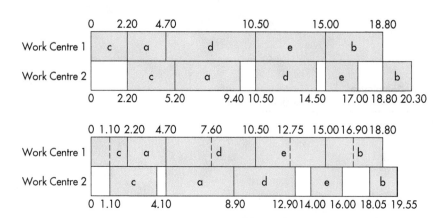

was achieved. Note that processing times at work centre 2 are generally smaller than at work centre 1 for jobs toward the end of the sequence. As a result, jobs e and b at work centre 2 were scheduled so that they were *centred* around the finishing times of e and b, respectively, at work centre 1, to avoid having to break the jobs due to waiting for the remainder of the split job from work centre 1.

Discussion and Review Questions

1. What is job scheduling? **LO1**

2. What is a Gantt chart? Name two uses of Gantt chart in scheduling. What is the advantage of using Gantt charts? **LO2 & 4**

3. What is loading? **LO2**

4. MRP assumes infinite loading. Explain. **LO2**

5. What is the assignment model? Briefly describe the Hungarian method for the assignment model. **LO2**

6. Briefly describe each of these priority rules: **LO3**

   a. FCFS   **b.** SPT   **c.** EDD   **d.** MST   **e.** Rush

7. Why are priority rules needed? **LO3**

8. Describe Johnson's rule. **LO3**

9. What is shop-floor control? Name two tools used in shop-floor control. **LO4**

10. What is the input/output control? **LO4**

11. Explain the theory of constraints. **LO5**

12. What is staff scheduling and what are the steps used in staff scheduling? **LO6**

13. What is meant by scheduling two consecutive days off and how is it done? **LO6**

14. What is shift scheduling and how is it done? **LO6**

15. How is airline pilot scheduling done? **LO6**

Taking Stock

1. What trade-off is involved in scheduling decisions? **LO1 & 3**

2. Who needs to be involved in setting job schedules? **LO1**

3. How has technology had an impact on scheduling? **LO1 & 6**

4. Some continuous 24/7 operations rotate the employee shifts on a weekly basis, e.g., day shift → evening shift → night shift → day shift etc, whereas others keep their employee shifts constant. What are the pros and cons of each approach? What ethical issues are involved in this decision? **LO6**

Critical Thinking Exercises

1. One approach that can be effective in reducing the impact on production bottleneck is to use smaller transfer lot sizes as in the theory of constraints. Explain how small transfer lot sizes can reduce the impact on the bottleneck operation. **LO5**

2. Doctors' and dentists' offices frequently schedule patient visits at regularly spaced intervals. What problems can this create? Can you suggest an alternative approach to reduce these problems? **LO6**

Experiential Learning Exercises

1. Visit a fast-food restaurant, a supermarket, a hospital, or another service and ask a manager about staff scheduling, covering these questions: **LO6**

   a. Who does it?
   b. How frequently is it done?
   c. Is any software used and, if so, which software?
   d. How easy or difficult is it?

   e. Are demand forecasts used?
   f. Is the manager generally satisfied with the outcome?
   g. Are employees satisfied?

2. How do you schedule your homework assignments? **LO1-3**

3. How does your city sequence/prioritize snow plowing? **LO3**

Internet Exercises

1. Visit http://www.preactor.com/getdoc/bdd42227-1d4b-4660-ab8b-99b0005de92b/North-America.aspx. Choose a case study not used in the chapter and summarize it. **LO1**

2. Visit http://www.taylor.com/industry/case_studies.php, choose a case study not used in the chapter, and summarize how Taylor software has helped the company. **LO1**

Problems

1. Use the assignment method to determine the best way to assign 3 workers to 3 jobs, given the following cost information. Calculate the total cost for your assignment. **LO2**

		JOB		
		A	B	C
	1	5	8	6
Worker	2	6	7	9
	3	4	5	3

2. Rework Problem 1, treating the numbers in the table as profits instead of costs. Calculate the total profit. **LO2**

3. Assign 5 trucks to 5 delivery routes so that total cost is minimized, given the cost data shown below. What is the total cost? **LO2**

		ROUTE				
		A	B	C	D	E
	1	4	5	9	8	7
	2	6	4	8	3	5
Truck	3	7	3	10	4	6
	4	5	2	5	5	8
	5	6	5	3	4	9

4. Develop an assignment plan for 3 workers that will minimize total cost, given the information shown below, and interpret your answer. **LO2**

		WORKER		
		A	B	C
	1	12	8	11
Job	2	13	10	8
	3	14	9	14
	4	10	7	12

5. Use the assignment method to obtain a plan that will minimize total processing cost in the following table under these conditions: **LO2**

   a. The combination 2-D is undesirable.
   b. The combinations 1-A and 2-D are undesirable.

		WORKER				
		A	B	C	D	E
	1	14	18	20	17	18
	2	14	15	19	16	17
Job	3	12	16	15	14	17
	4	11	13	14	12	14
	5	10	16	15	14	13

6. The following table contains information concerning four jobs that are waiting for processing at a machine. **LO3**

Job	Job Time (days)	Due Date (days)
A	14	20
B	10	16
C	7	15
D	6	17

   a. Sequence the jobs using priority rules (1) SPT, and (2) EDD.
   b. For each of the priority rules in part a, determine (1) the average flow time, and (2) the average days late.
   c. Is one priority rule superior to the other? Explain.

7. Using the information presented in the following table, identify the processing sequence that would result using priority rules (1) MST, (2) SPT, (3) EDD, and (4) CR. For each priority rule, determine (1) average flow time,

(2) average hours late, and (3) average WIP. Is one priority rule superior to the others? Explain. (*Hint:* First determine the total job time for each job by calculating the total processing time for the job and then adding in the setup time. All times are in hours.) (LO3)

Job	Processing Time (hr) per Unit	Units per Job	Setup Time (hr)	Due Hour
a	0.14	45	0.7	4
b	0.25	14	0.5	10
c	0.10	18	0.2	12
d	0.25	40	1.0	20
e	0.10	75	0.5	15

8. The following table shows orders to be processed at a machine. (LO3)

a. Determine the processing sequence using each of these priority rules: (1) CR, (2) MST, (3) SPT, (4) EDD.
b. Determine the performance of each rule using (1) average flow time, (2) average days late.
c. Is one rule superior to the others?

Job	Processing Time (days)	Due Date (days)
A	8	20
B	10	18
C	5	25
D	11	17
E	9	35

9. A production process uses a two-step operation. Tomorrow's work will consist of seven orders as shown below. Determine a job sequence that will minimize the total time required to fill the orders (i.e., the make-span) and determine the make-span. (LO3)

Time (hours)

Order	Step 1	Step 2
A	1.20	1.40
B	0.90	1.30
C	2.00	0.80
D	1.70	1.50
E	1.60	1.80
F	2.20	1.75
G	1.30	1.40

10. The times required to complete each of five jobs in a two-machine flow shop are shown in the following table. Each job must begin with machine A and end with machine B. (LO3)

a. Determine a sequence that will minimize the make-span.
b. Construct a load Gantt chart for the resulting sequence, and find machine B's idle time.
c. For the sequence determined in part *a*, can machine B's idle time be reduced by splitting some jobs in half? If so, which jobs? Split jobs *c* and e and draw the new load Gantt chart.

Time (hours)

Job	Machine A	Machine B
a	6	5
b	4	3
c	9	6
d	8	7
e	2	9

11. Given the operation times in the two-work-centre flow shop below:

a. Develop a job sequence that minimizes total idle time at Work Centre 2.
b. Construct a load Gantt chart for the activities at the two work centres, and determine work centre 2's idle time. (LO3)

Job Times (minutes)

	A	B	C	D	E	F
Work Centre 1	20	16	43	60	35	42
Work Centre 2	27	30	51	12	28	24

12. A two-person shoe repair operation uses a two-step sequence that all jobs follow (first work centre A then work centre B). For the group of jobs listed below, (LO3)

a. Find the sequence that will minimize the make-span.
b. Determine the amount of idle time for work centre B.
c. What jobs are candidates for splitting? Why? If jobs b and c are split in half, how much would the idle time of work centre B be reduced?

Job Times (minutes)

	a	b	c	d	e
Work Centre A	27	18	70	26	15
Work Centre B	45	33	30	24	10

13. The following schedules (in hours) were prepared by the production manager of a metal shop. Note that all jobs first go through cutting, then polishing. (LO3)

	CUTTING		POLISHING	
Job	Start	Finish	Start	Finish
A	0	2	2	5
B	2	6	6	9
C	6	11	11	13
D	11	15	15	20
E	15	17	20	23
F	17	20	23	24
G	20	21	24	28

Determine a sequence of jobs that will result in a shorter make-span. *Hint:* First calculate the job times.

14. A production manager must determine the processing sequence for seven jobs through the grinding and deburring departments. The same sequence will be followed in each department. The manager's goal is to move the jobs through the two departments as quickly as possible. The site supervisor of the grinding department wants the SPT rule to be used to minimize the work-in-process inventory in his department. **LO3**

PROCESSING TIME (HOURS)

Job	Grinding	Deburring
A	3	6
B	2	4
C	1	5
D	4	3
E	9	4
F	8	7
G	6	2

a. Prepare a schedule using the SPT priority rule for the grinding department (using the grinding times).
b. What is the total flow time in the grinding department for the SPT sequence? What is the make-span for the seven jobs in both the grinding and deburring departments (using the sequence found in part a)?
c. Determine a sequence that will minimize the make-span in both departments. Does using the SPT rule in the grinding department result in smallest make-span?

15. Suppose a body and paint shop has to work on four cars (A, B, C, and D) of a car rental agency. The manager estimated the job times required (in hours) as follows: **LO3**

Cars:	A	B	C	D
Body shop	6	9	7	8
Paint shop	3	5	4	6

The body and paint shop each have dedicated workers. A car has to finish body work before it can be painted. Assume that there are no other cars in the shops.

a. The rental agency is in a hurry to get its cars back. In what order should the shops work on the cars to minimize their make-span?
b. Draw a load Gantt chart for your sequence in part a, and determine the make-span.

16. A foreman has determined the expected processing times at a machine for a set of jobs and now wants to sequence them. Given the following information, do the following: **LO3**

a. Determine the processing sequence using (1) MST, (2) SPT, (3) EDD, and (4) CR. For each sequence, calculate the average days late, the average flow time, and the average WIP.
b. Which rule is the best?

Job	Job Time (days)	Due Date (days)
a	4.5	10
b	6.0	17
c	5.2	12
d	1.6	27
e	2.8	18
f	3.3	19

17. Given the information in the following table, determine a processing sequence that will minimize the average flow time. **LO3**

Job	Processing Time (days)	Due Date
A	5	8
B	6	5
C	9	10
D	7	12
E	8	10

18. Given the following information on job times and due hours, determine the processing sequence using priority rules (1) MST, (2) SPT, (3) EDD, and (4) CR. For each rule, find the average flow time and the average hours late. Which rule is the best? **LO3**

Job	Job Time (hours)	Due (hours)
A	3.5	7
B	2.0	6
C	4.5	18
D	5.0	22
E	2.5	4
F	6.0	20

19. A shop specializes in heat-treating gears. At 8 a.m. when the shop opened today, five orders were waiting to be processed. Assume that only one unit at a time can be heat-treated. **LO3**

Order	Order Size (units)	Per Unit Time in Heat Treatment (minutes/unit)	Due (minutes from now)
A	16	4	160
B	6	12	200
C	10	3	180
D	8	10	190
E	4	1	220

a. If the earliest due date (EDD) rule is used, what sequence should be used?
b. What will be the average minutes late for the sequence in part a?
c. What will be the average WIP in the shop for the sequence in part a?
d. Would the SPT rule produce better results in terms of average minutes late?

20. A manufacturer has accepted the following jobs for July. Today is Thursday, end of June. The nonworking days in July are July 1, 2, 3, 10, 17, 24, 30, and 31. **LO3**

Job	Date Order Received	Production Time Including Setup	Due Date	Due Date in Working Days From Now
A	6/4	6.25 days	11 July	7
B	6/7	2.5 days	8 July	5
C	6/12	8.25 days	25 July	19
D	6/14	3.5 days	19 July	14
E	6/15	9.5 days	29 July	23

Examine the following priority rules, summarizing your findings, and advise on which priority rule to use: FCFS, SPT, EDD, or CR.

21. The following table contains order-dependent setup times for three jobs. Which processing sequence will minimize the total setup time? **LO3**

		Initial Setup Time (hours)	Following Job's Setup Time (hours)		
			A	B	C
	A	2	—	3	5
Preceding Job	B	3	8	—	2
	C	2	4	3	—

22. The following table contains order-dependent setup times for three jobs. Which processing sequence will minimize the total setup time? **LO3**

		Initial Setup Time (hours)	Following Job's Setup Time (hours)		
			A	B	C
	A	2.4	—	1.8	2.2
Preceding Job	B	3.2	0.8	—	1.4
	C	2.0	2.6	1.3	—

23. The following table contains order-dependent setup times for four jobs. For safety reasons, job C cannot follow job A, nor can job A follow job C. Determine the processing sequence that will minimize the total setup time. (*Hint:* There are 12 sequences.) **LO3**

		Initial Setup Time (hours)	Following Job's Setup Time (hours)			
			A	B	C	D
	A	2	—	5	×	4
Preceding Job	B	1	7	—	3	2
	C	3	×	2	—	2
	D	2	4	3	6	—

24. Given the following standard hours of planned and actual inputs and outputs at a work centre, determine the WIP for each period. The beginning WIP is 12 hours of work. **LO4**

		Period				
		1	2	3	4	5
Input	Planned	24	24	24	24	20
	Actual	25	27	20	22	24
Output	Planned	24	24	24	24	23
	Actual	24	22	23	24	24

25. Given the following standard hours of planned and actual inputs and outputs at a work centre, determine the WIP for each time period. The beginning WIP is seven hours of work. **LO4**

		Period					
		1	2	3	4	5	6
Input	Planned	200	200	180	190	190	200
	Actual	210	200	179	195	193	194

		1	2	3	4	5	6
Output	Planned	200	200	180	190	190	200
	Actual	205	194	177	195	193	200

26. During each four-hour period, a small town police force requires the following number of on-duty police officers: eight from midnight to 4 a.m.; seven from 4 a.m. to 8 a.m.; six from 8 a.m. to noon; six from noon to 4 p.m.; five from 4 p.m. to 8 p.m.; and four from 8 p.m. to midnight. Each police officer works two consecutive four-hour shifts. Determine how to minimize the total number of police officers needed to meet the town's daily police requirements. **LO6**

27. Determine the minimum number of full-time workers needed and schedule their work given the following staffing requirements. Give the full-time workers two consecutive days off per week. **LO6**

Day	Mon	Tue	Wed	Thu	Fri	Sat	Sun
Staff needed	2	3	1	2	4	3	1

28. Determine the minimum number of full-time workers needed and schedule their work given the following staffing requirements. Give the full-time workers two consecutive days off per week. **LO6**

Day	Mon	Tue	Wed	Thu	Fri	Sat	Sun
Staff needed	3	4	2	3	4	5	3

29. Determine the minimum number of full-time workers needed and schedule their work given the following staffing requirements. Give the full-time workers two consecutive days off per week. **LO6**

Day	Mon	Tue	Wed	Thu	Fri	Sat	Sun
Staff needed	4	4	5	6	7	8	4

*30. A small grocery store needs the following number of cashiers during each day of a week for day (8 a.m. to 4 p.m.) and evening (4 p.m. to midnight) shifts. The store prefers to employ full-time cashiers who work eight hours a day, five days a week, with two consecutive days off. A half-time cashier works four hours a day up to five days a week (with no requirement for consecutive days off). Note that for each unit of cashier requirement, two half-time cashiers are needed because the periods are eight hours long. Determine the mix of full-time and half-time cashiers and schedule their work in order to minimize the total number of cashiers employed but meet the daily cashier requirements below. **LO6**

Cashiers needed	Mon	Tue	Wed	Thu	Fri	Sat	Sun
8 a.m.–4 p.m.	3	4	3	3	5	8	3

Cashiers needed	Mon	Tue	Wed	Thu	Fri	Sat	Sun
4 p.m.–12 a.m.	2	3	2	2	6	5	3

31. Refer to Example 6. Use the heuristic used in Example 6 to determine shifts for **LO6**

   a. Counter staff.

   b. Assembly Board staff.

32. Refer to Example 5. Find the optimal solution, i.e., the sequence of jobs that satisfies the due hours (i.e., end of the 8th hour) for all five jobs. (*Hint:* Switch a pair of jobs in the MST sequence.) **LO5**

MINI-CASE

Scotsburn Dairy—Operational Sequencing

The production scheduler of Scotsburn Dairy in Truro, NS, has just received a list of products and their desired lot size (the first week of MPS) from the operations coordinators to be produced next week. The aggregate plan has specified a 40-hour week (4 days of 10 hours each) for next week. In sequencing the production, she schedules the products in the same family (as determined during MPS), but also tries to assign allergens towards the end of a day, stronger flavours (e.g., mint) after weaker flavours, and keep availability of ingredients in mind. Suppose the following families, products, and their quantities have to be sequenced for production next week:

Family	Product	Quantity (in hours of production)
F1	Vanilla-1.89 L	9
	Butter scotch-1.89 L	3
F2	Neapolitan-1 L	2
	Neapolitan-1.65 L	2
	Neapolitan-1.89 L	4
F3	Maple Walnut-1 L	2
	Peanut butter fudge-1.89 L	3
F4	Chocolate-1.89 L	5
	Chocolate mint chip fudge-1.89L	2

The plant is running low in mint flavour but a shipment is expected later next week. Assume there is only one line. Sequence the production of these products.

For more information on the resources available from McGraw-Hill Ryerson, go to www.mheducation.ca/he/solutions.

CHAPTER 17
Project Management

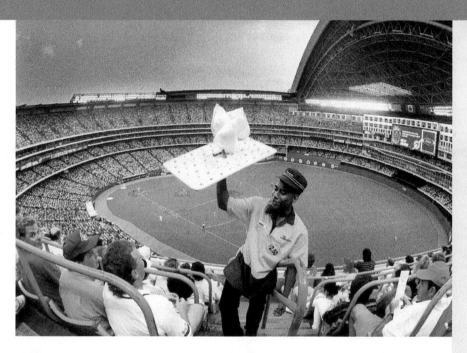

Projects are a unique aspect of business operations that require a special management approach. Unlike many other aspects of business, which tend to operate more routinely, projects often have uncertainties and risks that tend to make managing them more challenging, such as the Roger Centre.

The Rogers Centre, formerly known as Sky Dome, in downtown Toronto is the first stadium in the world to have a fully retractable rooftop. It was built in the late 1980s by general contractor Ellis Don Ltd. at a cost of C$570 million—a figure far exceeding the initial estimate of C$150 million. Primavera's Project Planner (now part of Oracle) was utilized to manage and control the various activities of thousands of tradespeople as they worked on the construction project. Despite serious setbacks such as soil contamination from a nearby water pumping station and a labour strike, the construction project was completed only two months behind schedule. What tools and techniques can be used to manage complex construction projects like the Rogers Centre? That is the topic of the current chapter.

Source: http://en.wikipedia.org/wiki/Rogers_Centre.

Learning Objectives

After completing this chapter, you should be able to:

LO1 Describe what a project is and discuss the nature of a project manager's job.

LO2 Explain what is involved in project planning, how to manage project risks, and what work breakdown structure is.

LO3 Explain what project scheduling is, how schedule/control Gantt charts can be used in project scheduling, and what PERT/CPM and precedence networks are.

LO4 Use PERT/CPM technique with deterministic activity durations to schedule projects, and solve typical problems.

LO5 Schedule activities with probabilistic activity durations, and solve typical problems.

LO6 Describe project "crashing" and solve typical problems.

LO7 Describe what is involved in project execution and control and explain what the earned value is.

LO8 Be able to use Microsoft® Project.

Project Manager

A **project** is a unique, large, one-time operation designed to accomplish a specific objective in a limited time frame. Examples of projects include constructing a store, redesigning a business process, merging two companies, putting on a play, designing new goods or services, and designing an information system. In the above examples, the specific objective is the store, the redesigned business process, the merged company, the play, etc. A related term is *program*. A *program* is a set of projects.

Consider the Olympic Games. They involve much more than the festivities, the excitement, national pride, and competition among athletes. They all involve a tremendous amount of planning, preparation, and coordinating work that needs to get done before and during the games. Athletes' living quarters and training facilities must be provided, competition schedules must be developed, arrangements for televising events must be made, equipment and crews must be coordinated, transportation and hotel accommodations must be made, and many other activities that go on behind the scenes must be planned and managed so that everything goes off smoothly.

Projects may involve considerable cost. Some have a long time horizon, and some involve a large number of activities that must be carefully planned and coordinated. All projects are expected to achieve the following **performance goals**: to be completed within time/schedule, cost/budget, and quality guidelines. To accomplish this, projects must be authorized, their objectives and scope must be established, a project manager should be appointed, and the project must be planned. Activities/tasks must be identified and time estimates made. Resource requirements must also be estimated and budgets prepared. Once underway, the project's progress must be monitored to ensure that project's performance goals will be achieved.

The project approach enables an organization to focus attention and concentrate efforts on accomplishing a narrow set of performance objectives within a limited time and budget framework. This can produce significant benefits compared with other approaches that might be considered. Even so, projects present managers with a host of problems that differ in many respects from those encountered with more routine activities. The problems of planning and coordinating project activities can be formidable for large projects, which typically have thousands of activities that must be carefully planned and monitored if the project is to proceed according to schedule and at a reasonable cost.

Projects go through a series of stages or *phases*—a life cycle—which include project initiation (conception, feasibility study/selection), planning and scheduling, execution, control, and closeout. During this life cycle, a variety of skills are needed. The circumstances are analogous to constructing a house. Initially an idea is presented and its feasibility is assessed, then plans must be drawn up by an architect, and approved by the owner and possibly a town's building permits department. Then a succession of activities occurs, each with its own skill requirements, starting with the site preparation; then laying the foundation; erecting the frame, roofing, constructing exterior walls; wiring and plumbing; installing kitchen and bathroom fixtures and appliances; and interior finishing and painting, and carpeting. Similar sequences occur on large construction projects, in R&D, information technology projects, and in virtually every other instance where projects are being carried out.

In a company, the project initiator/sponsor is usually a senior manager/VP. Project output or deliverable is a good such as a building/software or a service such as merging two databases.

A project is influenced by the company's strategy and policies, and "environment" (e.g., culture, information systems, human resources). The major document used in project initiation is the project *scope* (the work that needs to be accomplished to deliver a good or service, the specified objective).

Deciding which projects to implement is called *project portfolio selection*. This involves factors such as budget, availability of personnel with appropriate knowledge and skill, cost–benefit considerations, financial benefits, e.g., return on investment and net present value, and how the project will contribute to the company's strategy. The following steps for project selection have been suggested[1]:

1. Establish a project council (e.g., the executive committee).

2. Identify some project categories (e.g., long vs. short term, minor vs. major) and criteria (e.g., business value, customer satisfaction, process effectiveness, employee satisfaction).

project Unique, large, one-time operation designed to accomplish a specific objective in a limited time frame.

performance goals For a project: keeping the project within schedule, budget, and quality guidelines.

[1] R. L. Englund and R. J. Graham: "From Experience: Linking Projects to Strategy," *Journal of Product Innovation Management*, January 1999, 16(1), pp. 52–64.

SNC-Lavalin

SNC-Lavalin is a large design, engineering, construction, and project management company, based in Montreal, with 35 international offices. Founded in 1911, SNC-Lavalin has performed hundreds of large projects. An example is Phase 2 of the Alouette Aluminum Smelter project in Sept-Iles, Quebec, in 2005. The project increased the facility's capacity to 550,000 tons per annum, the largest aluminum smelter in North America.

SNC-Lavalin provided engineering, procurement, and construction management services. A subcontractor was ADF Group (http://www.adfgroup.com) of Terrebonne, near Montreal, that supplied engineering, fabrication, and installation of the steel structures for two new electrolysis halls, each about 1 km long. The project was completed within budget and time.

Source: http://www.snclavalin.com/expertise.php?lang=en&id=25&sub=1.

3. Collect project data.

4. Assess resources (e.g., labour, dollars) availability.

5. Prioritize the projects within categories.

6. Select projects to be funded.

7. Communicate the results to stakeholders and provide the reasons for selection or nonselection of each project.

For an application, see the "Pacific Blue Cross" OM in Action.

Project planning determines how the project is to be undertaken, and includes breaking down the job into smaller components, called *Work Breakdown Structure* (WBS), determining the resources needed and estimating their costs, scheduling the activities involved or subcontracting the work, planning risk management, and planning material purchases.

Project execution involves purchasing the material, and using the team members and subcontractors to perform the activities/tasks. Project control involves observing the project's progress, issuing performance reports on scope/schedule/cost/quality/risk, and making any necessary changes to the project.

Projects bring various people together, both from inside and outside the company. These stakeholders include the project team who perform the activities/tasks; project sponsor/initiator who initiates and gets approval for the project; and customer/users. The project is headed by a project manager, guided by the project sponsor.

Most team members, who have diverse knowledge and skills, will remain associated with the project for less than its full life. Some people go from project to project as their contributions become needed, and others are "on loan," either on a full-time or part-time basis, from their regular jobs.

Certain organizations are involved with projects on a regular basis; examples include consulting firms, architects, lawyers, publishers, and construction companies. For two examples, see the "SNC-Lavalin" OM in Action and the "Hatch" OM in Action. In these organizations, it is not uncommon for some employees to spend virtually all of their time on projects. These companies have a pure *project organization*.

matrix organization An organizational structure that temporarily groups together specialists from different departments to work on special projects.

However, most organizations use a **matrix organization** that temporarily groups together specialists from different departments to work on special projects. Each staff member, for example, a structural engineer or an accountant, works on one or more project(s) part time, but permanently belongs to his department. The project manager and the functional managers share the authority of assigning priorities and directing the work.

Finally, some organizations have set up a project management office (PMO) that acts as a department, housing project managers who use team members from functional departments just as in the matrix organization structure. For an example, see the "EMCO" OM in Action.

The Project Manager's Job

project manager The person responsible for planning, scheduling, executing, and controlling a project from inception to completion; meeting the project's requirements; and ensuring completion on time, within budget, and to the required quality standards.

The **project manager** is the person responsible for planning, scheduling, executing, and controlling a project from inception to completion; meeting the project's requirements; and ensuring completion on time, within budget, and to the required quality standards. The project manager bears the ultimate responsibility for the success or failure of the project. He or she must acquire adequate resources and personnel, and be capable of working through the team members to accomplish the objective of the project. The project manager is responsible for effectively managing each of the following:

1. The *work*, so that all of the necessary activities are accomplished in the desired sequence, and performance goals are met.
2. The *human resources*, so that those working on the project have direction and motivation.
3. *Communications*, so that everybody has the information they need to do their work (usually through regular meetings), and the customer/sponsor is well informed. Logs of actions, issues, and risks should be kept to manage the project, and to have as project history.
4. *Quality*, so that the specific objective is realized.
5. *Time*, so that the project is completed on schedule.
6. *Costs*, so that the project is completed within budget.

To effectively manage a project, a project manager must employ a certain set of skills. The skills include the ability to motivate and direct team members and build a team, make trade-off decisions in project performance goals, expedite the work when necessary, deal with obstacles and team conflicts, put out fires and solve problems, handle failure or fear of failure, and monitor time, budget, and technical details. For projects that involve fairly well defined work, those skills will often suffice. However, for projects that are less well defined, and thus have a higher degree of uncertainty, the project manager must also employ strong leadership skills. These include the ability to adapt to changing circumstances that may involve changes to project performance goals, technical requirements, and project team composition. As a leader, the project manager not only must be able to deal with these issues; but also able to recognize the need for change, decide what changes are necessary in consultation with stakeholders, and work to accomplish them.

OM in *ACTION*

Project Managers Have Never Been More Critical

Not many people can eloquently describe the changing role of project managers as well as Jonathan Gispan, who teaches the skill to managers at the Lockheed Martin Corporation division in King of Prussia, Pennsylvania. Gispan spent 38 years of his career working at GE Aerospace as a project manager.

Project managers have never been more critical, according to this veteran techie. The function's core responsibilities haven't changed, but the players and playing field are very different than they were five years ago.

Gispan views the project manager as the focal point of a complex relationship matrix that includes customers, workers, vendors, and bosses. "Project managers make things happen," he says. "Not only do they manage a project from start to finish, they also manage the people who make it happen."

The job requires a jack-of-all-trades who can both understand a problem and solve it. "Project managers must successfully manage the total lifecycle of a project," says Gispan. "The job requires a superorganized person who knows how to get a project completed quickly and inexpensively and boasts the advanced communication skills necessary to work closely with vendors, project teams, and senior management."

Project managers have always had to deal with changing relationships. The big change, according to Gispan, is the speed

of change, which has made the project manager's job more difficult. "The changes taking place now are faster and more dramatic than in the past," he says. "Customers are less inclined to give you money for development work, for example. They'd rather save money by using off-the-shelf capabilities. Budgets that used to be reasonably substantial and healthy are now tight." Gispan adds that corporate mergers and consolidations have complicated the picture. Project managers must deal with complex, often labyrinthine decision-making structures. Getting quick decisions requires work and persistence.

Further complicating the situation is a high worker attrition rate. "A decade ago, the attrition rate was about 3 percent; today it has jumped to almost 10 percent," Gispan explains. "It means project managers have to constantly put together new teams."

Through it all, the project manager must be clear-headed and keep a tight rein on projects. It sounds intimidating, yet Gispan sees it as a positive. "The current marketplace keeps you on your toes," he says. "Even though everything is changing at what seems like an overwhelming pace, it is best to view change as a motivator that allows you to keep pace with technology and get better at your job. The idea is not merely to cope with change but to thrive in it. It is more of an attitude than anything else."

What does it take to be a project manager? "You need a good technical base," says Karen Nichols, project manager at EWP Engineering, Inc., a consulting engineering company in Salt Lake City, UT. "That translates to at least five to seven years in the trenches."

(continued)

That's for starters. "But you also need to know how the business side of the equation works," says Nichols. "This is tough for some technical people because it requires the ability to understand how the two different sides of the business mesh. Project managers must also be familiar with accounting methods as well as sales and marketing strategies. In short, they must know how to manage a project so it makes a profit."

If you think you have what it takes, ask to work with a project manager. "It won't take you long to find out whether you have an aptitude and natural feel for the work," says Nichols. "Not everyone is happy–or capable of–juggling many balls in the air at once."

Once you get your feet wet, you can move up quickly, adds Gispan. "After you've proven to management that you're organized and can manage several tasks, it won't be long before you are managing everything associated with a program. Get good at it and you'll move up the ranks from project manager to general manager where you are running several company businesses."

And, don't be confused by job titles. Each company has its own unique title for the project manager role. Whatever the title, a project manager is easy to spot. "It's the person who negotiates with all the key players and makes things happen," says Gispan. "Technology companies would perish without them."

Source: Bob Weinstein, "Project Managers Have Never Been More Critical," *Rochester Democrat and Chronicle*, February 18, 1999. Copyright © 1999 *Rochester Democrat and Chronicle*. Reprinted by permission.

 OM in *ACTION*

Pacific Blue Cross

Pacific Blue Cross provides extended health and dental insurance to residents of British Columbia. When the new VP of Information Technology (IT) was appointed in 2003, she put in a gate governance process for approving larger projects (lasting over one month), changed the review boards for smaller projects (lasting less than a month), and created a PMO. Each large project is now sponsored by a VP who takes it to the executive committee. If it passes the first gate, cost/benefit analysis is performed on it with the help of the PMO. This result is brought to the executive committee again. If it passes gate 2, it is approved. However, projects costing over half a million dollars need to also go through gate 3, and those costing more than $1 million need

to also go through gate 4. Post-implementation review is gate 5. Smaller projects are prioritized by the department review boards that include department managers. The PMO consists of a manager, three project managers, and two to five contract project managers. All information about processes to follow for a project has been put online. The PMO regularly reports the status of projects to the executives. A "traffic light" report uses green, yellow, and red lights to show the status of each project in terms of time, budget, and performance. The reports are also put online.

Source: Dr. C. Aczel Boivie, "Red Light, Green Light; How One CIO Used Project Management Discipline and the Traffic Light Report to Align Her IT Department with Her Company's Business Goals," *CIO*, June 15, 2006, 19(17), p. 1.

 OM in *ACTION*   http://www.emcoltd.com

EMCO

EMCO is one of Canada's leading distributors and manufacturers of building plumbing products for residential, commercial, and industrial construction markets.

Before 1998, EMCO's information systems department had trouble estimating internal project durations, progress, and end dates. Red flags often came up too late to have a meaningful impact. Managing multiple projects simultaneously was difficult at best, posing serious resource allocation problems. The result: dissatisfied information systems customers.

In 1998, EMCO created a PMO. Fardin Maknoni, Senior Analyst, Project Management, heads up this department, which handles implementation and support of telecommunications, transaction processing (such as EDI), data processing, systems conversions, and financial system projects for the entire company.

The PMO adopted Deltek's (Welcom) Open Plan. According to Maknoni, "Open Plan was flexible and easy for everyone to use, and it had the features we needed. It allowed us to control

and centralize all of our projects." Here are some of the ways EMCO uses Open Plan:

- Before a project begins, managers create six to ten "what-if" scenarios in Open Plan. These allow them to effectively plan ahead, resolve schedule conflicts, and make baseline determinations (such as a project's start date).

- During a project, Open Plan generates weekly progress reports that include time sheets, action items, and project status.

- Time sheet information is uploaded to Open Plan from three sources: an internal data management system, Excel, and manual input.

- Various Gantt, PERT, and spreadsheet reports are created and filtered by criteria meaningful to different tiers of users.

- Progress-analysis reports give critical information to senior management to monitor projects and construct new project proposals.

Source: http://www.deltek.com/resource-center/~/media/pdf/case%20 studies/govcon/ipm/emco-op-cs.

A project manager should accept the political nature of his organization and use it to his advantage. He should be politically sensitive, i.e., realize that people are afraid of change because it might alter their established political relationships.[2]

The job of the project manager can be both difficult and rewarding. He or she must coordinate and motivate people who sometimes owe their allegiance to other managers in their functional areas. In addition, the people who work on a project possess specialized knowledge and skills that the project manager may lack. Nevertheless, the project manager is expected to guide and evaluate their efforts. Project managers often must function in an environment that is beset with uncertainties. Even so, budgets and time constraints are usually imposed, which can create additional pressures on project personnel. Finally, the project manager may not have the authority needed to accomplish all the objectives of the project. Instead, the manager sometimes must rely on persuasion and the cooperation of others to realize project goals.

Ethical issues often arise in connection with projects. Examples include the temptation to understate costs or to withhold information in order to get a project approved, pressure to alter or make misleading statements on status reports, falsifying records, compromising workers' safety, and approving substandard work. It is the responsibility of the project manager to maintain and enforce ethical standards.

The position of project manager has high visibility. The rewards of the job of project manager come from the creative challenges of the job, the benefits of being associated with a successful project (including promotion and monetary compensation), and the personal satisfaction of seeing it through to its conclusion.

Project Planning

Project planning involves further elaboration of the project scope (the work to be done) including breaking down the project into smaller components (deliverables, subprojects, work packages, and activities), risk management planning (the identification, analysis, and response plans to what may go wrong), estimating the required resources for the activities (employees, equipment, material), cost estimation (for each activity) and budgeting (calculating total cost per unit time, including subcontracting costs), human resource planning (including assigning team member roles and responsibilities), project scheduling (estimating activity durations, sequencing, and scheduling), quality planning, communications planning, and purchase planning.

project planning Analyzing the project into work packages and activities, estimating resources needed and durations, scheduling, etc.

It is important to determine the details of work to be done (scope), to formally obtain acceptance of the detailed scope from project customer/sponsor and later, during execution and control, to control the changes to the project scope. We will describe risk management planning, work breakdown structure (WBS), and project scheduling in more detail in the following sections. In many applications, the design of the good or service, which is the result of project management, is the part of the project performed by architects/engineers either within the firm or contracted from other firms.

Quality planning involves determining how product quality is to be assured and controlled. It includes deciding the quality policy, objectives, responsibilities, metrics, and tools such as checklists.

Communications planning involves determining the nature of information needed by stakeholders and how to satisfy these needs. It includes plans for information collection/storage, the technology and media used, nature of information distributed (e.g., project performance reports), and methods for accessing and updating the information. For an application, see the "Tim Hortons" OM in Action.

Purchase planning involves determining what to purchase, the statement of work or the specification of the item, supplier evaluation and selection, and the award of contract. The actual delivery and monitoring/controlling of supplier performance are part of the execution and control of the project.

---

[2] For more details, see J. K. Pinto and O. P. Kharbanda, "Lessons for an Accidental Profession," *Business Horizon*, March/April 1995, pp. 41–50.

Tim Hortons

In the early 2000s, Tim Hortons was in the middle of an aggressive expansion plan and needed a faster way to develop new restaurants. Therefore, the engineering services department started using Expesite project management software, which allowed them to use the Internet to communicate project documents (e.g., blueprints), monitor the schedule, track costs, and receive bids. The system cut the development process for a restaurant from 12 down to 11 months, and saved thousands of dollars a year for couriering blueprints back and forth between architects, engineers, and Tim Hortons' staff. The system has also increased process consistency and accountability (by regular reporting) across regions.

Source: M. Wilson, "Expediting Development," *Chain Store Age*, October 2006, 82(10), p. 92.

Risk Management Planning

Risks are inherent in projects. They relate to the occurrence of events that can have undesirable consequences, such as delays, increased costs, or an inability to meet technical specifications (quality/performance). In some instances, there is a risk that events will occur that will cause a project to be terminated. Although careful planning can reduce risks, no amount of planning can eliminate chance events due to unforeseen or uncontrollable circumstances.

The probability of occurrence of risk events is highest near the beginning of a project and lowest near the end. However, the cost associated with risk events tends to be lowest near the beginning of a project and highest near the end.

Good risk management entails identifying as many potential risks as possible, analyzing and assessing those risks, and planning a response to avoid, transfer, or mitigate the risk. Much of this takes place during planning of a project, although it is not unusual for this process to be repeated during the execution of project as experience grows and new information becomes available.

The first step for risk management planning is to identify the risks. Typically, there are numerous sources of risks, although the more experience an organization has with a particular type of work, the fewer and more identifiable the risks will be. Everyone associated with the project should have responsibility for identifying risks. Brainstorming sessions and questionnaires can be useful in this regard. Another approach to risk identification is to review the documents and analyze the assumptions, looking for inaccuracies, inconsistencies, and incompleteness. The list of risks and other information obtained in the following steps is usually stored in a *risk register*.

Once risks have been identified, each risk must be evaluated to determine its probability of occurrence and its potential consequences if it does occur. Both quantitative and qualitative approaches have merit. All stakeholders can contribute to this effort, and experts might also be called on. Experience with previous projects can be useful. Many tools might be applied, including scenario analysis, simulation, decision trees, and sensitivity analysis. There should be a response to risks with high probability and impact.

Risk response can take a number of forms. Much depends on the nature and scope of a project. First, the root cause of a risk is identified. It will help to categorize risks by either their source (this is called risk breakdown structure) or by the area of work (using the WBS). Risk response includes:

- Redundant (backup) systems, for example, an emergency generator could supply power in the event of an electrical failure.
- Using a less complex process or a more stable supplier.
- Frequent monitoring of critical project aspects with the goal of catching and eliminating problems in their early stages, before they cause extensive damage.
- Transferring risks, say by outsourcing a particular component of a project and requiring performance bonds.
- Risk-sharing, for example, as in an oil and gas consortium.
- Extending the schedule, creating contingency funds, reducing project scope, clarifying the requirements, obtaining information, and improving communications.

Work Breakdown Structure

Because a large project usually involves a large amount of work, it is decomposed into smaller components. **Work breakdown structure (WBS)** is a hierarchical listing of what must be done during the project; it is for a project what the product structure tree is for a product. This methodology establishes a logical framework for identifying the required activities for the project (see Figure 17-1). The first step in developing a work breakdown structure is to identify the major components of the project. These are the Level 2 boxes in Figure 17-1. The next step is to identify the major subcomponents for each of the major components–the Level 3 boxes. Then, each major supporting activity is broken down into a list of the activities that will be needed to accomplish it–the Level 4 boxes. (For purposes of illustration, only a portion of the Level 4 boxes are shown.) Usually there are many activities in the Level 4 lists. Large projects involve additional levels, but Figure 17-1 gives you some idea of the concept of the work breakdown structure.

work breakdown structure (WBS) A hierarchical listing of what must be done during a project.

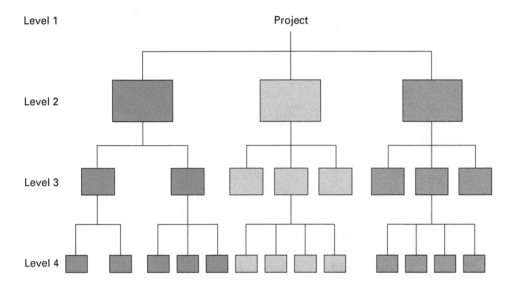

Level 1	Project
Level 2	
Level 3	
Level 4	

◀ **Figure 17-1**

A schematic example of a work breakdown structure.

Developing a good work breakdown structure can require substantial time and effort due to the uncertainties associated with a project and/or the size of the project. Typically the portion of time spent on developing the work breakdown structure greatly exceeds the time spent on actually developing a project schedule. The importance of a work breakdown structure is underscored by the fact that the activity list that results serves as the focal point for planning and doing the project. Moreover, the work breakdown structure is the basis for developing time and cost estimates.

A company can use its past experience to determine the WBS. Progressive elaboration can be pursued as the details of work packages become known (this is also called rolling wave planning). Each component in a WBS should be assigned a code for purpose of monitoring its performance.

Project Scheduling

Project scheduling involves determining the timing of activities of the project. It starts with the identification of the activities in the WBS, including their attributes (e.g., physical location to be performed, person/group/subcontractor responsible) and whether an activity is a milestone activity (signifying a review/test/approval decision).

Then, any sequential dependencies of every pair of activities should be identified.

Next, the resources (employees or subcontractors, equipment, material) needed for each activity should be identified. If the needed resources cannot be identified, the activity should be further decomposed.

Then, the duration of each activity can be estimated using information on the availability of resources. The risk register could possibly add some contingency time to the duration. As work is undertaken, more accurate estimates of costs and times become available. Analogous activities in the past can be used to estimate the activity duration. The 3-point estimates method, described

project scheduling Determining the timing of activities of the project.

later under "Probabilistic Activity Durations," can also be used to estimate the average and standard deviation of an activity's duration.

Finally, the schedule is developed using the activity duration estimates and the sequential dependencies of activities by the PERT/CPM technique (described later), for both one-point estimate (deterministic times) and 3-point estimates (probabilistic times). Attempts may be made to modify the schedule so that a more level use of resources takes place. If the project will be late, schedule compression methods such as project crashing (accelerating activities) and fast tracking (overlapping predecessor-successor activities) will be performed. The schedule will be displayed graphically using Gantt or PERT/CPM charts.

We will describe below the schedule/control Gantt chart, PERT/CPM technique using both deterministic and probabilistic times, and project crashing.

Gantt Chart

The schedule/control Gantt chart, defined in the previous chapter, can be used as a visual aid for scheduling and control of the activities of a project. It is a popular tool for scheduling and control of *simple* projects. It enables a manager to schedule the activities and then to monitor their progress over time by comparing their planned progress to their actual progress. Figure 17-2 illustrates the schedule/control Gantt chart for a bank's plan to establish a new branch. The chart indicates which activities are to occur, their planned duration, and when they are to occur. Then, as the project progresses, the manager is able to see which activities are ahead of schedule and which are behind. This enables the manager to direct attention where it is needed most in order to finish the project on time.

Figure 17-2 ▶

A schedule/control Gantt chart for establishing a new bank branch.

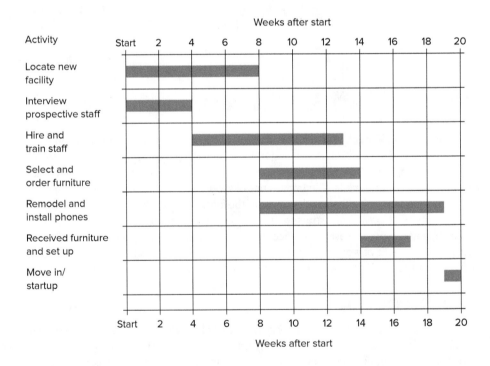

Aside from being a visual tool, an advantage of a schedule/control Gantt chart is its simplicity. However, schedule/control Gantt charts fail to reveal relationships among activities that can be crucial to effective project management. For instance, if one of the early activities in a project suffers a delay, it would be important for the manager to be able to easily determine which later activities are affected. Conversely, some activities may safely be delayed without affecting the overall project completion time. The schedule/control Gantt chart does not directly reveal this. On more complex projects, a *precedence network*, described later, is used for scheduling purposes.

PERT/CPM Technique

PERT (program evaluation and review technique) and **CPM** (critical path method) are two of the most widely used tools for scheduling and control of large-scale projects. By using PERT and CPM, managers are able to obtain:

1. A graphical display of project activities and their sequential relationship.
2. An estimate of how long the project will take.
3. An indication of which activities are most critical to timely project completion.
4. An indication of how long any activity can be delayed without delaying the project.

PERT and CPM were developed independently during the late 1950s. PERT evolved through the joint efforts of Lockheed Aircraft, the U.S. Navy Special Projects Office, and the consulting firm of Booz, Allen, Hamilton, in an effort to speed up the Polaris missile project. At the time, the U.S. government was concerned that the Soviet Union might be gaining nuclear superiority, and it gave top priority for the early completion of the project by the U.S. Department of Defense. The project was a huge one, with more than 3,000 contractors and thousands of activities. PERT was quite successful and was generally credited with shaving two years off the length of the project.

CPM was developed by J. E. Kelly of the Remington Rand Corporation and M. R. Walker of DuPont to schedule and control maintenance projects in chemical plants.

Although PERT and CPM were developed independently, they have a great deal in common. Moreover, many of the initial differences between them have disappeared as users borrowed certain features from one technique for use with the other. For example, PERT originally stressed probabilistic activity durations because the environment in which it was developed was characterized by high uncertainty. In contrast, the tasks for which CPM was developed were less uncertain, so CPM originally made no provision for variability of duration. To avoid confusion, we will not delve into this difference. For practical purposes, PERT and CPM are the same and we will use the term *PERT/CPM* to refer to either method.

Precedence Network

One of the main features of PERT/CPM is its use of a **precedence network** to depict project activities and their sequential relationships by use of arrows and nodes. There are two slightly different conventions for constructing these networks. Under the original convention, the *arrows* designate activities; under the new convention, the *nodes* designate activities. These are referred to as **activity-on-arrow (AOA)** and **activity-on-node (AON)** network, respectively.

Both types of networks are illustrated in Figure 17-3, using the new bank branch example of Figure 17-2. In the AOA network, the arrows represent both the activities and the sequence in which they must be performed (e.g., Interview precedes Hire and Train); in the AON network, the arrows show only the sequence in which activities must be performed, while the nodes represent the activities. Only AON precedence networks will be used in this chapter.

PERT Program evaluation and review technique, used for scheduling and control of large projects.

CPM Critical path method, used for scheduling and control of large projects.

precedence network Diagram of project activities and their sequential relationships by use of arrows and nodes.

activity-on-arrow (AOA) Network in which arrows designate activities.

activity-on-node (AON) Network in which nodes designate activities.

▼ **Figure 17-3**

Precedence networks for establishing a new bank branch.

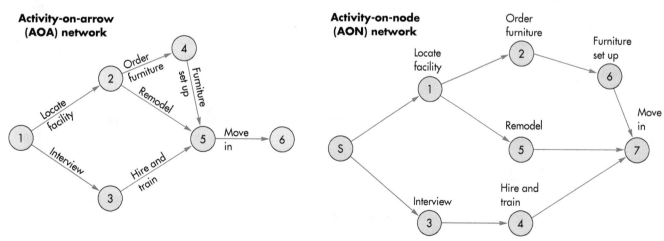

Activity-on-arrow (AOA) network

Activity-on-node (AON) network

Note that the AON network has a start node, S, which is actually not an activity but is added in order to have a single starting node. Also, an AON network should have only one ending node.

The relationships shown in Figure 17-3 are all of the finish-to-start type (i.e., an activity must finish before its immediate successor can start). Sometimes other types of relationships exist, such as start-to-start (an activity can start only after another has started), finish-to-finish, and start-to-finish. Also, it is possible to require a prespecified minimum delay (time buffer) in any of these relationships. In addition, some dependencies may be discretionary. Further, there may be external dependencies, e.g., an externally determined start or finish time for an activity. We will consider only finish-to-start relationships, which are most common, in this chapter. Developing and interpreting AON precedence networks requires some familiarity with network conventions; see Figure 17-4.

Figure 17-4 ▶

AON precedence network conventions.

INTERPRETATION	NETWORK RELATIONSHIP
Activities must be completed in sequence: first *a*, then *b*, and then *c*.	
Both *a* and *b* must be completed before *c* can start.	
Activity *a* must be completed before *b* or *c* can start.	
Both *a* and *b* must be completed before *c* or *d* can start.	

path A sequence of activities that leads from the start node to the end node.

critical path The longest path from start to end; determines the expected project duration.

critical activities Activities on the critical (longest) path.

path slack time Allowable slippage for a path; the difference between the length of the path and the length of the critical (longest) path.

Of particular interest are the *paths* or chains in a precedence network diagram. A **path** is a sequence of activities that leads from the start node to the end node. For example, in the AON network of Figure 17-3, S-1-2-6-7 is a path. Note that there are three paths in this network. One reason for the importance of paths is that they reveal *sequential relationships*. If one activity in a sequence is delayed (i.e., is late) or done incorrectly, all the following activities on that path will be delayed.

Another important aspect of a path is its length (i.e., duration). The length of a path can be determined by summing the expected duration of the activities on it. The path with the largest duration is of particular interest because it governs the project completion time. In other words, expected project duration equals the expected duration of the longest path. Moreover, if there are any delays along the longest path, there will be corresponding delays in the project completion time. Attempts to shorten project completion must focus on the activities on the longest path. Because of its influence on project completion time, the longest path is referred to as the **critical path**, and its activities are referred to as **critical activities**.

Paths that are shorter than the critical path can experience some delays and still not affect the overall project completion time as long as their duration does not exceed the length of the critical path. The allowable slippage for any path is called **path slack time**, and it reflects the difference between the length of the path and the length of the critical path. The critical path, then, has zero path slack time.

LO4

Deterministic Activity Durations

deterministic durations Durations that are fairly certain.

The main determinant of the way PERT/CPM networks are analyzed and interpreted is whether activity durations are *probabilistic* or *deterministic*. If durations are fairly certain, we say that the durations are **deterministic**. If durations are subject to variation, we say that the durations are **probabilistic**. Probabilistic durations must include an indication of the extent of probable variation.

This section deals with deterministic activity durations. The next section deals with probabilistic activity durations.

One of the best ways to gain an understanding of the nature of a precedence network and the critical path is to consider a simple example using an intuitive solution method.

Given the information provided below:

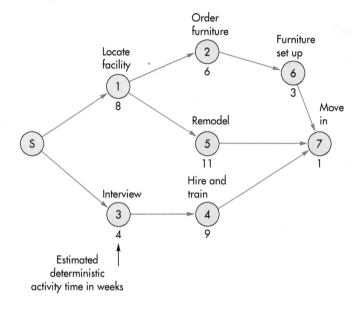

probabilistic durations
Durations that allow for variation.

◀ **Example 1**

Determine:

a. The length (duration) of each path.

b. The critical path.

c. The expected duration of the project.

d. The slack for each path.

a. As shown in the following table, the path durations are 18 weeks, 20 weeks, and 14 weeks.

b. The longest path (20 weeks) is S-1-5-7, so it is the critical path.

c. The expected duration of the project is equal to the length of the critical path (i.e., 20 weeks).

d. We find the slack for each path by subtracting its length from the length of the critical path, as shown in the right column of the following table. (*Note:* It is sometimes desirable to know the slack time of the activities. The next section describes a method for obtaining those slack times.)

SOLUTION

Path	Duration (weeks)	Path Slack (weeks)
S-1-2-6-7	$8 + 6 + 3 + 1 = 18$	$20 - 18 = 2$
S-1-5-7	$8 + 11 + 1 = 20^*$	$20 - 20 = 0$
S-3-4-7	$4 + 9 + 1 = 14$	$20 - 14 = 6$

*Critical path length.

Solution Technique

Many real-life precedence networks are much larger than the simple network illustrated in the preceding example; they often contain hundreds or even thousands of activities and exponentially more paths. Because the necessary calculations can become exceedingly time consuming, large networks are analyzed by a computer program and a solution technique that develops four values for each activity:

- ES, the *earliest* time the activity can *start*.
- EF, the *earliest* time the activity can *finish*.
- LS, the *latest* time the activity can *start* and not delay the project.
- LF, the *latest* time the activity can *finish* and not delay the project.

Once these values have been determined, they can be used to find:

1. Expected project duration
2. Activity slack times
3. The critical path

First, we calculate the earliest start and finish times for each activity, starting from the left at the start node and moving to the right of the precedence network (called a *forward pass*), using the following two simple rules:

1. The earliest finish time for any activity is equal to its earliest start time plus its expected duration, *t*:

$$EF = ES + t \qquad\qquad (17\text{-}1)$$

2. ES for an activity with one immediate predecessor is equal to the EF of that node. ES for an activity with multiple immediate predecessors is equal to the largest EF of those nodes. Let ES of the start node be zero.

Example 2 ▶ Calculate the earliest start time and earliest finish time for each activity in the network shown in Example 1.

SOLUTION

Begin by enlarging each node and placing the activity number and duration inside it as follows:

We determine and place the earliest start time, ES, and the earliest finish time, EF, for the activity inside each node as follows:

ES of the start node is 0. The start node in this example has zero duration. Therefore, $EF_S = ES_S + t = 0 + 0 = 0$. The EF of the start node becomes the ES of the nodes immediately following it. Thus, $ES_1 = 0$ and $ES_3 = 0$:

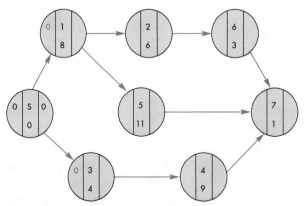

Next, use $EF = ES + t$ for each of the nodes 1 and 3; i.e., $EF_1 = 0 + 8 = 8$ and $EF_3 = 0 + 4 = 4$:

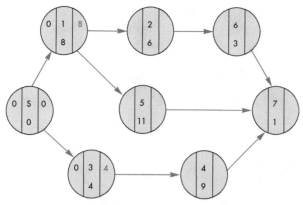

Now, because activity 1 has an EF of 8, both activities 2 and 5 (its immediate successor) will have ES of 8. Similarly, activity 4 will have ES of 4 because EF of node 3, its immediate predecessor, is 4:

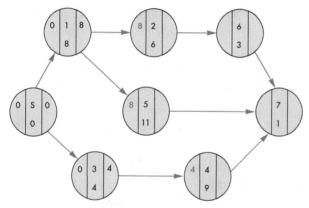

This permits calculation of the EFs for activities 2, 5, and 4: $EF_2 = 8 + 6 = 14$, $EF_5 = 8 + 11 = 19$, and $EF_4 = 4 + 9 = 13$.

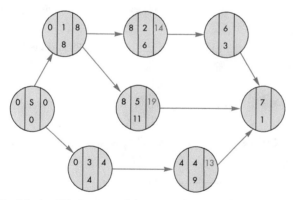

The ES for activity 6 is the EF of activity 2 (its immediate predecessor) which is 14. Using this value, we find $EF_6 = 14 + 3 = 17$.

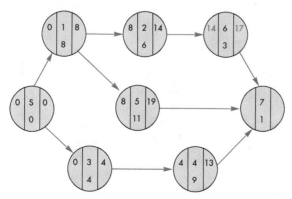

In order to determine the ES for activity 7, we must realize that activity 7 cannot start until *every* activity that immediately precedes it is finished. Therefore, the *largest* of the EFs for the three activities that immediately precede it determines ES_7. Hence, the ES for activity 7 is 19 (i.e., max (17, 19, 13)).

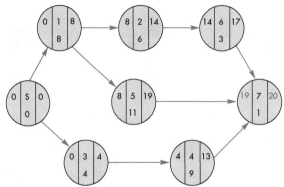

Finally, $EF_7 = 19 + 1 = 20$. Note that the EF for the end node is the expected project duration, 20 weeks.

Now, we calculate the latest start and finish times, starting from the right (i.e., the end node) and moving to the left of the precedence network (called a *backward pass*), using the following two simple rules:

1. The latest start time for any activity is equal to its latest finish time minus its expected duration:

   $$LS = LF - t \qquad (17\text{-}2)$$

2. For a node with one immediate successor, LF equals the LS of that node. For a node with multiple immediate successors, LF equals the smallest LS of those nodes. Let LF of the end node equal its EF.

Calculate the latest finish and latest start times of activities for the precedence network shown at the end of Example 2.

SOLUTION

We will add the LS and LF times to the nodes just below the ES and EF times, respectively, determined in Example 2.

Begin by setting the LF of the last activity (node 7) equal to the EF of that activity. Thus,

$$LF_7 = EF_7 = 20 \text{ weeks}$$

Obtain the LS for activity 7 by subtracting its duration, t, from its LF:

$$LS_7 = LF_7 - t = 20 - 1 = 19:$$

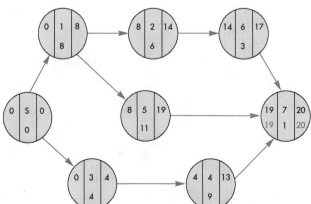

The LS of 19 for activity 7 now becomes the LF for each of the activities that immediately precede it. Thus, $LF_6 = LF_5 = LF_4 = 19$. Now subtract their activity time from their LF to obtain their LS. The LS for activity 4 is $19 - 9 = 10$, for activity 5 is $19 - 11 = 8$, and for activity 6 is $19 - 3 = 16$:

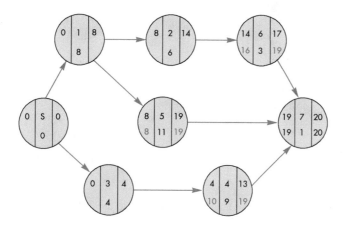

Next, the LS for activity 6, which is 16, becomes the LF for activity 2 (its immediate predecessor), and the LS for activity 4, which is 10, becomes the LF for activity 3 (its immediate predecessor). Using these values, we find the LS for each of these activities by subtracting their activity time from their LF. Therefore, LS for activity 2 is $16 - 6 = 10$, and for activity 3 is $10 - 4 = 6$:

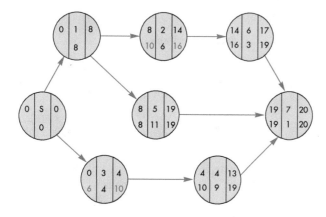

The LF for activity 1 is the *smaller* of the two LSs of the activities that immediately succeed it. Hence, the LF for activity 1 is 8 (i.e., min (8, 10)). The reason you use the smaller time is that activity 1 must finish at a time that permits both the immediately following activities to start no later than their LS.

Once we have determined the LF of activity 1, we find its LS by subtracting its time of 8 from its LF of 8. Hence, LS of activity 1 is 0:

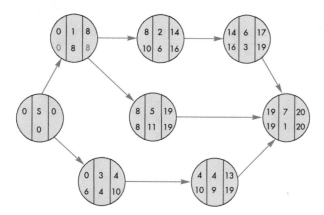

Next, the LF of activity S is the smaller of LS of activities 1 and 3, i.e., $LF_S = \min(0, 6) = 0$. Finally, $LS_S = LF_S - t = 0 - 0 = 0$:

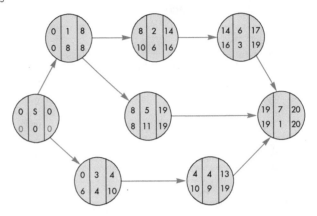

The rules for the above solution technique are reiterated in the following box.

Calculating Activity Slack Times. Activity slack times can be calculated in either of two ways:

$$\text{Slack} = \text{LS} - \text{ES} \quad \text{or} \quad \text{LF} - \text{EF} \tag{17-3}$$

The critical path consists of the activities with zero slack time.

Rules for the PERT/CPM Solution Technique

Forward Pass

Start at the left side of the precedence network (i.e., the start node) and work toward the right side.

For the start activity: ES = 0.

For each activity: ES + Activity duration = EF.

If an activity has a unique immediate predecessor: ES = EF of that activity.

If an activity has multiple immediate predecessors, set its ES equal to the largest EF of its immediate predecessors.

Backward Pass

Start at the right side of the precedence network (i.e., the end node) and work toward the left side.

Use the EF as the LF for the end activity.

For each activity: LS = LF − Activity time.

If an activity has a unique immediate follower: LF = LS of that activity.

If an activity has multiple immediate followers, set the activity's LF equal to the smallest LS of the immediate followers.

Example 4 ▶

Calculate activity slack times for the procedence network at the end of Example 3.

SOLUTION

Either the start times or the finish times can be used. Suppose we use the start times. Using ES calculated in Example 2 and LS calculated in Example 3, activity slack times are:

Activity	LS	ES	(LS − ES) Slack
S	0	0	0
1	0	0	0
3	6	0	6
2	10	8	2
5	8	8	0
4	10	4	6
6	16	14	2
7	19	19	0

Hatch

Hatch is a large Canadian design, consulting engineering, and project management firm specializing in power and energy projects. Hatch (previously Acres) has undertaken hundreds of projects since 1924, both within Canada and internationally. One project was a set of hydroelectric dams over Karun, a major river in southwest Iran, The challenging project started in 1977 and only recently the third dam was completed. The 2000-MW Karun III hydroelectric project includes a 205 metre-high arch dam, a huge underground powerhouse complex, power and water tunnels, and the world's largest concrete-lined plunge pool, all built on a limestone foundation in an area of high seismic activity.

Source: http://www.hatch.ca/project_management/projects/Karun.htm.

Example 4 indicates that activities S, 1, 5, and 7 are all critical activities, which agrees with the results of the intuitive approach demonstrated in Example 1.

Knowledge of activity slack times provides managers with information for planning the allocation of scarce resources and for directing control efforts toward those activities that are most susceptible to delaying the project. In this regard, it is important to recognize that activity slack times are based on the assumption that all of the activities on the same path will be started as early as possible and not exceed their expected times. Furthermore, if two activities are both on the same path (e.g., activities 2 and 6 in the preceding example) and have the same slack (e.g., two weeks), this will be the *total* slack available to both. In essence, the activities have *shared slack*. Hence, if the first activity uses all the slack, there will be zero slack left for all the following activities on that same path.

As noted earlier, this solution technique lends itself to computerization. This problem (Examples 2 to 4) will be solved using Microsoft Project at the end of chapter.

Probabilistic Activity Durations

The preceding discussion assumed that activity durations were known and not subject to variation. While this assumption is appropriate in some situations, there are many others where it is not. Consequently, these situations require a probabilistic approach.

The probabilistic PERT/CPM approach, called the **3-point estimates method**, involves *three* duration estimates for each activity instead of one:

1. **Optimistic duration**: The length of time under the best conditions; represented by t_o.
2. **Pessimistic duration**: The length of time under the worst conditions; represented by t_p.
3. **Most likely duration**: The most probable length of time; represented by t_m.

Managers or others with knowledge about the activity can make these duration estimates.

The **Beta distribution** is a family of continuous positive distributions used to describe the inherent variability of an activity's duration (see Figure 17-5). Although there is no real theoretical justification for using the Beta distribution, it has certain features that make it attractive in practice: The distribution can be symmetrical or skewed to either the right or the left depending on its shape parameters; the mean and variance of the distribution can be readily obtained from the three estimates listed above; and shape parameters can be chosen so that the distribution is unimodal with a high concentration of probability surrounding the most likely duration estimate.

Of special interest in probabilistic PERT/CPM are the average or expected duration for each activity t_e, and the variance of each activity's duration, σ_{act}^2. The expected duration of an activity, t_e, is an unequally weighted average of the three estimates:

$$t_e = \frac{t_o + 4t_m + t_p}{6} \tag{17-4}$$

3-point estimates method PERT/CPM when the activity durations are variable and are determined using three estimates: optimistic, most likely, and pessimistic.

optimistic duration The length of time under the best conditions (t_o).

pessimistic duration The length of time under the worst conditions (t_p).

most likely duration The most probable length of time (t_m).

Beta distribution A family of continuous positive distributions used to describe the inherent variability in activity durations.

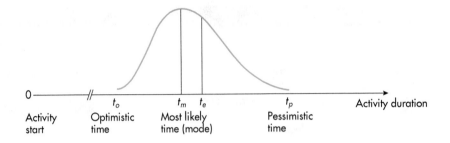

t_o — Activity start — Optimistic time

t_m t_e — Most likely time (mode)

t_p — Pessimistic time

Activity duration

The expected (average) duration of a path is equal to the sum of the expected duration of the activities on it:

$$\text{Path mean} = \sum(\text{expected duration of activities on the path}) \tag{17-5}$$

The standard deviation of each activity's duration is estimated as one-sixth of the difference between the pessimistic and optimistic estimates. (Analogously, almost all of the area under a Normal distribution lies within three standard deviations of the mean, which is a range of six standard deviations.) We find the variance by squaring the standard deviation. Thus,

$$\sigma^2_{\text{act}} = \left[\frac{(t_p - t_o)}{6}\right]^2 \quad \text{or} \quad \sigma^2_{\text{act}} = \frac{(t_p - t_o)^2}{36} \tag{17-6}$$

The size of the variance reflects the degree of uncertainty associated with an activity's duration: The larger the variance, the greater the uncertainty.

It is also required to calculate the standard deviation of the duration of a *path*. We can do this by summing the variances of the activity durations on the path and then taking the square root of that number; that is,

$$\sigma_{\text{path}} = \sqrt{\sum[(\text{variances of activity durations on path})]} \tag{17-7}$$

Example 5 illustrates these calculations.

Example 5

The precedence network for a project is shown below, with the three duration estimates for each activity (in weeks) over each node.

a. Calculate the expected duration for each activity and the expected duration for each path.

b. Identify the critical path (based on the expected durations).

c. Calculate the variance of each activity's duration and the standard deviation of each path's duration.

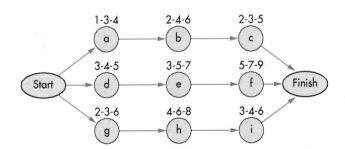

a. Because the start and finish activities do not take any time in this example, we can ignore
them in the following calculations:

Path	Activity	Durations t_o	t_m	t_p	$t_e = \dfrac{t_o + 4t_m + t_p}{6}$	Path Expected Duration
a-b-c	a	1	3	4	2.83 ⎫	
	b	2	4	6	4.00 ⎬	10.00
	c	2	3	5	3.17 ⎭	
d-e-f	d	3	4	5	4.00 ⎫	
	e	3	5	7	5.00 ⎬	16.00
	f	5	7	9	7.00 ⎭	
g-h-i	g	2	3	6	3.33 ⎫	
	h	4	6	8	6.00 ⎬	13.50
	i	3	4	6	4.17 ⎭	

b. The path that has the largest expected duration is the critical path. Because path d-e-f has the largest path expected duration, it is the critical path.

c.

Path	Activity	Durations t_o	t_m	t_p	$\sigma_{act}^2 = \dfrac{(t_p - t_o)^2}{36}$	σ_{path}^2	σ_{path}
a-b-c	a	1	3	4	$(4 - 1)^2/36 = 9/36$	$34/36 = 0.944$	0.97
	b	2	4	6	$(6 - 2)^2/36 = 16/36$		
	c	2	3	5	$(5 - 2)^2/36 = 9/36$		
d-e-f	d	3	4	5	$(5 - 3)^2/36 = 4/36$	$36/36 = 1.00$	1.00
	e	3	5	7	$(7 - 3)^2/36 = 16/36$		
	f	5	7	9	$(9 - 5)^2/36 = 16/36$		
g-h-i	g	2	3	6	$(6 - 2)^2/36 = 16/36$	$41/36 = 1.139$	1.07
	h	4	6	8	$(8 - 4)^2/36 = 16/36$		
	i	3	4	6	$(6 - 3)^2/36 = 9/36$		

Knowledge of the path's expected duration and standard deviation of duration enables a manager to calculate probabilistic estimates of the project completion time, such as these:

- The probability that the project will be completed by a specified time.
- The probability that the project will take longer than its scheduled completion time.

These estimates can be derived from the probability that various paths will be completed by the specified time or take longer than the scheduled completion time. Although activity durations are represented by Beta distribution, a path's duration is approximately a Normal distribution. This concept, called the central limit theorem, is illustrated in Figure 17-6.

Determining Path Probabilities

The probability that a given path will be completed in a specified length of time can be determined using the following formula:

$$z = \frac{\text{Specified length of time} - \text{Expected path duration}}{\text{Standard deviation of path duration}} \tag{17-8}$$

The resulting value of z indicates how many standard deviations of the path's duration the specified length of time is beyond the expected path duration. A negative value of z indicates that the specified time is *earlier* than the expected path duration. Once the value of z has been

Figure 17-6 ▲

Activity-duration distributions and the path-duration distribution.

determined, it can be used in Appendix B, Table B, to obtain the probability that the path will be completed by the specified time. Note that the probability is equal to the area under the Normal curve to the left of z, as illustrated in Figure 17-7.

A project is not completed until *all* of its activities, not only those on the critical path, have been completed. It sometimes happens that another path ends up taking more time to complete than the critical path, in which case the project runs longer than expected. Hence, it can be risky to focus exclusively on the critical path. This requires determining the probability that *all* paths will finish by a specified time. To do that, find the probability that each path will finish by the

Figure 17-7 ▶

The path probability is the area under the Normal curve to the left of z.

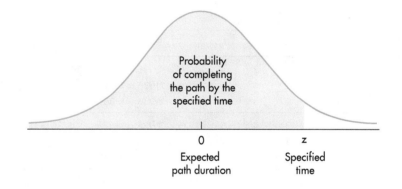

specified time, and then multiply those probabilities. The result is the probability that the *project* will be completed by the specified time. This assumes independence of path durations. The assumption of *independence* of path durations requires two conditions: (a) that the activity durations are independent of each other, and (b) that each activity is on only one path. For activity durations to be independent, the duration for one must not give any information about the duration of the other; if two activities were always early or late together, they would not be considered independent.

Example 6 ▶

Using the information from Example 5, answer the following questions:

a. Can the paths be considered independent? Why?

b. What is the probability that the project can be completed within 17 weeks of its start?

c. What is the probability that the project will be completed within 15 weeks of its start?

d. What is the probability that the project will *not* be completed within 15 weeks of its start?

SOLUTION

a. Yes, the paths can be considered independent, since no activity is on more than one path and we have no information suggesting that activity durations are interrelated.

b. To answer questions of this nature, we must take into account the degree to which the path-duration distributions "exceed" the specified completion time. This concept is illustrated in the following figure, which shows the three path-duration distributions, each centred on that path's expected duration, and the specified completion time of 17 weeks.

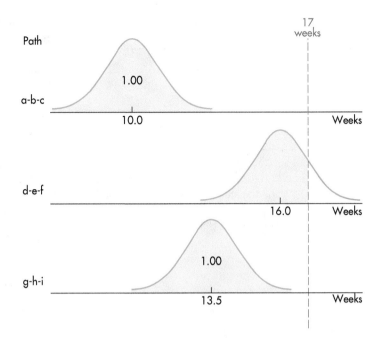

The coloured portion of each distribution corresponds to the probability that the path will be completed within the specified time. Observe that paths a-b-c and g-h-i are well enough to the left of the specified time so that it is highly likely that both will be finished by week 17. In such cases, we essentially need to consider only the distribution of path d-e-f in assessing the probability of completion by week 17. To do so, we must first calculate the value of z using formula 17-8 for this path:

$$z = \frac{17 - 16}{1.00} = +1.00$$

Turning to Appendix B, Table B with $z = +1.00$, we find that the area under the curve to the left of z is .8413. To check our intuition, the probabilities for the other two paths are also determined, and all three are summarized in the following table. *Note:* If the value of z exceeds $+3.50$, treat the probability of completion as being equal to 1.

Path	$z = \dfrac{17 - \textbf{Expected path duration}}{\textbf{Standard deviation of path duration}}$	Probability of Completion in 17 Weeks
a-b-c	$\dfrac{17 - 10}{.97} = +7.22$	1.00
d-e-f	$\dfrac{17 - 16}{1.00} = +1.00$	.8413
g-h-i	$\dfrac{17 - 13.5}{1.07} = +3.27$	.9995

Thus, Prob(project finishes by week 17) = Prob(path a-b-c finishes by week 17) ×
Prob(path d-e-f finishes week 17) ×
Prob(path g-h-i finishes by week 17)
$= 1.00 \times .8413 \times .9995 = .8409 \approx 84\%$

c. For a specified time of 15 weeks, the z values are:

Path	$z = \dfrac{15 - \text{Expected path duration}}{\text{Standard deviation of path duration}}$	Probability of Completion in 15 Weeks
a-b-c	$\dfrac{15 - 10}{.97} = +5.15$	1.0000
d-e-f	$\dfrac{15 - 16}{1.00} = -1.00$	.1587
g-h-i	$\dfrac{15 - 13.5}{1.07} = +1.40$	.9192

Paths d-e-f and g-h-i have z values that are less than $+3.50$. From Appendix B, Table B, the area to the *left* of $z = -1.00$ is .1587, and the area to the *left* of $z = +1.40$ is .9192. The path distributions are illustrated in the following figure. The joint probability of all paths finishing within 15 weeks is the product of their probabilities: $(1.00)(.1587)(.9192) = .1459$.

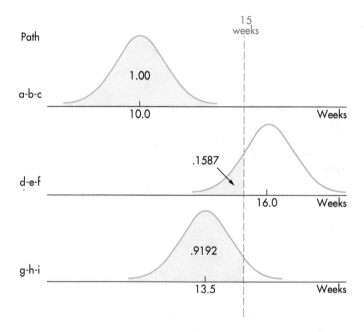

    d. The probability of not finishing within 15 weeks is the complement of the probability obtained in part *c*: $1 - .1459 = .8541$.

Using Simulation. The above discussion assumed that the paths of the project were *independent*, which requires that no activity be on more than one path. If an activity were on more than one path and it happened that the completion time for that activity far exceeded its expected time, all paths that include that activity would be affected and, hence, their durations would not be independent. If only a few activities are on multiple paths, particularly if the paths are *much* shorter than the critical path, the independence assumption may still be reasonable.

    Otherwise project schedulers often use *simulation* to find the desired probabilities. This amounts to a form of repeated sampling wherein many passes are made through the precedence network. In each pass, a random value for each activity's duration is selected from the probability distribution of its duration. After each pass, the project duration is determined. After a large number of such passes (e.g., several hundred), there is enough information to prepare a frequency distribution of the project duration. A project scheduler can use this distribution to make a probabilistic assessment of the project duration.

Project Crashing

LO6

Estimate of an activity's duration is usually made for a given level of resources. In many situations, it is possible to reduce the length of a project, i.e., "crash" the project, by using additional resources. The impetus to shorten projects may reflect efforts to avoid late penalties, to take advantage of monetary incentives for timely or early completion of a project, or to free resources for use on other projects. In new product development, shortening the time may lead to a strategic benefit: beating the competition to the market. In some cases, however, the desire to shorten the length of a project merely reflects an attempt to reduce the indirect costs associated with running the project, such as facilities, equipment, supervision, and personnel costs. Hence, a project manager may be able to shorten a project by increasing *direct* expenses to speed up the project, thereby realizing savings on indirect project costs. *Time–cost trade-off* can be used to identify those activities that will reduce the sum of the indirect and direct project costs.

Only activities on the critical path are potential candidates for crashing (i.e., shortening), because shortening non-critical activities would not have an impact on the project duration. From an economic standpoint, critical activities should be crashed according to crashing cost per period: crash those with the lowest crash cost per period first. Moreover, crashing should continue as long as the cost to crash is less than the benefits derived from crashing. We assume that the indirect costs are a linear function of project duration. Also, we assume (direct) crashing cost per period increases faster the more you crash the project. Figure 17-8 illustrates the basic relationship between indirect, direct, and total project costs due to crashing.

The general procedure for crashing is:

1. Obtain estimates of regular and crash durations and crash cost per period for each activity, and indirect project costs per period.

2. Determine the lengths of all paths.

3. Determine the critical activities.

4. Crash critical activities, starting from the cheapest, as long as crashing cost per period does not exceed the benefits of crashing. Note that two or more paths may become critical as the original critical path becomes shorter, so that subsequent improvements will require simultaneous shortening of two or more paths. In some cases, it will be more economical to shorten an activity that is on two (or more) of the critical paths than two (or more) activities on each critical path.

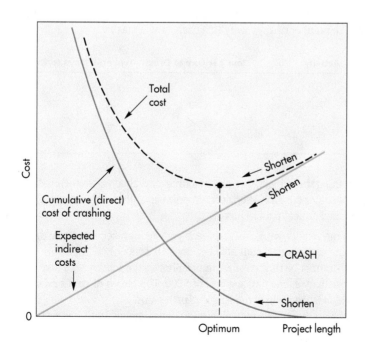

◀ Figure 17-8

Costs related to crashing activities; crashing activities reduces the indirect project costs but increases direct costs; the optimum amount of crashing results in minimizing the sum of these two types of costs.

Example 7 ▷

Using the following information and precedence network, develop the optimal project crashing. Indirect project costs are $1,000 per day.

Activity	Normal Duration (days)	Crash Duration (days)	Cost per Day to Crash
a	6	6	—
b	10	8	$500
c	5	4	300
d	4	1	700
e	9	7	600
f	2	1	800

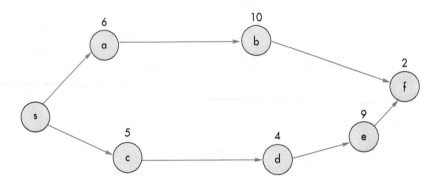

SOLUTION

a. Determine the critical path, its length, and the length of the other path:

Path	Length
s-a-b-f	6 + 10 + 2 = 18
s-c-d-e-f	5 + 4 + 9 + 2 = 20 (critical path)

b. Rank the critical activities in order of crashing cost per day, starting from the lowest, and determine the number of days for which each can be crashed.

Activity	Cost per Day to Crash	Available Days to Crash
c	$300	1
e	600	2
d	700	3
f	800	1

c. Begin shortening the project, one day at a time, and check after each reduction to see if the other path becomes critical. (After a certain point, the other path's length will equal the length of the shortened critical path.) Thus:

  i. Shorten the activity with cheapest crash cost per day, activity *c*, one day at a cost of $300. The length of the critical path now becomes 19 days.
  ii. Activity *c* cannot be shortened any more. Shorten the activity with next cheapest crash cost per day, activity *e*, one day at a cost of $600. The length of path *s-c-d-e-f* now becomes 18 days, which is the same as the length of path s-a-b-f.
  iii. The paths are now both critical; further improvements will necessitate shortening both paths.

The remaining activities for crashing and their costs are:

Path	Activity	Crash Cost (per day)	Available Days
s-a-b-f	a	—	0
	b	$500	2
	f	800	1
s-c-d-e-f	c	—	0
	e	$600	1
	d	700	3
	f	800	1

At first glance, it would seem that crashing f would not be advantageous, because it has the highest crashing cost per day. However, f is on both paths, so shortening f by one day would shorten *both* paths (and hence, the project) by one day for a cost of $800. The option of shortening the least expensive activity on each path would cost $500 for b for s-a-b-f and $600 for e for s-c-d-e-f, or $1,100 in total. Thus, shorten f by one day. The project duration is now 17 days.

iv. At this point, no additional crashing is cost-effective. The cost to crash b and e is a total of $1,100, and that would exceed the indirect project costs of $1,000 per day.

The crashing sequence is summarized below:

Path	n = 0	Length After Crashing n Days: 1	2	3
s-a-b-f	18	18	18	17
s-c-d-e-f	20	19	18	17
Activity crashed		c	e	f
Crash cost		$300	$600	$800

OM in ACTION

Warner Robins Air Logistics Center

Warner Robins Air Logistics Center (WR-ALC) in Southern Georgia repairs and overhauls U.S. Air Force transport planes such as C-5 Galaxy, C-17 Globemaster, C-130 Hercules, and F-15 fighter jets. Before year 2004, WR-ALC took an average of one year to overhaul a C-5 (resulting in 16-17 WIP) which was deemed to be too slow. Most of the time, a plane was waiting for mechanics, facilities, and/or parts. Then in 2004, WR-ALC implemented lean production, which reduced the throughput time to 240 days. However, this was still too long for the U.S. Air Force.

In 2005, WR-ALC implemented the Critical Chain project execution management. Aggressive times for each activity were determined, which added up to only 105 days, with 55 days of project buffer. Similarly, 100 or so non-critical chains each received their own buffers at their end (before feeding into the critical chain). Chains are prioritized daily based on the percentage of buffer time used divided by the percentage of the chain work completed. The activities on a chain receive the priority of their chain, and those with highest priorities are scheduled for the next five work days. Support services, including parts needed, are prepared/acquired for the schedule.

Also, the WIP is reduced to seven C-5 planes (from 12 in 2004). "Fixer Release Control" points (i.e., the points at which the director could permit the aircraft to move from one phase to the next) have been put in place after each major phase to control the WIP. Also, there is now a "hold" phase of 20 days after strip (i.e., disassembly)/repair phase to ensure that all parts needed have been refurbished before buildup (i.e., reassembly) phase can start. This will reduce the idle time and multitasking of mechanics. Supervisors roam the shop floor solving problems. Bottleneck activities are kaizened.

Source: M.M. Srinvasan, W.D. Best, and S. Chandrasekaran, "Warner Robins Air Logistics Center Streamlines Aircraft Repair and Overhaul," *Interfaces*, 37(1), January/February 2007, pp. 7–21.

Project Execution and Control

project execution Involves performance of activities planned.

Project execution involves the actual performance of the activities that were planned in project planning. The project manager directs, coordinates, and manages project activities and team members. The budgeted funds are expended to accomplish the project objective. Resources are obtained, managed, and used.

During execution, quality of the product is assured by applying the planned quality activities.

Team members who are not yet assigned are chosen; their skills are assessed, needed training instituted, and ground rules for team participation are set.

Any purchases or subcontracting plans, whose suppliers are not determined yet, are finalized, and contracts are negotiated. In a construction project, bid packages (e.g., for foundation, frame, roofing, etc.) go out.

The plan for information collection and distribution is executed using clear and timely information in appropriate form (written or oral, formal or informal, using software or manual, etc.). Unexpected requests for information by stakeholders are responded to.

An approach for project execution, especially when multiple projects are underway and require joint resources, is the *critical chain*, proposed by Eli Goldratt in 1997.[3] It is based on two psychological principles: (a) student's syndrome = a student tends to delay the start of an assignment until the last possible time, and (b) Parkinson's law = work expands to fill the time available for its completion. To combat these tendencies, which result in late projects, the critical chain approach does not disclose the due dates of activities to the project workers. Instead, activities are prioritized, scheduled accordingly, and done as soon as possible. Also, estimates of activity duration are examined to ensure that they are not being padded with safety time. Safety or buffer time is added at the end of the critical chain (critical path) and at the end of each feeder chain that feeds into the critical chain. Activity (and chain) priorities are determined daily based on the percentage of buffer time used divided by the percentage of the chain work completed (the activity with a larger ratio gets a higher priority). See the OM in Action "Warner Robins Air Logistics Center."

project control Comparing a project's progress against plans and taking corrective action if necessary.

Project control involves assessing a project's progress against plans and taking corrective actions, if necessary, in order to bring the project on track. Forecasts of costs and completion time are generated using trend analysis to determine the need for action.

Project control also involves controlling the changes to a project, e.g., to the project's scope. Replanning is usually necessary, but it should be kept to a minimum. Changes to the project's scope should be tightly controlled. If acceptable to the project manager, a change to the scope should be formally verified (i.e., authorized by the customer/sponsor). A common problem is that the customer/sponsor tends to frequently demand changes to the work required. The problem of uncontrolled changes to the project's scope is called *scope creep*.

To control a project's cost and schedule, various measures are used. Work performance information includes the completed and uncompleted deliverables, ongoing and completed activities, percentage of each activity completed, costs authorized/incurred, cost estimates to project completion time, and so on.

A common technique used for cost control is *earned value analysis*. After a project's time and cost are planned (called schedule baseline and cost baseline or budget), the progress of the project is measured, not by the budgeted cost of work scheduled (BCWS; also known as planned value, PV), but by budgeted cost of work performed (BCWP; also known as earned value, EV). The scheduled time overrun is measured by schedule "variance" = PV − EV, and the cost overrun is measured by cost "variance" = actual cost − EV. See Figure 17-9 for an overbudget project that is also behind schedule. Also, forecasts of cost estimate to completion (ETC) and cost estimate at completion (EAC) are made.

---
[3] Eliyahu M. Goldratt, *Critical Chain*, Great Barrington, MA: North River Press, 1997, pp. 246.

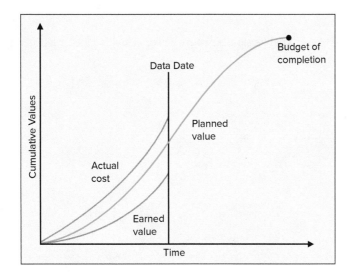

Cumulative cost values for a project that is over budget and behind schedule.

Quality control involves using quality tools such as control chart and cause and effect diagram in order to identify quality "variance," find its cause, and implement corrective actions.

The project team is managed by measuring team performance, providing feedback, resolving issues, and recognizing and rewarding good performance.

Software, e-mail, status review meetings, etc., are used to collect and report performance of project in the form of status reports, progress measurements, and forecasts. Communication with project stakeholders is managed by resolving issues promptly.

Risks are tracked and reassessed, and the response plans evaluated. Reserve analysis is performed to determine the adequacy of the contingency fund.

Contracts are managed by measuring the performance of suppliers, comparing them with the contract requirements, and taking corrective actions, if necessary. The relations with suppliers are managed by quickly resolving issues such as contested changes or late payments.

Finally, the project is completed and closed out. It is important to ensure that all contractors/teams have completed their work, and provided warranties/necessary paper works. Also, it is important to review the project for lessons learned and document these for future reference.

Project Management Software

Many project management software are available such as Microsoft Project and Deltek's (Welcom) EPM suite.

There are many advantages to using project management software. Among them are the following:

- It imposes a methodology and common project management terminology.
- It provides a logical planning structure.
- It enhances communication among team members.
- It flags the occurrence of a problem.
- It automatically formats reports.
- It generates multiple levels of summary reports and detailed reports.
- It enables "what-if" scenarios.
- It generates various charts, including basic schedule/control Gantt chart.

Using Microsoft® Project

Download a free 60-day Trial version of *Project Professional 2013*.[4] After registering, downloading, and installing the software, open it:

Next, enter the activity (or task) names and their duration. We will enter the data from Example 1. Click the cell under the Task Name and type in "Locate Facility," and press the Enter key. Continue entering the task names until all tasks are entered. Now, click on the cell below Duration and enter 8w (for 8 weeks), and press Enter. As you enter a duration, the Gantt chart on the right assigns a horizontal bar to the activity. Continue entering the durations until all durations are entered:

In order to see the whole Gantt chart, Click on the "View" tab on the top, then click "Entire Project." Note that the bars on the right and the pins under Task Mode are light blue. This indicates that the tasks are currently in Manually Scheduled Mode. This means that Microsoft Project will consider them as fixed tasks, and does not use them in its PERT/CPM solution method. We need

---

[4] http://www.microsoft.com/en-us/evalcenter/evaluate-project-professional-2013.

to change the Task Modes to Auto Scheduled by clicking on the cell to the left of each task name, then clicking on the blue arrow-down square, and finally clicking on the Auto Scheduled. As you do this, the colour of the pin and the bar on the right will change to dark blue. After all task modes have been changed to Auto Scheduled, the screen looks as follows. Note that in the present form, all the activities start the next day.

In order to enter the precedence relationships, click on the "Task" tab on the top, then select two activities with finish-start relationship (by keeping the control key pressed), and then clicking on the chain icon above the Schedule in the ribbon on the top to link the selected tasks. This will move the bar for the successor activity to the right of the bar for the Predecessor activity, and relate them with a short arrow. Continue with all the predecessor-successor pairs until all the precedence relationships have been specified. You can View to the Entire Project again to see the whole Gantt chart:

To see the precedence network, (in the "View" tab) click "Network diagram":

As you can see, the boxes for critical activities are pink.

Microsoft Project also permits us to define resources (i.e., employees and equipment) and to assign these to the activities. This is done by clicking on the "Resources" tab on the top. Also, Microsoft Project allows us to track the progress of activities. This is done by clicking on the "TASK" tab on the top, then on "Mark on Track," and finally "Update Tasks." As days pass, team members should enter the percentage of each activity completed. The software will indicate if any activity is behind schedule.

Deltek (Welcom)[5]

The Deltek (Welcom) Enterprise Project Management (EPM) software suite is an integrated toolset with modules supporting portfolio analysis, risk management, planning and scheduling, project collaboration, and complete earned value management. This modular, integrated toolset provides timely and selective information to all project participants from chief executives to project managers to team members.

Five products are included in the Deltek EPM suite: WelcomPortfolio™, WelcomRisk™, WelcomHome™, Open Plan®, and Cobra®. Each product can be used as standalone or configured in combination to meet customer requirements. The complete suite supports the full project life cycle from conception through to closure.

Deltek's WelcomPortfolio is a portfolio analysis tool that provides a structured approach to evaluating, selecting, and prioritizing projects so that resources are invested in the projects that best fit current business or organizational strategy. Scoring criteria such as net present value and return on investment are included in a library with the ability to edit or create new ones. Users can also utilize project risk scores generated in Deltek's WelcomRisk as additional scoring criteria.

Deltek's WelcomRisk is a risk management solution for the systematic identification, mitigation, and reporting of organizational and project risk on both threats and opportunities. Graphical reports allow executives to assess risk exposure across projects and track mitigation efforts. Project

---

[5] Courtesy of Deltek staff, 2006.

Typical project financial analysis with user-defined reporting criteria in WelcomPortfolio.

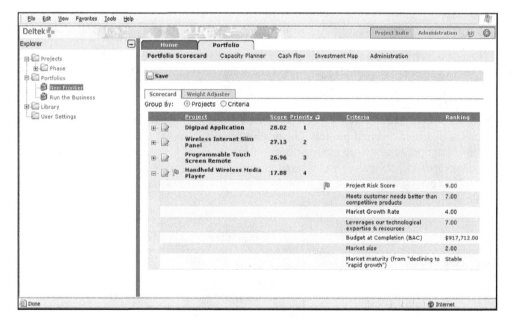

A typical portfolio of potential new projects with respective scores. Note the project risk score from Deltek's WelcomRisk is being used as a ranking criterion.

risks are identified, quantified, and tracked to minimize risk exposure. Team members play a collaborative role in identifying and mitigating risks using a formalized process.

WelcomRisk supports a typical five-step process to reduce risk. Risk planning is supported by identifying risk categories (i.e., development, production, technical, political), risk assessment is done by identifying impact types (on cost, quality, schedule, safety), the probability and severity impact of each risk, risk mitigation, and risk monitoring and control.

Risk planning involves determining a risk breakdown structure (also called a Risk Tree) and using it to calculate the risk of a project, working from bottom up using the risk scores. Risk assessment uses each risk, its cause, and potential consequences. The probability and impact severity is estimated and a risk score is generated for each risk event. The risk score is tracked over time and is expected to be reduced as a result of risk mitigation. Risk mitigation involves the steps to reduce the risk score. WelcomRisk has a library of generic response types, and can also recalculate the risk score given the mitigation steps undertaken. Risk Monitoring and Control uses reports such as Risk Tree and "waterfall" diagrams.

Typical risk tree (on the left) built from a project schedule with a corresponding matrix showing threats and opportunities on a project.

Deltek's Open Plan is an enterprise project management software that improves an organization's ability to complete multiple projects on time and on budget. Multiproject analysis, critical path planning, and resource management are supported.

Interproject constraints are easily modelled in Open Plan. Resource constraints and relationships can be created either at a high level between projects or at a more detailed level between specific activities in different projects. The relative priority of projects can be adjusted to ensure that important projects have access to resources first.

Deltek Open Plan's views can be tailored to create custom reports. For flexible program analysis, projects can be grouped into multi projects, with the ability for a project to belong to more than one multi project.

Open Plan's advanced Gantt chart view automatically shows constraining resources.

Typical Open Plan logic diagram (i.e., precedence network).

Deltek's Cobra is a robust cost management software for managing project costs, measuring earned value, and analyzing budgets, actual and forecast. Earned value is a means of putting a dollar value on project status. This allows managers to formulate a three-way comparison between budget, actual costs, and project status in order to evaluate the true health of each project. Simply analyzing budget versus actual costs often gives an incorrect picture of project status. For example, if a contract is 10 percent under budget, this might appear as if the contract is doing very well. Yet, when the project status or earned value is added to the analysis, it shows that only half of the originally planned work has been performed. Thus, the contract is behind schedule and the completed work has cost more than originally planned!

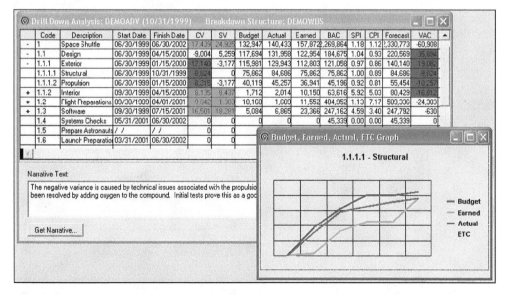

Cobra drill-down report highlights problem areas and an earned value curve.

Deltek's WelcomHome is a Web-based project management portal that provides all project participants with easy access to project information. It provides live access to schedules, budgets, action items, and project documents. WelcomHome also allows submission of progress and timesheet information using only a browser.

Graphical dashboards provide executives with high-level summaries at the program level. These views include cost, schedule, and outstanding item metrics in the form of bar charts, line graphs, and pie charts.

A customized project homepage in Deltek's WelcomHome.

Such instruments grouped together within a dashboard provide the user with an easy means of obtaining an overview of a project or program. Dashboards can also serve as an early warning system for potential problems (e.g., red, yellow, green indicators), helping busy executives make timely decisions and take corrective action. Each instrument can be expanded to show additional detailed metric information and can report at a project or program level.

Sample project metrics dashboard in WelcomHome.

Summary

- A project is a unique large one-time job requiring special activities by different people, established to realize a specific objective in a limited time span.
- Projects go through a life cycle that involves initiation, planning and scheduling, execution, control, and closeout.
- Most organizations are structured as a matrix, with members working for both projects and a functional department.
- A project manager is responsible for all project activities from inception to close-out, including meeting the project performance goals of being on time and within quality specifications and budget.
- Project planning involves finalizing the project scope, creating the work breakdown structure, risk management planning, scheduling, cost estimation and budgeting, and quality, communications, and purchase planning.
- Risk management planning involves risk identification, assessment, and response planning. Schedule/control Gantt charts are used to schedule simple projects.

- PERT/CPM is used to schedule complex projects. A precedence network depicts the sequential relationships that exist among activities. The solution reveals the longest (i.e., critical) path and the critical activities, i.e., those activities that must be completed on time to achieve timely project completion.
- For projects with variable activity durations, the 3-point estimates method can be used.
- It may be possible to shorten, or crash, the length of a project by shortening one or more of the critical activities. Typically, such gains are achieved by the use of additional resources, but the shortening will save indirect project costs.
- Project execution involves putting the project plans into action, buying materials and assigning team members, or subcontracting the work.
- Project control means taking measurements of project performance and taking corrective action if necessary. Microsoft Project and Deltek's (Welcom) EPM suite are two widely used types of project management software.

Key Terms

3-point estimates method
activity-on-arrow (AOA)
activity-on-node (AON)
Beta distribution
CPM
critical activities
critical path
deterministic durations
matrix organization

most likely duration
optimistic duration
path
path slack time
performance goals
PERT
pessimistic duration
precedence network
probabilistic durations

project
project control
project execution
project manager
project planning
project scheduling
work breakdown structure (WBS)

Solved Problems

Problem 1

The following list contains information related to the major activities of a research project. Use the information given to do the following:

a. Draw the precedence network.

b. Find the critical path by identifying all the start-to-end paths and calculating their lengths.

c. What is the expected duration of the project?

Activity	Immediately Precedes	Expected Duration (days)
a	c, b	5
c	d	8
d	i	2
b	i	7
e	f	3
f	m	6
i	m	10
m	End	8
g	h	1
h	k	2
k	End	17

Solution

a. In constructing precedence networks, these observations can be useful.

    i. Use pencil.

    ii. Start and end with a single node.

    iii. Try to avoid having paths cross each other.

    iv. Have arrows go from left to right.

    v. Activities with no predecessors are at the beginning (left side) of the network, immediately after the start node S.

    vi. Activities with multiple predecessors are located at path intersections.

    vii. Go down the activity list in order to avoid overlooking any activities.

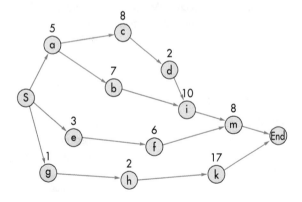

b. and c.

Path	Length (days)
s-a-c-d-i-m-End*	$5 + 8 + 2 + 10 + 8 = 33^\dagger$
s-a-b-i-m-End	$5 + 7 + 10 + 8 = 30$
s-e-f-m-End	$3 + 6 + 8 = 17$
s-g-h-k-End	$1 + 2 + 17 = 20$

* Critical path.
† Expected project duration.

Problem 2

Using the PERT/CPM solution technique, determine the ES, EF, LF, LS, and slack times for each activity in the following precedence network (durations are in days). Identify the activities that are on the critical path.

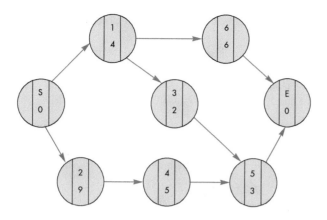

Solution

We will determine and place the ES, EF, LS, and LF times for each activity in its circle as follows:

We determine the earliest start and finish times, working from left to right, as shown in the following network. The explanations follow.

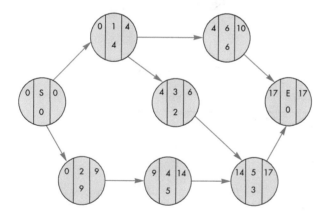

ES for the start node S is 0, by our convention. EF = ES + t = 0 + 0 = 0 for S. Then, activity 1 can start at 0 (i.e., its ES = 0). With a duration of 4 days, it can finish after 0 + 4 = 4 days (i.e., its EF = 4). Hence, activity 6 and 3 can start no earlier than day 4 (i.e., their ES = 4). Activity 6 has earliest finish of 4 + 6 = 10 days, and activity 3 has the earliest finish of 4 + 2 = 6 days. At this point, it is impossible to say what the earliest start is for activity 5; that will depend on which activity, 4 or 3, has the larger EF. Consequently, it is necessary to first calculate ES and EF along the lower path. Using an ES of 0 for activity 2, its EF will be 9, so activity 4 will have an ES of 9 and an EF of 9 + 5 = 14.

Considering that the two activities immediately preceding node 5 have EF times of 6 and 14, the earliest that activity 5 can start is the *larger* of these, which is 14. Hence, activity 5 has an EF of 14 + 3 = 17.

Now compare the EFs of the activities immediately preceding the End node. The larger of these, 17, is the ES_{End}, and EF_{End} = 17 + 0 = 17. This is also the expected project duration.

The LF and LS times for each activity can now be determined by working backward through the network (from right to left; see the following network). The LF for the End node is 17–the project duration. Then, $LS_{End} = LF_{End} - 0 = 17 - 0 = 17$.

Now, $LF_6 = LF_5 = LS_{End} = 17$. In the case of activity 5, the LS necessary for an LF of 17 is 17 − 3 = 14. This means that both activities 3 and 4 must finish no later than 14 days. Hence, their LF are 14. Activity 4 has an LS of $14 - 5 = 9$, making the LF of activity 2 equal to 9, and its LS equal to $9 - 9 = 0$.

Activity 3, with an LF of 14, has an LS of $14 - 2 = 12$. Activity 6 has an LF of 17 and therefore an LS of $17 - 6 = 11$. Since activity 1 precedes *both* of these activities, it can finish no later than the *smaller* of 11 and 12, which is 11. Hence, activity 1 has an LS of $11 - 4 = 7$.

Finally, LF of S is the smaller of LS of activities 1 and 2, which is min $(7, 0) = 0$. Hence, LS of S is $0 - 0 = 0$.

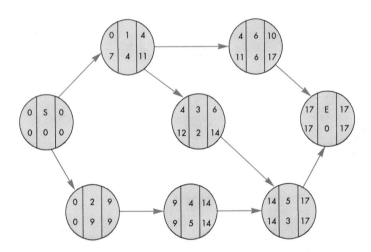

The slack time for an activity is the difference between either LF and EF or LS and ES. Thus,

Activity	LS	ES	Slack	or	LF	EF	Slack
S	0	0	0		0	0	0
1	7	0	7		11	4	7
6	11	4	7		17	10	7
3	12	4	8		14	6	8
2	0	0	0		9	9	0
4	9	9	0		14	14	0
5	14	14	0		17	17	0
E	0	0	0		0	0	0

The activities with zero slack times indicate the critical path. In this case the critical path is S-2-4-5-E.

When working on problems of this nature, keep in mind the following:

a. The ES time for a node with multiple immediate predecessors is the largest EF of the immediate predecessors.

b. The LF for a node with multiple immediate successors is the smallest LS of the immediate successors.

Problem 3

Expected durations (in weeks) and variances for the major activities of an R&D project are depicted on the following precedence network. Determine the probability that the project completion time will be:

a. Less than 50 weeks.

b. More than 50 weeks.

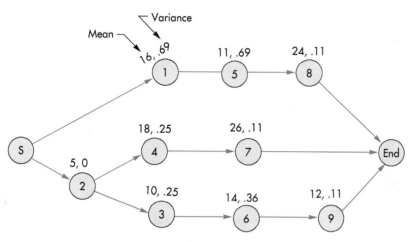

Solution

Because S and End have zero duration, we can ignore them in the following calculations. The mean and standard deviation for each path are:

Path	Expected Time (weeks)	Standard Deviation (weeks)
S-1-5-8-End	16 + 11 + 24 = 51	$\sqrt{.69 + .69 + .11} = 1.22$
S-2-4-7-End	5 + 18 + 26 = 49	$\sqrt{.00 + .25 + .11} = 0.60$
S-2-3-6-9-End	5 + 10 + 14 + 12 = 41	$\sqrt{.00 + .25 + .36 + .11} = 0.60$

a. Calculate the *z* value for each path for the length specified. Use:

$$z = \frac{50 - t_{path}}{\sigma_{path}}$$

The probability that each path will be completed in 50 weeks or less is shown on the following charts (probabilities are from Appendix B, Table B.) The probability that the project will be completed in 50 weeks or less depends on all three paths being completed in that time. Because *z* for path S-2-3-6-9-End is greater than +3.50, it is treated as having a probability of completion in 50 weeks of 1.00. The probability that *both* other paths will not exceed 50 weeks is the *product* of their individual probabilities of completion within 50 weeks. Thus, .2061(.9525) = .1963.

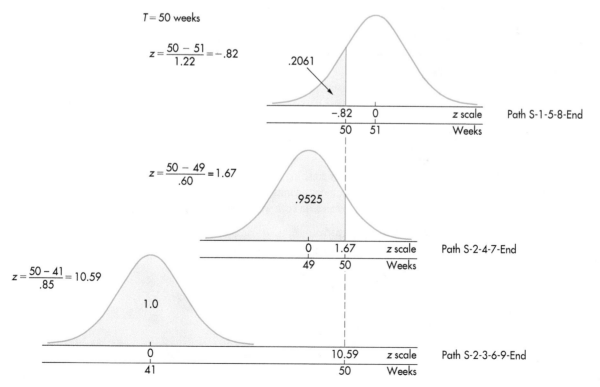

b. The probability that the project will exceed 50 weeks is the complement of this number, which is 1.000 − .1963 = .8037. (Note that this is not the product of the path probabilities of exceeding 50 weeks.)

Problem 4

Indirect cost for a project is $12,000 per week for as long as the project lasts. The project manager has supplied the crash cost and potential information and precedence network shown below. Use the information to:

a. Determine an optimum crashing plan.

b. Graph the total costs for the plan.

Activity	Crashing Potential (weeks)	Cost per Week to Crash
a	3	$11,000
b	3	3,000 first week, $4,000 after that
c	2	6,000
d	1	1,000
e	3	6,000
f	1	2,000

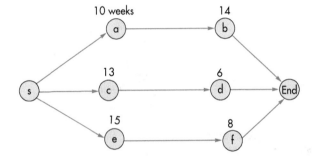

Solution

a. i. Calculate path lengths and identify the critical path:

Path	Duration (weeks)
s-a-b-End	24 (critical path)
s-c-d-End	19
s-e-f-End	23

ii. Rank critical activities according to crash costs:

Activity	Cost per Week to Crash	Available Weeks to Crash
b	$3,000 first week, $4,000 after that	3
a	11,000	3

Activity *b* should be shortened one week since it has the lower crashing cost per week. This would reduce indirect costs by $12,000 at a direct cost of $3,000, for a net savings of $9,000. At this point, paths s-a-b-End and s-e-f-End would both have length of 23 weeks, so both would be critical.

iii. Rank activities by crashing cost on the two critical paths:

Path	Activity	Cost per Week to Crash	Available Weeks to Crash
s-a-b-End	b	$4,000	2
. . . .	a	11,000	3
s-e-f-End	f	2,000	1
. . . .	e	6,000	3

Choose one activity (the least costly) on each path to crash: *b* on s-a-b-End and *f* on s-e-f-End, for a total cost of $4,000 + $2,000 = $6,000 and a net savings of $12,000 − $6,000 = $6,000. *Note:* There is no activity common to the two critical paths.

    iv. Check to see which path(s) might be critical: s-a-b-End and s-e-f-End would be 22 weeks in length, and s-c-d-End would still be 19 weeks.

    v. Rank activities on the critical paths:

Path	Activity	Cost per Week to Crash	Available Weeks to Crash
s-a-b-End	b	$4,000	1
. . . .	a	11,000	3
s-e-f-End	e	6,000	3
. . . .	f	(no further crashing possible)	0

Crash *b* on path s-a-b-End and *e* on path s-e-f-End one week each for a cost of $4,000 + $6,000 = $10,000, for a net savings of $12,000 − $10,000 = $2,000.

    vi. At this point, no further reduction is cost-effective: paths s-a-b-End and s-e-f-End would be 21 weeks in length, and one activity from each path would have to be shortened. This would mean activity a at $11,000 and e at $6,000 for a total of $17,000, which exceeds the $12,000 potential savings in indirect costs. Note that no further crashing for activity (b) is possible.

b. The following table summarizes the results, showing the length of the project after crashing *n* weeks:

Path	n = 0	1	2	3
s-a-b-End	24	23	22	21
s-c-d-End	19	19	19	19
s-e-f-End	23	23	22	21
Project crashed		b	b, f	b, e
Crashing costs ($000)		3	6	10

A summary of costs for the preceding schedule would look like this:

Project Length	Weeks Shortened	Cumulative Crashing Costs ($000)	Cumulative Indirect Costs ($000)	Total Costs ($000)
24	0	0	24(12) = 288	288
23	1	3	23(12) = 276	279
22	2	3 + 6 = 9	22(12) = 264	273
21	3	9 + 10 = 19	21(12) = 252	271
20	4	19 + 17 = 36	20(12) = 240	276

The graph of total cost is as follows.

Discussion and Review Questions

1. What are the phases of a project? **LO1**
2. Explain the difference between matrix and project organization. **LO1**
3. How should a company select its projects? **LO1**
4. What skills would a project manager need? **LO1**
5. What are some aspects of the project manager's job that make it more demanding than the job of a manager working in a more routine organizational framework? **LO1**
6. What does project planning involve? **LO2**
7. List the steps in risk management planning. **LO2**
8. What is a work breakdown structure, and how is it useful for project planning? **LO2**
9. What are some of the reasons an activity might take longer than expected? **LO2**
10. Compare a schedule/control Gantt chart and a precedence network. **LO3**
11. Identify the term used for each of the following:
    a. A sequence of activities in a project. **LO3**
    b. The longest sequence of activities in a project. **LO3**
    c. The technique used for probabilistic activity durations. **LO5**
    d. The difference in length of time of any path and the critical path. **LO4**
    e. The statistical distribution used to describe variability of an activity's duration. **LO5**
    f. The statistical distribution used to describe variability of project duration. **LO5**
    g. Shortening an activity by allocating additional resources. **LO6**
12. What are ES, EF, LF, and LS, and how are they calculated? **LO4**
13. What is a critical activity? **LO4**
14. Why might a probabilistic estimate of a project's completion time based solely on the variance of the *critical path* derived using the expected activity durations be misleading? Under what circumstances would it be acceptable? **LO5**
15. Define each of these terms used in the 3-point estimates method, and indicate how each is determined. **LO5**
    a. Expected activity duration.
    b. Variance of an activity duration.
    c. Standard deviation of a path's duration.
16. Describe the procedure for project crashing. **LO6**
17. Describe project execution. **LO7**
18. What is the critical chain method? **LO7**
19. What does project control involve? **LO7**
20. What is earned value analysis? **LO7**
21. How can Microsoft Project help to manage a project? **LO8**

Taking Stock

1. What trade-offs are associated with duration and cost of an activity? **LO6**
2. Who needs to be involved in project management? **LO1**
3. Explain briefly how Deltek's (Welcom) EPM software suite assists in project management. **LO8**

Critical Thinking Exercise

Project management techniques have been used successfully for a wide variety of projects, including the many NASA space missions, huge construction projects, implementation of major systems such as an ERP, production of movies, development of new goods and services, theatrical productions, and much more. Why not use them for managing the operations function of any business? **LO1**

Experiential Learning Exercise

Select a project you are currently working on, or one that you have recently worked on. **LO1**

a. List the project objective.
b. List the main activities.

c. List the project milestones, such as required progress reports or the completion of major tasks.

d. How important are (were) behavioural aspects of the project? For example, did the project team agree on project objective, individual work assignments, and so on?

e. Were there any unforeseen problems? If so, how were they resolved?

Internet Exercises

1. Visit http://www.taskcm.com/what-we-do and summarize what fast track scheduling is. **LO1 & 6**

2. Visit http://www.deltek.com, select customer successes under resource centre, choose a customer, and briefly summarize the benefits of using the software for the customer. **LO8**

3. Visit one of the following sites, choose a customer, and briefly summarize the benefits of the project (portfolio) management software to the customer: **LO8**

a. http://www.innotas.com/customers-case-studies.
b. http://www.amsrealtime.com/customers/clients.htm.

4. Visit http://mmmgrouplimited.com/careers/opportunities, choose Career Area = Project Management, and summarize the duties of a project manager in the MMM group. **LO1**

5. Visit http://www.stantec.com/default.htm, click on a Feature Project photo, click on "more information . . ." and summarize Stantec's project management role. **LO1**

Problems

1. For each of the following precedence networks, determine the critical path and the project duration by determining the length of each path. The numbers above the nodes represent activity durations (in days). **LO4**

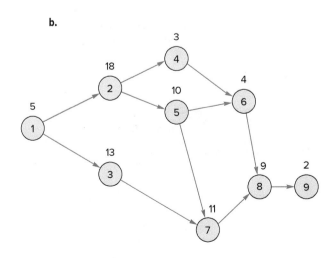

a.

b.

c.

2. Claire received a new word-processing software program for her birthday. She also received a cheque with which she intends to purchase a new computer. Claire's university instructor assigned a paper due next week. Claire decided that she will prepare the paper on the new computer. She made a list of the activities and their estimated durations. Claire's friend has offered to shop for, select, and purchase a computer, and install the software. **LO3 & 4**

a. Arrange the activities into two logical sequences.
b. Construct a precedence network.
c. Determine the critical path by determining the length of each path. What is the expected duration of the project?
d. What are some possible reasons for the project to take longer than expected?

Estimated Time (hours)	Activity (abbreviation)
.8	Install software (Install)
.4	Outline the paper (Outline)
.2	Submit paper to instructor (Submit)
.6	Choose a topic (Choose)
.5	Use a grammar-checker and make corrections (Check)
3.0	Write the paper using the word-processing software (Write)
2.0	Shop for a new computer (Shop)
1.0	Select and purchase a computer (Select)
2.0	Library research on chosen topic (Library)

3. The following information pertains to a project that is about to commence. Which activities would you be concerned with in terms of timely project completion? Explain. *Hint:* Determine the length of each path. **LO3 & 4**

Activity	Precedes	Estimated Duration (days)
A.................	B	15
B	C, D	12
C.................	E	6
D.................	End	5
E.................	End	3
F	G, H	8
G.................	I	8
H.................	J	9
I.................	End	7
J.................	K	14
K	End	6

4. Construct a precedence network for each of the following two projects. **LO3**

(1) Activity	Precedes Activity	(2) Activity	Precedes Activity
A	D	J	L, N
B	E, F	K	R
C	G	L	M
D	K	M	End
E	K	N	P
F	H, I	P	End
G	I	Q	S, T
H	End	R	V
I	End	S	V
K	End	V	End
		T	V, W
		W	End

5. For each of the problems listed below, determine the following values for each activity: the earliest start time, earliest finish time, latest finish time, latest start time, and activity slack time. Identify the critical activities, and determine the duration of the project. **LO4**

a. Problem 1*a*.
b. Problem 1*b*.
c. Problem 3.

6. Reconsider the precedence network of Problem 1a. Suppose that after 12 days, activities 1, 9, and 2 have been finished; activity 3 is 75 percent finished; and activity 10 is half finished. How many days after the original start time would the project finish? **LO4**

7. Three recent university graduates have formed a partnership and have opened an advertising firm. Their first project consists of activities listed in the following table. **LO5**

a. Draw the precedence network.
b. What is the probability that the project can be completed in 24 days or less? In 21 days or less?
c. Suppose that now is the end of the seventh day and that activities a and b have been completed while activity d is 50 percent completed. Three-point estimates for the remaining duration of activity d are now 5, 6, and 7 days. Activities c and h are ready to begin. Determine the probability of finishing the project by the end of (a) day 24 and (b) day 21.

Activity	Precedes	Duration in Days Optimistic	Most Likely	Pessimistic
a........	c	5	6	7
b........	h	8	8	11
c........	e	6	8	11
d........	f	9	12	15
e........	End	5	6	9
f........	g	5	6	7
g........	End	2	3	7
h........	i	4	4	5
i........	End	5	7	8

8. The new director of special events at a large university has decided to completely revamp the graduation ceremonies. Toward that end, a precedence network of the major activities has been developed. The network has five paths with expected durations and variances as shown in the following table. Graduation day is 16 full weeks from now. Assuming that the project begins now, what is the probability that the project will be completed before: **LO5**

a. Graduation day?
b. The end of week 15?
c. The end of week 13?

Path	Expected Duration (weeks)	Variance
A..........	10	1.21
B..........	8	2.00
C..........	12	1.00
D.........	15	2.89
E.........	14	1.44

9. Construct a precedence network for the information in the following table. What is the probability that a project will take more than 10 weeks to complete if the activity means and standard deviations (both in weeks) are as follows? **LO5**

Activity	Precedes	Mean	Standard Deviation
a	b	5	1.3
b	End	4	1.0
c	End	8	1.6

10. The project described in the following table is scheduled to be completed in 11 weeks. **LO6**

   a. Draw the precedence network.
   b. If you were the manager of this project, would you be concerned? Explain.
   c. If there is a penalty of $5,000 a week for each week the project is late, what is the probability of incurring a penalty of at least $5,000?

Activity	Precedes	Expected Duration (weeks)	Standard Deviation (weeks)
a	b	4	.70
b	End	6	.90
c	d	3	.62
d	End	9	1.90

11. The following precedence network displays the 3-point estimates for each activity of a project. Determine: **LO5**

   a. The expected duration for each path and its variance.
   b. The probability that the project will require more than 49 weeks.
   c. The probability that the project can be completed in 46 weeks or less.

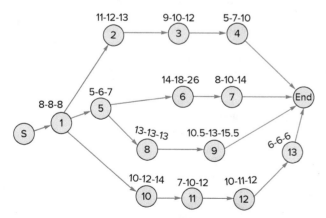

12. A project manager has compiled a list of major activities that will be required to install a computer information system in her company. The list includes 3-point estimates of durations (optimistic, most likely, pessimistic) for activities and the precedence relationships. **LO5**

Activity	Precedes	3-Point Estimates (weeks)
a	d, f	2-4-6
d	e	6-8-10
e	h	7-9-12
h	End	2-3-5
f	g	3-4-8
g	End	5-7-9
b	i	2-2-3
i	j	2-3-6
j	k	3-4-5
k	End	4-5-8
c	m	5-8-12
m	n	1-1-1
n	o	6-7-11
o	End	8-9-13

If the project is finished within 26 weeks of its start, the project manager will receive a bonus of $1,000; and if the project is finished within 27 weeks of its start, the bonus will be $500. Find the probability of each bonus.

13. The project manager of the construction of a domed stadium had hoped to be able to complete the construction prior to the start of the next season. After reviewing the activity duration estimates, it now appears that a certain amount of crashing will be needed to ensure project completion before the season opener. Given the following information, determine the minimum-cost crashing schedule that will shave five weeks off the project length. **LO6**

Activity	Precedes	Normal Duration (weeks)	Crashing Costs First Week	Crashing Costs Second Week
A	B	12	$15,000	$20,000
B	K	14	10,000	10,000
C	D, E, F	10	5,000	5,000
D	G	17	20,000	21,000
E	H	18	16,000	18,000
F	I	12	12,000	15,000
G	M	15	24,000	24,000
H	N, P	8	–	–
I	J	7	30,000	–
J	P	12	25,000	25,000
K	End	9	10,000	10,000
M	End	3	–	–
N	End	11	40,000	–
P	End	8	20,000	20,000

14. A construction project has indirect costs totalling $40,000 per week. Major activities in the project and their expected durations are shown in the following precedence network: **LO6**

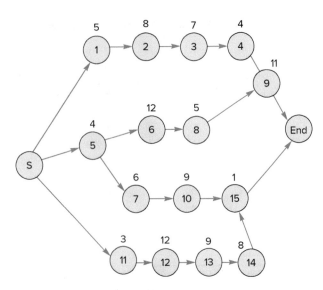

Crashing costs for each activity are:

Crashing Costs ($000)

Activity	First Week	Second Week	Third Week
1..........	$18	$22	$–
2..........	24	25	25
3..........	30	30	35
4..........	15	20	–
9..........	30	33	36
5..........	12	24	26
6..........	–	–	–
8..........	40	40	40
7..........	3	10	12
10..........	2	7	10
15..........	26	–	–
11..........	10	15	25
12..........	8	13	–
13..........	5	12	–
14..........	14	15	–

a. Determine the minimum-cost crashing plan that will take off six weeks from the project duration.

b. Plot the total cost curve against project duration. What is the optimum number of weeks to crash the project?

15. A company builds custom equipment. It has landed a contract with a major customer. Relevant data are shown below. The complication is that the delivery has been promised in 32 weeks and the company will have to pay a penalty of $375 for each week the equipment is late. **LO6**

Activity	Precedes	Normal Duration (weeks)	Crashing Costs 1st Week	Crashing Costs 2nd Week
K	L, N	9	$410	$415
L	M	7	125	–
N	J	5	45	45
M	Q	4	300	350
J	Q	6	50	–
Q	P, Y	5	200	225
P	Z	8	–	–
Y	End	7	85	90
Z	End	6	90	–

Develop the minimum cost crashing schedule.

16. The following is the list of activities, their immediate predecessor(s), and their expected duration used by a component supplier to automobile manufacturers to plan for QS 9000 (the auto industry version of ISO 9000) certification (registration).[6] **LO4**

The List of Activities in a QS-9000 Registration Project

Activity	Description	Immediate Predecessor(s)	Estimated Time (weeks)*
A	Appointment of QS-9000 taskforce	None	1
B	Preparation of a feasible plan	A	1
C	Delegation of responsibilities	B	1
D	Searching for a QS-9000 registrar	C	1
E	Preparation of three levels of documentation	C	12
F	QS-9000 awareness training	C	6
G	QS-9000 training of auditors and quality personnel	F	6
H	Preparing the plant for QS-9000 registrar	C	24
I	Conference with lead auditor	D	1
J	Examination of documentation	E, I	3
K	Internal audit of plant sections	G, H, J	12
L	Corrective actions of plant sections	K	12
M	Lead auditor and audit team audit plant	L	1

(continued)

[6] J. K. Bandyopadhyay, "The CPM/PERT Project Scheduling Approach to QS-9000 Registration: A Case Study at a United States Auto Parts Company," *International Journal of Management* 19(3), September 2002, pp. 455–463.

Activity	Description	Immediate Predecessor(s)	Estimated Time (weeks)*
N	Audit conference and corrective action plan	M	2
O	Implementation of corrective action plans	N	12
P	Lead auditor re-audits corrective actions	O	2
Q	Lead auditor's recommendation	P	1

* These are estimates of time and may vary based upon situation, company, and registrar.

a. Draw the precedence network.
b. Determine the earliest and latest times, and identify the critical activities and the project duration.

17. Use the following activities and their three duration estimates (in days) to do the following: **L05**

a. Determine the expected duration of the project.
b. Calculate the probability that the project will take at least 18 days.

Path	Activity	Durations		
		t_o	t_m	t_p
	a	4	5	6
a-b-c	b	7	8	10
	c	3	5	9
	d	7	8	11
d-e-f	e	2	3	4
	f	1	4	6

18. Consider the construction of a research building for Eli Lilly & Co., a pharmaceutical company, a few years ago. This 550,000 ft², 4-story (in 3 wings), $135 million building was planned to be completed in five years. It required special ventilation for 162 labs, purified water, and special drainage. Consider the following list of major activities/work packages (as seen by Eli Lilly), their expected duration, and their relationship to other activities/work packages for the Eli Lilly building. **L04**

Activity	Duration (in months)	Immediate Predecessor
A. project approval	3	—
B. decide general requirements	6	A
C. choose A/E firm	2	A
D. preliminary design	3	B, C
E. choose project management firm	2	B
F. decide detailed requirements	6	D, E
G. finalize design	6	F

Activity	Duration (in months)	Immediate Predecessor
H. schedule, budget, manual	4	F
I. start bid packages	2	G, H
J. excavate, foundation, steel structure	10	I
K. put up enclosures	7	J
L. HVAC, fire protection, plumbing	6	J
M. Electrical	5	J
N. Interior finishes	12	K, L, M
O. close out project	2	N

a. Draw the precedence network.
b. Determine the ES, EF, LF, and LS times.
c. What is the project duration?
d. What are the critical activities?

*19. A project consists of the following activities, normal durations (days), immediate predecessors, cost per day to crash ($000/day), and available days to crash.[7] **L06**

Activity	Normal Duration (days)	Immediate Predecessor(s)	Cost per Day to Crash ($000/day)	Available Days to Crash
A	8	—	9	5
B	8	—	2	4
C	6	—	4	3
D	9	A	6	7
E	20	A	3	7
F	11	B, D	1	5
G	9	B, D	7	5
H	12	C, G	8	7

a. Draw the precedence network.
b. Calculate the project duration using normal activity durations.
c. Determine the minimum-cost crashing plan that will take 16 days off the project duration.

20. Here is a list of activity times for a project as well as crashing costs for its activities. Determine the minimum-cost crashing if the goal is to shorten the project by three weeks. First construct a precedence network. **L06**

Activity	Precedes	Normal Duration (weeks)	Crashing Costs ($000)	
			1st Week	2nd Week
A	B	5	$8	$10
B	C	6	7	9
C	End	3	14	15
D	E	3	9	11
E	C	7	8	9
F	G	5	10	15
G	H	5	11	13
H	End	5	12	14

---

[7] N. Siemens, "A Simple CPM Time-cost Tradeoff Algorithm," *Management Science*, February 1971, 17(6), pp. B354–363.

MINI-CASE

Time, Please

"Smitty" Smith is a project manager for a large consumer electronics corporation. Although she has been with the company only four years, she has demonstrated an uncanny ability to bring projects in on time, meet technical specifications, and be close to budget.

Her latest assignment is a project that will involve merging two existing technologies. She and her team have almost finished developing the proposal that will be presented to a management committee for approval. All that remains to be done is to determine a duration estimate for the project. Smitty wants an estimated duration that will have a 95 percent probability of being met. The team has constructed a precedence network for the project. It has three paths. The expected durations and standard deviations for the paths are listed below.

Path	Expected Duration (weeks)	Standard Deviation (weeks)
A	10	4
B	14	2
C	13	2

Question

What project duration (in weeks) should Smitty include in the proposal?

CASE

Fantasy Products

Company Background

The Fantasy Products Company (disguised name) is a manufacturer of high-quality small appliances intended for home use. The company's current product line includes irons, a small hand-held vacuum, and a number of kitchen appliances such as toasters, blenders, waffle irons, and coffeemakers. Fantasy Products has a strong R&D department that continually searches for ways to improve existing products as well as developing new ones.

Currently, the R&D department is working on the development of a new kitchen appliance that will chill foods quickly much as a microwave oven heats them quickly, although the technology involved is quite different. Tentatively named The Big Chill, the product will initially carry a price tag of around $125, and the target market consists of upper-income consumers. At this price, it is expected to be a very profitable item. R&D engineers now have a working prototype and are satisfied that, with the cooperation from the production and marketing people, the product can be ready in time for the all-important Christmas buying season. A target date has been set for product introduction that is 24 weeks away.

Current Problem

Fantasy Products' Marketing Vice-President Vera Sloan has recently learned from reliable sources that a competitor is also in the process of developing a similar product, which it intends to bring out at almost the same time. In addition, her source indicated that the competitor plans to sell its product, which will be smaller than The Big Chill, for $99 in the hope of appealing to more customers. With the help of several of her key people who are to be involved in marketing The Big Chill, Vera has decided that in order to compete, the selling price for The Big Chill will have to be lowered to within $10 of the competitor's price. At this price level, it will still be profitable, although not nearly as profitable as originally anticipated.

However, Vera is wondering whether it would be possible to expedite the product introduction process in order to beat the competition to the market. If possible, she would like to get a six-week jump on the competition; this would put the product introduction date only 18 weeks away. During this initial period, Fantasy Products could sell The Big Chill for $125, reducing the selling price to $109 when the competitor's product actually enters the market. Since forecasts based on market research show that sales during the first six weeks will be about 400 units per week, there is an opportunity for $25 per unit profit if the early introduction can be accomplished. In addition, there is prestige involved in being first to the market. This should help enhance The Big Chill's image during the anticipated battle for market share.

Data Collection

Since Fantasy Products has been through the product-introduction process a number of times, Vera has developed a list of the tasks that must be accomplished and the order in which they must be completed. Although the duration and costs vary depending on the particular product, the basic process does not. The list of activities involved in product introduction and their precedence relationships are presented in Table 1. Duration and cost estimates for the introduction of The Big Chill are presented in Table 2. Note that some of the activities can be completed on a crash basis, with an associated increase in cost. For example, activity B can be crashed from 8 weeks to 6 weeks at an additional cost of $3,000 (i.e., $12,000 − $9,000). Assume that if B is crashed to 7 weeks, the additional cost will be $1,500 (i.e., $3,000/2).

Table 1 List of activities involved in product introduction and precedence relationships.

Activity	Description	Immediate Predecessor(s)
A	Select and order production equipment	—
B	Receive production equipment from supplier	A
C	Install and set up production equipment	B
D	Finalize bill of material	—
E	Order parts	D
F	Receive parts	E
G	First production run	C, F
H	Finalize marketing plan	—
I	Produce magazine ads	H
J	Script for TV ads	H
K	Produce TV ads	J
L	Begin ad campaign	I, K
M	Ship product to consumers	G, L

Table 2 Duration and cost estimates for introduction of The Big Chill.

Activity	Normal Duration (weeks)	Normal Cost	Crash Duration (weeks)	Normal & Crash Cost
A	3	$2,000	2	$4,400
B	8	9,000	6	12,000
C	4	2,000	2	7,000
D	2	1,000	1	2,000
E	2	2,000	1	3,000
F	5	0	5	0
G	6	12,000	3	24,000
H	4	3,500	2	8,000
I	4	5,000	3	8,000
J	3	8,000	2	15,000
K	4	50,000	3	70,000
L	6	10,000	6	10,000
M	1	5,000	1	5,000

Fantasy Products needs to decide whether to bring The Big Chill to market 18 weeks from now, as Vera Sloan is recommending. As the project management specialist in the R&D department, you have been asked to answer the following questions:

Questions

1. When would the project be completed using the normal durations?

2. Is it possible to complete the project in 18 weeks? What would be the associated additional cost? Which activities would need to be completed on a crash basis?

3. Is there some time frame shorter than the 18 weeks Vera has recommended that would make more sense in terms of profits?

Source: Adapted from an original case by R. J. Thieraus, M. Cunningham, and M. Blackwell, Xavier University, Cincinnati, Ohio.

CHAPTER 18
Waiting-Line Analysis

The chapter in this part covers the analysis of waiting lines. The occurrence of waiting lines in services indicates a temporary imbalance between demand and capacity. Waiting-line analysis can help managers reduce the impact of waiting lines on costs and effectiveness (i.e., customer service).

Learning Objectives

After completing this chapter, you should be able to:

LO1 Explain why waiting lines form, identify the goal of queuing (waiting-line) analysis, explain how waiting line models are used in bank teller staffing, and discuss how to deal with the perception of waiting.

LO2 Describe the system characteristics and measures of performance used in queuing.

LO3 List and distinguish among the queuing models studied in this chapter and understand and use some basic queuing relationships.

LO4 Discuss and use the single-server queuing models presented.

LO5 Discuss and use the multiple-server queueing models presented.

LO6 Discuss and use the finite-source queuing model presented.

The mission of Walt Disney theme parks is to "make people happy," and the folks at Disney World in Orlando are masters at doing that. They realize that waiting in lines at attractions does not add to the enjoyment of their customers. They also realize that customers waiting in lines are not generating the revenue that they would if they visited restaurants and souvenir shops. Hence, they have several reasons for wanting to reduce waiting times.

Walt Disney theme parks are leaders in effectively managing waiting lines. Disney analysts are so good that they present seminars to other companies on managing waiting lines. Their success can serve as a benchmark and provide valuable insights for a wide range of services.

Disney's methods are particularly relevant when circumstances make it impossible to quickly add capacity to alleviate waiting times. Here are some of the tactics Disney employs to achieve customer satisfaction:

- *Provide distractions.* Disney characters may entertain customers, videos provide safety information and build anticipation for the event, vendors move along some lines selling food and drinks, and other vendors sell souvenirs.

- *Provide alternatives to waiting in line.* Disney offers the "FastPass," which allows customers to reserve a time later in the day for a popular ride when they will be allowed to bypass the regular waiting line. Only one Fastpass is issued to a person at any time.

- *Keep customers informed.* Signs are clearly posted that give approximate waiting times from that point on, allowing the customers to make a decision on whether or not to join the line or not.

- *Exceed expectations.* Wait times are usually shorter than the posted times, thereby exceeding customers' expectations.

- *Other tactics.* Disney maintains a comfortable waiting environment: Waiting lines are often inside, protected from weather. Lines are kept moving, giving the impression of making progress.

This chapter will teach you how to manage waiting lines.

Source: Based in part on "Queuing: Featuring Disney World," McGraw-Hill Irwin OM Video Series.

Waiting Lines

Waiting lines occur when there is a temporary imbalance between supply (capacity) and demand. Waiting lines add to the cost of operation and they reflect negatively on customer service, so it is important to balance the cost of having customers wait with the cost of providing service capacity. Customer waiting lines occur when there is too little capacity to handle demand, but having more capacity than what is needed to handle demand means that there is idle (unproductive) capacity. From a managerial perspective, the key is to determine the balance that will provide an adequate level of service at a reasonable cost.

Those waiting in line would all agree that the solution to the problem is obvious: simply add more servers or do something to speed up service. Although both ideas may be potential solutions, there are certain subtleties that must be dealt with. For one thing, most service systems have the capacity to process customers over the long run. Hence, the problem of customers waiting is a short-term phenomenon. And at certain times the servers are idle, waiting for customers. Thus, by increasing the service capacity, the server idle time would increase even more. Consequently, in designing service systems, the designer must weigh the cost of providing a given level of service capacity against the cost of having customers wait for service. This planning and analysis of service capacity frequently lends itself to **queuing theory**, which is a mathematical approach for the analysis of waiting lines.

The modern queuing theory is based on studies about automatic dialing equipment made in the early part of the last century by Danish telephone engineer A. K. Erlang. Prior to the Second World War, very few attempts were made to apply queuing theory to operations. Since then, queuing theory has been applied to a range of operations problems.

The mathematics of queuing theory can be complex; for that reason, the emphasis here will not be on the mathematics but on the use of formulas and tables for analysis.

Waiting lines are commonly found wherever customers arrive randomly for a service. Some examples of waiting lines we encounter in our daily lives include the line at the supermarket

queuing theory
Mathematical approach to the analysis of waiting lines.

checkout, fast-food restaurant, hospital emergency department, college and university registration, airport check-in counter, movie theatre/concert, post office, call centre, government services, and the bank. In many situations, the "customers" are not people but orders waiting to be filled, trucks waiting to be unloaded, jobs waiting to be processed, equipment awaiting repairs, planes waiting to land or take off, and cars waiting at a traffic light or traffic jam.

One reason that queuing analysis is important is that customers tend to associate waiting with poor service quality, especially if the wait is long. Similarly, for an organization, having employees wait, such as a truck driver waiting to unload, is a waste.

Why Is There Waiting?

Many people are surprised to learn that waiting lines tend to form even though a system is under-loaded. For example, a fast-food restaurant may have the capacity to handle an average of 200 orders per hour and yet experience waiting lines even though the number of orders is only 150 per hour. In reality, customers arrive at random rather than at evenly spaced intervals and some orders take longer to fill than others. In other words, both arrival times and service durations exhibit a high degree of variability. As a result, the system at times becomes temporarily over-loaded, giving rise to waiting lines; at other times, the system is idle because there are no custom-ers. Thus, although a system may be *underloaded* from a *macro* standpoint, variabilities in arrival times and service durations imply that at times the system is *overloaded* from a *micro* standpoint. It follows that in systems where variability is minimal or non-existent (e.g., because arrivals can be scheduled and service durations are constant), waiting lines do not ordinarily form.

Goal of Waiting-Line Analysis

The goal of queuing analysis is to minimize total costs. There are two types of cost in a queuing situation: "cost" of customers waiting for service and cost of provision of capacity (e.g., determin-ing the number of cashiers at a supermarket or the number of repair people to handle equipment breakdowns). The cost of customers waiting, in addition to loss of goodwill, includes loss of busi-ness due to customers refusing to wait and going elsewhere. Also, if the "customers" are employ-ees, the salaries paid to employees while they wait for service (e.g., mechanics waiting for tools, truck drivers waiting to unload), are part of the cost of customers waiting.

Figure 18-1 shows the two costs and the total cost as a function of service capacity. Note that as capacity increases, its capacity cost increases. For simplicity, the increase is shown as a linear relationship. On the other hand, as capacity increases, the number of customers waiting and the time they wait tend to decrease at a faster rate; also the dissatisfaction of a typical customer is a

Figure 18-1 ▶

The goal of queuing is to minimize the sum of two costs: customers waiting cost and service capacity cost.

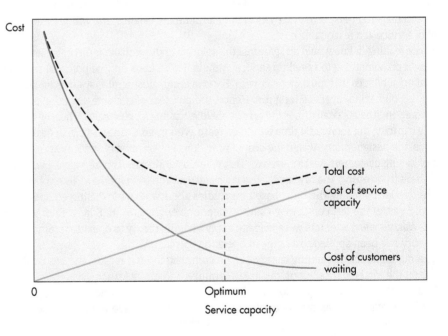

non-linear function of the waiting time (initially it is insignificant but increases at a faster rate as the wait time increases past a threshold); therefore, waiting cost decreases nonlinearly. Total cost is a U-shaped curve, and the goal of queuing analysis is to identify that level of service capacity that will minimize the total cost. (Unlike the situation in the EOQ model, the minimum point on the total cost curve is *not* necessarily where the two cost lines intersect.)

If pinning down the cost of customers waiting is difficult, another approach is to treat waiting times or line lengths as a policy variable: a manager simply specifies an acceptable level of waiting (e.g., average customer wait time of four minutes before service at a bank) and directs that enough capacity be established to achieve that level of waiting.

Queuing analysis is used in most services. As an example, we will briefly describe its use in bank teller staffing.

Queuing Analysis in Bank Teller Staffing[1]

Most banks have a staffing chart that suggests the minimum number of tellers required based on the forecast of number of customers expected (i.e., arrival rates) during each half-hour. These charts are derived by entering the following data into queuing theory formulas: forecast of average arrival rates, average customer service duration, and a customer service goal (such as an average wait time of approximately four minutes before being served). From branch to branch, the average customer service duration varies because of the type of transactions performed (e.g., retail vs. commercial), demographics, and the experience level of tellers. Most of these factors, and the time of day, also affect the customer arrival pattern at each branch during each half-hour. In addition, both service durations and arrival rates change over the years because of technological improvements. For example, Internet/telephone banking has reduced the need of customers to personally visit their bank.

To check the model assumptions, a sufficiently long data collection period is required; for example, the number of arrivals during each 15-minute period, the queue length at the end of each 15-minute period, and the number of tellers providing service could be recorded. Also, the service durations of at least 1,000 customers needs to be measured. Usually the distributions of number of arrivals and service durations match the assumed shapes (presented later).

The staffing requirements determined for each half-hour during each day of the following week are used to form feasible shifts and staff schedules (as presented in Chapter 16 on Staff Scheduling).

Psychology of Waiting

Despite management's best efforts, in some instances it is not feasible to shorten waiting times. Nevertheless, steps can be taken in certain situations that make the situation more acceptable to those waiting in line, particularly when the waiting line consists of people. The importance of doing so should not be underestimated.

Studies have shown a difference—sometimes a remarkable difference—between the actual time customers spend waiting and their perceived time. Several factors can influence the differences. One is the reason for being in line (e.g., waiting for police or fire personnel, waiting at the emergency room, having other appointments or a plane or train to catch). Aside from those situations, where the level of anxiety can make even short waits seem long, in many instances management can reduce their customers' perception of the waiting time. Some suggestions in this regard are:

- Determine the acceptable wait time for the operation.
- Try to keep the waiting time experienced by a customer consistent over time.
- Install distractions that entertain and involve customers. For example, provide magazines, TV, mirrors outside elevators, ask the customer to fill out a form, and use the lounge before eating. Make the wait comfortable.
- Inform the customer the cause of an abnormal wait and peak times.
- Keep the line moving continuously.

---

[1] Based on H. Deutsch and V.A. Mabert, "Queuing Theory and Teller Staffing; A Successful Application," *Interfaces* 10(5), October 1980, pp. 63–67.

David H. Maister on the Psychology of Waiting

David H. Maister's classic article on the psychology of waiting included these pearls of wisdom about waiting that can serve as a guide to system designers and to those operating a system in which waiting lines of people occur:

- Occupied time feels shorter than unoccupied time.

- People want to get started.

- Anxiety makes waits seem longer.

- Uncertain waits are longer than known, finite waits.
- Unexplained waits are longer than explained waits.
- Unfair waits are longer than equitable waits.
- The more valuable the service, the longer the customer will wait.
- Solo waits feel longer than group waits.

Source: David H. Maister, "The Psychology of Waiting Lines," davidmaister.com, September 8, 2008. Retrieved October 24, 2010.

- Use first come, first served discipline (fairness is important).
- Allow customers to serve themselves.
- Prepare the customers for service before the actual service. For example, encourage customers to print their boarding pass at home the night before their flight.
- Make people conscious of time only if they overestimate the wait time.
- Keep staff who are not serving customers out of sight.
- Try to segment customers by personality; some customers, the "watchers," actually like to spend time in lines, whereas the "impatients" need shorter lines. Some airlines and hotels have club memberships that provide express check-in and check-out for those who want it.
- Never underestimate the power of a friendly and attentive server.[2]

For example, see the "Six Flags" OM in Action.

(L02) Queueing System Characteristics and Performance Measures

There are numerous queuing models from which an analyst can choose. Naturally, much of the success of the analysis will depend on choosing the appropriate model. Model choice is dependent on the characteristics of the waiting line system under investigation. The main characteristics are:

1. Potential number of customers.
2. Number of servers and structure of queuing system.
3. Arrival and service patterns.
4. Queue discipline (i.e., order of service).

Figure 18-2 depicts a simple queuing system.

Figure 18-2

A simple queuing system.

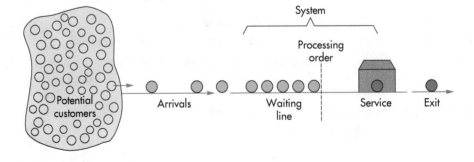

---

[2] K.L. Katz, B.M. Larson, and R.C. Larson, "Prescription for the Waiting-in-Line Blues: Entertain, Enlighten, and Engage," *Sloan Management Review*, Winter 1991, 32(2), pp. 44–53.

Hospital Wait Times

The Wait Time Alliance (WTA) recently gave Canada a failing grade on meeting performance targets regarding patient wait times. The alliance is composed of several medical groups, including the Canadian Association of Emergency Physicians and the Association of General Surgeons, whose job is to address physicians' concerns over patient access to health care. Canadians have long indicated that wait times are one of the most significant barriers to accessing health care services. Many developed countries with universal health systems provide quicker access to care compared to Canada. For example, 27 percent of Canadians reported waiting times in excess of four hours, compared with 5 percent in the United Kingdom and only 1 percent in the Netherlands.

While there has been considerable effort in the past decade to address the issue of long wait times for Canadians, there has been virtually no improvement. The following steps have been recommended to ensure all Canadians have more timely access to necessary medical care:

- Increased funding to health care providers can to be used to hire additional doctors and staff to clear up backlogs. With fewer patients waiting for service, average wait times will be reduced.

- Wait time guarantees establish maximum wait times for each procedure. When patient wait times exceed established thresholds, hospital administrators will be sanctioned and patients will be given the option to transfer to another health care provider.

- Reduce demand for specialty care by investing more heavily into primary care. Many procedures that can be performed by general practitioners are often referred to specialists, which increases waiting times and places further strain on the health care system.

Source: http://www.waittimealliance.ca/wp-content/uploads/2014/06/FINAL-EN-WTA-Report-Card.pdf.

Potential Number of Customers

The potential number of customers is either limited or is very large. In an **"infinite"-source** situation, the potential number of customers greatly exceeds system capacity. Examples are supermarkets, drugstores, banks, restaurants, theatres, amusement parks, and call centres. Theoretically, a large number of customers can request service at any given time. When the potential number of customers is limited, a **finite-source** situation exists. An example is the maintenance of machines in a company. The potential number of machines that might need repair at any given time is limited. A similar waiting situation occurs when an operator is responsible for loading and unloading a few machines and a nurse is responsible for a few patients.

"infinite" source
The potential number of customers greatly exceeds system capacity.

finite source The number of potential customers is limited.

Number of Servers and Structure of Queuing System

The capacity of a queuing system is a function of the capacity of each server and the number of servers. Each server can handle one customer at a time. (*Note:* A table of four is considered one "customer"). A queuing system can have either *single* or *multiple servers*. (*Note:* A group of servers working together as a team such as a surgical team is treated as a "single" server). Other examples of a single-server system are small grocery stores with one cashier, some theatres, and single-bay car washes. Multiple-server systems are commonly found in banks, at airline ticket counters, and at call centres.

Another distinctive characteristic is the number of steps or *phases* in a queuing system. For example, at most fast-food drive-throughs, cars first wait to order at the menu board, and then wait to pay at the pay window, and then wait to pick up the order at the pick-up window. Each stage constitutes a separate phase where queues can form.

Figure 18-3 illustrates some of the most common queuing systems. Because it would not be possible to cover all of these cases in sufficient detail in the limited amount of space available here, our discussion will focus on *single-phase* systems.

If the customers are homogeneous (i.e., similar), then a single line feeding into multiple servers is usually preferred to multiple independent lines each feeding to its own server. The reasons for this are as follows: First, the average wait time will be less because if there is an idle server, the customer waiting at the top of the line will be directed to the idle server right away. This does not happen in multiple independent lines, especially if the other lines cannot be observed. Even if a customer can see and jump to a shorter queue, this process will consume

Figure 18-3

Four common variations of queuing systems.

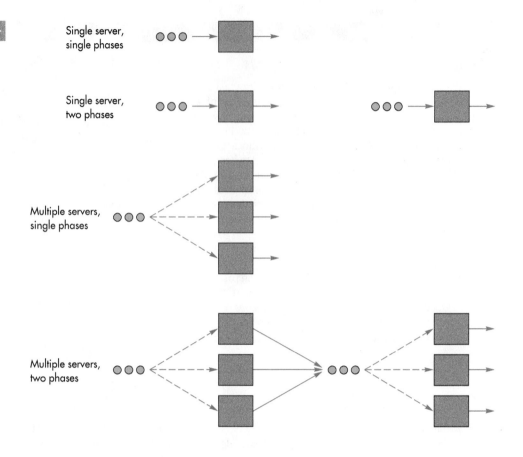

Single server, single phases

Single server, two phases

Multiple servers, single phases

Multiple servers, two phases

some time and does not guarantee getting to the server first. Second, the customers will be served first-come, first-served, which is more equitable and preferred by most customers. The disadvantages of a joint line are that it might appear too long, it may take a large space, servers may not work as fast as if they were responsible for their own line, and customers cannot choose their favourite server.

However, if the customers are heterogeneous (i.e., different), then separate lines could be advantageous. For example, a line for 10 items or less in a grocery store moves faster, resulting in shorter wait times for customers who do not buy a lot. This reduces the total variability of service durations, resulting in reduced average wait time for all customers. In some cases, the company can charge a higher price for providing a faster line; for example, the one-hour photo developing service is more expensive than the five-day economy service in The Real Canadian Superstore.

Arrival and Service Patterns

The most commonly used queueing models assume that the customer arrival *rate* (i.e., the number of arrivals per time unit) can be described by a Poisson distribution and that the service *duration* can be described by an Exponential distribution. **Poisson distribution** is a one-parameter discrete probability distribution of a number of events occurring in an interval of time, provided that these events occur with a known average rate and independently of the time since the last event. **Exponential distribution** is the continuous probability distribution of the times between events that happen continuously and independently at a constant average rate. Figure 18-4 illustrates these distributions.

Figure 18-5A illustrates how Poisson-distributed customer arrivals might occur during a three-day period. In some hours, there are three or four arrivals, in some other hours one or two arrivals, and in some other hours no arrivals.

Poisson distribution
A one-parameter discrete probability distribution of a number of events occurring in an interval of time, provided that these events occur with a known average rate and independently of the time since the last event.

Exponential distribution
The continuous probability distribution of the times between events that happen continuously and independently at a constant average rate.

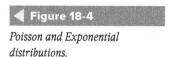

Poisson and Exponential distributions.

Figure 18-5B illustrates how Exponential service durations might appear for the same customers. Note that most service durations are very short but a few are relatively long.

Waiting lines are likely to occur when arrivals are bunched up and/or when service durations are particularly lengthy. For instance, note the long service duration of customer 7 on day 1 in Figure 18-5B. In Figure 18-5A, the seventh customer arrived just after 10 o'clock and the next two customers arrived shortly after that, making it very likely that a waiting line would form. A similar situation occurred on day 3 with the last three customers: the relatively long service duration for customer 13 (Figure 18-5B) and the short time before the next two arrivals (Figure 18-5A, day 3) would create (or increase the length of) a waiting line.

It is interesting to note that the Poisson and Exponential distributions are alternate ways of presenting the same basic information. That is, if service durations are Exponential, then the service rates (i.e., the number of services per time unit) are Poisson. Similarly, if the customer arrival rates are Poisson, then the inter arrival durations (i.e., the time between two consecutive arrivals) are Exponential. There is an inverse relationship between the means of these two distributions. For example, if a service facility can process 12 customers per hour, then average service duration is 1/12th of an hour or five minutes. And if the arrival rate is 10 per hour, then the average duration between two consecutive arrivals is six minutes.

Most models described in this chapter require that arrival and service rates be approximately Poisson or, equivalently, that interarrival and service durations be approximately Exponential. In practice, it is necessary to verify that these assumptions are met. Sometimes this is done by collecting data and plotting them, although the preferred approach is to use a chi-square goodness-of-fit test for that purpose. A discussion of the chi-square test is beyond the scope of this text, but it is covered in most statistics textbooks.

Research has shown that these assumptions are often appropriate for customer arrival rates but less likely to be appropriate for service durations. In situations where the assumptions are not reasonably satisfied, the alternatives would be to use (1) an approximate model or (2) a computer simulation.

Figure 18-5 ▶

*Examples of Poisson customer
arrivals (A) and Exponential
service durations (B).*

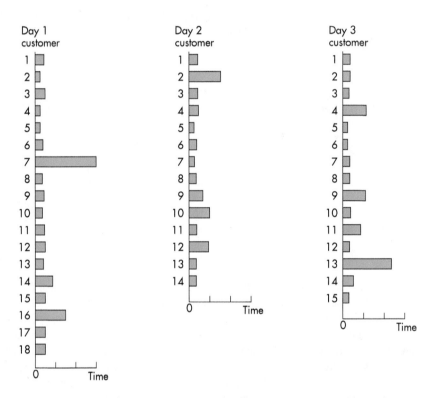

Queue Discipline (i.e., Order of Service)

queue discipline The order
in which customers are
served.

Queue discipline refers to the order in which customers are served. All but one of the models to
be described assumes that service is provided on a *first-come, first-served* (FCFS) basis. This is the
most commonly encountered rule at banks, stores, theatres, restaurants, four-way stop signs, registration lines, and so on. Examples of systems that do not serve on a FCFS basis include hospital emergency rooms, rush orders in a factory, and mainframe computer processing of jobs. In these and
similar situations, customers do not all represent the same waiting costs; those with the highest cost
(e.g., the most seriously ill) are processed first, even though other customers may have arrived earlier.

Performance Measures

Operations managers typically look at four measures when evaluating existing or proposed
queuing systems. Those measures are:

1. The average number of customers waiting, either in line (not counting those being served) or
   in the system (including those being served).

2. The average length of time customers wait, either in line or in the system.

server utilization The
proportion of time a server
will be busy.

3. **Server utilization**, i.e., the proportion of time a server will be busy.

4. The probability that an arriving customer will have to wait for service or will have to wait
   more than a specified length of time before being served.

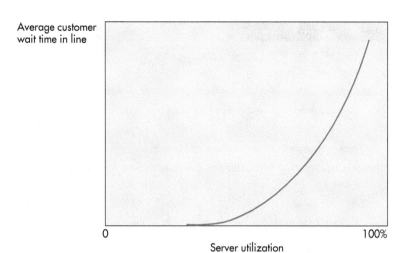

Average customer wait time in line

0   100%
Server utilization

◀ **Figure 18-6**

The average time customers wait in line increases non-linearly as the server utilization increases.

Of these measures, server utilization bears some elaboration. It reflects the extent to which the servers are busy rather than idle. On the surface, it might seem that the operations manager would want to seek 100 percent utilization. However, as Figure 18-6 illustrates, increases in server utilization are achieved at the expense of greater increases in the average customer wait time. In fact, average customer wait time becomes exceedingly large as server utilization approaches 100 percent. Also, 100 percent utilization of servers leads to burnout. Instead, a utilization of 80 to 90 percent is appropriate for most queueing systems.

Queuing Models: "Infinite" Source

Many "infinite"-source queuing models are available for a manager or analyst to choose from. The discussion here includes eight of the most basic and widely used models. All models discussed (except Model 7) assume Poisson arrival rates. Moreover, they assume that the average arrival and service rates are constant. If they are not, then the operating hours should be divided into subperiods within which the rates are fairly constant. For example, each hour or half-hour may have a different average arrival rate. In addition, the results are for the steady state condition, i.e., the transient behaviour of the queuing system at the opening hour are ignored. The eight "infinite"-source models described are:

1. Single server, Exponential service durations.
2. Single server, Exponential service durations, finite number in system.
3. Single server, constant service durations.
4. Single server, general service durations.
5. Multiple servers, Exponential service durations.
6. Multiple servers, Exponential service durations, finite number in system.
7. Multiple servers, general interarrival and service durations.
8. Multiple servers with priority, Exponential service durations.

To facilitate your use of queuing models, Table 18-1 provides a list of the symbols used for the "infinite"-source models.

Basic Relationships

There are certain basic relationships that hold for all "infinite"-source queuing models. Knowledge of these relationships can be very helpful in deriving the desired performance measures, given a few key values. Here are the basic relationships. Some are intuitive, others complex. For the latter, proof is omitted here.

Note: The average arrival and service rates, represented by λ and μ, respectively, must be in the same time units (e.g., per hour or per minute).

Table 18-1 ▶	Symbol	Represents
Symbols for "infinite"-source queueing models.	λ	Average arrival rate
	μ	Average service rate
	L_q	Average number of customers waiting in line for service
	L_s	Average number of customers in the system (waiting and being served)
	ρ	Server utilization
	W_q	Average length of time customers wait in line
	W_s	Average length of time customers spend in the system (waiting in line and being served)
	$1/\mu$	Average service duration
	P_o	Probability of zero customers in the system
	P_n	Probability of n customers in the system
	M	Number of servers
	r	Average number of customers being served at any time

Server utilization, ρ (rho), is equal to the ratio of demand (as measured by the average arrival rate) to capacity (as measured by the product of the number of servers, M, and the average service rate, μ):

$$\rho = \frac{\lambda}{M\mu} \tag{18-1}$$

The average number of customers being served (at any point in time), r, is equal to each server's utilization times the number of servers $= \rho M$, or:

$$r = \frac{\lambda}{\mu} \tag{18-2}$$

The average *number* of customers

waiting in line for service, L_q: L_q [Model dependent. Obtain using a table or formula.]

in the system (line plus being served), L_s: $\qquad\qquad L_s = L_q + r \tag{18-3}$

The average length of time customers

wait in line, W_q: $W_q = \dfrac{L_q}{\lambda}$ [Little's Formula] $\tag{18-4}$

spend in the system, W_s: $W_s = W_q + \dfrac{1}{\mu} = \dfrac{L_s}{\lambda}$ [Little's Formula] $\tag{18-5}$

All "infinite"-source models require that server utilization be less than 1.0; the models apply only to underloaded systems.

The average number of customers waiting in line, L_q, is a key value because it determines the other measures of system performance. Hence, L_q will usually be one of the first values you will want to determine in problem solving. Figure 18-7 can help you relate the symbols to the basic relationships in a queuing system.

 OM in *ACTION* http://www.sixflags.com

Six Flags

Six Flags uses a waiting system similar to Disney's Fastpass. It is called Flash Pass and uses a virtual queuing system by Lo-Q Company (http://www.lo-q.com). Each customer can rent a pager at the park entrance, called Q-Bot. Then, at some popular rides, the pager can be used to reserve the person's spot in the line. The person can go away and enjoy other rides. Ten minutes before her actual turn, she will be notified via the pager.

Sources: T. O'Brien, "Six Flags Debuts Queue Management," *Amusement Business* 113(9), March 5, 2001, pp. 1, 26; http://themeparks.about.com/cs/sixflagsparks/a/blfastlanea.htm.

	Line	+	Service	=	System
Customers	$\longrightarrow$ 000	$\rightarrow$	$\boxed{0}$	$\rightarrow$	
Average number waiting:	L_q	+	$\dfrac{\lambda}{\mu}$	=	L_s
Average time waiting:	$W_q = \dfrac{L_q}{\lambda}$	+	$\dfrac{1}{\mu}$	=	W_s

◄ **Figure 18-7**

Basic relationships.

Customers arrive at a bakery at an average rate of 18 per hour on weekday mornings. The arrival rate can be described by a Poisson distribution. Each server can serve a customer in an average of four minutes; service durations can be described by an Exponential distribution.

◄ **Example 1**

a. What are the average arrival and service rates?

b. Calculate the average number of customers being served at any time (assume that at least two servers will be working, resulting in server utilization < 1.0).

c. Suppose that the average number of customers waiting in line is 3.6. Calculate the average number of customers in the system (i.e., waiting in line or being served), the average length of time customers wait in line, and the average length of time customers spend in the system.

d. Determine the server utilization if there are $M = 2$, 3, or 4 servers.

a. The average arrival rate is given in the problem: $\lambda = 18$ customers per hour. Change the average service duration to a comparable *hourly* service rate by first restating the duration in hours and then taking its reciprocal. Thus, (4 minutes per customer)/(60 minutes per hour) = 1/15 hour per customer. Its reciprocal is $\mu = 15$ customers per hour, the average service rate.

SOLUTION

b. $r = \dfrac{\lambda}{\mu} = \dfrac{18}{15} = 1.2$ customers

c. Given: $L_q = 3.6$ customers,

$L_s = L_q + r = 3.6 + 1.2 = 4.8$ customers

$W_q = \dfrac{L_q}{\lambda} = \dfrac{3.6}{18} = .20$ hour, or $\times$ 60 minutes/hours

$= 12$ minutes

$W_s = W_q + \dfrac{1}{\mu} = .20 + \dfrac{1}{15} = .267$ hour, or 16 minutes

d. Server utilization is $\rho = \dfrac{\lambda}{M\mu}$.

For $M = 2, \rho = \dfrac{18}{2(15)} = .60$

For $M = 3, \rho = \dfrac{18}{3(15)} = .40$

For $M = 4, \rho = \dfrac{18}{4(15)} = .30$

Hence, as the system capacity, measured by $M\mu$, increases, the server utilization (for a given arrival rate) decreases.

LO4

Single-Server Models

Model 1: Single Server, Exponential Service Durations

The simplest model involves a system that has one server (or a single crew), the queue discipline is FCFS, and customer arrival rates can be approximated by a Poisson distribution and service durations by an Exponential distribution. The length of queue is not a constraint.

Table 18-2 lists some formulas for Model 1, which should be used in conjunction with formulas 18-1 through 18-5.

Table 18-2 ▶

Formulas for Model 1: single-server, Exponential service durations.

Performance Measure	Equation	
Average number in line	$L_q = \dfrac{\lambda^2}{\mu(\mu - \lambda)}$	(18-6)
Probability of zero customers in the system	$P_o = 1 - \left(\dfrac{\lambda}{\mu}\right)$	(18-7)
Probability of n customers in the system	$P_n = P_o\left(\dfrac{\lambda}{\mu}\right)^n$	(18-8)
Probability of fewer than n customers in the system	$P_{<n} = 1 - \left(\dfrac{\lambda}{\mu}\right)^n$	(18-9)
Probability that a customer waits at least t time units in queue	$P_{w\,in\,Q > t} = \dfrac{\lambda}{\mu}e^{-(\mu - \lambda)t}$	(18-10)

Example 2 ▶

A phone company is planning to open a kiosk in a new shopping mall, staffed by one sales agent. It is estimated that requests for phones, accessories, and information will average 15 per hour during peak period, and number of requests will have a Poisson distribution. Service durations are assumed to be Exponentially distributed. Previous experience with similar kiosks suggests that service duration should average about three minutes per request. Determine each of the following measures during the peak period:

a. Server utilization.

b. Percentage of time the sales agent will be idle.

c. The expected number of customers waiting in line to be served.

d. The average length of time customers will spend in the system.

e. The probability of zero customers in the system and the probability of four customers in the system.

f. The probability that a customer will have to wait.

g. The probability that a customer will have to wait more than 5 minutes.

SOLUTION

$\lambda = 15\,\text{per hour}$

$\mu = \dfrac{1}{\text{Average service duration}} = \dfrac{1\ \text{customer}}{3\ \text{minutes}} \times 60\ \text{minutes per hour}$

$= 20\ \text{customers per hour}$

a. $\rho = \dfrac{\lambda}{M\mu} = \dfrac{15}{1(20)} = .75$

b. Percentage idle time $= 1 - \rho = 1 - .75 = .25$, or 25 percent

c. $L_q = \dfrac{\lambda^2}{\mu(\mu - \lambda)} = \dfrac{15^2}{20(20 - 15)} = 2.25\ \text{customers}$

d. $W_s = \dfrac{L_q}{\lambda} + \dfrac{1}{\mu} = \dfrac{2.25}{15} + \dfrac{1}{20} = .20\ \text{hour, or 12 minutes}$

e. $P_0 = 1 - \dfrac{\lambda}{\mu} = 1 - \dfrac{15}{20} = .25$ and $P_4 = P_0\left(\dfrac{\lambda}{\mu}\right)^4 = .25\left(\dfrac{15}{20}\right)^4 = .079$

f. Probability that a customer will have to wait $= \rho = .75$

g. $P_{W\,in\,Q>t} = \dfrac{\lambda}{\mu}e^{-(\mu-\lambda)t}$

$\qquad = \dfrac{15}{20}e^{-(20-15)(5/60)}$

$\qquad = .494$

Note that t should be in the same time unit as λ and μ.

Model 2: Single Server, Exponential Service Durations, Finite Number in System

In many cases, the number of customers or calls that can fit in the queuing system is limited. Let $K =$ maximum number of customers (or calls) that can fit in the queuing system (in line and being served). If there are K customers already in the queuing system, the next customer will not be allowed to enter the system and has to balk (leave). In this case, P_0 and L_q can be calculated using the following two formulas. The probability of a customer balking is the same as probability of K customers in the system, P_k. The effective average arrival rate in this case is $\lambda(1 - P_k)$, and should be used to relate W_q to L_q.

$$P_0 = \left[\,1 + \frac{\left(\dfrac{\lambda}{\mu}\right)\left(1 - \left(\dfrac{\lambda}{\mu}\right)^K\right)}{\left(1 - \dfrac{\lambda}{\mu}\right)}\,\right]^{-1} \tag{18-11}$$

$$L_q = \frac{\left(\dfrac{\lambda}{\mu}\right)^2 P_0}{\left(1 - \dfrac{\lambda}{\mu}\right)^2}\left(1 - \left(\dfrac{\lambda}{\mu}\right)^K - K\left(1 - \dfrac{\lambda}{\mu}\right)\left(\dfrac{\lambda}{\mu}\right)^{K-1}\right) \tag{18-12}$$

$$P_K = \left(\dfrac{\lambda}{\mu}\right)^K P_0 \tag{18-13}$$

$$W_q = \frac{L_q}{\lambda(1 - P_K)} \tag{18-14}$$

Reconsider Example 2, but assume that if there are already four customers in the system (three in line and 1 being served), then no new customer will join the line. Calculate:

◀ **Example 3**

a. The average number in the line and compare it with Example 2.

b. The probability of balking.

c. The average time in the system and compare it with Example 2.

a. Recall $\lambda = 15$ per hour and $\mu = 20$ per hour. $K = 4$.

SOLUTION

$$P_0 = \left[\,1 + \frac{\left(\dfrac{15}{20}\right)\left(1 - \left(\dfrac{15}{20}\right)^4\right)}{\left(1 - \dfrac{15}{20}\right)}\,\right]^{-1} = .327785$$

$$L_q = \frac{\left(\dfrac{15}{20}\right)^2(.327785)}{\left(1 - \dfrac{15}{20}\right)^2}\left(1 - \left(\dfrac{15}{20}\right)^4 - 4\left(1 - \dfrac{15}{20}\right)\left(\dfrac{15}{20}\right)^3\right) = .7721 \text{ customers} < 2.25$$

customers in Example 2.

b. $P_K = \left(\dfrac{15}{20}\right)^4 (.327785) = 0.1037$ or 10%.

c. $W_s = \dfrac{L_q}{\lambda(1 - P_k)} + \dfrac{1}{\mu} = \dfrac{.7721}{15(1 - .1037)} + \dfrac{1}{20} = .10743$ hour or 6.4 minutes < 12 minutes

in Example 2.

Model 3: Single Server, Constant Service Durations

As noted previously, waiting lines are a consequence of random arrival and service rates. If we can reduce or eliminate the variability of either or both arrivals and services, then we can shorten the waiting line. A case in point is a queueing system with constant service durations (and Poisson arrival rates). The effect of constant service durations is to cut the average number of customers waiting in line in half (relative to Model 1):

$$L_q = \dfrac{\lambda^2}{2\mu(\mu - \lambda)} \qquad (18\text{-}15)$$

The average length of time customers wait in line, W_q, is also cut in half.

Example 4 ▶ Consider a single bay automatic car wash that takes five minutes to wash a car. On a typical Saturday morning, cars arrive at a mean rate of eight per hour, according to Poisson distribution. Find:

a. The average number of cars in line.

b. The average length of time cars spend in line and service (i.e., system).

SOLUTION

$\lambda = 8$ cars per hour
$\mu = 1$ per 5 minutes, or 12 cars per hour

a. $L_q = \dfrac{\lambda^2}{2\mu(\mu - \lambda)} = \dfrac{8^2}{2(12)(12 - 8)} = .667$ car

b. $W_s = \dfrac{L_q}{\lambda} + \dfrac{1}{\mu} = \dfrac{.667}{8} + \dfrac{1}{12} = .167$ hour, or 10 minutes

Model 4: Single Server, General Service Durations

For a general service durations with standard deviation $= \sigma_s$, it can be shown that:

$$L_q = \dfrac{\lambda^2(\mu^2 \sigma_s^2 + 1)}{2\mu(\mu - \lambda)} \qquad (18\text{-}16)$$

Note that when $\sigma_s = 0$, the above formula reduces to the L_q for Constant service durations (Model 3), and when $\sigma_s = \dfrac{1}{\mu}$, it reduces to the L_q for Exponential service durations (Model 1). Also, make sure that σ_s, λ and μ have the same time unit.

Example 5 ▶ At a small post office with one server, during the peak lunch period customers arrive according to Poisson distribution with an average rate of 30 customers per hour. Customers have a service time that is the sum of a constant 30 seconds and an Exponential service duration with average of 1 minute. Find:

a. The average number of customers in line during lunch time.

b. The average customer waiting time in line.

SOLUTION

$\lambda = 30$ customers per hour

$1/\mu = .5 + 1 = 1.5$ minutes per customer or $\mu = 60/1.5 = 40$ customers per hour

$\sigma_s = 1$ minute or $1/60 = .0166667$ hour (because the constant 30 seconds time has zero variance and the standard deviation of an Exponential distribution equals its mean). Note that service duration is *not* Exponentially distributed.

a. $L_q = \dfrac{\lambda^2(\mu^2\sigma_s^2 + 1)}{2\mu(\mu - \lambda)} = \dfrac{30^2(40^2(.016667)^2 + 1)}{2(40)(40 - 30)} = 1.625$ customers

b. $W_q = \dfrac{L_q}{\lambda} = \dfrac{1.625}{30} = 0.05417$ hour or 3.25 minutes.

Multiple-Server Models

Model 5: Multiple Servers, Exponential Service Durations

A multiple server system exists whenever there are two or more servers working individually to provide service to customers. Use of the model involves the following assumptions:

1. Poisson arrival rates with average λ and Exponential service durations with average $\dfrac{1}{\mu}$.

2. All M servers work at the same average rate.

3. Customers form a single waiting line.

Formulas for the multiple-server, Exponential service durations model are listed in Table 18-3. Obviously, the multiple-server formulas are more complex than the single-server formulas for L_q and P_0. Fortunately, you can also determine their values using Table 18-4, given values of λ/μ and M.

Performance Measure	Equation	
Average number of customers in line	$L_q = \dfrac{\lambda\mu\left(\dfrac{\lambda}{\mu}\right)^M}{(M-1)!(M\mu - \lambda)^2}P_0$	(18-17)
Probability of zero customers in the system	$P_0 = \left[\displaystyle\sum_{n=0}^{M-1}\dfrac{\left(\dfrac{\lambda}{\mu}\right)^n}{n!} + \dfrac{\left(\dfrac{\lambda}{\mu}\right)^M}{M!\left(1 - \dfrac{\lambda}{M\mu}\right)}\right]^{-1}$	(18-18)
Probability of n customers in the system	$P_n = \begin{cases}\dfrac{1}{n!}\left(\dfrac{\lambda}{\mu}\right)^n P_0 & \text{if } n \leq M \\[2ex] \dfrac{1}{M!\,M^{n-M}}\left(\dfrac{\lambda}{\mu}\right)^n P_0 & \text{if } n > M\end{cases}$	(18-19)
Average waiting time (before being served) for an arrival who is not immediately served	$W_a = \dfrac{1}{M\mu - \lambda}$	(18-20)
Probability that an arrival will have to wait for service	$P_W = \dfrac{W_q}{W_a}$	(18-21)
Probability that a customer waits at least t time units in queue	$P_{W\,\text{in}\,Q > t} = \dfrac{\left(\dfrac{\lambda}{\mu}\right)^M P_0}{M!\left(1 - \dfrac{\lambda}{M\mu}\right)}e^{-M\mu\left(1 - \frac{\lambda}{M\mu}\right)t}$	(18-22)

◀ **Table 18-3**

Formulas for the multiple-server, Exponential service durations model (M = number of servers).

To use Table 18-4, calculate the value of λ/μ and round it to two decimal places if $\lambda/\mu < 1$ and one decimal place if $\lambda/\mu \geq 1$. Then, simply read the values of L_q and P_0 for the appropriate number of servers, M. For instance, if $\lambda/\mu = 0.50$ and $M = 2$, the table provides a value of 0.033 for L_q and a value of .600 for P_0. These values can then be used to calculate other measures of system performance. Note that Table 18-4 can also be used for the single server, Exponential service durations model (Model 1) (use $M = 1$ values).

Table 18-4 ▶

Multiple-server, Exponential service durations model values for L_q and P_0, given values for λ/μ and M (number of servers).

λ/μ	M	L_q	P_o	λ/μ	M	L_q	P_o	λ/μ	M	L_q	P_o
0.15	1	0.026	.850		4	0.003	.427	1.8	2	7.674	.053
	2	0.001	.860	0.90	1	8.100	.100		3	0.532	.146
0.20	1	0.050	.800		2	0.229	.379		4	0.105	.162
	2	0.002	.818		3	0.030	.403		5	0.023	.165
0.25	1	0.083	.750		4	0.004	.406	1.9	2	17.587	.026
	2	0.004	.778	0.95	1	18.050	.050		3	0.688	.128
0.30	1	0.129	.700		2	0.277	.356		4	0.136	.145
	2	0.007	.739		3	0.037	.383		5	0.030	.149
0.35	1	0.188	.650		4	0.005	.386		6	0.007	.149
	2	0.011	.702	1.0	2	0.333	.333	2.0	3	0.889	.111
0.40	1	0.267	.600		3	0.045	.364		4	0.174	.130
	2	0.017	.667		4	0.007	.367		5	0.040	.134
0.45	1	0.368	.550	1.1	2	0.477	.290		6	0.009	.135
	2	0.024	.633		3	0.066	.327	2.1	3	1.149	.096
	3	0.002	.637		4	0.011	.367		4	0.220	.117
0.50	1	0.500	.500	1.2	2	0.675	.250		5	0.052	.121
	2	0.033	.600		3	0.094	.294		6	0.012	.122
	3	0.003	.606		4	0.016	.300	2.2	3	1.491	.081
0.55	1	0.672	.450		5	0.003	.301		4	0.277	.105
	2	0.045	.569	1.3	2	0.951	.212		5	0.066	.109
	3	0.004	.576		3	0.130	.264		6	0.016	.111
0.60	1	0.900	.400		4	0.023	.271	2.3	3	1.951	.068
	2	0.059	.538		5	0.004	.272		4	0.346	.093
	3	0.006	.548	1.4	2	1.345	.176		5	0.084	.099
0.65	1	1.207	.350		3	0.177	.236		6	0.021	.100
	2	0.077	.509		4	0.032	.245	2.4	3	2.589	.056
	3	0.008	.521		5	0.006	.246		4	0.431	.083
0.70	1	1.633	.300	1.5	2	1.929	.143		5	0.105	.089
	2	0.098	.481		3	0.237	.211		6	0.027	.090
	3	0.011	.495		4	0.045	.221		7	0.007	.091
0.75	1	2.250	.250		5	0.009	.223	2.5	3	3.511	.045
	2	0.123	.455	1.6	2	2.844	.111		4	0.533	.074
	3	0.015	.471		3	0.313	.187		5	0.130	.080
0.80	1	3.200	.200		4	0.060	.199		6	0.034	.082
	2	0.152	.429		5	0.012	.201		7	0.009	.082
	3	0.019	.447	1.7	2	4.426	.081	2.6	3	4.933	.035
0.85	1	4.817	.150		3	0.409	.166		4	0.658	.065
	2	0.187	.404		4	0.080	.180		5	0.161	.072
	3	0.024	.425		5	0.017	.182		6	0.043	.074

Table 18-4 (continued)

λ/μ	M	L_q	P_o
	7	0.011	.074
2.7	3	7.354	.025
	4	0.811	.057
	5	0.198	.065
	6	0.053	.067
	7	0.014	.067
2.8	3	12.273	.016
	4	1.000	.050
	5	0.241	.058
	6	0.066	.060
	7	0.018	.061
2.9	3	27.193	.008
	4	1.234	.044
	5	0.293	.052
3.0	4	1.528	.038
	5	0.354	.047
	6	0.099	.049
	7	0.028	.050
	8	0.008	.050
3.1	4	1.902	.032
	5	0.427	.042
	6	0.120	.044
	7	0.035	.045
	8	0.010	.045
3.2	4	2.386	.027
	5	0.513	.037
	6	0.145	.040
	7	0.043	.040
	8	0.012	.041
3.3	4	3.027	.023
	5	0.615	.033
	6	0.174	.036
	7	0.052	.037
	8	0.015	.037
3.4	4	3.906	.019
	5	0.737	.029
	6	0.209	.032
	7	0.063	.033
	8	0.019	.033
3.5	4	5.165	.015
	5	0.882	.026
	6	0.248	.029
	7	0.076	.030
	8	0.023	.030
	9	0.007	.030

λ/μ	M	L_q	P_o
3.6	4	7.090	.011
	5	1.055	.023
	6	0.295	.026
	7	0.019	.027
	8	0.028	.027
	9	0.008	.027
3.7	4	10.347	.008
	5	1.265	.020
	6	0.349	.023
	7	0.109	.024
	8	0.034	.025
	9	0.010	.025
3.8	4	16.937	.005
	5	1.519	.017
	6	0.412	.021
	7	0.129	.022
	8	0.041	.022
	9	0.013	.022
3.9	4	36.859	.002
	5	1.830	.015
	6	0.485	.019
	7	0.153	.020
	8	0.050	.020
	9	0.016	.020
4.0	5	2.216	.013
	6	0.570	.017
	7	0.180	.018
	8	0.059	.018
	9	0.019	.018
4.1	5	2.703	.011
	6	0.668	.015
	7	0.212	.016
	8	0.070	.016
	9	0.023	.017
4.2	5	3.327	.009
	6	0.784	.013
	7	0.248	.014
	8	0.083	.015
	9	0.027	.015
	10	0.009	.015
4.3	5	4.149	.008
	6	0.919	.012
	7	0.289	.130
	8	0.097	.013
	9	0.033	.014

λ/μ	M	L_q	P_o
	10	0.011	.014
4.4	5	5.268	.006
	6	1.078	.010
	7	0.337	.012
	8	0.114	.012
	9	0.039	.012
	10	0.013	.012
4.5	5	6.862	.005
	6	1.265	.009
	7	0.391	.010
	8	0.133	.011
	9	0.046	.011
	10	0.015	.011
4.6	5	9.289	.004
	6	1.487	.008
	7	0.453	.009
	8	0.156	.010
	9	0.054	.010
	10	0.018	.010
4.7	5	13.382	.003
	6	1.752	.007
	7	0.525	.008
	8	0.181	.008
	9	0.064	.009
	10	0.022	.009
4.8	5	21.641	.002
	6	2.071	.006
	7	0.607	.008
	8	0.209	.008
	9	0.074	.008
	10	0.026	.008
4.9	5	46.566	.001
	6	2.459	.005
	7	0.702	.007
	8	0.242	.007
	9	0.087	.007
	10	0.031	.007
	11	0.011	.077
5.0	6	2.938	.005
	7	0.810	.006
	8	0.279	.006
	9	0.101	.007
	10	0.036	.007
	11	0.013	.007
5.1	6	3.536	.004

Table 18-4

Table 18-4

(concluded)

λ/μ	M	L_q	P_o	λ/μ	M	L_q	P_o	λ/μ	M	L_q	P_o
	7	0.936	.005		8	0.483	.004	5.7	6	16.446	.001
	8	0.321	.006		9	0.178	.004		7	2.264	.002
	9	0.117	.006		10	0.066	.004		8	0.721	.003
	10	0.042	.006		11	0.024	.005		9	0.266	.003
	11	0.015	.006		12	0.009	.005		10	0.102	.003
5.2	6	4.301	.003	5.5	6	8.590	.002		11	0.038	.003
	7	1.081	.005		7	1.674	.003		12	0.014	.003
	8	0.368	.005		8	0.553	.004	5.8	6	26.373	.001
	9	0.135	.005		9	0.204	.004		7	2.648	.002
	10	0.049	.005		10	0.077	.004		8	0.823	.003
	11	0.017	.006		11	0.028	.004		9	0.303	.003
5.3	6	5.303	.003		12	0.010	.004		10	0.116	.003
	7	1.249	.004	5.6	6	11.519	.001		11	0.044	.003
	8	0.422	.005		7	1.944	.003		12	0.017	.003
	9	0.155	.005		8	0.631	.003	5.9	6	56.300	.000
	10	0.057	.005		9	0.233	.004		7	3.113	.002
	11	0.021	.005		10	0.088	.004		8	0.939	.002
	12	0.007	.005		11	0.033	.004		9	0.345	.003
5.4	6	6.661	.002		12	0.012	.004		10	0.133	.003
	7	1.444	.004								

Two new measures are given in Table 18-3: W_a and P_W. W_a is the average wait time for only those customers who have to wait. Note that $W_a > W_q$ because W_q also contains those customers who do not have to wait. P_W is the probability that a customer has to wait. These three terms are related through the following relationship:

W_q = average wait time if customer does not have to wait × probability of not waiting

  + average wait time if customer has to wait × probabitlity of waiting

$$= 0(1 - P_W) + W_a P_W \text{ or, } P_W = \frac{W_q}{W_a}$$

Example 6

A taxi company has seven cars stationed at an airport during late evening hours on weeknights. The company has determined that customers request taxis during these times at rates that follow Poisson distribution with a mean of 6.6 per hour. Service durations are Exponential with a mean of 50 minutes (including the return time to the airport). Find each of the performance measures listed in Table 18-3, and each taxi's utilization. Use $t = 5$ minutes in formula 18-22.

SOLUTION

$\lambda = 6.6$ per hour $M = 7$ taxis (servers)

$$\mu = \frac{1}{50 \text{ minutes} \div 60 \text{ minutes per hour}}$$
$$= 1.2 \text{ per hour}$$

$\lambda/\mu = \dfrac{6.6}{1.2} = 5.5$. From Table 18-4, for $\dfrac{\lambda}{\mu} = 5.5$ and M = 7 we get $L_q = 1.674$ and $P_0 = .003$

$$P_1 = \frac{1}{1!}(5.5)^1(.003) = 0.0165$$

$$P_2 = \frac{1}{2!}(5.5)^2(.003) = 0.0454$$

...

$$W_a = \frac{1}{M\mu - \lambda} = \frac{1}{7(1.2) - 6.6} = .556 \text{ hour, or } 33.36 \text{ minutes}$$

$$W_q = \frac{L_q}{\lambda} = \frac{1.674}{6.6} = .2536 \text{ hour, or } 15.22 \text{ minutes}$$

$$P_W = \frac{W_q}{W_a} = \frac{.2536}{.556} = .456$$

$$\rho = \frac{\lambda}{M\mu} = \frac{6.6}{7(1.2)} = .786$$

$$P_{w \, in \, Q > \frac{5}{60}} = \frac{\left(\frac{6.6}{1.2}\right)^7 (.003)}{7! \left(1 - \frac{6.6}{7(1.2)}\right)} e^{-7(1.2)\left(1 - \frac{6.6}{7(1.2)}\right)\left(\frac{5}{60}\right)} = \left(\frac{456.73}{1080}\right) e^{-.15} = 0.364$$

or 36.4%

OM in *ACTION*   http://www.llbean.com

L.L. Bean

L.L. Bean is a catalogue phone-order outdoors-clothing company. It has two large call centres in Maine that receive orders and answer questions. Like other call centres, capacity issues for these call centres range from "long" term (i.e., number of phone lines, called trunks, to install) to "medium" term (i.e., number of agents to employ) to short term (i.e., staff scheduling). L.L. Bean determines the number of trunks to install (on a biweekly basis), the number of stations and agents to employ (on a weekly basis), and the maximum size of queue and the number of staff on duty (on a half-hour basis). These are determined hierarchically using a search procedure. L.L. Bean uses the finite line-length version of the multiserver model (Model 6) for two of these (see the following diagram): (a) for determining the number of trunks s_t, (the line length is assumed to be zero, i.e., the number of calls in the trunks system = the number of trunks s_t); and (b) for determining

the number of agents on duty s_a and maximum queue size $K - s_a$ (after getting through but before talking to an agent). For each two-week period, a search procedure uses both the trunks model and agents queue model (for every half-hour within the two-week period) with various values of s_t, s_a, and K, $s_a \le K \le s_t$. For each set of values for s_t, s_a, and K, the probability of being blocked (getting a busy signal) and average customer connect time are determined. The set of value (s_t, s_a, and K) over all half-hour periods of the two-week period that minimizes the total cost of lost orders (due to being blocked), connect time, and staff pay is the optimal solution. A small number of calls, about 1–2 percent, abandon the queue system because of excessive wait. These are ignored in the optimization. Before the above method, L.L. Bean used the following target service goal to determine the values for s_t, s_a, and K: the percentage of calls that wait more than 20 seconds is at most 15 percent.

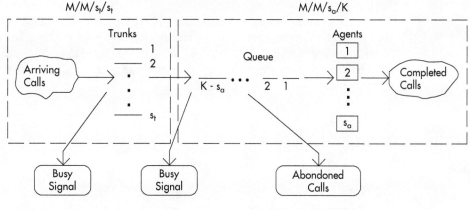

KEY:

s_t : number of trunks installed
s_a : number of agents on-duty
K : system capacity for calls waiting and in service

Source: P. Quinn, et al, "Allocating Telecommunications Resources at L. L. Bean, Inc.," *Interfaces*, 21(1), January–February 1991, pp. 75–91.

The Excel template provided on *Connect* can also be used to solve Example 6. After entering $\lambda = 6.6$ and $\mu = 1.2$ at the top of the template, the queuing statistics for 7 servers are shown in the $M = 7$ column of the table in the template. Note that Excel is a little more accurate because it carries several decimal digits. The template also provides queuing statistics for 8 through 12 servers, although these are not required for this example. In addition, the template can be used to increment λ and μ by a small amount, to perform sensitivity analysis.

Determining the Number of Servers Using Wait Time Standards

So far we have determined the performance measures of Model 5 using λ, μ and M. However, we can also do the reverse; that is, we can determine the number of servers M needed to achieve specified levels of various performance measures. This approach is illustrated in the following example.

Example 7 ▶

The taxi company of Example 6 also plans to have taxis at a new rail station. The expected customer requests for taxis there during weekday mornings is 4.8 per hour, and the average service time (including the return time to the rail station) is expected to be 40 minutes. How many taxis will be needed to achieve an average customer wait time in line of close to but not exceeding 10 minutes during weekday mornings?

SOLUTION

$\lambda = 4.8$ per hour

$$\mu = \frac{1}{\left(\frac{40}{60}\right)} = 1.5 \text{ per hour}$$

$M = ?$

$W_q(\text{desired}) = 10 \text{ minutes, or } .167 \text{ hour}$

Using $L_q = \lambda \, W_q$, $L_q = (4.8/\text{hour})(.167 \text{ hour}) = .8$. Thus, the average number waiting should be close to but not exceed .8. Referring to Table 18-4, with $\lambda/\mu = 4.8/1.5 = 3.2$, we obtain $L_q = 2.386$ for $M = 4$ and 0.513 for $M = 5$. Hence, five taxis will be needed during weekday mornings.

Determining the Number of Servers by Minimizing Total Cost

Instead of achieving a performance measure standard (e.g., the average wait time should be close to but not exceed 10 minutes), we can determine the number of servers by minimizing the sum of total average customer wait cost and total servers pay cost. Thus, the goal is:

Minimize total cost = Total average customer wait cost + Total servers pay cost

An iterative process is used to identify the number of servers that will minimize the total cost. The number of servers is incremented one unit at a time and the total cost is calculated at each increment. Because the total cost curve is U-shaped, the total cost will initially decrease as number of servers is increased and then it will eventually begin to increase. The optimal number of servers is the value just before the total cost increases.

Total average customer wait time in the system during an hour is equal to the average number of customers arriving during the hour multiplied by the average wait time per customer in the system; that is, λW_s. But this equals L_s by Little's formula. To save on calculations, we will use the formula $L_s = L_q + \dfrac{\lambda}{\mu}$ to obtain the total average customer wait time in the system.

Trucks arrive at a warehouse at an average rate of 15 per hour during business hours. A crew of four work together to unload the trucks at an average rate of five per hour. (Both distributions are Poisson.) Both the trucks and the warehouse belong to the same company. Recent changes in wage rates and truck and driver costs have caused the warehouse manager to re-examine the question of how many crews to use. The new rates are the following: a crew (of four) costs $100 per hour; truck and driver cost $120 per hour. Assuming there are enough unloading docks, how many crews should the manager use?

L_q values are from Table 18-4 using $\dfrac{\lambda}{\mu} = \dfrac{15}{5} = 3.0$

Crew Size	Crew Cost	$\left[L_s = L_q + \dfrac{\lambda}{\mu}\right]$ Total Average Wait Time in System per Hour	$[L_s \times \$120]$ Total Average Driver/Truck Wait Cost per Hour	Total Cost
4	$400	1.528 + 3.0 = 4.528	$543.36	$943.36
5	500	.354 + 3.0 = 3.354	402.48	902.48 (minimum)
6	600	.099 + 3.0 = 3.099	371.88	971.88
7	700	.028 + 3.0 = 3.028	363.36	1,063.36

Five crews will minimize the total cost. Because the total cost will continue to increase once the minimum is reached, it is not necessary to calculate the total cost for crew sizes larger than six.

One additional point should be made concerning the total cost approach. Because customer wait cost is often estimated, the apparent optimal solution may not represent the true optimum. If wait cost estimates can be obtained as *ranges* (e.g., between $40 and $50 per hour), total cost should be calculated using both ends of the range to see whether the optimal solution is different. If it is, management must decide whether to expend additional effort to obtain more precise cost estimates or to choose one of the two indicated optimal solutions.

Model 6: Multiple Servers, Exponential Service Durations, Finite Number in System

In many cases, the number of customers or calls that can fit in the queuing system is limited. Let K = maximum number of customers (or calls) in the queuing system (in line and being served). Obviously, $K \geq M$, the number of servers. If there are K customers already in the queuing system, the next customer will not be allowed to enter the system and has to balk (leave). The probability of this is P_K. Because P_K proportion of customers are lost, the effective average arrival rate is $\lambda(1 - p_K)$. The formulas in this case are as follows:

$$P_0 = \left[\sum_{n=0}^{M-1} \frac{\left(\frac{\lambda}{\mu}\right)^n}{n!} + \frac{\left(\frac{\lambda}{\mu}\right)^M \left(1 - \left(\frac{\lambda}{M\mu}\right)^{K-M+1}\right)}{M!\left(1 - \frac{\lambda}{M\mu}\right)} \right]^{-1}$$ (18-23)

$$L_q = \frac{\left(\frac{\lambda}{\mu}\right)^{M+1} P_0}{(M-1)!\left(M - \frac{\lambda}{\mu}\right)^2} \left(1 - \left(\frac{\lambda}{M\mu}\right)^{K-M+1} - (K - M + 1)\left(1 - \frac{\lambda}{M\mu}\right)\left(\frac{\lambda}{M\mu}\right)^{K-M}\right)$$ (18-24)

$$P_K = \frac{\left(\frac{\lambda}{\mu}\right)^K P_0}{M^{K-M} M!}$$ (18-25)

$$W_q = \frac{L_q}{\lambda(1 - P_K)}$$ (18-26)

Example 9 ▶

Reconsider Example 6, but assume that no more than 15 customers will wait for a taxi (the 16th customer will use the more expensive limousine service). Calculate:

a. The average number of customers waiting and compare it with Example 6.

b. The probability of balking.

c. The average time a customer is in the system, and compare it with Example 6.

SOLUTION

Recall that $\lambda = 6.6$ per hour, $\mu = 1.2$ per hour, and $M = 7$. Now, we also have $K = 15$.

a.

$$P_0 = \left[1 + \left(\frac{6.6}{1.2}\right) + \frac{\left(\frac{6.6}{1.2}\right)^2}{2} + \frac{\left(\frac{6.6}{1.2}\right)^3}{6} + \frac{\left(\frac{6.6}{1.2}\right)^4}{24} + \frac{\left(\frac{6.6}{1.2}\right)^5}{120} + \frac{\left(\frac{6.6}{1.2}\right)^6}{720} + \frac{\left(\frac{6.6}{1.2}\right)^7 \left(1 - \left(\frac{6.6}{8.4}\right)^9\right)}{7!\left(1 - \frac{6.6}{8.4}\right)} \right]^{-1}$$

$$= [1 + 5.5 + 15.125 + 27.7292 + 38.1276 + 41.9404 + 38.4453 + 124.8784]^{-1} = .003416$$

$$L_q = \frac{\left(\frac{6.6}{1.2}\right)^8 .003416}{6!\left(7 - \frac{6.6}{1.2}\right)^2}\left(1 - \left(\frac{6.6}{8.4}\right)^9 - 9\left(1 - \frac{6.6}{8.4}\right)\left(\frac{6.6}{8.4}\right)^8\right) = 1.070 \text{ customers} < 1.674 \text{ customers}$$

in Example 6.

b. $P_{15} = \frac{\left(\frac{6.6}{1.2}\right)^{15} .003416}{7^8 7!} = .015 \text{ or } 1.5\%. \text{ probability of balking.}$

c.

$$W_q = \frac{L_q}{\lambda(1 - P_K)} = \frac{1.070}{6.6(1 - .015)} = .1646 \text{ hour or } 9.88 \text{ minutes} < 15.22 \text{ minutes in Example 6.}$$

For an application of Model 6, see the "L.L. Bean" OM in Action.

Model 7: Multiple Servers, General Interarrival and Service Durations[3]

The solution to this model is difficult to obtain. Thus, we will provide an approximate solution.

Let σ_A = standard deviation of interarrival durations (i.e., the difference between arrival times of consecutive arrivals), and σ_S = standard deviation of service durations.

Then,

$$L_q \approx \frac{\rho^{\sqrt{2(M+1)}}}{1 - \rho} \times \frac{\mu^2\sigma_S^2 + \lambda^2\sigma_A^2}{2} \tag{18-27}[4]$$

An airport hotel receives groups of guests by airport shuttle vans. Each van may contain various numbers of guests arriving together. The average number of guests arriving per hour during work-day afternoons is forecast to be 30 and the standard deviation of interarrival time is estimated to be three minutes. The check-in process takes a constant time of one minute plus an Exponential time with a mean of two minutes. According to hotel policy, the average waiting time in line should not exceed three minutes. Are two employees at the check-in counter adequate during workday afternoons?

◀ **Example 10**

$\lambda = 30$ guests per hour, $\sigma_A = 3$ minutes $= .05$ hour

SOLUTION

$\mu = 60/3 = 20$ guests per hour, $\sigma_S = 2$ minutes $= .0333$ hour (*Note:* the constant part of service duration does not contribute to the standard deviation. The standard deviation of an Exponential distribution is equal to its mean).

$M = 2$.

$$\rho = \frac{\lambda}{M\mu} = \frac{30}{2(20)} = .75$$

$$L_q \approx \frac{.75^{\sqrt{2(2+1)}}}{1 - .75} \times \frac{20^2(.0333)^2 + 30^2(.05)^2}{2} = 2.6627$$

$$W_q = \frac{L_q}{\lambda} = \frac{2.6627}{30} = .08876 \text{ hour or } 5.3 \text{ minutes} > 3 \text{ minutes} \rightarrow \text{No, 2 check-in counter}$$

employees are not adequate.

---

[3] R.B. Chase et al., *Operations Management for Competitive Advantage*, 10th ed. (Boston: Irwin, 2004).

[4] We will evaluate the performance of this approximation by comparing it with the results of Examples 6 and 7.

In Example 6, $\lambda = 6.6$, $\mu = 1.2$, $M = 7$, and $\rho = .786$. It is well known that the standard deviation of an Exponential distribution equals its mean. Therefore, $\sigma_A = \frac{1}{\lambda}$ and $\sigma_s = \frac{1}{\mu}$. Substituting these in the L_q formula 18-27 results in:

$$L_q = \frac{0.786^{\sqrt{2(7+1)}}}{1 - 0.786} \times \frac{1 + 1}{2} = 1.784, \text{ which is very close to } L_q = 1.674 \text{ value obtained in Example 6.}$$

In Example 7, $\lambda = 4.8$, $\mu = 1.5$, $\rho = \frac{4.8}{5(1.5)} = .64$. Substituting these in the L_q formula 18-27 results in:

$$L_q = \frac{.64^{\sqrt{2(5+1)}}}{1 - .64} \times \frac{1 + 1}{2} = .592, \text{ which is very close to } L_q = .513 \text{ value obtained in Example 7 for } M = 5.$$

Model 8: Multiple Servers with Priority, Exponential Service Durations

In many queuing systems, processing occurs on a first-come, first-served (FCFS) basis. However, there are situations in which FCFS is inappropriate. The reason is that the waiting cost or penalty incurred may not be the same for all the customers. For example, in a hospital emergency waiting room, a wide variety of injuries and illnesses need treatment. Some may be minor (e.g., sliver in finger) and others may be much more serious, even life threatening. It is more reasonable to treat the most serious cases first, letting the nonserious cases wait until all serious cases have been treated. Similarly, computer processing of jobs on large mainframe computers often follows rules other than FCFS (e.g., shortest job first). In such cases, a **multiple-server-with-priority model** is useful for describing the queueing system.

multiple-server-with-priority model Customers (jobs) are processed not FCFS, but according to some measure of importance.

This model incorporates all of the assumptions of the multiple-server, Exponential service durations model (Model 5) except that it uses priority service rule instead of FCFS. Arrivals to the system are assigned a priority as they arrive (e.g., highest priority = 1, next priority class = 2, next priority class = 3, and so on). Let λ_k be the average arrival rate of priority class K. We have $\lambda = \Sigma\lambda_k$. An existing queue might look something like this:

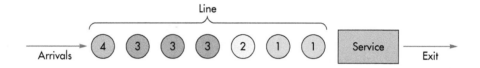

Within each class, waiting units are processed in the order they arrived (i.e., FCFS). Thus, in this sequence, the first 1 would be processed as soon as a server becomes available. The second 1 would be processed when that server or another one becomes available. We assume that each server can process any customer with any priority class and that the average service time is $\frac{1}{\mu}$ for any arrival. If, in the interim, another 1 arrived, it would be next in line *ahead of the first 2*. If there were no new arrivals, the only 2 would be processed by the next available server. At that point, if a new 1 or 2 arrived, it would be processed ahead of the 3s and the 4. We assume that any service already in progress would not be *preempted* or interrupted for another customer.

Obviously, a unit with a low priority could conceivably wait a rather long time for processing. In some cases, units that have waited more than a specified time are reassigned a higher priority.

Table 18-5 gives the appropriate formulas for the multiple-server-with-priority model.

Table 18-5 ▶	Performance Measure	Formula	Formula Number
Multiple-server-with-priority model.	Server utilization	$\rho = \dfrac{\lambda}{M\mu}$	(18-28)
	Intermediate values (L_q from Table 18-4)	$A = \dfrac{\lambda}{(1-\rho)L_q}$	(18-29)
		$B_k = 1 - \displaystyle\sum_{c=1}^{k} \dfrac{\lambda_c}{M\mu}$ $(B_o = 1)$	(18-30)
	Average wait time in line for units in *k*th priority class	$W_k = \dfrac{1}{A \cdot B_{k-1} \cdot B_k}$	(18-31)
	Average time in the system for units in the *k*th priority class	$W = W_k + \dfrac{1}{\mu}$	(18-32)
	Average number of the *k*th priority class waiting in line	$L_k = \lambda_k \times W_k$	(18-33)

A machine shop handles tool repairs in a large company. As each job arrives in the shop, it is assigned a priority based on urgency of the need for that tool: priority 1 is the highest and priority 3 is the lowest. Number of requests for repair per hour can be described by a Poisson distribution. Average arrival rates are $\lambda_1 = 2$ per hour, $\lambda_2 = 2$ per hour, and $\lambda_3 = 1$ per hour. The average service rate is one tool per hour for each mechanic, and the service rate has Poisson distribution. There are six mechanics in the shop. Determine the value of the following measures:

◄ **Example 11**

a.   The server utilization.

b.   The average time a tool in each of the priority classes will wait for repair.

c.   The average time a tool spends in the system for each priority class.

d.   The average number of tools waiting for repair in each class.

$$\lambda = \Sigma\lambda_k = 2 + 2 + 1 = 5 \text{ per hour}$$

SOLUTION

$$M = 6 \text{ servers}$$

$$\mu = 1 \text{ tool per hour}$$

a. $\rho = \dfrac{\lambda}{M\mu} = \dfrac{5}{6(1)} = .833$

b.   Intermediate values. For $\lambda/\mu = 5/1 = 5$ and $M = 6$, from Table 18-4, $L_q = 2.938$

$$A = \frac{5}{(1 - .833)2.938} = 10.19$$

$$B_0 = 1$$

$$B_1 = 1 - \frac{2}{6(1)} = \frac{2}{3} = .667$$

$$B_2 = 1 - \frac{2 + 2}{6(1)} = \frac{1}{3} = .333$$

$$B_3 = 1 - \frac{2 + 2 + 1}{6(1)} = \frac{1}{6} = .167$$

$$W_1 = \frac{1}{A \cdot B_0 \cdot B_1} = \frac{1}{10.19(1)(.667)} = .147 \text{ hour}$$

$$W_2 = \frac{1}{A \cdot B_1 \cdot B_2} = \frac{1}{10.19(.667)(.333)} = .442 \text{ hour}$$

$$W_3 = \frac{1}{A \cdot B_2 \cdot B_3} = \frac{1}{10.19(.333)(.167)} = 1.765 \text{ hours}$$

c. $W = W_k + 1/\mu$. In this case, $1/\mu = 1/1 = 1$. Thus:

Class	$W_k + 1 = W$ Hours
1	.147 + 1 = 1.147
2	.442 + 1 = 1.442
3	1.765 + 1 = 2.765

d.   The average number of units waiting for repair in each class is $L_k = \lambda_k W_k$. Thus:

Class	$\lambda_k W_k = L_k$ Units
1	2(.147) = .294
2	2(.442) = .884
3	1(1.765) = 1.765

Using the Excel template on *Connect*, the solution to Example 11 would appear as follows:

Note that the small differences between Excel and manual results are due to rounding.

Revising Priorities. If any of the wait times calculated in Example 11 are deemed too long by management (e.g., a wait time of .147 hour for tools in the first class might be too long), there are several options. One is to increase the number of servers. Another is to attempt to increase the service rate, say, by introducing new methods. If such options are not feasible, another approach is to re-examine the membership of each of the priority classes and relegate some jobs to lower priority classes. For example, if some repair requests in the first priority class can be reassigned to the second priority class, this will tend to decrease the average wait times for repair jobs in the highest priority class simply because the arrival rate of those items will be lower.

Example 12 ▶

The manager of the repair shop in Example 11, after consulting with the managers of the departments that use the shop's services, has revised the list of tools that are given the highest priorities. The revised average arrival rates are now: $\lambda_1 = 1.5$, $\lambda_2 = 2.5$, and λ_3 remains unchanged at 1.0. Determine the value of the following measures:

a. The server utilization.

b. The average waiting time for units in each priority class.

SOLUTION

$$\lambda = \sum \lambda_k = 1.5 + 2.5 + 1.0 = 5.0$$

$$M = 6$$

$$\mu = 1$$

Note that these values are the same as in the previous example.

a. $\rho = \dfrac{\lambda}{M\mu} = 5.0/6(1) = .833$, the same as in the previous example.

b. The value of A, since it is a function of M, μ, and λ, is the same as in the preceding example because these values are the same. Therefore, $A = 10.19$ and

$$B_0 = 1 \text{ (always)}$$

$$B_1 = 1 - \frac{1.5}{6(1)} = .75$$

$$B_2 = 1 - \frac{1.5 + 2.5}{6(1)} = .333, \text{ same}$$

$$B_3 = 1 - \frac{1.5 + 2.5 + 1.0}{6(1)} = .167, \text{ same}$$

Then

$$W_1 = \frac{1}{10.19(1)(.75)} = .131 \text{ hour}$$

$$W_2 = \frac{1}{10.19(.75)(.333)} = .393 \text{ hour}$$

$$W_3 = \frac{1}{10.19(.333)(.167)} = 1.765 \text{ hour}$$

Example 12 offers several interesting results. One is that through reduction of the average arrival rate of the highest priority class, the average wait time for units in that class has decreased. In other words, removing some members of the highest class and placing them into the next lower class reduced the average wait time for units that remained in the highest class. It is interesting that the average wait time for the second priority class also was reduced, even though units were added to that class. Although this may appear counterintuitive, the *total* average wait time (or total average number waiting) will remain unchanged. We can see this by noticing that the average *number* waiting (see Example 11, part *d*) is .294 + .884 + 1.765 = 2.943. In Example 12, using the average wait times just calculated, the average number waiting in all three classes in total is:

$$\sum_{k=1}^{3} \lambda_k W_k = 1.5(.131) + 2.5(.393) + 1.0(1.765) = 2.944.$$

Aside from a slight difference due to rounding, the totals are the same.

Another interesting observation is that the average wait time for customers in the third priority class did not change from the preceding example. The reason for this is that the *total* average arrival rates for the two higher-priority classes did not change and the average arrival rate for this class did not change.

Queuing Model: Finite Source

LO6

The finite-source model is appropriate for cases in which the calling population is limited. For instance, in a queuing system for breakdowns of five machines, the size of the calling population is five.

As in the "infinite"-source models, arrival rates are assumed to be Poisson and service durations Exponential. A major difference between the finite- and "infinite"-source models is that the arrival rate of customers (machines) in a finite situation is *affected by* the length of the waiting line; the arrival rate decreases as the length of the line increases simply because there is a decreasing proportion of the population that is out and can generate calls for service. When *all* of the population is waiting in line, the arrival rate is zero because no additional units can arrive.

Because the mathematics of the finite-source model can be complex, analysts often use a table (Table 18-6) in conjunction with simple formulas to analyze these systems. Table 18-7 contains a list of the key formulas and definitions. The inputs to the model are the average service duration *T*, the average run duration *U*, the number of servers *M*, and total number of machines *N*. The desired quantities of interest are the average wait time (before service) *W*, average number running *J*, the average number in line *L*, and the average number in service *H*. You will find it helpful to study the diagram of a run-wait-service cycle that is presented in Table 18-7.

Table 18-6 ▼

Finite-source model table; values for D and F, given values for X and M.

X	M	D	F	X	M	D	F	X	M	D	F	X	M	D	F
Population 5				.110	2	.065	.996	.220	3	.036	.997		1	.911	.569
.012	1	.048	.999		1	.421	.939		2	.229	.969	.360	4	.017	.998
.019	1	.076	.998	.115	2	.071	.995		1	.735	.765		3	.141	.981
.025	1	.100	.997		1	.439	.933	.230	3	.041	.997		2	.501	.880
.030	1	.120	.996	.120	2	.076	.995		2	.247	.965		1	.927	.542
.034	1	.135	.995		1	.456	.927		1	.756	.747	.380	4	.021	.998
.036	1	.143	.994	.125	2	.082	.994	.240	3	.046	.996		3	.163	.976
.040	1	.159	.993		1	.473	.920		2	.265	.960		2	.540	.863
.042	1	.167	.992	.130	2	.089	.993		1	.775	.730		1	.941	.516
.044	1	.175	.991		1	.489	.914	.250	3	.052	.995	.400	4	.026	.997
.046	1	.183	.990	.135	2	.095	.993		2	.284	.955		3	.186	.972
.050	1	.198	.989		1	.505	.907		1	.794	.712		2	.579	.845
.052	1	.206	.988	.140	2	.102	.992	.260	3	.058	.994		1	.952	.493
.054	1	.214	.987		1	.521	.900		2	.303	.950	.420	4	.031	.997
.056	2	.018	.999	.145	3	.011	.999		1	.811	.695		3	.211	.966
	1	.222	.985		2	.109	.991	.270	3	.064	.994		2	.616	.826
.058	2	.019	.999		1	.537	.892		2	.323	.944		1	.961	.471
	1	.229	.984	.150	3	.012	.999		1	.827	.677	.440	4	.037	.996
.060	2	.020	.999		2	.115	.990	.280	3	.071	.993		3	.238	.960
	1	.237	.983		1	.553	.885		2	.342	.938		2	.652	.807
.062	2	.022	.999	.155	3	.013	.999		1	.842	.661		1	.969	.451
	1	.245	.982		2	.123	.989	.290	4	.007	.999	.460	4	.045	.995
.064	2	.023	.999		1	.568	.877		3	.079	.992		3	.266	.953
	1	.253	.981	.160	3	.015	.999		2	.362	.932		2	.686	.787
.066	2	.024	.999		2	.130	.988		1	.856	.644		1	.975	.432
	1	.260	.979		1	.582	.869	.300	4	.008	.999	.480	4	.053	.994
.068	2	.026	.999	.165	3	.016	.999		3	.086	.990		3	.296	.945
	1	.268	.978		2	.137	.987		2	.382	.926		2	.719	.767
.070	2	.027	.999		1	.597	.861		1	.869	.628		1	.980	.415
	1	.275	.977	.170	3	.017	.999	.310	4	.009	.999	.500	4	.063	.992
.075	2	.031	.999		2	.145	.985		3	.094	.989		3	.327	.936
	1	.294	.973		1	.611	.853		2	.402	.919		2	.750	.748
.080	2	.035	.998	.180	3	.021	.999		1	.881	.613		1	.985	.399
	1	.313	.969		2	.161	.983	.320	4	.010	.999	.520	4	.073	.991
.085	2	.040	.998		1	.683	.836		3	.103	.988		3	.359	.927
	1	.332	.965	.190	3	.024	.998		2	.422	.912		2	.779	.728
.090	2	.044	.998		2	.177	.980		1	.892	.597		1	.988	.384
	1	.350	.960		1	.665	.819	.330	4	.012	.999	.540	4	.085	.989
.095	2	.049	.997	.200	3	.028	.998		3	.112	.986		3	.392	.917
	1	.368	.955		2	.194	.976		2	.442	.904		2	.806	.708
.100	2	.054	.997		1	.689	.801		1	.902	.583		1	.991	.370
	1	.386	.950	.210	3	.032	.998	.340	4	.013	.999	.560	4	.098	.986
.105	2	.059	.997		2	.211	.973		3	.121	.985		3	.426	.906
	1	.404	.945		1	.713	.783		2	.462	.896		2	.831	.689

▼ **Table 18-6**

(continued)

X	M	D	F	X	M	D	F	X	M	D	F	X	M	D	F
	1	.993	.357	.038	2	.046	.999		2	.216	.986		3	.169	.987
.580	4	.113	.984		1	.337	.982		1	.722	.867		2	.505	.928
	3	.461	.895	.040	2	.050	.999	.095	3	.049	.998		1	.947	.627
	2	.854	.670		1	.354	.980		2	.237	.984	.160	4	.044	.998
	1	.994	.345	.042	2	.055	.999		1	.750	.850		3	.182	.986
.600	4	.130	.981		1	.371	.978	.100	3	.056	.998		2	.528	.921
	3	.497	.883	.044	2	.060	.998		2	.258	.981		1	.954	.610
	2	.875	.652		1	.388	.975		1	.776	.832	.165	4	.049	.997
	1	.996	.333	.046	2	.065	.998	.105	3	.064	.997		3	.195	.984
.650	4	.179	.972		1	.404	.973		2	.279	.978		2	.550	.914
	3	.588	.850	.048	2	.071	.998		1	.800	.814		1	.961	.594
	2	.918	.608		1	.421	.970	.110	3	.072	.997	.170	4	.054	.997
	1	.998	.308	.050	2	.076	.998		2	.301	.974		3	.209	.982
.700	4	.240	.960		1	.437	.967		1	.822	.795		2	.571	.906
	3	.678	.815	.052	2	.082	.997	.115	3	.081	.996		1	.966	.579
	2	.950	.568		1	.454	.963		2	.324	.971	.180	5	.013	.999
	1	.999	.286	.054	2	.088	.997		1	.843	.776		4	.066	.996
.750	4	.316	.944		1	.470	.960	.120	4	.016	.999		3	.238	.978
	3	.763	.777	.056	2	.094	.997		3	.090	.995		2	.614	.890
	2	.972	.532		1	.486	.956		2	.346	.967		1	.975	.890
.800	4	.410	.924	.058	2	.100	.996		1	.861	.756	.190	5	.016	.999
	3	.841	.739		1	.501	.953	.125	4	.019	.999		4	.078	.995
	2	.987	.500	.060	2	.106	.996		3	.100	.994		3	.269	.973
.850	4	.522	.900		1	.517	.949		2	.369	.962		2	.654	.873
	3	.907	.702	.062	2	.113	.996		1	.878	.737		1	.982	.522
	2	.995	.470		1	.532	.945	.130	4	.022	.999	.200	5	.020	.999
.900	4	.656	.871	.064	2	.119	.995		3	.110	.994		4	.092	.994
	3	.957	.666		1	.547	.940		2	.392	.958		3	.300	.968
	2	.998	.444	.066	2	.126	.995		1	.893	.718		2	.692	.854
.950	4	.815	.838		1	.562	.936	.135	4	.025	.999		1	.987	.497
	3	.989	.631	.068	3	.020	.999		3	.121	.993	.210	5	.025	.999
Population 10					2	.133	.994		2	.415	.952		4	.108	.992
.016	1	.144	.997		1	.577	.931		1	.907	.699		3	.333	.961
.019	1	.170	.996	.070	3	.022	.999	.140	4	.028	.999		2	.728	.835
.021	1	.188	.995		2	.140	.994		3	.132	.991		1	.990	.474
.023	1	.206	.994		1	.591	.926		2	.437	.947	.220	5	.030	.998
.025	1	.224	.993	.075	3	.026	.999		1	.919	.680		4	.124	.990
.026	1	.232	.992		2	.158	.992	.145	4	.032	.999		3	.366	.954
.028	1	.250	.991		1	.627	.913		3	.144	.990		2	.761	.815
.030	1	.268	.990	.080	3	.031	.999		2	.460	.941		1	.993	.453
.032	2	.033	.999		2	.177	.990		1	.929	.662	.230	5	.037	.998
	1	.285	.988		1	.660	.899	.150	4	.036	.998		4	.142	.988
.034	2	.037	.999	.085	3	.037	.999		3	.156	.989		3	.400	.947
	1	.301	.986		2	.196	.988		2	.483	.935		2	.791	.794
.036	2	.041	.999		1	.692	.883		1	.939	.644		1	.995	.434
	1	.320	.984	.090	3	.043	.998	.155	4	.040	.998	.240	5	.044	.997

Table 18-6
(concluded)

X	M	D	F	X	M	D	F	X	M	D	F	X	M	D	F
	4	.162	.986		5	.135	.988		7	.058	.995		8	.072	.994
	3	.434	.938		4	.359	.952		6	.193	.979		7	.242	.972
	2	.819	.774		3	.695	.845		5	.445	.930		6	.518	.915
	1	.996	.416		2	.952	.617		4	.747	.822		5	.795	.809
.250	6	.010	.999	.330	6	.042	.997		3	.947	.646		4	.953	.663
	5	.052	.997		5	.151	.986		2	.998	.435		3	.996	.500
	4	.183	.983		4	.387	.945	.480	8	.015	.999	.650	9	.021	.999
	3	.469	.929		3	.723	.831		7	.074	.994		8	.123	.988
	2	.844	.753		2	.961	.600		6	.230	.973		7	.353	.954
	1	.997	.400	.340	7	.010	.999		5	.499	.916		6	.651	.878
.260	6	.013	.999		6	.049	.997		4	.791	.799		5	.882	.759
	5	.060	.996		5	.168	.983		3	.961	.621		4	.980	.614
	4	.205	.980		4	.416	.938		2	.998	.417		3	.999	.461
	3	.503	.919		3	.750	.816	.500	8	.020	.999	.700	9	.040	.997
	2	.866	.732		2	.968	.584		7	.093	.992		8	.200	.979
	1	.998	.384	.360	7	.014	.999		6	.271	.966		7	.484	.929
.270	6	.015	.999		6	.064	.995		5	.553	.901		6	.772	.836
	5	.070	.995		5	.205	.978		4	.830	.775		5	.940	.711
	4	.228	.976		4	.474	.923		3	.972	.598		4	.992	.571
	3	.537	.908		3	.798	.787		2	.999	.400	.750	9	.075	.994
	2	.886	.712		2	.978	.553	.520	8	.026	.998		8	.307	.965
	1	.999	.370	.380	7	.019	.999		7	.115	.989		7	.626	.897
.280	6	.018	.999		6	.083	.993		6	.316	.958		6	.870	.792
	5	.081	.994		5	.247	.971		5	.606	.884		5	.975	.666
	4	.252	.972		4	.533	.906		4	.864	.752		4	.998	.533
	3	.571	.896		3	.840	.758		3	.980	.575	.800	9	.134	.988
	2	.903	.692		2	.986	.525		2	.999	.385		8	.446	.944
	1	.999	.357	.400	7	.026	.998	.540	8	.034	.997		7	.763	.859
.290	6	.022	.999		6	.105	.991		7	.141	.986		6	.939	.747
	5	.093	.993		5	.292	.963		6	.363	.949		5	.991	.625
	4	.278	.968		4	.591	.887		5	.658	.867		4	.999	.500
	3	.603	.884		3	.875	.728		4	.893	.729	.850	9	.232	.979
	2	.918	.672		2	.991	.499		3	.986	.555		8	.611	.916
	1	.999	.345	.420	7	.034	.993	.560	8	.044	.996		7	.879	.818
.300	6	.026	.998		6	.130	.987		7	.171	.982		6	.978	.705
	5	.106	.991		5	.341	.954		6	.413	.939		5	.998	.588
	4	.304	.963		4	.646	.866		5	.707	.848	.900	9	.387	.963
	3	.635	.872		3	.905	.700		4	.917	.706		8	.785	.881
	2	.932	.653		2	.994	.476		3	.991	.535		7	.957	.777
	1	.999	.333	.440	7	.045	.997	.580	8	.057	.995		6	.995	.667
.310	6	.031	.998		6	.160	.984		7	.204	.977	.950	9	.630	.938
	5	.120	.990		5	.392	.943		6	.465	.927		8	.934	.841
	4	.331	.957		4	.698	.845		5	.753	.829		7	.994	.737
	3	.666	.858		3	.928	.672		4	.937	.684				
	2	.943	.635		2	.996	.454		3	.994	.517				
.320	6	.036	.998	.460	8	.011	.999	.600	9	.010	.999				

Source: L.G. Peck and R.N. Hazelwood, *Finite Queuing Tables* (New York: John Wiley & Sons, 1958). Reprinted by permission.

Formulas			Notation
Service factor	$X = \dfrac{T}{T + U}$	(18-34)	D = Probability that a machine will have to wait in line before service
Average number waiting	$L = N(1 - F)$	(18-35)	F = Efficiency factor: proportion of machines being serviced or running
Average waiting time	$W = \dfrac{L(T + U)}{N - L} = \dfrac{T(1 - F)}{XF}$	(18-36)	H = Average number of machines being serviced
Average number running	$J = NF(1 - X)$	(18-37)	J = Average number of machines running
Average number being serviced	$H = FNX$	(18-38)	L = Average number of machines waiting for service
			M = Number of servers
Number in population	$N = J + L + H$	(18-39)	N = Number of machines
			T = Average service duration
			U = Average run duration
			W = Average wait duration
			X = Service factor; proportion of average service duration to sum of average service and average run durations

Table 18-7

Finite-source model formulas and definitions.

Table 18-6 is an abbreviated finite-source model table used to obtain values of D and F, given X and M. (Most of the formulas require a value for F.) In order to use this table, follow this procedure:

1. Identify the values for

    a. N, population size.
    b. M, number of servers.
    c. T, average service duration.
    d. U, average run duration.

2. Calculate the service factor, $X = T/(T + U)$.

3. Locate the section of the finite-source model table for population size N. (Only values for $N = 5$ and 10 are shown here because of space limitation.)

4. Using the value of X as the point of entry, find the values of F and D that correspond to M.

5. Use the value of F to determine the values of the desired measures of system performance using the formulas in Table 18-7.

One operator loads and unloads a group of five machines. Service durations (i.e., one unloading and loading) are Exponentially distributed with a mean of 10 minutes per machine. Machines run for an average of 70 minutes between loading and unloading, and this duration is also Exponential. Find:

Example 13

a. The average number of machines waiting for the operator.
b. The expected number of machines running.
c. Average duration of downtime.
d. The probability that a machine will not have to wait for service.

SOLUTION

$N = 5$

$T = 10$ minutes

$M = 1$

$U = 70$ minutes

$$X = \frac{T}{T + U} = \frac{10}{10 + 70} = .125$$

From Table 18-6, with $N = 5$, $M = 1$, and $X = .125$, we obtain $D = .473$ and $F = .920$.

a. Average number waiting, $L = N(1 - F) = 5(1 - .920) = .40$ machine.
b. Expected number running, $J = NF(1 - X) = 5(.92)(1 - .125) = 4.025$ machines.
c. Downtime = Waiting time + Service time:

$$\text{Average waiting time } W = \frac{L(T + U)}{N - L} = \frac{.40(10 + 70)}{5 - .40} = 6.957 \text{ minutes}$$

Downtime = 6.957 minutes + 10 minutes = 16.957 minutes

d. Probability of not having to wait = 1 − Probability of having to wait

$$= 1 - D$$

$$= 1 - .473 = .527$$

Using the Excel template, the solution to Example 13 would appear as follows:

	A / B	C	D	E	F	G	H
1	Finite Source Waiting Line Model						
2	<Back						
3	Population Size	N =	5	5			
4	Number of servers	M =	1	2			
5	Average service time	T =	10	10			
6	Average time between service calls	U =	70	70			
7	P(wait) - from table	D =	0.4730	0.0820			
8	Efficiency factor - from table	F =	0.9200	0.9940			
9	Service factor	X =	0.125	0.125			
10	Average number waiting	L =	0.4000	0.0300			
11	Average waiting time	W =	6.9565	0.4829			
12	Average number running	J =	4.0250	4.3488			
13	Average number being serviced	H =	0.5750	0.6213			
14							
15		Per Time					
16		Unit					
17	Service cost =	10	10	20			
18	Downtime cost =	16	15.6	10.42			
19	Total Cost =		25.6	30.42			
20							
21							
22	Note: You must enter D and F (based on N, X, and M) from the table in the text.						
23							

Suppose that in Example 13, the operator is paid $10 per hour and machine downtime costs $16 per hour. Should the department add another operator if the goal is total cost minimization?

◀ **Example 14**

Compare the total cost of the present system with the total cost of the proposed system:

SOLUTION

M	Average Number Down, $N - J$	Average Down Cost (per hour), $(N - J) \times \$16$	Operator Cost (per hour)	Total Cost (per hour)
1	$5 - 4.025 = .975$	$15.60	$10	$25.60
2	.651	10.42	20	30.42

where $N - J$ for $M = 2$ is obtained as follows: For $X = .125$ and $M = 2$, from Table 18-6 $F = .994$; therefore $J = NF(1 - X) = 5(.994)(1 - .125) = 4.349$, and $N - J = 5 - 4.349 = .651$. Hence, the present system is superior because its total cost is less than the total cost of using two operators.

Summary

- Analysis of waiting lines can be an important aspect of the design of service systems.
- Waiting lines have a tendency to form in such systems even though, in a macro sense, the system is underloaded.
- The arrival of customers together and variability of service durations combine to create temporary overloads. By the same token, at other times the servers are idle.
- The goal is to minimize total customer wait and server costs, but a standard on a performance measure such as "average wait time < 3 minutes" is also used to determine the number of servers.
- A major consideration in the analysis of queuing systems is whether the number of

potential customers is limited (finite source) or unrestricted ("infinite" source).
- Nine queuing models are described, eight dealing with "infinite" source (four for single servers and four for multiple servers) and one dealing with finite source.
- Most models assume that customer arrival rates can be described by a Poisson distribution, that service durations can be described by an Exponential distribution, and customers are served FCFS.
- Basic relationships are given so that starting from the average queue length, other measures such as average wait time in the line or in the system and probability of having to wait can be determined.

Key Terms

Exponential distribution
finite source
"infinite" source

multiple-server-with-priority model
Poisson distribution
queue discipline

queuing theory
server utilization

Solved Problems

Problem 1

"Infinite"-source, Multiple servers, Exponential service durations (Model 5). One of the features of a new machine shop will be a well-stocked tool crib. The manager of the shop must decide on the number of attendants needed to staff the crib. Attendants will receive $9 per hour in wages and fringe benefits. Mechanics' time will be worth $30 per hour, which includes wages and fringe benefits. Based on previous experience, the manager estimates requests for tools will average 18 per hour with a

service capacity of 20 requests per hour per attendant. How many attendants should be on duty in order to minimize total mechanics wait cost and attendants' wages? Assume that arrival and service rates will be Poisson. (Also assume that the number of mechanics is very large, in order for the infinite-source model to be appropriate.)

Solution

$\lambda = 18$ per hour
$\mu = 20$ per hour

Number of Attendants, M	L_q^*	$L_q + \dfrac{\lambda}{\mu} = L_s$	$9M$: Attendant Cost (per hour)	$30L_s$: Mechanic Cost (per hour)	Total Cost (per hour)
1	8.1	8.1 + .9 = 9.0	$9	$270	$279
2	.229	.229 + .9 = 1.129	$18	$33.87	$52†
3	.03	.03 + .9 = .93	$27	$27.9	$55†

* L_q from Table 18-4, with $\lambda/\mu = 18/20 = .9$.

† Rounded.

Hence, two attendants will produce the lowest total cost.

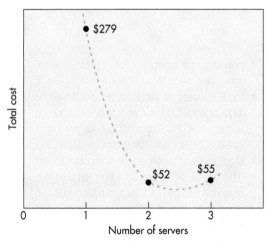

Problem 2

Infinite source. The following is a list of average service duration for three different operations:

Operation	Average Service Duration
A	8 minutes
B	1.2 hours
C	2 days

a. Determine the average service rate for each operation.
b. Would the calculated rates be different if these were interarrival durations rather than service durations?

Solution

a. The average service rate is the reciprocal of average service duration. Thus, the rates are:

   A: 1/8 per minute = .125 per minute, or × 60 = 7.5 per hour
   B: 1/1.2 per hour = .833 per hour
   C: 1/2 per day = .50 per day

b. No. In either case, the rate is simply the reciprocal of the duration.

Problem 3

Finite source. A group of 10 machines is loaded and unloaded by one of three servers. The machines run for an average of six minutes per cycle, and average time to unload and reload is nine minutes. Run and service durations can be described by Exponential distributions. While running, the machines produce a total of 16 units per hour if they did not have to pause to wait for a server and be loaded and unloaded. What is the average hourly output of each machine when waiting and serving are taken into account?

Solution

$T = 9$ minutes

$U = 6$ minutes; $X = \dfrac{T}{T + U} = \dfrac{9}{9 + 6} = .60$

$N = 10$ machines

$M = 3$ servers; *from* Table 18-6 (Population 10), *we obtain* $F = .500$, $D = .996$

Calculate the average number of machines running:

$J = NF(1 - X) = 10(.500)(1 - .6) = 2$

Determine the percentage of machines running, and multiply by output while running:

$\dfrac{J}{N} \times (16 \text{ per hour}) = \dfrac{2}{10} \times (16 \text{ units per hour}) = 3.2 \text{ units per hour}$

Discussion and Review Questions

Note: An asterisk indicates that a question or problem may be more challenging.

1. Give some examples of services where waiting lines are used. **LO1**

2. Why do waiting lines form even though the system is underloaded? **LO1**

3. What are the most common measures of system performance in queuing analysis? **LO2**

4. What information is necessary to analyze a queuing system? **LO2**

5. What effect would decreasing arrival and service variability have on the waiting line? **LO2 & 4**

6. What approach do supermarkets use to reduce waiting times? **LO2**

7. Contrast finite and "infinite" sources. **LO2**

8. In a multiple-server system, what is the rationale for having customers wait in a single joint line as is now done in many banks, rather than in multiple lines? **LO2**

9. What happens to the average wait time if a manager attempts to achieve a high capacity utilization? What happens if $\lambda \geq \mu$? **LO2**

10. Explain Little's formula: $L = \lambda W$. **LO3**

11. What is the difference between W_q and W_s? **LO3**

12. Will doubling the service rate of a single server system reduce the average waiting time in line by a factor of one-half? Explain briefly. **LO4**

13. Can a service duration be more variable than an Exponential distribution? Explain. **LO4**

14. Is Model 1 a special case of Model 5? Explain. **LO5**

15. Name two ways the number of servers can be determined. **LO5**

16. How can Model 6 be used to determine the maximum length of the line (size of waiting room)? **LO5**

17. Give an example where the distribution of interarrival times is not Poisson. **LO5**

18. A traffic light and the cars waiting at the traffic light on one side of the street form a queuing system. If there are two lines on this side of the street, what queuing model best describes this situation? **LO5**

19. Give an example of a situation where the finite-source model can be used. **LO6**

20. What are some psychological approaches to managing waiting lines, and why might a manger want to use them? **LO1**

Taking Stock

1. What general trade-off is involved in waiting-line decisions? **LO1**

2. Who needs to be involved in assessing the waiting cost if the customers are (a) the general public and (b) employees of the organization? **LO1**

3. How has technology (a) had an impact on analyzing waiting-line systems? (b) improved waiting-line performance? **LO1**

Critical Thinking Exercise

The owner of a restaurant implemented an expanded menu early last year. The menu was a success, drawing many more customers than the previous menu. But good news soon became bad news as long waiting lines began to deter customers, and business dropped off. Describe how waiting-line analysis can help the restaurant. **LO1 & 2**

Experiential Learning Exercise

Determine the average arrival rate and average service rate at one of these operations: a fast-food restaurant, supermarket, post office, or bank branch. **LO1 & 2**

a. For the arrival rate, observe for 15 one-minute intervals. Count the number of arrivals in each minute. Construct a frequency distribution for arrivals. Does it resemble a Poisson distribution? Calculate its mean.

b. Now determine the service durations. To do this, observe the service time of 15 customers (e.g., how many minutes a teller at a bank spent with each customer). Make a frequency distribution. Does it look like Exponential distribution? Calculate its mean.

Internet Exercises

1. Visit http://www.q-matic.com/ca, find a case study, and briefly describe how the Qmatic system helped the operation. **LO2**

Problems

1. $\lambda = 3$ customers/hour

$\mu = 5$ customers/hour

$M = 1$

a. What is the server utilization? **LO4**

b. What is the average number of customers waiting for service? **LO4**

c. What is the average time customers wait in line for service? **LO4**

2. Repair calls for Xerox copiers in a small city are handled by one repair person. Repair duration, including travel time, is Exponentially distributed with a mean of two hours per call. Requests for copier repairs come in at a mean rate of three per eight-hour day (assume Poisson). Assume infinite source. Determine: **LO4**

a. The average number of copiers waiting for repair.

b. Server utilization.

c. The amount of time during an eight-hour day that the repair person is not out on a call.

d. The probability of two or more copiers in the system (waiting to be or being repaired).

e. The probability that a copier waits more than four hours for repair to begin.

3. A vending machine dispenses hot chocolate or coffee. Service duration is 30 seconds per cup and is constant.

Customers arrive at a mean rate of 80 per hour (assume Poisson). Also assume that each customer buys only one cup. Determine: **LO4**

a. The average number of customers waiting in line.

b. The average time customers spend in the system.

c. The average number of customers in the system.

4. Many of a bank's customers use its automated teller machine (ATM). During the early evening hours in the summer months, customers arrive at the ATM at the rate of one every other minute (assume Poisson). Each customer spends an average of 90 seconds completing his or her transaction. Transaction times are Exponentially distributed. Assume that the length of queue is not a constraint. Determine: **LO4**

a. The average time customers spend at the machine, including waiting in line and completing transactions.

b. The probability that a customer will not have to wait upon arrival at the ATM.

c. Utilization of the ATM.

d. The probability that a customer waits four minutes or more in the line.

5. A small town with one hospital has two ambulances. Requests for an ambulance during weekday mornings average .8 per hour and tend to be Poisson. Travel and loading/unloading time averages one hour per call and follows an Exponential distribution. Find: **LO5**

a. Server utilization.

b. The average number of patients waiting.

c. The average time patients wait for an ambulance.

d. The probability that both ambulances will be busy when a call comes in.

6. The following information pertains to telephone calls to a call centre on a typical workday. Assume Poisson arrivals and Exponential service durations. **LO5**

Period	Average Incoming Rate (calls per minute)	Average Service Rate (calls per minute per operator)	Number of Operators
Morning	1.8	1.5	2
Afternoon	2.2	1.0	3
Evening	1.4	0.7	3

a. Determine the average time callers wait to have their calls answered for each period and the probability that a caller will have to wait during each period.

b. The call centre has seven leased phone lines (trunks). What is probability that a phone call will receive a busy signal during each of the three periods?

7. Trucks are required to check in a weigh station (scale) so that they can be inspected for weight violations. Trucks arrive at the station at the rate of 40 an hour in the mornings according to Poisson distribution. Currently two inspectors are on duty during those hours, each of whom can inspect 25 trucks an hour, according to Poisson distribution. **LO5**

a. How many trucks would you expect to see at the weigh station, including those being inspected?

b. If a truck were just arriving at the station, how many minutes could the driver expect to wait before being inspected?

c. How many minutes, on average, would a truck that is not immediately inspected have to wait before being inspected?

d. What is the probability that both inspectors would be busy at the same time (i.e., the probability that an arrival will have to wait for service)?

e. What condition would exist if there were only one inspector?

f. If only 13 trucks fit in the system, what is the probability that a truck cannot enter the system?

8. The manager of a new regional warehouse of a company must decide on the number of loading docks to request in order to minimize the sum of dock–crew and driver–truck costs. The manager has learned that each driver–truck combination represents a cost of $300 per day and that each dock plus crew represents a cost of $1,100 per day. **LO4 & 5**

a. How many docks should she request if trucks will arrive at average rate of four per day, each dock can handle an average of five trucks per day, and both rates are Poisson?

b. An employee has proposed adding new equipment that would speed up the service rate to 5.71 trucks per day. The equipment would cost $100 per day for each dock. Would this change the answer to part *a*? Should the manager invest in the new equipment?

9. The parts department of a large automobile dealership has a counter used exclusively for its own service mechanics requesting parts. The length of time between requests can be modelled by an Exponential distribution that has a mean of five minutes. A parts clerk can handle requests at an average rate of 15 per hour, and this can be modelled by a Poisson distribution. Suppose there are two parts clerks at the counter. **LO5**

a. On average, how many mechanics would be at the counter, including those being served?

b. If a mechanic has to wait, how long would the average wait be?

c. What is the probability that a mechanic would have to wait for service?

d. What percentage of time is a clerk idle?

e. If clerks represent a cost of $20 per hour and mechanics represent a cost of $30 per hour, how many clerks would be optimal in terms of minimizing total cost?

10. One field representative services five customers for a computer manufacturer. Customers request assistance at an average (Poisson-distributed) rate of once every four workdays. The field representative can handle an average (Poisson-distributed) of one call per day. Determine: **LO6**

a. The expected number of customers waiting.

b. The average length of time customers must wait from the initial request for service until the service has been completed.

c. The percentage of time the service rep will be idle, i.e., the probability that a customer will not have to wait.

d. By how much would your answer to part *a* be reduced if a second field rep were added?

11. Two operators handle adjustments for a group of 10 machines. Adjustment time is Exponentially distributed and has a mean of 14 minutes per machine. The machines operate for an average of 86 minutes after an adjustment (Exponentially distributed). While running, each machine can turn out 50 pieces per hour. Find: **LO6**

a. The probability that a machine will have to wait for an adjustment.

b. The average number of machines waiting for adjustment.

c. The average number of machines being serviced.

d. The expected hourly output of each machine, taking adjustments into account.

e. Machine downtime represents a cost of $70 per hour; operator cost (including fringe benefits) is $15 per hour. What is the optimum number of operators?

12. One operator services a group of five machines. Machine run time and service durations are both Exponential. Machines run for an average of 90 minutes after a service, and service duration averages 35 minutes. The operator receives $20 per hour in wage and fringe benefits, and machine downtime costs $70 per hour per machine. **LO6**

   a. If each machine produces 60 pieces per hour while running, find the average hourly output of each machine when waiting and service times are taken into account.

   b. Determine the optimum number of operators.

13. A milling department has 10 machines. Each machine operates an average of eight hours before requiring adjustment, which takes an average of two hours. Both distributions are Exponential. While running, each machine can produce 40 pieces an hour. **LO6**

   a. With one adjuster, what is the net average hourly output per machine?

   b. If machine downtime cost is $80 per hour and adjuster cost is $20 per hour, how many adjusters would be optimal?

14. Trucks arrive at the loading dock of a wholesale grocer at an average rate of 1.2 per hour in the mornings. A single crew consisting of two workers can load a truck in about 30 minutes. Crew members receive $10 per hour in wage and fringe benefits, and trucks and drivers reflect an hourly cost of $60. The manager is thinking of adding another member to the crew. The average service rate would then be 2.4 trucks per hour. Assume both arrival and service rates are Poisson. **LO4**

   a. Would the third crew member be economical?

   b. Would a fourth member be justifiable if the resulting average service capacity were 2.6 trucks per hour?

15. Customers arriving at a service centre are assigned to one of three categories (1, 2, and 3); category 1 is the highest priority. Records indicate that an average of nine customers arrive per hour and that one-third are assigned to each category. There are two servers, and each can process customers at an average rate of five per hour. Arrival and service rates can be described by Poisson distributions. **LO5**

   a. What is the utilization of a server?

   b. Determine the average wait time for customers in each class.

   c. Find the average number of customers in each class that are waiting for service.

16. A priority system is used to process customers, who are assigned one of two classes when they enter the processing centre. The highest-priority class has an average arrival rate of four per hour; the other class has an average arrival rate of two per hour. Both can be described as Poisson-distributed. There are two servers, and each can process customers in an average of six minutes (Exponentially distributed). **LO5**

   a. What is the server utilization?

   b. Determine the average wait time for each class.

   c. Determine the average number of customers of each class that would be waiting for service.

   d. If the manager could alter the assignment rules so that arrival rates of the two classes were equal, what would be the revised average wait time for each priority class?

17. A priority waiting system assigns arriving customers one of four classes (class 1 has the highest priority). Arrival rates of the classes have Poisson distribution and their average are: **LO5**

Class	Average Arrivals per Hour
1	2
2	4
3	3
4	2

Five servers process the customers, and each can handle an average of three customers per hour. The service rate is Poisson.

   a. What is the server utilization?

   b. What is the average wait time for service by customers in the various classes? How many are waiting in each class on average?

   c. If the average arrival rate of the second priority class could be reduced to three customers per hour by shifting some arrivals into the third priority class (which makes its average arrival rate 4 per hour), how would your answers to part *b* change?

   d. What observations can you make based on your answers to part *c*?

18. Referring to Problem 17, suppose that each server could handle an average of four customers per hour. Answer the questions posed in Problem 17. Explain why the impact of reassigning customers in part *c* is much less in this case than in Problem 17. **LO5**

19. During the morning hours at a catalogue sales department, phone calls come in at an average rate of 40 per hour. Calls that cannot be answered immediately are put on hold. The system can handle eight callers on hold. If additional calls come in, they receive a busy signal. The three customer service representatives who answer the calls spend an average of three minutes with a customer. Both arrival and service rates are Poisson. What is the probability that a caller will get a busy signal? **LO5**

20. Since the terrorist attack of September 11, 2001, getting into the United States became more difficult, and hence slower for Canadian cars and trucks at border crossings. This resulted in long line-ups. One such case occurred on the Ambassador Bridge connecting Windsor to Detroit.[5] There were nine U.S. customs booths at the Detroit side of the bridge. Each truck took approximately two minutes to get cleared. During the busy hours, about 300 trucks (i.e., one every 12 seconds) arrived at the booths. Assuming that the standard deviation of getting cleared is 1 minute per truck and the standard deviation of interarrival durations is 6 seconds, how many more U.S. Customs Booths were needed at the Ambassador Bridge to provide a reasonable average wait time (e.g., less than 10 minutes)? **LO5**

21. The number of customers coming to a bank between 1:00 and 1:30 p.m. of a "normal" day has a Poisson distribution with an average of 39 customers during the half hour. The length of time each customer spends with a teller is Exponential with an average of 45.5 seconds. The average time a customer spends in the line waiting is desired to be three minutes. The manager is wondering how many tellers are required during this time period. **LO5**

*22. Model 8300 Telemetry system used at Wesley Long Community Hospital, Greensboro, North Carolina, is a completely self-contained, wireless, one-patient cardiac monitor.[6] The system provides wireless transmission of a patient's heartbeat to a receiver either at a central station or at the bedside. A study was undertaken to analyze the service provided by the 18 currently held telemetry units and to investigate the cost/benefit of any additional units. During a 38-day reviewing period, there were 156 requests for service (telemetry units are requested and used 24 hours a day). The average service duration was 93.6 hours per patient. Both interarrival and service durations had Exponential distributions. **LO5**

a. What is the average arrival rate per day of patients needing telemetry?

b. What is the average service rate per day of patients needing telemetry?

c. If the average wait time before service is desired to be less than 5 hours, are 18 telemetry units enough? (*Hint:* For $\lambda/\mu = 16$ and M $= 18$, it can be shown that $L_q = 4.29$.)

*23. The number of calls coming into a child abuse hotline during the 5 p.m. to 9 a.m. period on weekdays had a Poisson distribution with an average of 1.67 calls per hour. Call lengths had Exponential distribution with

average of 5.4 minutes. It is considered important that a very high percentage of calls get through to the operator right away (as opposed to having to wait). If only one person is assigned to answer the phones, what is the probability that a call will have to wait because the operator is busy? **LO4**

*24. Becton-Dickinson manufactures medical supplies such as syringes.[7] In one plant it had 10 parallel syringe manufacturing lines. The problem was that syringes kept getting stuck in the lines, shutting the lines down. On average, a line got stuck again one minute after a blockage was removed (this time was distributed Exponentially). One operator was assigned to five lines (i.e., a total of two operators). The average time it took the operator to walk to the blocked line and fix the problem was 10 seconds (this time was distributed Exponentially). How long was a line expected to be down per hour? Assume that the two operators do not help each other. **LO6**

*25. Bendigo Health is a 672-bed hospital near Melbourne, Australia.[8] When the hospital administrators wanted to decide on the number of beds to set aside for a new program, transition care, some research staff suggested the use of queuing theory. Some hospital patients would qualify for the option of transition care before a group/nursing home is found for them. It is estimated that an average of $\lambda = 1.2$ patients per week would be eligible and interested for transition care (Poisson distribution). The average stay in transition care is estimated to be $(1/\mu) = 9.5$ weeks. If a bed is not available in transition care, the patient leaves for another facility (i.e., there is no wait). The research staff suggested the following method: first assume that the number of beds in transition care is infinite. Then, determine the average occupancy (i.e., the average number of patients in the system) $= 1.2(9.5) = 11.4$. Finally, use the fact that the distribution of number of patients in the system is Poisson with a mean of 11.4 to determine the probability that a bed will not be used, given various maximum number of beds. For example, "if the hospital allocates 9 beds to transition care, then in the long run there would be some empty beds on 19.84 percent of days, or about 1 day in 5." **LO5**

a. Use Excel to verify the 19.84% result. Note that the Poisson table at the end of the textbook goes up to only a mean of 9.5. *Hint:* use = poisson(8,11.4,TRUE) in Excel, which gives the cumulative Poisson probability of observing up to $x = 8$, given the average of 11.4. Note that a nine-bed transition care will have some empty beds if $x \leq 8$.

[5] D. Battagello, *Windsor Star Border Reporter*, November 9, 2004, http://web2.uwindsor.ca/math/hlynka/qreal.html.

[6] T. Scott and W.A. Hailey, "Queuing Model Aids Economic Analysis of Health Centre," *Industrial Engineering*, February 1981, pp. 56–61.

[7] M.A. Vogel, "Queueing Theory Applied to Machine Manning," *Interfaces*, 9(4), August 1979, pp. 1–7.

[8] A. Crombie, et al, "Planning the Transition Care," *Australian Health Review*, August 2008, 32(3), pp. 505–508.

b. An alternative method is to use the following (Erlang B) formula,[9] where p_n = probability of n patients in the system and K = maximum number of beds (*Note:* this system is a special case of Model 6 where the finite size K equals the number of servers M, i.e., beds in this case):

$$p_n = \frac{\dfrac{\left(\dfrac{\lambda}{\mu}\right)^n}{n!}}{\sum_{j=0}^{K}\left(\dfrac{\left(\dfrac{\lambda}{\mu}\right)^j}{j!}\right)}$$

Which method is more appropriate for this problem?

*26. Bay of Plenty Electricity (BOPE) is an electrical utility company in the Bay of Plenty, New Zealand.[10] BOPE has 21 company cars that the head-office employees share for company business. However, BOPE has to reduce its costs. Assuming that the average number of employees needing a car per work-hour is 4, the average time they need the car is 2.5 hours, and the average utilization of cars is desired to be 83 percent, how many cars does BOPE need? **LO5**

*27. A Greek electrical appliance manufacturer has three trucks that its various departments, such as production, receiving, mould shop, and maintenance shop, use as needed.[11] The users have expressed that they wait an average of about nine minutes before a truck arrives (travel time is negligible). A study over 17 days (a day has 15 work hours) recorded 1,172 requests for truck service (randomly distributed over time, implying that the number of requests per hour was Poisson). The average service time was 20.3 minutes with a standard deviation of 10.6 minutes. **LO5**

a. Calculate the approximate average wait time in the queue for the truck users by using Model 7. *Note:* Variance of a Poisson distribution is equal to its mean.

b. Give some possible reasons for the actual wait time in the queue being so much larger than your answer to part *a*.

*28. The Department of Psychiatry in Cambridge Hospital (CH), Massachusetts, wanted to know the effect of the number of its beds on demand for beds in the local public mental health hospital (PH).[12] A study was undertaken for one year that found that average number of in-state mental health patients arriving at CH was 1.44 per day, and average number of out-of-state mental health patients arriving at CH was .54 per day (both Poisson). CH had 46 beds for mental patients. If there was no free bed in CH, the patient was directed to PH. The average stay in CH was 37.1 days (the length of stay had close-to-Exponential distribution). Using the Erlang formula given in problem 24b above, calculate the probability that a patient finds CH full, i.e., P_{46}. **LO5**

29. A major New York bank commissioned a study to measure the service levels of its over 500 ATMs in New York.[13] The ATMs were located in pairs inside vestibules attached to bank branches. The team used the finite queue version of multiserver queuing model (i.e., Model 6) and suggested that the proportion of customers who balk (i.e., refuse to join the queue) should be used as the measure of service as opposed to the average wait time or average queue length. It was suggested that if the probability of balking during busiest times is greater than 5 percent, then a vestibule should be expanded and an additional ATM installed in it. Consider a specific vestibule with two ATMs in it. There is space for 10 people in the vestibule (2 being served, 8 in line); average service time is 1.28 minutes per customer (approximately Exponential), and average arrival rate is 86 customers per hour (approximately Poisson) during the busiest times of the week (noon–1pm or 1–2 pm weekdays). Determine the probability of balking at this vestibule. Should the vestibule be enlarged? **LO5**

30. The Columbia University Hospital wanted to know if it needed to have more than one operating room (OR) crew present during the night shift (11 p.m. to 7 a.m.).[14] If the probability that one crew is busy is greater than 1 percent, then a second OR crew would be required. During one year, 62 patients required emergency operation during the night shift. The average operation took 80.79 minutes. Does the hospital need a second OR crew during the night shift? **LO4**

[9] S.C. Graves, et al, "A Simple Stochastic Model for Facility Planning in a Mental Health Care System," *Interfaces*, 13(5), October 1983, pp. 101–110.

[10] J. Buchanan and J. Scott, "Vehicle Utilization at Bay of Plenty Electricity," *Interfaces*, 22(2), Mar–Apr 1992, pp. 28–35.

[11] G.P. Cosmetatos, "The Value of Queueing Theory–A Case Study," *Interfaces*, 9(3), May 1979, pp. 47–51.

[12] S.C. Graves, et al, "A Simple Stochastic Model for Facility Planning in a Mental Health Care System," *Interfaces*, 13(5), Oct 1983, pp. 101–110.

[13] P. Kolesar, "Stalking the Endangered CAT: A Queuing Analysis of Congestion at Automatic Teller Machines," *Interfaces*, 14(6), November–December 1984, pp. 16–26.

[14] J.B. Tucker, et al, "Using Queuing Theory to Determine Operating Room Staffing Needs," Journal of Trauma, 46(1), 1999, pp. 71–79.

MINI-CASE

Big Bank

The operations manager of a soon-to-open branch of a large bank is in the process of configuring teller operations. Currently some branches have a separate teller line for customers who have a single transaction, while other branches do not have separate lines. The manager wants to avoid complaints about long waits that have been received at some branches. Because the demographics differ from location to location, a system that works at one branch will not necessarily work at another. The manager has obtained data on processing times from the bank's home office, and is ready to explore different options for configuring operations.

One time that will get special attention is the noon hour on Friday. The plan is to have five tellers available then. Under consideration are the following options:

a. Have one waiting line and have the first person in line go to the next available teller.
b. Have two waiting lines: one teller for customers who have a single transaction and four tellers who would handle customers who have multiple transactions.

An average of 80 customers are served during the noon hour. The average service duration for customers with a single transaction is 90 seconds, while the average service duration for customers with multiple transactions is 4 minutes. Sixty percent of the customers are expected to have multiple transactions.

Question

If you were the manager, which option would you select? Why? Explain the disparity between the results for the two options. What assumptions did you make in your analysis?

MINI-CASE   http://www.lourdes.com

Lourdes Hospital

When doctors referred their patients to the Lourdes Hospital in Binghamton, New York, for various services such as X-rays, their office had a tough time getting through to the centralized appointment office of Lourdes. Most of the time, the line was busy. The installation of a call waiting system did not improve the situation, because callers were put on hold for indefinite lengths of time. The poor service had resulted in numerous complaints. One of the managers was put in charge of finding a solution, and a goal of answering at least 90 percent of calls without delay was set. The hospital was willing to employ more staff to receive calls. The manager studied this queuing problem by collecting data for 21 workdays during which additional staff was used to answer calls and no call received a busy signal or was put on hold. The number of calls per day ranged between 220 and 350, with no day-of-the-week seasonality. Most days, the number of calls was between 250 and 300. The average number of calls arriving during each 15-minute interval peaked at about 10 calls during 9:00–11:30 a.m. and 2:00–3:45 p.m. periods. The 944 service durations during the data collection period had a distribution similar to Exponential with a mean of 3.11 minutes. The manager also found out that

previously the 6.5 full-time-equivalent employees usually spent half their time doing other tasks and turned off their phones while busy with other tasks. Using the multiple servers queuing model and a service goal of at least 90 percent probability of not having to wait, the manager determined the number of staff required during each 15-minute interval. When the original staffing levels were compared with the model-determined ones, it was discovered that more staff were required earlier in the day and later in the afternoon, and fewer were needed around noon. The problem was solved by rearranging work shifts.

Question

During busy periods (9:00 a.m.–11:30 a.m. and 2:00 p.m.–3:45 p.m.), the central appointment office receives 40 calls per hour, on average. Each call takes an average of 3.11 minutes to serve. It is desired that at least 90 percent of calls is received without waiting. What is the minimum number of staff needed during these busy times?

Source: S.R. Agnihothri and P.F. Taylor, "Staffing a Centralized Appointment Scheduling Department in Lourdes Hospital," *Interfaces* 21(5), September–October 1991, pp. 1–11.

To access "Maintenance," the supplement to Chapter 18, please visit *Connect*.

Appendix A   Answers to Selected Problems

Chapter 2: Competitiveness, Strategic Planning, and Productivity

2. A crew size of two has the highest productivity (250 m² per person per week installed).

3. Week 1: 5.62.

   Week 2: 5.45.

   Week 3: 5.20.

   Week 4: 5.01.

   Multifactor productivity is decreasing.

6. 4.3% increase.

Chapter 3: Demand Forecasting

1. a. blueberry has no trend or seasonality; cinnamon has an increasing trend; cupcakes has 5-workday seasonality.

   b. blueberry = 33, cinnamon = 35, cupcakes = 47.

   c. For blueberry, could use an averaging technique such as moving average or exponential smoothing; for cinnamon, could use simple regression for linear trend; for cupcakes, could use the seasonality technique.

4. a. 22.   b. 20.75.   c. 20.72.

7. a. $Y_t = 195.47 + 7.00t$.

   $Y_{16} = 307.47$.

   b. 311.16.

11. a. Fri. = 0.79, Sat. = 1.34, Sun. = 0.87.

14. a.
Day	Relative
1...	0.900
2...	0.833
3...	0.916
4...	1.031
5...	1.412
6...	1.482
7...	0.426

17. b.
Jan	800
Feb	810
Mar	900
Apr	809.6

24. b. −0.985. A strong negative relationship between sales and price.

30. a.
	MSE	MAD	MAPE
Forecast 1......	9.4	2.8	.36%
Forecast 2	38.2	3.6	.46%

   Forecast 1 is superior.

Chapter 5: Strategic Capacity Planning

4. a. A: 8,000 units.

   B: 7,500 units.

   b. 10,000 units.

   c. A: $20,000.

   B: $18,000.

A's profit would be higher.

6. a. A: $74.

   B: $50.

   c. A: 0 to 66 minutes.

7. Vendor best for $Q \leq 63,333$. For larger quantities, produce in-house with process B.

9. 3 machines.

11. a. one machine: BEP = 80.   two machines: BEP = 152.

    b. one machine.

Chapter 6: Process Design and Facility Layout

1. a. 8.

   b. 3.6 minutes.

   c. (1) 50 units.

   (2) 30 units.

2. a.
Station	Tasks	Time
1	a	1.4
2	b, e	1.3
3	d, c, f	1.8
4	g, h	1.5

   b. 82%.

10.

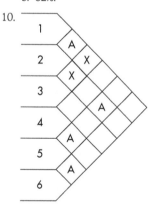

11.
4	3	1
5	8	6
7	2	

16. 3→A, 5→B, 1→C, 4→D, 6→E, 2→F.

Chapter 7: Work/Job Design and Measurement

2. a. 1.2 minutes.

   b. 1.14 minutes.

   c. 1.27 minutes.

4.

Task	OT
1	4.10
2	1.50
3	3.25
4	2.77

7. 5.85 minutes.

8. 7.125 minutes.

11. 57 observations.

12. 37 work cycles.

13. a. 12%.   b. 254 observations.

Chapter 8: Location Planning and Analysis

2. a. A: 16,854; B: 17,416; C: 17,753.   b. C, profit = $14,670.

4. a. B: 0 to 33; C: 34 to 400; A: 400+.   b. C.

   c. Expansion leads to more control, whereas subcontracting leads to more flexibility.

9. A (Score = 87.02).

11. (5, 4).

Chapter 9: Management of Quality

2.

	Res.	Com.
Noisy	10	3
Failed	7	2
Odour	5	7
Warm	3	4

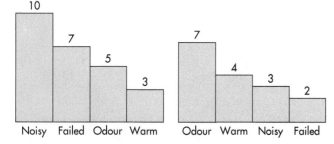

Chapter 10: Statistical Quality Control

1. a. 1.24%. b. 24.4 kg and 24.6 kg.

2. a. LCL: 1.991 litres.

   UCL: 2.009 litres.

  b. Yes, process is in control.

3. a. Mean: LCL is 2.96, UCL is 3.24.

   Range: LCL is .099, UCL is .801.

  b. Yes.

6. a.

1	2	3	4
.020	.010	.025	.045

  b. .025.

  c. Mean = .025, standard deviation = .011.

  d. LCL = .001, UCL = .049.

  e. .0456.

  f. Yes.

  g. Mean = .02, standard deviation = .0099.

  h. LCL = .0002, UCL = .0398. No.

8. a. UCL = 16.266, LCL = 0, Yes.   b. No change.

11. 35 pieces.

16. b. 4.5, .192.

  c. 4.5, .086.

  d. 4.242 to 4.758. The risk is .0026.

  f. None.

17. a. 1.11.   b. Capable.

20. H: C_{pk} = .9375, incapable, K: C_{pk} = 1.0, capable, T: C_{pk} = 1.07, capable.

Chapter 11: Supply Chain Management

1. Use 2-day freight ($29.38 saving).

Chapter 12: Inventory Management

3. a.

Item	Class
Z45	A
F95	A
K35	A
P05	B
F14	B
D45	B
K36	B
D57	B
K34	C
D52	C
M20	C
F99	C
N08	C
D48	C
M10	C

5. a. 228 packages.

  b. $228.04.

  c. Yes.

  d. Yes; TC = $310; save $81.96.

11. a. 1,633 bags.

  b. 490 bags.

  c. 3.27 days.

  d. 24.5 runs per year.

  e. $5,739.71.

15. a. 600 stones (total cost = $41,120).

  b. 150 stones.

19. 6,600 metres.

21. a. 91 kg.

  b. ROP = 691 kg.

30. a. EOQ = 126 cases.   b. ROP = 81.6 cases.

33. K033:581; K144:458; L700:−16 (do not order).

36. 25 dozens, service level = 73%.

38. 78.86 kg.

Chapter 13: Aggregate Operations Planning and Master Scheduling

11. Produce 25 units per month during overtime in months 2–4, and 20 units per month using part-time workers in months 2–4 and 5 units in month 5 using part-time workers, at total cost of $13,170.

20. Total cost = $124,960.

23. Projected on-hand, wk1 = 31, wk2 = 71, wk3 = 41, wk4 = 11, wk5 = 41, wk6 = 71, wk7 = 31, wk8 = 61.

Chapter 14: Material Requirements Planning and Enterprise Resource Planning

1. a. F = 2, G = 1, H = 1, J = 6, D = 10, L = 2, A = 4
2. a. E = 138.
    b. Week 5.
11. Order 160 units in Week 2; projected on-hand wk4 = 15, wk5 = 35, wk6 = 5, . . .

Week number		1	2	3	4	5	6	7	8	9
Quantity							100		100	100

Item: Golf cart LT = 1 week										
Gross requirements							100		100	100
Scheduled receipts										
Projected on-hand										
Net requirements							100		100	100
Planned-order receipts							100		100	100
Planned-order releases						100		100	100	

Item: Bases LT = 1 week										
Gross requirements							100		100	100
Scheduled receipts										
Projected on-hand	20	20	20	20	50	100	50	100	50	0
Net requirements										
Planned-order receipts				30	50	50	50	50	50	
Planned-order releases			30	50	50	50	50	50		

14. b. Production schedule for golf carts.
15. EPP = 79. Order 120 units in Month 2 and 60 units in Month 6.

Chapter 15: Just-in-Time and Lean Production

1. 4 or 5; fewer containers.
4. D-C-B-D-A-C-D-B-C-D.

Chapter 16: Job and Staff Scheduling

6. a. SPT = D-C-B-A,
        EDD = C-B-D-A.
    b.

	SPT	EDD
Avg. flow time	19.75	21
Avg. days late	6	6

    c. SPT.
9. B-A-G-E-F-D-C. Makespan = 11.7 hours.
21. A-B-C, total setup time = 7 hrs.

Chapter 17: Project Management

1. a. S-9-10-11-12-13-End: 31 days.
    b. 1-2-5-7-8-9: 55 days.
    c. S-1-2-3-4-End: 44 days.
3. critical path activities F, H, J, K.

8. a. .6881.   b. .3978.   c. .0203.
14. a. wk1: act. 4, wk2: act. 1, wk3: act. 4 and 13, wk4: act. 9 and 12, wk5: act. 9 and 11, wk6: act. 1, 5, and 13.

Chapter 18: Waiting-Line Analysis

6. a. Morning: .375 minute; .45.
        Afternoon: .678 minute; .54.
        Evening: .635 minute; .44.
    b. Morning: .01; Afternoon: .05; Evening: .03.
10. a. .995 customer.
    b. 2.24 days.
    c. 31.1 percent.
    d. .875 customer less.
16. a. 0.30.
    b. W1 = .52 min.
        W2 = .74 min.
    c. L1 = .034.
        L2 = .025.
    d. W1 = .49 min.
        W2 = .69 min.

Appendix B Tables

A. Areas under the Standardized Normal Curve, 0 to z, AP-4
B. Areas under the Standardized Normal Curve
    1. From $-\infty$ to $-z$, $z < 0$ AP-5
    2. From $-\infty$ to $+z$, AP-6
C. Cumulative Poisson Probabilities, AP-7

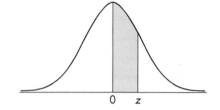

Table A ▼

*Areas under the Standardized
Normal Curve, 0 to z.*

z	.00	.01	.02	.03	.04	.05	.06	.07	.08	.09
0.0......	.0000	.0040	.0080	.0120	.0160	.0199	.0239	.0279	.0319	.0359
0.1......	.0398	.0438	.0478	.0517	.0557	.0596	.0636	.0675	.0714	.0753
0.2......	.0793	.0832	.0871	.0910	.0948	.0987	.1026	.1064	.1103	.1141
0.3......	.1179	.1217	.1255	.1293	.1331	.1368	.1406	.1443	.1480	.1517
0.4......	.1554	.1591	.1628	.1664	.1700	.1736	.1772	.1808	.1844	.1879
0.5......	.1915	.1950	.1985	.2019	.2054	.2088	.2123	.2157	.2190	.2224
0.6......	.2257	.2291	.2324	.2357	.2389	.2422	.2454	.2486	.2517	.2549
0.7......	.2580	.2611	.2642	.2673	.2703	.2734	.2764	.2794	.2823	.2852
0.8......	.2881	.2910	.2939	.2967	.2995	.3023	.3051	.3078	.3106	.3133
0.9......	.3159	.3186	.3212	.3238	.3264	.3289	.3315	.3340	.3365	.3389
1.0......	.3413	.3438	.3461	.3485	.3508	.3531	.3554	.3577	.3599	.3621
1.1......	.3643	.3665	.3686	.3708	.3729	.3749	.3770	.3790	.3810	.3830
1.2......	.3849	.3869	.3888	.3907	.3925	.3944	.3962	.3980	.3997	.4015
1.3......	.4032	.4049	.4066	.4082	.4099	.4115	.4131	.4147	.4162	.4177
1.4......	.4192	.4207	.4222	.4236	.4251	.4265	.4279	.4292	.4306	.4319
1.5......	.4332	.4345	.4357	.4370	.4382	.4394	.4406	.4418	.4429	.4441
1.6......	.4452	.4463	.4474	.4484	.4495	.4505	.4515	.4525	.4535	.4545
1.7......	.4554	.4564	.4573	.4582	.4591	.4599	.4608	.4616	.4625	.4633
1.8......	.4641	.4649	.4656	.4664	.4671	.4678	.4686	.4693	.4699	.4706
1.9......	.4713	.4719	.4726	.4732	.4738	.4744	.4750	.4756	.4761	.4767
2.0......	.4772	.4778	.4783	.4788	.4793	.4798	.4803	.4808	.4812	.4817
2.1......	.4821	.4826	.4830	.4834	.4838	.4842	.4846	.4850	.4854	.4857
2.2......	.4861	.4864	.4868	.4871	.4875	.4878	.4881	.4884	.4887	.4890
2.3......	.4893	.4896	.4898	.4901	.4904	.4906	.4909	.4911	.4913	.4916
2.4......	.4918	.4920	.4922	.4925	.4927	.4929	.4931	.4932	.4934	.4936
2.5......	.4938	.4940	.4941	.4943	.4945	.4946	.4948	.4949	.4951	.4952
2.6......	.4953	.4955	.4956	.4957	.4959	.4960	.4961	.4962	.4963	.4964
2.7......	.4965	.4966	.4967	.4968	.4969	.4970	.4971	.4972	.4973	.4974
2.8......	.4974	.4975	.4976	.4977	.4977	.4978	.4979	.4979	.4980	.4981
2.9......	.4981	.4982	.4982	.4983	.4984	.4984	.4985	.4985	.4986	.4986
3.0......	.4987	.4987	.4987	.4988	.4988	.4989	.4989	.4989	.4990	.4990

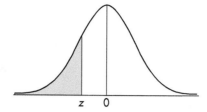

1. *Areas under the Standardized Normal Curve, from −∞ to z.*

.09	.08	.07	.06	.05	.04	.03	.02	.01	.00	z
.0002	.0003	.0003	.0003	.0003	.0003	.0003	.0003	.0003	.0003	−3.4
.0003	.0004	.0004	.0004	.0004	.0004	.0004	.0005	.0005	.0005	−3.3
.0005	.0005	.0005	.0006	.0006	.0006	.0006	.0006	.0007	.0007	−3.2
.0007	.0007	.0008	.0008	.0008	.0008	.0009	.0009	.0009	.0010	−3.1
.0010	.0010	.0011	.0011	.0011	.0012	.0012	.0013	.0013	.0013	−3.0
.0014	.0014	.0015	.0015	.0016	.0016	.0017	.0018	.0018	.0019	−2.9
.0019	.0020	.0021	.0021	.0022	.0023	.0023	.0024	.0025	.0026	−2.8
.0026	.0027	.0028	.0029	.0030	.0031	.0032	.0033	.0034	.0035	−2.7
.0036	.0037	.0038	.0039	.0040	.0041	.0043	.0044	.0045	.0047	−2.6
.0048	.0049	.0051	.0052	.0054	.0055	.0057	.0059	.0060	.0062	−2.5
.0064	.0066	.0068	.0069	.0071	.0073	.0075	.0078	.0080	.0082	−2.4
.0084	.0087	.0089	.0091	.0094	.0096	.0099	.0102	.0104	.0107	−2.3
.0110	.0113	.0116	.0119	.0122	.0125	.0129	.0132	.0136	.0139	−2.2
.0143	.0146	.0150	.0154	.0158	.0162	.0166	.0170	.0174	.0179	−2.1
.0183	.0188	.0192	.0197	.0202	.0207	.0212	.0217	.0222	.0228	−2.0
.0233	.0239	.0244	.0250	.0256	.0262	.0268	.0274	.0281	.0287	−1.9
.0294	.0301	.0307	.0314	.0322	.0329	.0336	.0344	.0351	.0359	−1.8
.0367	.0375	.0384	.0392	.0401	.0409	.0418	.0427	.0436	.0446	−1.7
.0455	.0465	.0475	.0485	.0495	.0505	.0516	.0526	.0537	.0548	−1.6
.0559	.0571	.0582	.0594	.0606	.0618	.0630	.0643	.0655	.0668	−1.5
.0681	.0694	.0708	.0721	.0735	.0749	.0764	.0778	.0793	.0808	−1.4
.0823	.0838	.0853	.0869	.0885	.0901	.0918	.0934	.0951	.0968	−1.3
.0985	.1003	.1020	.1038	.1056	.1075	.1093	.1112	.1131	.1151	−1.2
.1170	.1190	.1210	.1230	.1251	.1271	.1292	.1314	.1335	.1357	−1.1
.1379	.1401	.1423	.1446	.1469	.1492	.1515	.1539	.1562	.1587	−1.0
.1611	.1635	.1660	.1685	.1711	.1736	.1762	.1788	.1814	.1841	−0.9
.1867	.1894	.1922	.1949	.1977	.2005	.2033	.2061	.2090	.2119	−0.8
.2148	.2177	.2206	.2236	.2266	.2296	.2327	.2358	.2389	.2420	−0.7
.2451	.2483	.2514	.2546	.2578	.2611	.2643	.2676	.2709	.2743	−0.6
.2776	.2810	.2843	.2877	.2912	.2946	.2981	.3015	.3050	.3085	−0.5
.3121	.3156	.3192	.3228	.3264	.3300	.3336	.3372	.3409	.3446	−0.4
.3483	.3520	.3557	.3594	.3632	.3669	.3707	.3745	.3783	.3821	−0.3
.3859	.3897	.3936	.3974	.4013	.4052	.4090	.4129	.4168	.4207	−0.2
.4247	.4286	.4325	.4364	.4404	.4443	.4483	.4522	.4562	.4602	−0.1
.4641	.4681	.4721	.4761	.4801	.4840	.4880	.4920	.4960	.5000	−0.0

(continued)

2. *Areas under the Standardized Normal Curve, from −∞ to z.*

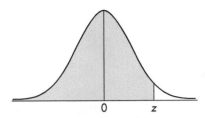

z	.00	.01	.02	.03	.04	.05	.06	.07	.08	.09
.0 . . .	.5000	.5040	.5080	.5120	.5160	.5199	.5239	.5279	.5319	.5359
.1 . . .	.5398	.5438	.5478	.5517	.5557	.5596	.5636	.5675	.5714	.5753
.2 . . .	.5793	.5832	.5871	.5910	.5948	.5987	.6026	.6064	.6103	.6141
.3 . . .	.6179	.6217	.6255	.6293	.6331	.6368	.6406	.6443	.6480	.6517
.4 . . .	.6554	.6591	.6628	.6664	.6700	.6736	.6772	.6808	.6844	.6879
.5 . . .	.6915	.6950	.6985	.7019	.7054	.7088	.7123	.7157	.7190	.7224
.6 . . .	.7257	.7291	.7324	.7357	.7389	.7422	.7454	.7486	.7517	.7549
.7 . . .	.7580	.7611	.7642	.7673	.7703	.7734	.7764	.7794	.7823	.7852
.8 . . .	.7881	.7910	.7939	.7967	.7995	.8023	.8051	.8078	.8106	.8133
.9 . . .	.8159	.8186	.8212	.8238	.8264	.8289	.8315	.8340	.8365	.8389
1.0 . . .	.8413	.8438	.8461	.8485	.8508	.8531	.8554	.8577	.8599	.8621
1.1 . . .	.8643	.8665	.8686	.8708	.8729	.8749	.8770	.8790	.8810	.8830
1.2 . . .	.8849	.8869	.8888	.8907	.8925	.8944	.8962	.8980	.8997	.9015
1.3 . . .	.9032	.9049	.9066	.9082	.9099	.9115	.9131	.9147	.9162	.9177
1.4 . . .	.9192	.9207	.9222	.9236	.9251	.9265	.9279	.9292	.9306	.9319
1.5 . . .	.9332	.9345	.9357	.9370	.9382	.9394	.9406	.9418	.9429	.9441
1.6 . . .	.9452	.9463	.9474	.9484	.9495	.9505	.9515	.9525	.9535	.9545
1.7 . . .	.9554	.9564	.9573	.9582	.9591	.9599	.9608	.9616	.9625	.9633
1.8 . . .	.9641	.9649	.9656	.9664	.9671	.9678	.9686	.9693	.9699	.9706
1.9 . . .	.9713	.9719	.9726	.9732	.9738	.9744	.9750	.9756	.9761	.9767
2.0 . . .	.9772	.9778	.9783	.9788	.9793	.9798	.9803	.9808	.9812	.9817
2.1 . . .	.9821	.9826	.9830	.9834	.9838	.9842	.9846	.9850	.9854	.9857
2.2 . . .	.9861	.9864	.9868	.9871	.9875	.9878	.9881	.9884	.9887	.9890
2.3 . . .	.9893	.9896	.9898	.9901	.9904	.9906	.9909	.9911	.9913	.9916
2.4 . . .	.9918	.9920	.9922	.9925	.9927	.9929	.9931	.9932	.9934	.9936
2.5 . . .	.9938	.9940	.9941	.9943	.9945	.9946	.9948	.9949	.9951	.9952
2.6 . . .	.9953	.9955	.9956	.9957	.9959	.9960	.9961	.9962	.9963	.9964
2.7 . . .	.9965	.9966	.9967	.9968	.9969	.9970	.9971	.9972	.9973	.9974
2.8 . . .	.9974	.9975	.9976	.9977	.9977	.9978	.9979	.9979	.9980	.9981
2.9 . . .	.9981	.9982	.9982	.9983	.9984	.9984	.9985	.9985	.9986	.9986
3.0 . . .	.9987	.9987	.9987	.9988	.9988	.9989	.9989	.9989	.9990	.9990
3.1 . . .	.9990	.9991	.9991	.9991	.9991	.9992	.9992	.9992	.9993	.9993
3.2 . . .	.9993	.9993	.9994	.9994	.9994	.9994	.9994	.9995	.9995	.9995
3.3 . . .	.9995	.9995	.9995	.9996	.9996	.9996	.9996	.9996	.9996	.9997
3.4 . . .	.9997	.9997	.9997	.9997	.9997	.9997	.9997	.9997	.9997	.9998

$$P(x \le c) = \sum_{x=0}^{x=c} \frac{\mu^x e^{-\mu}}{x!}$$

μ\x	0	1	2	3	4	5	6	7	8	9
0.05....	.951	.999	1.000							
0.10....	.905	.995	1.000							
0.15....	.861	.990	.999	1.000						
0.20....	.819	.982	.999	1.000						
0.25....	.779	.974	.998	1.000						
0.30....	.741	.963	.996	1.000						
0.35....	.705	.951	.994	1.000						
0.40....	.670	.938	.992	.999	1.000					
0.45....	.638	.925	.989	.999	1.000					
0.50....	.607	.910	.986	.998	1.000					
0.55....	.577	.894	.982	.998	1.000					
0.60....	.549	.878	.977	.997	1.000					
0.65....	.522	.861	.972	.996	.999	1.000				
0.70....	.497	.844	.966	.994	.999	1.000				
0.75....	.472	.827	.960	.993	.999	1.000				
0.80....	.449	.809	.953	.991	.999	1.000				
0.85....	.427	.791	.945	.989	.998	1.000				
0.90....	.407	.772	.937	.987	.998	1.000				
0.95....	.387	.754	.929	.984	.997	1.000				
1.0.....	.368	.736	.920	.981	.996	.999	1.000			
1.1.....	.333	.699	.900	.974	.995	.999	1.000			
1.2.....	.301	.663	.880	.966	.992	.998	1.000			
1.3.....	.273	.627	.857	.957	.989	.998	1.000			
1.4.....	.247	.592	.833	.946	.986	.997	.999	1.000		
1.5.....	.223	.558	.809	.934	.981	.996	.999	1.000		
1.6.....	.202	.525	.783	.921	.976	.994	.999	1.000		
1.7.....	.183	.493	.757	.907	.970	.992	.998	1.000		
1.8.....	.165	.463	.731	.891	.964	.990	.997	.999	1.000	
1.9.....	.150	.434	.704	.875	.956	.987	.997	.999	1.000	
2.0.....	.135	.406	.677	.857	.947	.983	.995	.999	1.000	
2.2.....	.111	.355	.623	.819	.928	.975	.993	.998	1.000	
2.4.....	.091	.308	.570	.779	.904	.964	.988	.997	.999	1.000
2.6.....	.074	.267	.518	.736	.877	.951	.983	.995	.999	1.000
2.8.....	.061	.231	.470	.692	.848	.935	.976	.992	.998	.999

(continued)

▼ Table C (concluded)

μ\x	0	1	2	3	4	5	6	7	8	9	10	11	12	13	14	15	16	17	18	19	20
3.0	.050	.199	.423	.647	.815	.916	.966	.988	.996	.999	1.000										
3.2	.041	.171	.380	.603	.781	.895	.955	.983	.994	.998	1.000										
3.4	.033	.147	.340	.558	.744	.871	.942	.977	.992	.997	.999	1.000									
3.6	.027	.126	.303	.515	.706	.844	.927	.969	.988	.996	.999	1.000									
3.8	.022	.107	.269	.474	.668	.816	.909	.960	.984	.994	.998	.999	1.000								
4.0	.018	.092	.238	.433	.629	.785	.889	.949	.979	.992	.997	.999	1.000								
4.2	.015	.078	.210	.395	.590	.753	.867	.936	.972	.989	.996	.999	1.000								
4.4	.012	.066	.185	.359	.551	.720	.844	.921	.964	.985	.994	.998	.999	1.000							
4.6	.010	.056	.163	.326	.513	.686	.818	.905	.955	.980	.992	.997	.999	1.000							
4.8	.008	.048	.143	.294	.476	.651	.791	.887	.944	.975	.990	.996	.999	1.000							
5.0	.007	.040	.125	.265	.440	.616	.762	.867	.932	.968	.986	.995	.998	.999	1.000						
5.2	.006	.034	.109	.238	.406	.581	.732	.845	.918	.960	.982	.993	.997	.999	1.000						
5.4	.005	.029	.095	.213	.373	.546	.702	.822	.903	.951	.977	.990	.996	.998	.999	1.000					
5.6	.004	.024	.082	.191	.342	.512	.670	.797	.886	.941	.972	.988	.995	.998	.999	1.000					
5.8	.003	.021	.072	.170	.313	.478	.638	.771	.867	.929	.965	.984	.993	.997	.999	1.000					
6.0	.002	.017	.062	.151	.285	.446	.606	.744	.847	.916	.957	.980	.991	.996	.999	.999	1.000				
6.2	.002	.015	.054	.134	.259	.414	.574	.716	.826	.902	.949	.975	.989	.995	.998	.999	1.000				
6.4	.002	.012	.046	.119	.235	.384	.542	.687	.803	.886	.939	.969	.986	.994	.998	.999	1.000				
6.6	.001	.010	.040	.105	.213	.355	.511	.658	.780	.869	.927	.963	.982	.992	.997	.999	.999	1.000			
6.8	.001	.009	.034	.093	.192	.327	.480	.628	.755	.850	.915	.955	.978	.990	.996	.998	.999	1.000			
7.0	.001	.007	.030	.082	.173	.301	.450	.599	.729	.830	.901	.947	.973	.987	.994	.998	.999	1.000			
7.2	.001	.006	.025	.072	.156	.276	.420	.569	.703	.810	.887	.937	.967	.984	.993	.997	.999	.999	1.000		
7.4	.001	.005	.022	.063	.140	.253	.392	.539	.676	.788	.871	.926	.961	.980	.991	.996	.998	.999	1.000		
7.6	.001	.004	.019	.055	.125	.231	.365	.510	.648	.765	.854	.915	.954	.976	.989	.995	.998	.999	1.000		
7.8	.000	.004	.016	.048	.112	.210	.338	.481	.620	.741	.835	.902	.945	.971	.986	.993	.997	.999	.999	1.000	
8.0	.000	.003	.014	.042	.100	.191	.313	.453	.593	.717	.816	.888	.936	.966	.983	.992	.996	.998	.999	1.000	
8.2	.000	.003	.012	.037	.089	.174	.290	.425	.565	.692	.796	.873	.926	.960	.979	.990	.995	.998	.999	1.000	
8.4	.000	.002	.010	.032	.079	.157	.267	.399	.537	.666	.774	.857	.915	.952	.975	.987	.994	.997	.999	1.000	
8.6	.000	.002	.009	.028	.070	.142	.246	.373	.509	.640	.752	.840	.903	.945	.970	.985	.993	.997	.999	.999	1.000
8.8	.000	.001	.007	.024	.062	.128	.226	.348	.482	.614	.729	.822	.890	.936	.965	.982	.991	.996	.998	.999	1.000
9.0	.000	.001	.006	.021	.055	.116	.207	.324	.456	.587	.706	.803	.876	.926	.959	.978	.989	.995	.998	.999	1.000
9.5	.000	.001	.004	.015	.040	.089	.165	.269	.392	.522	.645	.752	.836	.898	.940	.967	.982	.991	.996	.998	.999

Appendix C   Working with the Normal Distribution

The normal distribution is a theoretical distribution that approximates many real-life phenomena. It is widely used in many disciplines, including operations management. Consequently, having the ability to work with normal distributions is a skill that will serve you well.

The normal curve is symmetrical and bell-shaped, as illustrated in Figure C-1. Although the theoretical distribution extends in both directions, to plus or minus infinity, most of the distribution lies close to its mean, so values of a variable that is normally distributed will occur relatively close to the distribution mean.

▼ **Figure C-1**

The normal distribution.

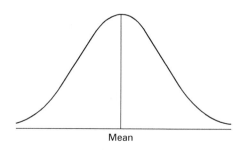

Mean

z Values

It is customary to refer to a value of a normally distributed random variable in terms of the number of standard deviations the value is from the mean of the distribution. This is known as its z value, or z score. In Figure C-2 you can see the normal distribution in terms of some selected z values. This particular distribution is referred to as the standard normal distribution. Notice that the z values to the left of (i.e., below) the mean are negative. Thus, a z value of -1.25 refers to a value that is 1.25 standard deviations below the distribution mean.

▼ **Figure C-2**

The standard normal distribution with selected values of z.

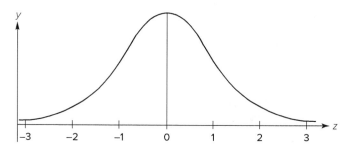

When working with a variable that is normally distributed, it is often necessary to convert an actual value of the variable to a z value. The z value can be computed using the following formula:

$$z = \frac{x - \mu}{\sigma}$$

where x = A specified value of a variable
μ = The distribution mean
σ = The distribution standard deviation

▼ **Example 1**

A normal distribution has a mean of 20 and a standard deviation of 2. What is the z value of 17.5?

SOLUTION
$x = 17.5$
$\mu = 20$
$\sigma = 2$
Using the formula for z, we find:
$$z = \frac{x - \mu}{\sigma}$$
$$z = \frac{17.5 - 20}{2} = -1.25$$

z Values and Probabilities

Once the z value is known, it can be used to obtain various probabilities by referring to a table of the normal distribution, such as the probability that a value will occur by chance that is greater than, or less than, that value. Note that the probability of *exactly* that value is zero, because there are an infinite number of values that could occur, so the probability of specifying in advance that any one particular value will occur is essentially equal to zero. z values can also be used to find the probability that a value will occur that is between $\pm z$. Two such cases are shown in Figure C-3. Note that the total area underneath the curve represents 100 percent of the probability, so knowing that the probability that a value will occur that is within the range, say, of $z = \pm 2$ is .9544, we can say that the probability that a value will occur that is outside of the range (e.g., either less than $z = -2$ or greater than $z = +2$) is equal to $1.0000 - .9544 = .0456$.

▼ **Figure C-3**

Areas under the normal curve between $z = \pm 2\sigma$ and $z = \pm 3\sigma$.

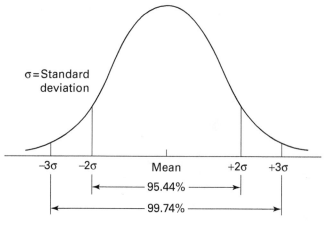

σ = Standard deviation

-3σ   -2σ   Mean   +2σ   +3σ

95.44%
99.74%

Tables of the Normal Distribution

Virtually all applications of the normal distribution involve working with a table of normal distribution probabilities. Tables make the process of obtaining probabilities and z values quite simple. This book has two slightly different normal distribution tables. Appendix B Table A has values for the right half of the distribution for the area under the curve (note the figure at the top of the table), which is the probability from the mean of the distribution ($z = 0$) to any other value of z, up to $z = +3.09$. Statistics books always have this version of the table, so you may already be familiar with it. A second table of normal probabilities is presented in Appendix B Tables B1 and B2. They show the area under the curve from negative infinity to any point z (see the figure at the top of the table), up to $z = +3.49$. In both tables, the values of z are shown in two parts. The integer and

first decimal are shown along the side of the table, while the second decimal is shown across the top.

Example 2

Using Appendix B Table B.2, find the area under the curve to the left of $z = 1.12$.

SOLUTION

$z = 1.12$ becomes 1.1
$$\begin{array}{r} + .02 \\ \hline 1.12 \end{array}$$

Find the row where $z = 1.1$ down the left-hand side of the table. Find the .02 column across the top of the table. The probability is at the intersection of the 1.1 row and the .02 column.

z	.00	.01	.02	.03	.04	.05	.06	.07	.08	.09
.0	.5000	.5040	.5080	.5120	.5160	.5199	.5239	.5279	.5319	.5359
.1	.5398	.5438	.5478	.5517	.5557	.5596	.5636	.5675	.5714	.5753
.2	.5793	.5832	.5871	.5910	.5948	.5987	.6026	.6064	.6103	.6141
.3	.6179	.6217	.6255	.6293	.6331	.6368	.6406	.6443	.6480	.6517
.4	.6554	.6591	.6628	.6664	.6700	.6736	.6772	.6808	.6844	.6879
.5	.6915	.6950	.6985	.7019	.7054	.7088	.7123	.7157	.7190	.7224
.6	.7257	.7291	.7324	.7357	.7389	.7422	.7454	.7486	.7517	.7549
.7	.7580	.7611	.7642	.7673	.7703	.7734	.7764	.7794	.7823	.7852
.8	.7881	.7910	.7939	.7967	.7995	.8023	.8051	.8078	.8106	.8133
.9	.8159	.8186	.8212	.8238	.8264	.8289	.8315	.8340	.8365	.8389
1.0	.8413	.8438	.8461	.8485	.8508	.8531	.8554	.8577	.8599	.8621
1.1	.8643	.8665	(.8686)	.8708	.8729	.8749	.8770	.8790	.8810	.8830
1.2	.8849	.8869	.8888	.8907	.8925	.8944	.8962	.8980	.8997	.9015
1.3	.9032	.9049	.9066	.9082	.9099	.9115	.9131	.9147	.9162	.9177
1.4	.9192	.9207	.9222	.9236	.9251	.9265	.9279	.9292	.9306	.9319

Note: You will find versions of both tables at the very end of the book for easy reference. The above table repeats Appendix B Table B.2, the positive values of z. For problems that involve negative values of z, refer to the portion of Appendix B Table B.1 on p. AP-5.

Finding the Probability of Observing a Value That Is Within $\pm z$ of the Mean or Outside of $\pm z$

Use Appendix B Table A for this type of problem:

Example 3

Find the area under the curve that is *within* two standard deviations of the mean.

SOLUTION

What the problems is asking for:

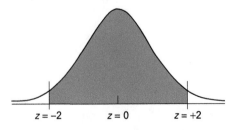

Appendix B Table A provides the right half of the area:

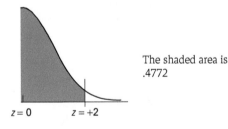

The shaded area is .4772

To find the total area between $\pm z = 2$, double the amount in the right half: $2(.4772) = .9544$.

Example 4

Find the area under the curve that is *outside* of two standard deviations from the mean.

SOLUTION

What the problem is asking for:

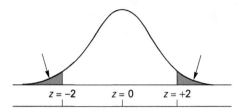

Appendix B Table A provides the right half of the area between the mean and $z = +2$. To find the area in the right tail, subtract the amount between the mean and $z = +2$ from .5000:

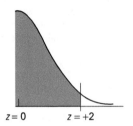

Area under the right side of the curve:	.5000
Subtract the area from $z = 0$ to $z = +2.00$:	$-.4772$
The area to the right of $z = +2.00$ is:	.0228

The same amount will be in each tail, so the total area in both tails is $2(.0228) = .0456$.

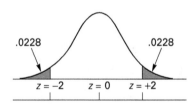

Another way to arrive at the same answer is to note that the area *within* two standard deviations of the mean is .9544, as shown previously, so the area outside of that is $1.0000 - .9544 = .0456$.

Finding the Area (Probability) That Is to the Left or to the Right of z

Use Appendix B Table B.2 for this type of problem (e.g., "What is the probability that the time will not exceed 22 weeks?").

▼ **Example 5**

A normal distribution has a mean of 20 and a standard deviation of 1.0. Find the probabilities:
a. A value that is 22 or less.
b. A value that is 22 or more.

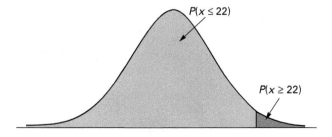

SOLUTION

First, determine the value of z for 22:

$$z = \frac{x - \mu}{\sigma} = \frac{22 - 20}{1} = +2.00$$

a. From Appendix B Table B, the area (probability) to the left of $z = +2.00$ is .9772.
b. Because the total area under the curve is 100 percent, or 1.0000, the area to the right of $z = +2.00$ is simply $1.0000 - .9772 = .0228$.

Points to Remember

1. The area under a normal curve represents probability.
2. The area under the curve is 100 percent, or 1.0000.
3. The area on either side of the mean is equal to half of the total, which is 50 percent, or .5000.
4. The curve extends to $\pm$ infinity, but 99.74 percent of the values will occur within ±3 standard deviations of the mean.
5. It is best to use Appendix B Table A for problems involving $\pm z$ (i.e., Chapters 7 and 10), and to use Appendix B Table B for problems involving one-sided probabilities such as the probability that x will be no more than a given (i.e., Chapters 4S, 13, and 17).
6. The probability of an exact value (e.g., 22 in Example 5) is zero. Therefore, $P(x \le 22) = P(x < 22)$.

Test Yourself

1. Suppose a normal distribution has a mean of 40 and a standard deviation of 5. Find the value of z for each of these values:
    a. 48   b. 30
    c. 34   d. 52.5
2. Using Appendix B Table A, find the area between $\pm z$ when z is:
    a. 1.00   b. 1.96
    c. 2.10   d. 2.50
3. Find the probability of observing a value that is beyond $\pm z$ when z is:
    a. 1.00   b. 1.80
    c. 1.88   d. 2.54
4. Use the appropriate Appendix B Table to find the probability of a value that does not exceed a z value of:
    a. .40   b. 1.27
    c. -1.32 d. 2.75
5. Find the probability of observing a value that is more than a z value of:
    a. .77   b. 1.65
    c. -1.32 d. 2.75

Answers

1. a. $+1.60$ b. -2.00
    c. -1.20 d. $+2.50$
2. a. .6826   b. .9500
    c. .9642   d. .9876
3. a. .3174   b. .0718
    c. .0602   d. .0110
4. a. .6554   b. .8980
    c. .0934   d. .9970
5. a. .2206   b. .0495
    c. .9066   d. .0030

Acknowledgements

Chapter 1

Page 12, Figure 1-6: Adapted from Table 13 in A.S. Sohal et al., "The Roles and Responsibilities of Production/Operations Managers In SMEs: Evidence from Canada," *Technovation* 21 (7), p. 437–448; **Page 13 (box):** Operations Management Students' Association, University of Saskatchewan, http://www.theomsa.com/events/2013-10.

Chapter 2

Page 33, Figure 2-2: Based on J.H. Sheridan, "America's Best Plants: Wilson Sporting Goods," *Industry Week* 241 (20), October 19, 1992, pp. 59–62; **Page 49 (unnumbered figure):** Canadian Pacific, *News Release—*January 29, 2014, Summary of Rail Data, p. 14.

Chapter 3

Page 58 (cartoon): © Mike Baldwin/Cornered/Cartoonstock.com. All rights reserved; **Page 82 (box):** InformationWeek, "i2 Says: 'You Too, Nike,'" March 1, 2001, http://www.informationweek.com/i2-says-you-too-nike-/d/d-id/1010113.

Chapter 4

Page 130 (unnumbered figure): Design Concepts, Inc., http://www.design-concepts.com/portfolio/industry/sports-recreation/wilson-youth-batting-helmet.

Chapter 5

Page 139 (unnumbered figures): Cisco, "Cisco IT Case Study: How Cisco IT Uses NetFlow to Improve Network Capacity Planning," Table 2, p. 4. All contents are Copyright © 1992–2007 Cisco Systems, Inc. All rights reserved. This document is Cisco Public Information; **Page 141 (unnumbered figure):** "Canada's Energy Future: Energy Supply and Demand Projections to 2035." Figure 4.9, p. 25. © Her Majesty the Queen in Right of Canada as represented by the National Energy Board 2011; **Page 144, Figure 5-3:** Slack, Nigel, and Lewis, Michael. *Operations Strategy*, 2nd Edition. © 2008 Pearson Education Ltd. (UK). Figure 3.8, p. 84.

Supplement 5S

Pages 168–171 (unnumbered figures): Syncopation Software, Inc., http://www.syncopation.com.

Chapter 6

Page 194 (unnumbered figure): Plant floor plan image courtesy of Shane Korol; **Page 197 (unnumbered figure):** Courtesy of Redpath Sugar, Ltd.; **Page 201, Figure 6-2:** Roger G. Schroeder, *Operations Management*, 1st ed., (Boston: McGraw-Hill/Irwin, 2000), p. 96. Reproduced with the permission of The McGraw-Hill Companies, Inc.; **Page 210, Figure 6-7:** Adapted from D. Fogarty and T. Hoffmann, *Production and Inventory Management*, (Cincinnati-South-Western Publishing, 1983), p. 472; **Page 211, Figure 6-9:** Mikell P. Groover, *Automation, Production Systems, and Computer-Aided Manufacturing*, 1st, © 1980. Figure 18.2, p. 540. Reprinted by permission of Pearson Education Inc., Upper Saddle River, NJ; **Page 213, Figure 6-11:** "Computer Integrated Manufacturing," Vol. 1 in Revolution in Progress series, Chapman and Hall, London, 1990. Adapted from R.U. Ayres, Morris A. Cohen, and Uday M. Apte, *Manufacturing Automation*, (Burr Ridge, IL: McGraw-Hill, 1997), p. 175; **Pages 236–237 (unnumbered figures):** Processed Plastic Co., http://www.processedplastic.com.

Chapter 7

Page 280, Figure 7-2: A. Freivalds, *Neibel's Methods, Standards, and Work Design*, 13e. Figure 2.14, p. 40. © 2013. Reprinted with permission of the McGraw-Hill Companies, Inc.; **Page 286 (unnumbered figures):** Canadian Centre for Occupational Health and Safety. "Supermarket Meat Department." http://www.ccohs.ca/oshanswers/occup_workplace/supermar.html.

Chapter 9

Page 359 (box): U.S. Department of Interior. "Report regarding the causes of the April 20, 2010, Macondo well blowout," http://docs.lib.noaa_documents/DWH_IR/reports/dwhfinal.pdf. Accessed February 10, 2014; **Page 363 (unnumbered figure):** http://www.hollandc.pe.ca/quality; https://sam.hollandcollege.com/AngelUploads/Content/Quality_Management_System/_assoc/9F99DA3DBED484E8C5DBA903BBD366/HC_Quality_Manual.pdf; **Page 365 (box):** Dairy Farmers of Canada, "Canadian Quality Milk On-Farm Food Safety Program: Reference Manual," June 2010. http://www.dairyfarmers.ca/content/download/886/6983/version/3/file/CQM+Reference+Manual-Jun2010.pdf; **Page 366 (unnumbered figures):** http://www.excellence.ca/en/certification/organizational-certification/about_pep.

Chapter 10

Page 408 (unnumbered figure): N.B. Riebling et al., "Toward Error Free Lab Work," *ASQ Six Sigma Forum Magazine* 4 (1), 2004, pp. 23–29. Fig. 6. Figure reprinted with permission from Six Sigma Forum Magazine. © 2004 American Society for Quality; **Page 409 (unnumbered figure):** Courtesy of State-Ease, Inc.; **Page 421 (top unnumbered figure):** H.E. Ganley and J. Moxey, "Making Informed Decisions in the Face of Uncertainty," *Quality Progress*, October 2000, 33 (10), pp. 76–78. Fig. 1. Copyright © 1993–2014 American Society for Quality. All rights reserved; **Page 421 (bottom unnumbered figures):** D.E. Lighter and C.M. Tylkowski, "Case Study: Using Control Charts to Track Physician Productivity," *Physician Executive*, September/October 2004, 30 (5), pp. 53–57.

Chapter 11

Page 429, Figure 11-2: Generated from The Beergame Portal, http://www.beergame.org. Copyright © Dr. Kai Riemer; **Pages 430–431 (unnumbered figures):** M. Brienzi and S. Kekre, "How Kodak Transformed Its Service Parts Supply Chain," *Supply Chain Management Review*, 9 (7), Oct. 2005, pp. 25–32. Used with permission of Supply Chain Management Review. Copyrighted 2014. Peerless Media LLC. 112052:814SH; **Page 436 (unnumbered figure):** Adapted from F.A. Kuglin, *Customer-Centered Supply Chain Management*. New York: AMACOM (American Management Association), 1998, p. 175; "IS in Action—Walmart Supply Chain," by Dennis Galletta, http://www.youtube.com/watch?v=SUe-tSabKag; **Page 438 (unnumbered figure):** © Voluntary InterIndustry Commerce Standards Association, http://www.vics.org; **Page 439, Table 11-1:** Based on information made available at http://www.supply-chain.org by the Supply Chain Council; **Page 443 (top box):** Microsoft Dynamics, "Teck's coal business unearths stronger procurement processes with Microsoft Dynamics," http://www.microsoft.com/en-ca/dynamics/customer-success-stories-detail.aspx?casestudyid=4000008850; **Page 443 (bottom box):** Mountain Equipment Co-op, http://www.mec.ca/AST/Navigation/MEC_Global/AboutMEC.jsp; **Page 444, Table 11-3:** Simchi-Levi, Philip Kaminsky, and Edith Simchi-Levi, *Designing and Managing the Supply Chain: Concepts, Strategies, and Case Studies*, New York: Irwin/McGraw-Hill, © 2000, p. 235; **Page 447 (top box):** OfficeMax/Grand & Toy, http://www.officemaxcanada.com/en/sites/core/aboutUs_corporateProfile.aspx; **Page 447 (bottom box):** Excellence Canada, "2011 CAE Recipient Profile—Cargill Value Added Meats—Canada," http://www.excellence.ca/en/awards2011-cae-recipients/2011-cae-profiles/2011-caeprofile-cvam.

Chapter 12

Page 468 (unnumbered figure): Get It/Wikimedia Commons; **Page 498, Figure 12-17:** Ronald H. Ballou, *Business Logistics: Supply Chain Management*, 5e. Figure 9.19, p. 371. © 2004 Reprinted by permission of Pearson Education Inc., Upper Saddle River, NJ; **Page 520 (unnumbered figure):** Floor plan courtesy of McGraw-Hill Ryerson, Ltd.

Chapter 13

Page 525, Figure 13-2: T.F. Wallace, *Sales & Operations Planning* (Cincinnati: T.F. Wallace & Co., 2001). Figures reprinted courtesy of T.F. Wallace & Co.; **Page 526, Figure 13-3:** T.F. Wallace, *Sales & Operations Planning* (Cincinnati: T.F. Wallace & Co., 2001). Figures reprinted courtesy of T.F. Wallace & Co.; **Page 531, Figures 13-5A and 13-5B:**

J.R. Edwards, et al., "Blue Bell Trims its Inventory," *Interfaces* 15(1), Jan/Feb 1985, pp. 34–52. The Institute for Operations Research and the Management Sciences (INFORMS). Reproduced with permission. Copyright, INFORMS, http://www.informs.org.

Chapter 14

Page 579, Figure 14-14: Stephen Love, *Inventory Control* (New York: McGraw-Hill, 1979), p.164. Reprinted by permission; **Page 604 (unnumbered figure):** Courtesy of Zurn Industries, LLC., http://www.content.zurn.com/web_documents/pdfs/repairparts/720A%2012-2.pdf.

Chapter 15

Page 607, Figure 15-1: Adapted from Thomas E. Vollmann, William L. Berry, and D. Glay Whybark. *Manufacturing Planning and Control Systems*, 4th ed. (McGraw-Hill/Irwin, 1997). Table 3.1, p. 77 and Figure 3.3, p. 75; **Page 611, Table 15-1:** Adapted from Edward M. Knod, Jr. and Richard J. Schonberger, *Operations Management: Meeting Customers' Demands*, 7th ed. (New York: McGraw-Hill, 2001).

Chapter 16

Page 634, Figure 16-1: R. Eade, "Cutting Lead Time through Smart Scheduling," *Manufacturing Systems* 11 (11), November, 1993. Figure reprinted with permission. Rhythm (Demand Consolidation, Capacity Optimized Planner, and Dynamic Scheduler) is at the core of Black & Decker's computer-integrated manufacturing system; **Page 637 (box):** Preactor®, Case Study: PLASTIQUE MICRON MOULDS ITS PLANNING FUTURE WITH PREACTOR, http://www.preactor.com/Case-Study/Case-Studies/Plastique-Micron#.U6-ll018Nv4; **Page 654 (top box):** http://www.Itworldcanada.com/article/chyma-links-doctors-across-canada/6747; http://www.prnewswire.com/news-releases/canadas-largest-urban-community-hospital-chooses-chymatm-on-call-physician-scheduling-technology-57319077.html.

Chapter 18

Page 753, Table 18-7: L.G. Peck and R.N. Hazelwood, *Finite Queuing Tables* (New York: John Wiley & Sons, 1958). Reprinted with by permission.

Photo Credits

Company Index

Note: Page numbers followed by n refer to notes.

Note: Boldface entries indicate key terms and the page numbers where they are defined; page numbers followed by n refer to notes.

Areas under the Standardized Normal Curve, from $-\infty$ to $+z$

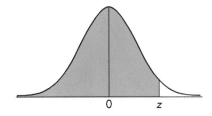

z	.00	.01	.02	.03	.04	.05	.06	.07	.08	.09
.0	.5000	.5040	.5080	.5120	.5160	.5199	.5239	.5279	.5319	.5359
.1	.5398	.5438	.5478	.5517	.5557	.5596	.5636	.5675	.5714	.5753
.2	.5793	.5832	.5871	.5910	.5948	.5987	.6026	.6064	.6103	.6141
.3	.6179	.6217	.6255	.6293	.6331	.6368	.6406	.6443	.6480	.6517
.4	.6554	.6591	.6628	.6664	.6700	.6736	.6772	.6808	.6844	.6879
.5	.6915	.6950	.6985	.7019	.7054	.7088	.7123	.7157	.7190	.7224
.6	.7257	.7291	.7324	.7357	.7389	.7422	.7454	.7486	.7517	.7549
.7	.7580	.7611	.7642	.7673	.7703	.7734	.7764	.7794	.7823	.7852
.8	.7881	.7910	.7939	.7967	.7995	.8023	.8051	.8078	.8106	.8133
.9	.8159	.8186	.8212	.8238	.8264	.8289	.8315	.8340	.8365	.8389
1.0	.8413	.8438	.8461	.8485	.8508	.8531	.8554	.8577	.8599	.8621
1.1	.8643	.8665	.8686	.8708	.8729	.8749	.8770	.8790	.8810	.8830
1.2	.8849	.8869	.8888	.8907	.8925	.8944	.8962	.8980	.8997	.9015
1.3	.9032	.9049	.9066	.9082	.9099	.9115	.9131	.9147	.9162	.9177
1.4	.9192	.9207	.9222	.9236	.9251	.9265	.9279	.9292	.9306	.9319
1.5	.9332	.9345	.9357	.9370	.9382	.9394	.9406	.9418	.9429	.9441
1.6	.9452	.9463	.9474	.9484	.9495	.9505	.9515	.9525	.9535	.9545
1.7	.9554	.9564	.9573	.9582	.9591	.9599	.9608	.9616	.9625	.9633
1.8	.9641	.9649	.9656	.9664	.9671	.9678	.9686	.9693	.9699	.9706
1.9	.9713	.9719	.9726	.9732	.9738	.9744	.9750	.9756	.9761	.9767
2.0	.9772	.9778	.9783	.9788	.9793	.9798	.9803	.9808	.9812	.9817
2.1	.9821	.9826	.9830	.9834	.9838	.9842	.9846	.9850	.9854	.9857
2.2	.9861	.9864	.9868	.9871	.9875	.9878	.9881	.9884	.9887	.9890
2.3	.9893	.9896	.9898	.9901	.9904	.9906	.9909	.9911	.9913	.9916
2.4	.9918	.9920	.9922	.9925	.9927	.9929	.9931	.9932	.9934	.9936
2.5	.9938	.9940	.9941	.9943	.9945	.9946	.9948	.9949	.9951	.9952
2.6	.9953	.9955	.9956	.9957	.9959	.9960	.9961	.9962	.9963	.9964
2.7	.9965	.9966	.9967	.9968	.9969	.9970	.9971	.9972	.9973	.9974
2.8	.9974	.9975	.9976	.9977	.9977	.9978	.9979	.9979	.9980	.9981
2.9	.9981	.9982	.9982	.9983	.9984	.9984	.9985	.9985	.9986	.9986
3.0	.9987	.9987	.9987	.9988	.9988	.9989	.9989	.9989	.9990	.9990
3.1	.9990	.9991	.9991	.9991	.9991	.9992	.9992	.9992	.9993	.9993
3.2	.9993	.9993	.9994	.9994	.9994	.9994	.9994	.9995	.9995	.9995
3.3	.9995	.9995	.9995	.9996	.9996	.9996	.9996	.9996	.9996	.9997
3.4	.9997	.9997	.9997	.9997	.9997	.9997	.9997	.9997	.9997	.9998

Areas under the Standardized Normal Curve, 0 to z

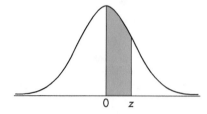

z	.00	.01	.02	.03	.04	.05	.06	.07	.08	.09
0.0	.0000	.0040	.0080	.0120	.0160	.0199	.0239	.0279	.0319	.0359
0.1	.0398	.0438	.0478	.0517	.0557	.0596	.0636	.0675	.0714	.0753
0.2	.0793	.0832	.0871	.0910	.0948	.0987	.1026	.1064	.1103	.1141
0.3	.1179	.1217	.1255	.1293	.1331	.1368	.1406	.1443	.1480	.1517
0.4	.1554	.1591	.1628	.1664	.1700	.1736	.1772	.1808	.1844	.1879
0.5	.1915	.1950	.1985	.2019	.2054	.2088	.2123	.2157	.2190	.2224
0.6	.2257	.2291	.2324	.2357	.2389	.2422	.2454	.2486	.2517	.2549
0.7	.2580	.2611	.2642	.2673	.2703	.2734	.2764	.2794	.2823	.2852
0.8	.2881	.2910	.2939	.2967	.2995	.3023	.3051	.3078	.3106	.3133
0.9	.3159	.3186	.3212	.3238	.3264	.3289	.3315	.3340	.3365	.3389
1.0	.3413	.3438	.3461	.3485	.3508	.3531	.3554	.3577	.3599	.3621
1.1	.3643	.3665	.3686	.3708	.3729	.3749	.3770	.3790	.3810	.3830
1.2	.3849	.3869	.3888	.3907	.3925	.3944	.3962	.3980	.3997	.4015
1.3	.4032	.4049	.4066	.4082	.4099	.4115	.4131	.4147	.4162	.4177
1.4	.4192	.4207	.4222	.4236	.4251	.4265	.4279	.4292	.4306	.4319
1.5	.4332	.4345	.4357	.4370	.4382	.4394	.4406	.4418	.4429	.4441
1.6	.4452	.4463	.4474	.4484	.4495	.4505	.4515	.4525	.4535	.4545
1.7	.4554	.4564	.4573	.4582	.4591	.4599	.4608	.4616	.4625	.4633
1.8	.4641	.4649	.4656	.4664	.4671	.4678	.4686	.4693	.4699	.4706
1.9	.4713	.4719	.4726	.4732	.4738	.4744	.4750	.4756	.4761	.4767
2.0	.4772	.4778	.4783	.4788	.4793	.4798	.4803	.4808	.4812	.4817
2.1	.4821	.4826	.4830	.4834	.4838	.4842	.4846	.4850	.4854	.4857
2.2	.4861	.4864	.4868	.4871	.4875	.4878	.4881	.4884	.4887	.4890
2.3	.4893	.4896	.4898	.4901	.4904	.4906	.4909	.4911	.4913	.4916
2.4	.4918	.4920	.4922	.4925	.4927	.4929	.4931	.4932	.4934	.4936
2.5	.4938	.4940	.4941	.4943	.4945	.4946	.4948	.4949	.4951	.4952
2.6	.4953	.4955	.4956	.4957	.4959	.4960	.4961	.4962	.4963	.4964
2.7	.4965	.4966	.4967	.4968	.4969	.4970	.4971	.4972	.4973	.4974
2.8	.4974	.4975	.4976	.4977	.4977	.4978	.4979	.4979	.4980	.4981
2.9	.4981	.4982	.4982	.4983	.4984	.4984	.4985	.4985	.4986	.4986
3.0	.4987	.4987	.4987	.4988	.4988	.4989	.4989	.4989	.4990	.4990